THE TRAVEL ATLAS

THE ULTIMATE ATLAS
FOR GLOBETROTTERS

Contents

Top to bottom: Alfama, one of Lisbon's oldest districts; 12th-century Ta Prohm temple at Angkor Wat, Cambodia; Monument Valley on the border of Utah and Arizona in the USA.

3

Foreword

I've often held up a copy of Arthur Ransome's 1930s children's book *Swallows & Amazons* as the inspiration for my own love of maps and, in turn, for the mapping in Lonely Planet's early guides. In fact, some of Lonely Planet's early hand-drawn maps looked remarkably like the imaginative *Swallows & Amazons* creations. The other enthusiasm I acquired from that book – sailing – didn't work out so well: as a sailor my sole virtue is that I don't get seasick, otherwise you certainly wouldn't want me in your crew.

Today, Lonely Planet's mapping is far more sophisticated than that early child-like cartography and far more precise as well. Early Lonely Planet mappers, like me, would also insist that it's far easier to do. After all, for almost anywhere in the world today, you can instantly access superbly accurate satellite mapping. In fact, for a spell, I could zero in on my aging mother's home and identify my bright yellow car sitting in her driveway. Since I generally visited her for lunch on a Saturday if I was in the country, I could even agree that the satellite must have gone over at exactly the right hour that week.

Convenient access to satellite mapping may make the first step of mapping far easier than in the 'old days', but that base map is only the first step. A map is absolutely no use – it's just a pretty photograph of some place on Earth – unless the information on that map is accurate and if there was one lesson we Lonely Planet mapping enthusiasts learned in the early days it was that you only found accurate information at ground level. It was remarkably like all the other information in the guidebooks: if it was going to be right then you had to go there and see it for yourself.

Field research

I had plenty of experiences that underlined how important research on the ground was. In 2006 I travelled across Afghanistan in a beat-up Toyota Hilux 4WD. Deliberately beat-up, I should add; my Afghan guide rejected the first vehicle we considered because it looked too new and shiny, too likely to attract unwanted Taliban attention. I had several maps of Afghanistan and they were often quite good for the roads, the rivers and the mountain passes. They were generally hopeless for village names and other vital mapping information. On the other hand I also had a copy of Rory Stewart's *The Places in Between*. Today, Rory is a British Member of Parliament and it's been suggested he might even become Prime Minister one day but in 2002 he was a penniless backpacker setting out to walk from Herat to Kabul, just after the Taliban had been (temporarily) booted out. My travels, beat-up though my 4WD may have been, were far more comfortable than his, but at every crossroad and junction I would find the names of the places we drove through were precisely as they appeared in his wonderful book. He had been and he had found out where he was, not from a satellite but by asking people at ground level.

That was an experience Lonely Planet guidebook writers could relate to over and over again. In those adventurous early days mapping was also an adventure. Of course, in the high-tech West, maps were no problem at all, but in many less developed parts of the world – the

places where the company earned its reputation – mapping had to start from step one. Was there something already available? Sometimes in India we had to go all the way back to Raj-era colonial British maps, although often they were restricted and hard to acquire... well, they wouldn't want the Pakistanis finding their way around India, would they? Sometimes you had to simply start at some convenient point – we'd call it a 'waypoint' in today's GPS jargon – take a compass heading down the main road and pace out along the street to the next junction, noting the name of the street and hotels, restaurants and points of interest as you passed by, of course. I clearly remember the first time I could map a town myself using GPS and simply driving up and down every street and then downloading the resulting route to my laptop. Times had moved on.

Even if you could find a good-looking base map to work from, it didn't mean it was accurate. It was often said you couldn't trust any

Soviet Union mapping; after all, they'd put an extra bend in the Moskva River so that it totally submerged the real location of the KGB headquarters, on the map at least. When I first visited Antarctica, I remember the Russian crew on the ex-Soviet ship, now operated by a Western adventure travel company, being clearly impressed by Lonely Planet's Russia mapping in the book I'd brought along. 'I've never seen such a good map of my hometown,' more than one crew member told me.

Politics

Having established precise base mapping and then ensured the information we added to the map was equally accurate, we would then run into mapping's political side. What's that sea off to the east of the Korean peninsula? To Koreans, north or south of the 38th parallel that separates North Korea from South Korea, that's the East Sea. Not to

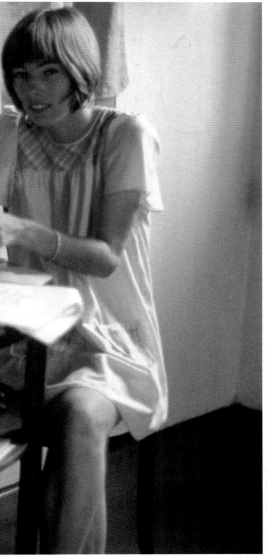

Left and above: Maureen Wheeler working on maps for *Southeast Asia on a Shoestring* in 1975 in a Singapore hotel; Tony Wheeler checking England's Wainwright's Way walking route.
Top right: The nightly india-Pakistan border-closing ceremony at Attari-Wagah.

the Japanese, who can get very upset with an atlas that suggests you're not sailing on the Sea of Japan. That often-fraught gulf which separates one oil-rich state, Saudi Arabia, from another, Iran? You can call it the Arabian Gulf or you can call it the Persian Gulf, but either way you're going to upset somebody. That little cluster of islands off the eastern side of the southern end of South America? Are they the Falkland Islands or the Islas Malvinas?

And then there's the India-Pakistan border. Simply saying 'on this side of this line you'll find citizens of Pakistan, on the other side they're Indians', isn't good enough for the government of India, which prefers that the borders be shown where they wish they actually were. Flying into Mumbai a few years ago, the immigration and customs form warned that along with weapons, drugs, pornography and all those other unwanted imports, the Indian government also took a very dim view of any map of India which showed the borders of India inaccurately. Which presumably means 'accurately', just not with the same accuracy they wanted to believe in. Arriving at my hotel I found myself in the lift with a young man wearing a T-shirt sporting a map of India. 'Is that T-shirt legal?' I wondered. Of course, China is just as touchy about cartography – don't even hint that Taiwan might not be part of China.

Despite all our modern mapping coverage, I continue to be delighted when I arrive somewhere that simply isn't covered. If there's something mapmakers hate even more than a place that's 'obscured by cloud', it's somewhere without a name on the map. Better an inaccurate place name than a blank seems to be the sentiment of many mapmakers, who then proceed to scatter names across the map like confetti – often with no hint that they're often almost fictitious. Plus, despite our ability to use satellites to map the world with incredible clarity – oh look, there's my car in front of my mum's house – sometimes the satellites don't show places with any clarity at all. A few years ago I made a little trek from Palestine, the West Bank, the Occupied Territories, even Judea and Samaria according to some more extreme viewpoints, into Israel, although even that name may be questionable in some parts of the world. I had to walk along the wall – a structure

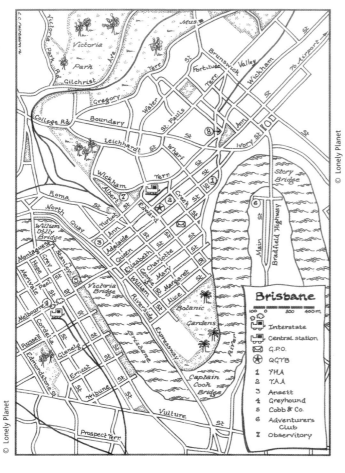

Left and below: Hand-drawn maps by Linda Fairbairn from the second edition of Lonely Planet's Australia guidebook; today Lonely Planet's Guides app offers on-the-go navigation.

first be bent into the shape of a map of Australia and the National Library's map collection includes a genuine, hand-crafted (by me) map-of-Australia car radio aerial.

Perhaps this travel atlas will be the start of a real mapping collection. The mapping may have changed dramatically from those early Lonely Planet guides, from small and hand-drawn to computer-generated and in a huge format, but isn't the end result exactly the same as the maps in those pioneering if primitive guidebooks? We included those original maps because we knew they'd provide invaluable aid, assistance and inspiration. If a picture is worth a thousand words, how much more valuable is a map?

By Tony Wheeler, co-founder of Lonely Planet
London, 2018

that also goes by a variety of names – cross through security into Israel, and then snake back towards where I'd come from in a little finger of Israel that sort of wiggled into that other place. Where exactly had I been? I mused when I got back to my hotel. I turned on my laptop and looked at satellite coverage and didn't find out.

The Israelis have an agreement with the US that Israel territory cannot be shown with any clarity. The resolution is deliberately degraded, when I zeroed in on my little trans-border (or trans-wall at least) stroll, all I saw was fuzz. On the other hand North Korea can be examined with wonderfully high resolution. I could pick out every ancient Korean War era MiG-15 lined up along the runway at the airport I'd flown into close to the northern border of the country.

Map love

I love maps and I'm very proud of all the work Lonely Planet has put in to being a leader in mapping. It was said that 'Lonely Planet reached places other guidebooks didn't' and that was equally true of Lonely Planet mapping. I've been a mapping enthusiast since an early age: I'm regularly mocked by my children about the family tale that I asked for a globe for a birthday present when I was eight. And then a filing cabinet in which to carefully organise and store my map collection. But I've never been a map (or guidebook) collector; there are no rare antique maps filed away in my library. However, the National Library of Australia does include a classic map of Australia in their collection, which they acquired from me after I'd used it in a mapping talk I gave. Back in the 1970s, car radio aerials were still a telescoping wire, popping up from a position on your car's front wing. Inevitably, age, accidents and vandals would take their toll and when your vehicle had achieved a sufficient state of decrepitude that a proper replacement was no longer justified, the standard repair, in Australia at least, was to take a wire coat-hanger, straighten out the hanger hook and jam it into the aerial base. The makeshift replacement would often give just as good reception as the original equipment. It probably made no difference to the reception, but the authentically dinky-die coat-hanger aerial would

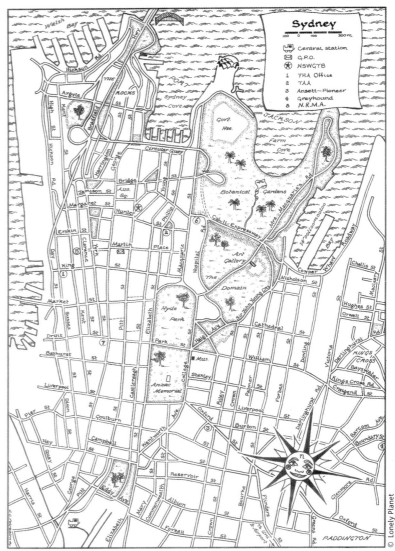

Introduction

We've all done it: traced a finger across a map and allowed our thoughts to wander. What else inspires such dreams of travel, of seeing sights outside of a screen, of encountering unfamiliar cultures, languages and traditions, of experiencing new sensations, sounds and tastes, as a map? If one map can compel us to imagine a journey filled with fresh adventures, then think what a book of more than 200 maps can do. This is the purpose of Lonely Planet's first atlas, a collection of our own cartography that covers much of the world and presents thousands of sights, experiences and itineraries. It is the ultimate atlas for globetrotters.

The Travel Atlas is our first atlas but it is only the latest in a very long lineage. Some of the earliest scientific maps date back to the first century, created by the polymath Claudius Ptolemy of Alexandria and collected in a series of books called the *Geography*, which is a precursor to the earliest atlases. (The Romans appear to have preferred what have been called 'illustrated itineraries' and decorative mosaic maps.) None of Ptolemy's original maps survive but, presciently, he also provided the tools with which others could recreate them, which is exactly what happened in the 13th and 14th centuries when versions of Ptolemy's maps – and others – began circulating.

These early maps were valuable and celebrated. As Jerry Brotton writes in *A History of the World in Twelve Maps*: 'for shamans, savants, rulers and religious leaders, maps of the world conferred arcane, magical authority on their makers and owners.' This is despite early mapmakers being content to embellish maps with rumours and legends where they were unsure of what lay beyond the boundaries of their knowledge. On the Mappa Mundi (world map) dating from around 1300 that is displayed in Hereford's cathedral in England – essentially a depiction of the world according to a 13th-century Christian – Noah's Ark is illustrated in Armenia. Beyond, into what we call Asia and Africa, as factual data was increasingly replaced by conjecture, cannibals, unicorns and griffins are depicted. Below the equator, the map assures its viewers, dwell a number of bizarre races, such as the one-legged Sciapodes.

Our idea of the modern atlas – a 'book of uniform maps by the same person, with the same look and feel, put together in a certain order' according to Tom Harper, the lead curator of antiquarian mapping at the British Library and author of *Atlas – A World of Maps* from the British Library – doesn't arrive until the 16th century, when it coincides with increasing demand for accurate maps due to the widening European gaze. The atlas, says Tom Harper, is rooted in the expansionist European world view and the beginnings of new empires: they showed a world as a place that was ripe for the taking.

The first time that the word 'atlas' was applied to a book was for a collection of maps published in 1595 by Gerard Mercator, a 16th-century German-Flemish cartographer. (In 2017 a later French edition of this beautifully illustrated book sold for £62,500 at Sotheby's auction house in London.)

For Mercator, geography was a way of reconciling theology and philosophy with reality. As 16th-century explorers sailed back from their adventures in the New World and Asia, it became increasingly clear that the Aristotelian world view (that the Earth was stationary and at the

centre of the universe) was no match for first-hand reports offering evidence to the contrary. Ground research superseded imagination.

Mercator, says Tom Harper, was the supreme editor, with a thirst for knowledge. 'He never strayed far from northern Europe but would bring together reports from an incredible number of correspondents. So he gathered information, stories, accounts of voyages and put it all together. A lot of the geography was spurious we now know but it wasn't at the time. He was basing his maps on the most reliable knowledge he had. They weren't errors – they were believed at the time.'

You can find the 1570 prototype of Mercator's *Atlas of Europe* in the British Library (now worth considerably more than the £500,000 that the library paid for it), together with a number of his letters to his correspondents, so you can understand his working processes. Each 16th-century expedition had its own cartographer. Similarly, when Lonely Planet was making its first maps in the 1970s, they too were researched on the ground (see the photograph of Maureen Wheeler crafting a map for *Southeast Asia on a Shoestring*).

Previous page: A statue of Gerard Mercator in Liverpool. **Left**: A map from Mercator's 1595 atlas of Europe. **Below**: A photo of a Martian crater taken by NASA's Mars Reconnaissance Orbiter in 2015.

'You'd naturally expect that every map started with someone actually going to a place and experiencing it, drawing it and ultimately having printed and published,' notes Tom Harper. 'But actually, throughout the history of cartography, mapmakers are pretty lazy [not Lonely Planet's – see 'how this book was made' on the facing page] and if they've got a good model to copy from, they copy it. The history of cartography is a process of invention and imitation. You have these milestones every few decades where someone does something new, based on original first-hand knowledge of something.' A reason for this is that maps, then as now, were immensely expensive to make. This meant that updates were few and far between.

By the time of Joan Blaeu's highly accomplished *Atlas maior* in the middle of the 17th century, world maps were much more recognisable, with several more decades of voyages to draw upon. Blaeu's atlas was also the first to present the Copernican solar system, in which our planet circled the sun. This pragmatism extended to the purpose of this new wave of Dutch mapping: commercial opportunities replaced unicorns and griffins at the edges of the world.

'One very important feature of these early atlases,' explains Tom Harper, 'is that they were not just about geography. The idea of an atlas was that it comprised a complete image and resource of the world: its geography, its natural history, its ethnography, everything was in there. We think of maps today as having just geographical content but that's actually relatively recent. In the 16th and 17th century, atlases were everything you needed to know about a country. There's more continuity with Lonely Planet publishing an atlas than you might suppose.'

Travel and exploration was also central to the conception of these early maps and atlases. Mercator's 1569 world map was his attempt at making life a little easier for navigators on the world's oceans by projecting more accurately a three-dimensional globe onto a two-dimensional map. Going back further, Hereford's Mappa Mundi points to another purpose for the map: pilgrimage. Routes of three important Christian pilgrimages – to Jerusalem, Rome and Santiago de Compostela in Spain – are shown, with towns along the way also noted. Even in 1300, maps were intended to aid and inspire not just bold explorers seeking the edges of knowledge but anybody who could read them. We know much more about the world today – and that there are sadly no unicorns out there – but *The Travel Atlas* still aims to inspire all readers to make a journey, whether it's near or far.

The present

Atlases are still being refined today. Google Earth is changing the potential of the atlas again: all the data with which Google has built its mind-boggling Maps database will no doubt guide self-driving cars and provide us with interactive displays in the not-too-distant future.

Technology allows us to photograph the world in pixel-perfect detail. But truth, as Tony Wheeler notes in his Foreword, remains difficult territory for maps. 'Wherever you are in the world you see a vision of the world according to where you are,' says Tom Harper. 'There's a myriad of truths. The implications of that are tricky.' There will always be debates among cartographers and editors about not only borders and names but also how different projections represent countries and continents (for the record, most of our country and regional mapping in this book uses the Albers equal-area conic projection, which minimises distortion).

On a more poetic level, the notion of the modern atlas has opened out considerably. 'Mapping in its widest sense,' Tom Harper argues, 'isn't just places but mapping other things: emotions, desires, thoughts.'

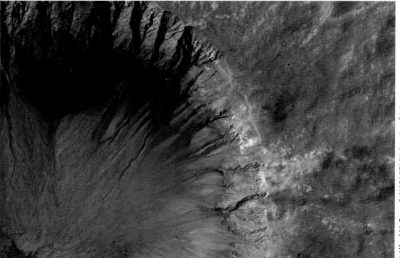

The future

The human impulse to map the unknown in order to understand it now takes us to the stars. 'People have been mapping the moon and the stars as long as they have been mapping the land,' says Tom Harper. 'The earliest globe is a star globe not an Earth globe. The equivalent of the search for the great southern continent in the 17th and 18th centuries is going into space today. ' Now scientists such as NASA's Dr Fred J. Calef III – also known as the Mars Science Laboratory's 'Keeper of the Maps' – have access to data from satellites to map Mars in astonishing detail. 'There's a global geologic map of Mars at the 'county' level, but at the 'city' or 'street' level most of the surface is unmapped. We can see any feature on Mars at the size of a large city building but only about five percent of Mars at the size of a desk,' explains Fred Calef.

However, map-making technology has advanced. Satellites that orbit Mars provide images that are assembled into a mosaic that becomes the base map of the planet. On Earth, GPS (Global Positioning System) is used to determine the exact locations of these images but on Mars radio signals are used instead. Other cartographic techniques are often the same as those used on Earth, although visits are limited to a few sites. 'Spacecraft are carrying higher resolution instruments,' says Fred Calef, 'but nothing beats being on the ground to know what's really going on.'

It's work that directly continues the tradition established by mapmakers such as Ptolemy and Mercator and is also represented by this book: 'We get to establish the base map for future explorers, whether robotic or human,' says Calef. 'A map can, and will, be used for generations, so it's important to get it right, but also make it accessible. There is a science and art to mapping with the former making it accurate and the latter making it readable. As with past cartographers, it requires a balance of both to make a good map.' For Calef, Venus is the next cartographic challenge: 'There hasn't been a new mission sent there to map the surface in decades, so we're still at the 'county' level of coverage. What amazing vistas remain unseen there? I want to know!'

Lonely Planet is always looking ahead but it might be a while before we send researchers to Venus. In the meantime, here's *The Travel Atlas*.

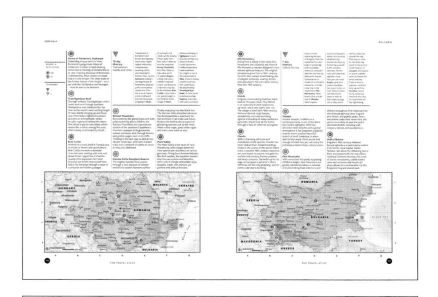

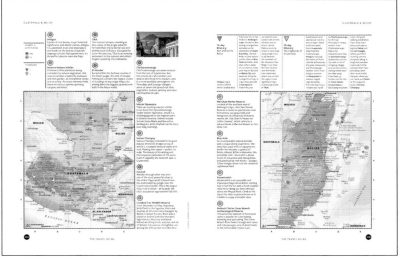

How to use this book

The Travel Atlas is organised by region, which may be a single large country (such as France or the USA) or a group of neighbouring countries. Within each region, the first map presents the entire area covered by that region, complete with the region's most frequented transport hubs and page references to more detailed maps of parts of the region and also to detailed city maps at the back of the book. Turn the page and you'll find a series of large-scale maps of areas within the region (the scale varies from map to map but is marked on each). These maps showcase some of the region's highlights, which are categorised according to whether they are sights, such as museums (in red), or activities, such as hiking, eating or shopping (in blue). We've also added one or two suggested itineraries (of varying durations) to each map, which recommend sights and experiences that are marked by a coloured ring.

Occasionally, there will be two smaller detailed maps on a spread, rather than one full-page map. In these instances, the maps will either be of adjoining regions (for example above, bottom right), in which case they will share places of interest and itineraries because travellers will be likely to move across both maps. Or they may be of entirely distinct regions or countries (for example above, top right) and will have separately numbered places of interest and their own itineraries.

The Travel Atlas concludes with detailed maps of 28 world cities and a comprehensive index. You'll find a key to the maps' symbols below the world map on the next spread.

How this book was made

At Lonely Planet we use ESRI ArcMap and Adobe Illustrator for the majority of map production. Moving to a GIS (Geographic Information System) enabled us to make multiple maps of the same location simultaneously, where every cartographer can immediately benefit from the work done by others, using consistent data and styles. It has vastly sped up map production; work on all Lonely Planet mapping is handled by a cadre of eighteen individuals, fifteen of whom worked directly on this product. We also have an in-house developer who creates and maintains world-class customised tools to support our team and improve production.

Our maps begin as satellite images, digitised using ArcMap and then processed from our database into files we can pass on to our writers. They undertake painstaking on-the-ground research to capture the vital human-scale information needed to flesh out our initial data preparation. Without our writers, our maps would be intricate works of art but hardly usable to find that perfect restaurant or sublime lookout.

The Travel Atlas you're reading now has been in the making – in a way – since 1997, when LP first began creating its mapping database using GIS. Without that technology, this book would have been almost impossible. We began conceptualising the product that would become *The Travel Atlas* at the end of 2014, and hands-on production began in late 2017, requiring hundreds of hours of map wrangling.

By Wayne Murphy, Cartographic Special Projects Coordinator

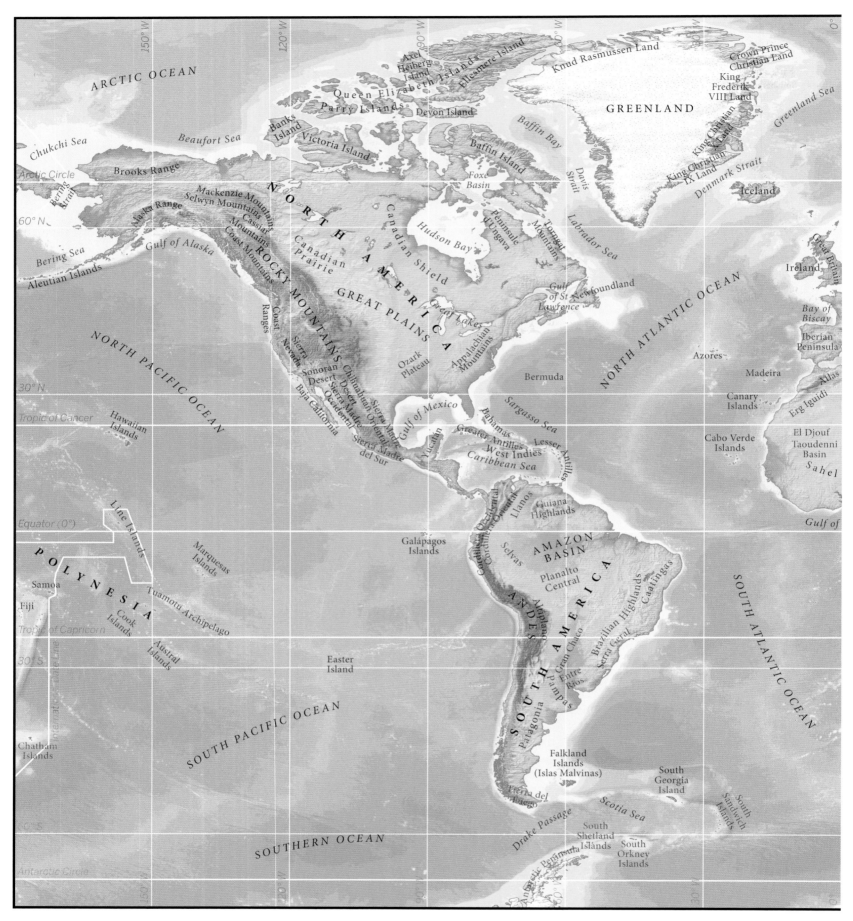

Map legend

These icons represent the main cartographic features and the references to points of interest and itineraries.

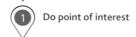

(1) Transport point of interest

(1) See point of interest

(1) Do point of interest

(1) Itinerary 1 start

(2) Itinerary 2 start

● Itinerary 1 point of interest

● Itinerary 2 point of interest

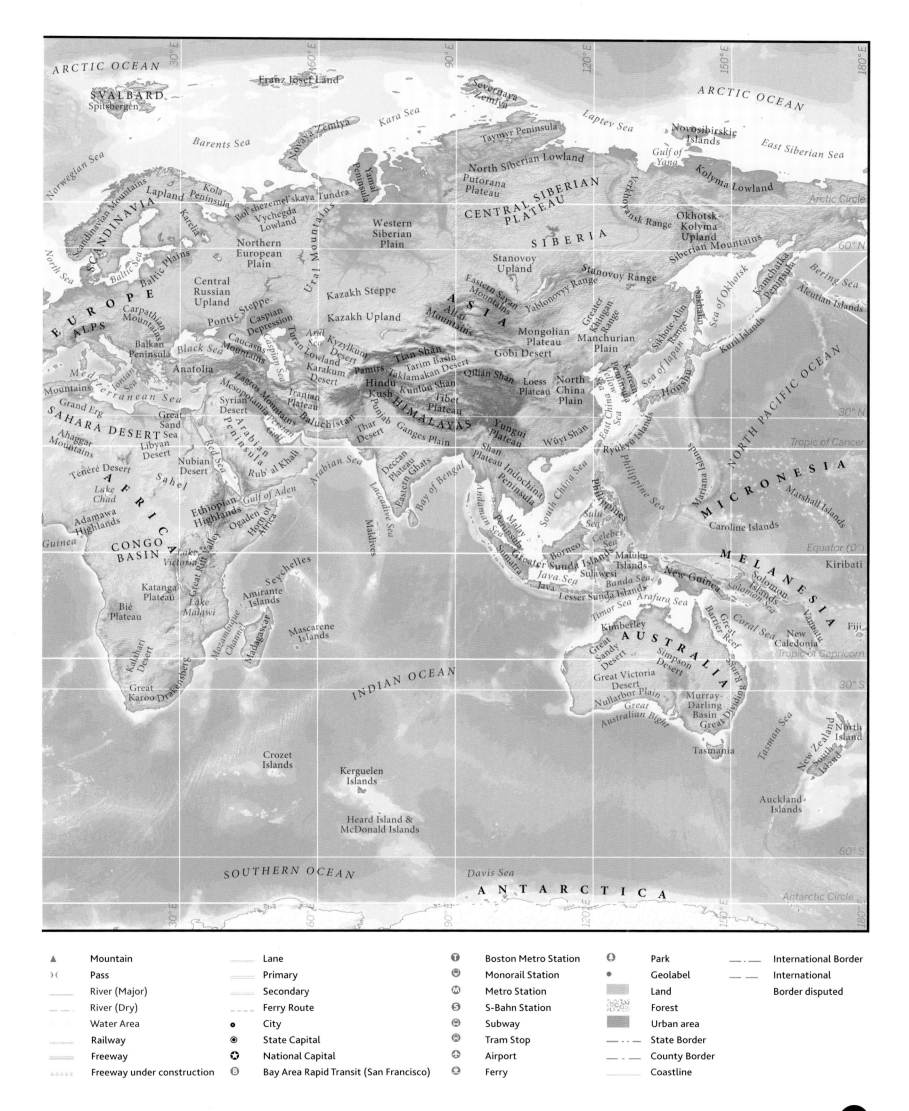

▲	Mountain	⋯⋯ Lane	Ⓣ	Boston Metro Station	Ⓟ	Park	— ‧ — International Border
)(	Pass	━━━ Primary	Ⓜ	Monorail Station	•	Geolabel	— — International
⎯⎯	River (Major)	━━━ Secondary	Ⓜ	Metro Station		Land	Border disputed
— ‧ —	River (Dry)	---- Ferry Route	Ⓢ	S-Bahn Station		Forest	
	Water Area	• City	Ⓢ	Subway		Urban area	
	Railway	◉ State Capital	Ⓡ	Tram Stop	— ‧ — ‧ State Border	
	Freeway	✪ National Capital	Ⓐ	Airport	— ‧‧ — County Border	
	Freeway under construction	Ⓑ Bay Area Rapid Transit (San Francisco)	Ⓕ	Ferry	⎯⎯ Coastline	

11

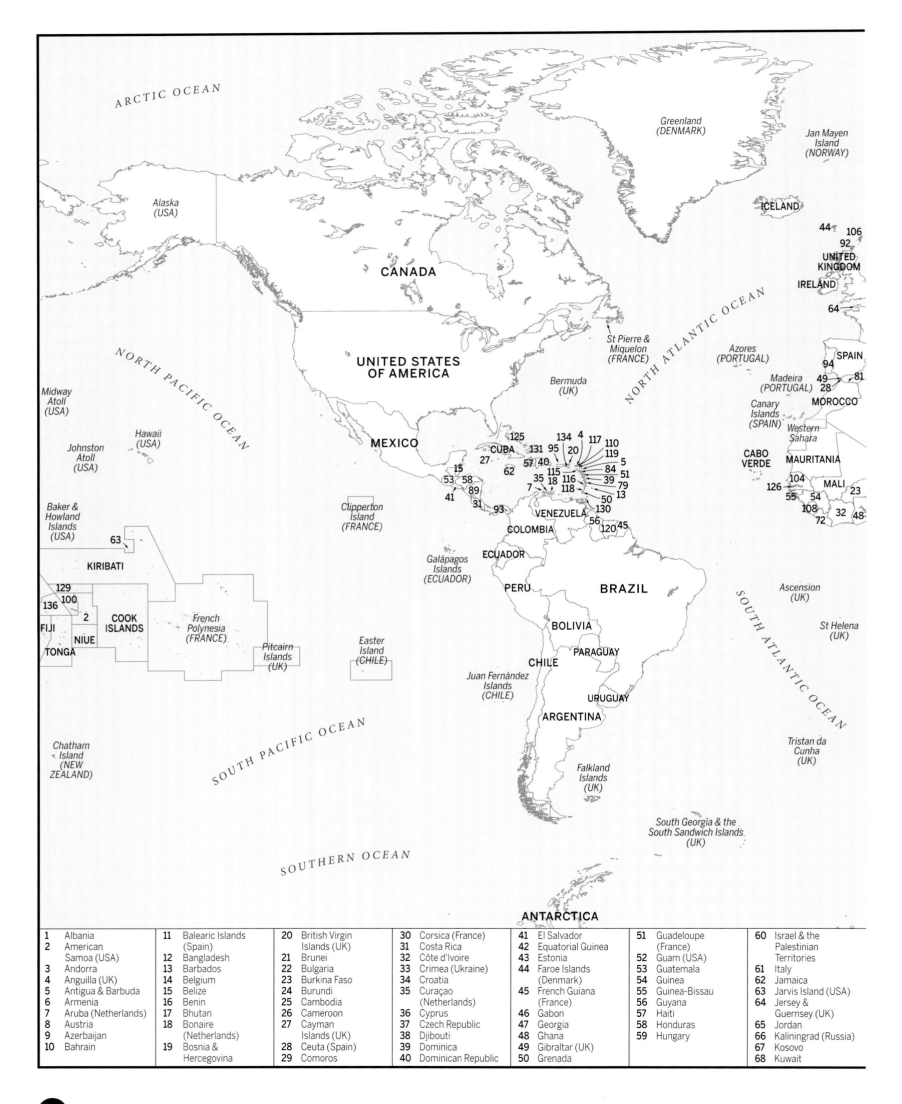

ARCTIC OCEAN

Greenland
(DENMARK)

Jan Mayen
Island
(NORWAY)

ICELAND

Alaska
(USA)

CANADA

44 106
92
UNITED
KINGDOM
IRELAND

64

St Pierre &
Miquelon
(FRANCE)

NORTH ATLANTIC OCEAN

Azores
(PORTUGAL)

SPAIN
94
Madeira   49   81
(PORTUGAL) 28
MOROCCO

UNITED STATES
OF AMERICA

Bermuda
(UK)

Midway
Atoll
(USA)

NORTH PACIFIC OCEAN

Hawaii
(USA)

Johnston
Atoll
(USA)

MEXICO

125
CUBA   131 95   134 4   117 110
27   57 40   20   119
62   35 115 84   5
53 58   18 116 51
7   50   39 79
41   89   118   13
31   93   130
VENEZUELA   56 120 45
COLOMBIA

Canary
Islands
(SPAIN)

Western
Sahara

CABO
VERDE

MAURITANIA

104
126   MALI 23
55   54
108   32 48
72

Baker &
Howland
Islands
(USA)

63

Clipperton
Island
(FRANCE)

Galápagos
Islands
(ECUADOR)

ECUADOR

Ascension
(UK)

KIRIBATI

129
136 100
2
FIJI
NIUE
TONGA

COOK
ISLANDS

French
Polynesia
(FRANCE)

Easter
Island
(CHILE)

PERU

BRAZIL

BOLIVIA

St Helena
(UK)

SOUTH ATLANTIC OCEAN

Pitcairn
Islands
(UK)

PARAGUAY

CHILE

Chatham
Island
(NEW
ZEALAND)

SOUTH PACIFIC OCEAN

Juan Fernández
Islands
(CHILE)

URUGUAY

ARGENTINA

Tristan da
Cunha
(UK)

Falkland
Islands
(UK)

South Georgia & the
South Sandwich Islands
(UK)

SOUTHERN OCEAN

ANTARCTICA

1	Albania	11	Balearic Islands (Spain)	20	British Virgin Islands (UK)	30	Corsica (France)	41	El Salvador
2	American Samoa (USA)	12	Bangladesh	21	Brunei	31	Costa Rica	42	Equatorial Guinea
3	Andorra	13	Barbados	22	Bulgaria	32	Côte d'Ivoire	43	Estonia
4	Anguilla (UK)	14	Belgium	23	Burkina Faso	33	Crimea (Ukraine)	44	Faroe Islands (Denmark)
5	Antigua & Barbuda	15	Belize	24	Burundi	34	Croatia	45	French Guiana (France)
6	Armenia	16	Benin	25	Cambodia	35	Curaçao (Netherlands)	46	Gabon
7	Aruba (Netherlands)	17	Bhutan	26	Cameroon	36	Cyprus	47	Georgia
8	Austria	18	Bonaire (Netherlands)	27	Cayman Islands (UK)	37	Czech Republic	48	Ghana
9	Azerbaijan	19	Bosnia & Hercegovina	28	Ceuta (Spain)	38	Djibouti	49	Gibraltar (UK)
10	Bahrain			29	Comoros	39	Dominica	50	Grenada
						40	Dominican Republic		

51	Guadeloupe (France)	60	Israel & the Palestinian Territories
52	Guam (USA)	61	Italy
53	Guatemala	62	Jamaica
54	Guinea	63	Jarvis Island (USA)
55	Guinea-Bissau	64	Jersey & Guernsey (UK)
56	Guyana	65	Jordan
57	Haiti	66	Kaliningrad (Russia)
58	Honduras	67	Kosovo
59	Hungary	68	Kuwait

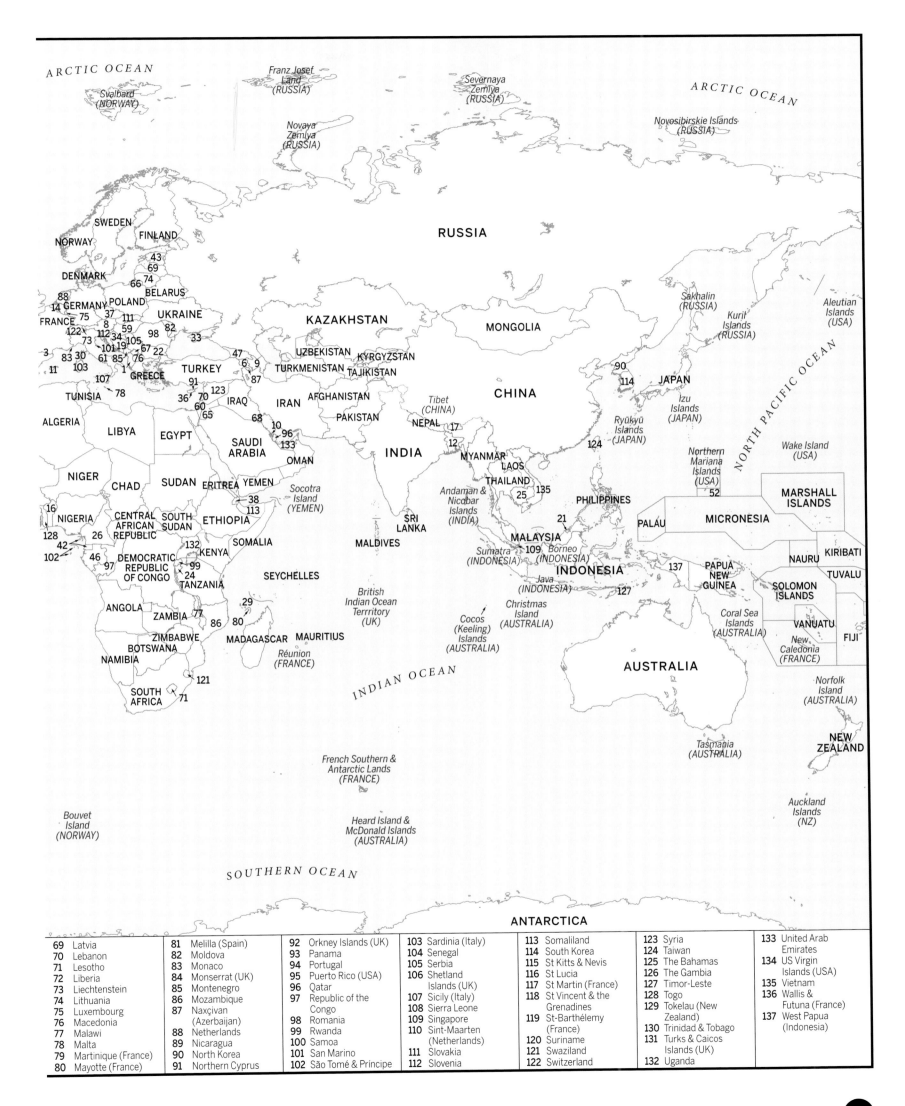

ARCTIC OCEAN

Svalbard
(NORWAY)

Franz Josef
Land
(RUSSIA)

Severnaya
Zemlya
(RUSSIA)

ARCTIC OCEAN

Novosibirskie Islands
(RUSSIA)

Novaya
Zemlya
(RUSSIA)

SWEDEN

FINLAND

NORWAY

RUSSIA

DENMARK

43
69
66 74
BELARUS

88
14 GERMANY POLAND
FRANCE 75 37 111 UKRAINE
122 8 34 59
73 112 105 98 82
3 101 19 67 22 33
83 30 61 85 76
11 103 1 GREECE TURKEY
107 91
TUNISIA 78 36 70 123
60 IRAQ
65

KAZAKHSTAN

UZBEKISTAN KYRGYZSTAN
47
6 9 TURKMENISTAN TAJIKISTAN
87

MONGOLIA

Sakhalin
(RUSSIA)

Kuril
Islands
(RUSSIA)

Aleutian
Islands
(USA)

90
114 JAPAN

Izu
Islands
(JAPAN)

ALGERIA LIBYA
EGYPT

IRAN AFGHANISTAN
68
10 96
133
SAUDI
ARABIA
OMAN

PAKISTAN

Tibet
(CHINA)

CHINA

NEPAL
17
12

Ryūkyū
Islands
(JAPAN)

124

NORTH PACIFIC OCEAN

Wake Island
(USA)

NIGER
CHAD SUDAN ERITREA YEMEN
38
113
16
NIGERIA CENTRAL SOUTH ETHIOPIA
AFRICAN SUDAN
128 26 REPUBLIC
42 132 SOMALIA
102 46 KENYA
97 DEMOCRATIC 99
REPUBLIC 24
OF CONGO TANZANIA

INDIA

MYANMAR
LAOS
THAILAND
Andaman & 135
Nicobar 25
Islands PHILIPPINES
(INDIA) 21

SRI
LANKA

MALDIVES

Socotra
Island
(YEMEN)

MALAYSIA
Sumatra 109 Borneo
(INDONESIA) (INDONESIA)

Northern
Mariana
Islands
(USA)
52

PALAU

MICRONESIA

MARSHALL
ISLANDS

NAURU KIRIBATI

137 PAPUA
NEW
GUINEA

TUVALU

SEYCHELLES

British
Indian Ocean
Territory
(UK)

Cocos
(Keeling)
Islands
(AUSTRALIA)

Christmas
Island
(AUSTRALIA)

INDONESIA
127

Java
(INDONESIA)

Coral Sea
Islands
(AUSTRALIA)

SOLOMON
ISLANDS

VANUATU

FIJI

ANGOLA
ZAMBIA 77
ZIMBABWE 86 80
BOTSWANA
NAMIBIA
121
SOUTH 71
AFRICA

29

MADAGASCAR MAURITIUS

Réunion
(FRANCE)

INDIAN OCEAN

AUSTRALIA

New
Caledonia
(FRANCE)

Norfolk
Island
(AUSTRALIA)

NEW
ZEALAND

French Southern &
Antarctic Lands
(FRANCE)

Tasmania
(AUSTRALIA)

Bouvet
Island
(NORWAY)

Heard Island &
McDonald Islands
(AUSTRALIA)

Auckland
Islands
(NZ)

SOUTHERN OCEAN

ANTARCTICA

69	Latvia	81	Melilla (Spain)	92	Orkney Islands (UK)	103	Sardinia (Italy)	113	Somaliland	123	Syria
70	Lebanon	82	Moldova	93	Panama	104	Senegal	114	South Korea	124	Taiwan
71	Lesotho	83	Monaco	94	Portugal	105	Serbia	115	St Kitts & Nevis	125	The Bahamas
72	Liberia	84	Monserrat (UK)	95	Puerto Rico (USA)	106	Shetland	116	St Lucia	126	The Gambia
73	Liechtenstein	85	Montenegro	96	Qatar		Islands (UK)	117	St Martin (France)	127	Timor-Leste
74	Lithuania	86	Mozambique	97	Republic of the	107	Sicily (Italy)	118	St Vincent & the	128	Togo
75	Luxembourg	87	Naxçivan		Congo	108	Sierra Leone		Grenadines	129	Tokelau (New
76	Macedonia		(Azerbaijan)	98	Romania	109	Singapore	119	St-Barthélemy		Zealand)
77	Malawi	88	Netherlands	99	Rwanda	110	Sint-Maarten		(France)	130	Trinidad & Tobago
78	Malta	89	Nicaragua	100	Samoa		(Netherlands)	120	Suriname	131	Turks & Caicos
79	Martinique (France)	90	North Korea	101	San Marino	111	Slovakia	121	Swaziland		Islands (UK)
80	Mayotte (France)	91	Northern Cyprus	102	São Tomé & Príncipe	112	Slovenia	122	Switzerland	132	Uganda
										133	United Arab Emirates
										134	US Virgin Islands (USA)
										135	Vietnam
										136	Wallis & Futuna (France)
										137	West Papua (Indonesia)

Britain & Ireland

CLIMATE CHARTS

LONDON

RAINFALL
INCH/MM
— 6/150
— 4/100
— 2/50
— 0

D N O S A J J M A M F J

TEMP
°C/°F
30/86
20/68
10/50
0/32
-10/-50

J F M A M J J A S O N D

EDINBURGH

RAINFALL
INCH/MM
— 10/250
— 8/200
— 6/150
— 4/100
— 2/50
— 0

D N O S A J J M A M F J

TEMP
°C/°F
40/104
30/86
20/68
10/50
0/32
-10/-14

J F M A M J J A S O N D

Buckingham Palace, Stonehenge, the Beatles, tartan kilts, St Patrick's Day and pints of Guinness: Britain and Ireland do icons like nowhere else and travel here is a fascinating mix of famous names and little-known discoveries. Britain comprises England, Wales, Scotland and Northern Ireland, with the latter three enjoying devolved governments of some type. Ireland, independent since the early 1920s, has a unique culture with a strong musical and literary heritage. Geographically, Britain and Ireland are separated by the Irish Sea and the Channel divides Britain from France. Britain's highest landscapes are in Scotland and to the north of Wales. These may be compact countries but don't underestimate the amount to see and do.

CASTLES
Centuries of tribal, familial and national conflict mean castles pepper these lands. Some of the most impressive are Cahir Castle in Ireland, Caernarfon Castle in Wales, Leeds and Warwick castles in England and Stirling Castle in Scotland.

LITERATURE
Be inspired by British and Irish writers. Take a Joycean tour of Dublin. London's literary heroes include Dickens. Oxford has fantasists such as JRR Tolkien and Philip Pullman, and Stratford was home to Shakespeare. Edinburgh inspired JK Rowling and Irvine Welsh.

WHISKY
The 'water of life' (*uisge beatha* in Gaelic) flows here. Scotland is a famed source: try distinctively briny Laphroig on Islay or Aberlour and Cardhu on Speyside. In Northern Ireland is Bushmills Old Distillery, while Wales has Penderyn Distillery.

FESTIVALS
Watch processions at the Shetlands' Up Helly Aa festival and burning effigies at Lewes' Bonfire Night. See a goat crowned at Puck Fair in Ireland, and longboats at Jorvik Viking Festival in York. Sing out at Eisteddfod, Wales or the legendary Glastonbury Festival.

SPORT
Britain has invented – or codified – many world sports. The home of golf is St Andrews in Scotland. The 'Cradle of Cricket' is Hambledon, a sleepy village in Hampshire, England. Rugby was invented at Rugby School. Soccer's first governing body was English.

GARDENS
Gardens are an obsession here. Some amazing green spaces are Cornwall's sub-tropical Lost Gardens of Heligan and Inverewe Garden, Scotland. Stourhead in Wiltshire, Powerscourt Garden in Ireland and London's Kew Gardens are all worth visiting.

Right: A view along Duddon Valley in Britain's Lake District.

Transport hubs

The two key transport hubs for Britain and Ireland are their capital cities. Few cities are as comprehensively connected to the world by air as London (and typically at competitive fares), which has two large airports at Heathrow and Gatwick. Onward travel around the British Isles requires leaving London by train in any direction (including mainland Europe) or driving. Dublin, the Irish capital, receives many more flights from the Americas these days. Although there are mainline train routes across Ireland – north, south, east or west – driving is an appealing option. In Britain, motorways run the length of the nation, north to south and also out to Wales and the south coast. Train travel is expensive so many people drive.

Below: Victoria Square in Belfast (left) and (right) the London Eye in the British capital.

London (see pp414-15 for city map)
One of the world's most visited cities, London has something for everyone. Most international visitors arrive via one of five airports: Heathrow to the west; Gatwick to the south; Stansted to the northeast; Luton to the northwest; or London City in the Docklands. An increasingly popular form of transport is the Eurostar – the Channel Tunnel train – between London and Paris or Brussels.

Cardiff
The Welsh capital has embraced the role with vigour. Cardiff Airport is 12 miles southwest of Cardiff, past Barry. Trains from major British cities arrive at Cardiff Central station, on the southern edge of the city centre.

Edinburgh (see pp406-7 for city map)
Scotland's capital, filled with quirky, come-hither nooks, begs to be discovered. It is well served by air, road and rail. Flight time from London is around one hour. There are fast and frequent rail connections to London, York, Newcastle and Glasgow.

Dublin (see pp404-5 for city map)
A small capital with a huge reputation, Dublin's mix of heritage and hedonism will not disappoint. Almost all airlines fly in and out of Dublin Airport, 13km north of the city centre. Ferries from the UK arrive at the Dublin Port terminal; ferries from France arrive in the southern port of Rosslare. Dublin is also the nation's rail hub with two main train stations: Heuston and Connolly.

Glasgow
Glasgow International Airport lies ten miles west of the city. Glasgow Prestwick Airport, 30 miles southwest, is used by low-cost carriers. The two main train stations are Glasgow Central station and Queen Street.

Birmingham
Renewal continues in Britain's second-largest city in its former industrial heartland. Birmingham Airport, eight miles east of the centre, has flights to cities in the UK and Europe as well as some long-haul routes. Most long-distance trains arrive at New St station.

Manchester
The uncrowned cultural capital of the north of England is both historic and hedonistic. Its international airport is 12 miles south of the city. Manchester Piccadilly is the main station for most mainline train services across Britain; Victoria Station serves destinations in the northwest.

Belfast
Belfast International Airport is located 18 miles northwest of Northern Ireland's transformed capital; flights serve the UK, Europe and the USA. George Best Belfast City Airport is located 3 miles northeast of the city centre. Car ferries to and from Scotland and England dock at Larne, 23 miles north of Belfast. For trains, Belfast Central Station is to the city's east.

Newcastle-upon-Tyne
Newcastle is on the main rail line between London and Edinburgh. Newcastle International Airport, seven miles north of the city, has direct services to UK and European cities.

© Andrew Montgomery / Lonely Planet

15°W 60°N 13°W 12°W 11°W 10°W 9°W 8°W 7°W 6°W 5°W 4°W 61°N 0° 1°E 2°E 3°E

Page 19

1

Norwegian Sea

Shetland Islands

Lerwick

59°N

2

Orkney Islands

Page 19

Kirkwall

58°N

ATLANTIC OCEAN

Outer Hebrides • Stornoway

Wick

3

57°N

Skye

Inverness

Loch Ness

SCOTLAND

Aberdeen

56°N

Ben Nevis (1344m)

Loch Lochy

Mull

Loch Awe

Perth Dundee

Greenock Glasgow ✪EDINBURGH

Page 27

Islay

Ayr

5

3

Page 21

5

NORTHERN IRELAND

Derry/Londonderry

Dumfries

Newcastle-upon-Tyne

Donegal

Lough Neagh

Larne

Carlisle

9

Sunderland

54°N

Lower Lough Erne

Omagh

Lisburn

✪**BELFAST**

Page 21

Middlesbrough

North Sea

Sligo

IRELAND

Isle of Man

Snaefell (620m)

Scarborough

53°N

Lough Corrib

Dundalk

✪Douglas

Lough Ree

Drogheda

Irish Sea

Blackpool

Leeds York

7

Bradford Hull

Galway

Page 25

Bolton

Huddersfield

Shannon

Holyhead

Liverpool ✪Manchester Sheffield

✪**DUBLIN**

4

Anglesey

Chester

ENGLAND

Shannon Limerick

Kilkenny

Snowdon (1085m)

Stoke-on-Trent

52°N

Tralee

Derby Nottingham

Carrauntoohil (1040m) Killarney

Waterford

Rosslare

Wolverhampton

Leicester Peterborough Norwich

Cork

Birmingham Coventry Northampton

WALES

6

Thames

Milton Keynes

Cambridge Ipswich

51°N

Swansea

Luton *Stansted*

CARDIFF Bristol

Oxford

LONDON

Southend-on-Sea

2

Bath

Swindon Reading

Heathrow ✪**1**

Bristol Channel

Gatwick

Brugge

Celtic Sea

Dover

BELGIUM

50°N

Exeter

Southampton Portsmouth

Calais

Bournemouth

Isle of Wight

Brighton

Lille

Isles of Scilly

Penzance

Plymouth

Pages 22-23

Land's End

English Channel

49°N

Dieppe

Pages 22-23

Cherbourg

Amiens

10

Channel Islands

Le Havre

Rouen

FRANCE

Caen

Seine

N 0 ___ 200 km 0 ___ 100 miles

A B C D E F G

SIGHTS &
ACTIVITIES

 SEE

DO

ITINERARY

1

2

1
Cairngorms National Park
Britain's largest, highest national park is a wild granite landscape that supports rare birdlife and alpine vegetation. The harsh mountain environment gives way lower down to scenic glens softened by open forests of Scots pine. It's prime hill-walking territory with many Munros (hills over 3000ft in elevation) to bag.

2
West Highland Way
The most popular long-distance walk in Britain reaches from Glasgow's outskirts to Fort William, the west coast's adventure capital. The 96-mile path takes a week to walk; hikers pass Loch Lomond. Fort William, at the foot of Ben Nevis, Britain's highest peak, is a magnet for mountain bikers.

3
Rosslyn Chapel
Scotland's most enigmatic chapel was built in the 15th century, and the ornate interior is a monument to the mason's art. As well as flowers, vines and angels, the carved stones depict the pagan 'Green Man'; other figures represent the Knights Templar. Note also carvings of plants from the Americas that predate Columbus' voyage of discovery.

4
Balmoral Castle
The upper valley of the River Dee was made famous by the monarchy – today's royal family still holiday at Balmoral Castle, built for Queen Victoria in 1855. Balmoral sparked the revival of the Scottish Baronial style of architecture of so many of Scotland's 19th-century country houses. Only the ballroom is open to the public but there are waymarked walks within the Estate.

Orkney: The interior of the Italian chapel was decorated by Italian prisoners of war in 1943.

5
Loch Ness
The cold waters of deep and narrow Loch Ness have been extensively searched for Nessie, an elusive monster. Keep an eye out from the quieter B862 road along the eastern shore and stop at the Dores Inn, a beautifully restored country pub specialising in quality Scottish produce.

6
Glen Coe
Scotland's most famous glen entered the history books in 1692 when the resident MacDonald clan was murdered by Campbell soldiers. Climb to the Lost Valley, a magical mountain sanctuary said to be haunted by the ghosts of MacDonalds who died here. Glen Coe's eastern approach is guarded by the rocky pyramid of Buachaille Etive Mor (the Great Shepherd of Etive).

7
Mull
Pack binoculars and hiking boots: Mull claims some of the finest scenery in the Inner Hebrides. Birds of prey soar over the ridges of Ben More, the black basalt crags of Burg and the white sand and emerald waters that fringe the Ross. Tobermory is the bright little port from which whale-watching boats depart.

8
Skye
Skye (*an t-Eilean Sgiathanach* in Gaelic) takes its name from the old Norse *sky-a*, meaning 'cloud island', a Viking reference to the mist-shrouded Cuillin Hills. It offers some of Scotland's finest (and most challenging) walking. The reward is a dram of the single malt whisky from local distillery Talisker.

9
Glasgow
Glaswegian architecture is a match for Edinburgh. Charles Rennie Mackintosh's sublime designs dot the city, his greatest being the Glasgow School of Art (1896–1909) until its devastating fire of 2018. The city's Gothic cathedral has a timelessness. Kelvingrove Art Gallery and Museum is a grand Victorian cathedral of culture with a bewildering variety of exhibits. And Zaha Hadid's modern Riverside Museum at the harbour covers the Clyde's shipbuilding heritage.

10
Orkney
Predating Stonehenge and the pyramids of Giza, extraordinary Skara Brae on Orkney is one of the world's most evocative and best-preserved prehistoric villages. Even the stone furniture has survived 5000 years. It's not Orkney's only ancient site: Maeshowe is a Stone Age tomb bearing Viking graffiti. Don't miss the WWII Italian chapel on Lamb Holm.

1
5-day itinerary
The Borders

Scotland's borders testify to a past of battles and bandits. From **Edinburgh** drive south to Sir Walter Scott's former home at **Abbotsford**, followed by a flying visit to the Border abbey of **Melrose** (the town is a charming place to overnight). Then head west to Moffat, passing the glorious scenery of **St Mary's Loch**, and continue to **Dumfries**, once home to national poet Robert Burns. Detour first to **Caerlaverock Castle** then again to refuel at the food town of **Castle Douglas** then bear northwest to **Alloway** (Burns' birthplace) then onto **Wemyss Bay** and the ferry to **Rothesay** to see the stately home of Mount Stuart. Return to the mainland and the city of **Glasgow**.

2
7-day itinerary
The Islands

This route is usually done by car, but it also makes a brilliant cycling tour (270 miles, including the 60 miles from Ullapool to Inverness train station, making both start and finish accessible by rail). From **Oban** it's a five-hour ferry trip to **Barra**; spend the night here (book ahead). On day two, after a visit to Kisimul Castle, take the ferry to **South Uist**. Walk the wild beaches of the west coast, sample the seafood and perhaps go fishing for trout. Continue through **Benbecula** and **North Uist**, birdwatching country. Overnight at Lochmaddy on North Uist (if camping, a night at Berneray is a must) before taking the ferry to **Harris**, whose west coast has some of Scotland's most spectacular beaches. The road continues north from Tarbert, where you'll find good hotels, through rugged hills to **Lewis**. Don't go directly to Stornoway, but loop west via the **Callanish Standing Stones** and Arnol Blackhouse museum. Spend a final night in **Stornoway**, then take the ferry to **Ullapool** for the scenic drive (or ride) to **Inverness**.

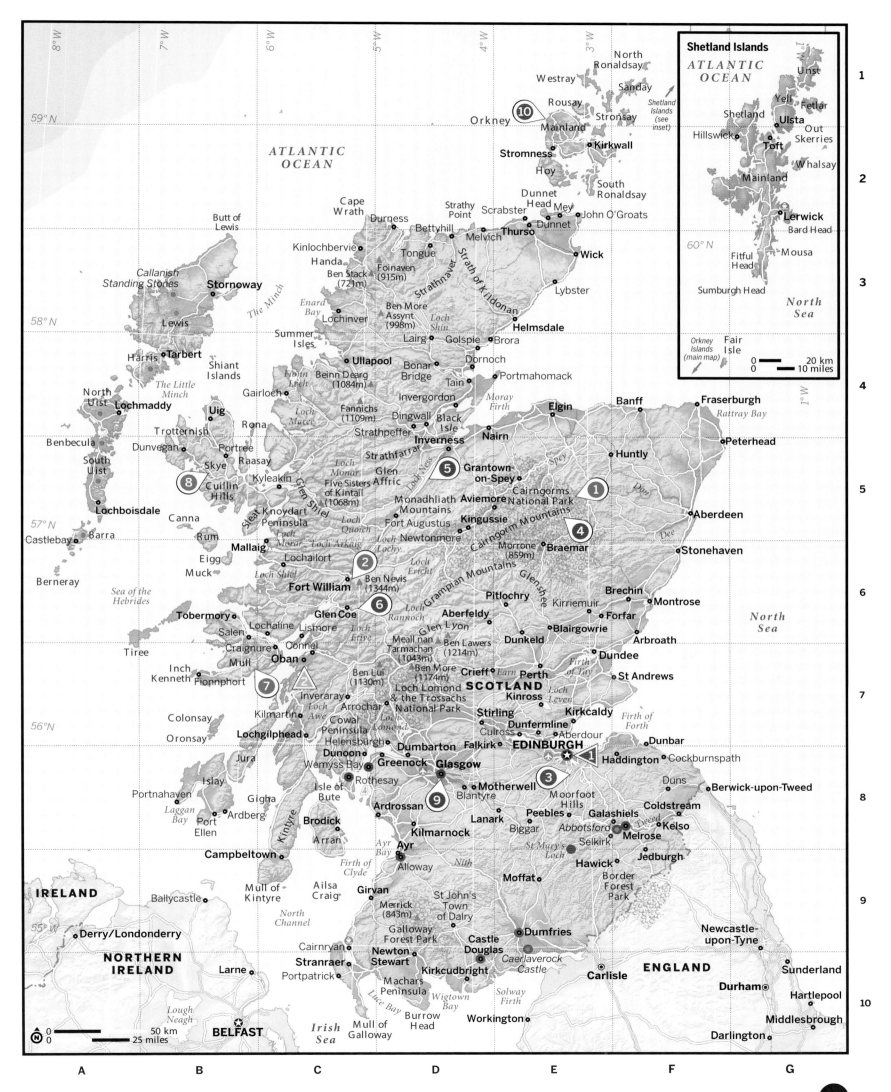

Shetland Islands

ATLANTIC OCEAN

Unst
Yell
Fetlar
Shetland
Hillswick
Ulsta
Out Skerries
Toft
Whalsay
Mainland
Shetland Islands (see inset)

60° N

Lerwick
Bard Head

Fitful Head
Mousa

Sumburgh Head

North Sea

Orkney Islands (main map)
Fair Isle

0   20 km
0   10 miles

ATLANTIC OCEAN

North Ronaldsay
Westray
Sanday
Rousay
Stronsay
Orkney ⑩ Mainland
Kirkwall
Stromness
Hoy
South Ronaldsay

Dunnet Head
Mey
John O'Groats
Scrabster
Strathy Point
Dunnet
Thurso
Wick
Melvich
Lybster

Cape Wrath
Durness
Bettyhill
Tongue
Foinaven (915m)
Strath of Kildonan
Helmsdale

Kinlochbervie
Handa
Ben Stack (721m)
Golspie
Brora
Strathnaver

Butt of Lewis

Callanish Standing Stones
Stornoway

The Minch

59° N

58° N

Enard Bay
Lochinver
Ben More Assynt (998m)
Loch Shin
Lairg
Bonar Bridge
Dornoch
Portmahomack
Tain

Lewis
Harris
Tarbert

Shiant Islands

Summer Isles
Ullapool

The Little Minch

North Uist
Lochmaddy
Uig
Rona

Gairloch
Beinn Dearg (1084m)
Loch Maree
Fannichs (1109m)
Dingwall
Strathpeffer
Black Isle
Invergordon
Moray Firth

Benbecula
Trotternish
Dunvegan
Portree
Raasay

Elgin
Banff
Fraserburgh
Rattray Bay

57° N

South Uist
Skye
⑧ Cuillin Hills
Kyleakin
Loch Monar
Five Sisters of Kintail (1068m)
Glen Affric
⑤ Grantown-on-Spey
Nairn
Peterhead
Huntly

Lochboisdale
Canna
Sleat
Knoydart Peninsula
Loch Quoich
Monadhliath Mountains
Aviemore
Cairngorms National Park ①
Kingussie
Spey
Aberdeen

Castlebay
Barra
Rum
Eigg
Muck
Mallaig
Lochailort
②
Loch Arkaig
Fort Augustus
Newtonmore
Morrone (859m)
Braemar ④
Stonehaven

Berneray
Sea of the Hebrides
Ben Nevis (1344m)
⑥ Glen Coe
Loch Ericht
Cairngorm Mountains
Dee

Tobermory
Lochaline
Lismore
Salen
Craignure
Mull
Connel
Oban
⑦
Fionnphort

Loch Shiel
Fort William
Loch Rannoch
Grampian Mountains
Aberfeldy
Glen Lyon
Dunkeld
Blairgowrie
Pitlochry
Kirriemuir
Forfar
Brechin
Montrose
Arbroath
Glenshee

Tiree
Inch Kenneth
Colonsay
Oronsay

Meall nan Tarmachan (1043m)
Ben Lawers (1214m)
Ben More (1174m)
Crieff
Dundee
St Andrews

56° N

②
Inveraray
Arrochar
Loch Awe
Kilmartin
Ben Lui (1130m)
Loch Lomond & the Trossachs National Park
Perth
Kinross
Firth of Tay

Cowal Peninsula
Helensburgh
Dumbarton
Stirling
Dunfermline
Kirkcaldy
Loch Leven
Firth of Forth

Lochgilphead
Dunoon
Greenock
Glasgow
Falkirk
Culross
Aberdour
Dunbar
EDINBURGH ★ ①
Haddington
Cockburnspath

Jura
Isle of Bute
Rothesay
⑨
Motherwell
Blantyre
Moorfoot Hills
Duns
Berwick-upon-Tweed

Islay
Gigha
Wemyss Bay
Ardrossan
Lanark
Peebles
Galashiels
Coldstream
Kelso

55° N

Portnahaven
Laggan Bay
Ardberg
Port Ellen
Kintyre
Brodick
Arran
Kilmarnock
Biggar
Abbotsford
Selkirk
Melrose
Jedburgh

Campbeltown
Ayr Bay
Ayr
Alloway
Nith
St Mary's Loch
Hawick
Border Forest Park

Ailsa Craig
Girvan
St John's Town of Dalry
Moffat

IRELAND
Ballycastle
Mull of Kintyre
Merrick (843m)
Galloway Forest Park

Derry/Londonderry
Cairnryan
Stranraer
Portpatrick
Newton Stewart
Kirkcudbright
Castle Douglas
Dumfries
Caerlaverock Castle
Carlisle
ENGLAND
Newcastle-upon-Tyne
Sunderland

NORTHERN IRELAND
Larne
Machars Peninsula
Wigtown Bay
Solway Firth
Durham
Hartlepool

Lough Neagh
Irish Sea
North Channel
Burrow Head
Luce Bay
Mull of Galloway
Workington
Middlesbrough

BELFAST
SCOTLAND
North Sea

0   50 km
0   25 miles

Darlington

A   B   C   D   E   F   G

1   2   3   4   5   6   7   8   9   10

SIGHTS &
ACTIVITIES

◉ SEE

◉ DO

ITINERARY

▽ 1

▽ 2

Peak District National Park:
Hayfield village and looking towards the classic Peak District scenery of Kinder Low's moorland.

1 Lake District National Park

Feel what inspired England's 19th-century Romantic poets among the craggy peaks, mountain tarns and chilly lakes of the Lake District. The park is awash with outdoor activities, from lake cruises to mountain walks (Scafell Pike, Catbells and Haystacks are classics). But many visit for the literary links: William Wordsworth lived in Dove Cottage by Grasmere; Beatrix Potter's Hill Top farmhouse sparked her tales.

2 Hadrian's Wall

Named after the emperor who commissioned it, Hadrian's Wall was one of Rome's greatest engineering projects. The 73-mile wall was built across Britain's narrow neck between AD 122 and 128 to separate Romans and Picts. Sections survive, punctuated by forts such as Housesteads.

3 Kirkgate Market, Leeds

Leeds embodies rediscovered northern self-confidence and it has the market to match: Kirkgate, Britain's largest covered market, selling fresh meat, fish and fruit and vegetables, and now including a popular street-food hall.

4 York

This city of cultural and historical wealth has lost little of its lustre. A ring of 13th-century walls encloses a medieval web of lanes with York Minster, one of the world's prettiest Gothic cathedrals, at its heart. York's Viking history is brought to life at the Jorvik Viking Centre. If trains are your thing, admire steam-powered Mallard and the Flying Scotsman at the National Railway Museum.

5 Whitby

Whitby is both a busy fishing port with a quayside fish market and a traditional seaside resort, complete with beach and amusement arcades. Overlooking it is a ruined abbey, the inspiration for part of Bram Stoker's Gothic horror story *Dracula* and now focal point for Whitby Goth Weekends.

6 Liverpool

Find the real Strawberry Fields and Penny Lane in the home of the Fab Four. Start at the Beatles Story on the Albert Dock: fans should book a tour to Mendips and 20 Forthlin Road, the childhood homes of John Lennon and Paul McCartney. Then shop for memorabilia in the Cavern Quarter.

7 Manchester

Explore Manchester's distinct blend of history and culture at the Manchester Art Gallery and the People's History Museum. Old Trafford may interest soccer fans. But what makes the north's uncrowned capital really fun is its swirl of hedonism: dine, drink and dance into happy oblivion.

8 Peak District National Park

This is one of the most popular walking

areas in England, with sweeping vistas of moors and dales. Ancient stone villages are folded into creases and hillsides are littered with stately homes. Mountaineers train in this area, which offers technical climbing on exposed tors (crags). Cyclists test themselves on off-road trails, while hikers hit the Pennine Way, which runs north from Edale to the Scottish Borders.

9 Alnwick Castle

Set in parklands designed by Lancelot 'Capability' Brown, the ancestral home of the duke of Northumberland has changed little since the 14th century. It's a favourite set for film-makers. Six rooms are open to the public, displaying incredible Italian paintings. Below the castle lies the maze of cobbled lanes of Northumberland's historic Alnwick.

10 Isle of Man

This semiautonomous island is home to the world's oldest continuous parliament, the Tynwald; a type of tail-less cat; and beautiful scenery that was designated a Biosphere Reserve by Unesco in 2016. The bucolic charm is shattered during the summer season of Tourist Trophy (TT) motorbike racing.

11 Castle Howard

Theatrical grandeur and audacity make this breathtaking stately home one of the world's most beautiful buildings. When the Earl of Carlisle hired his pal Sir John Vanbrugh to design his new home in 1699, he was hiring a man who had no formal training. Luckily, Vanbrugh hired Nicholas Hawksmoor, who was Christopher Wren's clerk of works. The result was this great baroque house, filled with treasures.

5-day itinerary
The Northeast

Tear yourself away from **Durham's** river and fabulous castle and cathedral and head north to **Beamish Open-Air Museum** to experience the Northeast's industrial age. Pass Anthony Gormley's **Angel of the North** sculpture on your way to nightlife capital **Newcastle-upon-Tyne**. After partying here, continue north to

Alnwick Castle (the inspiration for Harry Potter's Hogwarts). Then take the coast road, past beaches and more castles at Dunstanburgh and Bamburgh to **Lindisfarne**, the Holy Island, an otherworldly pilgrimage site and an important Celtic Christian centre founded in the 7th century. Return to Newcastle via wild **Northumberland National Park**.

10-day itinerary
The Northwest

Manchester is the gateway to England's Northwest. From this vibrant city head north through former industrial heartlands to **Haworth** on the edge of the Yorkshire Dales National Park. Home to the Brontë sisters in the 19th century, it lies on the south edge of moors and stone-walled fields. Overnight here, then take a short drive north to **Bolton Abbey**,

the atmospheric ruins of a 12th-century monastery, and onward to the handsome market town of **Harrogate**. Cross the **Yorkshire Dales National Park** diagonally, stopping for hikes and staying overnight in villages such as Grassington and Hawes. Cross the Cumbrian border and into the **Lake District National Park** via Kendal, an outdoor activities hub. If

you're not hiked out, seek some of Britain's most scenic views on foot. Otherwise, go boating on lakes such as Derwentwater or visit arts attractions such as Brantwood, the home of Victorian art critic John Ruskin, or Blackwell, an Arts and Crafts house, or places associated with Beatrix Potter and the Romantic Poets. Return south to Manchester on the M6 motorway.

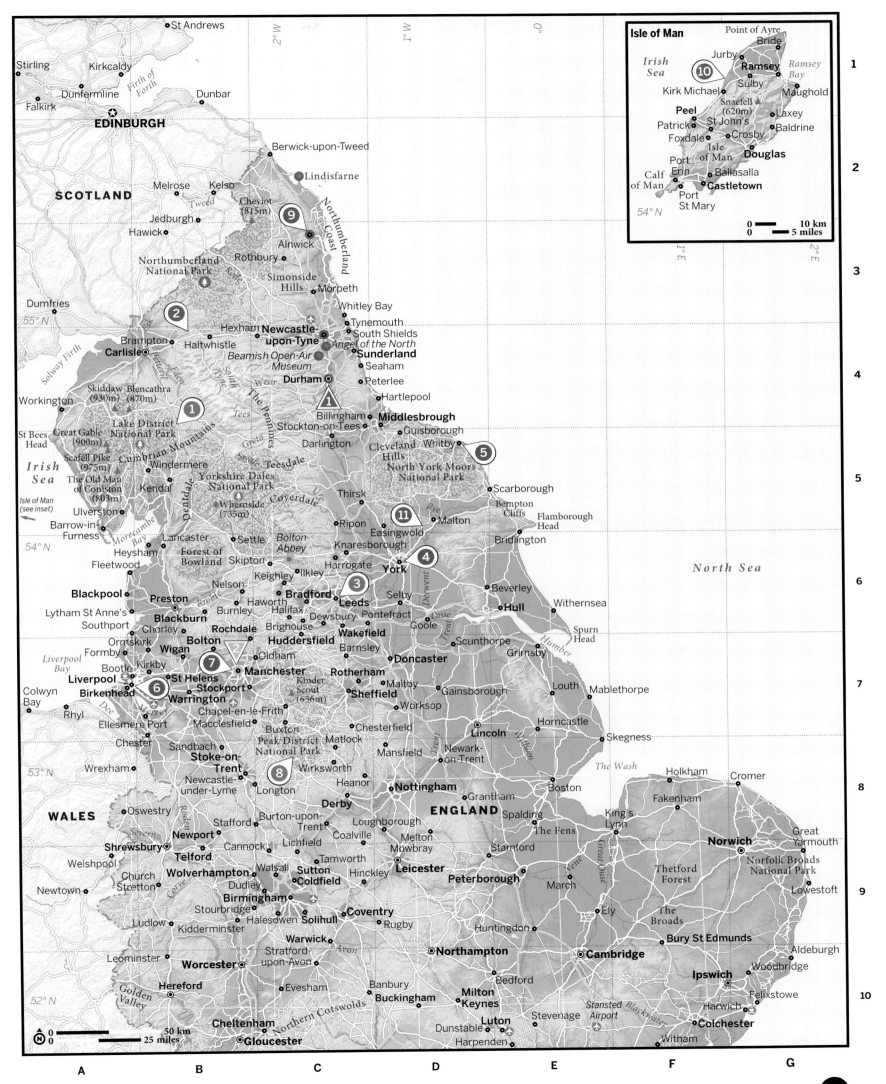

Isle of Man

Point of Ayre

Irish Sea

Jurby
Bride
Ramsey
Ramsey Bay
⑩
Sulby
Maughold
Kirk Michael
Snaefell
(620m)
Laxey
Peel
St John's
Baldrine
Patrick
Crosby
Foxdale
Isle
of Man
Douglas
Port
Erin
Ballasalla
Calf of Man
Port
St Mary
Castletown

54° N

0 ——— 10 km
0 ——— 5 miles

St Andrews

Stirling
Kirkcaldy
Firth of Forth
Dunbar
Dunfermline
Falkirk
EDINBURGH

Berwick-upon-Tweed

SCOTLAND
Melrose
Kelso
●Lindisfarne

Tweed
Jedburgh
Cheviot
(815m)
⑨
Hawick
Alnwick

Northumberland
National Park
Rothbury
Simonside
Hills
Morpeth

Northumberland Coast

Whitley Bay

Dumfries
②
Hexham
Tynemouth
South Shields

Brampton
Haltwhistle
Newcastle-upon-Tyne
Angel of the North
Sunderland

Carlisle
Beamish Open-Air Museum
Seaham

Solway Firth
South Tyne
Wear
Durham ⊙
Peterlee

Workington
Skiddaw
(930m)
Blencathra
(870m)
①①
Hartlepool

Great Gable
(900m)
Lake District National Park
The Pennines
Billingham
Middlesbrough

St Bees
Head
Scafell Pike
(975m)
Cumbrian Mountains
Stockton-on-Tees
Guisborough

Irish Sea
Windermere
Greta
Darlington
Cleveland
Hills
Whitby
⑤

The Old Man
of Coniston
(803m)
Teesdale
Swale
Teesdale
North York Moors National Park

Kendal
Yorkshire Dales
National Park
Scarborough

Ulverston
Whernside
(735m)
Coverdale
Ure
Thirsk
⑪
Bempton
Cliffs

Barrow-in-Furness
Morecambe Bay
Ripon
Easingwold
Rye
Malton
Flamborough
Head

54° N
Lancaster
Settle
Knaresborough
Bridlington

Heysham
Forest of
Bowland
Skipton
Harrogate
③
York
④

Fleetwood
Nelson
Keighley
Ilkley
North Sea

Blackpool
Preston
Bradford
Leeds
Selby
Beverley

Lytham St Anne's
Burnley
Halifax
Dewsbury
Pontefract
Hull

Southport
Haworth
Brighouse
Wakefield
Goole
Withernsea

Blackburn
Rochdale
Huddersfield
Barnsley
Ouse
Trent
Humber
Spurn
Head

Chorley
Bolton
Oldham
Doncaster
Scunthorpe
Grimsby

Ormskirk
Wigan
⑦②
Manchester
Rotherham
Maltby
Gainsborough
Louth
Mablethorpe

Formby
Kirkby
St Helens
Stockport
Kinder
Scout
(636m)
Sheffield
Worksop
Horncastle

Liverpool Bay
Bootle
⑥
Warrington
Chapel-en-le-Frith
Lincoln
Skegness

Liverpool
Birkenhead
Mersey
Macclesfield
Chesterfield
Newark-
on-Trent

Colwyn
Bay
Rhyl
Ellesmere Port
Buxton
Matlock
Witham
The Wash

Dee
Chester
Sandbach
Peak District National Park
Mansfield
Holkham
Cromer

Wrexham
Stoke-on-Trent
Wirksworth
Boston
Fakenham

53° N
Newcastle-
under-Lyme
Heanor
Nottingham
Grantham
King's
Lynn
Great
Yarmouth

WALES
Oswestry
⑧
Longton
Derby
Spalding
The Fens
Norwich

Stafford
Burton-upon-
Trent
Loughborough
Nene
Norfolk Broads
National Park

Welshpool
Newport
Shrewsbury ⊙
Cannock
Lichfield
Coalville
Melton
Mowbray
Stamford
Thetford
Forest
Lowestoft

Church
Stretton
Telford
Walsall
Tamworth
Leicester
ENGLAND
March
Great Ouse
Blackwater
The
Broads

Newtown
Wolverhampton
Dudley
Hinckley
Peterborough
Ely
Bury St Edmunds
Aldeburgh

Birmingham
**Sutton
Coldfield**
Avon
Huntingdon
Woodbridge

Ludlow
Stourbridge
Halesowen
Solihull
Coventry
Rugby
Northampton
Cambridge
Ipswich
Felixstowe

Kidderminster
Warwick
Bedford
Stansted
Airport
Harwich

Leominster
Stratford-
upon-Avon
Banbury
**Milton
Keynes**
Colchester

Worcester ⊙
Evesham
Buckingham
Stevenage
Witham

52° N
Hereford
*Golden
Valley*
Northern Cotswolds
Cheltenham
Luton
Dunstable
Harpenden

Gloucester ⊙

0 ——— 50 km
0 ——— 25 miles

A   B   C   D   E   F   G

1 2 3 4 5 6 7 8 9 10

SIGHTS &
ACTIVITIES

 SEE

DO

ITINERARY

▽ 1

▽ 2

① Bath

Bath's grand Georgian architecture – exemplified by the Royal Crescent, a terrace of town houses built between 1767 and 1775 – and one of the world's best-preserved Roman bathhouses have been drawing attention since the 18th century. The heart of Bath's Roman spa is the geothermally heated Great Bath.

② Oxford

The world's most famed university city is a wonderful place to wander. The elegant honey-toned buildings of the scattered colleges (not all are open to the public) wrap around tranquil courtyards, and spires twirl into the sky. Parks, pubs, rivers and museums, especially the Ashmolean and the Pitt Rivers, round out a weekend.

③ The Cotswolds

This tangle of golden villages, thatched cottages and old mansions of honey-coloured stone rolls across gentle hills and fields. Handsome Stow-on-the-Wold is still an important market town; Painswick is one of the Cotswold's most unspoiled towns; and bucolic Slad was the home of author Laurie Lee.

④ Stratford-upon-Avon

William Shakespeare was born in Stratford in 1564 and died here in 1616. Take in a play by the world-famous Royal Shakespeare Company at one of several theatres, where Lawrence Olivier, Judi Dench and Patrick Stewart have trodden the boards.

⑤ Cambridge

The tight-packed core of ancient colleges features such gems as Trinity College's Tudor gateway and vast Great Court, Kings College's Gothic chapel (its choir sings evensong during term time) and the Bridge of Sighs. 'The Backs' along the River Cam offer green spaces.

⑥ Stonehenge

Britain's most iconic archaeological site is not just a ring of monolithic stones but part of a complex of ancient monuments. No one knows for sure what drove prehistoric Britons to start building it around 3000BC, or how they managed to drag massive stones from many miles away.

⑦ Cornwall's North Coast

Immerse yourself in the classic Cornish combination of cliffs, sandy bays and white-horse surf. Newquay is the surfy, party hub but the coast also includes atmospheric Arthurian Tintagel Castle and the culinary capital of Padstow.

⑧ Portsmouth Historic Dockyard

The city's maritime heritage features three historic ships: HMS Victory was Lord Nelson's flagship at the Battle of Trafalgar (1805). The raising of the 16th-century warship the Mary Rose revealed Henry VIII's favourite ship. HMS Warrior is a floating Victorian-era fortress.

⑨ Brighton

Raves on the beach, Graham Greene, mods and rockers, party weekends, Green politics and the UK's biggest gay scene: bohemian Brighton is where Britain's seaside experience turns cool. Hit the Lanes for eclectic shopping.

⑩ Windsor Castle

The world's largest and oldest continuously occupied fortress, a vision of battlements and towers, is one of the Queen's principal residences. Take a tour of the gilded State Apartments and elegant chapels. The Changing of the Guard at 11am is a fabulous spectacle.

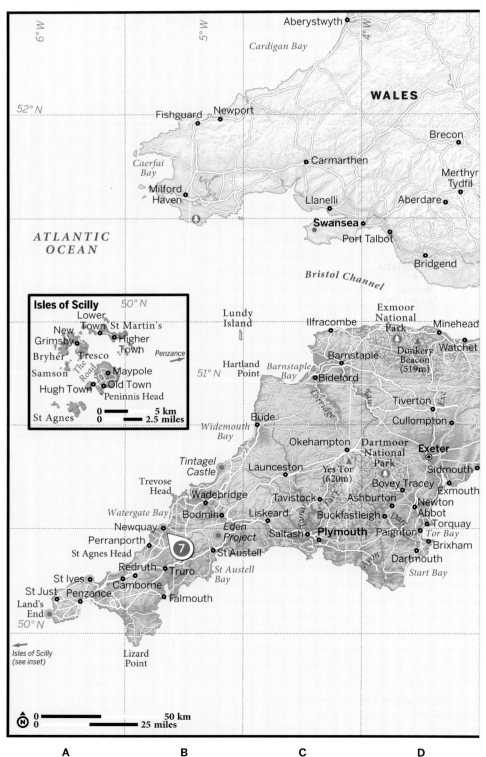

4-day itinerary
The Southeast

Leave **London** by its southwestern corner – both rail and road connections are good here. Head first for Jane Austen's house at **Chawton** and the collection of women's writing at nearby Chawton House Library. Continue southwest to **Winchester**, capital of an ancient kingdom. The beautiful cathedral is Jane Austen's resting place. Now bear east through the towns and villages of the South Downs National Park, stopping at **Singleton's** open-air museum of historic buildings and **Chichester**, a city with bracing beach walks on its doorstep. Continue to bohemian **Brighton** for a night out, then visit **Beachy Head**'s white cliffs – next stop France – before returning north to London.

10-day itinerary
The Southwest

The southwest of England takes some effort to reach, but repays in full with a green landscape of hills and moors, surrounded by sparkling seas. Start in **Bristol**, an enthralling port city, then saunter down through Somerset to **Glastonbury** – famous for its annual music festival and the best place to stock up on candles or crystals at any time of year. South of here is Dorset, where highlights include picturesque **Shaftesbury**. West is heathery **Exmoor National Park**, then it's onwards into Devon, where there's a choice of coasts, as well as **Dartmoor National Park**, which contains the highest hills in southern England. Cross into Cornwall to explore the space-age biodomes of the **Eden Project**. Nearby, but in another era entirely, is **Tintagel Castle**, the legendary birthplace of King Arthur. Depending on your tastes, you can hang ten in surf-flavoured party town **Newquay**, or browse the art galleries at **St Ives**. **Land's End** is the natural finish to this wild west meander, where the English mainland comes to a full stop. Sink a drink in the First & Last Inn at nearby Sennen.

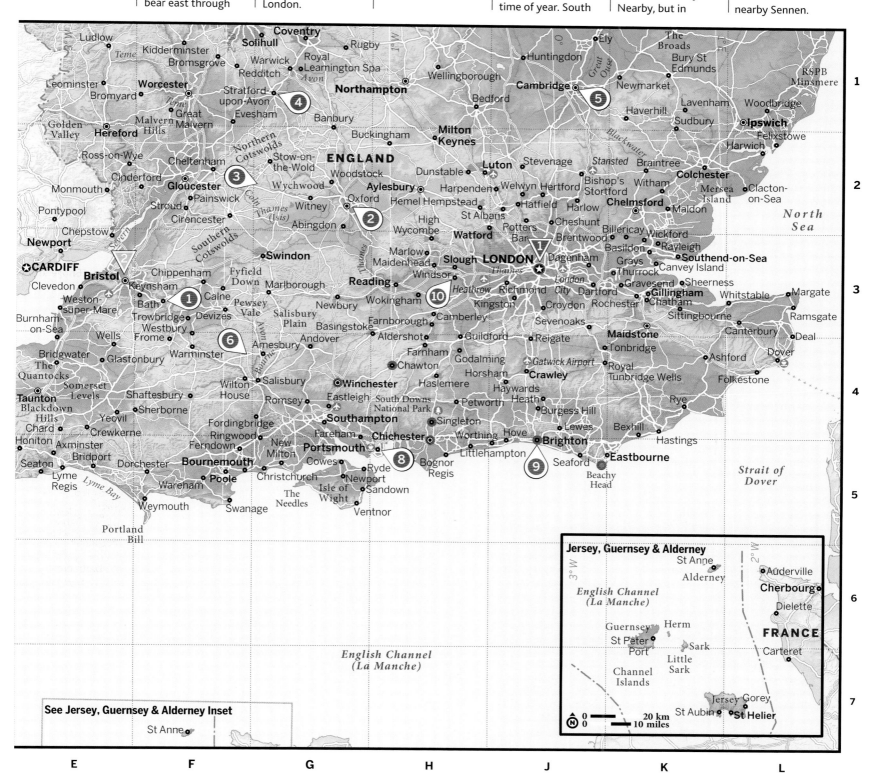

SIGHTS & ACTIVITIES

 SEE
 DO

ITINERARY

▽ 1
▽ 2

Snowdonia National Park: Mt Snowdon is the highest peak in Wales and England.

Cardiff Castle
Compact Cardiff, the Welsh capital since 1955, is caught between an ancient fort and an ultramodern waterfront. Once owned by the Bute family, this is a collection of disparate castles scattered around a green, encompassing practically the whole history of Cardiff, from its Norman shell keep and the 13th-century Black Tower to the faux-Gothic towers and turrets added by the third Marquess of Bute.

Isle of Anglesey Coastal Path
At 276 sq miles, the Isle of Anglesey is Wales' largest island and almost all of its coast has been designated as an Area of Outstanding Natural Beauty. Explore it on the Isle of Anglesey Coastal Path, a waymarked 125-mile route passing through a watery landscape of coastal heath, salt marsh, clifftops and beaches.

Tintern Abbey
For 200 years travellers have visited the misty River Wye as it meanders along the border with England, where the haunting ruins of Tintern Abbey inspired poets and artists such as Wordsworth and Turner. The sprawling monastic complex was founded in 1131 by the Cistercian order and occupied until Henry VIII evicted the monks in 1536.

Snowdonia National Park
From Mt Snowdon's 1085m summit, the views stretch to Ireland over fine ridges that swoop down to sheltered *cwms* (valleys) and deep lakes. Six paths of varying length and difficulty lead to the top, all taking around six

hours return (the most straightforward is the Llanberis Path). If you're not able to climb a mountain, those industrious Victorians have gifted an alternative: the Snowdon Mountain Railway.

St David's Cathedral
Charismatic St Davids, Britain's smallest city, surrounded on three sides by sea, has a magnificent 12th-century cathedral that marks Wales' holiest site: the birth and burial place of the nation's patron saint. St Davids has been a place of pilgrimage for 1500 years. Hidden in a hollow, the cathedral is intentionally unassuming but the atmosphere inside is one of great antiquity.

Hay-on-Wye
Hay-on-Wye – an attractive town on the banks of the River Wye – hosts, in the words of Bill Clinton, 'the Woodstock of the mind', a festival of literature and culture founded in 1988 that has expanded to cover all aspects of the creative arts.

Conwy Castle
A visit to Britain's most complete walled town should be high on the itinerary for anyone with a crush on things historic. Caernarfon is more complete, Harlech more dramatically positioned and Beaumaris more

technically perfect, yet out of the four castles that comprise the Unesco World Heritage Site, Conwy is the prettiest to gaze upon. Its crenellated turrets and towers call to mind fairy tales rather than subjugation.

Carreg Cennen, Brecon Beacons
On the western edge of the Brecon Beacons National Park, with its mountain plateaus of grass and heather rising above wooded, waterfall-splashed valleys, lie the brooding ruins of Wales' ultimate romantic castle, dating back to Edward I's conquest of Wales in the late 13th century.

Portmeirion
Is this a surreal dream vision or an actual village? Set on its own tranquil peninsula, Portmeirion is a fantastical collection of buildings with an Italian influence, masterminded by the Welsh architect Sir Clough Williams-Ellis. Starting in 1925, he collected bits and pieces from disintegrating mansions and set them alongside his own creations at this weird and wonderful seaside utopia. It was the set for cult TV series, *The Prisoner*, and hosts the acclaimed Festival No.6.

Pembrokeshire Coast National Park
The Pembrokeshire coast is a living geology lesson: stratified limestone is pushed up vertically and then eroded into arches, blowholes and sea stacks; red and grey cliffs play leapfrog with sandy beaches. Watersports are a big deal along this wild, rugged coastline with sailing, surfing, windsurfing, kite surfing, diving and kayaking operators, as well as Pembrokeshire's home-grown invention, coasteering.

6-day itinerary
North Wales

Start in historic **Ruthin** and take the back road south through the Clwydian Range to **Llangollen** and its World Heritage-listed aqueduct. From here, head west on the A5, swapping Denbighshire for Snowdonia National Park. **Betws-y-Coed** is a pretty base for walks and mountain biking. Shadow the River Conwy north, pausing at Bodnant

Estate and Garden before the quaint town of **Llandudno**. Hop to **Conwy** to find a medieval world between its walls. The A55 hugs the coast as it bears southwest past Bangor. Cross the Menai Strait to the Isle of Anglesey; stay at **Beaumaris** and circle the druids' sacred island. Then loop back to **Llanberis** to ascend Mt Snowdon by foot or train.

9-day itinerary
South Wales

Head west from the Welsh capital **Cardiff** to **Swansea** for a Dylan Thomas fix. Then spend a day on the beach-lined **Gower Peninsula** before proceeding to ancient **Carmarthen**, Merlin's town. Settle into the seaside vibe at candy-striped **Tenby**, Wales' most appealing resort town and the gateway to **Pembrokeshire Coast National**

Park. Check out the mighty castle at Pembroke and head on through Haverfordwest and the pretty port of **Solva** to **St Davids**, a sweet city in a magical setting. Near beachy Newport, neolithic and Iron Age sites await discovery in the surrounding hills. From **Cardigan**, follow the Teifi Valley along the border of Ceredigion,

stopping at **Cenarth** and the National Woollen Museum. There are gardens, manor houses and castles to explore here. Head on to the market town of **Llandovery**. Cross the River Usk and cut down towards **Blaenavon**, a small town with a coal-mining legacy. Backtrack to **Abergavenny**, home to good country restaurants and pubs.

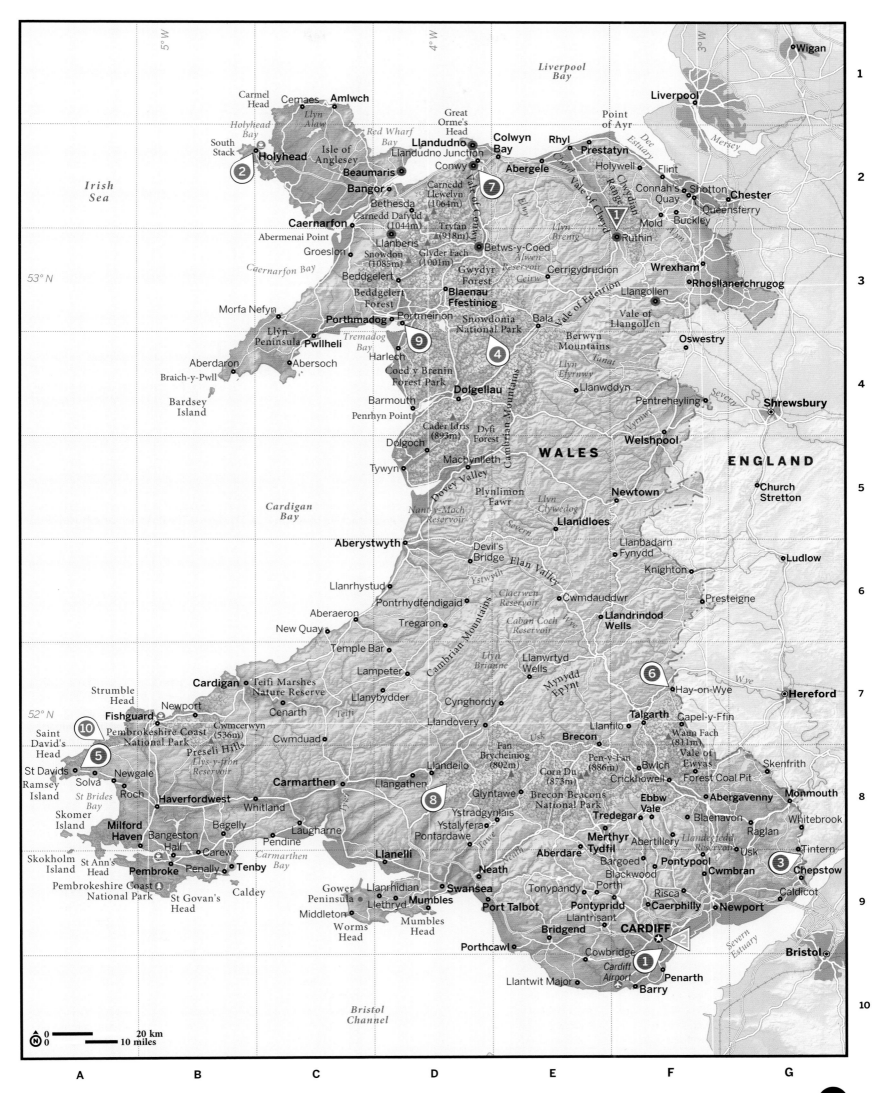

Wigan

Liverpool Bay

Liverpool

Carmel Head
Cemaes
Amlwch
Llyn Alaw
Holyhead Bay
Red Wharf Bay
Great Orme's Head
Point of Ayr
Llandudno
Colwyn Bay
Rhyl
Prestatyn
Dee Estuary
South Stack
Holyhead
Isle of Anglesey
Llandudno Junction
Conwy
Abergele
Holywell
Flint
Connah's Quay
Shotton
Chester
Beaumaris
Bangor
Vale of Conwy
Chwydian Range
Vale of Clwyd
Mold
Buckley
Queensferry
Carnedd Llewelyn (1064m)
Bethesda
Caernarfon
Carnedd Dafydd (1044m)
Tryfan (918m)
Betws-y-Coed
Elwy
Llyn Brenig
Ruthin
Connah's Quay
Wrexham
Abermenai Point
Groeslon
Llanberis
Snowdon (1085m)
Glyder Fach (1001m)
Gwydyr Forest
Cerrigydrudion
Rhosllanerchrugog
Caernarfon Bay
Beddgelert
Blaenau Ffestiniog
Reservoir Ceirw
Alwen
Llangollen
Oswestry
Morfa Nefyn
Beddgelert Forest
Portmeirion
Snowdonia National Park
Bala
Vale of Edeirion
Vale of Llangollen
Porthmadog
Llangollen
Llŷn Peninsula
Pwllheli
Tremadog Bay
Harlech
Berwyn Mountains
Aberdaron
Abersoch
Coed y Brenin Forest Park
Llanwddyn
Pentreheyling
Shrewsbury
Braich-y-Pwll
Barmouth
Dolgellau
Cambrian Mountains
Llyn Efyrnwy
Tanat
Bardsey Island
Penrhyn Point
Cader Idris (893m)
Dyfi Forest
WALES
Welshpool
Severn
53° N
Dolgoch
Machynlleth
Newtown
ENGLAND
Tywyn
Dovey Valley
Cambrian Mountains
Church Stretton
Cardigan Bay
Plynlimon Fawr
Llyn Clywedog
Nant-y-Moch Reservoir
Severn
Llanidloes
Aberystwyth
Devil's Bridge
Llanbadarn Fynydd
Ludlow
Llanrhystud
Elan Valley
Ystwyth
Knighton
Pontrhydfendigaid
Claerwen Reservoir
Cwmdauddwr
Presteigne
Aberaeron
Tregaron
Caban Coch Reservoir
Llandrindod Wells
New Quay
Cambrian Mountains
Wye
Temple Bar
Llyn Brianne
Lampeter
Llanwrtyd Wells
Hay-on-Wye
Hereford
Cardigan
Teifi Marshes Nature Reserve
Cynghordy
Mynydd Epynt
Strumble Head
Cenarth
Teifi
Llandovery
Talgarth
Capel-y-Ffin
52° N
Newport
Llanybydder
Llanfilo
Fishguard
Cwmcerwyn (536m)
Cwmduad
Llandeilo
Brecon
Waun Fach (811m)
Saint David's Head
Pembrokeshire Coast National Park
Preseli Hills
Llangathen
Fan Brycheiniog (802m)
Corn Du (873m)
Pen-y-Fan (886m)
Bwlch
Vale of Ewyas
Skenfrith
St Davids
Llys-y-frân Reservoir
Crickhowell
Forest Coal Pit
Solva
Newgale
Carmarthen
Glyntawe
Brecon Beacons National Park
Ramsey Island
Roch
Haverfordwest
Whitland
Ystradgynlais
Ebbw Vale
Abergavenny
Monmouth
Skomer Island
Begelly
Pendine
Pontardawe
Merthyr Tydfil
Blaenavon
Raglan
Whitebrook
Milford Haven
Bangeston Hall
Carew
Carmarthen Bay
Ystalyfera
Abertillery
Llandegfedd Reservoir
Usk
Tintern
Skokholm Island
St Ann's Head
Penally
Tenby
Llanelli
Aberdare
Tredegar
Bargoed
Pontypool
Cwmbran
Chepstow
Pembroke
Caldey
Gower Peninsula
Llanrhidian
Tawe
Tonypandy
Blackwood
Caldicot
Pembrokeshire Coast National Park
St Govan's Head
Llethryd
Mumbles
Swansea
Neath
Neath
Porth
Risca
Caerphilly
Newport
Middleton
Port Talbot
Llantrisant
Llantrisant
Pontypridd
Worms Head
Mumbles Head
Bridgend
CARDIFF
Severn Estuary
Bristol
Porthcawl
Cowbridge
Penarth
Llantwit Major
Cardiff Airport
Barry

Irish Sea

Bristol Channel

0   20 km
0   10 miles
N

SIGHTS & ACTIVITIES

◉ SEE
◉ DO

ITINERARY

▽ 1
▽ 2

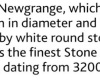

① Brú na Bóinne, County Meath
This Neolithic necropolis – the Boyne Palace – houses tombs across several sites, including Newgrange, which is a grass dome 80m in diameter and 13m high supported by white round stone walls. Beneath is the finest Stone Age tomb in Ireland, dating from 3200BC.

② Wicklow
South of Dublin, the Military Rd marches along the spine of the wild Wicklow Mountains, crossing gorse-, bracken- and heather-clad moors, bogs and hills, dotted with corrie lakes. Hiking trails head into the hills. Here, haunting Glendalough (Gleann dá Loch, 'Valley of the Two Lakes') is a significant monastic site, founded in the late 6th century by St Kevin.

③ Galway City
The brightly painted pubs of arty Galway (Gaillimh) heave with live music: Róisín Dubh is the best place for bands; Tig Cóilí excels at trad sessions. Although steeped in history, the city buzzes with a contemporary vibe, thanks in part to students. It was designated the European Capital of Culture for 2020.

④ Connemara
The filigreed coast of Connemara ('Inlets of the Sea') features stunning hidden beaches and seaside hamlets. Its beautiful interior, traversed by the N59, is a kaleidoscope of rusty bogs, lonely valleys and shimmering black lakes, laced by stone walls. Hiking and biking trails abound but hiring a tour guide may aid appreciation of the region.

The Giant's Causeway: The hexagonal basalt columns were formed by molten lava from the planet's core.

⑤ The Giant's Causeway
When you see this rock formation you'll realise why the ancients believed the close-packed stone columns were the work of giants. Reach Northern Ireland's only Unesco World Heritage site via a 45-minute stroll from Bushmills.

⑥ Aran Islands
These isles have a desolate beauty, with wildflowers, grazing livestock and surf-pounded cliffs. Ancient forts here are some of Ireland's oldest archaeological sites. Visit for a day or explore for longer: Inishmore (Irish: Inis Mór) is home to the only town, Kilronan. Inishmaan (Inis Meáin) preserves age-old traditions, and Inisheer (Inis Oírr), the smallest island, has a sense of enchantment.

⑦ Cliffs of Moher, County Clare
Sunsets seen from these 214m-tall cliffs turn the sky shades of amethyst, rose-pink and garnet-red. Their fame brings crowds, but heading south, past the Moher Wall, a 5.5km trail runs along the cliffs to Hag's Head – few venture this far, yet the views are uninhibited.

⑧ The Burren
Stretching across northern Clare, this limestone plateau has fantastic opportunities for walking and climbing. Its villages include the music hub of Doolin and charming Ballyvaughan; south lies a dolmen, the Portal Tomb.

⑨ Strandhill
Surfing is the main draw for many visitors to this long, red-gold beach and its great Atlantic rollers. Surf schools offer tuition and gear. There are also excellent walks along the beach.

⑩ Skellig Michael
George Bernard Shaw described Skellig Michael as the most fantastic rock in the world. Its landscape made it a perfect Jedi temple in recent Star Wars movies. Skellig Michael (Archangel Michael's Rock) is the larger of the two Skellig Islands and a Unesco World Heritage site: Christian monks survived here from the 6th to the 13th century.

⑪ Dingle Peninsula
A highlight of the Wild Atlantic Way, the Dingle Peninsula (Corca Dhuibhne) is the Irish mainland's westernmost point. Fuchsia-fringed *boreens* (lanes) link prehistoric ring forts and beehive huts; early Christian chapels, crosses and holy wells; hamlets and abandoned villages. It is a beacon for creative types.

⑫ Titanic Quarter, Belfast
Belfast's shipyards are transformed and the star of this sleek quarter is the prow-shaped edifice of the Titanic Belfast centre, covering the ill-fated liner's construction here. The list of attractions includes beautifully restored Victorian architecture, a glittering waterfront and a fantastic food scene.

▽1

3-day itinerary Around Dublin

Venture out of Dublin for seaside towns, monastic ruins and palatial 18th-century mansions. From the pretty port of **Howth** (take a stroll first) drive north to **Brú na Bóinne**, a pre-Celtic necropolis. Return south to **Celbridge** and magnificent Castletown House, Ireland's largest Georgian estate, commissioned by its wealthiest man.

South, in the town of **Blessington**, is Russborough House, another Palladian pleasure palace. Turning southeast, **Glendalough** is a spectacular glacial valley with an important monastic site. North towards Dublin, **Enniskerry** is home to Powerscourt Estate. Finish at **Sandycove**, a smart suburb of Dublin with beaches and good restaurants.

▽2

5-day itinerary Around Galway

From the busker-packed streets of **Galway** city, this route takes you around County Clare and the Aran Islands to trad music pubs and venues. After catching some *céilidhs* in Galway, drive south to **Ennis**, a medieval town bursting with musical pubs; if you have time, take a class in music or dance at Cois na hAbhna. Turn west to **Miltown Malbay**, a Victorian resort with beautiful walks along isolated beaches. Northeast is **Ennistimon**, a characterful country village with several old pubs and live music. Loop towards Doolin, a centre of Irish music thanks to a trio of lively pubs, via the towns of **Kilfenora** and **Lisdoonvarna**. You'll want to enjoy **Doolin's** tuneful diversions before taking a ferry to **Inishmór** in the Aran Islands. Sing songs as the turf fires warm the pub, and seek out the ancient fort of **Dún Aengus**. Wind up on **Inisheer**, the smallest of the Arans, with its mystical air and end-of-the-world landscapes. The *bodhrán* (traditional Irish drum) rules here with a summer school every June.

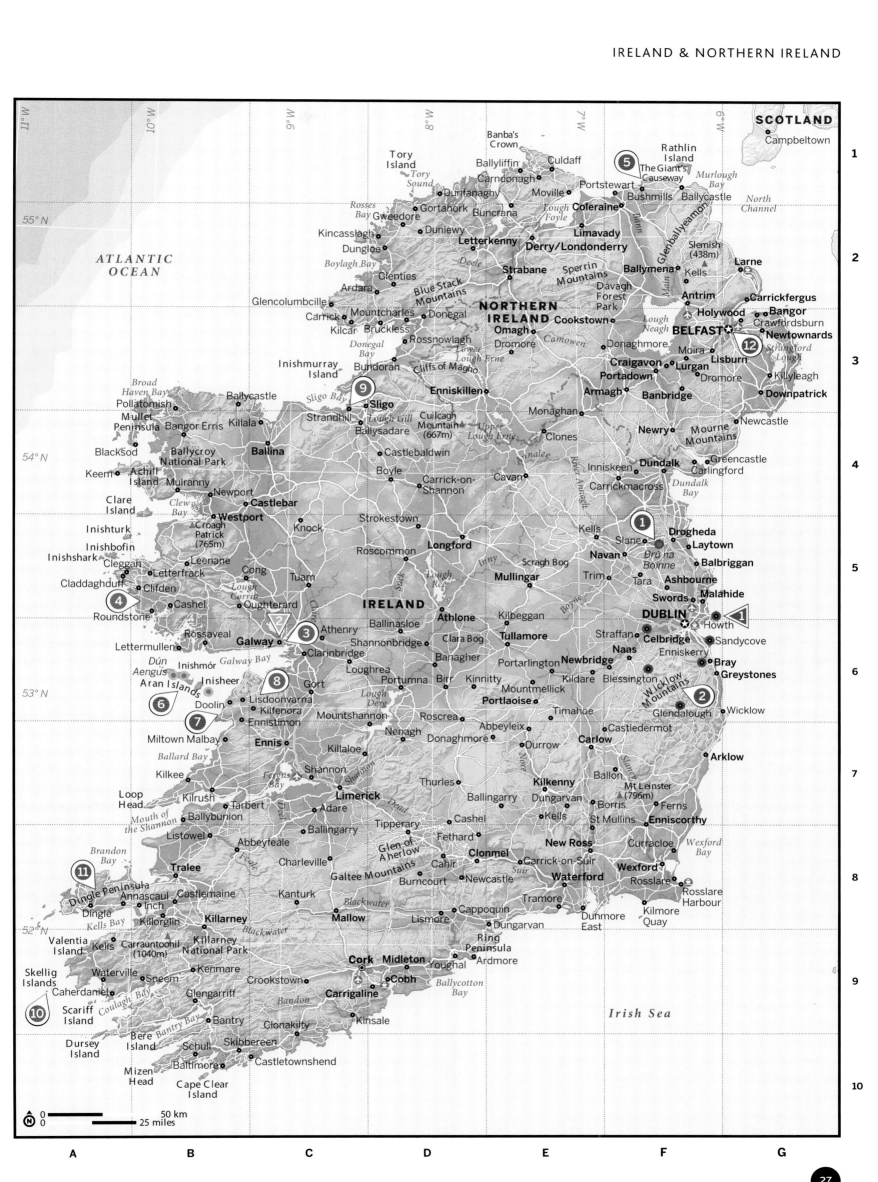

SCOTLAND
Campbeltown

1

Banba's
Crown
Tory
Island
Ballyliffin
Culdaff
Rathlin
Island
5
The Giant's
Causeway
Murlough
Bay
*Tory
Sound*
Carndonagh
Moville
Portstewart
Bushmills
Ballycastle
*North
Channel*

Dunfanaghy
Gortahork
Buncrana
Coleraine

*Rosses
Bay*
Gweedore
*Lough
Foyle*

ATLANTIC
OCEAN

55° N
Kincasslagh
Dunlewy
Letterkenny
Limavady
Slemish
(438m)
Larne

Dungloe
Derry/Londonderry
Ballymena
Kells

2

Boylagh Bay
Glenties
Strabane
Sperrin
Mountains
Davagh
Forest
Park
Antrim
Carrickfergus

Ardara
Blue Stack
Mountains
Donegal
NORTHERN
IRELAND
Cookstown
Holywood
Bangor
Crawfordsburn

Glencolumbcille
Carrick
Mountcharles
Omagh
Donaghmore
BELFAST
Newtownards
12

Kilcar
Bruckless
*Lough
Neagh*
Moira
Lisburn
*Strangford
Lough*

Pollatomish
Killala
Rossnowlagh
Dromore
Craigavon
Lurgan
Dromore
Killyleagh

3

*Donegal
Bay*
Bundoran
Cliffs of Magho
*Lower
Lough Erne*
Portadown
Banbridge
Downpatrick

Mullet
Peninsula
Bangor Erris
Inishmurray
Island
9
Sligo
Enniskillen
Armagh
Newry
Newcastle

Blacksod
Strandhill
Lough Gill
Cuilcagh
Mountain
(667m)
*Upper
Lough Erne*
Monaghan
Mourne
Mountains
Greencastle

54° N
Keem
Achill
Island
Ballycroy
National Park
Mulranny
Ballina
Ballysadare
Castlebaldwin
Clones
Inniskeen
Dundalk
Carlingford

4

Clare
Island
Newport
Castlebar
Boyle
Carrick-on-
Shannon
Cavan
River Anagh
Carrickmacross
*Dundalk
Bay*

Inishturk
*Clew
Bay*
Knock
Croagh
Patrick
(765m)
WESTPORT
Strokestown
Kells
1
Drogheda

Inishbofin
Inishshark
Cleggan
Letterfrack
Leenane
Cong
Roscommon
Longford
Scragh Bog
Navan
*Brú na
Bóinne*
Laytown

Claddaghduff
Clifden
*Lough
Corrib*
Tuam
Mullingar
Trim
Tara
Ashbourne
Balbriggan

5

4
Cashel
Oughterard
IRELAND
Athlone
Kilbeggan
Swords
Malahide

Roundstone
7
3
Athenry
Ballinasloe
Tullamore
Straffan
DUBLIN
Howth
1

Rossaveal
Galway
Clarinbridge
Shannonbridge
Clara Bog
Newbridge
Naas
Celbridge
Sandycove

Lettermullen
Galway Bay
Gort
Loughrea
Banagher
Portarlington
Kildare
Enniskerry
Bray

Dún
Aengus
Inishmór
Inisheer
8
Doolin
Portumna
Birr
Kinnitty
Blessington
Glendalough
2
Greystones

Aran Islands
6
Lisdoonvarna
Kilfenora
*Lough
Derg*
Mountmellick
*Wicklow
Mountains*
Wicklow

53° N
7
Ennistimon
Mountshannon
Roscrea
Portlaoise
Timahoe
Castledermot

Miltown Malbay
Ennis
Killaloe
Nenagh
Abbeyleix
Durrow
Carlow
Arklow

Ballard Bay
Shannon
Donaghmore
Kilkenny
Ballon
Mt Leinster
(796m)

Kilkee
*Fergus
Bay*
Thurles
Ballingarry
Dungarvan
Borris
Ferns

Loop
Head
Kilrush
Tarbert
Limerick
Kells
St Mullins
Enniscorthy

7

*Mouth of
the Shannon*
Ballybunion
Adare
Tipperary
Cashel
Fethard
New Ross
Curracloe
*Wexford
Bay*

Listowel
Ballingarry
Cahir
Clonmel
Carrick-on-Suir
Waterford
Rosslare

*Brandon
Bay*
11
Tralee
Charleville
Glen of
Aherlow
Burncourt
Clonmel
Newcastle
Wexford
Rosslare
Harbour

8

Dingle Peninsula
Annascaul
Inch
Castlemaine
Kanturk
Galtee Mountains
Tramore
Kilmore
Quay

Dingle
Killorglin
Kells Bay
Blackwater
Lismore
Cappoquin
Dunmore
East

52° N
Valentia
Island
Kells
Carrauntoohil
(1040m)
Killarney
Mallow
Dungarvan

Skellig
Islands
Waterville
Sneem
Kenmare
Killarney
National Park
Crookstown
Blackwater
Ring
Peninsula
Ardmore

Caherdaniel
Glengarriff
Cork
Midleton
Youghal
*Ballycotton
Bay*

9

10
Scariff
Island
Coulagh Bay
Bantry Bay
Bantry
Clonakilty
Carrigaline
Cobh
Irish Sea

Dursey
Island
Bere
Island
Schull
Skibbereen
Kinsale

Mizen
Head
Baltimore
Castletownshend

10

Cape Clear
Island

0   50 km
0   25 miles
N

A   B   C   D   E   F   G

France & Benelux

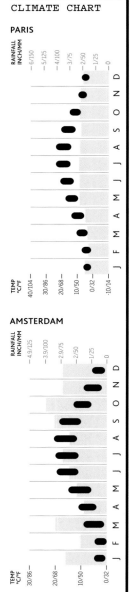

PARIS

RAINFALL INCH/MM

TEMP °C/°F

AMSTERDAM

RAINFALL INCH/MM

TEMP °C/°F

Combined, France, Belgium, Netherlands and Luxembourg (Benelux) represent world-class art and architecture; tumultuous history (ancient and modern); food and drink to delight every epicurean; exciting cities; and beautiful, varied landscapes. Highlights range from museums and monuments to rustic villages and national parks. Equally enthralling, however, are the distinct traditions and culture of every region across all four countries: it will be the local communities that supply some of the most memorable moments of a trip here. Geographically, France dominates the region with two major mountain ranges and a lengthy coastline. The hills subside in size through Belgium towards lowland Netherlands.

BEACHES
With a coastline embraced by the Atlantic (for surf and bracing dips) and the Mediterranean (for sun and swims), France's best beaches include Quiberon in Brittany, the Île d'Oléron, Biarritz and chic Plage des Sablettes at Menton on the Côte d'Azur.

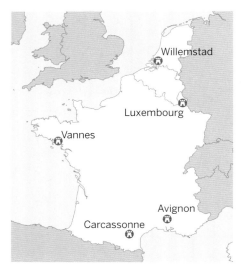

FORTIFIED TOWNS
If you love a well-built fort, this corner of Europe is for you. Star-shaped Willemstad in the Netherlands is a stand-out; Luxembourg is a defensive stronghold; Vannes is a well-preserved walled town; and Carcassone and Avignon in France's south amaze all.

WINE
Explore France's famed wine regions – such as the fizz of Champagne, ethereal Burgundy, Bordeaux's big names, the Rhône's reds and the deliciously strange but hip wines of the Jura – and you might meet the *vignerons* who make the wine.

CANALS
Give this region the time it deserves by slowing down and seeing it from a narrowboat on the pretty River Leie through Belgium; the Canal du Midi, Canal du Nivernais or the northern Canal de la Somme in France; or by floating the waterways of Amsterdam.

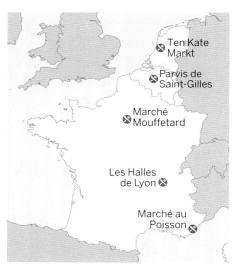

FOOD MARKETS
Taste local specialities at the region's best food markets, include Marché Mouffetard in Paris; the daily food market at Parvis de Saint-Gilles in Brussels; Ten Kate Markt in Amsterdam; renowned Les Halles de Lyon; and Marseille's Marché au Poisson.

GREAT OUTDOORS
Explore France's mountains and rivers: hit the French Alps around the Trois Vallées and climbing centre Chamonix for summer and winter sports. Hikers and bikers will love the Vosges, the Gorges du Verdon and the Parc National des Pyrénées.

Clockwise from top left: Pont de Pierre bridge in Bordeaux; tasting wine in Burgundy; Biarritz's beach; market treats.

Transport hubs

In one of the best-connected corners of Europe, state-of-the-art trains speed from city to city, crossing borders seamlessly. Major transport hubs include Paris and Brussels but all cities will have sophisticated train stations and online ticketing. Getting around by road may mean encountering congestion in this densely populated part of the continent. Tolls are also charged on many major routes. Parking also tends to be expensive and competitive. Most large cities have airports with low-cost airlines offering options for onward travel around Europe. Paris Charles de Gaulle and the Netherland's Schiphol airports are the international gateways for this region. Several ports along the coast link to the UK.

TRANSPORT

B6, C8, D5,
D9, E2, E3,
F2, F7, F9,
F10, G6, G9

A5, B4, B5,
C4, D3, D4,
E2, E3, E9,
F9, G9

Below: Beachfront Nice (left) at dusk and (right) looking along Groenburgwal canal in Amsterdam.

Amsterdam (see pp384-5 for city map)
Most visitors access Amsterdam via Schiphol International Airport, which has copious air links worldwide, including many low-cost European airlines. Trains arrive at Centraal Station, which has good links with several European cities.

Rotterdam
The Netherlands' huge international airport, Schiphol, is equidistant by high-speed train to both exhilarating Rotterdam and Amsterdam. The Hague Airport, serving 40 European destinations, is 6km northwest. Rotterdam Centraal Station has fast trains to Brussels, Paris and London.

Antwerp
Belgium's second city and biggest port is a capital of cool. Tiny Antwerp Airport, 4km southeast of the city and accessible on bus 14, has limited flights. But the gorgeous main train station, Antwerpen-Centraal, has high-speed services to the Netherlands and beyond.

Brussels
Belgium's fascinating capital is well-connected with its EU friends. Brussels Airport is 14km northeast of the centre. Bruxelles-Midi is the main station for international connections: the Eurostar and Thalys high-speed trains stop here.

Luxembourg City
One of Europe's most scenic capitals, draped across the deep gorges, Luxembourg can be easily reached by train, with good connections to northern Europe. Flights to and from Luxembourg's international airport are mostly limited to European hops.

Paris (see pp420-1 for city map)
Few roads don't lead to Paris, one of the most visited destinations on earth. Most major airlines fly through one of its three airports, and European train and bus routes cross it. It is the central point in the French rail network with six train stations that connect different parts of France and Europe. Most trains – and all Trains à Grande Vitesse (TGV) – require advance reservations.

Lyon
France's third largest city offers today's urban explorers a wealth of enticing experiences. Lyon-St-Exupéry Airport, 25km east of the city, has 40 airlines serving more than 100 destinations. There are two mainline train stations and a TGV station at the airport.

Toulouse
The enchanting old town of Toulouse is a gateway to the southwest. Eight kilometres northwest, Toulouse-Blagnac Airport has flights to Paris and other large French cities, as well as European hubs. The city is served by TGVs, which run east and west.

Nice
With its mix of real-city grit and old-world opulence, Nice is the unofficial capital of the Côte d'Azur. Nice-Côte d'Azur Airport is France's second airport and has flights to Europe, North Africa and the US. The city also has excellent train connections to almost everywhere on the coast, plus an excellent intercity bus service.

Map Labels

United Kingdom / Ireland area

Liverpool, Manchester, Hull, Nottingham, Leicester, Norwich, Birmingham, Cambridge, WALES, ENGLAND, Gloucester, Oxford, Colchester, Swansea, CARDIFF, Bristol, Bath, LONDON, Bristol Channel, Exeter, Southampton, Brighton, Bournemouth, Portsmouth, Plymouth, Dover, Irish Sea

English Channel (La Manche)

Netherlands / Belgium / Germany area

NORTH SEA, Frisian Islands, Waddenzee, Groningen, Emden, Bremer-haven, Bremen, Oldenburg, Leeuwarden, Lingen, Emmen, NETHERLANDS, Den Helder, Zwolle, Hengelo, Bielefeld, Alkmaar, Almere, Apeldoorn, Münster, AMSTERDAM, Utrecht, Amersfoort, GERMANY, Den Haag (The Hague), Arnhem, Rotterdam, Dordrecht, Duisburg, Dortmund, 's-Hertogenbosch, Breda, Venlo, Düsseldorf, Middelburg, Bergen op Zoom, Eindhoven, Essen, Ostend, Ghent, Antwerp, Genk, Cologne, Bruges, Leuven, Bonn, Wetzlar, Calais, Dunkirk, BRUSSELS, Liège, Koblenz, Kortrijk, BELGIUM, Lille, Namur, Wiesbaden, Arras, Mons, Charleroi, Bitburg, Mainz, Abbeville, St-Quentin, Bastogne, Trier, LUXEMBOURG, Amiens, Laon, Charleville-Mézières, Dieppe, Beauvais-Tillé, Soissons, Reims, LUXEMBOURG CITY, Saarbrücken, Compiègne, Verdun, Metz, Mannheim, Châlons-sur-Marne, St-Dizier, Nancy, Karlsruhe, Charles de Gaulle, Strasbourg, Orly, Offenburg, Freiburg, Mulhouse, Koblenz, Basel-Mulhouse-Freiburg, Basel

France area

Channel Islands, Guernsey, Jersey, Cherbourg, Le Havre, Rouen, Beauvais, Roscoff, St-Malo, Caen, Seine, PARIS, Brest, St-Brieuc, Chartres, Troyes, Quimper, Alençon, Sens, Rennes, Laval, Le Mans, Orléans, Auxerre, Lorient, Angers, Tours, FRANCE, Dijon, St-Nazaire, Nantes, Vierzon, Bourges, Besançon, Biel, BERN, Nantes-Atlantique, Loire, SWITZERLAND, Poitiers, Lausanne, La Rochelle, Montluçon, Mâcon, Thonon-les-Bains, Montreux, Limoges, Lyon, Geneva, Chamonix, Aosta, Angoulême, Clermont-Ferrand, Saint-Exupéry, Mont Blanc (4307m), Périgueux, Chambéry, Ivrea, Brive-la-Gaillarde, Grenoble, ALPS, ITALY, Bordeaux, Le Puy-en-Velay, Valence, Turin, Mérignac, Bergerac, Pinerolo, Bra, Garonne, Rodez, Orange, Cuneo, Montauban, Alès, San Remo, Blagnac, Albi, Nîmes, MONACO, Mont-de-Marsan, Arles, Aix-en-Provence, MONACO, Nice, Bayonne, Montpellier, Cannes, Côte d'Azur, Pau, Tarbes, Béziers, Marseille, TOULOUSE, Carcassonne, Narbonne, Toulon, Corsica (see p76), Bay of Biscay, PYRENEES, Golfe du Lion, MEDITERRANEAN SEA

Spain area

Santander, San Sebastián, Bilbao, Pamplona, Monte Perdido (3355m), Pico de Aneto (3404m), ANDORRA, ANDORRA LA VELLA, Vitoria, SPAIN, Jaca, Perpignan, Figueres, Burgos, Logroño, Huesca, Ebro

Page references

Page 45
Page 43
Pages 32-33
Page 35
Pages 40-41
Page 39
Pages 36-37

0 — 200 km
0 — 100 miles

SIGHTS &
ACTIVITIES

 SEE

DO

ITINERARY

▽ 1

▽ 2

Rouen

With its soaring Gothic cathedral, beautifully restored medieval quarter, excellent museums and vibrant cultural life, Rouen is one of Normandy's most engaging destinations. The city's main throughfare in the old city runs from the cathedral west to Place du Vieux Marché and is where 19-year-old Joan of Arc was executed for heresy in 1431.

Bayeux

The celebrated and embroidered Bayeaux Tapestry, commissioned for the opening of Bayeux cathedral in 1077, depicts the conquest of England by William the Conqueror in 1066 from an unashamedly Norman perspective. The 68.3m-long cartoon strip tells the dramatic, bloody tale with verve and vividness.

Mont St-Michel

One of France's most iconic images is the slender spires, stout ramparts and rocky slopes of Mont St-Michel rising dramatically from the sea – or towering over sands laid bare by the receding tide. The bay around Mont St-Michel is famed for having Europe's highest tidal variations; the difference between low and high tides – only about six hours apart – can reach 15m.

Le Havre

A Unesco World Heritage Site, Le Havre is a love letter to modernism, evoking, more than any other French city, France's postwar energy and optimism. The 107m-high Église St-Joseph was built with concrete from 1951 to 1959. Some 13,000 panels of coloured glass make the interior particularly striking when it's sunny.

St-Malo

The enthralling mast-filled port town of St-Malo has a dramatically changing landscape with one of the world's greatest tidal ranges. Château de St-Malo holds the Musée d'Histoire de St-Malo, which looks at the life and history of the city.

Carnac

Predating Stonehenge by around 100 years, the Carnac (Garnag in Breton)

area offers the world's greatest concentration of megalithic sites. There are 3000 of these upright stones, erected between 5000 and 3500 BC.

Pointe de Pen-Hir

Three kilometres southwest of Camaret, this headland is bounded by sea cliffs. On a peninsula known for breathtaking scenery, this might be the most impressive lookout of them all.

Côte d'Albâtre

Stretching for 130km, the vertical, bone-white cliffs of the Côte d'Albâtre

(Alabaster Coast) are strikingly reminiscent of the limestone cliffs of Dover, just across the Channel. On the plateau above the cliffs, walkers can follow the long-distance GR21 hiking trail, which runs parallel to the coast from Le Tréport to Le Havre.

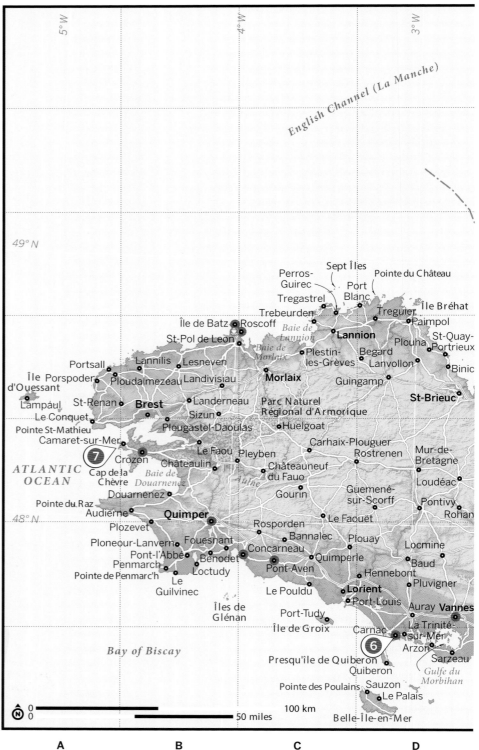

D-Day Beaches

A guided minibus tour can be an excellent way to get a sense of the D-Day beaches and their place in history. Tours by Le Mémorial – Un Musée pour la Paix depart from the museum and take in Pointe du Hoc, Omaha Beach, the American cemetery and the artificial port at Arromanches.

8-day itinerary
Breton Coast

On this maritime-flavoured drive, taking you from St-Malo to Vannes, you'll experience serene seaside towns, sparkling beaches, dramatic storm-lashed headlands and the world's greatest concentration of megalithic sites. Start in **St-Malo** where you can stroll along the ramparts for panoramic views over the walled city. Via the charming old town in **Dinan** take the slow coastal road to **Roscoff**, from where you can set sail for the peaceful **Île de Batz**. Your next stop is the **Crozon Peninsula**, one of the most scenic spots in Brittany. Carry on to **Quimper**, **Concarneau** and **Pont-Aven** before reaching **Carnac**. With its enticing beaches and a pretty town centre, Carnac would be a popular tourist town even without its collection of magnificent megalithic sites, which predate Stonehenge by around 100 years. From here, opt for the beautiful coastal route to Carnac Plage and La Trinité-sur-Mer then head inland to Auray. Make your way to the arty and alternative streets of **Vannes**, and explore the web of narrow alleys around the 13th-century Gothic Cathédrale St-Pierre.

5-day itinerary
Tour des Fromages

Sate all your cheese cravings, explore the backstreets of Rouen, build sandcastles and conquer real castles. Start in **Camembert** and learn the secrets of this cheese at the Président farm. Next stop is the **Livarot**, home to perhaps France's best cheese museum. Meander via **Les Jardins du Pays d'Auge** to unpretentious **Pont l'Évêque** and its cheese shops. Then buy Norman cider and calvados at Distillerie Christian Drouin. A short drive will lead you to your first sea views and Normandy's charming seaside town, **Honfleur**. Next is the market town of **Neufchâtel-en-Bray**, and then on to see the ruins of Château Gaillard in **Les Andelys**. Less than an hour away is your last stop, **Rouen**, with a beautifully restored medieval quarter and Gothic cathedral.

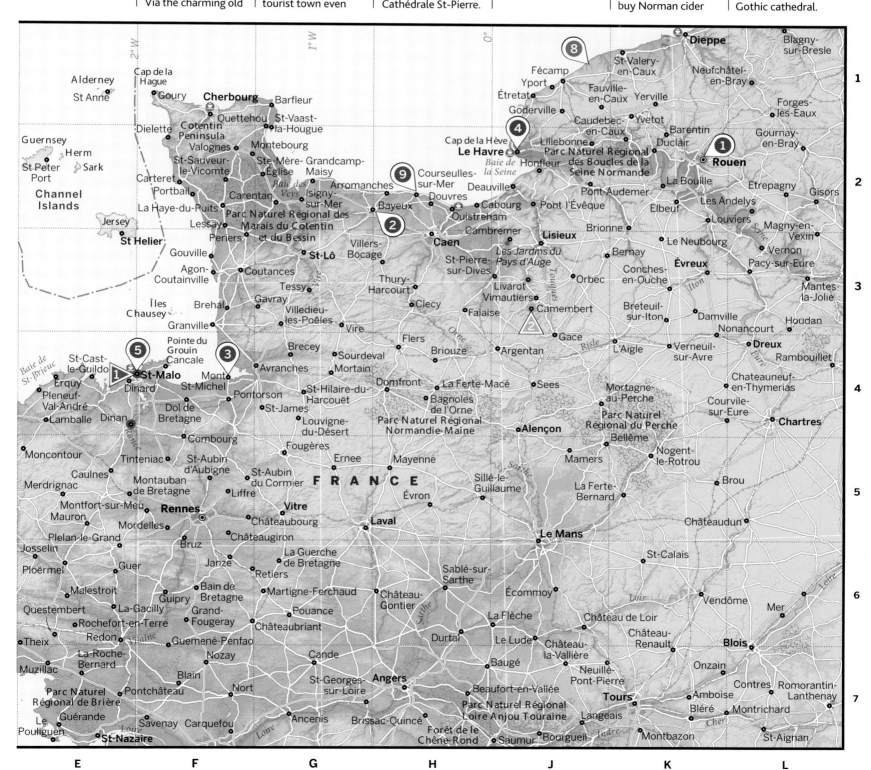

SIGHTS & ACTIVITIES

◉ SEE
◉ DO

ITINERARY

▽ 1
▽ 2

1 Musée des Beaux-Arts, Dijon

Housed in Dijon's monumental Palais des Ducs, these sprawling galleries constitute one of France's most outstanding museums. The star attraction is the Salle des Gardes, which houses the ornate late-medieval sepulchres of dukes John the Fearless and Philip the Bold.

2 Cathédrale Notre Dame, Reims

Site of the 1429 coronation of Charles VII, with Joan of Arc at his side, Reims' resplendent Gothic cathedral is over eight centuries old. To get the most impressive first view, approach the cathedral from the west, along rue Libergier.

3 Centre Pompidou-Metz

Designed by Japanese architect Shigeru Ban, with a curved roof resembling a space-age Chinese hat, the architecturally innovative Centre Pompidou-Metz is the star of Metz' art scene. The satellite branch of Paris' Centre Pompidou draws on Europe's largest modern-art collection to stage ambitious temporary exhibitions.

4 Troyes

The lively centre of Troyes is graced with one of France's finest ensembles of half-timbered houses and Gothic churches. It's one of the best places in France to get a sense of what Europe looked like back when Molière was penning his finest plays and the three musketeers were swashbuckling.

Burgundy: Sample the fruits of the winemakers' labour in Beaune, wine capital of Burgundy.

5 Essoyes

It's easy to see why Renoir loved Essoyes: it's one of the area's comeliest villages, with neat stone houses and a riverfront that glows golden in the late afternoon sun. The town's Atelier Renoir has displays zooming in on the hallmarks of Renoir's work (the female form, the vibrant use of colour and light), alongside original pieces such as his antiquated wheelchair.

6 Palais Rohan, Strasbourg

Built in 1732 by French architect Robert de Cotte, of Versailles fame, this opulent 18th-century residence in the heart of Strasbourg is replete with treasures, from Palaeolithic artefacts to masterpieces by El Greco and Sandro Botticelli.

7 Beaune

The unofficial capital of the Côte d'Or, this thriving town's *raison d'être* is wine: making it, tasting it, selling it, but most of all, drinking it. La Cave de l'Ange Gardien is home to Beaune's most convivial wine-tasting experience. From here it's easy to set out on wine-tasting expeditions through Burgundy, visiting famous villages such as Nuits-Saint-George and Vosne-Romanée.

8 Lyon

Deep within the Vieux Lyon and Croix Rousse neighbourhoods, dark *traboules* (secret passages) wind their way through apartment blocks, under streets and into courtyards. In all, 315 passages link 230 streets, with a combined length of 50km. Recover after your explorations at one of Lyon's famed *bouchons* (rustic restaurants).

9 Colmar

If you see just one thing in Colmar, make it the Petite Venise (Little Venice) quarter. Canal connection aside, it doesn't resemble the Italian city in the slightest, but it's truly lovely in its own right, whether explored on foot or by rowboat. The bright-painted town is also the gateway to the Alsace wine region, with villages such as Turckheim and Saint-Hippolyte offering tastings of the local Riesling and Pinot Noir wines.

10 Parc Naturel Régional du Vercors

This 2062-sq-km wildlife-rich nature park offers gently rolling pastures, highland plateaus, chiselled limestone peaks and pastoral hamlets, drawing families and outdoor enthusiasts seeking fresh air and low-key activities such as cross-country skiing, snowshoeing, hiking (on a whopping 3000km of trails), mountain biking and caving.

11 Les Trois Vallées

This is the big one: vast, fast and a contender for largest ski area in the world. Indeed, it's impossible to tire of all this terrain: depending on how it's reckoned, there are more than 600km of pistes and 180 lifts linking eight resorts and three parallel valleys. Mountain bikers arrive in the summer.

▽1 5-day itinerary — The Alps

Explore the French Alps after the snow has melted and you'll be pleasantly surprised. Warm up with old-town ambling, and warm-weather swimming in fairy-tale **Annecy**. Day two, shift to **Chamonix** at the foot of Mont Blanc, Europe's highest peak. Hike along trails in the chic Alpine villages of **St-Gervais** and **Megève**. Let the adrenalin rip, or push on via the ancient Savoyard stronghold of Chambéry to the **Parc National de la Vanoise**, for spectacular mountain biking in Les Trois Vallées. A fitting finale to your Alpine foray is the stunning drive through the **Parc National des Écrins** to **Briançon**, perhaps the loveliest of all the villages in the French Alps.

▽2 5-day itinerary — The Jura

On this trip through the mountains and vineyards of the Jura, you'll clamber over magnificent citadels, explore deep forests of beech, oak and fir, taste the region's famous yellow wine and relax into its unhurried culture. First, seek out the Vauban citadel and the stellar Musée des Beaux Arts in **Besançon** (birthplace of Victor Hugo and the Lumière brothers). Then taste the alchemical golden wine, *vin jaune*, in the bucolic village of **Arbois**. Carry on, stopping in **Pupillin** and **Poligny**. In the pocket-sized medieval village of **Château-Chalon** overlook a carpet of vineyards known for their legendary *vin jaune*. Next, head to one of the least-known corners of France and explore the high-mountain bliss of the **Parc Naturel Régional du Haut-Jura**. The park stretches from Chapelle-des-Bois in the north almost to the western tip of Lake Geneva. Check out the Maison du Parc in the village of **Lajoux**. From here, head to the small ski resort of **Mijoux** for some fabulous panoramas of Lake Geneva, framed by the French Alps and Mont Blanc.

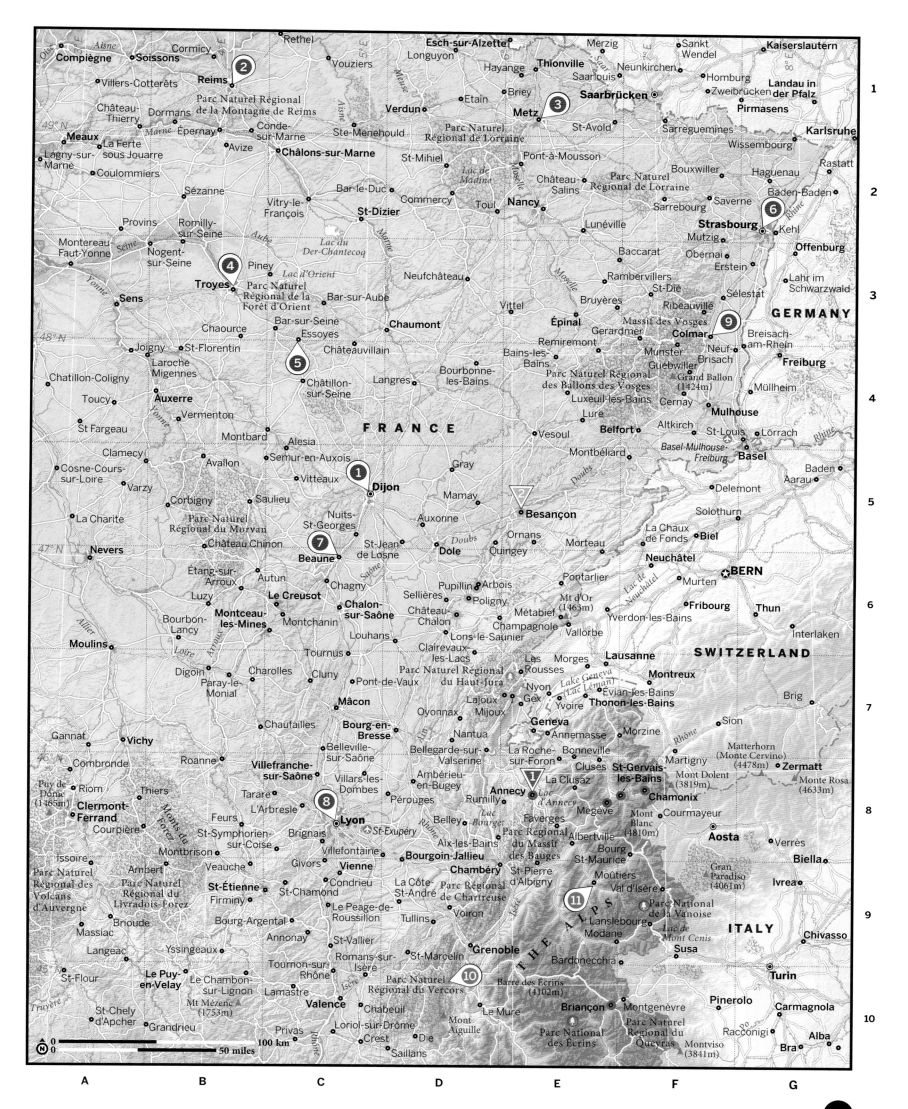

1

49° N

Compiègne
Soissons
Cormicy
Rethel
Vouziers
Esch-sur-Alzette
Longuyon
Merzig
Sankt Wendel
Kaiserslautern

2
Reims
Villers-Cotterêts
Hayange
Thionville
Neunkirchen
Homburg
Zweibrücken
Landau in der Pfalz

Château-Thierry
Dormans
Épernay
Condé-sur-Marne
Ste-Menehould
Verdun
Étain
Briey
Saarbrücken
St-Avold
Sarreguemines
Pirmasens
Karlsruhe

Parc Naturel Régional de la Montagne de Reims

3
Metz

Meaux
La Ferté-sous-Jouarre
Châlons-sur-Marne
St-Mihiel
Pont-à-Mousson
Parc Naturel Régional de Lorraine
Bouxwiller
Haguenau
Rastatt
Wissembourg

Lagny-sur-Marne
Coulommiers
Avize
St-Dizier
Commercy
Toul
Nancy
Château-Salins
Sarrebourg
Saverne
Baden-Baden

2

Sézanne
Bar-le-Duc
Lac de Madine
Parc Naturel Régional de Lorraine

Provins
Vitry-le-François
Lunéville
Strasbourg **6**
Kehl

Montereau-Faut-Yonne
Romilly-sur-Seine
Nogent-sur-Seine
Seine
Lac du Der-Chantecoq
Mutzig
Offenburg

4
Piney
Baccarat
Obernai
Erstein

Troyes
Lac d'Orient
Bar-sur-Aube
Neufchâteau
Rambervillers
St-Dié
Sélestat
Lahr im Schwarzwald

3

Sens
Parc Naturel Régional de la Forêt d'Orient
Vittel
Bruyères
Ribeauvillé
48° N

Chaource
Bar-sur-Seine
Chaumont
Épinal
Massif des Vosges
Colmar **9**
GERMANY

Joigny
St-Florentin
Essoyes
5
Châteauvillain
Gerardmer
Neuf-Brisach
Breisach-am-Rhein

Auxerre
Laroche Migennes
Châtillon-sur-Seine
Langres
Bourbonne-les-Bains
Remiremont
Munster
Guebwiller
Freiburg

Toucy
Vermenton
Bains-les-Bains
Parc Naturel Régional des Ballons des Vosges
Grand Ballon (1424m)
Müllheim

4

St Fargeau
Montbard
FRANCE
Luxeuil-les-Bains
Cernay
Mulhouse

Clamecy
Alesia
Vesoul
Lure
Altkirch
St-Louis
Lörrach

Cosne-Cours-sur-Loire
Avallon
Semur-en-Auxois
Gray
Belfort
Basel-Mulhouse-Freiburg
Baden

Varzy
Vitteaux
1 Dijon
Montbéliard
Basel
Aarau

Corbigny
Saulieu
Nuits-St-Georges
Mamay
Doubs
Delemont

5

La Charité
Parc Naturel Régional du Morvan
Auxonne
Besançon **2**
Solothurn

Nevers
Château Chinon
7
St-Jean de Losne
Ornans
Morteau
La Chaux de Fonds
Biel

47° N
Beaune
Dole
Quingey
Neuchâtel
BERN

Étang-sur-Arroux
Autun
Chagny
Sellières
Pupillin
Arbois
Pontarlier
Lac de Neuchâtel
Murten
Fribourg
Thun

Luzy
Le Creusot
Château-Chalon
Poligny
Mt d'Or (1463m)
Yverdon-les-Bains
Interlaken

6

Bourbon-Lancy
Montceau-les-Mines
Montchanin
Chalon-sur-Saône
Champagnole
Vallorbe

Moulins
Louhans
Lons-le-Saunier
Clairevaux-les-Lacs
SWITZERLAND

Digoin
Charolles
Cluny
Tournus
Parc Naturel Régional du Haut-Jura
Les Morges
Lausanne

Paray-le-Monial
Pont-de-Vaux
Les Rousses
Montreux

7

Gannat
Vichy
Chaufailles
Mâcon
Bourg-en-Bresse
Lajoux
Nyon
Lake Geneva (Lac Léman)
Évian-les-Bains
Thonon-les-Bains
Brig

Combronde
Roanne
Belleville-sur-Saône
Nantua
Gex
Geneva
Morzine
Sion

Puy de Dôme (1465m)
Riom
Villefranche-sur-Saône
Villars-les-Dombes
Oyonnax
Mijoux
Annemasse
Bonneville
Matterhorn (Mont Cervino) (4478m)
Zermatt

Clermont-Ferrand
Thiers
Tarare
Ambérieu-en-Bugey
Bellegarde-sur-Valserine
La Roche-sur-Foron
Martigny
Mont Dolent (3819m)
Monte Rosa (4633m)

8

Courpière
L'Arbresle
8
Pérouges
1
Annecy
La Clusaz
St-Gervais-les-Bains
Mont Blanc (4810m)
Courmayeur

Issoire
Feurs
St-Symphorien-sur-Coise
Brignais
Lyon
Villars-les-Dombes
Rumilly
Lac d'Annecy
Megève
Aosta
Verrès

Ambert
Montbrison
Veauche
Givors
St-Exupéry
Belley
Lac du Bourget
Favergès
Albertville
Bourg
St-Maurice
Biella

Parc Naturel Régional des Volcans d'Auvergne
Parc Naturel Régional du Livradois-Forez
St-Étienne
St-Chamond
Vienne
Bourgoin-Jallieu
Aix-les-Bains
Parc Régional du Massif des Bauges
Moûtiers
Gran Paradiso (4061m)
Ivrea

9

Massiac
Brioude
Firminy
Condrieu
La Côte-St-André
Chambéry
St-Pierre d'Albigny
Val d'Isère
Parc National de la Vanoise
ITALY

Langeac
Bourg-Argental
Le Peage-de-Roussillon
Tullins
Voiron
Parc Régional de Chartreuse
11
Lanslebourg
Chivasso

Yssingeaux
Annonay
St-Vallier
St-Marcelin
Grenoble
THE ALPS
Modane
Lac de Mont Cenis
Susa

Le Puy-en-Velay
Le Chambon-sur-Lignon
Tournon-sur-Rhône
Romans-sur-Isère
Parc Naturel Régional du Vercors
10
Bardonecchia
Turin

St-Flour
St-Chely d'Apcher
Lamastre
Chabeuil
Valence
Barre des Écrins (4102m)
Briançon
Montgenèvre
Pinerolo
Carmagnola

Mt Mézenc (1753m)
Grandrieu
Privas
Crest
Die
Saillans
Loriol-sur-Drôme
Mont Aiguille
Le Mure
Parc National des Écrins
Parc Naturel Régional du Queyras
Montviso (3841m)
Bra
Alba

10

0   100 km
0   50 miles

A   B   C   D   E   F   G

SIGHTS &
ACTIVITIES

 SEE

 DO

ITINERARY

▽ 1

▽ 2

Le Panier, Marseille

Marseille's ancient Le Panier neighbourhood is a history-woven quarter, a mishmash of lanes hiding artisan shops and terraced houses strung with drying washing. In Greek Massilia, it was the site of the *agora* (marketplace), hence its name, which means 'the basket'. During WWII the quarter was dynamited and afterwards rebuilt.

Fondation Vincent van Gogh, Arles

The colourful sun-baked houses of Arles might evoke a sense of déjà vu because you've seen them already on a Van Gogh canvas – the artist painted 200-odd works around town. A visit to the Fondation Vincent van Gogh in Arles is a must, as much for its contemporary architecture and design as for the art it showcases.

Casino de Monte Carlo

Peeping inside Monte Carlo's legendary marble-and-gold casino is a Monaco essential. The building, open to visitors every morning, is Europe's most lavish example of belle-epoque architecture.

Musée Granet, Aix-en-Provence

Aix (pronounced like the letter X) is a pocket of left-bank Parisian chic deep in Provence. The Musée Granet sits right near the top of France's artistic must-sees, housing works by some of the most iconic artists, including Picasso, Matisse, Van Gogh and, perhaps most importantly of all in Aix, nine works by local boy Cézanne.

Palais des Papes, Avignon

The largest Gothic palace ever built, the Palais des Papes in Avignon was erected by Pope Clement V, who abandoned Rome in 1309 as a result of violent disorder following his election. It served as the seat of papal power for seven decades. The palatial fortress has been inscribed as a World Heritage site by Unesco since 1995.

La Cité, Carcassonne

Built on a steep spur of rock, Carcassonne's rampart-ringed fortress dates back over two millennia. The fortified town is encircled by two sets of battlements and 52 stone towers.

Promenade des Anglais, Nice

With its mix of real-city grit, old-world opulence, year-round sunshine and stunning seaside location, Nice is the unofficial capital of the Côte d'Azur. The most famous stretch of seafront in Nice – if not France – is this vast paved promenade, which gets its name from the English expat patrons who paid for it in 1822. It runs for the whole 4km sweep of the Baie des Anges.

Marché Forville, Cannes

When it comes to shopping with taste, forget the designer fashion houses. For local folklore, head to Cannes' Marché Forville, a busy food market a couple of blocks back from the port. It is one of the most important markets in the region and the supplier of choice for restaurants – and for your beach picnic. On Monday the food stalls are replaced by an all-day *brocante* (flea market).

Pont du Gard

The scale of the extraordinary three-tiered Pont du Gard is huge: the bridge is 48.8m high, 275m long and graced with 52 arches. The Gard River flows from the Cévennes mountains all the way to the aqueduct, passing through the dramatic Gorges du Gardon. Canoeing beneath the Pont du Gard is an unforgettable experience.

5-day itinerary
Lavender Route

Get out among the purple haze and navigate hilltop villages and pretty valleys on this drive. Start in **Coustellet** and visit the working lavender farm at Musée de la Lavande. Head for **Gordes** then turn off to the photogenic Abbaye Notre-Dame de Sénanque. Next, drive to **St-Saturnin-lès-Apt** and climb to the ruins for knockout views. From here, make your way to the hilltop town of **Sault** (stop for nougat). The next 25km features dense, fragrant forest and views of **Mont Ventoux**. Via **Banon**, head to **Forcalquier** and then to **Mane**. On its outskirts is the 13th-century priory, Prieuré de Salagon – wander the medieval herb garden. Finally, head to the dreamy **Plateau de Valensole**, home to the greatest concentration of lavender farms.

7-day itinerary
Riviera Cruising

What glitzier opening could there be to a Côte d'Azur drive than **Cannes**. Once you've had your fill, head to **Mougins**, home of Picasso from 1961 until his death. Next stop is the beach resort of **Juan-les-Pins** and around the penisula to pretty **Antibes**. From here make your way to the hilltop village of **Biot** and linger in the town square. A short drive will lead you to **St-Paul de Vence**, a beautifully preserved village closed to traffic. Jump on the A8 to **Nice** – there's a real thrill following the Baie des Anges and the beach vibe is instantly intoxicating. After Nice, head to the picturesque village of **Villefranche-sur-Mer**, overlooking the Cap Ferrat peninsula. Head down the narrow isthmus towards **Cap Ferrat**. Leave the car and the crowds behind and enter the fragrant and leafy, walled realm of the ultrawealthy. The best way to experience the Cap (besides an invite from Bill Gates or Bono) is to grab a trail map from the tourist office. There are some 14km of easygoing eucalyptus-scented paths skirting the Côte's coastline.

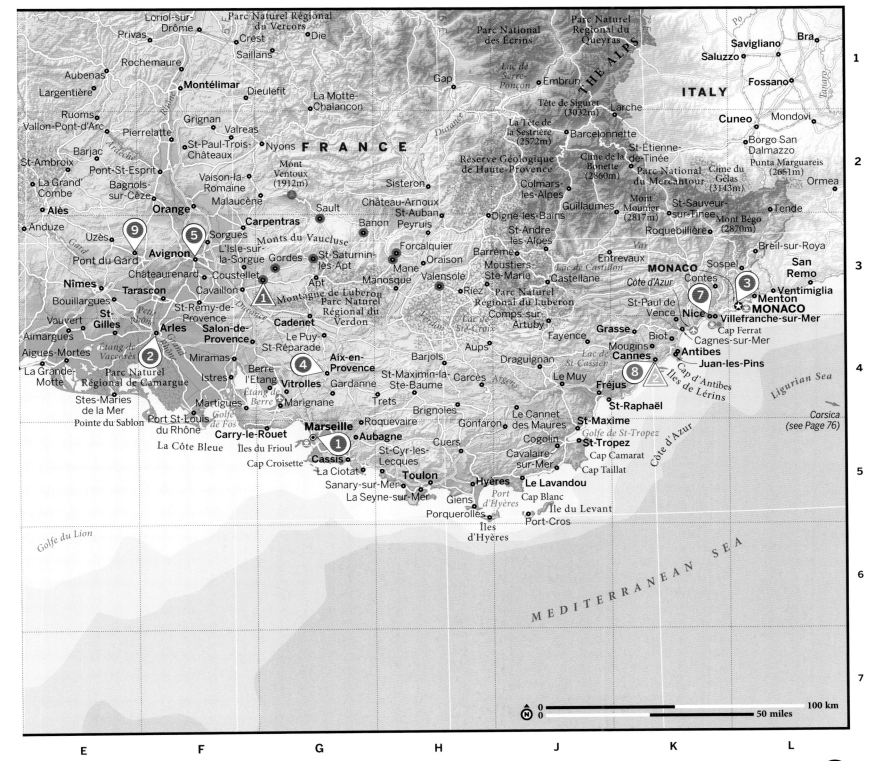

SIGHTS & ACTIVITIES

 SEE

DO

ITINERARY

1

2

Biarritz: Go bathing at Le Grand Plage (the big beach), which is backed by casinos and hotels.

① La Cité du Vin, Bordeaux

Over 15 years, Bordeaux has shed its languid, *Belle au Bois Dormant* (Sleeping Beauty) image. World-class architects have recently designed a bevy of striking buildings including the decanter-shaped La Cité du Vin. The curvaceous gold building glitters in the sun and its 3000 sq metres of exhibits are equally sensory and sensational.

② Dune du Pilat

This colossal sand dune (sometimes referred to as the Dune de Pyla), 8km south of Arcachon, stretches from the mouth of the Bassin d'Arcachon southwards for 2.7km. Already Europe's largest, the dune is growing eastwards 1.5m a year – it has swallowed trees, a road junction and even a hotel, so local lore claims. The view from the top – approximately 115m above sea level – is magnificent.

③ Aquarium La Rochelle

La Rochelle's modern aquarium is home to 12,000 marine animals and 600 different species. Visits begin by descending in an old 'submarine' to the ocean floor. One floor up, the Galerie des Lumières is particularly magical.

④ Parc Naturel Interrégional du Marais Poitevin

A tranquil bird-filled wetland dubbed the *Venise Verte* (Green Venice), covering 800 sq km, the marshlands are interspersed with villages and woods threaded by canals and bike paths. There are two main bases from which to punt out across the waterways: Coulon and Arçais.

⑤ Cordes-sur-Ciel

One of the most spellbinding *bastides* (fortified towns) in Toulouse's surrounds, Cordes-sur-Ciel's cobbled pathways wiggle their way up to its soaring vantage point over meadows banking the Tarn River. Legend has it that 13th-century Count Raimon VII of Toulouse originally picked a different site for his northern fortress, but a mysterious force undid construction work each night. Furious at the supernatural forces tampering with his efforts, a workman hurled his trowel in the air; when it landed on a faraway hilltop, it was taken as a sign from the divine that this should be the location for the fortified town.

⑥ Maison Natale de Pierre Fermat, Beaumont-de-Lomagne

In a region of identically pretty towns, Beaumont-de-Lomagne's mathematical heritage offers something a little different. It is the birthplace of 17th-century maths genius and polymath Pierre de Fermat, whose life and works spring to life through puzzles and games at a small museum in his birth house.

⑦ Les Halles Victor Hugo, Toulouse

The beating heart of Toulouse's food scene is this covered market, packed with local producers busily selling cheeses, fresh pasta, meats and takeaway nibbles from sushi to spicy curries. For a great-value local dining experience, join streams of hungry market-goers at one of the tiny restaurants on the first floor. Don't miss the cassoulet.

⑧ Armagnac Ryst-Dupeyron, Condom

While the historic centre needs only a day to explore, Condom is in the midst of Armagnac country, where a potent local brandy has been produced for centuries. This mellow town is a superb base from which to visit distilleries, abbeys and historic ramparts. The best place to start your Armagnac tasting is this turn-of-the-century cellar.

⑨ Biarritz

Once the almost exclusive haunt of the rich, Biarritz is now known more as the capital of European surfing. The city's main beach, Grande Plage, is good from mid-low tide on a moderate swell, but the 4km-long stretch of beaches that make up Anglet to the south are usually more consistent. Head south to Saint-Jean-de-Luz for a quieter, family-friendly seaside town and beach.

⑩ St-Martin-de-Ré, Île de Ré

Bathed in the southern sun, Île de Ré is one of the most delightful places on France's west coast. For an authentic taste of island life, pick up the cycling path to Ars-en-Ré – either on foot or by bike. Within seconds of hitting the coast, the path brushes past a twinset of oyster farmer *cabanes* (huts), whose doors are open to the culinary curious. Snag a table overlooking oyster beds and tuck into freshly shucked oysters, courtesy of Auberge de la Mer.

5-day itinerary
Atlantic Coast to the Pyrenees

Known as La Ville Blanche (the White City), begin in **La Rochelle,** one of France's most attractive cities. From here, head to **St-Émilion** for fine wine. Hit the road for a 2.5-hour drive to ritzy **Biarritz.** The town boomed as a resort in the mid-19th century due to regular visits by Napoléon III. Your next stop is **Gavarnie;** park here and venture to the Cirque de Gavarnie. This mountain amphitheatre is one of the region's most famous sights, sliced by waterfalls and ringed by sawtooth peaks, many of which top out at over 3000m. From here it's a 3-hour drive to vibrant **Toulouse,** known as La Ville Rose, situated at the confluence of the Canal du Midi and the Garonne River.

5-day itinerary
Heritage Wine Country

Start your trip in gourmet **Bordeaux.** Barista-run coffee shops, gourmet food trucks, an exceptional dining scene and more fine wine than you could ever possibly drink will make it hard to leave. When you can, head to **Arsac** and La Winery, part giant wine shop, part grape-flavoured theme park, and part wine museum. From here, your next stop is **Pauillac,** at the heart of the wine country. Essential is lunch at Café Lavinal, a mind-blowing village bistro in Bages, about 2km south. Next is **Blaye;** getting here involves splashing over the Gironde River on a car ferry. Pay a visit to the Citadelle de Blaye, inscribed onto the Unesco World Heritage List in 2008. Drive an hour or so to celebrated **St-Émilion,** easily the most alluring of all the region's wine towns. Next, take a break from the grape and head to the seaside to eat oysters in the area around **Gujan Mestras.** From here take a short drive to the seaside town of **Arcachon** and prepare yourself for the epic sand dune, the **Dune du Pilat,** near Pyla-sur-Mer.

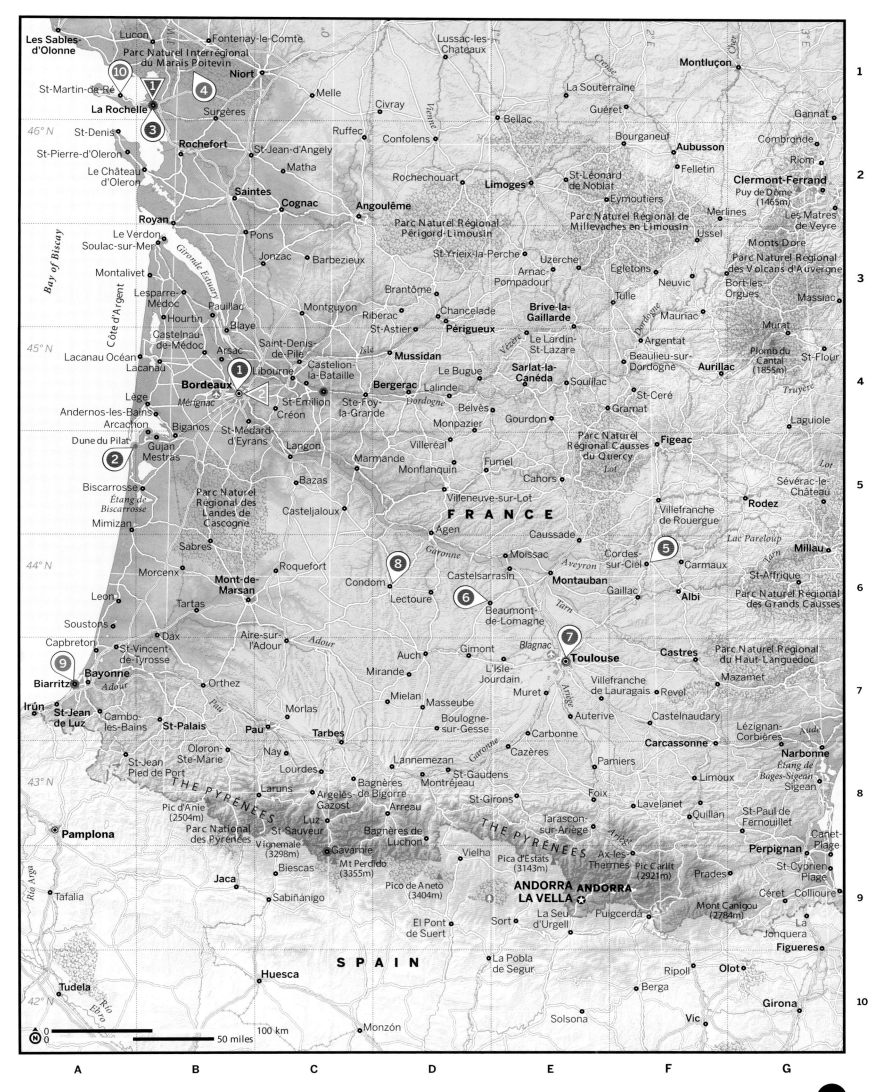

Les Sables-d'Olonne
Luçon
Fontenay-le-Comte
Lussac-les-Châteaux
Montluçon

Parc Naturel Interrégional du Marais Poitevin
St-Martin-de-Ré
Niort
Melle
La Souterraine
Guéret
Gannat

St-Denis
La Rochelle
Surgères
Civray
Bellac
Bourganeuf
Aubusson
Combronde

46° N
Rochefort
St-Jean-d'Angély
Ruffec
Confolens
Felletin
Clermont-Ferrand
Riom

St-Pierre-d'Oléron
Matha
Rochechouart
Limoges
St-Léonard de Noblat
Eymoutiers
Merlines
Puy de Dôme (1465m)
Les Maîtres de Veyre

Le Château d'Oléron
Saintes
Cognac
Angoulême
Parc Naturel Régional Périgord-Limousin
Parc Naturel Régional de Millevaches en Limousin
Ussel
Monts Dore
Parc Naturel Régional des Volcans d'Auvergne

Royan
Pons
Jonzac
Barbezieux
St-Yrieix-la-Perche
Uzerche
Egletons
Neuvic
Bort-les-Orgues
Massiac

Le Verdon
Soulac-sur-Mer
Brantôme
Arnac-Pompadour
Tulle
Mauriac
Murat

Montalivet
Lesparre-Médoc
Pauillac
Riberac
Chancelade
St-Astier
Périgueux
Brive-la-Gaillarde
Le Lardin-St-Lazare
Argentat
Beaulieu-sur-Dordogne
Plomb du Cantal (1855m)
St-Flour

45° N
Hourtin
Blaye
Montguyon
Mussidan
Le Bugue
Sarlat-la-Canéda
Souillac
Aurillac

Lacanau Océan
Castelnau-de-Médoc
Arsac
Saint-Denis-de-Pile
Isle
Bergerac
Lalinde
Gourdon
St-Céré
Gramat
Laguiole

Lacanau
Libourne
Castelion-la-Bataille
Ste-Foy-la-Grande
Dordogne
Belvès
Monpazier
Parc Naturel Régional Causses du Quercy

Lège
Bordeaux
Mérignac
St-Emilion Créon
Villeréal
Marmande
Cahors
Figeac
Sévérac-le-Château

Andernos-les-Bains
Arcachon
Biganos
St-Médard-d'Eyrans
Langon
Monflanquin
Fumel
Lot

Dune du Pilat
Gujan Mestras
Parc Naturel Régional des Landes de Cascogne
Bazas
Casteljaloux
Villeneuve-sur-Lot
F R A N C E
Villefranche de Rouergue
Lac Pareloup
Rodez
Millau

Biscarrosse
Étang de Biscarrosse
Agen
Caussade
Cordes-sur-Ciel
Carmaux

Mimizan
Sabres
Garonne
Moissac
Aveyron
Gaillac
Albi
St-Affrique
Parc Naturel Régional des Grands Causses

44° N
Morcenx
Roquefort
Condom
Castelsarrasin
Montauban
Tarn

Leon
Mont-de-Marsan
Lectoure
Beaumont-de-Lomagne
Gimont
Blagnac

Soustons
Tartas
Aire-sur-l'Adour
Adour
Auch
Toulouse
Castres
Parc Naturel Régional du Haut-Languedoc

Dax
Mirande
L'Isle-Jourdain
Muret
Villefranche de Lauragais
Revel
Mazamet

Capbreton
St-Vincent-de-Tyrosse
Mielan
Masseube
Auterive
Castelnaudary

Bayonne
Biarritz
Orthez
Morlas
Boulogne-sur-Gesse
Carbonne
Lézignan-Corbières
Narbonne

Irún
St-Jean de Luz
Cambo-les-Bains
St-Palais
Pau
Tarbes
Lannemezan
Garonne
Cazères
Pamiers
Carcassonne
Aude

Oloron-Ste-Marie
Nay
Lourdes
Bagnères-de-Bigorre
St-Gaudens
Montréjeau
Foix
Limoux
Étang de Bages-Sigean
Sigean

43° N
THE PYRENEES
Larens
Argelès-Gazost
Arreau
St-Girons
Lavelanet
Quillan
St-Paul de Fernouillet

Pic d'Anie (2504m)
Parc National des Pyrénées
Luz-St-Sauveur
Bagnères de Luchon
THE PYRENEES
Tarascon-sur-Ariège
Ariège
Perpignan
Canet-Plage

Vignemale (3298m)
Gavarnie
Mt Perdido (3355m)
Vielha
Pica d'Estats (3143m)
Ax-les-Thermes
Pic Carlit (2921m)
Prades
St-Cyprien Plage

Biescas
Pico de Aneto (3404m)
ANDORRA LA VELLA
ANDORRA
Mont Canigou (2784m)
Céret
Collioure

Jaca
Sabiñánigo
La Seu d'Urgell
Puigcerdà
La Jonquera

El Pont de Suert
Sort
Figueres

Tudela
S P A I N
La Pobla de Segur
Ripoll
Olot

Huesca
Berga
Girona

Monzón
Solsona
Vic

Bay of Biscay
Côte d'Argent
Gironde Estuary
Rio Arga
Rio Ebro
Pamplona
Tafalia

0
0
100 km
50 miles

A   B   C   D   E   F   G

SIGHTS & ACTIVITIES

 SEE

 DO

ITINERARY

1

2

Château de Chenonceau

Spanning the languid Cher River atop a supremely graceful arched bridge, Chenonceau is one of France's most elegant châteaux. It's hard not to be moved and exhilarated by the glorious setting, the formal gardens, the magic of the architecture and the château's fascinating history, shaped by a series of powerful women. The interior is decorated with rare furnishings and a fabulous art collection that includes works by Tintoretto, Correggio, Rubens, Murillo, Van Dyck and Ribera (look for an extraordinary portrait of Louis XIV).

École Nationale d'Équitation, Saumur

One of the world's premier equestrian academies, the École Nationale d'Équitation in Saumur is home to the Cadre Noir, an elite group of riding instructors that's also an equestrian display team. One-hour tours take you behind the scenes at the prestigious school.

Cycling in the Loire

There's nothing quite like pedalling through the fertile Loire Valley, sprinkled with hundreds of France's most extravagant fortresses and the villages and vineyards that surround them. Le Loire à Vélo maintains 800km of signposted routes from Cuffy (near Nevers) righ through to the Atlantic. It's part of the Eurovelo 6 bike route that you can follow eastwards all the way to the Bulgarian coast of the Black Sea.

Le Clos Lucé, Amboise

It was on the invitation of François I that Leonardo da Vinci (1452–1519), aged 64, took up residence at this grand manor house (built 1471). An admirer of the Italian Renaissance, the French monarch named Da Vinci 'first painter, engineer and king's architect', and the Italian spent his time here sketching, tinkering and dreaming up ingenious contraptions. Fascinating models of his many inventions are on display inside the home and around its lovely gardens.

Château de Chambord

One of the crowning achievements of French Renaissance architecture, the Château de Chambord – with 440 rooms, 365 fireplaces and 84 staircases – is by far the largest, grandest and most visited château in the Loire Valley. Begun in 1519 by François I as a weekend hunting lodge, it quickly grew into one of the most ambitious – and expensive – architectural projects ever attempted by a French monarch.

Hot-air ballooning

Floating silently over fields, vineyards and châteaux in a hot-air balloon – what could be more romantic? Spend an hour aloft and then quaff a celebratory glass of bubbly (or two). Art Montgolfières is one of the best operators.

Carré Cointreau Distillery, Angers

The orange-flavoured liqueur Cointreau has its origins in the experiments of two brothers: sweet-maker Adolphe Cointreau and Édouard-Jean Cointreau, who founded a factory in Angers in 1849 to produce fruit-flavoured liqueurs. In 1875 Édouard-Jean's son (also called Édouard) hit upon a winning formula combining sweet and bitter oranges, flavoured with intensely orangey peel. Every one of the 15 million bottles produced annually is distilled according to the same top-secret recipe at this factory, 3km east of Angers' city centre.

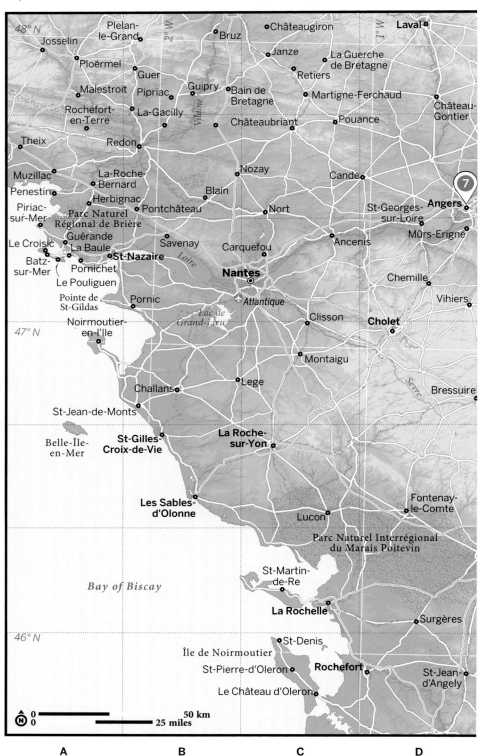

3-day itinerary
Caves & Cellars of the Loire

This tour explores the best of the western Loire Valley, home to *habitations troglodytiques* (cave dwellings) and some of France's finest food and wine. Start your tour in sophisticated **Saumur**, one of the Loire Valley's great gastronomic and viticultural centres. A meander along the D947 will lead you to **Turquant**, a showcase for the creative adaptation of historic troglodyte dwellings. Carry on via the Château de Montsoreau, **Candes-St-Martin** (one of France's prettiest villages), the Abbaye Royale de Fontevraud and then on to the riverside village of **Chinon** – an ideal place for an overnight stop. Zigzag from **Chinon** through rolling farmland to **La Devinière** and the Musée Rabelais, then to Château de Brézé, **Doué-la-Fontaine** and the museum-village of **Rochemenier**, where you can explore ancient cave-dwelling traditions. From here head to **Brissac-Quincé** and visit France's tallest castle, Château de Brissac. Heading back towards Saumur along the Loire's sandy banks, make your last stop **St-Hilaire-St-Florent**, home to a number of wineries and cave-based attractions.

5-day itinerary
Châteaux of the Loire Valley

Admire nine of the Loire's spectacular châteaux. Start in **Chinon** and explore its castle, Forteresse Royale de Chinon. Head for **Langeais** via the Château d'Ussé, to the most medieval of the Loire châteaux, Château de Langeais. Backtrack south for the gardens of the Château de Villandry. Next stop is romantic **Azay-le-Rideau**. From here head (via Saché) for the elegant **Château de Chenonceau**. Go north to **Amboise** and the Château Royal d'Amboise, perched on an escarpment above town. **Blois'** chateau, home of seven French kings, is next, 35km northeast of Amboise. Cross the Loire for perfectly proportioned **Cheverny**. Last to visit is **Chambord**, for its château superstar, the royal hunting lodge Château de Chambord.

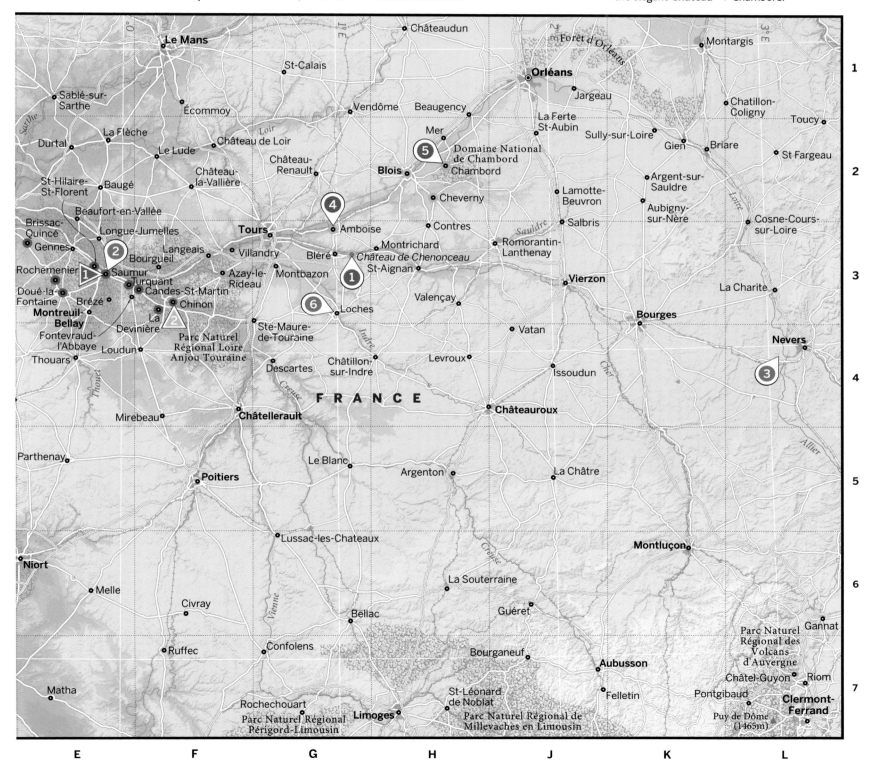

SIGHTS &
ACTIVITIES

◉ SEE

◉ DO

ITINERARY

▽ 1

▽ 2

Château de Versailles

Louis XIV transformed his father's hunting lodge into the monumental Château de Versailles in the mid-17th century, and it remains France's most famous and grand palace. Situated in the leafy, bourgeois suburb of Versailles, southwest of central Paris, the Baroque château was the kingdom's political capital and the seat of the royal court from 1682 until 1789.

Maison et Jardins de Claude Monet

The tiny country village of Giverny is a place of pilgrimage for devotees of impressionism. Monet lived here from 1883 until his death in 1926, in a rambling house – surrounded by flower-filled gardens – that's now the immensely popular Maison et Jardins de Claude Monet.

Palais du Tau, Reims

A Unesco World Heritage Site, this lavish former archbishop's residence was where French princes stayed before their coronations – and where they threw sumptuous banquets afterwards. Now a museum, it displays truly exceptional statuary, liturgical objects and tapestries from the cathedral.

Cathédrale Notre Dame, Amiens

The largest Gothic cathedral in France (it's 145m long), this magnificent edifice was begun in 1220 to house the skull of St John the Baptist. Connoisseurs of architecture rave about the soaring Gothic arches, unity of style and immense interior, but for locals the highlight is a 17th-century statue known as the Ange Pleureur (Crying Angel).

Château de Versailles: The mesmerising Hall of Mirrors in the Palace of Versailles.

Musée des Beaux-Arts, Orléans

Orléans' five-storey fine-arts museum is a treat, with an excellent selection of Italian, Flemish and Dutch paintings (including works by Correggio, Velázquez and Bruegel) as well as a huge collection of work by French artists such as Léon Cogniet, Orléans-born Alexandre Antigna, and Paul Gauguin, who spent some of his youth here.

Château de Chantilly

In the elegant town of Chantilly, the Château de Chantilly is a storybook vision amid an artificial lake and magnificent gardens, housing a superb collection of paintings within the Musée Condé.

Fontainebleau

Fresh air fills your lungs on arrival in the smart town of Fontainebleau. It's enveloped by the 200-sq-km Forêt de Fontainebleau, which is as big a playground today as it was in the 16th century. Cycle through the forest with a bike from A la Petite Reine.

Épernay

The self-proclaimed capital of Champagne and home to many of the world's most celebrated Champagne houses, Épernay is the best place for touring cellars and sampling bubbly. Prestigious Moet & Chandon offers frequent one-hour tours that are among the region's most impressive, offering a peek at part of its 28km labyrinth of caves (cellars).

Lille

Capital of the Hauts-de-France région, Lille may be France's most underrated metropolis. Recent decades have seen the city transform from an industrial centre into a glittering cultural and commercial hub. Highlights include its enchanting old town with magnificent French and Flemish architecture, renowned art museums, stylish shopping, outstanding cuisine, a nightlife scene bolstered by 67,000 university students, and some 1600 designers in its environs.

Disneyland Paris

Located 32km east of Paris lies a land of fantasy populated by larger-than-life characters. It took almost €4.6 billion to establish Europe's first Disney theme park. Today the resort comprises the Disneyland Park theme park, the film-oriented Walt Disney Studios Park, and the hotel-, shop- and restaurant-filled Disney Village. Disneyland Park has five themed pays (lands): Main Street USA; Frontierland, home of the Big Thunder Mountain ride; Adventureland; Fantasyland, crowned by Sleeping Beauty's castle; and the high-tech Discoveryland. Star Wars Land is due to arrive in 2022.

3-day itinerary
Champagne

This fizz-filled trip, starting and ending at the prestigious Champagne centres of Reims and Épernay, really slips under the skin of these Unesco-listed vineyards. Begin in **Reims**, the start of the 70km Montagne de Reims Champagne Route, the prettiest of the three signposted road routes which wind their way through the Champagne vineyards. Several big names have their caves (wine cellars) near Reims; Mumm is in central Reims. From here head to **Verzenay** and then on to the village of **Verzy**, home to several small vineyards. Next stop is the village of **Hautvillers**, a hallowed name among Champagne aficionados: it's where a Benedictine monk by the name of Dom Pierre Pérignon is popularly believed to have created Champagne in the late 16th century. From here, make your way to **Épernay**, the self-proclaimed capitale du champagne and home to many of the most illustrious Champagne houses. Beneath the streets are an astonishing 110km of subterranean cellars.

3-day itinerary
Northern Coast

Take off from the port of **Calais**. Head west to **Cap Blanc-Nez**. Here, dunes give way to cliffs affording views of the Bay of Wissant, the Flemish countryside and the distant chalk cliffs of Kent. It's an 8km descent to the village of **Wissant**. From here, head for **Cap Gris-Nez**, topped by a lighthouse and a radar station that tracks the 500 ships that pass daily. Next, go to **Audinghen**, **Ambleteuse**, see the Dunes de la Slack and press on to France's key fishing port, **Boulogne-sur-Mer**. Head south to **Le Touquet-Paris-Plage** and then on to **Parc du Marquenterre Bird Sanctuary**, where 300 bird species have been observed. Next stop is laid-back **Le Crotoy** before a short drive to your last stop, **St-Valery-sur-Somme**.

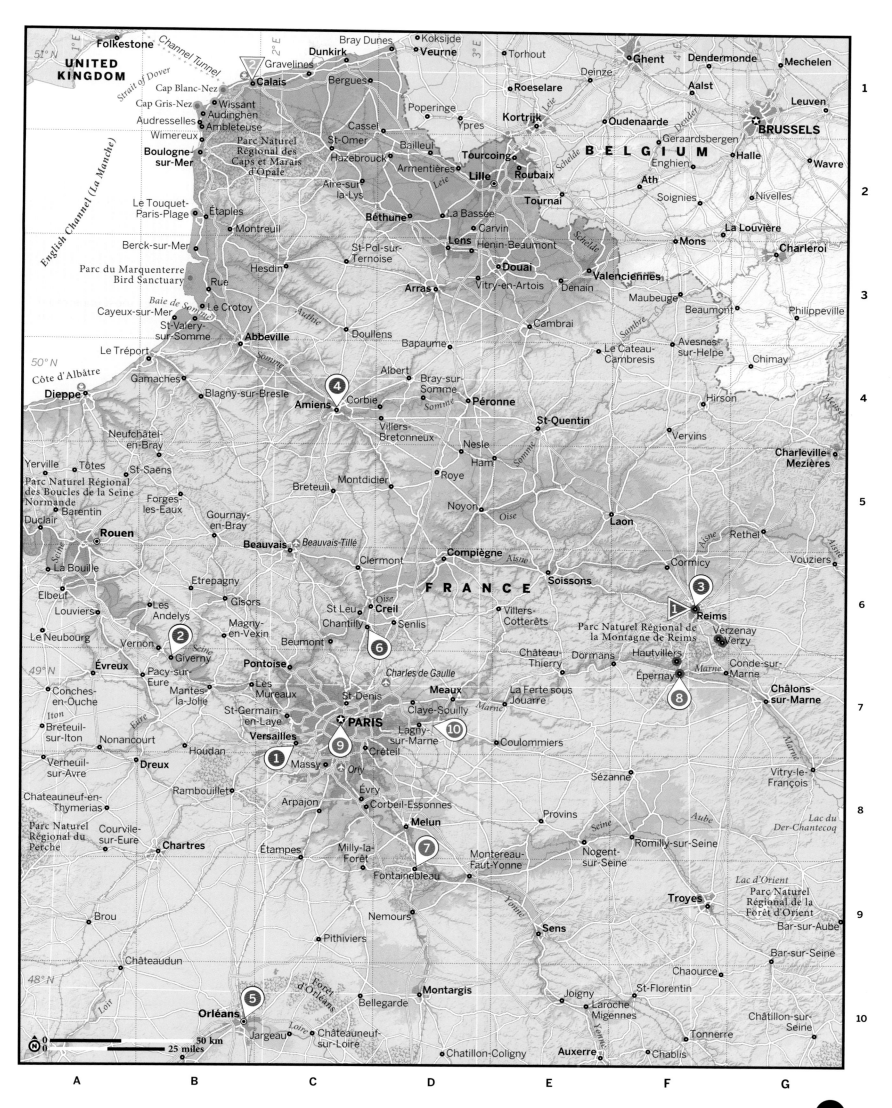

SIGHTS & ACTIVITIES

◉ SEE
◉ DO

ITINERARY

▽ 1
▽ 2

Bruges: See the beautiful Belgian city from its many quiet waterways.

① Groningen
A student population of around 40,000 ensures Groningen's hedonistic nightlife and thriving music scene, alongside the museums demanded by its more mature, established residents (think professors). Stop by in January to catch a series of concerts by up-and-coming bands during the Eurosonic Noorderslag festival.

② Frisian Islands
The crescent of islands over Friesland form a natural barrier between the Frisian coast and the open North Sea, hemming in the mudflats of the Waddenzee. Each boasting a web of hiking and cycling trails, the elongated islands all have a dual character: villages on the Waddenzee side and broad swaths of beach and dunes on the seaward side. Visitors can hop between the islands on a classic century-old Eilandhopper clipper.

③ Edam
In the 16th century Willem van Oranje bestowed on Edam the right to hold a Kaasmarkt, which, at its peak, sold 250,000 rounds of cheese annually. On Wednesdays in summer the town now holds a market event, with displays of traditional dress and plenty of cheese.

④ Mons Memorial Museum
This superb museum focuses on Mons' experience of the two world wars. With excellent visuals throughout, it gets the balance just right between military history, personal testimony of civilians and soldiers, and thought-provoking items on display.

⑤ Keukenhof Gardens
Situated 1km west of Lisse, Keukenhof is the world's largest bulb-flower garden. Spring brings an explosion of colour to the glorious tulip-, daffodil- and hyacinth-filled grounds, which open just eight weeks a year.

⑥ Hoge Veluwe National Park
The marshlands, forests, heath and drift sands would be reason enough to visit this 5500ha national park, the largest in the Netherlands, but its brilliant museum – with works by some of the greatest painters of several centuries, from Bruyn the Elder to Picasso – makes it simply unmissable.

⑦ Luxembourg City
Much of Luxembourg's charm is gained from simply strolling the Chemin de la Corniche. Hailed as Europe's 'most beautiful balcony' it winds along the course of the 17th-century city ramparts with views across the river canyon towards the hefty fortifications of the Wenzelsmauer (Wenceslas Wall).

⑧ Rotterdam
Rotterdam is a vast open-air museum of modern and contemporary design with architectural wonders such as the new home of the Museum Rotterdam, the Timmerhuis, and the eye-popping Markthal Rotterdam. There's also the Unesco World Heritage status 'glass palace', Van Nelle Fabriek, and 45-degree-tilted cube-shaped apartments, Kijk-Kubus Museum-House.

⑨ Bruges
Taking a canal tour of the fairy-tale medieval town is a must. Yes, it's touristy, but what isn't in Bruges? Viewing the city from the water gives it a different feel than by foot. Cruise down Spiegelrei towards Jan Van Eyckplein and it's possible to imagine Venetian merchants entering the city centuries ago and meeting under the turret of the Poortersloge building. Then check out the chocolate shops.

⑩ Antwerp
Antwerp may seem far more sartorially laid-back than fashion heavyweights Paris or Milan, but it punches above its weight. Few places in the world have such a convenient and covetable concentration of fashion stores. Ann Demeulemeester's flagship store is a stunning fashion stage set, and Dries Van Noten's Het Modepaleis is worth a pilgrimage even if you're just window shopping.

⑪ Gravensteen, Ghent
Flanders' quintessential 12th-century stone castle comes complete with moat, turrets and arrow slits. It's all the more remarkable considering that during the 19th century the site was converted into a cotton mill. Meticulously restored since, the interior sports the odd suit of armour, a guillotine and torture devices.

▽ **3-day itinerary** Historic Cities

Three of the cities in this itinerary are so close together that an hour's train ride is enough to get between any of them. **Brussels** has a Grand Place that's one of the world's most beautiful squares. Don't miss the unique 1958 Atomium. Medieval architecture and canalside charm make **Bruges** one of Europe's most romantic getaways. Less tourist-oriented, grittier yet somehow more satisfying, is magical **Ghent**, whose intimate medieval core is complemented by a lively student vibe and some wonderful museums. Return to Brussels and take a train northbound to explore the Dutch capital of **Amsterdam**, with its Golden Age canals, narrow lanes and masterpiece-laden art galleries.

▽ **7-day itinerary** Belgian Beer Tour

In Belgium you can be a complete boozehound but look very cultured as you tour medieval monasteries and historic towns, trying a drop of the local brew out of politeness along the way. Sign up a patient designated driver – some of these monster brews tip the scales at 10% ABV or more. Start your pilgrimage in **Brussels**, where you can pay your respects at L'Arbre d'Or, the venerable brewers' guild on the Grand Place. Next head north to **Mechelen**'s legendary Het Anker.Then, head into western Flanders, Belgium's hop-growing country, tasting **Westvleteren**'s fabled Trappist beer at Sint-Sixtus. Head southeast to Dubuisson at **Pipaix** and arrange a visit to the charming nearby steam brewery. The enticingly rural Botte du Hainaut is home to the legendary Chimay Trappist beer. Belgium's deep southeast holds lovely **Orval**'s brewery-monastery. On your way back north, drop by the rural hamlet of **Achouffe** for La Chouffe's magnificent beer.

© Matt Munro / Lonely Planet

Spain & Portugal

Passionate, sophisticated and devoted to the good life, Spain stirs the soul. The landscape ranges from the peaks of the Pyrenees and the Picos de Europa to the green hills of Asturia and Cantabria, sunbaked plains of Andalucía and sprawling beach resorts of the Mediterranean coast. Throw in history-heavy cities, hilltop villages and a rich Moorish legacy and you've got one of Europe's most enticing destinations. Across the border, Portugal's beauty unfolds in all its startling variety, with more than 800km of coast to explore – including some of Europe's most stellar surf breaks, as well as a wealth of dune-covered beaches, sandy islands and blue seas.

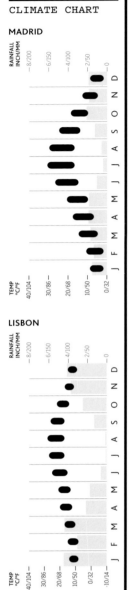

CLIMATE CHART

MADRID

LISBON

FOOD & WINE

Food is a national obsession in Spain, and an experience to savour – whether that means trying tapas in an earthy bar deep in the *barrios* of Madrid, or savouring a Michelin-starred meal prepared by one of the country's famously experimental chefs. But don't forget the wine: tasting your way around the vineyards of La Rioja, Ribera del Duero and Portugal's Douro Valley is a vintage experience.

FESTIVALS

It might involve being pummeled with tomatoes in Buñol, watching the pageantry of Semana Santa in Seville or Lorca, or getting swept up by flamenco in Cádiz, but one thing's for sure – Spain is a nation that knows how to party. The best thing to do is find a fiesta and join in with the fun. In Portugal the Saints' festivals – St Anthony's in Lisbon, St John's in Porto – are highlights of the calendar.

ARCHITECTURE

Almost eight centuries of Muslim rule has left Spain with Europe's finest accumulation of Islamic architecture, especially in the former Moorish heartland of Al-Andalus (Andalucía), which encompassed Granada, Córdoba and Seville. But there is a wonderful Christian legacy, too: Catholicism is central to Spanish identity, and cathedrals form the spiritual heart of many Spanish towns.

BEACHES

With such a surfeit of stunning beaches, it's no surprise that Spain remains one of Europe's top summer holiday destinations. While the hordes descend on the Costa Blanca and Costa del Sol, many more unspoiled beaches await further afield: from the windy sands of the Costa de la Luz to Andalucia's flawless Cabo de Gata. Portugal competes with the family-friendly Algarve and golden Ilha de Tavira.

Right: The Alhambra in southern Spain began life as a citadel, before becoming the seat of Granada's Nasrid emirs.

Transport hubs

Spain is one of Europe's top holiday destinations and is well linked to other European countries by air, rail and road. Regular ferries run to the UK, Italy, the Canary Islands, Morocco and Algeria, and high-speed trains serve major Spanish and other European cities. An increasingly popular destination, Portugal is well connected to North America and European countries by air. There are also handy overland links by bus and train to and from Spain.

Madrid

Madrid's Barajas Airport is one of Europe's busiest and is served by almost 100 airlines. Direct flights connect the city with destinations across Europe. Flight times are less than one hour to Lisbon and around two hours to London, Paris and some Moroccan cities. Within Spain, Madrid is also the hub of the country's outstanding bus and train network. Bus routes radiate to all four corners of the country, and the expansion of Spain's high-speed rail network has dramatically cut travel times between Madrid and the rest of the country.

Barcelona (see pp388-9 for city map)

Most travellers enter Barcelona through El Prat airport, although some budget airlines use Girona–Costa Brava or Reus airports. Travelling by train is a pricier but more romantic way of reaching Catalonia from other European cities. The TGV takes around around seven hours to reach Barcelona from Paris. High-speed Tren de Alta Velocidad Española (AVE) trains connect Madrid and Barcelona in under three hours.

Valencia

Valencia's airport is 10km west of the centre along the A3, towards Madrid. All fast trains use Valencia Joaquín Sorolla station, 800m south of the old town. It's linked with Estación del Norte, 500m away, by free shuttle bus. Trasmediterránea and Baleària operate ferries to Ibiza and Mallorca, and less frequently Menorca and Algeria.

Seville

Seville Airport, 7km east of the city, has flights to/from Spanish cities and destinations across Europe including London, Paris, Amsterdam, Dublin, Frankfurt and Rome. Seville's principal train station, Estación Santa Justa, is 1.5km northeast of the centre. High-speed AVE trains go to/from Madrid and Córdoba.

Bilbao

Direct flights connect Bilbao with London, Paris, Lisbon, Frankfurt and Amsterdam, as well as Barcelona, Madrid and other Spanish cities. The airport is conveniently located 12km northeast of the city. You can also reach Bilbao by train from other parts of Spain, including Madrid (from 5 hours) and Barcelona (around 7 hours).

Lisbon

Situated around 6km north of the centre, the ultramodern Aeroporto de Lisboa operates direct flights to major international hubs including London, New York, Paris and Frankfurt. Lisbon is also linked by train to other key Portuguese cities.

Ibiza

Ibiza's airport is 7km southwest of Ibiza Town. The island receives a huge range of direct flights from mainland Spanish cities and a host of UK and European destinations. Arriving by sea from Barcelona, Valencia and Mallorca is another option: most ferries use the new Estació Marítima de Botafoc, across the harbour from central Ibiza Town and its old Estació Marítima.

Palma

Most visitors to Mallorca fly into Palma's international airport, 8km east of Palma de Mallorca and Spain's third busiest airport. It's possible to arrive by ferry from points along the Spanish coast (Alicante, Barcelona, Denia and Valencia). The neighbouring islands of Ibiza and Menorca are also linked to Mallorca by air and ferry.

Right: Seville's Metropol Parasol (left) and (right) colourful buildings in Lisbon, Portugal.

© Margaret Stepien / Lonely Planet

© Matt Munro / Lonely Planet

SIGHTS & ACTIVITIES

 SEE

 DO

ITINERARY

▽ 1

▽ 2

Alhambra, Granada

The Alhambra is Granada's love letter to Moorish culture. Set against a backdrop of brooding Sierra Nevada peaks, this fortified palace complex started life as a walled citadel before going on to become the opulent seat of Granada's Nasrid emirs. Their showpiece palaces, the 14th-century Palacios Nazaríes, are among the finest Islamic buildings in Europe.

Seville

Seville's historic centre is an intoxicating mix of Mudéjar palaces, baroque churches and medieval lanes. Flamenco clubs keep this centuries-old tradition alive whilst aristocratic mansions recall the city's past as a Moorish capital. The Unesco-listed Real Alcázar complex is a breathtaking spectacle – and a location for *Game of Thrones* – while the colossal Gothic cathedral contains the tomb of explorer Christopher Columbus.

Mezquita, Córdoba

Córdoba's magnificent mosque is a grand symbol of the time when Islamic Spain was at its cultural and political peak, and Córdoba, its capital, was western Europe's most cultured city. In the Mezquita's interior, mesmerising rows of horseshoe arches stretch away in every direction. The most intricate surround the gold-mosaic-decorated portal of the *mihrab* (prayer niche).

The Sherry Triangle

In the vineyards of western Cádiz province, fortified white wine has been produced since Phoenician times, and enjoyed by everyone from Christopher Columbus to Francis Drake. Its oaky essence is best savoured in the Sherry Triangle towns of Jerez de la Frontera, El Puerto de Santa María and Sanlúcar de Barrameda.

White Towns of Cádiz

In northeastern Cádiz province lies a string of fortified *pueblos blancos* that once guarded the Moorish-Christian border. Now, they're a delight to explore, with moody streets twisting past whitewashed houses to crumbling castles and churches. Most spectacular is Arcos de la Frontera, followed by Zahara de la Sierra, Grazalema, Olvera and Setenil de las Bodegas.

Sierra Nevada

From the Spanish for 'snowy mountains', much of this range is protected by the 859-sq-km Parque Nacional Sierra Nevada, including Spain's highest peak, 3479m Mulhacén. The white villages along the southern slopes, known as Las Alpujarras, are famous for their crafts and flat-roofed, Berber-style houses, as well as their numerous hiking and horse-riding opportunities.

Málaga

Picasso's home town is becoming an art heavyweight to rival Madrid or Barcelona. The central sight is the Museo Picasso Málaga, with 200-plus works cataloguing the artist's career, but you can also visit the house where Picasso was born in 1881.

Costa de la Luz

If Andalucía has a hallmark outdoor activity, it's kitesurfing, a daredevil sport given extra oomph by the stiff winds that enliven the choppy waters off the Strait of Gibraltar, especially along the beaches of the Costa de la Luz. The main base is Tarifa, a whitewashed coastal town that often feels more Moroccan than Spanish. A little northwest, El Palmar has Andalucía's best surfing waves.

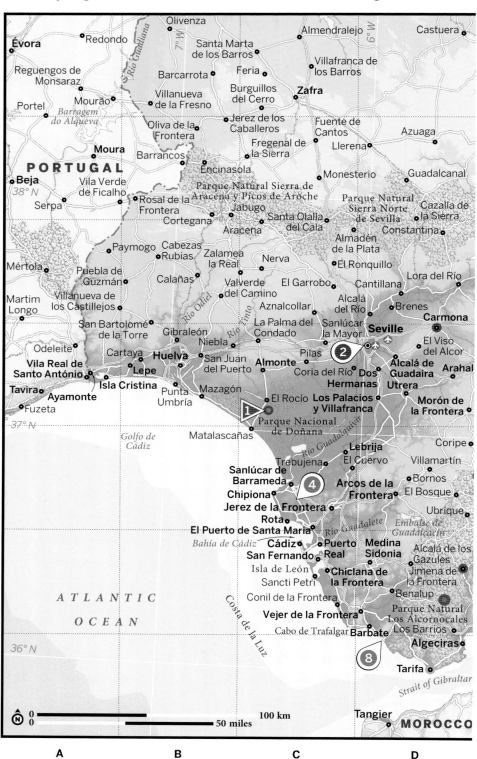

14-day itinerary
The West of Andalucía

Already seen the Alhambra and hiked the Sierra Nevada? Then it's time to go west. Start in Huelva province's **Parque Nacional de Doñana**, arguably Andalucía's finest natural attraction. Visit **Carmona**, with its Alcázar, and **Osuna**, with its grand palaces. Sidestep west to white towns **Zahara de la Sierra** and **Grazalema**. Exciting stops en route east from Ronda to Málaga could be **El Chorro gorge** (home to the Caminito del Rey path) or ancient **Antequera**. Lively port city **Málaga** has great seafood and excellent galleries and museums. With time, you can head southwest to some of Cádiz province's less-trodden spots, including **Jimena de la Frontera**, a good base for hiking in the **Parque Natural Los Alcornocales**.

21-day itinerary
Andalucía's Coastline

Lapping five of its eight provinces, the Andalucian coastline is one of the region's delights. Most coastal towns are linked by bus. Start with Almería's protected, underdeveloped **Cabo de Gata**, a combination of cliffs, salt flats and sandy beaches. Tracking west, **Almería** is worth a stop for its Moorish Alcazaba. Granada's Costa Tropical is precipitous and authentic: **Almuñécar** makes a great base and low-key **La Herradura** offers water sports. Further west, **Nerja** in Málaga province has tempered its development, and excellent inland hiking beckons in **La Axarquía**. **Málaga** deserves three days thanks to its fine gastronomy and art and museum scene. **Marbella** is the most interesting stop on the over-touristed Costa del Sol, though **Mijas** also merits a day trip. Southwest, the British-owned promontory of **Gibraltar** guards the jaws of Europe. Extending northwest from kitesurfing capital **Tarifa**, Cádiz' Costa de la Luz harbours water sports, coastal hikes, Roman ruins, white-sand beaches and international-flavoured cuisine.

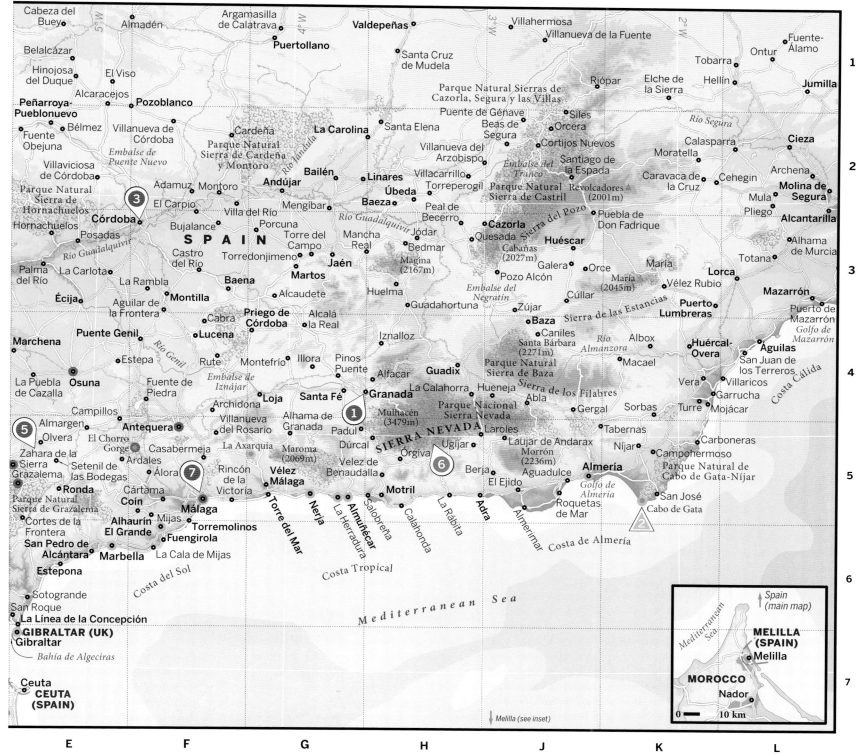

SIGHTS &
ACTIVITIES

 SEE

 DO

ITINERARY

▽ 1

▽ 2

Dalt Vila, Ibiza

All-night raver, boho-cool hippy, blissed-out beach lover – Ibiza has its devoted fans, but there's more to this sun-kissed island than meets the bleary eye. A Unesco World Heritage site and the one must-see sight on Ibiza, the walled enclave of Dalt Vila occupies the highest ground in Ibiza Town. It contains a roster of cultural sights huddled between centuries-old mansions, jasmine-draped balconies and steep, cobbled streets.

Parc Natural de Ses Salines, Ibiza

These ancient, shimmering salt pans are a haven for local and migrating birdlife on Ibiza. Platja de Ses Salines, also within the natural park, is a breathtaking sweep of pale sand that's also home to the island's best *chiringuitos* (beach bars).

Trucador Peninsula, Formentera

With sugar-white sands and perfectly turquoise water, the pencil-slim Trucador Peninsula rivals the world's finest beaches. Dreamy Platja Illetes slinks along the west side of this sliver of land; on its east coast (just a few steps away) is equally gorgeous Platja Llevant.

Menorca

Menorca's sublime beaches are some of the Balearics' best, and authorities have taken important measures to preserve their natural beauty: you often have to park and walk the final 1km to 3km (15 to 30 minutes) to reach the shore. In 1993, Unesco declared Menorca a Biosphere Reserve, aiming to preserve areas, such as the Parc Natural S'Albufera des Grau wetlands, and its sprinkling of mysterious Bronze Age sites.

Illa de Cabrera

The only national park in the Balearics, Parc Nacional Marítim-Terrestre de l'Arxipèlag de Cabrera is a special place. Illa de Cabrera is the largest of 19 uninhabited islands that make up the marine park – its wild headlands and secluded beaches are protected by laws that limit the number of daily visitors. Boat excursions to the island from Colònia de Sant Jordi stop off at Sa Cova Blava, an exquisitely blue marine cave.

Catedral de Mallorca

Mallorca has a sunny personality thanks to its beaches, mountains and soulful hill towns. The island's architectural tour de force is Palma Catedral, resembling a vast ship moored at the city's edge. On the seaward side, the flying buttresses are extraordinary. A kaleidoscope of stained-glass windows and a flight of fancy by Gaudí inhabit the interior.

Cap de Formentor, Mallorca

This narrow, precipitous peninsula forms one of the most dramatic mountain ranges in southern Europe, its peaks swathed in forests of Aleppo pines plunging to some of the most beautiful and isolated beaches on the island. However you travel the road running its length, prepare for drama and photo ops at every bend.

Serra de Tramuntana, Mallorca

Mallorca's northwest coast is remarkably wild, ensnared by scarred limestone peaks and cliffs that loom over brilliant blue sea. Honey-coloured villages such as Deià and Sóller sit high atop the sheer hillsides, surrounded by vegetable gardens, citrus orchards and olive groves, arranged in steep terraces that in some cases date back at least to the Moorish occupation.

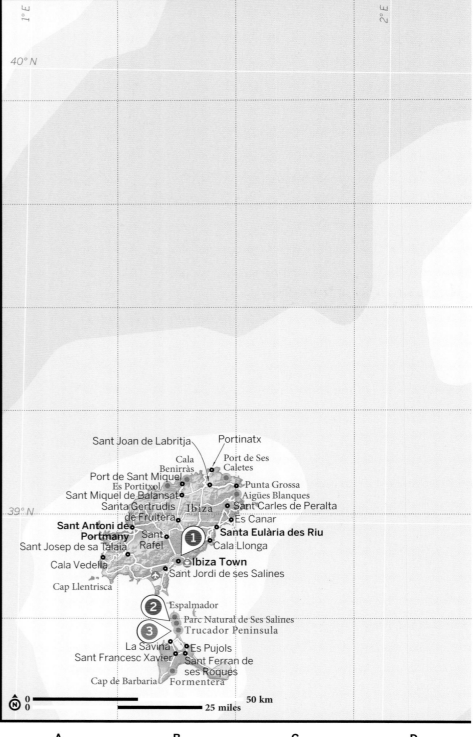

7-day itinerary
Mallorca

With just a week it's best to stay put on one island and explore by car or scooter: **Mallorca** is the obvious choice. Spend the first few days in stately **Palma**, then head north into the **Serra de Tramuntana**. Don't miss hilltop **Valldemossa**, with its Carthusian monastery, and ochre-stoned **Deià**, set against the backdrop of the Puig des Teix (1062m).

Detour via the lively town of **Sóller** to view its Modernista architecture, then track the coast to **Cap de Formentor**, before veering south via beaches and bays to the quiet town of **Artà**, centred around its 14th-century hilltop fortress. Turn west via the monastery at **Petra**, pausing for some wine tasting in the nearby vineyards before returning to Palma.

14-day itinerary
Three Balearics

With a couple of weeks, you'll be able to explore two or even three Balearic islands. Begin with a few days on **Mallorca**, then catch a ferry to **Ibiza Town**. Though famous (read: notorious) for its hardcore hedonist nightlife, there's more to Ibiza than its raucous reputation. Away from the clubs and bars of the capital's centre, you'll find hilltop Dalt Vila and

its stately cathedral. Along the north coast are stunning beaches such as **Cala Benirràs** and **Aigües Blanques**, which attract a bohemian crowd, and private quiet coves such as **Es Portitxol** or **Port de Ses Caletes**. A visit to the old hippy-hangout village of **Sant Carles de Peralta** is also worthwhile. Then it's another short ferry trip over to **Formentera**,

where more beach-lounging and sea-swimming await on the **Trucador Peninsula**. The astoundingly beautiful back-to-back beaches of Illetes and Llevant are a vision of paradise worthy of the Caribbean. They form part of the **Parc Natural de Ses Salines**, which stretches north to the uninhabited island of **Espalmador**.

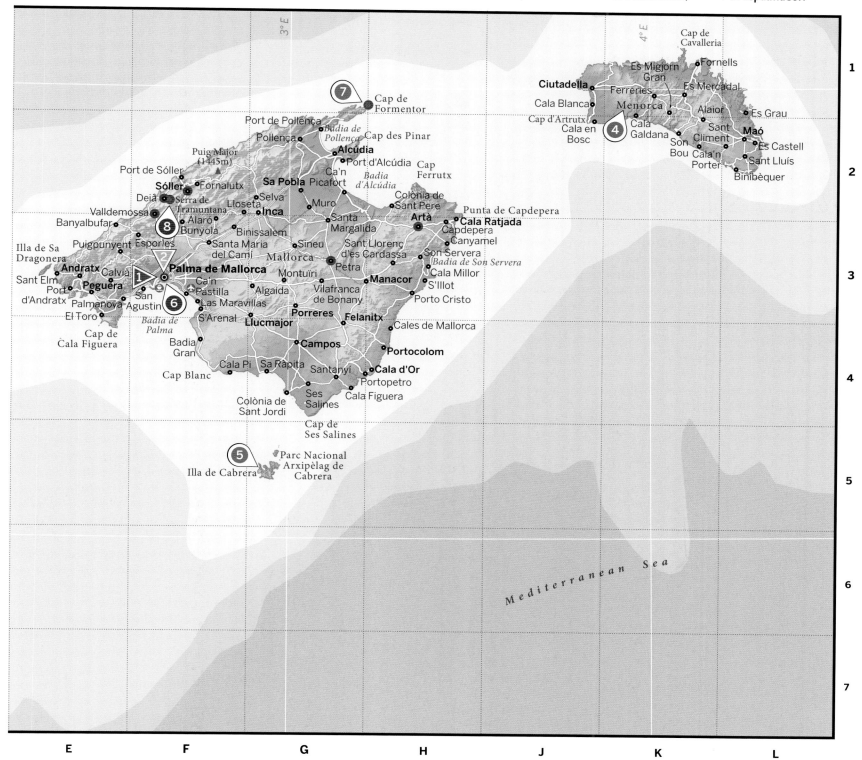

Art Museums of Madrid

Madrid is one of the fine arts capitals of the world. The Museo del Prado, housing works by Goya, Velázquez and El Greco, is the kingpin, but also within a short stroll are the Centro de Arte Reina Sofía, showcasing Picasso's Guernica, plus works by Dalí and Miró. The renowned Museo Thyssen-Bornemisza is nearby, too.

Segovia

Set amid the hills of Castilla, Segovia has two buildings that set it apart: the multiturreted Alcázar, which inspired a Disneyland castle, and a Roman aqueduct of granite blocks held together without mortar that is still standing after almost 2000 years.

Aranjuez

Aranjuez was founded as a royal pleasure retreat but by the 18th century its 300-plus rooms had turned the palace into a sprawling complex. The gardens are filled with species brought back by botanists and explorers from Spanish colonies.

④ Cáceres

Protected by defensive walls, the medieval core of Cáceres, known as the Monumental City, has survived

14-day itinerary
The Spanish Interior

The Spanish interior may not fit the stereotype of sun, sand and sangría, but we love it all the more for that. This route takes in a mix of lesser-known cities and historic villages. From **Madrid**, head to some of the loveliest towns of the Spanish heartland, all of which can be easily visited by train. **Segovia** is a must-see, with its Disney-esque castle and Roman aqueduct. **Ávila** is one of the best-preserved medieval bastions in Spain, surrounded by imposing city walls comprising eight monumental gates, 88 watchtowers and more than 2500 turrets. Vibrant **Salamanca**'s Plaza Mayor is another unforgettable highlight, especially when it's illuminated at night to impressive effect. Back in Madrid, hire a car and head south on the trail of Don Quijote. **Consuegra**'s nine windmills are the best examples of the novel's 'monstrous giants', but there are older versions in **Campo de Criptana**. **El Toboso** has a library with more than 300 editions of the book in various languages, and a statue of the hero.

almost intact. Cobbled streets climb among stone walls lined with palaces, mansions, arches and churches, while the skyline is decorated with turrets, spires, gargoyles and storks' nests.

Toledo

Toledo was known as the 'city of three cultures' in the Middle Ages, a place where – legend has it – Christian, Muslim and Jewish communities peacefully coexisted. The town appears in the canvases of El Greco, the painter with whom the city is synonymous.

Cuenca

An Unesco World Heritage Site, Cuenca's old centre is a stage set of medieval buildings, many painted in bright colours, stacked on a promontory at the meeting of two deep river gorges. Two of its famous *casas colgadas* (hanging houses) have transformed their interiors into modern galleries.

Consuegra

In Consuegra you can get a classic shot of nine of the region's characterful *molinos de viento* (windmills) flanking the town's 12th-century castle. The windmills of La Mancha were made famous in Miguel de Cervantes' novel *Don Quijote*. Track down the Plaza Mayor, with its pretty first-floor balconies.

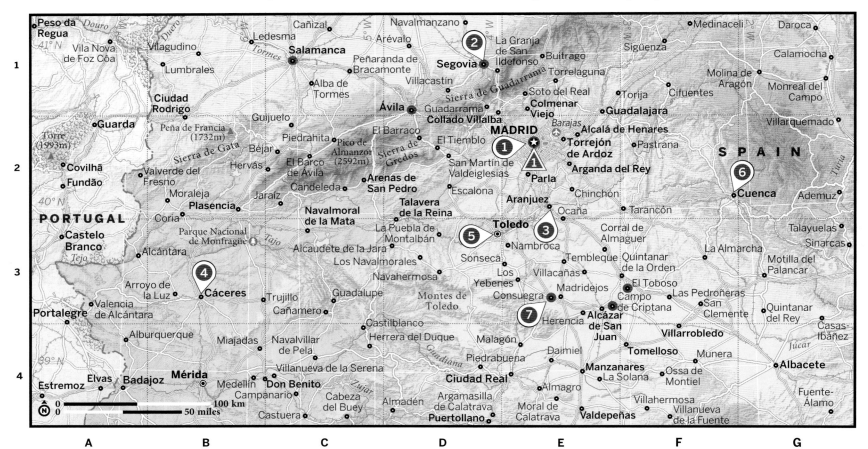

Murcia

Officially twinned with Miami, Murcia is a sizeable but laid-back provincial capital. Like Valencia, it is famous for its *huerta*, a zone of market gardens dating back to Moorish times, which supply the city's restaurants with fresh produce and drive a thriving tapas scene.

Cartagena

Pick an era to explore in Cartagena. Its magnificent Modernista buildings. include the Palacio Consistorial (town hall); Casa Cervantes; Casa Llagostera; the zinc-domed Gran Hotel; the strawberries-and-cream confection of Casa Clares; and the Palacio Aguirre, now a space for modern art.

Castillo de Xàtiva

Xàtiva's castle is arguably the most evocative in the Valencia region. Behind its crumbling battlements you'll find flower gardens, tumbledown turrets, towers, dungeons and a Gothic chapel. The views are sensational.

Lorca

The market town of Lorca is known for hosting Spain's most flamboyant Semana Santa (Holy Week) festivities, when the town is divided into two

10-day itinerary
Adventure from Valencia

Valencia is easily the equal of Madrid or Barcelona in terms of its nightlife: it's best sampled in the lively *barrio* (neighbourhood) of Russafa, with its fabulous tapas, cafe and bar scene. Next, hire a car and head south. Trudge up to the magnificent hilltop of **Castillo de Xàtiva** (pack a picnic), then take a breath and delve headlong into the crazy nightlife of

Alicante, drinking till dawn in the wall-to-wall weekend bars of the old quarter (known as El Barrio) around Catedral de San Nicolás, then sunbathing away your hangover on the beach. Take a couple of days to explore the underrated city of **Murcia**, then head back in time amongst the fascinating Roman and Carthaginian sites of **Cartagena**. Conclude with a few days in the **Parque Regional de Sierra Espuña**, tackling the peaceful trails and enjoying the unspoiled beauty of these wild Spanish hills.

tribes: Blanco (White) and Azul (Blue), the colours of the brotherhoods that have competed since 1855 to stage the most lavish display.

Buñol

The last Wednesday in August marks Spain's messiest festival, La Tomatina, which attracts more than 20,000 visitors. At 11am, 100 tonnes of squishy tomatoes are tipped from trucks to the crowd, and everyone joins in an anarchic tomato battle.

Valencia

The cultural highlight of Spain's third-largest city is the Ciudad de las Artes y las Ciencias, a series of buildings by the world-famous local architect Santiago Calatrava, including an opera house, science museum, 3D cinema and aquarium. Famous as the home of paella, the city is surrounded by its *huerta*, a fertile area of market gardens.

Morella

This outstanding example of a medieval fortress town is perched on a hilltop, crowned by a castle and girdled by an intact rampart wall more than 2km long. It's the ancient capital of Els Ports, the 'Mountain Passes', a rugged region offering scenic drives, strenuous cycling and first-rate walks.

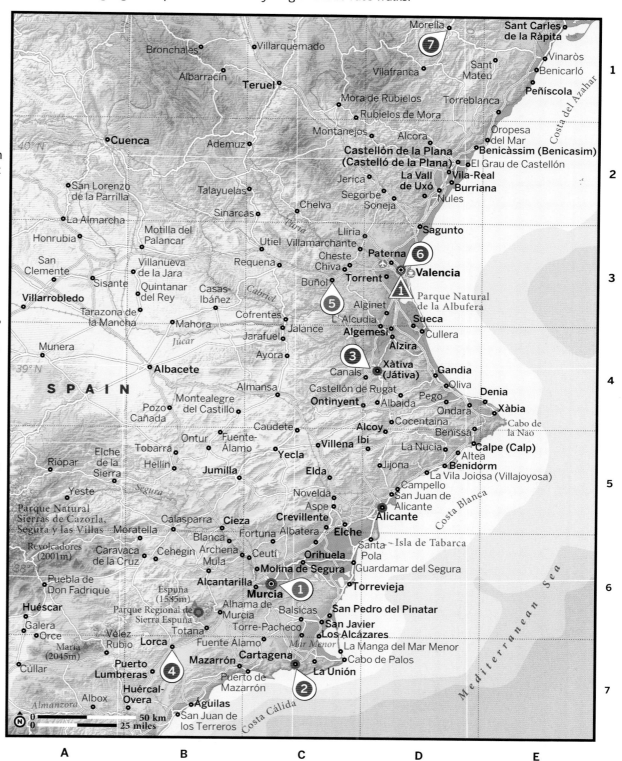

SIGHTS &
ACTIVITIES

 SEE

 DO

ITINERARY

 1

 2

① Cadaqués

This easygoing whitewashed village gleams above the cobalt-blue waters of a rocky bay on Catalonia's most easterly outcrop. It's best known for its links with the surrealist artist Salvador Dalí, who spent family holidays here during his youth and lived much of his later life at nearby Port Lligat, where the Dalí family's otherworldly seaside home stands.

② Girona

Northern Catalonia's largest city, Girona is a jewellery box of museums, galleries, Modernista mansions and Gothic churches, strung around a web of cobbled lanes, medieval walls and one of the country's finest Jewish quarters. With the world's second-widest Gothic nave, the town's cathedral is also a formidable sight.

③ Parc Nacional d'Aigüestortes i Estany de Sant Maurici

Catalonia's only national park extends 20km east to west, and just 9km north to south. Though small, this mountain park sparkles with over 200 lakes and countless streams and waterfalls. It comprises two east–west valleys framed by jagged peaks of granite and slate.

④ Olot

This bustling town is the regional capital of La Garrotxa, a landscape of cone-shaped hills chiselled by geological activity up to 700,000 years ago, which now forms the Parc Natural de la Zona Volcànica de la Garrotxa.

⑤ Tarragona

In this effervescent port city, Roman history collides with beaches, bars and a tempting seafood scene. The biggest lure is the town's Roman ruins, including a mosaic-packed museum and a seaside amphitheatre.

⑥ Ruta del Cister

The Cistercian Route weaves between Tarragona and Lleida, linking a trio of ancient monasteries: Santa Maria de Poblet, Santes Creus and Santa Maria de Vallbona. All three can be visited in a single day's drive from Lleida or, more conveniently, Tarragona.

⑦ Zaragoza

The multi-domed Basílica del Pilar reflected in the Río Ebro is a potent symbol of Spain's fifth-largest city, home to a lively tapas and bar scene, and many artworks by Francisco de Goya, who was born nearby in 1746.

⑧ Valles de Hecho and Ansó

Little known to non-Spaniards, these enchanting valleys in Aragón's far northwest corner were carved out by the Río Aragón Subordán and Río Veral. A walkers' paradise, they lie partly within the 270-sq-km Parque Natural de los Valles Occidentales.

⑨ Albarracín

Positioned on a rocky promontory created by the Río Guadalaviar, the town of Albarracín is famous for its pink-hued medieval houses. The colour comes from the unusual hue of the local gypsum.

⑩ Parque Nacional de Ordesa y Monte Perdido

This is where the Spanish Pyrenees take your breath away. The park extends south from a dragon's back of peaks along the French border, and includes Monte Perdido (3355m), the third-highest peak in the Pyrenees.

10-day itinerary
Into the Hills

Rent a car in **Barcelona** and travel west to **Zaragoza**, one of Spain's most vibrant cities, with a wealth of monuments and great tapas. Head north for the hills to the small village of **Loarre**, home of the Castillo de Loarre, a multi-towered Requonquista-era castle with panoramic views. Stop for a day or two in the Pyrenees village of **Hecho** and walk a section of the Camino de Santiago before heading to **Sos del Rey Católico**, which looks for all the world like a Tuscan hill town. Drive south for an overnight stop in dramatic **Daroca**, then on to **Teruel**, remarkable for its old town's Mudéjar architecture. Visit **Albarracín**, one of Spain's most spectacular – and colourful – villages.

14-day itinerary
Catalonia Cruise

A lifetime in **Barcelona** may not be enough, but drag yourself away and you'll discover that the wider Catalonia region is just as fascinating. You'll need a minimum of two days in Barcelona to soak up Gaudí, taste the city's culinary excellence and wander its old town. Rent a car and head north, passing through **Tossa de Mar** and its castle-backed bay, then **Calella de Palafrugell** and **Tamariu**, two beautifully sited coastal villages, before heading inland to spend the night in **Girona**. The next day is all about Salvador Dalí, from his fantasy castle **Castell de Puból** to his extraordinary theatre-museum in **Figueres**, and then his one-time home, the lovely seaside village of **Cadaqués**. The next morning leave the Mediterranean behind and drive west in the shadow of the Pyrenees. Your reward is a couple of nights in **Taüll**, gateway to the magnificent **Parc Nacional d'Aigüestortes i Estany de Sant Maurici**. A loop south via **Lleida** then east has you back in Barcelona by mid-afternoon on your final day.

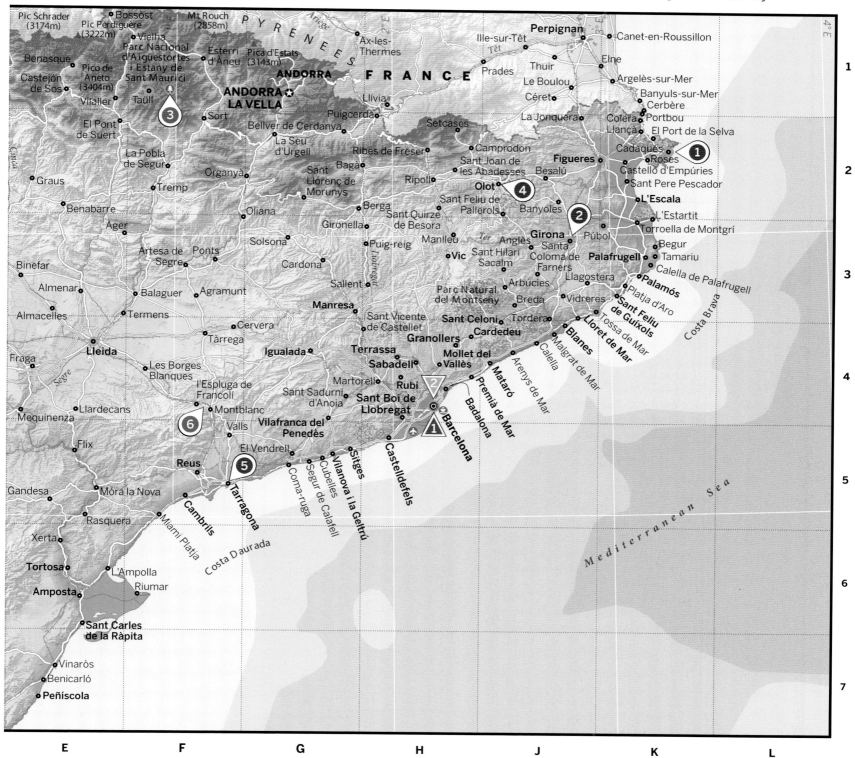

SIGHTS & ACTIVITIES

 SEE

 DO

ITINERARY

▼ 1

▽ 2

Museo Guggenheim Bilbao

Once blighted by industrial decay, Bilbao's fortunes were transformed by its magnificent, titanium-clad art museum by superstar architect Frank Gehry. Its treasures include a massive flower-covered doggy sculpture by Jeff Koons that has become a Bilbao icon in its own right, plus a maze-like installation by Richard Serra and a 9m bronze and steel spider that looks like it scuttled out of a Dalí painting.

Picos de Europa

The Picos de Europa offer Spain's finest walking country. There are three massifs: the eastern Macizo Ándara, with a summit of 2444m; the western Macizo El Cornión, rising to 2596m; and the Macizo Central (or Macizo de los Urrieles), reaching 2648m. The 671-sq-km Parque Nacional de los Picos de Europa covers all three.

San Sebastián

San Sebastián has a deserved reputation as one of the world's great dining destinations. Chefs here have turned bar snacks into an art form. Sometimes called 'high cuisine in miniature', *pintxos* (Basque tapas) are piles of flavour often mounted on a slice of baguette. The city also has an alluring coastline, focusing on Playa de la Concha, its backyard beach.

Pamplona

Capital of the fiercely independent Kingdom of Navarra and home to a famous bull-running festival, Pamplona makes a fascinating place to explore, with its grand cathedral, archaeological treasures and 16th-century fortifications.

Santiago de Compostela

The capital of Galicia and the final stop on the Camino de Santiago pilgrimage trail, Santiago is a city imbued with a millennium's worth of journeys. Today some 300,000 Camino pilgrims venture here each year, heading for journey's end at the famous cathedral.

Burgos

The extraordinary Gothic cathedral of Burgos looms large over the city and skyline. Beneath its majestic spires of lies the tomb of Burgos' favourite and most roguish son, El Cid.

Asturian Coast

This green northern region and its jagged coast is strung with colourful fishing ports, such as Ribadesella and Cudillero, and more than 200 beaches. Asturias' cultured capital, Oviedo, is both historic and coolly contemporary. It was at Covadonga that the Spanish nation came into being 1300 years ago.

Altamira

Dating from 35,000 to 13,000 years old, the paintings of bison, horses, deer and other animals in the Cueva de Altamira, 2.5km southwest of Santillana del Mar, are Spain's finest examples of prehistoric art. The original cave was closed to protect the artworks, but a replica now enables everyone to appreciate them.

La Rioja

All wine fanciers know the vintages of La Rioja, where the vine has been cultivated since Roman times. Vineyards cover the hinterland of Río Ebro and around the town of Haro: many are centuries old, such as López Heredia, while others such as Viña Real are much younger and favour more modern wine styles.

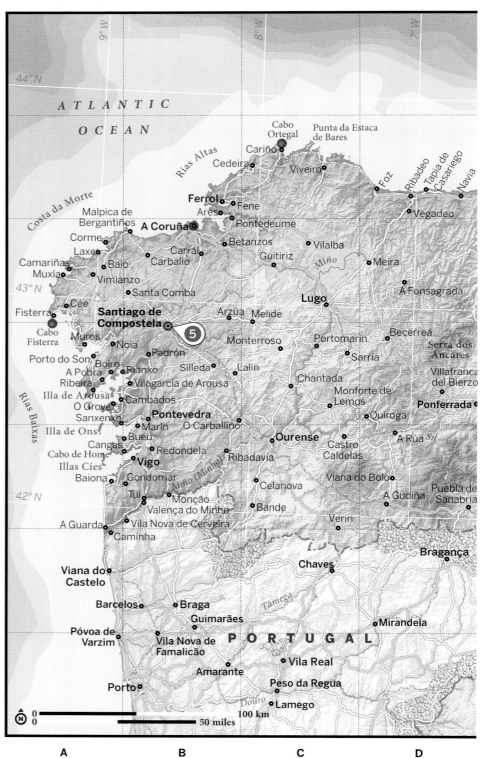

10-day itinerary
Along the North Coast

The Mediterranean Coast gets the crowds, but the country's northern coastline is equally lovely. Begin in **San Sebastián**, with its dramatic setting and fabulous food. West by train is **Bilbao** and its showpiece Museo Guggenheim Bilbao. Hire a car to explore Cantabria's cobblestone **Santillana del Mar**, the rock art at **Altamira** and the village of **Ribadesella**, followed by the valleys of the **Picos de Europa**. After a night in **Oviedo**, tackle Galicia's coastline, punctuated with fishing villages and stunning cliffs. Don't miss **Cabo Ortegal**, dynamic **A Coruña** and windswept **Cabo Fisterra**. Finish in **Santiago de Compostela**, a place of pilgrim footfalls and a cathedral of singular power.

14-day itinerary
Picos de Europa

Spain's wildest countryside awaits in the mountains of the Picos de Europa; a car is the only way to go here. Start with a trip on the **Teleférico de Fuente Dé**, a precipitous cable car that whizzes up to the superb heights of the southeastern Picos. Circle north, stopping in **Arenas de Cabrales** to taste some of Asturias' ultra-tangy cheese, then veer south to hike through the **Garganta del Cares**, Spain's most famous gorge, with sheer limestone walls that rise to a kilometre high in places. There's more fine trekking in store nearby around the lovely **Lagos de Covadonga**, where a web of trails wind through the western massif's twinkling, high-altitude lakes. At **Bulnes**, board the eerie mountain-traversing funicular or brave the uphill hike to this roadless, cliff-framed hamlet. Continue on to **Covadonga** for a trip through Spanish history in a holy village that was the launchpad of the 800-year Reconquista. From **Arriondas**, kayak your way downriver along the rushing Río Sella, then round things off with some well-deserved R&R in the pretty city of **Oviedo**.

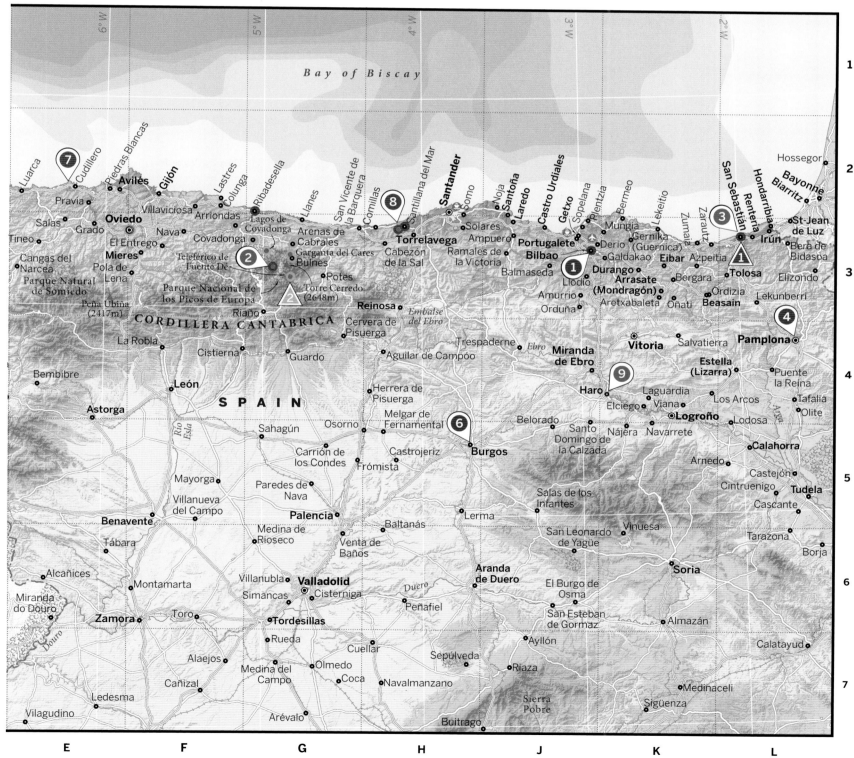

SIGHTS &
ACTIVITIES

 SEE

DO

ITINERARY

 1

 2

1 The Alfama, Lisbon

With its labyrinthine alleyways, hidden courtyards and curving, shadow-filled lanes, Lisbon's Alfama district is a magical place to delve into the soul of the city. You'll pass breadbox-sized grocers, brilliantly tiled buildings and cosy taverns filled with easygoing chatter, accompanied by the scent of chargrilled sardines and the mournful rhythms of fado drifting in the breeze.

2 Sintra

With its rippling mountains, dewy forests, exotic gardens and glittering palaces, Sintra is like a page torn from a fairy tale. Its Unesco World Heritage–listed centre, Sintra-Vila, is dotted with pastel-hued manors tucked into luxuriant hills that roll down to the blue Atlantic.

3 Porto

Laced with pedestrian laneways, Porto is blessed with baroque churches, epic theatres and sprawling plazas. Its Ribeira district – a Unesco World Heritage Site – is just a short walk across a landmark bridge from Vila Nova de Gaia's centuries-old port wineries, where you can sip the world's best port.

4 Cabo de São Vicente

Five kilometres from Sagres, Europe's southwesternmost point is a barren headland, the last piece of home Portuguese sailors saw as they set off into the unknown. A red lighthouse houses the small but excellent Museu dos Faróis, showcasing Sagres' role in Portugal's maritime history.

Alto Douro: The Douro wine region is the oldest demarcated wine region in the world.

5 Alto Douro

Heading upriver from Peso da Régua, terraced vineyards blanket every hillside, with whitewashed *quintas* (estates) perched above the Douro. This dramatic landscape is the by-product of 2000 years of winemaking. Countless vintners receive guests for tours, tastings and overnight stays.

6 Parque Natural da Ria Formosa

This system of lagoons and islands stretches for 60km along the Algarve coastline from west of Faro to Cacela Velha, enclosing *sapal* (marsh), *salinas* (salt pans), creeks and dune islands. The marshes are an important area for migrating and nesting birds. It is the favoured nesting place of the little tern and the rare purple gallinule.

7 Évora

Megaliths are found all over the ancient landscape around Évora. These prehistoric structures, built around 5000 to 7500 years ago, dot the European Atlantic coast, but here in Alentejo there are an astounding number of Neolithic remains: dolmens (Neolithic stone tombs; *antas* in Portuguese), menhirs (individual standing stones) and cromeleques, organised sets of standing stones.

8 Beiras Villages

From schist-walled communities spilling down terraced hillsides to spiky-edged sentinels that guarded the eastern border against Spanish incursions, the inland Beiras are filled with picturesque villages like Piódão, Trancoso, Sortelha, Monsanto and Idanha-a-Velha.

9 The Algarve

Along Portugal's south coast, the Algarve is home to a wildly varied coastline. There are sandy islands reachable only by boat, dramatic cliff-backed shores, rugged beaches and people-packed sands. To escape the hordes, plan a low-season visit, when prices dive and crowds disperse.

10 Barcelos

The Minho is famous for its sprawling outdoor markets, but the largest and oldest is the Feira de Barcelos, held every Thursday on the banks of the Rio Cávado. Most outsiders come for the yellow-dotted *louça de Barcelos* ceramics and the gaudy figurines à la local potter Rosa Ramalho, while villagers are more interested in the chickens, linen, baskets and ox yokes.

11 Ilha de Tavira

This island is a magnet for sunseekers, beach bums, nature lovers (and naturists) thanks to kilometre after kilometre of golden beach. Not only that, it's part of the protected Parque Natural da Ria Formosa. Outside the high season, the island feels wonderfully remote and empty, but during July and August it's jammed.

10-day itinerary
Heart of Portugal

This journey explores Portugal's interior. From **Lisbon** head 200km southeast to the historic village of **Castro Verde**. Drive east to **Mértola**, a medieval settlement perched above the placid Rio Guadiana. From **Mértola**, drive north to Beja, a lively town with a walled centre, intriguing museums and a 13th-century castle. Keep north to reach **Évora**, a good base for visiting Neolithic sites. Travel northeast to the marble town of **Vila Viçosa**, home to a staggering palace. Next are the clifftop towns of **Castelo de Vide** and **Monsanto**. End in **Vila Nova de Foz Côa**, a gateway to some of Iberia's most impressive petroglyphs, followed by a detour to the vineyards of the Douro.

14-day itinerary
Southern Beauty

This trip follows Portugal's southern rivers, beaches and ridges. From **Lisbon** head to the **Costa da Caparica** and its bevy of beaches. Next steer down to **Praia do Meco** for more sandy action and seafood. Keep going south to reach the desolate cliffs of **Cabo Espichel** and a night in **Sesimbra**, a fishing village turned resort. Continue east, stopping for a picnic on the forest-lined shores of **Parque Natural da Arrábida**. Stay in **Setúbal** for more seafood feasting and a dolphin-watching boat trip along the **Sado Estuary**. From Setúbal, take the ferry across to **Tróia**, then continue south to overnight in **Vila Nova de Milfontes**, a lovely seaside town with fine beaches and charming places to stay. Follow the coast to **Aljezur**, with its unspoilt, cliff-backed sands, and into the rustic town of **Carrapateira**, with more wild, untouched beaches. Soon, you'll reach the southern coast at pretty, laid-back **Sagres**, another surfers' town. Visit the sea-cliff fortress, then wind up at the surreal cliffs of **Cabo de São Vicente**, Europe's last stop.

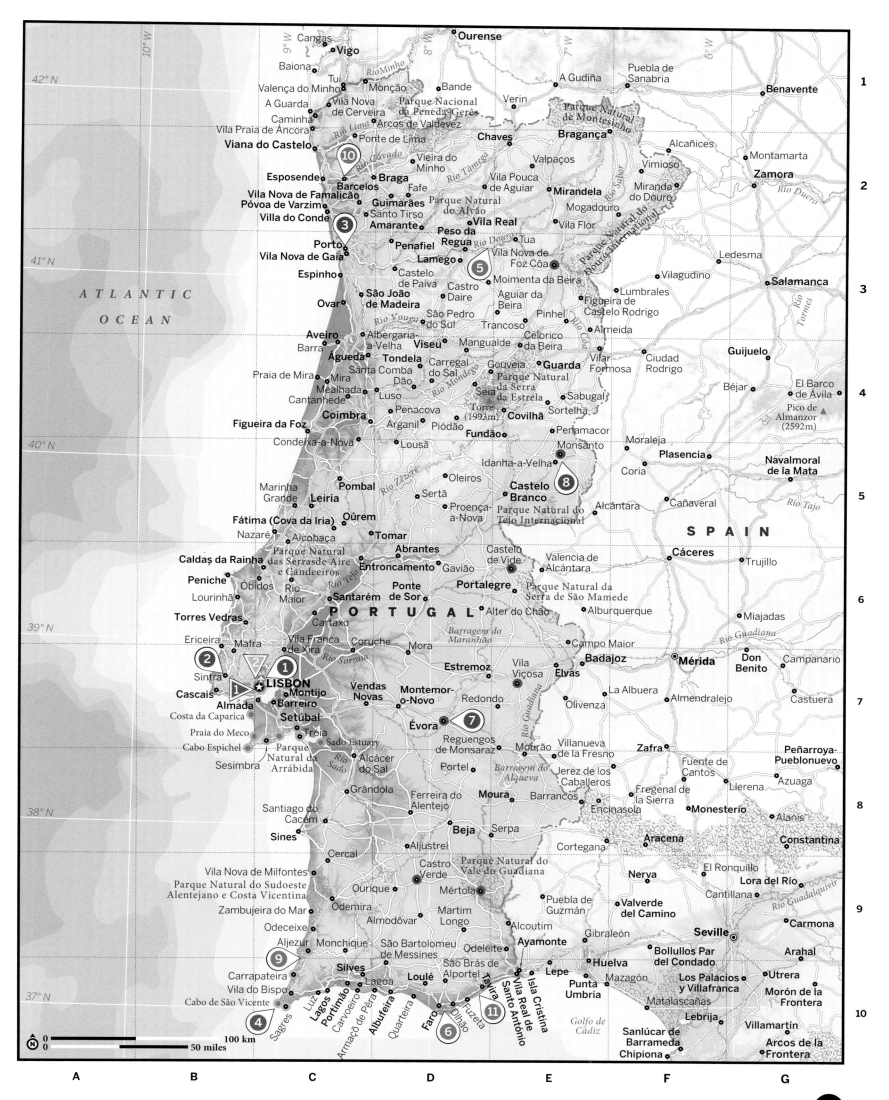

ATLANTIC
OCEAN

SPAIN

PORTUGAL

Italy, Corsica & Malta

Home to many of the world's greatest works of art, architecture and gastronomy, Italy elates, inspires and moves like nowhere else. Epicentre of the Roman Empire and birthplace of the Renaissance, this European virtuoso groans under the weight of its cultural cachet: this is, after all, the land of Dante, Michelangelo, Titian and Verdi. But not to be outdone, nature puts on her own performance: from icy mountains to glacial lakes, fiery craters, sparkling coastline and idyllic islands, Italy is a geographical textbook writ large. Out in the Mediterranean lie three islands of note: Italian-owned Sardinia; its craggy, French-owned neighbour Corsica; and fiery, independent Malta. All are worthy of their own island expedition.

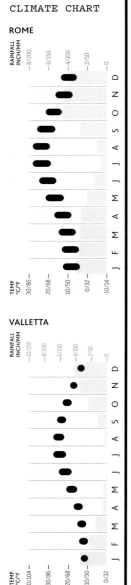

WINE

Vino has been a cornerstone of Italian life since at least the Roman era. The oldest known wine in Italy is Chianti Classico, but there are plenty of other regions to taste and savour: Barolo, Montepulciano, Valpolicella, Soave and the South Tyrol, to name a few.

FOOD

Italian food encompasses many regional cuisines, from the rustic flavours of Tuscany to the seafood of Sicily, the ragùs of Bologna and Piedmont's mountain dishes. What unites them all is tradition, flavour and, above all, a passion for food.

ART

Italy's stunning art and architecture have long seduced visitors. From Venice's *palazzi* and Florence's churches and galleries to Michelangelo's extraordinary ceiling fresco in Rome's Sistine Chapel, it's Elysium for art-lovers.

HILLTOP TOWNS

Perched on crags, clinging to cliffs, teetering over drops, Italy's hill-towns were built for reasons of defence and devotion – but nowadays it's the views that steal the show. There are scores to explore: coastal Ravello, medieval Spello, towering San Gimignano.

COASTLINE

Surrounded on three sides by sea, few countries boast a coastline as long and varied. Aside from the Mediterranean, it's worth exploring the south and east too – and don't forget the sands of Sicily, Sardinia and the Aeolian Islands, nor Corsica and Malta further afield.

NATURE

Wild mountains, active volcanoes, bird-rich wetlands and fragrant forests: this is a region rich with natural resources, and incredibly diverse. Hike the Dolomites, ski the Aosta Valley, explore the Apennines, swim the Amalfi Coast or scale Mt Etna.

Right: The aquamarine waters surrounding Italy's Aeolian Islands offer glorious swimming and snorkelling.

Transport hubs

A plethora of airlines link Italy with the rest of the world, and cut-rate carriers have driven down the cost of flights from other European countries. Excellent rail and bus connections, especially with northern Italy, offer efficient overland transport, while car and passenger ferries run to ports throughout the Mediterranean. Aside from the coastal roads linking Italy with France and Slovenia, arriving in Italy overland involves tunnels through the Alps (open year-round) or mountain passes (seasonally closed or requiring snow chains). Having a car is great for reaching rural areas, but it's generally best to avoid driving in Italian cities.

Below: Milan's Stazione Centrale (left) and (right) Venice's Grand Canal as seen from the Rialto Bridge.

Rome (see pp426-7 for city map)
Rome has two airports: Leonardo da Vinci, better known as Fiumicino, and Ciampino. Long-distance trains run to Stazione Termini from many European destinations. The port of Civitavecchia, 80km northwest of Rome, has ferries to Sardinia, Sicily and other Mediterranean destinations.

Milan
Northern Italy's main airport, Malpensa is 50km northwest of Milan. Linate Airport, 7km east of the centre, handles many domestic and European flights. Stazione Centrale receives high-speed trains from France, Switzerland and Germany, plus most Italian cities.

Venice
Most people arrive by train, plane and, more controversially, cruise ship. Airlines mainly use Marco Polo Airport, 12km outside Venice, but budget carriers also use Treviso Airport. Direct trains connect to major Italian cities, as well as France, Germany, Austria, Switzerland, Slovenia and Croatia.

Florence
Florence has two useful airports: Florence Airport, 5km northwest, and Pisa International Airport, 80km west. Florence is on the Rome–Milan line: trains run to Stazione Campo di Marte or Stazione di Santa Maria Novella, both in central Florence.

Bologna
Bologna is a major train junction for northern Italy, with most services arriving at Bologna Centrale station. High-speed trains to Florence take only 37 minutes, with other fast connections to Venice, Milan, Rome and Naples. Guglielmo Marconi airport is 8km northwest of the city.

Naples
Naples International Airport (Capodichino), 7km northeast, is southern Italy's main airport. The city's train station is also southern Italy's rail hub and on the main Milan–Palermo line. Non-resident vehicles are banned in much of central Naples, though there is no need for a car as a visitor.

Sicily
Sicily's main airports are Palermo's Falcone-Borsellino Airport, 30km west of the city, and Fontanarossa Airport, 7km outside Catania. Ferries cross the Strait of Messina (the 3km stretch of water that separates Sicily from the mainland) and also sail from Genoa, Livorno, Civitavecchia, Naples, Salerno, Cagliari (Sardinia), Malta and Tunisia.

Malta
Malta is well connected to Europe and North Africa by air. All flights arrive at Malta International Airport, 8km south of Valletta. Malta also has regular sea links with Sicily (Pozzallo and Catania), central Italy (Civitavecchia) and northern Italy (Genoa).

Corsica
Corsica is connected by regular year-round flights to French mainland airports, and in summer to other European countries. The island has five ferry ports serving the French and Italian coasts, including Sardinia. Journey times vary greatly.

© Justin Foulkes / Lonely Planet

Zürich
Biel
Bodensee
Leoben
Szombathely
Dunaújváros
VADUZ
Innsbruck
Page 69
AUSTRIA
Graz
Veszprém
BERN
Lucerne
LIECHTENSTEIN
Wolfsberg
Siófok
Lac de Neuchâtel
Villach
Klagenfurt
Szekszárd
SWITZERLAND
Page 67
Inn
Grossglockner (3798m)
Maribor
Murska Sobota
Nagykanizsa
HUNGARY
Lausanne
Finsteraarhorn (4274m)
St Moritz
Zernez
Cortina d'Ampezzo
Villach
Tarvisio
Velenje
Ptuj
Kaposvár
Rhein
Locarno
Bellinzona
Bolzano
Drau
Triglav (2864m)
Bled
Kranj
Celje
Varaždin
Pécs
Lake Geneva
Zermatt
Rhône
Lago di Como
Sondrio
Trento
Udine
Gorizia
SLOVENIA
LJUBLJANA
Bjelovar
Virovitica
Sombor
Geneva
Chamonix
Monte Rosa (4634m)
Lago Maggiore
Lugano
Lecco
Lago di Garda
Vicenza
Treviso
Trieste
Koper
Postojna
Novo Mesto
ZAGREB
Daruvar
Slatina
Osijek
Mont Blanc (4807m)
Aosta
Ivrea
Varese
Como
Bergamo
Brescia
Verona
Padua
Venice
Marco Polo
Rijeka
CROATIA
Našice
Vukovar
FRANCE
Turin
Novara
Malpensa
Milan
Pavia
Linate
Cremona
Mantua
Chioggia
Marco Polo
Krk
Senj
Cres
Rab
Karlovac
Sisak
Slavonski Brod
Đakovo
Asti
Piacenza
Ferrara
Pag
Bihać
Doboj
Brčko
Alessandria
Parma
Modena
Bologna
Ravenna
Cres
Zadar
Banja Luka
Bijeljina
Tuzla
Alba
Cuneo
Genoa
Savona
Guglielmo Marconi
Forlì
Rimini
BOSNIA HERZEGOVINA
Jajce
Zenica
La Spezia
Pistoia
SAN MARINO
Pesaro
Zadar
Knin
MONACO
Nice
MONACO
San Remo
Pisa
Florence
SAN MARINO
Ancona
Split
Šibenik
SARAJEVO
Konjic
Foča
Durmitor (2522m)
Cannes
Livorno
Arezzo
Brac
Hvar
Mostar
Ligurian Sea
Siena
ITALY
Perugia
APPENNINES
Ascoli Piceno
Vis
Korčula
Nikšić
Page 76
Monte Cinto (2706m)
Bastia
Elba
Lago Trasimeno
Corno Grande (2912m)
Pescara
Adriatic Sea
Mljet
Calvi
Corsica
Grosseto
Terni
Lago di Bolsena
Viterbo
L'Aquila
Vasto
Dubrovnik
Herceg Novi
Ajaccio
Civitavecchia
Lago di Bracciano
Monte Viglio (2156m)
Page 73
Corsica (FRANCE)
Page 71
VATICAN CITY
ROME
Leonardo da Vinci (Fiumicino)
Ciampino
Campobasso
Sassari
Olbia
Barletta
Bari
Alghero
Nuoro
Caserta
Benevento
Foggia
Monopoli
Naples
Vesuvio (1281m)
Salerno
Matera
Ostuni
Brindisi
Oristano
Sardinia
Punta la Marmora (1834m)
Ischia
Potenza
Taranto
Lecce
Sardinia (ITALY)
Tyrrhenian Sea
Cagliari
Page 77
Cosenza
Crotone
Mediterranean Sea
Aeolian Islands
Catanzaro
Ionian Sea
Lipari Town
Vibo Valentia
Falcone-Borsellino
Messina
Reggio di Calabria
Trapani
Palermo
Milazzo
Marsala
Sicily
Monte Etna (3322m)
Bizerte
Caltanissetta
Enna
Cap Bon
Fontanarossa
Catania
Skikda
Annaba
Beja
Agrigento
Gela
Syracuse
Guelma
TUNIS
Pantelleria
Ragusa
Pozzallo
Souk-el Arba
Kairouan
Susah
Linosa
Gozo
Page 75
ALGERIA
Aïn Beida
TUNISIA
Mahdia
Lampedusa
MALTA
VALLETTA
Malta
Souk Ahras
Mediterranean Sea

N
0   200 km
0   100 miles

© Matt Munro / Lonely Planet

SIGHTS & ACTIVITIES

 SEE

DO

ITINERARY

 1

 2

① Cinque Terre
Cinque Terre's five famous coastal villages date from the early medieval period, and are bisected by fields and gardens that have been shaped over the course of nearly two millennia. A network of more than 30 numbered hiking paths links the quintet.

② Turin
Innovative and industrious, Turin is best-known for producing Italy's most iconic car – the Fiat. It remains an industrial hub, but is now also known for contemporary art, thanks to the Castello di Rivoli Museum, which has one of Italy's top modern art collections. Meanwhile, the Palazzo dell'Accademia delle Scienze houses the most important hoard of Egyptian treasures outside Cairo.

③ Barolo
The 1800-hectare parcel of land around this lovely hilltop village yields arguably the finest red wines in all of Italy. Barolo has been a viticultural hub for at least four centuries, and many wineries around the town offer tutored tastings.

④ Genoa
Italy's largest sea port ruled much of the Mediterranean during the 12th to the 13th centuries, when it was modestly known as 'The Most Serene Republic of Genoa'. Its old city is a twisting maze of *caruggi* (narrow streets), while the Unesco-listed, Enlightenment-era Palazzi dei Rolli were built for Genoa's wealthiest merchants and citizens.

Cinque Terre: These five villages are built into a mountainous and picturesque kink of the Italian Riviera.

⑤ Parco Nazionale del Gran Paradiso
Italy's oldest national park, the Gran Paradiso, was created in 1922 after Vittorio Emanuele II gave his hunting reserve to the state, ostensibly to protect the endangered ibex. The park incorporates several valleys around its eponymous 4061m peak (Italy's seventh highest), affording fine hiking.

⑥ Courmayeur
Among Italy's busiest ski resorts, Courmayeur's *pièce de résistance* is its proximity to Mont Blanc, Western Europe's highest mountain at 4810m. The Funivie Monte Bianco cable car travels three quarters of the way up the mountain in state-of-the-art, 360-degree rotating cabins, then heads across the glaciers into France.

⑦ Alba
Once a powerful city-state, Alba's prestige now rests almost entirely on its gastronomic reputation – particularly its white truffles, dark chocolate and wine. The town's annual autumn truffle fair draws huge crowds and the odd truffle-mad celebrity, while the vine-striped Langhe Hills radiate out from the town, replete with a bounty of grapes, hazelnut groves and wineries.

⑧ Monte Rosa
The Monte Rosa ski area consists of three valleys: Champoluc in the Valle d'Ayas, Gressoney in the Val de Gressoney and Alagna Valsesia in the Valsesia. These valleys have a low-key resort scene, but the skiing is white-knuckle, with some of Europe's best off-piste and heli-skiing areas.

⑨ Lago di Como
Set in the shadow of the snow-covered Rhaetian Alps, Lake Como (aka Lake Lario) is the most spectacular of the three major Italian Lakes. Measuring around 160km, it's strewn with villages, including exquisite Bellagio and Varenna, as well as fabulous mansions such as Villa Carlotta with its 8 hectares of gardens.

⑩ San Remo
Italy's answer to Monte Carlo is a sun-dappled resort with a casino, ostentatious villas and lashings of Riviera-style grandeur. Known colloquially as the City of Flowers, San Remo also stages an annual music festival and the world's longest professional one-day cycling race, the 298km Milan–San Remo classic.

⑪ Golfo di Poeti
Renamed for the English poets Lord Byron and Percy Bysshe Shelley, who escaped here in the 1820s, this beautiful bay had inspired writers and artists as far back as Petrarch and Dante. Its forest-fringed sandy coves are beautiful, but the highlight is a trio of pastel-tinted, classically Italian towns – Lerici, San Terenzo and Tellaro.

10-day itinerary
Around Piedmont

The under-explored Piedmont region deserves a dedicated detour, though you'll need your own wheels. Begin in **Turin** with some art and architecture, then head southeast to taste some sparkling wine in the workaday town of **Asti**, and some truffle-flavoured cuisine in the well-heeled **Alba**. There's more gastronomy to savour in nearby **Bra**, the spiritual home of the Slow Food movement, and in **Barolo**, the region's most celebrated winemaking area. Continue on to **Cuneo**, famous for its rum-filled chocolates, and finish up by working off the extra calories with a few days, hiking in the **Limone Piemonte & the Maritime Alps**.

14-day itinerary
Mountains to the Med

Start amongst the mountains and canyons of the craggy **Valle d'Aosta**. Don't miss a trip on the incredible Mont Blanc cable car, and pass at least two days tramping the trails of the **Parco Nazionale del Gran Paradiso** – possibly the finest hiking to be had in all of Italy. Stop in for a visit at the 19th-century **Forte di Bard**, an imposing fortress set amongst lofty mountain peaks, en route to a few days in **Turin**. From here, it's a day's drive to the old city-state of **Genoa**, gateway to the Italian Riviera and the glittering Med coastline. Everyone knows about (and wants to hike) the paths of the **Cinque Terre**, so try and visit outside summer when the trails are at their most tranquil. Further along the coast, the **Golfo di Poeti** is rich with literary heritage: Byron and Shelley sought inspiration here. Visit the lovely gardens at **Lerici**, hike along the coast to **San Terenzo**, a seaside village with a Genoese castle, and finish in **Porto Venere**, looking out from the glorious coastal viewpoint favoured by Lord Byron.

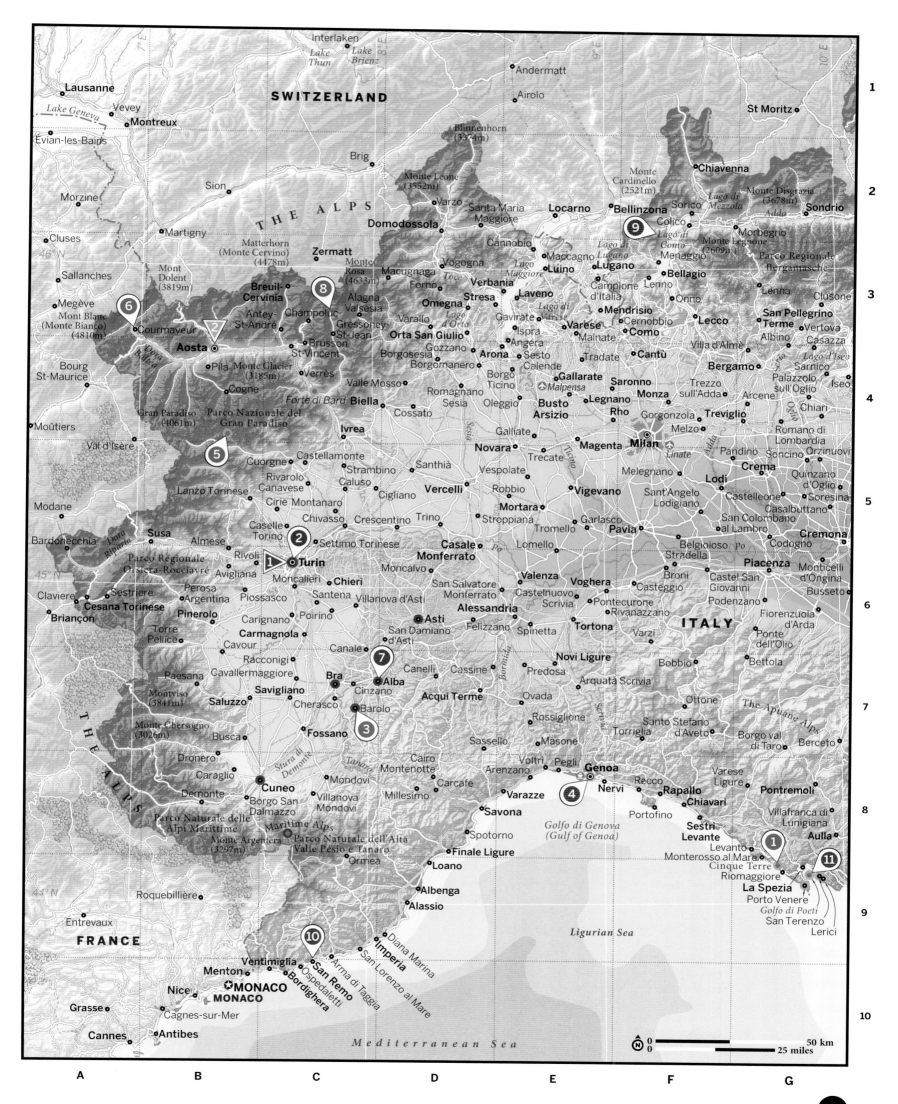

SWITZERLAND

Lausanne
Vevey
Montreux
Evian-les-Bains
Morzine
Cluses
Sallanches
Megève
Moûtiers
Val d'Isère
Modane
Bardonecchia
Susa
Claviere
Sestriere
Cesana Torinese
Briançon
Torre Pellice
Paesana
Montviso (3841m)
Busca
Dronero
Caraglio
Demonte
Entrevaux
FRANCE
Roquebillière
Menton
Nice
Grasse
Cagnes-sur-Mer
Cannes
Antibes

Interlaken
Lake Thun
Lake Brienz
Brig
Sion
Martigny
THE ALPS
Matterhorn (Monte Cervino) (4478m)
Zermatt
Mont Dolent (3819m)
Mont Blanc (Monte Bianco) (4810m)
Courmayeur
Bourg St-Maurice

Andermatt
Airolo
Blinnenhorn (3374m)
Monte Leone (3552m)
Varzo
Domodossola
Santa Maria Maggiore
Monte Rosa (4633m)
Macugnaga
Alagna Valsesia
Gressoney-St-Jean
Brusson
St-Vincent
Verrès
Monte Glacier (3185m)
Pila
Cogne
Gran Paradiso (4061m)
Parco Nazionale del Gran Paradiso
Forte di Bard
Biella
Cossato
Ivrea
Castellamonte
Strambino
Caluso
Cuorgne
Rivarolo Canavese
Lanzo Torinese
Ciriè Montanaro
Chivasso
Caselle Torino
Settimo Torinese
Rivoli
Avigliana
Moncalieri
Almese
Rivalta
Piossasco
Santena
Villanova d'Asti
Pinerolo
Perosa Argentina
Carignano
Poirino
Carmagnola
Cavour
Racconigi
Cavallermaggiore
Saluzzo
Savigliano
Cherasco
Fossano
Monte Chersogno (3026m)
Cuneo
Borgo San Dalmazzo
Villanova Mondovi
Mondovi
Parco Naturale delle Alpi Marittime
Monte Argentera (3297m)
Parco Naturale dell'Alta Valle Pesio e Tanaro
Ormea
Ventimiglia
San Remo
Ospedaletti
Bordighera
MONACO
MONACO

Breuil-Cervinia
Antey-St-André
Champoluc
Aosta
Verrès
Forno
Vogogna
Omegna
Stresa
Varallo
Orta San Giulio
Borgosesia
Gozzano
Borgomanero
Arona
Valle Mosso
Romagnano
Sesia
Oleggio
Galliate
Novara
Vercelli
Robbio
Cigliano
Crescentino
Trino
Santhià
Vespolate
Mortara
Stroppiana
Casale Monferrato
Moncalvo
San Salvatore Monferrato
Valenza
Alessandria
Felizzano
Castelnuovo Scrivia
Spinetta
Tortona
Voghera
ITALY
Asti
San Damiano d'Asti
Canale
Alba
Cinzano
Barolo
Bra
Canelli
Cassine
Acqui Terme
Novi Ligure
Predosa
Ovada
Rossiglione
Masone
Arquata Scrivia
Cairo Montenotte
Carcare
Sassello
Millesimo
Spotorno
Savona
Finale Ligure
Loano
Albenga
Alassio
Diana Marina
Imperia
Arma di Taggia
San Lorenzo al Mare
Arenzano
Voltri
Pegli
Varazze
Genoa
Nervi
Recco
Rapallo
Chiavari
Portofino
Sestri Levante
Levanto
Monterosso al Mare
Cinque Terre
Riomaggiore
La Spezia
Porto Venere
Golfo di Poeti
San Terenzo
Lerici
Aulla
Villafranca di Lunigiana
Pontremoli
Varese Ligure
Borgo val di Taro
Berceto
Bobbio
Ottone
Torriglia
Santo Stefano d'Aveto
Golfo di Genova (Gulf of Genoa)
Ligurian Sea
Mediterranean Sea

Locarno
Cannobio
Luino
Maccagno
Lugano
Campione d'Italia
Verbania
Laveno
Mendrisio
Cernobbio
Varese
Como
Malnate
Ispra
Angera
Sesto Calende
Gallarate
Saronno
Busto Arsizio
Legnano
Rho
Monza
Gorgonzola
Melzo
Magenta
Milan
Linate
Vigevano
Pavia
Belgioioso
Melegnano
Sant'Angelo Lodigiano
Lodi
Garlasco
Lomello
Tromello
Casteggio
Broni
Stradella
Pontecurone
Rivanazzano
Varzi
Bellinzona
Bellagio
Lenno
Onno
Lecco
Como
Villa d'Alme
Bergamo
Treviglio
Pandino
Crema
Soncino
Romano di Lombardia
Orzinuovi
Quinzano d'Oglio
Soresina
Casalbuttano
San Colombano al Lambro
Codogno
Castelleone
Cremona
Piacenza
Monticelli d'Ongina
Castel San Giovanni
Podenzano
Busseto
Fiorenzuola d'Arda
Ponte dell'Olio
Bettola
The Apuane Alps
St Moritz
Chiavenna
Monte Cardinello (2521m)
Monte Disgrazia (3678m)
Sondrio
Sorico
Colico
Morbegno
Monte Legnone (2609m)
Lago di Mezzola
Adda
Parco Regionale Bergamasche
Lago di Como
Menaggio
Lenna
Clusone
San Pellegrino Terme
Vertova
Albino
Casazza
Lago d'Iseo
Sarnico
Palazzolo sull'Oglio
Iseo
Trezzo sull'Adda
Arcene
Villa d'Alme
Chiari

THE ALPS
Maritime Alps
Stura di Demonte
Tanaro
Bormida
Scrivia
Po

Parco Regionale Orsiera-Rocciavrè
Dora Riparia
Turin
Chieri

N   0 _____ 50 km
     0 _____ 25 miles

SIGHTS &
ACTIVITIES

 SEE

DO

ITINERARY

1

2

The Dolomites:
A network of via ferrata, some dating from WWI, crisscross the range.

Venice

An Escher-esque maze of narrow streets and atmospheric waterways, Venice is one of the world's great cities. Through its heart runs the *palazzi*-lined Grand Canal, leading straight to the two key sights: the Palazzo Ducale and Basilica di San Marco. At the world-famous Galleria dell'Accademia, the development of Venetian art from the 14th to 18th centuries is explored, with works by Bellini, Titian, Tintoretto, Veronese, Canaletto and more.

Verona

Best known for its Shakespeare associations (*Romeo & Juliet* was set here), Verona's main attraction is historical, not fictional. Built of pink-tinged marble in the 1st century AD, the city's Roman amphitheatre survived a 12th-century earthquake, and is now a legendary open-air opera house, with seating for 15,500 people.

Bologna

Hard-working and high-tech, Bologna is home to the world's oldest university, as well as many terracotta medieval buildings adorned with miles of porticoes. It's also sometimes known as La Grassa (the fat one) thanks to its rich food culture – ragù, or bolognese sauce, was concocted here.

Modena

Beside the Po River, Modena is one of Italy's great gastronomic centres – it's the source of balsamic vinegar, for one. Museums explore the city's links with opera singer Luciano Pavarotti and supercar supremo Enzo Ferrari.

Trieste

Tumbling down to the Adriatic and almost surrounded by Slovenia, Trieste is isolated from the rest of the Italian peninsula. Once a free port under Austrian rule, the city blossomed under the 18th- and 19th-century Habsburgs. It's home to handsome belle époque cafes and bars – as well as its very own wind, *la bora*.

Ravenna

Spread out over several churches and baptisteries around Ravenna is one of the world's most dazzling collections of early Christian mosaic artwork, enshrined since 1996 on Unesco's World Heritage list.

Parma

Parma's specialities need no introduction: *prosciutto di Parma* and *parmigiano reggiano*. But the city has non-edible attractions too, including its cathedral and its octagonal pink-marble baptistery, both hailing from the 12th century.

The Dolomites

The jagged peaks of the Dolomites, or Dolomiti, span the provinces of Trentino and Alto Adige. The mountains offer incredible skiing, including the legendary 40km Sella Ronda through Val Gardena, Val Badia, Arabba and Val di Fassa.

Parco Nazionale dell' Appennino Tosco-Emiliano

Established in 2001, this 260-sq-km parcel of land straddles Tuscany and Emilia-Romagna. Running along the spine of the Apennine mountains, the park is notable for its hiking, beech forests and small population of wolves.

Brisighella

This storybook village is perched on the Tosco-Romagna Apennine mountains. Brisighella boasts a trio of 12th-century structures – La Rocca, La Torre and Il Monticino – as well as a photogenic 700-year-old walkway, the Via degli Assini (Donkey's Street).

Alpe di Siusi

Europe's largest mountain plateau, the green pastures of the Alpe di Siusi end at the base of the Sciliar Mountains, not far from the Austrian border. To the southeast lies the Catinaccio range; its German name, 'Rosengarten', refers to the eerie pink hue given off by the dolomite rock at sunset.

Padua

A medieval city-state and home to Italy's second-oldest university, Padua has its own version of the Sistine Chapel: the Cappella degli Scrovegni, with a striking cycle of Giotto frescoes, which tell the story of Christ from Annunciation to Ascension.

7-day itinerary
Venice to Verona

Villas, frescoes, star-struck lovers and cult wines; this journey serves up a northeast feast. Begin in **Venice**, sampling art, architecture and seafood. Make like a Venetian on a boat trip along the Brenta Riviera, marvelling at the Tiepolo frescoes of Villa Pisani Nazionale and snooping around Palladio's Villa Foscari. Boat trips end in **Padua** where you can overnight overlooking the Basilica di Sant'Antonio. Hop on the train to **Vicenza** to see Palladio's *palazzi* and the fresco-covered Villa Valmarana 'ai Nani'. Finish in **Verona** with visits to the Basilica di San Zeno Maggiore and modern art displays at the Galleria d'Arte Moderna Achille Forti.

14-day itinerary
Northeast Adventures

Laced with cross-cultural influences, wines, charcuterie and Alpine landscapes, this lesser-known corner of the country is ripe for discovery. After three days in **Venice**, head east via the Roman ruins of **Aquileia** and the medieval heart of **Grado**. Take two days in **Trieste** for its gilded cafes, literary heritage and central European air, then catch a ferry to **Muggia**, the only Italian settlement on the Istrian peninsula. On day seven, head inland for celebrated whites in the Collio wine region. Spend two days in **Udine**, dropping in on the Museum of Modern and Contemporary Art and sidestepping to **Cividale del Friuli**, home to Europe's only surviving example of Lombard architecture. Pit-stop in **San Daniele del Friuli** for Italy's best prosciutto before encountering breathtaking mountain scenery on your way to ski town **Cortina d'Ampezzo**. Allow two days to hit the slopes, on winter skis or in summer hiking boots. Head south for afternoon bubbles in the prosecco heartland of **Conegliano** before wrapping things up in Venice.

SIGHTS & ACTIVITIES

 SEE

 DO

ITINERARY

▽ 1

▽ 2

Florence
Packed with extraordinary art and architecture, this small city on the Arno river has hardly changed since the Renaissance. Its most iconic landmark is the Duomo, designed by Sienese architect Arnolfo di Cambio and topped by a red-tiled cupola by Filippo Brunelleschi. Equally stunning is the Uffizi Gallery and its unparalleled collection of Italian Renaissance art.

Chianti
The vineyards in this postcard-perfect part of Tuscany produce the grapes used in namesake Chianti and Chianti Classico: world-famous reds sold under the Gallo Nero (Black Cockerel/Rooster) trademark. Scores of wineries offer tours of their vineyards followed by cellar visits and tasting sessions.

Piazza del Campo, Siena
This sloping piazza has been Siena's civic and social centre since the mid-12th century. Built on the site of a Roman marketplace, once a year it is the venue for Siena's famous horse race, Il Palio, in which the city's 17 *contrade* (town districts) compete for the coveted *palio* (silk banner).

④

San Gimignano
The 14 towers of this walled town rise like a medieval Manhattan. Originally an Etruscan village, the settlement was named after the bishop of Modena, San Gimignano. Today it's thronged with day trippers, lured by a palpable sense of history, intact medieval streetscapes and enchanting rural setting.

Florence: The Duomo's *campanile* (bell tower) has 414 steps and staggering views from the top.

Piazza dei Miracoli, Pisa
Meaning 'Field of Miracles', Pisa's central square is among the world's most beautiful urban spaces. Ringed by marvellous buildings, it's the renowned Leaning Tower that draws all eyes. Tilting 3.9 degrees off the vertical, the 56m-high tower was already listing when it was unveiled in 1372, the result of weak sub-soil.

⑥

Necropoli di Tarquinia
This remarkable 7th-century BC necropolis is one of Italy's most important Etruscan sites. Some 6000 tombs have been excavated in this area since digs began in 1489, of which 140 are painted and 20 are currently open to the public.

⑦

Assisi
The Basilica di San Francesco is Assisi's crowning glory. It's divided into the Basilica Superiore, with a cycle of Giotto frescoes, and the older Basilica Inferiore, with frescoes by Cimabue, Pietro Lorenzetti and Simone Martini. The tomb of St Francis is also here.

Sistine Chapel, Vatican
Home to two of the world's most famous works of art – Michelangelo's ceiling frescoes (1508–12) and his *Giudizio Universale* (Last Judgment; 1536–41) – the Sistine Chapel forms part of the Vatican Museums (which also feature sculpture and papal history). Michelangelo's ceiling design covers the entire 800-sq-m surface.

Grotte di Frasassi
In September 1971 a team of climbers stumbled across a hole in the hill country around Genga. On closer inspection, this 'hole' turned out to be one of the biggest cave systems in Europe. The fast-flowing River Sentino has gouged out this karst wonderland, which can be admired on a 75-minute tour through its warren of chambers and tunnels.

10-day itinerary
Tuscany, Umbria & Le Marche

Begin with two cultured days in **Florence**, then enjoy a couple more in decadent style in **Chianti**, tasting the area's wine. Head east, pit-stopping in tiny **Sansepolcro** to meditate on Pietro della Francesca's trio of masterpieces. Overnight in the Umbrian hilltop town of **Gubbio**. Spend the following day exploring the town's Gothic streets, then drive into Le Marche for a guided tour of the **Grotte di Frasassi** cave system. Head back into Umbria to **Assisi**, taking in the frescoes of the Basilica di San Francesco and the hiking trails flanking Monte Subasio. End your trip with some time in the university city of **Perugia**, enjoying brooding Gothic architecture and Bacio chocolates.

4-day itinerary
Etruscan Tuscany and Lazio

To begin exploring this ancient, lesser-known region, head first for Porto Ercole, one of the two towns on **Monte Argentario**, a rugged promontory just off the southern Tuscan coast. Its hillside historic centre is a charming place for a stroll, and from the top there are magnificent views. Drive on to **Sovana** for the Parco Archeologico della Città del Tufa, to see some of Tuscany's most significant Etruscan tombs. Next, head southeast to **Pitigliano**, a lovely knot of twisting stairways, cobbled alleys and stone houses, surrounded by dramatic gorges on three sides. Make a stop-off at **Bolsena**, the main town on Lago di Bolsena, Italy's largest volcanic lake, before overnighting in the town of **Viterbo**, an important medieval centre founded by the Etruscans. From here, head southwest towards **Tarquinia**, the pick of Lazio's Etruscan towns. Its highlight is the 7th-century-BC Necropolis and its extraordinary frescoed tombs. Round off your trip in **Cerveteri** with its fascinating ancient burial complex.

Adriatic
Sea

The Apuane Alps

Monte Vecchio
(1982m)

Pavullo nel
Frignano

Casola
Valsenio

Faenza

Cervia

Bellaria

Igea Marina

Aulla
Fivizzano
Pievepelago
Sestola
Montese
Vergato
Lagaro
Brisighella
Forli
Forlimpopoli
Viserba
Parco Regionale
delle Alpi Apuane
Parco Nazionale dell'
Appennino Tosco Emiliano
Porreta
Terme
Castiglione
dei Pepoli
Firenzuola
Modigliana
Cesena
Rimini
Carrara
Castelnuovo di
Garfagnana
San Marcello
Pistoiese
Marradi
Savignano sul
Rubicone
Rivazzurra
Marina di Carrara
Barga
Vernio
Barberino
di Mugello
Borgno
San Lorenzo
Parco Nazionale delle
Foreste Casentinesi,
Monte Falterona
e Campigna
Santa Sofia
Verucchio
Riccione
Massa
Seravezza
Bagni di Lucca
Montemurlo
Cattolica
Forte dei
Marmi
Pietrasanta
Camaiore
Borgo a Mozzano
Pistoia
Dicomano
Monte Falterona
(1654m)
Bagno di
Romagna
Urbino
Calcinelli
SAN MARINO
Pescia
Lucca
Montecatini
Terme
Prato
Sesto
Fiorentino
Rufina
Stia
Pratovecchio
SAN
MARINO
Fossombrone
Viareggio
Lago di
Massaciuccoli
Lamporecchio
Altopascio
Vinci
Montelupo
Florence
Pontassieve
Poppi
Pieve di
Santo Stefano
Pesaro
Torre del Lago
Pisa
Fucecchio
Empoli
San Casciano
in Val di Pesa
Rignano
sull'Arno
Figline Valdarno
Bibbiena
Anghiari
Sansepolcro
Fermignano
Ligurian
Sea
Marina di Pisa
Cascina
Pontedera
Montespertoli
Tavarnelle
Val di Pesa
Greve in
Chianti
San Giovanni
Valdarno
San Giustino Valdarno
San Giustino
Città di
Castello
Pietralunga
Cagli
Tirrenia
Ponsacco
Castelfiorentino
Certaldo
Chianti
Panzano
in Chianti
Montevarchi
Arezzo
Montone
Sasso
Ferrato
Livorno
Antignano
Gabbro
Casciana
Terme
Montaione
San Gimignano
Poggibonsi
Radda in
Chianti
ITALY
Castiglion
Fiorentino
Umbertide
Grotte di
Frasassi
Quercianella
Volterra
Saline
Colle di
Val d'Elsa
Siena
Monte
San
Savino
Lucignano
Cortona
Gubbio
Sigillo
Fabriano
Castiglioncello
Rosignano Solvay
Vada
Cecina
Pomarance
Rapolano
Terme
Bettolle
Camucia
Castel
Rigone
Passignano
Nocera
Umbra
Marina di Cecina
Castelnuovo
Valle di Cecina
Riserva
Naturale
Alto Merse
Monteroni
d'Arbia
Asciano
Sinalunga
Terontola
Lago
Trasimeno
Magione
Perugia
Bastia
Umbra
Spello
Donoratico
Buonconvento
Montepulciano
Castiglione
del Lago
San
Feliciano
Assisi
San Vincenzo
Suvereto
Venturina
Massa
Marittima
Montalcino
San Quirico
d'Orcia
Pienza
Chiusi
Panicale
Torgiano
Deruta
Cannara
Foligno
Roccastrada
Chianciano
Terme
Città della Pieve
Montegiove
Bevagna
Montefalco
Trevi
Piombino
Follonica
Bagno di
Gavorrano
Ribolla
Castelnuovo
dell'Abate
Sarteano
Marsciano
Bastardo
San Giacomo
Marciana
Marina
Portoferraio
Punta Ala
Montepescali
Monte Amiata
(1738m)
Abbadia
San Salvatore
Piancastagnaio
Ficulle
Monte Castello
di Vibio
Todi
Spoleto
Monte
Capanne
(1019m)
Elba
Rio Marina
Porto Azzurro
Capoliveri
Castiglione
della
Pescaia
Grosseto
Archidosso
Santa Fiora
Orvieto
Baschi
Avigliano
Acquasparta
San
Gemini
Parco
Regionale del
Coscerno
Aspra
Marina di
Campo
Alberese
Arcille
Sempronio
Scansano
Sorano
Bagnoregio
Guardea
Amelia
Ferentillo
Pianosa
Parco Regionale
della Maremma
Magliano
in Toscana
Manciano
Pitigliano
Lago di
Bolsena
Bolsena
Montefiascone
Bomarzo
Orte
Terni
Narni
Pianosa
Talamone
Albinia
Orbetello
Ansedonia
Tuscania
Viterbo
Bagnaia
Calvi dell'
Umbria
Rieti
Montecristo
Porto Santo Stefano
Monte Argentario
Porto Ercole
Vetralla
Lago di
Vico
Caprarola
Civita
Castellana
Giglio Porto
Giglio
Promontorio
dell'Argentario
Tarquinia
Trevignano
Romano
Tyrrhenian
Sea
Civitavecchia
Bracciano
Lago di
Bracciano
Santa
Marinella
Cerveteri
Guidonia
Tivoli
Ladispoli
CITTÀ DEL
VATICANO
VATICAN CITY
ROME
Palestrina
Leonardo da Vinci
Ciampino
Frascati
Rocca di
Priora
Fiumicino
Ostia
Antica
Marino
Lido di Ostia
Albano Laziale
Lago Albano
Monte Cavo
(949m)
Pomezia
Genzano
di Roma
Velletri
Cisterna
di Latina
Aprilia

0   50 km
0   25 miles

SIGHTS &
ACTIVITIES

 SEE

 DO

ITINERARY

▽ 1

▽ 2

Amalfi Coast
Deemed an outstanding example of a Mediterranean landscape by Unesco, the Amalfi Coast is a nail-biting scene of precipitous crags, cliff-clinging abodes and verdant woodland. Its string of towns reads like a Hollywood cast list: jet-set favourite Positano, ancient Amalfi, mountaintop Ravello and handsome Sorrento. Turquoise seas and postcard-perfect piazzas aside, the region is home to some of Italy's finest hotels and restaurants, and it's also a top spot for hiking.

Lecce
If Puglia were a movie, Lecce would be cast in the starring role. Bequeathed with a generous stash of baroque buildings by its 17th-century architects, the city's architecture even has its own moniker, *barocco leccese* (Lecce baroque), characterised by gargoyles, asparagus columns and cavorting gremlins.

Pompeii
The ruins of ancient Pompeii make for one of the world's most engrossing archaeological experiences. The town wasn't simply blown away by Vesuvius in AD 79, but buried under a layer of *lapilli* (burning fragments of pumice stone), the disaster conserving an amazing slice of Roman life: millennia-old houses, temples, shops, cafes, amphitheatres, and even a brothel.

Amalfi Coast:
Colourful villages cling to sheer cliffs that drop into the Tyrrhenian Sea.

Matera
Matera may be the third-longest continuously inhabited human settlement in the world. Natural caves in the tufa limestone attracted the first inhabitants around 7000 years ago. More elaborate structures were built atop them. Today, looking across the gorge to Matera's huddled *sassi* (cave dwellings) it seems you've been transported back to the ancient Holy Land. Indeed, the 'Città Sotterranea' (Underground City) has often been used for biblical scenes in films and TV.

Alberobello
Alberobello resembles an urban sprawl – for gnomes. More than 1500 beehive-shaped houses known as *trulli* cover the hillsides, white-tipped as if dusted by snow. These dry-stone buildings are made from local limestone; none date back further than the 14th century, but amazingly, many are still actually used as family dwellings.

Naples
Italy's third-largest city can feel anarchic, but beyond the grime and graffiti lie frescoes, sculptures and panoramas galore. Its *centro storico* is filled with palaces, castles and churches, and the Museo Archeologico Nazionale contains the *Toro Farnese* (Farnese Bull), the largest sculpture to have survived from antiquity. But it's Neopolitan food that steals visitors' hearts (and stomachs) – especially at street markets such as Porta Nolana or La Pignasecca.

Mt Vesuvius
Guilty of decimating Pompeii and Herculaneum in AD 79, 1281m Mt Vesuvius looms over the Bay of Naples. Though well behaved since 1944, it remains mainland Europe's only active volcano. Its slopes are part of the Parco Nazionale del Vesuvio, an area laced with nature trails, and at the summit, you can peer into its unnervingly silent mouth.

Capri
The most famous (and fashionable) of the Bay of Naples islands, Capri's craggy coast is studded with more than a dozen sea caves, including the *Grotta Azzurra* (Blue Grotto), bathed in eerie iridescent light. Getting to the cave is an experience in itself: on a little wooden rowboat, complete with singing captain.

Valle d'Itria
The great limestone plateau of the Murgia is riddled with holes and ravines through which small streams and rivers gurgle. At the heart of the Murgia lies the Valle d'Itria, a green valley criss-crossed by dry-stone walls, vineyards, almond and olive groves and luxury *masserias* (working farms).

Procida
The Bay of Naples' smallest island is also its best-kept secret. Mercifully off the mass-tourist radar, Procida remains refreshingly real. August aside – when mainlanders flock to its shores – its narrow, sun-bleached streets are the domain of the locals. It's an ideal place to explore on foot.

14-day itinerary
The Southern Coastline

Crank up the romance along Italy's most beautiful coastline. Rev things up with three days in **Naples**, day-tripping to **Caserta** to explore Italy's largest royal palace. On day four, head south to the Amalfi Coast, allowing for two nights in Positano, followed by a day in **Amalfi** and Ravello on your way to **Salerno**.

Come day seven, continue to the World Heritage-listed temples of **Paestum**, then through the **Parco Nazionale del Cilento e Vallo di Diano** to coastal jewel **Maratea**. Spend two nights in town, followed by lunch in **Tropea** (one of Calabria's most beautiful coast towns) on your way to stately **Villa San Giovanni**.

14-day itinerary
Perfect Puglia

Start your explorations in **Bari**, roaming its ancient historic centre and Romanesque basilica. Strike south, via Polignano a Mare to the **Grotte di Castellana**, Italy's longest network of subterranean caves. From here, a two- to three-day drive south will take you through the Valle d'Itria towns, including **Alberobello**, with its hobbit-like *trulli* houses, wine-producing Locorotondo, baroque **Martina Franca** and chic, whitewashed **Ostuni**. Next is **Lecce**, dubbed 'Florence of the South' for its operatic architecture. Hire a bike and spend at least three or four days here before moving on to **Galatina**, its basilica bursting with astounding frescoes. Head east to the fortified port of **Otranto** and the beaches of the Baia dei Turchi, then push south along the wild, vertiginous coastline to **Santa Maria di Leuca**, the tip of the Italian stiletto. Conclude in the island city of **Gallipoli**, feasting on sea urchin and octopus in its elegant town centre.

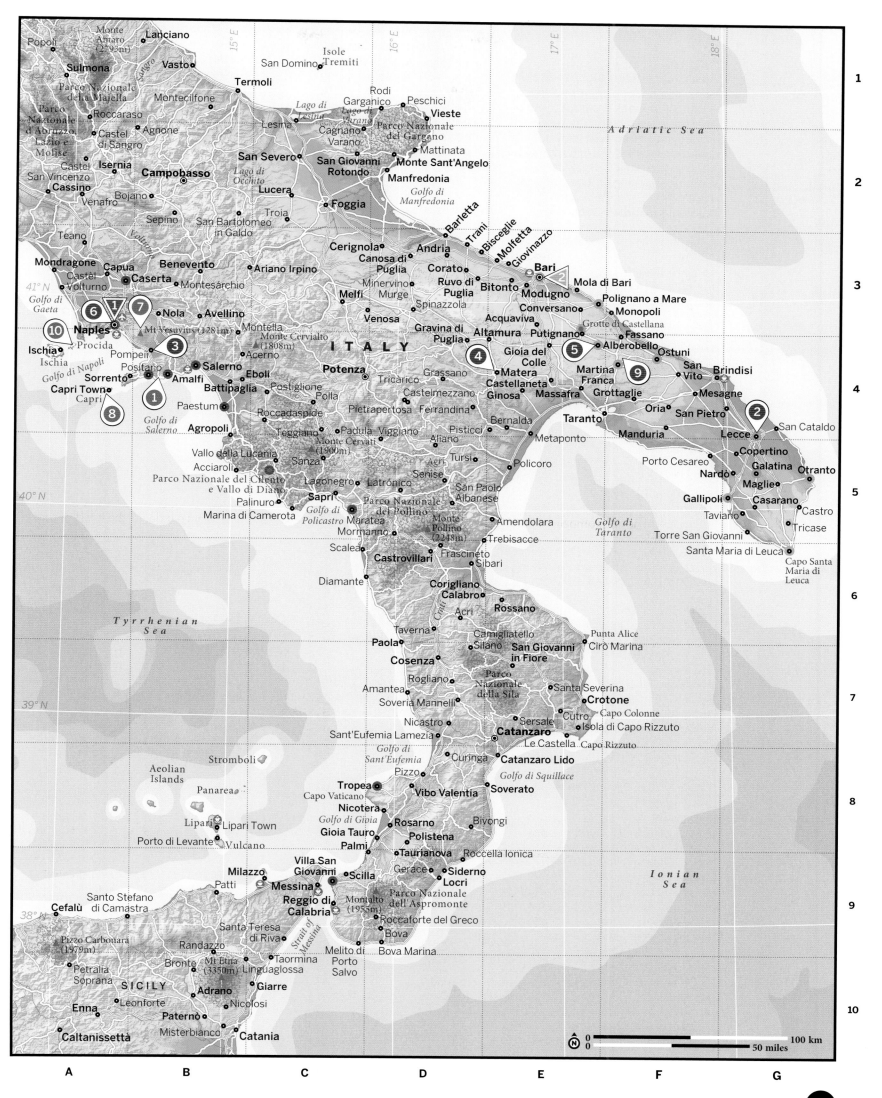

Popoli

Monte
Amaro
(2793m)

Lanciano

Sulmona

Vasto

Parco Nazionale
della Majella

Montecilfone

San Domino

Isole
Tremiti

Roccaraso

Agnone

Termoli

Adriatic Sea

Parco Nazionale
d'Abruzzo,
Lazio e
Molise

Castel
di Sangro

Lesina

*Lago di
Lesina*

Rodi
Garganico

Peschici

Vieste

Castel

Isernia

Bojano

*Lago di
Occhito*

San Severo

Cagnano
Varano

*Lago di
Varano*

Parco Nazionale
del Gargano

Mattinata

San Vincenzo

Cassino

Campobasso

Lucera

San Giovanni
Rotondo

Monte Sant'Angelo

Venafro

Sepino

San Bartolomeo
in Galdo

Troia

Foggia

Manfredonia

*Golfo di
Manfredonia*

Teano

Mondragone

Castel
Volturno

Capua

Caserta

Benevento

Montesárchio

Ariano Irpino

Cerignola

Canosa di
Puglia

Barletta

Andria

Trani

Bisceglie

Molfetta

Giovinazzo

Bari

Mola di Bari

*Golfo di
Gaeta*

Naples

Nola

Avellino

Melfi

Minervino
Murge

Corato

Ruvo di
Puglia

Bitonto

Modugno

Polignano a Mare

Monopoli

Ischia

Procida

Mt Vesuvius (1281m)

Montella

Monte Cerviatto
(1808m)

Venosa

Spinazzola

Gravina di
Puglia

Acquaviva

Altamura

Putignano

Conversano

Grotte di Castellana

Fassano

Alberobello

Ostuni

Pompeii

Positano

Salerno

Eboli

Acerno

ITALY

Potenza

Grassano

Matera

Gioia del
Colle

Martina
Franca

Grottaglie

San
Vito

Brindisi

Sorrento

Amalfi

Battipaglia

Tricarico

Castellaneta

Massafra

Mesagne

Capri Town

Paestum

Postiglione
Polla

Castelmezzano

Ferrandina

Ginosa

Oria

San Pietro

*Golfo di
Salerno*

Agropoli

Roccadaspide

Pietrapertosa

Bernalda

Taranto

Manduria

Lecce

San Cataldo

Teggiano

Padula

Viggiano

Pisticci

Metaponto

Porto Cesareo

Copertino

Vallo della Lucania

Monte Cervati
(1900m)

Sanza

Aliano

Agri

Tursi

Policoro

Nardò

Galatina

Otranto

Acciaroli

Parco Nazionale del Cilento
e Vallo di Diano

Lagonegro

Latrónico

Senise

San Paolo
Albanese

Gallipoli

Casarano

Maglie

Palinuro

Sapri

Parco Nazionale
del Pollino

Amendolara

*Golfo di
Taranto*

Taviano

Castro

Marina di Camerota

*Golfo di
Policastro*

Maratea
Mormanno

Monte
Pollino
(2248m)

Trebisacce

Torre San Giovanni

Tricase

Santa Maria di Leuca

Scalea

Frascineto
Sibari

Capo Santa
Maria di
Leuca

Diamante

Castrovillari

Corigliano
Calabro

Acri

Rossano

*Tyrrhenian
Sea*

Taverna

Camigliatello
Silano

Punta Alice

Ciro Marina

Paola

San Giovanni
in Fiore

Cosenza

Rogliano

Parco
Nazionale
della Sila

Santa Severina

Amantea

Soveria Mannelli

Santa Severina

Crotone

Nicastro

Sersale

Cutro

Isola di Capo Rizzuto

Sant'Eufemia Lamezia

Catanzaro

Le Castella

Capo Rizzuto

*Golfo di
Sant'Eufemia*

Curinga

Catanzaro Lido

Golfo di Squillace

Pizzo

Soverato

Stromboli

Tropea

Vibo Valentia

Aeolian
Islands

Panarea

Capo Vaticano

Nicotera

Golfo di Gioia

Rosarno

Bivongi

Lipari

Lipari Town

Gioia Tauro

Polistena

Porto di Levante

Vulcano

Palmi

Taurianova

Roccella Ionica

Milazzo

Villa San
Giovanni

Scilla

Gerace

Siderno

Locri

*Ionian
Sea*

Patti

Messina

Santo Stefano
di Camastra

Cefalù

Santa Teresa
di Riva

Reggio di
Calabria

Parco Nazionale
dell'Aspromonte

Montalto
(1955m)

Roccaforte del Greco

Bova

Pizzo Carbonara
(1979m)

Randazzo

*Strait of
Messina*

Melito di
Porto
Salvo

Bova Marina

Petralia
Soprana

Bronte

Mt Etna
(3350m)

Taormina

Linguaglossa

Giarre

SICILY

Adrano

Leonforte

Nicolosi

Enna

Paternò

Misterbianco

Caltanissetta

Catania

0 ——— 100 km

0 ——— 50 miles

SIGHTS &
ACTIVITIES

SEE
DO

ITINERARY

1
2

Mt Etna

Dominating eastern Sicily, at 3329m Mt Etna is Europe's largest active volcano. Eruptions occur frequently from the four summit craters, as well as from fissures and old craters on the mountain's flanks. Seismic activity is monitored around the clock at 120 stations; assuming it's open, you can ride a cable-car to the summit, hike trails or book a 4WD tour.

Aeolian Islands

The seven Aeolian Islands rise off Sicily's northeastern coast. Lipari is the largest; Panarea and Salina have become chic getaways; and tiny Filicudi and Alicudi remain remote. The islands' volcanic origins are most obvious on Vulcano and Stromboli, where you can peer into active craters and relax on the black-sand beaches.

Palermo

Sicily's capital and main port, Palermo recounts 3000 years of history. Phoenicians, Greeks, Byzantines, Arabs, Normans and Spanish have all left their mark on the city's varied architecture, but also on its street food, which is best sampled at the madcap markets of Ballarò and del Capo.

Agrigento

Sicily's most enthralling archaeological site encompasses the ancient city of Akragas. Largely dating from the 5th and 6th centuries BC, the site's impressive temples include the Tempio di Hera, the Tempio di Ercol and the Tempio della Concordia, which provided the model for Unesco's logo.

Syracuse

Founded in 734BC, Syracuse was once the largest city in the ancient world. The star attraction is the Parco Archeologico della Neapolis and its ancient Greek amphitheatre, while across the water, Ortygia is a labyrinth of alleyways, piazzas, *palazzi* and a fascinating old Jewish Quarter.

Noto

Around 40km southwest of Syracuse, Noto is one of several baroque towns in the island's southeastern corner. Rebuilt in the wake of a 1693 earthquake, the *pièce de résistance* is Corso Vittorio Emanuele, flanked by wonderful *palazzi* and churches.

Valletta

Malta's Lilliputian capital was built by the Knights of St John on a peninsula 1km by 600m. While it retains much of its 16th-century elegance, the Renzo Piano–designed City Gate, Parliament Building and Opera House have transformed Valletta's landscape.

Hal Saflieni Hypogeum

These mysterious underground burial chambers are around 5000 years old. Amazingly preserved, the sacred spaces are hollowed from the rock – painted ochre patterns decorating the ceilings of some areas are still visible. Covering some 500 sq metres, the site is thought to date from around 3600 to 3000 BC, and an estimated 7000 bodies may have been interred here.

The Blue Lagoon

Just offshore from Malta, the island of Comino is famous for this spectacular, white-sand cove. The blue is so intense it's as if you've stepped into an over-saturated postcard. Swimming and snorkelling are top-notch, but try to head here in the afternoon, by which point most people have left.

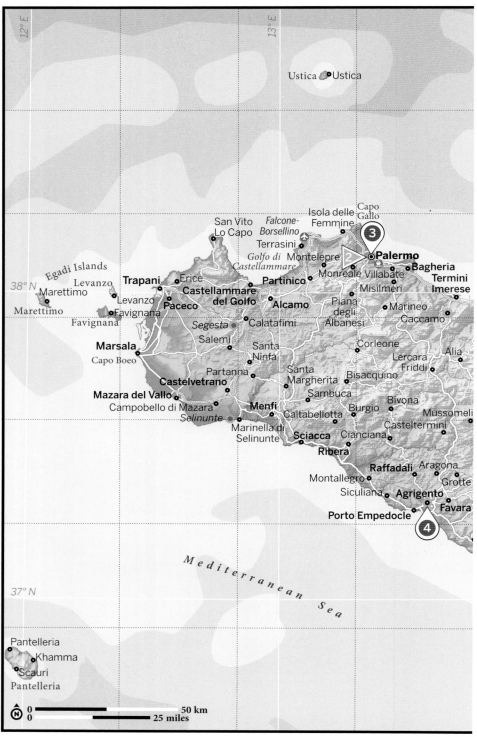

7-day itinerary
Essential Malta

Malta's diminutive dimensions (27km by 14.5km) mean that you can cover a lot of ground by car. Begin in **Valletta** – explore the narrow streets, walk around the fortifications, and visit sights such as St John's Co-Cathedral and the Grand Master's Palace. From here, head on to the Tarxien Temples and Hal Saflieni Hypogeum, close to Valletta in the suburb of Paola. Take a boat trip to the **Blue Grotto** and the magnificent clifftop temples of **Ħaġar Qim** and **Mnajdra**, followed by outings to **Mdina** and **Rabat**. Factor in time for some beach-lounging at **Golden Bay**, combined with a clifftop walk or maybe some scuba diving, before ending on a high with a day trip to Comino's spectacular **Blue Lagoon**.

14-day itinerary
Circling Sicily

This two-week round tour offers an introduction to Sicily's wonders – archaeological sites, baroque hill towns, Arab-Norman churches and castles, volcanoes and beaches. Begin in **Palermo**. After spending some time exploring the capital's diversity of architectural treasures, head southwest to the temples at **Segesta**, **Selinunte** and **Agrigento**. Next, cut east across the island to the Unesco-listed **Val di Noto**, where the baroque beauties of Ragusa, Modica and Noto are all obligatory stops. From here it's on to **Syracuse**, a highlight of any trip to Sicily: split your time between the pedestrian-friendly ancient island city of Ortygia and the vast classical ruins of the Parco Archeologico. Continue up the coast to bustling **Catania** and circle Mt Etna to reach **Taormina**, whose abundant attractions include its ancient Greek theatre and gorgeous beaches. Finally, loop back to Palermo via **Cefalù** – where the beautiful beach and 12th-century cathedral will vie for your attention – and **Caccamo**, home to one of Sicily's most spectacularly sited Norman castles.

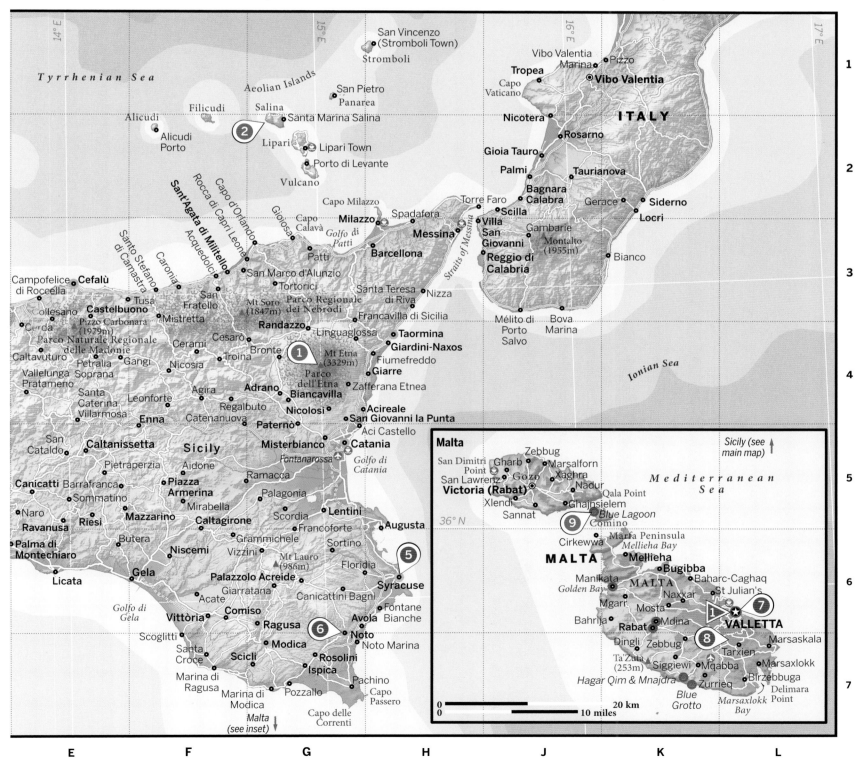

SIGHTS &
ACTIVITIES

 SEE

 DO

ITINERARY

 1

 2

Bonifacio

Just a short hop from Sardinia, Bonifacio has a distinctly Italianate feel. Sun-bleached townhouses, dangling washing lines and murky chapels cram the web of alleyways in the old clifftop citadel.

Terra Vecchia, Bastia

A spiderweb of lanes, Terra Vecchia is Bastia's heart and soul. Place de l'Hôtel de Ville hosts a lively weekend market, and the baroque Chapelle de l'Immaculée Conception has an elaborately painted barrel-vaulted ceiling.

3 Filitosa

Northwest of Propriano, a collection of extraordinary carved Bronze Age menhirs was discovered in 1946. Several have detailed faces, anatomical features (such as ribcages) and even swords and armour, suggesting they commemorate warriors or chieftains.

4 Gorges de Spelunca

One of Corsica's deepest natural canyons, this gorge offers splendid hiking and freshwater swimming. A short, signposted trail leads through the heart of the gorge, or a longer section connects the towns of Ota and Évisa.

5 Aiguilles de Bavella

The Col de Bavella (Bavella Pass; 1218m) is overlooked by the pointy rock pillars known as Aiguilles de Bavella (Bavella Needles). *Mouflon* (mountain sheep) frequent the area.

6 Îles Lavezzi

In summer, various companies organise boat trips to these uninhabited islets, famous for their white beaches and azure water. The 65-hectare Île Lavezzi, which gives its name to the whole archipelago, is the most accessible of the islands.

7 Calanques de Piana

These sculpted cliffs rear up from the Golfe de Porto in staggering scarlet pillars, teetering columns, towers and irregularly shaped boulders of pink, ochre and ginger. A switchbacking clifftop road runs between Porto and the village of Piana, but the vista is best seen from the sea.

8 Plage de Palombaggia

This is the Corsican beach you've been daydreaming about: sparkling turquoise waters, long stretches of white sand edged with pine trees and breathtaking views over the Îles Cerbicale.

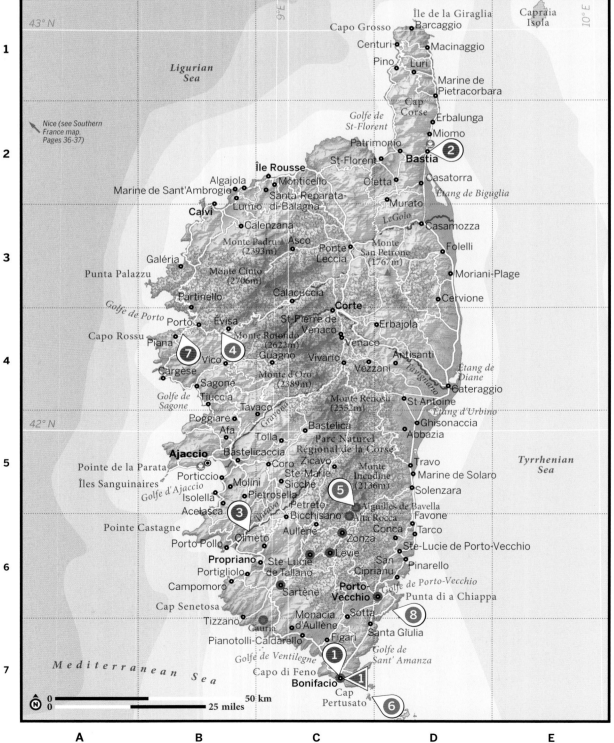

5-day itinerary Southern Corsica

Start your trip in **Bonifacio**, Corsica's most dramatic town, perched on chalky cliffs that plunge into the sea. Head north towards the traditional village of **Sartène** – taking a small detour to the beautiful prehistoric sites of **Cauria** – before continuing into the mountainous region of **Alta Rocca**. From here, visit the prehistoric sites of Pianu di Livia, and explore the picturesque villages of **Levie** and **Ste-Lucie de Tallano**. Take a day to do some canyoning, hiking or mountain biking in the spectacular landscape of the **Aiguilles de Bavella**. Spend the night in **Zonza** to recover, before driving down to **Porto-Vecchio** the next day and flopping on one of its paradisiacal beaches: Plage de Palombaggia or Plage de San Ciprianu get our vote. Finish with a feast of fresh pasta or seafood at one of the town's lovely harbourside restaurants.

Alghero

One of Sardinia's most beautiful medieval cities, Alghero's *centro storico* is a tightly knit enclave of cobbled lanes, Gothic *palazzi* and cafe-lined piazzas, all enclosed by honey-coloured sea walls.

Bosa

Seen from a distance, Bosa's rainbow townscape resembles a vibrant Paul Klee canvas, with pastel houses stacked on a steep hillside, tapering up to a stark, grey castle. In front, fishing boats bob on a glassy, palm-lined river.

Gola Su Gorropu

Dubbed Europe's Grand Canyon, this mighty ravine boasts soaring, 400m-high rock walls and massive boulders. At its narrowest, the gorge is just 4m wide. The endemic endangered *Aquilegia nuragica* plant grows here, and sometimes it's possible to spot *mouflon* and golden eagles.

Grotta di Nettuno

Whether you glide in by boat or take the 654-step staircase that zigzags down the cliff, your first sight of this cathedral-like grotto is unforgettable: forests of stalactites and stalagmites are reflected in pools of water.

Nuraghe Su Nuraxi

Defensive watchtowers, sacred sites, prehistoric community centres…the purpose of Sardinia's 7000 Bronze Age *nuraghi* is unknown. Most famous is the beehive complex of Nuraghe Su Nuraxi, a Unesco World Heritage Site.

Costa Smerelda

This glorious coastline is famous as a millionaire's playground, home to flashy marinas and mega-yachts. Starting at the Golfo di Cugnana, the Costa stretches 55km north to the Golfo di Arzachena. The 'capital' is the yachtie haven of Porto Cervo.

Parco Nazionale dell'Asinara

Dangling off the northwestern tip of the island, this coastal wilderness is a haven for the unique *asino bianco* (albino donkey), as well as peregrine falcons, *mouflon*, wild boar and loggerhead turtles. Guided walking and cycling tours explore the area.

Tiscali

Hidden in a mountain-top cave deep in the Valle Lanaittu, this mysterious nuraghic village dates from the 6th century BC and was populated until Roman times, before being rediscovered in the late 19th century.

7-day itinerary
Sardinia's South

Kick off with two days in soulful **Cagliari**, wandering the winding lanes, lounging on Poetto beach and visiting the Pisan towers and Museo Archeologico Nazionale. Day three whisks you on a serpentine coastal drive east. Tiptoe off the map for a spell in the lushly forested heights of **Monte dei Sette Fratelli**. On day four, dive into the iridescent water of the **Capo** Carbonara marine reserve, or simply bliss out on the flour-white beaches at **Costa Rei**. Spend a few days swinging west of Cagliari, perhaps taking in the Phoenician ruins of **Nora** before more chilled time on the lovely pine-flanked coves of the Costa del Sud – **Chia** is the go-to beach for windsurfing, flamingo-spotting and dune walking. Wind up your trip in Sardinia's southwestern corner: hop across to the ravishing **Isola di San Pietro** for coastal walks and a lunch of freshly caught tuna.

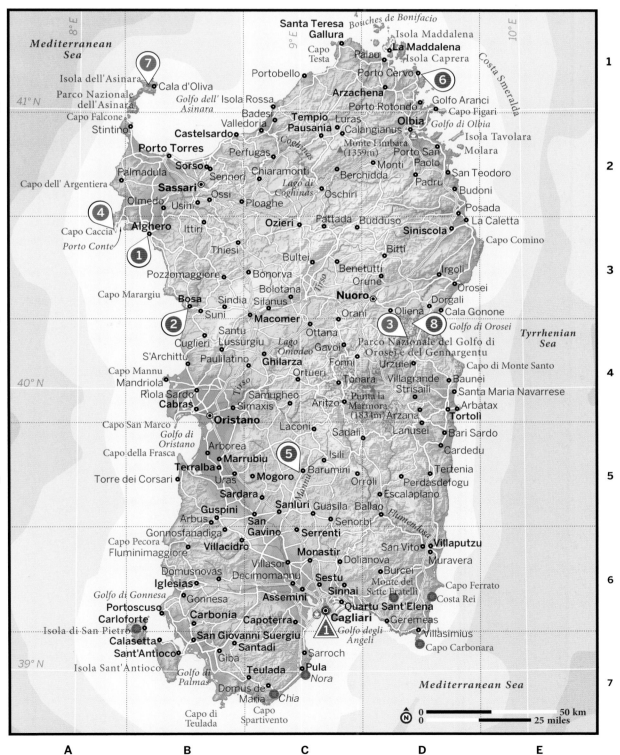

Central Europe

With its snowy mountains, half-timbered towns, medieval castles and mineral baths, Central Europe is at once natural and refined, folksy and cultured. This strategic corner of Europe has been squabbled over by practically all of Europe's great empires down the centuries, and it's a place where history's legacy lurks around every corner – whether that means the baroque palaces of Salzburg and Vienna, the sturdy fortresses of the Czech Republic or the Cold War remnants of Berlin. But Mother Nature has worked her magic here too: from the icy spike of the Matterhorn to the stately Danube and the sprawling Black Forest, Central Europe is a non-stop parade of stirring scenery.

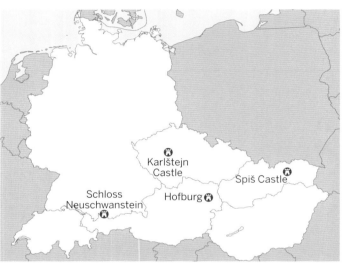

CASTLES

Defence was long a priority here at the crossroads of Europe. In some countries it seems that at the top of every cliff you'll find a castle ruin, chateau or palace. Central Europe's range from the famous, such as the Czech Republic's Karlštejn Castle, Vienna's Hofburg and Bavaria's madcap Schloss Neuschwanstein, to lesser-known gems such as Spiš Castle in Slovakia. All have their own story to tell.

BATHS

If there's one thing the nations of Central Europe have in common, it's their love of a good hot soak. Thermal waters bubble under parts of Germany and the Czech Republic, and beneath all of Hungary and Slovakia. The queen of the spa towns, Budapest, has thermal bathhouses dating back to Turkish times, while Baden-Baden in Germany and Karlovy Vary in the Czech Republic are also magnets for bathers.

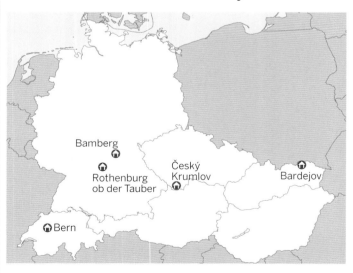

OLD TOWNS

Teutonic half-timbered villages (Bamberg), fairy-tale Renaissance architecture (Český Krumlov), medieval walled towns (Rothenburg ob der Tauber)…if you're looking for old-world appeal, you're in the right place. Germany and the Czech Republic have their fair share of masterpieces, but you can find lanes and quaint townscapes throughout the region – from Bern, Switzerland to Bardejov, Slovakia.

NATURE

The great outdoors holds sway in this mountainous region. The Alps rise to their highest in Switzerland, with Toblerone-like peaks such as the Matterhorn, and march on through southern Germany and across Austria. In Slovakia the High Tatras range contains a web of stunning mid-elevation trails. Rivers provide equally bucolic landscapes: cruise Austria's Danube River or enjoy terraced vineyards in Rhineland.

Right: The Matterhorn straddles the border between Switzerland and Italy and soars above the ski resort of Zermatt.

Transport hubs

The heart of Europe is, unsurprisingly, incredibly easy to access from practically everywhere. Frankfurt is mainland Europe's largest, busiest and best-connected international airport, as well as a centre for international rail connections. Fast, frequent trains link all the major cities, and thanks to the Schengen agreement, which allows for cross-border travel without passport checks for European Union citizens, travelling between countries is a breeze.

Berlin (see pp392-3 for city map)

Flights mainly land at the city's Tegel and Schönefeld airports, although a new central airport (Berlin Brandenburg) is currently being developed. Lufthansa and practically all the other major European airlines operate direct flights to Berlin from throughout Europe. Travel to Berlin by train and bus is a viable alternative, thanks to Germany's high-speed trains and the Eurostar to Belgium, northern France and the UK.

Frankfurt

Frankfurt Airport is Germany's main gateway for transcontinental flights, and a key European hub, with connections to most of the world's major cities, both within Europe and from the USA, Asia, South America, the Middle East and Africa. Frankfurt's train station, about 1km west of the Altstadt, is also Germany's busiest, with convenient trains to pretty much everywhere in Germany, and all major European capitals too.

Vienna

Vienna is the main transport hub for Austria, although flights to smaller cities like Graz, Salzburg and Innsbruck are often cheaper than those to the capital. Austria benefits from its central location within Europe by having excellent rail connections to all important destinations.

Budapest

Ferenc Liszt International Airport is 20km southeast of Budapest. Hungary is well connected with all seven of its neighbours by road and rail, while long-distance services run from Keleti station as far as London (via Munich and Paris), Stockholm (via Hamburg and Copenhagen), Moscow, Rome and Istanbul (via Belgrade).

Prague (see pp422-3 for city map)

Prague's Václav Havel Airport is an important hub for Central Europe, with daily flights to cities throughout Europe, the UK, the Middle East, and Asia. International trains connect German cities like Berlin and Dresden with Prague. From here, fast trains head southeast to Brno, and onward to Austria, Slovakia and Hungary.

Bratislava

Bratislava and Košice are Slovakia's main entry points. Bratislava Airport, 9km northeast of the city, has the most flights. Direct trains connect Bratislava to Austria, the Czech Republic, Poland, Hungary and Russia; from Košice, trains connect to the Czech Republic, Poland, Ukraine and Russia. Entering Slovakia from the EU is a breeze, but custom checks make arriving from Ukraine tedious.

Vaduz

It is not possible to travel to Liechtenstein by air (or by sea, since the country doesn't have a coastline). So, the best way to arrive is by road: Vaduz is only 1km from the Swiss border and there are no immigration formalities. If you don't have a car, Vaduz is easily reached by bus, both from within Liechtenstein and from Buchs or Sargans in Switzerland, or Feldkirch in Austria.

Zürich

Landlocked Switzerland is well linked to its neighbours, especially by train. Border formalities are minimal thanks to the Schengen Agreement. Zürich is Switzerland's busiest international terminus, with trains to Munich and Vienna, and onward connections to cities in Eastern Europe. Numerous flights serve the principal airports in Zürich and Geneva.

Right: Germany's fairytale Schloss Neuschwanstein (left) and (right) the U-Bahn in Berlin.

SWEDEN
Malmö
Odense
Zealand
Fyn
Bornholm
Lolland Falster
Puttgarden
Sassnitz
Kiel
Rostock
Cuxhaven
Lübeck
Bremerhaven
Hamburg
Schwerin
Bremen
Szczecin

DENMARK

Baltic Sea

Šilutė
TaSovetskurage
Kaliningrad
KALININGRAD
(RUSSIA)
Marijampolė
Alytus
VILNIUS
LITHUANIA

Słupsk
Gdynia
Gdańsk
Koszalin
Elbląg
Olsztyn
Grudziądz
Bydgoszcz
Toruń

Hrodna
Białystok

Hanover
Wolfsburg
Braunschweig
Potsdam
Magdeburg
Bielefeld
Hildesheim
Paderborn
Göttingen
Kassel

BERLIN
Schönefeld
Tegel
Gorzów
Wielkopolski
Poznań
Płock
WARSAW
Brest

BELARUS

POLAND
Warta
Zielona Góra
Kalisz
Łódź
Radom
Lublin

Erfurt
Jena
Offenbach
Würzburg
Heilbronn

GERMANY
Halle
Leipzig
Dresden
Chemnitz
Ústí nad Labem
Liberec
Wałbrzych
Legnica
Wrocław
Opole
Częstochowa
Kielce

Pages 84-85

Václav Havel
PRAGUE
Plzeň
Pardubice
Hradec Králové
Katowice
Kraków
Rzeszów
Lviv
Tarnów

CZECH REPUBLIC
Ostrava
Olomouc
Rybnik
Bielsko-Biała

Page 93

UKRAINE

CARPATHIAN MOUNTAINS
Gerlach
(2655m)
Prešov
Uzhhorod

Pages 82-83
Nuremberg
Regensburg
Stuttgart
Reutlingen
Ulm
Augsburg
Munich
Ingolstadt
Donau
(Danube)
České Budějovice
Český Krumlov
Brno
Zlín
TATRA MOUNTAINS
SLOVAKIA
Košice

Linz
Pöchlarn St Pölten
Donau
(Danube)
VIENNA
Eisenstadt
Neusiedler
See
Győr
BRATISLAVA
Miskolc
Nyíregyháza
Baia Mare

Lake Constance
Bregenz
Zugspitze
(2963m)
LIECHTENSTEIN
VADUZ
Innsbruck
Grossglockner
(3798m)
Kapfenberg
BUDAPEST
Ferenc Liszt
Debrecen
Oradea

THE ALPS
Zernez
Bolzano
Jesenice
Klagenfurt
Wolfsberg
Graz
HUNGARY
Kecskemét
Lake Balaton

AUSTRIA
Salzburg
Chiemsee
Inn

ITALY
Trento
Belluno
Udine
Triglav
(2864m)
LJUBLJANA
Maribor
SLOVENIA
Pécs
Szeged
Mures
Arad
ROMANIA
Subotica
Timişoara

Bergamo
Lago di
Como
Vicenza
Coneglian
Treviso
Trieste
ZAGREB
CROATIA
Osijek
SERBIA
Page 92

Brescia
Lago di Garda
Padua
Venice
Verona
Gorizia
Kočevje
Petrinja
Zrenjanin
Novi Sad
TRANSYLVANIAN ALPS

Adriatic Sea

SIGHTS &
ACTIVITIES

 SEE

DO

ITINERARY

1

2

Eisriesenwelt

Billed as the world's largest accessible ice caves, Eisriesenwelt spans 30,000 sq metres and 42km of narrow passages burrowing deep into the heart of the mountains. Guided tours explore the icy passages, with carbide lamps illuminating otherworldly ice sculptures, frozen columns and lakes.

Grossglockner Road

A stupendous feat of 1930s engineering, the 48km Grossglockner Road swings around 36 switchbacks, passing jewel-coloured lakes, forested slopes and above-the-clouds glaciers from Bruck in Salzburgerland to Heiligenblut in Carinthia.

Hofburg, Vienna

Nothing symbolises Austria's heritage more than its Hofburg, headquarters of the Habsburgs from 1273 to 1918. The oldest section is the 13th-century Schweizerhof (Swiss Courtyard), named after the Swiss guards who used to protect its precincts. The palace now houses the Austrian president's offices and a raft of museums.

Stift Melk

Of the many abbeys in Austria, Stift Melk is the most famous. The monastery church dominates the complex with its twin spires and high octagonal dome. The interior is baroque gone barmy, with regiments of smirking cherubs, gilt twirls and polished faux marble.

Krimmler Wasserfälle

At 380m high, this is Europe's highest waterfall. It's best seen from the Wasserfallweg (Waterfall Trail) whose path zigzags up through moist, misty forest to viewpoints that afford close-ups of the three-tiered falls and a shower in its fine spray.

Mozart's Geburtshaus, Salzburg

Wolfgang Amadeus Mozart, Salzburg's most famous son, was born in this yellow townhouse in 1756 and spent his first 17 years here. Today it is a Mozart-themed museum: highlights include the mini-violin he played as a toddler, plus a lock of his hair and buttons from his jacket.

Salzkammergut

The Salzkammergut is a region of alpine and subalpine lakes, picturesque valleys, rolling hills and rugged mountains rising to almost 3000m. Remote wilderness for the most part, there are countless opportunities for boating, swimming and fishing.

Semmeringbahn

This 42km stretch of mountain railway begins at Gloggnitz and rises 455m to 896m at Semmering Bahnhof. A major feat of engineering for its time, it still impresses with its hairpin bends, 15 tunnels and 16 viaducts.

The Wachau

The dramatic stretch of the River Danube between Krems an der Donau and Melk is characterised by vineyards, wine-producing villages, forested slopes and fortresses. Today, the region is a Unesco World Heritage site.

St Anton am Arlberg

The zenith of Austria's alpine skiing covers a vast terrain of slopes, with fantastic backcountry opportunities and exhilarating descents, including the Kandahar run on Galzig. State-of-the-art cable cars connect St Anton to over-the-mountain Lech and Zürs.

10-day itinerary
Tyrol

Wherever you go in Tyrol, you'll be confronted by big, in-your-face, often snow-dusted mountains. Start in laid-back **Innsbruck**. Stroll the historic Altstadt (old town), taking in its galleries, Habsburg treasures and nightlife. On the third day, hop on the funicular to the Nordkette, or eyeball Olympic ski jump, Bergisel. From Innsbruck, go south for scenic skiing in the **Stubai Glacier** or west to the exquisite baroque abbey in **Stams**. Day five takes in the rugged **Ötztal**, where you can dip into prehistory at Ötzi Dorf and thermal waters at Aqua Dome spa. Spend the next couple of days rafting near **Landeck**, exploring the Rosengartenschlucht gorge at **Imst**, or hiking and skiing in **St Anton am Arlberg**.

14-day itinerary
Vienna to Innsbruck

This is the grand tour of Austria's cities, loaded with culture – abbeys, palaces, art – and the alpine landscapes for which the country is renowned. Start in the regal capital, **Vienna**, lapping up Habsburg life in Klimt-crammed Schloss Belvedere or opulent Schloss Schönbrunn, before heading west along the Danube Valley to **Krems an der Donau** for cutting-edge galleries and wine tastings. Factor in a trip to the spirit-lifting Benedictine abbey-fortress in **Melk**, too. Next head on to **Linz**, an industrial city that has rediscovered its creative mojo, with edgy galleries like Lentos and Ars Electronica. From here, mountain-rimmed **Hallstatt** and the lakes of the **Salzkammergut** are within easy reach.

Onwards from Hallstatt, you could venture to **Salzburg**, a pristine, castle-topped baroque city, for a Mozart and *Sound of Music* fix. Alternatively stop off in peaceful lakeside **Zell am See**, where hiking trails thread among some of Austria's highest peaks, before continuing to **Innsbruck** for a dose of culture, hiking, skiing – or whatever else takes your fancy.

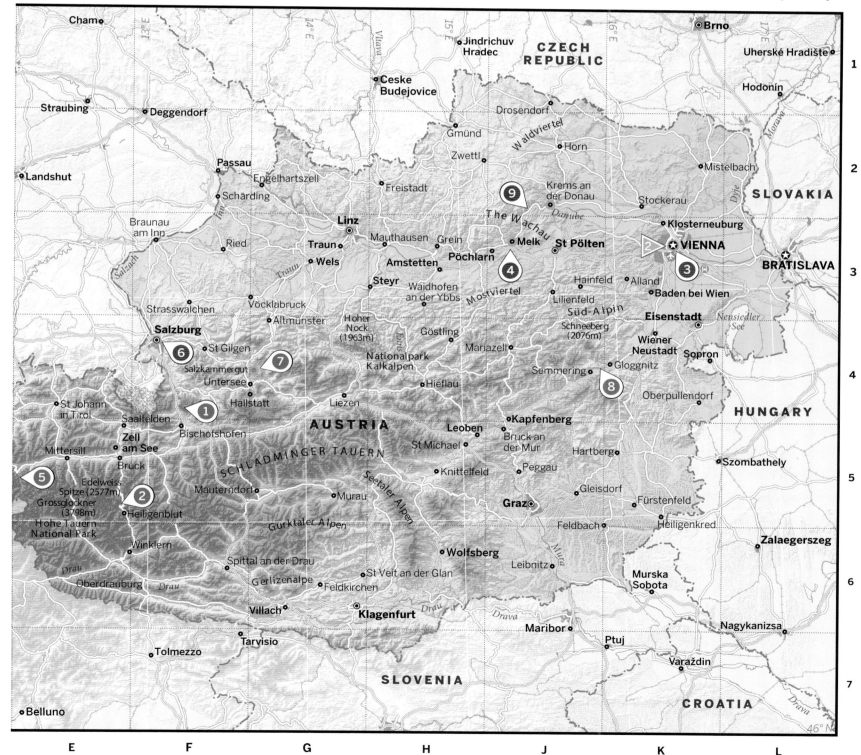

Český Krumlov

In Bohemia's deep south, Český Krumlov is like Prague in miniature – a Unesco World Heritage Site with a stunning castle above the Vltava River, an attractive old town square and Renaissance and baroque architecture. Northwest of the town centre you can ride a clanking electric wagon through an abandoned graphite mine.

Karlštejn Castle

Around 30km southwest of Prague, this fortress started life in 1348 as a hideaway for the crown jewels of Holy Roman Emperor Charles IV. After falling into disrepair, it has been restored to such fairy-tale perfection that it wouldn't look out of place on Disneyland's Main Street.

Telč

The Unesco heritage town of Telč, perched on the border between Bohemia and Moravia, possesses one of the country's best-preserved historic squares, lined by Renaissance and baroque burghers' houses with yellow, pink and green facades.

Plzeň

Plzeň's main attraction is the tour of the Pilsner Urquell Brewery, in operation since 1842. Entry is by guided tour: highlights include a trip to the cellars and a glass of unpasteurised nectar at the end.

Třeboň

A favourite holiday resort for Czech families, Třeboň is a picturesque maze of baroque and Renaissance buildings clustered around a sleepy chateau, with leafy parkland strung along a waterside setting. It lies at the centre of a scenic landscape of lakes, woods, canals and wetlands, and is perhaps the best place in the country to sample the national dish of fried carp.

Olomouc

Set in a broad, fertile stretch of the Morava River basin, Olomouc is a youthful, laid-back university town, with the largest trove of historical architecture outside Prague. The local cheese, Olomoucký sýr, is reputedly the smelliest in the Czech Republic.

Valtice-Lednice

This Unesco-protected landscape is a popular weekend destination for Czechs thanks to its two royal palaces and glorious countryside. The two towns are about 10km apart; cycle paths explore the surrounding southern Moravian wine country.

Karlovy Vary

The Czech Republic's best-known spa town was put on the map by Tsar Peter the Great, who visited in the 18th century. Day trippers come here for treatments and to sip the supposedly health-restoring sulphurous waters.

Kutná Hora

The silver-rich city of Kutná Hora was made the seat of Wenceslas II's royal mint in 1308. Nearby, the Sedlec Ossuary contains the bones of around 40,000 people, fashioned into macabre decorations by woodcarver František Rint in the 19th century.

Konopiště Chateau

Dating from 1300, Konopiště was the country retreat of Archduke Franz Ferdinand d'Este, whose assassination triggered WWI. The chateau's neo-Gothic face-lift was instigated by the Archduke in the 1890s.

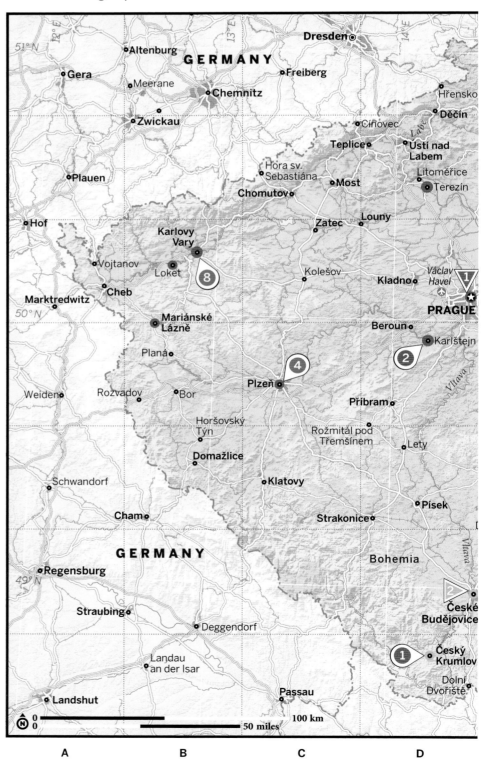

10-day itinerary
Czech Classics

Begin in **Prague** and take your time enjoying one of Europe's most beautiful cities, factoring in day trips to the photogenic cluster of turrets at **Karlštejn Castle**, and heart-rending **Terezín**, a former concentration camp for European Jews during the Holocaust. Next, head west to the gorgeous spa town of **Karlovy Vary** to sample the sulphurous spring waters and stroll among its elegant colonnades. Plan on a day trip from here to picture-postcard **Loket** with its riverside castle. Allow a morning to explore the spa town of **Mariánské Lázně** before continuing southeast to **Plzeň** for a tour of the famous brewery where Pilsner Urquell is made – arguably one of the finest lagers in the world.

14-day itinerary
Moravia & Beyond

Continue the beer theme at **České Budějovice**, home of the Budvar brewery. From here, it's an easy 50-minute drive to **Český Krumlov**; spend one day wandering around its picturesque streets and castle, and a second taking a boat trip along the Vltava River. Next you enter Moravia and arrive in the gorgeous Renaissance town of **Telč**, where you can stroll over narrow bridges spanning ancient fish ponds and tour the ornate chateau. Move on to **Brno**, the buzzing capital of Moravia and the country's second city, and spend a day exploring its museums and cafe culture before continuing to **Mikulov**, in the heart of South Moravian wine country. Allow a day here to visit a local winery, and rent a bicycle to explore the hills. Afterwards, move on to **Olomouc**, and its lovely old town square, good museums, microbreweries and restaurants. Finish in **Kutná Hora**, whose magnificent cathedral of St Barbara is almost a match for Prague's St Vitus. Don't miss the weird 'bone church' at Sedlec ossuary, surely one of the Czech Republic's oddest sights.

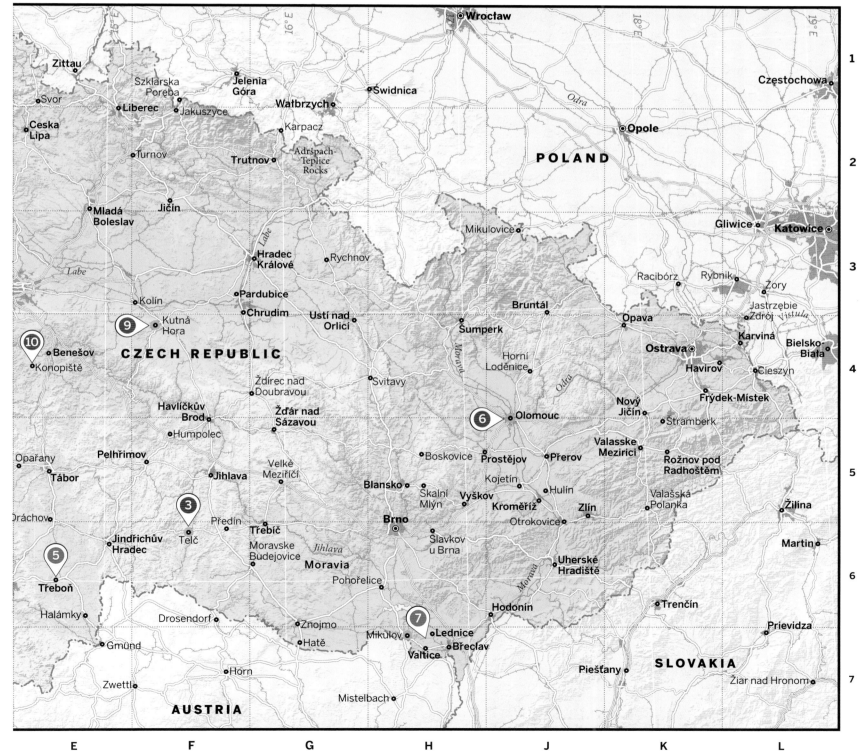

Kloster Chorin
About 60km northeast of Berlin, Kloster Chorin is a romantically ruined monastery near a little lake and surrounded by a lush park. Built by Cistercian monks over six decades starting in 1273, it is widely considered one of the finest red-brick Gothic structures in northern Germany. It makes an enchanting setting for concerts, theatre, markets and festivals.

Sanssouci Palace, Potsdam
Frederick the Great's famous summer palace, this rococo gem was designed by Georg Wenzeslaus von Knobelsdorff in 1747. Standout features include the Konzertsaal (Concert Hall), the intimate Bibliothek (library) and the Marmorsaal (Marble Room), modelled on the Pantheon in Rome.

Dresden
Once known as 'Florence on the Elbe', Dresden was bombed to rubble during WWII, but its architectural gems have been rebuilt – including the fabulous, domed Frauenkirche and the Residenzschloss, Dresden's Renaissance city palace. Daniel Libeskind's dramatic Military History Museum provides historical context.

Lübeck
A 12th-century gem boasting more than 1000 historical buildings, Lübeck was one of the founding cities of the Hanseatic League, and was known as the 'Queen of the Hanse'. Behind its landmark Holstentor (gate) are streets lined with medieval merchants' homes and spired churches.

Dresden: The domes of the Frauenkirche and the Academy of Fine Arts overlook the Elbe River.

Hamburg
Germany's biggest port was rebuilt after WWII and is known for its multicultural neighbourhoods and lively nightlife, epitomised by the Reeperbahn red-light district. In Hanseatic times, merchants grew rich along the city's canals, and from 1874 to 1876, St Nikolai church was the world's tallest building; mostly destroyed in WWII, it is now called Mahnmal St-Nikolai.

Schwerin
Picturesquely sited around seven lakes (or possibly more, depending on how you tally them), the centrepiece of the capital of Mecklenburg-Western Pomerania is its Schloss (castle), built in the 14th century during the city's six centuries as the former seat of the Grand Duchy of Mecklenburg.

Rügen Island
Einstein, Bismarck and Thomas Mann have all sought relaxation in the fashionable resorts of Germany's largest island. The most celebrated seaside resort is Binz, with 19th-century villas, blue water and white sand. The Jasmund National Park further north is a ruggedly beautiful area where jagged white-chalk cliffs plunge into jade-coloured sea.

Harz Mountains
Straddling three German states (Lower Saxony, Saxony-Anhalt and Thuringia) the Harz Mountains contain delightful historical villages like Goslar, Quedlinburg and Wernigerode, from where you can catch an old-world steam train to the top of the 1142m Brocken, the highest peak in the Harz.

Spreewald
A lacework of channels and canals hemmed in by forest, the Spreewald is Berlin's back garden. Visitors come to this Unesco biosphere reserve in droves to hike, fish, punt, canoe or kayak. Lübben and Lübbenau are the main tourist towns. The Spreewald is also the home of the Sorb ethnic minority, and produces over 40,000 tonnes of gherkins every year!

Naturpark Holsteinische Schweiz
Sprawling over 753 sq km between Lübeck and Kiel to the north, the name of this verdant landscape translates as 'Holstein Switzerland' – a nod to the park's undulating green hills, golden fields, wildflower-strewn meadows and some 200 lakes, of which 70 are over one hectare in size.

Lüneberg
With an off-kilter church steeple, buildings leaning on each other and houses with swollen 'beer-belly' facades, Lüneberg's wobbly angles and uneven pavements are the result of centuries of salt extraction, shifting the ground beneath the town and causing subsidence that has tilted many buildings sideways.

7-day itinerary
Hanseatic Highlights

This tour of northern Germany's mercantile cities is as easily done by train as by car. Kick off in **Hamburg**, a maritime city that cradles a historic centre, converted docklands, the red-brick Speicherstadt (warehouse district) and a famously seedy red-light district. Venture on to enchanting **Lübeck**, where the landmark Holsten Gate is a photo op favourite, and pastoral **Schwerin**, hemmed in by crystalline lakes. Continue eastwards to **Wismar**, one of the prettiest towns on the Baltic Coast before steering north to **Stralsund**. This vibrant city is a leading example of Backsteingotik (classic red-brick Gothic gabled architecture) and an unmissable stop.

7-day itinerary
Berlin & beyond

Base yourself in **Berlin** for a few days, factoring in enough time to tick off the main architectural highlights, delve into the city's history, nightlife and art scene, and explore the Cold War sites of East Berlin. Next, add a one-day excursion to park-and-palace-filled **Potsdam**, the capital and crown jewel of the federal state of Brandenburg, and a Unesco World Heritage Site since 1990. Allow at least another day or two for pottering around the canal-laced **Spreewald**, preferably in your own kayak or canoe. Then detour to **Görlitz** on the Polish border, Germany's most Eastern city and Saxony's most magical town, with nearly 4200 heritage buildings covering an entire encyclopedia of European architectural styles, from the Renaissance to the 19th century. Set aside a couple of days to get acquainted with the cultural riches of **Dresden**, including the Frauenkirche, then continue on to **Weimar** and **Erfurt** to walk in the footsteps of some of Germany's greatest intellects – from Luther and Goethe to Gropius.

Kölner Dom, Cologne
Cologne's geographical and spiritual heart is the magnificent Kölner Dom. With its soaring twin spires, this is the Mt Everest of cathedrals, jam-packed with art and treasures. Climb the 533 steps up the Dom's south tower to experience what was once Europe's loftiest view – until Gustave Eiffel built a certain tower in Paris, that is.

Münster
A lively city of 50,000 students and some 500,000 bicycles, Münster is a suprisingly appealing city. Cultural highlights include the LWL-Museum für Kunst und Kultur and its collection of vibrant German Expressionist paintings Take time to sample the slew of pubs and restaurants.

Aachen
Aachen's mineral springs have been favoured from Roman times, but it was the Emperor Charlemagne, who really put the city on the map when he made Aachen the geographical and political capital of his vast Frankish Empire in 974. He is buried in the town's stunning cathedral, where more than 30 German kings were crowned.

Bremen
Bremen is best known for its fairy-tale character, a unique expressionist quarter and one of Germany's most exciting football teams. It's also a European leader in science and technology. The beautiful Altstadt is a highlight, there are excellent museums covering science and modern art and you can also tour Beck's Brewery.

Moselle Valley: The world's steepest vineyard (reputedly) is found on the banks of the Moselle.

East Frisian Islands
An archipelago off the coast of Lower Saxony, the seven East Frisian are Wangerooge, Spiekeroog, Langeoog, Baltrum, Norderney, Juist and Borkum. Their long sandy beaches and sea air make them a nature-lovers' paradise. 'Paddle and pedal' stations allow visitors to combine kayaking or canoeing with cycling.

Bonn
The capital of West Germany between 1949 and 1991, Bonn's main claim to fame is as Beethoven's birthplace. The composer was born here in 1770, and his family home displays original scores, letters, paintings and instruments, including his last grand piano, as well a collection of enormous ear trumpets which he used to combat his increasing deafness.

Rhine Valley
Between Rüdesheim and Koblenz, the River Rhine cuts through the Rhenish mountains, meandering between steep vineyards and hillside castles. In 2002, Unesco designated 65 kilometres of riverscape, the Oberes Mittelrheintal, as a World Heritage Site. Hiking or cycling is the best way to explore the scenery, or you can take a boat cruise along the river.

Düsseldorf
North Rhine–Westphalia's capital is one of Germany's wealthiest cities. The best views are from the Rheinturm, a 240m tower, which has an observation deck at 168m along with cafes, bars and a revolving restaurant. Check out the Altstadt, 'the longest bar in the world', and the dynamic harbour area.

Frankfurt am Main
Glinting with glass, steel and concrete skyscrapers, Frankfurt-on-the-Main (pronounced 'mine') is unlike any other German city. A conurbation of 5.5 million inhabitants, 'Mainhattan' is a high-powered finance and business hub, home to one of the world's largest stock exchanges and the headquarters of the European Central Bank.

Burg Vischering, Lüdinghausen
Located 30km to the south of Münster, Burg Vischering is the quintessential medieval moated castle, and the oldest in Westphalia (1271). Surrounded by ramparts and ditches, the complex consists of an outer and main castle, the latter now a museum. Cue visions of knights and damsels.

Moselle Valley
Wending between vine-covered slopes, the Moselle (Mosel in German) is narrower than its neighbour, the Rhine, and has a more intimate charm. The German section flows for 195km from Trier to Koblenz, its banks lined by half-timbered medieval villages, crumbling castles, elegant *Jugendstil* (art nouveau) villas, and ancient wine warehouses.

7-day itinerary
The Fairy-Tale Road

The Brothers Grimm travelled through Germany in the early 19th century documenting folklore. Their route now forms the 600km Märchenstrasse (Fairy-Tale Road). Start in **Hanau**, the brothers' birthplace, then move on to **Steinau**, where the brothers spent their youth, followed by **Kassel**, which has a Grimm-themed museum. The brothers worked as professors in **Göttingen** before being expelled in 1837 for their liberal views. Detour to **Bodenwerder**, where the Münchhausen Museum is dedicated to Baron von Münchhausen, infamous for telling outrageous tales, and finish in **Hamelin** (Hameln), forever linked with the Pied Piper.

14-day itinerary
Romans, Rivers & Rieslings

Start in **Cologne**, where you can stand in awe of the twin-spired Kölner Dom, explore engaging museums dedicated to chocolate, contemporary art or sports, and spend an evening guzzling Kölsch beer in a Rhenish tavern. Make a day trip to **Bonn** to visit Beethoven's birthplace before heading west to **Aachen** to walk in the footsteps of Charlemagne and munch on a crunchy *Printen* cookie. Change gear and swoop south to half-timbered **Bernkastel-Kues**, the starting point for a relaxing mosey along the Moselle River, which runs its serene, serpentine course past steep vineyards to meet the Rhine at Koblenz. Swoon over crisp rieslings in fairy-tale **Beilstein**, then compare them with wines grown in the slate-rich Rhine soil. Follow the Rhine south as it curves past villages like **Boppard** and **Bacharach**, craggy cliffs crowned by medieval castles and vineyards. Wrap up in **Mainz** with its grand cathedral and fabulous museum dedicated to local hero Johannes Gutenberg.

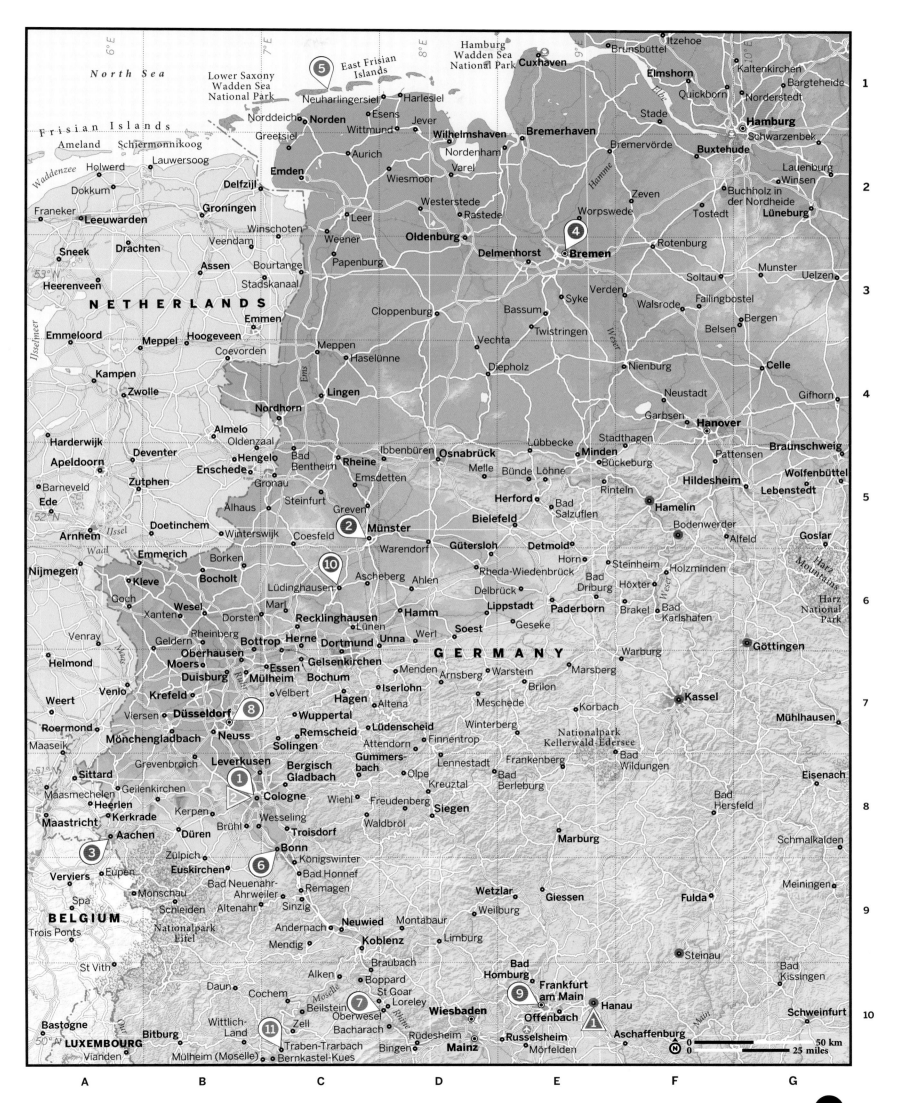

North Sea

Hamburg Wadden Sea National Park

Lower Saxony Wadden Sea National Park

East Frisian Islands

Frisian Islands

Ameland
Schiermonnikoog

Waddenzee

NETHERLANDS

GERMANY

BELGIUM

LUXEMBURG

Harlesiel
Neuharlingersiel
Norddeich
Norden
Greetsiel
Emden
Esens
Wittmund
Jever
Aurich
Wiesmoor
Wilhelmshaven
Nordenham
Varel

Cuxhaven
Itzehoe
Brunsbüttel
Elmshorn
Kaltenkirchen
Quickborn
Norderstedt
Bargteheide
Stade
Hamburg
Schwarzenbek
Lauenburg
Winsen
Lüneburg

Bremerhaven
Bremervörde
Buchholz in der Nordheide
Tostedt
Buxtehude

Oldenburg
Delmenhorst
Bremen
Worpswede
Zeven
Rotenburg
Munster
Uelzen

Leer
Weener
Papenburg
Cloppenburg
Bassum
Syke
Verden
Walsrode
Nienburg
Belsen
Bergen
Celle
Gifhorn

Westerstede
Rastede

Meppen
Haselünne
Vechta
Twistringen
Diepholz
Neustadt
Garbsen
Hanover
Braunschweig

Lingen
Nordhorn

Bad Bentheim
Rheine
Emsdetten
Ibbenbüren
Osnabrück
Lübbecke
Minden
Stadthagen
Pattensen
Wolfenbüttel
Lebenstedt

Almelo
Oldenzaal
Gronau
Steinfurt
Greven
Warendorf
Melle
Bünde Löhne
Bückeburg
Rinteln
Hildesheim
Hamelin
Bodenwerder
Alfeld
Goslar

Harz Mountains

Harz National Park

Göttingen

THE TRAVEL ATLAS

89

SIGHTS &
ACTIVITIES

◉ SEE
◉ DO

ITINERARY

▽ 1
▽ 2

Black Forest

Home of the cuckoo clock, the Schwarzwald (Black Forest) gets its name from its dark, slightly sinister evergreen canopy: this is where Hansel and Gretel met the wicked witch. The 3700-sq-km Naturpark Südschwarzwald contains the forest's highest peak, Feldberg (1493m).

Baden-Baden

The grand dame of German spa towns, Baden-Baden's curative waters have long attracted royals and the rich and famous. Grand colonnaded buildings, turreted art-nouveau villas and a palatial casino spread across the hillsides, while its temple-like thermal baths put the Baden (bathe) in Baden.

Bamberg

Bamberg's entire Altstadt is a Unesco World Heritage Site. The town is bisected by rivers and canals and was built by archbishops on seven hills, earning it the sobriquet of 'Franconian Rome'. No fewer than ten breweries make Bamberg's famous smoked beer.

Berchtesgaden National Park

Framed by six mountain ranges, Berchtesgaden National Park is criss-crossed by hiking circuits. Away from the trails, the infamous Eagle's Nest served as a mountain-top aerie for Hitler, while the Dokumentation Obersalzberg museum chronicles the region's sinister Nazi past.

Nuremberg

Bavaria's second-largest city is an energetic place. For centuries the preferred residence of German kings, and the birthplace of artist Albrecht Dürer, the city became infamous for the Nazi war trials that occurred here after WWII. The medieval Kaiserburg and the Atlstadt's churches were restored after Allied bombing.

Schloss Heidelberg

Heidelberg's ruined Renaissance castle cuts a romantic figure, especially lit up at night. Attractions include the world's largest wine cask and fabulous views. It's reached via a cobbled trail or by taking the Bergbahn (cogwheel train) from Kornmarkt station.

Rothenburg ob der Tauber

A medieval gem, this town is the top tourist stop along the 'Romantic Road'. With its cobbled lanes, higgledy-piggledy houses and towered walls, the town's urban conservation orders here are the strictest in Germany.

Oktoberfest, Munich

The world's favourite beer fest runs for 16 ethanol-fuelled days on the Theresienwiese (Theresa's Meadow), with troops of crimson-faced oompah bands, armies of traditionally garbed locals and foreigners guzzling their way through seven million litres of lager.

Schloss Neuschwanstein

The model for Disney's *Sleeping Beauty* castle, this fairy-tale pile designed by King Ludwig II was inspired by the operas of Richard Wagner. Building started in 1869 but the castle was unfinished. The Sängersaal (Minstrels' Hall) depicts scenes from *Tannhäuser*.

Königssee

Cradled by steep mountain walls 5km south of Berchtesgaden, the emerald-green Königssee is Germany's highest lake (603m). Electric boat tours go to St Bartholomä, a quaint onion-domed chapel on the western shore.

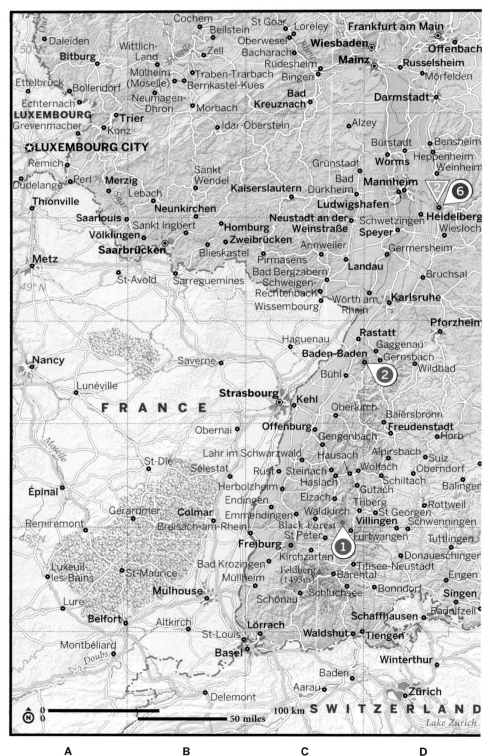

7-day itinerary
German Greats

Start in **Nuremberg**, investigating the city's Third Reich legacy, followed by day trips to medieval **Bamberg**, and elegant **Regensburg**, a university town overlooking the Danube. Visit the enchanting **Altmühltal Nature Park**, best explored slowly on foot, by bike or by boat. Make a study of **Munich** for a few days, finding time for modern art at Alte Pinakothek, jewel-encrusted bling at the Schatzkammer der Residenz, and brews at the city's beer halls. Conclude in **Berchtesgaden**, where you can contemplate the spot where Hitler planned world domination – the infamous Eagle's Nest – before exploring trails in the surrounding national park.

10-day itinerary
Bavaria, the Black Forest & Baths

Begin in **Heidelberg**, Germany's oldest university town, where you shouldn't miss a tour of the imposing hilltop castle. Take a day's break from culture in **Baden-Baden**, the legendary spa resort. From here go cuckoo for the **Black Forest**, an intoxicating mosaic of forest-cloaked hills, glacial lakes, snug valleys and half-timbered villages such as Gengenbach, Schiltach, and Triberg. Stop in **Freiburg**, a sunny university town. From here cut east to the vast **Lake Constance** and follow its scenic northern shore, perhaps stopping in **Meersburg**, at the prehistoric *Pfahlbauten* (pile dwellings) or in **Friedrichshafen**, the birthplace of the Zeppelin airship. Overnight in lovely **Lindau**, a teensy, alley-laced island. You're now in Bavaria, en route to the fabled **Schloss Neuschwanstein** in Füssen and on to **Garmisch-Partenkirchen**, where a train and cable car whisks you up the Zugspitze, Germany's highest Alpine peak. Finish with a visit to the fabulous Residenzmuseum in **Munich**, followed by a few local brews in a beer hall.

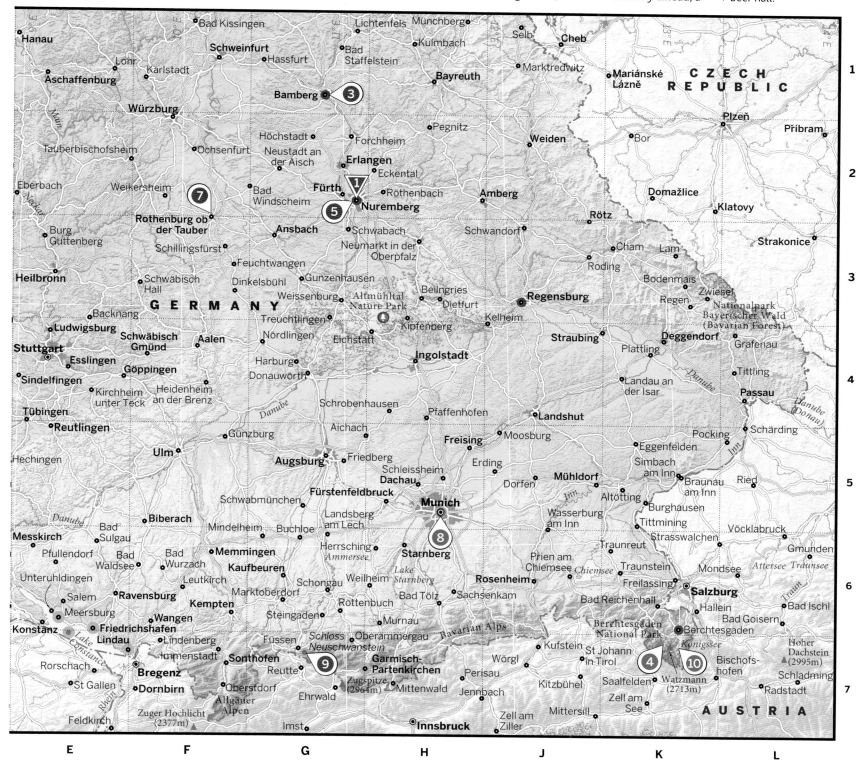

SIGHTS &
ACTIVITIES

◉ SEE

◉ DO

ITINERARY

▽ 1

▽ 2

Budapest
The history of Hungary's capital officially begins in 1873, when Buda and Óbuda on the west bank of the Danube merged with Pest on the east. The city is now celebrated for its hilltop castle and lively nightlife, particularly its graceful cafes and music halls, as well as for its thermal waters; the historic Rudas Baths date back to the 16th century and 'taking the waters' has been a Budapest experience since Roman times.

Lake Balaton
Extending roughly 80km like a lopsided paprika pepper, Lake Balaton is Europe's biggest and shallowest body of water. In summer, its beaches are popular with swimmers and sunbathers, while waterside towns like Keszthely and Balatonfüred draw history-lovers. Tihany, on a peninsula jutting 4km into the lake, is home to an abbey church.

Hortobágy National Park
Lying 40km west of Debrecen, this 810-sq-km national park centres around the village of Hortobágy, once famous for its *csikósok* (cowboys), who now perform in *puszta* horse shows. The park is home to hundreds of bird species, as well as plants more usually found by the coast. It was added to Unesco's World Heritage list in 1999.

▽

7-day itinerary
West Hungary

This road trip of Hungary's west has something for everyone: castles, churches, palaces, thermal spas, rolling hills and Hungary's biggest lake. From stately **Budapest** head north through the Danube Bend region to the former artist colony of **Szentendre**, before carrying on to **Esztergom**, Hungary's most sacred city, with both an important basilica and a castle. Head southwest to **Pannonhalma**, where the awesome (and still very much active) abbey is on Unesco's World Heritage List. **Lake Balaton's** scenic northern coast road of is your next port of call, with stops at Balatonfüred and Tihany; the latter boasts a beautiful Benedictine abbey and some lovely hillside walks. Follow the north shore of Lake Balaton and head southwest for **Őrség National Park**, where Hungary's westernmost region converges with Austria and Slovenia in forest and farmland. Turn to the southeast and make tracks for **Pécs**, the jewel of the south, before returning to the capital.

Hollókő
Nestled in a valley, the two-street village of Hollókő has changed little since the 17th and 18th centuries, when most of its 67 whitewashed houses were built. It's a bastion of traditional Hungarian culture, particularly the folk art of the Palóc people.

Eger
Beautiful baroque architecture gives Eger a relaxed, almost Mediterranean feel; it is flanked by northern Hungary's most beautiful range of hills, the Bükk, and is home to some of Hungary's best wines, including the celebrated Bull's Blood.

Pécs
This popular city harbours Turkish architecture and early Christian and Roman tombs. Its Mosque Church is thought to be the largest Ottoman structure in Hungary, while the Hassan Jakovali Mosque has survived the centuries in excellent condition.

Szeged
The cultural capital of the Great Plain and Hungary's third-largest city, Szeged straddles the Tisza River and is filled with eye-popping art nouveau masterpieces. Theatre, opera, classical and pop music take centre stage in the summer Szeged Open-Air Festival.

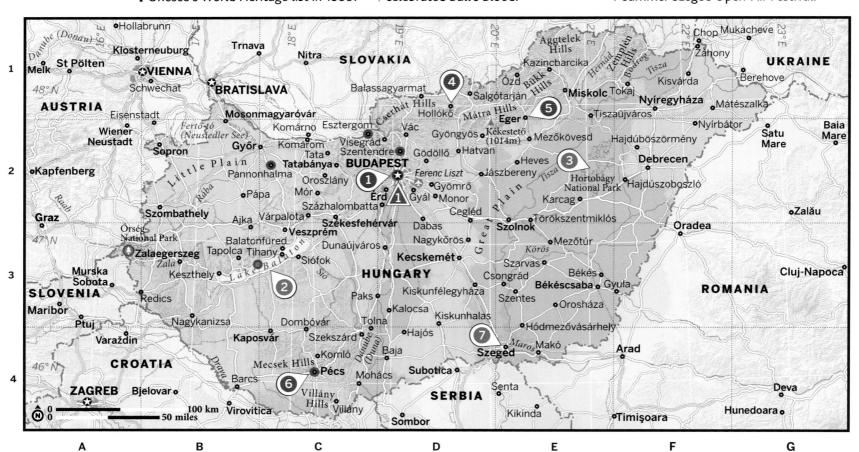

Bratislava
Bratislava banks the Danube River by the Austrian border. Its castle presides over a pastel-hued old town and the square of Hlavné Námestie, backed by a concrete jungle. Its parks are threaded with hiking and biking trails.

High Tatras
The High Tatras (Vysoké Tatry), the tallest range in the Carpathian Mountains, tower over Eastern Europe. Some 25 peaks measure above 2500m, but the massif is only 25km wide and 78km long, with pristine snowfields and Slovakia's biggest ski resorts.

Spiš Castle
One of Slovakia's most impressive medieval fortifications, 12th-century Spiš Castle spreads over four hectares, making it one of the largest in Central Europe. A residence for Hungarian royals and nobles, its highlights are the views from the 22m-high tower, and a museum of medieval history.

Slovenský Raj National Park
Sporting some of the most thrilling hiking terrain in Slovakia, this mountain park offers treks involving scaling metal ladders or balancing on footbridges over cascades.

7-day itinerary
Bratislava to the High Tatras

Beyond the big city of Bratislava, Slovakia's highlights are its castles and untamed mountain scenery. This route starts in the capital, weaving east via castles to the High Tatras. Three days is enough to enjoy **Bratislava**'s main sights – Bratislava Castle, Hlavné Nam, Soviet oddities – and excursions to Devín Castle and Danubiana Meulensteen Art Museum. On day four, head east towards the High Tatras. Break up the journey in **Trenčín**, arranged prettily beneath a hilltop castle. On day five, continue to **Orava Castle**, Gothic lair of foregone nobles and fiends. Rejoin the road going east and turn off to **Starý Smokovec** for your final two days. On day six, board the funicular to **Hrebienok** for trails among waterfalls beneath forbidding Slavkovský štít (2452m). Finally, bolt south and day-hike **Slovenský Raj National Park**. Treks in this pristine reserve involve hanging onto ladders and balancing on walkways: a heart-pounding experience sure to be remembered.

Banská Štiavnica
Gold, silver and minerals brought great wealth to Slovakia's oldest mining centre, and it grew into Hungary's third-largest town. Medieval castles, burghers' houses and sacred sights contributed to the old centre's Unesco listing in 1993.

Danubiana Meulensteen Art Museum
On a promontory jutting into the Danube, the Meulensteen has a world-class collection of Slovakian art: Viera Kraicová's bold nudes, ghoulish end-of-days tableaux by Vincent Hložník, and the realist-abstractionist mash-ups of Rudolf Fila.

SNP Museum, Banská Bystrica
The dark history of wartime Slovakia is explored within this ark of concrete and glass, with two halves framing a war memorial and sculpture. Inside, exhibits relate the build-up to WWII through to anti-fascist resistance, as well as the brutal subesquent reprisals.

Vlkolínec
This tiny mountain hamlet is somewhere between medieval Europe and a Hobbit village. Among its 45 buildings are pastel-painted cottages, an 18th-century timber bell tower and dozens of woodcarved sculptures representing village life and folklore.

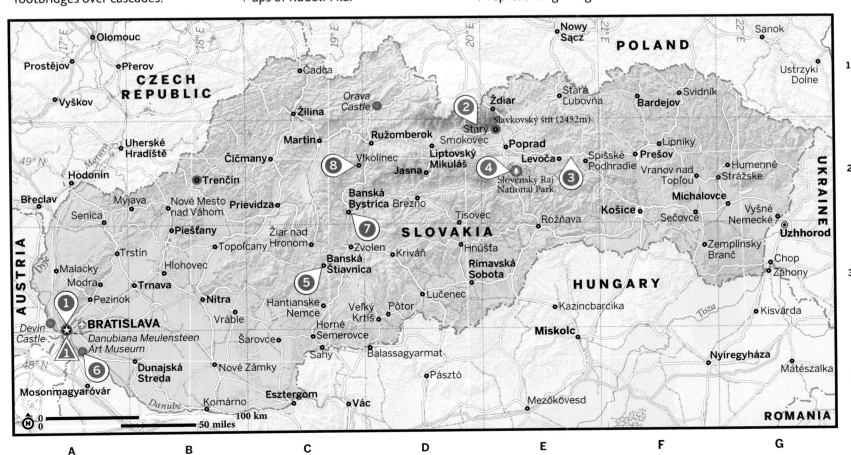

SIGHTS &
ACTIVITIES

◉ SEE
◉ DO

ITINERARY

▽ 1
▽ 2

The Matterhorn
Some 3000 alpinists summit Switzerland's iconic 4478m-high peak each year, but a short cut is provided by the Matterhorn Glacier Paradise – Europe's highest-altitude cable car. It climbs to 3883m, from where 14 glaciers and 38 mountain peaks over 4000m can be seen from the Panoramic Platform.

Aletsch Glacier
This mesmerising glacier in the Upper Valais is tantamount to a 23km-long, five-lane highway of ice powering between mountain peaks at altitude. Its ice is glacial blue and 900m thick at its deepest point. The view of Aletsch from Jungfraujoch is legendary.

Lake Geneva
Known by francophones as Lac Léman but to everyone else as Lake Geneva, this is Western Europe's largest lake. Half belongs to France, the rest to Switzerland; the mighty Alps loom over all of it. Boats putter across the lake, and guided tours visit the famous CERN research centre, unravelling the mysteries of particle physics.

Château de Chillon
From the Montreux waterfront, fairy-tale Chemin Fleuri (Floral Path) snakes dreamily along the lake for 4km to the magnificent stone hulk of lakeside Château de Chillon. This oval-shaped 13th-century fortress is a maze of courtyards, towers and halls filled with arms, period furniture and artwork.

Glacier Express
One of Europe's mythical train journeys starts and ends in two of Switzerland's best-known mountain resorts – Zermatt and St Moritz. Highlights include the stretch from Disentis/Mustér to Andermatt, across the Oberalp Pass (2033m).

Swiss National Park
The first national park in the Alps (founded 1914) covers 172 sq km and is a stunning collection of peaks, glaciers, woodlands, pastures, waterfalls, high moors and lakes. Conservation issues and climate change are explored at the national park centre.

Grindelwald
Hiking or skiing beneath the 'Big Three' – Eiger (3970m), Mönch (4107m) and Jungfrau (4158m) – is the highlight of a visit to this stunning Alpine village, one of Switzerland's oldest ski resorts.

Zürich
Regularly recognised as one of the world's most liveable cities, Switzerland's largest and wealthiest metropolis has an arty edge and a bewitching old centre. The city's chocolate-makers are legendary, and often make use of Alpine ingredients like hay, cassis, violets and elderflower.

Furstensteig
Liechtenstein's most famous trail is a rite of passage. The 12km hike, including the Drei Schwestern (Three Sisters) track, takes about five hours, beginning in Gaflei and ending in Planken. In places the path is narrow and falls away to a sheer drop.

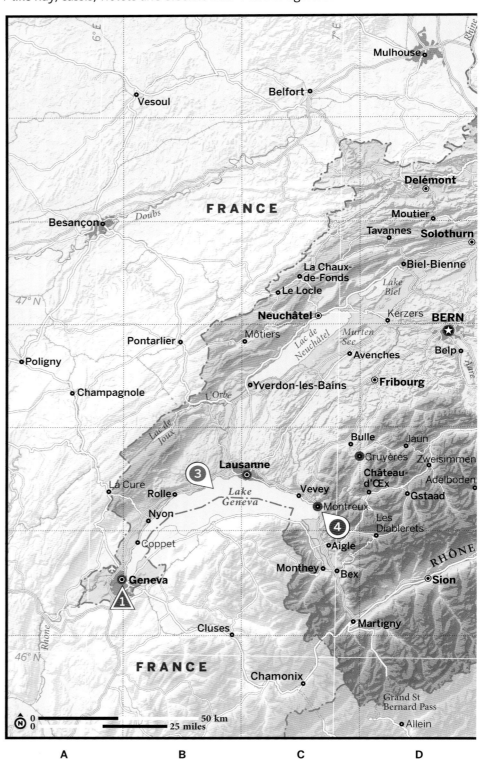

Schloss Vaduz
Vaduz Castle looms over Liechtenstein's capital from the hill above and, although closed to the public, is worth the climb for the vistas. Trails ascend the hill from the end of Egertastrasse.

10-day itinerary
Geneva to Zürich

This 385km trip is doable by car or public transport. Landing in **Geneva**, explore Switzerland's most cosmopolitan big city, then trundle along the lakeshore to **Lausanne**, a lakeside city with a lively cafe scene and sweet old town. Continue along the Swiss Riviera to magical **Montreux**, famous for its annual jazz festival. Head north next to **Gruyères**, land of chateaux, cheese and meringues. Further north, visit the pretty Swiss capital **Bern**, then the lakeside towns around **Interlaken** for skiing, hiking and outdoor pursuits. Swing north to another bewitching lakeside star, **Lucerne**. Conclude your trip in Switzerland's most hip 'n' happening city, **Zürich**, with some chocolate-tasting and laid-back sightseeing.

14-day itinerary
Graubünden & Ticino

This circular route of Switzerland's scenic southeast is best done by car, but can be picked up at any point along the route. From **Chur**, head north for a detour to pretty **Maienfeld** and its vineyards. Spin east to ski queens **Klosters** and **Davos**, then surge into the Engadine Valley, with pretty towns like **Guarda** and **Scuol** (and its tempting thermal baths). The road then ribbons southeast to the Austrian border, which you cross to head south through a slice of Austria and Italy before veering back into Switzerland to contemplate frescoes at **Müstair**. Continue southwest to chic **St Moritz**. Climb the Julier Pass mountain road and drop down the Via Mala gorges. The southbound road then crosses into Ticino and Bellinzona. Steam on past lakeside **Locarno** and up the enchanting Valle Maggia. Backtracking to **Bellinzona**, the main route takes you along the Valle Leventina before crossing the St Gotthard Pass to **Andermatt**. Nip into the monastery of **Disentis/Mustér** before plunging into designer spa waters in **Vals**, the last stop before you arrive back in Chur.

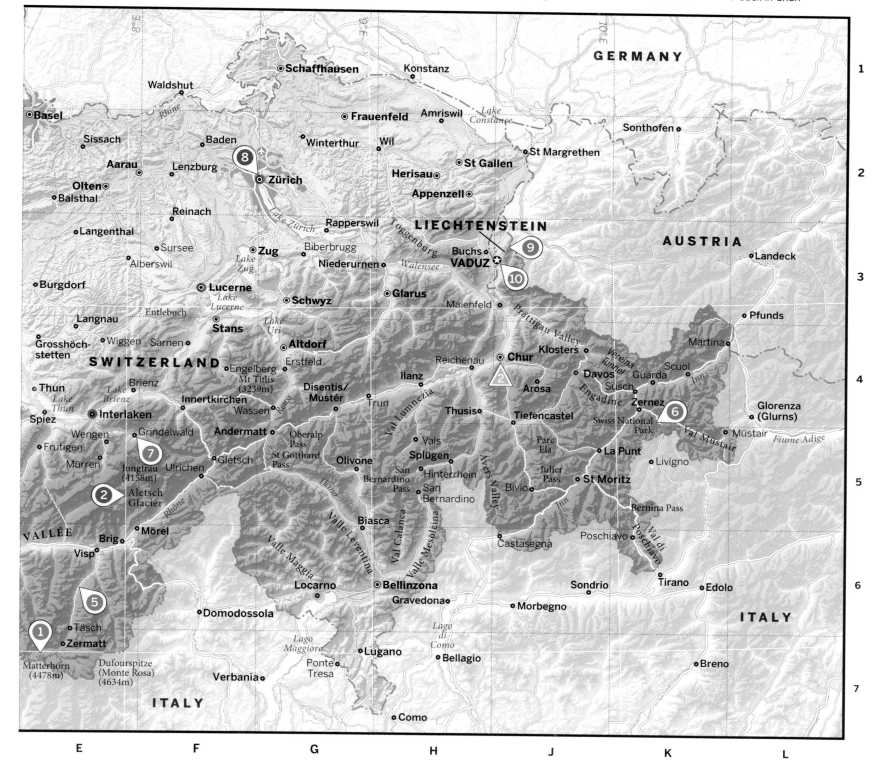

Southeastern Europe

Thousands of islands scattered from the Adriatic to the Aegean Sea lure beach lovers to Southeastern Europe, particularly Croatia and Greece. The craggy mountain peaks of the Dinaric Alps, stretching across the Balkan Peninsula from Slovenia to Albania, are made for hiking and biking. Throughout the region, sun-bleached ruins, cobblestoned walled towns, old bazaars and fresco-rich monasteries are remnants of turbulent history – this was the meeting place of Roman, Byzantine, Ottoman and Austro-Hungarian Empires. Travel here is also a culinary adventure, with typically Mediterranean flavours and up-and-coming indigenous wines. Ferry and hydrofoil connections let you reach the most far-flung of islands.

CLIMATE CHART

ATHENS

RAINFALL
INCH/MM
—8/200
—6/150
—4/100
—2/50
—0

D N O S A J J M A M F J

TEMP
°C/°F
40/104—
30/86—
20/68—
10/50—
0/32—

SARAJEVO

RAINFALL
INCH/MM
—4.9/125
—3.9/100
—2.9/75
—2/50
—1/25
—0

D N O S A J J M A M F J

TEMP
°C/°F
40/104—
20/68—
0/32—
-20/-4—

BEACHES

Dazzling beaches grace the coastlines and islands across Southeastern Europe, rivalling any in the world for dropping your jaw. Some of the most famous stretches of sand are Crete's pink Elafonisi Beach, tongue-shaped Zlatni Rat on Croatia's Brač Island, mythical Aphrodite's Rock and Beach in Cyprus, white rocky Drymades in Albania, and Montenegro's Sveti Stefan, with fabulous views of the eponymous islet.

GASTRONOMY

The region's culinary treats are astounding, with fresh local produce inland and bounty plucked from the sea. Foodie highlights include truffles on Croatia's Istrian peninsula, seafood and olives across the Greek islands, *pršut* (smoke-dried ham) in Montenegro's highlands, *haloumi* cheese (made from goat's or ewe's milk) in Cyprus, and Macedonia's slow-food scene, from foraged mushrooms to fire-hued peppers.

HIKING

This region is latticed by hiking trails which pass through some of the continent's most remote and dramatic mountain scenery. Memorable experiences include the trek to the top of Mt Triglav, Slovenia's highest peak, the hike from Valbona to Theth in the Albanian Alps, walking in Crete's Samaria Gorge, and the stretch of the Via Dinarica trail between Bosnia's Sutjeska and Montenegro's Durmitor national parks.

OLD TOWNS

You won't find cobbled squares, weaving back streets and crumbling walls quite like this anywhere else. Not to be missed are the Adriatic Coast's gorgeous walled towns of Dubrovnik in Croatia and Kotor in Montenegro, the spectacular Ottoman mansions of Albania's Gjirokastra, the historic Knights' Quarter of Rhodes Town in Greece, and sublime Ohrid on Macedonia's eponymous lake.

Right: The first set of walls to enclose the city of Dubrovnik was constructed in the 9th century.

© Mark Read / Lonely Planet

Transport hubs

TRANSPORT

A1, B2, B3,
C2, C4, D4,
E6, J8

A2, A3, B3,
C4, C5, C6,
D6, E6, F6,
F7

Southeastern Europe's main hub for transcontinental flights is Athens. The region's other capital cities are well connected to the rest of Europe (increasingly by low-cost carriers), with seasonal routes added in summer to major tourist destinations like Dubrovnik in Croatia, Crete's Iraklio or Pafos in Cyprus. Regular ferries link Greek and Croatian islands to each other and the mainland, while buses are the fastest and most reliable way to travel around the rest of this vast region.

Athens
The Greek capital offers spectacular ancient sights, world-class museums and bustling social life played out in open-air restaurants and bars. Eleftherios Venizelos International Airport, 27km east of Athens, has flights to destinations around Europe, as well as to Cairo, İstanbul, Tel Aviv, New York and Toronto. Most ferry services to the islands leave from the massive port at Piraeus, southwest of Athens.

Larnaka
Larnaka revolves around its seaside location, while the old Turkish quarter of Skala is a slice of bygone Cyprus. Larnaka International Airport is the busiest airport on the island, with direct flights to major European cities, plus destinations in the Middle East and North Africa. Regular daily buses go to Pafos, Lemesos and the capital Nicosia.

Belgrade
The exuberant nightlife of Serbia's capital makes it one of Europe's most happening cities, where remnants of Habsburg and Ottoman legacies contrast with relics of ex-Yugoslavia. Nikola Tesla Airport has direct flights to cities across Europe as well as New York and the Middle East. There are frequent domestic and international buses, while the Belgrade–Bar railway runs to Montenegro's Adriatic Coast.

Zagreb
Croatia's coastal attractions aside, Zagreb has culture, architecture, gastronomy and everything else that makes a quality capital city. Zagreb Airport is Croatia's busiest, with a range of international and domestic services and a new terminal unveiled in 2017. Excellent bus services run to most coastal destinations and link Zagreb to all neighbouring countries.

Ljubljana
Slovenia's small, green capital boasts gorgeous art-nouveau architecture and an active clubbing and cultural scene. Jože Pučnik Airport has regular flights to and from the region and the rest of Europe. Bus and train stations are next to each other, with services to places both within Slovenia and abroad.

Sarajevo
The restored historic centre of Bosnia's capital is full of welcoming cafes, *caravanserai*-restaurants, mosques and churches. Sarajevo International Airport has flights to Europe, Dubai and Istanbul. The two bus stations service domestic locations, neighbouring Balkan countries and Western Europe.

Skopje
Macedonia's capital is a quirky contrast of the delightful Čaršija (old Turkish bazaar) and the super-sized new riverside monuments. Skopje International Airport has direct flights to many cities throughout Europe, Turkey and the Gulf. Buses and trains run locally and internationally.

Tirana
Albania's lively, colourful capital is a pleasure to explore. Nënë Tereza International Airport is an increasingly busy air hub. Regular buses head to neighbouring countries, while *furgon* (minibuses) service Albania. Tirana has no official bus station; buses leave from various stops around the city centre.

Podgorica
Montenegro's capital is pint-sized but worth a visit. Podgorica Airport continues to gain new routes (including low-cost carriers), while buses run to major local towns as well as Dubrovnik.

Above: Bridge over the Miljacka River, Sarajevo (left); the view across Athens from the Acropolis (right).

THE TRAVEL ATLAS

© Pete Seaward / Lonely Planet

© Adrienne Pitts / Lonely Planet

BUDAPEST
Debrecen
Baia Mare
MOLDOVA
UKRAINE
Melitopol
Szolnok
HUNGARY
Cluj-Napoca
Iaşi
Tiraspol
CHIŞINĂU
Kherson
Sea of Azov
Page 103
Bacău
Odesa
Pécs
Szeged
Târgu Mureş
Dzhankoy
Kerch
Subotica
Timişoara
ROMANIA
Cahul
Osijek
Novi Sad
Reşiţa
Braşov
Yevpatoriya
Simferopol
SERBIA
Zrenjanin
Transylvanian Alps
Izmayil
Sevastapol
Yalta
Tuzla
BELGRADE
Pitești
Ploieşti
Danube
Danube Delta
Craiova
BUCHAREST
Constanţa
Kragujevac
Călăraşi
Black Sea
SARAJEVO
Čačak
Page 106
Ruse
Dobrich
MONTENEGRO
Niš
Danube
Pleven
BULGARIA
Varna
Peja (Peć)
KOSOVO
PRISTINA
Veliko Târnovo
PODGORICA
Prizren
SOFIA
Balkan Mountains
Burgas
Shkodra
Puka
SKOPJE
Kjustendil
Stara Zagora
Bafra
Lezhë
Tetovo
MACEDONIA (FYROM)
Haskovo
Edirne
Zonguldak
Durrës
TIRANA
Bitola
Vardar
Serres
Xanthi
Komotini
Tekirdağ
İstanbul
Kocaeli (İzmit)
Amasya
Elbasan
Kavala
Alexandroupoli
Sea of Marmara
Bolu
Korçë
Thessaloniki
Thasos
Samothraki
Çanakkale
Bursa
Eskişehir
ANKARA
Kırıkkale
Vlorë
Katerini
Gökçeada (Imvros)
Limnos
Balıkesir
ALBANIA
GREECE
Larissa
Skyros
TURKEY
Kayseri
Corfu Town (Kerkyra)
Ioannina
Pindus Mountains
Aegean Sea
Lesbos
Uşak
Afyon
Corfu (Kerkyra)
Volos
Sporades
Manisa
Lamia
Skyros
Chios
İzmir
Konya
Lefkada
Agrinio
Halkida
Samos
Karaman
Patra
Page 104
ATHENS
Ikaria
Söke
Denizli
Zakynthos
Peloponnese
Kea
Andros
Tinos
Samos
Pyrgos
Tripoli
Kythnos
Syros
Mykonos
Antalya
Kalamata
Sparta
Serifos
Paros
Naxos
Kalimnos
Kos Town
Myrtoön Sea
Sifnos
Cyclades
Amorgos
Kos
NORTHERN CYPRUS
Milos
Santorini (Thira)
Astypalea
Dodecanese Islands
Rhodes Town
NICOSIA
Larnaka
Kythira
Karpathos
Rhodes
REPUBLIC OF CYPRUS
Page 107
Sea of Crete
Hania
Iraklio
Sitia
Lemesos
Crete
Page 105
Mediterranean Sea

C   D   E   F   G   H   J

Dubrovnik's Old Town

A sense of awe never fails to descend when you set eyes on the beauty of Dubrovnik's Old Town. It's hard to imagine anyone becoming jaded by the city's white limestone streets and baroque buildings, or failing to be inspired by a walk along the ancient city walls that protected a sophisticated republic for centuries. The view over the Old Town's terracotta roofs and the shimmering Adriatic is sublime.

Plitvice Lakes National Park

This glorious expanse of forested hills and crystalline lakes is linked by a series of hundreds of waterfalls and cascades. It takes over six hours to explore the 18km of footbridges and pathways on foot; or take the park's free boats and buses from April to October. Spring, when the falls are flush with water, and autumn, when changing leaves put on a colourful display, are the best times to visit.

Istrian gastronomy

Croatia's heart-shaped peninsula just south of Trieste in Italy, Istria is acclaimed for its gastronomy – starring net-fresh seafood, prime white truffles, wild asparagus, top-rated olive oils and award-winning wines. Farmhouses open their doors to visitors, rustic taverns serve up slow-food delights and Croatia's top winemakers offer tastings in their cellars.

Diocletian's Palace, Split

Split's 4th-century Diocletian's Palace, one of the most impressive Roman ruins in existence, is the city's living heart. The labyrinthine streets hide passageways and courtyards, some deserted, others thumping with music from bars and cafes, while the locals hang out their washing overhead, kids play football amid the ancient walls, and grannies sit in their windows watching the action below.

Zlatni Rat Beach

Zlatni Rat on Brač island extends like a tongue into the sea for about 500m, drawing crowds of visitors in summer. Made up of smooth white pebbles, its elegant tip is constantly shuffled by the wind and waves. Pine trees provide shade and rocky cliffs rise sharply behind it, making the setting one of the loveliest in Dalmatia. This is a windsurfing hot spot, with most of the action taking place west of Bol town centre. The *maestral* (strong westerly wind) blows from April to October.

Ljubljana

Ljubljana is one of Europe's greenest capitals. The Ljubljanica River's leafy banks are given over to pedestrians and cyclists. Take the funicular up to Ljubljana Castle for amazing views. The Old Town below is lined with baroque townhouses, 19th-century wooden shopfronts, quiet courtyards and cobbled alleys. On the much-loved Dragon Bridge, look out for winged bronze dragons, the symbol of Ljubljana.

Lake Bled

With the peaks of the Julian Alps as backdrop, Bled is Slovenia's most popular resort. Its greatest attraction is the emerald lake, whose tiny, tear-shaped island with a picture-postcard church beckons from the shore. Perched atop a steep cliff, the 11th-century Bled Castle has towers, ramparts, moats and a terrace offering magnificent views.

Triglav National Park

Triglav is a spectacular world of rocky mountains – its centrepiece is Mt Triglav (2864m), Slovenia's highest peak – as well as gorges, lakes, canyons, caves, rivers, waterfalls and meadows. Climbing Mt Triglav is a rite of passage for patriotic locals and curious tourists (ideally with a guide). The best months for climbing are August and September.

Soča River

Rafting the aquamarine Soča River (Grades I to IV), northwest of Lake Bled, provides all the adrenaline of a mountain climb, with the added advantage of a cooling swim on a hot summer day. The town of Bovec in the Soča Valley is the base for rafting, but agencies in Bled organise excursions too. The rafting season is April to October.

Vipava Valley

The fertile Vipava Valley is an excellent place to tour by car or bike, with idyllic rural scenery and family-owned wineries. The maritime climate and steep slopes make ideal conditions for wine production. Top tipples include fresh whites from the indigenous *zelen* and *pinela* grapes.

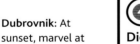

Dubrovnik: At sunset, marvel at the interplay of light on the old stone buildings.

7-day itinerary
Essential Slovenia

This whistlestop tour takes in the highlights of Slovenia's alpine, karst and coastal regions. Spend two nights in the green capital **Ljubljana** to soak up its architecture, restaurants and beautiful riverside setting. Next, catch a bus or train north to serene **Lake Bled** in the Julian Alps, overnighting to allow time for lakeside ambles and taking a *pletna* (gondola) to Bled Island. The following day return south via Ljubljana to the karst cave at **Postojna** to see its stalagmite and stalactite formations. Then it's just a hop by bus to the Adriatic coastal resorts: if you're seeking romance, choose **Piran**; if it's sun and fun, **Portorož** is the centre of the action.

10-day itinerary
Croatian Capital to the Coast

Take in Croatia's heavyweights, from the hip capital to the gems of the Dalmatian coast. Set aside two days to delve into **Zagreb's** booming cafe culture, cutting-edge arts scene, simmering nightlife and great museums. En route south by bus, spend a day at the Unesco-listed **Plitvice Lakes National Park**, exploring its verdant chain of turquoise lakes and cascading waterfalls. Continue south to the buzzing Dalmatian city of **Split** for a two-day fling focused on the splendid Diocletian's Palace. Next, catch the catamaran to chic **Hvar Town** for a taste of its happening nightlife and some sunbathing on the **Pakleni Islands**, immediately offshore. Hvar has year-round connections to **Korčula Island**, whose highly photogenic walled town juts out into the Adriatic on its own little peninsula and drips with history. In summer, there are direct fast ferries from here to magnificent **Dubrovnik**. Spend the final two days exploring the Old Town's marble-paved *Stradun* (streets), vibrant street life and fine architecture.

Kapfenberg
Leoben
Pápa
Érd
Dabas

AUSTRIA
Graz
Szombathely
Várpalota
Székesfehérvár

Wolfsberg
Zalaegerszeg
Veszprém
Dunaújváros

Villach
Klagenfurt
Ravne na Koroškem
Murska Sobota
Lenti
HUNGARY
Siófok
Kiskunhalas

Tarvisio
Triglav (2864m)
Jesenice
Bled
Slovenj Gradec
Slovenska Bistrica
Maribor
Ptuj
Čakovec
Nagykanizsa
Kaposvár
Szekszárd
Komló
Baja

Jože Pučnik Airport
Kranj
Kamnik
Velenje
Žalec
Celje
Varaždin
Pécs
Mohács

M Vogel (1922m)
Škofja Loka
Trbovlje
Hrastnik
Ivanec
Križevci
Đurđevac
Barcs
SERBIA
Sombor

Nova Gorica
LJUBLJANA
Idrija
Domžale
Zagorje ob Savi
Litija
Sava
Krapina
Medvednica Nature Park
ZAGREB
Bjelovar
Čazma
Virovitica
Slatina
Donji Miholjac
Beli Manastir
Apatin
Kula

Gorizia
Vrhnika
Ajdovščina
Grosuplje
Novo Mesto
Brežice
Zaprešić
Velika Gorica
CROATIA
Kutina
Pakrac
Slavonska Požega
Đakovačka Breznica
Đakovo
Vinkovci
Osijek
Dalj
Bačka Palanka

Monfalcone
Sežana
Postojna
Kočevje
Jastrebarsko
Metlika
SLOVENIA
Samobor
Karlovac
Petrinja
Sisak
Hrvatska Kostajnica
Novska
Nova Gradiška
Slavonski Brod
Županja
Šid

Golfo di Trieste
Trieste
Ilirska Bistrica
Črnomelj
Crna Mlaka
Glina
Bosanska Gradiška
Bosanski Brod
Derventa
Brčko

Piran
Izola
Koper
V Planik (1272m)
Obruč (1376m)
Bosiljevo
Duga Resa
Kupa
Žirovnica
Novi Grad
Bosanska Krupa
Prijedor
Doboj
Bijeljina

Umag
Buje
Buzet
Rijeka
Opatija
Vrbovsko
Ogulin
Slunj
Plitvice Lakes National Park
Bihać
Banja Luka
Sava
Loznica

Rovinj
Kanfanar
Istria
Beli
Krk
Crikvenica
Plaški
Bosansko Petrovac
BOSNIA & HERCEGOVINA
Tuzla
Vlasenica

Brijuni Islands
Labin
Baška
Cres
Senj
Brinje
Jablanac
Otočac
Plješivica
Žepče
Zenica
Srebrenica

Pula
Verudela Peninsula
Kvarner
Zeča
Rab
Lopar
Žuta Lokva
Šatorina (1623m)
Gospić
Ožeblin (1657m)
Una
Jajce

Lošinj
Mali Lošinj
Pag Town
Vaganski vrh (1757m)
Livno
SARAJEVO
Goražde

Ilovik
Silba
Premuda
Molat
Vir
Paklenica National Park
V Crnopac (1402m)
Gračac
Konjic
Foča

Dugi Otok
Sestrunj
Ugljan
Iž
Pašman
Božava
Zadar
Benkovac
Obrovac
Krka
Knin
Pljevlja

Kornat
Žut
Biograd
Krka National Park
Peručko Lake
Čikola
Livno

Ancona
Vodice
Kaprije
Žirje
Šibenik
Primošten
Sinj
Aržano
Imotski
Mostar
Konjic

Osimo
Trogir
Split
Omiš
Brela
Makarska
Drvenik

Civitanova Marche
Šolta
Supetar
Brač
Neretva
Metković
Gacko

Porto San Giorgio
Pakleni Islands
Hvar
Hvar

San Benedetto del Tronto
Jabuka
Svetac
Vis
Vela Luka
Korčula Island
Korčula Town
Orebić

Ascoli Piceno
Giulianova
Biševo
Pomena
Sobra
Dubrovnik
Nikšić
MONTENEGRO

Teramo
ITALY
Adriatic Sea
Lastovo
Mljet National Park
Mljet
Herceg Novi
Risan
Morača Canyon

Penne
Pescara
Rose
Tivat
PODGORICA

Chieti
Ortona
Cetinje
Budva

Celano
Sulmona
Vasto
Lanciano
Isole Tremiti
Bar

Termoli
Lago di Lesina
Vieste
Ulcinj

1 Sarajevo

The stone-flagged alleys of the ancient Baščaršija quarter give Sarajevo's Old Town a certain Turkish feel. They are full of souvenir shops flogging slippers, carpets, copperware, woodwork and jewellery. Another Sarajevo delight is exploring its many cafes; there's a special concentration around Ferhadija.

2 Vrbas Canyons

Between Jajce and Banja Luka in western Bosnia, the Vrbas River descends through a series of gorges and reservoir lakes that together form one of the country's foremost adventure-sport playgrounds. This is a popular place for canyoning, hiking, kayaking and top-class rafting.

3 Mostar's Old Bridge

The 16th-century arched Stari Most (Old Bridge) on the emerald Neretva River was built by Suleyman the Magnificent. Following its bombardment during the Bosnian war, it was laboriously reconstructed in 2004 and is now a World Heritage Site famed for the spectacle of bridge diving.

4 Sutjeska National Park

The glorious canyon-land scenery of

Sutjeska National Park is a spectacular place to explore on foot. There's a network of waymarked hiking trails; two of the most popular treks lead to Mt Maglić (2386m), Bosnia's highest peak.

5 Kotor's Old Town

Wedged between brooding mountains and a moody corner of the bay, Kotor is hemmed in by staunch walls snaking improbably up the surrounding slopes. The atmospheric Old Town is a medieval maze of museums, churches, cafe-strewn squares and Venetian palaces.

6 Lake Skadar National Park

Birdwatching in dolphin-shaped Lake Skadar is a joy. The blissfully pretty area of steep mountains, island monasteries and floating meadows of water lilies is one of the most important reserves for wetland birds in Europe. The endangered Dalmatian pelican nests here along with 256 other species, including a quarter of the global population of pygmy cormorants.

7 Tara Canyon

Slicing through the mountains at the northern edge of the impossibly rugged Durmitor National Park, the Tara River forms one of the world's deepest canyons (1300m). Rafting the canyon is suitable for both white-water novices and experienced foam-hounds. Though not the world's most white-knuckled ride, it does have some rapids.

8 Sveti Stefan Island

Sveti Stefan is the jewel in the Adriatic Coast's crown. A fortified island village connected to the mainland by a narrow causeway, its 15th-century stone villas overlook an impeccable pink-sand beach and turquoise waters.

Mostar's Old Bridge: The Balkans' most famous bridge forms a stone arc between reincarnated medieval towers.

© Alexandre Ehrhard / 500px

7-day itinerary
Vojvodina to Hercegovina

Travel between Serbia and Bosnia and taste wine along the way. Start in **Novi Sad**, the capital of the Vojvodina region, soaking up its laid-back vibe and exploring the Petrovaradin Citadel. Take a day trip to the hills of **Fruška Gora**, famous for medieval monasteries and ancestral vineyards. Move on south to **Tara National Park** to board the Šargan Eight vintage train that chugs through mountain scenery. Cross into Bosnia and enjoy a cruise on the Drina River's canyons around historic **Višegrad**. Catch a bus to **Mostar** to admire the Balkans' most celebrated bridge and browse the old bazaar's craft shops. Save the last day for historic **Trebinje** and some of Hercegovina's best wines, notably at Tvrdoš Monastery.

10-day itinerary
Via Dinarica and the Adriatic

Some of the Balkans' best scenery is found along the Via Dinarica hiking trail and the Adriatic coast. Spend at least two days in Bosnia's capital **Sarajevo** to enjoy its vibrant cafe culture and mix of Turkish and Austro-Hungarian historical influences. Take a day trip to fabled **Lukomir**, the most remote of Sarajevo's highland villages, for a short hike. The road south leads into the glorious canyons of **Sutjeska National Park**. The cross-border hike from Sutjeska into the rugged **Durmitor National Park** is the Via Dinarica's classic leg. From here, head south to Montenegro's old royal capital of **Cetinje**, home to the country's most impressive collection of museums spanning centuries of history. The white-knuckle back-road drive from Cetinje to **Kotor** provides jaw-dropping views of the bay and the Adriatic beyond. Devote a couple of days to hanging out in Kotor's atmospheric, Venetian-inspired old town, then pop over to romantic **Perast** and catch a boat to the Our-Lady-of-the-Rock island. Finally, head south along the coast to buzzy, minaret-studded **Ulcinj** and its sandy beach.

Belgrade
Belgrade's chaotic history unfolds on its ancient Kalemegdan Fortress, destroyed and rebuilt 40 times, and in the fascinating museums like the Museum of Yugoslavia. It's also one of the world's top party cities, famous for the Sava and Danube riverbarge clubs, known as *splavovi*. The once-derelict Savamala quarter is Belgrade's hip HQ.

Subotica
Sugar-spun art-nouveau marvels make Subotica a delightful destination. Once an important hub of the Austro-Hungarian Empire, the town attracted some of the region's most influential architects and artists; their excellently preserved handiwork is today the town's biggest drawcard.

Djerdap National Park
The sprawling Djerdap is home to the formidable Iron Gates gorge, whose cliffs dip and dive for 100km along the Danube and guard the prehistoric settlement of Lepenski Vir. The EuroVelo 6 cycling path runs through here, while bus-and-boat tours from Belgrade pass through the gorge.

Uvac Canyon
The spectacular meanders of Uvac River are a feat of nature that's best admired by hiking up to one of the nature reserve's lookouts. Boat trips with a park ranger also take in part of the 2093m-long Ice Cave. The canyon is home to the mighty (and endangered) griffon vulture.

1. The Acropolis, Athens

Regal on its hilltop, the Acropolis remains the quintessential landmark of Western civilisation. Whether you explore it early in the morning or soak up the view from a dinnertime terrace, you'll be mesmerised by its beauty, history and sheer size. Beyond the Parthenon are quieter spots like the exquisite Temple of Athena Nike and the Theatre of Dionysos. Nearby, the Acropolis Museum showcases the surviving treasures of the Acropolis.

2. Meteora

Magnificent Meteora beckons pilgrims, hikers and rock climbers from around the world. Soaring pillars of rock jut heavenward, with monasteries perched on their summits. Built as early as the 14th century, these were home to hermit monks fleeing persecution. The rope ladders that monks once used to reach the top have long been replaced by steps carved into the rock, and six monasteries remain open to resident monks and visitors alike.

3. Thessaloniki's gastronomy

Taste-test your way through Greece's gastronomic capital. There are excellent restaurants all over town, and you can eat your way through each neighbourhood. Along Egnatia, up in Ano Poli, in Ladadika and around the

Meteora: Moni Agias Varvaras Rousanou is home to around 15 nuns and contains superb frescoes.

waterfront, you'll find quality local ingredients and traditional recipes used in innovative ways. Don't miss the *zaharoplasteia* (patisseries) for Ottoman-inspired sweets.

4. Mykonos nightlife

Mykonos is the great glamour island of Greece and happily flaunts its sizzling St-Tropez-meets-Ibiza style and party-hard reputation. Each major beach has at least one bar which gets going during the day, while the whitewashed Cycladic maze of Mykonos Town (aka Hora) hosts a catwalk cast of thousands. The scene is most intense in July and August, but bring funds – the high life doesn't come cheap.

5. Santorini

This remarkable island, shaped by the fire of prehistoric eruptions, has made the celebratory sunset its own. On summer evenings, the clifftop towns of Fira and Oia are packed with visitors

awed by the vast blood-red canvas of the cliff face. You can catch the sunset without the crowds from almost anywhere along the cliff edge. If you miss sundown, face east at first light for some fairly stunning sunrises.

6. Palace of Knossos

Rub shoulders with the ghosts of the mighty Minoans. Knossos was their Bronze Age capital over 4000 years ago. Their extraordinary wealth of frescoes, sculptures, jewellery and structures lay buried under the Cretan soil until the site's excavation in the early 20th century. Despite a controversial partial reconstruction, Knossos remains one of the most important archaeological sites in the Mediterranean.

7. Iraklio Wine Country

In central Crete, almost two dozen wineries are embedded in a landscape of round-shouldered hills, sunbaked slopes and lush valleys. Winemakers cultivate many indigenous Cretan grape varietals, such as Kotsifali, Mandilari and Malvasia; many estates now offer wine tours and tastings. A visit here is especially pretty during the spring bloom and the late-summer harvest.

8. Corfu's Old Town

Imbued with Venetian grace and elegance, Corfu's Old Town is a tight-

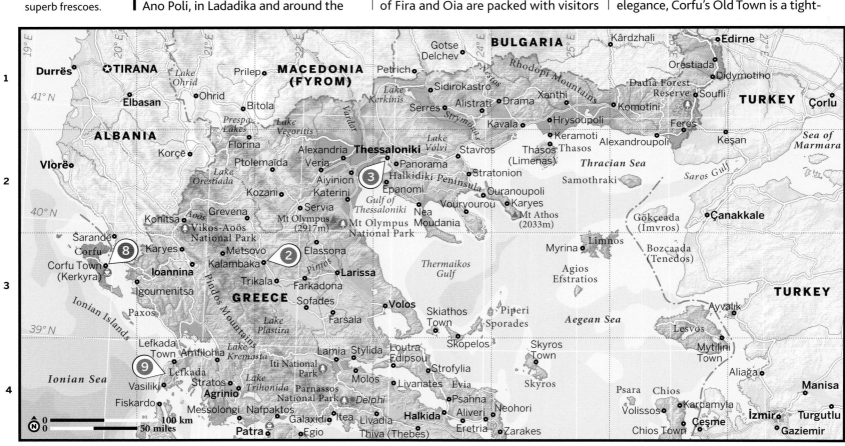

© Justin Foulkes / Lonely Planet

10-day itinerary
Athens and the Cyclades

It's possible to island-hop in just 10 days. Spend a couple of days in **Athens** taking in its ancient sights, lively markets, contemporary art scene and brilliant nightlife. Catch a ferry from Rafina for a day or two on chic **Mykonos** and enjoy the stylish bars and beaches full of sun worshippers. Take a day trip to sacred **Delos** and explore its ancient ruins. Hop on a ferry to **Naxos**, the greenest of the Cyclades, with its Venetian-walled old town, quaint villages and sugar-soft beaches. Move on to **Paros**, whose cobbled capital is filled with trendy boutiques and great dining. Lastly, visit spectacular **Santorini** for lovely sunsets, excellent wineries and volcanic beaches, along with the Minoan site of Akrotiri. From here you can catch a flight back to Athens.

7-day itinerary
Crete

This route is a roller-coaster ride through the natural wonders of Greece's largest island, as well as its historical treasures. Kick off your trip in **Iraklio**, checking out the museums and soaking up its cafe culture. Then head to the **Palace of Knossos** where the mysterious Minoans ruled over 4000 years ago. Spend a day enjoying the fruits of the **Iraklio Wine Country**, dotted with vineyards that produce 70% of Crete's wine. Next, head west to soulful **Rethymno**, where you can spend a day wandering the maze of Venetian lanes. Then swing down south to **Moni Preveli**, a working monastery on a hill with sweeping views of the Libyan Sea, and palm-studded **Preveli Beach** down below. Finally, make your way to **Hania**, a lively city wrapped around a romantic Venetian harbour and evocative old quarter. For your last day, when you've had your fill of history, either take the early bus to **Samaria Gorge** and trek one of Europe's most famous canyons, or hop over to the western tip of the island at **Elafonisi**, which beckons with pink-shimmering sandy beaches.

---

packed warren of winding lanes, some bursting with fine restaurants, lively bars and intriguing shops, others timeless back alleys where washing lines stretch between balconies. It holds some majestic architecture including the splendid Liston arcade, and high-class museums along with 39 churches.

Lefkada
Lefkada's rugged coastline offers some amazing beaches, stunning little bays and inlets, as well as windy conditions that attract kitesurfers and windsurfers from all over the world. The harbour village of Vasiliki, complete with stony beach, is one of the top places to learn windsurfing in Greece, thanks to its breezy conditions.

Rhodes' Old Town
Rhodes' Old Town lies sealed like a time capsule behind a double ring of imposing 12m-thick ramparts and a deep moat now filled with lush gardens. Getting lost in its twisting, cobbled alleyways with stone mansions, soaring archways and lively squares is a must. Explore the medieval Knights' Quarter, the old Jewish Quarter or the Hora (Turkish Quarter). Wander along the top of the city walls, with the sea on one side and a bird's-eye view into this living museum on the other.

Preveli Beach
With its heart-shaped boulder standing just offshore, lapped by the bluest waves, Crete's Preveli Beach (also known as Palm Beach) is one of Greece's most celebrated strands. Bisected by a freshwater river and flanked by rugged cliffs concealing sea caves, Preveli is a thick ribbon of soft sand on the Libyan Sea, with clear pools of water along its palm-lined riverbank that are perfect for refreshing dips (cross an ankle-deep river to reach the sandiest stretch). The beach lies under the sacred gaze of Moni Preveli, a magnificent monastery perched high above.

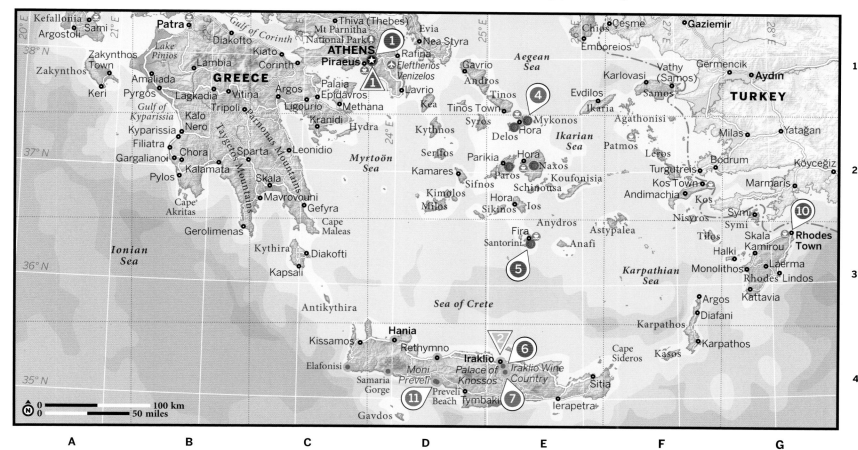

SIGHTS &
ACTIVITIES

SEE

DO

ITINERARY

1

2

Accursed Mountains

Hiking in the Accursed Mountains shows off some of Albania's most impressive scenery, deep tradition and local pride. The two main villages with tourist infrastructure are Theth and Valbona, and a superb day hike (roughly five hours) links the two. The trail begins a couple of kilometres beyond Valbona and is marked, with places to stop on the way for food and drinks.

Ksamil Beach

One of the most popular beaches on the Albanian Riviera, the last virgin stretch of the Mediterranean coast, is Ksamil (17km south of Saranda). It has three small islands within swimming distance of the shore and dozens of beachside bars and restaurants that open in the summer. A short bus ride away are the ancient ruins of Butrint.

Gjirokastra's Old Town

Gjirokastra is a magical hillside town described beautifully in Ismail Kadare's novel *Chronicle in Stone*. There has been a settlement here for 2500 years; these days it's the town's impressive Ottoman-era houses that attract visitors. The bazaar is crammed with shops supporting local artisans, while the eerie hilltop castle is definitely worth the walk up from the Old Town.

Lake Ohrid

Three-million-year-old Lake Ohrid was once home to a prehistoric pile-dwelling settlement, elaborately reconstructed by archaeologists as the Museum on Water in the Bay of Bones. Both beginners and certified divers can see the animal remains and fragmented vessels that have been found here, at depths between 5m and 8m.

Skopje

The riverside area of Skopje has the look of a set design for an ancient civilisation. Towering warrior statues gaze down on you and gleaming Italianate power buildings make visitors feel very small indeed. Marble-clad museums have mushroomed alongside hypnotic new mega-fountains. The building frenzy is the result of the 'Skopje 2014' government project.

Mavrovo National Park

Hiking in Mavrovo National Park offers plenty of scenic views – gorges, pine forests, karst fields and waterfalls – and the chance to climb Macedonia's highest peak, Mt Korab (2764m). The park is also home to one of the country's most revered (and accessible) monasteries, Sveti Jovan Bigorski, and the atmospheric villages of Galičnik and Janče, separated by a mountain ridge.

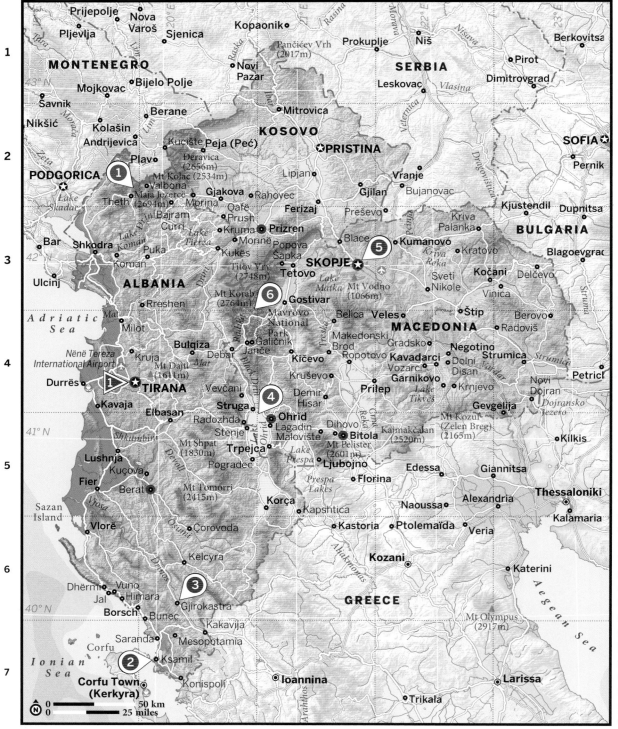

10-day itinerary
Offbeat Balkans

Start this ramble through some of the more offbeat pockets of the Balkans with a couple of days in Albania's colourful capital **Tirana**, checking out a few fascinating museums and the Blloku quarter's nightlife. Head south to **Berat**, a striking old town of Ottoman houses in a rugged montain setting. Backtrack to Tirana and catch a bus to Kosovo's picturesque **Prizren**, with a mosque- and church-filled old town and a fortress on the hill above it. Catch another cross-border bus to Macedonia's capital **Skopje** to marvel at its heady mix of quirky statues and Ottoman and Byzantine heritage. Move on to **Bitola** for a taste of the country's love affair with local foraging. Browse its food market and sample seasonal highlights paired with local *vranec* (red wine). End the trip in sublime **Ohrid**, exploring its historic quarter, relaxing in traditional cafes and swimming in the eponymous lake.

Pafos Archaeological Site
The sprawling ancient city in the southerly resort of Pafos dates to the late 4th century BC; what is seen today is believed to be only a modest part of what remains to be excavated. The major highlight of the ruins are the intricate, colourful Roman floor mosaics at the heart of the original complex, first unearthed in 1962 – they are based on ancient Greek myths.

Kyrenia's Old Harbour
Backdropped by jagged mountains and overlooked by a golden-stoned castle, Kyrenia's Old Harbour evokes bygone Cyprus. Where merchant ships once fought for space, bobbing *gülets* (traditional wooden ships) now moor, ushering on day trippers. Hugging the waterfront, tall stone-cut buildings which once stored raw carob are reinvented as cafes and restaurants.

Aphrodite's Rock and Beach
Myth has it that this is where the goddess of love emerged from the sea. The romantic connections and cliff-fringed coastal view make it Cyprus' most famous photo stop, particularly at sunset. Stroll along the pretty pebble beach, lapped by delightfully cool water and loomed over by its striking sea stack, to admire Aphrodite's dramatic choice of an entrance up close.

10-day itinerary
Southern Cyprus

Take in southern Cyprus' beaches, sweeping history, mountain vistas, rural villages and urban buzz, all in one swoop. Fly into **Larnaka** for a day of beach time. Brush off the sand to discover the history behind this beach resort by checking out its Byzantine church, old Turkish quarter and fort. Then travel to the capital **Nicosia (Lefkosia)** and delve into the historic Old Town, framed by Venetian walls and crammed with art galleries, museums and contemporary cafe life. Next, head for the hills. The slopes of the **Troödos Mountains** hide a clutch of churches, home to fabulous frescoes which fizz with Byzantine-era flair. Pull on your hiking boots to traverse a mountain trail or two. Roll back to the coast, basing yourself in buzzing **Lemesos (Limassol)** while exploring the Commandaria region's village idylls. Then veer west to **Pafos**. Check out the swag of ancient mosaics and ruins here and take a quick trip north to escape the crowds and flop on the sand at **Lara Beach**, before catching a flight off the island from Pafos.

Troödos Mountains
The Troödos Mountains comprise an expanse of flora, fauna and geology across pine forests, waterfalls, rocky crags and babbling brooks. Mt Olympus (1952m) provides spectacular views of the southern coastline and a respite from summer heat. Ramblers, campers, flower-spotters and birdwatchers alike will be absorbed by the ridges, peaks and valleys along the island's most diverse hiking and nature trails.

Larnaka Bay
The waters surrounding the Cypriot coastline are a wreck-diving dream. The battered husks of sunken ships which never made it to port are now patrolled by shoals of flitting fish. Larnaka Bay's *Zenobia,* which capsized in 1980, is rated as one of the world's top-five wreck dives. Exploring it, complete with cargo decks of trucks, is one of the island's eeriest adventures.

Omodos wine villages
The far-reaching vineyards of the *krasohoria* (wine villages) dominate the slopes surrounding Omodos. Over 50 boutique wineries are spread across six or seven traditional villages, with a vast array of wines and grapes for the connoisseur's choice. The most famous indigenous varieties derive from the *mavro* (dark-red grape) and *xynisteri* (white grape) vines.

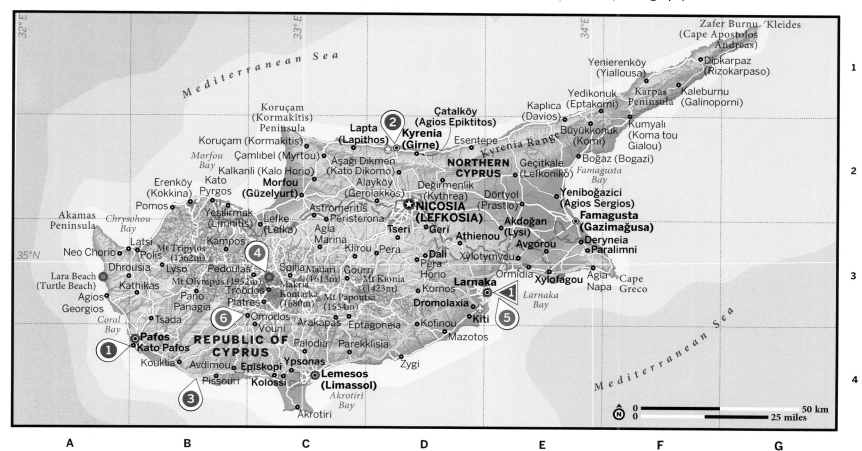

Eastern Europe & Baltics

CLIMATE CHART

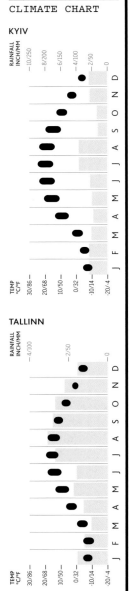

Squeezed between Russia and Scandinavia, the three countries on the Baltic Sea (Estonia, Latvia and Lithuania) share similar history and geography. They might be small but you can still enjoy pristine nature – forests, lakes and a stunning coastline – all to yourself, or explore the cobbled lanes of medieval capitals. Further south, from Poland to Bulgaria, you'll find echoes of history spent behind the Iron Curtain alongside a living heritage of folklore, and hushed monasteries competing for attention with hip nightlife. The great outdoors – from Romania's soaring Carpathian Mountains and Bulgaria's Black Sea beaches to the European bison of the continent's last primeval forest in Belarus and the birdlife of Ukraine's Danube Delta – begs to be explored.

CASTLES
Eastern Europe's history stretches far beyond communism. Live out medieval fantasies in Romania's Bran Castle (of *Dracula* fame), the Teutonic knights' Malbork Castle in Poland, Ukraine's castle town of Kamyanets-Podilsky, or the 16th-century Mir Castle in Belarus.

OUTDOOR ACTIVITIES
Eastern Europe offers outdoor thrills for a fraction of their cost in the West. Try cycling in Lithuania's Curonian Spit National Park, sail Poland's Great Masurian Lakes, go caving in Romania's Apuseni Nature Park, or ski in Bulgaria's Pirin Mountains – the choice is yours.

MONASTERIES
The heartland of Orthodox Christianity is Eastern Europe. You can admire ancient frescoes at Moldova's Orheiul Vechi cave monastery, the painted monasteries of Bucovina in Romania, Bulgaria's splendid Rila Monastery, and Ukraine's holy Kyevo-Pecherska Lavra.

FOLKLORE
Folk culture and festivals are what sets Eastern Europe apart. Don't miss the traditional villages of Maramureş in Romania, rose festivals in Bulgaria's Valley of Roses, folk art on Lithuania's Hill of Crosses, and Poland's open-air museum of folk architecture in Sanok.

Above and right: Romanian shepherd tending his flock (above) and (right) Bran Castle, once home of Vlad the Impaler.

Transport hubs

It's never been easier to reach Eastern Europe, especially from major Western European cities. There's a vast range of routes by air, thanks to low-cost carriers, with budget flights (particularly from the UK) now reaching airports from Tallinn in Estonia to Plovdiv in Bulgaria. The region has long been easily accessible by rail and bus, with hubs like Warsaw in Poland particularly well connected. Depending on the countries involved, the relative efficiency of train and bus links can vary. Journeys between Schengen area countries (the Baltics and Poland) will be uninterrupted at border crossings. In some countries, buses may be quicker and more reliable than trains.

TRANSPORT

B5, C2, C3, C4, C9, D4, D7, D8, E6

B3, B4, C1, C3, D9, E7

Below: Snow dusting the roofs of Tallinn (left) and (right) Blackheads House, Rīga.

Tallinn
The old town of Estonia's capital, with its medieval lanes and hidden bars, is captivating. Tallinn Airport is well connected to other Baltic and European destinations. There are direct trains to St Petersburg and Moscow, and ferries to Helsinki, St Petersburg, Mariehamn and Stockholm. International buses depart from Tallinn's Central Bus Station.

Rīga
Latvia's cosmopolitan capital offers a surplus of art-nouveau architecture and is a joy to explore. Rīga International Airport has direct flights to cities across Europe, including Tallinn and Vilnius. Buses and trains also connect Rīga to St Petersburg, Moscow and Warsaw, and ferry services shuttle passengers to Swedish and German ports.

Vilnius
The capital of Lithuania has Europe's largest baroque old town at its heart. Vilnius International Airport and bus station have connections to Rīga and Tallinn and other major European cities.

Warsaw
Poland's capital has a dramatic history; fine museums reflect that complex past. Most international flights arrive at Frédéric Chopin Airport. Warsaw Modlin Airport, 35km north of the city, handles budget flights. International and domestic trains and buses are serviced by Warszawa Zachodnia bus terminal and Warszawa Centralna train station.

Minsk
Belarus' capital is a showcase of Stalinist architecture. Minsk-2 International Airport is well connected by direct flights to Europe, the Middle East and the former Soviet Union. Several daily buses run to Vilnius and Warsaw. There are train services to Russia, Ukraine, Lithuania, Poland and Moldova.

Kyiv
The capital of Ukraine offers hip urban art alongside ancient golden-domed churches. Boryspil International Airport handles most international flights. Kyiv Zhulyany International Airport serves domestic routes and budget carriers.

Chişinău
Moldova's pleasant capital boasts tree-lined streets and parks made for strolling. Chişinău International Airport has good connections to Western Europe and the former Soviet Union. Daily buses head to Bucharest, Kyiv, Moscow and Odesa. Only a handful of international trains serve Chişinău.

Bucharest
The Romanian capital is far more than a gateway to Transylvania – it's trendy, dynamic and fun. Henri Coandă International Airport has connections with many European capitals and large cities, plus the Middle East. Train and long-haul bus services are frequent, though bus travel can be faster.

Sofia
Bulgaria's laid-back capital has eclectic architecture that lends an almost exotic feel. Sofia Airport has good links with many European cities, as well as some in the Middle East. The city is also easily accessible by bus and rail from all neighbouring Balkan countries.

© Matt Munro / Lonely Planet

NORWAY

SWEDEN

Sarpsborg
Karlstad
Uddevalla
Göteborg (Gothenburg)
Halmstad
DENMARK
COPENHAGEN
Malmö

Falun
Gävle
Mälaren
Örebro
Uppsala
Nyköping
Visby
Gotland
Växjö
Kalmar
Öland
Bornholm

Gulf of Bothnia
Åland
Mariehamn

Pori
Hämeenlinna
Turku (Åbo)
HELSINKI

Salmaa
Lahti
Lappeenranta
Kouvola
Kotka
Vyborg

Lake Onega
Lake Ladoga
St Petersburg
Gatchina

Lake Beloye
Lake Kubenskoye
Vologda

Sukhona

Page 113

TALLINN
Keila-Joa
ESTONIA
Türi
Pärnu
Elva
Tartu

Narva
Gulf of Finland

Veliky Novgorod
Lake Il'men

Rybinsk Reservoir
Yaroslavl
Ivanovo
Gorky Reservoir
Kostroma

RUSSIA

Hiiumaa
Saaremaa

Lake Peipsi
Lake Pskovskoye

Lake Ладога

Volkhov

Vladimir

Page 119

Kattegat
Vänern
Vättern

Baltic Sea

Ventspils
Gulf of Riga
Valmiera
Pskov

Liepāja
RĪGA
Jelgava
LATVIA
Rēzekne
Velikie Luki

Tver
Vladimir

Oka

MOSCOW

Page 115

Szczecin Lagoon
Słupsk
Gdynia
Gdańsk
Elbląg
Olsztyn

Koszalin
Szczecin
GERMANY
Bydgoszcz
Gorzów Wielkopolski
Poznań

Telšiai
Šiauliai
Klaipėda

Sovetsk
Kaliningrad
Marijampolė

Jēkabpils
Panevėžys
Daugavpils

LITHUANIA
Utena
Tauragė
Kaunas
VILNIUS
Alytus
Maladzechna
MINSK

Daugava

Vitsebsk
Lepel

Barysau

Smolensk

Ryazan

Novomoskovsk

Kaluga
Tula

Tambov
Lipetsk

Cottbus
Zielona Góra
POLAND
Płock
Warsaw Modlin
WARSAW
Frédéric Chopin

Legnica
Wrocław
Wałbrzych
PRAGUE
CZECH REPUBLIC

Toruń
Kalisz
Łódź
Radom

Hrodna
Białystok
Brest

Mahileu (Mogilev)
BELARUS
Slutsk
Salihorsk
Homel

Bryansk
Oryol

Voronezh

Odra
Warta
Vistula

Opole
Częstochowa
Kielce
Lublin

Lutsk
Rivne

Chernihiv
Kyivske Reservoir

KYIV

Kursk

Belgorod

Pripyat
Desna
Seym

Sumy

Rybnik
Katowice
Kraków

Ostrava
Bielsko-Biała
Tatras Mountains
Prešov
Košice

Tarnów
Rzeszów
Lviv
Ternopil
Khmelnytsky

Zhytomyr
Kyiv Zhulyany
Boryspil

Vinnytsya
Cherkasy
Kremenchutske Reservoir

Kharkiv
Poltava

Luhansk

Dnipro (Dnieper)

SLOVAKIA
VIENNA
AUSTRIA
BRATISLAVA
Győr
Graz

Gerlach (2655m)
Miskolc

Ivano-Frankivsk
Yaremche
Gora Goverla (2058m)
Chernivtsi

Kropyvnytsky

Kremenchuk
Slovyansk
Horlivka
Bryanka
Krasny Luch

Danube
Tisa

BUDAPEST
HUNGARY
Maribor
SLOVENIA
ZAGREB
CROATIA

Lake Balaton
Kecskemét
Pécs
Szeged

Debrecen
Oradea
Cluj-Napoca
Târgu Mureş

Baia Mare
Satu Mare

Bălţi
MOLDOVA
Botoşani
Iaşi
CHIŞINĂU

UKRAINE

Dnipro
Zaporizhzhya
Donetsk

Kryvy Rih
Nikopol
Kakhovske Reservoir

Rostov-on-Don

Mariupol
Berdyansk

Don

Drava
Sava
Mures

Subotica
Arad
Timişoara
ROMANIA
Sibiu
Moldoveanu (2543m)

Bacău
Tiraspol
Bendery
Kherson
Mykolaiv
Odesa

Sea of Azov

Novi Sad
Banja Luka
BELGRADE

Transylvanian Alps
Braşov
Buzău
Galaţi

Olt

CRIMEA
Krasnodar
Kuban

BOSNIA & HERCEGOVINA
SARAJEVO
Split
Mostar
Brač
Hvar
Korčula

Kragujevac
SERBIA
Kruševac
Craiova

Danube
Ploieşti
BUCHAREST
Henri Coandă
Ruse
Constanţa

Simferopol
Sevastopol
Yalta

Dubrovnik
MONTENEGRO
PODGORICA

Niš
Leskovac
BULGARIA

Pitesti
Pleven
Dobrich

Black Sea

Lake Skadar
PRISTINA
KOSOVO
SOFIA

Balkan Mountains
Stara Zagora
Burgas

Varna

Page 116

Adriatic Sea
SKOPJE
Musala (2925m)
Plovdiv

MACEDONIA
Page 117
TIRANA
Durrës

Serres
Komotini
Edirne

Çorlu
İstanbul

Zonguldak
Karabük

Samsun

Ordu

Bari
Taranto
ITALY
Brindisi
Lecce

ALBANIA
Vlorë
Kozani

Thessaloniki

Thasos
Samothraki

Tekirdağ
Sea of Marmara
Bursa

Kocaeli (İzmit)
Bolu

ANKARA

Çorum
Tokat
Sivas

Ionian Sea
Crotone

Corfu (Kerkyra)
Corfu Town (Kerkyra)
Ioannina
Larissa
GREECE

Mt Olympus (2917m)
Limnos
Lesbos
Aegean Sea

Gökçeada (Imvros)
Bandırma
Balıkesir
Uludağ Tepe (2543m)
Eskişehir

İnegöl
Kırıkkale

TURKEY

N
0   250 miles
0   500 km

A   B   C   D   E   F   G

1 2 3 4 5 6 7 8 9 10

© Sarah Coghill / Lonely Planet

SIGHTS & ACTIVITIES

 SEE

DO

ITINERARY

▽ 1

▽ 2

Tallinn's Old Town

The medieval jewel of Tallinn's Old Town is Estonia's most fascinating locality. Picking your way along the narrow, cobbled streets is like strolling into the 15th century. You'll pass the ornate stone facades of Hanseatic merchants' houses, wander into hidden medieval courtyards, and find footworn stone stairways leading to sweeping views of the red-roofed city.

Lahemaa National Park

The 'Land of Bays' is unspoiled, rural Estonia. A microcosm of the country's natural charms, the park takes in a stretch of deeply indented coast with several peninsulas and bays, plus pine-fresh hinterland encompassing forest, lakes, rivers and peat bogs. There's an extensive network of forest trails for walkers, cyclists and horse riders.

Saaremaa

Saaremaa ('island land') is synonymous with space, spruce and fresh air, and is perfect for unwinding. Estonia's largest island is substantially covered in forests of pine, spruce and juniper, while its windmills, lighthouses and tiny villages seem largely unbothered by the passage of time. The regional capital Kuressaare, on the south coast, is a natural base for visitors.

④

Vilnius

Vilnius is a city of immense allure that draws tourists like moths to a flame with its easy charm and golden glow. It's centred around Europe's largest baroque old town, with a skyline pierced by countless Orthodox and Catholic church steeples, cobbled alleys, crumbling corners, majestic hilltop views and artists' workshops.

⑤

Curonian Spit National Park

Curonian Spit is refreshingly wild and undeveloped, with beautiful beaches, sandy dunes and sweet-smelling pine forests populated by deer, elk and wild boar. Hit the Juodkrantė–Nida cycling path, go swimming in the Baltic Sea, or explore hardy human settlements on this thin spit of sand and spruce.

Hill of Crosses

One of Lithuania's most inspiring sights is the legendary Hill of Crosses. The sound of the thousands of crosses (which appear to grow on the hillock) tinkling in the breeze is wonderfully eerie. Planted since at least the 19th century, the crosses were bulldozed by the Soviets, but people added more, risking their lives or freedom to express their national and spiritual fervour.

Dzūkija National Park

Mushrooming is a booming business in Dzūkija National Park, which in August and September is carpeted with little white and yellow buttons. The forests lining the Varėna–Druskininkai highway and the Zervynos forests, known for sand dunes and beehive hollows, make rich mushroom-hunting grounds, too. Berrying is another trade and tradition; red bilberries ripen in August and cranberries in September. Look for locals selling at roadsides, with freshly picked forest goodies on car bonnets.

Rīga

The Gothic spires that dominate Rīga's cityscape might suggest austerity, but it's art nouveau (also known as Jugendstil) that forms the flesh and the spirit of the city. More than 750 buildings in Rīga boast this flamboyant and haunting style, and the number continues to grow as myriad restoration projects get underway. Alberta Iela street is at the heart of Rīga's art-nouveau district.

Kurzeme Coast

Kurzeme is miles and miles of jaw-dropping natural beauty. The region's sandy coastline is tailor-made for an off-the-beaten-track adventure. Enchantingly desolate and hauntingly beautiful, a journey to Cape Kolka feels like a trip to the end of the earth. Slītere National Park is a rugged, often tundra-like expanse, home to wild deer, elk, buzzards and beavers.

Jūrmala

The Baltic's version of the French Riviera, Jūrmala is a long string of townships with Prussian-style villas. Jūrmala's main attraction is its colourful art-nouveau wooden houses, distinguishable by frilly awnings, detailed facades and elaborate towers. There are over 4000 wooden structures found throughout Jūrmala; get your fill on a leisurely stroll along Jūras iela.

Hill of Crosses: Some of the crosses are finely carved folk-art masterpieces.

10-day itinerary
Capital Drop-in

Ten days is just enough to get a feel for each of the Baltic's capitals. Start in **Vilnius** (Lithuania) to appreciate the sumptuous baroque architecture and take in the city's rich Jewish history. A side trip to the castle at **Trakai** is a must before visiting Latvia's capital, **Rīga**. Haggle for huckleberries at the Central Market and admire the glorious art-nouveau architecture soaring above. Take a day trip to **Sigulda**, where you can crank up the adrenaline choosing from its clutch of adventure sports. Next it's on to Estonia and **Tallinn**, a fairy-tale of quaint medieval houses. Indulge in the city's world-class culinary scene, then end the trip with a day at **Pärnu** for a spot of beach-lazing.

14-day itinerary
Best of the Baltic

If you only have limited time but are keen on seeing the best of what each Baltic state has to offer, this route ticks off many of the big-ticket destinations. Inaugurate your tour in **Tallinn** and roam the magnificent medieval streets of the Estonian capital's Old Town. Delve into the city's treasure trove of gastronomic delights before trekking out to **Lahemaa National Park**. The electric nightlife in the university town of **Tartu** awaits. Afterwards, skip south into Latvia to take in the crumbling castles of Cēsis and Sigulda in **Gauja National Park**. Spend the night at one of the posh manor houses nearby, then plough through to reach **Rīga**, home to a dizzying array of decorated facades. Next, head south to **Rundāle** to visit the opulent palace, the Baltic's version of Versailles. From here hop the border into Lithuania and stop for a look at the **Hill of Crosses** in Šiauliai. Continue on to **Aukštaitija National Park**, with its lakes and hiking paths, and stop overnight in Labanoras, before ending the trip in flamboyant, baroque **Vilnius**.

© gorsh13 / Getty Images

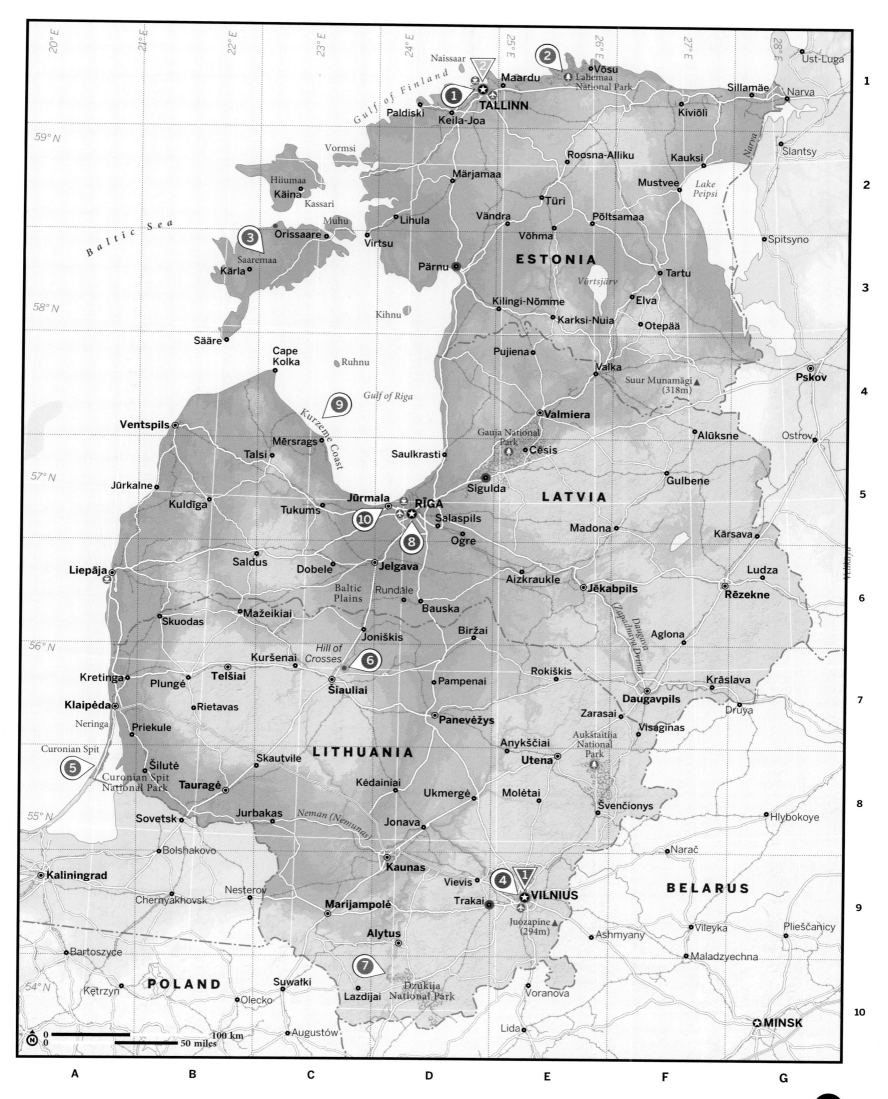

Ust-Luga
Narva
Sillamäe
Kiviõli
Slantsy
Kauksi
Mustvee
Spitsyno
Lake Peipsi
Roosna-Alliku
Tartu
Põltsamaa
Elva
Otepää
Pskov
Ostrov
Alūksne
Gulbene
Kārsava
Ludza
Rēzekne
Krāslava
Druya
Daugavpils
Visaginas
Hlybokoye
Narač
Vileyka
Plieščanicy
Ashmyany
Maladzyechna
Voranova
Lida
MINSK

Võsu
Lahemaa National Park
Maardu
TALLINN
Paldiski
Keila-Joa
Naissaar

Gulf of Finland

59° N
Vormsi
Hiiumaa
Käina
Kassari
Muhu
Orissaare
Virtsu
Lihula
Märjamaa
Vändra
Türi
Võhma

Baltic Sea

Saaremaa
Kärla
Säära
Kihnu
Pärnu
Kilingi-Nõmme
Karksi-Nuia

ESTONIA
Vörtsjärv
Pujiena
Valka
Suur Munamägi (318m)

58° N

Cape Kolka
Ruhnu
Gulf of Riga
Ventspils
Mērsrags
Talsi
Saulkrasti
Valmiera
Gauja National Park
Cēsis

Kurzeme Coast

57° N
Jūrkalne
Kuldīga
Tukums
Jūrmala
RĪGA
Salaspils
Sīgulda
Madona
LATVIA

Liepāja
Saldus
Dobele
Jelgava
Ogre
Aizkraukle
Jēkabpils
Bauska
Rundāle
Baltic Plains
Mažeikiai
Skuodas
Joniškis
Biržai
Pampenai
Rokiškis
Daugava (Zapadnaya Dvina)
Aglona

56° N
Kretinga
Plungé
Telšiai
Kuršenai
Hill of Crosses
Šiauliai
Panevėžys
Zarasai
Aukštaitija National Park

Klaipėda
Neringa
Rietavas
Skautvile
Kėdainiai
Ukmergė
Utena
Molėtai
Švenčionys

Curonian Spit
Priekule
Šilutė
Curonian Spit National Park
Tauragė
LITHUANIA
Anykščiai

55° N
Sovetsk
Jurbakas
Neman (Nemunas)
Jonava

Kaliningrad
Bolshakovo
Kaunas
Vievis
VILNIUS
Juozapine (294m)
Chernyakhovsk
Nesterov
Marijampolė
Trakai

BELARUS

POLAND
Bartoszyce
Suwalki
Lazdijai
Dzūkija National Park
Alytus
Kętrzyn
Olecko
Augustów
Lida

0   100 km
0   50 miles

A   B   C   D   E   F   G

SIGHTS & ACTIVITIES

 SEE
◉ DO

ITINERARY

▽ 1
▽ 2

Białowieża National Park:
Once hunted to extinction, the European bison has been reintroduced to several countries.

1 Warsaw
Warsaw's museums reflect Poland's complex past. The city's revolt against Nazi rule is powerfully retold at the Warsaw Rising Museum. Poland's long Jewish presence is related with energy at the Museum of the History of Polish Jews. Beautiful music can be heard at the Chopin Museum, while the Neon Museum is a riot of communist colour.

2 Great Masurian Lakes
Sip a cocktail on the deck of a luxury yacht, take a dip, or don a lifejacket, grab your paddle and slide off into a watery adventure on one of the interconnected lakes that make up this mecca for Polish sailing and water-sports fans. In winter, when the lakes freeze over, cross-country skis replace water skis on the steel-hard surface.

3 Wieliczka Salt Mine
The deep salt mine of Wieliczka is an eerie world of pits and chambers, carved by hand from salt blocks. The salt-hewn formations include chapels with altarpieces and figures, and there are even underground lakes. The 300km-long labyrinth of tunnels is distributed over nine levels; some 22 chambers connected by galleries can be toured.

4 Tatras Mountains
The Tatras mountain range is awe-inspiring yet approachable, with peaks that even ordinary folk – with a bit of extra effort – can conquer. In summer, the clouds part to reveal the stern rocky visage rising up over the dwarf pines below. The best approach to the peaks is from the mountain resort of Zakopane.

5 Toruń
Toruń is a magnificently preserved, walled Gothic city by the swirling Vistula. Wandering through the Old Town, crammed with museums, churches, grand mansions and squares, is a treat. The city also has Copernicus connections – the illustrious astronomer allegedly first saw the light of day in one of Toruń's Gothic townhouses.

6 Białowieża National Park
That bison on the label of bottles of Żubr beer or Żubrówka vodka starts to make a lot more sense once you've visited the Białowieża National Park. It holds one of Europe's last vestiges of primeval forest, which you can tour in the company of a guide. A nearby small reserve is home to another survivor: the once-mighty European bison.

7 Sanok
Poland's biggest *skansen* (open-air museum of folk architecture) is in Sanok in the Carpathians. These great gardens of log cabins and timbered chalets make for a wonderful ramble and are testament to centuries of peasant life in Poland. Apart from the museums, you'll find remnants of old wooden churches and other buildings sprinkled throughout the mountains.

8 Karkonosze National Park
Slung between Mt Wielki Szyszak to the west and Mt Śnieżka to the east, Karkonosze is a treat for mountain bikers. Its leafy expanse is threaded by several biking trails, passing impressive lofty cliffs carved by ice-age glaciers. Covering some 450km, the trails are easily accessed from the mountain towns of Szklarska Poręba or Karpacz.

9 Malbork Castle
Medieval mother ship of the Teutonic order, Malbork Castle is a mountain of bricks held together by a lake of mortar. It was home to the all-powerful order's grand master and later to visiting Polish monarchs. If you came to Poland to see castles, this is the place to go; catch it just before dusk when the slanting sunlight burns the bricks kiln-crimson.

10 Słowiński National Park
The season may be brief and the sea one of Europe's nippiest, but if you're looking for a dose of sand, head to the Baltic's cream-white beaches. To flee the masses at the many coastal resorts, head out for the shifting dunes of the Słowiński National Park, where the Baltic's constant bluster sculpts mountains of sifted grains.

11 Kazimierz, Kraków
Once a lively blend of Jewish and Christian cultures, Kazimierz has become one of Kraków's nightlife hubs. Its narrow streets and distressed facades hide small bars ranging from grungy to glamorous. The centre of action is Plac Nowy, which was once home to the quarter's meat market.

▽ 1

7-day itinerary
Cities of the West

Western Poland straddles a region hotly contested between Poland and Germany over the centuries. **Wrocław** makes a logical start and merits at least two days. This was the former German city of Breslau; its architecture retains a Germanic flavour with a Polish pulse. Next, make your way to **Poznań**, where the Polish kingdom got its start a millennium ago. Today it's a thriving commercial hub with a large student population. The beautifully preserved Gothic town of **Toruń** is a short bus or train ride away. It boasts enchanting red-brick architecture and traditional gingerbread biscuits. End in **Gdańsk**, once part of the Hanseatic League and shaped by a rich maritime and trading past.

▽ 2

14-day itinerary
Eastern Borderlands

Poland's eastern border region feels especially remote. This swathe of natural splendour will appeal to wanderers who prefer the solitude of nature to the city bustle. Start with a couple of days in **Kraków**, one of Europe's most perfectly preserved medieval cities. Then head to **Sanok**, with its *skansen* and icon museum, and continue deeper into the **Bieszczady National Park**, which has about a dozen well-marked hiking trails. Turn north and take the back roads to the Renaissance town of **Zamość**, via sleepy Przemyśl. Continue on to **Chełm** to see the underground chalk tunnels and then to the big-city comforts of **Lublin**, once nicknamed the 'Jewish Oxford'. Head north through rural backwaters to **Białowieża National Park** to see its primeval forest and bison herd. Continue north via the provincial city of Białystok to the hamlet of **Tykocin**, with its unforgettable synagogue. On from here is a wealth of parks, and beyond, the **Great Masurian Lakes**, offering fine boating possibilities.

SIGHTS & ACTIVITIES

 SEE

 DO

ITINERARY

 1

▽ 2

Palace of Parliament, Bucharest

Depending on your point of view, Bucharest's gargantuan Palace of Parliament is either a mind-blowing testament to the folly of dictatorship or an awe-inspiring showcase of Romanian craftsmanship. Most visitors conclude that it's a bit of both. The sheer scale of the former 'House of the People' – on a par with the Taj Mahal or the Pentagon – must be seen to be believed.

Transfăgărășan Road

The high-altitude Transfăgărășan, which twists and turns through southern Transylvania, was celebrated by *Top Gear* as the world's most exciting length of road. Boldly charging up and down one of Romania's highest mountains provides an unforgettable, white-knuckle experience behind the wheel. The climax is glacial Lake Bâlea, which hovers like a mirror among the rocks, often totally enshrouded by clouds.

Bran Castle

Perched on a rocky bluff in Transylvania, in a mass of turrets and castellations, Bran Castle overlooks a desolate mountain pass swirling with mist and dense forest. Legend has it Vlad the Impaler (the inspiration for Count Dracula) was briefly imprisoned here; follow his footsteps through a maze of courtyards and hidden passages.

10-day itinerary
Transylvania's Castles and Cities

Transylvania is Romania's best-known and arguably most scenic region, replete with rocky mountaintops, haunting castles and characterful, historic cities. Fly into **Bucharest**, taking in the huge Palace of Parliament, pleasant parks and excellent restaurants. Then hire a car or hop on a train northward into the mountains, stopping in **Sinaia** to overnight and check out the dreamy Peleş Castle. From here, take a cable car into the unspoiled **Bucegi Mountains** for a hike. Drive or take a bus north to explore **Braşov**, a lively hub with a cobbled medieval centre. Use Braşov as a base for a day trip to the infamous **Bran Castle**. If you have a car, spend a night in the fortified Saxon village of **Viscri** before continuing to **Sighişoara** (Count Dracula's birthplace), whose dramatic citadel epitomises medieval splendour. Head southwest for a night or two in the cultural hub of **Sibiu**. If you're driving (and it's summer), veer south along the breathtaking **Transfăgărășan Road**. Or head north to bohemian **Cluj-Napoca,** crammed with cafes and clubs.

Retezat Mountains

Bejewelled by 80 glacial lakes and with peaks towering above 2000m, the Retezat Mountains are a spectacular stretch of the southern Carpathians. Marmots scamper in its grasslands, wolves and bears slink through forests, and golden eagles nest on its cliffs. Trekking is the best way to absorb this vibrant landscape, with well-marked trails and a network of cabins en route to keep you sheltered.

Danube Delta Biosphere Reserve

The mighty Danube River passes through a vast expanse of remote wetland in eastern Romania before finally emptying into the Black Sea. The Danube Delta Biosphere Reserve has developed into a sanctuary for fish and fowl of all stripe and colour. Birders will thrill to the prospect of glimpsing species such as the roller, white-tailed eagle, great white egret and even a bee-eater or two.

Mara Valley

The Mara Valley is the heart of rural Maramureş, with villages famed for their spectacular churches and carved gateways. Rising from forested hillsides like dark needles, the exquisite wooden churches are austere and beautiful, with roofs of shingle and Gothic-style steeples. Inside, rich interiors are painted with biblical frescoes.

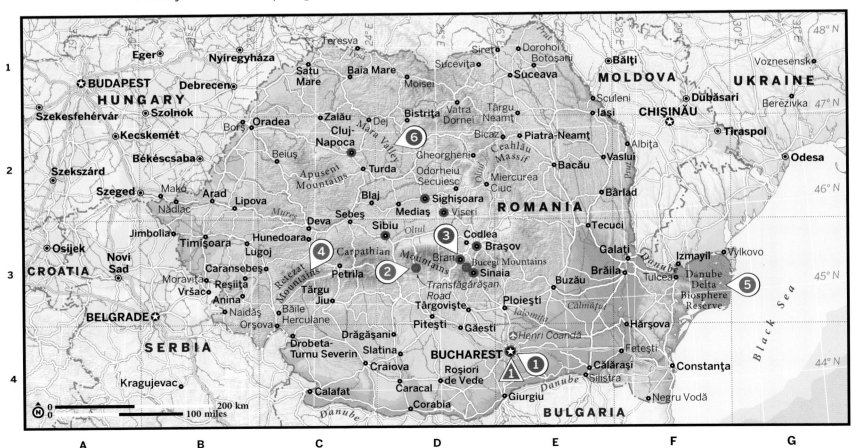

Rila Monastery

Rising from a valley in the misty Rila Mountains, the colourful and revered Rila Monastery remains Bulgaria's most storied spiritual treasure. The original monastery grew from a 10th-century hermit's hut; today's breathtaking mix of elegant archways, soaring domes and apocalyptic frescoes dates mostly from the 19th century.

Melnik

Bulgaria's winemaking tradition dates back to Thracian times. Tiny Melnik is an especially fruitful location to sip wine, and a very scenic one, too. The village is lined with 19th-century National Revival–style houses, wonderfully restored and rising against a backdrop of steep sandstone pyramids, which look all the better through a haze of cabernet sauvignon.

Plovdiv

With a charming old town and revitalised artistic quarter, Plovdiv has never looked finer. Ancient buildings nestle in the centre of this seven-hilled town, colourful 19th-century mansions are now house-museums and galleries, and the 2nd-century Roman stadium still hosts concerts. The build-up for its reign as European Capital of Culture 2019 has left the city gleaming, and its events calendar is bursting.

7-day itinerary
Sofia to the Sea

Spend a week exploring the best of Bulgaria, from the capital to the coast. Begin in pleasingly laid-back **Sofia**, where you shouldn't miss the shimmering Aleksander Nevski Cathedral and a couple of worthwhile museums, and take a day trip to the resplendent **Rila Monastery**. Next, board a bus or train east to **Plovdiv**, Sofia's sassier cousin and Europe's oldest continuously inhabited city. Devote two days to immersing yourself in the romantic old town, Roman ruins and bohemian nightlife. From here you can reach **Burgas**, your first stop on the Black Sea coast, by bus or train. Nature lovers can bird-watch, kayak or take an impromptu plunge into a salt pool at the four lakes just outside the city. Then hop on a bus for the short trip south to the ancient Greek harbour of **Sozopol**, and explore its quaint cobbled lanes and attractive sandy beaches. If you're here in summer, catch the ferry up north to **Nesebâr**, famed for its numerous medieval churches, and spend the last day sightseeing.

Sozopol

Ancient Sozopol, huddled on a narrow peninsula, is one of the Black Sea Coast's highlights. With two attractive town beaches and a genial atmosphere, it has long been a popular seaside resort; another beautiful stretch of sand, Smokinya, is about 4km further south. Once you've had enough of beach fun, you can enjoy the picturesque town's lively cultural scene.

Pirin Mountains

With more than 100 peaks surpassing 2000m in height, Pirin Mountains are greatly admired by hikers. A network of marked hiking trails links huts and shelters throughout Pirin National Park, which boasts glinting lakes, fragrant pine forests and granite peaks. Bears and wolves make their home here, but you're more likely to spot the park's abundant birdlife, including wall-creepers, falcons and woodpeckers.

Veliko Târnovo

Bulgaria's 19th-century National Revival splendour is particularly evident in its former royal capital, Veliko Târnovo. Set above the ribboning Yantra River and topped with the marvellous medieval Tsarevets Fortress, this town of Soviet monuments, cobblestoned lanes and centuries-old handicraft shops allows for a memorable trip into Bulgaria's long and storied past.

SIGHTS &
ACTIVITIES

 SEE

○ DO

ITINERARY

▽ 1

▽ 2

 Lviv
Moody and elegant, with quaint cobbles and rattling trams, Lviv is the beating cultural heart of Ukraine. The Unesco-listed city exudes the same authentic Central European charm as pre-tourism Prague or Kraków once did. Incense billows through magnificent medieval churches, while cosy coffeehouses lure you in with old-world ambience and the scent of arabica.

 Odesa
By day Odesa's museums and beaches provide ample distraction, but the city really comes alive at night. With its dance temples and chill-out zones just steps from the Black Sea, Arkadia Beach is the place to strut and pose until the wee summer hours. Odesa also has a stomping alternative scene, with hip venues serving up cool ales to the sound of indie bands and local DJs.

 Kamyanets-Podilsky
Ringed by the dramatic gorge of the Smotrych River, Kamyanets-Podilsky is supremely easy on the eye. Stroll through the cobbled quarters of the 11th-century Old Town, past beautifully renovated churches, crumbling palaces and forgotten pieces of the once beefy defences, to the town's impossibly picturesque fortress.

 The Carpathians
The Carpathians' wooded slopes, stony trails, flower-filled pastures and snaking valleys add up to prime hiking territory. Ukraine's highest peak, Mt Hoverla (2061m), is a fairly easy trek from nearby villages. This is rural Ukraine at

Danube Delta Biosphere Reserve: Around 300 species of bird make the Danube Delta home.

its best, where tiered wooden churches dot hillsides, and horse-drawn carts clip-clop along potholed roads.

 Kyiv
Ukraine's ancient capital boasts timeless treasures. The postcard-friendly Andriyivsky uzviz is the bohemian haunt of artists. Magnificent Kyevo-Pecherska Lavra has a cluster of gold-domed churches, baroque edifices and orchards. And Kyiv's recent hip, creative boom is embodied in urban art, vintage cafes and street markets.

 Danube Delta Biosphere Reserve
Danube Delta in Ukraine's southwest is Europe's largest wetland. Boat tours through the delta's unique waterways offer some astoundingly beautiful scenery, colourful birdlife, memorable days out on the water and serene evenings in Vylkovo, fancifully nicknamed the 'Ukrainian Venice' thanks to its network of canals.

 Brest Fortress
Don't come to Belarus' Brest Fortress expecting a medieval turreted affair – this is a moving Soviet memorial to a devastating WWII battle. Little remains of the original fortress on the Bug and

Mukhavets rivers, just a whisper from the Belarus–Poland border. The epic Courage monument – a huge stone soldier's head projecting from a massive rock – is flanked by a skyscraping obelisk and an eternal flame.

 Belavezhskaya Pushcha
Belavezhskaya Pushcha National Park is the oldest wildlife refuge in Europe and the pride of Belarus. Surviving primeval forest is all that remains of a canopy that eight centuries ago covered northern Europe. At least 55 mammal species call this park home, but the area is most celebrated for its 300 or so European bison, the continent's largest land mammal. You have a chance to spot them in the wild on a park tour.

 Orheiul Vechi
Occupying a remote, rocky ridge over the Răut River, Orheiul Vechi (Old Orhei) is Moldova's most important historical site and a place of stark natural beauty. The complex is famous for its fantastic Cave Monastery, burrowed by 13th-century monks inside a cliff above the river, but it also includes baths, fortifications, and ruins ranging from the earliest days of the Dacian tribes over 2000 years ago.

 Cricova
Dedicated oenophiles know Eastern Europe's great wine secret: Moldova offers some of the region's top grapes. Of its many vineyards, Cricova is the best known. Some 60km of the 120km-long underground limestone tunnels (dating from the 15th century) are lined wall-to-wall with bottles. Tour them by car, or linger in their chandeliered chambers for a tasting session.

7-day itinerary
Ukraine and Belarus

The quintessential Ukrainian experience starts in **Kyiv**, the cradle of Slavic civilisation. Two days are just enough to absorb the mix of gold-domed Orthodox churches and raucous nightlife. Take a guided day trip to **Chornobyl** to see the sarcophagus now in place over the nuclear reactor and the ghost town of Pripyat. Back in Kyiv, catch an overnight sleeper train to **Lviv**, a former Habsburg city with gorgeous architecture and seductive cafe culture. Hop on a bus across the border to Belarus and spend two days getting to know **Minsk**, whose Stalinist skyline belies a lively, friendly city. End the journey with a day trip to **Belavezhskaya Pushcha** for a chance to spot European bison in the wild.

10-day itinerary
Ukraine and Moldova

Start with a few days in Ukraine's capital, **Kyiv**, to admire its ancient Unesco-listed sights and experience the creative wave that has swept across the city in recent years. Then jump aboard an express train heading east to the spa town of **Myrhorod**, where you can take the waters. Rent a car or charter a taxi for a day and tour the nearby **Gogol** Circuit, visiting sites associated with the famous author. Your next stop is **Odesa**, the cosmopolitan Black Sea port city of neoclassical buildings and crowded sandy beaches. After a couple of days here, make your way to Moldova by either bus or train. Use the capital **Chişinău** as your base for a few days. Spend the first day strolling the pleasant parks of this fast-changing city and checking out its museums and excellent restaurants. The following day head out to the stunning, serene cave monastery at **Orheiul Vechi**. End the trip in style by taking a tour on your final day to one of the big-name vineyards around Chişinău – Cricova or Mileştii Mici – for some excellent wine tasting.

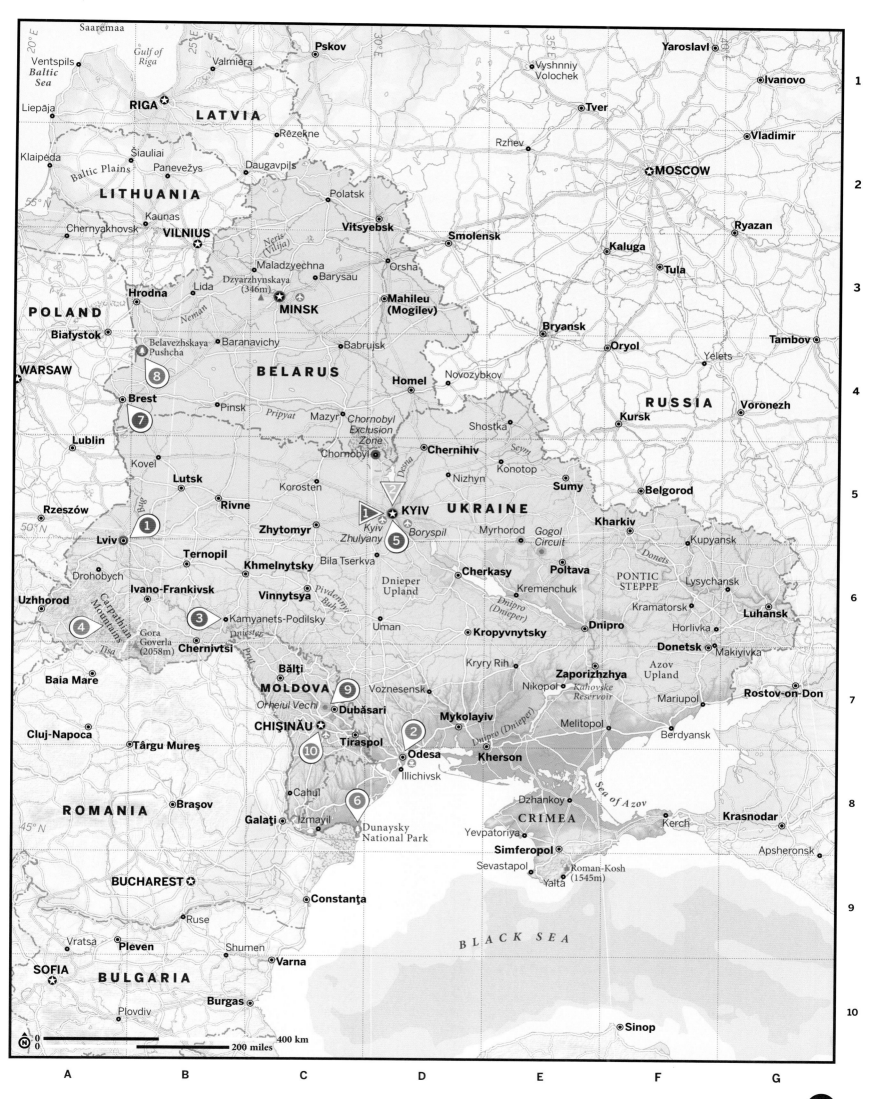

The Nordic Countries

Endless day, perpetual night. Rocking festivals, majestic aurora borealis. With effortlessly chic cities and remote forests, the Nordic nations attract style-gurus and wilderness-hikers alike. Some of Europe's wildest wild places are here. From soaring fjord walls in Norway to the volcanic brutality of Iceland, from the awe-inspiring colours of autumn's forest palette to charming Baltic islands, from sparkling summer lakes to Arctic snowscapes, there's a feast of natural beauty. It's an indication of how the Nordic nations value their natural environments that the region has well over a hundred national parks; as well as being crucial drivers of conservation, many also offer the best chance to appreciate deep Nordic nature.

CLIMATE CHART

COPENHAGEN

RAINFALL INCH/MM

TEMP °C/°F

STOCKHOLM

RAINFALL INCH/MM

TEMP °C/°F

NATURE
Epic wilderness – forests, lakes, volcanoes and fjords – make nature here a viscerally pleasurable experience. The national parks are a major draw, whether that means reindeer-spotting in Hardangervidda or hiking the trails of Abisko, but there are countless ways to explore nature in the raw: kayaking through Geirangerfjord, camping on an icecap near Kangerlussuaq or crossing Svalbard by dog-sled.

MODERN ARCHITECTURE
Stolid Nordic stereotypes dissolve in the region's taste for experimental architecture. This region is a boon for architecture buffs: for starters, check out the futuristic lines of Copenhagen's opera house, Tromsø's luminous Arctic Cathedral, Oslo's playful Barcode skyscrapers, the ethereal Louisiana Art Museum or Reykjavík's rocket-shaped Hallgrímskirkja. Architecture doesn't get more fun.

Right: Looking out over Ålesund, a port town in Norway's far north.

HISTORY
From the ancient vessels at Oslo's Viking Ship Museum to the more domestic Viking culture investigated at Ribe in Denmark, the Nordic nations have a wealth of fascinating Viking sites. Later, Scandinavia's royal families left behind many castles and palaces, such as Drottningholm (dubbed Sweden's Versailles); Renaissance Frederiksborg; and Kronborg, the model for Hamlet's Elsinore.

DESIGN
If good design makes the practical beautiful, then Scandinavia rules the roost. The Dansk Design Centre in Copenhagen and Stockholm's Swedish Design Museum provide a good primer on Scandi design. Then there's the town of Billund, Denmark, the spiritual home of Lego, and Älmhult, Sweden, where Scandinavia's most successful design export, Ikea, began its world-dominating journey.

Transport hubs

Despite its fjords and snow, Scandinavia is easily accessed from the rest of Europe and beyond. There are direct flights from numerous destinations into Sweden, Norway, Denmark and Finland, with a smaller (but growing) choice to Iceland. Denmark, Sweden and Norway can be reached by train from Western Europe, while Baltic and North Sea ferries are another good option for getting to these Nordic countries. Flights to Greenland are much more limited.

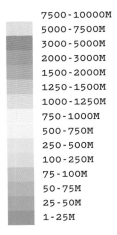

Stockholm
Stockholm Arlanda Airport is served by major European and North American cities. Direct access to Sweden by land is possible from Norway, Finland and Denmark (via the Öresund toll bridge). Stockholm is the hub for national trains run by Sveriges Järnväg, with services to most of Scandinavia. Ferry routes from Stockholm travel to Turku and Helsinki (Finland), Tallinn (Estonia) and Riga (Latvia).

Oslo
Norway is well linked to other European countries by air. Oslo's Gardermoen International Airport receives the largest number of flights, and there are regular bus and rail services to Oslo from Sweden and Finland, with less regular services to/from Russia. All trains run to/from Oslo S in the city centre. Ferries connect Oslo with Denmark daily, and in the summer, Kiel (Germany).

Copenhagen (see pp400-1 for city map)
Copenhagen has worldwide air links, and train, road and bridge connections exist to Germany and Sweden. Ferries run to/from several countries including Norway, Sweden, Germany, Poland (via Sweden), Iceland and the Faroe Islands.

Helsinki
Helsinki-Vantaa Airport, 19km north of the city, is Finland's main air terminus. International ferries sail to Stockholm, Tallinn, St Petersburg and German destinations. The train is the fastest, cheapest way to reach Finland's other major towns; Helsinki's central station is the nation's main hub. There are also daily trains to the Russian cities of Vyborg, St Petersburg and Moscow (you'll need a Russian visa).

Right: Snowmobile on frozen waters of Mohnbukta, near Longyearbyen (left) and (right) the Oslo–Bergen train route, Norway.

Reykjavík
Keflavík, Iceland's main airport, is 48km southwest of Reykjavík. It's served by a growing number of airlines (including budget carriers) from Europe and North America. The smaller Reykjavík Domestic Airport handles domestic flights and those to Greenland and the Faroes. By sea, Smyril Line operates a weekly car ferry from Hirtshals (Denmark) through Tórshavn (Faroe Islands) to Seyðisfjörður in East Iceland.

Svalbard
Unless you're travelling on an organised boat cruise from the Norwegian mainland, the only way to reach Svalbard is by air, with either SAS or Norwegian, from Tromsø or Oslo. Plans for international flights that go directly to Longyearbyen are under discussion.

Lofoten Islands
Lofoten's main airports are in Svolvær and Leknes. There are now direct flights at least twice a week from Oslo to Svolvær and Leknes, as well as more frequent flights from the small town of Bodø, on mainland Norway's west coast. The cheapest way to get to Lofoten is usually via ferry, either from Bodø or Skutvik, or via the Hurtigruten. Once you've arrived on Lofoten, it's easy to get around by bus or car; the main islands are linked by a network of bridges, tunnels and the E10 highway.

Nuuk
There are no roads to speak of in Greenland, so travel here is exclusively done by air or sea. The national carrier, Air Greenland, flies to the main international airport in Kangerlussuaq from Copenhagen. There are also direct flights to Nuuk from Reykjavík with Air Iceland Connect.

THE TRAVEL ATLAS

© Jonathan Gregson / Lonely Planet

© Justin Foulkes / Lonely Planet

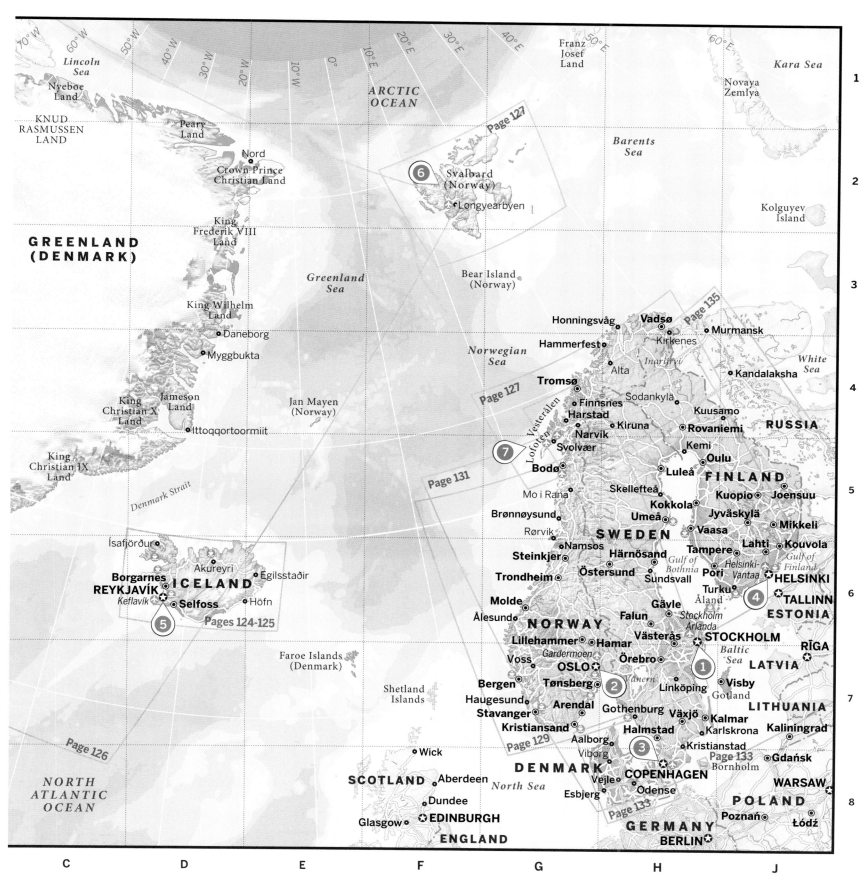

1

ARCTIC OCEAN

70°W · 60°W · 50°W · 40°W · 30°W · 20°W · 10°W · 0° · 10°E · 20°E · 30°E · 40°E · 50°E · 60°E

Lincoln Sea

Nyeboe Land

Kara Sea

Novaya Zemlya

Franz Josef Land

KNUD RASMUSSEN LAND

Peary Land

Nord

Crown Prince Christian Land

Page 127

Barents Sea

2

Svalbard (Norway) **6**

Longyearbyen

Kolguyev Island

GREENLAND (DENMARK)

King Frederik VIII Land

Greenland Sea

Bear Island (Norway)

3

Daneborg

King Wilhelm Land

Myggbukta

Page 135

Honningsvåg · Vadsø · Murmansk

Norwegian Sea

Hammerfest · Kirkenes

White Sea

Alta · *Inarijärvi* · Kandalaksha

King Christian X Land

Jameson Land

Jan Mayen (Norway)

Tromsø · Finnsnes · Sodankylä · Kuusamo

Page 127

Ittoqqortoormiit

Harstad · Kiruna · **Rovaniemi** · **RUSSIA**

4

Narvik · Kemi

King Christian IX Land

Svolvær · **Oulu**

7 Bodø · **Luleå** · **FINLAND**

Denmark Strait

Page 131

Mo i Rana · Skellefteå · **Kuopio** · **Joensuu**

5

Brønnøysund · **Kokkola** · **Jyväskylä**

Rørvik · Umeå · **Vaasa** · **Mikkeli**

Ísafjörður

SWEDEN

Namsos · **Härnösand** · **Tampere** · **Lahti** · **Kouvola**

Akureyri · Egilsstaðir

Steinkjer · *Gulf of Bothnia* · **Pori** · Helsinki-Vantaa

Borgarnes · **ICELAND** · **Trondheim** · Östersund · Sundsvall · **Turku** · **HELSINKI**

REYKJAVÍK · Höfn · *Åland* · **4** · **TALLINN**

Keflavík · **Selfoss** · **Molde** · **Gävle** · Stockholm · **ESTONIA**

6

5 · Pages 124-125 · Ålesund · Falun · Arlanda

NORWAY · Västerås · **STOCKHOLM** · **RĪGA**

Faroe Islands (Denmark) · **Lillehammer** · Hamar · *Baltic Sea*

Voss · *Gardermoen* · **Örebro** · **1** · **LATVIA**

Shetland Islands · **OSLO** · **2** · *Vänern* · Linköping · **Visby**

Bergen · Tønsberg · *Gotland* · **LITHUANIA**

7

Haugesund · Gothenburg · **Växjö** · **Kalmar** · **Kaliningrad**

Stavanger · Arendal · Karlskrona

Kristiansand · **Halmstad** · Kristianstad

Page 126 · Aalborg · **3** · Page 133 · **Gdańsk**

Viborg · Bornholm

DENMARK · **COPENHAGEN** · **WARSAW**

Wick · Page 129 · Vejle · **POLAND**

NORTH ATLANTIC OCEAN

SCOTLAND · Aberdeen · *North Sea* · Esbjerg · Odense · **BERLIN** · Poznań · Łódź

8

Dundee · Page 133

Glasgow · **EDINBURGH** · **GERMANY**

ENGLAND

C · D · E · F · G · H · J

SIGHTS &
ACTIVITIES

 SEE

 DO

ITINERARY

 1

 2

Reykjavík Old Harbour
The world's most northerly capital combines colourful buildings, quirky, creative people, eye-popping design, wild nightlife and a capricious soul. In the Old Harbour, educate yourself at the Saga Museum, or learn about the area's maritime history.

Blue Lagoon
Set in a magnificent black-lava field, the milky-teal water of this famous geothermal lagoon is rich in blue-green algae, mineral salts and silica mud. The 38°C water comes from the futuristic Svartsengi geothermal plant.

Þingvellir National Park
Iceland's most important historical site, set in a rift valley at the meeting of the North American and Eurasian tectonic plates. It was here that Vikings established the world's first parliament, the Alþingi, in AD 930.

Geysir
The original hot-water spout after which all other geysers are named, the Great Geysir has been active for perhaps 800 years but can require patience. Luckily, you rarely have to wait more than five to 10 minutes for the nearby Strokkur geyser to shoot a great 15m to 30m plume into the air.

Gullfoss
Iceland's most famous and popular waterfall, Gullfoss (Golden Falls) is a spectacular double cascade. It drops 32m, kicking up walls of spray before thundering down a narrow ravine.

Snæfellsnes Peninsula
West Iceland is a microcosm of what the country has to offer. Snæfellsnes is a favourite for birding, whale watching, lava-field hikes and horse riding. Inland lies Langjökull glacier and its unusual ice cave.

LAVA Centre, Hvolsvöllur
A full-blown multimedia experience exploring volcanic and seismic life. Highlights include an earthquake simulator and a fog of smoke resembling volcanic ash.

Dettifoss
With the greatest volume of any waterfall in Europe, Dettifoss is nature at its most awesome: 400 cu metres of water thunders over its edge every second in summer, creating a plume of spray that can be seen 1km away.

Vatnajökull
Iceland's largest ice-cap dominates the island's south. Take a guided hike on icy glacial tongues, or travel up into the whiteness on snowmobile or super-Jeep tours. Nearby Jökulsárlón is a glacial lagoon where wind and water sculpt icebergs into fantastical shapes.

Húsavík
This is Iceland's whale-watching capital, where up to 11 species come to feed in summer. Visit between June and August for a near-100% chance of a sighting.

Drangey
Guarding the mouth of Skagafjörður, the 180m-high, sheer cliffsides of this rocky islet serve as nesting sites for around a million seabirds – puffins, guillemots, gannets, kittiwakes, fulmar and shearwaters. Three-hour boat trips depart from a small harbour beside Grettislaug, at Reykir.

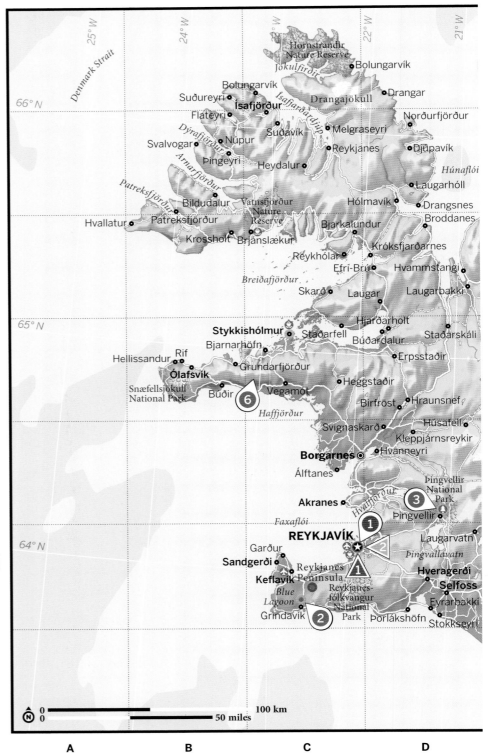

4-day itinerary
Reykjavík & Beyond

From **Reykjavík**, drive out to the **Reykjanes Peninsula** to experience the steaming earth near Valahnúkur or Krýsuvík. Then travel down the coast for seafood in Eyrarbakki or Stokkseyri. Base yourself near **Hella**, and explore the lush waterfall-rimmed **Fljótshlíð valley** on horseback, or try to spot the Northern Lights in the colder months.

At **Fimmvörðuháls**, hike from Skógar up through the ridge between two ice caps (and the site of the Eyjafjallajökull eruption in 2010) then into **Þórsmörk**, a forested valley dotted with wild Arctic flowers. Take a super-Jeep tour or amphibious tour if you're tight on time. Then it's back to Reykjavík for a couple of late nights experiencing the city's pubs and bars.

10-day itinerary
The Ring Road

From **Reykjavík**, head clockwise to **Borgarnes** for its fascinating Settlement Centre. Then zip up to **Stykkishólmur**, an adorable village overlooking an islet-studded bay. Continue to the **Tröllaskagi Peninsula** before gliding through **Akureyri**, Iceland's unofficial northern capital. Head to the geological treasure chest of the **Mývatn**

region next, with a stop at mighty **Dettifoss** waterfall. Push eastwards, detouring to **Borgarfjörður Eystri** for summer puffins galore. Take a break in pretty **Seyðisfjörður**, and stop in **Höfn** for langoustines, then jump on a snowmobile to discover the ice cap at **Vatnajökull**. Don't miss the glacial lagoon at **Jökulsárlón**. Warm

up your hiking legs in **Skaftafell**, then head south across lava fields to **Vík** and the nearby basalt-columned beach. Continue westwards, passing the enormous waterfall at **Skógafoss**, then veer away to check out the Golden Circle: **Gullfoss**, **Geysir** and **Þingvellir National Park**. Roll back into Reykjavík for a geothermal dip in the **Blue Lagoon**.

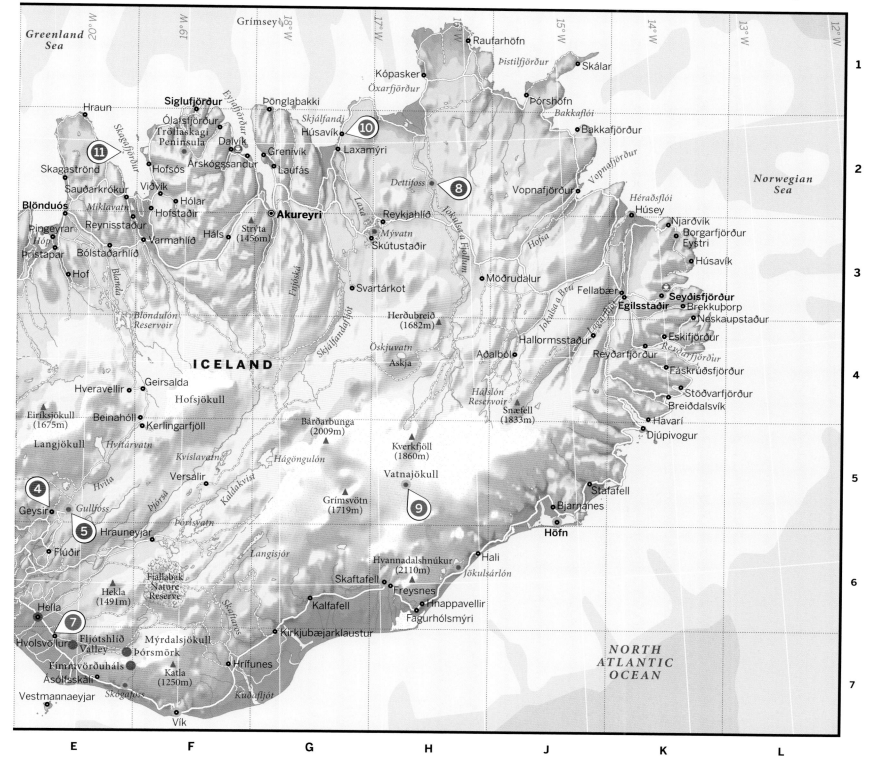

Nuuk

Nuuk is Greenland's capital and its most cosmopolitan town. It commands a grand fjord system and is backed by a splendid panorama of mountains. At the Greenland National Museum, one room contains the spooky sight of a trio of mummified 15th-century women and a six-month-old child.

Qaqortoq

Qaqortoq Museum is housed in a tar-blackened 1804 building, once the Julianehåb colony manager's house. The beautifully restored top floor was once used for guests. Explorer Knud Rasmussen stayed in the red room, and the blue room hosted famous American aviator Charles Lindbergh. The Tele-Museum traces Greenland's role in the development of transatlantic communications.

Nanortalik

Astonishingly grand spires of granite soar straight out of Greenland's southernmost fjords, a magnet for climbers. Most visits start from Nanortalik, whose old town has been preserved as a picturesque living museum. The main fjords are Tasermiut or shorter, more spectacular Torssuqatoq, which culminates with the photogenic village of Aappilattoq.

Kangerlussuaq

Standing at a lonely crossroads in Kangerlussuaq, you'll feel right at the edge of the world. This isolated settlement borders the icecap covering 80% of Greenland, where the relatively stable and green part of the country transforms abruptly into a desert of permanent ice. It's one of the best places to spot wildlife, thanks to an introduced population of around 10,000 musk oxen, along with caribou, snow hares and Arctic foxes.

Ilulissat Kangerlua

The Greenland of travel fantasies. Ilulissat's rainbow-coloured houses are scattered at the mouth of a 40km ice fjord. A phenomenal 35 billion tonnes of icebergs pass through here each year, calved from the Jakobshavn Glacier. It's easily explored on a short hike from town – though the bus-sized 'bergs are best seen on a boat tour.

Qasigiannguit

The Qasigiannguit Museum has an excellent collection of finds dating from the Saqqaq culture to the present-day Inuits. Exhibits give a detailed picture of life in Greenland's earliest Stone Age settlements, and include a large number of tools and the northernmost discovery of the now extinct great auk.

7-day itinerary Greenland

Begin your ends-of-the-earth adventure in **Nuuk**, Greenland's capital. Get yourself acquainted with local culture with a visit to Katuaq Cultural Centre, the National Museum and the Nuuk Art Museum, followed by a self-guided tour of the city's surprising street art. Then, hop on a flight to **Kangerlussuaq**, where the green landscape gives way to icy expanse and wildlife-spotting opportunities abound. Here, you can take a pleasure flight over the ice-cap or – if you're after a more visceral experience of life on the ice – make an expedition on foot and spend the night in a traditional ice cave (surprisingly, it's warmer than it sounds). Conclude the trip in **Ilulissat**, with a visit to the town's intriguing museum, followed by a couple of unforgettable days kayaking down the spectacular ice-fjord of Ilulissat Kangerlua, and whale-watching around **Disko Bay**.

SIGHTS & ACTIVITIES

◉ SEE
◉ DO

ITINERARY

▽ 1
▽ 2

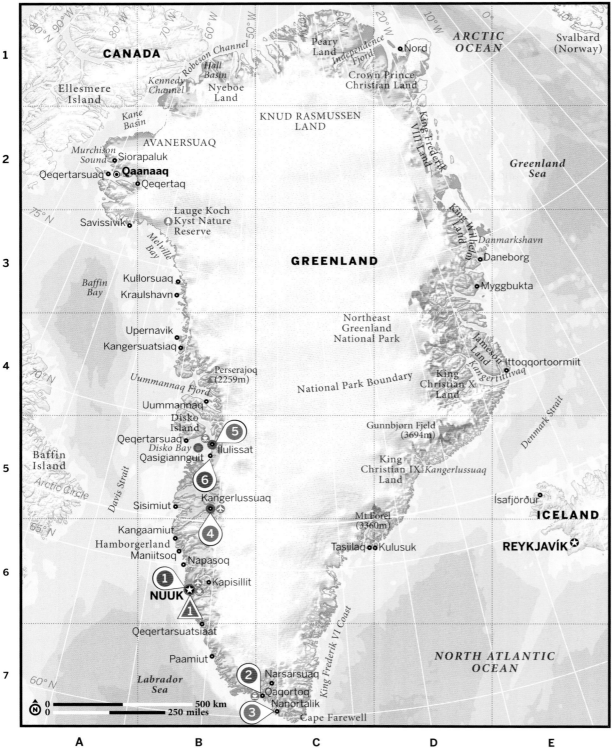

Andenes

Andenes is northern Norway's main base for whale-watching. In summer catch sight of majestic sperm whales. In winter, when herrings migrate to the seas here, orcas, humpback and fin whales are all possible.

Tromsø

At 400km north of the Arctic Circle and 69°N, the small town of Tromsø bills itself as Norway's gateway to the Arctic. Surrounded by chilly fjords and craggy peaks, Tromsø was a launch pad for several Arctic expeditions, but these days it's one of Norway's top spots to see the northern lights.

Lofoten Islands

You'll never forget your first approach to Lofoten. The islands spread their craggy physique against the sky like some spiky sea dragon. On each are sheltered bays, sheep pastures and picturesque villages. Some of the best views are from the E10 road, which runs along the islands from tip to toe.

Alta

The cliffs around the town of Alta are incised with late–Stone Age carvings, dating from 6000 to 2000 years ago, including hunting scenes, fertility symbols, bear, moose, reindeer and boats. The town is also home to the daringly designed Northern Lights Cathedral, a swirling pyramid structure clad in rippling titanium sheets.

Karasjok

Sami Norway's indisputable capital is home to the Sami Parliament and library, NRK Sami Radio, a wonderful Sami museum and a Sami theme park. This is also one of the best places in Norway to go dog-sledding in winter.

Knivskjelodden

Here's a secret: Nordkapp isn't actually continental Europe's northernmost

14-day itinerary
The Far North

The mystique of the extreme north has drawn explorers for centuries – a frozen wilderness that inspires awe. Tromsø's Polar Museum captures the spirit of Arctic exploration, and its Arctic Cathedral wonderfully evokes the landscapes of the north, while the surrounding peaks host a wealth of summer and winter activities. You could also visit lovely Senja from here. Next head east for the rock carvings of Alta, then even further to Nordkapp: almost as far north as you can go in Norway without setting out to sea. Then head inland to Karasjok and Kautokeino, to the heartland of the Sami people, the indigenous inhabitants of this icy region, and expert reindeer wranglers. Finally, complete your Arctic adventure with an unforgettable trip to Svalbard: you'll need to backtrack to Tromsø and fly north to the archipelago. This is one of Europe's last great wildernesses. Allow at least five days to soak up the Arctic sights, whether from the seat of a snowmobile or, better still, the back of a dog sled.

point. That award belongs to Knivskjelodden, an 18km-return-trip hike away – less dramatic, inaccessible by vehicle, and to be treasured all the more for it.

Svalbard

Svalbard is the Arctic North as you always dreamed it would be. This archipelago of snow-drowned peaks, vast icefields and forbidding icebergs is an elemental place where the endless Arctic night and perpetual sunlight of summer carry a deep kind of magic. The main settlement, Longyearbyen, offers a taste of what lies beyond: boat trips, glacier hikes, snowmobile expeditions and husky-sledding. Look out for polar bears.

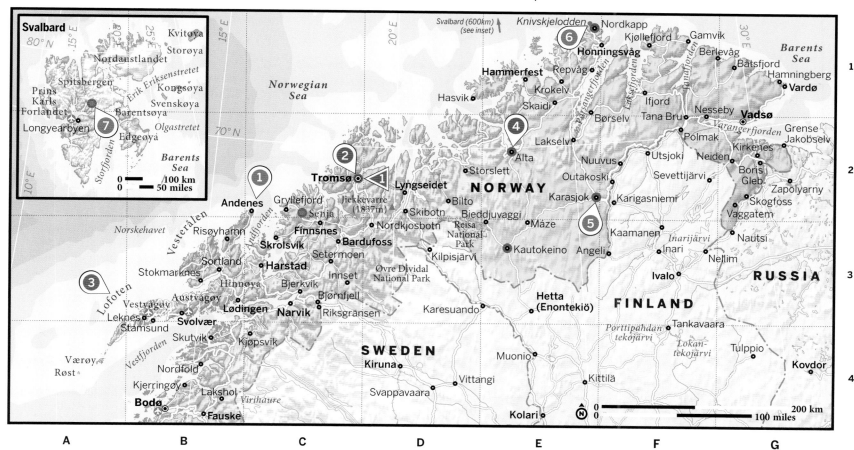

SIGHTS & ACTIVITIES

 SEE

 DO

ITINERARY

 1

 2

Bergen: Unesco-listed Bryggen is Bergen's oldest quarter.

1 Oslo
One of the world's greenest cities, Norway's capital is bursting at the seams with top-notch museums, art galleries and a glacier-white opera house that could make even Sydney jealous. The redeveloped waterfront district also boasts daring architecture, a grade-A modern-art gallery, exciting new restaurants and even a beach.

2 Geirangerfjord
The world-famous, Unesco-listed, oft-photographed fjord that every visitor to Norway has to tick off their bucket list. It is one of the world's great natural features, a majestic combination of huge cliffs, tumbling waterfalls and deep blue water that's guaranteed to make a lasting imprint on your memory.

3 Hurtigruten Ferry
There are few better ways to drink in the scenery of the fjords than aboard the iconic Hurtigruten ferry, which has been plying Norway's waters since 1894. Every day of every year, there is at least one Hurtigruten boat shuttling along the 5200km of coastline between Bergen and Kirkenes.

4 Preikestolen
As clifftop lookouts go, Preikestolen (Pulpit Rock) has few peers. Perched atop an almost perfectly sheer cliff that hangs more than 600m above the waters of gorgeous Lysefjord, it's one of Norway's signature – and most essential – sights. The hike to reach it takes two hours and involves a full-day trip from Stavanger.

5 Bergen
Surrounded by seven hills and seven fjords, Bergen is a beguiling city. During the early Middle Ages, it was a member of the Hanseatic League and Norway's capital – a heritage preserved in the wooden houses of Bryggen, a Unesco World Heritage Site.

6 Jotunheimen National Park
With a name meaning 'Home of the Giants', Jotunheimen is Norway's most spectacular wilderness destination. Hundreds of hiking routes lead past lakes, waterfalls, glaciers and all of Norway's highest peaks over 2300m.

7 Dovrefjell-Sunndalsfjella
Bleak and dramatic, Dovrefjell-Sunndalsfjella National Park is a high, cold plateau of undulating mountains buried under a thick blanket of snow for much of the year. The park provides an Arctic-like habitat for reindeer, wolverines and musk oxen.

8 Urnes Stave Church
Covered in elaborate carvings of intertwining vines and battling beasts, this 12th-century church looks like a forgotten set from *Lord of the Rings*. It's Norway's oldest place of worship.

9 Flåmsbana Railway
This 20km-long engineering wonder hauls itself up 864m of altitude gain through 20 tunnels. At a gradient of 1:18, it's the world's steepest railway without cable or rack wheels. It takes 45 minutes to climb to Myrdal on the bleak Hardangervidda plateau.

10 Trollstigen
This twisting, sky-topping corkscrew road is the most famous stretch of tarmac in Norway. Completed in 1936, the Troll's Ladder spirals up the mountainside through 11 hairpin bends and a 1:12 gradient.

11 Folgefonna
Established in 2005, this 545-sq-km national park encompasses mainland Norway's third-largest icefield. The ice is 400m thick in places, and can be explored on guided glacier walks.

12 Lysefjord
All along the 42km-long 'Light Fjord', the granite rock glows with an ethereal light and even on dull days it's offset by almost-luminous mist. It makes one of the country's most compelling locations for a fjord cruise.

13 Voss
Sitting on a sparkling lake not far from the fjords, this small town has earned a world-renowned reputation as Norway's adventure capital, offering white-water rafting, kayaking, bungee jumping and just about anything you can do from a parasail.

7-day itinerary
Oslo to Bergen

After a couple of days exploring the fine galleries and museums of **Oslo**, take the spectacular Oslo–Bergen railway over the beautifully desolate **Hardangervidda plateau**, home to Norway's largest herd of wild reindeer and numerous hiking trails. At **Myrdal**, catch the Flåmsbana Railway down to **Flåm**, from where fjord cruises head up the incomparable Nærøyfjord. Travel via **Gudvangen**, sleep overnight in **Stalheim**, and then press on to adrenalin-fuelled **Voss**. Trains then continue to **Bergen**, arguably Norway's prettiest city, where you'll need at least two days to explore its historic wooden waterfront, wild mountains and plentiful bars and restaurants.

14-day itinerary
Into the Fjords

Nothing defines Norway so much as its fjords. You'll need a vehicle for this trip, but it's worth taking as much time as you can spare. Begin in oil-rich **Stavanger** and take a day trip to **Lysefjord**, including the hike up to the signature lookout of **Preikestolen** (Pulpit Rock). A long day's drive north brings you to **Hardangerfjord**, and a string of villages you'll never want to leave, among them Utne and Eidfjord. Continue on to **Flåm**, or better still, the far lovelier **Aurland**, for a couple of fjordside nights surrounded by extraordinary views. Don't miss the vista from the gravity-defying Stegastein viewpoint. Wind your way north to pretty **Solvorn** on Lustrafjord, and climb up and over the stunning Sognefjellet Rd through **Jotunheimen National Park**, famous for its hiking possibilities. Overnight in **Lom**, known for its stave church. Then it's on to **Geirangerfjord**, up another epic mountain road, the Trollstigen, down to **Åndalsnes** and then out along the coast to end in quiet **Ålesund** with its art-deco buildings.

20° E

1

Værøy
Røst

Vestfjorden

Virihaure

Bodø ◉
Saltstraumen
Saltnes
Fauske
Sulitjelma
Kvikkjokk

Storvik
Røkland

Ørnes ◉
Holand
Storjord

Jøkmokk

Arctic Circle

Jektvik

Kilboghamn

Stokkvågen
Mo i
Rana
Arjeplog

Nesna

Hornavan

*Norwegian
Sea*

Sandnessjøen

Tjøtta
Mosjøen
Tärnaby
Sorsele
Arvidsjaur

Forvik

Røssvatnet

Anndalsvågen
Hattfjelldal
Umnäs
Storuman
Storuman

Brønnøysund ◉
Tosbotn

65° N

Vennesund
Holm

Limingen

Gutvik

Namsskogan

Kittelfjäll
Vilhelmina
Lycksele

Rørvik

Tunnsjøen

Grøndalselv

Høylandet

Gäddede

Åsele

Namsos ◉
Grong

Fossli
Snåsa
*Gressåmoen
National Park*
Strömsund

Hoffstad
Følling
Snåsavatnet

Årnes
*Beitstad
fjorden*
Steinkjer ◉

Frøya
Brekstad
Rødsjo
Sund
Verdalsøra

Kvenvær
Hitra
Trondheimsfjorden
Levanger

Stjørdal
Åre
Långsele

Dyrnesvågen
Smøla
Orkanger
Trondheim ◉
Heimdal
Storlien
Östersund ◉
Bollstabruk

Kristiansund
Averøya
Kvernes

Storsjön

N O R W A Y
Støren
Nesjøen

Bud
Sylte
Eidsvåg

Härnösand ◉

Molde ◉
Sunndalsøra
Osen
Berkåk
Glåmos
Aursund
Funäsdalen
Ånge
Sundsvall

Andalsnes
Oppdal
Røros
Synnervika

Ålesund
Spjelkavik
Gjøra
*Snøhetta
(2286m)*
*Dovrefjell-
Sundalsfjella*
Tynset
Femunden
Sveg

Ørsta
Volda
②
Stranda
Hjerkinn
⑦
Alvdal

Måløy
Nordfjordeid
Geirangerfjord
Dombås
*Rondane
National Park*
Isterfossen
Idre
Ljusdal

Bremanger
Stryn
Grotli
Lom
Atna

Nordfjorden
Byrkjelo
Skjåk
Otta
*Glittertind
(2452m)*
Vinstra
Koppang
Särna
Bollnäs

Florø
Norddal
*Galdhøpiggen
(2469m)*
Ringebu

Naustdal
Skei
*Jotunheimen
National Park*
Trysil

Sande
Solvorn
⑧
⑥
Beitostølen

Høyanger
⑨
Lillehammer
Rena
Mora
Siljan
Rättvik

Lavik
Sognefjorden
Gudvangen
Aurland
Fagernes
Gävle

Sævrasvåg
Stalheim
Flåm
Dokka
Hamar
Elverum

⑤
Dale
Voss
Myrdal
Gol
Gjøvik
Stange
Malung
Falun

Norheimsund
⑬
Mjøsa
Vansbro
Borlänge
Gysinge
Sandviken

③
⑪
Odda
Geilo
Brandbu
Eidsvoll
Ludvika

Bergen ◉
Hardangerfjord
Rødberg
Jevnaker
Roa
Gardermoen
Kongsvinger
Hagfors

Leirvik
Utåker
*Hardangervidda
National Park*
Hønefoss
Kopparberg
Sala
Uppsala

60° N
*Hardangervidda
Plateau*
Vikersund
Tyrifjorden
Jessheim
Lillestrøm

Sauda
Rjukan
⭐
Oslo ◉
Västerås

Haugesund
Røldal
Hovden
Åmot
Drammen
①
Mysen
Arvika
Mälaren

Nedstrand
Sand
Seljord
Kongsberg
Moss
Ørje

④
Blåsjøen
Bykle
Brunkeberg
Bø
Horten
Sarpsborg
Karlstad
Örebro
Hjälmaren
Eskilstuna

Stavanger ◉
Sinnes
Preikestolen
Fyresdal
Skien
Tønsberg
Fredrikstad

Sandnes
Lysefjord
Porsgrunn
Sandefjord
Åmal

Nærbø
⑫
Byglandsfjord
Kragerø
Mariestad
Nyköping

Tonstad
Evje
Risør
Vänern
Motala

Egersund
Skagerrak
Uddevalla
Lidköping
Linköping

Flekkefjord
Kvinesdal
Vennesla
Tvedestrand
Vänersborg
Skövde
Mjölby

Lyngdal
Arendal
Grimstad
*Baltic
Sea*

Vigeland
Kristiansand
Falköping

Alingsås

*North
Sea*

S W E D E N

*Gulf of
Bothnia*

A B C D E F G

2

3

4

5

6

7

8

9

10

SIGHTS & ACTIVITIES

 SEE

 DO

ITINERARY

▽ 1

▽ 2

1. Stockholm

The nation's capital calls itself 'beauty on water', and it doesn't disappoint. Stockholm's glittering waterways reflect slanted light onto spice-hued buildings, and the crooked cobbled streets of Gamla Stan are perfect to wander. Don't miss the stunning Vasamuseet (Viking Ship Museum).

2. Visby

It's hard to overstate the beauty of the Hanseatic port of Visby, in itself justification for making the ferry trip to Gotland. Inside its medieval walls are cobbled streets, fairy-tale cottages draped in flowers and haunting ruins with superb Baltic views.

3. Gothenburg

The humble sibling to confident Stockholm, Gothenburg is a city of slick museums, industrial landscapes, pleasant parks, can-do designers and cutting-edge food. For a unique way of arriving, jump on a boat along the 190km of the Göta Canal.

4. Inlandsbanan

This historic, summer-only railway line passes small mining towns, deep green forests, herds of reindeer and the occasional elk. Built during the 1930s and rendered obsolete by 1992, the line has more than enough charm to make up for its lack of speed.

5. Abisko National Park

Easy access to spectacular scenery makes Abisko (Ábeskovvu in Sami) one of Lappland's highlights. The 75-sq-km national park spreads out from the southern shore of lake Torneträsk. In winter, people come to see the northern lights; in summer to hike and to bask in the midnight sun.

6. Foteviken Viking Reserve

If you mourn the passing of big hairy men in longboats, find solace at this 'living' reconstruction of a late–Viking Age village. Around 22 authentic reconstructions of houses with reed or turf roofs have been built, and the residents live as the Vikings did, eschewing modern conveniences and adhering to old traditions.

7. Kiruna

This small town is home to two phenomena that have made the north of Sweden famous: the aurora borealis, which dance across the night sky from October to March, and the Icehotel, a manmade ice palace that is now a year-round phenomenon.

8. Stockholm Archipelago

Exactly how many there are is debatable (the consensus is 24,000), but whatever the number, Stockholm's islands are a wonderland of deep forests, fields of wildflowers and picturesque red wooden cottages.

9. Glasriket

In the 'Kingdom of Crystal' skill and brawn combine to produce stunning (and often practical) works of art. Watch glass-blowers spin bubbles of molten crystal into fantastic creatures, bowls, vases and sculptures.

10. Gammelstad

Sweden's largest church town, medieval Gamelstad feels almost lost in time. The village's stone Nederluleå Church is glorious, and 420 wooden houses where rural pioneers stayed overnight on their weekend pilgrimages still remain.

Abisko National Park: Nordic skier in Abisko, Sweden.

▽ 1

7-day itinerary Around Stockholm

Start in sophisticated **Stockholm**, whose many attractions include the Kungliga Slottet (Royal Palace), Gamla Stan (Old Town), Skansen (an open-air museum that presents Sweden in miniature), and the nightlife of Södermalm. Next, check out the cathedral and palace at **Uppsala** and delve into early Swedish history via the burial mounds and museum at **Gamla Uppsala**. On the way back, explore **Sigtuna**, with its old-world buildings, cafes and church ruins. Move on to the sculpture museum at Millesgården, or visit Greta Garbo's memorial at Unesco-recognised cemetery Skogskyrkogården. Finally, enjoy some island-hopping in the **Stockholm Archipelago**.

▽ 2

10-day itinerary Stockholm to Gothenburg

From **Stockholm**, make your way west via the lively college town of **Örebro**, known for its moat-protected castle and beautiful city park. Continue southwest, between lakes Vänern and Vättern into **Gothenburg**. Sweden's second city is easily worth a few days of exploration: grown-ups will love the nostalgia-fest that is Mölndals Museum, while the kids will go crazy for Liseberg amusement park, one of Sweden's most visited tourist attractions. Don't miss the cool, retrofitted space at Röda Sten, a gritty power-station-turned-gallery. From Gothenburg, explore the craggy coastline and rickety fishing villages of the **Bohuslän Coast**. Check out the Bronze Age rock carvings on the **Tanum plain**, then try making sense of them with the help of the **Vitlycke Museum**. Cross the bridge from Stenungsund (on the Swedish mainland) to **Tjörn**, island favourite of landscape artists and sailors alike. Wander the tiny villages admiring sailboats, have a summer barbecue on the deck of a youth hostel or make a meal of it at renowned Åstols Rökeri, famous for its smoked fish.

© Johner Images / Getty Images

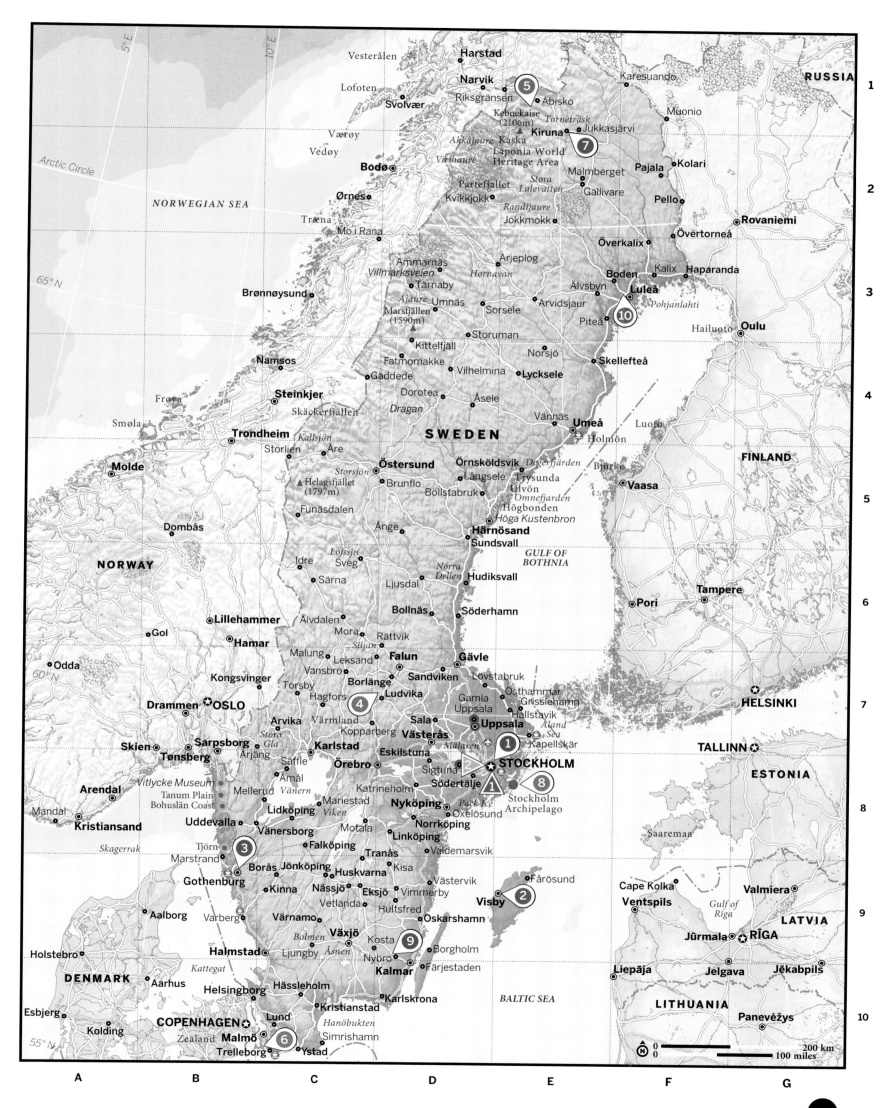

SIGHTS & ACTIVITIES

 SEE

 DO

ITINERARY

 1

 2

1. Aarhus

Denmark's second city is compact, photogenic and terrific to explore. It has a booming dining scene, thriving nightlife, transformed waterfront, woodland trails, beaches, and one of the country's top art museums, crowned by *Your Rainbow Panorama* – a 360-degree rooftop walkway offering technicolor city views.

2. Legoland, Billund

Billund is the home town of the Lego Company. Here, the Legoland theme park and the new Lego House (designed to resemble gigantic Lego bricks) celebrate the iconic toy in ways that will delight your child (and your inner child). Among the attractions are Lego models of Danish cities, miniature versions of the Statue of Liberty, the Acropolis and an Egyptian temple, and even classic scenes from *Star Wars*.

3. Bornholm

Sunny Bornholm lies in the Baltic Sea, closer to Germany and Sweden than Denmark. This magical island is beloved for its sandy beaches, cycle paths, *rundekirke* (round churches), artistic communities and harbourside villages – as well as Denmark's finest Michelin-starred restaurant, Kadeau.

4. Kronborg Slot

This fabulous 16th-century castle in Helsingør was the model for Elsinore Castle in Shakespeare's *Hamlet*. Once a grandiose toll house for ships travelling between Denmark and Sweden, it now hosts summer performances of Shakespeare's plays.

Ribe: The crooked cobblestone streets of Ribe date from the late 9th century

5. Ærø

Just 30km long and 9km wide, Ærø is Denmark's loveliest isle. Steeped in time, it's an idyllic slice of island life: visit for seafaring heritage, bike lanes, cobblestoned villages, sandy beaches and photogenic bathing huts.

6. Ribe

Compact, postcard-perfect Ribe is Denmark's oldest town and encapsulates the country's golden past with an imposing 12th-century cathedral, cobbled streets, half-timbered houses and water meadows.

7. Roskilde

Five Viking ships, discovered at the bottom of Roskilde Fjord, are displayed at the Vikingeskibsmuseet, but this coastal town is best-known for its annual rock festival.

8. Grenen

Denmark's most northerly point is a neat finger of sand a few metres wide. Here, the waters of the Kattegat (an arm of the Baltic Sea) and Skagerrak (part of the North Sea) clash, and you can put one foot in each sea – but not too far. Bathing is forbidden because of the ferocious tidal currents.

9. Skagen

Northern Jutland wows with its magnificent light and shifting sands. The area's main draw is the island of Skagen, a civilised haven of restaurants and art museums, and a wild place where nature calls the shots.

10. Silkeborg

Lakeside Silkeborg offers forests and waterways that are perfect for cycling, rambling and canoeing. The Museum Silkeborg contains one of Denmark's best-known 'bog bodies', the 2400-year-old Tollund Man.

11. Frederiksborg Slot

This gigantic, Dutch Renaissance–styled fortress-palace rises proudly out of photogenic moat-lake Slotsø. The oldest part dates from the reign of Frederik II, after whom it is named, and the 80-plus rooms are overloaded with furniture, tapestries and portraiture.

12. Vikingemuseet Ladby

Near Kerteminde, this site preserves the only known Viking-era ship grave in Denmark, hidden within a grassy burial mound. The ship's remnants are preserved in an airtight display with the bones of sacrificed cattle.

13. Møns Klint

One of Denmark's most iconic landscapes, Møn's tree-topped white cliffs rise sharply up to 128m above an azure sea with milky-blue shallows coloured by chalky run-off. Descend the cliffs by a series of wooden stairways.

10-day itinerary
Classic Denmark

Start in **Copenhagen** and soak up the cultural riches of the capital. From there, it's a short hop west to **Roskilde** to investigate Denmark's royal and Viking heritage. Further west, **Odense** offers up fairy-tale charm thanks to its famous son, Hans Christian Andersen. Continue to history-soaked **Ribe**, Denmark's oldest town, oozing chocolate-box appeal. From here, enjoy Lego-themed treats in **Billund**, then cruising and canoeing in **Silkeborg**. Head north to **Skagen** for art, beaches and seafood, and stop by cosmopolitan **Aarhus**, the country's second city. From here, take a ferry to northern Zealand to return to Copenhagen.

14-day itinerary
Denmark in Depth

Spend a couple of days seeing the classic **Copenhagen** sights, then venture further afield for the superb modern art collection at Louisiana Museum in **Humlebæk**, as well as the magnificent castles of Kronborg Slot at **Helsingør** and Frederiksborg at **Hillerød**. Head south to potter around pretty, historic **Køge**, then catch a ferry out to **Bornholm** for a couple of leisurely days exploring the island's bike trails, sandy beaches and gastronomic treats. Back on Zealand, head south to **Møn**, with some of the country's most exalted scenery – the white-chalk cliffs rise sharply over a sapphire sea. Head back across southern Zealand to reach the island of **Funen** and its many sights. **Odense** is a must-see for its connections with home-town-hero Hans Christian Andersen, but it's also worth visiting the Viking ship grave at **Ladby** and the Renaissance splendour at **Egeskov Slot**. A day or two on the old seafaring island of **Ærø** will recharge your batteries before retracing your steps to the capital.

SIGHTS & ACTIVITIES

 SEE

 DO

ITINERARY

 1

2

Finnish Lakeland:
The sun setting over sparkling lakeland waters in Finland.

1 Lapland
Lapland casts a powerful spell. The midnight sun, the Sami people, the aurora borealis and roaming reindeer are all components – as is Santa Claus himself, who 'officially' resides here. Spanning 30% of Finland's land area, Lapland is home to just 3% of its population. It's ripe for exploring on foot, skis or sled. At Nuorgam, the northernmost point, you're above Iceland and most of Canada and Alaska.

2 Urho Kekkonen National Park
Saariselkä Wilderness, incorporating the 2538-sq-km Urho Kekkonen National Park, extends to the Russian border. It's a fabulous slice of Finland, home to bears, wolverines and golden eagles, plus thousands of free-grazing reindeer. It's also a brilliant trekking area, with a network of wilderness huts amid forest, marshland and low fells.

3 Helsinki
Entwined with the Baltic's bays, inlets and islands, Helsinki is awash with architecture and groundbreaking design. The city's alternative chic is best explored by browsing the vast variety of design shops around its centre, while stunning examples of Finland's art nouveau movement, National Romanticism, grace the city.

4 Rauma Old Town
The largest wooden old town in the Nordic countries, Vanha Rauma deserves its Unesco World Heritage status. Its 600 houses might be museum pieces, but they also form a living centre of cafes, shops, museums and artisans' workshops. Rauman *giäl*, the local dialect that mixes up a host of languages, is still spoken here.

5 Inari
This tiny village is Finland's most significant Sami centre. The village sits on Lapland's largest lake, Inarijärvi, with more than 3000 islands in its 1084-sq-km area. One of Finland's most absorbing museums, Siida, offers a fine overview of Sami culture.

6 Karelia
The brown bear is Finland's national animal. Around 1000 live in the northeast across the Finnish–Russian border. Operators run bear hides close to the frontier; sit out a silent night's vigil watching as bruins snuffle out elk carcasses and chunks of salmon.

7 Turku
Finland's second city actually served as the capital until 1812. The majestic Turun Linna (Turku Castle) and Tuomiokirkko (cathedral), both dating from the 13th century, are a testament to the city's storied past. Contemporary Turku is even more enticing, a hotbed of experimental art, music festivals, boutiques and innovative restaurants.

8 Finnish Lakeland
Most of Finland could be dubbed lakeland, but around here it seems there's more aqua than terra firma. It's almost obligatory to get waterborne, whether it be while practising your paddling skills in a canoe or by hopping aboard a historic steamboat.

9 Åland Archipelago
Paradisical Åland is best explored by bicycle. Bridges and ferries link many of its 6000 islands. En route you can pick wild strawberries, wander castle ruins, sunbathe on a slab of red granite, visit a medieval church or quench your thirst at a cider orchard.

10 Hanko
On a long, sandy peninsula, Hanko (Swedish: Hangö) grew up as a well-to-do Russian spa town in the late 19th century. It's crammed with opulent seaside villas, while 30km of beaches provide swimming and sunbathing.

11 Kuopio
Kuopio is the quintessential summery lakeside town. At Jätkänkämppä, you can experience a communal *savusauna* (smoke sauna). Bring a swimsuit – locals and brave tourists plunge into the lake even when it's covered with ice.

12 Kemi
An important deep-water harbour and heavy-industry town, Kemi is also home to two of Finland's blockbuster winter attractions – a snow castle and an ice-breaker cruise.

1 7-day itinerary Essential Finland
Kick off in capital **Helsinki**, prowling the Design District, exploring the archipelago and day tripping to see historic **Porvoo's** wooden buildings. Next head to **Lappeenranta** on Finland's largest lake. Then – go by boat in summer – it's on to **Savonlinna**, where the castle hosts an opera festival. From there, head to the heart of the Lakeland, **Kuopio**, another segment doable by lake boat. The high latitudes can be felt once you get to **Oulu** – depending on the season, the sun barely sets or barely rises. In winter stop in **Kemi** to see the snow castle and take an icebreaker cruise. Finally head to **Rovaniemi**, a great base for enjoying Lapland's outdoor possibilities.

2 10-day itinerary Lapland
Rovaniemi is Lapland's capital (and a good spot to hire a car). Santa Claus is the big crowd-puller here, while the excellent Arktikum museum is the perfect introduction to these northern latitudes. Cut eastward to **Ruka**, a lively winter ski resort and activity base. Here, there's walking to be done in **Oulanka National Park**, including the Karhunkierros, one of Finland's best treks. You can also canoe some great river routes and go bear-watching from nearby **Kuusamo**. From Ruka, head north until you reach **Urho Kekkonen National Park**, one of Europe's great wildernesses. Take some time out for a hike across the fells, or try gold-panning at **Tankavaara's** Kultamuseo. Still further on, **Inari** is one of Lapland's most intriguing towns and the capital of Finland's Sami people. Last stop is the wild **Lemmenjoki National Park**, where treks, river trips, gold-panning and yet more Sami culture await – and if time allows, there's trekking to be done in **Kevo Strict Nature Reserve**.

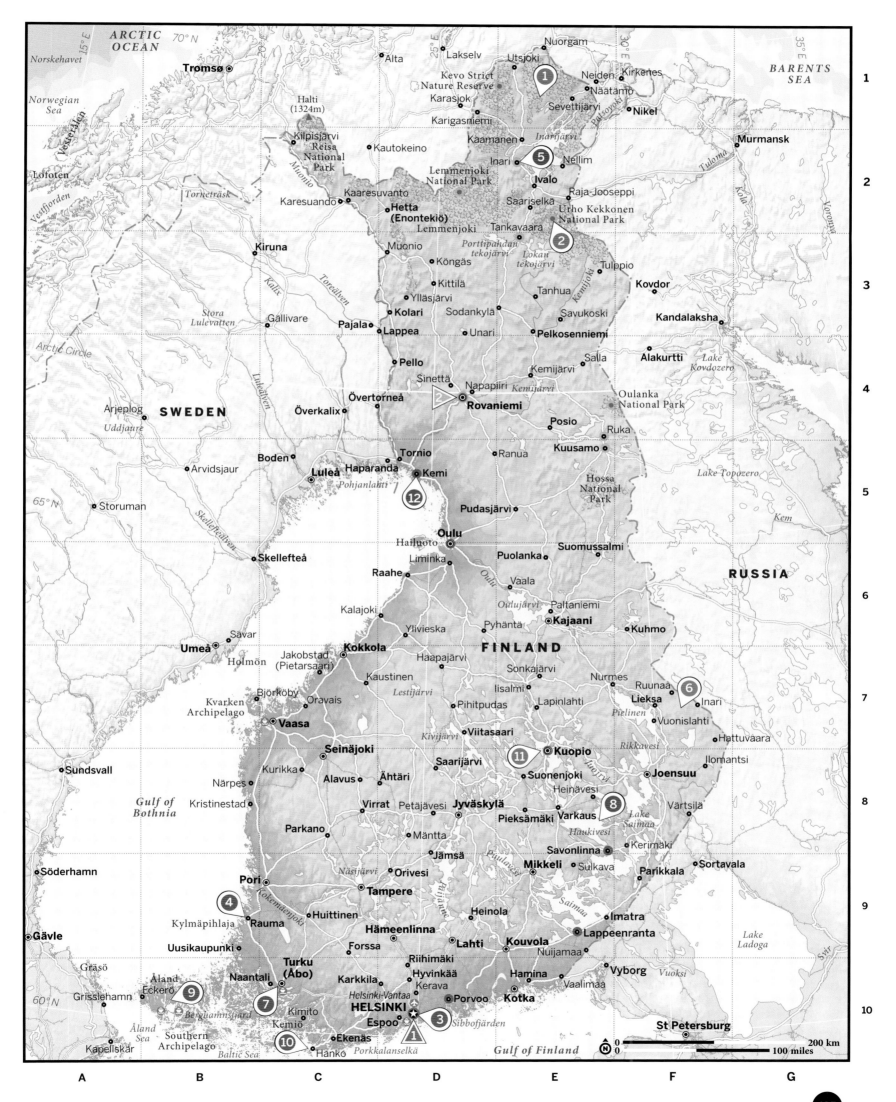

ARCTIC OCEAN

Norskehavet

Norwegian Sea

BARENTS SEA

Tromsø

Vesterålen

Lofoten

Vestfjorden

Halti (1324m)

Alta

Lakselv

Nuorgam

Utsjoki

①

Neiden

Kirkenes

Näätämö

Nikel

Kevo Strict
Nature Reserve

Karasjok

Sevettijärvi

Kilpisjärvi
Reisa
National
Park

Karigasniemi

Kaamanen

Inarijärvi

Murmansk

Kautokeino

Inari

⑤

Nellim

Muonio

Lemmenjoki
National Park

Ivalo

Raja-Jooseppi

Kiruna

Torneträsk

Karesuando

Kaaresuvanto

Hetta
(Enontekiö)

Saariselkä

Tankavaara

Urho Kekkonen
National Park

②

Muonio

Lemmenjoki

*Porttipahdan
tekojärvi*

*Lokan
tekojärvi*

Tulppio

Kovdor

Köngäs

Kittilä

Tanhua

Savukoski

Kandalaksha

Kalix

Toreälven

Ylläsjärvi

Sodankylä

Gällivare

Kolari

Pajala

Lappea

Unari

Pelkosenniemi

Salla

Alakurtti

*Lake
Kovdozero*

*Stora
Lulevatten*

Pello

Sinettä

Napapiiri

Kemijärvi

Kemijärvi

Övertorneå

②

Rovaniemi

Oulanka
National Park

Kemijoki

Arjeplog

Uddjaure

SWEDEN

Överkalix

Luleälven

Posio

Ruka

Kuusamo

Boden

Tornio

Kemi

Ranua

Arvidsjaur

Haparanda

⑫

Pohjanlahti

Hossa
National
Park

Lake Topozero

Luleå

Pudasjärvi

Storuman

Kem

Oulu

Hailuoto

Liminka

Puolanka

Suomussalmi

RUSSIA

Skellefteå

Raahe

Vaala

Oulu

Oulujärvi

Paltaniemi

Kalajoki

Pyhäntä

Kajaani

Kuhmo

Ylivieska

Sävar

Umeå

Holmön

Jakobstad
(Pietarsaari)

Kokkola

Haapajärvi

Sonkajärvi

Iisalmi

Nurmes

Ruunaa

⑥

Lieksa

Inari

Björköby

Kvarken
Archipelago

Oravais

Kaustinen

Lestijärvi

Pihtipudas

Lapinlahti

Pielinen

Vuonislahti

Vaasa

Seinäjoki

Viitasaari

Kivijärvi

⑪

Kuopio

Rikkavesi

Hattuvaara

Ilomantsi

Kurikka

Alavus

Saarijärvi

Suonenjoki

Joensuu

Orajärvi

Sundsvall

Närpes

Ähtäri

Heinävesi

Vårtsilä

Kristinestad

*Gulf of
Bothnia*

Virrat

Petäjävesi

Jyväskylä

Varkaus

⑧

*Lake
Saimaa*

Parkano

Mäntta

Pieksämäki

Haukivesi

Söderhamn

Näsijärvi

Jämsä

Savonlinna

Kerimäki

Orivesi

Mikkeli

Sulkava

Parikkala

Sortavala

Pori

④

Huittinen

Tampere

Päijänne

Saimaa

Imatra

Kylmäpihlaja

Rauma

Heinola

Lappeenranta

*Lake
Ladoga*

Gävle

Uusikaupunki

Hämeenlinna

Lahti

Kouvola

Nuijamaa

Gräsö

Forssa

Riihimäki

Hamina

Vyborg

Vaalimaa

Åland

Eckerö

⑨

Naantali

Turku
(Åbo)

Karkkila

Hyvinkää

Vuoksi

Grisslehamn

Berghamnsfjord

⑦

Kimito

Helsinki-Vantaa

Kerava

Porvoo

Kotka

St Petersburg

*Åland
Sea*

Kemiö

⑩

Espoo

③

Sibbofjärden

Kapellskär

Southern
Archipelago

⑩

Ekenäs

HELSINKI

①

Hanko

Porkkalanselkä

Gulf of Finland

Baltic Sea

0 — 200 km
0 — 100 miles

Russia, the Caucasus & Central Asia

With its blue-domed cities, kinetic bazaars and remote yurtstays, Central Asia encapsulates the romance of the Silk Road. Mass tourism has yet to make its mark here, lending an authentic sense of discovery to each trip. As a forgotten region emerging as a geopolitical pivot point, this is one of Asia's most absorbing corners. And then there's Russia: 'a riddle, wrapped in a mystery, inside an enigma', as Churchill famously put it. It's what makes the world's largest country so fascinating – along with its historic cities, idyllic countryside, epic train rides and vodka-fuelled nightlife.

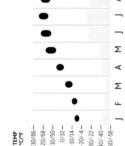

HISTORY
Central Asia's page-turning history awaits at every turn. Moscow and St Petersburg are rich repositories of eye-boggling national treasures, while ancient cities such as Khiva, Bukhara, Turkestan and Bishkek retain a flavour of the Silk Road. Whether it's marvelling at the Narikala Fortress in Tbilisi or Armenia's Unesco-listed Geghard Monastery, this is a place where you'll be haunted by history.

ADVENTURE TRAVEL
For centuries, Central Asia has been synonymous with the middle of nowhere – and beyond the big cities, you'll still likely have the place to yourself. You could be trekking through the Charyn Canyon in Kazakhstan, horse-trekking to Lake Son-Köl in Kyrgyzstan, summiting Mt Kazbek in Georgia or hiking Russia's Great Baikal Trail – wherever you head, wilderness awaits.

Right: The fairytale theme park of the Kremlin in Izmaylovo, Moscow contains shops, restaurants, museums and monuments.

LANDSCAPES
As you'd expect for a country that spans 13% of the globe, Russia's terrain is wildly varied, from tundra to taiga (forest) and steppe (grasslands). Nature-lovers should head for Kamchatka, the Altai and the wild Caucasus mountains, while the adventurous could take a road trip along the epic Pamir Highway, climb peaks in Kazbegi or Karakol, or sleep out in the *jailoo* (summer pasture) around Lake Son-Köl.

CULTURES
Central Asia is a cauldron of cultures, from gold-toothed Turkmen in shaggy, dreadlocked hats to high-cheekboned Kyrgyz herders. Hospitality is a defining feature of this region, whether it's staying in a traditional yurt in Kochkor, shopping for bargains at Kumtepa Bazaar, soaking with the locals in an Almaty bathhouse or meeting eagle-hunters on the shores of Lake Issyk-Köl.

Transport hubs

Getting to Central Asia is half the fun, whether it's part of an overland Silk Road trip or crossing formerly forbidden border posts. Air connections are improving steadily throughout the region, with Tashkent (Uzbekistan) and Almaty (Kazakhstan) the main hubs. The long-distance rail connections are mostly with Russia, from Moscow or the Trans-Siberian Railway to Tashkent, Almaty, Bishkek (Krygyzstan) and Astana (Kazakhstan).

TRANSPORT

A5, B3, B6,
C5, C6

A5, A6, B5,
H6

Moscow
Most travellers arrive in Moscow by air, flying into one of the city's four international airports: Domodedovo, Sheremetyevo, Vnukovo or Zhukovsky. The vast majority of international flights go in and out of Domodedovo and Sheremetyevo, both of which are about an hour from the city centre by car or train. Rail riders will arrive at one of Moscow's central train stations: Kievsky or Belorussky vokzal if you're coming from Europe.

St Petersburg
Travel between Moscow and St Petersburg has never been easier: several airlines fly into Pulkovo International Airport in St Petersburg (75 to 90 minutes). There are about a dozen overnight trains travelling between Moscow and St Petersburg. Most depart between 10pm and 1am, arriving the following morning between 6am and 8am.

Tashkent
The main international gateways to Tashkent are Moscow and Istanbul, through there are direct flights from most European and Asian cities. If arriving by air, your grand entrance into Uzbekistan will most likely take place at Tashkent International Airport. A few flights from Russia arrive in regional hubs such as Samarkand, Bukhara and Urgench. Land crossings are theoretically possible, but probably not worth the hassle and bureaucracy.

Astana
As long as you have your visa organised, you should have no problems getting into Kazakhstan. Astana and Almaty Airport have direct connections to Europe, Asia and Central Asia, as well as the Gulf States. Kazakhstan's 6846km border with Russia has 18 'multilateral' road crossings (open to all nationalities), and around 15 rail crossings. If you can face the red tape, crossings from China, Kyrgyzstan, Turkmenistan and Ukbekistan are also possible.

Bishkek
Most visitors will arrive in Kyrgyzstan by air at Bishkek's Manas International Airport, though many still travel overland as part of larger Silk Road itineraries. There are two land routes to Kashgar in Xinjiang, China, three possible routes into Kazakhstan, and one into Uzbekistan and Tajikistan.

Ashgabat
The only international airport in Turkmenistan is Ashgabat. Visitors with visas can enter Turkmenistan from all bordering countries; Uzbekistan and Iran are the most frequently used. There are no international train or bus services to or from Turkmenistan. You can also enter Turkmenistan at Turkmenbashi by ferry from Baku in Azerbaijan, although the ferry is notoriously unreliable.

Yerevan
Zvartnots Airport, 11km from Yerevan, is Armenia's major airport, with regular flights to and from Russia, Ukraine, Iran, France, Austria, Turkey, the UAE and Georgia. Trains to Georgia and Gyumri depart from the atmospheric Soviet-era Yerevan train station.

Tbilisi
Tbilisi International Airport is 15km east of the city centre. Direct flights head to/from more than 40 international destinations spread from Paris to Ürümqi (China). Many flights arrive and depart at unholy early-morning hours. Tbilisi's main train station is Georgia's railway hub.

Right: Old Tbilisi at sunset (left) and (right) Russia's Izmaylovo Kremlin.

THE TRAVEL ATLAS

© MiGol / Shutterstock

© Yuliya Baturina / 500px

ALASKA
(USA)

Pages 140-141

ARCTIC OCEAN

Svalbard
(Norway)

Nome

Arctic Circle

1

Barents Sea

International Date Line

Murmansk

2

White Sea

Novaya Zemlya

Kara Sea

Laptev Sea

Bering Sea

Arkhangelsk

3

Mt Narodnaya
(1895m)

Mt Klyuchevskaya
(4750m)

Magadan

Perm

Kamchatka Peninsula

4

Ural Mountains

Yekaterinburg

RUSSIA

SIBERIA

Chernyshevskiy

Yakutsk

Sea of
Okhotsk

Petropavlovsk-
Kamchatsky

Ufa

Tyumen

Chelyabinsk

Lensk

Kostanay

Omsk

Tomsk

Krasnoyarsk

Sakhalin

Kuril
Islands

5

KAZAKHSTAN
ASTANA ✪ ④

Novosibirsk

Kemerovo

Pavlodar

Severobaikalsk

Vanino

Yuzhno-
Sakhalinsk

Zhezkazgan

Ekibastuz

Barnaul

Novokuznetsk

Karagandy

Semey

Lake
Baikal

Irkutsk

Chita

Khabarovsk

Kyzylorda

Ust-Kamenogorsk

Belukha
(4506m)

Ulan Ude

Sapporo

6

Lake
Balkhash

Ölgii

Erdenet

Darkhan

TASHKENT ✪ ⑤

Almaty

BISHKEK ③

Ürümqi

MONGOLIA

ULAANBAATAR ✪

Hā'ěrbīn

Vladivostok

Fergana

Chángchūn

Sendai

KYRGYZSTAN

Chŏngjin

DUSHANBE ✪
TAJIKISTAN

Shěnyáng

Sea of Japan

Niigata

7

Peshawar

N KOREA

Hamhūng

JAPAN ✪ TŌKYŌ

ISLAMABAD ✪

BĚIJĪNG ✪

PYŎNGYANG ✪

Nagoya

Gujranwala

Tiānjīn

Dàlián

SEOUL ✪

Ōsaka

Lahore

Tàiyuán

Shíjiāzhuāng

S KOREA

Daegu

Hiroshima

INDIA

CHINA

Qīngdǎo

Gwangju

Busan

DELHI ✪

Zhèngzhōu

Fukuoka

NEPAL

Xī'ān

Yellow River
(Huáng Hé)

Nánjīng

Yellow Sea

PACIFIC
OCEAN

8

Jaipur

Pages 144-145

Héféi

Shànghǎi

Lucknow

Pokhara

Wǔhàn

Sūzhōu

Ningbo

Kanpur

KATHMANDU ✪

Chéngdū

Hángzhōu

C   D   E   F   G   H   J

SIGHTS & ACTIVITIES

◉ SEE
◉ DO

ITINERARY

▽ 1
▽ 2

Moscow

Red Square and the Kremlin are the historical, geographic and spiritual heart of Moscow, as they have been for nearly 900 years. The fortress, onion domes of St Basil's Cathedral and granite mausoleum of Vladimir Ilych Lenin are the city's key historical sights.

St Petersburg

St Petersburg is a treasure trove of art, culture and canals. You can spend days exploring the 360 rooms of the Hermitage, seeing everything from Egyptian mummies to Picassos, while the Russian Museum houses the world's best collection of Russian art. Don't miss an evening at the Bolshoi.

Grand Palace of Peterhof

Hugging the Gulf of Finland, 29km west of St Petersburg, Peterhof is known as the 'Russian Versailles'. The palace and buildings are surrounded by gardens and fountains, but what you see today is largely a reconstruction.

Yekaterinburg

The political capital of the Urals is overflowing with history and culture: gem rush, miners' mythology, the execution of the Romanovs, the rise of Russia's first president, Boris Yeltsin, and infamous gangster feuds of the 1990s.

Great Baikal Trail

Enthusiasts began work in 2003 on the first section of the Great Baikal Trail. Every summer, volunteers flock to Lake Baikal's shores to develop the 2000km-long trail network.

Vladivostok

With a hilly setting, striking architecture and numerous islands and bays, Vladivostok's name means 'Master the East'. It's the unofficial capital of the Russian Far East.

Kazan

Kazan ('cooking pot' in Tatar) is the capital of the Tatarstan Republic. Kul Sharif Mosque is named after the imam who died defending Kazan against Ivan the Terrible in 1552. The museum inside tells the story of Islam on the Volga.

Suzdal

A royal capital when Moscow was a cluster of cowsheds, Suzdal has preserved its idyllic character. The cathedral, wooden churches and kremlin (the grandfather of Moscow's) are straight out of storybook Russia.

Volgograd

In February 1943, when the city was known as Stalingrad, it was here that the German advance was halted and eventually turned back for good. An enormous victory monument, the Mamaev Kurgan, bears the names of 7200 fallen soldiers.

Volga Delta

The Volga River winds for 3530km through Russia's heartland. The Volga Delta is the natural highlight: 70km south of Astrakhan, the river bursts into thousands of streams, creating an ecosystem teeming with wildlife, including the Caspian flamingo.

Ulan-Ude

With its Asian features, cosy city centre and Mongol-Buddhist culture, the Buryat capital is one of Eastern Siberia's most likeable cities. It's a base for day trips and, for many travellers, a taster for what's to come in Mongolia.

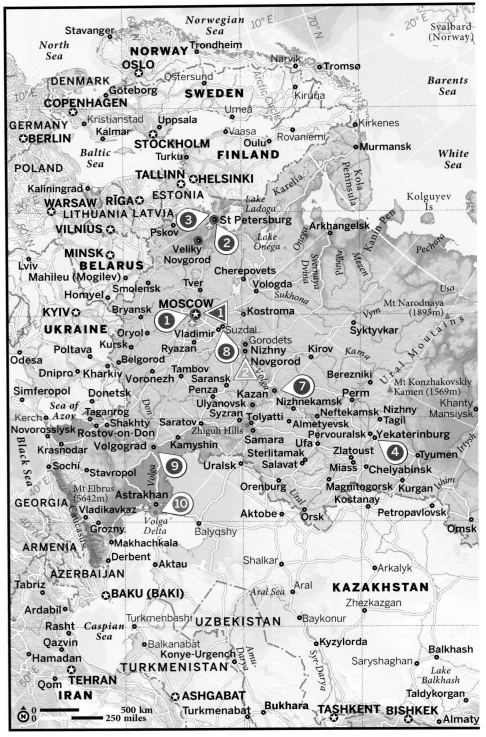

7-day itinerary
Two Capitals

Unsurprisingly, Moscow and St Petersburg are top of the wish list for most Russian first-timers. Start in **Moscow** with visits to the Kremlin, Red Square, Tretyakov Gallery and the Bolshoi Theatre. Stretch your legs in Gorky Park and along the Moscow River. Catch the train towards St Petersburg, with a stop at tourist-friendly **Veliky Novgorod** and its riverside kremlin and museum of wooden architecture. The historic heart of **St Petersburg** offers the Hermitage and Russian Museum, a river cruise, and the Mariinsky and Mikhailovsky Theatres. With time, you could also venture out to the palace at Peterhof, an easy half-day trip from the city.

14-day itinerary
Along the Volga to Astrakhan

Follow the mighty Volga as it flows east from Russia's capital to the Caspian Sea. From Moscow, head east towards **Nizhny Novgorod** where the river can be viewed from above on a cable-car ride. Consider making a day trip by hydrofoil to nearby **Gorodets**, known for its folk arts. The next stop is the intriguing Tatarstan capital of **Kazan** with its World Heritage Site–listed kremlin, which includes an enormous mosque and a satellite branch of St Petersburg's Hermitage. The Volga continues to guide you south past Lenin's birthplace of **Ulyanovsk** and the port city of **Samara**, from where you could go hiking in the rocky **Zhiguli Hills**. The 17-hour train journey to **Volgograd**, entirely rebuilt after Russia's bloodiest battle of WWII, is worth it to see the amazing 72m-tall statue of Mother Russia, Mamaev Kurgan. The Volga spills into the Caspian Sea at **Astrakhan**, the jumping-off point for the **Volga Delta** – home to lots of wildlife, including rare flamingos and the even rarer sturgeon, the source of Beluga caviar.

SIGHTS & ACTIVITIES

◉ SEE

◉ DO

ITINERARY

▽ 1

▽ 2

Tbilisi

Tbilisi has come a long way since the Rose Revolution of 2003, but the Old Town is still redolent of an ancient Eurasian crossroads, with its lanes, balconied houses, leafy squares and handsome churches, overlooked by the 17-centuries-old Narikala Fortress. Many buildings date from after the Persian sacking of 1795, contrasting with some eye-catching new architecture.

Davit Gareja

On the border with Azerbaijan, this Georgian monastery complex is surrounded by a lunar, semidesert landscape that turns green and blooms with flowers in early summer. The site comprises about 15 monasteries. Most are long abandoned, and visitors usually just see two – Lavra, now restored and reinhabited by monks, and Udabno, which has beautiful frescoes.

Svaneti

Beautiful, wild and mysterious, Svaneti is so remote that it was never tamed by any ruler. Picturesque villages and snow-covered, 4000m-plus peaks provide a superb backdrop to the many walking trails. Svaneti's emblem is the *koshki* (defensive stone tower). Around 175, most built between the 9th and 13th centuries, survive today.

Mt Kazbek

This 5047m extinct volcano has much folk history: Prometheus was supposedly chained up here for stealing fire from the gods, while the Betlemi (Bethlehem) cave was said to contain Christ's manger, Abraham's tent and a dove-rocked golden cradle. Today thousands of people attempt the summit each year; perhaps half of those who try do not reach the top.

Yerevan

Armenia's capital is a city full of contradictions, where top-of-the-range Mercedes sedans share the roads with Ladas so old they should be in museums. Few traces of the city's ancient past remain, with most of the building stock dating from the Soviet era. The Cafesjian Center for the Arts, housed in a flight of stone steps known as the Cascade, is Yerevan's major cultural attraction.

Geghard Monastery

Named after the lance that pierced Christ's side at the crucifixion, this World Heritage–listed monastery is carved out of the Azat River Gorge. Legend has it as founded in the 4th century and its oldest surviving cave church dates back to the 7th century.

Tatev

This rural village sprouted around its famous fortified monastery, accessible via hike or cable car. Perched on the edge of a rocky canyon, the monastery offers jaw-dropping views over to the peaks of Karabakh.

Baku

On the Caspian Sea, Azerbaijan's capital rings an ancient core with dazzling 21st-century architecture – including the blue-glass Flame Towers, ranging from 28 to 33 storeys high, and Zaha Hadid's fluid Heydar Aliyev Cultural Centre, formed of waves and peaks that seem to melt together.

Quba

Venture to these remote hinterlands for sheepy Caucasian foothills, dramatic canyons, mountain panoramas and fascinating villages with their own unique languages.

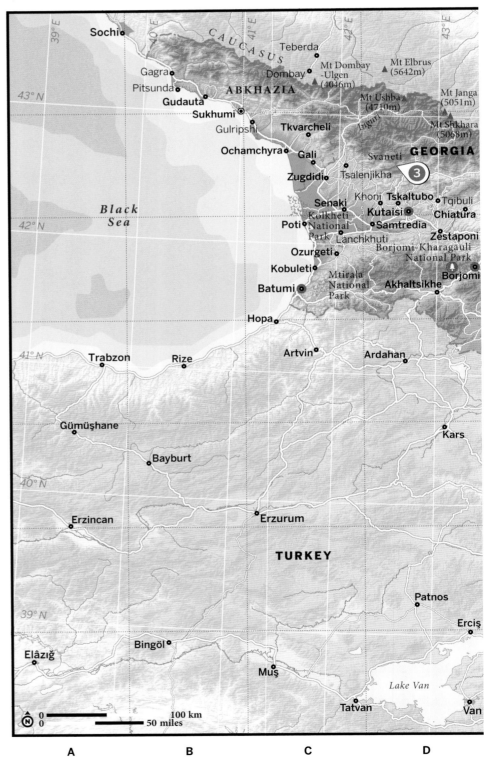

21-day itinerary
Georgia by foot

One of the best ways of exploring this spectacular country is on foot (with the aid of a horse if needed) as hiking routes often link villages. From a base at **Telavi** in Kakheti, get driven along the summer-only road to **Omalo** in remote Tusheti and hike four days to **Shatili**. Then get driven to **Roshka** and make the strenuous day-hike to Juta en route to

Kazbegi. Return to **Tbilisi** to recharge before another summery fix of fun at the Black Sea resort of **Batumi**, visiting **Uplistsikhe**, Stalin's home town of **Gori** and historic **Kutaisi**. Take the route back to Akhaltsikhe via the old-world spa town of **Borjomi**, gateway to the **Borjomi-Kharagauli National Park** where great hiking awaits on 11 mapped trails with accommodation.

14-day itinerary
Highlights of the Caucasus

It's possible to get a basic taste of all three countries in two weeks if you organise an Azerbaijian visa well in advance. Arrive in **Bakı** and pass a couple of days exploring the art galleries and Old City core, plus make an excursion to **Qobustan** and the mud volcanoes. Take the night train to lovely **Şəki** then hop west via **Zaqatala** and into

Georgia's grape-growing region, Kakheti, believed to be the birthplace of wine. Stop in **Sighnaghi** and drive on to the Georgian capital via the **Davit Gareja** cave monasteries. Spend three nights in lovely **Tbilisi**, including an excursion to the old Georgian capital **Mtskheta**. Next head up to **Kazbegi** for two or three days' walking in the Great

Caucasus. Return to Tbilisi and venture south to Armenia, hopping to the border via Marneuli and Sadakhlo then taking a taxi to the World Heritage monasteries of **Haghpat** and **Sanahin**. Continue from **Alaverdi** to the capital **Yerevan** with its wine bars and museums. Add excursions to **Garni Temple** and to **Geghard** and **Khor Virap** monasteries.

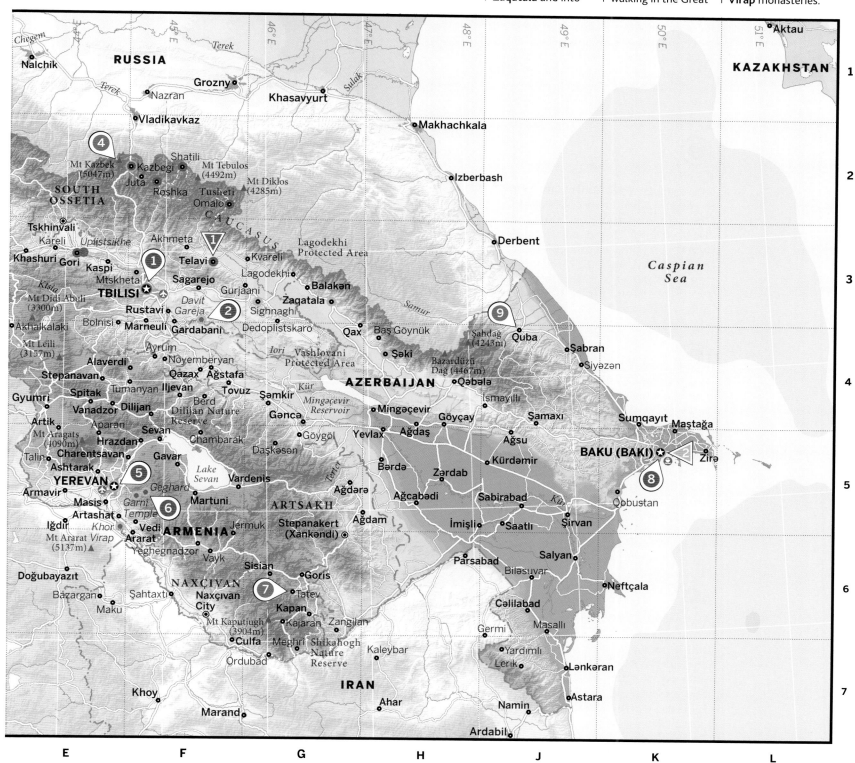

SIGHTS &
ACTIVITIES

 SEE

 DO

ITINERARY

 1

2

Samarkand

The Registan, which translates as 'Sandy Place' in Tajik, was medieval Samarkand's commercial centre and the plaza was probably a wall-to-wall bazaar. This ensemble of majestic, tilting *medressas* – a near-overload of majolica, azure mosaics and vast, well-proportioned spaces – is the city's centrepiece, and arguably the most awesome sight in Central Asia.

Bukhara

Central Asia's holiest city has buildings spanning a thousand years of history. When it was built in 1127, the Kalon Minaret was probably the tallest building in Central Asia – 47m high with 10m-deep foundations. The Ark, a royal town-within-a-town, is Bukhara's oldest structure, occupied from the 5th century until 1920. For centuries the residence of the emirs of Bukhara, it's now 80% ruins.

Khiva

Khiva's Ichon-Qala (inner walled city) is one of the highlights of Uzbekistan. The historic heart of Khiva (Xiva) has been so well preserved that it's sometimes criticised as lifeless – a 'museum city'. But walk through the city gates and wander the fabled Ichon-Qala in all its monotone, mud-walled glory and it's hard not to feel like you are stepping into another era.

Charyn Canyon

The region from Almaty to Lake Balkhash in Kazakhstan is known as Zhetisu (Russian: Semirechie), meaning Land of Seven Rivers. Over millions of years, the swift Charyn (Sharyn) River has carved a 150m- to 300m-deep canyon into the otherwise flat steppe 200km east of Almaty, and time has weathered this into weird and colourful rock formations. It's Kazakhstan's answer to the Grand Canyon.

Turkestan

Kazakhstan's most sacred Muslim shrine is the astounding Yasaui Mausoleum. It is home to Kozha Akhmed Yasaui, the first great Turkic Muslim holy man. The main chamber is capped with an 18m-wide turquoise dome, above a 2000kg metal *kazan* (cauldron) for holy water.

Lake Son-Köl (

The jewel of central Kyrgyzstan is the high-alpine Lake Son-Köl, fringed with summer pastures and Kyrgyz yurt camps. You can hike or drive, but the best option is a horse trek, overnighting in yurtstays.

Pamir Highway

This epic Soviet-built highway runs from the valleys of Badakhshan via the Pamir plateau and the 'wild east' town of Murgab to Alay Valley. En route it passes ancient tombs, hot springs, Kyrgyz yurt camps and spectacular mountain scenery.

Fan Mountains

Lying 30km east of Penjikent in Tajikistan, the rugged, glaciated Fan Mountains are one of Central Asia's premier trekking destinations. Studded with turquoise lakes and burnished with wind-blown, high-altitude vistas they beg to be walked, hiked and climbed.

Karakum Desert

Central Asia's hottest desert is a sun-scorched expanse of dunes and sparse vegetation. The Darvaza Gas Craters date from Soviet-era gas exploration in the 1970s. One has been set alight, and is visible from miles away.

14-day itinerary
Silk Road Cities

This loop route covers almost all of Central Asia's greatest sites. Fly into **Tashkent** and get a feel for the big city before taking a flight to **Urgench** and a bus or taxi ride to **Khiva**. Then hop in a taxi for a day trip to the crumbling Elliq-Qala desert cities of **Karakalpakstan**. Next, it's train or taxi to **Bukhara's** atmospheric bazaars and backstreets. To get off the beaten track make a detour to **Nurata** and then overnight at either a yurt camp at **Lake Aidarkul** or a mountain village homestay at **Sentyab**. From here take the golden (actually tarmac) road to **Samarkand**. Admire the glories of the Registan and Shah-i-Zinda and add on a day trip to **Shakhrisabz**, birthplace of Timur (Tamerlane).

21-day itinerary
Over the Torugart

This trip takes in fabulous mountain scenery, traditional life in the pastures and the rollercoaster ride over the Torugart Pass to Kashgar. Kick off in cosmopolitan **Almaty**, with visits to Panfilov Park and the Central State Museum and a soak in the Arasan Baths. It's an easy four-hour drive to Kyrgyzstan's capital **Bishkek**, from where you can head east to the blue waters and sandy beaches of **Issyk-Köl**, the world's second-largest alpine lake. Hire transport to take you to the colourful, eroded **Charyn Canyon** and on to the Kyrgyz border through the Karkara Valley to **Karakol** for some trekking. In **Kochkor** take advantage of the Community Based Tourism (CBT) programme and spend time in a yurt or homestay on the *jailoos* (summer pasture) around **Lake Son-Köl**. From here head onwards to **Naryn** and then the Silk Road caravanserai of **Tash-Rabat**, where you can stay overnight in yurts, and perhaps ride up to a pass overlooking **Chatyr-Köl**. From Tash-Rabat it's over the **Torugart Pass** and into China to wonderful **Kashgar** for its epic Sunday Market.

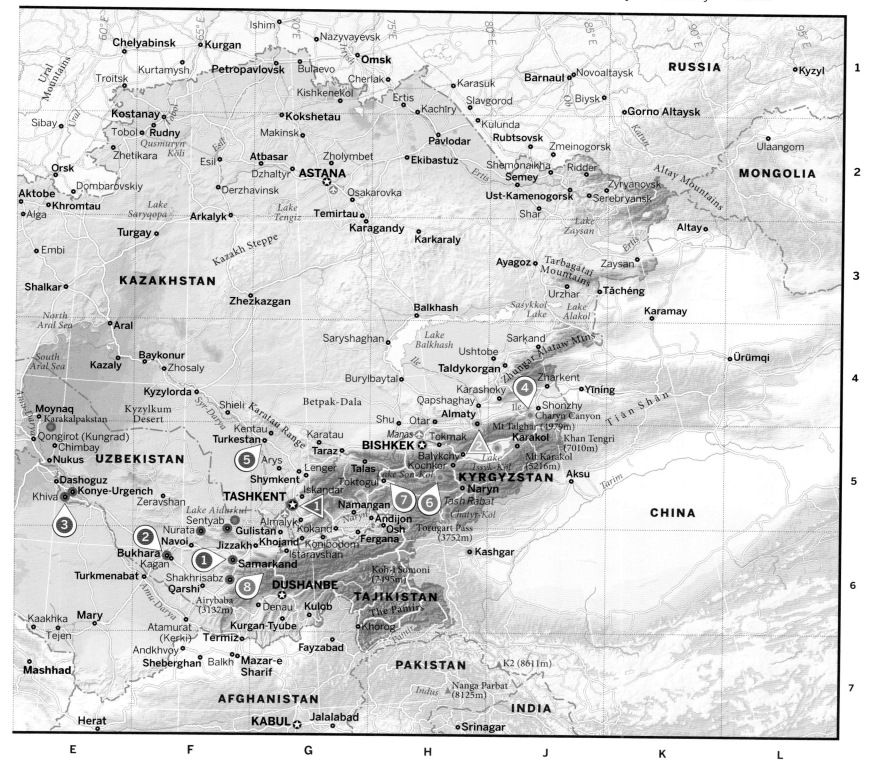

The Middle East

The Middle East is a grand epic, a cradle of civilisations and a beautiful, complicated land that's home to some of the planet's most hospitable people. This is where humankind first built cities and learned to write, and it was from here that Judaism, Christianity and Islam all arose. Deserts sprawl across many of the countries of the Middle East, but they're rarely home to the sandy landscapes of childhood imaginings. Beyond the vast desert of the Arabian Peninsula, stony gravel plains are the defining feature. Four mighty rivers run through the region: the Euphrates and Tigris, said to have flowed into the Garden of Eden, and both the world's lowest and longest rivers, the River Jordan and the fabled River Nile.

CLIMATE CHART

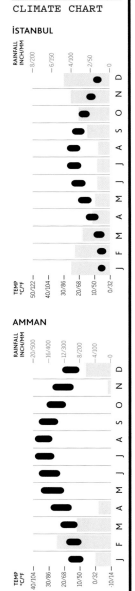

İSTANBUL

AMMAN

RELIGION
The Middle East is where it all began for three monotheistic religions: Judaism, Christianity and Islam. Religious icons abound – Jerusalem's Dome of the Rock and Church of the Holy Sepulchre, Esfahan's Masjed-e Jameh and Masjed-e Shah mosques and İstanbul's Aya Sofya.

ARCHITECTURE
From tombs to ruins, temples to ziggurats, the Middle East is awash with amazing architecture. Wander along Jerusalem's old walls, hike past ancient Petra, gaze out from the ramparts of Masada or marvel at the sheer grandeur of the ruins of Ephesus.

SOUQS & BAZAARS
Master the art of haggling here: shop for carpets in İstanbul's Grand Bazaar, teapots in Esfahan's Bazar-e Bozorg, spices and silks in Tabriz Bazaar, sweets in Lebanon's Saida Souq or antiques in Oman's Mutrah Souq – just be sure to bargain with a smile.

LANDSCAPES
The Middle East is famous for arid landscapes – best seen in Wadi Rum, the 'Empty Quarter' and Cappadocia – but there are surprises too, like the snows on top of Iran's Mt Damavand, the natural springs of Mujib Biosphere Reserve, and the fish-rich Red Sea.

Left to right: A Bedouin guide leads his two dromedary camels over the dunes of Wadi Rum; interior of Aya Sofya museum.

Transport hubs

Once the land of desert nomads and trains of camel caravans, these days most visitors to the Middle East arrive rather less romantically aboard a jumbo jet. Overland travel is still possible, however, especially from the west – although sadly, the same cannot be said for the east; check current travel advisories before you travel. Border crossings can be excruciatingly slow: patience, politeness and good humour are your best hopes for speeding up the process.

İstanbul

İstanbul's main airport, Atatürk International Airport, is located in Yeşilköy, 23km west of Sultanahmet, but construction on a new airport 50km north is underway. Germany, Austria and Greece have direct buses to İstanbul. If you're arriving overland, expect to be held up at the border for two to three hours – or longer if your fellow passengers don't have their paperwork in order. Day trips on ferries to Greece are popular: remember your passport, and check you have a multiple-entry Turkish visa.

Dubai and Abu Dhabi

Dubai International and Abu Dhabi International are the UAE's main airports. Passenger flights have also started using Dubai's new megasized Al Maktoum International. The UAE shares borders with Oman and Saudi Arabia, but only Gulf Cooperation Council (GCC) citizens are permitted to cross into Saudi Arabia. The handiest border crossings for non-GCC citizens headed for Oman are the Hili checkpoint in Al Ain, the Hatta checkpoint east of Dubai and the tiny coastal Khatmat Malaha crossing south of Fujairah. Visas for Oman must be purchase online in advance.

Amman

Queen Alia International Airport, about 35km south of Amman, is the country's main gateway. The only other international airport is at Aqaba, where some carriers stop en route to Amman. Flights to Sharm El Sheikh in Egypt are handled from here. It's easy to reach Jordan by land from Israel and the Palestinian Territories. Most overland travellers arrive by bus or taxi, though it's also possible to bring your own vehicle. Note that currently it's not possible to get a visa on arrival in Jordan at King Hussein Bridge or at Wadi Araba. There are two main boat services to Egypt, leaving from Aqaba, and arriving in either Nuweiba or Taba (check travel advisories).

Tel Aviv

Most visitors arrive in Israel via Ben Gurion Airport; Ramon International Airport, in Eilat, is scheduled to open in 2018. It is relatively easy to enter Israel from Jordan and Egypt, but procedures at the four crossings regularly change – check before travel. Israel issues visa on arrival, but going the other way, you may need to pre-apply for Jordanian visas. You will need cash and infinite patience.

Muscat

There is only one truly international airport in Oman, and that is Muscat International Airport, although there are some direct flights to Salalah. Oman borders the UAE, Saudi Arabia and Yemen. Current practicalities mean, however, that you can only enter UAE.

Beirut

With the land border with Israel closed and the Syrian border off-limits, most travellers to Lebanon arrive and depart by air. Beirut–Rafic Hariri International Airport is Lebanon's only airport and main entry point into the country.

Tehran

International sanctions have made Iran increasingly isolated, but it is nevertheless fairly straightforward to get into the country on a plane, by train from Turkey or over border crossings from the north. Tehran's Imam Khomeini International Airport (IKIA) sees most of Iran's international air traffic. Crossing from Turkey is easy and from Armenia, Azerbaijan and Turkmenistan is doable with varying degrees of hassle.

Left to right:
Muslim woman wearing traditional *hijab*; Tel Aviv by night.

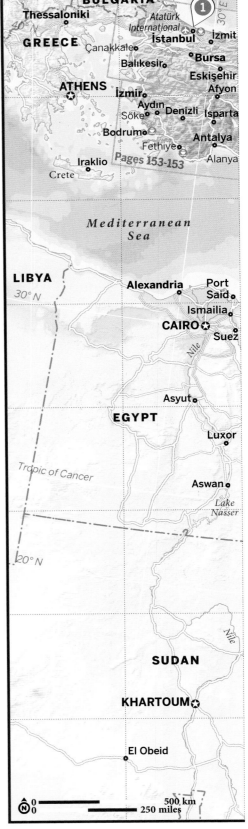

© Mansoreh / Shutterstock

© SJ Travel Photo and Video / Shutterstock

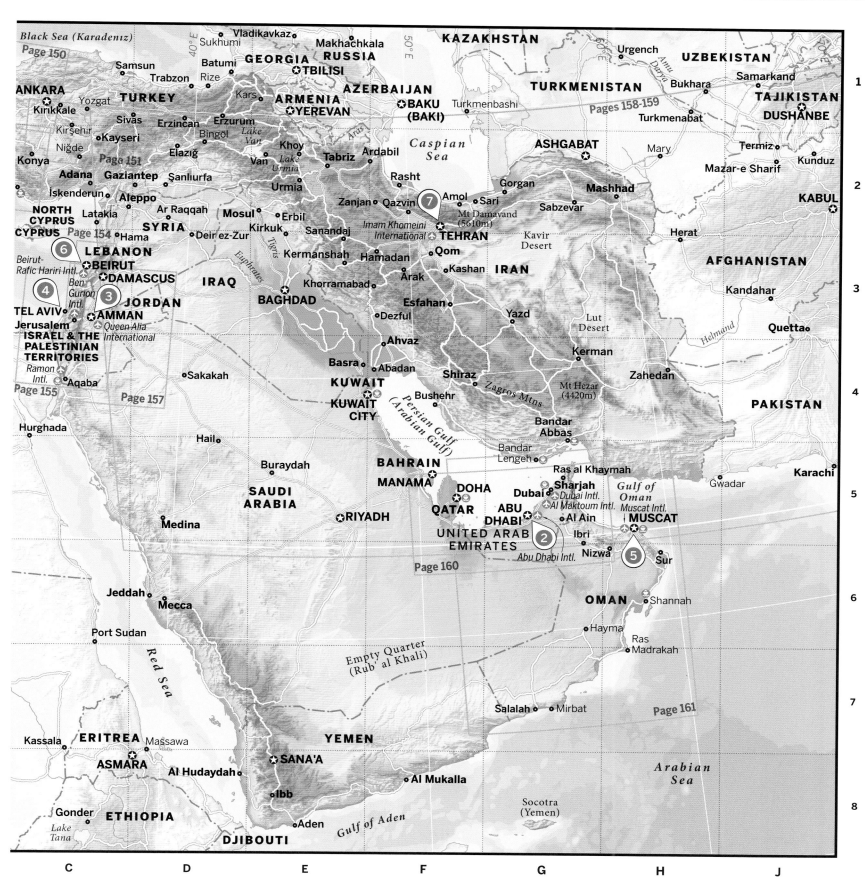

Black Sea (Karadeniz)
Page 150

Vladikavkaz
Sukhumi
Makhachkala
KAZAKHSTAN
Urgench
UZBEKISTAN

Samsun
Batumi
GEORGIA
Rize
RUSSIA
Amu Darya
Bukhara
Samarkand

ANKARA
Trabzon
TBILISI
AZERBAIJAN
TURKMENISTAN
Pages 158-159
TAJIKISTAN

Kırıkkale
Yozgat
TURKEY
Kars
ARMENIA
BAKU
(BAKI)
Turkmenbashi
Turkmenabat
DUSHANBE

Kırşehir
Sivas
Erzincan
Erzurum
YEREVAN
Caspian
Sea
ASHGABAT
Mary
Termiz
Kunduz

Niğde
Kayseri
Bingöl
Lake
Van
Khoy
Tabriz
Ardabil
Rasht
Gorgan
Mashhad
Mazar-e Sharif

Konya
Page 151
Elazığ
Van
Lake
Urmia
Zanjan
Qazvin
⑦
Amol
Sari
Sabzevar
KABUL

Adana
Gaziantep
Şanlıurfa
Urmia
Mt Damavand
(5610m)
Kavir
Desert
Herat
AFGHANISTAN

İskenderun
Ar Raqqah
Mosul
Erbil
Sanandaj
Imam Khomeini
International
TEHRAN

NORTH
CYPRUS
Latakia
Aleppo
SYRIA
Kirkuk
Kermanshah
Hamadan
Qom
IRAN
Kandahar

CYPRUS
Page 154
Hama
Deir ez-Zur
Arak
Kashan

⑥
LEBANON
Khorramabad
Esfahan
Yazd
Lut
Desert
Quetta

Beirut-
Rafic Hariri Intl.
BEIRUT
DAMASCUS
IRAQ
BAGHDAD
Dezful
Kerman
Zahedan

④
③
Ben
Gurion
Intl.
JORDAN
AMMAN
Ahvaz
Mt Hezar
(4420m)
PAKISTAN

TEL AVIV
Jerusalem
Queen Alia
International
Basra
Abadan
Shiraz
Zagros Mtns
Bandar
Abbas

ISRAEL & THE
PALESTINIAN
TERRITORIES
Sakakah
KUWAIT
Bushehr
Bandar
Lengeh
Karachi

Ramon
Intl.
Aqaba
Page 157
KUWAIT
CITY
Persian Gulf
(Arabian Gulf)
Ras al Khaymah
Gwadar

Page 155
Hurghada
Hail
BAHRAIN
MANAMA
Sharjah
Dubai Intl.
Al Maktoum Intl.
Gulf of
Oman
Muscat Intl.

Buraydah
DOHA
Dubai
ABU
DHABI
Al Ain
②
MUSCAT
⑤

SAUDI
ARABIA
QATAR
UNITED ARAB
EMIRATES
Abu Dhabi Intl.
Ibri
Nizwa
Sur

Medina
RIYADH
Page 160
Ibri

Jeddah
Mecca
OMAN
Shannah

Port Sudan
Red
Sea
Empty Quarter
(Rub' al Khali)
Hayma
Ras
Madrakah

Salalah
Mirbat
Page 161

Kassala
ERITREA
Massawa
YEMEN
Arabian
Sea

ASMARA
Al Hudaydah
SANA'A
Al Mukalla
Socotra
(Yemen)

Gonder
ETHIOPIA
Ibb
Aden
Gulf of Aden
DJIBOUTI

THE TRAVEL ATLAS

① Selimiye Mosque, Edirne

Designed by Ottoman architect Mimar Koca Sinan (1497–1588), this exquisite World Heritage–listed mosque is Edirne's most cherished building. Built between 1569 and 1575 by order of Sultan Selim II, the mosque features four striking 71m-high minarets and was positioned in the centre of an extensive *külliye* (mosque complex).

② Ankara

Turkey's 'other' city may not have showy Ottoman palaces or regal facades, but Ankara thrums to a vivacious, youthful beat. The superb Museum of Anatolian Civilisations contains artefacts from just about every archaeological site in Anatolia.

③ Safranbolu

Safranbolu's old town, known as Çarşı, is a vision of red-tiled roofs and alleys full of candy stores, timber-framed mansions and traditional shops. Having first found fame as a source of the precious spice saffron, Safranbolu has been a World Heritage site since 1994.

④ Gallipoli

The Gallipoli (Gelibolu) Peninsula is infamous for the bloody battles fought here in 1915 between the Allied and

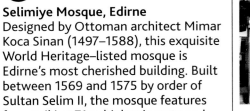

Ottoman armies, which resulted in more than half a million casualties. Today, the battlefields are covered in pine forests and fringed by beaches. Taking a guided tour is the best way to understand the various sites.

⑤ Ruins of Troy

Layers of history are revealed as you explore this ancient ruined city. Resembling an overgrown archaeological dig, it takes some imagination to reconstruct, although you can still make out the remains of fortifications, gates, walls, shrines and sanctuaries. Informative audioguides help visitors to interpret the site.

⑥ Hattuşa

The mountainous site of Hattuşa was once the capital of the Hittite kingdom, which stretched from Syria to Europe. At its zenith this was a city of 15,000 inhabitants with defensive walls over 6km in length, studded with watchtowers and secret tunnels – it's now encircled by a hilly, 5km loop trail.

⑦ Bergama

Bergama's celebrated acropolis is sited on a hill northeast of the town. Chief among the ruins are the Temple of Trajan, the vertigo-inducing 10,000-seat Hellenistic theatre, the Altar of Zeus and the whimsical mosaic floors in Building Z.

⑧ Beylerbeyi Palace, İstanbul

This opulent 1865 building was built for Sultan Abdül Aziz (r 1861–76). Look out for the marble bathing pavilions by the water's edge; one was for men, the other for women of the harem.

⑨ Thrace

In his epic poem, the *Iliad*, Homer wrote about the honey-sweet black wine of Thrace. Generations of farmers have capitalised on the region's climate to grow grapes for wine. An official route takes in several of the best Thracian vineyards.

⑩ Konya

The home town of the whirling dervish orders and a bastion of Seljuk culture, Konya is a mix of ancient mosques, tea gardens and a maze-like market district. Most people come to visit the Mevlâna Museum, the former lodge of the whirling dervishes.

Safranbolu: The old town is a warren of timber-framed mansions, many now boutique hotels.

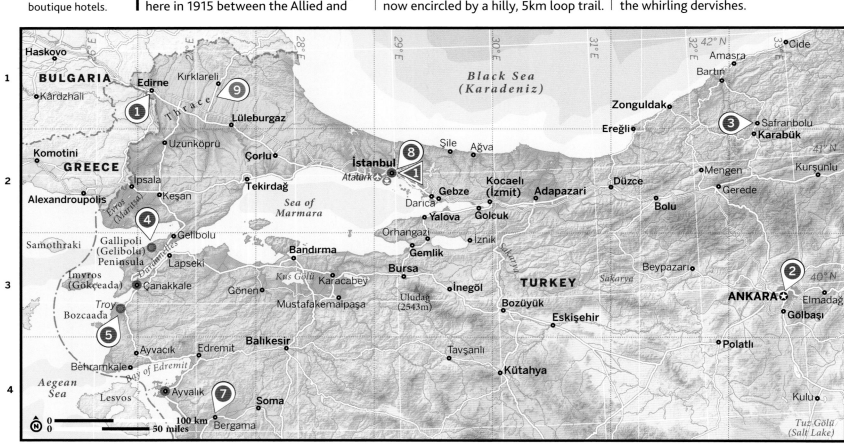

© Oguz Dikbakan / Shutterstock

3-day itinerary
İstanbul to Ephesus

You'll need at least three days in **İstanbul** to cover the Aya Sofya, Topkapı Palace and the Blue Mosque, but there's a sultan's treasury of other sights and activities, including a cruise up the Bosphorus, nightlife around İstiklal Caddesi, and the Grand Bazaar. From İstanbul, take a bus to **Çanakkale**, a lively student town on the Dardanelles. A tour of the nearby **Gallipoli Peninsula**'s poignant WWI battlefields is a memorable experience, as is a visit to ancient **Troy**, immortalised by Homer in the *Iliad*. From Çanakkale, it's a 3½-hour bus ride to **Ayvalık**, with its atmospheric old Greek quarter and fish restaurants. From here, it's easy to travel onwards to Selçuk, the most useful base for visiting Ephesus.

10-day itinerary
Cappadocia

From İstanbul, catch a bus or hop on the fast train to the capital, **Ankara**. Two sights here give an insight into Turkish history, ancient and modern: the Anıt Kabir, Atatürk's hilltop mausoleum, and the Museum of Anatolian Civilisations, a restored 15th-century *bedesten* (covered market) packed with finds from the surrounding steppe. Tying in with the latter, a detour east takes in the evocative ruins of **Hattuşa**, the Hittite capital in the late Bronze Age. To explore the rest of Cappadocia, base yourself in a cave hotel in **Göreme**, surrounded by valleys of fairy chimneys. The famous rock formations line the roads to sights including Göreme's rock-cut frescoed churches and the Byzantine underground cities at **Kaymaklı** and **Derinkuyu**. Alongside the hot-air balloon trips, valley walks and horse riding, schedule some time to just sit and appreciate the fantastical landscape – ideally in *çay*-drinking villages such as **Mustafapaşa**, with its stone-carved Greek houses and 18th-century church – before returning to İstanbul.

Güllüdere Vadısı
The trails that loop around Güllüdere Vadısı (Rose Valley) provide some of the finest fairy chimney–strewn vistas in Cappadocia. As well as this, though, they hide fabulous, little-visited rock-cut churches boasting fresco fragments and intricate carvings.

Derinkuyu
Derinkuyu underground city has large, cavernous rooms and tunnels arrayed on seven levels. At the bottom, look up the ventilation shaft to see just how far down you've gone.

Ala Dağlar National Park
This national park is famous for its trekking routes, which snake through craggy limestone ranges and across a high plateau dotted with lakes. The elusive Caspian snowcock makes its home in the high reaches of the Taurus.

Uçhisar Castle
This tall volcanic-rock outcrop is visible for miles around. Riddled with tunnels, it was used for centuries by villagers as a place of refuge. Stairs climb to the peak for panoramic views over the Cappadocian countryside.

Zelve
First a monastic settlement and then a village (abandoned in the 1950s due to rock collapse), Zelve's three interconnecting valleys feature crumbling cave-habitations, an old mill and several abandoned chapels.

Ihlara Valley
Southeast of Aksaray, the Ihlara Valley scythes through the stubbly fields in a sea of greenery. Once called Peristrema, the valley was a favourite retreat of Byzantine monks, who cut churches into the base of its cliffs.

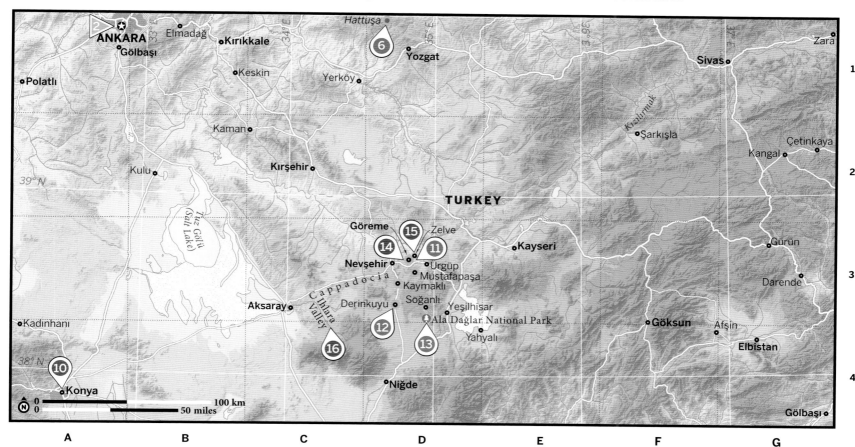

SIGHTS &
ACTIVITIES

● SEE

● DO

ITINERARY

▼ 1

▽ 2

Ephesus

Considered the best-preserved ruins in the Mediterranean, Ephesus (Efes) is a tribute to Greek artistry and Roman architectural prowess. Ancient Ephesus was a great trading city and the marble-coated Curetes Way provides myriad photo opportunities – not least the Library of Celsus with its two storeys of columns, and the Terraced Houses, their vivid frescoes and sophisticated mosaics giving insight into the daily lives of the city's elite.

Pamukkale

Famed for its intricate series of travertines (calcite shelves), and crowned by the ruined Roman and Byzantine spa city of Hierapolis, the 'Cotton Castle' is one of Turkey's most unusual treasures. Explore ruins such as the Roman theatre and soak your feet in the thermal water filling the crystal travertines, then tiptoe down to Pamukkale village past a line of the saucer-shaped formations. An optional extra is a dunk in Hierapolis' Antique Pool amid toppled marble columns.

Lycian Way

This long-distance trail runs for 500km between Fethiye and Antalya across the Teke Peninsula, once the stamping ground of the ancient and mysterious Lycian civilisation. The route leads through pine and cedar forests, past dramatic 3000m-high mountains, stunning coastal views and ancient cities such as Pınara, Xanthos, Letoön and Olympos.

Datça and Bozburun Peninsulas

Stretching from Marmaris towards the Greek island of Symi, these mountainous peninsulas form a scenic line between the Aegean and Mediterranean, with stunning azure coves, hidden archipelagos and craggy, thickly forested peaks overlooking it all. From *gület*-building Bozburun village to the ruins of Knidos at the tip of the Datça Peninsula, they mix holiday charm with rustic tranquility.

Olympos

Known in Turkish as Yanartaş, or 'Burning Rock', the Chimaera is a cluster of small flames that naturally blaze on Mt Olympos. Ancient peoples attributed them to a monster's breath – part lion, part goat, part snake. The mythical hero Bellerophon supposedly killed the Chimaera by mounting the winged horse Pegasus and pouring molten lead into the monster's mouth.

Kekova

This island is home to the remains of Lycian Simena, submerged following a series of severe earthquakes in the 2nd century AD. Most of what you can still see is a residential part of ancient Simena. From a kayak or glass-bottomed boat, it's possible to catch a ghostly glimpse of amphorae, building foundations and staircases disappearing into the depths.

Afrodisias

Out in the Anatolian hinterland among Roman poplars, green fields and warbling birds, the remote site of Afrodisias boasts two of western Turkey's most photogenic relics. The tetrapylon, a monumental gateway, welcomed travellers when Afrodisias was the capital of Roman Caria, and the 30,000-seat stadium echoes with the roars of long-gone spectators. Today, there's an excellent museum to explore, and the site itself is relatively untended, with some of its side paths disappearing into thickets and bramble, which creates the exotic sensation of discovering lost ruins.

5-day itinerary
İzmir and Ephesus

After a few days in İstanbul, either fly or take a bus to İzmir, spend a day or two exploring its museums and bazaar, and then catch the bus or train straight down to **Selçuk**. Time your visit to coincide with Selçuk's sprawling Saturday market, and pair the magnificent ruins of **Ephesus** with a trip to the mountaintop village of **Şirince**. Next,

hit the southern Aegean coast at cruise port **Kuşadası**, where you can sign up for a 'PMD' day trip to see a trio of sites: the ruins of **Priene**, **Miletus** and **Didyma**. These sites, respectively two ancient port cities and a temple to Apollo, make extremely interesting additions to an Ephesus visit, giving a much fuller picture of the region in centuries past.

10-day itinerary
Onwards to Antalya

Kuşadası makes a good launch pad for further explorations. Spend a day or two nibbling calamari and sipping cocktails on the chi-chi **Bodrum Peninsula** and cross the Gulf of Gökova by ferry to the **Datça Peninsula**. With their fishing villages and forested mountains, Datça and the adjoining **Bozburun Peninsula** are excellent for exploring by scooter. Continuing along

the Mediterranean coast, beautiful **Ölüdeniz** is the spot to paraglide from atop **Baba Dağ** (Mt Baba; 1960m) or just lie low on the beach. You're now within kicking distance of the 509km-long **Lycian Way**. Hike for a day to overnight in heavenly **Faralya**. Also on the Lycian Way, laid-back **Kaş'** pretty harbourside square buzzes nightly. Boat trips depart from here to

the sunken Lycian city at **Kekova**. From Kaş, it's a couple of hours to **Olympos**, famous for the Chimaera flames. A 1½-hour bus journey reaches the city of **Antalya**. Its Roman-Ottoman quarter, Kaleiçi, is worth a wander, set against a jaw-dropping mountain range. From Antalya you can either fly back to İstanbul or head onwards into Cappadocia.

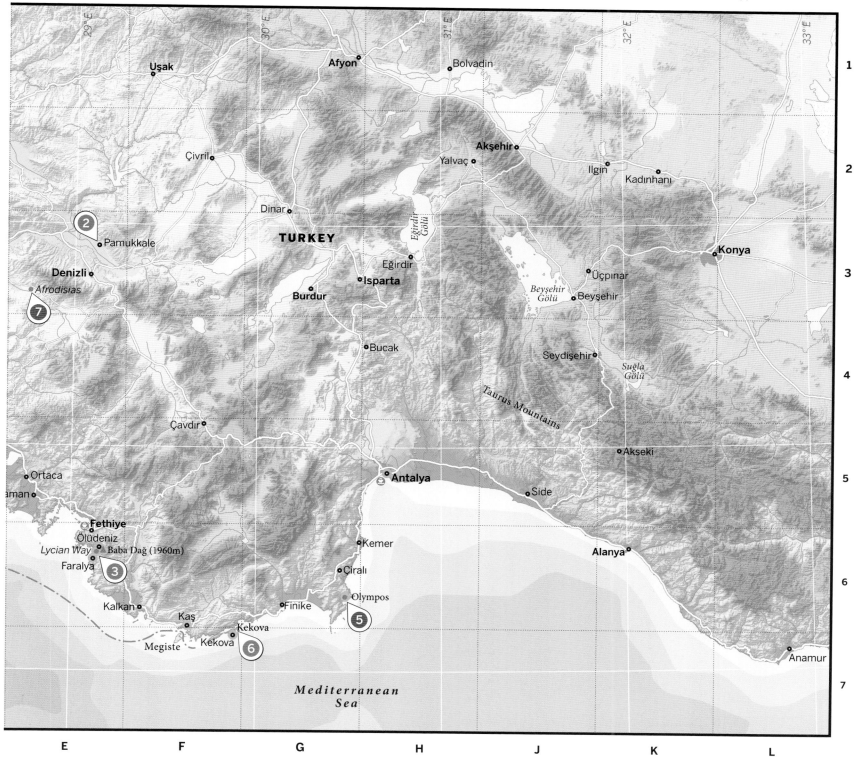

SIGHTS & ACTIVITIES

 SEE

 DO

ITINERARY

▼ 1

▽ 2

① Beirut
Fast-paced, fashion-conscious and friendly, Beirut was once known as the 'Paris of the East'. Its nightlife is legendary: hotspots include the hipster hangouts of Gemmayzeh and Mar Mikhaël and the student district of Hamra. South of the Mohammed Al Amin Mosque is Rue de Damas (Damascus St), once the Green Line between warring East and West Beirut.

② Baalbek
Known as the Heliopolis or 'Sun City' of the ancient world, Baalbek's ruins comprise the most impressive ancient site in Lebanon and are arguably the best preserved in the Middle East. The monumental Temple of Jupiter impresses by its sheer scale, while the adjacent Temple of Bacchus is astoundingly well preserved, with exquisite carved decoration.

③ Jeita Grotto
The Jeita Grotto cave system extends 6km into the mountains northeast of Beirut. The extraordinary upper cavern, accessed via a cable car from the ticket office, has coloured lights that showcase the stalactites and stalagmites in all their crystalline glory. The flooded lower caves are explored by rowing boat.

④ Qadisha Valley
This World Heritage-listed valley is home to Lebanon's finest mountain scenery, from rock-cut monasteries to red-roofed villages. The Qadisha River runs along the valley bottom, and Lebanon's highest peak, Qornet As Sawda (3090m), soars overhead.

⑤ Tyre
Once famous for its purple dye made from murex sea snails (Tyrian purple), Tyre has a wonderful seaside location and extensive Roman ruins. The town's foundations date back to approximately 2750 BC.

⑥ Shouf Biosphere Reserve
Comprising 5% of Lebanon's land area, this is the largest natural cedar reserve in the country and has more than 250km of hiking trails. Some of the trees are thought to be around 2000 years old. The reserve incorporates the Ammiq Wetland, which once covered parts of the Bekaa Valley.

⑦ Bekaa Valley
Heavily cultivated over millennia fertile, pastoral Bekaa Valley is now known for its plentiful vineyards, which have gained an international reputation for their wines.

▼1

7-day itinerary
The Full Lebanese

Spend at least a full day in **Beirut**, indulging in the capital's funky bars and cooler-than-cool cafe scene. A day trip to the marvellous ruins at **Baalbek** should occupy another day and could incorporate a winery visit and a tasting or two in the **Bekaa Valley**. Next, head west, visiting the fairytale cave of **Jeita Grotto** before continuing to pretty **Byblos**, where ancient ruins are sprinkled beside an azure sea. On the fourth day, head up to the breathtaking **Qadisha Valley** for a long, hot nature hike. From here, make for **Tripoli** to explore its super-atmospheric old town, before heading south for two days to explore **Saida** and **Tyre**, two Mediterranean cities that both bear tumultuous pasts and an astonishing wealth of ancient remains. Conclude the trip by travelling north along the coast to **Deir Al Qamar** to soak up the small-town atmosphere and the wonders of the Beiteddine Palace.

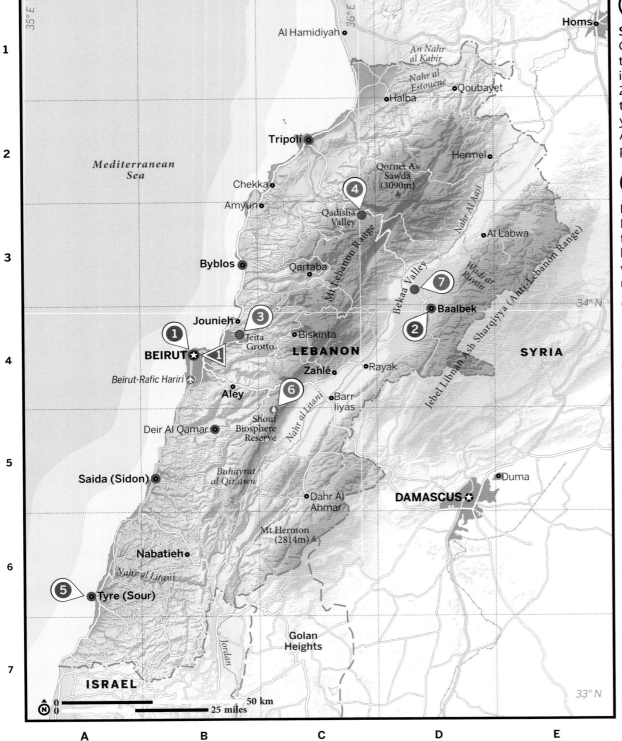

Temple Mount, Jerusalem
Known to Muslims as Al Haram Ash Sharif (The Noble Sanctuary) and to Jews as Har HaBayit (Temple Mount), this elevated cypress-planted plaza in Jerusalem's Old City is home to two of Islam's most sacred buildings – the Dome of the Rock and Al Aqsa Mosque.

Baha'i Gardens, Haifa
The 19 terraces of Haifa's Baha'i Gardens incorporate the gold-domed Shrine of the Báb and tier after tier of flower beds, lawns, sculptures and fountains, all cascading down the slopes of Mt Carmel.

Dead Sea
The lowest place on earth, the Dead Sea (431m below sea level) brings together natural beauty, ancient history and modern mineral spas. At the oasis of Ein Gedi you can hike through steep canyons to crystal-clear pools and tumbling waterfalls.

Masada
This isolated desert mesa is where the last Jewish resistance to Roman rule was crushed in AD 73 after a bloody siege. A Unesco World Heritage Site since 2001, the remains of the 10th Legion's siege bases are still visible.

14-day itinerary
Essential Israel

Spend your first four days in **Jerusalem**, including a couple of days wandering the alleys of the Old City, exploring the Western Wall and the adjacent Temple Mount/Al Haram Ash Sharif, and following the Via Dolorosa to the Church of the Holy Sepulchre. Break out your swimsuit and hiking shoes for a full-day excursion down to the **Dead Sea** and up the storied stronghold of **Masada**. Next, head to the Mediterranean coast for three days around **Tel Aviv**, dividing your time between strolling, cycling, lounging on the beach and fine dining. Next, head up the coast for a peek at Roman-era **Caesarea** before pushing on to **Haifa**. Check out the views from atop Mt Carmel and the Baha'i Gardens before a day trip to the walled city of **Akko** and the grottoes of Rosh HaNikra. After a day in **Nazareth**, head to **Tiberias** to explore the shores of the Sea of Galilee before returning to Jerusalem.

Bethlehem
Revered by Christians as Jesus' birthplace, Bethlehem's ancient buildings and alleyways look as they did centuries ago. The separation wall, which divides the city from Jerusalem, has become a canvas for street artists.

Makhtesh Ramon
An asymmetrical canyon formed by 200 million years of erosion, this majestic gash features pink-hued rock formations, a sandstone floor studded with ammonite fossils, and wildlife including oryx, gazelles, leopards, ibex, vultures and onagers (wild horses).

Golan Heights
In the 'Galilee Panhandle', hikers can take on the alpine peaks of Mt Hermon or follow the cliff-lined wadis of the Banias and Yehudiya Nature Reserves on their way to the Sea of Galilee.

Mar Saba Monastery
Built into a cliff face above a wadi, this copper-domed hermitage was founded in 439 CE and is still home to 15 monks. It's worth visiting for its wall paintings and to see the remains of St Saba (439–532 AD), but women will have to be content with the view from the adjacent hillside.

SIGHTS & ACTIVITIES

◉ SEE

◉ DO

ITINERARY

▽ 1

▽ 2

Petra

A honeycombed landscape of tombs, carved facades, pillars and sandstone cliffs, the Ancient City of Petra lies half-hidden in the wind-blown landscape in southern Jordan. Protected as a Unesco World Heritage Site, guided visits are provided by Bedouin tribespeople and the residents of neighbouring Wadi Musa.

Wadi Rum

With its burnished sandstone cliffs and vivid-coloured dunes, Wadi Rum is everything you'd expect of a quintessential desert. Today, it's possible to get a glimpse of the traditional Bedouin way of life (with a few more creature comforts) at camps scattered across this desert wilderness.

Jordan Trail

Around 650km from top to toe, the newly established 36-day Jordan Trail covers the entire length of Jordan and threads through some of the country's most iconic landscapes, including Petra and Wadi Rum. The trail is segmented into eight legs averaging around 80km each.

④

Ajloun Forest Reserve

This forest reserve was established in 1988 to protect rare oak, carob, pistachio and strawberry-tree forests. Nearby, the Al Ayoun Trail combines community-run hikes with village homestays, while in Umm Qais, classes are offered in foraging, cooking, beekeeping and basket weaving.

Jordan Trail: Walk through landscapes seen in many Hollywood films.

⑤

Jerash

The ruined city of Jerash is Jordan's largest Roman site. Its ceremonial gates, colonnaded avenues, temples and theatres speak of a time when this was an important imperial centre. From the well-preserved hippodrome, it's easy to imagine chariots tearing around the track.

⑥

Mujib Biosphere Reserve

Encompassing the canyonesque landscape of Wadi Mujib, this reserve was established for the captive breeding of the Nubian ibex, and supports a variety of flora and fauna, including Syrian wolves, striped hyenas, caracals and Blandford's fox.

⑦

Karak Castle

The Levant is dotted with crusader castles. Karak Castle, commanding the semi-arid hills above the King's Highway, is the most atmospheric. Reconstruction and excavation work is ongoing: bring a torch (flashlight).

⑧

Qasr Kharana

The plains of eastern Jordan are home to the 'desert castles': early Umayyad pleasure palaces, bathhouses and hunting lodges. Qasr Kharana is the most photogenic. A painted inscription mentions AD 710, making it one of the earliest forts of the Islamic era.

⑨

The Red Sea

The Red Sea is home to some of the most beautiful underwater seascapes in the world: pristine reefs, crumbling wrecks and kaleidoscopic coral gardens. Snorkelling and diving can be arranged through dive centres around the lively seaside city of Aqaba.

⑩

Amman

Feel the pulse of modern Jordan than in Amman with its international restaurants, trendsetting nightlife and fashionable shopping. But don't sleep through the capital's historic treasures, including fine Roman ruins and the excellent Jordan Museum.

7-day itinerary
Footsteps of Kings

This route follows the ancient caravan route of the King's Highway. Begin in modern Jordan in the souqs of **Amman**. On day two, piece together a biblical history in **Madaba** and, like Moses, survey the Promised Land from **Mt Nebo**. Spend day three following the King's Highway, visiting the Crusader castles in **Karak** and **Shobak**. Rise early on day four to experience the Siq at **Petra** and climb to a High Place for lunch. On day five, attempt the back trail to Petra and watch the sunset at Petra's Monastery. Proceed to seaside **Aqaba**, and wash off the desert dust in the Red Sea before returning to Amman (via the Desert Highway) on day seven; with an early start, a desert lunch is possible at **Wadi Rum** en route.

14-day itinerary
Border to Border

This 14-day route assumes entry by ferry from Egypt and exit by bus to Israel. Check travel advisories as the security situation is changeable. Begin by exploring **Aqaba**'s souqs and snorkelling in the **Red Sea**, then go in search of 'El Lawrence' in magnificent **Wadi Rum**. Catch the minibus to **Petra**, factoring in a hike to the High Places and at least one sunset. Head north to **Amman** on a Desert Highway bus; don't miss the Roman ruins and citadel. Take an overnight trip to **Azraq Fort**, Lawrence's winter hideout. Nearby **Azraq Wetland Reserve** is a miraculous oasis surrounded by the black Badia (stone desert). Move on to the Roman ruins of **Jerash**, followed by a visit to **Ajloun**'s crumbling castle and nature reserve. Thanks to the Al Ayoun Trail and village homestays, Ajloun also offers a rare chance to really engage with rural life in the Middle East. Travel up to peaceful **Umm Qais** for a spot of basket weaving before heading along the **Jordan Valley** to the border with Israel and the Palestinian Territories where the journey ends.

© Tom Mackie / Lonely Planet

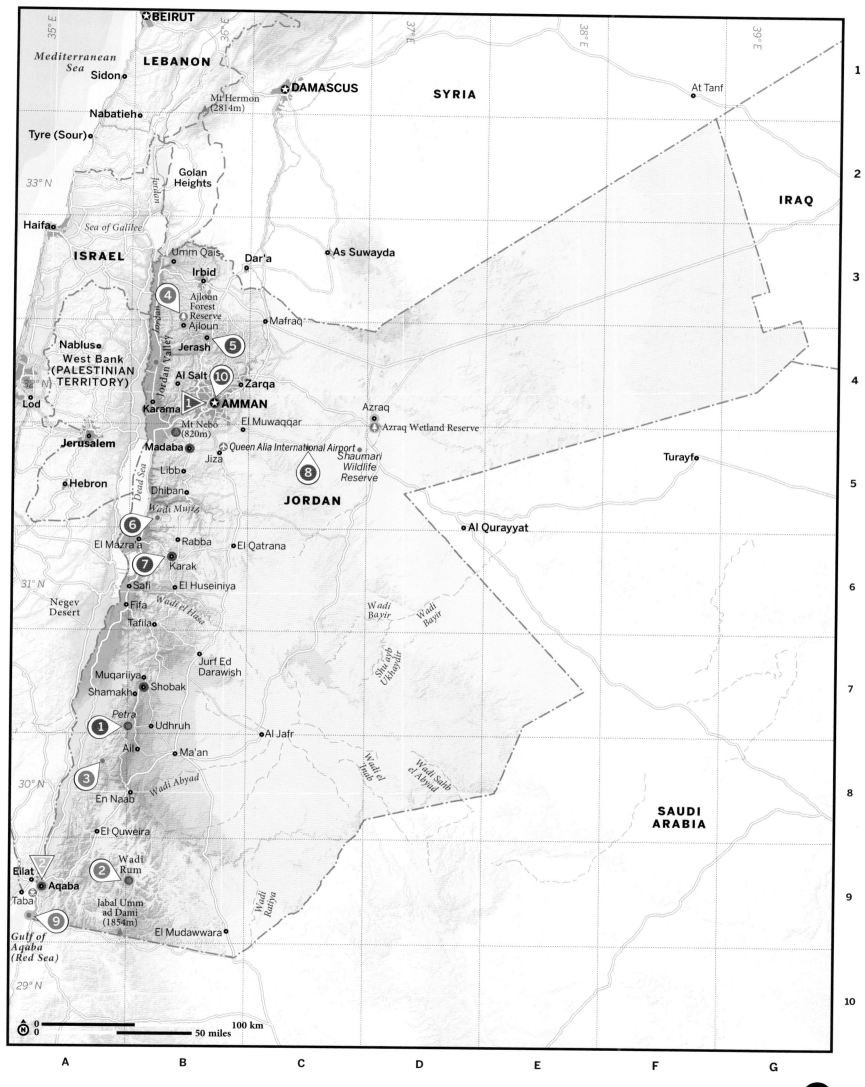

Mediterranean
Sea

35° E

BEIRUT

LEBANON

36° E

DAMASCUS

37° E

SYRIA

38° E

39° E

At Tanf

1

Sidon

Nabatieh

Mt Hermon
(2814m)

33° N

Tyre (Sour)

IRAQ

2

Golan
Heights

Haifa

Sea of Galilee

Umm Qais

Dar'a

As Suwayda

Irbid

3

ISRAEL

4

Ajloun
Forest
Reserve

Ajloun

Mafraq

Nablus

West Bank
(PALESTINIAN
TERRITORY)

Jerash

5

32° N

Al Salt

10

Zarqa

4

Lod

Karama

1

AMMAN

Azraq

Jordan Valley

Jordan

Mt Nebo
(820m)

El Muwaqqar

Azraq Wetland Reserve

Jerusalem

Madaba

Queen Alia International Airport

Turayf

Hebron

Libb

Jiza

Shaumari
Wildlife
Reserve

5

Dhiban

8

Wadi Mujib

JORDAN

Dead Sea

6

Rabba

El Qatrana

El Mazra'a

7

Karak

Al Qurayyat

Negev
Desert

Safi

El Huseiniya

31° N

Fifa

6

Wadi el Hasa

Tafila

Wadi
Bayir

Wadi
Bayir

Jurf Ed
Darawish

Muqariiya

Shobak

Shu'ayb
U'khaydir

Shamakh

7

Petra

1

Udhruh

Ail

Al Jafr

Ma'an

3

Wadi Abyad

Wadi el
Naab

Wadi Sahb
el Abyad

30° N

En Naab

8

El Quweira

SAUDI
ARABIA

Eilat

2

Wadi
Rum

2

Aqaba

Wadi
Ratiya

Taba

Jabal Umm
ad Dami
(1854m)

9

9

El Mudawwara

Gulf of
Aqaba
(Red Sea)

29° N

N

0

0

100 km

50 miles

A   B   C   D   E   F   G

SIGHTS &
ACTIVITIES

 SEE

 DO

ITINERARY

▽ 1

▽ 2

① Tehran

The capital's museums and palaces provide great insights into Iran's past, but don't miss the city's hip cafes and contemporary art galleries. Even government-sponsored institutions such as the Iran Holy Defense Museum and Qsar Garden Museum make inventive use of contemporary art.

② Naqsh-e Jahan Square, Esfahan

This square is home to perhaps the most majestic collection of buildings in the Islamic world: the perfectly proportioned blue-tiled dome of the Masjed-e Shah, the supremely elegant Masjed-e Sheikh Lotfollah and the indulgent and lavishly decorated Ali Qapu Palace. The square and the nearby teahouses throng with life.

③ Persepolis

Persepolis is Iran's premier ancient city. Built by kings Darius and Xerxes as the ceremonial capital of the Achaemenid empire, a visit to the World Heritage-listed ruins testifies to Alexander the Great's merciless destruction of that empire. Don't miss the monolithic tombs at nearby Naqsh-e Rostam.

④ Tabriz

Tabriz' historical heritage and Silk Road pedigree is evident in the World Heritage–listed Bazar-e Tabriz, the world's largest covered bazaar, and the Blue Mosque, which was constructed for ruler Jahan Shah in 1465. It was once famous for its intricate turquoise mosaics, but was badly damaged in an earthquake in 1773.

⑤ Mashhad

Imam Reza's Holy Shrine is enveloped in a vast series of sacred precincts collectively known as the Haram-e Razavi, or Haram for short. This magical city-within-a-city sprouts dazzling clusters of domes and minarets in blue and pure gold behind fountain-cooled courtyards and magnificent arched arcades.

⑥ Alborz Mountains

Iran has more than 20 ski fields and most of the action is conveniently concentrated around Tehran. The Dizin and Shemshak resorts are the picks too.

⑦ Alamut Valley

The Alamut Valley is home to the fabled Castles of the Assassins. Nestled on knolls and pinnacles lie the remnants of more than 50 ruined fortresses, once the lairs of the medieval world's most feared religious cult.

⑧ Garmeh

Surrounded by date palms clustered around a small warm-water spring clouded with fish, Garmeh is the classic desert oasis. The 1500-year-old mud-brick village is a base for camel treks and hikes to local hot-water springs and mountain villages.

⑨ Mt Damavand

At 5671m, the dormant volcano of Mt Damavand is the Middle East's highest mountain and appears on the IR10,000 note. The main climbing season is from June to September, or May to October for experienced climbers.

⑩ Yazd

A desert gem of winding lanes, blue-tiled domes, soaring minarets, covered bazaars and old courtyard homes topped by *badgirs* (windtowers) and watered by *qanats* (underground water channels). Many of these have been converted into evocative hotels.

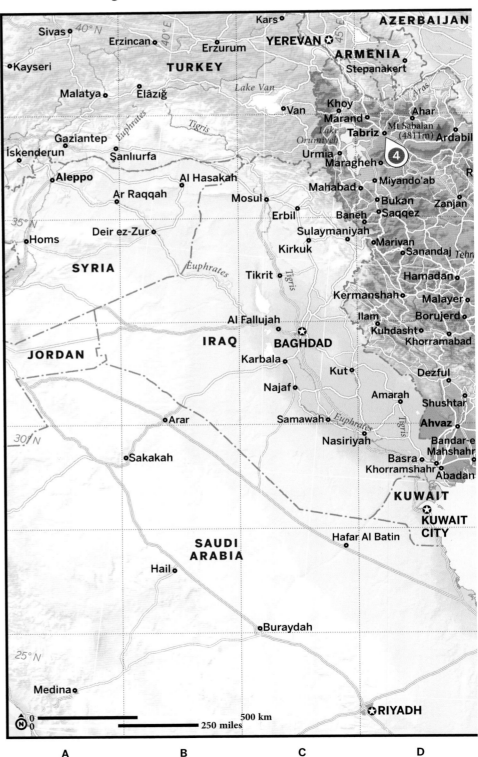

14-day itinerary
Classic Iran

Two weeks is just enough time to see the jewels of Iran's rich history. Start in **Tehran** with two days visiting the Golestan Palace, the Treasury of National Jewels and Tehran Bazaar. Take a bus to **Kashan**, where you can explore the bazaar, view Qajar-era houses and chill out in the Bagh-e Fin garden. Stop to check out the mosque in **Natanz** en route to **Esfahan** and its wonderful mosques and bazaars. Head to the desert trading city of **Yazd** to wander the maze of lanes and climb to the Zoroastrian Towers of Silence. Stop in the desert village of **Fahraj** before visiting ancient **Pasargadae** and **Persepolis**. Spend two days in **Shiraz** to see the Zand-era gardens, bazaar and old city. From here, fly back to Tehran.

12-day itinerary
Desert Detour

If you've ever dreamt of the oasis towns of *The Thousand and One Nights*, this trip is for you. It's doable by taking infrequent buses, but the odd taxi *dar bast* (private) can reduce waiting time. Avoid the summer heat by travelling between October and April. Start in **Esfahan** and take a bus to Toudeshk for a night and a morning in the shifting sands of the **Varzaneh Desert**, before continuing to see the traditional houses of **Na'in**. Then take the bus east to Khur, where you get a taxi to **Farahzad** and/or **Garmeh** for desert homestays that redefine hospitality; plan for three days. From Garmeh, head east via Tabas and the remarkable 'forgotten' villages of **Old Deyhuk** and **Esfandiar**, continuing on to **Birjand** with its impressive fortress-restaurant. From there don't miss an oasis night at **Deh Salm** before crossing the **Lut Desert** with its extraordinary Kaluts (giant 'sandcastles'). After some bazaar browsing in **Kerman** and a daytrip to **Rayen Fortress**, end your trip in a traditional hotel in **Yazd**, perhaps with a side trip to the Zoroastrian fire temple at **Chak Chak**.

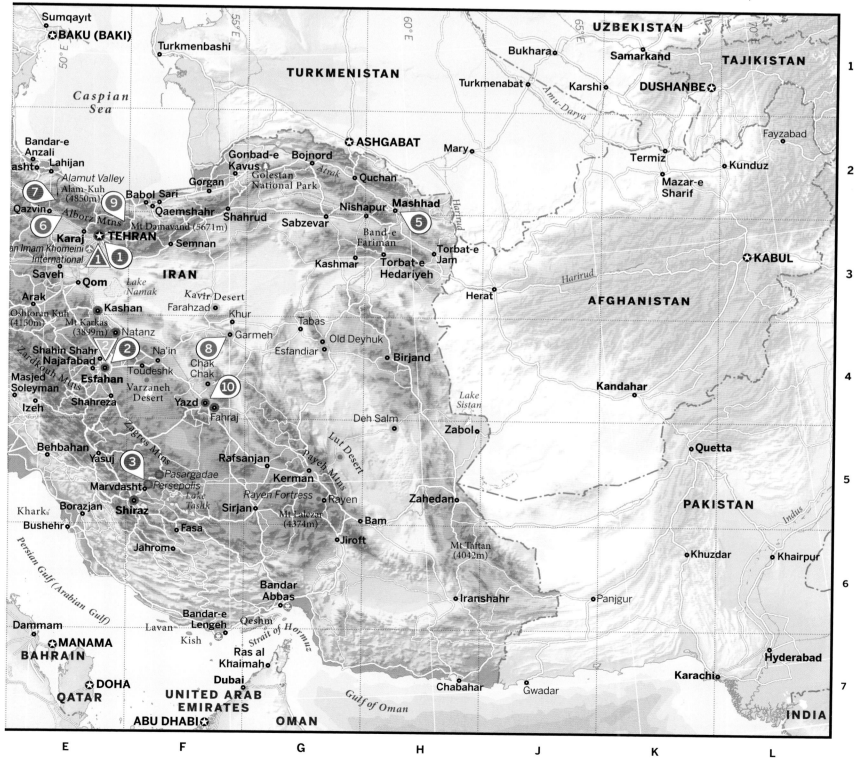

SIGHTS &
ACTIVITIES

 SEE

 DO

ITINERARY

 1

▽ 2

 1

Burj Khalifa, Dubai
Slicing through Dubai's superhighways, the Burj Khalifa is shaped like a deep-space rocket and at 828m is the world's tallest building. Clad in 28,000 glass panels, it also features the highest outdoor observation deck, the most floors, the highest occupied floor and a lift (elevator) with the longest travel distance. The building was opened in January 2010.

 2

Abu Dhabi
The world's largest hand-loomed carpet, the fastest rollercoaster, the highest high tea, the tower with the greatest lean, the largest cluster of cultural buildings of the 21st century – UAE capital Abu Dhabi isn't afraid to challenge world records. Don't miss the Sheikh Zayed Grand Mosque and and the high-octane Ferrari World.

 3

Liwa Oasis
Approximately 250km south of Abu Dhabi, the Liwa Oasis is a 150km arc of villages and farms hugging the edge of Saudi Arabia's Empty Quarter (Rub' al Khali), an endless landscape of undulating sand dunes, shimmering in shades of gold, apricot and cinnamon. The dunes here are like shifting mountain ranges of sand, with green farms creating an occasional and unexpected patchwork effect.

 ▽

7-day itinerary
Dubai to Al Ain

If you're a first-timer in the UAE, especially if your time is short, it makes sense to base yourself in downtown **Dubai**. Spend day one checking off the iconic sights on a bus tour, then head up to the Burj Khalifa at sunset for what has to be one of the world's most mindblowing human-made views. If time allows, it's worth doing some shopping around Dubai Mall. The next day, take a cab to **Sharjah** for a glimpse into the UAE's past in the Heritage Area, stocking up on souvenirs at the Central Souq and enjoying dinner at a local restaurant. From Sharjah, head south to the UAE's second city, **Abu Dhabi,** to marvel at the Sheikh Zayed Grand Mosque, zoom around the motorhead temple of Ferrari World and learn about the new Cultural District on Saadiyat Island. For contrast, make for the desert next to face a huge dune, magical silence and plenty of camels, preferably on an overnight trip. Wrap up with a day in **Al Ain** and its zoo and Unesco–recognised heritage sites.

 4

Al Ain
The birthplace of the United Arab Emirates' founding father Sheikh Zayed was once a vital stop on the caravan route between Oman and the Gulf. Nowadays visitors flock to its forts, museums, zoo and one of the UAE's last camel markets.

 5

Jebel Jais
At 1934m, Jebel Jais is the highest peak in the UAE. Since 2015 a mountain road has corkscrewed almost to the top, delivering great visual drama: eroded cliffs, deep canyons and warped escarpments around nearly every bend.

 6

Al Wathba Race Track
Sporting colourful nosebags and matching blankets, camels are the stars at the Al Wathba Race Track, 45km southeast of Abu Dhabi. Owners often drive alongside the track cheering their beloved animals along.

 7

Museum of Islamic Civilization, Sharjah
Everything about Islam is addressed in this museum in a converted souq on Sharjah's waterfront. Galleries explore different aspects of the Islamic faith, including the ritual of the hajj, scientific accomplishments and 1400 years of Islamic art and artefacts.

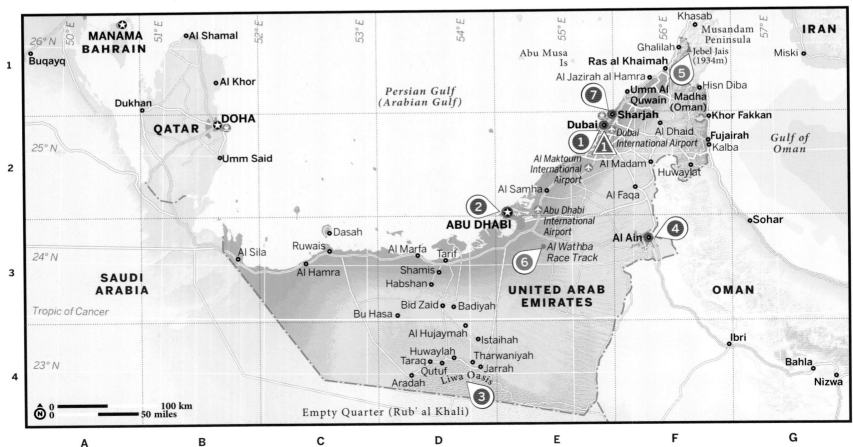

Jebel Shams

Oman's highest mountain, Jebel Shams (Mountain of the Sun; 3009m), is best known for the view into the deep Wadi Ghul, the Grand Canyon of Arabia, with vertical cliffs of 1000m and more. At the top, you can haggle with carpet sellers for a goat-hair rug. Weaving is men's work on Jebel Shams: spinning the wool is women's responsibility.

Bahla Fort

One of the most comprehensive walled cities in the world, Bahla's walls extend for several kilometres and are said to have been designed 600 years ago by a woman. Part and parcel of the battlements is the impressive fort, built by the Bani Nebhan tribe who were dominant from the 12th to the 15th centuries. After many years of painstaking restoration, the site was granted Unesco World Heritage Site status in 1987.

Sharqiya (Wahiba) Sands

These dunes are home to the Bedu, who still practise their traditional nomadic lifestyle. Bedouin women wear elaborate costumes with peaked masks and an *abeyya* (full-length robe) of gauze. Accommodation takes the form of tented or *barasti* camps that offer the full desert experience.

14-day itinerary
Iconic Oman

Begin with a mountain tour in the old city of **Nizwa**. Climb the beanstalk to **Jebel Akhdar**, famed for giant pomegranates and hailstones. Hike the rim of Oman's Grand Canyon for a spot of carpet-buying on **Jebel Shams**. Engage with *jinn* (genies) at the remarkable tombs and forts of **Bat**, **Bahla** and **Jabrin**. Take the scenic route to Muscat via a dizzying mountain drive to **Rustaq**, and wash the dust off in the sparkling sea at **Sawadi**. Once in **Muscat**, rise with the dawn to see fishermen bring in the weird and wonderful at **Mutrah**'s fish market. Join the ebb and flow of the city's residents by strolling the corniche, then duck under the overhanging balconies into Mutrah Souq to lose your way among the pink, plastic and implausible. Spare an hour for the sights of Muscat proper, the walled heart of the capital, before relaxing in one of the city's spa resorts.

Ras al Jinz

Ras al Jinz (Ras al Junayz), the easternmost point of the Arabian Peninsula, is an important turtle-nesting site for the endangered green turtle. Over 20,000 females return annually to the beach where they hatched in order to lay their eggs.

Musandam Peninsula

Guarding the southern side of the strategically important Strait of Hormuz, the Musandam Peninsula is dubbed the 'Norway of Arabia' for its beautiful khors (rocky inlets), small villages and mountain-hugging roads.

Mutrah Souq

Mutrah's celebrated souq retains the chaotic interest of a traditional Arab market, albeit under modern timber roofing. Shops selling Omani and Indian artefacts jostle among textile, hardware and jewellery stores.

Masirah

With its palm oases and sandy beaches, Masirah is the typical desert island. Flamingos, herons and oyster-catchers patrol the coast by day, and ghost crabs march ashore at night. The island is home to a rare shell, the Eloise, and large turtle-nesting sites.

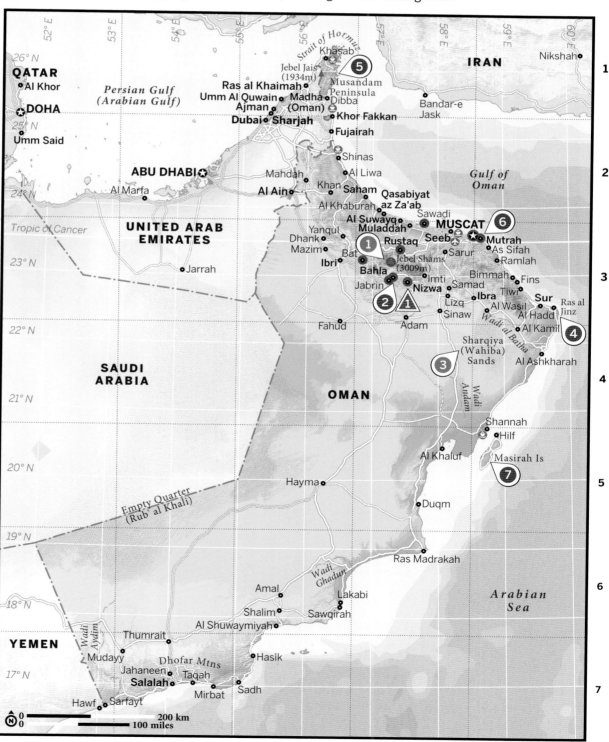

Northern Africa

The northern half of the great continent of Africa is as diverse as any region on the planet, with landscapes climbing from the sandy shores of the Mediterranean and West Africa to the high-altitude peaks of the Atlas and Simien Mountains. And in between it all? The vastness of the mighty Sahara Desert, some nine million sq km in size alone. Northern Africa's culture and history are no less compelling – explore Egypt's pyramids, North Africa's many Roman ruins, Ethiopia's rock-hewn churches and Île de Gorée's sobering Maison des Esclaves in Senegal. Or stay in the present, soaking up the atmosphere in frenetic markets, squares and music festivals. And you'd be wrong to think Africa's famed wildlife is limited to its south and east.

CLIMATE CHART

CAIRO

RAINFALL
INCH/MM
8/200
6/150
4/100
2/50
0

D N O S A J J M A M F J

TEMP
°C/F
50/122
40/104
30/86
20/68
10/50
0/32

MARRAKESH

RAINFALL
INCH/MM
8/200
6/150
4/100
2/50
0

D N O S A J J M A M F J

TEMP
°C/F
40/104
30/86
20/68
10/50
0/32

HISTORY
Pharaohs, Romans and colonial slave traders have all left their mark, but so have ancient sub-Saharan empires that ruled over vast tracts of this region and grew rich by trading widely in gold and salt: the ancient empires of Songhaï, Mali, Ghana, Aksum, Egypt and Ethiopia to name but a few.

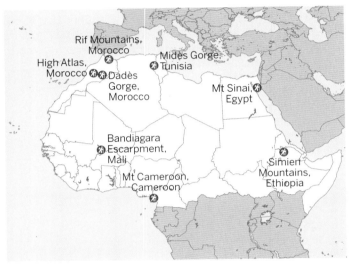

TREKKING
Trails – some new, some age-old – criss-cross stunning landscapes: the High Atlas, Rif Mountains and Dadès Gorge in Morocco; Midès Gorge in Tunisia; Mt Sinai in Egypt; the Simien Mountains in Ethiopia; the Bandiagara Escarpment in Mali; and Cameroon's Mt Cameroon among others.

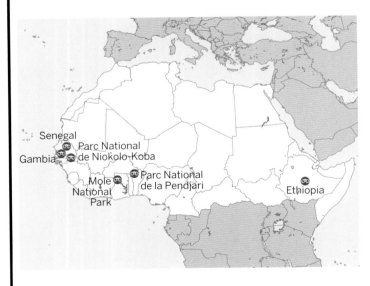

WILDLIFE
Elephants and other safari species roam Ghana's Mole National Park, Senegal's Parc National de Niokolo-Koba, Chad's Zakouma National Park and Benin's Parc National de la Pendjari. The latter is also known for its big cats. Birdlife is particularly prolific in Senegal, the Gambia and Ethiopia.

CULTURE
Perhaps more than anything else, it's this region's people and the richness of their culture that are its greatest asset: the enigmatic tribes of the Omo Valley; the welcoming Berbers in North Africa; the intriguing Dogon people of Mali; and the nomadic Tuareg in the Sahara.

Right: Cross shaped Bet Giyorgis church in Lalibela, Ethiopia.

Transport hubs

Northern Africa can be accessed by air, sea and land. Airports in Cairo, Casablanca, Lagos and Addis Ababa are the main air hubs, though it's possible to fly into most capital cities directly from Europe. Ferries link Egypt with Jordan, and Morocco (and North Africa's Spanish enclaves of Ceuta and Melilla) with southern Europe. Once landed, there are innumerable ground transport options between cities, regions and countries, including some to Central and East Africa.

ELEVATION KEY

7500-10000M
5000-7500M
3000-5000M
2000-3000M
1500-2000M
1250-1500M
1000-1250M
750-1000M
500-750M
250-500M
100-250M
75-100M
50-75M
25-50M
1-25M

TRANSPORT

A5, C2, C6,
D6, G3, H6

A5, B5, C2,
D2, E2, G3,
G4

① Cairo

Cairo is chaos at its most magnificent, infuriating and beautiful. This mega-city's constant buzz and noise is a product of its 22-or-so million inhabitants. Car horns bellow tuneless symphonies amid avenues of faded 19th-century grandeur, while donkey carts rattle down dusty lanes lined with colossal Fatimid and Mamluk monuments. Towering over it all are the Pyramids of Giza. Cairo International Airport is the country's main entry point and is served by most international carriers.

② Casablanca

Casablanca is the best representation of modern Morocco. This is where money is being made, where young Moroccans come to seek their fortunes. Mohammed V International Airport is 30km southeast of the city. Regular flights leave to most countries in Western Europe, as well as to West Africa, North Africa, the Middle East and North America.

③ Lagos

The economic and cultural powerhouse of Nigeria thanks to an influx of oil money, Lagos has an exploding arts and music scene. If you're headed to Nigeria, you'll have no choice but to jump right in. Murtala Muhammed International Airport is roughly 10km north of the city and is well linked throughout the continent.

④ Addis Ababa

Since its establishment in the late 19th century, Addis Ababa has always seemed like a magical portal, a gateway to another world. Bole International Airport, on the south side of the city has flight links across Europe, Africa, the Middle East and the Americas.

⑤ Dakar

Dakar is a city of extremes, where horse-cart drivers judder over swish highways and gleaming SUVs squeeze through tiny sand roads; where elegant ladies dig skinny heels into dusty walkways and suit-clad businessmen kneel down for prayer in the street. The city's new Aéroport International Blaise Diagne, some 50km southeast of the city, has been a decade in making.

⑥ Accra

Ghana's beating heart probably won't inspire love letters, but you might just grow to like it. The capital's hot, sticky streets are perfumed with sweat, fumes and yesterday's cooking oil. Kotoka International Airport, just 5km north of the ring road, is the main international gateway to the country.

⑦ Douala

Sticky and frenetic, it's not likely to be your first choice for a honeymoon. But by any measurement but political power this is Cameroon's main city. It's the primary air hub and a leading business centre with a major port.

⑧ Tangier

Guarding the Strait of Gibraltar, Tangier has for centuries been Europe's gateway to Africa. Its blend of cultures and influences is still unique but cultural life is buzzing here in a way it hasn't done since the 1950s. Numerous daily ferries serve Spain from Tangier Port in town and Tanger Med terminal, which is 48km east (linked by bus).

⑨ Nuweiba

Nuweiba lacks a defined centre or cohesive ambience. It functions primarily as a port for ferries from Aqaba in Jordan.

Right: A bushbuck in Mole National Park, Ghana (left) and (right) Djemaa El Fna in Marrakesh.

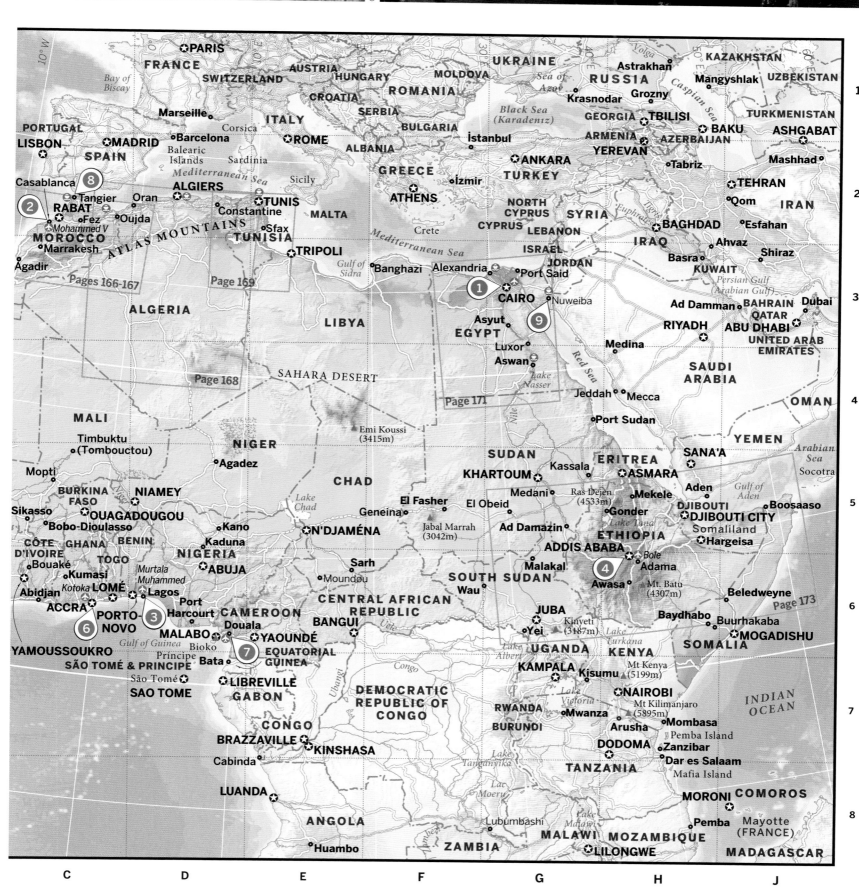

SIGHTS &
ACTIVITIES

 SEE

 DO

ITINERARY

▽ 1

▽ 2

Djemaa El Fna, Marrakesh
Dorothy and Toto had their Oz; Alice had her wonderland; and now you can experience the out-of-this-world pandemonium that is Djemaa El Fna. This chaotic hub is the heart and soul of Marrakesh, where snakes are charmed by day, music troupes shimmy and shake at night and visitors look on wide-eyed.

Essaouira
Essaouira's walled medina dates from the late 18th century. It is an outstanding and well-preserved example of European military architecture in North Africa. For the visitor, the lanes, souqs, street vendors, leafy plazas and whitewashed houses with ornate wooden doors make it a wonderfully charming place to stroll.

Fez
Fez's ancient medina can seem like it's in a state of perpetual mayhem, but its charms are many. Seemingly blind alleys lead to squares with exquisite fountains and streets bursting with aromatic food stands, rooftops unveil a sea of minarets, and stooped doorways reveal the workshops of tireless artisans.

Anti Atlas Mountains
The arid, pink- and ochre-coloured Anti Atlas are the last significant mountains before the Sahara and they offer some wonderful trekking. The quartzite massif of Jebel L'Kest lies about 10km north of Tafraoute, and the twin peaks of Adrar Mqorn are 10km southeast.

Volubilis
The Roman ruins of Volubilis sit in the middle of a fertile plain and its most amazing features are the many beautiful mosaics preserved in situ. The better-known monuments are in the northern part of the site, furthest from the entrance in the south. Incredibly, only about half of the 40-hectare site has been excavated.

Al-Hoceima
Quiet, safe, relaxing and hassle-free, this seaside resort is full of proud and genial Berbers and the town has a surprisingly independent outlook.

Dadès Gorge
The Dadès Gorge presents a dramatic landscape: ancient rust-red and mauve mountains stripped back to zigzagging layers of strata and knobbly rock formations. A rush of springtime water puddles in the valley where irrigation channels siphon it off to fields of wheat and orchards of fig, almond and olive trees. A series of crumbling kasbahs and *ksour* (castles) line the valley.

Hammam experience, Marrakesh
For an authentic Moroccan spa experience, head to one of Marrakesh's hammams for a steam and a scrub.

Erg Chigaga
Exploring the Sahara by camel – whether on an overnight excursion or a longer desert safari – is one of the desert's most rewarding wilderness experiences. Some of Morocco's most evocative stretches of Saharan sand are found around Erg Chigaga, near M'Hamid and Zagora.

Chefchaouen
Beautifully perched beneath the raw peaks of the Rif, Chefchaouen is one of the prettiest towns in Morocco, an artsy, blue-washed mountain village that feels like its own world.

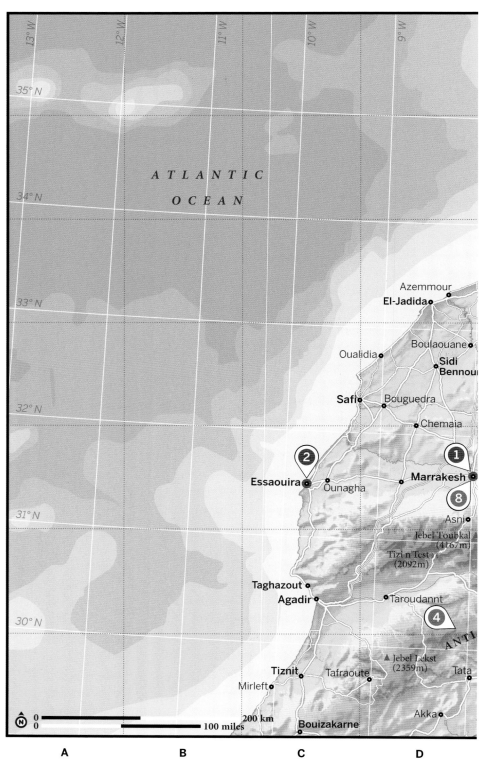

14-day itinerary
Essential Morocco

Touch down in **Casablanca**, the commercial capital with the stupendous Hassan II Mosque, then head by train to venerable **Fez**, with its ancient medina. Next, cross the Middle Atlas via **Midelt**, continuing all the way to **Merzouga**, Morocco's gateway to the Sahara. Saddle up your camel and sleep under the stars amid the perfectly

sculpted **Erg Chebbi**. Shadowing the High Atlas as you head west brings you to **Todra Gorge** for a day's hiking. From here, head past **Ouarzazate** to **Aït Benhaddou**, with its fairy-tale-like kasbah. En route to the artsy seaside medina and fishing port **Essaouira**, check into a riad in **Marrakesh** and spend as many sunsets as possible on Djemaa el-Fna.

14- to 21-day itinerary
The Med and the Mountains

Start in **Tangier**, ideally arriving by ferry across the Strait of Gibraltar to feel the thrill of passing from Europe to Africa. After a few days taking in the history, nightlife and restaurants, skip inland to **Tetouan**, the old capital of Spanish Morocco, with its charming blend of Arab medina and Andalucían architecture. The Spanish left a lighter imprint on nearby

Chefchaouen, nestled in the Rif Mountains with its gorgeous blue-painted medina. Head out on a multi-day trek if you fancy, via riverside **Akchour** to fishing village **Bou Ahmed**. Alternatively, continue east along the coast to the proud, modern seaside resort of **Al-Hoceima**, gateway to the dry canyons and limestone cliffs of the **Al-Hoceima**

National Park. Walk to the park along the coast, or do some hiking and mountain biking. There's more fine scenery in the verdant Beni-Snassen Mountains, with their gorges, caves, mesa and Barbary sheep. In the **Zegzel Gorge**, pluck a cumquat and see why the Romans remarked on this small citrus fruit. From here, head to **Oujda** to refresh yourself before finishing in Fez.

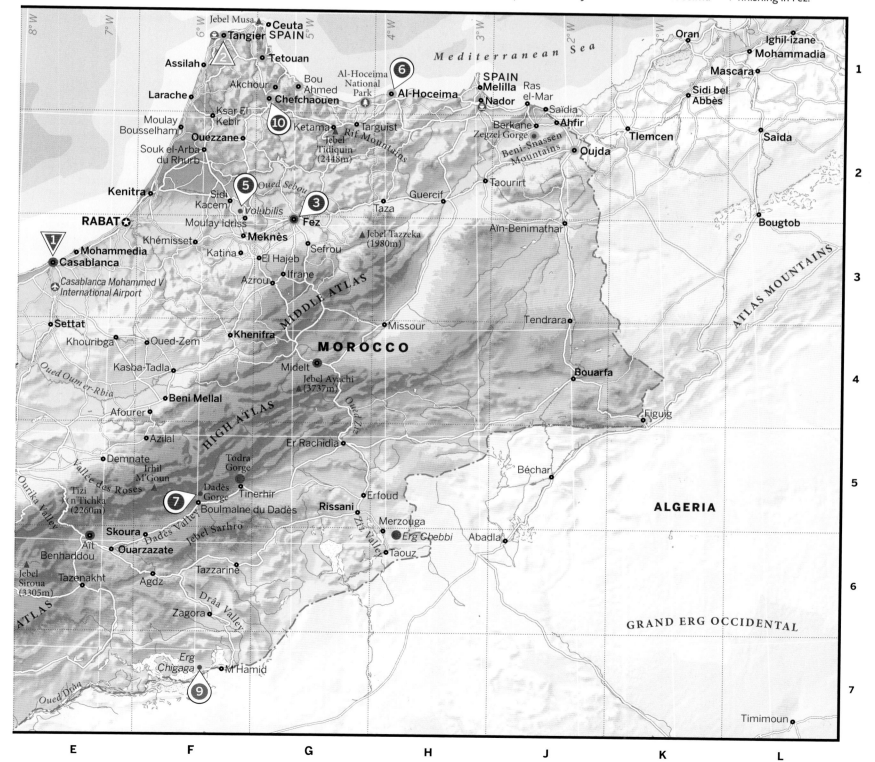

Algiers

The heart of Algiers is its ancient Casbah, a steep and narrow maze of streets just west of the Place des Martyrs. There are several magnificent Ottoman palaces to explore here, most concentrated around the Djemaa Ketchoua at the end of Rue Ahmed Bouzrina; the finest is the Dar Hassan Pacha.

Timimoun

The largest oasis in the Grand Erg Occidental, the dusty desert city of Timimoun is an enchanting place. Its characteristic architecture, red-mud buildings studded with spikes, hints at sub-Saharan Africa. The main street bustles in the morning and evening; the locals are a diverse mix that includes Haratines, Berbers and the descendants of Malian merchants and slaves. It's also the base for the Sebkha Circuit, a 75km to 90km drive that takes in the dunes of the Grand Erg Occidental.

Djemila

The spectacular ruined Roman town of Djemila is one of the world's great archaeological sites. Linger in the temples and markets, stroll through the bath chambers, or just lie down in the shade of villa walls and conjure up the sounds of those long gone days.

Ghardaïa

Ghardaïa is one of five towns clustered within the river valley of the M'Zab, which skirts the edge of the Sahara. Peek at the pristine medieval town, bargain for a boldly patterned carpet in the main square and then swim in the shade of date palms.

Timgad

One of the finest Roman sites in existence, these ruins stretch almost as far as the eye can see. Its preservation is incredible – take the time to walk around slowly, inhabit the place and Timgad will spring to life. The original Roman town was designed as a perfect square, 355m long on each side.

Tlemcen

Tlemcen, a former Islamic capital, close to the (closed) border of Morocco, is one of the most beautiful towns in Algeria. With its sand-red old city walls, elegant minarets and palaces filled with graceful arches and Moorish atmosphere, Tlemcen looks like the love child of Marrakesh and Cordoba – without the other tourists. Buildings of note include: the Grand Mosque, one of North Africa's most important Islamic buildings; the 12th-century citadel of Mechouar; and the mosque and tomb of Sidi Boumediene, which is one of Algeria's most beautiful complexes and a place of huge spiritual significance for Algerians.

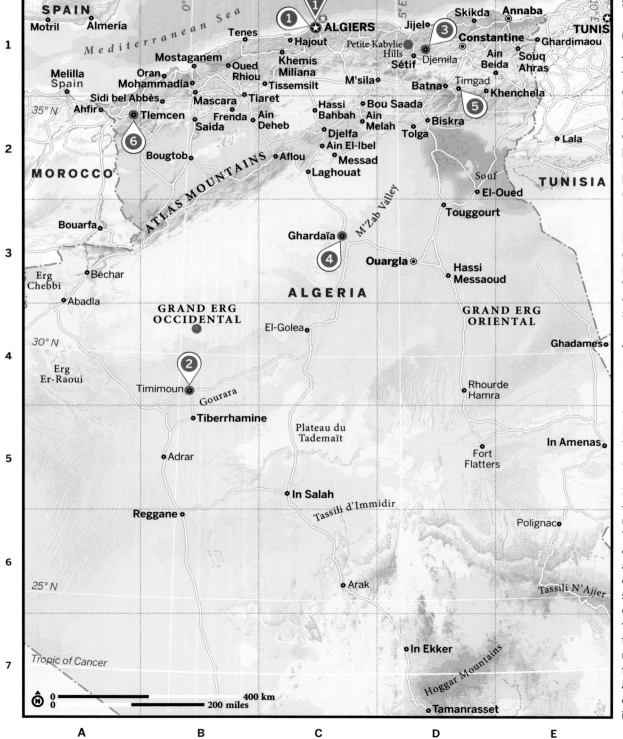

▽

7- to 10-day itinerary
The Best of Algeria

Start in **Algiers** – it never fails to make an impact. The capital is a city of rare beauty and of thrilling, disorientating and sometimes brutal contrast. Next, travel to **Djemila** for its incredible ruins, which are all that remains of the ancient Roman town of Cuicul. Tucked into the handsome **Petite Kabylie** hills, it is one of the most perfect expressions of the meeting of Roman power and African beauty. Continue into the Oued M'Zab river valley to see the medieval town of **Ghardaïa**. Get a taste of the Sahara from Timimoun, where trips into the Grand Erg Occidental are possible. Stop in **Tlemcen**, a former Islamic capital that is rich in architecture and one of Algeria's most striking towns, before returning to Algiers.

Ksar Haddada

Marvel at the maze of small alleyways and courtyards in this former *ksar* (castle) – a place of pilgrimage for Star Wars fans following its appearance in *Star Wars I: The Phantom Menace*.

Midès

The dramatic Midès Gorge, used as a setting for many movies such as *The English Patient*, makes for a rewarding 4.5km trek between Tamerza and the oasis village of Midès. If you'd rather let your eyes do the walking, the views down into the rocky depths from the latter are stunning.

Carthage

The ancient Punic and Roman site of Carthage lies over a wide area northeast of Tunis. Wander the vestiges of Roman baths, houses, cisterns, basilicas and streets, before listening to live music in the open-air Roman theatre by night.

Sidi Bou Saïd

With cascading bougainvillea and geraniums against gleaming whitewash, bright-blue window grills, cobbled streets, Ottoman and the Andalusian architecture and glimpses of coast, the cliff-top village of Sidi Bou Saïd is one of Tunisia's prettiest spots. Previous visitors include Paul Klee, Edith Sitwell and André Gide.

Mahdia

Occupying a narrow peninsula jutting out into the Mediterranean, Mahdia is blessed with a spectacular setting and a wonderful old-world charm. A walk anywhere along Ave 7 Novembre or Rue du Borj, both of which hug the narrow peninsula, offers wonderful views of the shimmering Mediterranean.

Djerba

The small island of Djerba is fringed with soft, sandy beaches and warm Mediterranean waters. The charms also abound inland – you'll find a warren of shops selling every imaginable handicraft; a maze of cobbled streets; and a history of ethnic and religious diversity more pronounced than in the rest of the country.

Tunis

This sprawling maze of ancient streets and alleyways is a national treasure. It's home to numerous cave-like souqs selling everything from shoes to shisha pipes, as well as lavishly tiled cafes, backstreets full of artisans at work, and residential areas punctuated by grand, brightly painted doorways. The beach is never far away as the suburbs stretch out along deep-blue seafronts.

14-day itinerary
Mosques, Medinas and a Colosseum

Begin in **Tunis**, Tunisia's laid-back, cosmopolitan capital. Day trip to ancient **Carthage** and the enchanting whitewashed village of **Sidi Bou Saïd**. Next head south to **Sousse**, where the buzzing Ville Nouvelle stretches along the popular beach, and the sandcastle medina contains some of Tunisia's finest architecture. From here you can visit **Monastir**, with its superb *ribat* (fort) and mausoleum to Habib Bourguiba; the mystical holy city of Kairouan; and the amazingly well-preserved Roman colosseum towering over El Jem. It's worth staying at least overnight in **Mahdia**, the perfect antidote to busy resorts and towns. Further down the coast, **Sfax** has Tunisia's best-preserved medina.

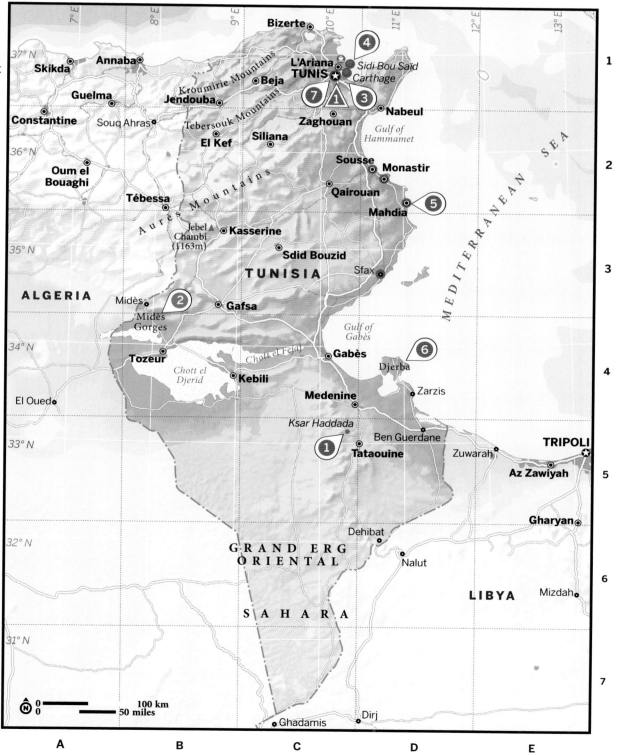

SIGHTS & ACTIVITIES

- SEE
- DO

ITINERARY

▽ 1
▽ 2

1. Pyramids of Giza, Cairo

The last remaining wonder of the ancient world; for nearly 4000 years, the extraordinary shape, impeccable geometry and sheer bulk of the Giza Pyramids have endured the shifting sands and the test of time. Built as massive tombs on the orders of the pharaohs, they were constructed by teams of workers tens-of-thousands strong.

2. Egyptian Museum, Cairo

One of the world's most important collections of ancient artefacts, the Egyptian Museum holds the glittering treasures of Tutankhamun and other great pharaohs. You'll also find grave goods, mummies, jewellery, eating bowls and toys of Egyptians whose names are lost to history. To walk around the museum is to embark on an adventure through time.

3. Nile River, Aswan

There are few things more relaxing than hiring a felucca boat in Aswan before sunset and sailing between the islands, the desert and the huge black boulders, listening to the flapping of a sail and to Nubian boys singing from tiny dugouts.

4. Abu Simbel temple complex

The Great Temple of Ramses II and the Temple of Hathor, which make up this complex, are among the most spectacular monuments in Egypt. In a modern marvel of engineering, the structure was moved lock, stock and barrel to the position it sits upon today during the High Dam construction.

Siwa Oasis: Temple of the Oracle (left) amongst ruined mud buildings.

5. Temples of Luxor

Luxor is often called the world's greatest open-air museum, but that doesn't do justice to this extraordinary place. Nothing in the world compares to the scale and grandeur of the monuments that have survived from ancient Thebes.

6. White Desert National Park

Upon first glimpse of the 300-sq-km national park, you'll feel like Alice through the looking glass. Walk through the blinding-white chalk rock spires that sprout almost supernaturally from the ground, each frost-coloured lollipop licked into a surreal landscape of familiar and unfamiliar shapes by the dry desert winds.

7. Dahab

Enjoy some of the planet's most spectacular diving and snorkelling by plunging into the Red Sea off the Sinai Peninsula (based out of the dive town of Dahab). Descend into the depths of the infamous Blue Hole, a gaping sinkhole in the reef that drops straight down – some say as far as 130m. Other incredible dive sites for aquatic treasures nearby include the Canyon, Eel Garden, Bells, Gabr El Bint and Lighthouse Reef.

8. Siwa Oasis

Even though there are some fascinating sights hidden in the dense palm greenery of this oasis, Siwa's main attraction is its serene atmosphere. Siwa is different from Egypt's other oases, more remote, more relaxed and more beautiful. Hang out with Siwans, have a picnic, ride a donkey cart, explore the dunes by 4WD and soak it all up.

9. Mt Sinai

Rising up out of the desert and jutting above the other peaks surrounding St Katherine's monastery is the 2285m Mt Sinai. Known locally as Gebel Musa, the mountain is revered by Christians, Muslims and Jews, all of whom believe that God delivered his Ten Commandments to Moses at its summit. The mountain is easy and beautiful to climb, and offers a taste of the magnificence of southern Sinai's high mountain region.

10. Alexandria

Founded in 331 BC by Alexander the Great, this city is the stuff of legend. Its towering Pharos lighthouse, marking the ancient harbour's entrance, was one of the Seven Wonders of the World, and its Great Library was considered the archive of ancient knowledge. Alas, the Pharos collapsed and the Great Library was torched. Part of the ancient city disappeared under the sea and part under the modern city. Today the grand modern library of Alexandria sits amid faded remnants of the once-grand seafront Corniche, as a symbol of the city's latest incarnation as Egypt's cultural capital.

▽1 14-day itinerary
Treasures of the Nile

After seeing the Pyramids of Giza and the Egyptian Museum in **Cairo**, head south to **Luxor** to visit the Karnak and Luxor temples and the brilliant Luxor Museum, as well as strolling through the souq. Use the next few days to cycle around the west bank where the major sights include the Valley of the Kings, the Ramesseum and the Memorial Temple of Hatshepsut. Save some energy for less-visited sights such as Medinat Habu, the Tombs of the Nobles and Deir Al Medina. In the second week arrange sailing up the Nile to **Aswan** on a budget-friendly felucca or a luxurious *dahabiyya*. From Aswan you can visit the temples at **Abu Simbel**, perched on the edge of Lake Nasser.

▽2 14-day itinerary
Desert Escape

The Western Desert offers a wonderful mix of lush oasis gardens, stunning desert landscapes and interesting ancient monuments. Begin your trip with a bus from **Cairo** or **Asyut** to **Al Kharga Oasis**, and explore the Al Kharga Museum of Antiquities as well as the Graeco-Roman temples and tombs. From Al Kharga, head northwest to **Dakhla Oasis** to see the fascinating, hive-like mudbrick settlements of Balat and Al Qasr. Next, hop north to the small and quaint **Farafra Oasis**. From there you may be able to make a two- or three-day trip to camp in the stunning **White Desert National Park**, and then head for the closest oasis to Cairo, **Bahariya**. The desert road from Bahariya to **Siwa Oasis** may be closed, so you might have a long detour via Cairo. Worth the trouble? Certainly. Perched on the edge of the Great Sand Sea, and surrounded by some staggeringly beautiful desert, Siwa is renowned for its dates as well as for the Temple of the Oracle where Alexander the Great was declared son of the god Amun.

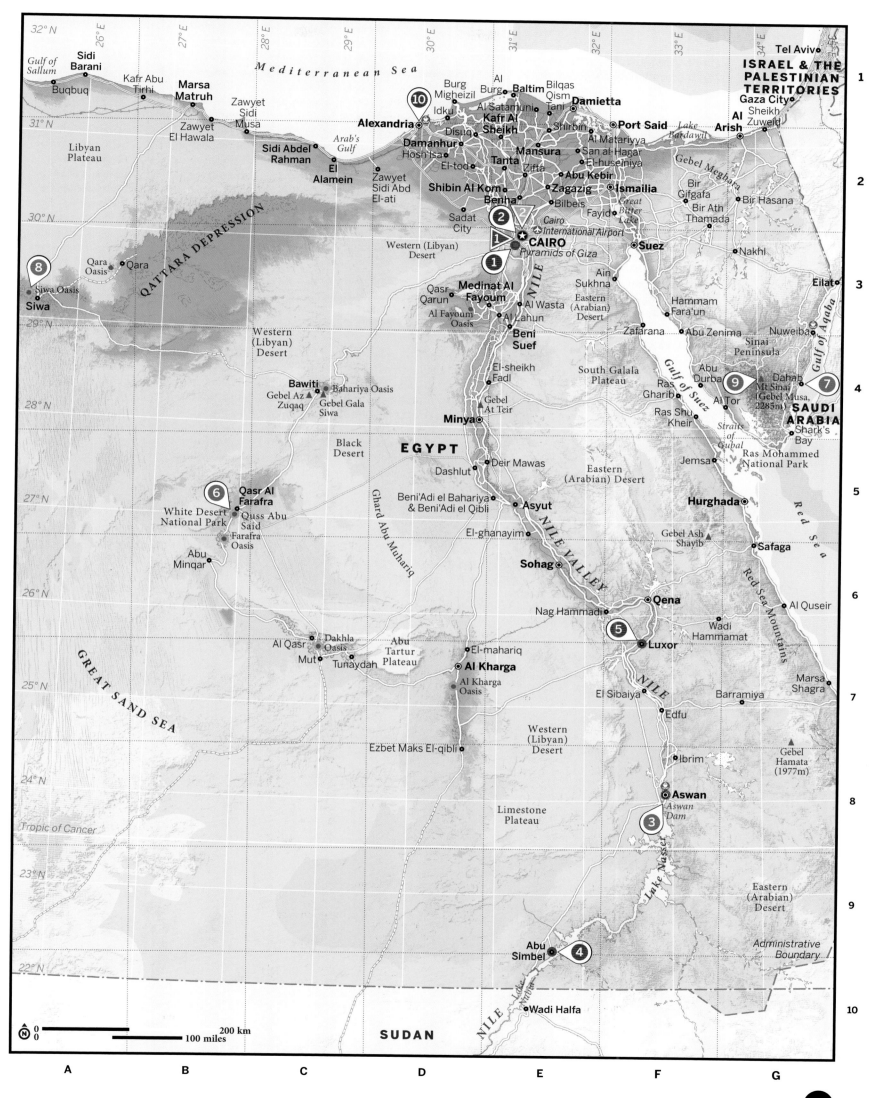

Mediterranean Sea

Gulf of Sallum

Sidi Barani

Buqbuq

Kafr Abu Tirhi

Marsa Matruh

Zawyet Sidi Musa

Zawyet El Hawala

Libyan Plateau

Sidi Abdel Rahman

El Alamein

Zawyet Sidi Abd El-ati

Arab's Gulf

Hosh 'Isa

Damanhur

El-tod

Burg Migheizil

Idku

Al Burg

Al Satamuni

Baltim

Bilqas Qism

Tani

Damietta

Qara Oasis

Qara

QATTARA DEPRESSION

Western (Libyan) Desert

Western (Libyan) Desert

8

Siwa Oasis

Siwa

Alexandria

Kafr Al Sheikh

Disuq

Tanta

Zifta

Shirbin

Mansura

San al-Hagar

El-huseiniya

Al Matariyya

Port Said

Lake Bardawil

Al Arish

Gaza City

Sheikh Zuweid

ISRAEL & THE PALESTINIAN TERRITORIES

Tel Aviv

Gebel Meghara

Bir Gifgafa

Bir Ath Thamada

Bir Hasana

Shibin Al Kom

Benha

Zagazig

Bilbeis

Ismailia

Fayid

Great Bitter Lake

2

Cairo International Airport

Sadat City

1

CAIRO

Pyramids of Giza

Suez

Nakhl

1

Ain Sukhna

Eilat

Qasr Qarun

Medinat Al Fayoum

Al Wasta

Eastern (Arabian) Desert

Hammam Fara'un

Gulf of Aqaba

Al Fayoum Oasis

Al Lahun

Beni Suef

Zafarana

Abu Zenima

Nuweiba

Sinai Peninsula

Dahab

7

El-sheikh Fadl

South Galala Plateau

Ras Gharib

9

Abu Durba

Mt Sinai
(Gebel Musa, 2285m)

SAUDI ARABIA

Bawiti

Gebel Az Zuqaq

Bahariya Oasis

Gebel Gala Siwa

Gebel At Teir

Al Tor

Ras Shu Kheir

Straits of Gubal

Shark's Bay

Minya

EGYPT

Black Desert

Ghard Abu Muhariq

Deir Mawas

Dashlut

Eastern (Arabian) Desert

Jemsa

Ras Mohammed National Park

6

Qasr Al Farafra

White Desert National Park

Quss Abu Said

Farafra Oasis

Beni'Adi el Bahariya & Beni'Adi el Qibli

Asyut

Gebel Ash Shayib

Hurghada

Abu Minqar

El-ghanayim

Safaga

Sohag

Red Sea

Al Qasr

Dakhla Oasis

Mut

Tunaydah

Abu Tartur Plateau

El-mahariq

Nag Hammadi

Qena

Wadi Hammamat

Al Quseir

GREAT SAND SEA

Al Kharga

Al Kharga Oasis

5

Luxor

Red Sea Mountains

Marsa Shagra

Ezbet Maks El-qibli

Western (Libyan) Desert

El Sibaiya

NILE

Barramiya

Edfu

Tropic of Cancer

Limestone Plateau

Ibrim

Gebel Hamata (1977m)

Aswan

Aswan Dam

3

Eastern (Arabian) Desert

Administrative Boundary

Abu Simbel

4

Lake Nasser

NILE

Wadi Halfa

SUDAN

N

0

0

200 km

100 miles

SIGHTS &
ACTIVITIES

 SEE

 DO

ITINERARY

 1

 2

Parc National du Delta du Saloum

This lush national park of Senegal is a water-filled wonderland with mangroves, salt marshes, islands and woodland. Birds are abundant, with the delta harbouring species like the dwarf flamingo, goliath heron and dimorph egret. The best way to experience the park is to get out on the water by *piroque* (traditional canoe).

Île de Gorée

This island, offshore from Senegal's capital of Dakar, is an internationally famous symbol for the tragedy of the Atlantic slave trade. Though relatively few slaves were shipped from here, the island was a place where much of the trade was orchestrated. The Maison des Esclaves is a poignant reminder of this dark time.

Abuko Nature Reserve

There are 5km of walking paths through this 106-hectare reserve in the Gambia, as well as a field station with views over a watering hole that's often a good place for wildlife-watching. Among the 52 mammal species calling Abuko home are bushbucks, duikers, porcupines and three types of monkey. It's one of the region's best bird-watching haunts too, with more than 250 species (migratory and resident) present.

7- to 10-day itinerary
Senegal's North Coast

Absorb the urban delights of **Dakar** for a couple of days before sailing to Île de Gorée for some sobering slave-trade history. From there return to the mainland and venture north to **Lac Rose**. This lagoon surrounded by dunes has a magic trick – the otherworldly pink hues that sometimes colour its waters. Next follow your compass north along the coast to the charming city of **Saint-Louis** (West Africa's first French settlement) to take in its historical charm. Wander among its crumbling colonial architecture, and absorb the peaceful ambience. Bird-lovers should head to **Parc National de la Langue de Barbarie**, a short distance from town. The park includes part of the Langue de Barbarie peninsula and the estuary of the Senegal River. It is home to many water birds, swelled from November to April by migrant birds from Europe. True twitchers may detour to **Parc National des Oiseaux du Djoudj** before returning to Saint-Louis for a return flight.

Saint-Louis Jazz Festival

The most internationally renowned festival in West Africa is held annually in early or mid-May in this Senegalese city. It attracts jazz greats from around the world, with the main event usually happening at the Quai des Arts or on an open-air stage in Place Faidherbe, plus fringe events all over town.

Île de N'Gor, Dakar

This tiny island just off Dakar's north shore has a few calm beaches and some legendary surf. Most visitors just come for the day, to relax on the beaches and stroll the sandy lanes of the village.

Parc National des Oiseaux du Djoudj

With almost 300 species of bird, this 160-sq-km park in Senegal is one of the most important bird sanctuaries in the world. Flamingos, pelicans and waders are most plentiful, and large numbers of migrating birds travel here in November.

Wassu Stone Circles

This 1200-year-old arrangement of megaliths in the Gambia captures your attention and commands your respect. The stones, weighing several tonnes each, stand between 1m and 2.5m in height. Archaeologists believe the sites may have been used as burial grounds.

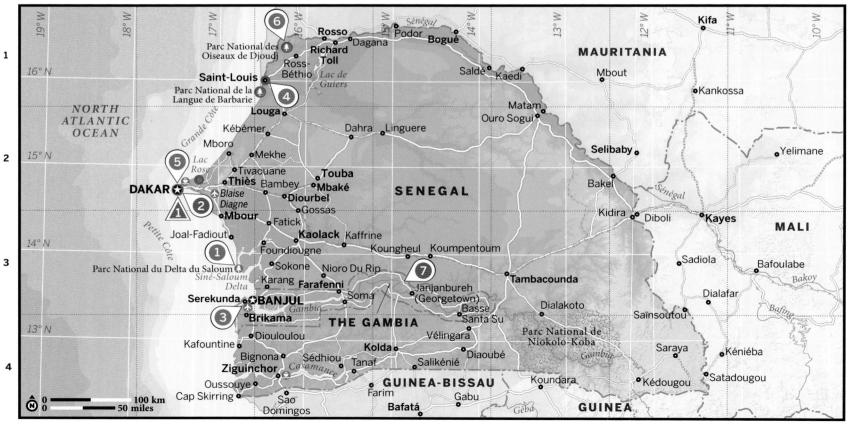

Bet Giyorgis, Lalibela

Found in the ancient city of Lalibela, this church represents the apogee of Ethiopia's millennia-old rock-hewn tradition. Bet Giyorgis (St George's Church) is Lalibela's masterpiece. Its 15m-high, three-tiered plinth in the shape of a Greek cross is a perfectly proportioned shape, one that miraculously required no internal pillars. Petra – eat your heart out.

Simien Mountains

This massive 4000m-high plateau, riven with gullies and pinnacles, offers tough but immensely rewarding trekking along the ridge that falls sheer to the plains far below. It's not just the scenery (and altitude) that will leave you speechless, but also the excitement of sitting among a group of gelada monkeys, or watching magnificent walia ibex joust on precipitous rock ledges.

Royal Enclosure, Gonder

It's not what Gonder is, but what Gonder was that's so enthralling. The towering walls of its numerous 16th-century castles and palaces have been both bathed in blood and painted in the pomp of royalty. Today the wealth and brutality are gone, but the memories linger in this amazing World Heritage site.

14-day itinerary
Historical Circuit

The historical sights along this loop north of Addis Ababa are monumental in both scale and detail – this is Ethiopia at its best. You'll need your own vehicle and driver to manage this in two weeks. After a few days in **Addis Ababa**, head north to palm-fringed **Bahir Dar**. Spend the next day at **Lake Tana** exploring some of the centuries-old island monasteries. Next wander the Royal Enclosure in in **Gonder**. Looming 100km north are the **Simien Mountains**, one of Ethiopia's most stunning national parks – spend a couple of days trekking. Push on to **Aksum** where pre-Christian tombs underlie splendid 1800-year-old *stelae* (obelisks). After two days, venture to the 3000-year-old ruins of Ethiopia's first capital, **Yeha**, and to the cliff-top monastery of **Debre Damo**. Then head south to search out Tigray's precarious rock-hewn churches. Drive south to **Lalibela**: its rock-hewn churches have poignantly frozen 12th- and 13th-century Ethiopia in stone. After three or so days here, it's back to Addis Ababa.

Aksum

Aksum has been described as 'the last of the great civilisations of Antiquity to be revealed to modern knowledge.' Today it still holds most of its secrets. An exploration of its ruined tombs and palaces will surely spark excitement.

Harar

With its 368 alleyways squeezed into just 1 sq km, Harar is more reminiscent of Fez in Morocco than any other city in the Horn. Its countless mosques and shrines, animated markets, crumbling walls and charming people will make you feel as if you've floated right out of the 21st century.

Lower Omo Valley

Despite the close confines of this valley, there are 16 ethnic groups, each often dramatically different from the others. Historians believe this region served for millennia as a kind of cultural crossroads for Cushitic, Nilotic, Omotic and Semitic peoples.

Tigray

Tigray's landscapes seem to spring from some hard-bitten African fairy tale. The luminous light bathes sharp peaks that rise out of a semi-desert. And the 120-odd rock-hewn churches here, some clinging to cliffs, are as intriguing as the region is beautiful.

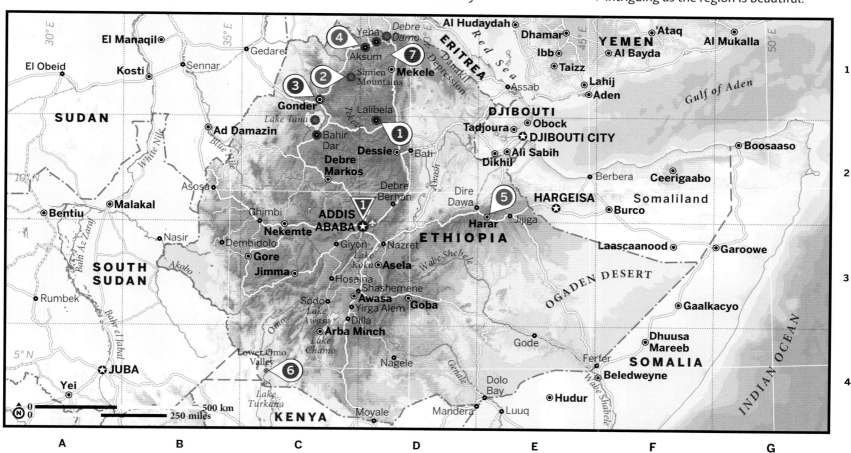

Southern & East Africa

The Masai Mara, Serengeti, Okavango Delta, Kalahari, Cape Town, Kilimanjaro and Zanzibar: Southern and East Africa's big name destinations roll easily off the tongue and inspire thoughts of romance and grand adventures at first utterance. This is the Africa of childhood longings, a wild realm of extraordinary landscapes, peoples and wildlife in one of our planet's most beautiful corners. And yet, despite visitors arriving with a lifetime's worth of expectations and fanciful preconceptions, these two regions still have innumerable secrets and the power to disarm, charm and surprise the most hardened travellers. Put simply, this is Africa at its most memorable.

CLIMATE CHART

ANTANANARIVO

RAINFALL
INCH/MM

20/500
16/400
12/300
8/200
4/100
0

D
N
O
S
A
J
J
M
A
M
F
J

TEMP
°C/°F

40/104
30/86
20/68
10/50
0/32
-10/14

JOHANNESBURG

RAINFALL
INCH/MM

12/300
8/200
4/100
0

D
N
O
S
A
J
J
M
A
M
F
J

TEMP
°C/°F

40/104
30/86
20/68
10/50
0/32

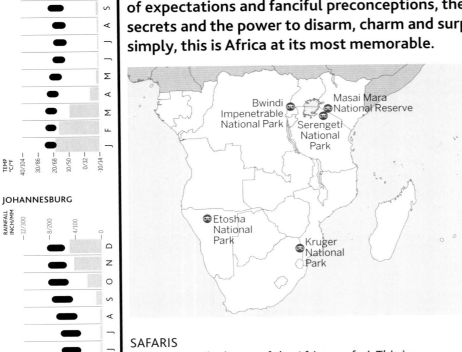

SAFARIS
Welcome to the home of the African safari. This is untamed Africa, where iconic species roam. Follow the great wildebeest migration in the Masai Mara (Kenya) and Serengeti (Tanzania); spot rhino in Etosha (Namibia) and Kruger (South Africa); and track gorillas in Bwindi (Uganda).

MOUNTAIN TREKS
Climbing to the top of Africa on Kilimanjaro is a dream for many, but no less rewarding are treks on glacier-clad Mt Kenya or in Uganda's Rwenzoris. The Chimanimani Mountains straddling Mozambique and Zimbabwe, and the Drakensberg range in South Africa, are also fantastic choices.

BEACHES
Pristine coastlines, turquoise waters and miles of inland lakeshore mean there are no excuses not to wet your toes. Drop your towel in the Quirimbas Archipelago (Mozambique), Zanzibar (Tanzania), Kilifi (Kenya), Lake Malawi (Malawi) and Cape Town (South Africa).

PEOPLES
Though it's wildlife that often lures travellers to the region, it's usually the warmth of the people that captures their hearts. Share some time with the Maasai (Kenya and Tanzania), San (Botswana), Himba (Namibia), Chewa (Malawi), Shona (Zimbabwe) and Karamojong (Uganda).

Right: The Maasai people, known for their red-checked *shuka* robes, inhabit Kenya and northern Tanzania.

Transport hubs

ELEVATION KEY

7500-10000M
5000-7500M
3000-5000M
2000-3000M
1500-2000M
1250-1500M
1000-1250M
750-1000M
500-750M
250-500M
100-250M
75-100M
50-75M
25-50M
1-25M

Southern and East Africa are well-connected to the rest of the world by air, most commonly through Johannesburg and Cape Town in South Africa and Kenya's capital, Nairobi. Arriving by land is limited to overland epics, the easiest being via Ethiopia. Independent sea travel is very much uncharted territory, though several cargo-shipping companies sail between Europe and South Africa, with cabins for public passengers. Once here, ground transport is widespread.

TRANSPORT

B3, C6, C8,
D5, E5, E6,
E7, F2, F3,
H5

C8, D8, E7,
F3, G2, G3,
H4

Right: Cape Town from above (left) and (right) the Blue Train en route from Johannesburg to Cape Town.

Johannesburg
Exciting urban-renewal projects are transforming this city, which is the vibrant heart of South Africa. The wealth divide remains stark, however, and crime rates remain a problem. Still, Jo'burg is an incredibly friendly, unstuffy city and there's a lot to see and do. OR Tambo International Airport, about 25km east of central Johannesburg, is the continent's best-connected (and busiest) airport.

Cape Town (see pp396-7 for city map)
A coming-together of cultures, cuisines, seascapes and landscapes crowned by the magnificent Table Mountain, there's nowhere quite like this South African city. Cape Town International Airport, 22km east of the city centre, is Africa's second-busiest airport. The city is now featured on various international cruises and is a staging post for the luxury Blue Train.

Nairobi
East Africa's most cosmopolitan city and the capital of Kenya, Nairobi is an exciting, maddening concrete jungle. Reviled and loved in equal measure, its charms include a vibrant cultural life, fabulous places to eat and exciting nightlife. Jomo Kenyatta International Airport, 15km southeast of the city, is East Africa's most important air hub.

Entebbe
On the shores of gorgeous Lake Victoria in Uganda, Entebbe is an attractive, verdant town that once served as the capital city. It's the relaxed pace of life and nearby natural attractions that give the city its charm. Until the Entebbe Express Hwy debuts in 2019, the city (and Uganda's only international airport) remains a 90-minute drive south of the country's modern capital, Kampala.

Dar es Salaam
This Tanzanian city has grown from a sleepy fishing village into a thriving tropical metropolis of over four million people. Yet it manages to maintain a low-key feel. Julius Nyerere International Airport is Tanzania's hub airport, serving numerous domestic routes and a handful of flights to Europe and the Middle East.

Windhoek
The capital of Namibia is the sort of place that divides travellers, with those who love it for the respite it offers from the rigours of life on the African road facing off against those who don't find it African enough. They're both right. Hosea Kutako International Airport, which is about 40km east of the city centre, serves international flights, with Frankfurt being the main destination outside of Africa.

Maputo
With its Mediterranean-style architecture, waterside setting and wide avenues lined with jacaranda and flame trees, the capital of Mozambique is easily one of Africa's most attractive cities. Its international airport regularly serves Nairobi and Johannesburg, with limited flights to Lisbon, Portugal.

Maun
Tiny Maun is the gateway to the Okavango Delta and is thus Botswana's tourism hub. International flights serve Johannesburg, Victoria Falls (Zimbabwe) and Livingstone (Zambia).

Livingstone
The friendly town of Livingstone is set just 11km from Victoria Falls in Zambia. Its airport is well linked to Southern Africa's capitals.

© Quality Master / Shutterstock

© Michael Heffernan / Lonely Planet

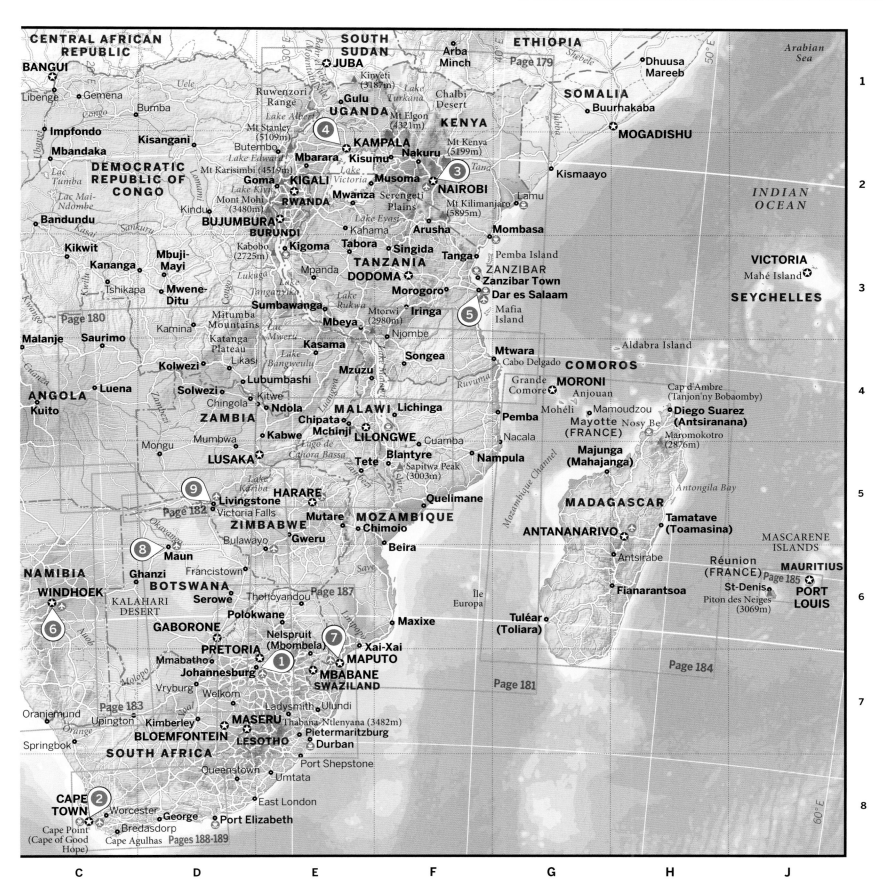

SIGHTS &
ACTIVITIES

 SEE
 DO

ITINERARY

 1
2

Lamu Town: Dhow trips from Lamu are a fun way to take in the Kenyan coast.

Bwindi Impenetrable National Park

Sheltering almost half of the world's surviving mountain gorillas, Bwindi Impenetrable National Park is one of East Africa's most famous national parks, as well as its most evocatively named. Set over 331 sq km of improbably steep mountain rainforest, it's home to an estimated 340 gorillas: undoubtedly Uganda's biggest tourist drawcard.

Zanzibar Town

For most visitors to Tanzania, Zanzibar Town means Stone Town, the historic quarter where you can wander through a maze of narrow streets, losing yourself in centuries past. Each twist and turn brings something new – a former palace, a Persian bathhouse, a tumbledown ruin or a coral-stone mansion with carved doors and latticework balconies.

The great migration

The Masai Mara (Kenya) and Serengeti (Tanzania) ecosystem is a huge expanse of rolling grassland, specked with flat-topped acacia trees. Every year hundreds of thousands of wildebeest and zebra make a remarkable migration from the Serengeti's short-grass plains to the Masai Mara and back, crossing several crocodile-filled rivers in the process. It's a spectacle like no other.

Jinja

The source of the Nile near Jinja in Uganda is one of the most spectacular rafting destinations in the world, with many Grade IV and V class rapids.

Nile Trail

Walk or cycle the 227km Nile Trail from Gisenyi at the northern end of Lake Kivu to Cyangugu (Rusizi) at the lake's southern extremity. Rwanda is renowned for its hills, so you'll have to be extremely fit to tackle this.

Lake Turkana

The first sight of this sparkling Jade Sea (travelling north from South Horr) will take your breath away. The world's largest permanent desert lake, it has a shoreline that's longer than Kenya's entire Indian Ocean coast. South Island stands proudly before you, while Teleki Volcano's geometrically perfect cone lurks on Turkana's southern shore. The first village on the eastern shore is tiny Loyangalani, which will assault all your senses in one crazy explosion of clashing colours, feather headdresses and blood-red robes of the great northern tribes: Turkana and Samburu, Gabbra and El Molo.

Kibale National Park

This 795-sq-km park in southwestern Uganda is a lush tropical rainforest, and is believed to have the highest density of primates in Africa. It's one of the best places in the world to track wild chimpanzees, with five groups habituated to human contact.

Kilwa Kisiwani

Today, 'Kilwa on the Island' is a quiet Tanzanian fishing village, but in its heyday it was the centre of a vast trading network linking the Shona kingdoms and the goldfields of Zimbabwe with Persia, India and China. It's a truly significant Swahili ruin.

Mt Kenya

Africa's second-highest mountain might just be its most beautiful. Here, mere minutes from the equator, glaciers carve out the throne of Ngai, the old high god of the Kikuyu. The two tallest peaks can only be reached by mountaineers with technical skills, but Point Lenana (4985m), the third-highest peak, can be reached by trekkers.

Lamu Town

Arguably the most complete Swahili town in existence, Lamu seems almost ethereal as you approach it from the water, hidden by a forest of dhow masts. Up close, the illusion shatters and the Kenyan town becomes a hive of activity – from the busy waterfront, with carts wheeled to and fro, to the pungent labyrinth of alleyways.

Mt Kilimanjaro

Standing atop Africa – on what is one of Tanzania's (and the continent's) most magnificent sights – is one of the greatest travel experiences in Africa. Trekking routes climb through cultivated farmlands on the lower slopes, through lush rainforest to alpine meadows, and finally across a lunar landscape to the summit (5896m).

14- to 21-day itinerary
Classic East Africa

Start on Zanzibar to experience **Stone Town**'s many cultural rewards, then move to the beaches for diving, snorkelling and chill time. Hop to Kilimanjaro International Airport, visit **Arusha** and its eponymous national park for a day or two, then head west to the incredible **Ngorongoro Crater** and the

famed **Serengeti National Park** for fabulous wildlife and iconic East African landscapes. Next fly north to **Nairobi** before continuing by road to the rhino-haven of **Lake Nakuru National Park**. Push west to Uganda for whitewater rafting in **Jinja** and gorilla trekking in **Bwindi Impenetrable National Park**. Finish in **Kampala**.

21-day itinerary
Swahili Coast

From Dar es Salaam travel south to the historic Swahili ruins at **Kilwa Kisiwani** before stopping at the pretty, palm-fringed **Lindi**, and the tiny Swahil village of **Mikindani**. Return northwards, tasting the treasures of three remarkable islands: **Mafia**, a rich melting pot of historical influences; **Zanzibar**, for Stone Town, incredible beaches

and spice tours; and **Pemba**, a hilly, lush and relatively undeveloped island that is surrounded by some of East Africa's best diving sites. Return to the mainland, with your first stop being **Pangani** – it's an intriguing step back into the coast's history. Continue north and cross into Kenya to explore **Kisite Marine National Park**'s

dolphin-filled waters and croc-lined mangroves. Next, pause at **Tiwi Beach** for a rest before delving into the culture and history of **Mombasa**. Next stop is the charming town of Kilifi and the impressive **Gede Ruins**. Finish in **Lamu Town**, a Swahili heritage gem with oodles of charm. From here fly back to **Nairobi** for your journey home.

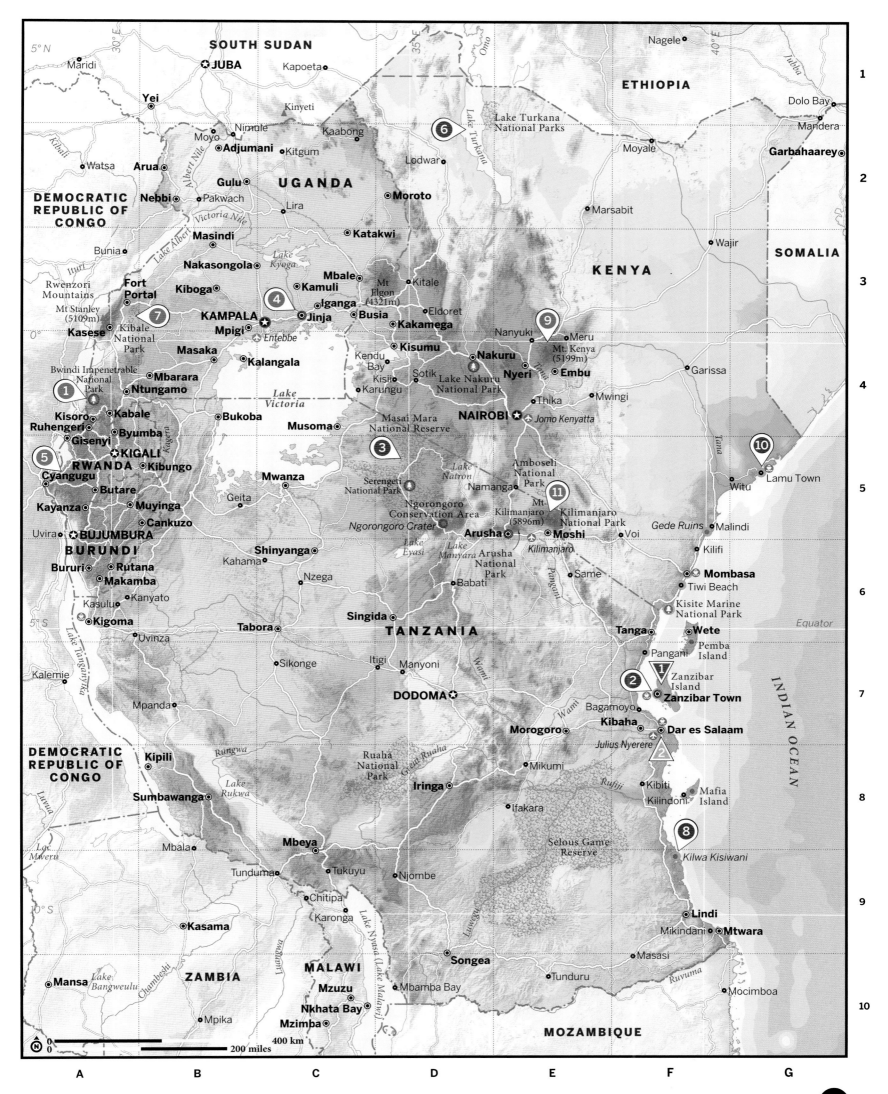

SIGHTS & ACTIVITIES

 SEE

DO

ITINERARY

 1

2

Victoria Falls

Taking its place alongside the Pyramids and the Serengeti, Victoria Falls (Mosi-oa-Tunya – the 'smoke that thunders') is one of Africa's original blockbusters. And although Zimbabwe and Zambia share it, this mile-wide waterfall is a place all of its own.

Lower Zambezi National Park

One of the Africa's premier wildlife-viewing areas, this park covers a large stretch of wilderness area along the northeastern bank of the Zambezi River. Drifting silently in a canoe past the riverbank allows you to get eye-to-eye with drinking buffaloes, elephants and even lions. Further excitement comes when navigating around hippos and crocodiles.

South Luangwa National Park

This park is the birthplace of the walking safari, and there is arguably still no place better to do it. Well-trained guides take you quietly through the bush for unforgettable – and exposed – encounters with the park's wildlife, large and small: impalas, pukus, giraffes, hippos, leopards and elephants – the list goes on. For scenery, variety and density of animals, South Luangwa is also one of the best parks in Zambia, if not all Africa.

14-day itinerary
Wildlife & Waterfalls

Start in **Lusaka**, then journey southeast to **Lower Zambezi National Park**, one of Africa's finest wilderness regions, to spot animals while canoeing along the Zambezi River. Navigate yourself southwest to **Siavonga** on sparkling, scenic Lake Kariba and relax by the water. From Siavonga, retrace your steps northwest, before continuing westwards to **Lochinvar National Park**, renowned for birding and its lechwe (antelope with curved horns) population. The next stop is historical **Livingstone**, gateway to thundering **Victoria Falls**, where adventurous excursions await: serene canoe trips above the falls or whitewater rafting the churning Zambezi down below. Next head northeast to **Kafue National Park**, accessing it via its south Dundumwezi Gate. Spend the first night overlooking **Lake Itezhi-Tezhi**, then allow a few days to head north in the park, enjoying excellent birding and abundant wildlife. From here it's a day's travel back to Lusaka.

Zambezi River

This is one of the best whitewater rafting destinations in the world, both for experienced rafters and newbies. You'll find plenty of Grade IV and V rapids. Expect very long rides with huge drops and big kicks; it's not for the faint-hearted.

Kasanka National Park

The fruit bat migration, which has to be seen to be believed, occurs in November and December. With the arrival of nearly 10 million bats, it's the biggest mammal gathering anywhere in the world, and can blanket the sky.

Kafue National Park

Covering more than 22,500 sq km, this park is the largest in Zambia and one of the biggest in the world. With terrain ranging from the lush riverine forest of the Kafue River to the vast grassland of the Busanga Plains, the park rewards wildlife enthusiasts with glimpses of carnivores and their nimble prey, including a good chance of sighting lions and leopards, and if you're lucky cheetahs, elephants, zebras and numerous species of antelope. There are some 500 species of birds, too. Kafue is one of the few parks in Zambia that's easily accessible by public transport, with a handful of camps just off the main highway.

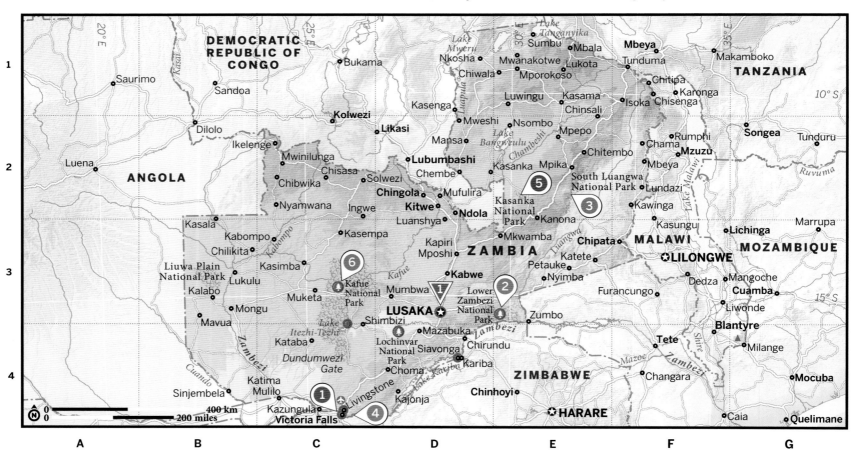

Mozambique Island

Dhows shifting silently through shallow seas, bruised colonial buildings withering elegantly in the tropical heat, and the voices of a church choir competing with the muezzin's call to prayer. Mozambique Island, the former capital, is a fragrant melange of African, Portuguese, Swahili, French and Goan flavours – it's one of the cultural highlights of Africa.

Nyika National Park

Towering over 2000m above sea level, the 3200-sq-km Nyika National Park is easily one of Malawi's most bewitching experiences. Turning burnt amber in the afternoon sun, the highland grass flickers with the stripes of zebras and is punctuated by glittering boulders. Its network of gravel roads is ideal for exploring by mountain bike.

Likoma Island

Lake Malawi's blissful Likoma Island measures just 17 sq km, but it has an abundance of pristine beaches and the attendant snorkelling, diving and water sports. The island's flat and sandy south is littered with baobabs and offers an uninterrupted panoramic view of Mozambique's wild coast.

14-day itinerary
Beaches & Islands

The beach town of **Pemba** in northern Mozambique makes a good starting point. Hit nearby **Murrébuè** for kitesurfing, white sand and ocean vistas. Next, set off for enchanting **Ibo Island** in the Quirimbas Archipelago, with its massive star-shaped fort, silversmiths and crumbling colonial-era mansions. Travel south via Nampula to **Mozambique Island**, where historical treasures, cultural riches and sea breezes pervade. Now pass through Nampula (again) to catch the train west to **Cuamba** – it's a scenic trip and offers fascinating glimpses of local life. Overnight in Cuamba, then continue straight on to Lake Malawi. **Cape Maclear** is the first stop, with snorkelling, kayaking and relaxing on order. From here turn north to **Nkhata Bay**, with detours to the islands of Chizumulu and Likoma for scenery and a relaxed cultural vibe. Finally travel south to finish your trip in **Blantyre**.

The Quirimbas Archipelago

Hidden like pirate treasure off Mozambique's north coast, these islands conceal a multitude of secrets. From Medjumbe's brilliant coral reefs and Vamizi's powdery white-sand beaches to Quilaluia's ancient baobabs and Ibo's historical gems shaped by Portuguese, Swahili, Indian and African cultures, there's plenty enjoy.

Majete Wildlife Reserve

Majete is Malawi's only Big Five park. It's a rugged wilderness of hilly woodland and savannah that hugs the west bank of the Shire River.

Mt Mulanje

Mt Mulanje towers over 3000m high, and its stunning scenery – dense green valleys and rivers that drop from sheer cliffs to form dazzling waterfalls – easy access, clear paths and well-maintained huts make it a fine hiking area worthy of a few days.

Bazaruto National Park

Dolphins swim through the Bazaruto Archipelago's clear waters, along with 2000 types of fish, plus loggerhead, leatherback and green turtles. Most intriguing are the elusive dugongs. Diving is best from May to September.

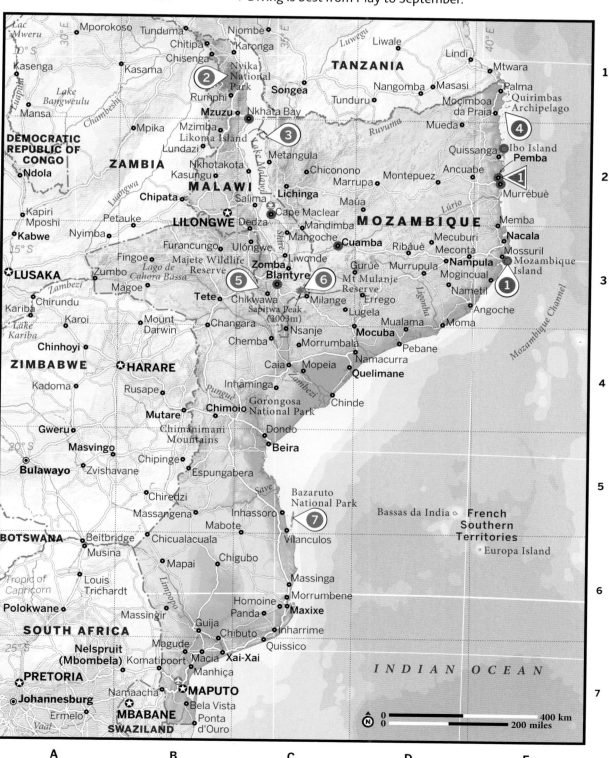

SIGHTS & ACTIVITIES

- SEE
- DO

ITINERARY

- 1
- 2

① Etosha National Park

Etosha National Park, covering more than 20,000 sq km, is one of the world's great wildlife-viewing venues. Etosha's appeal lies in its ability to bring the animals straight to you. Its many waterholes attract a host of animals – rhinos, lions, elephants, springboks, gemsboks etc – who come not two by two but by the hundreds.

② Namib-Naukluft National Park

Deadvlei is the most alluring pan in the Sossusvlei section of the Namib-Naukluft National Park – and one of Southern Africa's greatest sights. Sprouting from it is a seemingly ghost-like forest of petrified trees, with their parched limbs casting shadows across the bleached-white canvas. The backdrop of mountainous orange dunes and cobalt skies only adds to the allure. The view from Big Daddy dune is worth the climb.

③ Fish River Canyon

At 160km in length, up to 27km in width, and reaching a depth of 550m, Fish River is one the world's largest canyons. The monumental five-day, 85km hike from Hobas to Ai-Ais is a magical route that follows the sandy riverbed past a series of ephemeral pools. The exposed rock and lack of plant life are quite startling and invoke thoughtful reflection.

④ Spitzkoppe

The 1728m-high Spitzkoppe rises mirage-like above the dusty plains of southern Damaraland. Gawk at its spellbinding peaks at sunset and sunrise, unless you're hellbent on tackling the summit yourself.

⑤ Skeleton Coast Park

This treacherous coast – a foggy region with rocky and sandy coastal shallows, rusting shipwrecks and soaring dunes – has long been a graveyard for unwary ships and their crews, hence its forbidding name. Reach it via the salt road from Swakopmund.

⑥ Kolmanskop

This enigmatic ghost town being swallowed by the sands of the Namib was originally constructed as the Consolidated Diamond Mines headquarters. The sight of the deserted town is truly surreal.

⑦ Cape Cross Seal Reserve

In a corner of the world where land-based predators or tusked giants get most of the attention, this writhing mass of 100,000 sea mammals is one of the continent's most memorable wildlife-watching experiences.

▽ 14-day itinerary

Essential Namibia

Begin in **Windhoek**, one of Southern Africa's more agreeable capitals. From here, head north in your 4WD to the **Erongo Mountains** for a night or two. Follow it with two nights in the **Okonjima Nature Reserve**, then it's on to **Etosha National Park**, one of Africa's greatest parks, with fabulous wildlife-watching – three nights here is a bare minimum. Tracking southwest, head down into **Damaraland**, home to some of the most dramatic scenery anywhere in the country – Twyfelfontein, Brandberg and Spitzkoppe are all highlights; plan on at least three days. Take in the seals at **Cape Cross**, sandboard down a dune near **Swakopmund** then head via **Sesriem Canyon** for two nights in the dunes of **Sossusvlei** en route back to Windhoek.

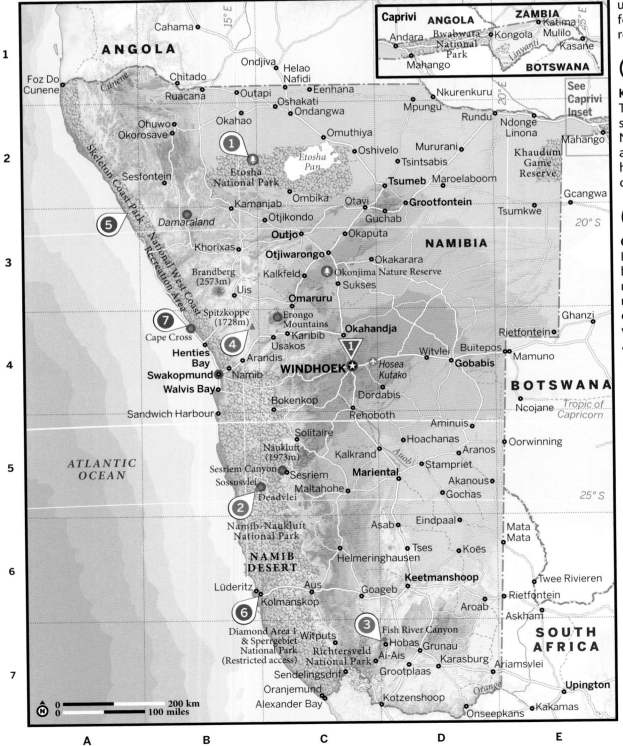

Okavango Delta
The Okavango is an astonishing, beautiful, wild place, and there's something special about drifting slowly down its reed-lined channels in a *mokoro* (traditional dugout canoe). You become a part of a land that belongs to crocodiles, hippos, rich birdlife and elephants.

Kuru Art Project, D'kar
This art project provides opportunities for local artists to create and sell paintings and other artwork; it's worth spending an hour or two leafing through the various folios.

Chobe National Park
There are more elephants in Chobe National Park – tens of thousands of them – than anywhere else on earth. And these are big elephants, really big. Venture onto the Chobe River at sunset to watch as most of Africa's charismatic megafauna come to drink.

Tsodilo Hills
The Tsodilo Hills rise abruptly from the northwestern Kalahari. These lonely chunks of quartzite schist are dramatic and beautiful, distinguished by streaks of vivid natural hues – mauve, orange, yellow, turquoise and lavender. Sheltering more than 4000 prehistoric rock paintings, the hills are a site of huge spiritual significance for the region's original inhabitants, the San.

Makgadikgadi Pans National Park
The Sowa, Nxai and Ntwetwe Pans together make up the 12,000-sq-km Makgadikgadi Pans, the largest such network in the world. The parched, white salt pans were once part of a 'super lake' of more than 60,000 sq km. Today, responsible operators operate quad biking forays along the edges of the pans.

Central Kalahari Game Reserve
Think desolation, desert silences and the sound of big cats roaring in the night – this is big-sky country, home to black-maned Kalahari lions, a full suite of predators and an utterly wonderful sense of remoteness. Covering 52,800 sq km, it's also one of Africa's largest protected areas.

Kgalagadi Transfrontier Park
One of the most beautiful expanses of the Kalahari is found here. Salt pans and sand dunes provide habitat for desert-adapted wildlife including big cats, meerkats, abundant birdlife and desert favourites such as gemsboks. This border-crossing park is one of the most underrated in Botswana and South Africa.

14-day itinerary
Best of Botswana

Fly into **Maun**, staying just long enough to pick up your pre-booked vehicle and take a scenic flight to get a sense of the delta in all its vast glory. Drive into **Moremi Game Reserve**, with a couple of nights in each of Xakanaxa Campsite, Savuti Campsite and Linyanti Campsite. Spend the next two days recharging the batteries in **Kasane**, with a sunrise and a sunset foray along the Chobe Riverfront. A day-trip to **Victoria Falls** is an enthralling option from here. Next, drive to **Gweta** and stay overnight, long enough for an encounter with meerkats, then plan a night by the Boteti River in **Makgadikgadi Pans National Park**. With some hard driving, you could make a dash for the **Central Kalahari Game Reserve**, camping in Deception Valley and **Motopi** on your way back to Maun.

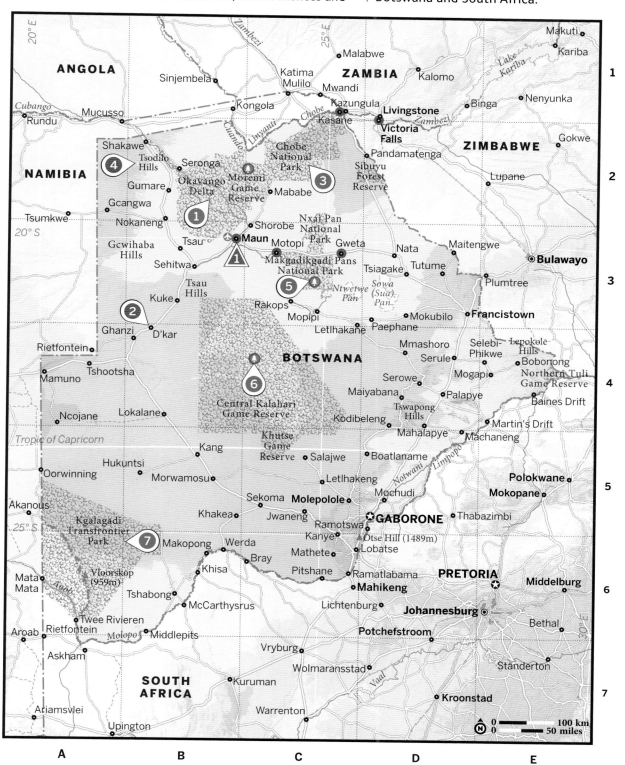

SIGHTS &
ACTIVITIES

◉ SEE

◉ DO

ITINERARY

▽ 1

▽ 2

① Parc National de Marojejy

One of Madagascar's great undiscovered parks, Marojejy is a primordial place, where the astonishing 'angel of the forest', the silky sifaka (lemur), inhabits misty mountains, and spectacular views of the Marojejy Massif peek through the canopy. World-class treks are the best way to explore.

② Ambohimanga

Poised atop a hill is this fortress-palace. Its walls were constructed using cement made from sand, shells and egg whites – 16 million eggs were required to build the outer wall alone.

③ Parc National de l'Isalo

Isalo is like a museum dedicated to the art of the desert canyon. It contains sculpted buttes, vertical rock walls and deep canyon floors shot through with streams, lush vegetation and pools for swimming. Explore by mountain bike, foot, horse or via ferrata.

④ Parc National de Ranomafana

Containing 400 sq km of oddly shaped rolling hills carpeted in jungle and fed by rushing streams, this park supports 29 mammal species, including 12 species of lemur. On a typical day's walk, you are likely to see between three and five species, including the famed golden bamboo lemur.

⑤ Andilana, Nosy Be

Far and away the island of Nosy Be's best beach, Andilana, at the isle's northwest tip, is a long stretch of pearly white sand, with water that's true turquoise and clear as gin. It's ideal for swimming and chilling for an afternoon, with gorgeous sunsets. It ignites on Sundays, when French expats and Malagasy come for a lazy day in the sun. Families lay out picnics, tuck into a crate of beers, turn on their stereo, and swim and dance until the sun drops.

⑥ Parc National des Tsingy de Bemaraha

Formed over centuries by the wind and water, and often towering several hundred metres into the air, the serrated limestone pinnacles known as tsingy within this park would definitely look at home in a Dalí painting. Get a bird's-eye-view from rope bridges, walkways and the fixed cables and ladders that make up the via ferrata.

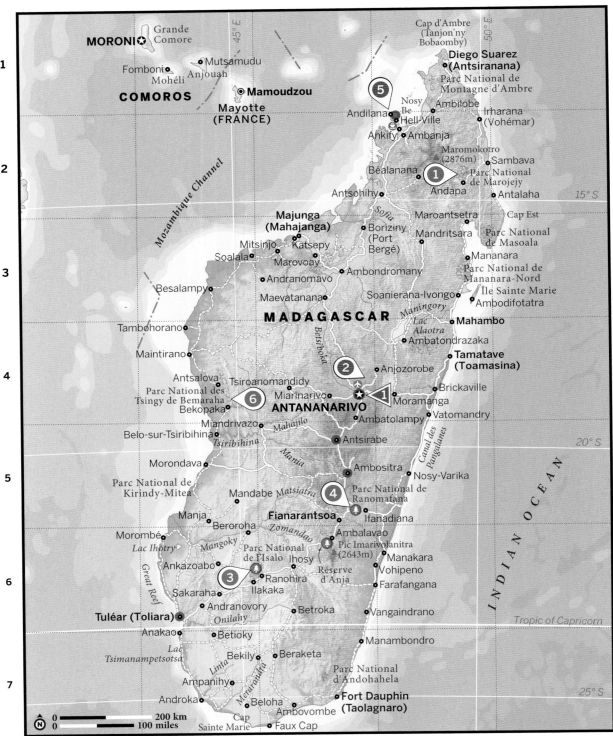

▽1 14-day itinerary
Essential Madagascar

Head down from **Antananarivo** to **Antsirabe**, with its wide colonial streets and colourful rickshaws. Then wind your way to **Parc National de Ranomafana** through the highland's scenic landscapes, stopping en route at the arts-and-crafts capital, **Ambositra**. Next is a day hiking and searching for lemurs in Ranomafana's rainforest. Follow this with a drive to the superb **Parc National de l'Isalo**, stopping in **Réserve d'Anja** on your way to see ring-tailed lemurs. Spend two days exploring Isalo's stunning desert canyons before visiting **Tuléar** (make sure to stop at Arboretum d'Antsokay en route). Now fly to **Nosy Be** (via Antananarivo) for some beach time and unrivalled snorkelling around Nosy Komba and Nosy Tanikely. Visit Réserve Naturelle Intégrale de Lokobe before flying back to the capital.

Black River Gorges National Park

Mauritius' biggest and best national park is a wild expanse of rolling hills and thick forest covering roughly 2% of the island's surface. Numerous trails criss-cross the park like unravelling shoestrings and provide wonderful hiking possibilities. A guide will help you navigate to the best viewpoints.

Eureka Plantation Mansion

Arguably the finest Creole plantation mansion left on Mauritius, Eureka is situated in the cooler climes of Moka. Built in the 1830s, it's now a museum and veritable time machine providing insight into the island's plantation past.

Passe St Jacques

Filled with fabulous underwater formations, Passe St Jacques, near Baie du Cap, is one of Mauritius' best drift-dive sites. Its highlight is the dazzling aggregation of grey reef sharks, barracudas, snappers and trevallies.

Grand Baie

Sailing north on a catamaran from Grand Baie to Coin de Mire, Île Plate and Îlot Gabriel is something special. Snorkel the lagoon between the islands, watch for wildlife and take in the extraordinary scenery.

14-day itinerary
Jaunt around Mauritius

This itinerary takes you from the stunning coast of Mauritius southeast to the dramatic mountain landscapes of the interior and far southwest. Start along the beautiful sands of Pointe d'Esny. Snorkel the sparkling azure lagoon at **Blue Bay**, eco-explore **Île aux Aigrettes**, then slip up to sleepy Mahébourg for the Monday market.

Drive north along the coast. Embrace the fisherfolk lifestyle in **Trou d'Eau Douce**, then glide through the crystal lagoon to **Île aux Cerfs**. Pass through the sky-reaching sugar cane before emerging at gorgeous **Cap Malheureux**. In **Grand Baie**, hop on a catamaran bound for the scenic northern islands, then treat yourself to a meal in lively Trou aux Biches.

A day-trip loop could then take in the botanical gardens and sugar factory at **Pamplemousses** and lovely **Château Labourdonnais**. Emerge on the west coast for a spot of diving in **Flic en Flac**, then base yourself around Black River. From here, try canyoning in **Black River Gorges**, biking in **Chamarel** or climbing the iconic **Le Morne Brabant**.

Sir Seewoosagur Ramgoolam Botanical Gardens

One of the world's best botanical gardens, its centrepiece is a pond filled with giant Victoria amazonica water lilies (their flowers open white one day and close red the next). Share the grounds with enclosures of giant tortoises as well as abundant birdlife.

St-Denis

Absorb the rootsy Creole music of *maloya* – sung in patois – in Réunion's capital. The French influence on St-Denis's colonial architecture is equally enthralling – check out Maison Kichenin and the Préfecture.

Piton de la Fournaise

Réunion's famous feature, Piton de la Fournaise is simply a must-do for walkers. From Pas de Bellecombe, it's possible to hike up to Balcon du Dolomieu, a viewpoint on the northeastern side of the Dolomieu Crater rim, from where you can gaze down to the bottom of the caldera.

Rivière Langevin

Expect lots of slippery dips, exhilarating water jumps, short swims and fun scrambles in a picturesque Réunion landscape. Canyoning outings last from one hour to four or five hours.

Parc National des Tsingy de Bemaraha: Fittingly, the Malagasy word *tsingy* means 'walking on tiptoes'.

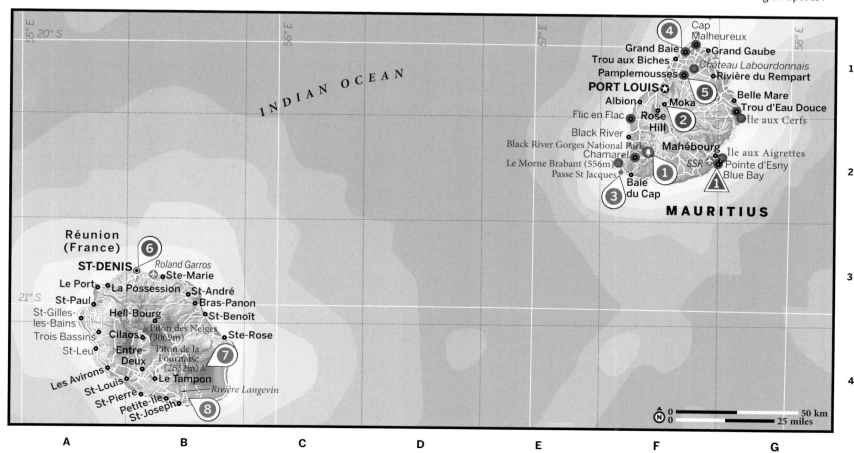

SIGHTS &
ACTIVITIES

◉ SEE
◉ DO

ITINERARY

▽ 1
▽ 2

Kruger National Park

Kruger is one of the world's greatest wildlife-watching destinations. All of Africa's signature safari species – elephant, lion, leopard, cheetah, rhino, buffalo, giraffe, hippo, crocodile and zebra – are here and share the bushveld with a supporting cast of 137 other mammals and over 500 varieties of birdlife.

Apartheid Museum, Johannesburg

This museum illustrates the rise and fall of South Africa's era of segregation and oppression. It uses a broad variety of media to provide a chilling insight into the architecture and implementation of the apartheid system, as well as inspiring stories of the struggle towards democracy.

uKhahlamba-Drakensberg Park

The jagged, green Drakensberg range is one of the best hiking destinations in Africa. Valleys, waterfalls, rivers, caves and the escarpment, which rises to an impressive 3000m, provide spectacular wilderness experiences. The trails are accessed through any of the park's entrances – Royal Natal National Park (renowned for its day walks), Cathedral Peak, Monk's Cowl, Injisuthi and Giant's Castle.

KwaZulu-Natal

Voortrekkers vs Zulus, British vs Boers and Zulus vs British – the history of KwaZulu-Natal (KZN) is intrinsically linked to its battlefields, the stage on which many of South Africa's bloodiest chapters were played out.

Kruger National Park: Elephant populations in South Africa have risen from an estimated 120 animals in 1920 to 10,000 today.

KwaZulu-Natal's South Coast

Aliwal Shoal is one of the best dive sites in the world – its ledges, caves and pinnacles are home to everything from wrecks to rays, turtles, 'raggies' (ragged-tooth sharks), tropical fish and soft corals. Further south, near Shelly Beach, the extraordinary Protea Banks dive site is *the* place to see sharks.

Blyde River Canyon

This reserve centres on the 30km-long Blyde River Canyon, where epic rock formations tower above the forested slopes and eagle's-eye views abound.

Durban

Bunny chow is Durban's ultimate takeaway food, where the container (a loaf of bread) is part of the meal and the utensils are your hands. The hollowed-out loaf is filled with curry (the city has the largest population of people of Indian descent outside of India).

Venda Region

This enigmatic region is the traditional homeland of the Venda people, and it's a place where myth and legend continue to play a major role in everyday life. The distinctive local artwork is famous nationwide.

---

iSimangaliso Wetland Park

This park stretches for 220 glorious kilometres from the Mozambique border to the southern end of Lake St Lucia. With the Indian Ocean on one side and a series of lakes on the other, iSimangaliso protects five distinct ecosystems and a wealth of diverse wildlife that ranges from antelopes and zebras to whales and dolphins.

Mapungubwe National Park

Stunningly stark, arid, rocky landscapes reverberate with cultural intrigue and wandering wildlife at Mapungubwe National Park. As much about wildlife as history, the park contains South Africa's most significant Iron Age site, plus animals ranging from black and white rhinos to the rare Pel's fishing owl and meerkats.

Hluhluwe-iMfolozi Park

Rivalling Kruger National Park in its beauty and variety of landscapes, Hluhluwe-iMfolozi Park is one of South Africa's best-known, most evocative parks. There's plenty of wildlife, including lions, elephants, rhinos (black and white), leopards, giraffes, buffaloes and African wild dogs.

Golden Gate Highlands National Park

This park is known for its dramatic, golden-hued sandstone cliffs, abundant wildlife (including elands, baboons, zebras and wildebeest) and centuries-old cave paintings by the San people. The landscape is breathtaking, and best experienced on multi-day hikes.

14-day itinerary
Wildlife and Nature

Strike out south from **Durban** to explore the underwater riches of **Aliwal Shoal** and **Protea Banks**. From here enjoy safari wildlife at the **Hluhluwe-iMfolozi Park** and **iSimangaliso**. The latter also offers wetland and aquatic species. Close up elephant encounters rule the roost at **uMkhuze Game Reserve's**

hides, while rhino sightings dominate proceedings at Swaziland's **Mkhaya Game Reserve**. Walk, mountain bike or cycle with wildlife at **Mlilwane Wildlife Sanctuary** before hiking and zip-lining at **Malalotja Nature Reserve**. Return to South Africa to gaze into **Blyde River Canyon** and to experience Big Five action at **Kruger National Park**.

14-day itinerary
Eastern Wander

Linger a few days in the dynamic metropolis of **Johannesburg**, seeing how urban regeneration is transforming the inner city and creating hipster enclaves. Visit Africa's most famous township, **Soweto**, and see where Nobel Peace Prize winners Nelson Mandela and Archbishop Desmond Tutu lived. Next cross the

Free State, taking scenic Rte 712 past Sterkfontein Dam to **Clarens**, an arty town with galleries, a microbrewery and surroundings worthy of an impressionist landscape. Nearby is **Golden Gate Highlands National Park**, with its many hiking trails. Just outside the park, the day-long Sentinel Hiking Trail climbs the iconic Amphitheatre

to the top of the **Drakensberg Escarpment**. Now, spend a couple of days enjoying the spectacular day walks in **Royal Natal National Park**. Continuing across KwaZulu-Natal, take in the twee Midlands region around **Howick**, with its art studios, before revelling in **Durban's** beaches and Indian restaurants.

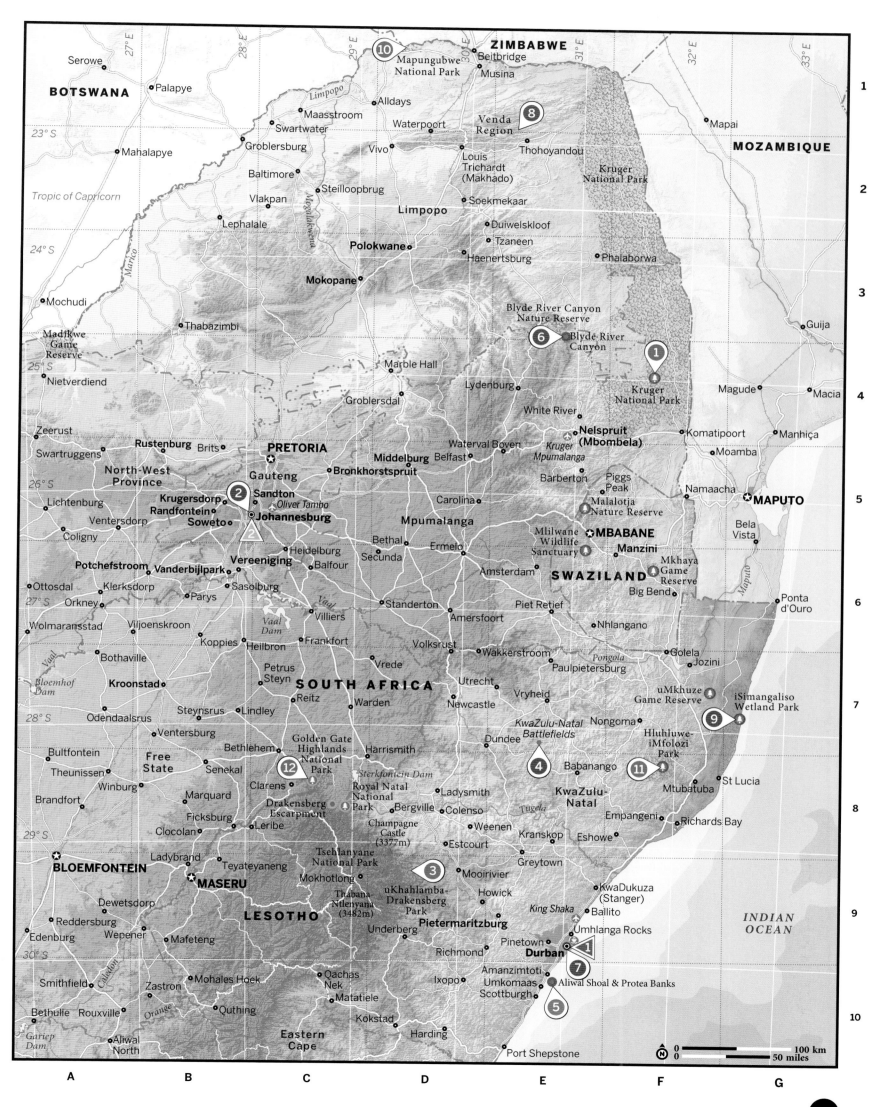

BOTSWANA

Serowe
Palapye
Mahalapye
Mochudi
Madikwe Game Reserve
Tropic of Capricorn

ZIMBABWE
Beitbridge
Musina
10 Mapungubwe National Park
Alldays
Maasstroom
Swartwater
Waterpoort
8 Venda Region
Thohoyandou
Groblersburg
Vivo
Louis Trichardt (Makhado)
Steilloopbrug
Vlakpan
Soekmekaar
Lephalale
Duiwelskloof
Tzaneen
Limpopo
Haenertsburg
Phalaborwa
Polokwane
Mokopane
Thabazimbi
Marble Hall
Blyde River Canyon Nature Reserve
6 Blyde River Canyon
Lydenburg
1 Kruger National Park
Groblersdal
White River
Zeerust
Rustenburg
Brits
PRETORIA
Middelburg
Belfast
Waterval Boven
Nelspruit (Mbombela)
Komatipoort
North-West Province
Gauteng
Sandton
Bronkhorstspruit
Barberton
Piggs Peak
Namaacha
MAPUTO
Lichtenburg
2 Krugersdorp
Randfontein
Oliver Tambo
Carolina
Malalotja Nature Reserve
Ventersdorp
Soweto
Johannesburg
Mpumalanga
Mlilwane Wildlife Sanctuary
MBABANE
Bela Vista
Coligny
2
Bethal
Ermelo
Manzini
Potchefstroom
Vanderbijlpark
Vereeniging
Heidelburg
Balfour
Secunda
Amsterdam
SWAZILAND
Mkhaya Game Reserve
Ottosdal
Klerksdorp
Sasolburg
Big Bend
Ponta d'Ouro
Orkney
Parys
Vaal Dam
Standerton
Amersfoort
Piet Retief
Nhlangano
Wolmaransstad
Viljoenskroon
Koppies
Heilbron
Frankfort
Volksrust
Wakkerstroom
Golela
Jozini
Bothaville
Bloemhof Dam
Villiers
Vrede
SOUTH AFRICA
Utrecht
Paulpietersburg
Pongola
Kroonstad
Petrus Steyn
Reitz
Warden
Vryheid
uMkhuze Game Reserve
9 iSimangaliso Wetland Park
Odendaalsrus
Steynsrus
Lindley
Newcastle
Nongoma
Hluhluwe-iMfolozi Park
Bultfontein
Ventersburg
KwaZulu-Natal Battlefields
Dundee
4 Babanango
11
Theunissen
Bethlehem
Golden Gate Highlands National Park
Harrismith
Mtubatuba
St Lucia
Winburg
12
Clarens
Sterkfontein Dam
Ladysmith
KwaZulu-Natal
Brandfort
Marquard
Senekal
Royal Natal National Park
Bergville
Colenso
Empangeni
Richards Bay
Ficksburg
Leribe
Champagne Castle (3377m)
Weenen
Kranskop
Eshowe
Clocolan
Drakensberg Escarpment
Estcourt
Tugela
BLOEMFONTEIN
Ladybrand
Tsehlanyane National Park
Mooirivier
Greytown
MASERU
Teyateyaneng
Mokhotlong
Thabana-Ntlenyana (3482m)
3 Howick
KwaDukuza (Stanger)
Dewetsdorp
Reddersburg
uKhahlamba-Drakensberg Park
King Shaka
Ballito
Edenburg
Wepener
Mafeteng
Underberg
Pietermaritzburg
Umhlanga Rocks
Smithfield
Zastron
Mohales Hoek
Richmond
Pinetown
Durban
7
LESOTHO
Qachas Nek
Matatiele
Amanzimtoti
Umkomaas
Aliwal Shoal & Protea Banks
Bethulie
Rouxville
Quthing
Kokstad
Harding
Scottburgh
5
Gariep Dam
Aliwal North
Eastern Cape
Port Shepstone
INDIAN OCEAN
Mapai
MOZAMBIQUE
Guija
Magude
Macia
Moamba
Manhiça
Guija
Kruger National Park
Kruger Mpumalanga

N
0   100 km
0   50 miles

SIGHTS & ACTIVITIES

 SEE

 DO

ITINERARY

1

2

1 Table Mountain, Cape Town

Around 600 million years old, and a canvas painted with the rich diversity of the Cape floral kingdom, Table Mountain is truly iconic. You can admire this showstopper from multiple angles, but you really can't say you've visited Cape Town until you've stood on top of it.

2 Cape Winelands

The Winelands region, famed around the globe for its superb vineyards, sits just northeast of Cape Town. The magnificent mountain ranges around Stellenbosch and Franschhoek provide ideal microclimates for the vines and there are hundreds of estates dotting the hillsides. A tasting tour will likely form the backbone of your visit.

3 Robben Island

Used as a prison from the early days of the VOC right up until 1996, this Unesco World Heritage Site is preserved as a memorial to those (such as Nelson Mandela) who spent many years incarcerated here. Tours last around four hours, including ferry rides from Cape Town.

4 Jeffrey's Bay

Once just a sleepy seaside town, 'J-Bay' is now one of the world's top surfing destinations. Boardies from all over the planet flock here to ride waves such as the famous Supertubes. June to September are the best months for experienced surfers, but novices can learn at any time of year.

5 Prince Albert

Cape wine is justifiably celebrated but for food to accompany it this charming village in the Karoo, accessible on a day trip from Oudtshoorn or the coast, is the place to be. Although encircled by harsh country, the town is green and fertile, producing soft fruits and olives. A slew of farms, producers, markets and restaurants offers tasting experiences.

6 Hermanus

Hermanus is one of the world's best land-based whale-watching locations. Southern right whales arrive from June to December. A cliff path with lookouts runs 10km from New Harbour.

7 Cederberg Wilderness Area

The 830-sq-km Cederberg Wilderness Area harbours San rock art, craggy mountains, clear streams and numerous trails perfect for hiking. As well as hiking, the Cederberg is popular with rock climbers, star gazers and photographers.

8 Knysna

Knysna is probably the Garden Route's most famous town, and for good reason. Take to the gorgeous lagoon for water sports, hike the ancient forests in search of elephants and dine on the town's famous oysters.

9 Langebaan

The town of Langebaan is known for its water sports, particularly kitesurfing and windsurfing on its lagoon.

10 Kirstenbosch National Botanical Garden, Cape Town

There's been European horticulture on the picturesque eastern slopes of Table Mountain since the 17th century. Today it's a spectacular showcase for the Cape Floral Kingdom, which was declared a World Heritage site for its incredible biodiversity. Take in the view from the treetop walkway known as the Boomslang.

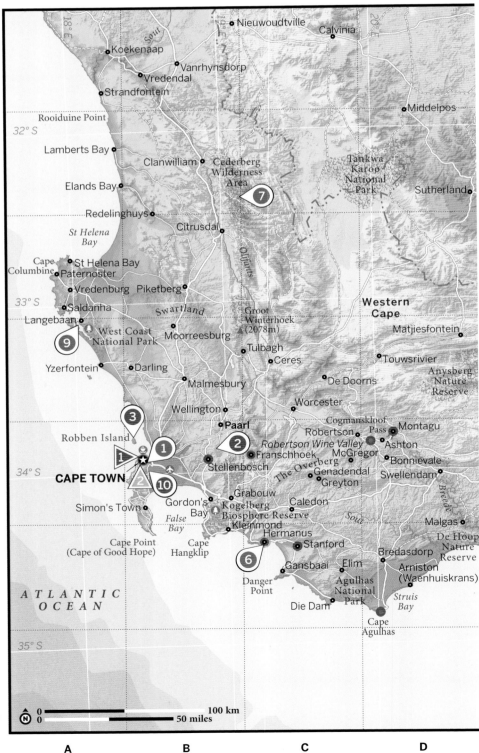

18-day itinerary
Cape Cruise

After a few days in **Cape Town** museum-hopping and scaling Table Mountain, head to **Stellenbosch** and **Franschhoek** in the Winelands. Next hit the coast to whale watch at **Hermanus**, before you move on to **Stanford**, **Cape Agulhas** (Africa's southernmost point), Cogmanskloof Pass, **Montagu** and the **Robertson Wine Valley**. Now travel along Rte

62 between rolling mountains dotted with charming towns such as **Calitzdorp**. Cross the Swartberg range from Oudtshoorn to the Great Karoo and **Prince Albert** where the nearby N1 highway leads back to Cape Town; alternatively, backtrack south to the ever-popular Garden Route, with stops at **Wilderness**, **Knysna** and **Plettenberg Bay**.

7-day itinerary
Alternative Cape

From **Cape Town**, head north to the **West Coast National Park**, which offers an accessible, southern look at the spring wildflower bloom on the shores of Langebaan Lagoon. Overnight in the park's Duinepos chalets or Paternoster, with art galleries and restaurants among its whitewashed cottages. Veer inland to **Tulbagh**, where there are some

superb wineries surrounded by mountain ranges. Further into the Winelands, **Franschhoek** distils the area's refined, European charm, with its French Huguenot heritage, vineyards and restaurants. Cross the Franschhoek Pass and hit the N2 through the Overberg region to the delightful village of **Greyton**, with its thatched cottages, restaurants,

mountain views, and neighbouring 18th-century Genadendal Mission Station. The 14km Boesmanskloof Trail leads hikers to **McGregor**, a New Age village in the Breede River Valley. From Greyton, return to Cape Town via **Hermanus**. Finish the journey on the stunning, coastal Route 44, which winds around Cape Hangklip and skirts **Kogelberg Nature Reserve**.

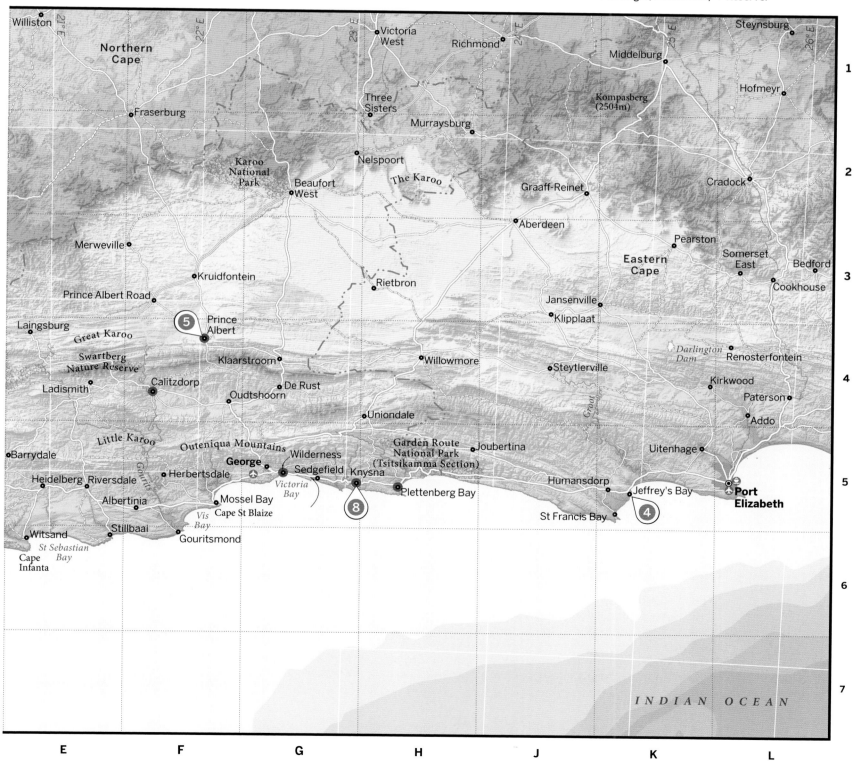

Indian Subcontinent

CLIMATE CHART

DELHI

RAINFALL INCH/MM
32/800 · 24/600 · 16/400 · 8/200 · 0

D N O S A J J M A M F J

TEMP °C/°F
40/104 · 30/86 · 20/68 · 10/50 · 0/32

KOLKATA

RAINFALL INCH/MM
32/800 · 24/600 · 16/400 · 8/200 · 0

D N O S A J J M A M F J

TEMP °C/°F
40/104 · 20/68 · 0/32 · -20/-4

A mesmerising medley of countries and cultures, deities and dynasties, the Indian subcontinent is united by the shared experience of British colonialism. So, while India has its temples, Sri Lanka has its stupas, Pakistan and Bangladesh have their mosques and Nepal has its mighty mountains, all share a love of the Sunday newspapers, government forms filled out in triplicate and a good cup of tea. India, Nepal, Pakistan and Bhutan come together in the rucked-up ridges of the Himalaya, while Sri Lanka floats in the idyllic blue of the Indian Ocean, alongside the atolls of Maldives. Shared across them are the relics of untold empires: ruined cities, desert forts and some of the most iconic palaces and religious buildings on the planet.

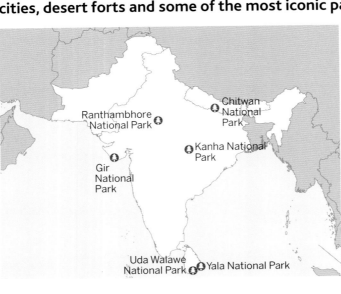

JUNGLES
The subcontinent gave the world the word 'jungle' and in reserves such as India's Ranthambhore National Park and Sri Lanka's Yala, wildlife encounters are intense. Seek tigers in India's Kanha National Park, Asiatic lions in Gir, rhinos in Nepal's Chitwan or wild elephants in Sri Lanka's Uda Walawe.

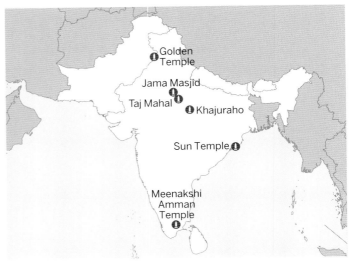

TEMPLES
Four of the world's great religions arose here, leaving behind such architectural masterpieces as Amritsar's Golden Temple, Madurai's Meenakshi Amman Temple, Konark's Sun Temple, and the erotic temples of Khajuraho. Later Muslim conquerors added Delhi's Jama Masjid and the Taj Mahal.

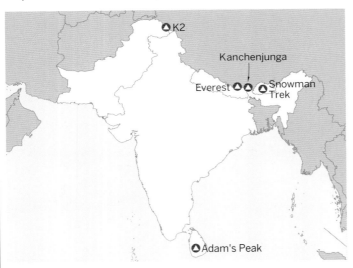

MOUNTAINS
The Himalayan mountain range slices across this region, taking in lots of the world's tallest summits. Trek the slopes of Everest in Nepal, gaze on Kanchenjunga in Nepal or K2 in Pakistan, attempt the Snowman Trek in Bhutan or set your sights lower on the pilgrimage to Adam's Peak in Sri Lanka.

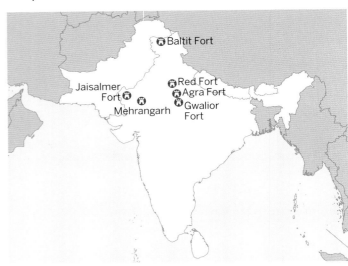

FORTS
Untold empires have marched across the subcontinent, from the British to the Mughals, leaving fortresses infused with the spirit of the *Arabian Nights*. Topping the list are Delhi's Red Fort, Jodhpur's Mehrangarh, epic eponymous forts in Agra, Gwalior and Jaisalmer, and Baltit in Pakistan's Karakoram.

Right: Devi Jagadambi Temple in Khajuraho, India, built between the 10th and 12th centuries.

Transport hubs

The Indian subcontinent is in the middle of an aviation revolution, as more and more airports open up to budget airlines, making this one of the cheapest places in the world to fly, hopping from gateway hubs such as Delhi, Mumbai, Kolkata and Bengaluru to every corner of the subcontinent. For terrestrial travel, take your pick from buses, boats, inexpensive chartered jeeps and taxis, and perhaps the most extensive and atmospheric rail network in the world.

ELEVATION KEY

	7500-10000M
	5000-7500M
	3000-5000M
	2000-3000M
	1500-2000M
	1250-1500M
	1000-1250M
	750-1000M
	500-750M
	250-500M
	100-250M
	75-100M
	50-75M
	25-50M
	1-25M

TRANSPORT

D3, D5, E8,
F3, G3, G4,
E7

C5, D7, D8,
E7, E8, F6,
G4

Delhi (see pp402-3 for city map)
India's busiest airport is the gateway to north India, with the great cities of Rajasthan and Uttar Pradesh and the Himalaya all within easy reach. Many visitors link up Delhi, Jaipur and Agra by train from New Delhi Railway Station, but other easy hops by rail include Amritsar, Shimla and Varanasi.

Mumbai
Western India opens up from Mumbai's comfortable and modern Chhatrapati Shivaji International Airport, with legions of budget airlines offering flights across the nation. Savvy travellers arrive by rail, into imposing Chhatrapati Shivaji Terminus, perhaps Asia's grandest colonial building.

Bengaluru
India's fast-growing air hub has pipped Chennai as the doorway to India's steamy south. From Bengaluru City and Yeshvantpur railway stations, trains rumble towards Goa, Kerala, Tamil Nadu, historic Hampi and the temple towns of the south.

Kolkata
Named for a Bengali freedom fighter, Kolkata's Netaji Subhash Chandra Bose International Airport is the portal not only to Bengal and eastern India, but to lofty Darjeeling, Sikkim and the little-explored tribal states of India's Northeast. By land, a multitude of trains roll daily into Kolkata (Chitpur), Howrah and Sealdah stations.

Kathmandu
Though new airports are under construction in the plains, Kathmandu's oversubscribed Tribhuvan International Airport currently receives all international flights. Domestic airlines link the capital to Pokhara, the Terai and trekking trailheads high in the Himalaya. For overland travel on to India and Tibet, buses and jeeps are the only option.

Colombo
Sri Lanka has two international airports, but most airlines use Colombo's Bandaranaike International Airport in preference to eerily quiet Mattala Rajapaksa International. Trains and buses link Colombo to the coast and the interior, climbing dramatically up through the Hill Country to Sri Lanka's ancient cities.

Dhaka
Numerous carriers, many from the Middle East, serve Dhaka's Hazrat Shahjalal International Airport, the nation's main air hub. From here, buses, trains and a flotilla of boats transport travellers around the waterlogged delta. For atmosphere, take a ride on the Rocket, Dhaka's unmistakable paddlewheel steamer.

Male
Velana International Airport takes up most of the island of Hulhule, a short ferryboat ride from the pint-sized Maldivian capital. Covering just 1.95 sq km, Male can easily be explored on foot, while ferries, speedboats and seaplanes wait to whisk guests to luxury resorts and inhabited islands around the atolls.

Paro
Tucked between mountains, Bhutan's international airport is approached by one of the most dramatic flight paths on earth. Only Bhutanese carriers fly to Paro, and visitors must come on a pre-arranged tour, so a vehicle and guide will be waiting to whirl you to Thimphu or other parts of the country.

Right: Taking a rickshaw in Delhi (left) and (right) Chhatrapati Shivaji Terminus in Mumbai.

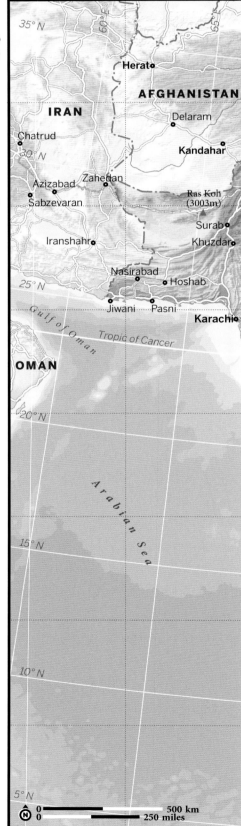

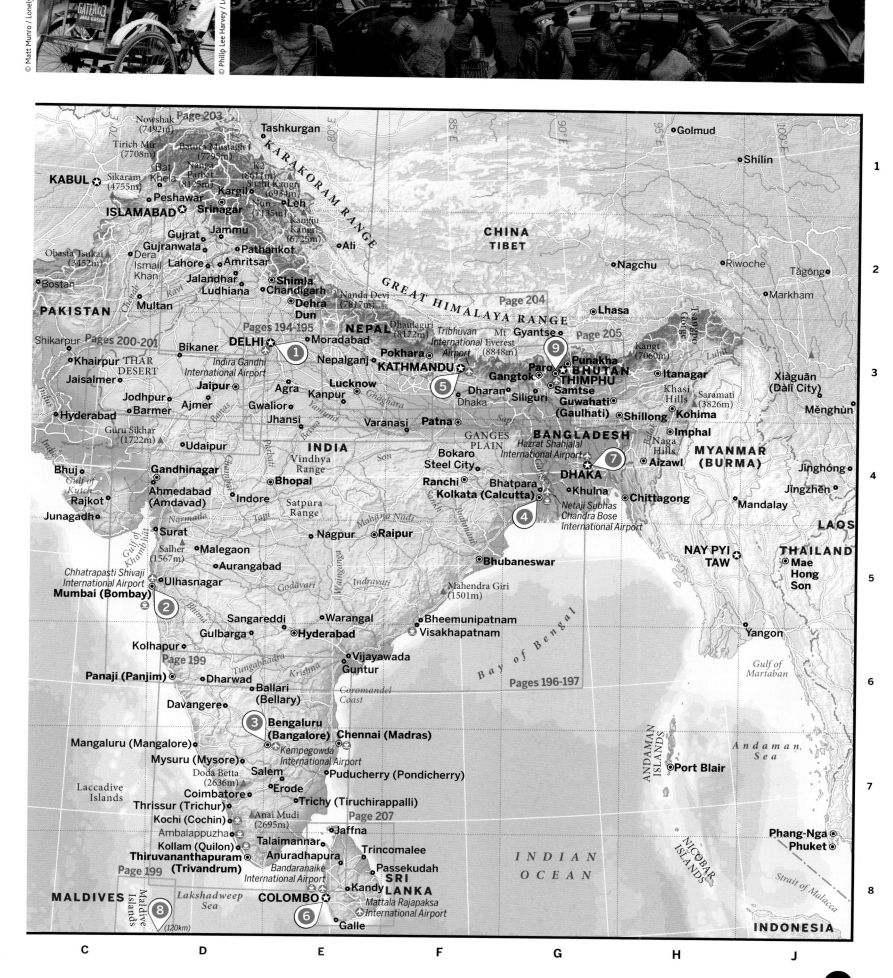

SIGHTS &
ACTIVITIES

 SEE

DO

ITINERARY

1

2

Keoladeo National Park, Bharatpur

This bird sanctuary and national park has long been recognised as one of the world's most important bird breeding grounds. In a good monsoon season, over one third of the park can be submerged, hosting 360 bird species.

Suraj Mahl's Palace, Deeg

At the centre of Deeg – a dusty tumult of a town north of Bharatpur – the incongruously glorious Suraj Mahl's Palace is edged by stately formal gardens. It's one of India's most beautiful and carefully proportioned palace complexes, full of stuffed tigers, faded sofas and royal heirlooms.

Taj Mahal, Agra

Poet Rabindranath Tagore described the Taj as 'a teardrop on the cheek of eternity'. Widely considered the most beautiful building in the world, this eye-wateringly graceful mausoleum was built by the Mughal Emperor Shah Jahan as a memorial for his wife, Mumtaz Mahal, who died in childbirth in 1631.

Jama Masjid, Fatehpur Sikri

Dominating the ruins of Akbar's model city at Fatehpur Sikri, this beautiful, immense mosque was completed in 1571, blending elements of Persian and Indian design. The spectacular 54m-high Buland Darwaza (Victory Gate) was built to commemorate Akbar's military triumphs in Gujarat.

Sangam, Allahabad

The *sangam* in Allahabad marks the auspicious point where two of India's holiest rivers, the Ganges and the Yamuna, meet the Saraswati, a mythical third river recorded in ancient Hindu texts. Every 12 years, as many as 100 million pilgrims flock here for the Kumbh Mela, the largest human gathering on earth.

Orchha Home-stay, Orchha

Started by the non-profit organisation Friends of Orchha, this unique homestay program offers a chance to stay with local people and experience traditional village life. You'll be sleeping on *charpoys* (rope beds) in humble homes, but the close interaction with villagers is priceless.

Gwalior Fort

Stretched along a 3km-long plateau overlooking Gwalior, this iconic fort is full of palaces, temples, museums and historic buildings, including the Scindia School, founded in 1897 for the education of Indian nobility.

Dashashwamedh Ghat, Varanasi

The ceremonial steps of Varanasi's most atmospheric ghat dip down to the waterside in a cascade of noise and colour. Dashashwamedh is mobbed by devotees, holy men, flower sellers, boat owners and touts, yet it still exudes a powerful sense of spirituality.

Sarnath

Near the sacred city of Varanasi, and surrounded by a ghost town of ruined Buddhist monasteries, the great stupa at Sarnath marks the site of the deer park where Siddhartha Gautama, the historical Buddha, gave his first sermon.

The Residency, Lucknow

The British Residency's cannon-scarred ruins are a reminder of the human cost of India's First War of Independence in 1857. Thousands were killed on both sides during the 90-day Siege of Lucknow, as Indian soldiers mutinied against their colonial commanders.

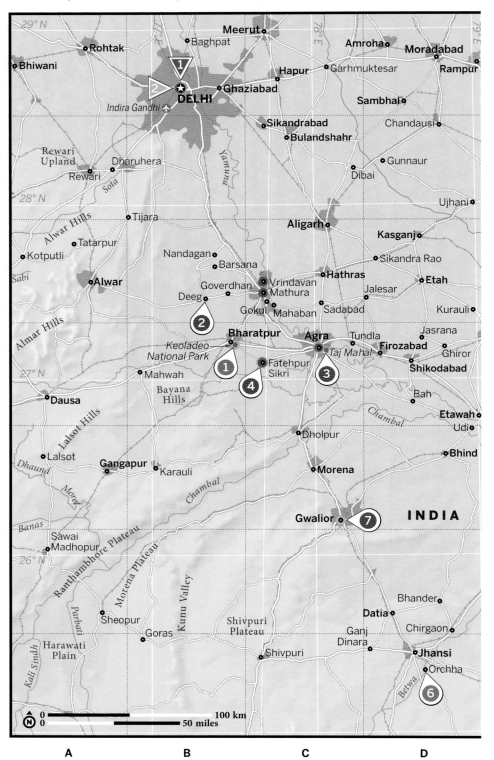

6-day itinerary
Mughal Rambles

The plains around Delhi and Agra were the crucible of the Mughal Empire. Start in **Delhi**, with a wander round medieval streets laid out by Shah Jahan, stopping in at the Jama Masjid and the Red Fort, seat of the last Mughal, Bahadur Shah Zafar. Next, roll south through **Mathura** and **Vrindavan**, childhood playgrounds of the Hindu god Krishna, to **Fatehpur Sikri**, the great city that Akbar built and abandoned to the desert winds. Complete the Mughal odyssey at **Agra**, where Akbar raised his grand fort and where Shah Jahan crafted the breathtaking Taj Mahal as a monument to love. A short train ride will whisk you back to Delhi at the end of the trip.

9-day itinerary
Once Across the Plains

Encompassing old, new and futuristic, with a population larger than Australia's, Delhi is the gateway to India's northern plains, forged by gods and scarred by empires. Start with a short stay in **Delhi**, browsing the ancient bazaars of Chandni Chowk and the ruins of India's first Islamic city at Qutb Minar. Next take the train south to Bharatpur, leaping off point for **Keoladeo National Park**, a watery playground for spoonbills, ibis, eagles and cranes. Rumble on to **Fatehpur Sikri** and **Agra**, for Mughal encounters and a day spent in awe at the Taj Mahal, then cut south to **Gwalior**, whose princely past lives on in the grand halls of Gwalior Fort and the Jai Vilas Palace. Now make haste for **Allahabad**, and pay your respects at the confluence of three holy rivers – the Ganges, Yamuna and mythical Saraswati. Reboard the train bound for **Varanasi**, India's most sacred city, and spend at least a day in the company of pilgrims and holy men on the *ghats* (sacred steps) that flank the Ganges River, before flying back to Delhi to close the circle.

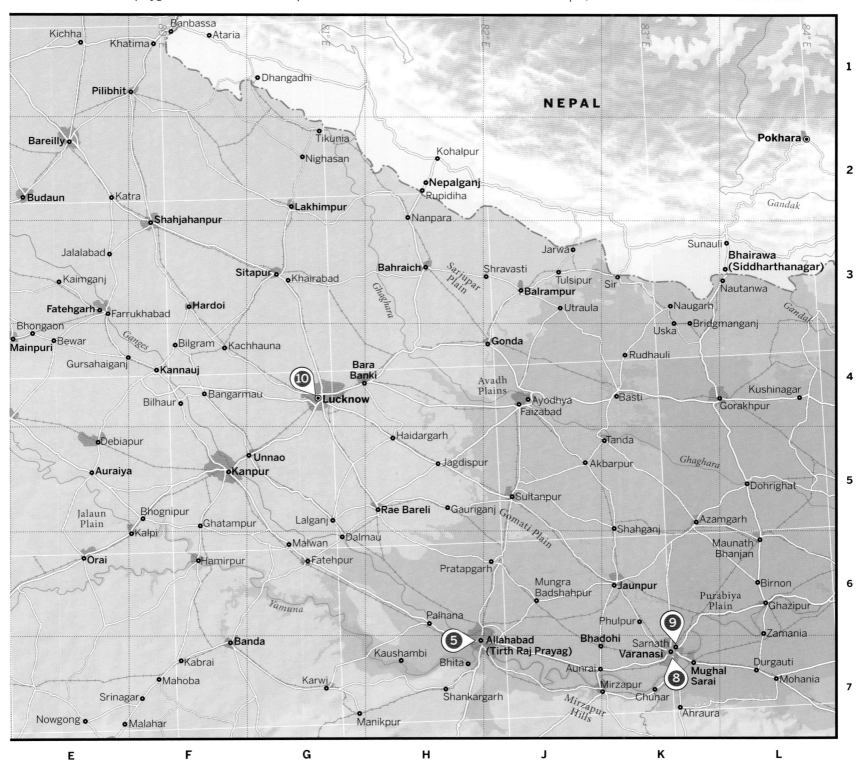

SIGHTS &
ACTIVITIES

 SEE

DO

ITINERARY

1

2

Elephanta Temple, Mumbai

Boats sail out daily (except Mondays) from Mumbai's Gateway of India bound for the rock-cut temples on Elephanta Island. Unesco-listed, the caves are famous for their vivid depictions of Hindu deities, including a three-faced statue of Shiva as the destroyer, creator and preserver of the universe.

Chhatrapati Shivaji Maharaj Terminus, Mumbai

Imposing and overflowing with people, this train station is Mumbai's most extravagant colonial building. Formerly known as Victoria Terminus, the station is a meringue of Gothic, Hindu and Islamic styles whipped into a Daliesque dream of buttresses, domes and spires.

Ajanta Caves

Set in a remote river valley, the cave temples of Ajanta were among the first monastic institutions in the subcontinent. Excavated from the 2nd to the 6th century BC, the site was lost for almost a millennium, until 1819 when a British hunting party stumbled across the jungle-choked caverns.

Ellora Cave Temples

The might of the hammer and chisel is clear at the Unesco World Heritage–listed Ellora cave temples, located 30km from Aurangabad. The pinnacle of Indian rock-cut architecture, the caves were chipped out over five centuries by generations of Buddhist, Hindu and Jain monks.

Lakshmana Temple, Khajuraho

Arguably the best preserved erotic temples of Khajuraho, the Lakshmana Temple took 20 years to build and was completed in about AD 954. View Khajuraho's most orgiastic carvings, including one gentleman proving that a horse can be a man's best friend.

Kipling Lodge, Kanha National Park

Just 3km from Kanha National Park's Khatia gate, this laid-back wildlife lodge is hosted by one of India's most dedicated tiger campaigners, film-maker, photographer and writer Belinda Wright. Thronged by wildlife, the lodge's profits are channelled to community causes.

Falaknuma Palace, Hyderabad

One of India's most charismatic heritage hotels, the former residence of the sixth Nizam of Hyderabad offers a taste of the opulent lifestyle enjoyed by the rulers of India's princely states. Built in 1884, the palace is a neoclassical masterpiece, full of heirlooms.

Sun Temple, Konark

Conceived as the cosmic chariot of the sun god Surya and towed by seven stone horses on 24 cartwheels, this vast 13th-century temple is lit by the sun at dawn, noon and sunset, illuminating the presiding deity.

Victoria Memorial, Kolkata

Had it been built for an Indian princess rather than a colonial queen, this would surely be considered one of India's greatest buildings. Today the white marble pavilion houses an even-handed museum of colonial history.

Sunderbans Tiger Reserve

The 2585-sq-km Sunderbans Tiger Reserve has 100-plus royal Bengal tigers who lurk in the depths of its mangrove forests, which also shelter everything from Gangetic dolphins and giant saltwater crocodiles to fishing eagles and luminescent kingfishers.

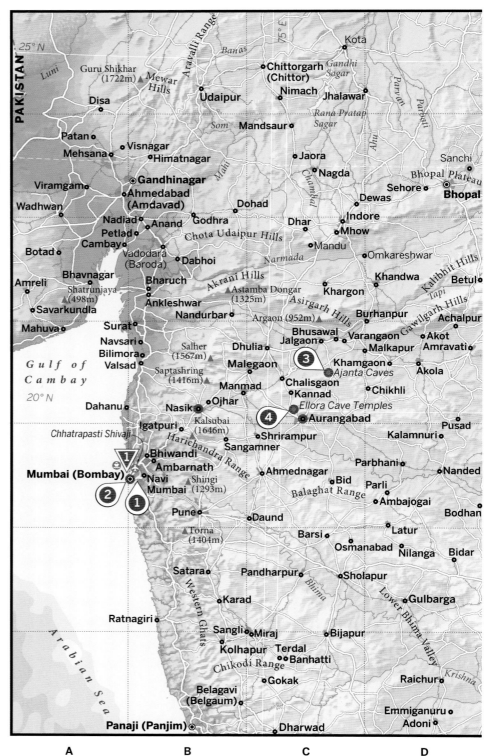

7-day itinerary
A Profusion of Temples

Travellers arriving in **Mumbai**'s modern metropolis will find religious history close at hand. Start with a boat ride across the harbour to the Elephanta Caves, carved in the 5th century (don't miss the effigy of Shiva as the creator and destroyer of the universe). From Mumbai, ride the rails northeast to **Aurangabad**, whose marble Bibi-qa-Maqbara pays homage to the Taj Mahal, then bus it to the **Ajanta Caves**, hewn by Buddhist masons over seven centuries. For all its magnificence, Ajanta was eclipsed by the nearby **Ellora Cave Temples**, where carvings of gods and angels represent the zenith of Indian temple art. Loop back to Mumbai via **Nasik**, gateway to Maharashtra's flourishing winelands.

10-day itinerary
Prowling Madhya Pradesh

A trip around Madhya Pradesh is a journey through jungles, faiths and legends. Start off in **Khajuraho**, where the masons of the Chandela dynasty created some of India's finest symphonies in stone. Risk a blush at the erotic carvings gracing the well-preserved Lakshmana Temple and **Kandariya-Mahadev Temple**, then delve into Madhya's tiger-teeming jungles at nearby **Panna National Park**, where you also stand a good chance of spotting leopards and sloth bears. More wildlife adventures await nearby at the **Bandhavgarh Tiger Reserve**, second only to Rajasthan's Ranthambhore for tiger encounters. Continue the safari further south at **Kanha National Park**, then roll on to **Sanchi**, whose Great Stupa was commissioned by the Buddhist emperor Ashoka in the third century BC. Move on to busy **Bhopal**, more notable for its rich Islamic history and tribal museum than for its tragic 20th-century industrial disaster, then complete the loop with a short hop back to Khajuraho.

SIGHTS &
ACTIVITIES

 SEE

DO

ITINERARY

1

2

Basilica of Bom Jesus, Old Goa
Old Goa's most famous monument, the 16th-century Basilica of Bom Jesus contains the tomb of the Portuguese missionary St Francis Xavier, the so-called Apostle of the Indies. The saint's 'incorrupt' body is displayed in a glass coffin behind the baroque facade.

Anjuna Flea Market
Goa's famous market was founded by hippies on the overland trail, who convened every Wednesday to trade pairs of jeans and jewellery to fund their travels. Today, the merchandise comes from all over India, from Keralan spices to Tibetan prayer flags.

National Gallery of Modern Art, Bengaluru
Housed in the former holiday home of the Maharaja of Mysuru in Bengaluru, this world-class art museum showcases an impressive permanent collection of works by Indian artists.

Mysuru Palace
The palace of the Wodeyar maharajas is actually a facsimile; the original palace was gutted by fire in 1897 and reconstructed in 1912. The Indo-Saracenic interior is a kaleidoscope of stained glass and mirrors and gaudy colours, and is illuminated on Sundays and holidays by 100,000 light bulbs.

Gomateshvara Statue, Sravanabelagola
The great statue of Gomateshvara at Sravanabelagola only comes into

Nagarhole National Park: A tiger peers out from amid trees.

view once you brave the 614 steps that climb the granite massif looming over the village. At 17m, the naked deity is said to be the world's tallest monolithic statue, and every 12 years millions of devotees douse the deity with coloured holy water.

Nagarhole National Park
West of the Kabini River, this 643-sq-km wildlife sanctuary provides a lush home for tigers, leopards, elephants and a host of other signature species. Herds of wild elephants gather on the riverbanks to drink, making this one of the best viewing locations in India.

Vittala Temple, Hampi
Rising to the northeast of Hampi Bazaar, the 16th-century Vittala Temple was never finished or consecrated, but its sculptural work – including an intricate stone chariot in the courtyard – remains the pinnacle of Vijayanagar art and a highlight of Hampi's ruins.

Alappuzha (Alleppey)
Explore Kerala's jungle-fringed backwaters by houseboat. From these floating homes (some in a better state of repair than others) paddy fields and

village life passes by at mesmerising pace. The chaotic town of Alappuzha (also known as Alleppey) offers the greatest choice of houseboat.

Periyar Wildlife Sanctuary
South India's most popular wildlife sanctuary, Periyar encompasses 777 sq km of wild forest and lakes, home to bison, wild boar, monkeys, nearly 1000 elephants and some 40 hard-to-spot tigers. Skip touristy boat cruises in favour of a trek led by tribal villagers.

Kerala Kathakali Centre, Kochi
Kathakali – Kerala's ancient tradition of dance-opera – is best experienced at a religious ceremony, but performances can last all night. For a taster, visit Kochi's intimate, wood-lined theatre, which introduces visitors to the rituals of Kathakali, including the painstaking application of vivid make-up.

Meenakshi Amman Temple, Madurai
The abode of the triple-breasted warrior goddess Meenakshi represents the peak of South Indian temple architecture. Founded in the 17th century, this is not so much a temple as a virtual city in Madurai, ringed by 12 gopurams (pyramidal towers), each encrusted with a staggering array of gods, goddesses, demons and heroes.

Old Friday Mosque, Male
The oldest mosque in the country, dating from 1656, the Hukuru Miskiiy was crafted from coral stone, chiselled with verses from the Quran. The interior is famed for its fine lacquer work and elaborate woodcarvings.

8-day itinerary
A Slice of the South

Bengaluru offers a calm counterpoint to chaotic Delhi and manic Mumbai. See Indian art at the National Gallery of Modern Art and fill up at restaurants, bars and microbreweries, then take the train southwest to historic **Mysuru** – until recently Mysore – the seat of the Wodeyar maharajas. Tour the staterooms of Mysuru Palace

then book onto the night sleeper to Hosapete, gateway to **Hampi**, temple-laden capital of the ancient kingdom of Vijayanagar. Explore for a few serene days, then take the train to **Panaji**, Goa's capital. Old Goa is strewn with Portuguese relics – the Basilica of Bom Jesus is a jewel – and spend a day on the sand at Anjuna before flying back to Bengaluru.

10-day itinerary
Cultured Kerala

Human-scale **Thiruvanantha-puram** (Trivandrum) is the doorway to Kerala's beaches and backwaters, but explore its towering temples and Victorian-era museums (the eccentric Napier Museum stands out) before rushing to the coast. Indulge your inner beach bum at **Varkala**, just north of Trivandrum,

then let the salt dry in your hair on the train trip to **Alappuzha** (Alleppey), embarkation point for a couple of peaceful days of drifting through Kerala's backwaters. Another train ride will transport you to **Kochi**; take your time seeing the historic Pardesi synagogue and Mattancherry Palace and attend

a performance of the ancient Keralan dance-opera known as kathakali. Now it's time to head inland for a jeep safari in **Wayanad Wildlife Sanctuary**, where wild elephants roam the steamy jungles. Finish off in **Kannur**, enjoying the lavish colours of a theyyam (ceremonial dance) performance at a local temple.

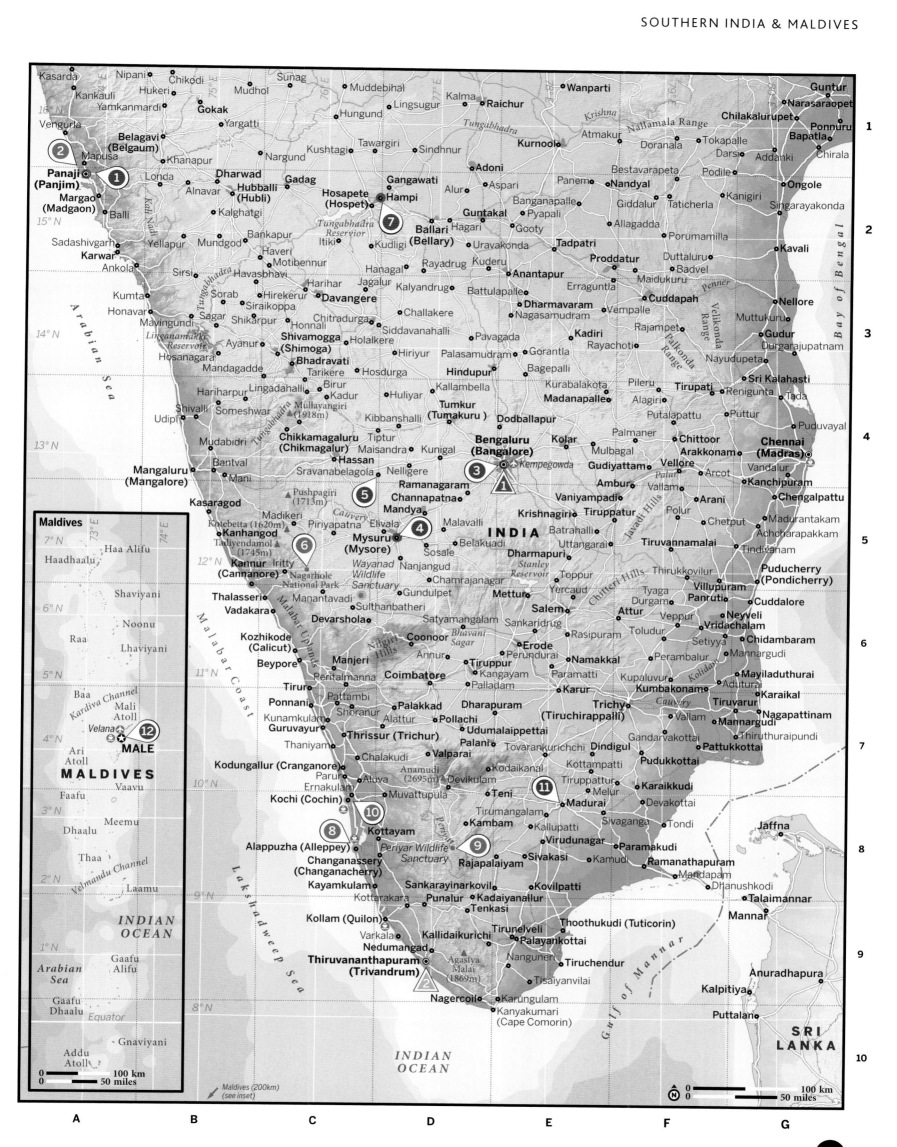

SIGHTS & ACTIVITIES

◉ SEE

◉ DO

ITINERARY

▽ 1

▽ 2

1 City Palace, Jaipur
A beguiling complex of courtyards, gardens and palace buildings, the City Palace blends Rajasthani and Mughal architecture. Parts of the palace now contain museums displaying some of the maharaja's finest treasures.

2 Jantar Mantar, Jaipur
The celestial observatory founded by Maharaja Jai Singh II in 1728 is a bizarre collection of geometric sculptures, all built for the purpose of measuring the heavens. Paying for a local guide is recommended if you wish to learn how each fascinating instrument works.

3 Amber Fort
Amber Fort, northeast of Jaipur, is a jumble of palaces and forts, hewn from yellow and pink sandstone and white marble. The women's quarters were designed so that the maharaja could make secretive nocturnal visits to his wives and concubines.

4 Pushkar Camel Fair
During the full moon of Kartika in October or November, a staggering 200,000 livestock traders converge on Pushkar, bringing with them some 50,000 camels, horses and cattle. The holy city becomes an extraordinary swirl of colour, sound and movement, thronged with musicians, mystics, livestock and devotees.

5 Ranthambhore National Park
Rajasthan's most famous national park preserves 1334 sq km of wild jungle and crocodile-filled lakes hemmed in by rocky ridges, enclosing the 10th-century ruins of Ranthambhore Fort. With more than 50 resident tigers lurking among the ruins, it's the best place to spot big cats in Rajasthan.

6 Chittorgarh
Rising from the plains like a rock island, Chittorgarh is the largest fort complex in India, and its history epitomises the romanticism, chivalry and tragedy of the Rajputs. Three times, Chittorgarh was attacked by a more powerful enemy, and each time, its men rode out from the fort to certain death, while women and children immolated themselves on huge funeral pyres.

7 Lake Pichola, Udaipur
At the heart of Udaipur, limpid Lake Pichola reflects the grey-blue mountains on its surface. The City Palace extends for nearly 1km along the lake's east shore, and floating amid the waters is the romantic Lake Palace.

8 Mehrangarh, Jodhpur
Rising above Jodhpur's skyline, Mehrangarh is one of India's most magnificent forts. Still run by the Jodhpur royal family, it is packed with history. Its walls bear the tragic handprints of royal widows who threw themselves on their maharajas' pyres.

9 Jaisalmer Fort
Jaisalmer's fortress is a living Indian city, with 3000 people residing within its sandstone walls. Hidden in its honeycomb of lanes are ornate merchants' houses and ancient temples, all created from the same golden stone.

10 Junagarh, Bikaner
Bikaner's landmark fortress was constructed between 1589 and 1593 by Raja Rai Singh, a general in the army of the Mughal emperor Akbar, but Junagarh is more noteworthy for its lavish interior decor than for military brute force.

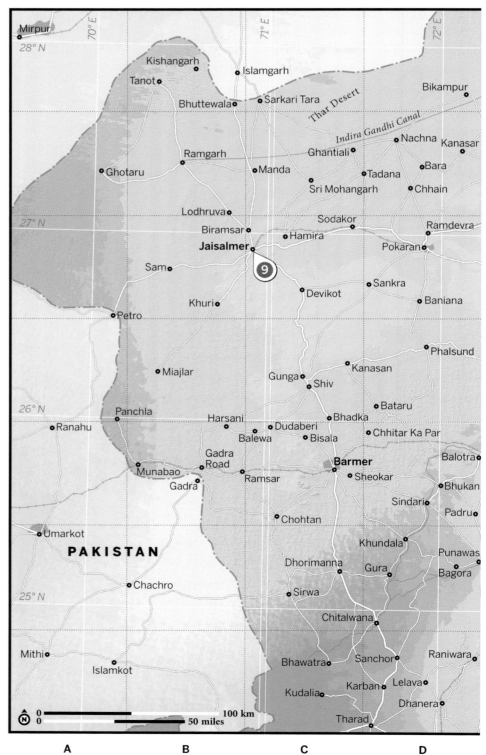

200

7-day itinerary
Rajasthan's Golden Triangle

The deserts of Rajasthan tell stories of feuding empires and epic, tragic acts of chivalry. Start your search for the soul of Rajasthan in **Jaipur**, where the City Palace and Hawa Mahal hint at the lavish lifestyle of the city's maharajas. It was Maharaja Jai Singh II who created Jantar Mantar observatory to monitor the stars. From Jaipur, take the train to **Ajmer** junction, to see the *dargah* (tomb) of the Sufi saint, Khwaja Muin-ud-din Chisthti, and then bus it to **Pushkar**, famed for its temples, sacred water tank and lively camel fair. Travel on to **Bundi**, pausing at the frescoed ruins of Bundi Palace, before cutting north to **Ranthambhore National Park** to spot tigers. Back in Jaipur, gaze over the city from the Heaven-Piercing Minaret.

10-day itinerary
Coloured Cities of Rajasthan

Rajasthan is alive with colour, from the turbans sported by proud Rajput gentlemen and India's most vivid bazaars to the lapis lazuli walls of its painted cities. From **Jaipur**, the Pink City – so named for the pink paint-job given to the old town in 1876 to welcome Queen Victoria – take the train southwest to magical **Udaipur**, the White City and a bastion of Rajasthani tradition, whose gleaming marble City Palace rises above the waters of placid **Lake Pichola**. Relive your favourite moments from *Octopussy*, filmed at Udaipur's Lake Palace in 1983, then move on to **Mt Abu**, Rajasthan's only hill station, crowned by the lavishly decorated Delwara Temples, two of Jainism's most revered monuments. Take the train on from Abu Road station to **Jodhpur**, the Blue City, painted kingfisher-blue by its Brahmin inhabitants. For superlative views, look down from the battlements of the magnificent Mehrangarh fort and descend to its base to wander the old city. One last train ride will speed you back to Jaipur.

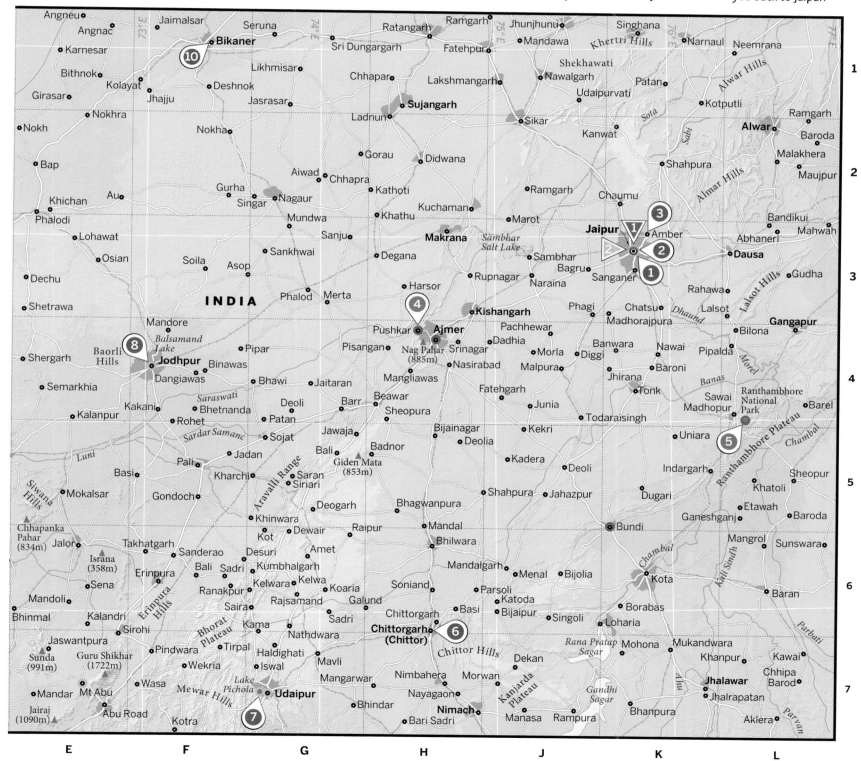

Golden Temple, Amritsar
The Sikh religion's most important shrine, encased in engraved gold panels, floats serenely atop the healing waters of the Amrit Sarovar, a vast ceremonial tank excavated by the fourth Sikh guru in 1577. Thronged day and night, priests keep up a continuous chant from the Sikh holy book.

Border Closing Ceremony, Attari-Wagah
Every afternoon at sunset, Indian and Pakistani border guards engage in a display of military showmanship that verges on pure theatre. Officially, the purpose of the ceremony is to formally close the border for the night, but what actually occurs is a bizarre mix of competitive marching, chest beating and almost comical high-stepping.

 Nek Chand's Rock Garden, Chandigarh
This sprawling sculpture garden was the fantasy of a local transport official who spent almost 20 years creating sculptures using discarded junk left over from the construction of Chandigarh. Entering is like falling down a rabbit hole into the depths of one man's imagination.

 Leh Palace
Bearing an obvious similarity to Lhasa's Potala Palace, this dun-coloured edifice was raised in the 17th century but its chambers have been unoccupied since the Ladakhi royal family were exiled in 1846. Climb to the uppermost rooftops for giddying views across to the mountains.

Golden Temple: The temple complex is surrounded by Amrit Sarovar, a giant pool said to have healing powers.

 Tabo Monastery
Founded in AD 996, reputedly by Ringchen Zangpo, the Great Translator, and filled with vivid murals and sculptures of protector deities and bodhisattvas, the monastery at Tabo is reckoned to be the oldest continuously functioning Buddhist monastery in India.

 Dal Lake, Srinagar
Over 15km around, Dal Lake is the jewel of Srinagar, a serene sheet of water reflecting the misty peaks of the Pir Panjal mountains. Gaily painted *shikaras* (taxi boats) skiff around as travellers soak up the view from the balconies of wooden houseboats.

 Tsuglagkhang, McLeod Ganj
At the heart of the Tibetan refugee settlement at McLeod Ganj, the revered Tsuglagkhang is the concrete equivalent of the Jokhang temple in Lhasa, built by Tibetan exiles. Note the statue of Avalokitesvara, bodhisattva of compassion, represented on earth by the Dalai Lama.

 Great Himalayan National Park
India's 754-sq-km Great Himalayan National Park reaches the 6000m-plus peaks of the Great Himalaya mountain range. Thick forests at lower altitudes give way to alpine meadows and high-altitude glaciers, offering stunning hiking and trekking opportunities.

 Shimla
Now Himachal's capital, Shimla was once British India's summer capital, an escape from the heat of the plains. The narrow-gauge Kalka to Shimla railway opened in 1906 to ferry colonial elites to this hill station. Its grand Viceregal Lodge can still be toured.

 Lahore Fort
Given its current form in 1566, Lahore Fort is the star attraction of the Old City. Within the walls you'll find a succession of stately palaces, halls and gardens built by Mughal emperors Akbar, Jehangir, Shah Jahan and Aurangzeb, comparable to the great forts at Delhi and Agra in India.

 Baltit Fort, Karimabad
Perhaps the most evocative fortress in the Karakoram range, Baltit Fort rises improbably against a sheer wall of snowy mountains. The oldest parts of the fort date from the 13th century, but Nazim Khan (r 1892–1938) was responsible for the wallpaper, fireplaces and tinted windows.

 Central Karakoram National Park
Pakistan's largest protected area, the Central Karakoram National Park contains most of Pakistan's highest peaks, including mighty K2 (8611m), second only to Mt Everest. Wild and inhospitable, it's the preserve of mountaineers on organised trips.

6-day itinerary
Delhi to Lahore

A pre-arranged Pakistani visa will see off administrative troubles on the Grand Trunk Road between India and Pakistan. Start by touring **Delhi's** Mughal monuments, then leave the tourist trail at **Patiala**, whose Qila Mubarak was the playground of a playboy maharaja. Take the bus on to surreal **Chandigarh** and marvel at the sculptures in Nek Chand's Rock Garden. Another bus whisks you to **Amritsar**, where the Golden Temple gleams. It's a short hop to Pakistan's border at **Attari-Wagah**, closed nightly with a display of military pomp. Trucks accompany you on the Grand Trunk to **Lahore**, mirroring Delhi with its fort, mosques and manic markets. Return by air to Delhi.

14-day itinerary
Rain Shadow of the Himalaya

No rain falls in the shadow of the Himalaya, where Buddhist monasteries cling to the sides of moisture-starved valleys. Embark from the historic hill station of **Shimla**, where the British-era hotels shimmer with the ghosts of the Raj, then put your vertigo to the test during the bus ride through lofty Kinnaur to wind-scoured Spiti. Pause at **Tabo**, whose dun-coloured monastery hides a treasure trove of Buddhist art, then follow precarious mountain roads on to **Keylong**. Another epic drive through frozen deserts will deliver you to **Leh**, capital of Buddhist Ladakh. Climb to the palace for humbling mountain views, then hopscotch along a chain of Buddhist monasteries (the Choskhor Temple at Alchi is particularly splendid) to **Kargil**, Ladakh's second city. One more climb over breathless passes will drop you down into **Srinagar**, for a houseboat stay on serene Dal Lake before you fly onwards to Delhi or beyond.

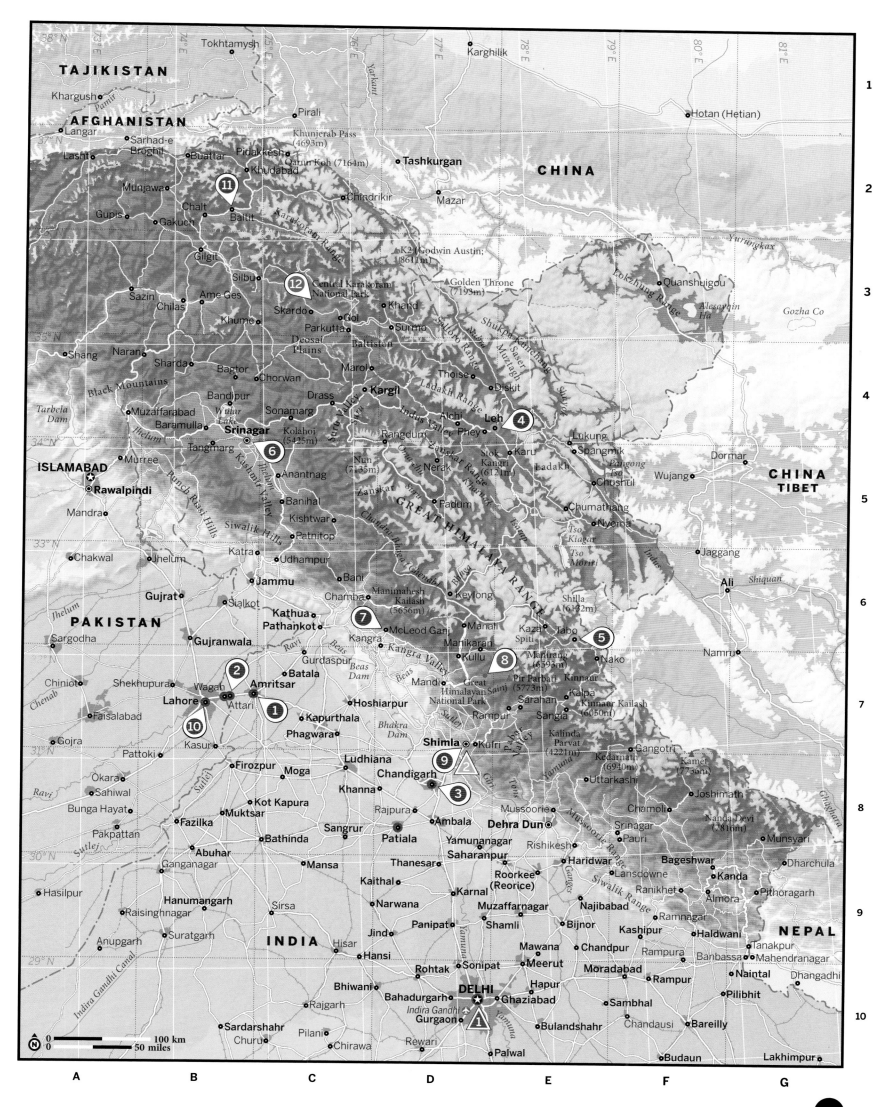

SIGHTS &
ACTIVITIES

SEE

DO

ITINERARY

 1

2

Swayambhunath Stupa, Kathmandu
Reached via a vertiginous stairway crowded with monkeys, climbing up the side of a conical hilltop, the whitewashed dome of Swayambhunath Stupa rises to a gilded spire, from where the eyes of Buddha keep watch over the valley.

Bodhnath Stupa, Bodhnath
No other stupa in Nepal comes close to Bodhnath. From its whitewashed dome to its golden tower, painted with the all-seeing eyes of the Buddha, the monument was laid out according to ancient Buddhist geometric principles, and Tibetan Buddhist pilgrims swirl around its base in a human tide.

Durbar Sq, Kathmandu
Kathmandu's stunning Durbar Square was where the city's medieval kings were crowned, and it formed the centre of their power and influence. Founded in the 17th century, the square bore the full force of the 2015 earthquake, but an astonishing amount of medieval architecture survived, from graceful, multi-tiered temples to the elegant precincts of the royal palace.

Durbar Sq, Patan
The concentrated mass of temples at

7-day itinerary
Once Around the Valley

Every journey in Nepal should start in **Kathmandu**, shaken by earthquakes but still standing proud after 14 centuries. Wander the old streets, dropping in on medieval masterpieces such as Durbar Square and Itum Bahal. Climb the monkey-crowded steps to the hilltop stupa of Swayambhunath, then join a tide of Tibetan pilgrims at magnificent **Bodhnath**, Nepal's most sacred Buddhist site. Continue on foot via the walking trail to **Sankhu** and the carving-filled Changu Narayan Temple, then drop downhill to historic **Bhaktapur**, whose ancient streets are a living museum of Nepali culture. Take a bus to the top of the ridge at **Nagarkot** for giddying views of eight Himalayan ranges, then travel back past Bhaktapur to gorgeous **Patan**, whose temple-crammed Durbar Square marks the high point of Newari architecture. Kathmandu is within walking distance, so take a gentle stroll through the backstreets, passing the fair-trade shops at Kupondol.

the heart of Patan's Durbar Square is perhaps the most stunning display of Newari architecture in all of Nepal. Temple construction went into overdrive during the Malla period (14th to 18th centuries), filling the skyline with tiled pagoda roofs and stone shikhara towers.

Ultimate Descents, Nepal
The rivers that drain down from the Himalaya provide some of the world's most spectacular white-water rafting and kayaking, from the snaking Trisuli to the foamy rage of the Marsyangdi. Ultimate Descents is one of the veterans of Nepali rafting and kayaking, and trips include nights beneath the stars on riverside beaches.

Chitwan National Park
World Heritage–listed Chitwan National Park protects more than 932 sq km of forests, marshland and grassland, providing a home for one-horned rhinos, deer, monkeys, and a healthy population of royal Bengal tigers. Traditionally, safaris were on elephant-back, but these days, visitors prefer to visit on foot or by jeep.

Janaki Mandir, Janakpur
Paying homage to the Mughal Baroque architecture of the Indian plains, the turreted and domed Janaki Mandir marks the spot where Lord Rama married Sita in the Ramayana.

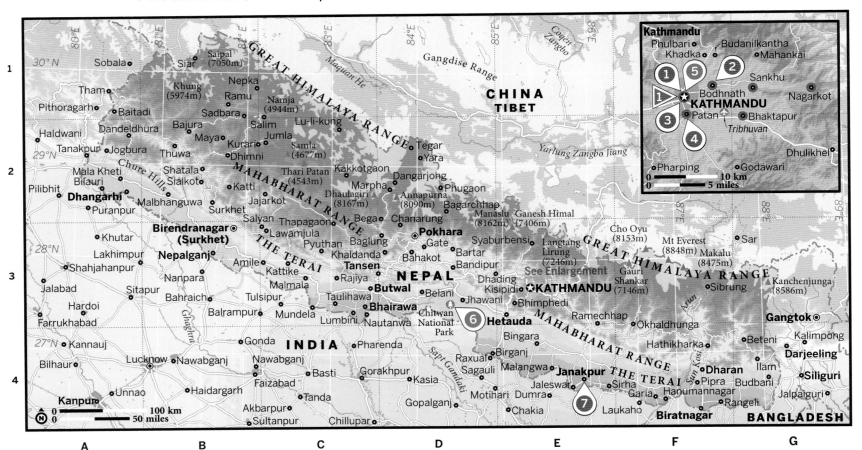

Tiger Hill

To watch the dawn break over a spectacular 250km stretch of Himalayan horizon, rise early and take a jeep out to Tiger Hill, 11km south of Darjeeling. From this famous viewpoint, the skyline is dominated by 8598m Khangchendzonga, the world's third-highest peak, painted into pastel colours by the pale morning light.

Rumtek

Sprawling along a forested ridge to the southeast of Gangtok, Rumtek is Sikkim's most spiritually significant monastery, and home-in-exile of the Kagyu sect of Tibetan Buddhism. The gompa was built in the 1960s to replace Tibet's Tsurphu Monastery, but the 17th Karmapa is still to be enthroned following a dispute over the reincarnation of his predecessor.

Tawang

Founded in 1681, magical Tawang Gompa is reputedly the world's second-largest Buddhist monastery after Drepung Monastery in Lhasa. The gleaming white gompa is famed in Buddhist circles for its priceless library filled with sacred scriptures, many with gold-washed pages. Come at dawn to see monks performing early-morning prayers and local farmers handing out grain to the assembled novices.

9-day itinerary
Himalayan Highlights and Cultured Kingdoms

With its airport and train station, **Siliguri** is the leaping-off point for the remarkable eastern Himalaya. Start with a jeep ride through tea plantations to lofty **Darjeeling**, for tea-tasting and views of 8598m Khangchendzonga from Tiger Hill. Joy-ride on Darjeeling's charming toy train then take another jeep to **Kalimpong**, for hikes to flower nurseries, viewpoints and mural-filled gompas (Buddhist monasteries). Continue north to **Gangtok** and drop into revered **Rumtek**, seat of the exiled Kagyu sect of Tibetan Buddhism. A bone-shaking bus ride will bring you back through Siliguri to **Phuentsholing**, where, with a prearranged tour, you can enter Bhutan and ascend to **Thimphu**, the kingdom's atmospheric capital. Catch the Weekend Market, then branch west to **Paro** and hike up to precariously perched Taktshang Goemba, Bhutan's signature landmark. Depending on your budget, consider a few more days in Bhutan around serene **Punakha** to visit its dzong (fortress), before retracing your steps back to Siliguri.

Taktshang Goemba

The 'Tiger's Nest Monastery' is one of the Himalaya's most incredible sites, perched on the side of a cliff 900m above the Paro Valley. According to legend, Guru Rinpoche flew here on the back of a flying tiger on one of his supernatural Himalayan excursions.

Punakha Dzong

Set at the confluence of two holy rivers, Punakha Dzong is arguably the most beautiful dzong (fortress monastery) in all of Bhutan, especially in spring when lilac-coloured jacaranda trees bring a lush sensuality to its towering, whitewashed walls.

Thimphu

Thimphu hosts the most captivating public market in Bhutan, if not the whole Himalaya. Its weekend bazaar fills the west bank of the Wang Chhu river with vendors trading everything from traditional Bhutanese handicrafts to dried fish, yak legs, and disks of *datse* (Bhutanese soft cheese).

Trongsa Dzong

Perhaps the most dramatically located dzong in Bhutan, Trongsa Dzong is a handsome sprawl of whitewashed chapels and prayer halls, perched high above the plunging valley of the Mangde Chhu river.

SIGHTS &
ACTIVITIES

SEE
DO

ITINERARY

1
2

National Museum, Colombo
A 9th-century stone Buddha greets you with an enigmatic smile as you enter Sri Lanka's premier cultural institution. In galleries dating back as far as 1877, you'll encounter art, carvings and statuary from Sri Lanka's ancient and recent past.

Galle Fort Walks
Home to hundreds of historic houses, churches, mosques, temples and civic buildings, Galle Fort is an experience to savour, taste and touch. Author and photographer Juliet Coombe brings the old city alive on excellent walking tours, exploring the city's myths, legends and black magic traditions.

Mirissa
Blue whales are similar to holidaying humans: they love the coast of Sri Lanka, and Mirissa in particular. Recommended boat operator Raja & the Whales uses a trimaran for whale-spotting trips and follows international wildlife-welfare guidelines.

Yala National Park
With trumpeting elephants, monkeys, peacocks and leopards sliding like shadows through the undergrowth, Yala National Park is *The Jungle Book* brought to life. Spanning 1268 sq km of woodland and grasslands, this is a playground for wildlife.

Temple of the Sacred Tooth Relic, Kandy
A vibrant symbol of Sri Lankan spirituality, the golden-roofed Temple of the Sacred Tooth houses Sri Lanka's most important Buddhist relic – a tooth of the historical Buddha. The sacred relic is kept in a gold casket shaped like a *dagoba*, at the centre of a captivating complex of temples, shrines and museums.

Cave Temples, Dambulla
A home in exile for King Valagamba of Anuradhapura, the caves of Dambulla were filled with rock-cut temples in the first century BC. Lavish paintings were added later by King Nissanka Malla, creating Sri Lanka's most important powerhouse of religious art.

Handungoda Tea Estate
At the heart of Sri Lanka's tea country, this exquisite tea plantation in the hills above Koggala is owned by Herman Gunaratne, one of the legends of the island's tea industry. On highly informative tours, visitors get to sample and investigate the production of over 25 delectable varieties of tea.

Sigiriya
Rising from the central plains, the enigmatic rocky outcrop of Sigiriya is perhaps Sri Lanka's most dramatic sight. Vertiginous stone stairways climb past remarkable frescoes to a flat-topped summit that contains the ruins of an ancient civilisation.

Polonnaruwa
For three centuries Polonnaruwa was a royal capital, and the Buddhist rulers of the Chola and Sinhalese kingdoms left behind a mesmerising garden of temples, stupas, brick-walled monasteries and other historic treasures, spilling out from the jungle.

Minneriya National Park
Dominated by the ancient Minneriya Wewa reservoir, Minneriya's 88.9 sq km of scrub, forest and wetlands provide shelter for an astonishing variety of wildlife. Wild elephants come together here in vast groups, often numbering 200 or more, for the phenomenon known as 'the Gathering' from April to October.

Sri Maha Bodhi, Anuradhapura
The sacred bodhi tree at Anuradhapura was grown from a cutting brought from Bodhgaya in India, where the Buddha attained enlightenment. It is said to be the oldest historically authenticated tree in the world, tended by an uninterrupted succession of guardians for over 2000 years.

Arugam Bay
The famous, long point break at the southern end of Arugam Bay serves up consistently good surf from April to September. Some breaks are best left to the experienced, but for newbies, the Safa surf shop run by surfer Fawas Lafeer offers well thought-out lessons from local instructors.

Galle Fort: Within the walls of the fort, Galle Lighthouse guards against the rocks at the southern end of the Galle promontory.

7-day itinerary
Colombo to the Hills

Before reclining on one of Sri Lanka's blissful beaches, explore the jungle-cloaked interior. Kick off in **Colombo**, where the old Dutch Hospital and the National Museum spin a tale of feuding European powers. Ride the rails uphill to **Kandy**, famed for its Esala Perahera festival and the temple that enshrines a tooth of the historical Buddha. Take the bus on to **Nuwara Eliya** and sample the brews at the Pedro Tea Estate, before climbing to the eerie plateau of **Horton Plains National Park**, for a hike to World's End and views across the hill country. You may have time for a pilgrimage to **Adam's Peak** – revered by Buddhists, Hindus and Christians – then return to Colombo and the coast.

10-day itinerary
Sri Lanka's Ancient Cities

Sri Lanka's tropical hills are dotted with the ruined remains of ancient civilisations. Start in elegant **Kandy**, where pilgrims queue for a grace-giving glimpse at the Temple of the Sacred Tooth Relic, then take a bus to **Dambulla**, whose cave temples overflow with swirling carvings and Buddhist art treasures. A short hop northeast will drop you at the base of mighty **Sigiriya**, a soaring rocky outcrop crowned by the ruins of King Kasyapa's pleasure palace. Continue to **Minneriya National Park**, where wild elephants often gather in herds of a hundred or more. Make your next stop **Polonnaruwa**, blessed with stunning temples and *dagobas* (stupas) from the 10th century. Admire the Rankot Vihara and Val Vihara, then complete the old city tour with a bus ride to **Anuradhapura**, home to the legendary Sri Maha Bodhi – a direct descendant of the sacred tree under which Buddha attained enlightenment.

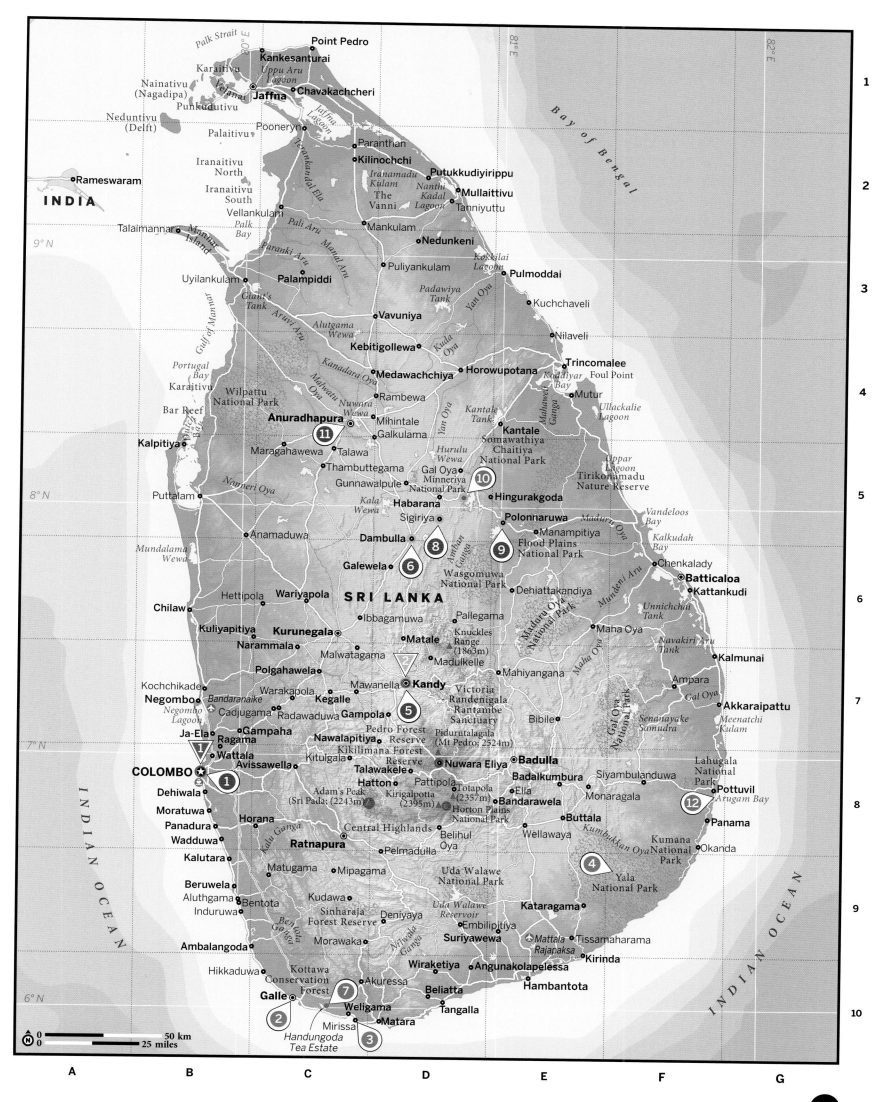

Palk Strait

Point Pedro

Kankesanturai

Karaitivu

Uppu Aru Lagoon

Nainativu (Nagadipa)

Jaffna

Chavakachcheri

Punkudutivu

Neduntivu (Delft)

Pooneryn

Jaffna Lagoon

Palaitivu

Paranthan

Rameswaram

Kilinochchi

Iranaitivu North

Iranamadu Kulam

Putukkudiyirippu

INDIA

Iranaitivu South

The Vanni

Nanthi Kadal Lagoon

Mullaittivu

Vellankulam

Mankulam

Tanniyuttu

Talaimannar

Palk Bay

Mannar Island

Faranki Aru

Puliyankulam

Nedunkeni

Kokkilai Lagoon

Uyilankulam

Giant's Tank

Aruvi Aru

Pali Aru

Manal Aru

Palampiddi

Padawiya Tank

Yan Oya

Pulmoddai

9°N

Gulf of Mannar

Portugal Bay

Vavuniya

Kuchchaveli

Karaitivu

Alutgama Wewa

Kebitigollewa

Kanadara Oya

Kuda Oya

Nilaveli

Bar Reef

Wilpattu National Park

Medawachchiya

Rambewa

Horowupotana

Trincomalee

Kaddiyar Bay

Foul Point

Kalpitiya

Malwatu Oya

Nuwara Wewa

Anuradhapura

Mihintale

Galkulama

Yan Oya

Kantale Tank

Mutur

Ullackalie Lagoon

⑪

Mahaweli Ganga

Kantale

8°N

Nameri Oya

Maragahawewa

Talawa

Hurulu Wewa

Somawathiya Chaitiya National Park

Uppar Lagoon

Tirikonamadu Nature Reserve

Puttalam

Thambuttegama

Kala Wewa

Gunnawalpule

Gal Oya

Minneriya National Park

⑩

Hingurakgoda

Vandeloos Bay

Mundalama Wewa

Anamaduwa

Habarana

Sigiriya

Polonnaruwa

Maduru Oya

Manampitiya

Flood Plains National Park

Kalkudah Bay

Dambulla

⑧

Amban Ganga

⑨

Chenkalady

Galewela

⑥

Wasgomuwa National Park

Batticaloa

Hettipola

Wariyapola

SRI LANKA

Dehiattakandiya

Kattankudi

Chilaw

Ibbagamuwa

Pallegama

Unnichchai Tank

Kuliyapitiya

Kurunegala

Matale

Knuckles Range (1863m)

Maha Oya

Navakiri Aru Tank

Kalmunai

Narammala

Malwatagama

Madulkelle

Maduru Oya National Park

Maha Oya

Polgahawela

Mawanella

⑦

Kandy

Mahiyangana

Ampara

Gal Oya

Akkaraipattu

Kochchikade

Negombo

Warakapola

Kegalle

⑤

Victoria Randenigala Rantambe Sanctuary

Bibile

Gal Oya National Park

Senanayake Samudra

Meenatchi Kulam

Bandaranaike

Cadjugama

Radawaduwa

Gampola

Negombo Lagoon

Nawalapitiya

Pedro Forest Reserve

Piduruntalagala (Mt Pedro: 2524m)

Ja-Ela

①

Ragama

Kikilimana Forest Reserve

Kitulgala

Wattala

Avissawella

Talawakele

Nuwara Eliya

Badulla

Badalkumbura

Siyambulanduwa

Lahugala National Park

7°N

COLOMBO

①

Hatton

Pattipola

Totapola (2357m)

Ella

Monaragala

Pottuvil

Arugam Bay

Dehiwala

Adam's Peak (Sri Pada: (2243m)

Kirigalpotta (2395m)

Bandarawela

⑫

Moratuwa

Horana

Horton Plains National Park

Buttala

Panama

Panadura

Central Highlands

Belihul Oya

Wellawaya

Kumbukkan Oya

Kumana National Park

Wadduwa

Ratnapura

④

Yala National Park

Okanda

Kalutara

Matugama

Mipagama

Uda Walawe National Park

Beruwela

Kalu Ganga

Kudawa

Kataragama

Aluthgama

Bentota

Sinharaja Forest Reserve

Deniyaya

Uda Walawe Reservoir

Induruwa

Embilipitiya

9

Morawaka

Nilwala Ganga

Suriyawewa

Mattala Rajapaksa

Tissamaharama

Ambalangoda

Benota Ganga

Kirinda

Hikkaduwa

Kottawa Conservation Forest

⑦

Wiraketiya

Angunakolapelessa

INDIAN OCEAN

Galle

②

Akuressa

Beliatta

Hambantota

Weligama

Matara

③

Mirissa

Tangalla

Handungoda Tea Estate

0 — 50 km
0 — 25 miles

A   B   C   D   E   F   G

Northeast Asia

Home to the world's oldest civilisations, holiest temples, grandest landscapes and greatest cities – not to mention some of its weirdest food – the nations of Northeast Asia have enough attractions to sustain lifetimes of travel. Take China, a riveting jumble of dialects, landscapes, cultures and topographical extremes, it's like several different countries rolled into one. Japan and South Korea are just as varied, nations where ancient traditions are fused with modern life as if it were the most natural thing in the world. Then there's Taiwan, a green island combining outdoor adventures, dynamic cities and spirited traditions, and Tibet, a land of monasteries, mountains and some of the friendliest people you will ever meet.

CLIMATE CHART

BĚIJĪNG

RAINFALL INCH/MM
—12/300
—8/200
—4/100
—0

D N O S A J J M A M F J

TEMP °C/°F
40/104
30/86
20/68
10/50
0/32
-10/14
-20/4
-30/22
-40/40

TOKYO

RAINFALL INCH/MM
—16/400
—12/300
—8/200
—4/100
—0

D N O S A J J M A M F J

TEMP °C/°F
40/104
30/86
20/68
10/50
0/32
-10/14

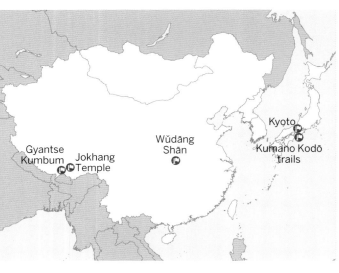

SACRED PLACES
Religion informs life here: be it Buddhism, Shinto, Taoism, Confucianism or Shugendo. Find peace in the temples of Kyoto, take a pilgrimage along the Kumano Kodō trails, commune with the spirit of Taoist martial arts in Wǔdāng Shān, climb the 32m-high chorten in Gyantse Kumbum, or light a butter lamp in Jokhang, Lhasa's most sacred temple.

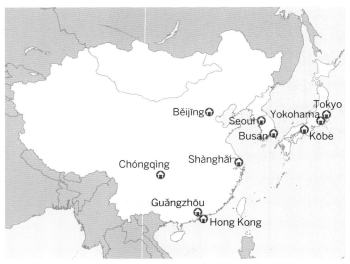

CITIES
If it's urban excitement you're after, Northeast Asia holds many of the world's mightiest metropolises – both the well-known (Běijīng, Shànghǎi, Tokyo, Seoul, Hong Kong) and lesser-visited (Guǎngzhōu, Chóngqìng, Yokohama, Kōbe and Busan, to name a few). Home to multiple millions, they offer a non-stop, neon-lit adrenaline hit.

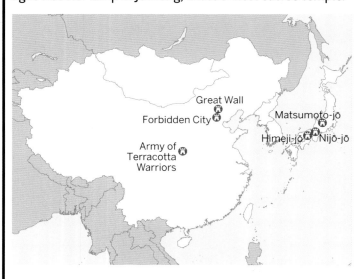

ANCIENT HISTORY
While much of Northeast Asia is about looking to the future, this is also a place in thrall to the past. Cradle of several of the world's oldest civilisations, it's a place to indulge your history buff like no other – whether you're walking the battlements of the Great Wall, pondering the past in the Forbidden City, marvelling at the Terracotta Warriors, or time-travelling into feudal-era Japan at the castles of Himeji-jō, Nijō-jō and Matsumoto-jō.

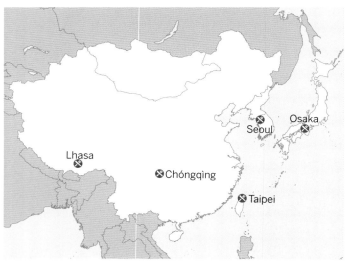

CUISINE
If there's one thing the diverse peoples of Northeast Asia share, it's a love of food. Melt over a Chóngqìng hotpot, sample okonomiyaki pancakes in Osaka, taste bibimbap and kimchi in Seoul, sup beef noodle soup and stinky tofu in Taipei – the flavours are myriad. Tibetan cuisine is more of an acquired taste, and generally more about survival than pleasure but, who knows, you might come away from Lhasa with a taste for *tsampa* porridge and yak-butter tea.

Right: The bright lights of Japan's capital surrounding its Tokyo Tower.

Transport hubs

Major cities including Běijīng, Shànghǎi, Osaka, Tokyo, Seoul and Hong Kong host some of the world's busiest airports, with flight connections across the globe, so northeast Asia is invariably easy to get to. Once in Asia, you can catch an onward flight to Taipei and Lhasa. Japan and China have two of the world's busiest, biggest rail systems, making travel a breeze, whether you opt for a futuristic bullet-train or a long-distance slow-coach.

ELEVATION KEY

7500-10000M
5000-7500M
3000-5000M
2000-3000M
1500-2000M
1250-1500M
1000-1250M
750-1000M
500-750M
250-500M
100-250M
75-100M
50-75M
25-50M
1-25M

TRANSPORT

F4, F7, G4, G5, G6, H4, J4

F4, F5, F6, F7, G4, G5, G7, H4, H5, J3

① Běijīng (see pp390-1 for city map)
Most travellers fly to Běijīng Capital International Airport. The only trains from overseas to Běijīng come from Mongolia, North Korea, Russia and Vietnam, as well as Hong Kong and Lhasa in Tibet. High-speed 'bullet' trains travel to cities such as Tiānjīn, Shànghǎi, Hángzhōu and Qīngdao. The massive, multi-line Běijīng subway system is modern, safe, cheap, easy to use – and incredibly crowded.

② Shànghǎi
Shànghǎi is China's second-largest international air hub (or third including Hong Kong); most travellers arrive at Pǔdōng International Airport. The city is also a hub for China's gargantuan rail service, with high-speed G-class trains to Běijīng, Hángzhōu, Nánjīng and Sūzhōu, plus long-distance services to Kowloon in Hong Kong, and even Lhasa in Tibet. Shànghǎi's metro has 14 lines serving 366 stations over 617km.

③ Hong Kong (see pp408-9 for city map)
More than 100 airlines operate from Hong Kong International Airport. The ultramodern Mass Transit Railway (MTR) is the quickest way to get to most urban destinations. Ferries link the China Ferry Terminal in Kowloon and the Hong Kong–Macau Ferry Terminal on Hong Kong Island with towns on the Pearl River Delta, including Macau. Fast trains travel to Guǎngzhōu, Běijīng and Shànghǎi.

④ Tokyo (see pp436-7 for city map)
Tokyo has two international airports. Narita Airport is the primary gateway to Tokyo; most budget flights end up here. Haneda Airport, closer to the city centre, is where most domestic flights arrive. Tokyo Station is the main point of entry for travellers coming via shinkansen (bullet train) from other parts of Japan. The city's rail network includes JR lines, a subway system and commuter lines that depart in every direction for the suburbs. Trains run with formidable punctuality.

⑤ Osaka
Two airports serve Osaka: Kansai International Airport for all international and some domestic flights; and the mainly domestic Itami Airport, also confusingly called Osaka International Airport. Shin-Osaka Station is on the Tōkaidō-Sanyō shinkansen line (between Tokyo and Hakata in Fukuoka), and also has regular trains to Kyoto, Kōbe and Nara.

⑥ Taipei
Taiwan is an island, so air is the most common means of arrival, into Taiwan Taoyuan International Airport. But arrival by sea is an option too: there are daily ferries from/to Xiàmén (Fujian province, China) and Kinmen Island, plus Matsu Island and Fúzhōu (Fujian province, China).

⑦ Seoul (see pp430-1 for city map)
Most international flights leave from Incheon International Airport, connected to Seoul by road (80 minutes) and train (60 minutes). Ferries link a dozen Chinese ports with Incheon, and four Japanese cities to Busan.

⑧ Lhasa
The usual route to Lhasa is to fly from Kathmandu in Nepal. You can also drive from Kathmandu along the Friendship Hwy. In theory, it is possible to fly from Chinese cities (Chéngdū, Kūnmíng, Xī'ān or Běijīng), but bureaucratic obstacles to entering Tibet from China make this fraught with complexity.

Right: A Běijīng rickshaw driver takes a break (left) and (right) a high-speed train in Shànghǎi.

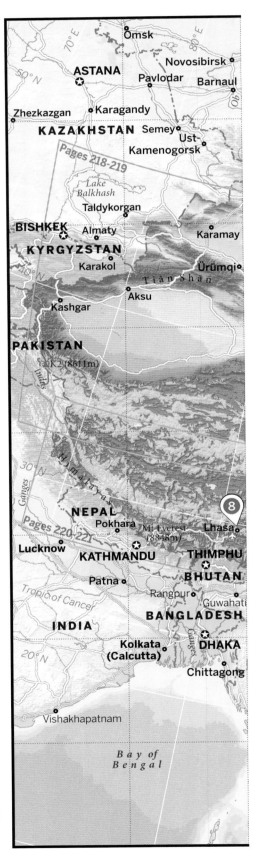

© Matt Munro / Lonely Planet

© ArtisticPhoto / Shutterstock

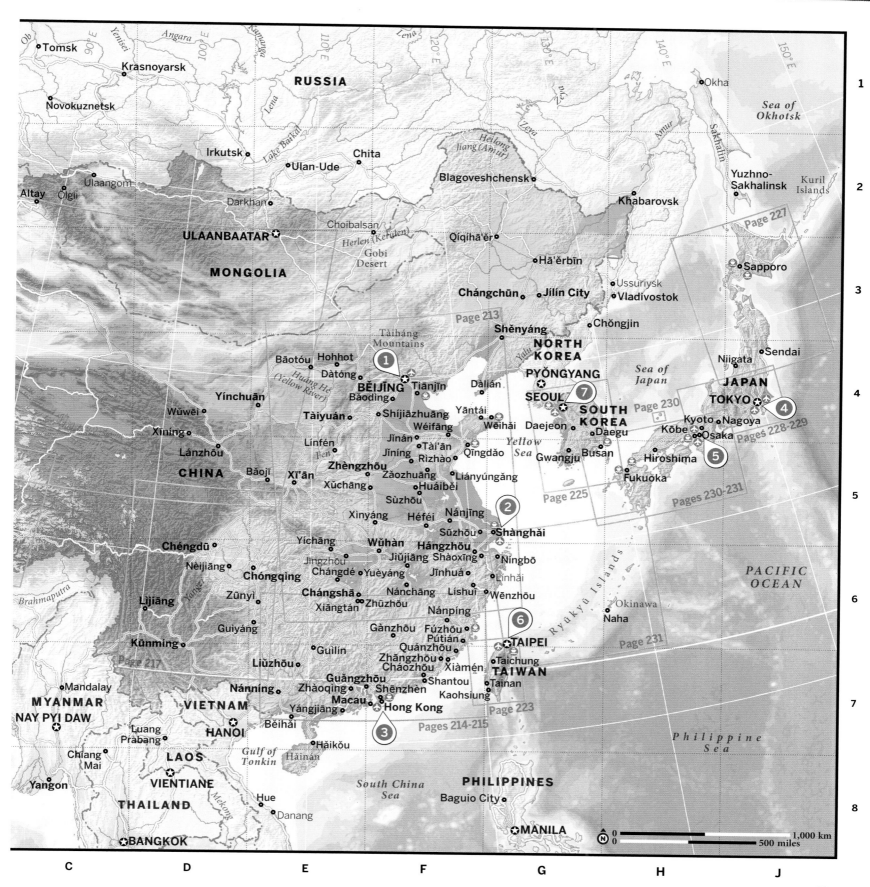

RUSSIA

Tomsk
Krasnoyarsk
Novokuznetsk
Altay
Ulaangom
Ölgii

Irkutsk
Ulan-Ude
Chita
Darkhan
Choibalsan
ULAANBAATAR
MONGOLIA
Gobi Desert

Blagoveshchensk
Qíqíhā'ěr
Hā'ěrbīn

Khabarovsk

Sea of Okhotsk

Okha

Yuzhno-Sakhalinsk
Kuril Islands

Sapporo

Chángchūn
Jílín City
Vladivostok
Ussuriysk
Chŏngjin
Shěnyáng

NORTH KOREA
PYŎNGYANG

Sea of Japan

Niigata
Sendai

Tàiháng Mountains
Bāotóu
Hohhot
Dàtóng
Huang He (Yellow River)
BĚIJĪNG
Tiānjīn
Bǎoding
Dàlián
Yāntái
Wēihǎi
SEOUL
SOUTH KOREA
Daejeon
Daegu

JAPAN
TOKYO

Yínchuān
Wǔwēi
Xīníng
Lánzhōu
Tàiyuán
Shíjiāzhuāng
Wéifāng
Jǐnán
Línfén
Fen
Jīníng
Tài'ān
Rizhào
Qīngdǎo
Yellow Sea
Gwangju
Busan
Kyoto
Nagoya
Kōbe
Osaka
Hiroshima

CHINA
Bǎojī
Xī'ān
Zhèngzhōu
Xǔchāng
Zǎozhuāng
Huáiběi
Liányúngǎng
Fukuoka

Sùzhōu
Xìnyáng
Héféi
Nánjīng
Sūzhōu
Shànghǎi

Chéngdū
Yíchāng
Wǔhàn
Hángzhōu
Jiǔjiāng
Shàoxīng
Níngbō
Nèijiāng
Jingzhōu
Chángdé
Yuèyáng
Jīnhuá
Línhǎi
Lìjiāng
Chóngqìng
Zūnyì
Chángshā
Nánchāng
Líshuǐ
Wēnzhōu
Xiāngtán
Zhūzhōu

PACIFIC OCEAN

Ryūkyū Islands
Okinawa
Naha

Kūnmíng
Guiyáng
Guìlín
Nánpíng
Gànzhōu
Fúzhōu
Quánzhōu
Pútián

Liǔzhōu
Zhāngzhōu
Cháozhōu
Xiàmén
TAIPEI
Taichung
TAIWAN
Tainan

Guǎngzhōu
Zhàoqìng
Shēnzhèn
Shantou
Kaohsiung

Mandalay
Nánníng
Yángjiāng
Macau
Hong Kong

MYANMAR
NAY PYI DAW
VIETNAM
Běihǎi

Luang Prabang
HANOI
Chiang Mai
LAOS
VIENTIANE
Hǎikǒu
Hǎinán
Gulf of Tonkin
South China Sea

PHILIPPINES
Baguio City

THAILAND
Hue
Danang
BANGKOK
MANILA

Philippine Sea

0   1,000 km
0   500 miles

Brahmaputra
Yangtze
Mekong

Yenisei
Ob
Angara
Lena
Katanga
Lake Baikal
Herlen (Kerulen)
Heilong Jiang (Amur)
Amur
Zeya
Ussuri
Sakhalin

90° E
100° E
110° E
120° E
130° E
140° E
150° E

1
2
3
4
5
6
7
8

C   D   E   F   G   H   J

Page 227
Page 213
Page 230
Pages 228-229
Page 225
Pages 230-231
Page 231
Pages 214-215
Page 223
Page 217

THE TRAVEL ATLAS

SIGHTS &
ACTIVITIES

 SEE

 DO

ITINERARY

 1

▽ 2

The Great Wall:
The Jiankou section of the Wall is surrounded by dramatic mountain scenery and panoramic views.

Jīnshānlǐng, The Great Wall
China's greatest engineering triumph, the Great Wall winds from its scattered Manchurian remains in Liáoníng province to wind-scoured rubble in the Gobi desert. Various sections near Běijīng, such as Bādáling and Mùtiányù, have been restored and are now heavily touristed, but the Jīnshānlǐng section sees fewer tourists.

Ming Tombs
The Unesco-protected Ming Tombs are the final resting place for 13 of the 16 Ming dynasty emperors. Each tomb is a huge temple-like complex guarding an enormous burial mound at its rear, back onto the southern slopes of Tiānshòu Mountain. Only three of the 13 tombs are open to the public, and only one has had its underground burial chambers excavated, leaving you wondering how many priceless treasures must still be buried here.

Army of Terracotta Warriors
This subterranean life-size army of thousands has stood guard over the soul of China's first unifier, Qin Shi Huang, for more than two millennia. Discovered by chance in 1974 by peasants drilling a well, the underground vault eventually yielded thousands of terracotta soldiers and horses in battle formation. Famously, no two faces in the army are alike.

The Bund, Shànghǎi
Symbolic of concession-era Shànghǎi, the Bund was the city's Wall Street. Originally a towpath for dragging barges of rice, the Bund (an Anglo-Indian term for the embankment of a muddy waterfront) was transformed into a grandiose sweep of powerful banks and trading houses.

Pǔtuóshān
The Zhōushān Archipelago's most celebrated isle and one of China's four sacred Buddhist mountains, Pǔtuóshān is the abode of Guanyin, the eternally compassionate Goddess of Mercy. With pine groves, beaches, temples and grottoes, it is very popular, even though it is only accessible by boat.

Huángshān
With its mist-shrouded granite peaks and twisted pines, Huángshān's beauty has inspired legions of poets and painters – but these days, it's tourists who flock here for the views. There are three routes to the summit: the short, hard way (eastern steps); the longer, harder way (western steps); and the very short, easy way (cable car).

Garden of the Master of the Nets
Off Shiquan Jie, this pocket-sized garden is considered one of Sūzhōu's best preserved. Laid out in the 12th century, it was restored in the 18th century by a retired official turned fisherman (hence the name). The labyrinth of courtyards, with windows framing parts of the garden, gives the illusion of a much larger area.

The Yangzi
Taking a boat down the Yangzi River – China's longest and most scenic waterway – isn't just an escape from marathon train journeys and bus rides, but a chance to experience an astonishing panorama. Along the way, river cruises pass major landmarks such as the Three Gorges, Ming Mountain and White Emperor City.

Tài Shān
This sacred mountain has been worshipped since at least the 11th century BC. To scholars it is known as Dōng Yuè, the Eastern Great Mountain, one of China's five holiest Taoist peaks. Qin Shi Huang, the first emperor, chose its summit to proclaim the unified kingdom of China in 219 BC.

Píngyáo
While other 'ancient' Chinese cities have been badly over-restored, Píngyáo remains largely intact: red-lantern-hung lanes set against night-time silhouettes of town walls, courtyard architecture, and a brood of temples, towers and old buildings.

Yúngāng Caves
This cave complex contains 51,000 sacred statues carved by the Turkic-speaking Tuǒbà, who drew their designs from Indian, Persian and even Greek influences which swept along the Silk Road. Work began in AD 460, continuing for 60 years before all 252 caves had been completed.

▽

10-day itinerary
Shànghǎi to Běijīng

This trip can be done entirely by train. Begin by delving into the hectic streets of **Shànghǎi**: factor in the Bund, the futuristic skyscraper district of **Pǔdōng** and shopping in the French Concession. Catch a train to **Sūzhōu**, famous for its beautiful gardens. Continue to **Hángzhōu**, one of China's most popular holiday spots thanks to its vistas of West Lake, green hills and spotlessly clean streets. Next comes **Nánjīng**, a former imperial capital still ringed by a magnificent city wall. Stop off in **Xī'ān**, the terminus of the Silk Road and the home of the legendary Terracotta Warriors, before hopping on a bullet train for a few days, seeing the big-ticket sights in **Běijīng**.

▽

21-day itinerary
Běijīng to the Silk Road

Běijīng is central to this tour, so give yourself five days to take in the Forbidden City, size up the Great Wall, the Summer Palace and the city's *hútòng* (residential alleyways). The splendour of the **Yúngāng Caves** outside the rebuilt ancient city of **Dàtóng** should put you in a Buddhist mood, sharpened by a few nights on monastic **Wǔtái Shān**. Make a three-day stopover in **Píngyáo**, an age-old walled town, followed by the historic walled city of **Kāifēng** in **Hénán**, once the traditional home of a small community of Chinese Jews; move on to **Luòyáng** and the Buddhist spectacle of the **Lóngmén Caves** and the **Shàolín Temple**, also within reach. A few days of sightseeing in **Xī'ān** brings you face-to-face with the Army of Terracotta Warriors and gives you time for the Taoist mountain of **Huá Shān**. Xī'ān traditionally marked the start of the Silk Road which you can follow through **Gānsù** province all the way to the oasis town of **Dūnhuáng**, and beyond (if you wish).

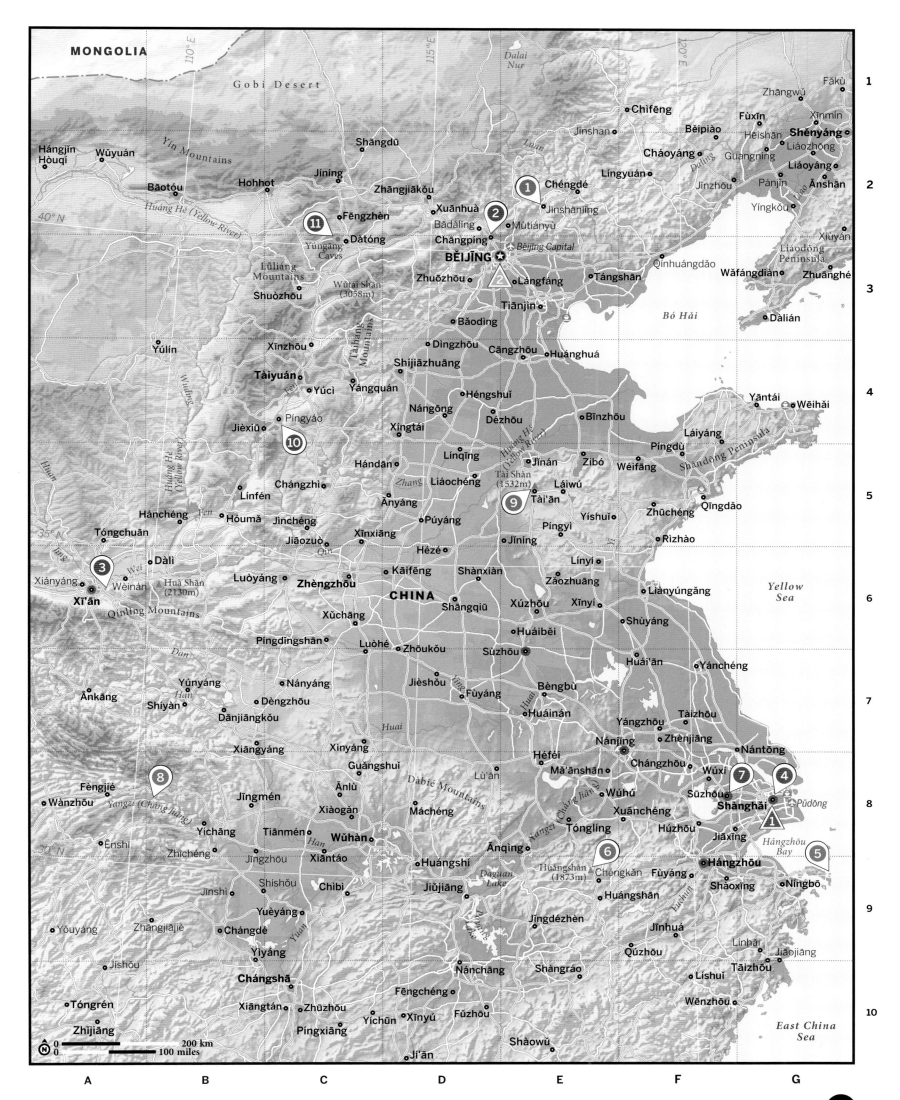

MONGOLIA

Gobi Desert

110° E

115° E

120° E

Dalai Nur

Fǎkù 1

Zhāngwǔ

Chìfēng

Jinshan

Fùxīn Xīnmín

Běipiào Hēishān **Shěnyáng**

Liáozhōng

Hángjǐn Wǔyuán Hohhot Jíníng Shàngdū Chéngdé

Hòuqí

Bāotóu Zhāngjiākǒu Cháoyáng Guǎngníng Liáoyáng

① Línyuán Liáoyáng

Jǐnzhōu Pánjǐn Ānshān

Yin Mountains Fēngzhèn Xuānhuà ② Mùtiányù Yíngkǒu

40° N *Huáng Hé (Yellow River)* Bādálǐng Qínhuángdǎo Xiùyán

Dàtóng Chāngpíng *Liáodōng Peninsula*

⑪ Yúngāng Caves *Běijīng Capital* Wǎfángdiàn Zhuānghé

Lǚliáng Mountains **BĚIJĪNG** ★

Shuòzhōu Wǔtái Shān (3058m) Zhuōzhōu ② Lángfáng Tángshān *Bó Hǎi*

Tiānjīn Dàlián

Bǎodìng

Yúlín Xīnzhōu Dìngzhōu Cāngzhōu Huánghuá

Taihang Mountains Shíjiāzhuāng

Tàiyuán Yángquán Héngshuǐ Bīnzhōu Yāntái Wēihǎi

Yùcì Nángōng Dézhōu Láiyáng

Jièxiū Píngyáo Xíngtái *Huáng Hé (Yellow River)* Píngdù *Shandōng Peninsula*

⑩ Hándān Línqīng Jǐnán Zibó Wéifāng Qīngdǎo

Chángzhì Liáochéng *Tài Shān (1532m)* Láiwú Zhūchéng

Línfén Ānyáng ⑨ Tài'ān

Hánchéng Hóumǎ Jìnchéng Xīnxiāng Púyáng Yíshuǐ Rìzhào

Tóngchuān Dàlì Jiāozuò Hézé Jǐníng Píngyì

Jīng Línyí

Xiányáng ③ Wèinán Luòyáng **Zhèngzhōu** Kāifēng Shànxiàn Zǎozhuāng Liányúngǎng *Yellow Sea*

Xī'ān Huà Shān (2130m) **CHINA** Shàngqiū Xúzhōu Xīnyí

Qinling Mountains Xúchāng Huáiběi Shùyáng

Píngdǐngshān Luòhé Zhōukǒu Sùzhōu Huái'ān Yánchéng

Dan Yúnyáng Nányáng Jièshǒu Fùyáng Bèngbù Yángzhōu Tàizhōu

Ānkāng Dèngzhōu *Huai* Huáinán Zhènjiāng Nántōng

Shíyàn Dānjiāngkǒu Nánjīng Chángzhōu Wúxī ⑦ ④

Han Xiāngyáng Xìnyáng Guǎngshuǐ Lù'ān Héféi Mǎ'ānshān Súzhōu **Shànghǎi** *Pǔdōng*

⑧ Jīngmén Ānlù *Dàbié Mountains* Wúhú Xuānchéng Húzhōu ①

Fèngjié *Yangzi (Cháng Jiāng)* Xiàogǎn Tónglíng Jiāxīng *Hángzhōu Bay*

Wànzhōu Yíchāng Tiānmén **Wǔhàn** Ānqìng ⑥ Fùyáng **Hángzhōu** ⑤

30° N Ēnshī Zhīchéng Jīngzhōu Xiàntáo Huángshí *Dàguān Lake* Huángshān (1873m) Chéngkǎn Shàoxīng Níngbō

Shíshǒu Chìbì Jiǔjiāng Huángshān *Fùchūn*

Jīnshì Jǐngdézhèn Jǐnhuá Línhǎi

Yōuyáng Yuèyáng Zhāngjiājiè Chángdé Qúzhōu Jiāojiāng

Yìyáng Nánchāng Shàngráo Lǐshuǐ Tàizhōu

Jíshǒu **Chángshā** Fēngchéng

Tóngrén Xiāngtán Zhūzhōu Yíchūn Xīnyú Fúzhōu Wēnzhōu 10

Zhìjiāng Píngxiāng Yíchūn Xīnyú Shàowǔ

Jí'ān *East China Sea*

N 0   200 km
0   100 miles

A   B   C   D   E   F   G

Lóngjǐ Rice Terraces

This part of Guǎngxī is famous for its vistas of terraced paddy fields cascading in swirls down the valley. For centuries, the villagers of Lóngjǐ (literally 'Dragon's Back') have been cultivating rice in this way, using dikes, ponds and dams to control water.

2

Yángshuò

The countryside of Yángshuò, especially around the Lí River and its tributaries, has inspired generations of Chinese painters with its scenery of wallowing water buffalo and farmers tending crops against a backdrop of limestone peaks. The area's riverside villages can be explored by boat or bike, or you can take a bamboo-raft trip down the Lí River.

3

Gǔlàng Yǔ

At the turn of the 20th century, Gǔlàng Yǔ was an international enclave where consulates from Europe, America and Japan managed their affairs among banyan trees and vine-strewn villas. In 2017, the island was inscribed as a Unesco World Heritage Site thanks to its fusion of architectural styles and heritage of cross-cultural exchange.

Taipa Village, Macau

Taipa has modernised fast in recent years, but remnants of the past linger in this old-world village. A warren of alleys hold traditional Chinese shops and restaurants, while the main roads are punctuated by colonial villas, churches and temples.

Fújiàn Tǔlóu

The Hakka and the Minnán (Fujianese) people have lived in circular earthen structures known as *tǔlóu* for centuries. Many are still inhabited and welcome visitors. Remarkable for their ingenuity, their rural setting lends an ethereal quality that's often hard to find in modern China.

Méizhōu

Populated by the Hakka people, Méizhōu is home to China's largest cluster of 'coiled dragon houses' or *wéilóngwū:* horseshoe-shaped dwellings evocative of a dragon napping at the foot of a mountain.

Sun and Moon Twin Pagodas

Set against the scenery of Shān Lake, the Sun and Moon Twin Pagodas are the highlight of Guìlín's two central lakes. The octagonal, seven-storey Moon Pagoda is connected by a tunnel to the 41m-high Sun Pagoda.

Kāipíng

Found 140km southwest of Guǎngzhōu, Kāipíng is home to the Unesco-crowned *diāolóu*, eccentric watchtowers featuring a fusion of Eastern and Western architectural styles. Out of approximately 3000 originally built, only 1833 remain.

Po Lin Monastery and Big Buddha

On the island of Lantau, near Hong Kong, Po Lin Monastery is known for the Tian Tan Buddha, or 'Big Buddha', 23m high (34m with podium). Built in 1993, it's the tallest seated bronze Buddha statue in the world.

Chen Clan Ancestral Hall

An ancestral shrine, Confucian school and 'chamber of commerce' for the Chen clan, this compound was built in 1894 by the residents of 72 villages in Guǎngdōng. There are 19 buildings in the Lǐngnán style, featuring carvings, statues, paintings and scrollwork.

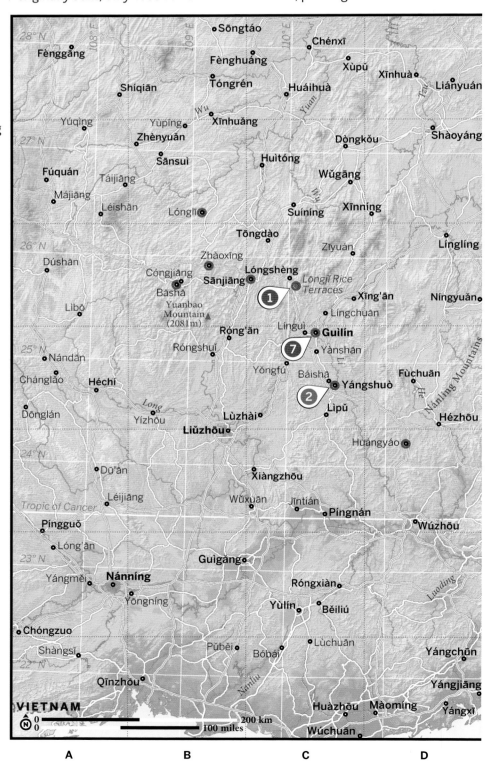

14-day itinerary
Best of South China

Four days' wining and dining in **Hong Kong** and **Macau** should whet your appetite, before you head inland to **Guìlín** and three days' immersion in the dreamy karst landscape of **Yángshuò**. Cycle the riverside paths, take a bamboo raft downriver and soak up the scenery. Join a local tour from Yángshuò to the picturesque village of **Huángyáo**, the star of countless movies thanks to its well-preserved period architecture. From here, backtrack to Guìlín and then journey north to the **Lóngjī Rice Terraces** and the wind-and-rain bridges and ethnic hues of **Sānjiāng**. From here, you can creep over the border to explore the minority-rich villages of eastern Guìzhōu, including **Lónglǐ**, **Bāshā** and **Zhàoxīng**.

14-day itinerary
Around Guǎngdōng

After exploring all the varied delights in the crazy metropolises of Hong Kong and Macau, head out to **Kāipíng** to clamber among the dramatic forest of watchtowers, a fusion of East–West architecture. Next up is **Fóshān**, the hometown of two icons of kung fu, Wong Fei Hung and Ip Man (Bruce Lee's master). It was here that the Wing Chun style of kung fu was developed. Nearby is Guǎngzhōu, where you can visit the amazing Chen Clan Ancestral Hall, a meeting place for members of the Chen lineage, the most predominant in Guǎngdōng province. Continue on to **Méizhōu**, where you will be awed by the strange crouching dragons and outlandish flying saucers of traditional Hakka architecture. Make a detour via the old towns of **Bǎihóu** and **Cháyáng**, then finish up in **Cháozhōu** to see the Guangji Bridge – originally a 12th-century pontoon bridge over the Hán River, now a faux-ancient passageway, with 24 pagoda-topped piers and 18 wooden boats hooked up every morning. From here, you can head back to Hong Kong or on to **Shànghǎi**.

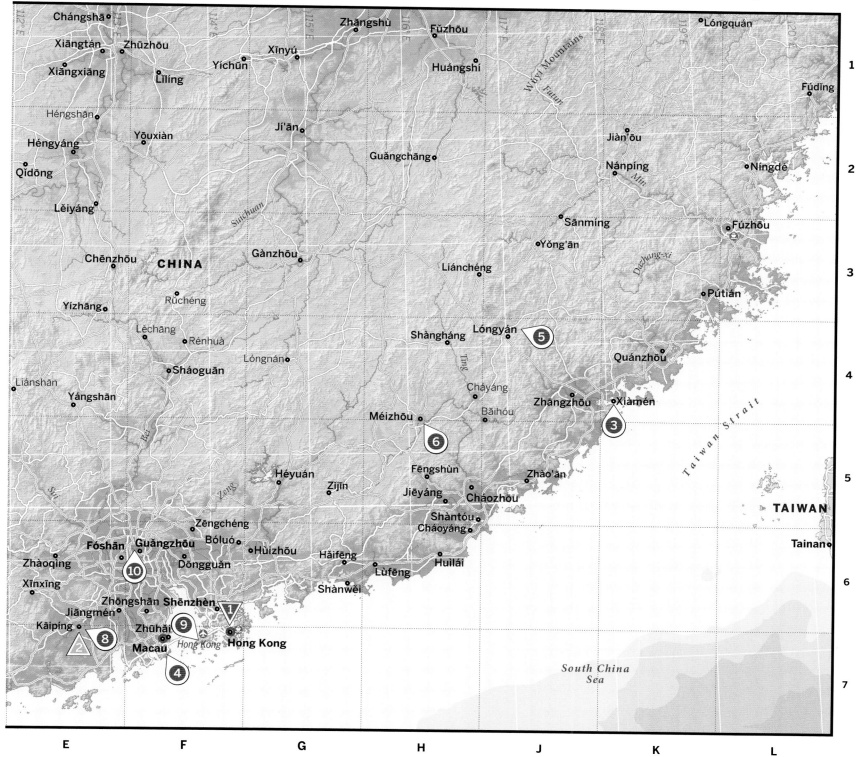

SIGHTS & ACTIVITIES

 SEE

 DO

ITINERARY

 1

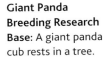 2

1. Tiger Leaping Gorge
One of the deepest gorges in the world, this vast ravine measures 16km long and provides the unmissable trek of southwest China. Of the two trails, the higher one is the more spectacular, even if parts of the path are dicey (especially in the rainy season).

2. Bamboo Temple, Kūnmíng
This serene temple is as interesting to sculptors as sightseers. Raised during the Tang dynasty, it was rebuilt in the 19th century by master Sichuanese sculptor Li Guangxiu and his many apprentices, who fashioned 500 *luóhàn* (arhats or noble ones) in a mishmash of realism and exaggerated surrealism.

3. Giant Panda Breeding Research Base
This reserve 18km north of Chéngdū's city centre is the easiest way to glimpse Sìchuān's most famous residents outside of a zoo. Home to nearly 120 giant and 76 red pandas, the base focuses on getting these notoriously shy creatures to breed. March to May is the 'falling in love period' (wink wink).

4. Éméi Shān
A misty retreat from Sìchuān basin's heat, Éméi Shān (3099m) is one of China's four sacred Buddhist Mountains. A farmer built the first Buddhist temple in the 1st century, marking Buddhism's arrival in the Eastern world. Many of the more than 150 temples on the mountain have suffered fires or looting over the centuries, but around 30 have been maintained and restored.

Giant Panda Breeding Research Base: A giant panda cub rests in a tree.

5. Four Sisters Mountain
A national park since 1994 and a Unesco World Heritage Site since 2006, Four Sisters Mountain is famous for its natural scenery. At 6250m the fourth of the Four Sisters, pyramid-shaped Yāomèi Fēng, is the second-highest peak in Sìchuān. The park has plenty of hiking and rock climbing.

6. Lè Shān
With fingernails dwarfing a human, the world's largest ancient Buddha draws many tourists to this riverside town. The 1200-year-old Grand Buddha sits in repose, carved from a cliff face overlooking the confluence of three restless rivers: the Dàdù, Mín and Qīngyì. The Buddhist monk Haitong conceived the project in AD 713, hoping Buddha would protect the boats and calm the rivers' capricious currents.

7. Dàlǐ's Three Pagodas
This celebrated trio of pagodas are among the oldest standing structures in southwestern China. The tallest of the three, Qiānxún Pagoda, has 16 tiers that reach a height of 70m. Originally erected in the mid-9th century by engineers from Xī'ān, it is flanked by two smaller 10-tiered pagodas, each of which are 42m high.

8. Dàzú Buddhist Caves
The Unesco-protected rock carvings of Dàzú are one of China's four great Buddhist cave-sculpture sites, along with Dūnhuáng, Luòyáng and Dàtóng. The Dàzú sculptures are the most recent and in the best condition. Scattered over some 40 sites are thousands of cliff carvings and statues, dating from the Tang (9th century) to the Song dynasty (13th century).

9. Wǔlóng County Geology Park
About 20km from the town of Wǔlóng, this fairy-tale landscape of gorges, karst peaks, natural bridges and mossy caves lies deep within the mountains about three hours from Chóngqìng. The park has three main areas: Qingkou Tiankeng Scenic Area, Furong Cave and Three Natural Bridges, which you can gaze at in awe from beneath.

10. Ānjū Ancient Town
Established in 588 AD, Ānjū is a riverfront village of wonderful Ming and Qing dynasty buildings. Once an important centre of scholarship, it is now protected as an 'ancient town', a place of crumbling lanes where chickens roam and the smell of homemade noodles perfumes the air.

11. Chóngqìng
One of China's most booming metropolises, Chóngqìng City dates back to the ancient Ba kingdom, but very little remains of the old city. It's famous for hotpot – a fiery cauldron of *làjiāo* (chillies) and *huājiāo* (Sìchuān peppers) into which vegetables, tofu, fish and meat are dipped.

10-day itinerary
Introduction to Yúnnán

Begin by exploring north Yúnnán's Naxi town of **Lìjiāng**. Then pick up the trail of the Jīnshā River on a hike along **Tiger Leaping Gorge**. Discover the scattered villages and old towns around Lìjiāng, including **Shāxī** and **Shùhé** on the old Tea Horse Road, and be blown away by the views of **Yùlóng Xuěshān**. In the warmer months, detour northeast towards west Sìchuān and **Lúgū Lake** on the provincial border; during the winter months this entire area is snowbound, but in summer it's a lovely place to relax. Return to Lìjiāng to fly to **Chóngqìng**, home of the spicy and searing Chóngqìng hotpot and gateway to the marvellous Three Gorges.

14-day itinerary
Chóngqìng and Sìchuān

Start in booming **Chóngqìng** with a bus trip to the stunning landscapes of **Chìshuǐ** on the Guìzhōu border to chill, unwind and explore before returning by bus to Chóngqìng. You'll need around three days in Chóngqìng for the main sights, and for a side journey to visit the Buddhist Caves at **Dàzú** and a trip to the Yangzi River village of **Sōnggài** for an insight into rural China. Then hop on a bus to **Chéngdū** to enjoy some spicy Sìchuān cuisine and to say hello to the city's most famous residents at the Giant Panda Breeding Research Base. Chéngdū makes a great base for exploring the region's top sights. Start with a trip to the lush, forested peaks of **Éméi Shān**.

Getting a feel for the place takes at least a day or two. Wander the wooden temples, meet macaques and stay overnight in a monastery guesthouse. From here it's a short (and regular) bus trip to **Lè Shān**'s Grand Buddha. Next catch a flight west from Chéngdū to Dàochéng for a few days exploring the magnificent **Yàdīng Nature Reserve**.

© Feng Wei Photography / Getty Images

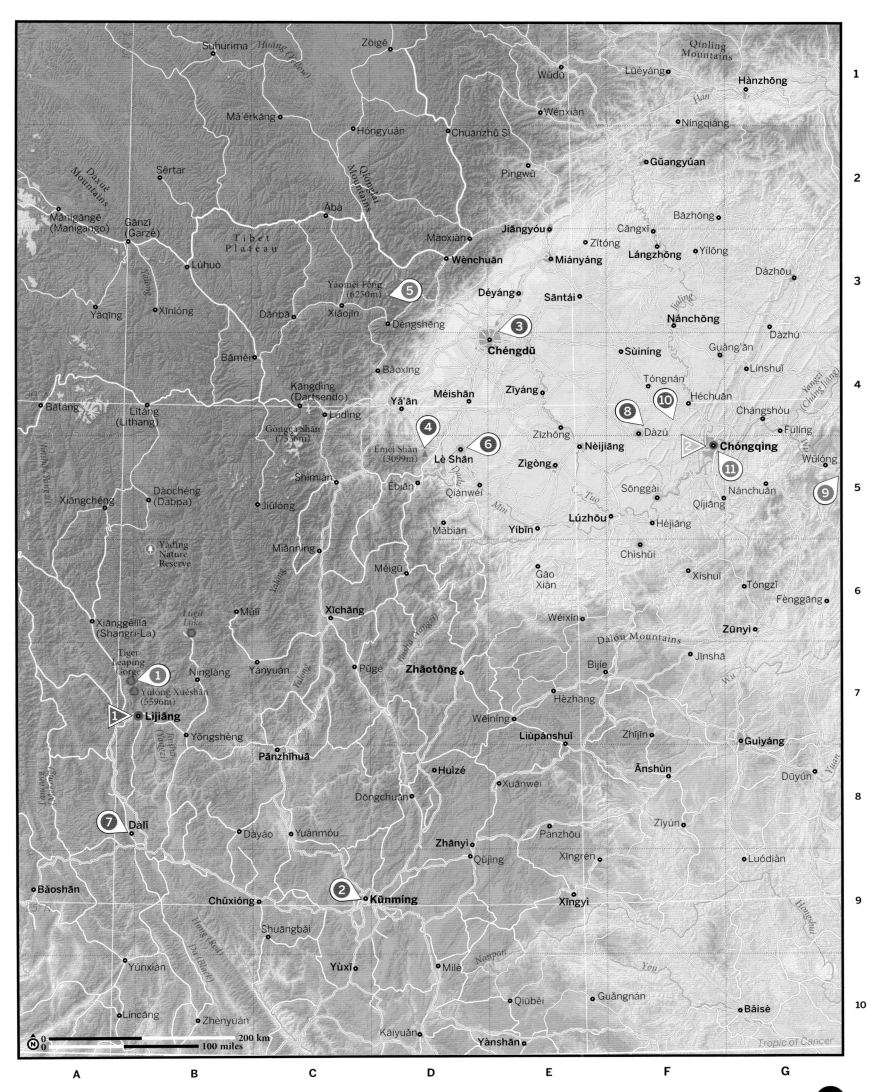

Suhurima
Huáng (Yellow)
Zöigê
Wǔdū
Lüèyáng
Hànzhōng
Hán

Mǎ'ěrkāng
Wénxiàn
Níngqiáng

Hóngyuán
Chuǎnzhǔ Sì
Gǔangyúan

Dàxuě Mountains
Sêrtar
Āba
Pingwǔ
Bāzhōng

Mǎnigàngě
(Manigango)
Gānzī
(Garzê)
Tibet Plateau
Màoxiàn
Jiāngyóu
Zìtóng
Lángzhōng
Yílóng
Cāngxī

Lúhuò
Yǎomèi Fēng
(6250m) ⑤
Wènchuān
Miányáng
Dázhōu

Yǎqīng
Xīnlóng
Dānbā
Xiǎojīn
Déyáng
Sāntái
Nánchōng
Dàzhú

Bāměi
Dèngshēng
Chéngdū ③
Guǎng'ān
Línshuǐ

Bǎoxīng
Kāngdìng
(Dartsendo)
Yǎ'ān
Méishān
Zīyáng
Tóngnán ⑩
Héchuān
Jiālíng

Bātáng
Lìtáng
(Lithang)
Lúdìng
④
Gònggā Shān
(7556m)
Emei Shān
(3099m) ⑥
Lè Shān
Zizhōng
⑧
Dàzú
② **Chóngqìng**
Chángshòu
Yangzi (Cháng Jiāng)

Xiāngchéng
Dàochéng
(Dabpa)
Shímián
Ébiān
Qiánwèi
Nèijiāng
⑪
Wúlóng

Jiǔlóng
Zigòng
Sōnggài
Qíjiāng
Nánchuān ⑨

Yàdīng Nature Reserve
Miǎnníng
Méigū
Mǎbiān
Yíbīn
Lúzhōu
Héjiāng
Chìshuǐ
Xīshuǐ
Tóngzǐ
Fènggāng

Xiānggélǐlā
(Shangri-La)
Lúgū Lake
Mùlǐ
Xīchāng
Gāo Xiàn
Wéixín
Dàlóu Mountains
Zūnyì

Tiger Leaping Gorge
Nínglàng
Yányuán
Pǔgé
Zhāotōng
Bìjié
Jīnshā

① Yùlóng Xuěshān
(5596m)
Wéiníng
Hèzhāng
Guìyáng

① **Lìjiāng**
Yǒngshèng
Liùpánshuǐ
Zhíjīn

Pānzhīhuā
Huìzé
Xuānwēi
Ānshùn
Dūyún

⑦ **Dàlǐ**
Dàyáo
Yuánmóu
Dōngchuān
Pánzhōu
Zīyún
Luódiàn

Bǎoshān
Chǔxióng
Zhānyì
Xīngrén

Shuāngbǎi
Qǔjìng
Xīngyì
② **Kūnmíng**

Yúnxiàn
Hong (Red)
Yùxī
Mǐlè
Nánpán
You

Líncāng
Zhènyuán
Kāiyuǎn
Qiūběi
Guǎngnán
Bǎisè
Hòngshuǐ

0 — 200 km
0 — 100 miles
Yànshān
Tropic of Cancer

A   B   C   D   E   F   G

1   2   3   4   5   6   7   8   9   10

SIGHTS &
ACTIVITIES

 SEE

DO

ITINERARY

1

2

Jiāyùguān Fort

A classic image of western China, this fort guarded the narrow pass between the snowcapped Qílián Shān peaks and the Hēi Shān (Black Mountains) of the Mǎzōng Shān range. Built in 1372, it was named the 'Impregnable Defile Under Heaven' and was the last major stronghold of imperial China.

Bǐnglíng Sì

Inaccessibility means Bǐnglíng Sì is one of the few Buddhist grottoes in China to have survived the 20th century unscathed. During a period spanning 1600 years, sculptors dangling from ropes carved 183 niches and sculptures into the steep canyon walls.

Labrang Monastery

With its squeaking prayer wheels (3km in total), hawks circling overhead and the throb of Tibetan longhorns resonating from the surrounding hills, Labrang is a monastery town unto itself. Many of the chapel halls are illuminated in a yellow glow by yak-butter lamps, their strong-smelling fuel scooped out from voluminous tubs.

Shipton's Arch

This extraordinary natural rock arch (the Uyghur name means simply 'mountain with a hole in it') is one of the tallest on earth. The first Westerner to describe it was Eric Shipton, the last British consul-general in Kashgar, in 1947. Successive expeditions failed to find it until a team from National Geographic rediscovered the arch in 2000, 80km northwest of Kashgar.

Mògāo Grottoes

The Mògāo Grottoes are considered one of the most important collections of Buddhist art in the world. At its peak during the Tang dynasty (618–907), the site housed 18 monasteries, more than 1400 monks and nuns, and countless artists, translators and calligraphers.

Jiāohé Ruins

Established as a garrison town during the Han dynasty, this 1600-year-old city is a window into China's ancient past. Get an overview of the site at the central governor's complex, then continue to the 'stupa grove' with its 10m-tall pagoda surrounded by 100 smaller ones.

Kanas Lake

Pinched between Mongolia, Russia and Kazakhstan, Kanas Lake is famous for a legendary monster (China's answer to Nessie), long a fixture of scary stories around yurt campfires. She appears every year or two, bringing journalists and conspiracists in her wake.

Grand Sunday Bazaar, Kashgar

Closer to Tehran and Damascus than to Běijīng, Kashgar has been the epicentre of regional trade for more than two millennia. Uyghur craftsmen hammer and chisel away as they have done for centuries, traders haggle in the boisterous bazaars and donkey carts trundle through the alleyways. The Sunday livestock market is a must-see.

Yǎdān National Park

This weird, eroded desert landscape sits in the middle of the Gobi Desert's greater nothingness. A former lake bed that eroded in spectacular fashion some 12,000 years ago, the strange rock formations provided the backdrop to the last scenes of Zhang Yimou's film *Hero*. Tours are confined to group minibuses (with regular photo stops) to preserve the natural surrounds.

14-day itinerary
Lánzhōu to Jiāyùguān

From **Lánzhōu**, first head southeast to **Tiānshuǐ** to check out the Buddhist grottoes at Màijī Shān. Return to Lánzhōu, then ramble along the fringes of the Tibetan world in the Buddhist monastic settlements of **Xiàhé** and **Lángmùsì**. The Hèxī Corridor draws you on to the ancient Great Wall outpost of **Jiāyùguān**, via the Silk Road stopover town of **Wǔwēi**, and the Great Buddha Temple with its outsize effigy of a reclining Sakyamuni in **Zhāngyè**. Finish your trip with a walk along the wind-blasted ramparts of **Jiāyùguān Fort**, the last major stronghold of imperial China, and a memorable hike along some of the most westerly remnants of the Great Wall.

21-day itinerary
West Along the Silk Road

This trip heads into China's wild west and the far reaches of the Silk Road. Start in **Dūnhuáng**, one of China's tidiest towns, with the mighty sand dunes of the Singing Sands Mountains pushing up from the south, and some intriguing sights in the surrounding desert. The town is also the hopping-off point for China's hoard of Buddhist art, the spellbinding **Mògāo Grottoes**. From Dūnhuáng you can access the northwestern Uyghur province of Xīnjiāng via the melon town of **Hāmì** before continuing to **Turpan**, China's Death Valley; at 154m below sea level, the world's second-lowest depression and the hottest spot in China. Consider spending the night in a yurt or camping on the shores of mountainous **Tiān Chí**. Thread your way through Silk Road towns by rail to the Central Asian outpost of **Kashgar**, or get there via the Marco Polo–journeyed southern Silk Road, along the cusp of the **Taklamakan Desert**. From Kashgar, hatch plans to conquer the **Karakoram Hwy** or, in the other direction, head back into China proper.

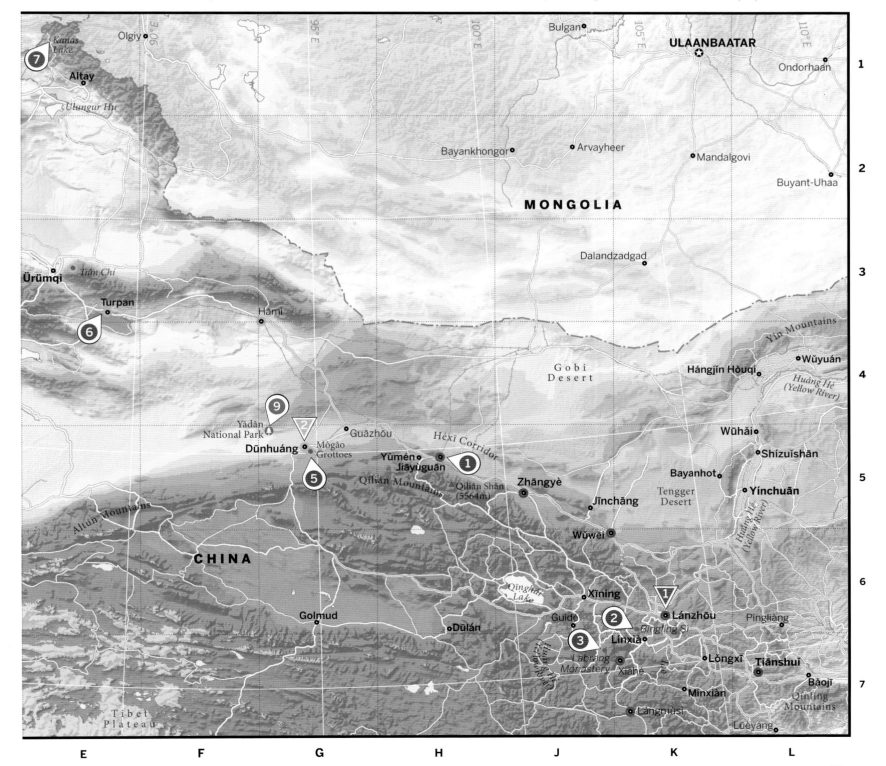

Mt Kailash

Worshipped by more than a billion Buddhists and Hindus, Asia's most sacred mountain rises from the Barkha plain like a giant four-sided 6714m chorten (Buddhist stupa). The three-day pilgrim path around the mountain erases the sins of a lifetime.

Jokhang Temple, Lhasa

The 1300-year-old Jokhang Temple is the spiritual heart of Tibet: the continuous waves of awestruck pilgrims prostrating themselves outside are a testament to its timeless allure. The central golden Buddha image here is the most revered in all of Tibet. The Barkhor, a *kora* (pilgrim circuit), winds clockwise around the periphery of the Jokhang Temple.

Potala Palace, Lhasa

The magnificent Potala Palace, once the seat of the Tibetan government and the winter residence of the Dalai Lamas, is Lhasa's cardinal landmark. An architectural wonder even by modern standards, the palace rises 13 storeys from 130m-high Marpo Ri (Red Hill) and contains more than 1000 rooms.

Mt Everest Base Camp

While two-week-long trekking routes on the Nepal side offer only fleeting glimpses of the peak, in Tibet you can drive on a paved road right up to unobstructed views of Mt Everest's north face, framed in the prayer flags of Rongphu Monastery. Bring headache tablets and pray for clear skies.

Samye Monastery

Tibet's first monastery is a collection of chapels, chörtens and shrines arranged around a medieval Tibetan-, Chinese- and Indian-style temple. The 1200-year-old site is where Guru Rinpoche battled demons to introduce Buddhism to Tibet.

Nam-tso

The waters of sacred Nam-tso, the second-largest saltwater lake in China, are a miraculous shade of turquoise blue and shimmer in the rarefied air of 4730m. Most people come here for the scenery and for the short but pilgrim-packed *kora*.

Gyantse Kumbum

Commissioned in 1427, this 32m-high chörten contains incredible early Tibetan art. The snail-shell-shaped building conceals dim alcoves full of painted buddhas and Tantric demons (*kumbum* means '100,000 images').

Sera Monastery

About 5km north of Lhasa, Sera was founded in 1419 by a disciple of Tsongkhapa as one of Lhasa's two great Gelugpa monasteries. About 600 monks are now in residence; monk debating takes place from 3pm to 5pm in a garden near the assembly hall.

Ganden Monastery

50km east of Lhasa, this monastery, founded in 1417 by Tsongkhapa, was the first of the Gelugpa Buddhist order. About 400 monks study here; reconstruction has been underway since the its near-total destruction during the Cultural Revolution.

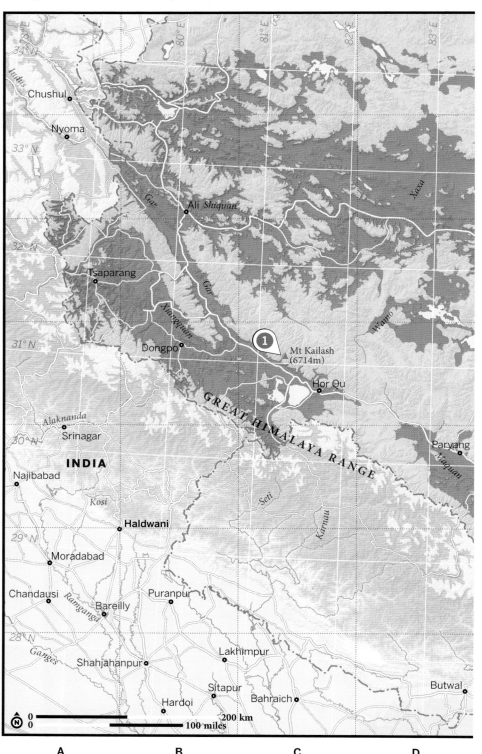

Drepung Monastery

At 8km west of Lhasa, 15th-century Drepung was one of three 'pillars of the Tibetan state', with Sera and Ganden monasteries. It was purportedly the world's largest monastery, with 7000 resident monks at its peak.

SIGHTS & ACTIVITIES

● SEE
● DO

ITINERARY

▼ 1
▼ 2

10-day itinerary
Lhasa and Around

There's enough in **Lhasa** to occupy at least five days. Must-sees include the Potala Palace, Jokhang Temple and Barkhor pilgrimage circuit. The huge monasteries of Drepung and Sera lie on the edge of town and offer worthwhile pilgrim circuits. An overnight return trip to the salt lake of **Nam-tso** offers a break from peering at Buddhist deities.

If you add three days you can loop back to Lhasa from Nam-tso via the little-visited monastery at **Reting**, the amazing cliff-side **Sili Götsang** hermitage and the atmospheric **Drigung Til Monastery**, perhaps visiting Ganden Monastery en route. If time allows, explore the monasteries between Reting and Drigung Til, or around Nyima Jiangre.

14-day itinerary
Yarlung Tsangpo Valley loop

This valley is less than an hour from Lhasa but offers a wealth of surprisingly off-the-beaten-track sights. From Lhasa, stop first at **Dorje Drak Monastery**, with its views of sand dunes and the river. Make the overnight trip up the Drak valley to the nunnery and caves of Drak Yangdzong, where you can join pilgrims as they traverse ladders and

squeeze through tunnels. Next up is **Samye Monastery**, one of Tibet's great highlights. Take in the morning views from Hepo Ri and continue to the city of **Tsetang** to pick up permits. Allow at least a day to visit the Yarlung Valley via **Trandruk Monastery**, photogenic **Yumbulagang** and the ruins of **Rechung-puk**. Headed back

towards Lhasa, stop at **Mindroling**, one of Tibet's most important Nyingmapa-school gompas. Nearby **Dranang Monastery** offers Pala-era wall murals, while history buffs can hike to the ruins of **Jampaling chörten**, a monument to the destruction of the Cultural Revolution. From here Lhasa's Gongkar airport is less than an hour away.

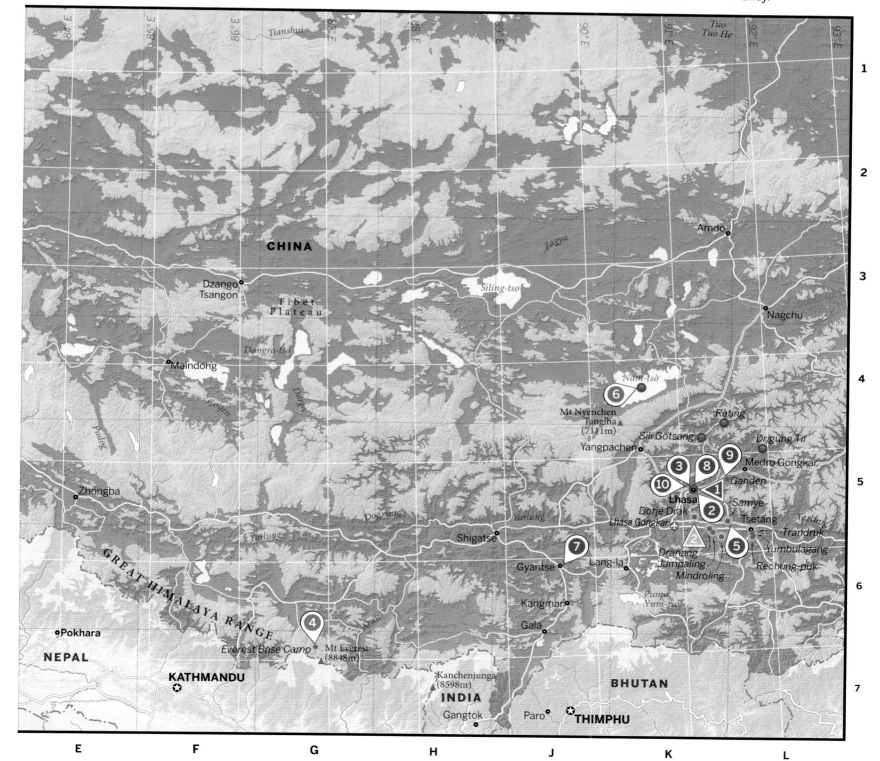

SIGHTS & ACTIVITIES

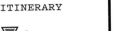

◉ SEE
◉ DO

ITINERARY

▽ 1
▽ 2

1. Taroko Gorge

Taiwan's top tourist draw is a walk-in Chinese painting. Rising above the froth of the blue-green Liwu River, the marble walls swirl with the colours of a master's palette. Walk along the Swallow Grotto to see the gorge at its most sublime or brave the Jhuilu Old Trail, a vertigo-inducing path 500m above the canyon floor.

2. Sun Moon Lake

Sun Moon Lake is the largest body of water in Taiwan and has a watercolour background, ever-changing with the seasons. Although the area is packed with tour groups these days, it's still easy to get away from the crowds on the trails and cycling paths. Don't miss the region's high-mountain oolong tea: it's some of the world's finest.

3. National Palace Museum, Taipei

Home to the world's largest collection of Chinese art, this vast museum covers treasures in painting, calligraphy, statuary, bronzes, lacquerware, ceramics, jade and religious objects. With 700,000 pieces spanning every Chinese dynasty, only a tiny fraction is on display, but the most popular items, such as the famous jade cabbage, are always on show.

4. Miaokou Night Market, Keelung

Probably the most famous night market in Taiwan, Miaokou became known for food during the Japanese era, when merchants sold snacks at the mouth of the Dianji Temple. Nowadays, Miaokou remains a centre for street snacks, especially seafood.

Sun Moon Lake: A scenic bike path follows the water's edge at Sun Moon Lake.

5. Kenting National Park

Featured as a location in Ang Lee's *Life of Pi* in 2012, this park sprawls over Taiwan's southern tip, attracting visitors who come to swim, surf, hike, snorkel and dive. The beaches are wonderful, and mountains, hill terraces and deserts cover the rest of the park.

6. Cat Village, Houtong

This former coal-mining village has revived itself in the 21st century by tapping into cats. Villagers here traditionally kept cats because houses were built on the hillside where rats were rampant. After the closure of the coal mines, the area went into a decline and many villagers left. About 10 years ago, cat lovers organised efforts to take care of the strays.

7. Snow Mountain

The first recorded climb of Snow Mountain was in 1915 – it was then called Mt Silvia, and is now variously spelled Syueshan, Shueshan and Xueshan. Since then Taiwan's second highest peak has attracted teams and solo hikers from all over the world. The trail, from the ranger station trailhead in Wuling to the summit, is 10.9km, but due to terrain and altitude, requires two days (with a third for the return).

8. Beitou Hot Springs

A 30-minute MRT ride north of Taipei, Beitou Park was one of the largest hot-spring spas under Japanese rule. Today's park, about a third of its former size, is still a lovely wooded space with old stone bridges, heritage buildings and a hot-spring stream running through the centre.

9. Tainan

Traditional culture continues to thrive in Tainan, the oldest city in Taiwan. The district of Anping has a rich concentration of relics and temples. Begin a tour at the Grand Matsu Temple, once the palace of Ning Jin, the last king of the Ming dynasty. Outside, young Tainanese make art and coffee in former canal-side houses.

10. Longshan Temple, Taipei

Longshan Temple, one of the city's top religious sites, is devoted to the Guanyin Buddha. Built in 1738 and then rebuilt in the 1850s, the temple retains much of its southern architectural roots. The swallowtail roof is particularly elegant.

11. Yushan National Park

Covering 3% of the landmass of Taiwan, Yushan sits at the junction of the Philippine and Eurasian plates. The landscape is strikingly rugged, marked by thick forests, deep valleys, high cliffs and rocky peaks. Among these peaks, 30 are over 3000m, and one, the eponymous Yushan (Jade Mountain), is the highest mountain in Northeast Asia at 3952m. It attracts hikers from all over the world.

▽ **1**

7-day itinerary
Taipei and the North

Start in **Taipei** by visiting the National Palace Museum and the Longshan and Bao'an Temples. Take the gondola to mountainous Maokong and check out a traditional teahouse. Soak in the hot springs of **Beitou** and take a stinky tofu tour along the old street of Shenkeng. From Taipei, catch a bus to the old mining towns of **Jiufen** and Jinguashi, then on to **Ruifang**. Travel on the Pingxi Branch Rail Line down an 18km wooded gorge to photograph frontier villages and hike paths cut into steep crags. Round off the trip by heading back up the coast, stopping to see the bizarre rocks of **Yeliu**, the sculptures at **Juming Museum** and the colonial houses of seaside Tamsui.

▽ **2**

21-day itinerary
Total Taiwan Loop

After seeing the sights in **Taipei** and spending a day or two cycling and hiking in **Wulai**, hop on a train to **Hualien** and visit marble-walled Taroko Gorge. Take a train to **Yuli** and hike the nearby Walami Trail, then recuperate at Antong Hot Springs. Next, head to Taitung and catch a flight or ferry to **Lanyu**, a tropical island with pristine coral reefs and a unique indigenous culture. Back on the mainland, another train ride – across Taiwan's fertile southern tip – takes you to **Kaohsiung**, Taiwan's buzzing second-largest city. For beaches and coastline head down to **Kenting National Park**. Continue by train up the coast to the old capital of **Tainan** for temple touring, then rent a vehicle to drive up the **Dongshan Coffee Road** to the hot-mud springs in **Guanziling**. Continue into the mountains to explore the **Alishan National Scenic Area** and hike around **Tatajia** in the shadow of Yushan, Taiwan's highest mountain. Drive from Yushan to scenic **Sun Moon Lake**, and conclude in **Lukang**, home to master lantern, fan and tin craftspeople.

© Frank Chen / Getty Images

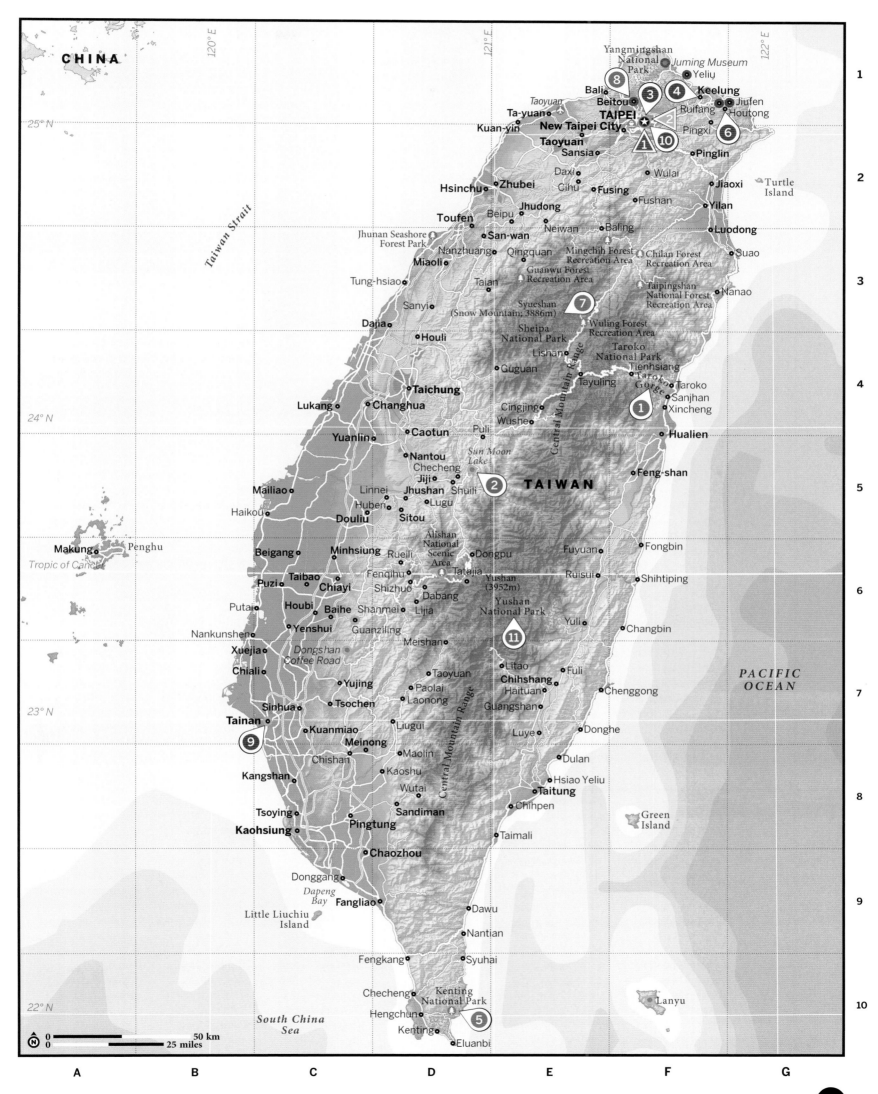

CHINA

Taiwan Strait

120° E

121° E

122° E

Yangmingshan
National
Park

Juming Museum

25° N

8   Bali   Beitou   Yeliu
      Ta-yuan   3   4   Keelung
                                Jiufen
      Kuan-yin   TAIPEI   Ruifang   Houtong
              New Taipei City   2   Pingxi   6
      Taoyuan   1   10
      Sansia   Pinglin

              Daxi   Wulai
Hsinchu   Zhubei   Cihu   Fusing   Jiaoxi   Turtle
              Gihu   Fushan   Island
      Toufen   Beipu   Jhudong
              San-wan   Neiwan   Baling   Yilan
      Nanzhuang   Luodong
Jhunan Seashore   Qingquan   Mingchih Forest   Chilan Forest   Suao
Forest Park   Miaoli   Recreation Area   Recreation Area
      Guanwu Forest
      Recreation Area
      Tung-hsiao   Taian   Taipingshan   Nanao
              Syueshan   7   National Forest
      Sanyi   (Snow Mountain; 3886m)   Recreation Area
      Dajia   Sheipa   Wuling Forest
      Houli   National Park   Recreation Area
              Lishan   Taroko
      Taichung   National Park
              Guguan   Tienhsiang
                  Tayuling   Taroko
      Lukang   Changhua   Gorge   Taroko
                              Sanjhan
24° N   Yuanlin   Cingjing   1   Xincheng
      Caotun   Wushe   Hualien
              Puli
      Nantou
      Checheng   Sun Moon   Feng-shan
Mailiao   Jiji   Lake   TAIWAN
      Linnei   Jhushan   Shuili   2
Haikou   Huben   Lugu
      Douliu   Sitou
      Makung   Penghu
Tropic of Cancer   Alishan
              National   Fuyuan   Fongbin
Beigang   Minhsiung   Scenic   Dongpu
      Rueili   Area   Ruisui   Shihtiping
Puzi   Taibao   Fenqihu   Yushan
Chiayi   Shizhuo   Tatajia   (3952m)
Putai   Houbi   Baihe   Dabang   Yushan   Yuli   Changbin   PACIFIC
Nankunshen   Shanmei   Lijia   National Park   OCEAN
      Yenshui   Guanziling   Meishan   11
Xuejia   Dongshan   Litao   Fuli
Chiali   Coffee Road   Taoyuan   Chihshang
              Yujing   Paolai   Haituan   Fuli
Sinhua   Tsochen   Laonong   Guangshan   Chenggong
Tainan   Kuanmiao
9   Meinong   Liugui   Luye   Donghe
      Chishan
Kangshan   Maolin   Dulan
      Kaoshu   Wutai   Hsiao Yeliu
Tsoying   Sandiman   Taitung   Green
Kaohsiung   Pingtung   Chihpen   Island
      Chaozhou
              Taimali
Donggang
Dapeng   Fangliao   Dawu
Bay
Little Liuchiu   Nantian
Island
      Fengkang   Syuhai
Checheng   Kenting
South China   Hengchun   National Park   Lanyu
Sea   Kenting   5
      Eluanbi

0   50 km
0   25 miles

A   B   C   D   E   F   G

SIGHTS & ACTIVITIES

◉ SEE
◉ DO

ITINERARY

▽ 1
▽ 2

Hwaseong: The wall of the fortress incorporates gates, pavilions, observation towers and fire-beacon platforms.

1. Bukhansan National Park

Granite-studded Bukhansan National Park is so close to Seoul that it's possible to visit by subway. Popular with hikers and rock-climbers, the park offers sweeping mountaintop vistas, maple leaves, rushing streams and remote temples.

2. Jeju-do

The volcanic landscape of Jeju-do, the largest of South Korea's many islands, is best seen on foot. The Jeju Olle Trail is a network of 26 half- to full-day hiking routes that meander around the island's coast, part of the hinterland and three other islands. The summit of Hallasan, the country's highest peak, provides spectacular views.

3. DMZ

The 4km-wide, 240km-long buffer known as the Demilitarized Zone (DMZ) separates North and South Korea. Lined by tank traps, electrical fences, landmines and armies in full battle readiness, it is one of the world's scariest – and most surreal – tourist attractions, with observatories allowing you to peek into North Korea.

4. Hwaseong, Suwon

Sitting at the base of Mt Paldal, King Jeongjo's palace was constructed in the late 18th century as a place for him to stay on his visits. It has been meticulously reconstructed and restored after being destroyed during the Japanese Occupation and later heavily damaged by war. A walk around the 5.7km-long wall takes you through four grand gates.

5. Boryeong Mud Festival

Every July, thousands of people converge on the seaside town of Boryeong and jump into gigantic vats of mud. The official line is that the local mud has restorative properties, but one look around and it's clear that no one really cares for much except having a messy old good time.

6. Jeonju Hanok Maeul

This *maeul* (village) has more than 800 *hanok* (traditional wooden houses), one of the largest such concentrations in the country. The slate-roof houses are home to traditional arts – artisans craft fans, hand-make paper and brew *soju* (local vodka). It is also the birthplace of *bibimbap* (rice, egg, meat and vegetables with chilli sauce).

7. Bulguk-sa, Gyeongju

On a series of stone terraces about 16km southeast of Gyeongju, set among gnarled pines and iris gardens, this temple is the crowning glory of Shilla architecture and is on the Unesco World Cultural Heritage list. The excellence of its carpentry, the skill of its painters (particularly the interior woodwork and the eaves of the roofs) and the subtlety of its landscapes all contribute to its magnificence.

8. Seoraksan National Park

One of the most iconic parks on the Korean Peninsula, and a Unesco Biosphere Protection site, Seoraksan National Park boasts oddly shaped rock formations, dense forests, abundant wildlife, hot springs and Shilla-era temples. Seorak-san (Snowy Crags Mountain) is the third-highest mountain in South Korea; its highest peak is 1708m Daecheong-bong.

9. Guin-sa, Sobaeksan National Park

A templestay at Guin-Sa is the perfect antidote to fast-paced modern Korea. Participants are completely immersed in the monastic lifestyle, from the simple cotton uniform provided to 3am meditation sessions and the performance of hundreds of bows in front of the Buddha.

10. Jagalchi Fish Market, Busan

Anyone with a love of seafood and a tolerance for powerful odours should visit the country's largest fish market. Outer lanes teem with decades-old stalls and rickety food carts selling seafood, including red snapper, flounder and creepy-crawly creatures with undulating tentacles.

11. Hahoe Folk Village

The closest thing Korea has to a time machine, the charming Hahoe Folk Village is a window into how Korea looked, felt, sounded and smelled before the 20th century. More than 200 people live here, maintaining traditional ways and customs and inviting people to spend the night in their *minbak* (private homes).

14-day itinerary
South Korean Highlights

Spend four or five days in **Seoul**, including a day trip north to the **DMZ**. Next head east to **Chuncheon** to cycle around Uiam Lake and sample the famous chicken dish, *dakgalbi*. Dine on seafood in **Sokcho** then hike around the peaks and waterfalls of **Seoraksan National Park**. Follow the coast to **Gangneung** to view well- preserved Joseon-era buildings. From Samcheok explore **Hwanseongul** and **Daegeumgul** caves, as well as **Haesindang Park**, which is packed with phallic sculptures. Delve into Korea's past at **Hahoe Folk Village** and **Gyeongju**, ancient capital of the Shilla kingdom, and home to the World Heritage-listed grotto at Seokguram.

21-day itinerary
West to East

This cross-country itinerary explores South Korea's more natural side. From Incheon International Airport it's a hop to the idyllic island of **Muuido**, from where you can walk to So-Muuido or relax on lovely beaches. Take a bus to **Suwon** to stride around the ramparts of the fortress wall. Your next stops are **Gongju** and **Buyeo**, the ancient capitals of the Baekje kingdom, Korea's oldest dynasty. After enjoying the mud skincare spa of **Daecheon Beach**, continue north by bus to Anmyeondo, the largest island in the **Taean Haean National Marine Park**, with many beaches and trails. Travel inland to Daejeon to soak at **Yuseong Hot Springs**. Continue to **Cheongju** to learn about the world's oldest printed book, then move on to scenic **Songnisan National Park**, home to a 33m-tall gold-plated Buddha statue. Take a two-hour scenic ferry trip across **Chungju Lake** to **Danyang**, small-town Korea at its most charming, and finish at the temple complex of **Guin-sa** within **Sobaeksan National Park**.

© Panya Khamtuy / 500px

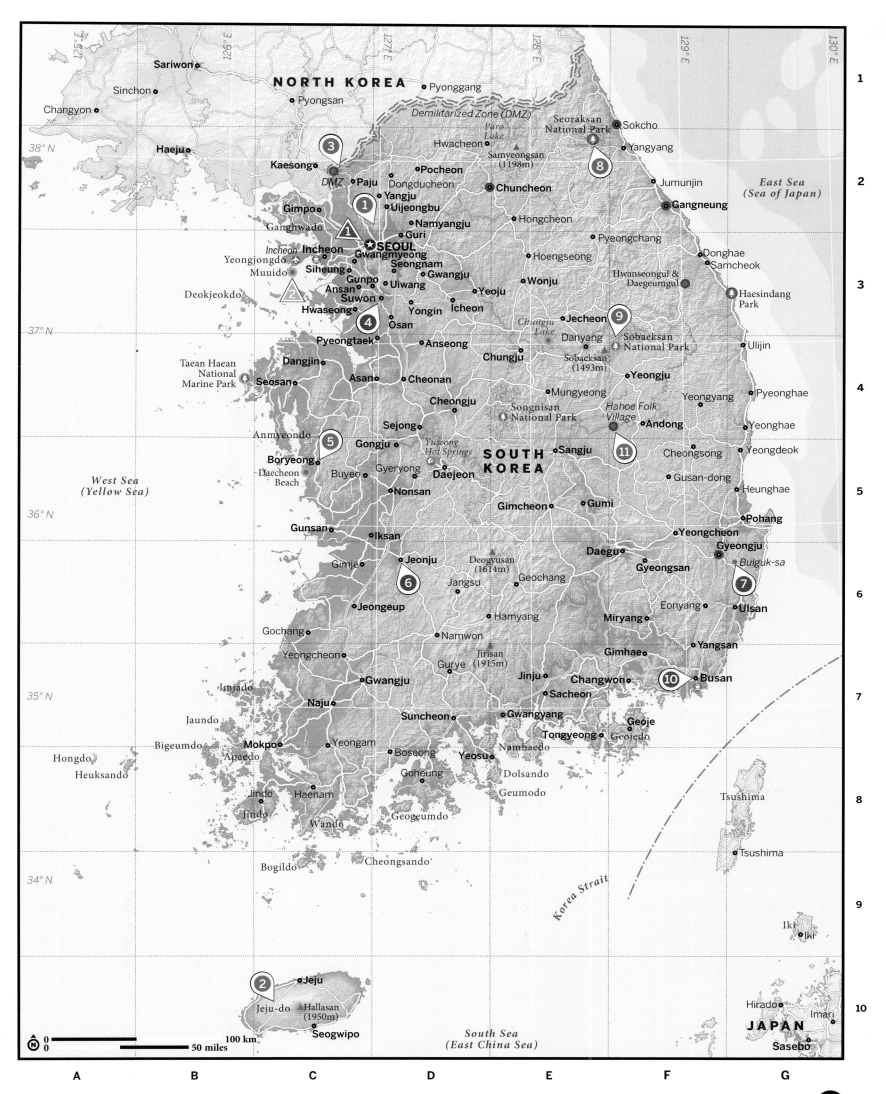

NORTH KOREA

Sariwon

Sinchon

Changyon

Pyonggang

Pyongsan

Demilitarized Zone (DMZ)

38° N

Haeju

Kaesong

DMZ

Paju

Hwacheon

Paro Lake

Samyeongsan
(1198m)

Seoraksan
National Park

Sokcho

Yangyang

*East Sea
(Sea of Japan)*

Pocheon

Dongducheon

Chuncheon

Jumunjin

Gangneung

Gimpo

Yangju

Uijeongbu

Namyangju

Hongcheon

Pyeongchang

Donghae

Samcheok

Ganghwado

★ **SEOUL**

Guri

Hoengseong

Wonju

Hwanseongul &
Daegeumgul

Haesindang
Park

Incheon

Incheon

Gwangmyeong

Seongnam

Gwangju

Yeoju

Yeongjongdo

Siheung

Gunpo

Uiwang

Deokjeokdo

Muuido

Ansan

Suwon

Yongin

Icheon

*Chungju
Lake*

Jecheon

Danyang

Sobaeksan
National Park

Ulijin

37° N

Hwaseong

Osan

Anseong

Chungju

Sobaeksan
(1493m)

Yeongju

Yeongyang

Pyeonghae

Pyeongtaek

Taean Haean
National
Marine Park

Dangjin

Asan

Cheonan

Mungyeong

Songnisan
National Park

Hahoe Folk
Village

Andong

Yeonghae

Seosan

Cheongju

Yeongdeok

Cheongsong

Anmyeondo

Sejong

Gongju

*Yusong
Hot Springs*

**SOUTH
KOREA**

Sangju

Gusan-dong

Heunghae

Boryeong

Buyeo

Gyeryong

Daejeon

Daecheon
Beach

Nonsan

Gimcheon

Gumi

Pohang

West Sea
(Yellow Sea)

36° N

Gunsan

Iksan

Gimje

Jeonju

Deogyusan
(1614m)

Geochang

Daegu

Yeongcheon

Gyeongju

Bulguk-sa

Jangsu

Gyeongsan

Eonyang

Ulsan

Jeongeup

Hamyang

Miryang

Gochang

Namwon

Jirisan
(1915m)

Gimhae

Yangsan

Yeongcheon

Gurye

Jinju

Changwon

Busan

35° N

Imjado

Gwangju

Sacheon

Naju

Suncheon

Gwangyang

Geoje

Jaundo

Yeongam

Tongyeong

Geojedo

Bigeumdo

Mokpo

Boseong

Namhaedo

Hongdo

Apaedo

Yeosu

Dolsando

Heuksando

Jindo

Haenam

Goheung

Geumodo

Jindo

Geogeumdo

Wando

Tsushima

34° N

Bogildo

Cheongsando

Tsushima

Korea Strait

Iki

Iki

JAPAN

2

Jeju

Jeju-do

Hallasan
(1950m)

Hirado

Imari

Seogwipo

*South Sea
(East China Sea)*

Sasebo

0 — 100 km
0 — 50 miles

| A | B | C | D | E | F | G |

225

SIGHTS &
ACTIVITIES

 SEE

 DO

ITINERARY

 1

2

Niseko:
Snowcapped Mount
Yotei in Japan's
powder capital,
Niseko.

1. Daisetsuzan National Park

Japan's largest national park was designated in 1934 and covers more than 2300 sq km. Daisetsuzan literally means 'Big Snow Mountain', but the park is also home to volcanoes, onsen, lakes, forests – and wild brown bears. For experienced hikers, the park offers an amazing opportunity to experience Japanese wilderness, staying at bare-bones huts along the way.

2. Sapporo

Japan's fifth-largest city, and the prefectural capital of Hokkaidō, Sapporo offers far and away the best nightlife on the island. The action centres on Susukino, home to craft-beer bars, hostess bars, flashy nightclubs and jazz cafes.

3. Noboribetsu

You can smell the sulphur around Noboribetsu from miles away. There are countless springs here, sending up mineral-rich waters for Hokkaidō's most famous onsen. The source of the waters is Jigoku-dani, a hissing, steaming volcanic pit that is said to be the home of the *oni* (demon) Yukujin.

4. Yamadera

Founded in AD 860 and immortalised by haiku master Matsuo Bashō, Yamadera is home to many special temple buildings, including the 'Temple of Standing Stones', which rests atop a rock-hewn staircase weathered over centuries. At the foot of the mountain is the sacred flame Konpon-chūdō, said to have been transported from Kyoto many centuries ago.

5. Niseko

Hokkaidō is dotted with world-class ski resorts, but the reigning prince of powder is Niseko. There are four interconnected resorts with more than 800 skiable hectares along the eastern side of the mountain, Niseko Annupuri.

6. Kakunodate

Established in 1620 by Ashina Yoshikatsu, the lord of the Satake clan, Kakunodate has arguably the best-preserved *buke yashiki* (samurai district) in the country; most of its buildings are still in perfect order, creating a living relic of feudal Japan.

7. Towada-ko

Hemmed in by coastlines and forests, Towada-ko is the largest crater lake in Honshū (52km in circumference). Once the site of violent volcanic eruptions; today, the only action is the quiet trickle of the Oirase Keiryū (mountain stream). In summer, it makes for an unrivalled open-water swim.

8. Shiretoko National Park

The peninsula of Shiretoko-hantō was known in Ainu as 'the end of the world'. This magnificent national park is one of Japan's last remaining sections of true wilderness, with access to pristine lakes, waterfalls and hidden hot springs. The classic two-day hiking traverse covers 25km from Iwaobetsu Onsen to Kamuiwakka-yu-no-taki.

9. Dewa Sanzan

The three peaks of Dewa Sanzan are said to symbolise the cycle of life: Haguro-san (Birth), Gas-san (Death) and Yudono-san (Rebirth). Hiking all three takes two days and is possible from June to September. Sometimes, you might see white-clad *yamabushi* (Shugendō mountain priests), dressed in chequered jackets and pantaloons.

10. Akan National Park

Designated in 1934 and covering 905 sq km, Akan was one of Japan's first national parks. It's home to volcanic peaks, several caldera lakes, Sakhalin spruce forests, wild sika deer, natural onsen and an Ainu *kotan* (village).

11. Nyūtō Onsen

Named for the bosom-shaped hills nearby (*nyūtō* means 'nipple'), Nyūtō Onsen offers the practice of *konyoku* (mixed-gender bathing) surrounded by nature in all its glory – and afterwards, you can swim in the crisp waters of Tazawa-ko lake.

12. Aizu-Wakamatsu

A former feudal capital, this town on the Bandai Plateau is rich in history, with a castle, Buddhist temple complex and many old-fashioned craft shops in the district of Nanoka-machi-dōri – plus a number of famous sake breweries that do tours and tastings.

10-day itinerary
Northern Honshū

From Tokyo, catch a fast train north to **Yamadera** to stoke your inner Shintō spirit in the place where the poet Matsuo Bashō penned his best-known works. Follow the *yamabushi* mountain priests through the fabled peaks of **Dewa Sanzan**, then step back into the samurai era at **Kakunodate**, where you'll find some of the finest feudal architecture anywhere in the country. Soak your travel-weary bones at one of the numerous hot springs in the mountains above Tazawa-ko, collectively known as **Nyūtō Onsen**, and finish up on the shores of **Towada-ko** crater lake, one of the finest places in Japan for a (summertime) swim.

14-day itinerary
Wild Hokkaidō

Snow falls early in Hokkaidō, Japan's northernmost island, so this is a summer trip. Start in **Hakodate**, Hokkaidō's southernmost port, which has a charming 19th-century city centre. You can arrive via *shinkansen* (bullet train) from Tokyo. Pick up a car and drive to **Shikotsu-Toya National Park** to take in caldera lakes and an active volcano. The city of **Asahikawa** is the gateway to **Daisetsuzan National Park**, Japan's largest and a mostly untouched wilderness of dense forest, mountains and outdoor onsen. Continue east to **Shiretoko National Park** for hikes through primeval woods and more hidden hot springs. **Akan National Park** is famous for its blue caldera lakes, Kussharo-ko and Mashu-ko. This is also the best place to learn about the indigenous Ainu people. Finally wend down to **Kushiro-shitsugen National Park**, home to the endangered Japanese red-crowned crane. From Kushiro it's easy work on the expressway back to New Chitose Airport, south of Sapporo.

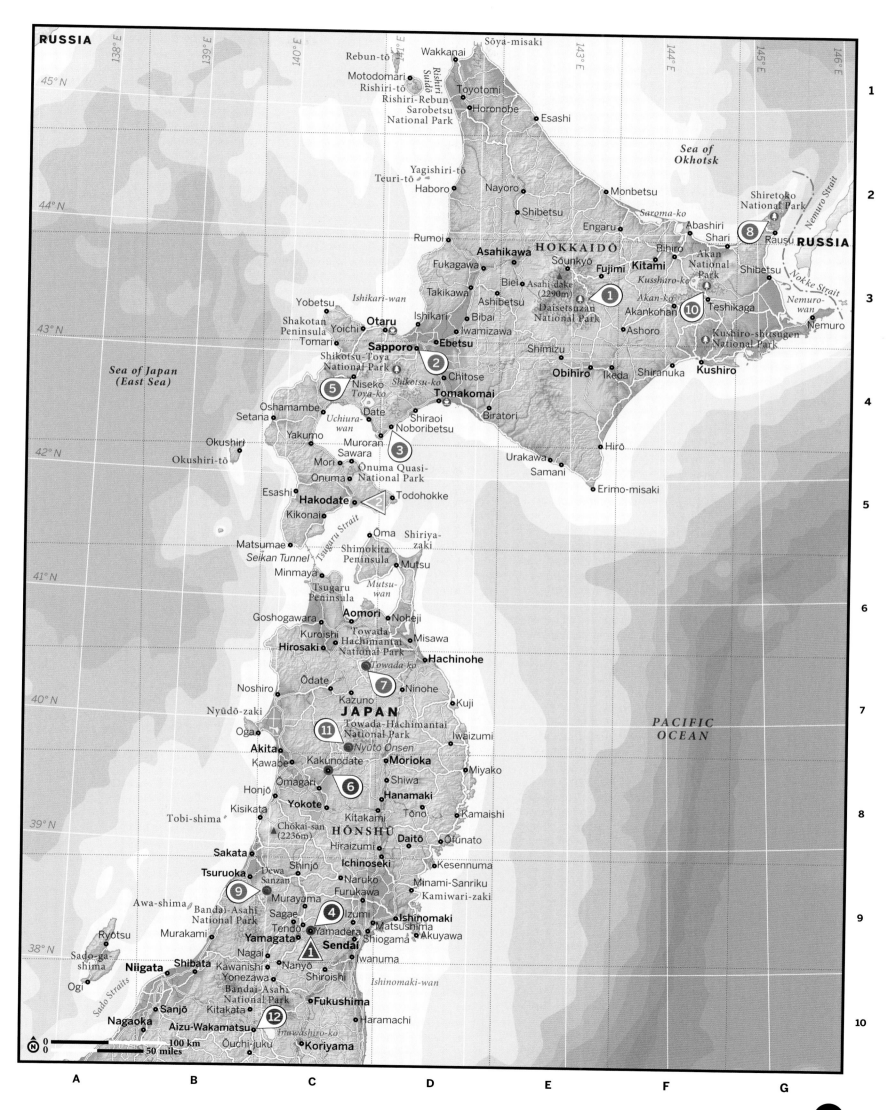

SIGHTS &
ACTIVITIES

 SEE

 DO

ITINERARY

 1

 2

Mt Fuji

The Japanese proverb 'He who climbs Mt Fuji once is a wise man, he who climbs it twice is a fool' remains as valid as ever. Scaling Japan's highest peak (an active volcano) is a great achievement but the apocalyptic-looking landscape is a world away from the mountain's serene snow-capped profile seen from afar. Almost all hikers start from hiking stations halfway up; allow five to six hours to reach the top and three hours to descend, plus 1½ hours for circling the 4km crater.

Kyoto

Kyoto, Japan's imperial capital for a thousand years, is home to more than a thousand temples: some monumental, some subtle, all fascinating. While famous temples draw big crowds, the majority see few visitors: such as Ryōan-ji, with its stark Zen rock garden, or Daitoku-ji a complex of lanes, subtemples and *kare-sansui* (dry landscape) gardens.

Tōdai-ji Temple, Nara

Japan's first permanent capital, Nara's star attraction is the Daibutsu (Great Buddha), with origins going back to AD 728. The Daibutsu statue itself is one of the largest bronze figures in the world. The present statue, recast in the Edo period, stands just over 16m high and consists of 437 tonnes of bronze and 130kg of gold.

Kenroku-en Gardens, Kanazawa

Ranked as one of the top three gardens in Japan, this Edo-period garden draws its name (meaning 'combined six') from a Sung-dynasty garden in China that dictated six attributes for perfection: seclusion, spaciousness, artificiality, antiquity, abundant water and broad views. Developed from the 1620s to the 1840s, it was first opened to the public in 1871.

Matsumoto-jō

This is Japan's oldest wooden castle and one of four castles designated National Treasures – the others are Hikone, Himeji and Inuyama. The three-turreted *donjon* (main keep) was completed around 1595, earning the nickname Karasu-jō (Crow Castle). You can climb to the top, with impressive views on each level.

Nakasendō

In the thickly forested Kiso Valley, there exist several sections of the twisty post road, or Nakasendō, that have been carefully restored for walkers. The most impressive is the 7.8km stretch between Magome and Tsumago.

Kamikōchi

Kamikōchi is a base for day trippers, hikers and climbers who come to make forays into the Japan Alps. Snowcapped peaks, bubbling brooks, wild monkeys, wildflowers and ancient forests are accessible on trails that range from easy day trips to multi-day treks.

Hida

The villages of Ogimachi and Ainokura are famed for their *gasshō-zukuri* buildings, with steeply slanted thatch roofs that prevent snow accumulation. The name comes from the Japanese word for prayer, because the shape resembles hands clasped together.

Nikkō

Enshrining the glories of the Edo period (1600–1868), the various temple sites of Nikkō are scattered among hilly woodlands. A highlight is Tōshō-gū, a brilliantly decorative shrine in a beautiful natural setting.

10-day itinerary
Tokyo Circular

This is a classic route, taking advantage of Japan's seamless rail system. Start with a couple of days in the madcap metropolis of **Tokyo**, getting a taste of big-city Japan – the skyscrapers, the bustle and all that endless neon. Then hop on the bullet train for **Kyoto**. You'll need two or three days to sample the best of Kyoto's temples and gardens. From here you can make side trips to **Nara**, home of the Daibutsu (Great Buddha), and **Osaka**, famous for its vivid nightscape and street food. Take a detour to the mystical mountain monastery Kōya-san (where you can spend the night in a Buddhist temple) before heading back via the mountain onsen of **Hakone** to the bright lights of Tokyo.

14-day itinerary
Kyoto, Kanazawa & the Japan Alps

This route highlights Japan's traditional culture and its natural beauty. Spend the first few days in **Kyoto**, exploring the city's temples, shrines and gardens. Next take the train to **Kanazawa**, known for excellent seafood, but also for its artisan traditions and its strolling garden, Kenroku-en. Hire a car and head for the mountains of **Hida**. The villages of **Shirakawa-gō** and **Gokayama** in this area are famed for their farmhouses with dramatically angled thatched roofs. In the World Heritage–listed village of **Ainokura**, you can spend the night in one. Continue to **Takayama**, a charming old post town with well-preserved wooden buildings. For beautiful alpine scenery and a spot of hiking, head next to **Kamikōchi**; then, for rustic onsen (hot springs), to **Shin-Hotaka Onsen**. From here drive east to one of Japan's best original castles, **Matsumoto-jō**. Near Nagano, pretty **Obuse**, another well-preserved mountain town, is home to the Hokusai Museum. End your trip in **Nagano** with a visit to the city's impressive temple, Zenkō-ji.

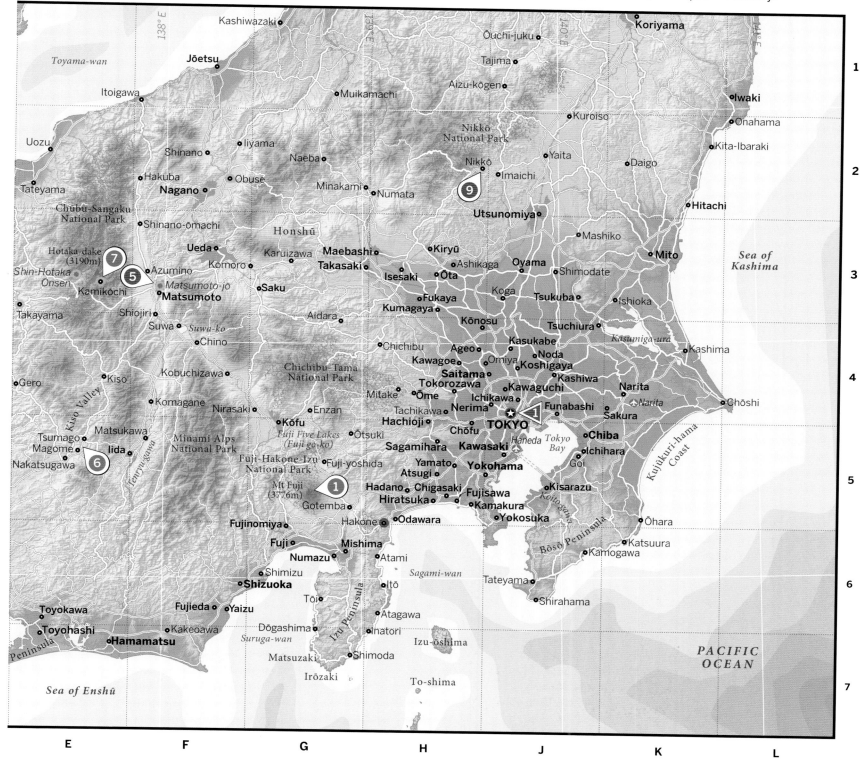

Hiroshima

On 6 August 1945, Hiroshima became the target of the world's first atomic-bomb attack. The city's Peace Memorial Park is a reminder of that day, a leafy space criss-crossed by walkways and dotted with memorials. The tree-lined Pond of Peace leads to the cenotaph, which holds the names of all the known victims of the bomb.

Himeji-jō

Japan's most magnificent castle is nicknamed Shirasagi-jō (White Egret Castle) for its lustrous white plaster exterior and stately hilltop form. There's a five-storey main *tenshū* (keep) and three smaller keeps, all surrounded by moats and defensive walls punctuated with openings for firing guns and shooting arrows.

Naoshima

This island offers a unique opportunity to see some of Japan's best contemporary art in gorgeous natural settings. In Honmura, half a dozen traditional buildings have been turned over to contemporary artists to use as the setting for creative installations, often incorporating local history.

Miyajima

The island of Miyajima's star attraction is the oft-photographed vermilion *torii* (shrine gate) of Itsukushima-jinja, which seems to float on the waves at high tide – traditionally ranked as one of the three best views in Japan.

Shimanami Kaidō

The Setouchi Shimanami Kaidō (Shimanami Sea Route) is a chain of bridges linking Onomichi with Imabari via six Inland Sea islands. Besides being remarkable feats of engineering (the Kurushima-kaikyō trio at the Imabari end are among the longest suspension bridges in the world), the bridges make it possible to cycle the whole way across – a total route of roughly 70km.

Shikoku

The birthplace of the founder of the Shingon Buddhist sect Kōbō Daishi, Shikoku is synonymous with natural beauty and spiritual perfection. It's also home to the 88 Sacred Temples of Shikoku, Japan's most famous pilgrimage – a 1400km route that takes between 40 and 60 days to complete.

Izumo Taisha

Izumo Taisha, also known as Izumo Ōyashiro, is perhaps the oldest Shintō shrine. It is dedicated to Ōkuninushi, God of marriage and bringer of good fortune; there are references to Izumo in the Kojiki, Japan's oldest book.

Yakushima

The mountainous Okinawan island of Yakushima is home to the ancient cedar trees known as *yakusugi*. Hiking is the best way to see them: the most popular hike is to the 3000-to-7000-year-old Jōmon-sugi, while the Shiratani-unsuikyō hike passes waterfalls, moss-lined rocks and *yakusugi* to the overlook at Taiko-iwa.

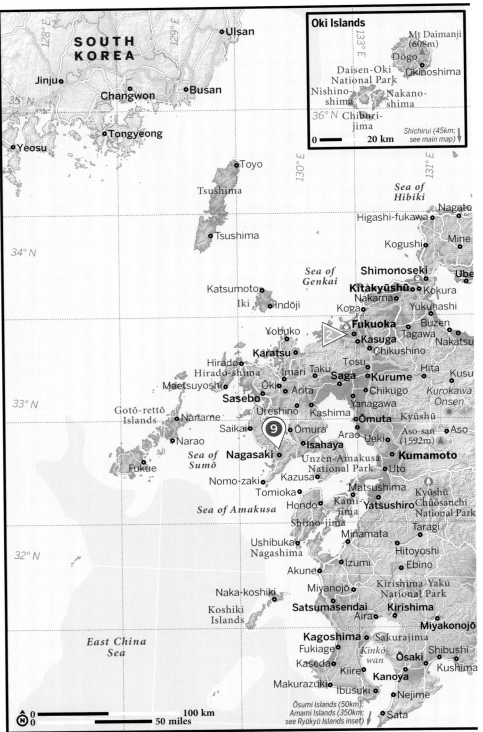

Nagasaki

Synonymous with the dropping of the second atomic bomb, Nagasaki's Atomic Bomb Museum is a sombre experience. It recounts the city's destruction through photos and artefacts, including mangled rocks, trees, furniture, pottery and clothing, first-hand accounts from survivors, and a clock stopped at 11.02 – the time of the bombing.

7-day itinerary
Western Honshū to Hiroshima

Starting in **Kōbe**, one of Japan's most attractive and cosmopolitan cities, head west to see the country's best castle, **Himeji-jō**. Stop in **Onomichi** for a temple hunt (there are some 25 to find), en route to **Hiroshima**, the first city destroyed by an atomic bomb. Pay your respects at the moving Peace Memorial Park, but don't overlook the city's buzzy nightlife and excellent museums. Further down the coast is the island of **Miyajima**, with its photogenic floating shrine. You can spend a memorable night in a *ryokan* (traditional inn) here. End with a visit to **Izumo Taisha**, second in importance only to Ise-jingū. There is evidence that the shrine towered as high as 48m above the ground during the Heian period.

14-day itinerary
Kyūshū Cruising

Considered off the beaten track, the island of Kyūshū is great for seeing another side of Japan. Fly into **Fukuoka** from Tokyo and spend a day in this hip city, known for its food stalls and pork-bone ramen. Hire a car to work your way down the coast via the pottery towns of **Karatsu** and **Arita**. History, of course, weighs heavily on **Nagasaki**, the second Japanese city destroyed by an atomic bomb, but there's a cosmopolitan food scene and interesting architecture to experience, too. Cut into the heartland to **Kurokawa Onsen**, one of Japan's best onsen towns. Travel south, past the active volcano **Aso-san** and the castle town **Kumamoto** (still recovering from a 2016 earthquake) to **Kagoshima** on the Shimabara Peninsula, a city known for its *shōchū* (strong distilled liquor) and the smoking volcano of Sakurajima. South of Kagoshima are the hot sand baths of **Ibusuki**. Return the car and catch a speedboat from Kagoshima to **Yakushima**, an island with primeval, moss-strewn forests and seaside onsen. If you have time, head to Kagoshima for a ferry out to the idyllic **Okinawa Islands**.

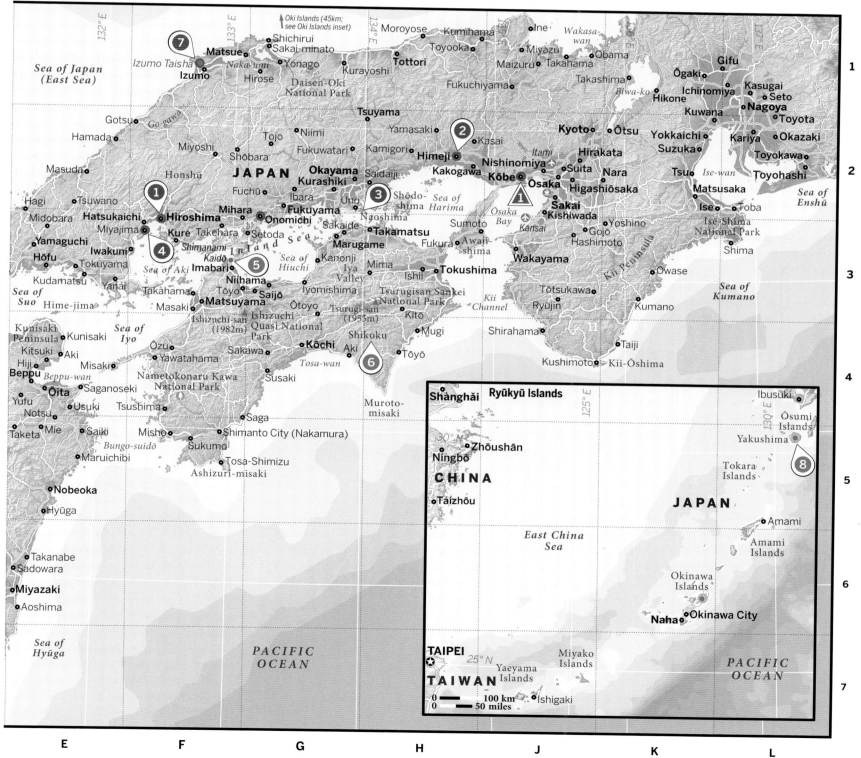

Mainland Southeast Asia

Wrapped in rainforests, edged by islands, crowned by volcanoes, studded with lost civilisations: this is Southeast Asia as you've always imagined it. In this region of rivers, oceans and islands, you're as likely to travel by boat as by road, following trade routes that were old when the great powers of Europe were young. Millennia of monsoons have created cultures defined by the seasons and by the annual flooding of rivers, which double as super-highways through impenetrable jungles. Every aspect of life here has a spiritual dimension, from the food people eat to the religious geometry that dictates the layout of temples. In short: it's an incredible mix of ancient and modern, urban and natural, sacred and secular.

CLIMATE CHART

BANGKOK

RAINFALL INCH/MM
—20/500
—16/400
—12/300
—8/200
—0

TEMP °C/°F
40/104
30/86
20/68
10/50
0/32

J F M A M J J A S O N D

HANOI

RAINFALL INCH/MM
—32/800
—24/600
—16/400
—8/200
—0

TEMP °C/°F
40/104
30/86
20/68
10/50
0/32

J F M A M J J A S O N D

TEMPLES
Religion is central to life here, as it has been for centuries. The sprawling, creeper-clad ruins of great religious centres such as Angkor Wat, Wat Phu and Ayutthaya seem straight out of *Indiana Jones*, but you'll find stunning temples everywhere you look.

Ayutthaya
Wat Phu
Angkor Wat

Chiang Mai
Vientiane
Yangon
Bangkok
Phnom Penh
Ho Chi Minh City

Hanoi
Vang Vieng
Hue
Battambang
Phuket

Cham Islands
Myeik Archipelago
Koh Rong
Ko Samui
Ko Phi Phi

Right: Longtail boat anchoring at Thailand's Ao Noi beach (left) and (right) monks wandering through temple ruins of Ta Prohm at Angkor.

CITIES
A madcap mix of skyscrapers, hawker stalls, markets and malls, megacities such as Bangkok, Ho Chi Minh City, Yangon and Phnom Penh are a definite highlight here – but don't overlook the gentler charms of elegant, temple-rich cities like Vientiane or Chiang Mai.

FOOD
Southeast Asia is one giant cooking pot, home to some of the world's great cuisines. Epicurean experiences abound: sample pad Thai in Phuket, spicy *láhp* salad in Vang Vieng, royal rice cakes in Hue, *bun cha* in Hanoi or rice noodle soup in Battambang.

ISLANDS
Archipelagos speckle Southeast Asia's seas, and there's an island for every traveller: from party islands such as Ko Phi-Phi and Ko Samui to backpacker hangouts like Cambodia's Koh Rong and remote gems such as the Cham Islands and Myeik Archipelago.

Transport hubs

Flying to this corner of southeast Asia is the easiest option. The only overland possibilities from outside the region are from China into Vietnam or Laos. Travel agencies can sometimes arrange crossings from India into Myanmar, although this requires a special permit. The major gateway in this region is Bangkok, which has frequent links with most of the other major cities. If you're planning on border hopping, do your homework: some border crossings (like Thailand to Laos) are well trodden, but others can be troublesome and bureaucratic. Often it's easier – and cheaper – just to catch a flight rather than trying to negotiate a land crossing.

Below: Nam Xong River in Vang Vieng, Laos (left) and (right) streetlife in Hanoi, Vietnam.

① Bangkok (see pp386-7 for city map)
Located 30km east of Bangkok, Suvarnabhumi Airport (pronounced 'sù-wan-ná-poom') is Thailand's main air hub. The city's train station is called Hualamphong, but long-distance buses and private minivans are the main ways to get around the country. In the city itself, there's a choice of taxi, tuk-tuk, the MRT metro, the BTS Skytrain and canal boats.

② Chiang Mai
Chiang Mai has good domestic air connections to the rest of Thailand, and with Kuala Lumpur (Malaysia), Yangon (Myanmar) and destinations around China. Trains run five times daily on the main line from Bangkok and the city's bus terminal has onward services to northern destinations such as Pai and Mae Hong Son. There is also a regular international bus to Luang Prabang in Laos

③ Phnom Penh
The majority of visitors enter or exit Cambodia by air through the gateways of Phnom Penh or Siem Reap. Lots of travellers also arrive in Cambodia via the numerous land borders shared with Thailand, Vietnam and Laos; frequent buses travel to Phnom Penh from Ho Chi Minh City. Visas are now available at all the land crossings with Laos, Thailand and Vietnam. To get around Cambodia, bus is by far the most popular form of transport.

④ Hanoi
Hanoi is one of Vietnam's major entry points with plenty of direct international flights. Vietnam Airlines flies to destinations throughout the rest of Vietnam. Trains connect with southern China and to cities along the whole length of the country to HCMC – though buses are generally an easier option for China. The city's traffic is notoriously bad; promisingly an eight-line metro system is planned.

⑤ Ho Chi Minh City (HCMC)
Ho Chi Minh City is served by Tan Son Nhat International Airport, located 7km northwest of central Ho Chi Minh City. A number of airlines offer domestic routes from HCMC. The busy Moc Bai/Bavet border crossing is the fastest land route between Ho Chi Minh City and Phnom Penh in Cambodia.

⑥ Vientiane
Vientiane has air connections with nearby countries including Thailand, Vietnam, Cambodia, Malaysia, China and South Korea. It's also straightforward to cross into Thailand via the Thai–Lao Friendship Bridge over the Mekong River, using the regular Thai–Lao International Bus. Rivers are the lifeblood of Laos, making boat journeys an important part of the transport network, along with the ubiquitous buses and minivans.

⑦ Yangon
Yangon International Airport is Myanmar's main international gateway and the hub for domestic flights. Yangon is also a useful launchpad for exploring the rest of the country: trains run to destinations including Bagan, Mandalay and Nay Pyi Taw, but long-distance buses still provide the backbone of the country's transport network.

Page 241

Yibin · Luzhou
Zunyi · Zhijiang
Xichang · ZHAOTANG · Lupanshui · Guiyang · Shaoyang
PLATEAU OF TIBET
Hkakabo Razi (5889m)
HIMALAYAS
Putao
Dibrugarh
BHUTAN
Lijiāng · Panzhihua · Huize · Anshun · Guilin
INDIA
Dispur
Myitkyina · Bǎoshān · DÀLĪ · Zhanyi · Xingyi · Yishan · CHINA
Khasi Hills
YUNGUI PLATEAU
Tengchong · Kūnmíng · Chuxiong · Yuxi · Zhanyi · Liuzhou
BANGLADESH
Imphal
Tamu
Agartala
Mt Kennedy (2703m)
Kalaymyo · Mogok · Lashio
MYANMAR
Loi Leng (2673m)
Simao · Gejiu · Mengzi · Wenshan · Nanning · Hechi
Page 240
Page 236
Chittagong
Mowdok Mual (1052m)
Ye-U · Shwebo · Monywa · Kyaukme
INDOCHINA PENINSULA
Phongsali
Fansipan (3143m) · Hekou · VIETNAM · Chóngzuǒ · Qinzhou · Maoming
Mandalay
Dien Bien Phu · Son La · Son Tay · Mong Cai · Beihai · Zhanjiang
Mt Victoria (3053m)
Nyaung U · Myingyan · Meiktila
Mong La · Kyaingtong
Luang Namtha (Namtha) · Udomxai (Muang Xai) · Sam Neua (Xam Neua)
Hoang Lien Mountains · HANOI · Haiphong · Cam Pha · Halong City · Cat Ba Island
Qiongzhou Strait
Haikou
Kyaukpadaung · Magwe
Mrauk-U · Mt Popa (1518m) · Nyaungshwe
Huay Xai (Hoksay) · Pak Beng · Luang Prabang · Phonsavan · Nam Dinh
Hainan Island
Sittwe
Chiang Rai
Hongsa · Sainyabuli (Sayaboury) · Phu Bia (2820m) · Do Luong · Dien Chau
Page 244
Page 237
Allanmyo · NAY PYI TAW · Loikaw
Doi Inthanon (2580m) · Chiang Mai · Nan · Phon Hong · Paksan · Vinh · Ky Anh
Taunggok · Pyay · Pyu · Taungoo
Lampang · Phrae · Wattay · VIENTIANE · Nakhon Phanom · Thakhek · Dong Hoi
Sanya
Letpadan · Hinthada · Yandoon · Bago
Tak · Phetchaburi · Udon Thani · Sakhon Nakhon · Hue
Gulf of Tonkin
Patthein · Yangon · Thongwa · Thaton · Khon Kaen · Savannakhet · Muang Phin · Dong Ha
Page 238
Mawdwin Point · Mawlamyine · Ye
Nakhon Sawan · THAILAND · Ubon Ratchathani · Salavan · Sekong (Muang Lamam) · Hoi An · Tam Ky
Mouths of the Ayeyarwady
Singburi · Nakhon Ratchasima (Khorat) · Pakse · Attapeu (Samakhi Xai) · Ngoc Linh (2598m)
Dawei · Suphanburi · Saraburi · Prachinburi
Samraong · Stung Treng · Ban Lung · Kon Tum · Pleiku · Quy Nhon
Pages 246-247
BANGKOK · Suvarnabhumi · Sisophon · Siem Reap · Kompong Thom · Chuo Yang Sin (2420m)
Kanchanaburi · Ratchaburi · Chonburi · Battambang · Pursat · Kratie · Sen Monorom · Nha Trang
Phetchaburi · Pattaya · Rayong · Chanthaburi · Kompong Chhnang · Hon Quan · Dalat
Hua Hin · Trat · Phnom Aural (1813m) · PHNOM PENH · Tay Ninh · Tan Son Nhat · Phan Rang
Myeik · Prachuap Khiri Khan · Koh Kong · Takeo · Svay Rieng · Ho Chi Minh City · Phan Thiet
Port Blair · Myeik Archipelago · Koh Sdach · Koh Rong · Sihanoukville · Kep · My Tho · Vung Tau
ANDAMAN ISLANDS
Andaman Sea
Chumphon · Ko Tao · Koh Tonsay · Rach Gia · Can Tho · Soc Trang · Pages 242-243
Ranong · Ko Pha-Ngan · Ko Samui · Ca Mau · Bac Lieu · Con Dao Islands · Page 239
Surin Islands · Surat Thani
Similan Islands · Khao Laung (1780m) · Càu Mau Point
NICOBAR ISLANDS
Phang-Nga · Nakhon Si Thammarat
SOUTH CHINA SEA (EAST SEA)
Phuket Town · Krabi · Trang · Phatthalung
Ko Lanta · Ko Libong · Thaleh Luang · Songkhla
Great Nicobar
Satun · Kangar · Yala · Pattani
Banda Aceh · Page 249 · Butterworth · Sungai Kolok
INDONESIA · Lhokseumawe · MALAYSIA · Kuala Terengganu

Bay of Bengal
Gulf of Martaban
Gulf of Thailand

400 km
200 miles

© kwanchai_k photograph / Getty Images, © Matt Munro / Lonely Planet

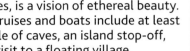

1 Halong Bay

Towering limestone pillars and tiny islets topped by forest rise from the emerald waters of the Gulf of Tonkin. Designated a World Heritage site in 1994, Halong Bay's scatter of islands, dotted with wind- and wave-eroded grottoes, is a vision of ethereal beauty. Most cruises and boats include at least a couple of caves, an island stop-off, and a visit to a floating village.

2 Hanoi

The streets of Vietnam's capital surge with scooters, and layers of history reveal periods of French and Chinese occupation. In the Old Quarter, farmers hawk their wares, while city folk breakfast on noodles, practise t'ai chi or play chess. Sampling the city's street food is an essential experience, as is tasting a cup of Vietnamese coffee in a traditional Old Quarter cafe.

3 Ba Be National Park

Often referred to as the Ba Be Lakes, this area was established as a national park in 1992. The hundreds of wildlife species here include 65 mammals, 353 butterflies, 106 species of fish, four kinds of turtle, and the highly endangered Vietnamese salamander. The region is home to 13 tribal villages, most belonging to the Tay minority.

Halong Bay: Boats cruise between the towering limestone pillars of Vietnam's Halong Bay.

4 Sapa

Established as a hill station by the French in 1922, Sapa today is the tourism centre of the northwest. This is northern Vietnam's premier trekking base, from where hikers launch themselves into rice terraces and hill-tribe villages that seem a world apart.

5 Bac Ha Market

Sleepy Bac Ha wakes up for the riot of colour and commerce that is its Sunday market, when the lanes fill to choking point and villagers flock in from the hills and valleys.

6 Mai Chau

Set in an idyllic valley hemmed in by hills, the Mai Chau area is a patchwork of rice fields speckled by tiny Thai villages where visitors can sleep for the night in traditional stilt houses. The villagers are mostly White Thai, distantly related to tribes in Thailand, Laos and China.

7 Ha Giang

Ha Giang is the final frontier in northern Vietnam, a landscape of limestone pinnacles and granite outcrops. The trip between Yen Minh and Dong Van, and across the Mai Pi Leng Pass to Meo Vac is mind-blowing.

8 Cat Ba Island

The largest island in Halong Bay is a superb base for adventure sports – including mountain-biking, trekking, kayaking and rock-climbing on the karst pillars. Almost half the island (354 sq km) and 90 sq km of adjacent sea became a national park in 1986.

9 Co To Island

Despite being the furthest inhabited island from the mainland, Co To Island has boomed in the last few years. It is home to some of Bai Tu Long Bay's best beaches and its widest spread of accommodation and restaurants, but receives few foreign tourists.

10 Meo Vac

Meo Vac is a charming district capital hemmed in by karst mountains. It's reached by the spectacular Mai Pi Leng Pass, which is cut into the cliffside with a view of hills tumbling down to the waters of the Nho Que River.

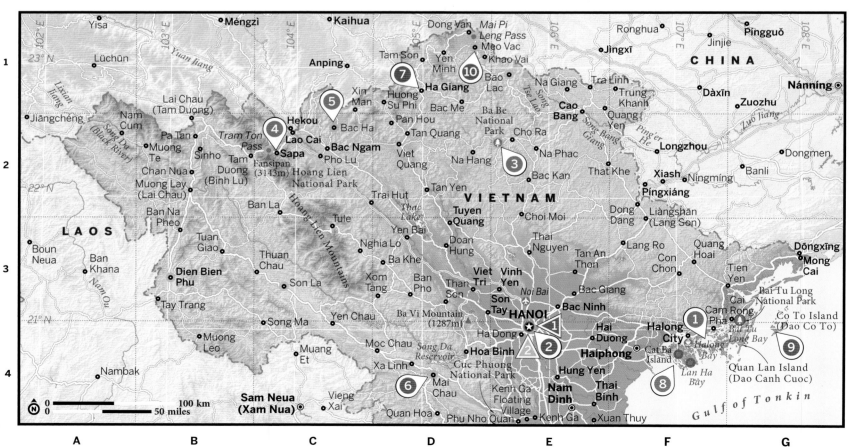

10-day itinerary
Hanoi to Cat Ba Island

Spend a few days delving into the sights of **Hanoi**: wandering the Old Quarter, visiting the temples of Bach Ma and Hai Ba Trung, and sampling street food along Pho Cam Chi and Đuong Thuy Khue. From Hanoi, take an organised trip out to **Cat Ba Island**, which has developed fast in recent years but is still largely wild, with jungle-covered hills and waterfalls.

From the island, you can arrange sailing and kayaking trips to **Lan Ha Bay**, dotted with 300 karst islands fringed by white beaches, and without the crowds of nearby Halong Bay. If time allows, you can arrange custom trips to explore the islands of **Bai Tu Long National Park**, another gem that's still relatively lightly touristed – at least for now.

21-day itinerary
Northern Mountains

Northern Vietnam's mountains and minority villages are ideal for two wheels, though can also be tackled by public transport. Leaving **Hanoi**, head west to **Mai Chau**, home to the White Thai people, for an introduction to ethnic minority life. Northwest, a logical overnight stop is **Son La**, a sleepy town with good minority restaurants. Continue to **Dien**

Bien Phu, where the French colonial story ended in defeat. Tour the military sights and new museum then continue up the **Tram Ton Pass** to Sapa, a place with infinite views (on a clear day!) and an array of minority peoples. Travel on to experience **Bac Ha's** markets, then into Ha Giang province, passing through towns such as Yen Minh, Dong Van and Meo Vac. There's no

public transport to reach the vertiginous **Mai Pi Leng Pass** and **Meo Vac** so you'll need to hire a *xe om* or car. The route then loops down to the riverside junction town of **Bao Lac**. Local buses run from Bao Lac to Cao Bang and on to **Ba Be National Park**, a super place to do some trekking or kayaking. Travel back to Cao Bang for the trip back south to Hanoi.

Hue
Pronounced 'hway', the capital of the Nguyen emperors resonates with the glories of imperial Vietnam. Most sights lie within the moats of its Citadel and Imperial Enclosure.

Vinh Moc
Vinh Moc literally went underground in response to unremitting American bombing. More than 90 families disappeared into three levels of tunnels running for almost 2km.

Phong Nha-Ke Bang National Park
Designated a World Heritage site in 2003, these are the oldest karst mountains in Asia, formed 400 million years ago. Riddled with hundreds of cave systems, many of extraordinary scale, they are a speleologists' heaven.

Kenh Ga
Kenh Ga (Chicken Canal) is named after the wild chickens that lived here. Today, locals watch over fish-breeding pens or trade boat-to-boat, and children commute to school by river.

Cuc Phuong National Park
Cuc Phuong spans two limestone mountain ranges and three provinces. Its highest peak is Dinh May Bac (Silver Cloud Peak) at 656m. In 1962 Ho Chi Minh declared this Vietnam's first national park, saying: 'Forest is gold'. Unfortunately, poaching and habitat destruction plague the park.

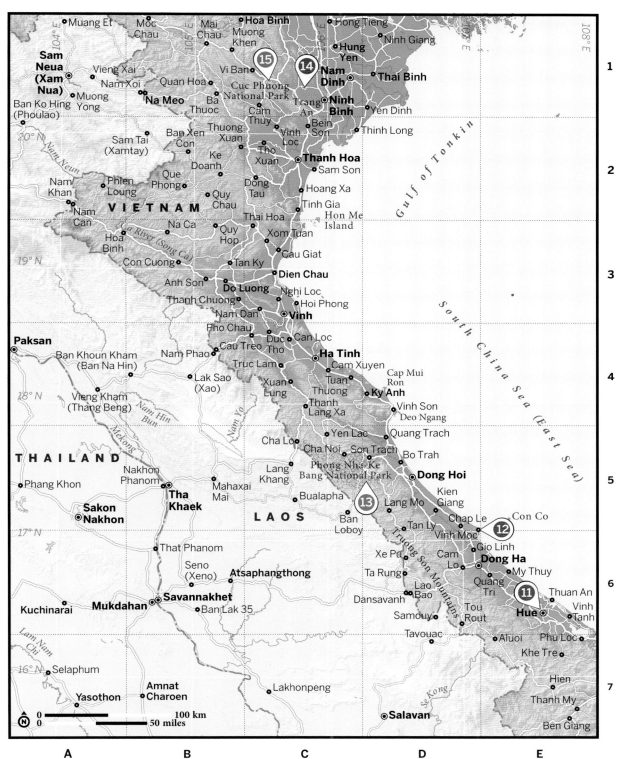

SIGHTS &
ACTIVITIES

 SEE

DO

ITINERARY

1

2

 1

Ho Chi Minh Highway

This legendary route formed the major supply link for the North Vietnamese and Viet Cong in the American War. The epic mountain road can be explored by car, 4WD, motorbike or even bicycle.

 2

Dalat

Dalat is dotted with French-colonial villas and farms cultivating strawberries, coffee and flowers, rather than the usual rice crop. It's Vietnam's honeymoon capital, as well as a centre for adventure sports: canyoning, mountain-biking, white-water rafting and trekking.

 3

Son My Memorial

This tranquil spot is infamous for a massacre committed by US troops that killed 504 villagers. A poignant memorial centres on a sculpture of an elderly woman holding up her fist in defiance, a dead child in her arms.

 4

Danang

For decades a provincial backwater, Danang is now home to gleaming new hotels, apartments, restaurants and the landmark new D-City. Book an after-dark tour to see Danang at its neon-lit best. The city's street-food scene also deserves close investigation.

 5

Hoi An

Hoi An is Vietnam's most graceful and historic town. Once a major port, it boasts the grand architecture and beguiling riverside setting that befits its heritage. Its Old Town has preserved Japanese merchant houses, Chinese temples and tea warehouses.

 6

My Son

The site of Vietnam's most extensive Cham remains, the temple complex of My Son enjoys an enchanting setting in a jungle valley, overlooked by Cat's Tooth Mountain (Hon Quap). About 20 structures survive.

 7

Kon Tum

A relaxed ambience, friendly locals, river setting and relatively traffic-free streets make Kon Tum a great stop for exploring the local hill-tribe villages, of which there are 700 or so – mostly Bahnar, but also Sedang and Jarai.

 8

Ganh Da Dia

A smaller version of Ireland's Giant's Causeway, Ganh Da Dia is a spectacular outcrop of hundreds of interlocked columns of volcanic rock. It's possible to bathe in the tiny rock cove beside it.

 9

Lak Lake

The largest natural body of water in the central highlands, Lak Lake (Ho Lak) is surrounded by bucolic scenery. You can get paddled out onto its reed-covered expanse in a longboat, and visit three minority villages, all occupied by M'nong people.

 10

Cham Islands

The Cham Islands offer superb diving and snorkelling, with 135 species of soft and hard coral. Though a marine park, fishing and the collection of birds' nests (for soup) are key industries.

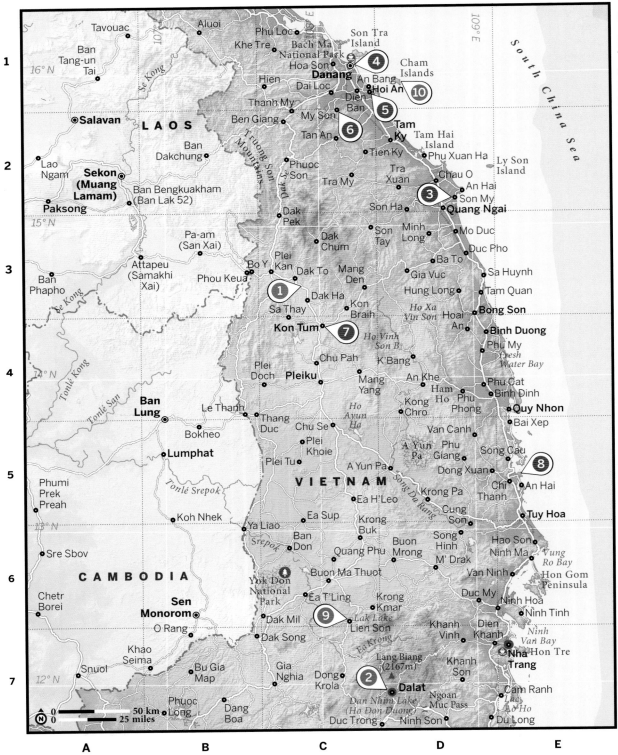

14-day itinerary
Vietnam's Southeast Coast

This coastal trip can easily be done by bus or motorbike. Starting in **Ho Chi Minh City**, head east to the busy beach resorts of **Mui Ne**, Vietnam's kitesurfing capital. Continue to the twin towns of Phan Rang and Thap Cham, from where you can visit the impressive ancient **Po Klong Garai Cham Towers**, dating from the 13th century. From here, veer inland to

Dalat, an attractive colonial town that's become a centre for adrenaline-fuelled adventure sports. Back out on the coast lies **Nha Trang**, a high-rise, high-energy beach resort known for its party scene. Move on through Buon Ma Thot to finish the trip by exploring the forested trails of **Yok Don National Park**, Vietnam's largest nature reserve.

14-day itinerary
Deep South

If beaches are high on your agenda it's best not to plan this trip during the rainy season (May to October). After a couple of days enjoying the urban delights of **Ho Chi Minh City**, head into the Mekong Delta, stopping at **Ben Tre** to explore canalside lanes by bike and islands by boat. Then hop on-board a cargo ship to **Tra Vinh** and take in the town's colourful

pagodas. Next, it's a short trip to **Can Tho** for floating markets, the city museum and a temple or two. Then head to **Phu Quoc Island** for three days of well-earned beach time. From Phu Quoc, fly (or bus it) back to HCMC, then head north into the south-central highlands via a night in **Cat Tien National Park**, home to gibbons, crocodiles and bountiful birds. Next

up it's the romantic hill station of **Dalat** for adventure sports such as canyoning, mountain-biking or kayaking. The road trip from Dalat down to **Mui Ne** negotiates highland ridges, valleys and pine forests: it's best seen from a motorbike. End the trip in this tropical, laid-back idyll, exploring towering sand dunes, learning to kitesurf or taking a sailing course.

Ho Chi Minh City
HCMC is a high-octane city of commerce and culture. Highlights include the War Remnants Museum, the French colonial cathedral and the Jade Emperor Pagoda. HCMC is also Vietnam's culinary capital, from local street food to fine French dining.

Can Tho
The epicentre of the Mekong Delta, Can Tho is the perfect base for visiting nearby floating markets such as Cai Rang, the biggest floating market in the Mekong Delta.

Phu Quoc
Phu Quoc has morphed from a sleepy island backwater to a busy beach escape. Its local claim to fame is the production of fish sauce (*nuoc mam*). For visitors, it's a place to dive, kayak and explore back roads by motorbike.

Cat Tien National Park
The 720-sq-km Cat Tien National Park comprises an amazingly biodiverse region of lowland tropical rainforest. The hiking, mountain biking and birdwatching are fantastic: look out for wild gibbons and crocodiles.

Con Dao Islands
Long the preserve of political prisoners and undesirables, these 15 islands are now known for their striking natural beauty. Con Son, the largest, is ringed with beaches, reefs and bays, and remains partially covered in forests.

Cu Chi Tunnels
The tunnel network of Cu Chi became legendary during the 1960s. More than 250km of tunnels honeycomb the ground, with space for living, storage, weapon factories, field hospitals, command centres and kitchens.

Hoi An: The sun sets over the ancient town of Hoi An, Vietnam.

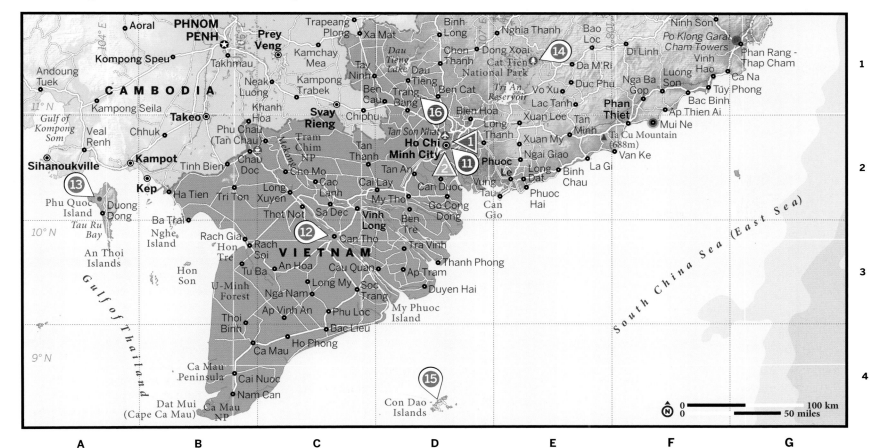

Luang Prabang
This city of temples is rich in royal history. Luang Prabang's best-known monastery is Wat Xieng Thong, centred on a 1560 ordination hall. Its roofs sweep low to the ground and there's a stunning 'tree of life' mosaic set on its western exterior wall.

Vang Vieng
Vang Vieng sits under soaring karst cliffs beside the Song River and is the undisputed adventure capital of Laos. Tubing, climbing, kayaking, cycling, motorbiking, hot-air ballooning and hiking are all possibilities here.

Vieng Xai
Vieng Xai was home to the Pathet Lao communist leadership during the US bombing campaign of 1964–73. Guided tours explore the seven most important war-shelter cave complexes.

Wat Phu
Stretching 1400m up the slopes of Phu Pasak, Wat Phu is contemporaneous with the Angkor-era sites near Siem Reap in Cambodia. The site's pavilions, Shiva-lingam sanctuary and enigmatic crocodile stone give it a mystical atmosphere. The complex was made a World Heritage Site in 2001.

Si Phan Don
In southern Laos the Mekong bulges to a breadth of 14km, the widest point along its 4350km journey. If you count every islet that emerges in the dry months, the area's name (which means the 'Four Thousand Islands') isn't that much of an exaggeration. Grab a kayak, spot rare Irrawaddy dolphins, and round off with a sunset boat trip.

Vientiane
This former French trading post beguiles with glittering temples, elegant boulevards, street-food stalls and gastronomic eateries. Cheap food on the hop can be grabbed from vendors around the old quarter, and braziers that fire up grilled chicken and Mekong fish on skewers. Noodles of all kinds are popular in Laos, and Vientiane has the greatest variety.

Luang Namtha
Trekking around Phongsali is considered some of the most authentic in Laos and involves the chance to stay with the colouful Akha people. Luang Namtha is the most accessible base for ecotreks in the Nam Ha National Protected Area (NPA), one of the best trekking spots in the Mekong region. Phongsali shelters below the peak of Phu Fa ('Sky Mountain'; 1625m) rising majestically in the background.

SIGHTS & ACTIVITIES

⊙ SEE
◉ DO

ITINERARY

▼ 1
▽ 2

14-day itinerary
Along the Mekong

This classic southern route takes you through the heartland of lowland Lao culture. Start in **Vientiane**, the country's capital, and soak up the sights, shopping, cuisine and nightlife. Make a side trip to the backpacker mecca of **Vang Vieng**, surrounded by craggy, cave-studded limestone peaks. Head south to **Tha Khaek**, the archetypal sleepy town on the Mekong,

and **Savannakhet** for its old French architecture and street stalls. Roll on southward to **Champasak Town**, gateway to the area's most important archaeological site, **Wat Phu**, an Angkor-style temple ruin. Pass through the coffee capital of **Paksong**, and consider stopping at the village of **Kiet Ngong** to visit the elevated archaeological site of Phu Asa. Head on to **Si Phan Don**, an archipelago of idyllic river islands where the farming and fishing life have changed little in centuries.

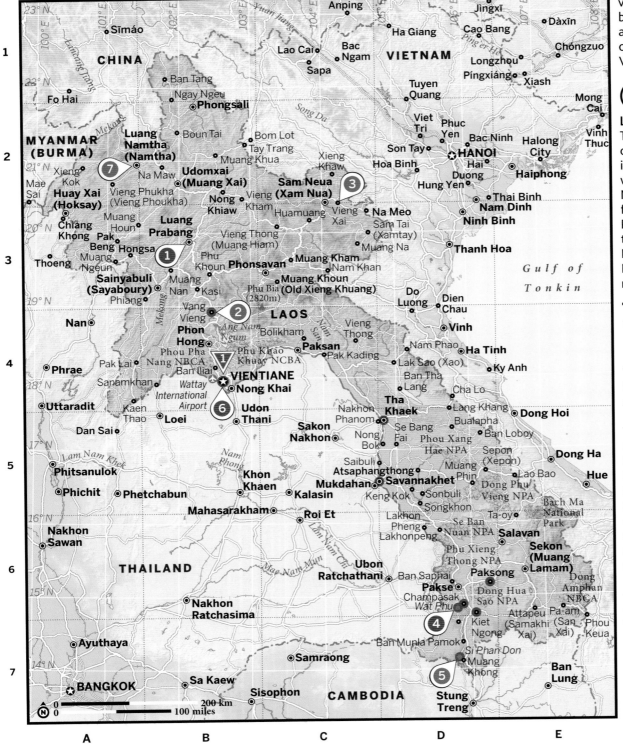

Shwedagon Pagoda, Yangon
One of Buddhism's most sacred sites, the 325ft *zedi* (stupa) here is adorned with 27 metric tons of gold leaf, along with thousands of diamonds and other gems, and is believed to enshrine eight hairs of the Gautama Buddha as well as relics of three former buddhas.

Inle Lake
This vast, serene lake – 22km long and 11km wide – is fringed by marshes and floating gardens, where stilt-house villages and Buddhist temples rise above the water. Intha fisherfolk propel their boats along via their unique technique of leg-rowing.

Bagan
In a 230-year building frenzy until 1287 and the Mongol invasions, Bagan's kings commissioned more than 4000 Buddhist temples. Despite numerous earthquakes, many are still standing. Bikes are ideal for exploring, but the best way to appreciate Bagan's size is from a hot-air balloon.

Myeik Archipelago
This chain of 800 barely populated islands with white-sand beaches set in a turquoise sea offers Myanmar's best diving and island-hopping.

Sagaing
A former royal capital, Sagaing is dominated by low hills covered by numerous white and gold stupas. The cave monastery of Tilawkaguru has impressive preserved cave paintings.

Mrauk U
Mrauk U (pronounced 'mrau-oo') is Myanmar's second-most-famous archaeological site. The area's temples are dispersed throughout a landscape of small villages, rice paddies, hillocks and grazing cows. In the 16th century, wide-eyed Western visitors compared the city to London or Venice.

Mawlamyine
A time capsule of the Raj, Mawlamyine has changed little since the colonial era. The former capital of British Burma, Mawlamyine mixes historic architecture, imposing churches, hilltop temples and a busy harbour.

Kalaw
With an almost Himalayan atmosphere, Kalaw is one of the best places in Myanmar for upcountry treks. Hiking through the Danu, Pa-O and Taung Yo villages which link Kalaw with Inle Lake gives a real insight into the lives of the local hill peoples.

14-day itinerary
Burma Days

Myanmar's top locations form the bedrock of this plan, which includes a train and boat ride. Fly into **Yangon** and start with a walking tour around the historic downtown, chill out beside Kandawgyi Lake and visit Shwedagon Paya at sunset. Board the overnight sleeper train to **Mandalay**. In three or four days you can see the old capital's sights as well as make day trips to places such as **Mingun**, home to a giant earthquake-cracked stupa; **U Bein Bridge** at Amarapura; and **Monywa**, where you can climb inside the world's tallest standing buddha. Catch the fast boat from Mandalay to **Bagan**; set aside three days to explore the thousands of ancient temples here. Fly to beautiful **Inle Lake**, where motor-powered dugout canoes take you to floating markets. Day-trip to the **Shwe Oo Min cave** near Pindaya to see 8000 buddha images or arrange some light trekking.

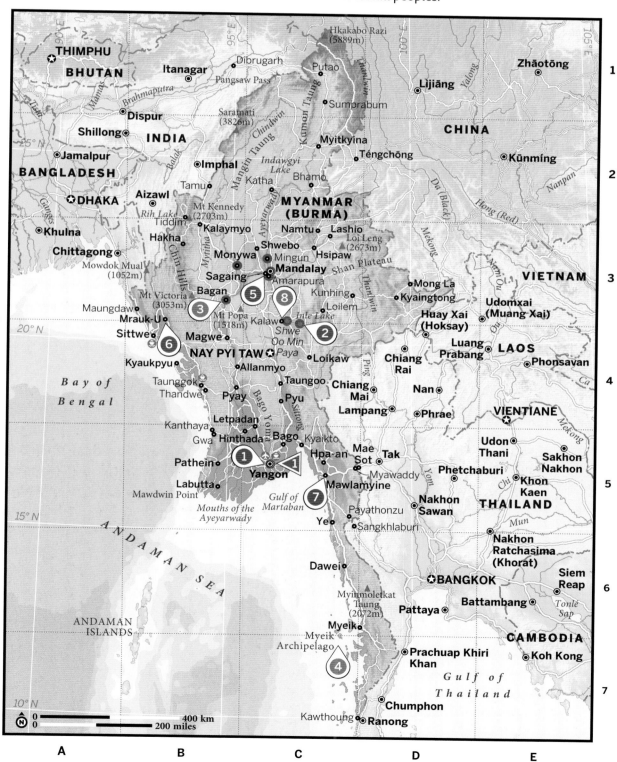

SIGHTS &
ACTIVITIES

 SEE

 DO

ITINERARY

 1

2

Angkor Wat

Angkor is home to the most spectacular collection of temples on earth, including the world's largest religious building, Angkor Wat. The Khmers packed the equivalent of all Europe's cathedrals into an area the size of Los Angeles: don't miss overgrown Ta Prohm, the jungle ruin of Beng Mealea and the Mayan-style pyramid temple of Koh Ker.

Siem Reap

Siem Reap has reinvented itself as the epicentre of chic Cambodia, with everything from backpacker party pads to hip hotels. Food tours provide an insider's view of Siem Reap cuisine, and the city's nightlife is legendary, centring around heaving 'Pub St'.

③ National Museum, Phnom Penh

Located just north of the Royal Palace, the National Museum is housed in a graceful terracotta structure of traditional design (built from 1917 to 1920), with an inviting courtyard garden. The museum is home to the world's finest collection of Khmer sculpture: a millennium and more's worth of masterful Khmer design.

④ Southern Islands

Paradise fantasies await. Off the coast of Sihanoukville, Koh Rong and hippyish Koh Tuch village are party central; the rest of the island is fringed by sand and clad in jungle. Just south is Koh Rong Sanloem, with tropical resorts and bays. Along the coast lies the Koh Sdach archipelago and undeveloped Koh Kong.

⑤ Mondulkiri Province

Upland Mondulkiri is home to the hardy Bunong people. Wildlife is a big draw here with the chance to 'walk with the herd' at Elephant Valley Project or spot douc monkeys or gibbons in the Seima Protected Forest.

Battambang

Battambang is one of the country's best-preserved colonial-era towns. Streets of French shophouses host everything from fair-trade cafes to art galleries. Beyond the town are temples which lack the crowds of Angkor Wat.

Prasat Preah Vihear

The mother of all mountain temples, Prasat Preah Vihear stands atop the Dangkrek Mountains between Cambodia and Thailand. The foundation stones stretch to the edge of the cliff, and the views across northern Cambodia are incredible.

Sambor Prei Kuk

Cambodia's most impressive group of pre-Angkorian monuments, Sambor Prei Kuk encompasses more than 100 mainly brick temples scattered through the forest. It is Cambodia's third Unesco World Heritage Site.

Kratie

Riverside Kratie (pronounced 'kra-cheh') is the most popular place in Cambodia to see endangered Irrawaddy dolphins, which live in the Mekong in ever-diminishing numbers. The town also has a vast riverfront and a legacy of French-era architecture.

Osoam

In isolated Osoam, the community centre organises hiking, dirt-bike and boat trips in the surrounding countryside, as well as day trips to Phnom Samkos, where elephants can be spotted. Homestays are available.

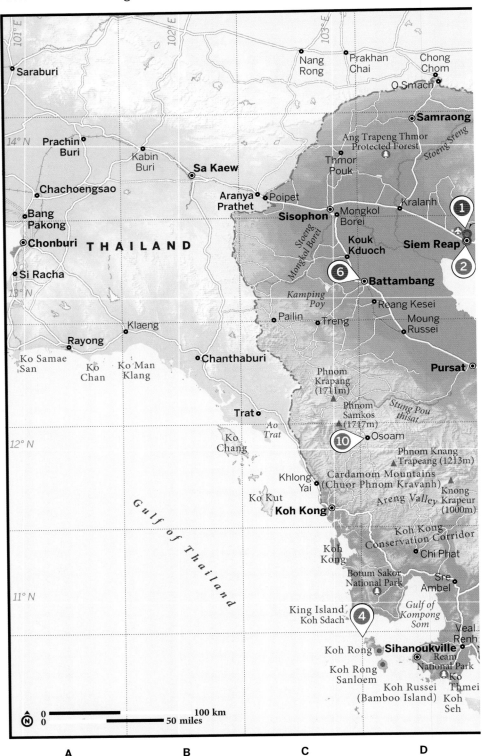

7-day itinerary
A Tale of Two Cambodian Cities

If time is tight, focus on the big hitters of Phnom Penh and Siem Reap. Start out in **Phnom Penh** to relive the glories of the past at the National Museum and the Royal Palace, then discover a darker past with a visit to the Tuol Sleng Genocide Museum and the Killing Fields of Choeung Ek. From the capital, hop the short flight to **Siem Reap**, or opt for the improved overland route to see more of the Cambodian countryside. Spend a couple of days touring the nearby temples of **Angkor**, including headline names such as Angkor Wat, Bayon and Ta Prohm. Allow some time to catch the support acts, like beautiful **Banteay Srei** and immense **Preah Khan**.

14-day itinerary
Best of Cambodia

This is the ultimate journey, via temples, beaches and the capital. Public transport serves most of this route, although some side trips will require chartered transport or a motorbike trip. Hit **Phnom Penh** for starters, delving into the city's eclectic cuisine from fine-dining Khmer restaurants to street food. Take a fast boat to the hilltop temple of **Phnom Da**, and then continue south to the colonial-era town of **Kampot**, which makes a good base for this area. From here, visit the seaside town of **Kep** (and Rabbit Island, just off the coast) and nearby cave pagodas. Go west to the bling beach town of **Sihanoukville**, the jumping-off point to explore Cambodia's idyllic islands, **Koh Rong** and **Koh Rong Sanloem**. Then backtrack via Phnom Penh to **Kompong Thom** and visit the pre-Angkorian brick temples of **Sambor Prei Kuk**. Finish the trip at Siem Reap: if you've already seen Angkor Wat, then consider venturing further afield to **Kbal Spean**, jungle-clad Beng Mealea or even **Prasat Preah Vihear**, a mountain temple perched on the Thai border.

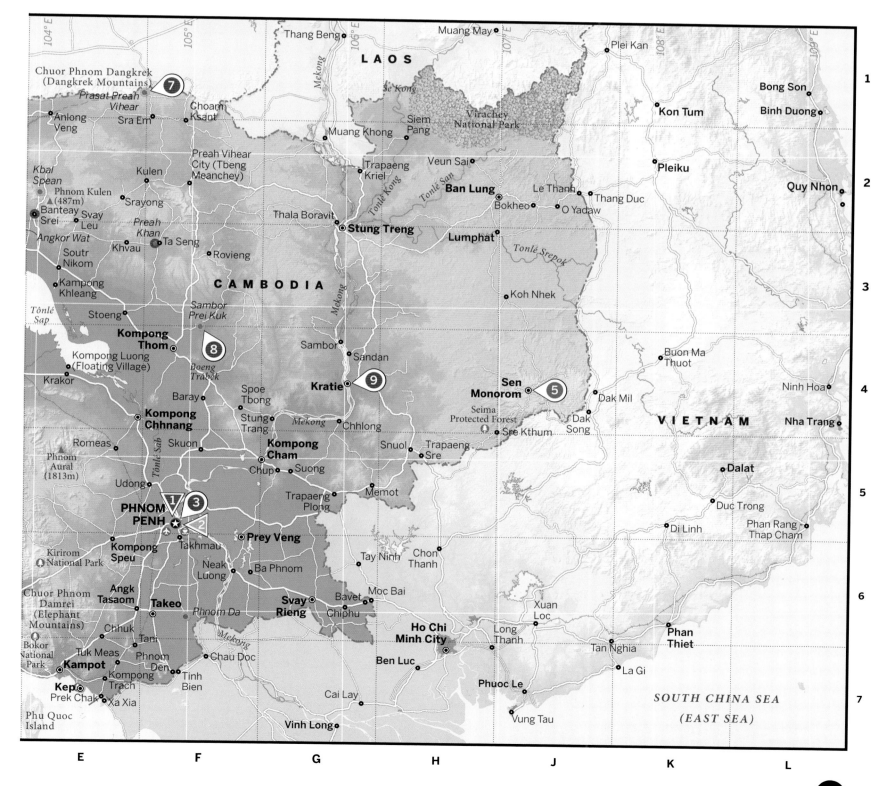

SIGHTS &
ACTIVITIES

 SEE

DO

ITINERARY

 1

2

 10-day itinerary
Into Isan

Thailand's rural northeast (known as Isan) tracks the Mekong River, which divides Thailand and Laos. Start in the charming town of **Nong Khai**, an easy border-crossing point. If the pace here is too fast, follow the river road east to **Bueng Kan**, a dusty speck of a town with a temple built on a rocky outcrop, several homestays and forays into wild-elephant territory. Pass through **Nakhon Phanom** for its river promenade and tiny **That Phanom**, with its famous Lao-style temple. For a little urban Isan, check out **Ubon Ratchathani**, surrounded by the **Pha Taem National Park**.

 21-day itinerary
Thailand's North

Temple-heavy **Chiang Mai** is an ideal beginning, and base, for northern culture and exploration. Next is **Soppong**, a mecca for caving. Continue to **Mae Hong Son** to immerse yourself in a remote region that is more akin to Myanmar than Bangkok. The last stop along this route is **Mae Sariang**, a small riverside town with a good reputation for sustainable trekking. Return to civilisation in Chiang Mai and plot your next campaign towards **Chiang Rai**. More mountains await northwards in **Chiang Dao**, a more sober alternative to backpackery **Pai**. Next, take the back door to Chiang Rai through the riverside village of **Tha Ton** before zigzagging up the mountain ridge to **Doi Mae Salong**, a Yunnanese tea settlement. Slide into **Chiang Rai** for a hill-tribe homestay and culturally sensitive treks and continue on to the towns of **Chiang Saen** and **Sop Ruak**, formerly Ground Zero of the infamous Golden Triangle. Bypass the crowds with a stop in **Phayao**, a pleasant northern town for temple-spotting, before returning to where you started in Chiang Mai.

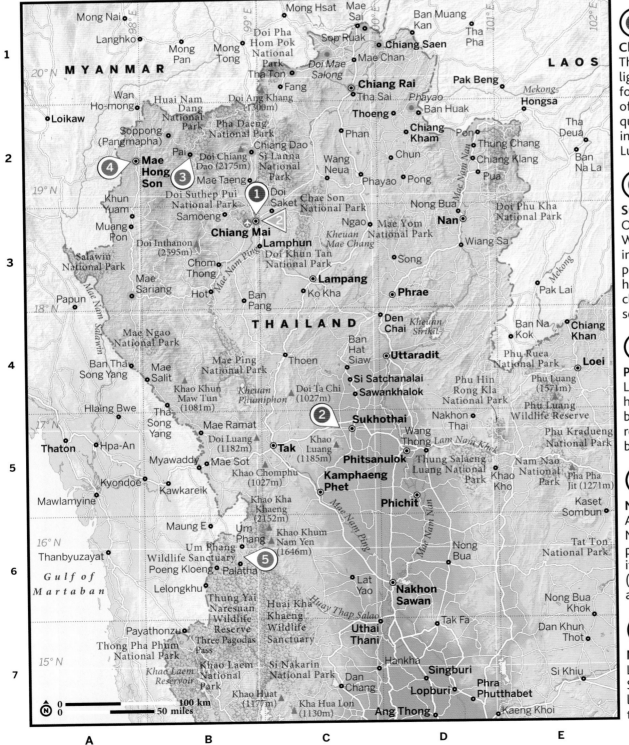

 Chiang Mai
Thailand's northern capital feels light years away from Bangkok. The former capital of the Lanna people offers monasteries, manic markets, quiet streets and numerous temples, including Wat Phra Singh, Wat Chedi Luang and Wat Phra That Doi Suthep.

 Sukhothai Historical Park
One of Thailand's most impressive World Heritage Sites, this temple park includes 21 historical sites and four ponds within its walls. The temples here are typified by the lotus-bud chedi, featuring a conical spire on a square structure and three-tiered base.

 Pai
Live music, bars and fresh-air activities have made this tiny town a serious backpacker destination, but its Shan roots can still be seen in its temples, backstreets and afternoon market.

 Mae Hong Son
Accessible by winding mountain roads, Mae Hong Son is Thailand's remotest province. Forested and mountainous, it is a crossroads for ethnic hill tribes (mostly Karen, Hmong, Lisu and Lahu), and a popular base for hill trekking.

 Nam Tok Thilawsu
Located in the Um Phang Wildlife Sanctuary, this waterfall is Thailand's largest, measuring 200m high and up to 400m wide during the rainy season.

Khao Yai National Park

This park is home to elephants, monkeys, gibbons, hornbills, pythons, bears, a million bats and even a few wily tigers. Wildlife sightings are at the mercy of chance, but hiking in the jungle guarantees a good day out.

Wat Phu Thok

A network of rickety staircases and walkways built in, on and around a giant sandstone outcrop, Wat Phu Thok is one of the region's wonders. Precarious paths lead past shrines and *gù·đì* (monk's huts) scattered around the mountain.

Prasat Phanom Rung

Crowning the summit of a spent volcano, this sanctuary sits 200m above the paddy fields below. The temple was erected as a Hindu monument to Shiva between the 10th and 13th centuries.

Red Lotus Sea

This pink water lily lake is now one of Isan's top attractions, but few Westerners make it there. Boats can be hired to go out into the middle of the lake to see the bloom, and the earlier the better as the flowers are completely shut by noon.

Pha Taem National Park

Pha Taem is named after and centred on a large cliff above the Mekong River. The cliff's ancient rock paintings have become Ubon icons. The rocky scenery elsewhere in the park is also wonderful, particularly Nam Tok Saeng Chan, a rainy-season waterfall flowing through a natural rock hole.

Nam Nao National Park

Nam Nao is one of Thailand's most wildlife-rich parks, although its remote location means it never gets busy. With a little luck you might see elephants, gaur, Asian jackals, porcupines and barking deer.

Phimai Historical Park

Prasat Phimai is among the most impressive Khmer ruins in Thailand, both in its grand scale and its intricate

details. Though built as a Mahayana Buddhist temple, the carvings feature Hindu deities, and elements later used at Angkor Wat.

Chiang Mai: Wat Phra That Doi Suthep, one of northern Thailand's most sacred temples.

Ban Ta Klang

Long known for its dubious elephant shows, this little Suai village is now home to modern ethical elephant encounter programmes, where the elephants are well cared for and there is no riding or tricks.

Suan Hin Pha Ngam

The 'Beautiful Rock Garden' is a strange patch of eroded rocks known as 'Thailand's Kunming', due to a slight resemblance with the Stone Forest in Kunming, China. The highlight is a guided walk through the labyrinthine paths in the heart of the forest.

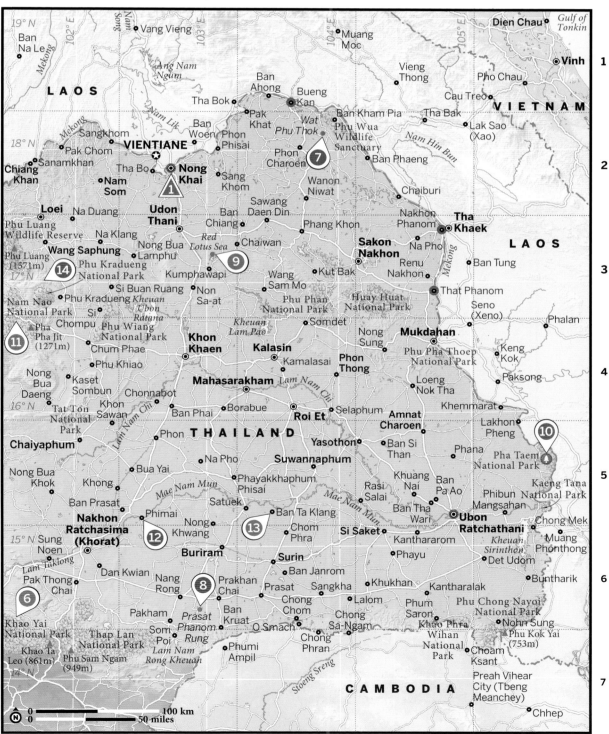

© structuresxx / Shutterstock

Ayuthaya

Enigmatic temple ruins are strewn across Ayuthaya, whispering of its days as a royal capital. The city was the capital of Siam from 1350 until 1767, when it was brutally sacked by the Burmese. Now, crumbling temples and stupas evoke visions of lost grandeur.

Kanchanaburi

Kanchanaburi has a dark history: during WWII, Japanese forces used Allied prisoners of war to build a rail route between Thailand and Myanmar. The 300m-long Death Railway Bridge cost thousands of imprisoned labourers their lives. Its centre was destroyed by Allied bombs in 1945; only the outer curved spans are original.

Tham Phraya Nakhon

The most-visited attraction in Khao Sam Roi Yot National Park is this revered cave, sheltering a royal *săh·lah* (pavilion) built for Rama V in 1890 – prettily bathed in morning light by about 10.30am. The trail to the cave is a 430m long, steep and rocky stairway. You'll almost certainly meet macaques and dusky langur on the way up.

Erawan National Park

Splashing in cerulean pools under Erawan Falls is the highlight of this 550 sq km park. Seven tiers of waterfall tumble through the forest – bathing beneath these crystalline cascades is popular with locals and visitors.

Thong Pha Phum National Park

Crossing a serrated mountain range along the Myanmar border, this national park is one of the most beautiful but least-known places in Thailand. Marbled cats, palm civets, serow (Asian mountain goats) and Fea's muntjac often wander through visitor areas.

Tha Kha Floating Market

This authentic floating market near Amphawa sees a handful of vendors coalesce along an open rural *klorng* (canal, also spelt *khlong*) lined with coconut palms and old wooden houses. Boat rides can be arranged along the canal, and there are lots of tasty snacks and fruits for sale.

Nam Tok

Central Thailand has countless raft resorts and waterside hotels, but Nam Tok corners riverbank chic. Guests glide on a longboat to reach thatched-roof chalets set amid lush gardens.

Hua Hin

Thailand's original beach resort is a delightful mix of city and sea with a cosmopolitan ambience, tasty street eats and a long blond beach. Its night market in particular is an attraction in itself, drawing visitors and locals to eat and shop at its lively stalls.

Phetchaburi

This provincial capital is often called a living Ayuthaya. It has an antique hilltop palace, sacred cave shrines and bustling temples, and the old shophouse neighbourhood is filled with DIY businesses run by Thai aunties and grannies.

Kaeng Krachan National Park

Thailand's largest (2915 sq km) national park shelters animal life including wild elephants, tigers, leopards, tapir, gaur (wild cattle), white-handed gibbons, dusky langurs and black giant squirrels.

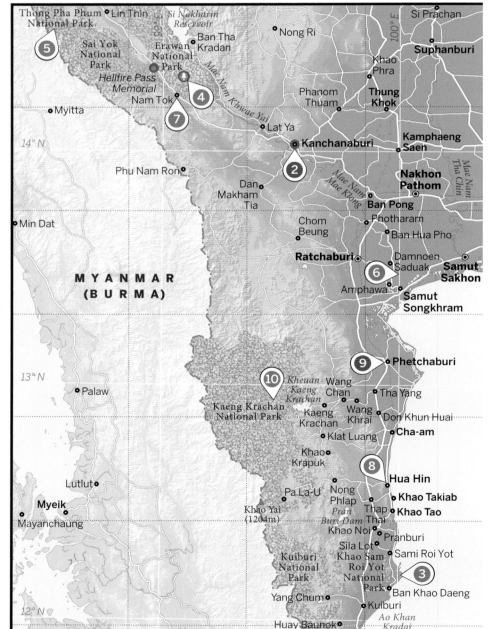

7-day itinerary
Two Capitals

If time is not on your side, you can still manage to explore jungles, temples and Thai culture – all within easy reach of **Bangkok**. After spending a couple of days delving into the temples and hectic markets in the capital, embark on the scenic train ride to **Kanchanaburi.** Here, enjoy a quick dip in the seven-tiered waterfalls of **Erawan National Park** before visiting

the **Hellfire Pass Memorial**, a poignant tribute to the many thousands of prisoners of war (and indentured labourers) who died during the construction of the infamous Death Railway to Myanmar during WWII. Next, jump in a minivan bound for **Ayuthaya** and cycle around the ruins of this erstwhile capital, before circling back to Bangkok.

10-day itinerary
Eastern Seaboard

This trip explores the eastern seaboard and islands southeast of **Bangkok**. From the capital, take a bus south to the lively coastal town of **Si Racha**. Explore the picturesque waterfront, then delve into the town's sushi restaurants and karaoke bars. Hop over for a day on the island of **Ko Si Chang** for a chilled out fishing-village atmosphere

then travel south to experience the full-on resort vibe of **Pattaya**. Pass through Rayong en route to the island of **Ko Samet**, once the doyen of backpacker destinations, now a flashpacker hangout par excellence. The north coast beaches have been developed, but the southern side and jungled interior remain surprisingly quiet. Back on the mainland,

continue west to **Chanthaburi**, where wonderfully restored waterfront buildings show how Chinese, French and Vietnamese have influenced local life – and architecture. Finish the tour on **Ko Kut**, often feted as the perfect Thai island. The supersoft sands are like talcum powder, the water lapping the bays is clear and there are more coconut palms than buildings.

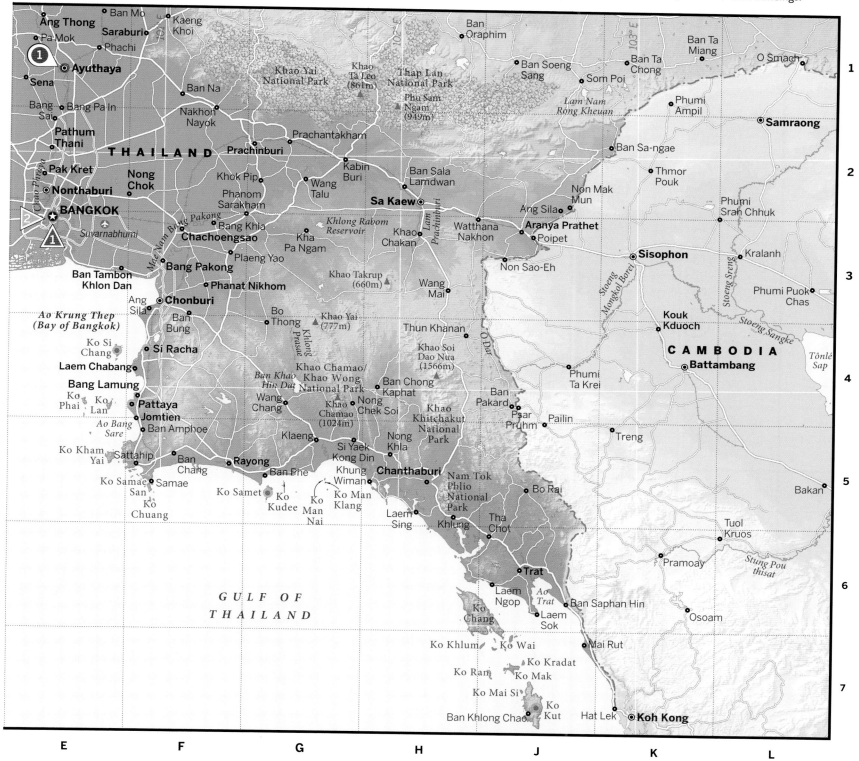

SIGHTS & ACTIVITIES

◉ SEE

◉ DO

ITINERARY

▽ 1

▽ 2

 Phuket
Loved for its luxury resorts, plush beach clubs, island-chic boutiques and Patong's after-hours nightlife, Phuket is Thailand's largest and most developed island.

 Khao Sok National Park
This deep, dark jungle hugs the midsection of southern Thailand. The ancient rainforest is filled with long, sweaty hiking routes and plentiful wildlife, and after trying out tubing, kayaking and rafting, you can sleep on floating lake-top huts at Chiaw Lan.

 Ko Phi-Phi
With their bleached beaches and jungle interiors, Phi-Phi Don and Phi-Phi Leh are the darlings of the Andaman Coast. Phi-Phi Don is a hedonistic party paradise, while smaller Ko Phi-Phi Leh is undeveloped and hotel-free.

 Ko Pha-Ngan
World-famous for its debauched Full Moon Parties and all-night electronic madness, Ko Pha-Ngan is Thailand's premier party island. Just offshore is Sail Rock, one of the gulf's best dive sites, visited by elusive whale sharks.

 Trang Islands
Covered in verdant jungle and lined with pure white sand beaches, the Trang Islands are less developed than the other Andaman islands and have far smaller populations. This is real honeymooners' territory.

Similan and Surin Islands: An idyllic beach spot on the Surin Islands.

 Ao Phang-Nga
The limestone-tower-studded bay of Ao Phang-Nga Marine National Park is best explored by sea kayak. Many sea caves here are inscribed with prehistoric rock art, and the secluded beaches are perfect for picnics.

 Similan and Surin Islands
Largely untouched by development, the marine national parks of the Similan and Surin Islands are two of Thailand's real treasures. Superbly clear water make the islands two of the very best places in the country to don a scuba mask and delve into the underwater world.

 Railay
Over 1000 rock-climbing routes cover Railay's sheer limestone walls, delivering unbeatable vistas across some of Thailand's best beach scenery. Seasoned climbers stay for months.

 Ko Samui
Whether you're sun-seeking, hammock dozing, feasting, beach partying or relaxing in a spa, Ko Samui has it covered. With an area of just under 230 sq km, Thailand's third largest island is a luxurious retreat.

 Ang Thong Marine National Park
These 40-something dream-inducing islets inspired Alex Garland's cult novel *The Beach*. They are characterised by sheer limestone cliffs, hidden lagoons and perfect peach-coloured sands.

 Ko Tarutao Marine National Park
Ko Tarutao Marine National Park encompasses 51 islands blanketed by well-preserved rainforest teeming with fauna, surrounded by healthy coral reefs and radiant white beaches. Ko Lipe is the main tourist base.

 Ko Phayam
Part of Laem Son National Park, Ko Phayam is fringed with beaches and is becoming increasingly popular as a family destination. The island's coasts are dotted with rustic bungalows, small-scale resorts, sand-side restaurants and barefoot beach bars.

 Ko Lanta
Once the domain of sea gypsies, Lanta has morphed from a luscious Thai backwater into a getaway for visitors who come for the divine long beaches and nearby dive spots of Hin Daeng, Hin Muang and Ko Haa.

 Ko Yao Yai and Ko Yao Noi
These neighbouring islands ('Big' and 'Little') are surrounded by Ao Phang-Nga's beautiful karst scenery. A boat ride from Phuket, they're surprisingly undeveloped, with unspoilt shorelines, friendly Muslim fishing villages and varied birdlife.

14-day itinerary
Easy Island-Hopping

For a quick island hit from **Phuket**, jump on a boat bound for **Ko Phi-Phi**, a party island that stays up all night and still looks fantastic in the morning. From here you can head back to the mainland and explore the gorgeous coastline of **Krabi** (be sure to take a longboat to Railay beach, regarded as one of the finest in Thailand) or ferry straight to laid-back **Ko Lanta** to collapse in a hammock and drink in the bucolic island life. Continue south by ferry past the beautiful **Trang Islands**, where you could spend weeks island-hopping and beach-lounging at increasingly popular but still relatively undeveloped **Ko Lipe**. Catch a speedboat back to the mainland when you're ready to begin your journey home.

21-day itinerary
Island Classics

The journey through Thailand's Upper Gulf is pockmarked with long, sandy stretches of coastline; start your itinerary at **Ban Krut** to find a secluded strip of sand and a laidback beach scene. Now for some island time: first stop **Ko Tao** (via Chumphon). Sign up for a dive course or enjoy a few days of snorkelling before island-hopping to **Ko Pha-Ngan** for Full Moon Party fun. Retire to the resort island of **Ko Samui** for some pampering and more partying, from where it's a short ferry ride to transport hub Surat Thani. Buses leave hourly for **Khao Sok National Park**, where you can enjoy some jungle time in one of the world's oldest rainforests before making the short transfer to **Khao Lak**, a sleepy beach resort that serves as the perfect base for dive trips to the **Similan and Surin Islands**. Once you surface, finish on the lively island of **Phuket** – Thailand's largest – and don't miss a day trip out to explore the idyllic *hongs* (islets) dotted around the bay of **Ao Phang-Nga**.

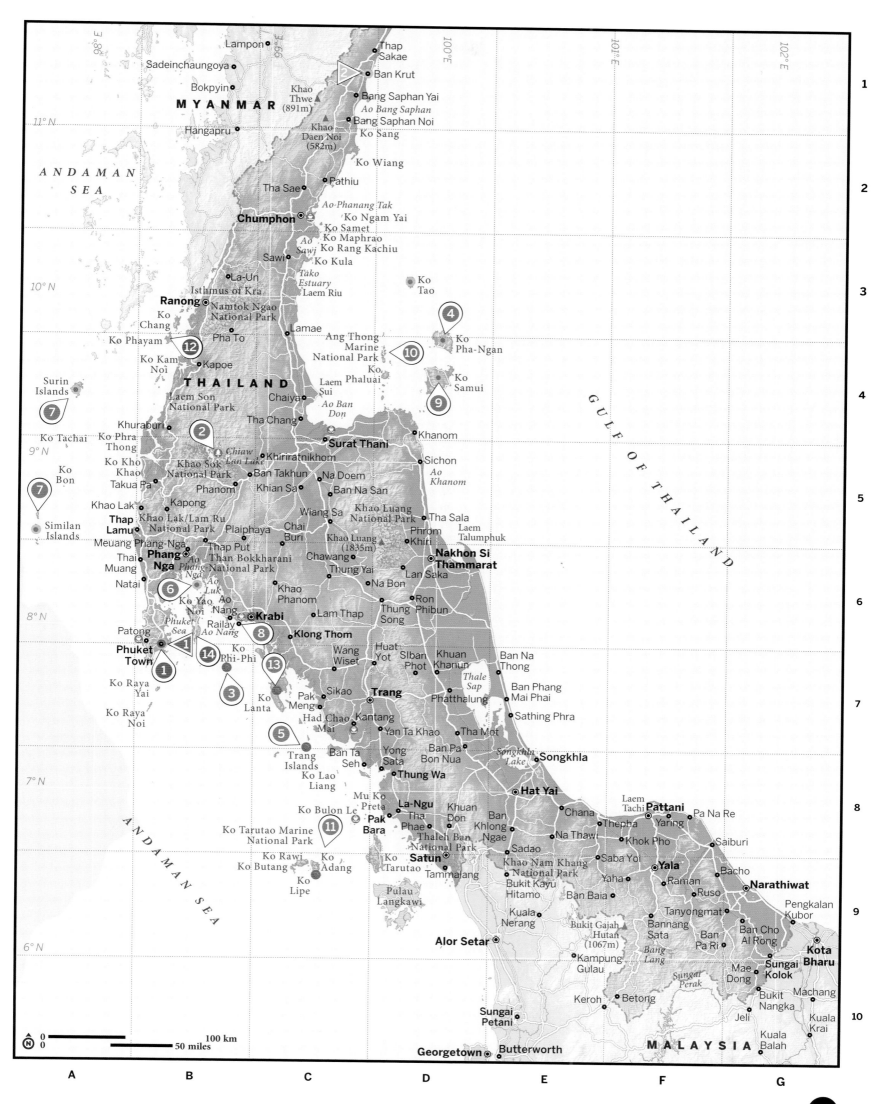

Lampon

Sadeinchaungoya

Bokpyin

MYANMAR

Hangapru

Thap
Sakae

Ban Krut

Bang Saphan Yai

Ao Bang Saphan

Khao
Thwe
(891m)

Bang Saphan Noi

Khao
Daen Noi
(582m)

Ko Sang

*ANDAMAN
SEA*

Ko Wiang

Tha Sae

Pathiu

Ao Phanang Tak

Chumphon

Ko Ngam Yai

*Ao
Sawi*

Ko Samet
Ko Maphrao
Ko Rang Kachiu

Sawi

Ko Kula

Ko
Tao

La-Un

Isthmus of Kra

*Tako
Estuary*

Laem Riu

Ang Thong
Marine
National Park

Ranong

Namtok Ngao
National Park

Lamae

⑩

④

Ko
Pha-Ngan

Ko
Chang

⑫

Pha To

Ko Phayam

Kapoe

THAILAND

Ko Kam
Noi

Ko
Phaluai

⑨

Ko
Samui

*Surin
Islands*

⑦

Laem Son
National Park

Chaiya

Laem
Sui

*Ao Ban
Don*

Ko Tachai

Khuraburi

②

*Chiaw
Lan Lake*

Tha Chang

Khanom

Ko Phra
Thong

Khiriratnikhom

Surat Thani

Ko Bon

Ko Kho
Khao

Khao Sok
National Park

Ban Takhun

Na Doem

*Ao
Khanom*

Sichon

⑦

Takua Pa

Phanom

Khian Sa

Ban Na San

Khao Lak

Kapong

Wiang Sa

Khao Luang
National Park

Tha Sala

*Similan
Islands*

**Thap
Lamu**

Khao Lak/Lam Ru
National Park

Plaiphaya

Chai
Buri

Khao Luang
(1835m)

Phrom
Khiri

Laem
Talumphuk

Meuang Phang-Nga

Thap Put

Chawang

**Nakhon Si
Thammarat**

Thai
Muang

**Phang
Nga**

*Ao
Than Bokkharani
Phang-National Park
Nga*

Thung Yai

Lan Saka

Natai

*Ao
Luk*

⑥

Ko Yao
Noi

Ao
Nang

Khao
Phanom

Na Bon

Ron
Phibun

Patong

*Phuket
Sea*

Railay

Ao Nang

Krabi

Lam Thap

Thung
Song

**Phuket
Town**

①

⑧

Ko
Phi-Phi

⑭

Klong Thom

Wang
Yot

Huat
Wiset

Slban
Phot

Khuan
Khanun

Ban Na
Thong

Ko Raya
Yai

③

⑬

Sikao

Trang

Phatthalung

*Thale
Sap*

Ban Phang
Mai Phai

Ko Raya
Noi

Ko
Lanta

Pak
Meng

Kantang

Yan Ta Khao

Tha Mot

Sathing Phra

⑤

Had Chao
Mai

*Songkhla
Lake*

*Trang
Islands*

Ban Ta
Seh

Yong
Sata

Ban Pa
Bon Nua

Songkhla

Ko Lao
Liang

Thung Wa

Ko Bulon Le

Mu Ko
Preta

La-Ngu

Khuan
Don

Ban
Khlong
Ngae

Hat Yai

Chana

*Laem
Tachi*

Pattani

Pa Na Re

Ko Tarutao Marine
National Park

⑪

**Pak
Bara**

Tha
Phae

Thaleh Ban
National Park

Thepha

Yaring

Saibur

Ko Rawi

Ko
Adang

Satun

Ko
Tarutao

Tammalang

Sadao

Khao Nam Khang
National Park

Bukit Kayu
Hitamo

Saba Yoi

Khok Pho

Saiburi

Yala

Bacho

Ko Butang

Ko
Lipe

*Pulau
Langkawi*

Ban Baia

Yaha

Raman

Narathiwat

Kuala
Nerang

Bannang
Sata

Ban
Pa Ri

Ban Cho
Al Rong

Pengkalan
Kubor

Alor Setar

Bukit Gajah
Hutan
(1067m)

*Bang
Lang*

Tanyongmat

**Kota
Bharu**

Kampung
Gulau

Mae
Dong

**Sungai
Kolok**

*Sungai
Perak*

Keroh

Betong

Bukit
Nangka

Machang

*ANDAMAN
SEA*

**Sungai
Petani**

Georgetown

Butterworth

MALAYSIA

Jeli

Kuala
Balah

Kuala
Krai

0   100 km
0   50 miles

GULF OF THAILAND

1
2
3
4
5
6
7
8
9
10

A   B   C   D   E   F   G

11° N
10° N
9° N
8° N
7° N
6° N

98° E
100° E
101° E
102° E

Maritime Southeast Asia

Entwined by centuries of shared history, culture and language, Southeast Asia's maritime nations offer steamy jungles packed with wildlife, beautiful beaches, culinary sensations and multi-ethnic culture. If you're an island-hopper, this is surely paradise: Indonesia alone has more than 17,000 islands to explore, with thousands more in the Philippines and Malaysia. But there's one island that tops them all in terms of natural diversity: Borneo, home to some of the world's oldest forests and most precious (and endangered) wildlife. Don't overlook the lesser-visited places either: the pocket-sized sultanate of Brunei, for example, or the remote island nations of Nusa Tenggara and Timor-Leste.

CLIMATE CHART

JAKARTA

RAINFALL
INCH/MM
24/600
16/400
8/200
0

J F M A M J J A S O N D

TEMP
°C/°F
40/104
30/86
20/68
10/50
0/32

MANILA

RAINFALL
INCH/MM
20/500
16/400
12/300
8/200
4/100
0

J F M A M J J A S O N D

TEMP
°C/°F
40/104
30/86
20/68
10/50
0/32

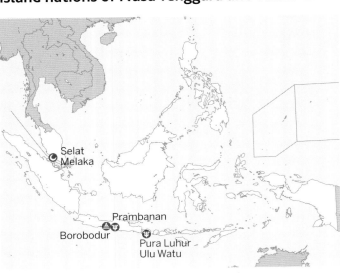

HOLY PLACES
Three of the world's great religions – Buddhism, Islam and Hinduism – co-exist here, often sharing or reappropriating the same sacred spaces. These range in scale, from huge, sprawling monuments such as Borobudur and Prambanan to smaller-scale sites like Pura Luhur Ulu Watu and Selat Melaka, but every village has its own shrines and temples.

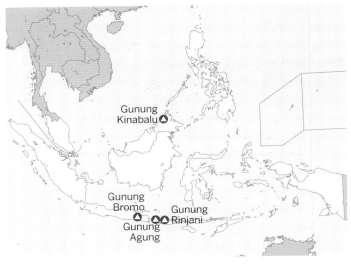

VOLCANOES
This region sits on the Pacific 'Ring of Fire', a crack in the Earth's crust caused by friction between tectonic plates. It's home to countless volcanoes, including the sacred mountains of Rinjani, Bromo, Agung and Kinabalu, plus scores of unnamed others. Some lie dormant, while others are extremely – and often dangerously – active.

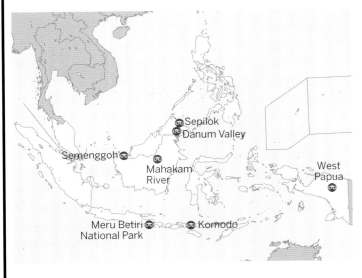

WILDLIFE
Thanks to its magnificent rainforests, maritime Southeast Asia boasts astonishing natural diversity. It's the only place in the world to see wild orangutans, which can be easily spotted in reserves such as Semenggoh, Sepilok and the Danum Valley in Malaysia. But that's just the start. There are proboscis monkeys along the Mahakam River, giant lizards on Komodo, the world's longest snake in Java's Meru Betiri National Park and birds of paradise in West Papua.

ISLANDS
There are said to be so many islands in the seas around Southeast Asia that they're impossible to count. Hundreds of different archipelagos are waiting to be explored by speedboat, longtail or kayak: from well-established island getaways like the Tunku Abdul Rahman Marine Park, Langkawi and the Gili Islands, to little-visited chains such as the Alor Archipelago, the Raja Ampat Islands and the Karimunjawa Islands.

Clockwise from top left: Stupas at Borobudur, Java; orangutans at Semenggoh Wildlife Centre; a traditional Malay wedding ceremony; beach at Gili Air Island.

Transport hubs

Several major air hubs (including Kuala Lumpur, Singapore and Manila) mean that flying to this side of Southeast Asia is both easy and affordable. Travelling around the widely scattered islands of Malaysia and Indonesia can generally be achieved by a combination of flights, ferries and passenger boats. To reach Borneo and Brunei, flights from Singapore, KL or Jakarta are the usual route, but ferry crossings are possible, too.

Singapore (see pp432-3 for city map)
Singapore is one of Asia's major air hubs, serviced by both full-service and budget airlines. Changi Airport, 20km northeast of the city centre, is an international gateway, with frequent flights to all corners of the planet. You can also catch trains and buses to Malaysia and Thailand, and ferries to several Malaysian and Indonesian islands.

Kuala Lumpur (KL) (see pp412-13 for city map)
Kuala Lumpur International Airport has flights to pretty much everywhere on the globe. The city has rail connections to Singapore in the south and Thailand in the north, with stops at Butterworth (for Penang) and Alor Setar (for Langkawi). Long-distance buses connect KL with cities all over Malaysia and beyond; most of these now leave from the Terminal Bersepadu Selatan.

Kota Kinabalu (KK)
Sabah's main city is well served by flights to Asian cities including Brunei, Shenzhen, Jakarta, Manila, Singapore and Taipei. Passenger boats connect KK to Pulau Labuan with onward service to Brunei. There is also a cross-border bus to Brunei. The 19th-century North Borneo Railway has recently been restored; now a heritage line mainly used by tourists, it chugs once a day from KK to Papar.

Kuching
Sarawak's main gateway has air links with Singapore, Kuala Lumpur, Penang, Kota Kinabalu, and Bandar Seri Begawan (BSB). Flights also go to the West Kalimantan city of Pontianak, which can also be reached overland by a very long bus ride, passing through the Tebedu-Entikong crossing, 80km south of Kuching.

Jakarta
Jakarta is the main international gateway to Indonesia. It's a hub for domestic and international flights as well as train services from across Java. Trains are convenient and cheap; buses travel to more out-of-the way areas. Jakarta's notorious traffic means there are no great options for getting around that avoid long delays. The Jakarta MRT, a new subway system currently under construction, is sorely needed to ease the congestion.

Denpasar
Denpasar is a hub of public transport in Bali – you'll find buses and minibuses from here bound for all corners of the island. Bali's Ngurah Rai International Airport is actually 12km south of Denpasar, closer to Kuta. Island-hoppers can catch frequent ferries between eastern Java and Bali, between Bali and Lombok, and between Lombok and Pulau Sumbawa.

Manila
Most people enter the Philippines via Manila Ninoy Aquino International Airport (NAIA), by far the best connected in the country. Boats and ferries are unsurprisingly the main way to reach many of the Philippines' countless islands, but there is only one international ferry open to foreigners – from Zamboanga to Sandakan in the Malaysian state of Sabah.

Brunei Darussalam
The tiny sultanate of Brunei is tucked into the northeast corner of Borneo. There are regular flights to Malaysia, the Philippines, Thailand, Australia and Singapore; express buses also run over the border into Sabah and Sarawak. The crossing is generally hassle-free if your documents are in order, but there are lots of checkpoints to negotiate.

Right: Passengers aboard a jeepney in Banaue, Philippines (left) and (right) Singapore's city skyline.

© Antonio V. Oquias / Shutterstock

© Matt Munro / Lonely Planet

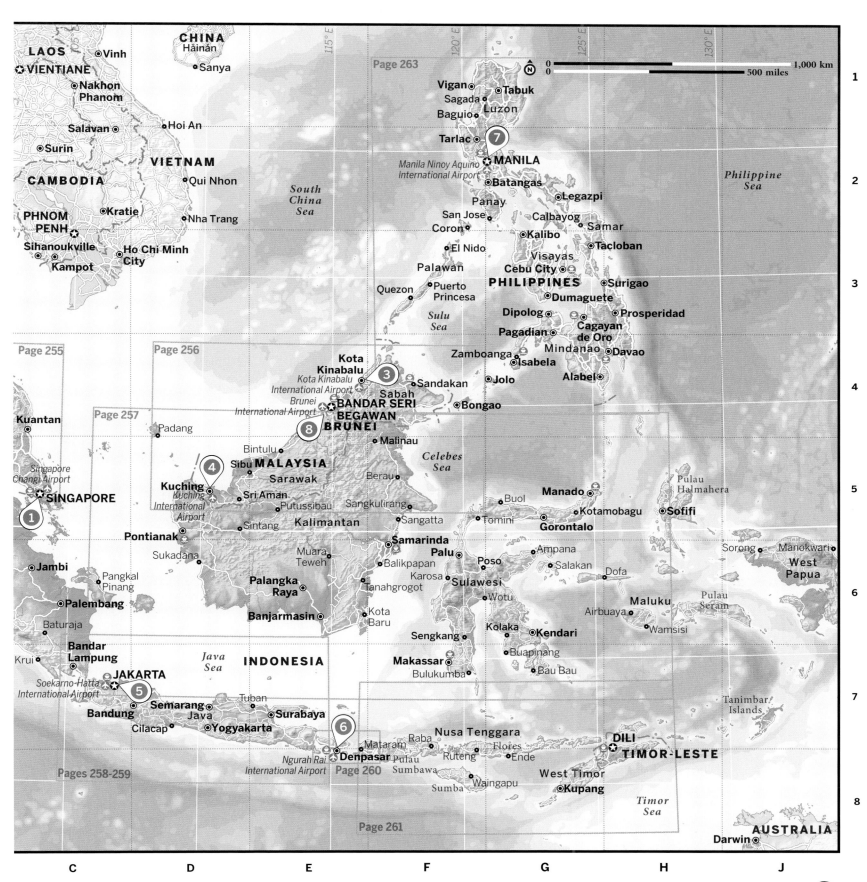

SIGHTS &
ACTIVITIES

◉ SEE
◉ DO

ITINERARY

▽ 1
▽ 2

1 Kuala Lumpur

Dominated by the 452m-high Petronas Towers, Malaysia's sultry capital is packed with historic monuments, steel-clad skyscrapers, lush parks, megasized shopping malls, bustling street markets and lively nightspots. The city's atmospheric Chinatown neighbourhood along the River Klang epitomises multicultural Malaysia.

2 George Town

Declared a World Heritage Site in 2008, Pulau Penang's prettiest city is a movie set mishmash of Chinese temples in Little India, mosques in Chinatown, and Western-style skyscrapers gleaming above British Raj–era architecture. Many of the city's shophouses have been turned into museums, hotels and restaurants.

3 Cameron Highlands

Tea plantations unfurl across valleys in Malaysia's largest hill station, named after explorer Sir William Cameron, who mapped the area in 1885. The area developed during the British colonial period, and is now one of Malaysia's top active destinations, with hiking, nature trekking and ecotourism.

4 Taman Negara National Park

Malaysia's oldest, largest and most popular national park straddles Pahang, Kelantan and Terengganu. Since 1939, the park has been a haven for tropical flora and a vast variety of wildlife, including elephants, tigers, leopards and flying squirrels. It is also home to the peninsula's highest peak, 2187m Gunung Tahan.

Taman Negara National Park: The rainforest in this park is the oldest in the world.

5 Ipoh

This pleasant, mid-sized town is an attractive city break destination. Food-lovers visit for its famous white coffee, beancurd pudding and the excellent restaurants in the Little India district. The old town's laneways are lined with period buildings housing cafes and shops, many splashed with street art.

6 Pulau Perhentian

The seas around the Perhentian Islands draw a variety of colourful marine life, from sharks and tropical fish to turtles and urchins. Coral beds lie close to shore, providing fantastic snorkelling.

7 Batu Caves

Only 13km from Kuala Lumpur, these limestone caves harbour Hindu temples where murals of mythic scenes gleam behind stalactites, bats flutter in the shadows, and troops of monkeys prey on hapless tourists.

8 Pulau Langkawi

Dominating an archipelago of more than one hundred islands, Pulau Langkawi is synonymous with sandy shores, jungle-cloaked valleys and bargain shopping (the 478.5-sq-km island has been duty-free since 1987).

9 Kota Bharu

A centre for Malaysian crafts, Kota Bharu's shops and markets sell items such as batik, *kain songket* (fabric with gold thread), silverware, hand-carved puppets and kites. Both the Central Market and the Bazaar Buluh Kubuh are great for local goods.

10 Pulau Tioman

Sitting like an emerald dragon guarding the waters of the South China Sea, Tioman Island offers every shade of paradise. There's cascading waterfalls, rigorous jungle hikes and laid-back villages facing onto idyllic beaches – and at 20km long and 11km wide, the island never feels crowded.

11 Jonker Walk Night Market

Food hawkers, trinket sellers and fortune tellers pile into Jln Hang Jebat for Melaka City's weekly extravaganza of street food and shopping. Graze on barbecued quail eggs and *kuih* (sticky-rice sweets) as you squeeze between souvenir stands, T-shirt stalls and even the occasional impromptu performance of Chinese karaoke.

12 Gardens by the Bay, Singapore

Spanning 101 hectares, Gardens by the Bay is Singapore's hottest horticultural asset. The park is home to almost 400,000 plants, not to mention contemporary architecture. Two giant conservatories rise beside Marina Bay, one home to ancient olive trees, the other to a towering, tropical mountain. To the north are the Supertrees: futuristic, botanical giants connected by a commanding Skyway.

14-day itinerary
The Northern Peninsula

Explore **Kuala Lumpur** before heading to the east coast resort of **Cherating**. Move on to **Kuala Terengganu**, with its pretty Chinatown and the Kompleks Muzium Negeri Terengganu. Next come the **Perhentian Islands**, accessed from Kuala Besut (Pulau Perhentian Besar tends to be less crowded than

Pulau Perhentian Kecil). Back on the mainland, visit **Kota Bharu**, for its museums and market, then head to the remote **Royal Belum State Park** in northern Perak. Access Malay culture in Kedah's capital **Alor Setar** before taking the ferry from Kuala Perlis to **Pulau Langkawi** for sunbathing, island-hopping and jungle exploration.

21-day itinerary
Colonial Footsteps

The southern end of Malaysia's peninsula is easily accessed from **Singapore**, the logical start and finish to this trip. After soaking up the island state's attractions, and popping over the causeway to Johor Bahru for street food and duty-free booze, meander down to the lethargic riverside town of **Muar**. It has a well-preserved

colonial-era district that's worth a look, and can be used as a base for assaults on **Gunung Ledang**, Johor's highest mountain, located within the Gunung Ledang National Park. Recover in Unesco World Heritage Site–listed **Melaka** where you can spend several days enjoying the enduring Portuguese and Dutch influence. Explore the last

remaining stands of lowland forest on the peninsula in **Endau-Rompin National Park**. To complete the trip, stunning **Pulau Tioman** is the absolute epitome of an island paradise. Alternatively, indulge in some island-hopping and diving around the 64 gems of the **Seribuat Archipelago** before retracing your steps and flying back to Singapore.

© ElenaMirage / Getty Images

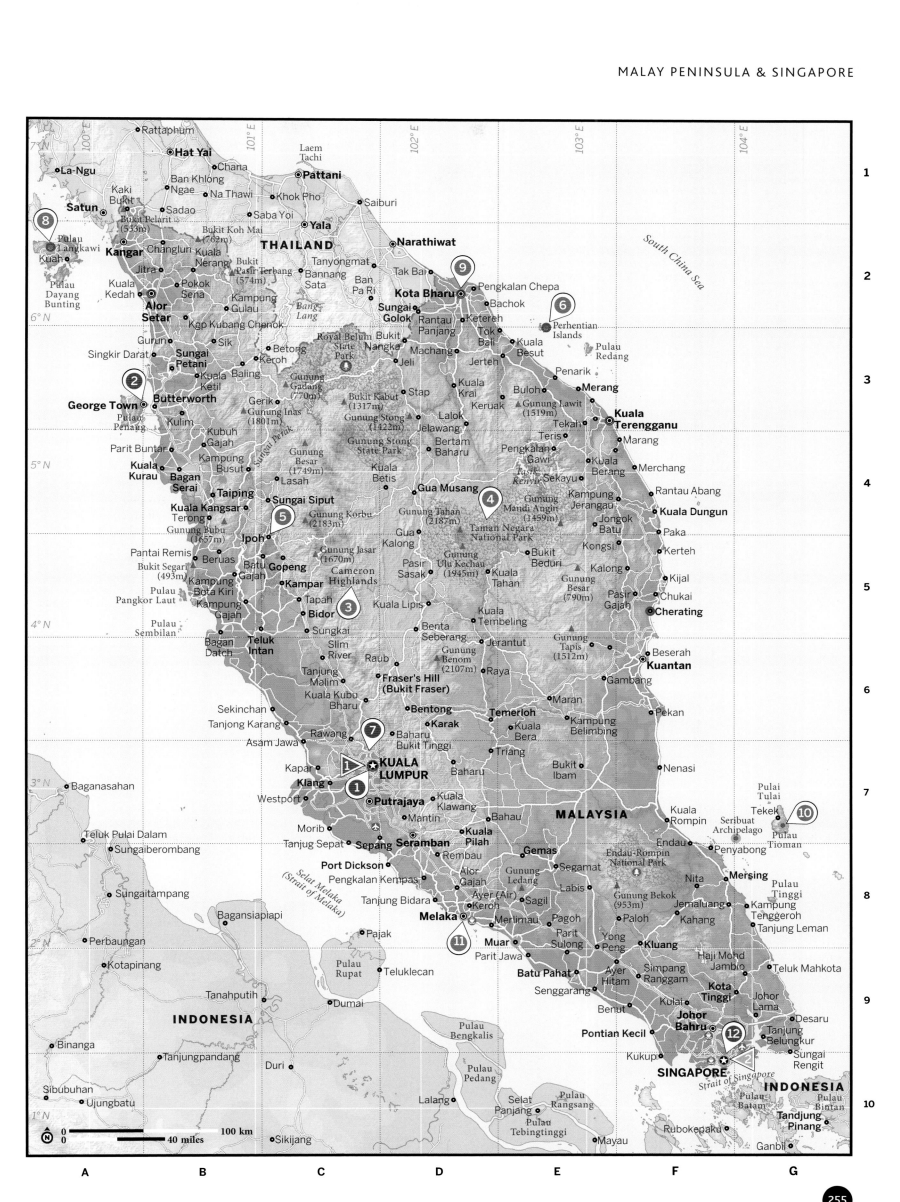

SIGHTS & ACTIVITIES

 SEE

 DO

ITINERARY

 1

 2

① Mt Kinabalu

At 4095m, Gunung Kinabalu, as it is known in Malay, is the highest mountain on the world's third-largest island, and Malaysia's first Unesco World Heritage Site. It attracts thousands of climbers, and increases in height by about 5mm a year.

② Sepilok Orangutan Rehabilitation Centre

Covering 40 sq km of the Kabili-Sepilok Forest Reserve, this world-famous centre welcomes orphaned and injured orangutans for rehabilitation before returning them to forest life.

③ Kelabit Highlands

The air is clean and cool, the rice fields impossibly green and the trekking – from longhouse to longhouse – is some of the best in Borneo. Reaching Sarawak's remote northeastern corner requires 12 hours by logging road or a flight in a 19-seat turboprop.

④ Gunung Mulu National Park

This national park is home to the biggest caverns on earth, including the Deer Cave, from which clouds of bats emerge at dusk. It also harbours natural oddities such as the Pinnacles formation on Mt Api.

▽ 14-day itinerary
Sarawak Highlights

Featuring stops at incredible caves and traditional longhouses, this trip across Sarawak is truly memorable. Fly into **Kuching** and take day trips to nearby national parks such as **Gunung Gading** and **Bako** in search of orangutans, proboscis monkeys and exotic flora. Then hop on an express ferry to the river port of **Sibu**, the gateway to the mighty Batang Rejang (Rejang River). Board an early-morning express boat and head upriver to **Kapit**, a trading centre founded in the days of the White Rajahs. If the river is high enough, continue to back-of-beyond **Belaga** for hikes to Orang Ulu longhouses. A jarring 4WD ride will get you down to **Similajau National Park**, which stretches along the coast for 30km. Hop on a bus heading northeast to Batu Niah Junction, a few kilometres from the caves, chirping bat colonies and archaeological sites of **Niah National Park**. Fly from Miri into Borneo's interior for visits to **Gunung Mulu National Park** and the green **Kelabit Highlands**.

⑤ Danum Valley Conservation Area

Flowing over 440 sq km of central Sabah, the Danum Valley Conservation Area is one of the world's most complex ecosystems. Its precious dipterocarp forest provides a habitat for rare species including orangutan, pygmy elephant, clouded leopard and marbled cat. A new species of plant is found here by scientists every week.

⑥ Kuching

Borneo's most sophisticated city combines an atmospheric old town, romantic waterfront, fine cuisine and buzzing nightlife. Several of Sarawak's sites are easy to visit on day trips.

⑦ Maliau Basin

The Maliau Basin Conservation Area (MBCA) is known as 'Sabah's Lost World'. This 25km-wide basin is home to Borneo's oldest and most pristine dipterocarp rainforest. It lay undiscovered until a pilot almost crashed into the crater walls in 1947, and was unexplored until the 1980s.

⑧ Ulu Temburong

Set in 500-sq-km of pristine rainforest covering southern Temburong, this is a highlight of any visit to Brunei. The forests teem with life, including 400 kinds of butterfly. Only about 1 sq km of the park is accessible.

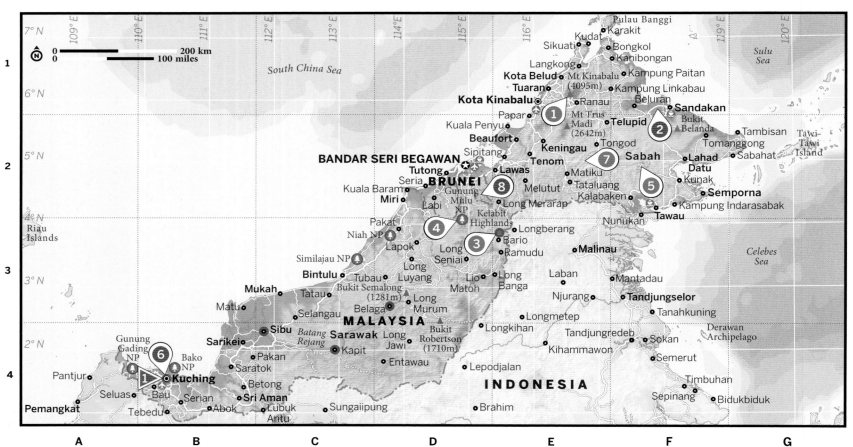

Tanjung Puting

Though remote, Tanjung Puting is the most popular destination for seeing wild orangutans in Kalimantan. The park is best seen from a *klotok*, a ramshackle, multistorey liveaboard boat that travels up Sungai Sekonyer from Kumai to the rehabilitation centre at Camp Leakey.

Derawan Archipelago

Of the 31 named islands, the four most accessible to visitors are the crowded weekend getaway of Derawan, peaceful Maratua atoll, and the wildernesses of Sangalaki and Kakaban. The scuba diving and snorkelling rank among the best in Indonesia.

Sungai Mahakam

The second-largest river in Indonesia, the Mahakam is a microcosm of Kalimantan. As you float upriver, you'll pass river barges, centuries-old villages and impossibly tall trees, as well as coal mines, logging camps and oil palm plantations.

Loksado

Loksado is nestled in the foothills of the Meratus Mountains. Base yourself here for treks to mountain peaks, waterfalls, or remote Dayak villages.

21-day itinerary
Around Kalimantan

Kalimantan is big and cloaked in jungle, with many places accessible only by boat. Start at **Balikpapan** (where you can get your visa) before flying to **Berau**. From there, explore the **Derawan Archipelago**, home to world-class diving. Back in Berau, head south to **Samarinda**, gateway to the Sungai Mahakam (Mahakam River). Head upriver via **Tenggarong** and its *keraton* (palace) to **Muara Muntai**, where you can hire a *ces* (longtail canoe) for a backwater journey to **Mancong**. Take a bus south to the market village of **Kandangan** where you can hop on a pick-up truck bound for **Loksado**, in the foothills of the Meratus Mountains, for hiking, bamboo rafting or relaxing. Experience **Banjarmasin**'s floating market before flying to Pangkalan Bun and nearby **Tanjung Puting National Park** for wildlife – and orangutan – watching. Finish by flying to Putussibau to see Kalimantan's oldest longhouses and wildest forests in the **Kapuas Hulu**, then float through the wetlands of **Danau Sentarum National Park**.

Merabu

The Dayak Lebo village of Merabu became the first in the Berau District to gain recognition of their village forest, and now offers ecotourism – including orangutan-spotting safaris, expeditions to Lake Tebo and visits to Goa Beloyot, a cliff-side cavern full of ancient stencilled handprints.

Pulau Bunaken

This 808-hectare island is part of the 891-sq-km Bunaken Manado Tua Marine National Park. It's a diving hotspot, with more than 300 types of coral and 3000 fish species inhabiting its vertical underwater walls.

Tangkoko-Batuangas Dua Saudara Nature Reserve

Due to its 88-sq-km of rainforest, Tangkoko is prime wildlife-spotting territory, from black macaques, cuscuses and tarsiers to maleo birds and red-knobbed hornbills. Its ferocious midges, called gonones, leave victims scratching furiously.

Tana Toraja

With its vibrant tribal culture, the highland region of Tana Toraja is fascinating. Traditional tribal funeral ceremonies can still be seen here; it's customary to bring a gift for the family and to wear black or dark clothes.

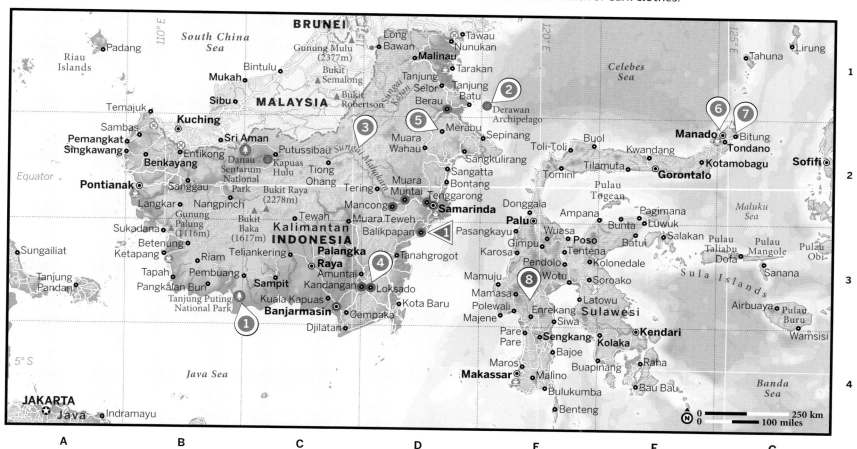

SIGHTS &
ACTIVITIES

◉ SEE

◉ DO

ITINERARY

▽ 1

▽ 2

Borobodur

The world's largest Buddhist temple, Borobodur is built from two million blocks in the form of a massive stupa. Standing on a 118m by 118m base, its six square terraces are topped by three circular ones, with four stairways leading through carved gateways to the top. Viewed from the air, the structure resembles a 3D tantric mandala (symbolic circular figure). Some 432 Buddha images stare out from chambers above the galleries.

Gunung Bromo

Rising from the ancient Tengger caldera, Gunung Bromo (2329m) is one of three volcanoes to have emerged from a vast crater, stretching 10km across. Flanked by the peaks of Kursi (2581m) and Batok (2440m), the smouldering cone of Bromo stands in a sea of ashen, volcanic sand. To the south, Gunung Semeru (3676m), Java's highest peak and one of its most active volcanoes, throws its shadow – and occasionally ash – over the scene.

Kawah Ijen

The fabled Ijen Plateau is a vast volcanic region dominated by the three cones of Ijen (2368m), Merapi (2800m) and Raung (3332m). It's possible to hike up to its sulphur crater lake and experience the unworldly 'blue fire' phenomenon.

Karimunjawa Islands

The dazzling archipelago of Karimunjawa consists of 27 coral-fringed islands, only five of which are inhabited, that lie about 90km north of Jepara. The main island, Pulau Karimunjawa, is home to Javanese, Bugis and Madurese families who live off fishing, tourism and seaweed cultivation. The archipelago is divided into zones to protect the ecosystem.

Prambanan

Comprising the remains of some 244 temples, World Heritage–listed Prambanan is Indonesia's largest Hindu site. The highlight is the central compound, where its eight main and eight minor temples rise up majestically like ornate 9th-century skyscrapers. Erected in the middle of the 9th century, little is known about its early history.

Ujung Kulon National Park

On the southwestern tip of Java, this national park is the last refuge of the one-horned Javan rhinoceros, one of the globe's most critically endangered mammals – only 50 to 60 remain.

Yogyakarta

Yogyakarta (pronounced 'Jogjakarta') is Java's cultural centre. It is still headed by its sultan, whose *kraton* (walled city palace) remains the hub of traditional life, although the modern city is home to over 3.3 million people. It remains a stronghold of batik, gamelan and traditional ritual.

Meru Betiri National Park

Covering 580 sq km between Jember and Banyuwangi districts, this coastal rainforest is known for its abundant wildlife, although the Java tiger is now almost certainly extinct.

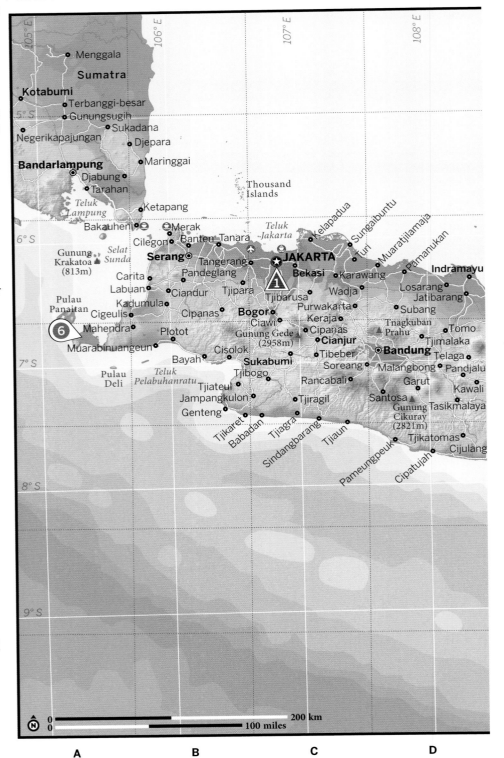

Candi Sukuh

Sitting 900m above the Solo plain, this enigmatic temple rests on a large, truncated pyramid of rough-hewn stone and has some fascinating reliefs and Barong statues. A fertility cult was once practised here: several explicit carvings have led it to be dubbed the 'erotic' temple.

10-day itinerary
Java Jaunt

Indonesia's most populous island mixes the nation's future and past with incredible natural beauty. Begin in **Jakarta** and wrap your senses around the dizzying smells, sounds, sights and people of Indonesia's teeming capital. Linger long enough to binge on Bintang beer and shopping, then head to **Batu Karas** for classic laid-back beach vibes or go for the resorts of nearby **Pangandaran**. After you've worshipped the sun for a week or so, catch the train to **Yogyakarta**, Java's cultural capital. Dabble in batik, amble through the bustling *kraton* and part with your rupiah at one of the vibrant markets. Round things off with a day trip to majestic **Borobudur**, unquestionably one of Asia's most awe-inspiring temples.

14-day itinerary
Backcountry Java

This itinerary heads a bit further off the regular tourist trail to explore some of Java's more out-of-the-way sights. Starting in **Yogyakarta**, catch a bus to the enigmatic Hindu temples of **Prambanan**, then on to the laid-back city of **Solo** – arguably the epicentre of Javanese identity and tradition, and one of the least Westernised cities on the island. From here, travel by motorbike or bus to explore awesome **Bromo-Tengger-Semeru National Park**, spending a memorable night sleeping on the lip of Tengger crater. Next, head to the southeast coast and arrange a 4WD tour to visit **Meru Betiri National Park**, a remote area of magnificent coastal rainforest and abundant wildlife. If you're really lucky, you might just catch a glimpse of the amazing giant squirrel, but sadly, the Java tiger is now thought to be extinct. Finally, follow the coast to **Alas Purwo National Park**, where there are wild leopards to spot and amazing surf to brave at G-Land. The park is hard to reach by public transport, so motorbikes or guided tours are the best way to go.

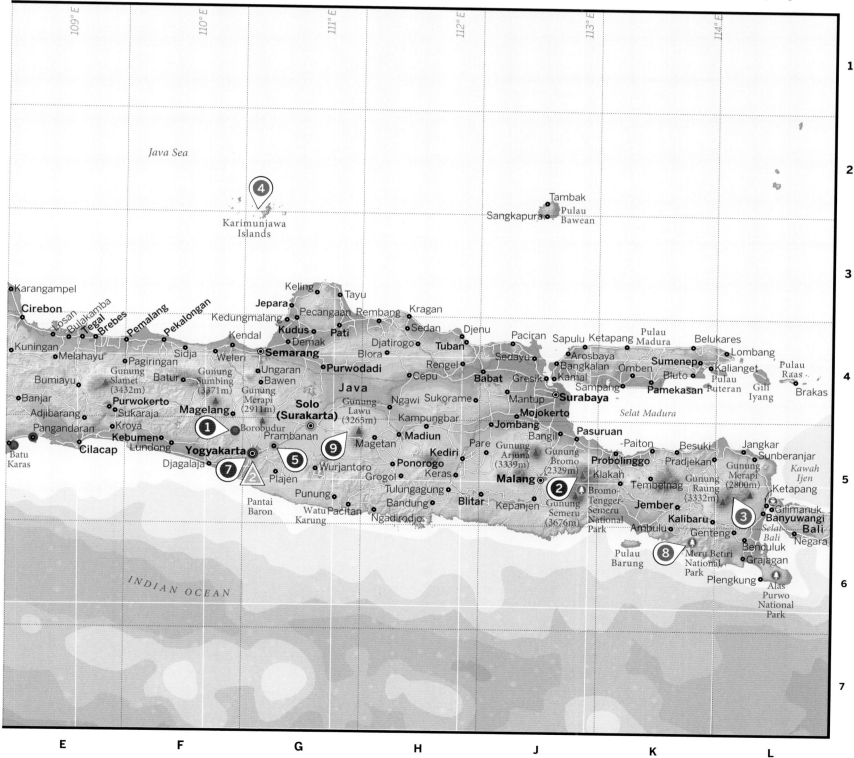

SIGHTS &
ACTIVITIES

 SEE

DO

ITINERARY

1

2

Komodo National Park: These mountainous islands are laced with trails and patrolled by Komodo dragons.

1 Ubud

The artistic heart of Bali exudes spiritual appeal. Performances showcasing the island's culture take place nightly. Museums and galleries honour those who have been inspired here, while rice fields offer perfect spots to sit in the lotus position.

2 Kuta and Legian

Kuta and Legian are the epicentre of mass tourism in Bali. Their grit and wall-to-wall cacophony have become notorious. Tourism in Bali began on Kuta Beach, where surf crashes to shore in long symmetrical breaks. Rent surfboards or crash on the sand.

3 Jatiluwih

At Jatiluwih, centuries-old rice terraces have received Unesco World Heritage status. Water runs through channels and bamboo pipes from one plot to the next. The twisting road leading in and out of town offers the best panorama.

4 Pura Luhur Ulu Watu

One of Bali's holiest temples, Pura Luhur Ulu Watu is perched precipitously top tall, sheer cliffs in Bali's southwest. Shrines and sacred sites are strung along the limestone precipice.

5 Pulau Menjangan

One of Bali's many legendary dive sites, Pulau Menjangan is a protected island offering more than a dozen areas for diving, all with plentiful tropical fish, soft corals, great visibility, caves and steep drops. Whales, whale sharks and manta rays may be seen here.

6 Bukit Peninsula

The west coast of the Bukit Peninsula in south Bali is dotted with wonderful beaches, such as Balangan Beach, Bingin and Padang Padang. Families run surfer bars built on bamboo stilts over the tide.

7 Mt Rinjani

Dominating northern Lombok is Gunung Rinjani, a volcano sacred to Hindus and Sasaks. Hiking it involves planning, guides, stamina and sweat. The route climbs to a caldera overlooking the crater lake and the mini-cone of Gunung Baru.

8 Selong Blanak

Southern Lombok's coastline has a wild savage beauty and few visitors. When you set eyes on pristine Selong Blanak beach, you'll understand the hype. Enjoy a perfect swath of sand and clear, turquoise-tinged water.

9 Gili Islands

Fringed by white sand and coconut palms, the Gilis are a vision of paradise. Each island has its own character. Gili Trawangan (aka Gili T) is the most cosmopolitan, with a raucous party scene and upscale dining. Gili Air has the strongest local character, while little Gili Meno is the smallest and quietest of all.

1 14-day itinerary

The Best of Bali and Lombok

Start your trip in **Seminyak**, allowing three days to experience the charms of Kerobokan, the beaches of Canggu and the wild nights of Kuta. Head north, driving through the rice terraces of **Jatiluwih** and on to **Pura Luhur** **Batukaru**, a holy temple up in the clouds. Head northwest to the beach resorts at **Pemuteran**, from where you can snorkel or scuba Bali's best dive site at **Pulau Menjangan**. Driving inland, spend a few days soaking up Balinese culture in **Ubud**, where you can enjoy nightly performances of traditional dance and music. Visit the monuments at **Gunung Kawi**, then head to Padangbai and catch a fast boat to the **Gili Islands** for snorkelling, swimming and sunbathing.

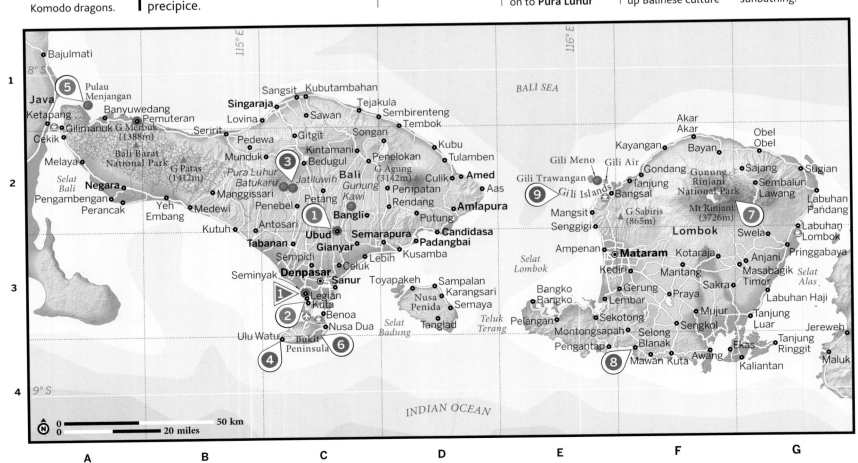

© Ali Trisno Pranoto / Getty Images

21-day itinerary
Island to Island

Begin on **Sumbawa** and admire the beautiful coastline and surf breaks that dot the island such as **Maluk** and **Pantai Lakey**. Catch the ferry to **Labuanbajo** on Flores, the fast-growing hub for exploring nearby **Komodo National Park**. Enjoy dragons and beautiful little island beaches. Flores is a rugged volcanic island with thriving ancient cultures and dramatic terrain which more and more travellers are exploring via the fast-improving Trans-Flores Hwy. Stop in **Bajawa** to explore volcanoes and villages, then use mountainside **Moni** as a base for visiting the vivid waters at Kelimutu. Stop off at the lovely beaches near **Paga**. Now take a ferry south to isolated and timeless **Sumba**, where some superb beaches are just starting to attract visitors. After indulging in sun and isolation, fly to **Kupang** in West Timor. Visit entrancing ancient villages like None, Boti and Temkessi in the surrounding areas to the east, then catch a flight to **Dili** in Timor Leste. Take a few days to explore the reefs, mountains and ancient traditions of Asia's newest country.

Komodo National Park
Between Sumbawa and Flores, Komodo Island's savannah-clad hills and mangrove forests are home to the legendary Komodo dragon, or *ora*. The world's largest lizard, it can reach 3m in length and eats deer and buffalo.

Alor Archipelago
Isolated from the outside world and one another by rugged terrain, the 200,000 inhabitants of this tiny volcanic archipelago are divided into 100 tribes speaking eight languages and 52 dialects.

Flores
Named by 16th-century Portuguese colonists, the island of Flores features smoking volcanoes, rice fields and hidden beaches, and is still little explored by Western visitors. Most inhabitants are nominally Catholic, but are still part of ancient island cultures.

West Sumba
People of West Sumba still inhabit *kampung* – high-roofed hilltop houses surrounding ancestors' tombs. Rituals and ceremonies here often involve animal sacrifices.

Ataúro
In 2016, this island was highlighted by Conservation International for having the most biodiverse waters in the world. Many of the reefs are accessible from the shore. It's 24km from neighbouring Dili.

Mt Ramelau
Hatubuilico is the main base for climbing Mt Ramelau (2963m). From the village to the Na'i Feto Ramelau (Virgin Mary) statue at the top takes three hours; from the summit, south and north coasts are visible.

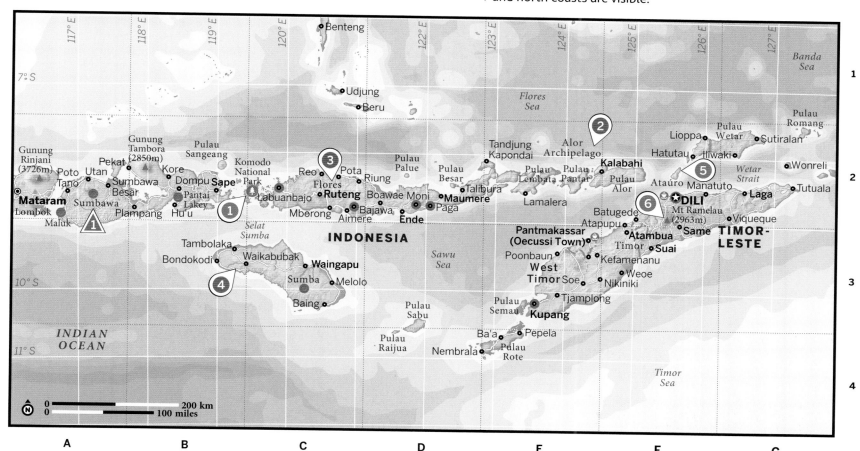

SIGHTS & ACTIVITIES

 SEE

 DO

ITINERARY

 1

 2

Bacuit Archipelago
A short *bangka* (boat) ride from the easygoing coastal town of El Nido, Bacuit Bay blends imposing limestone escarpments, palm-tree-lined beaches and coral reefs. Overnight island-hopping trips offer an opportunity to bed down in remote fishing villages.

Ifugao Rice Terraces
In North Luzon, even the sheerest cliffs have been tilled into rice paddies. Five of Ifugao's rice terraces are on Unesco's World Heritage list; they are best seen one to two months before harvest, when they change from green to gold.

Calamian Islands
This group of islands in the far north of Palawan is an adventurer's paradise, with wreck diving, kayaking, island-hopping and motorbiking. Busuanga is the largest and most developed island.

Bohol
While most visitors to this central Visayan island are divers bound for Alona Beach, the real charms lie inland along its perfectly paved jungle roads, perfect for motorbiking (look out for cuddly tarsiers). The island was rocked by an earthquake in 2013.

5

Kalibo
This town hosts the nation's biggest Mardi Gras. A mix of Catholic ritual, social activity, indigenous drama and tourist trap, it's a week-long street party raging from sunrise to sundown, peaking on the third Sunday of January.

Cebu: Snorkelling with a green sea turtle near Moalboal.

Manila
There's more to this megacity than just traffic and noise. Manila's nightlife is second to none. From the bongo-infused hipster hang-outs of Quezon City and Cubao X to the sizzling bars and chichi nightclubs of Makati and the Fort, there's something for everyone.

Cebu
Cebu is the most densely populated island in the Philippines and draws almost two million foreign travellers a year. The island's prime attractions are its white-sand beaches and diving, especially at Malapascua, where thresher sharks are present year-round.

8

Camiguin
Relatively unspoiled, Camiguin ('cah-mee-geen') is notable for its imposing silhouette. With more than 20 cinder cones 100m-plus high, Camiguin has more volcanoes per square kilometre than any other island on earth.

Puerto Galera
Puerto Galera is one of the Philippines' greatest dive sites and a beautiful place with gorgeous bays and offshore islands, and an interior of jungle-clad mountains and hill-tribe villages.

Siquijor
It may be best known for healers and witch doctors, but this Visayan island's real magic lies in its ring road – 72km of nearly traffic-free coastal bliss. It's brilliant to experience by motorbike, taking in blazingly white beaches, ancient churches, mysterious banyan trees and natural fish spas.

Sagada
Sagada is the closest thing the Philippines has to a backpacker mecca. A former refuge for intelligentsia, the village is known for its centuries-old coffins high up along limestone cliffs. Sagadans are of Applai (northern Kankanay) ancestry; during *begnas* (Kankanay community celebrations), chickens are sacrificed, gongs are played and merriment ensues.

12

Siargao
This laid-back island is the Philippines' top surf destination. The legendary Cloud Nine break is the hub but waves abound elsewhere; head to tranquil Pacfico in the north for an undeveloped experience, or take a surf safari to seldom-visited spots.

Bicol Peninsula
Southeast Luzon is adventure-travel central. The CamSur Watersports Complex specialises in wakeboarding. Daet in Camarines Norte is a burgeoning surf and kitesurfing destination. Near Legazpi you can climb the perfect cone of Mt Mayon, ride an ATV around its base or snorkel alongside the gentle whale sharks of Donsol – an unforgettable highlight.

14-day itinerary
A Philippines Primer

In two weeks you can cover stunning seascapes, white-sand beaches and lively islands. Fly into the capital city, **Manila**, then on to Busuanga in Palawan's **Calamian Islands**. Visit majestic Coron Island, dive the WWII wrecks and snorkel until you drop. Camp overnight on an offshore island such as Calumbuyan, Pass or North Cay.

Next, take a ferry to Palawan's other crown jewel, **El Nido**, home to some of Indonesia's finest beaches and jumping-off point for island-hopping in the **Bacuit Archipelago**. Enjoy El Nido's drinking and dining scene – a warm-up for your final stop: **Boracay**, where the party never stops. Relax on White Beach before flying back to Manila.

21-day itinerary
Luzon

Not a beach person? The mountains of the main island offer rice terraces, trekking and hill tribes. Head north from Manila to **Baguio**, gateway to the Cordillera Mountains. Visit the city's museums for background on the area's ethnographic make-up. From Baguio, take a bus to **Kabayan**, centre of Ibaloi culture and base for

hikes in Mt Pulag National Park. Next, **Sagada** beckons. This tranquil backpacker village with cool climes, a laid-back vibe and top-notch hikes is tough to leave. Take a jeepney to **Bontoc** and explore the amphitheatre-like rice terraces of Maligcong on a day trip. Continue north to **Tinglayan**, a base for treks into indigenous Kalinga

villages where the contemporary world feels far away. Head back to **Bontoc**, then continue to **Banaue** and Batad, site of Luzon's most famous rice terraces. Hikes will keep you busy, and you can sleep in homestays. With R&R in mind, catch a bus south to **San Jose** (you might have to overnight here) to jump on another bus to the surfing town of **Baler**.

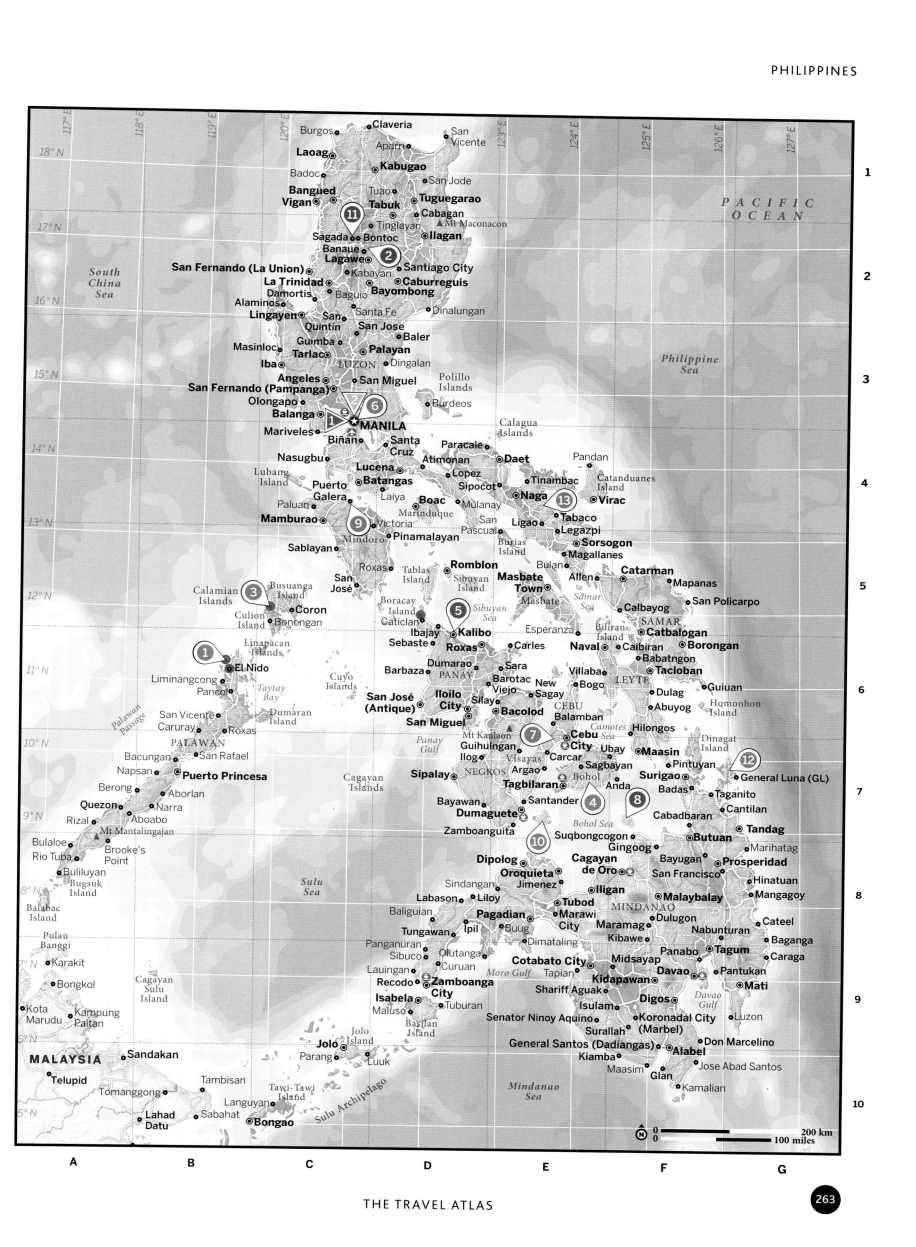

Claveria
San Vicente
Burgos
Laoag Aparri
Badoc **Kabugao** San Jode
Banged Tuao **Tuguegarao** Cabagan
Vigan Tabuk Tinglayan
⑪ **Ilagan** ▲ Mt Maconacon
Sagada Bontoc
Banaue ②
Lagawe **Santiago City**
San Fernando (La Union) Kabayan **Caburreguis**
La Trinidad **Bayombong**
Damortis Baguio Santa Fe Dinalungan
Alaminos
Lingayen San, Santa Fe
Quintin **San Jose**
Masinloc Guimba Baler
Tarlac **Palayan**
Iba Dingalan
Angeles LUZON Polillo
San Fernando (Pampanga) San Miguel Islands
Olongapo Burdeos
Balanga ② ⑥
Mariveles ① ★ **MANILA**
Biñan Santa
Nasugbu Cruz Atimonan Calagua
Lucena Paracale Islands
Batangas Lopez **Daet** Pandan
Puerto Sipocot Tinambac Catanduanes
Galera Laiya **Naga** ⑬ Island
Paluan **Boac** Mulanay ⑬ **Virac**
Mamburao Marinduque San
⑨ Victoria Pascual Ligao **Tabaco**
Pinamalayan Burias **Legazpi**
Sablayan Mindoro Island **Sorsogon**
Roxas Tablas **Magallanes**
San Island **Romblon** Bulan
José Sibuyan Allen
Calamian Busuanga Island **Masbate** **Catarman**
Islands Island ③ **Town** Mapanas
Culion Coron Boracay Masbate Sámar San Policarpo
Island Bonongan Island ⑤ Sibuyan Sea Calbayog SAMAR
Gaticlan Sea
Linapacan Ibajay **Kalibo** Esperanza Biliran **Catbalogan**
① Islands Sebaste **Roxas** Island **Borongan**
El Nido Cuyo **Roxas** Carles Naval Caibiran Babatngon
Liminangcong Islands Dumarao PANAY Sara **Tacloban**
Pancol Barbaza Barotac New LEYTE Guiuan
San Vicente Dumaran Viejo Sagay Villaba Homonhon
Caruray Island **San José** Silay Bogo Dulag Island
Roxas (Antique) **Iloilo** CEBU Abuyog
PALAWAN **City** Balamban Hilongos Dinagat
Bacungan **Bacolod** Mt Kanlaon Camotes Island
Napsan San Rafael **San Miguel** ▲ Sea
Puerto Princesa Guihulngan ⑦ **Cebu** Ubay ⑫
Berong Aborlan Sipalay Ilog **City** Carcar Sagbayan **Maasin** Pintuyan **General Luna (GL)**
Quezon Narra Visayas **Surigao** Taganito
Rizal Aboabo NEGROS **Tagbilaran** Bohol Anda Badas Cantilan
Bulaloe ▲ Mt Mantalingajan Bayawan Santander ④ ⑧
Rio Tuba Brooke's **Dumaguete** ⑧ Cabadbaran
Buliluyan Point Zamboanguita Bohol Sea **Tandag**
Bugsuk ⑩ Suqbongcogon Marihatag
Island Dipolog Gingoog **Butuan**
Balabac **Oroquieta** Bayugan **Prosperidad**
Island Jimenez Cagayan San Francisco Hinatuan
Pulau Labason Liloy **Iligan** de Oro Mangagoy
Banggi Sindangan **Tubod** MINDANAO Dulugon **Malaybalay** Cateel
Karakit Baliguian **Pagadian** Maramag Kibawe **Tagum** Baganga
Kota Marawi Panabo
Marudu Tungawan Ipil City Kibawe **Davao** Pantukan
Kampung Panganuran Buug Dimataling **Kidapawan** Caraga
Bongkol Paitan Sibuco Olutanga **Cotabato City** Midsayap **Mati**
Cagayan Sulu Lauingan Curuan Moro Gulf Tapian Shariff Aguak **Digos**
Island Recodo **Zamboanga** Isulam Koronadal City Luzon
Isabela **City** Tuburan Senator Ninoy Aquino (Marbel)
Maluso Surallah Don Marcelino
Jolo Basilan General Santos (Dadiangas) **Alabel**
Sandakan Jolo Island Kiamba Jose Abad Santos
MALAYSIA Parang Luuk Maasim Glan
Telupid Kamalian
Tambisan Tawi-Tawi
Tomanggong Island
Languyan Mindanao
Bongao Sea

MALAYSIA
Telupid
Tambisan
Tomanggong
Languyan
Lahad
Datu Sabahat **Bongao**

0 ⬆N 200 km
0 100 miles

Australia & New Zealand

Both Australia and New Zealand are natural wonderlands with tropical rainforests to the north, snow-laden mountains in the south, iron-rich deserts and fertile farmland, all surrounded by surging oceans. The islands – fragments of ancient Gondwana – teem with surreal wildlife but while the kangaroos and the kiwis might draw first-time visitors, it is the delights of life in and around both nations' supremely civilised cities that keep people coming back. Explore the laneways of Melbourne, Sydney and Auckland to sample global cuisines and world-beating home-produced wine, beer and coffee. Then tap into the indigenous cultures of Australia and New Zealand to discover the deeper stories of these wild lands of the southern hemisphere.

CLIMATE CHART

SYDNEY

RAINFALL INCH/MM
20/500 16/400 12/300 8/200 4/100 0
D N O S A J J M A M F J

TEMP °C/F
40/104 30/86 20/68 10/50 0/32

AUCKLAND

RAINFALL INCH/MM
6/150 4/100 2/50 0
D N O S A J J M A M F J

TEMP °C/F
30/86 20/68 10/50 0/32

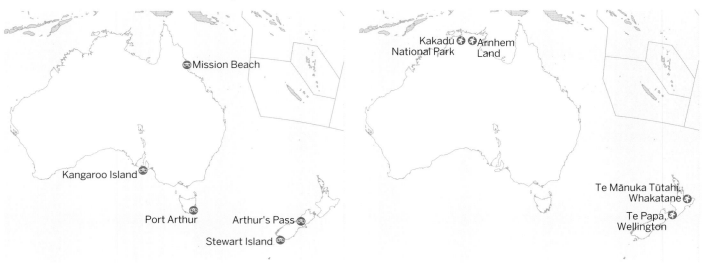

WILDLIFE

Quirky creatures abound on these islands. Seek out kiwis on Stewart Island or climb Arthur's Pass on the South Island to meet a mischievous kea. Tasmanian devils have a sanctuary near Port Arthur on Tasmania; the cassowary prowls Mission Beach and many marsupials thrive on Kangaroo Island.

INDIGENOUS CULTURE

Learn more about Australia and New Zealand's indigenous culture at a *marae* (meeting place) such as Te Mānuka Tūtahi in Whakatane. See Māori carvings at Te Papa museum. In Australia, immerse yourself in Aboriginal reserve Arnhem Land and view rock art in Kakadu National Park.

Clockwise from top left: a Tasmanian devil; a vineyard at Renwick in New Zealand's Marlborough region; Sydney's Spice Alley food court; New Zealand's Mt Aspiring National Park.

HIKING

Pull on a pair of walking boots to explore the wonderful landscapes here. New Zealand's famed Great Walks include the Abel Tasman along the Nelson coast and the Routeburn Track in Fiordland. The Overland Track traverses Tasmania and the Larapinta Trail is a 20-day undertaking.

WINE

World-class wines flow out of New Zealand and Australia. Watch the sunset with a glass of chardonnay in Margaret River. Savour pinot noir in the Tamar Valley or Central Otago or riesling in Clare Valley. And don't miss the Pyrenees' cabernet sauvignon or Marlborough's sauvignon blanc.

Transport hubs

Australia and New Zealand, separated by the Tasman Sea, are a long way from most countries, if not each other. Most people arrive on these islands by jet, although cruise ships dock at some of the city ports. Major transport hubs in Australia are invariably the state capitals; there's an extensive and surprisingly affordable rail network across the land. In New Zealand, Wellington, Christchurch and Queenstown join Auckland as key centres for train and air travel.

TRANSPORT

A5, C2, D5, E2, E6, E7, F4, F5, J6

A5, D6, E2, E6, F3, F4, F5, H7, J6, J7

1 Cairns
Qantas, Virgin Australia and Jetstar, and a handful of international carriers, arrive in and depart from Cairns Airport. Most Great Barrier Reef trips from Cairns depart the Marlin Wharf.

2 Brisbane
Brisbane Airport is Australia's third-busiest airport and the main international airport serving southeast Queensland. Roma St station hosts long-distance trains north or inland.

3 Sydney (see pp434-5 for city map)
Numerous airlines fly to Sydney from destinations throughout Australia, Asia, Oceania, Europe (with a stopover), North America and elsewhere. Trains chug into Sydney's Central Station from as far north as Brisbane (13½ hours), as far south as Melbourne (11½ hours) and as far west as Perth (four days). Cruise ships and ferries dock at Circular Quay.

4 Canberra
Canberra Airport's only international connections are with Singapore and Wellington, but the Australian capital is well connected domestically. There are also train and bus links to Sydney and Melbourne, and Canberra is the gateway to the Australian Alps.

5 Melbourne (see pp416-17 for city map)
Most visitors to Victoria arrive via Melbourne Airport, which is well connected to the city by shuttle bus and taxi. The Spirit of Tasmania ferry crosses Bass Strait from Melbourne to Devonport, Tasmania, at least nightly. Southern Cross station is the terminus for intercity and interstate trains.

6 Hobart
Hobart's 'international' airport has only domestic flights, with services operated by Qantas, Virgin Australia, Jetstar and Tiger Air. There's no public transport to Hobart airport.

7 Darwin
The gateway to the Northern Territory has an international airport that also receives domestic flights from across the region. Regular long-distance bus services also head up and down the Stuart Hwy; and there's a daily service to Kakadu. The Ghan train departs Darwin for Adelaide weekly from Berrimah Rd (shuttles from the city).

8 Adelaide
International, interstate and regional flights via a number of airlines service Adelaide Airport. The Ghan train departs for Darwin, the Indian Pacific for Perth and the Overlander for Melbourne, tickets for all three are sold by Great Southern Rail.

9 Perth
Perth Airport is served by numerous airlines, including Qantas, and there are daily flights to and from international and Australian destinations, including the world's first non-stop flight from Australia to London. Regular bus services run up and down the coast and the Indian Pacific train crosses the country.

10 Auckland
The Kiwi capital is the main international gateway to New Zealand, and a hub for domestic flights. Auckland Airport is 21km south of the city centre and its domestic terminal offers connections to dozens of towns, cities and islands.

Right: The Ghan runs between Adelaide, Alice Springs and Darwin (left) and (right) the iconic Sydney harbour.

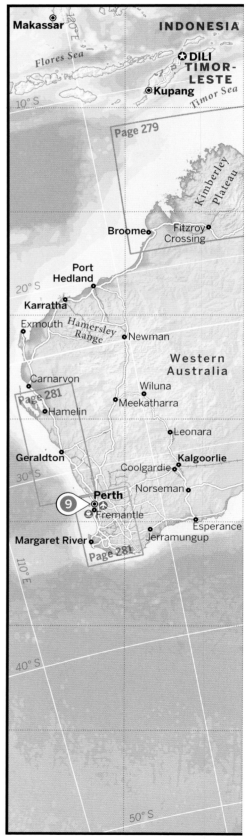

© Matt Munro / Lonely Planet

© Rudy Balasko / Shutterstock

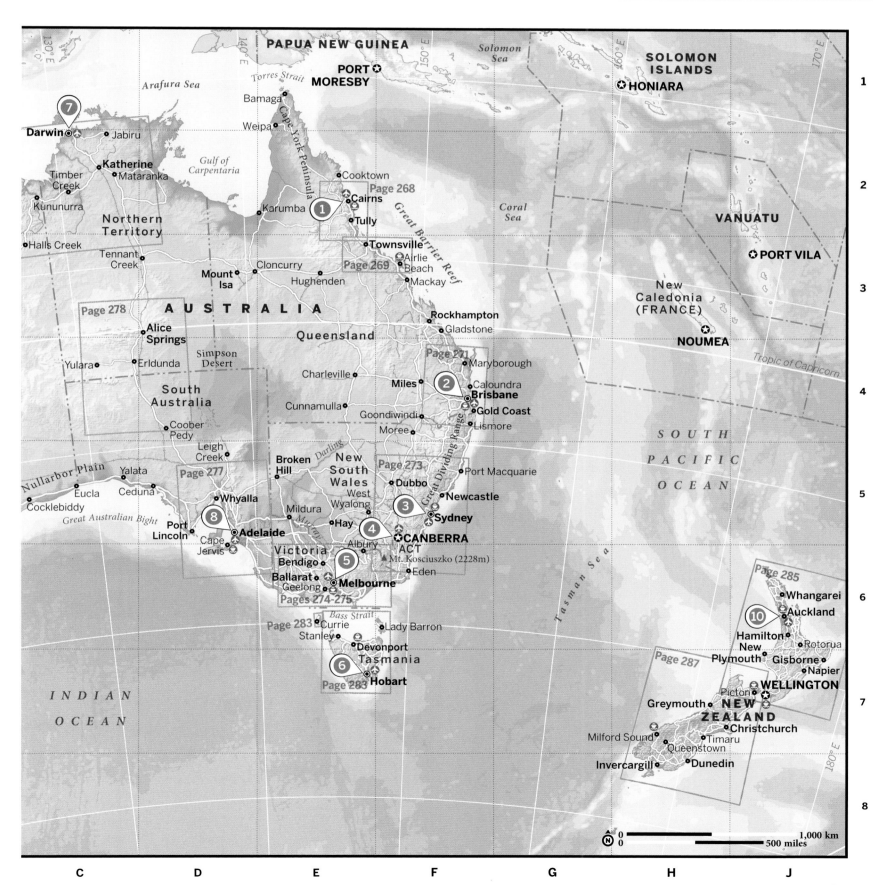

	C	D	E	F	G	H	J

PAPUA NEW GUINEA

Solomon Sea

SOLOMON ISLANDS

Arafura Sea

Torres Strait

PORT MORESBY

HONIARA — 1

Bamaga

Weipa

7
Darwin

Jabiru

Cape York Peninsula

Coral Sea

VANUATU — 2

Katherine
Mataranka

Gulf of Carpentaria

Karumba

Cooktown
Page 268
Cairns
Tully

Timber Creek

Kununurra

Northern Territory

Townsville
Airlie Beach
Page 269
Mackay

Great Barrier Reef

PORT VILA

Halls Creek

Tennant Creek

Cloncurry

Hughenden

New Caledonia (FRANCE) — 3

Mount Isa

AUSTRALIA

Page 278

Rockhampton
Gladstone

NOUMEA

Alice Springs

Queensland

Charleville

Page 271
Maryborough
Caloundra
2 Miles **Brisbane** — 4
Gold Coast

Yulara
Erldunda

Simpson Desert

South Australia

Cunnamulla

Goondiwindi
Moree
Lismore

Tropic of Capricorn

Coober Pedy

Leigh Creek

Darling

New South Wales

Page 273

Port Macquarie

S O U T H

Nullarbor Plain

Eucla
Cocklebiddy
Ceduna
Yalata

Broken Hill

Dubbo

West Wyalong

3 Newcastle
Sydney — 5

Great Dividing Range

P A C I F I C

Page 277
Whyalla

Mildura

Murray

Hay

4

CANBERRA
ACT

O C E A N

Great Australian Bight

Port Lincoln

8 **Adelaide**

Cape Jervis

Victoria
Bendigo
Ballarat
Geelong

Albury

Mt. Kosciuszko (2228m)
Eden

Page 285

5 **Melbourne**

Pages 274-275

Tasman Sea

10 Whangarei
Auckland — 6

Page 283
Currie
Stanley

Bass Strait

Lady Barron

Hamilton
New Plymouth
Gisborne
Rotorua

I N D I A N

Devonport
6 **Tasmania**

Page 287

Napier

Page 283 **Hobart**

WELLINGTON — 7

Greymouth

Picton

O C E A N

NEW ZEALAND

Milford Sound
Timaru
Christchurch

Queenstown

Invercargill
Dunedin

N
0 — 1,000 km
0 — 500 miles

— 8

SIGHTS &
ACTIVITIES

◉ SEE
◉ DO

ITINERARY

▽ 1
▽ 2

Cairns

Cairns (pronounced 'cans') has come a long way since its origins as a goldfields port. It's now one of Queensland's main tourist centres, and a major launch pad for expeditions to the Great Barrier Reef. There's no beach in town, but the magnificent Esplanade Lagoon makes up for it.

Kuranda

Tucked away in thick rainforest, arty, alternative Kuranda is one of Cairns' most popular day trips. Just getting here is an experience in itself: choose between driving a forest road, chugging up on a train or soaring over the treetops on Australia's longest gondola cableway.

Daintree National Park

The Daintree is the accessible section of the huge coastal rainforest in the Wet Tropics World Heritage Area. It has amazing biodiversity with swamp and mangrove forest habitats, eucalypt woodlands, native birds and tropical rainforest. Once threatened by logging, it's now protected.

Cape Tribulation

Cape Trib lies at the end of the

winding road from the Daintree River and, with its two beaches (Myall and Cape Tribulation), laid-back vibe, rainforest walks and compact village, it's a slice of backpacker paradise. Crocs and cassowaries roam wild, and activities range from hiking to jungle surfing.

Bloomfield Track

The fabled 80km outback track from Cape Tribulation to Cooktown features creek crossings and mountain climbs, with diversions including waterfalls, Aboriginal tours, walking trails and the Lion's Den pub near the northern end. It's mostly sealed; there's just 32km of 4WD-only road between the Bloomfield River and Cape Tribulation.

Great Barrier Reef

Stretching more than 2000km along Queensland's coast, the world's largest coral reef dazzles with turtles, rays, reef sharks and 1500 species of fish. Whether you dive on it, snorkel over it, or explore it via glass-bottom boat, this undersea kingdom and its 900 coral-fringed islands are unforgettable. Many visitors arrange trips from Cairns, with local operators offering diving courses and snorkelling trips.

Chillagoe–Mungana Caves

This national park boasts 400-million-year-old limestone caves, indigenous rock art, eerie outcrops and the looming ruins of Chillagoe's old smelters. Three of the park's 500-odd caves can be visited on ranger-guided tours: Donna, Trezkinn and Royal Arch.

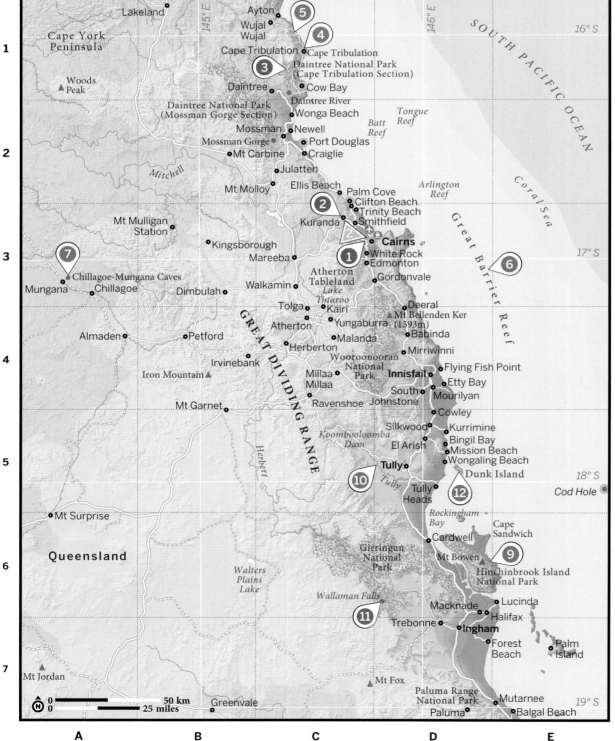

7-day itinerary
Out to the Islands

Fly into lively **Airlie Beach** to arrange a multi-day trip out to the Whitsundays. Make sure your itinerary includes **Whitsunday Island** itself for a memorable swim off sublime **Whitehaven Beach**, a night or two at an island resort and an overnight kayaking trip. Back in Airlie, track north around three hours to **Townsville**, Queensland's third-biggest city. Promenade along the waterfront, check out the excellent aquarium, clamber up Castle Hill and enjoy the local dining scene. Experienced divers might want to book a dive on the famous wreck of the SS *Yongala*. Wind up your journey on **Magnetic Island**, an unpretentious isle with easy-going beach villages, plenty of wildlife and bushwalking tracks.

10-day itinerary
Cairns to Daintree

Ten days is just about enough time to explore the best of the Far North. Start at **Cairns**, Australia's reef-diving capital, and book a snorkelling or dive trip to the Great Barrier Reef. If you have the time, consider a live-aboard expedition to **Cod Hole**. A short drive north of Cairns is the resort town of **Palm Cove**, good for decompressing for a day or two, then another hour north lies **Port Douglas**. This uptempo holiday hub has great places to eat, drink and bronze on the beach. Continuing north, the next stop is **Mossman Gorge**, where lowland rainforest surrounds the photogenic Mossman River. Take a guided walk and cool off in a waterhole. Further north is **Daintree River**, where you can go on a crocodile-spotting cruise then stop for lunch at **Daintree Village**. Head back to the river and cross by ferry to drive north to the Daintree Discovery Centre to learn about this extraordinary jungle wilderness. Nearby, **Cow Bay** is perfect for beach-combing. Last stop is **Cape Tribulation**, a magnificent natural partnership between rainforest and reef.

Whitsunday Islands
Seen from above, the Whitsundays are like a stunning organism under the microscope. There are 74 islands: five have resorts, but most are uninhabited, offering back-to-nature beach camping and bushwalking. Whitehaven Beach is the finest beach in the Whitsundays while Airlie Beach, is the coastal hub and major gateway.

Hinchinbrook Island
Australia's largest island national park (399 sq km) is a holy grail for walkers thanks to the formidable 32km Thorsborne Trail. Only 40 walkers are allowed at a time; crocs, mosquitoes, and the need to draw your own water add to the challenge.

Tully River
The Tully provides white water year-round thanks to the river's hydroelectric floodgates: rafting trips are timed to coincide with the daily release of the gates, resulting in Grade IV rapids foaming almost on cue.

Wallaman Falls
Located in Girringun National Park, 51km west of Ingham, the country's longest single-drop waterfalls look their best in the wet season, though they are spectacular at any time. A steep but worthwhile track (2km) takes you to the bottom of the falls.

Dunk Island
Known to the Djiru Aboriginal people as Coonanglebah ('the island of peace and plenty'), this is pretty much the ideal tropical island, with jungle, beaches and impossibly blue water. The circuit track (9.2km) is the best way to see the island's wildlife, and there's snorkelling over bommies (coral pinnacles) at Muggy Muggy.

Cape Tribulation:
The Daintree River mouth near Cape Tribulation, Queensland.

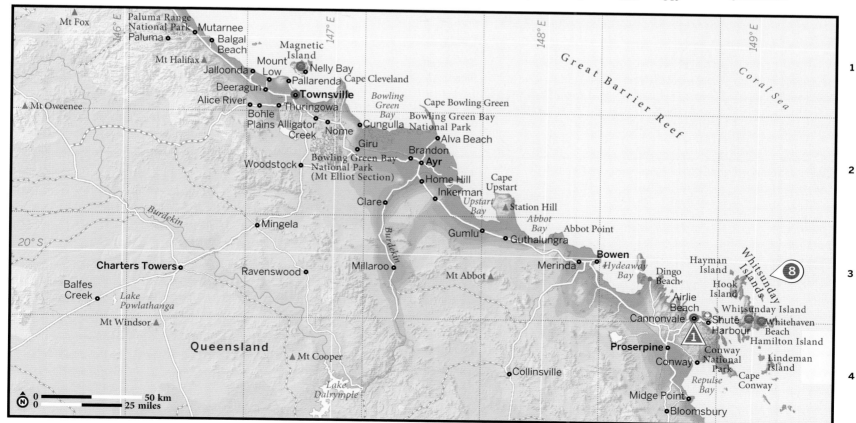

SIGHTS & ACTIVITIES

 SEE

DO

ITINERARY

 1

2

Brisbane

No longer happy to settle for 261 days of sunshine a year, Queensland's capital has an ever-expanding booty of street art, galleries, bookshops, cocktail bars and award-winning microbreweries. The Gallery of Modern Art is Australia's biggest contemporary gallery, and there are panoramic city views from Mt Coot-tha Lookout.

Gold Coast

Brash, trashy, hedonistic, overhyped… Queensland's Gold Coast is all these things, but it's still one of Australia's best-known beach destinations. Clean sand, warm water and surf breaks are the main draws, plus Australia's biggest theme parks – roller-coaster nirvana.

Byron Bay

Known for its epic surf breaks and bohemian lifestyle, Byron Bay is one of the key towns on the NSW coast. The main beaches can be busy, but quieter sands can be found around Cape Byron and Tallow Beach nearby.

Sunshine Coast

The Sunshine Coast – the 100 golden kilometres stretching from the tip of Bribie Island to the Cooloola Coast – is aglow with perfect beaches, coveted surf and a laid-back, sun-kissed populace. Resort towns dot the coast.

Noosa National Park: Morning surfers at Noosa Head Beach.

Noosa National Park

Near the town of Noosa, this pocket of wilderness is accessed via a boardwalk along the coast. Koalas are often

spotted in the trees near Tea Tree Bay, and dolphins are commonly seen from the rocky headlands around Alexandria Bay. There are also idyllic bays and great surf spots.

Lamington National Park

Escape the coast and climb to this national park, which features a 300-million-year-old volcanic landscape that is home to ancient tracts of Gondwana rainforest. The ferns, pines and a cool climate support an ecosystem in which songbirds flourish. On a wildlife tour look out for the performance spaces of the satin bowerbird, as well as pademelons and possums. The park is also the starting point of the 54km-long Gold Coast Hinterland Great Walk, which descends to Springbrook National Park.

Fraser Island

The vast, 120km-long sandbar of Fraser Island is a primal utopia, home to a profusion of wildlife including the purest strain of dingo in Australia.

The best way to explore is in a 4WD – cruising up the seemingly endless Seventy-Five Mile Beach and bouncing along sandy inland tracks.

Hervey Bay

For most of the year, Hervey Bay is a soporific seaside village, but in mid-July, when migrating humpback whales arrive, thousands of tourists come here to see them. It's one of the world's top whale-watching spots, but it's vital to go with an eco-accredited operator.

Glass House Mountains

These volcanic plugs rise from the subtropical plains 20km northwest of Caboolture. In Dreaming legend, they belong to a family of mountain spirits. To explorer James Cook, their shapes recalled the conical glass-making furnaces of his native Yorkshire.

Great Sandy National Park

Extending from Lake Cootharaba north to Rainbow Beach, this 540-sq-km section of national park offers wide beaches, pristine bushland, heathland, mangroves and rainforest, all rich in birdlife. The drive along the beach from Noosa North Shore to Double Island Point is a memorable one.

Toowoomba

This sprawling country hub is an unlikely hotbed of street art. The First Coat Art & Music Festival has generated an ever-growing number of murals around town – take a walking tour to discover more than 50. Toowoomba's Carnival of Flowers is a spring festival featuring food and drink.

7-day itinerary
Queensland to NSW

Kick-start your trip in big city **Brisbane**, then head south on the Gold Coast, stopping to experience the party-prone pleasure dome of **Surfers Paradise**, then moving on to gently hip **Burleigh Heads**, with its great beer and coffee. Continue south to laid-back **Coolangatta** on the New South Wales border, before moving on to **Byron Bay** in northern NSW. Despite big summer crowds and big development money, the town remains a hippie haven with great pubs, restaurants, beaches and the famous Pass point break. Don't miss inland day trips to pretty **Bangalow** and Australia's near-mythical alternative-lifestyle hangout, **Nimbin**.

14-day itinerary
North from Brisbane

A car is essential for this trip – and preferably a 4WD if you're including Fraser Island. Start in booming **Brisbane**, a city growing so fast it can be difficult to navigate. Its urban charms (great restaurants, arts scene, coffee and bars) meld seamlessly with the natural environment (cliffs, parklands and the Brisbane River). Spend two nights here, then truck north to the **Glass House Mountains** for panoramas and rock climbing. Nearby is the superb **Australia Zoo**. Next comes the laid-back Sunshine Coast: sunny **Caloundra** has cafes, eateries, street art and beaches, and a short hop north is **Noosa**, a classy resort town with sublime beaches, a lush national park and a first-class foodie scene. Take a detour into the **Great Sandy National Park**, cruising up the coast to **Rainbow Beach**, then hop across to the gigantic sandbar of **Fraser Island**; you'll require a 4WD to explore its lakes, creeks, giant dunes and rainforests. Catch a boat back to the mainland, and conclude with whale-watching in **Hervey Bay**.

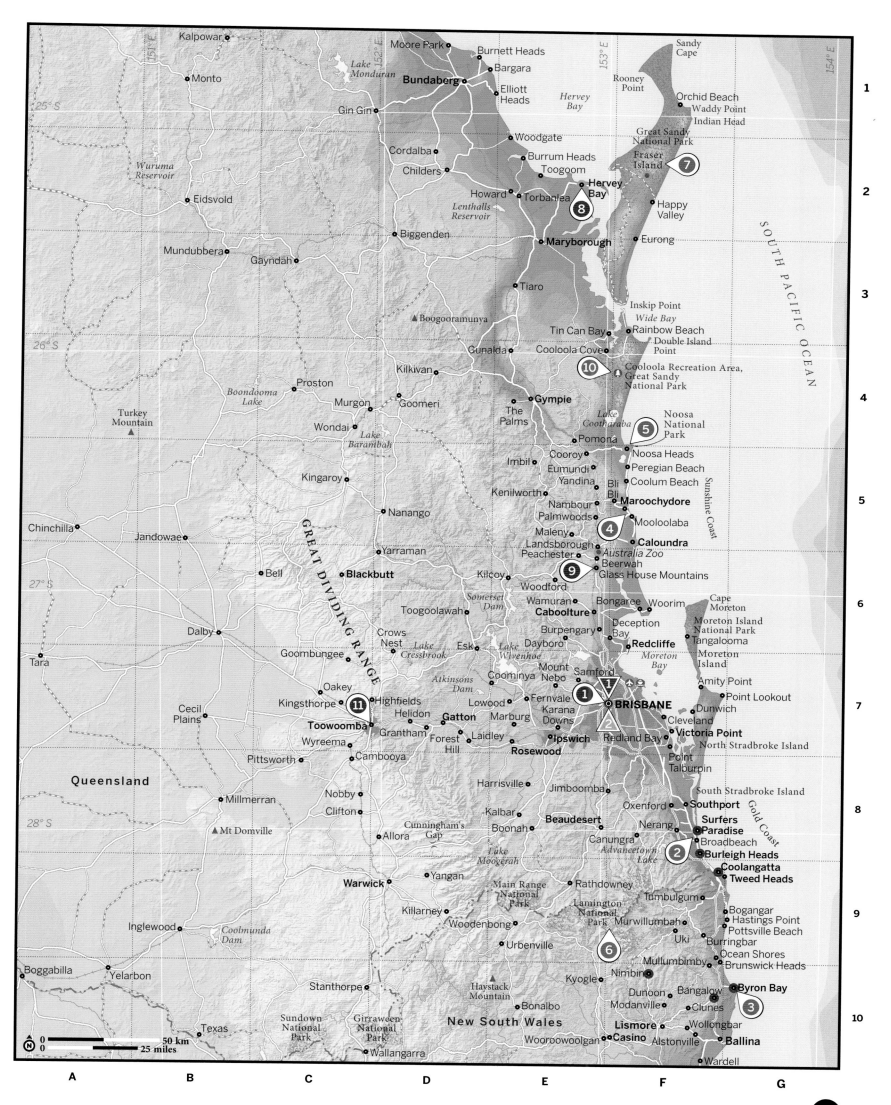

Kalpowar

Monto

Lake
Monduran

Moore Park

Burnett Heads

Bargara

Bundaberg

Elliott
Heads

Gin Gin

*Hervey
Bay*

Sandy
Cape

Rooney
Point

Orchid Beach
Waddy Point
Indian Head

Eidsvold

Wuruma
Reservoir

Woodgate

Cordalba

Childers

Burrum Heads
Toogoom

Great Sandy
National Park
Fraser
Island

⟨7⟩

Mundubbera

Gayndah

Howard

Torbanlea

*Lenthalls
Reservoir*

**Hervey
Bay**

⟨8⟩

Happy
Valley

Biggenden

Maryborough

Eurong

Tiaro

Boogooramunya

Turkey
Mountain ▲

*Boondooma
Lake*

Proston

Murgon

Goomeri

Kilkivan

Gunalda

Tin Can Bay

Inskip Point
Wide Bay

Rainbow Beach
Double Island
Point

Cooloola Cove

⟨10⟩

Cooloola Recreation Area,
Great Sandy
National Park

Gympie

Wondai

*Lake
Barambah*

The
Palms

*Lake
Cootharaba*

Noosa
National
Park

⟨5⟩

Pomona

Cooroy

Noosa Heads

Kingaroy

Imbil

Eumundi

Peregian Beach

Kenilworth

Yandina

Coolum Beach

Nanango

Bli
Bli

Nambour

Maroochydore

Palmwoods

⟨4⟩

Mooloolaba

Sunshine Coast

Bell

Yarraman

Maleny

Landsborough

Australia Zoo

Caloundra

Blackbutt

Peachester

Chinchilla

Jandowae

Kilcoy

Beerwah
Glass House Mountains

⟨9⟩

Woodford

*Somerset
Dam*

Wamuran

Bongaree

Woorim

*Cape
Moreton*

GREAT DIVIDING RANGE

Toogoolawah

Caboolture

*Moreton Island
National Park*

Tangalooma

Dalby

Goombungee

Crows
Nest

*Lake
Cressbrook*

Esk

*Lake
Wivenhoe*

Burpengary

Dayboro

Deception
Bay

Redcliffe

Moreton
Island

*Moreton
Bay*

Tara

Coominya

Mount
Nebo

Samford

⟨1⟩

Amity Point

Oakey

Kingsthorpe

⟨11⟩

Highfields

*Atkinsons
Dam*

Lowood

Fernvale

Karana
Downs

⟨1⟩

BRISBANE

Point Lookout

Dunwich

Cecil
Plains

Helidon

Gatton

Marburg

⟨2⟩

Cleveland

Toowoomba

Grantham

Forest
Hill

Laidley

Victoria Point

North Stradbroke Island

Wyreema

Ipswich

Redland Bay

Pittsworth

Cambooya

Rosewood

Point
Talburpin

Harrisville

Jimboomba

South Stradbroke Island

Nobby

Kalbar

Oxenford

Southport

Millmerran

Clifton

Cunningham's
Gap

Boonah

Beaudesert

Nerang

**Surfers
Paradise**

Gold Coast

Mt Domville ▲

Allora

Canungra

Broadbeach

⟨2⟩

Burleigh Heads

*Lake
Moogerah*

*Advancetown
Lake*

Coolangatta
Tweed Heads

Queensland

Warwick

Yangan

Main Range
National
Park

Rathdowney

Tumbulgum

Bogangar
Hastings Point
Pottsville Beach

Killarney

Woodenbong

*Lamington
National
Park*

Murwillumbah

Uki

Burringbar
Ocean Shores
Brunswick Heads

Inglewood

*Coolmunda
Dam*

Urbenville

⟨6⟩

Mullumbimby

Kyogle

Nimbin

Dunoon

Bangalow

Byron Bay

Boggabilla

Yelarbon

Stanthorpe

Haystack
Mountain

Bonalbo

Modanville

Clunes

⟨3⟩

Texas

Sundown
National
Park

Girraween
National
Park

New South Wales

Lismore
Casino

Wollongbar

Alstonville

Ballina

Wooroowoolgan

Wallangarra

Wardell

SOUTH PACIFIC OCEAN

0   50 km
0   25 miles

N

1

2

3

4

5

6

7

8

9

10

A   B   C   D   E   F   G

SIGHTS & ACTIVITIES

 SEE

 DO

ITINERARY

 1

 2

Blue Mountains: The Three Sisters rock formation above Jamison Valley.

1 Blue Mountains National Park

Beginning 65km inland from Sydney, these mountains are named after the slate-coloured haze exuded by the eucalypts that cloak the landscape. There are eight conservation areas, offering excellent bushwalks (hikes), Aboriginal engravings and countless canyons and cliffs.

2 Hunter Valley

The Hunter is one big gorge fest: gourmet restaurants, beer, chocolate, cheese, olives and above all, wine. Its vineyards are refreshingly attitude-free, making the valley a popular weekend getaway for Sydney city-dwellers.

3 Snowy Mountains

The 'Snowies' form part of the Great Dividing Range along the NSW–Victoria border. They include the highest peak on the Australian mainland, Mt Kosciuszko (2228m). This is Australia's only true alpine area; skiing is usually possible from June until October at resorts such as Thredbo (although mountain bikers now take to the slopes in summer). Hikers are spoiled for choice, with routes lacing the region, including to the summit of Mt Kosciuszko.

4 Warrumbungle National Park

Just 35km west of Coonabarabran, this 232-sq-km park has spectacular granite domes, bushwalking trails, plentiful wildlife and brilliant wildflowers during spring. It's one of NSW's most beautiful parks, although a bushfire swept through in 2013. It's also Australia's first Dark Sky Park.

5 Montague Island (Baranguba)

Nine kilometres offshore from Narooma, this small, pest-free island is home to seabirds and fur seals. Little penguins nest here, especially from September to February, while seals (and whales) are most numerous from September to November. Informative guided tours are conducted by the island's park rangers.

6 Jervis Bay

This large, sheltered bay combines snow-white sand, crystalline waters, dolphins and migrating whales, which visit from May to November. In 1995 the Aboriginal community won a land claim in the Wreck Bay area and now jointly administers Booderee National Park at the southern end of the bay.

7 Wollemi National Park

In 1994 a tree long thought extinct was discovered in a gorge in this national park. It was a Wollemi pine, a member of a 200-million-year-old plant family; the last fossil record of the Wollemi pine dates from around two million years ago. Today you can see Wollemi pines in botanic gardens around the world, but there's no subsitute for exploring this park and imagining dinosaurs around the next corner.

8 Eden

Eden's origins are as a whaling town, but now that the migrating humpback whales and southern right whales are left in peace, this has become one of Australia's best whale-watching locations. Whales can often be seen during their southern migration during September, October and November.

9 Ben Boyd National Park

Ben Boyd was an entrepreneur who failed spectacularly to build an empire around Eden in 1850. This 105-sq-km park protects some of his follies, along with a coastline peppered with beaches. Scenic highlights include the Disaster Bay lookout and Green Cape Lightstation.

10 Canberra

Australia's youthful capital was founded in 1913, designed by American architect Walter Burley Griffin as a model city with open public spaces and broad boulevards. Highlights are the National Gallery of Australia, the National Portrait Gallery and the Australian Parliament House (which can be toured). Hike (or drive) up Mt Ainslie for an eagle's eye view of the city and its geometry.

11 Namadgi National Park

From the Ngunnawal word for the mountains southwest of Canberra, this national park offers bushwalking, biking, fishing and horse riding, along with the opportunity to view Aboriginal rock art.

1 7-day itinerary
South of Sydney

This driving tour covers the coast south of NSW's main city to the Victorian border. Begin in **Sydney**, taking in the view from the harbour: the gorgeous Sydney Opera House and colossal Sydney Harbour Bridge are unmissable. Heading south, zip through the surprisingly wild **Royal National Park** to the elevated Grand Pacific

Drive, continuing to the lively town of **Wollongong** and its nearby beaches, and the coastal town of **Kiama**. Nearby, the Illawarra Fly Treetop Walk and Zipline traverse the rainforest canopy. Continuing south, meander through the seaside towns of **Ulladulla** and **Narooma**, ending with whale-watching at **Eden** near the Victorian border.

2 14-day itinerary
Sydney to Canberra

From **Sydney**, head west into the **Blue Mountains** along the Bells Line of Road, which runs from North Richmond all the way to Lithgow, and makes a much more scenic alternative to the main highway. Spend a few days in the mountains, visiting pretty towns like **Leura** and **Blackheath**, as well as the busy mountain town of

Katoomba. Circle back through the big city and then head south along the coast, overnighting in **Wollongong** or **Kiama** before veering west through the pretty heritage towns of **Berry** and **Kangaroo Valley**, with sleepy main streets, cafes and craft shops. Continue up into the Southern Highlands, perhaps stopping at **Fitzroy Falls** on

the way to the twin towns of **Bowral** and **Mittagong**, boyhood home of cricketing legend Sir Donald Bradman (the town has an interesting cricketing museum). From here, it's onto the main highway all the way west to **Canberra**, Australia's often overlooked capital, with its sophisticated dining and drinking scene and lots of Arts and Crafts architecture.

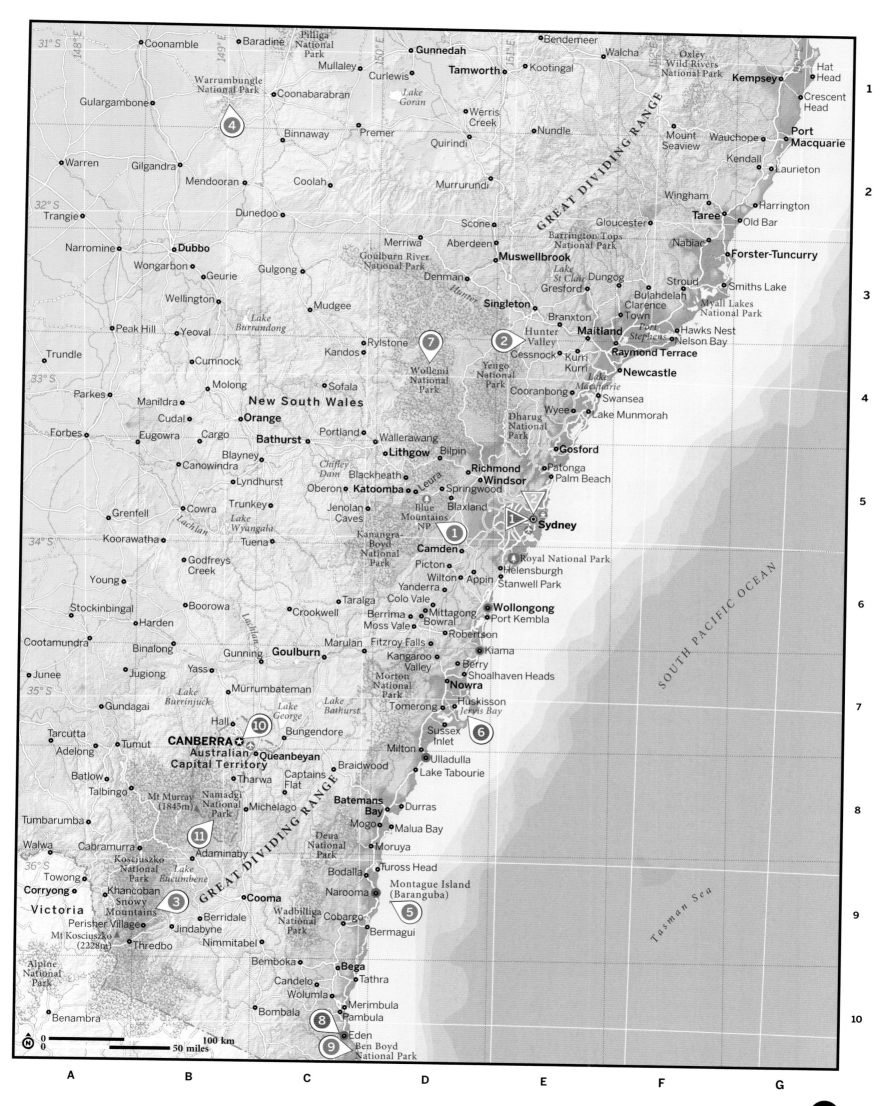

31°S
148°E
149°E
150°E
151°E

Coonamble
Baradine
Pilliga National Park
Bendemeer
Walcha
Oxley Wild Rivers National Park
Kempsey
Hat Head
1

Gulargambone
Warrumbungle National Park
Mullaley
Curlewis
Gunnedah
Tamworth
Kootingal
Crescent Head

Binnaway
Coonabarabran
Premer
Werris Creek
Nundle
Mount Seaview
Wauchope
Port Macquarie

Warren
Gilgandra
Mendooran
Coolah
Quirindi
Murrurundi
Kendall
Laurieton

32°S
Trangie
Dunedoo
Scone
Wingham
Harrington
2

Narromine
Dubbo
Wongarbon
Gulgong
Merriwa
Aberdeen
Barrington Tops National Park
Gloucester
Taree
Old Bar

Geurie
Mudgee
Goulburn River National Park
Denman
Muswellbrook
Lake St Clair
Dungog
Gresford
Stroud
Nabiac
Forster-Tuncurry

Wellington
Hunter
Singleton
Bulahdelah
Clarence Town
Smiths Lake
Myall Lakes National Park
3

Peak Hill
Yeoval
Lake Burrandong
Rylstone
Kandos
Branxton
Maitland
Port Stephens
Hawks Nest

Trundle
Cumnock
Sofala
Wollemi National Park
Hunter Valley
Cessnock
Kurri Kurri
Raymond Terrace
Nelson Bay

Parkes
Molong
Yengo National Park
Newcastle

New South Wales
33°S

Manildra
Orange
Cooranbong
Lake Macquarie
Swansea
4

Forbes
Eugowra
Cargo
Cudal
Bathurst
Portland
Wallerawang
Dharug National Park
Wyee
Lake Munmorah

Blayney
Canowindra
Lyndhurst
Chifley Dam
Blackheath
Lithgow
Bilpin
Gosford

Grenfell
Trunkey
Oberon
Katoomba
Leura
Richmond
Windsor
Springwood
Patonga
Palm Beach
5

Cowra
Lake Wyangala
Jenolan Caves
Blue Mountains NP
Blaxland
Sydney

34°S
Kooarawatha
Tuena
Kanangra-Boyd National Park
Camden
Royal National Park

Young
Godfreys Creek
Picton
Helensburgh
Stanwell Park

Stockinbingal
Boorowa
Crookwell
Taralga
Wilton
Appin
Yanderra
6

Harden
Binalong
Lachlan
Berrima
Colo Vale
Mittagong
Bowral
Wollongong
Port Kembla

Cootamundra
Gunning
Marulan
Moss Vale
Robertson
Kiama

Junee
Jugiong
Yass
Goulburn
Fitzroy Falls
Kangaroo Valley
Berry
Shoalhaven Heads

35°S
Gundagai
Lake Burrinjuck
Murrumbateman
Lake George
Lake Bathurst
Morton National Park
Nowra
Huskisson
7

Tarcutta
Tumut
Hall
Bungendore
Tomerong
Jervis Bay

Adelong
CANBERRA
Queanbeyan
Braidwood
Milton
Sussex Inlet

Batlow
Australian Capital Territory
Tharwa
Captains Flat
Ulladulla
Lake Tabourie
8

Talbingo
Mt Murray (1845m)
Namadgi National Park
Michelago
Batemans Bay
Durras

Tumbarumba
Adaminaby
Deua National Park
Mogo
Malua Bay

Walwa
Cabramurra
Kosciuszko National Park
Lake Eucumbene
Moruya

36°S
Corryong
Khancoban
Snowy Mountains
Berridale
Cooma
Wadbilliga National Park
Bodalla
Tuross Head
Montague Island (Baranguba)

Victoria
Perisher Village
Jindabyne
Cobargo
Narooma
9

Mt Kosciuszko (2228m)
Thredbo
Nimmitabel
Bermagui

Alpine National Park
Bemboka
Bega

Candelo
Tathra

Benambra
Bombala
Wolumla
Merimbula
Pambula

GREAT DIVIDING RANGE

SOUTH PACIFIC OCEAN

Tasman Sea

N
0   100 km
0   50 miles

Eden
Ben Boyd National Park
10

A   B   C   D   E   F   G

SIGHTS &
ACTIVITIES

◉ SEE

◉ DO

ITINERARY

▽ 1

▽ 2

Great Ocean Road

Running along Victoria's southern coastine, this highway zooms past world-class surfing breaks, pockets of rainforest and quiet seaside towns. The limestone pillars known as the Twelve Apostles are a dramatic feature, along with the lighthouse at Cape Otway. Wild koalas can often be seen in the eucalyptus trees around here.

Grampians National Park

Rising from the western Victorian plains, the rocky Grampians are a haven for bushwalkers, rock climbers and nature lovers. Explorer Major Thomas Mitchell named the ranges after the mountains in Scotland, but long before he arrived, Aboriginal people painted rock art in the area's many caves.

Phillip Island

This small island is best-known for the parade of penguins (the world's smallest, Eudyptula minor), which waddle out of the ocean into their sandy burrows every night. The island also has great surf beaches, several wildlife parks and a MotoGP circuit.

Sovereign Hill, Ballarat

For a brief time in the mid-19th century, more than a third of the world's gold came out of Victoria. This attraction in Ballarat presents the town as it would have looked in the 1860s; much of the equipment is original, as is the mine shaft, and you can try your hand at gold-pannning.

Wilsons Promontory

The Prom, as it's affectionately known, is the southernmost section of mainland Australia, and once formed part of a land bridge to Tasmania. It's now a national park with more than 80km of walking tracks, swimming and surf beaches and abundant wildlife.

Mornington Peninsula

The boot-shaped land between Port Phillip Bay and Western Port Bay has been Melbourne's summer playground since the 1870s. Today, much of the farmland has been replaced by vineyards and orchards – but it retains areas of native bushland, too.

Murray River

At 2400km, the mighty Murray River is Australia's longest inland waterway, and arrayed along its banks are some of Victoria's most historic towns. Australia's earliest explorers travelled along the river, and later, paddle steamers plied its waterways. It's now known for wineries, orchards, bush camping, and river red gum forests.

Gippsland Lakes

This area of lakes forms the largest inland waterway system in Australia, with the three main interconnecting lakes – Wellington, King and Victoria – stretching from Sale to beyond Lakes Entrance. The lakes are actually saltwater lagoons, separated from the ocean by the Gippsland Lakes Coastal Park and the strip of sand dunes known as Ninety Mile Beach.

⑨

The High Country

The Great Dividing Range – Australia's eastern mountain spine – curls around eastern Victoria, peaking in the spectacular High Country. It's a mountain playground, attracting skiers and snowboarders in winter and bushwalkers and mountain bikers in summer. The 94km Murray to Mountains Rail Trail is a great way to explore the scenery.

10-day itinerary
The Great Ocean Road

The Great Ocean Road is one of Australia's best road trips. The road begins in earnest at **Torquay**, one of the world's great surf capitals, and the gateway to the legendary swells of **Bells Beach**. Further down the coast, drop in at **Anglesea** then tour the lighthouse at **Aireys Inlet** before stopping for a night or two in **Lorne**, with its fine beach and

waterfalls. Detour to **Kennett River** for koala-spotting, then relax around **Apollo Bay** for a night or two. Look out for koalas and visit the lighthouse at **Cape Otway**, then it's on to **Port Campbell National Park** and the Twelve Apostles before overnighting in **Port Campbell**. Look for whales off the coast of **Warrnambool**, and finish in quaint **Port Fairy**.

14-day itinerary
Gold Fever

This trip explores the once-prosperous towns of Victoria's gold country, via the the otherworldly Grampians. You'll need your own transport. Begin in **Halls Gap**, a central base for hiking amongst the sandstone and granite rock formations of the the **Grampians National Park**. From here, drive north and enter the gold country via the

former mining town of **Castlemaine**, a picturesque place with late 19th-century architecture, attractive gardens and great nightlife. Next comes **Maldon**, a well-preserved relic of the gold-rush era, with many fine buildings constructed from local stone. Detour north to **Bendigo**, which boasts one of Victoria's finest regional art galleries and an

excellent museum exploring the town's Chinese heritage (the undoubted highlights are the imperial dragons, including Old Loong, the oldest in the world). End the trip in **Ballarat**, another historic gold town with a superb art gallery, stunning streetscapes and the fascinating Sovereign Hill historic park, which really brings the gold rush era to life.

SIGHTS &
ACTIVITIES

◉ SEE

◉ DO

ITINERARY

▽ 1

▽ 2

Kangaroo Island

A booming destination for wilderness and wildlife fans, KI is a veritable zoo of seals, birds, dolphins, echidnas and (of course) kangaroos. The island remains rurally paced and underdeveloped; wine and fresh produce is a highlight.

Flinders Ranges National Park

'The Flinders' is an ancient range of peaks and escarpments rising north of Port Augusta for 400km to Mt Hopeless. Before Europeans, the Flinders were prized by the Adnyamathanha peoples for their ochre deposits, which had medicinal and ritual uses. The colours are remarkable, shifting from mauve mornings to midday chocolates and ochre sunsets.

Adelaide

Once known as the staid 'City of Churches', Adelaide has become a much livelier place in recent years, with great galleries, markets, gardens, bars and, of course, one of the world's prettiest cricket grounds, the Adelaide Oval. Adelaide especially excels at food and wine – check out the National Wine Centre of Australia near the Botanic Garden. For arts and culture, the Art Gallery of South Australia is in a beautiful location, and don't forget to mark the Adelaide Fringe festival and the WOMADelaide music festival in your diary.

Eyre Peninsula

The vast, straw-coloured triangle of Eyre Peninsula is Australia's big-sky country. The wild western flank is an important breeding ground for

Kangaroo Island:
The sheltered, shallow waters of Snelling Beach on Kangaroo Island's north coast.

Australian sea lions, great white sharks and southern right whales – Head of Bight is a great place to spot them. The Coffin Bay National Park has wild, remote beaches that can only be reached by 4WD.

Clare Valley

Wine buffs should barrel through Barossa to reach the cool, green plateau of the Clare Valley, where some of the world's most highly regarded Riesling (and not to mention excellent cool-climate Shiraz) is made. It's an idyllic place to explore family-owned cellar doors, aided by the Riesling and Rattler Trails if pedal power is preferred. Some of the key wineries include Grosset, Skillogalee, Adelina and Jim Barry.

Yorke Peninsula

For history buffs, the northwestern end of boot-shaped 'Yorkes' – just under two hours northwest of Adelaide – has a trio of towns called the Copper Triangle: Moonta (the mine), Wallaroo (the smelter) and Kadina (the service town). Settled by Cornish miners, this area drove the regional economy following a copper boom in the 1860s.

Mannum

The unofficial houseboat capital of the world is a pretty town on the Murray River, about 30km upstream from Murray Bridge. This broad, slow-swirling river is part of Australian legend. It flows from the Australian Alps to its mouth south of Adelaide. Renting a houseboat to meander along a stretch of the river is a popular way to pass a weekend; most towns along the river here offer houseboats.

Shiraz Trail

This 8km walking/cycling track runs through the renowned wine country of McLaren Vale, following an old railway line to Willunga. The trail continues another 29km to Marino Rocks as the Coast to Vines Rail Trail. There are plenty of fantastic local vineyards to visit, including Wirra Wirra, Woodstock and Chapel Hill.

Naracoorte Caves National Park

For more than half a million years, fossilized animal bones have accumulated in the 28 limestone caves here, creating one of the world's most important fossil records. Many of the caves also contain impressive stalactites and stalagmites, while the Wonambi Fossil Centre recreates the rainforest that covered this area 200,000 years ago.

Robe

Robe is a cherubic little fishing port that's become a very popular holiday hotspot for Adelaidians and Melburnians. It's known for its food and wine (especially around the up-and-coming Mount Benson Wine Region), and the Little Dip Conservation Park features lakes, wetlands, dunes, and beaches.

10-day itinerary
Fine Wines and the Flinders Ranges

This short trip allows you to experience South Australia's main city as well as its finest wines. As ever, a car is pretty much essential. After spending a few days exploring the eat-streets and old stone pubs of **Adelaide**, head north to the **Barossa Valley** to taste some of the area's world-beating red wines; if you're here on a Saturday, you can also visit the Barossa morning market. Tour through the **Clare Valley** for sweet rieslings and mineral-rich reds, then head on to hike in the rust-coloured **Flinders Ranges National Park**. A central feature is the 80-sq-km expanse of **Ikara** (Wilpena Pound), a sunken elliptical valley ringed by gnarled ridges and semi-desert.

14-day itinerary
Adelaide to Kangaroo Island

This trip heads south of Adelaide along the Fleurieu Peninsula, a popular weekend retreat for city-dwellers in search of some beach time. Start in **Adelaide**, allowing at least two days to see the city sights, then travel out to seek some of the beaches dotted around the Gulf St Vincent, from suburban Christies Beach onto Maslin Beach and Port Willunga, the best swimming spot along this stretch of coast. Detour inland to **McLaren Vale** – a renowned wine region producing vintages every bit as good as the better-known Barossa Valley. If you like, stop also in **Willunga**, an arty town with some excellent restaurants and a great farmers market. Continue southwest via the white-sand beach of **Carrickalinga** en route to **Cape Jervis**, where you can catch a ferry over to **Kangaroo Island**. Spot seals at **Seal Bay**, visit wineries wineries in **Penneshaw** and on the **Dudley Peninsula**, and check out the rock formations and remote lighthouses of **Flinders Chase National Park**, on the island's west tip.

© Greg Brave / Shutterstock

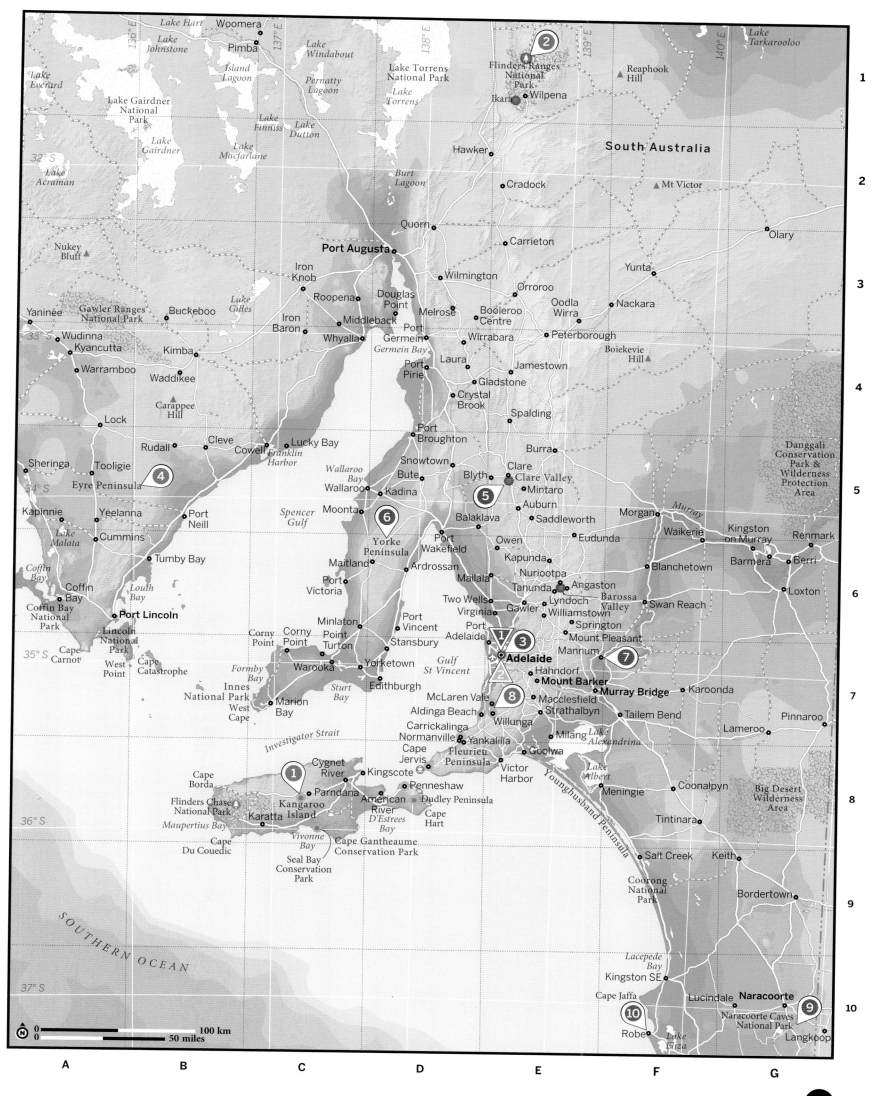

Lake Tarkarooloo

Lake Hart Woomera

Pimba

Lake Johnstone

Island Lagoon

Lake Windabout

Lake Torrens National Park

Flinders Ranges National Park

Reaphook Hill

②

Lake Everard

Lake Gairdner National Park

Pernatty Lagoon

Lake Torrens

Ikara Wilpena

1

Lake Acraman

Lake Finniss

Lake Dutton

Lake Macfarlane

Burt Lagoon

South Australia

Hawker

Cradock

Mt Victor

2

Quorn

Carrieton

Olary

Nukey Bluff

Port Augusta

Wilmington

Yunta

3

Iron Knob

Orroroo

Oodla Wirra

Nackara

Yaninee

Gawler Ranges National Park

Buckeboo

Lake Gilles

Roopena

Douglas Point

Melrose

Booleroo Centre

Peterborough

Boiekevie Hill

Wudinna Kyancutta

Iron Baron

Middleback

Whyalla

Port Germein

Wirrabara

Jamestown

Danggali Conservation Park & Wilderness Protection Area

Warramboo

Waddikee

Germein Bay

Laura

4

Carappee Hill

Port Pirie

Gladstone

Spalding

Crystal Brook

Lock

Burra

Rudall Cleve

Cowell

Lucky Bay

Franklin Harbor

Port Broughton

Snowtown

Clare

Sheringa Tooligie

Eyre Peninsula

④

Wallaroo Bay

Bute

Blyth

Clare Valley

Mintaro

Morgan

Murray

5

Kapinnie Yeelanna

Port Neill

Wallaroo

Kadina

Balaklava

Auburn

Saddleworth

Waikerie

Kingston on Murray

Renmark

Lake Malata

Cummins

Spencer Gulf

Moonta

⑥

Owen

Eudunda

Barmera

Berri

Coffin Bay

Tumby Bay

Louth Bay

Yorke Peninsula

Maitland

Port Wakefield

Kapunda

Nuriootpa

Blanchetown

Loxton

6

Coffin Bay National Park

Coffin Bay

Port Lincoln

Port Victoria

Ardrossan

Mallala

Two Wells

Tanunda Angaston

Barossa Valley

Swan Reach

Lincoln National Park

Cape Carnot

West Point

Minlaton

Stansbury

Port Vincent

Gawler Lyndoch

Virginia

Williamstown

Springton

Springton

Port Adelaide

① ③

Mount Pleasant

⑦

7

Corny Point

Corny Point

Warooka

Yorketown

Point Turton

Edithburgh

Gulf St Vincent

Adelaide

Mannum

Cape Catastrophe

West Cape

Formby Bay

Sturt Bay

②

Hahndorf

Mount Barker

Murray Bridge

Karoonda

Innes National Park

Marion Bay

McLaren Vale

⑧

Macclesfield

Tailem Bend

Lameroo

Pinnaroo

West Cape

Aldinga Beach

Strathalbyn

Carrickalinga

Willunga

Normanville

Yankalilla

Milang

Lake Alexandrina

Cape Jervis

Fleurieu Peninsula

Goolwa

Lake Albert

Coonalpyn

Big Desert Wilderness Area

8

Cape Borda

Cygnet River

Kingscote

Penneshaw

Victor Harbor

Meningie

①

Flinders Chase National Park

Parndana

American River

Dudley Peninsula

Younghusband Peninsula

Tintinara

Karatta

Kangaroo Island

D'Estrees Bay

Cape Hart

Maupertius Bay

Vivonne Bay

Cape Gantheaume Conservation Park

Salt Creek

Keith

Cape Du Couedic

Seal Bay Conservation Park

Coorong National Park

Bordertown

9

Lacepede Bay

Kingston SE

SOUTHERN OCEAN

Cape Jaffa

Lucindale

Naracoorte

⑨

⑩

Naracoorte Caves National Park

10

Robe

Lake Eliza

Langkoop

A B C D E F G

SIGHTS &
ACTIVITIES

◉ SEE

◉ DO

ITINERARY

▽ 1

▽ 2

① Alice Springs

This quintessential outback town won't win a beauty contest, but it serves as the gateway to Uluru-Kata Tjuta National Park and the rugged MacDonnell Ranges. Activities here range from stargazing to outback desert safaris. It's also a good place to learn about Aboriginal Australia.

② Uluru (Ayers Rock)

Probably Australia's most recognisable landmark, the hulking mountain of Uluru is 3.6km long and rises a towering 348m from the surrounding scrubland (867m above sea level).

Sacred Aboriginal sites are located around the base of Uluru; entry is restricted by Anangu law.

③ Kata Tjuta (the Olgas)

About 35km west of Uluru, this striking group of 36 domed boulders stand shoulder to shoulder, forming deep valleys and steep-sided gorges. Kata Tjuta means 'many heads'; the tallest rock, Mt Olga (546m) is about 200m higher than Uluru.

④ Kings Canyon

The yawning chasm of Kings Canyon in Watarrka National Park is one of central Australia's most dramatic natural features. The 100m-high walls are extraordinarily smooth, and above the canyon rim are fascinating 'beehive' formations.

⑤ Coober Pedy

This remote town became an opal-mining mecca a century ago, and it's now a rather unlikely tourist draw thanks to its fabulously desolate desert landscape. It's also a favourite location for film-makers, who've come here to shoot end-of-the-world epics like *Mad Max III*, *Red Planet*, *Ground Zero* and *Pitch Black*.

⑥ MacDonnell Ranges

The weather-beaten MacDonnell Ranges, stretching 400km across the desert, are a hidden world of gorges, rare wildlife and Aboriginal heritage, all within a day's travel from Alice Springs. Hike through the gorge of Standley Chasm, and see more than 12,000 red cabbage palms in the out-of-the-way Palm Valley.

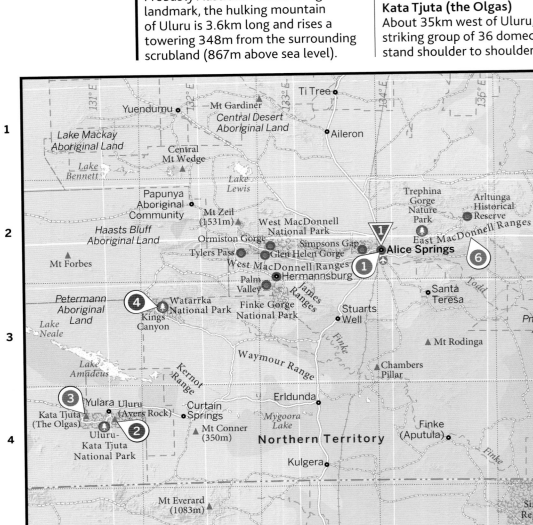

▽ 14-day itinerary
The Red Centre

This is the essence of the outback: rocky outcrops; fascinating wildlife; and an endless horizon. You'll need wheels (preferably a 4WD) to make this journey. Start in **Alice Springs**, a frontier town with the trappings of civilisation. Take a day trip along the East MacDonnell Ranges to **Trephina Gorge Nature Park** and **Arltunga Historical Reserve**. Next, head in the opposite direction to explore the West MacDonnells, visiting **Simpsons Gap**, **Ormiston Gorge** and **Glen Helen Gorge** (overnight here). Get an early start and make for **Tylers Pass** for vast views, then loop back to Alice Springs, detouring to **Palm Valley** and **Hermannsburg** along the way. Track south down the Stuart Hwy then west on the Lasseter Hwy to oasis-like **Watarrka National Park** and Kings Canyon. Saving the best until last, make the obligatory pilgrimage to **Uluru-Kata Tjuta National Park**.

© Mmartin / Shutterstock

Darwin

Australia's only tropical capital city, Darwin is closer to Bali than Bondi. The city's cosmopolitan mix – more than 50 nationalities are represented here – is typified by lively markets held throughout the dry season, while museums and galleries explore the area's rich Aboriginal heritage.

Kakadu National Park

Encompassing almost 20,000 sq km within a few hours' drive of Darwin, Kakadu's unique ecosystem contains billabongs bursting with wildlife, especially saltwater crocs and native birds. It's also an important crucible of Aboriginal culture, with 25,000-year-old rock paintings that can be visited with the help of an Indigenous guide.

Katherine Gorge

A series of 13 sandstone gorges have been carved out by the Katherine River on its journey from Arnhem Land to the Timor Sea. Katherine Gorge forms the backbone of the 2920-sq-km Nitmiluk National Park, about 30km from Katherine.

Litchfield National Park

This national park, 115km from Darwin, is a world of striking rock formations,

10-day itinerary
The Top End

This overland route gets you to the heart of the Top End, via some of Australia's finest wild places (you'll definitely need a car). Gone are the days when **Darwin** was a brawling frontier town; right now it's all about museums, galleries of Indigenous art and great food. A few hours south on the Stuart Hwy you'll run into national parks: **Litchfield**, famous for its waterfalls, bush hikes and cooling swimming holes; and World Heritage–listed **Kakadu**, a wetland of international significance, with millennia-old Aboriginal rock art as well as a full line-up of native Australian wildlife. Make sure you pop across the croc-rich East Alligator River to **Gunbalanya (Oenpelli)** for great Aboriginal art. Further south, spend a day in **Katherine**, the regional 'big smoke'. Be sure to have a meal at Marksies Camp Tucker before ending up in **Nitmiluk (Katherine Gorge) National Park**, where the Katherine River cuts its way through thirteen jagged ravines.

high cliffs, waterfalls, great hiking and croc-free swimming. The big attraction is Wangi Falls, which spill into a swimming hole bordered by rainforest.

Broome

Broome clings to a strip of red pindan on the western edge of the Kimberley Range. Surrounded by the mangroves and mudflats of Roebuck Bay, it's a resort town: famous Cable Beach is synonymous with camels, and an evening ride along the sand is a highlight for many visitors.

Dampier Peninsula

Stretching north from Broome, the Dampier Peninsula offers deserted beaches, mangrove bays and crimson cliffs. This remote country is home to the Ngumbarl, Jabirr Jabirr, Nyul Nyul, Nimanburu, Bardi Jawi and Goolarabooloo peoples. Access is by 4WD, along the largely unsealed 215km-long Cape Leveque Rd.

Mimbi Caves

One of the Kimberley's best-kept secrets, this vast subterranean labyrinth sits on Gooniyandi land, 90km southeast of Fitzroy Crossing. The cave walls display significant Aboriginal rock art and some of the most impressive fish fossils in the southern hemisphere. Indigenous-owned Girloorloo Tours runs trips here.

Kings Canyon:
Visitors can climb high on these red cliffs for fabulous aerial views of Watarrka National Park.

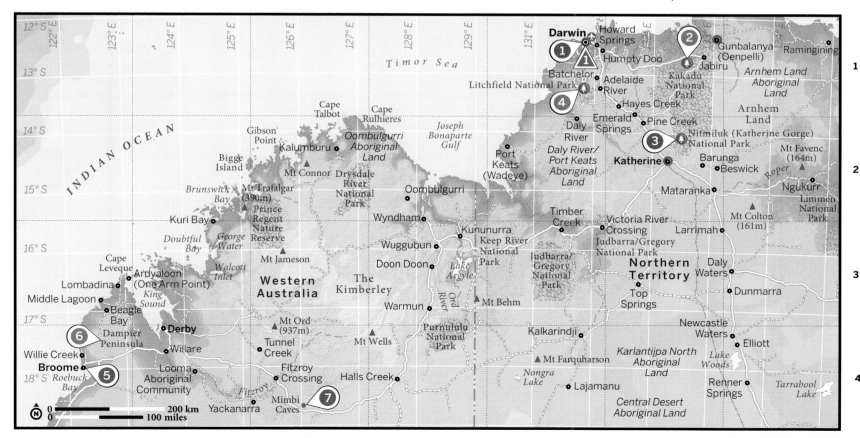

SIGHTS &
ACTIVITIES

 SEE

 DO

ITINERARY

▽ 1

▽ 2

1 Perth
Laid-back, liveable Perth has wonderful weather, beautiful beaches and an easy-going character. Its many attractions include a superb aquarium, the grand sweep of Kings Park and the outstanding Art Gallery of Western Australia, which has a significant indigenous collection.

2 Fremantle
Creative, relaxed and open-minded: Fremantle combines working-class roots with hippie leanings and hipster sensibilities. It's a cosy home for artists, performers and more than a few eccentrics, not to mention a line-up of Victorian and Edwardian buildings, creating a heritage precinct that's unique among Australia's cities.

3 Pinnacles Desert
It could be mistaken for the surface of Mars, but scattered among the dunes of Nambung National Park, thousands of ghostly limestone pillars rise from the plain like a vast, petrified alien army. Staying overnight in nearby Cervantes allows you to experience the full spectrum of colour changes at dawn, sunset and full moon, when most tourists are back in their hotels.

4 Margaret River Wine Region
With vineyard restaurants, artisan food producers and surf beaches, the Margaret River region is worthy of a detour. The best wineries are focused around Cowaramup and Wilyabrup, and the road south to the windswept Cape Leeuwin Lighthouse at Augusta is studded with underground caves.

Rottnest Island:
Seals playing at Cathedral Rocks on Rottnest Island.

5 Monkey Mia
Part of Unesco-protected Shark Bay, this small beach resort is known for its wild Indo-Pacific bottlenose dolphins, which turn up for a feed each morning in the shallow waters offshore. Rangers talk you through the history of the dolphin encounters.

6 Dwellingup
This small, characterful, forest-shrouded township lies on both the Bibbulman Track hiking trail and the Munda Biddi Trail, which meanders from Mundaring to Albany for 1000km, making it one of the world's longest off-road cycling routes. As a result, Dwellingup has become an activity hub, with a Forest Heritage Centre to introduce the local flora and fauna.

7 Valley of the Giants
The area around Walpole is home to some of Australia's largest, oldest and most magnificent tingle trees. A 600m-long ramp rises from the valley, allowing visitors to walk 40m up into the canopy of the giant trees.

8 King George Sound
After whaling ended in 1978, whales slowly began returning to the waters of Albany. Now southern right and humpback whales gather near the bays and coves of King George Sound from July to mid-October. You can sometimes spot them from the beach. Whales migrate along the Western Australia coast from May to December, often coming close to shore. And a Bremer Bay Canyon, east of Albany, the southern hemisphere's largest pod of orca hunts.

9 National Anzac Centre, Albany
Opened for Albany's Anzac centenary commemorations in late 2014, this terrific museum remembers the men and women who left by convoy from Albany to fight in WWI. Excellent multimedia installations provide realism and depth to the exhibitions.

10 Rottnest Island
Although only 19km offshore from Fremantle, 'Rotto' is a car-free slice of paradise, ringed by beaches and bays. Cycling around the 11km-long, 4.5km-wide island, you're bound to spot quokkas, the island's only native land mammals, and perhaps New Zealand fur seals, dolphins and whales.

11 Leeuwin-Naturaliste National Park
Not all national parks in WA are remote: this park is highly accessible. In spring it explodes with colourful wildflowers, including many orchids.

▽1

10-day itinerary
Perth to Shark Bay

Perth is the obvious launch pad for Western Australia. After exploring the city, head north along the coast to otherworldly **Nambung National Park**, home to the rock formations of the Pinnacles Desert. Next, it's out along the **Batavia Coast**, littered with shipwrecks and rich in marine life. Break the drive with beach time around

Dongara-Port Denison, then allow yourself a day or two to explore sun-drenched **Geraldton**, surrounded by excellent beaches. If you wish, stop off in the seaside towns of **Horrocks** and **Port Gregory** en route to see the soaring cliffs and gorges of **Kalbarri National Park**. End by communing with dolphins at Shark Bay's **Monkey Mia**.

▽2

14-day itinerary
From Coast to Forest and Back

Start in **Perth** and exhaust all of your urban urges in its great pubs, galleries, bars and restaurants. Be sure to fit in an afternoon in the relaxed port of **Fremantle**, south of the city. Then head south via the stunning beaches of **Cape Naturaliste**, before camping out in **Margaret River** (a three-hour hop from Perth). Go surfing and winery-hopping

before continuing south to **Augusta** and magnificent **Cape Leeuwin**, where whales drop by. Meander through the giant old-growth forests of the southwest and rest a while in **Pemberton**. Take time to sample its excellent chardonnays and pinot noirs and at least a day or two to explore the nearby national parks. Continue

east to the peaceful inlet of **Walpole**: a great base for the Walpole Wilderness Area and the Valley of the Giants. For some well-earned beach time, head to **Denmark** where the **William Bay National Park** offers sheltered swimming, before finishing in **Albany** with its historic architecture, world-class diving and moving Anzac Museum.

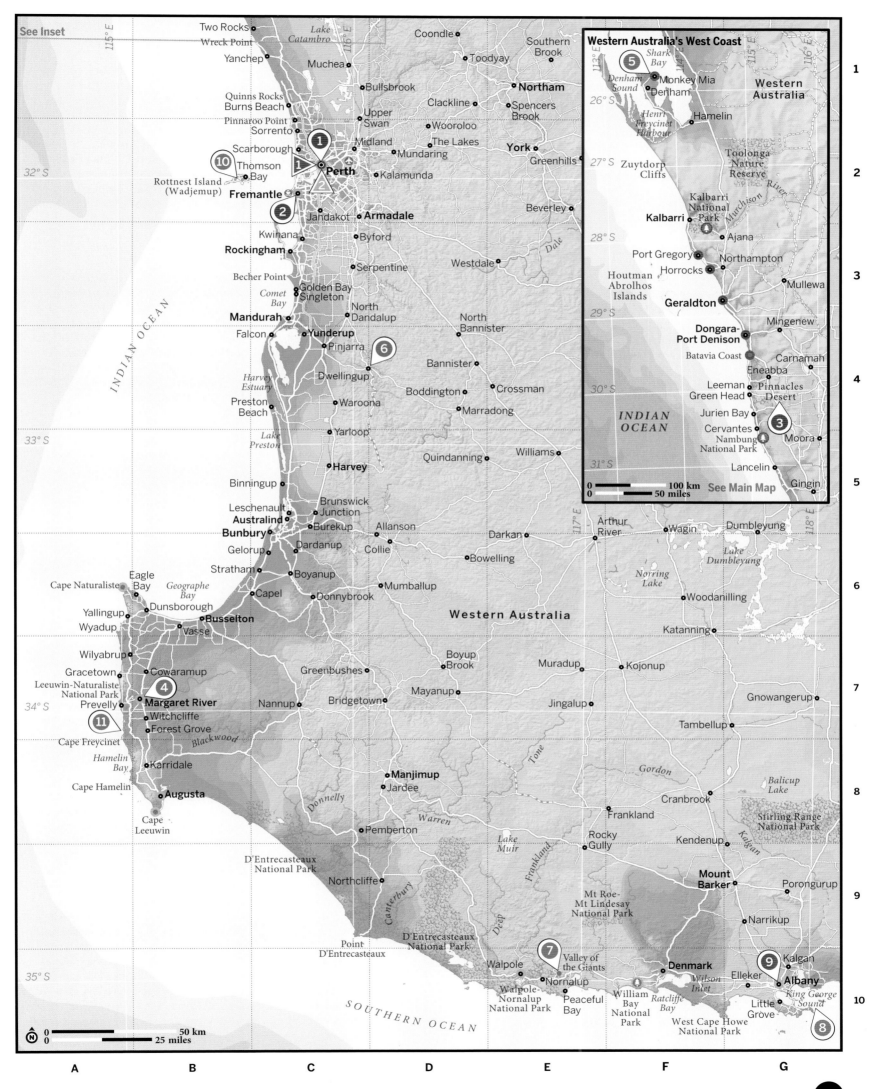

See Inset

115° E

116° E

Two Rocks
Wreck Point
Yanchep
Muchea
Lake Catambro
Coondle
Southern Brook
Toodyay

Quinns Rocks
Burns Beach
Bullsbrook
Northam
Clackline
Spencers Brook
Pinnaroo Point
Sorrento
Upper Swan
Wooroloo
The Lakes
York
Scarborough
Midland
Mundaring
Greenhills
1
Thomson Bay
Perth
Kalamunda
Rottnest Island (Wadjemup)
Fremantle
Jandakot
Armadale
Beverley
2
Kwinana
Byford
Rockingham
Serpentine
Westdale
Becher Point
Golden Bay
Singleton
North Dandalup
North Bannister
Comet Bay
Mandurah
Yunderup
Pinjarra
6
Falcon
Dwellingup
Bannister
Crossman
Harvey Estuary
Waroona
Boddington
Preston Beach
Yarloop
Marradong
Lake Preston
Quindanning
Williams
32° S
33° S
Harvey
Binningup
Brunswick Junction
Allanson
Leschenault
Australind
Burekup
Darkan
Bunbury
Gelorup
Dardanup
Collie
Bowelling
Stratham
Boyanup
Mumballup
6
Cape Naturaliste
Eagle Bay
Geographe Bay
Capel
Donnybrook
Western Australia
Yallingup
Dunsborough
Wyadup
Busselton
Vasse
Greenbushes
Boyup Brook
Muradup
Kojonup
Wilyabrup
Gracetown
Cowaramup
Greenbushes
Mayanup
Leeuwin-Naturaliste National Park
Prevelly
4
Margaret River
Nannup
Bridgetown
Jingalup
11
Witchcliffe
Forest Grove
34° S
Cape Freycinet
Blackwood
Hamelin Bay
Karridale
Manjimup
Jardee
Cape Hamelin
Augusta
Donnelly
Warren
Cape Leeuwin
Pemberton
D'Entrecasteaux National Park
Northcliffe
Lake Muir
Rocky Gully
Canterbury
Point D'Entrecasteaux
D'Entrecasteaux National Park
35° S
SOUTHERN OCEAN
Walpole
7
Valley of the Giants
Nornalup
Walpole-Nornalup National Park
Peaceful Bay
William Bay National Park
Denmark
Mount Barker
Cranbrook
Stirling Range National Park
Kendenup
Porongurup
Narrikup
Mt Roe-Mt Lindesay National Park
Albany
Little Grove
West Cape Howe National Park

INDIAN OCEAN

Western Australia's West Coast

5
Shark Bay
Denham Sound
Monkey Mia
Denham
26° S
Hamelin
Henri Freycinet Harbour
Zuytdorp Cliffs
Western Australia
Toolonga Nature Reserve
27° S
Kalbarri
Kalbarri National Park
Ajana
Port Gregory
Northampton
Horrocks
Mullewa
Houtman Abrolhos Islands
28° S
Geraldton
Mingenew
Dongara-Port Denison
Batavia Coast
Carnamah
Eneabba
29° S
Leeman
Green Head
Pinnacles Desert
Jurien Bay
3
Cervantes
Nambung National Park
Moora
INDIAN OCEAN
30° S
Lancelin
Gingin
31° S

0 ___ 100 km
0 ___ 50 miles
See Main Map

SIGHTS & ACTIVITIES

 SEE

 DO

ITINERARY

 1

 2

1 Hobart

Hobart is Australia's southernmost state capital and Tasmania's most cosmopolitan town. Don't miss history-rich Battery Point, the Saturday-morning Salamanca Market, and the astonishing MONA (Museum of Old & New Art), where ancient antiquities are provocatively displayed beside contemporary works.

2 Port Arthur Historic Site

In 1830 Governor Arthur chose Port Arthur as a 'natural penitentiary' to confine prisoners who had committed further crimes in the colony. Connected to the mainland by Eaglehawk Neck, its poignant sites include the Isle of the Dead cemetery and the much-feared Separate Prison, built to punish prisoners through isolation and sensory deprivation.

3 Franklin River

Rafting the wild Franklin River in Tasmania's remote southwest may be the ultimate wilderness journey. River trips here involve up to 10 days on the water, navigating white water rapids through deep gorges, sleeping at backcountry forest camps.

4 Freycinet National Park

Freycinet is a photogenic assembly of pink granite mountains, azure bays and white-sand beaches (including the much-photographed Wineglass Bay). The park was named after French navigator Louis de Freycinet and proclaimed in 1916, making it (along with Mt Field) Tasmania's oldest national park. Black cockatoos, yellow

Cradle Mountain:
A boatshed on Tasmania's Dove Lake, overlooked by Cradle Mountain beyond.

wattlebirds, honeyeaters and Bennett's wallabies bounce between the bushes.

5 Bay of Fires (Larapuna)

Larapuna/Bay of Fires is a 29km-long sweep of powder-white sand that's featured on plenty of 'Most Beautiful Beaches in the World' lists. To refer to the Bay of Fires as one beach, though, is a mistake: it's actually a string of them, studded by lagoons and headlands, backed by coastal bush.

6 Bathurst Harbour

In Tasmania's deep south, the hushed, mirror-still waterways of Bathurst Harbour and Port Davey are a watery wilderness of tannin creeks, white quartzite beaches and underwater kelp forests. You can fly in by light plane to the gravel airstrip at Melaleuca – an adventure in itself – then kayak and camp your way around.

7 Bruny Island

Windswept Bruny Island is a sparsely populated microcosm of Tasmania. Plentiful wildlife includes penguins, seals and marine birds, but the island has become known for its food scene, producing handmade cheeses, oysters, smoked seafood, fudge, berry products, craft beer, and wines from Australia's most southerly vineyard.

8 Cradle Mountain

A precipitous comb of rock carved out by millennia of ice and wind, crescent-shaped Cradle Mountain is Tasmania's most recognisable mountain peak. For unbelievable panoramas over Tasmania's alpine heart, take the all-day hike (and scramble) to the summit and back. The Overland Track, Tasmania's legendary six-day alpine hike, starts here and ends at Lake St Clair.

9 Tasman Peninsula

An epic trail on the Tasman Peninsula southeast of Hobart, the Three Capes Track takes hikers on a four-day, 46km cliff-top tour from Port Arthur Historic Site to Cape Pillar, Cape Hauy and Fortescue Bay. Accommodation en route is in architect-designed huts; reservations are needed.

10 Maria Island National Park

A ferry ride off the East Coast, Maria Island is like an island zoo without the fences. On bushwalks here you might spot wombats, kangaroos, pademelons, echidnas, Tasmanian devils or a forty-spotted pardalote, one of Tasmania's rarest birds.

11 Stanley

Almost completely encircled by the sea, the little fishing village of Stanley is a tight clutch of heritage buildings sited at the foot of an enormous volcanic 'plug' called the Nut (accessed via trails and a gondola). Maritime heritage abounds here, along with boutique hotels and classy Mod Oz restaurants.

10-day itinerary
Cradle Country

Get started in Tasmania's 'second city', **Launceston**. Check out Cataract Gorge and the Queen Victoria Museum & Art Gallery. From Launceston, explore the **Tamar Valley**: seahorses, gold mines, lighthouses and wineries. Loop south through historic **Evandale** before doing some caving at **Mole Creek Karst**

National Park. Skate southwest via the lunar landscapes of **Queenstown** to ride the West Coast Wilderness Railway to **Strahan**. Head north through the Arthur Pieman Conservation Area to check the surf at **Marrawah**; then clamber up the Nut in north coast **Stanley**. The beach at **Boat Harbour** is the perfect journey's end.

14-day itinerary
Central Tasmania

This tour takes in Tasmania's agricultural heartland as well as its alpine core. Get started in lively **Hobart**, then head northwest to **Mt Field National Park** for waterfalls and bushwalking – just a hint of the vast wilderness beyond. From Mt Field, day trip through the hop fields of the gorgeous **Derwent Valley**, passing

pretty Westerway, little Ellendale and historic Hamilton, before continuing to soporific **Bothwell** in the Central Highlands, where you can tee off at Ratho, Australia's oldest golf course. Back east in the Midlands, you can sip some fine Tasmanian whisky at Redlands Distillery in **Kempton**. **Oatlands** offers more Georgian

sandstone buildings than any other Australian town, and **Campbell Town** makes a handy stop en route to the laid-back city of **Launceston**. Continue north to the chilled-out fishing town of **Bicheno** for some penguin-spotting, then unwind among the rocky lagoons and headlands of the impressive **Bay of Fires (Larapuna)**.

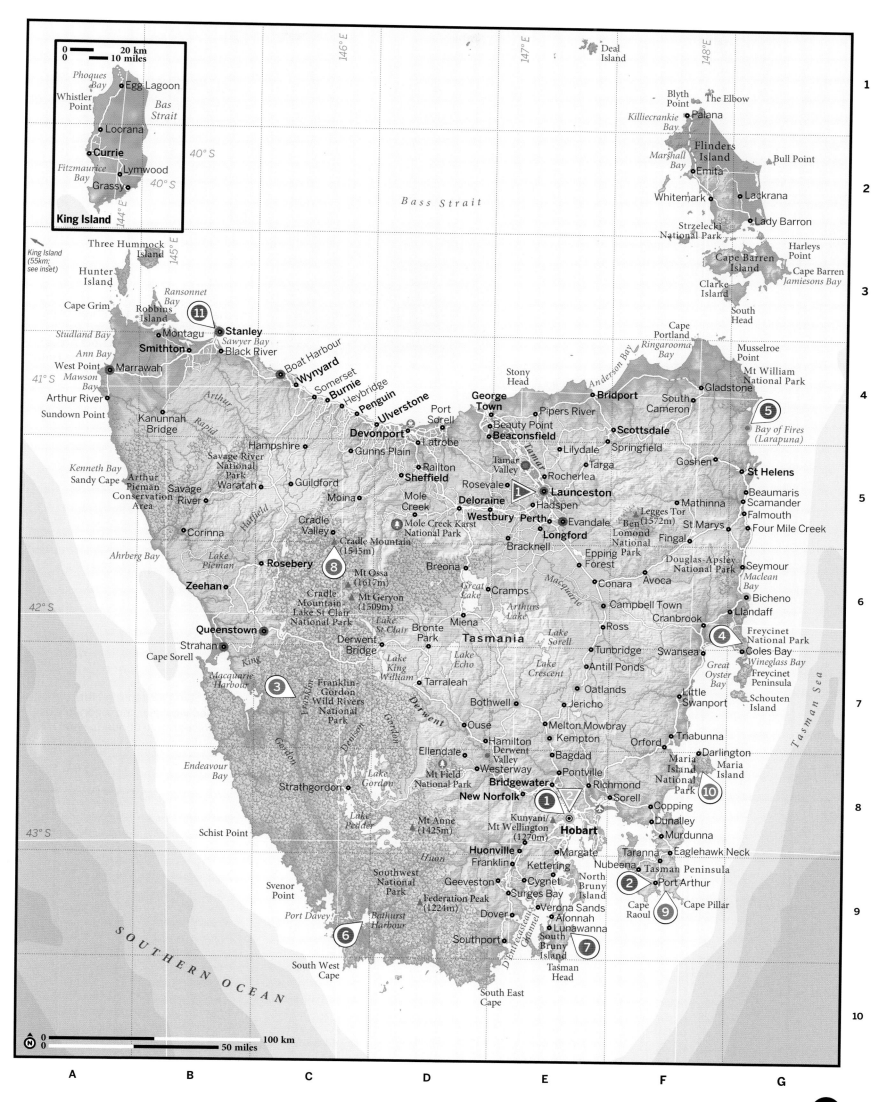

Inset — King Island

0   20 km
0   10 miles

Phoques Bay

Egg Lagoon

Whistler Point

Bas Strait

Loorana

Currie

40° S

Lymwood

Fitzmaurice Bay

Grassy

King Island

Main map

King Island (55km; see inset)

146° E   147° E   148° E

Deal Island

1

Blyth Point   The Elbow

Killiecrankie Bay   Palana

Marshall Bay

Flinders Island

Bull Point

Emita

Bas Strait

Whitemark   Lackrana

2

Strzelecki National Park

Lady Barron

Jamiesons Bay

Cape Barren Island

Harleys Point

Clarke Island

Cape Barren

3

South Head

Three Hummock Island

Hunter Island

Ransonnet Bay

Cape Grim

Robbins Island

Montagu   **Stanley**

Studland Bay   *Sawyer Bay*   Black River

Boat Harbour

Smithton

Wynyard

Somerset

Burnie

Heybridge

Cape Portland

Ringarooma Bay

Musselroe Point

Mt William National Park

41° S

Ann Bay

West Point   Marrawah

Mawson Bay

Arthur River

Sundown Point

Penguin

Ulverstone

Port Sorell

Stony Head

George Town

Pipers River

Beauty Point

Beaconsfield

Bridport

Scottsdale

South Cameron

Gladstone

5

Arthur

Kanunnah Bridge

Savage River National Park

Hampshire

Gunns Plain

Devonport

Latrobe

Springfield

Bay of Fires (Larapuna)

4

Kenneth Bay

Sandy Cape

Arthur Pieman Conservation Area

Savage River

Waratah

Guildford

Moina

Sheffield

Railton

Mole Creek

Deloraine

Lilydale

Rocherlea

Rosevale

Tamar Valley

1

Launceston

Hadspen

Targa

Goshen

St Helens

5

Corinna

Cradle Valley

Cradle Mountain (1545m)

8

Mt Ossa (1617m)

Mole Creek Karst National Park

Westbury   **Perth**

Evandale

Longford

Bracknell

Ben Lomond (1572m)

Legges Tor

St Marys

Beaumaris

Scamander

Falmouth

Four Mile Creek

Ahrberg Bay

Lake Pieman

Rosebery

Mt Geryon (1509m)

Cradle Mountain-Lake St Clair National Park

Breona

Great Lake

Epping Forest

Fingal

Douglas-Apsley National Park

Maclean Bay

Seymour

6

Zeehan

42° S

Queenstown

Strahan

Cape Sorell

Macquarie Harbour

Derwent Bridge

Bronte Park

Lake St Clair

Tasmania

Miena

Cramps

Arthurs Lake

Macquarie

Campbell Town

Ross

Conara

Avoca

Cranbrook

Llandaff

Bicheno

Freycinet National Park

Coles Bay

Wineglass Bay

Freycinet Peninsula

Great Oyster Bay

4

Swansea

Lake Sorell

Tunbridge

Antill Ponds

Little Swanport

Schouten Island

7

King

Franklin-Gordon Wild Rivers National Park

3

Lake King William

Lake Echo

Lake Crescent

Tarraleah

Oatlands

Bothwell

Jericho

Tasman Sea

Endeavour Bay

Gordon

Denison

Gordon

Derwent

Ouse

Hamilton

Derwent Valley

Melton Mowbray

Kempton

Bagdad

Orford

Triabunna

Darlington

Maria Island

Lake Gordon

Strathgordon

Ellendale

Westerway

Mt Field National Park

Pontville

Richmond

Sorell

Maria Island National Park

10

8

Schist Point

Lake Pedder

Mt Anne (1425m)

Bridgewater

New Norfolk

1   2

Kunyani/ Mt Wellington (1270m)

⊙ **Hobart**

Copping

Dunalley

Murdunna

43° S

Huon

Huonville

Franklin

Margate

Kettering

Geeveston

Cygnet

Surges Bay

Taranna

Nubeena

North Bruny Island

Eaglehawk Neck

Tasman Peninsula

Southwest National Park

Federation Peak (1224m)

Dover

Verona Sands

Alonnah

Lunawanna

2

Port Arthur

Cape Raoul

9

Cape Pillar

9

Svenor Point

Port Davey

Bathurst Harbour

6

Southport

D'Entrecasteaux Channel

South Bruny Island

7

Tasman Head

South West Cape

SOUTHERN OCEAN

South East Cape

10

0   100 km
0   50 miles

N

A   B   C   D   E   F   G

SIGHTS & ACTIVITIES

◉ SEE

◉ DO

ITINERARY

▽ 1

▽ 2

Auckland

Regularly dubbed one of the world's most liveable cities, Auckland is set around two harbours, punctuated by volcanic cones and surrounded by fertile farmland. The city's west coast beaches are popular with surfers, while kayakers and sailors explore the many islands of the Hauraki Gulf.

Bay of Islands

Turquoise waters and 150 undeveloped islands make this vast bay north of Auckland popular for many water-based outdoor activities – yachting, big-game fishing, kayaking, diving or cruising around in the company of whales and dolphins. As the site of NZ's first permanent British settlement (at Russell), it is also the birthplace of European colonisation in the country.

Waitomo Caves

Dotted across the Waitomo region are countless shafts dropping into more than 300 mapped cave systems. The best-known is the Glowworm Cave, whose main chamber, The Cathedral, has walls covered with thousands of glowworms. Tours through the tunnels are conducted in subterranean boats.

Rotorua

One of New Zealand's most active volcanic areas, Rotorua is famous for its geysers, bubbling mud and pervasive sulphurous smell. The features of Wai-O-Tapu (Sacred Waters) include the 65m-wide Champagne Pool, the lime-hued Devil's Bath and the 20m-high Lady Knox Geyser.

Wellington: The Wellington Cable Car runs between downtown Wellington and the suburb of Kelburn.

Tongariro Crossing

This popular crossing is lauded as NZ's finest one-day walk with more than 100,000 trampers finishing it yearly. It takes between six to eight hours to complete the 19.4km walk amid steaming vents and springs, rock formations, moonscape basins, scree slopes and vast views – the most memorable across the Emerald Lakes.

Coromandel Peninsula

The Coromandel Peninsula juts into the Pacific east of Auckland, forming the eastern boundary of the Hauraki Gulf. The east coast has some of the North Island's best white-sand beaches, including Cathedral Cove and Hot Water Beach, where you can dig your own natural, geothermally heated pool in the sand.

Hawke's Bay

Wine has been crafted in the Hawke's Bay region since 1851, with dozens of vineyards now joining famous long-standing local wineries such as Mission Estate and Church Road. The emphasis is on excellent Bordeaux-style reds and chardonnay, and many wineries also incorporate good vineyard restaurants.

Napier

Modern Napier is a charismatic city with the air of an affluent English seaside resort – but in 1931 it was all but flattened by a devastating earthquake. Rebuilt in the popular architectural styles of the time, the city retains a unique concentration of art-deco buildings.

Wellington

One of the world's coolest little capitals, windy Wellington is famed for a vibrant arts and music scene, fuelled by excellent espresso and more restaurants per head than New York. Its highlights include a superb history museum, lovely botanical gardens and buildings belonging to New Zealand's national parliament.

Whanganui National Park

Curling 290km from Mt Tongariro to the Tasman Sea, the Whanganui is the longest navigable river in New Zealand. In 2017 it was the first river in the world to became legally recognised as a person, acknowledging its spiritual importance as an ancestor to the Māori people. Visitors traverse it by canoe, kayak, jetboat and bike.

Huka Falls

These dramatic waterfalls mark where NZ's longest river, the Waikato, is slammed into a narrow chasm, making a dramatic 11m drop into a surging crystal-blue pool at a rate of 220,000 litres per second. From the footbridge you can see the full force of this torrent that the Māori called Hukanui (Great Body of Spray).

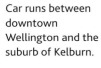

10-day itinerary
The Grand Circuit

Kick off in action-packed **Auckland**, then head the long way round the **Coromandel Peninsula** to explore its beaches and quiet coastal towns. Hold your nose around the bubbling pools of **Rotorua**, stopping overnight at laid-back **Whakatane** before taking the coastal road around isolated **East Cape** to beachy **Gisborne**. At **Napier**, pause

to admire the architecture and acclaimed Hawke's Bay wineries. After a couple of days and nights exploring the capital, **Wellington**, branch out west to **New Plymouth**, a charming city in the shadow of Mt Taranaki, with a brilliant art gallery. Last comes the glowworm-lit **Waitomo Caves** and the chilled-out little surf town of **Raglan**.

14-day itinerary
Central Highlights

This easy route covers a quick circular northern tour from **Auckland**. Ideally it's best done by car. Spend three days in the city exploring its volcanoes, beaches, bars and eateries, and taking day trips to **Waiheke Island** and the west coast beaches. Head north to sleepy **Tutukaka** for a day's diving around the **Poor Knights Islands**.

Continue on to the **Bay of Islands** for a dose of Māori and colonial history, pretty coves and coastal scenery. Drop by **Doubtless Bay** for another lazy beach day and to feast on fish and chips on the wharf at **Mangonui**. The following morning, take a long, leisurely drive up to **Cape Reinga** at the very tip of the country – the most sacred site

in traditional Māori spirituality. Venture south, skirting the windswept expanses of **Ninety Mile Beach**, before hitting Ahipara. Continue south via the Hokianga Harbour and stop for the night at **Opononi**. Allow yourself time to pay homage to the majestic trees of the **Waipoua Forest** before commencing the long, scenic drive back to Auckland.

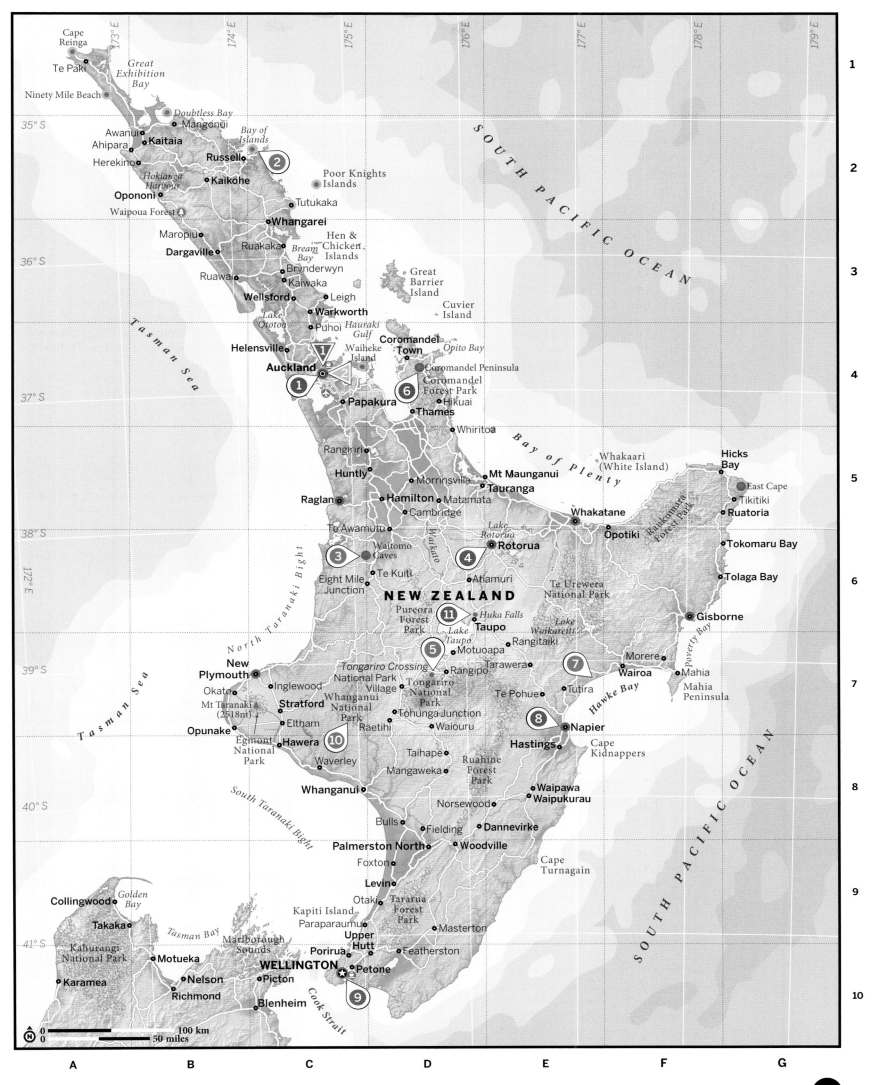

Cape Reinga
Te Paki
Great Exhibition Bay
Ninety Mile Beach
173° E
35° S
Doubtless Bay
Awanui
Mangonui
Ahipara
Kaitaia
Herekino
Bay of Islands
Russell
174° E
2
Kaikohe
Opononi
Hokianga Harbour
Poor Knights Islands
Tutukaka
Waipoua Forest
Whangarei
Maropiu
Hen & Chicken Islands
Dargaville
Bream Bay
36° S
Ruakaka
Brynderwyn
Great Barrier Island
Ruawai
Kaiwaka
175° E
Lake Ototoa
Wellsford
Leigh
Cuvier Island
Warkworth
Puhoi
Hauraki Gulf
Helensville
1
Coromandel Town
Opito Bay
Auckland
Waiheke Island
37° S
6
Coromandel Peninsula
1
Papakura
Coromandel Forest Park
Hikuai
Thames
Whiritoa
Rangiriri
176° E
Bay of Plenty
Whakaari (White Island)
Hicks Bay
Huntly
Morrinsville
Mt Maunganui
East Cape
Tikitiki
Raglan
Hamilton
Matamata
Tauranga
Ruatoria
Cambridge
Whakatane
Te Awamutu
38° S
Lake Rotorua
Ōpotiki
172° E
Waitomo Caves
3
Rotorua
4
Tokomaru Bay
Te Kuiti
NEW ZEALAND
177° E
Eight Mile Junction
Atiamuri
Tolaga Bay
Te Urewera National Park
Pureora Forest Park
Huka Falls
11
Taupo
Lake Waikareiti
Gisborne
5
Lake Taupo
Motuoapa
Rangitaiki
Poverty Bay
39° S
New Plymouth
Tongariro Crossing National Park
Rangipo
Tarawera
7
Morere
Wairoa
Inglewood
Village
Tongariro National Park
Te Pohue
Tutira
Mahia
Okato
Hawke Bay
Mahia Peninsula
Mt Taranaki (2518m)
Stratford
Whanganui National Park
Tohunga Junction
Waiouru
8
Napier
Opunake
Eltham
Raetihi
Hastings
Cape Kidnappers
Egmont National Park
Hawera
10
Taihape
Ruahine Forest Park
Waverley
Mangaweka
178° E
Whanganui
Norsewood
Waipawa
Waipukurau
40° S
South Taranaki Bight
Bulls
Fielding
Dannevirke
Palmerston North
Woodville
Foxton
Cape Turnagain
179° E
Collingwood
Golden Bay
Levin
Otaki
Tararua Forest Park
Kapiti Island
Masterton
Takaka
Tasman Bay
Paraparaumu
Kahurangi National Park
Motueka
Upper Hutt
Featherston
Porirua
Karamea
Nelson
Picton
WELLINGTON
Petone
Cook Strait
9
Richmond
Blenheim
0 — 100 km
0 — 50 miles

A B C D E F G
1
2
3
4
5
6
7
8
9
10

SIGHTS & ACTIVITIES

 SEE

DO

ITINERARY

1

2

Kaikoura

A peninsula town backed by the snow-capped Seaward Kaikoura Range, this is the top place in New Zealand to spot marine megafauna – particularly whales and dolphins – plus albatross, petrels and other seabirds. Wildlife-watching trips and kayaking expeditions depart from the harbour.

Abel Tasman Coast Track

This is arguably NZ's most beautiful Great Walk – 60km of sparkling seas, golden sand, quintessential coastal forest, and hidden surprises such as Cleopatra's Pool, attract around 30,000 overnight trampers and kayakers per year. The tidal differences here are among the greatest in New Zealand, up to a staggering 6m.

Queenstown

Famous as the birthplace of bungee jumping, Queenstown is NZ's adventure capital – with activities such as mountain biking, paragliding, alpine heli-skiing, zip-lining, skydiving, rafting and 4WD tours. Thanks to its setting near Lake Wakatipu, the Shotover River and the Remarkables, Mother Nature has created an unparalleled natural playground here.

Fox and Franz Josef Glaciers

Located within Westland Tai Poutini National Park, the twin glaciers of Franz Josef and Fox are the most accessible of the park's 60-odd glaciers They can both be explored on a guided glacier hike or a sightseeing heli-tour, but the ice is melting frighteningly fast due to climate change.

Aoraki: New Zealand's highest peak (left), with Lake Pukaki in the foreground.

Milford Sound

New Zealand's most famous fjord, Milford Sound (Piopiotahi) was gouged out by glaciers during the last ice age. It is backed by the 1692m-high summit of Mitre Peak (Rahotu). Cruises traverse its length, and during rainfall, dozens of waterfalls curtain the cliffs.

Marlborough Sounds

The Marlborough Sounds are a maze of peaks, bays, beaches and waterways, formed when the sea flooded valleys after the last ice age. They are very convoluted: Pelorus Sound is 42km long but has 379km of shoreline.

Aoraki (Mt Cook)

At 3724m, mighty Mt Cook is the tallest peak in Australasia. It is the centrepiece of its own 700-sq-km national park, more than one third of which has a blanket of permanent snow and glacial ice. Of the 23 NZ mountains over 3000m, 19 are here.

Otago Peninsula

Only half an hour's drive from downtown Dunedin, this small sliver of land is home to the South Island's most accessible diversity of wildlife, including albatross, penguins, fur seals and sea lions. The peninsula's only town is petite Portobello.

TranzAlpine Railway

This famous train traverses the Southern Alps through Arthur's Pass National Park, from the Pacific Ocean to the Tasman Sea. Dramatic landscapes span its 223km length, from the flat, alluvial Canterbury Plains, through alpine gorges, an 8.5km tunnel and beech-forested valleys.

Marlborough Wine Region

Marlborough produces around three quarters of the country's wine. With 244 sq km of vines (more than 28,000 rugby pitches), it has perfect conditions for cool-climate grapes: sauvignon blanc, pinot noir, chardonnay, riesling, gewürztraminer, pinot gris and even bubbly.

Dunedin

The 'Edinburgh of the South' is immensely proud of its Scottish heritage, never missing an opportunity to break out the haggis and bagpipes on civic occasions (the city even has its own tartan). The country's oldest university provides plenty of student energy to sustain the local bars.

Stewart Island (Rakiura)

New Zealand's 'third island' is home to spectacular wildlife, including NZ's shy feathered icon, the kiwi. The 269-hectare Ulva Island has been a bird reserve since 1922. The island also has challenging hiking: the 32km, three-day Rakiura Track is one of New Zealand's nine 'Great Walks'.

10-day itinerary
South Island Classics

This tour takes in the South Island's essential sights. Begin in **Christchurch**, a cultured city that's gradually recovering post-earthquake. Continue through the **Marlborough Wine Region** and the harbour town of **Picton** before whiling away a day or two in the **Marlborough Sounds**. Detour west past artsy **Nelson** and eco-friendly **Golden Bay**. Take an ice walk onto **Franz Josef** or **Fox Glacier**, then go crazy in adventurous **Queenstown**, before taking a cruise along **Doubtful Sound**. Visit Scottish-flavoured **Dunedin**, then detour through the **Waitaki Valley** to glimpse the snowy heights of **Aoraki (Mt Cook)**, before rolling back into Christchurch.

14-day itinerary
The South Island's Wild Side

Cast adrift from ancient Gondwanaland, and uninhabited by humans until around 800 years ago, the South Island boasts a remarkable range of land and sea creatures. From **Christchurch**, travel to **Akaroa** to swim with Hector's dolphins, New Zealand's smallest and rarest. Squeeze in a return trip up the coast to **Kaikoura** for whale-watching and swimming with NZ fur seals, before travelling south to **Oamaru**, with a little blue penguin colony which comes alive at dusk. From Oamaru, continue south to the **Otago Peninsula** to spot more little blue penguins, as well as their extremely rare, shuffling cousin, the yellow-eyed penguin (hoiho). Join a tour to meet seals and sea lions before admiring the royal albatross colony on nearby **Taiaroa Head**. Continue south to the rugged and isolated **Catlins Conservation Park**, where penguins, Hector's dolphins and sea lions are all regular visitors at **Curio Bay**. Leave the South Island at **Bluff** for a few days of kiwi-spotting on wild and idiosyncratic **Stewart Island (Rakiura)**.

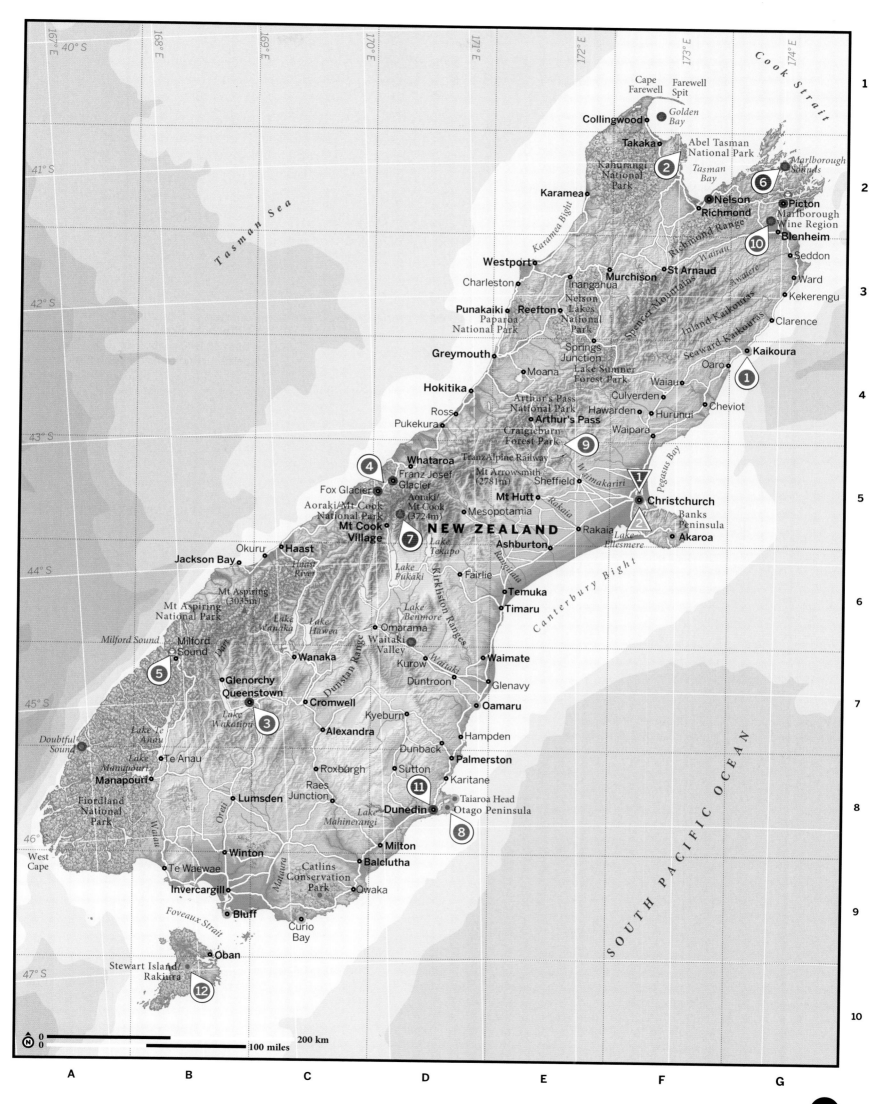

1

2

3

4

5

6

7

8

9

10

Cook Strait

Cape Farewell
Farewell Spit
Collingwood
Golden Bay
Takaka
Abel Tasman National Park
Tasman Bay
②
⑥
Marlborough Sounds
Kahurangi National Park
Karamea
Nelson
Richmond
Picton
Marlborough Wine Region
⑩
Blenheim
Seddon
Westport
Murchison
St Arnaud
Richmond Range
Wairau
Ward
Charleston
Inangahua
Spencer Mountains
Kekerengu
Nelson Lakes National Park
Awatere
Punakaiki
Reefton
Paparoa National Park
Inland Kaikouras
Clarence
Greymouth
Springs Junction
Lake Sumner Forest Park
Seaward Kaikouras
Oaro
Kaikoura
Moana
①
Hokitika
Arthur's Pass National Park
Culverden
Waiau
Ross
Hawarden
Hurunui
Cheviot
Pukekura
Arthur's Pass
Waipara
Craigieburn Forest Park
⑨
TranzAlpine Railway
④
Whataroa
Mt Arrowsmith (2781m)
Sheffield
Pegasus Bay
Franz Josef Glacier
Waimakariri
Fox Glacier
Aoraki/ Mt Cook
Mt Hutt
①
Christchurch
Aoraki/Mt Cook National Park
Mt Cook (3724m)
Mesopotamia
Rakaia
Banks Peninsula
Mt Cook Village
⑦
NEW ZEALAND
②
Okuru
Haast
Lake Takapo
Rakaia
Akaroa
Jackson Bay
Ashburton
Lake Ellesmere
Haast River
Lake Pukaki
Fairlie
Mt Aspiring (3035m)
Canterbury Bight
Mt Aspiring National Park
Lake Wanaka
Lake Hawea
Kirkliston Ranges
Temuka
Timaru
Milford Sound
Lake Benmore
Omarama
Dart
Wanaka
Waitaki Valley
Milford Sound
⑤
Waitaki
Waimate
Glenorchy
Queenstown
Cromwell
Kurow
Duntroon
Glenavy
Lake Wakatipu
③
Dunstan Range
Kyeburn
Oamaru
Doubtful Sound
Lake Te Anau
Alexandra
Lake Manapouri
Te Anau
Roxburgh
Dunback
Hampden
Manapouri
Raes Junction
Sutton
Palmerston
Karitane
⑪
Fiordland National Park
Lumsden
Dunedin
Taiaroa Head
Otago Peninsula
Waiau
Oreti
Lake Mahinerangi
⑧
West Cape
Winton
Milton
Mataura
Catlins Conservation Park
Balclutha
Invercargill
Owaka
Bluff
Foveaux Strait
Curio Bay
SOUTH PACIFIC OCEAN
Oban
Stewart Island/ Rakiura
⑫

Tasman Sea

167° E
168° E
169° E
170° E
171° E
172° E
173° E
174° E

40° S
41° S
42° S
43° S
44° S
45° S
46° S
47° S

N
0
0
200 km
100 miles

A   B   C   D   E   F   G

Pacific Islands

The South Pacific's paradisiacal reputation can be traced back to European explorers returning home with tales of fertile soils, beautiful islanders and simple ways. These island nations have modernised since the late 1700s, but their allure remains undiminished. You'll still find gin-clear waters, smiling locals and gardenia-scented air. But what's most amazing is how untainted by tourism most islands are. Blame it on remoteness, blame it on airfares... but few people who fantasise about the South Seas ever actually make the journey. Getting off the tourism grid and playing Robinson Crusoe is the true gift of the South Pacific.

CLIMATE CHART

PORT MORESBY

RAINFALL INCH/MM
—24/600
—16/400
—8/200
—0
D N O S A J J M A M F J

TEMP °C/°F
40/104—
30/86—
20/68—
10/50—
0/32—

SUVA

RAINFALL INCH/MM
—16/400
—12/300
—8/200
—4/100
—0
D N O S A J J M A M F J

TEMP °C/°F
40/104—
30/86—
20/68—
10/50—

TRADITIONAL DANCE AND MUSIC
The South Pacific knows how to put on a show (generally accompanied by a grand feast). In Fiafia (Samoa), watch fire dancing and traditional 'slap' dancing. On Vanuatu, there's the Rom Dance, a feet-pounding, hypnotic magical performance. In the Cook Islands, locals shake their hips, juggle fire and sing traditional songs at 'island nights'. And in Fiji, *meke* dances are a highlight of many village visits.

BEACHES
You could spend a lifetime sunbathing in the South Pacific and still only see a fraction of its breathtaking beaches. Some are straightforward to reach, like the white sands of Aitutaki Lagoon (Cook Islands), the Yasawas (Fiji) and Tikehau (French Polynesia). Others, such as the remote beaches of Ofu (American Samoa) or Ouvéa (New Caledonia), feel fantastically far-flung.

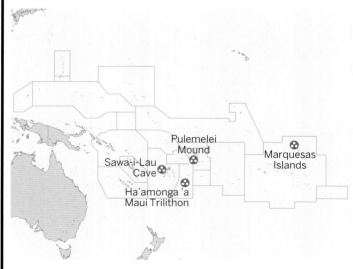

ARCHAEOLOGY AND HISTORY
Indulge your inner Indiana Jones in the South Pacific. See giant moss-covered *tiki* (sacred statues) on the Marquesas Islands; visit the Pulemelei Mound in Samoa, Polynesia's largest ancient structure; marvel at the Ha'amonga 'a Maui Trilithon on Tonga, the 'Stonehenge of the South Pacific'; and ponder the cryptic carvings, paintings and inscriptions of unknown age and meaning in Fiji's Sawa-i-Lau cave.

DIVING AND SNORKELLING
With incredible reefs, clear water and myriad marine life, the South Pacific offers a wealth of underwater adventures. Dive corals on Vanuatu's Espiritu Santo and WWII wrecks on the Solomon Islands; swim with sharks and dolphins on Rangiroa (French Polynesia); flip your fins with manta rays on Fiji's Barefoot Manta Island; or snorkel in the Piscine Naturelle on the Île des Pins (New Caledonia).

Right: The shoreline of Samoan island 'Upolu, formed by a volcano rising from the floor of the Pacific Ocean.

© Richard Vandewalle / 500px

Transport hubs

Due to the vast expanse of open ocean, and the relatively small number of travellers visiting the region, getting to the South Pacific can be both time-consuming and expensive. Airlines flying between the US, Australia, New Zealand and Japan stop off at a number of South Pacific destinations. Smaller local airlines hop between the islands, but the most memorable way to arrive is aboard your own yacht – or, for the less romantically inclined, cruise ship.

ELEVATION KEY

7500-10000M
5000-7500M
3000-5000M
2000-3000M
1500-2000M
1250-1500M
1000-1250M
750-1000M
500-750M
250-500M
100-250M
75-100M
50-75M
25-50M
1-25M

TRANSPORT

B5, D6, E5,
E6, F6, G6

B5, D5, D6,
E5, E6, F6,
G6

Fiji
Fiji's central location makes it one of the South Pacific's main air hubs, often visited as a stopover for flights travelling from Australia or New Zealand to the northern hemisphere. Most visitors arrive at Nadi International Airport (NAN). The national carrier is Fiji Airways, which code-shares with several major airlines and flies from Viti Levu to many outer islands. Seaplanes and helicopters are an option for the Mamanuca and Yasawa island groups; some are also visited by ferry or cargo ship.

Tahiti
Faa'a International Airport is the aviation centre of French Polynesia. All international flights arrive here, and Air Tahiti flights to the other islands leave from here. Flights within each archipelago hop from one island to the next, but most connections between archipelagos are via Faa'a ('fa-ah-ah'). All passenger boats to other islands moor at the Gare Maritime in Pape'ete.

Cook Islands
Rarotonga has international flights to Auckland, Sydney, Los Angeles and Tahiti. It's also a frequent port of call for South Pacific cruise ships. Air Rarotonga, the only domestic airline in the Cook Islands, has several daily flights to Aitutaki, and several weekly flights between Rarotonga and the rest of the Southern Group. Flights to the Northern Group are more erratic.

Tonga
Most visitors fly into Tonga's only international airport on the main island of Tongatapu. From there, air is the fastest and most comfortable way to head to the other islands. Chathams Pacific is the domestic airline, and offers various local air passes.

Samoa
Flights to Samoa arrive at Faleolo Airport, 35km west of Apia, usually in the early hours of the morning. Fagali'i Airport, on Apia's eastern outskirts, is mainly used for flights to/from American Samoa. Direct flights head to Samoa from American Samoa, Fiji, Auckland, Brisbane and Sydney. If you're flying from the northern hemisphere, flights via Honolulu are likely to be the most straightforward.

Vanuatu
The easiest way to reach Vanuatu is by flying from Auckland, Brisbane or Sydney. There are regular flights, but costs vary depending on whether you fly direct or with stopovers: some flights island-hop via Nadi or Suva (Fiji), Honiara (Solomon Islands) and/or Noumea (New Caledonia). Any which way, you'll land at the island's main airport at Port Vila.

Papua New Guinea
Port Moresby's Jacksons Airport is where most visitors will arrive. Air Niugini, PNG's national airline, offers fairly frequent flights to several Australian cities (sometimes as code-shares with Qantas) as well as Bali, Japan, Philippines, Singapore, Fiji, China and the Solomon Islands. PNG and the Solomons are popular stopping points for cruising yachts heading through Asia or the Pacific.

New Caledonia
Tontouta international airport is 45km northwest of Noumea. Aircalin (Air Calédonie International) has good code-share agreements, especially with Air France, which allows flight connections to pretty much anywhere. Many cruise ships visit New Caledonia, docking at Noumea's *gare maritime* (boat terminal).

Right: Fiji's crimson-crowned fruit dove (left) and (right) flying over the Cook Islands.

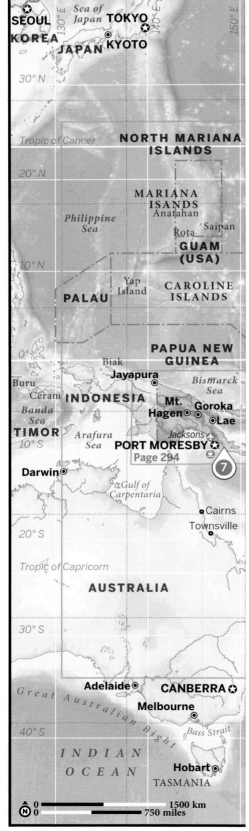

Page 294

© Sjo / Getty Images

© Pete Seaward / Lonely Planet

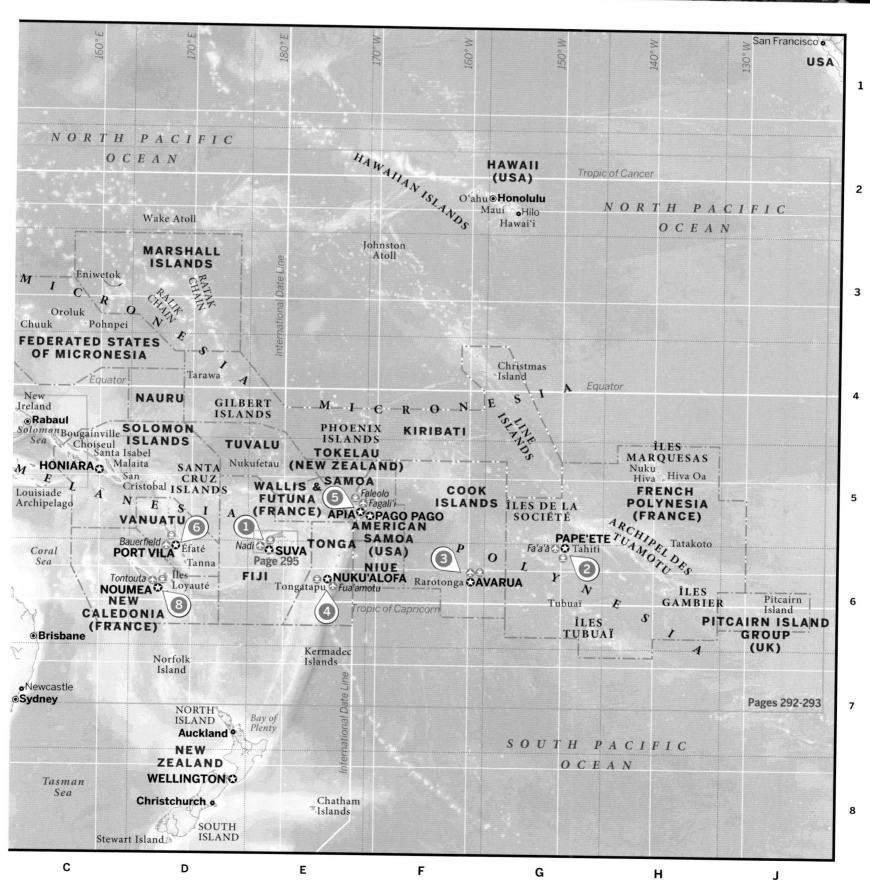

USA

San Francisco

NORTH PACIFIC
OCEAN

HAWAIIAN ISLANDS

HAWAII
(USA)

Tropic of Cancer

O'ahu Honolulu
Maui
Hawai'i Hilo

NORTH PACIFIC
OCEAN

Wake Atoll

Johnston
Atoll

MARSHALL
ISLANDS

RATAK CHAIN

RALIK CHAIN

Eniwetok

M I C R O N E S I A

Oroluk
Chuuk   Pohnpei

FEDERATED STATES
OF MICRONESIA

Equator

Tarawa

NAURU

GILBERT
ISLANDS

M I C R O N E S I A

Christmas
Island

Equator

LINE ISLANDS

New
Ireland
Rabaul
Solomon
Sea   Bougainville
Choiseul
Santa Isabel
HONIARA   Malaita
Louisiade   San
Archipelago   Cristobal

SOLOMON
ISLANDS

TUVALU

Nukufetau

PHOENIX
ISLANDS

KIRIBATI

M E L A N E S I A

SANTA
CRUZ
ISLANDS

TOKELAU
(NEW ZEALAND)

ÎLES
MARQUESAS

Nuku
Hiva   Hiva Oa

WALLIS &
FUTUNA
(FRANCE)

SAMOA

Faleolo
Fagali'i

APIA   PAGO PAGO

AMERICAN
SAMOA
(USA)

COOK
ISLANDS

ÎLES DE LA
SOCIÉTÉ

FRENCH
POLYNESIA
(FRANCE)

ARCHIPEL DES TUAMOTU

Tatakoto

VANUATU

Bauerfield
PORT VILA   Éfaté
Coral   Tanna
Sea

Nadi
SUVA
Page 295

TONGA

NIUE

PAPE'ETE

Fa'a'a   Tahiti

P O L Y N E S I A

Rarotonga   AVARUA

Tubuaï

ÎLES
GAMBIER

Pitcairn
Island

NOUMEA
NEW
CALEDONIA
(FRANCE)

Tontouta
Îles
Loyauté

FIJI

NUKU'ALOFA

Tongatapu   Fua'amotu

Tropic of Capricorn

ÎLES
TUBUAÏ

PITCAIRN ISLAND
GROUP
(UK)

Brisbane

Newcastle
Sydney

Norfolk
Island

Kermadec
Islands

International Date Line

Pages 292-293

NORTH
ISLAND   Bay of
Plenty
Auckland

NEW
ZEALAND
WELLINGTON

Tasman
Sea

Christchurch

Chatham
Islands

SOUTH PACIFIC
OCEAN

Stewart Island

SOUTH
ISLAND

International Date Line

160° E   170° E   180°   170° W   160° W   150° W   140° W   130° W

C   D   E   F   G   H   J

Tahiti

What Tahiti lacks in white-sand beaches, it makes up for in mountains, black-sand beaches, blue lagoons and a distinctly Polynesian buzz. In July, catch the country's most spectacular festival; the percussion- and dance-heavy Heiva. For luxury, stay in a private lagoon bungalow on nearby Bora Bora, the 'Pearl of the Pacific'.

Cook Islands

The Cook Islands are among the South Pacific's most accessible destinations. Rarotonga is the main island, with snorkelling, hiking, markets and an uptempo nightlife. Elsewhere, 'Atiu offers birdlife and cave systems; Aitutaki is awash with deserted islets and a stunning lagoon; and Ma'uke and Mitiaro offer village homestays.

Vanuatu

Staring into the lava-spouting mouth of a volcano is exactly as nerve-wracking as it sounds. At Mt Yasur in Vanuatu, it's possible to camp at the base, then climb the crater to watch the volcano light up the night. For more adventure, head to Ambrym island to scale the volcanoes of Mt Marum and Mt Benbow.

Tonga

The Kingdom of Tonga ticks along at its own pace: church-life is all pervasive, chickens and pigs have right-of-way, and there's nothing that can't wait until tomorrow. Gorgeous beaches, low-key resorts and affable locals await you.

Samoa

Samoa's *fale* (open-air huts on stilts) hover all along the island's sands. Traditionally, guests sleep on the floor and privacy is found by pulling down thatched louvres. *Fale* are basic, but the views are a million bucks.

Pitcairn Islands

The Pitcairn Islands – the last British Overseas Territory in the Pacific – comprise Pitcairn plus uninhabited Oeno, Henderson and Ducie. It was here that Captain Bligh was set adrift by Fletcher Christian and the other mutineers on HMS *Bounty*.

Cook Islands:
Rarotonga offers watersports opportunities aplenty.

Solomon Islands

The Solomon Islands serve up history by the bucketful: WWII battlefields, Sherman tanks, Japanese field guns and downed aircraft. Underwater, sunken wrecks of planes, battleships and tanks provide impressive dive sites.

American Samoa

These little-known islands belong to, but aren't a part of, the United States. Tutuila is home to Pago Pago, a fishing town beside a stunning natural harbour. For more escapism, head to the remote Manu'a Islands, believed to be the birthplace of Polynesia.

New Caledonia

With its World Heritage–listed lagoons, New Caledonia is the South Pacific with a French twist, especially around Noumea. Head out to the Loyalty Islands to experience tribal accommodation and Kanak culture.

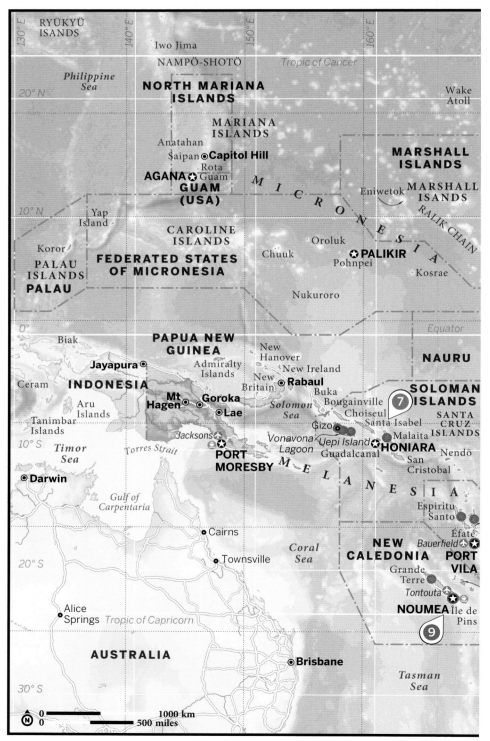

21- to 28-day itinerary
Melanesian Meander

After island-hopping in **Tahiti**, fly into New Caledonia's capital **Noumea**. Explore the mangroves, forests and barren vistas of **Grande Terre**, then jet into Vanuatu's **Port Vila** with its rich English and French colonial history. Swim at the Mele Cascades and sip kava before swaying into the Port Vila nightlife. See the active **Mt Yasur** volcano on Tanna island, then continue to **Pentecost** where yam farmers invented bungee jumping, then on to **Espiritu Santo** for world-class diving. Fly on to the Solomon Islands: boat around **Vonavona Lagoon**, snorkel off **Uepi Island,** chill out in **Gizo**, and wrap up in **Malaita** where locals summon sharks and live on artificial islands.

30-day itinerary
The Northern Loop

With a month of island time, Polynesia delivers a bounty of tropical delights. Kick things off in **Apia**, Samoa's capital: check out the Robert Louis Stevenson Museum, explore Upolu and spend at least one night on the beach in a traditional *fale*. Take the ferry to **Savai'i** for cave tunnels, lava fields and white beaches, then visit the forest-engulfed Pulemelei Mound, Polynesia's largest ancient monument. Fly to **Nuku'alofa** in Tonga: eyeball the Royal Palace en route to lively Talamahu Market. To the north, the **Ha'apai Group** offers beachy living in thatched *fale*, while the Vava'u Group delivers active adventures like sea kayaking, diving and sailing. Whiz through Auckland Airport en route to **Rarotonga** in the Cook Islands. Here, hike the cross-island track, snorkel at sublime Muri Beach, and catch a plane to exquisite **Aitutaki**. Explore the caves of the *makatea* (raised coral islands) of **'Atiu**, **Mangaia** and **Ma'uke**. From Rarotonga, fly to **Pape'ete**, the chic capital of the French Pacific, and squeeze in a visit to sleepy **Huahine** and the Polynesian spiritual capital of **Ra'iatea**.

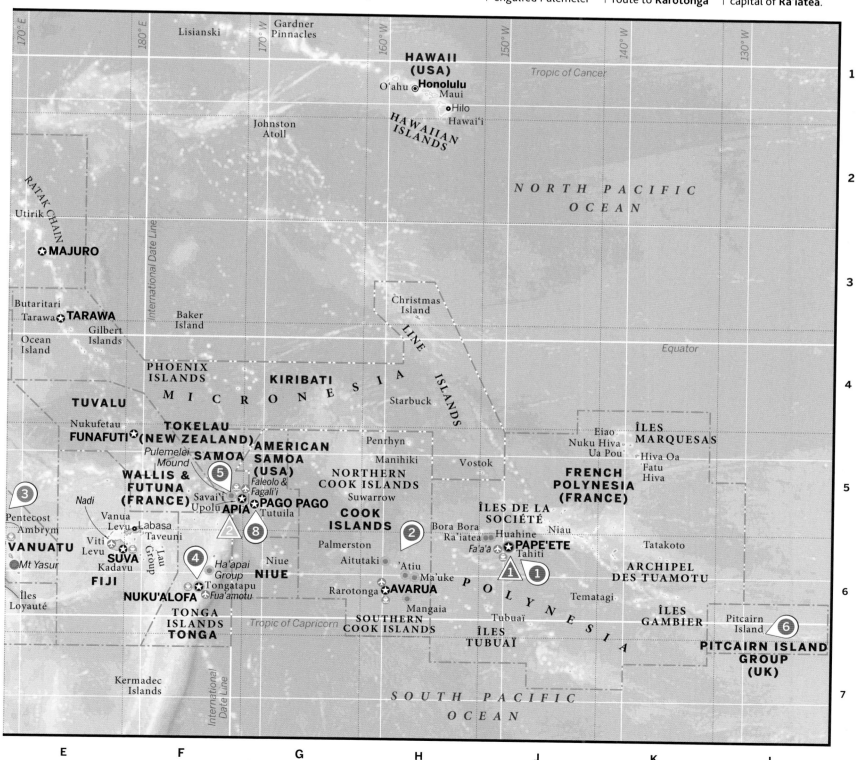

Kokoda Track

During WWII, Australians, Americans and Japanese fought for their lives along the infamous 96km Kokoda Track. These days, an average of 4000 trekkers (95% of them Australian) grit their teeth and tackle the same mountains for fun. Most walk as part of an organised group.

SIGHTS & ACTIVITIES

◉ SEE

◉ DO

ITINERARY

▽ 1

▽ 2

Sepik River

The mighty Sepik is PNG's most famous geographical feature. Its scale, along with the *haus tambarans* (spirit houses), stilt villages, crocodile-headed canoes and flower-clogged lakes, make a visit unforgettable.

Goroka Show

The Goroka Show is held over the Independence Day weekend (mid-September) at the National Sports Institute's Sports Oval. It attracts *singsing* (celebratory dance/festival) groups, bands and cultural activities.

Milne Bay

At the eastern end of mainland PNG, the Owen Stanley Range plunges into the sea, and more than 435 islands give the province 2120km of coastline, connected by a myriad of banana boats, for want of better infrastructure.

14-day itinerary
The Papua Highlands

Take in the highlights of the Highlands and the coast on this two-week tour. Spend a day absorbing the highlights of **Port Moresby** before flying up to pretty **Madang**. Spend a couple of days diving or snorkelling and exploring nearby islands before taking a short flight or a PMV bus up the Highlands (Okuk) Hwy to **Goroka** and see the Goroka Show. Don't forget to visit the mudmen of Asaro just outside Goroka. Continue through **Kundiawa** up to Kegsugl for the amazing three- or four-day trek up **Mt Wilhelm**. After admiring the view of both coasts, make the descent for travel onward to **Mt Hagen**, enjoying the scenery and a game of Highlands darts. For a chance to spot birds of paradise spend a couple of days at Kumul Lodge on the road up to Wabag. Head to **Tari** to see the beautiful Tari Basin, a superb sight that's worth the extra expense. Don't miss the Huli wigmen in all their feathered glory. From Tari fly back to Port Moresby and, if time allows, spend a final day relaxing and reflecting on **Loloata Island**.

Kimbe Bay

On a dive around Kimbe Bay you might see anything from a tiny glass prawn to a pod of killer whales. The marine biodiversity is stunning, with more than 413 types of hard coral and 860 species of fish vying for your attention.

Rabaul

On 19 September 1994 Mt Tavurvur erupted, spewing huge amounts of ash over Rabaul and the Simpson Harbour and Karavia Bay area. It buried much of the city in brown and black ash, and is still active. At the Vulcanology Observatory, there are views over the bay and the volcanoes.

Kiunga

Seeing PNG's rich bird life is becoming easier thanks to birding lodges and local guides. Kiunga is especially popular: the best birding is between April and October when the birds are beginning their breeding cycles.

Trobriand Islands

Despite the many anthropologists, missionaries, TV crews and tourists who have travelled here, the Trobriands remain one of Papua's most culturally intact places, with a strict matrilineal social system, decorated yam houses, exquisite carvings and colourful festivals of clan prestige.

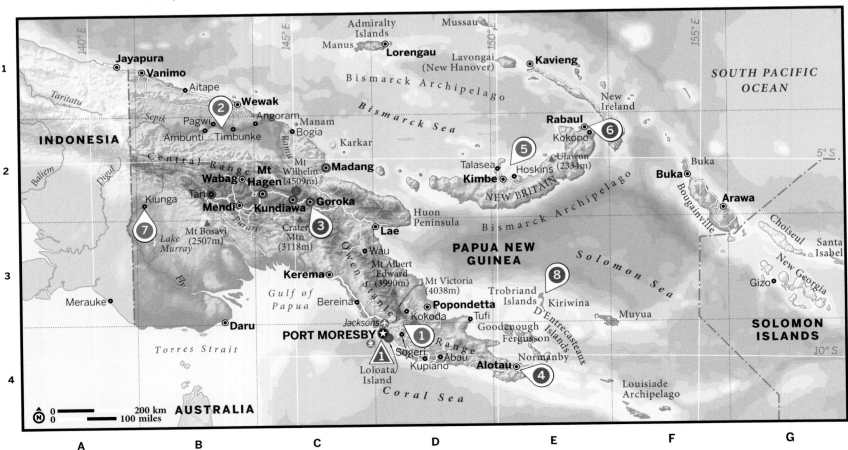

Suva
Steamy Suva is a mix of contemporary and colonial Fiji. Gracious buildings line a lively waterfront, while downtown boasts shopping malls and handicraft stalls. Don't miss the municipal market, the national museum and cocktails at the Grand Pacific Hotel.

Navala Village
In the Nausori Highlands, Navala village is the place to see indigenous life up close. All its 200 buildings are constructed using woven bamboo walls, thatched roofs and ropes made of fibre. Visitors are welcomed with a traditional kava ceremony.

Sawa-i-Lau Cave
A lone limestone island among the volcanic Yasawas, Sawa-i-Lau hides a mystery within its hollow caverns: carvings, paintings and inscriptions of unknown age and meaning. They're accessible with a torch and a guide by swimming through a short underwater passage from the cave's main chamber.

Garden of the Sleeping Giant
This 20-hectare plantation is a botanic bonanza, abloom with more than 2000 varieties of orchids, plus indigenous flora and other tropical beauties.

14-day itinerary
The Yasawas and Mamanucas

This trip is best undertaken with a Bula Pass (which lasts from five to 21 days) for the *Yasawa Flyer* ferry. Climb on board at **Port Denarau** and head first to **Beachcomber Island**. Popular with party people (and increasingly families), this is a great place to soak up the first of your island rays. Head on to **Mana** island for a sharky scuba dive at the Supermarket and a day trip aboard a schooner to **Monuriki**, where *Cast Away* was shot. Say goodbye to the resorts of the Mamanucas and hello to a genuine look at local life, Yasawas-style, with a homestay at **Waya** island. After a couple of days of village food – and a steep host-led hike up a volcanic plug on neighbouring **Wayasewa** – you're now ready to keep up with the manta rays that ply the passage between **Nanuya Balavu** and **Drawaqa** islands; resorts in the area run snorkel trips here in season. Further north, take a well-earned rest with a frolic in the **Blue Lagoon** before hopping in a water taxi to the magnificent **Sawa-i-Lau Cave**.

Yasawa Islands
Ringed by reefs, the 20-odd Yasawa Islands beckon with lagoons, volcanic landscapes and beaches. There are no roads, cars, banks or shops, and locals live in small villages, surviving on agriculture and tourism. Ferries, cruise ships and seaplanes link the islands.

Taveuni
Taveuni's tangled, steamy interior is reminiscent of a prehistoric jungle, covered by a riotous quilt of palms, monster ferns and tropical wildflowers. Its dense rainforest is a magnet for birdlife. At 1241m, cloud-shrouded Mt Uluigalau is Fiji's highest summit.

Namosi Highlands
Geology looms large in the spectacular Namosi Highlands. Sheer canyon walls crowd the Wainikoroiluva River, providing the backdrop for Fiji's most scenic river-rafting trip, taken aboard a *bilibili* (bamboo raft).

Vanua Levu
Fiji's second-largest island is a world away from the more-touristed ones. Savusavu is a yachtie haven, Labasa is a low-key capital and the rest of the island is given over to plantations, villages, waterfalls and forest-swathed mountains that are home to the rare silktail bird and *tagimaucia* flower.

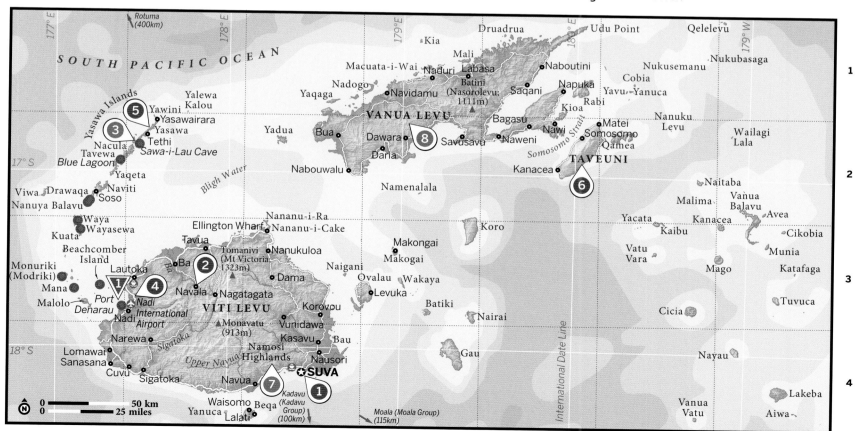

Canada

The human story of Canada begins about 15,000 years ago when Aboriginal people began carving thriving communities from the abundant wilderness. Today, Aboriginal people make up 4.3% of Canada's total population, split between First Nations (those of North American Indian descent), Métis (those with 'mixed blood' ancestry) and Inuit (those in the Arctic). After being discovered by European explorers, Canada was colonised by French and British settlers before declaring independence in 1867. The globe's second-biggest country, Canada is best known for the endless variety of its landscapes: sky-high mountains, glinting glaciers, spectral rainforests and remote beaches are all here, spread across six time zones.

CLIMATE CHART

VANCOUVER

RAINFALL INCH/MM
—8/200
—6/150
—4/100
—2/50
—0

TEMP °C/°F
30/86
20/68
10/50
0/32
-10/14
-20/4
-30/22

MONTRÉAL

RAINFALL INCH/MM
—8/200
—6/150
—4/100
—2/50
—0

TEMP °C/°F
30/86
20/68
10/50
0/32
-10/14
-20/4
-30/22

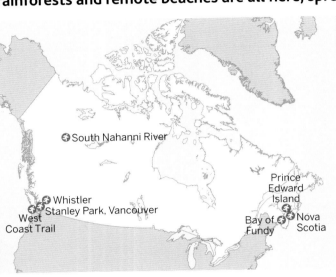

OUTDOOR ACTIVITIES

Whether it's snowboarding Whistler's mountains, surfing Nova Scotia's swells or kayaking the white-frothed South Nahanni River in the Northwest Territories, adventures abound. You could hike the coast of the Bay of Fundy or the epic West Coast Trail, but there are gentler options, too, like strolling Vancouver's Stanley Park or swimming off Prince Edward Island's pink-sand beaches.

CULTURE

Sip a *café au lait* and tear into a flaky croissant at a pavement bistro in Montréal; head to an Asian night market and slurp noodles in Vancouver; join a wild Celtic fiddling party on Cape Breton Island; kayak between rainforest-cloaked Aboriginal villages on Haida Gwaii; or learn all about indigenous culture at Haida Heritage Centre or Squamish Lil'wat Cultural Centre, both in British Columbia.

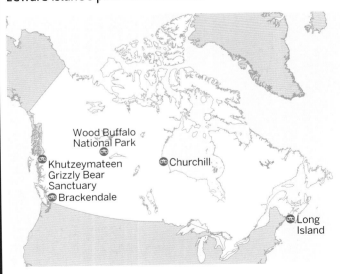

Right: Driving in the shadow of the Canadian Rockies in Kananaskis Country, Alberta.

WILDLIFE

On land, in the water and in the air, Canada teems with camera-worthy critters. You could watch grizzlies in the wild at Khutzeymateen Grizzly Bear Sanctuary in BC; spot right whales, blue whales and humpbacks off Long Island in Nova Scotia; watch polar bears on the tundra in Churchill, Manitoba; follow moose and wolves in Alberta's Wood Buffalo National Park; or spy eagles in Brackendale, BC.

NATIONAL PARKS

If there's one thing Canada excels at, it's national parks: all 44 of them. The first was Banff, founded way back in 1885, but national parks now cover 3% of Canada's land mass – from the boreal forests of the Cape Breton Highlands to the fjords of Gros Morne and the peaks and glaciers of Kluane. Eight new parks have been established since 2000, including Sable Island, Qausuittuq and Torngat Mountains.

Transport hubs

Canada is a vast country, so it takes a long time to get there from anywhere outside North America – and often an equally long time to get from one place to another. Thankfully, an extensive domestic air network cuts down travel times, although a more scenic alternative is to take the train: most Canadian cities are linked by the excellent rail network. Arriving over the US border is another option, but check visa requirements and be prepared for long waits.

Toronto
Most Canadian airlines and international carriers arrive at Canada's busiest airport, Toronto Pearson International Airport, 27km northwest of downtown Toronto: it's a giant and attracts one of the highest airport taxes in the world. Overland, a couple of Amtrak trains travel from Buffalo and New York. You can make a land crossing into Ontario from the southwest at Detroit–Windsor.

Vancouver
Vancouver is only an hour from several US border crossings, so many visitors arrive by car. Those that don't tend to arrive via Canada's second-busiest airport, Vancouver International Airport, lies 13km south of downtown in the city of Richmond. Some people also arrive on Alaska-bound cruise ships that dock on the city's waterfront, or by train: Cross-Canada rail operations service the city, which is the main gateway for destinations throughout British Columbia (BC). US trains and intercity buses trundle in from Seattle to Pacific Central Station.

Montréal
It's easy to drive to Montréal from elsewhere in Canada or the US, or take the train or intercity coach from cities such as Toronto or New York. Gare Centrale is the hub of VIA Rail, Canada's vast rail network, which links Montréal with cities across the country. Located west of downtown, Pierre Elliott Trudeau International Airport has frequent connections to the US, Europe, the Caribbean, Latin America, Africa and the rest of Canada.

Québec City
Québec City is a great weekend trip from Montréal, and many travellers arrive by car, bus or rail. The drive is about three hours. VIA Rail's trains take only slightly longer (3¼ hours). Highway networks connect Québec's capital with the rest of the province. Québec City has frequent air connections to Canadian and US destinations, as well as less frequent flights to Mexico and the Caribbean.

Halifax
The main gateway for the provinces of Nova Scotia, New Brunswick and Prince Edward Island, Halifax Stanfield International Airport is 32km northeast of town on Hwy 102. There are multiple daily flights to Toronto, Calgary and Vancouver. VIA Rail operates an overnight train to Montréal. Local buses travel up into Québec, Nova Scotia and North Sydney on Cape Breton Island (for ferry connections to Newfoundland).

Calgary
Famous for its annual cowboy-themed stampede, Calgary is a useful access point for both the Rockies and the rest of Alberta. Calgary International Airport is about 15km northeast of the centre, off Barlow Trail, and has good connections with the rest of Canada and the US, as well as European and Asian hubs. Inexplicably, Calgary welcomes no passenger trains (which bypass the city in favour of Edmonton and Jasper); you'll have to catch a Greyhound or Red Arrow bus instead.

Whitehorse
To get to the Yukon and those destinations further to the north, you will most likely pass through the town of Whitehorse, which is linked by air to Vancouver, Kelowna, Calgary and Edmonton. By road, the Alaska Hwy runs from Dawson Creek, British Columbia, while the Stewart–Cassiar Hwy travels from northwest BC and then joins the Alaska Hwy near Watson Lake.

Right: Vancouver's Yaletown and Burrard Bridge by night (left) and (right) the Québec city skyline.

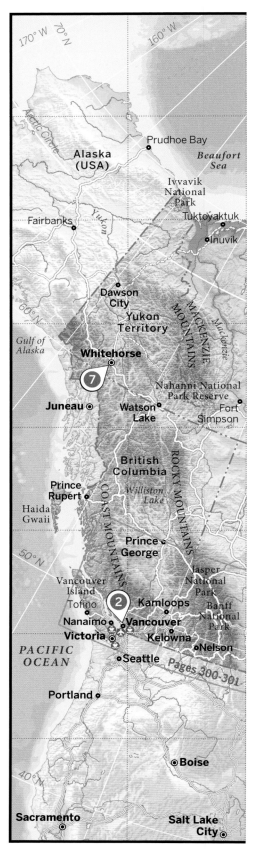

© dohitsch / Shutterstock

© Nino H. Photography / Getty Images

ARCTIC
OCEAN

GREENLAND
(DENMARK)

ICELAND

1

150° W 140° W 80° N 130° W 120° W 110° W 100° W 90° W 80° W 70° W 60° W 50° W 40° W 30° W 20° W Denmark Strait

Prince
Patrick
Island

Ellesmere
Island

Axel
Heiberg
Island

Melville
Island

Bathurst
Island

Cornwallis
Island

Devon
Island

2

Banks
Island

Viscount Melville Sound

Somerset
Island

Baffin
Bay

Prince
of Wales
Island

Sirmilik
National
Park

Amundsen Gulf

Prince Albert Sound

Victoria
Island

Boothia
Peninsula

Gulf of
Boothia

Baffin Island

Auyuittuq
National
Park

Davis Strait

3

Tuktut Nogait
National Park

Colville
Lake

King
William
Island

Prince
Charles
Island

Nettilling
Lake

Great Bear
Lake

Melville
Peninsula

Northwest
Territories

Nunavut

Foxe
Basin

Amadjuak
Lake

Iqaluit

Hudson Strait

Labrador
Sea

4

Lac la
Martre

Back

Thelon

Baker
Lake

Southampton
Island

Ungava
Bay

Yellowknife

Dubawnt
Lake

Yathkyed
Lake

Coats
Island

Mansel
Island

George

Newfoundland & Labrador

Great Slave
Lake

5

Wood Buffalo
National Park

Wholdaia
Lake

Kasba
Lake

Hudson
Bay

Labrador

Caniapiscau

Lake
Clare

Lake
Athabasca

Cree
Lake

Reindeer
Lake

Churchill

Wapusk
National
Park

Smallwood
Reservoir

Alberta

Churchill
Lake

Southern
Indian
Lake

Belcher
Islands

Réservoir
Robert
Bourassa

Réservoir
Manicouagan

Île
d'Anticosti

St John's

Corner Brook

Newfoundland

6

Saskatchewan

Lac la
Ronge

Thompson

Churchill

Nelson

James
Bay

Québec

Page 305

Edmonton

Manitoba

Akimiski
Island

Lac
Mistassini

Gulf of
St Lawrence

Channel-Port
aux Basques

Calgary

Prince
Albert

Saskatoon

Lake
Winnipeg

Moosonee

PEI

Charlottetown

6

Medicine
Hat

Moose
Jaw

Yorkton

Lake
Winnipegosis

Ontario

Réservoir
Gouin

Rivière-
du-Loup

New
Brunswick

Halifax
Stanfield

Page 304

7

Swift
Current

Regina

Brandon

Lake
Manitoba

Winnipeg

Thunder
Bay

Lake
Nipigon

Lake
Abitibi

Page 303

Québec
City

Fredericton

Saint
John

Halifax

Nova
Scotia

Helena

Missouri

Sudbury

North
Bay

Pierre Elliott
Trudeau

Montréal

Yarmouth

Bismarck

UNITED STATES
OF AMERICA

Sault
Ste Marie

Lake
Superior

Page 302

Georgian
Bay

Lake
Huron

OTTAWA

Kingston

Boston

ATLANTIC
OCEAN

8

Minneapolis

Toronto

Lake
Ontario

Lake
Michigan

Toronto Rearson

London

Niagara Falls

Detroit

Lake
Erie

New York

Chicago

0 500 km
0 250 miles

C D E F G H J

Stanley Park, Vancouver

Canada's finest urban park sits on Vancouver's doorstep: a 404-hectare temperate rainforest that's lined with multitudinous hiking and biking trails. An 8.8km sea wall promenade runs around the edge of the park.

Vancouver Island

Measuring 500km long and 100km wide, Vancouver Island is studded with small, quirky communities, many founded on logging or fishing. The BC capital Victoria is a centre for whale watching, while Tofino is known for its surf. The island has great hikes such as the West Coast and Cape Scott Trails.

Lake Louise, Banff National Park

Named for Queen Victoria's fourth daughter, Lake Louise is famous for its intensely blue water and glistening glaciers. It's best seen by canoe. Nearby Moraine Lake sits in the Valley of the Ten Peaks, surrounded by 3000m mountains, and provides another of Canada's best-known views.

Jasper National Park

As the largest of Canada's Rocky Mountain parks – covering 10,878 sq km – Jasper is perfect for spotting native wildlife in solitude. Mountain lions, wolves, caribou, beaver and bear roam freely, while natural wonders like Miette Hot Springs and Maligne Canyon are easily accessible, and many more are just a hike away.

Icefields Parkway

The Icefields Parkway is often referred to as the 'world's most spectacular road'. Stretching for 230km from Lake Louise all the way to Jasper, the road climbs through diverse Rocky Mountain scenery, from surging rivers and high-alpine glaciers to mountain passes and blue lakes.

Okanagan Valley

The 180km-long Okanagan Valley is home to orchards of peaches and apricots, and scores of excellent wineries whose vines spread across the terraced hills, soaking up some of Canada's sunniest weather. The best times to visit are late spring and early autumn, when the crowds lessen.

Head-Smashed-In Buffalo Jump

For thousands of years, the Blackfoot people used the cliffs near Fort Macleod to hunt buffalo by driving them over a cliff edge. A trail leads to the spot where the buffalo plummeted. An interpretive centre explores the site's history.

Whistler

This scenic alpine village was the host mountain for the 2010 Winter Olympics, and is the location of some of North America's most popular terrain for skiing and snowboarding – and in the summer, mountain biking.

National Music Centre, Calgary

The most recent addition to downtown Calgary's attractions is the copper-clad National Music Centre, which chronicles Canada's musical history with interactive displays – there's more to it than Alanis Morissette.

Waterton Lakes National Park

Established in 1895, this 525-sq-km reserve is a sanctuary for numerous iconic Canadian animals – grizzlies, elk, deer and cougar – along with 800-odd wildflower species. Highlights include cruises on serene Waterton Lake and plenty of high-alpine hiking.

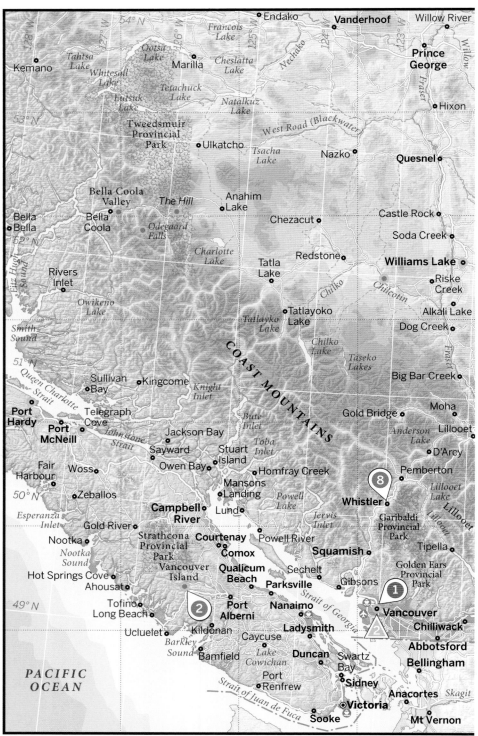

7-day itinerary
Rocky Mountains

Begin in **Edmonton** spending some time shopping, perusing museums and pottering around Old Strathcona. Then hit Hwy 16 for a half-day weave to **Jasper**. Check in for three nights and plan your wildlife watching around the region's lakes and mountains. Next it's time to move southwards via the **Icefields Parkway**. Stop en route at the **Columbia Icefield** and take a hike or truck tour on the **Athabasca Glacier**. Continue south to **Lake Louise**: snap photos and wander the shoreline, saving time for a visit to the equally dazzling Moraine Lake a short drive away. Heading onwards, soon you'll arrive in **Banff**, where you can spend your days hiking flower-covered alpine trails and marvelling at the epic landscapes.

14-day itinerary
British Columbia

Start your journey in **Vancouver**, then catch the ferry over to **Vancouver Island**. Head north on Hwy 19, taking an eastward detour to **Telegraph Cove**. Continue north on Hwy 16 and check in to **Port Hardy**, making time for an oceanfront hike. Catch an early morning ferry back to the mainland, looking out for eagles, whales and seals en route. Find yourself a rustic retreat for a few nights in the **Bella Coola Valley**, hiking trails alongside huge old cedars and to pounding **Odegaard Falls**. Go for a float on the river and lose count of the grizzlies you spy along the shore. When you leave, tackle **The Hill**, a thrill-ride for drivers, and head east through the lonely **Chilcotin** area, stopping at the many little lakes along the way. At **Williams Lake** say yee-ha to cowboy country, then turn south on the Cariboo Hwy (Hwy 97), aka the **Gold Rush Trail**. From Lytton, head out for white-water rafting on the **Thompson** and **Fraser Rivers**. After these chilly waters, warm up with a soak in **Harrison Hot Springs**. From here, it's an easy drive back to Vancouver on Hwy 1.

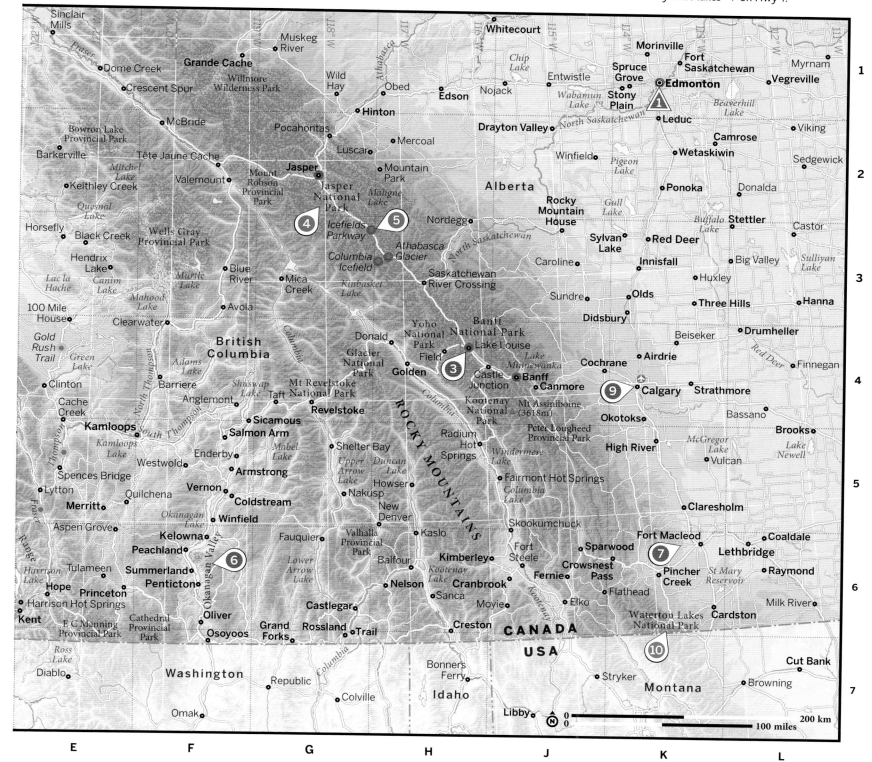

SIGHTS & ACTIVITIES

 SEE

DO

ITINERARY

▼ 1

▽ 2

1 Algonquin Provincial Park

Established in 1893, Ontario's oldest and second-largest park is a sight for city-sore eyes, with over 7600 sq km of thick pine forests, jagged cliffs, trickling crystal streams, mossy bogs and thousands (thousands!) of lakes. An easily accessible outdoor gem, this rugged expanse is a must-visit for canoeists, hikers and seekers of pine-fresh air.

2 Ottawa

The gargantuan Gothic Parliament buildings anchor the downtown core of Canada's stately capital. It has several world-class museums: make time for the National Gallery of Canada, the Canadian Museum of History and the Canadian War Museum. In winter, the Rideau Canal becomes one of the world's largest ice-skating rinks – an impressive 7.8km long.

3 Niagara Falls

Niagara is not the tallest of waterfalls, but in terms of volume, there's nothing like it – more than a million bathtubs of water plummet down every second. It spans Ontario and New York State. On the US side, Bridal Veil Falls and the adjacent American Falls crash on to mammoth fallen rocks; across the border, the Horseshoe Falls plunge into the Maid of the Mist Pool.

Niagara Falls:
Seen here from the US side, the thunderous Niagara draws thousands of onlookers every day.

4 Bruce Peninsula

The Bruce is a 100km limestone outcrop of craggy shorelines and woodlands at the northern end of the Niagara Escarpment. The finger-like protrusion separates Georgian Bay from warmer Lake Huron. Owen Sound is the largest centre, while wreck-diving mecca Tobermory sits at the tip of the peninsula.

5 Stratford

In 1953 the first performance of what has become the Stratford Festival (the largest Shakespeare festival of its kind) was born, creating an industry which continues to support the town today.

6 Blue Mountain

Hands down the best skiing and snowboarding in Ontario, from the folks who brought you Whistler and Mont-Tremblant: freestyle terrain, half pipes, jump-on jump-off rails, 16 lifts and over 35 runs.

7 Thousand Islands

The 'Thousand Islands' are a constellation of over 1800 rugged islands dotting the St Lawrence River from Kingston to Brockville. The Thousand Islands Parkway and the St Lawrence Bikeway bicycle path wind out along the shoreline.

8 Killarney Provincial Park

Killarney is one of the finest kayaking destinations in the world. Paddlers can explore over 50 lakes here, including two deep, clear gems on either side of La Cloche ('the bell') Mountains.

9 Muskoka Lakes

Originally a centre for lumber production and shipbuilding, this area is now 'cottage country': a place for families to enjoy the water and, for many, to retire. Ontario's most extravagant cottages are here, many located along fabulous 'Millionaires' Row' on Lake Muskoka.

10 Canadian Canoe Museum, Peterborough

With the world's largest collection of canoes and kayaks, this museum documents Canada's history of water navigation, from its Aboriginal origins to exploration and fur trading.

© Tony Shi Photography / Getty Images

5-day itinerary
Québec

Start with a leisurely stroll within **Québec City**'s walls in the Old Upper Town, before searching for the ultimate *table d'hôte* in the Old Lower Town. On day two, in **Montréal**, work the calories off on a hike up Parc du Mont-Royal. Descend through Mile End or the Plateau Mont-Royal, where you'll be spoiled for choice for dinner and drinks. On day three,

escape the city for a scenic drive through the Laurentians to **Mont-Tremblant**. Spend the next couple of days rambling through Charlevoix. Stop for lunch in **Baie St Paul** or **La Malbaie**, then head to welcoming **Tadoussac**, where you could easily pass another few days by whale watching in the bay or simply cruising the fjord and watching the scenery scoot by.

7-day itinerary
Ontario

Begin your Ontarion adventure with two days in **Toronto**. Visit Yonge–Dundas Square, then scan the scene from atop the CN Tower and explore Queen Street West and Kensington Market. Next day, focus on King St: from the Entertainment District to St Lawrence Market and the Distillery District. On your third day, take a tour to cram **Niagara**

Falls into a single day. Come day four, head west to the villages of **Elora** and **Fergus**, step back in time to the Mennonite community of **St Jacobs** and move on to arty-foodie **Stratford** for the night, catching a play before returning to Toronto. Next, spend one night enjoying the rustic charm of a Prince Edward County B&B. Stop by **Sandbanks**

Provincial Park for a swim, then overnight in **Kingston**. Journey on to **Gananoque** for a cruise around the Thousand Islands, then continue along the St Lawrence River through quaint **Brockville** and historic **Upper Canada Village**. Finally, turn north to **Ottawa**, the nation's capital, for museums, restaurants, bars and the Unesco-listed, 185-year-old **Rideau Canal**.

Old City, Montréal
With its cobblestoned streets, grand plazas, history museums and period buildings, the old city is where Montréal began and where its heart still lies. The city's nightlife and live music scene are rightly renowned.

La Citadelle, Québec City
Covering 2.3 sq km, North America's largest fort was begun by the French in the 1750s and completed by the British in 1850 to defend against an American invasion that never came. A one-hour tour takes in its main historical sites.

Tadoussac
This small town is a hub for whale watching. Zodiacs zip out in search of the behemoths, while smaller whales such as belugas and minkes can often be glimpsed from the shore.

The Laurentians
Also known as Les Laurentides in French, this region of mountains, lakes and crystal rivers draws Montréal day-trippers. Village destinations include St-Sauveur-des-Monts and pretty Val-David but four-season playground Mont-Tremblant is the crown jewel.

Baie St Paul
An easy day-trip from Québec City, Cirque du Soleil's bohemian hometown overlooks the St Lawrence and Gouffre Rivers. It has a great wining-and-dining scene, and cosy *gîtes* provide overnight accommodation.

Parc National du Bic
The headlands and foggy coastline here have been inhabited by Aboriginal peoples for 9000 years. Nowadays visitors come to spot marine birds, seals, deer and one of North America's highest-density porcupine populations.

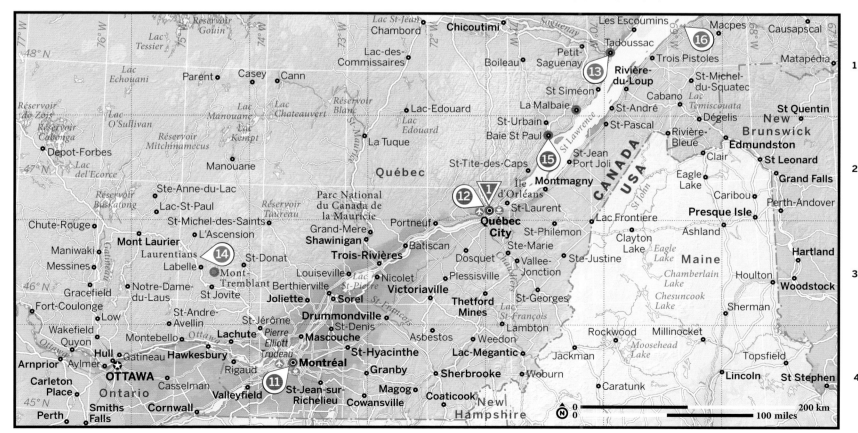

SIGHTS &
ACTIVITIES

 SEE

DO

ITINERARY

 1

2

Cape Breton Highlands

Established in 1936 and encompassing 20% of Cape Breton's land mass, this coastal national park is Nova Scotia's jewel in the crown. It's accessible via the famous Cabot Trail, one-third of which runs through the park.

2 Bay of Fundy

The Bay of Fundy is home to the highest tides in the world, with a tidal range of a whopping 15m. The spectacle is best seen at Hopewell Rocks, where erosion has formed bizarre sandstone sculptures known as 'flowerpots', resembling arches, mushrooms and ice-cream cones.

3 Peggy's Cove

One of the most visited fishing villages in Canada, Peggy's Cove and its red-and-white lighthouse exude seaside calm, despite the non-stop parade of tour buses. Lower Prospect offers similar scenery without the crowds.

New Glasgow

Gourmet lobster suppers have been a tradition in this fishing town since 1958, a sumptuous celebration of its crustacean-fishing heritage. The feasts include chowder, mussels, salads, breads and home-made desserts.

7-day itinerary
Nova Scotia

Soak up some music and culture in **Halifax** then travel to much-snapped **Peggy's Cove**. Don't forget your sunscreen in **Mahone Bay**, where the sun shines on great craft shopping and sea kayaking. Move on slightly south to Lunenburg, a World Heritage site known for its colourful buildings and Bluenose schooner. The **Kejimkujik National Park** offers a range of terrain from coastal beaches (in the section of park known as the Kejimkujik Seaside Adjunct) to inland rivers, which are the perfect spot to float a canoe and drift through the woods. Cross the province to **Annapolis Royal** to stay at a heritage bed and breakfast; explore its fort by day and graveyard by night. The next day visit the wineries around the fabulous college town of **Wolfville** and the Grand Pré National Historic Site, before stopping to enjoy an indulgent meal at a vineyard restaurant. Lastly, explore the **Fundy coast** around Parrsboro and Advocate Harbour, or head to **Maitland** to get the endorphins going by rafting the tidal bore.

Charlottetown

The bucolic area around Charlottetown provided the backdrop to the *Anne of Green Gables* books, loved by children around the world. The town has a pretty waterfront and a well-preserved old town, while Point Prim lighthouse offers stirring coastal views.

Grand Manan Island

From jagged cliffs and marshland to spruce forests and lighthouses, Grand Manan has incredible natural diversity along its 30km length. There are dozens of trails to wander and coves to explore, but no fast-food restaurants or traffic.

Louisbourg National Historic Site

Built to protect French interests, this fortress was erected from 1719 to about 1745, but was burned to the ground by British troops in 1760. The site re-creates the fortress as it was in 1744, complete with costumed guides.

Halifax

The capital of Nova Scotia, Halifax's waterfront is characterised by street buskers, brewpubs and portside restaurants. Out in the bay, container ships, frigates and sailboats chug across the water, and the Dartmouth ferry enjoys great views back to Halifax's boxy downtown.

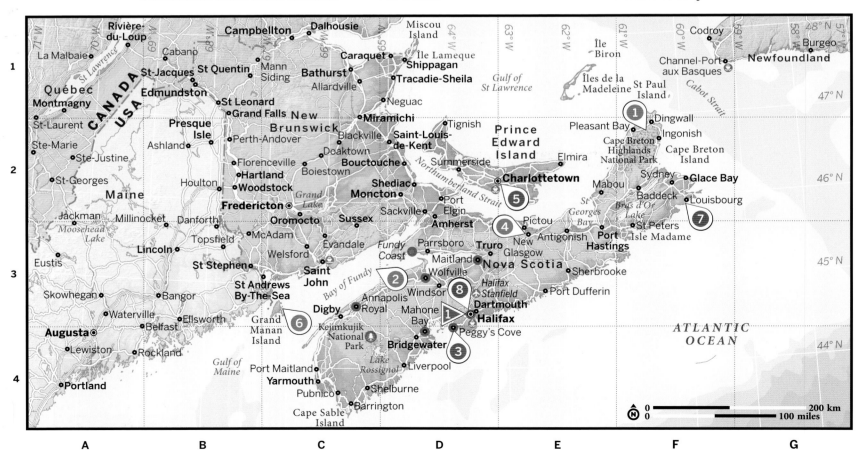

Gros Morne National Park

This 1800-sq-km coastal park is the remnant of a mountain chain formed 1.2 billion years ago. Its geology is a rare example of continental drift, with exposed deep ocean crust and mantle. Hiking, sea kayaking and sightseeing cruises are the top activities here.

St John's

North America's oldest city sits on the slopes of a snug harbour, with jelly-bean-coloured terraced houses lining the hilly streets. Highlights include Signal Hill, with its sweeping views of the harbour, and hoisting a pint (or shot of rum) in a pub along George St.

L'Anse aux Meadows

Viking explorer Leif Eriksson, the first European to set foot in North America, lived here circa AD 1000. Eight wood-and-sod buildings (now just outlines in the turf) and three replica buildings are all that remain of the settlement.

Witless Bay Ecological Reserve

North America's largest Atlantic puffin colony resides on the four islands of this marine reserve. About 260,000 pairs nest here during late spring and summer, as well as kittiwakes, storm petrels and the penguin-like murres.

Red Bay National Historical Site

In the mid-16th century, Basque whalers came to the Strait of Belle Isle to hunt right and bowhead whales for their oil. Basque artifacts and a restored *chalupa* (whaling boat) can be viewed at this World Heritage Site.

Viking Trail

The Viking Trail, aka Rte 430, connects Gros Morne National Park and L'Anse aux Meadows, but it's an attraction in its own right, holding close to the sea as it heads north past the ancient burial grounds of Port au Choix and the ferry jump-off to Labrador.

Twillingate Island

This area of Notre Dame Bay gets an influx of whales and icebergs every summer, both of which can be seen on boat trips. Comprised of two barely separated islands, Twillingate is linked to the mainland via short causeways.

St-Pierre and Miquelon

Twenty-five kilometres offshore from the Burin Peninsula floats a little piece of France. The islands of St-Pierre and Miquelon aren't just French-like with their berets, baguettes and Bordeaux, they *are* France, governed and financed by the *tricolore*.

5-day itinerary
Newfoundland

Start in the historic town of **St John's** by visiting Signal Hill and Cape Spear. Both are historic sites, but they also offer walking trails and views where you just may see an iceberg, a whale or both if you're really lucky. At night sample some of St John's eateries, funky shops and music-filled pubs. After a couple of days of 'big city' life, move onward through the **Avalon Peninsula**. Catch a cruise to see whales and puffins at the amazing Witless Bay Ecological Reserve, or stop in for a wander around **Ferryland,** one of North America's earliest settlements, founded in 1621. Then it's on to **Cape St Mary's Ecological Reserve**, a major seabird colony, with tens of thousands of northern gannet, black-legged kittiwake and common murre. End the last day or two soaking up the historic eastern communities of **Trinity** and **Bonavista** and the cliffside hikes in-between.

USA

Swamps in the Deep South, snow-capped mountains and red-rock deserts of the west, forests and plains from the Atlantic to the Pacific: this is a vast nation of extraordinary geographic variety, riven by volcanoes and great rivers. America's landscape – almost 4 million sq miles of it – has influenced great works of art, literature and music over the centuries and the US continues to inspire all who visit or inhabit it. Peppered with diverse, thrilling cities, from authentic Austin to the neon artifice of Las Vegas, it's a country that compels visitors to hit the road to discover for themselves that America, paraphrasing Walt Whitman, contains multitudes.

CLIMATE CHART

NEW YORK CITY

RAINFALL INCH/MM
10/250
8/200
6/150
4/100
2/50
0

J F M A M J J A S O N D

TEMP °C/°F
50/122
40/104
30/86
20/68
10/50
0/32
-10/14
-20/4

LOS ANGELES

RAINFALL INCH/MM
6/150
4/100
2/50
0

J F M A M J J A S O N D

TEMP °C/°F
40/104
30/86
20/68
10/50
0/32

MUSIC
Name the 20th-century genre and it may well have its roots in the US. Country music still thrives in Nashville; jazz rings through New Orleans; hip hop was born in New York; soul music flourished in Motown (Detroit); and Nirvana were the flannel-wearing figureheads of grunge in Seattle.

ADVENTURE
The US has no shortage of spectacular settings for outdoor activities. Rafting the Grand Canyon in Arizona; mountain biking the slick rock in Utah; hiking 14,000ft peaks in Colorado; heli-skiing in Alaska; and surfing in Hawaii are all top wishlist activities for adventurous types.

ARCHITECTURE
The US is a treasure chest of architectural wonders. Tick off everything from the first skyscraper in Chicago to modernism in Palm Springs, original colonial structures on Elfreth's Alley in Philadelphia, art deco designs in Miami and Santa Fe-style in New Mexico.

SPECTATOR SPORTS
Iconic sports events in the US are some of the best entertainment in the country. Join the crowd for college American football in Alabama, baseball at Fenway Park in Boston, basketball at Madison Square Garden in New York City and auto racing at the Indy 500 in Indianapolis.

Right: The unmistakable ripples and striations of the Grand Canyon, with the Colorado River cutting through.

Transport hubs

America's busiest airports are distributed evenly across the nation (the top five serve Atlanta, Chicago, Los Angeles, Dallas and New York). From these gateways, the US remains the land of the automobile (fuel and car rental costs are relatively low) although some 30 Amtrak rail routes allow for leisurely long-distance travel to more than 500 destinations. Cruise ships arrive at ports in Miami and Fort Lauderdale and also along the east and west coasts.

San Francisco (see pp428-9 for city map)
Three international airports serve the Bay Area: San Francisco International, Oakland International and Norman y Mineta San Jose International. The Transbay Transit Center is the primary bus terminal and trains regularly pass through the Caltrain station and the Ferry Building in San Francisco.

Los Angeles
Southern California's main gateway is Los Angeles International Airport – the terminals are all linked with a free LAX shuttle. Amtrak runs numerous trains through LA's Union Station, including the Pacific Surfliner along the coast.

Miami
As a major international airline hub, many travellers to the US go through Miami International Airport. Travelling by car is easy; it's common to include Florida in a larger US road trip.

Atlanta
Most international visitors arrive in the South's so-called capital via Hartsfield–Jackson International Airport. Atlanta is at the intersection of three interstate highways, making travelling by car to nearby states easy.

New York (see pp418-19 for city map)
New York City wears many crowns, and offers up an irresistible feast for all. Three busy airports – John F Kennedy International, LaGuardia and Newark Liberty International – provide flights to just about anywhere. Port Authority Bus Terminal has buses to most major US cities and Penn Station is the departure point for all Amtrak trains.

Chicago (see pp398-9 for city map)
The Windy City has two airports – O'Hare International Airport and Midway. Chicago's Union Station is a hub for regional and national Amtrak train services.

Seattle
Sea-Tac International has domestic flights and direct connections to Asia and a handful of European cities.Three rail routes – to Oregon and California, Vancouver and Chicago – converge at Seattle's King Street Station.

Houston
Houston has two airports, George Bush Intercontinental and William P Hobby. The Sunset Limited Amtrak train stops in Houston three times a week en route between New Orleans and Los Angeles.

Washington, DC
With two airports and numerous bus and train routes, DC makes it easy to get north and south along the eastern seaboard. Dulles International serves international and domestic flights and Reagan National handles domestic.

Denver
Denver is the best place to fly into to hit the western states on your road trip. Denver International is the largest airport in the country and numerous interstates criss-cross the city. Amtrak's California Zephyr stops in the new Union Station.

Las Vegas
No passenger rail services serve Las Vegas, but its McCarran International Airport is one of the US's busiest hubs.

Right: A streetcar in San Francisco (left) and (right) a view of Chicago from the 'L' Train.

ALEUTIAN ISLANDS

40°N

PACIFIC OCEAN

Tropic of Cancer

Pages 334-335

Honolulu

Hawaii (USA)

20°N

N 0 _____ 1000 km
   0 _____ 500 miles

A   B

© Matt Munro / Lonely Planet, © Dan Welldon / Lonely Planet

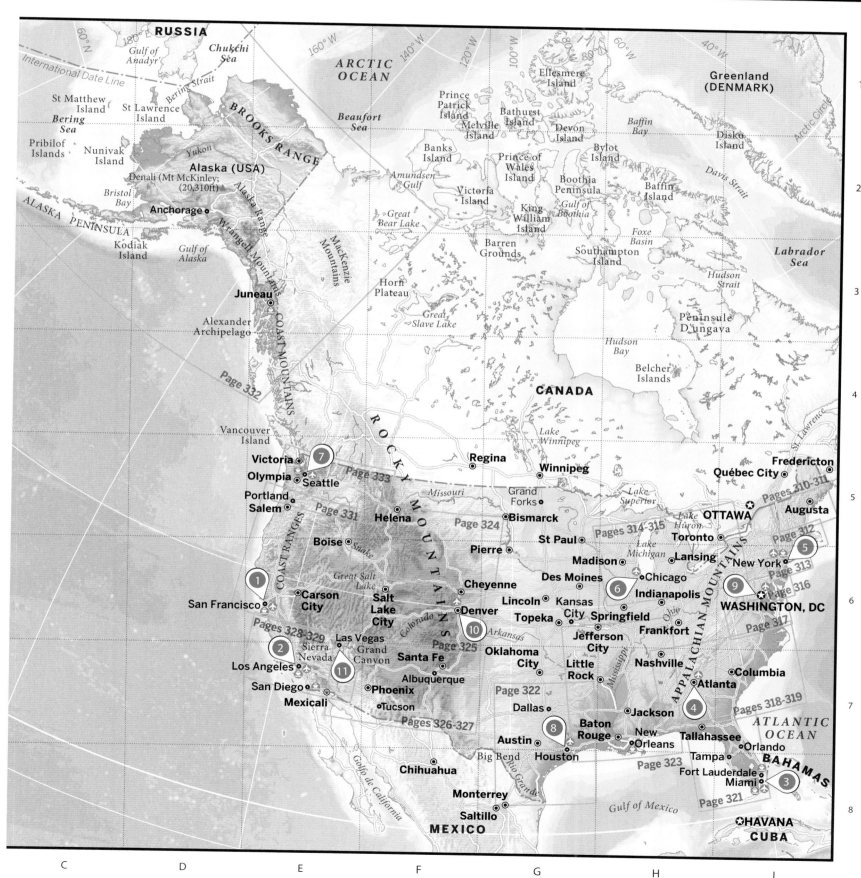

RUSSIA

Gulf of
Anadyr'

Chukchi
Sea

International Date Line

ARCTIC
OCEAN

Greenland
(DENMARK)

Ellesmere
Island

St Matthew
Island

St Lawrence
Island

Bering
Sea

Beaufort
Sea

Prince Patrick
Island

Bathurst
Island

Melville
Island

Devon
Island

Baffin
Bay

Disko
Island

Davis Strait

Pribilof
Islands

Nunivak
Island

Yukon

Banks
Island

Prince of
Wales
Island

Boothia
Peninsula

Baffin
Island

Alaska (USA)

Denali (Mt McKinley;
(20,310ft)

Amundsen
Gulf

Victoria
Island

King
William
Island

Gulf of
Boothia

Bristol
Bay

Anchorage

Labrador
Sea

ALASKA
PENINSULA

Kodiak
Island

Gulf of
Alaska

Wrangell Mountains

Alaska Range

MacKenzie
Mountains

Great
Bear Lake

Barren
Grounds

Southampton
Island

Foxe
Basin

Hudson
Strait

Juneau

Horn
Plateau

Great
Slave Lake

Hudson
Bay

Belcher
Islands

Péninsule
D'ungava

Alexander
Archipelago

COAST MOUNTAINS

CANADA

Vancouver
Island

ROCKY MOUNTAINS

Page 332

Page 333

Regina

Winnipeg

Lake
Winnipeg

Fredericton

Québec City

Pages 310-311

Victoria

Olympia   Seattle

Missouri

Grand
Forks

Lake
Superior

OTTAWA

Augusta

Portland
Salem

Page 331

Helena

Page 324

Bismarck

St Paul

Pages 314-315

Lake
Huron

Toronto

Page 312

Boise

Snake

Pierre

Madison

Lake
Michigan

Lansing

New York

Page 313

COAST RANGES

Sierra
Nevada

Great Salt
Lake

Cheyenne

Des Moines

Chicago

Indianapolis

WASHINGTON, DC

Page 316

San Francisco

Carson
City

Salt
Lake
City

Colorado

Denver

Lincoln

Kansas
City

Springfield

Frankfort

Ohio

Page 317

Pages 328-329

Las Vegas

Grand
Canyon

Santa Fe

Page 325

Arkansas

Jefferson
City

Nashville

APPALACHIAN MOUNTAINS

Los Angeles

Albuquerque

Oklahoma
City

Little
Rock

Mississippi

Columbia

San Diego

Phoenix

Page 322

Atlanta

Pages 318-319

Mexicali

Tucson

Dallas

Jackson

Tallahassee

ATLANTIC
OCEAN

Pages 326-327

Austin

Baton
Rouge

New
Orleans

Orlando

Chihuahua

Big Bend

Houston

Page 323

Tampa

Fort Lauderdale

BAHAMAS

Rio Grande

Miami

Monterrey

Golfo de California

Page 321

Gulf of Mexico

Saltillo

HAVANA

MEXICO

CUBA

1

2

3

4

5

6

7

8

C   D   E   F   G   H   J

SIGHTS &
ACTIVITIES

◉ SEE

◉ DO

ITINERARY

▽ 1

▽ 2

Coastal Maine Botanical Gardens, Boothbay

These magnificent gardens are one of the state's most popular attractions. The waterfront kingdom has 270 acres, with groomed trails winding through forest, meadows and ornamental gardens. The storybook-themed children's garden offers interactive fun.

Fort Williams Park, Cape Elizabeth

Stroll around the ruins of the fort, checking out the WWII bunkers and gun emplacements that still dot the rolling lawns. Don't miss Portland Head Light, commissioned by President George Washington.

Marginal Way, Ogunquit

Tracing the 'margin' of the sea, Ogunquit's famed mile-long footpath winds above the crashing grey waves and allows for some excellent real-estate admiring.

Acadia National Park

The only national park in all of New England, Acadia offers unrivalled coastal beauty and activities for both leisurely hikers and thrill seekers.

Farnsworth Art Museum, Rockland

The excellent collection here spans 200 years of American art, focusing on artists with a Maine connection – look for works by the Wyeths, Edward Hopper, Louise Nevelson and more.

Portland

Maine's 'can-do' attitude and seafood bounty have combined to create one of the country's best cities in which to eat. Local tours take you through the scene, from food trucks to fine dining.

Franconia

This tranquil town sports splendid mountain views and a poetic attraction: Robert Frost's farm.

Black Heritage Trail of New Hampshire, Portsmouth

Twenty-four bronze plaques around Portsmouth commemorate centuries of black history, from the arrival of the first enslaved people at Prescott Park wharf in the 1680s to the formation of civil rights group Scorr in the 1960s.

Mt Washington Cog Railway

Since 1869, coal-fired, steam-powered locomotives have climbed this scenic 3.5-mile track up a steep mountainside trestle (a three-hour round trip).

Brattleboro Farmers Market

Offering a crash course in Vermont food, the market has more than 50 local vendors. Live music and an active crafts scene round off the experience.

Stowe Recreation Path

This easy 5.5-mile path offers a fabulously accessible four-season escape for all ages. It rambles through woods, meadows and outdoor sculpture gardens along the river, with sweeping views of Mt Mansfield in the distance.

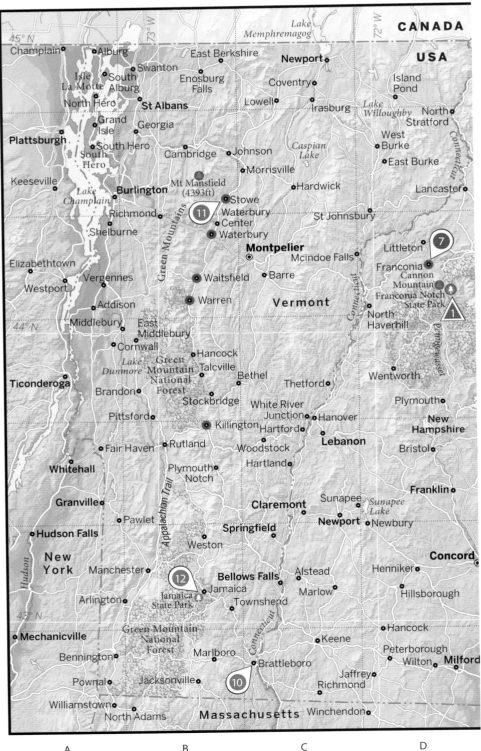

Jamaica State Park

Thanks to its long riverside hiking trail and campsites right next to the rushing West River, this state park is especially popular with kayakers and rafters for annual white-water weekends in late September.

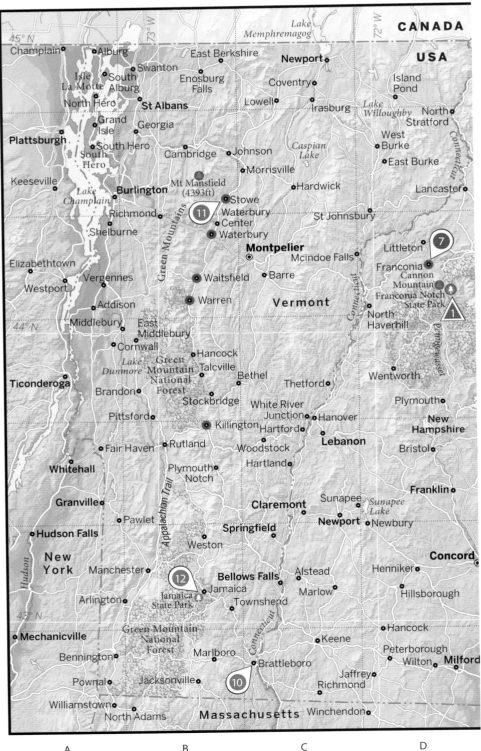

7-day itinerary
Mountain Majesty

Follow this route for some pure mountain air. Start at **Franconia Notch State Park,** where you can hike down the Flume or ride a tramway up **Cannon Mountain**. Sleep at one of many welcoming inns in **Franconia**. Stop at **Bretton Woods** and take **Mt Washington Cog Railway** to the top of New England's highest peak. Drive west across the White Mountain National Forest to **Killington** for skiing or mountain biking. Continue north on scenic VT 100. Don't miss **Warren** and **Waitsfield**, excellent for browsing art galleries and antique shops. Sidle up to **Stowe**, where **Mt Mansfield** is the outdoor capital of northern Vermont. End by indulging in some Ben & Jerry's ice cream from the factory in **Waterbury**.

10-day itinerary
Coastal New England

New England is intrinsically tied to the sea. Start with a frolic in the waves at Crane Beach in **Ipswich** and feast on fried clams in **Essex**. Walk the boardwalk at **Hampton Beach** and admire the old houses in historic **Portsmouth**. Continuing into Maine, spend a day or two exploring **Portland**. Eat, drink and shop the Old Port District and check out the Portland Museum of Art. Don't leave town without snapping a photo of the Portland Head Light on **Cape Elizabeth**. Continuing north, stroll around lovely **Boothbay Harbor**, perhaps stopping for a seafood lunch on the harbour. Don't miss a stop in pretty **Camden**, where you can take a windjammer cruise up the rocky coast. When you return to dry land, clamber to the top of Mt Battie in **Camden Hills State Park** for sweeping views of Penobscot Bay. End your trip in beautiful **Bar Harbor** and **Acadia National Park**, which are highlights of the New England coast. You'll have no problem occupying yourself for a few days exploring Mt Desert Island's beautiful scenery while hiking, biking, kayaking, camping and more.

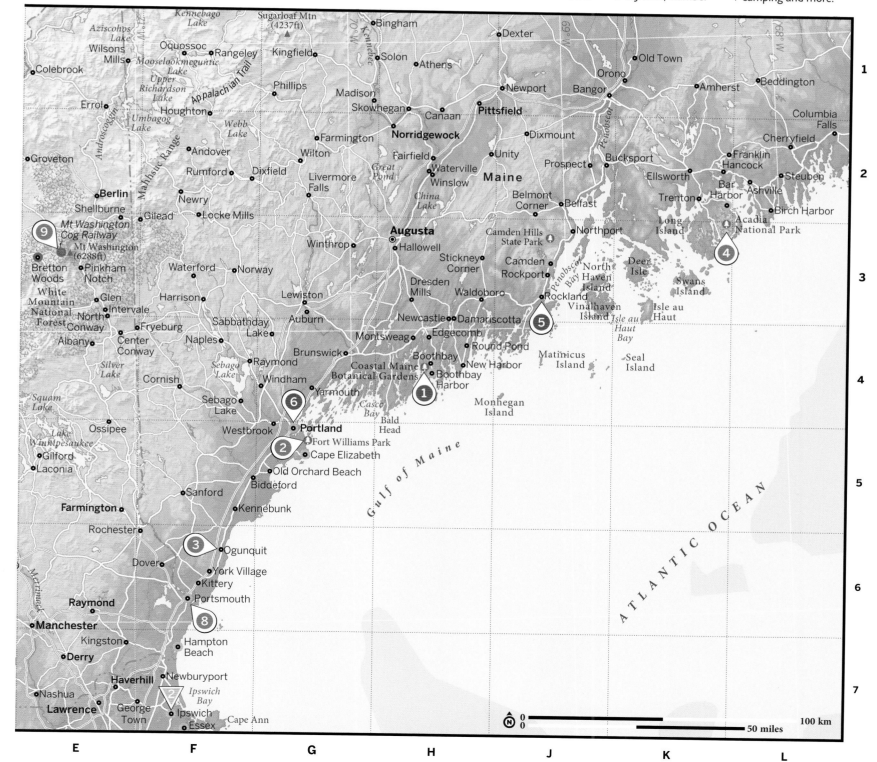

SIGHTS & ACTIVITIES

1

Essex Steam Train and Riverboat Ride
All aboard for the most scenic – and most popular – train ride in New England, between Essex and Deep River in Connecticut. Add on a riverboat ride for the ultimate day of old-fashioned fun.

SIGHTS & ACTIVITIES

 SEE

DO

ITINERARY

 1

2

2

Yale University, New Haven
Wander the hallowed halls and verdant campus of this legendary Ivy League school with a free guided tour. Notable alums include Noah Webster, Eli Whitney, Sonia Sotomayor, Hillary Clinton, George W Bush and Angela Bassett.

3

Seaport Museum, Mystic
Step into New England's whaling past at this unique 17-acre museum, which recreates an entire New England whaling village. Interpreters give demonstrations on oystering and whaleboat launching, as well as traditional crafts.

4

Cliff Walk, Newport
Newport is known for its glitzy mansions and dramatic ocean views – get both at once with this 3.5-mile walk that hugs the rugged coast and allows for a peek into some very elite backyards.

Cape Cod National Seashore: The oldest lighthouse on Cape Cod dates from 1857.

5

Narragansett
Can you say you've been to the Atlantic Coast if you don't try a lobster roll? We say no, and Narragansett is one of the best places to get this buttery, decadent seafood fix. In this part of the world, that's really saying something.

6

Lime Rock Race Track
No, this isn't NASCAR country, but one of the USA's most beautiful race tracks is right here in Connecticut. Paul Newman is among the many thrill-seekers to have sped around the seven turns of this picturesque 1.5-mile track. Events run from May to September.

7

Independence Hall and Liberty Bell, Philadelphia
You can feel the history inside Philadelphia's modest Independence Hall, where the Declaration of Independence was approved in 1776. Outside, the hallowed Liberty Bell, which tolled on the first public reading of the Declaration, resides in all its cracked glory.

8

Minute Man National Historical Park
British troops followed this route into Concord, Massachusetts, on the night of Paul Revere's famous midnight ride. Walk the 5-mile Battle Road Trail to see battle sites and the place where Revere was captured in April 1775.

5-day itinerary
Hudson Valley

Painters, presidents and captains of industry were beguiled by the beauty of this region. Start in **NYC** at the Cloisters, to gaze at medieval tapestries. Then head north to **Tarrytown**, where Washington Irving's home awaits. Next is **Harriman State Park**, 72 sq miles of wilderness. Follow the river past **West Point US Military Academy**. Next up is **Beacon**, an art world star thanks to Dia: Beacon. In **Hyde Park**, the Franklin D Roosevelt Home and the beaux-arts Vanderbilt Mansion offer daily tours. Aircraft aficionados shouldn't miss the **Old Rhinebeck Aerodome**, with a collection of pre-1930s planes. Finish off in **Hudson** by visiting the restored Hudson Opera House and Olana, the 'Persian fantasy' home of artist Frederic Church.

7-day itinerary
Coastal Charm

A week of whale watching, maritime museums and sailing boats will leave you feeling pleasantly waterlogged. Begin in **Gloucester**, founded in 1623 by English fisherfolk and home of the Maritime Gloucester Museum. Then drive on to **Salem**, famous for the witch trials but also full of grand homes that once belonged to sea captains. Next up is **Marblehead**, the state's premier yachting port, dotted with colourful Colonial homes. In **Boston**, plunge further into history along the Freedom Trail and stroll along the Rose Kennedy Greenway to take in the waterfront as well as city views. Head south to **New Bedford**, the setting of *Moby-Dick* and home to the excellent, hands-on New Bedford Whaling Museum. Continue on to **Newport** to take in the magnificent mansions and steep cliffs, before moving on to **Mystic** and its Seaport Museum, which launched many a clipper ship in the 19th century. End your trip in **New Haven** with a tour of Yale and its campus and a ride on the Shore Line Trolley, which is the oldest operating suburban trolley car in the country.

Newport Mansions
During the 19th century, the wealthiest New Yorkers chose Newport as their summer playground, building fabulous mansions along Bellevue Ave that can be toured today, in all their Gilded Age glory.

Freedom Trail, Boston
Follow the red-brick road through the city centre to discover Boston's most famous Revolutionary War-era sights, from Boston Common to the USS *Constitution* and Bunker Hill.

Cape Cod National Seashore
Beaches, dunes, salt marshes and trails – unspoiled and wild beauty awaits on this 40-mile stretch of coast, one of the region's outdoor treasures.

Kaaterskill Falls
Nearly 100ft higher than Niagara Falls, New York's most thundering waterfall captured the imagination of regional artists and sparked early tourism in the area. Today the stunning view is easily accessible to all courtesy of a viewing platform.

Plimoth Plantation, Plymouth
One of the earliest British settlements has been recreated here in painstaking detail. Amid replica period-style buildings, historic interpreters live, work and play like it's 1627.

Dia: Beacon, Beacon
An impressive collection of contemporary art is housed here, in a 300,000-sq-ft former Nabisco box-printing factory. Look for the likes of Louise Bourgeois and Gerhard Richter on the walls.

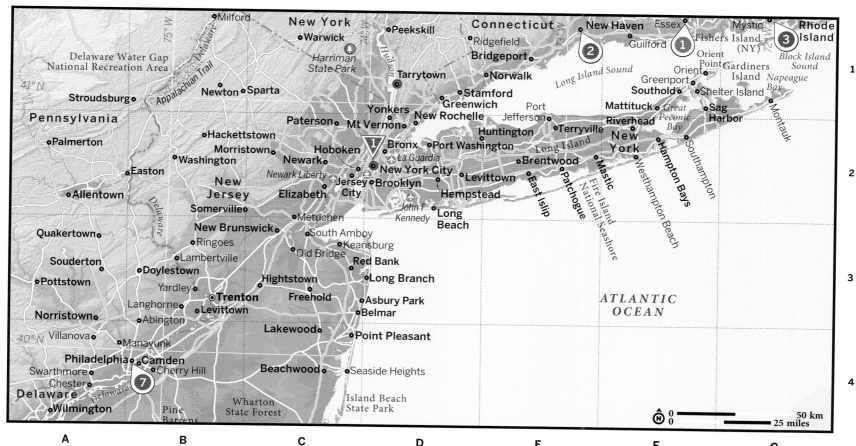

SIGHTS & ACTIVITIES

 SEE

 DO

ITINERARY

1

2

Fisher Building, Detroit

From the soaring vaulted ceilings, featuring an array of intricate, hand-painted patterns, to the sparkling mosaics and the gleaming marble on the walls, this 1928 stunner by Albert Kahn was dubbed 'Detroit's largest art object' and provides endless visual inspiration.

Sleeping Bear Dunes National Lakeshore

Eye-popping lake views over water blue enough to be in the Caribbean and miles of unspoiled beach – it's all here, along with lush forests, terrific day hikes and glass-clear waterways for paddling.

Fishtown, Leland

In the early 1900s, tiny commercial fishing villages lined the shores of the Great Lakes. Fishtown is one of the few that has been preserved. Wander among the shanties and see fish being cleaned and smoked.

Old Mission Peninsula

Winery-hop amid stunning views of Grand Traverse Bay. Michigan's excellent wines taste even better when imbibed in one of the many vineyards that pepper the peninsula.

Mackinac Island

The most important date on this 3.8-sq-mile island is 1898 – the year cars were banned in order to encourage tourism. Today all travel is by horse or bicycle; even the police use bikes to patrol the town.

Ohio's Amish Country

Rural Wayne and Holmes Counties are home to the USA's largest Amish community,and visiting is like entering a pre-industrial time warp. Many here adhere to rules prohibiting the use of electricity and motorized vehicles.

Dane County Farmers Market, Madison

Shop for produce and Wisconsin cheese in the shadow of the Madison Capitol building, at one of the country's most picturesque farmers markets.

Milwaukee's Third Ward

Go on a gastropub crawl in one of the USA's biggest beer cities. The bars are as good as you've heard, and there are some surprising flavours to be found in this under-the-radar Great Lakes city as well.

Buffalo City Hall

This 32-storey art-deco masterpiece, beautifully detailed inside and out and opened in 1931, towers over downtown. It's worth joining the free tour at noon to get the full scoop on the building's history and access to its open-air observation deck.

Niagara Falls

Great plumes of icy mist rise for hundreds of feet as the waters collide, like an ethereal veil. Thousands of daily onlookers delight in the spectacle of more than six million cubic feet of water passing its crest every minute.

Cleveland Rock and Roll Hall of Fame & Museum

Cleveland's top attraction is like an overstuffed attic bursting with groovy finds: Jimi Hendrix's Stratocaster, John Lennon's Sgt Pepper suit and a 1966 piece of hate mail to the Rolling Stones.

7-day itinerary
Lake Michigan

Lake Michigan's coastline offers a wide range of experiences, from world-class cities to natural wonders. Start in **Traverse City**. Wineries dot the **Old Mission Peninsula** north of town, and offer great bayside views. Then head to Fishtown in **Leland** one of the last remaining Great Lakes fishing villages, and the undulating golden waves of the **Sleeping Bear Dunes National Lakeshore**. Then it's on to **Ludington State Park** – climb the lighthouse for excellent views of the lake. Follow the lakeshore to **Holland**. Founded by (you guessed it) the Dutch, its tulips are a sight to behold in the spring. Take in more sun and sand on the 15-mile **Indiana Dunes National Lakeshore** – look out for blue herons.

12-day itinerary
Cities of the Great Lakes

The industrial past of the Great Lakes region created many of the USA's most dynamic cities. Start in **Milwaukee**, one of the brewing capitals of the country. Hit the Calatrava-designed art museum or the badass Harley-Davidson Museum, and wander the Third Ward for some stylish eats. Head south to **Chicago** for a peek at Millennium Park, Navy Pier and an architecture tour. Then drive around the lower curve of Lake Michigan and over to **Grand Rapids**, the second largest city in Michigan, where more than 20 local breweries await. Sample local cuisine at Downtown Market, a bustling food hall. From there, cut across the bottom of the Michigan mitten to **Detroit**. Tour top-notch art-deco architecture like the Guardian and Fisher buildings and take in the Detroit Institute of Art and the Motown Museum. From here, cruise the coast of Lake Erie to **Cleveland**, where you can take in a baseball game or check out the arts and music scene, before heading to the Rust Belt city of **Buffalo** and rounding things off at the famous thunder of **Niagara Falls**.

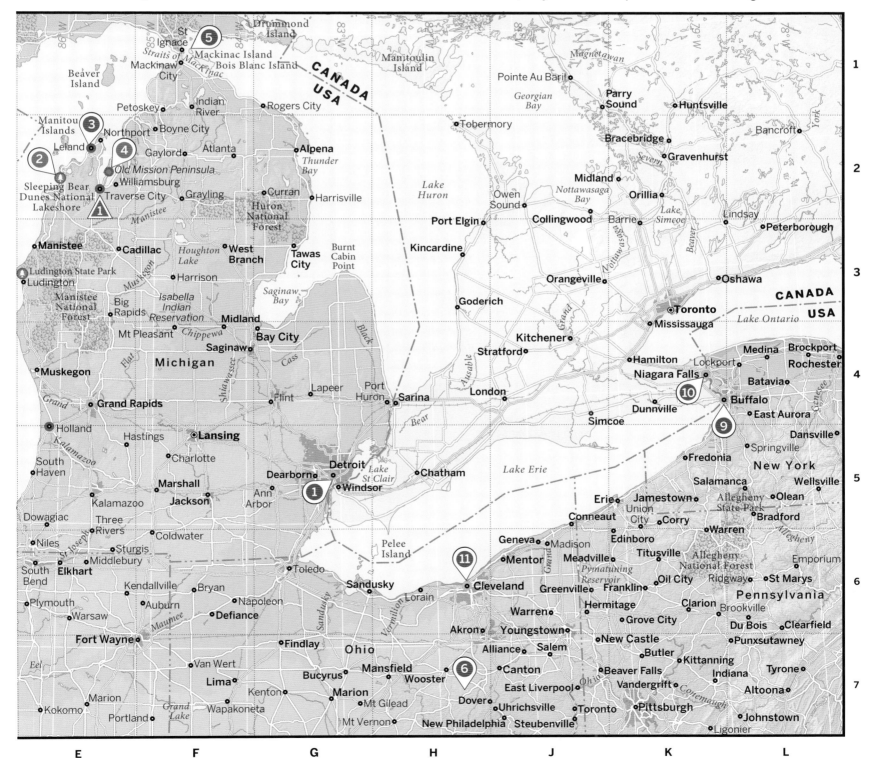

SIGHTS &
ACTIVITIES

 SEE

DO

ITINERARY

▽ 1

▽ 2

Shenandoah National Park: The stunning Skyline Drive is even more spectacular in the leaf-peeping season.

1 Lincoln Memorial, Washington, DC
Anchoring the Mall's west end is the hallowed shrine to Abraham Lincoln, who gazes peacefully across the Reflecting Pool. Look for the engraving that marks the spot MLK gave his 'I Have a Dream' speech (it's on the landing 18 stairs from the top).

2 Gettysburg National Military Park
The museum at the visitor centre is a must-see, particularly for the awe-inspiring cyclorama – a life-size, 360-degree painting of Pickett's Charge, a lethal assault on the Battle of Gettysburg's last day. In the park, you can explore on your own, on a bus tour or – recommended – on a two-hour, guide-led tour in your own car.

3 C&O Canal National Historic Park
A marvel of engineering, the C&O Canal was designed to stretch alongside the Potomac River from Chesapeake Bay to the Ohio River. The park's protected 185-mile corridor includes a 12ft wide towpath, hiking and bicycling trail.

4 Rehoboth Beach
As the closest stretch of sand to Washington, DC, Rehoboth Beach is often dubbed 'the Nation's Summer

Capital'. Escape the crowds by wandering the downtown side streets: you'll find a mix of gingerbread houses, tree-lined thoroughfares, posh restaurants and child-friendly amusements, plus a wide beach fronted by a mile-long boardwalk.

5 Harriet Tubman Underground Railroad National Historic Park
Learn more about the life of Harriet Tubman, who led hundreds of people to freedom from slavery, at great personal risk, on the Underground Railroad.

6 Hammond Harwood House, Annapolis
Of the many historical homes in Annapolis, the 1774 HHH is the one to visit. It has a superb collection of decorative arts, including furniture, paintings and ephemera dating from the 18th century, and is one of the

finest existing British Colonial homes in America. Knowledgeable guides help bring the past to life.

7 Museum of the American Revolution, Philadelphia
This massive, multimedia-rich, new museum will have you virtually participating in the American Revolution, from interactive dioramas to 3D experiences that take you all the way from contentment under British rule to the rejection of it. Don't miss George Washington's battlefield tent, a true national treasure.

8 Fort McHenry National Monument and Historical Shrine, Baltimore
On September 13 and 14, 1814, this fort successfully repelled a British navy attack during the Battle of Baltimore. After a long night of bombs bursting in the air, Francis Scott Key saw, 'by dawn's early light', the

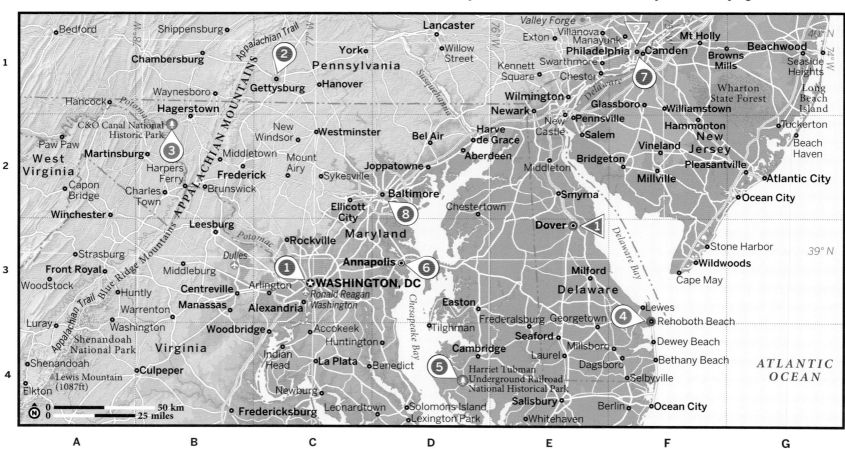

© Matt Munro / Lonely Planet

7-day itinerary
Beaches, Bikes & Hikes

Set off from **Dover** and enjoy **Rehoboth Beach**. Then travel south to **Assateague Island National Seashore** and **Chincoteague Island**, where you might be lucky enough to see wild horses. Get a dose of history at the new **Harriet Tubman Underground Railroad National Historical Park**, which honours Tubman's heroic rescue of dozens of people from slavery. Then hop on two wheels to explore the miles of greenway in **C&O Canal National Historic Park**. Move on to the peaks and valleys of **Shenandoah National Park**. Don't miss the winding **Skyline Drive**. Finish in **Charlottesville**, home to the University of Virginia and Thomas Jefferson's marvellous home, Monticello.

12-day itinerary
American History

The Mid-Atlantic States hold some of the USA's most important historical sites. Start in **Philadelphia**, city of Benjamin Franklin and Independence Hall. You'll need at least a couple of days – don't forget to try the cheesesteak! Then move on to **Valley Forge** and **Gettysburg**, battlefields from two different wars that marked major milestones for a nation. Next, head to **Baltimore** to discover some of the country's maritime heritage and a few literary sites, like the home of Edgar Allan Poe. Now you're ready to see **Washington, DC**, with its mass of monuments and museums. Spend a few days here to take it all in. For a small-town change of pace, don't miss **Fredericksburg** – George Washington grew up here. Today the main street is a pleasant amble of bookshops, pubs and cafes. Next stop is **Richmond**, steeped in Civil War history. End your trip by revisiting the USA's earliest days in the **Historic Triangle**, with the site of the battle of Yorktown and the historical interpretation centres of **Jamestown** and **Colonial Williamsburg**.

---

tattered flag still waving. Inspired, he penned 'The Star-Spangled Banner', which was set to the tune of a popular drinking song.

Shenandoah National Park
One of the country's most spectacular national parks, Shenandoah is a natural marvel: in spring and summer the wildflowers explode, in fall the leaves burn bright red and orange, and in winter a starkly beautiful hibernation period sets in. Spot white-tailed deer, black bears and wild turkeys and don't miss the Skyline Drive, the breathtaking road that follows the Blue Ridge Mountains.

(10) Assateague Island National Seashore
A low-key barrier island, Assateague is a place to relax. In the Maryland section of the national seashore, you can cycle along a 4-mile trail, check out the exhibits at the visitor centre, catch a ranger talk or simply unwind on the beach. You might even spot some of the famed wild horses.

(11) Virginia's Historic Triangle
Welcome to America's birthplace. Nowhere else in the country has such a small area played such a pivotal role in the nation's history. The nation's roots were planted in Jamestown, the first permanent English settlement in the New World; the flames of the American Revolution were fanned at the colonial capital of Williamsburg; and Independence was won at Yorktown.

(12) Virginia Museum of Fine Arts, Richmond
Stop in for a remarkable collection of European works, sacred Himalayan art and one of the largest Fabergé egg collections on display outside Russia. Don't miss Andy Warhol's *Triple Elvis* or the striking new *Chloe* sculpture by Jaume Plensa.

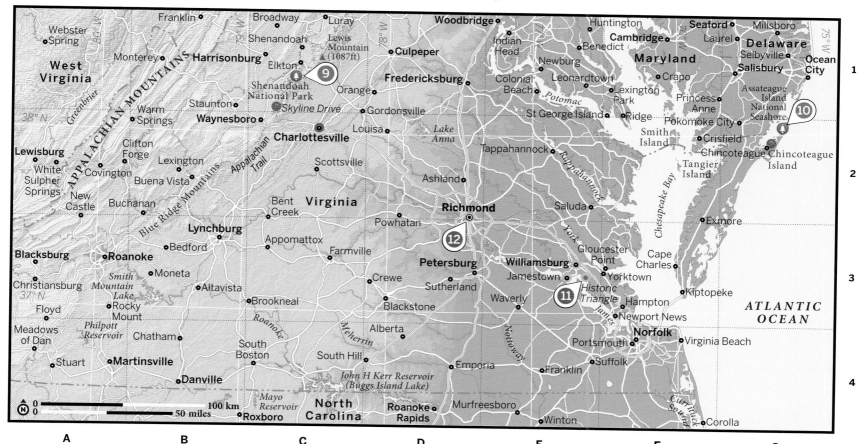

SIGHTS &
ACTIVITIES

 SEE

DO

ITINERARY

1

2

Great Smoky Mountains National Park

This is the country's most visited park and one of the world's most diverse geographic areas: landscapes range from deep, dim spruce forest and sunny meadows carpeted with daisies to wide, coffee-brown rivers.

Birmingham Civil Rights Institute

A maze of moving exhibits tells the story of racial segregation in America and the Civil Rights movement, with a focus on activities in and around Birmingham. There's extensive information on the 16th Street Baptist Church (located across the street), which was bombed in 1963.

East Nashville

Come here to appreciate the creativity of Nashville's passionate artisans. Shop the pop-up retailers, sample the speciality chocolate, try a dish from a farm-friendly eatery, and sip seasonal brews. For lush natural distractions, hit Shelby Bottoms Park.

Beaufort

On Port Royal Island, darling Beaufort ('byoo-furt') is often used as a set for Hollywood films. The streets of the historic district are lined with antebellum homes and magnolias dripping with Spanish moss. The riverfront downtown has lots of linger-worthy cafes and galleries.

Asheville

The undisputed 'capital' of the North Carolina mountains, Asheville is one of the coolest small cities in the South. Although it's still an overgrown mountain town that holds on tight to its traditional roots, a large population of artists and hardcore hippies keep things here progressive and sustainable.

Cumberland Island

The southernmost barrier island in the state of Georgia can only be accessed by boat, and it makes for a lovely, peaceful departure from all traces of the modern world. Wild horses roam around, sea turtles hatch here, and ruins still stand, just begging to be discovered.

Blue Ridge Parkway

Take in sublime sunsets, watch for wildlife and lose all sense of time while gazing at the wilderness surrounding this 469-mile roadway, which traverses the southern Appalachian Mountains of Virginia and North Carolina.

Atlanta BeltLine

The Atlanta BeltLine is a sustainable redevelopment project that is repurposing an existing rail corridor into 33 miles of multi-use trails. Walk, bike, run, drink and eat your way through the BeltLine's Eastside Trail, its hippest, most developed stretch.

Martin Luther King Jr birthplace, Atlanta

This historic site provides a deep dive into the life, work and legacy of the Baptist preacher and international civil rights leader. Free, first-come, first-served guided tours of King's childhood home take about 30 minutes.

Charleston

This is a place for seduction by Southern hospitality – Charleston will charm the sweat right off your brow. Its cannons, cemeteries and carriage rides conjure an earlier era and the romanticism combines with great food.

7-day itinerary
The Coastal South

Charleston is a city to savour – stroll past Rainbow Row and enjoy shrimp and grits on a local verandah. Then head on to **Walterboro** to peruse the South Carolina Artisans Center. Swing down to **Savannah** for the city's historic centre, photogenic Forsyth Park, and the SCAD Museum of Art. Further south lies the barrier island of **Jekyll** – check out the Sea Turtle Center and its historic winter cottages. On your loop back north, rent a kayak on **Little St Simons Island**; further along, stop in charming **Beaufort** before heading east to **St Helena Island**, the heart of Gullah Country. Take the Edisto Island Scenic Byway, a route replete with marshes and moss-draped oaks, stopping to camp at the **Edisto Beach State Park**.

12-day itinerary
Southeastern Cities

Start with two days in hilly, shady **Birmingham**, which was a battleground at the heart of the Civil Rights movement. Now it's home to a great dining and drinking scene and some innovative beautification projects. Head north to **Nashville**, taking a few days to enjoy the sonic history of Music City. The music scene today is as vibrant as ever, and half a dozen burgeoning neighbourhoods are packed tight with unique shops and distilleries. Ping over to leafy **Chattanooga** with its miles of waterfront trails, world-class rock climbing and growing arts districts, before turning east to **Atlanta**, the capital of the South, where you'll find a palpable Hollywood influence and iconic African American history. Swing up to photogenic **Greenville** to explore its lively downtown wrapped around the picturesque Reedy River. Then head on to cool **Asheville**, which offers easy access to outdoor adventures of all kinds, while downtown's historic art-deco buildings hold stylish restaurants, decadent chocolate shops and microbreweries.

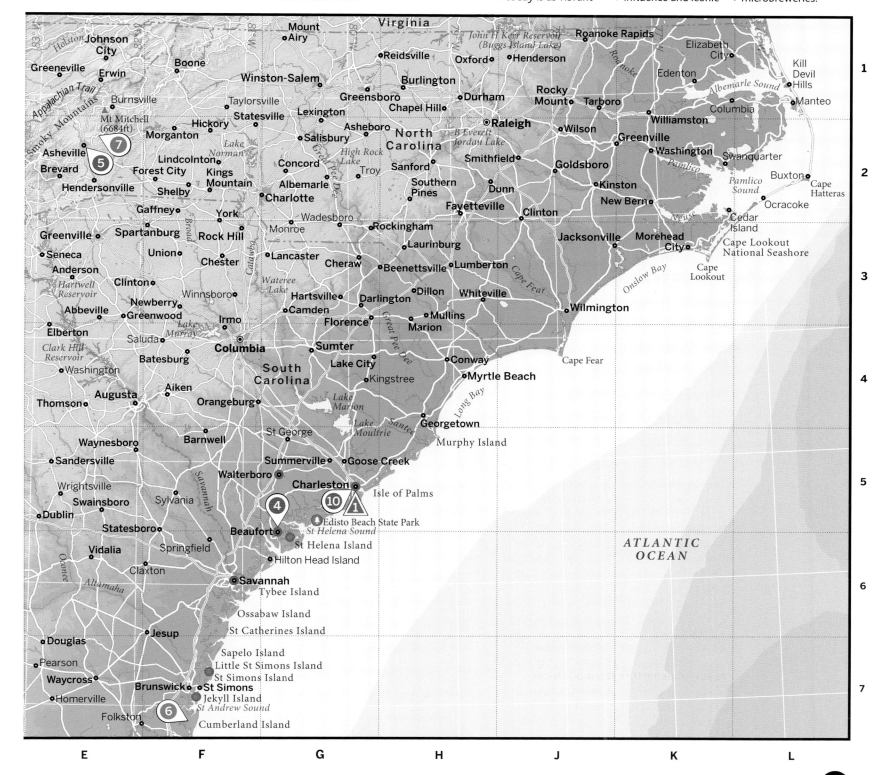

SIGHTS & ACTIVITIES

 SEE

 DO

ITINERARY

 1

 2

 Ponce de Leon State Park
Soak in one of Florida's loveliest and least-touristed springs. The clear, almost luminescent waters are studded with knobby trees and surrounded by ladders for easy swimming access.

 Amelia Island
This moss-draped, sun- and sand-soaked blend of the Deep South and Florida coast has been inhabited for more than 4000 years, and has been a holiday destination since the 1890s.

 Hemingway House, Key West
Key West's literary luminary, Ernest Hemingway, lived in this Spanish Colonial house from 1931 to 1940. The descendants of his favourite six-toed cats basically run the grounds, but they're indifferent to human visitors.

 Art deco, Miami Beach
The world-famous art-deco district of Miami Beach is pure exuberance: an architecture of bold lines, whimsical tropical motifs and a brilliant palette. Among the 800 deco buildings listed on the National Register of Historic Buildings, no design is the same.

Everglades National Park: These wetlands provide an important habitat for manatee, alligator and the Florida panther.

 Everglades National Park
There is no wilderness in America quite like this. Called the 'River of Grass' by Native American inhabitants, the Everglades are not just a wetland, a swamp, a lake, a river, or a grassland, but all of the above, twisted together.

 St Augustine
Visit the oldest occupied European settlement in the US, with Spanish-style architecture and narrow streets. Its large National Historic Landmark District is a deservedly popular destination.

 Walt Disney World® Resort
Since 1951, this magical theme park has been earning the title 'Happiest Place on Earth'. It's an integral part of most Florida vacations.

 Ringling Museum Complex, Sarasota
The 66-acre winter estate of railroad, real-estate and circus baron John Ringling is one of the Gulf Coast's premier attractions and also Florida's state art museum. Nearby, Ringling's Circus Museum documents his theatrical successes.

 Tarpon Springs
Watch the sponge boats line up to deliver their bounty on the docks and sink your teeth into an authentic gyro in this historic Greek community, settled in the early 20th century by divers from the Dodecanese Islands.

 Kennedy Space Center
Whether you're mildly interested in space or a die-hard science-fiction fan, a trip to the Space Center is awe-inspiring. Visitors can experience a virtual moonwalk, try a shuttle simulator and walk under a real rocket.

 Grayton Beach State Park
With acres of marble-coloured dunes rolling to the water's edge, this state park's beauty is genuinely mind-blowing. Locals flock here to watch the sunset and to wakeboard on the unique coastal dune lakes.

 Homosassa Springs
This unique spring system is an excellent place to see a gentle manatee in the wild, harvest scallops in season and catch Atlantic tarpon – dozens of hopeful fishing boats dot the river each summer.

5-day itinerary
The Glorious Gulf

The Gulf Coast is a less flashy side of Florida, but offers great value and stunning landscapes. Set off from **Pensacola**, near the Alabama state line. The best beaches here are on a barrier island in the bay – check out historic **Fort Pickens** while you're there. Travel down scenic Hwy 98 along the Gulf, which takes you through vacation hotspots like **Fort Walton Beach**, **Destin** and **Seaside**. The white sands and small-town beachy vibes are strong here. It's worth detouring from the Gulf's charms for a quick dip at **Ponce de Leon Springs State Park**, where vivid blue spring waters bubble up year-round. Then get back on Hwy 98 to finish your trip in **Apalachicola**, an old-fashioned bayside town that backs up onto a sprawling National Forest with spring-fed lakes.

5-day itinerary
Space Coast to the Everglades

Start your trip at the world-class **Kennedy Space Center**, to see the Space Shuttle Atlantis and other NASA artifacts. Nearby Merritt Island National Wildlife Refuge is one of the country's best birding spots. From there, head south – I-95 is fastest, but Hwy 1 has the best views – through an endearing collection of beach towns like **Melbourne**, **Vero Beach** and **Lauderdale-by-the-Sea**. Pick a favourite, grab a fresh seafood lunch and spend the afternoon working on your tan. Soon you'll be in **Miami**, where the art-deco architecture is all curves and colours and the beaches are as hot as the nightlife. Your last stop is the **Everglades National Park**. The drive here from Miami will take you past several Cuban-style fruit stands; order a coffee or freshly squeezed juice to keep you going. Don't miss quaint **Everglades City**, home of the Everglades Rod & Gun Club. Stop in for lunch and travel back in time within its wood-panelled walls and an oh-so-Southern back porch. Kayak through the brackish water of these swamps – but keep an eye out for 'gators!

Georgia

Marianna
Chattaoohchee
Cairo · Thomasville · Valdosta
Havana · Quitman
Blountstown · Quincy
Lake Talquin · Monticello
Greenville · Jasper
Tallahassee · Madison · White Springs
Lamount · Falmouth
Dead Lake · **Live Oak**
Wewahitchka · St Marks · **Perry** · Mayo
Apalachicola · Carrabelle · Eastpoint
Apalachee Bay
St Vincent Island · St George Sound
St George Island

See Florida Panhandle Inset

St Joseph Bay
St Vincent Island · *St George Island*

Kingsland
St Marys
Fernandina Beach
Yulee · Amelia Island
Callahan
Jacksonville
Jacksonville Beach

ATLANTIC OCEAN

Lake City · Olustee
Fort · Lake Butler
White · Green Cove Springs
Branford · Starke
High Springs · **St Augustine**
Cross City · Newberry · **Gainesville** · Interlachen
Trenton · **Palatka**
Chiefland · Micanopy · Orange Satsuma
Bronson · Williston · Lake · Crescent City
Otter Creek · Silver Springs · *Crescent Lake* · Flagler Beach
Cedar Key · Dunnellon · Belleview · Ocala · *Lake George*
Waccasassa Bay · Weirsdale · Ocala National Forest · **Daytona Beach**
DeLand · **New Smyrna Beach**
Homosassa Springs · **Inverness** · Lady Lake · *Mosquito Lagoon*
Umatilla · Canaveral National Seashore
Crystal Bay · Leesburg · **Eustis** · **Sanford** · Titusville
Brooksville · Bushnell · Mount Dora · **Orlando** · Kennedy Space Center
Weeki Wachee · Groveland · Clermont · Walt Disney World Resort · **Cape Canaveral**
Spring Hill · **Dade City** · **Kissimmee** · Cocoa · Cocoa Beach
New Port Richey · Zephyrhills · **Florida** · **St. Cloud**
Tarpon Springs · Davenport · Haines City · Holopaw · Melbourne
Dunedin · **Tampa** · Winter Haven · **Melbourne Beach**
Clearwater · **Plant City** · Lake Kissimmee
St Petersburg · **Bartow** · Lake Wales · Kenansville · *Blue Cypress Lake* · *Sebastian Inlet*
St Pete Beach · Brewster · Forstproof · **Vero Beach**
Ruskin · Fort Meade · **Avon Park** · Wauchula
Bradenton · **Fort Pierce**
Sarasota · Gardner · *Lake Clay* · Brighton · Okeechobee · **Stuart**
Arcadia · Childs · Indian Town
Venice · Punta Gorda · Fort Ogden · Palmdale · Port Mayaca · **Jupiter**
Englewood · *Lake Okeechobee* · Canal Point · **West Palm Beach**
Charlotte Harbour · La Belle · Clewiston · **Lake Worth**
Pine Island · Fort Myers · Belle Glade · **Boynton Beach**
Fort Myers Beach · Immokalee · **Delray Beach**
Sunniland · Big Cypress National Preserve · **Boca Raton**
Naples · Coral Springs · Lauderdale-by-the-Sea
Everglades City · **Fort Lauderdale**
Marco · Ochopee · Monroe Station · **Hollywood**
Cape Romano · 10,000 Islands · Chokoloskee · *Tamiami* · **Miami Beach**
Everglades National Park · **Miami** · Key Biscayne
Gulf of Mexico · Goulds · *Biscayne Bay*
Shark Point · *Whitewater Bay* · **Homestead** · Florida City · Biscayne National Park
Cape Sable · Flamingo · Key Largo
Biscayne National Park · Tavernier · *Florida Bay* · Islamorada
Marathon · Grassy Key
Key West · Big Pine Key · *Florida Keys*

Florida Panhandle

Alabama
Flomaton · Geneva · Hartford · Ashford
Crestview · **Florida** · Graceville
Milton · Bonifay · **Marianna** · *Lake Seminole*
Defuniak Springs · Ponce de Leon Springs State Park · Chattaoohchee
Fort Walton · Niceville · Valparaiso · Blountstown
Pensacola · Beach · Destin · *Apalachicola*
Gulf Breeze · Gulf Islands National Seashore · Seaside · *Dead Lake*
Fort Pickens · Pensacola Beach · Panama · **Lynn Haven** · Wewahitchka
City Beach · **Panama City**
Gulf of Mexico · St Joseph Bay · Eastpoint
St Vincent Island · Apalachicola
St George Island

0 ———— 100 km
0 ———— 50 miles

0 ———— 100 km
0 ———— 50 miles

SIGHTS &
ACTIVITIES

 SEE

 DO

ITINERARY

1

2

1 Pioneer Plaza, Dallas

For a Texas-sized photo op of the largest bronze monument on earth, head to Pioneer Plaza. Its showpiece is a collection of 40 bronze larger-than-life longhorns, amassed as if they were on a cattle drive.

2 Padre Island National Seashore

To say this 70-mile-long protected coast is windswept is an understatement: Bird Island Basin, on the lagoon side of the park, is a hub for windsurfers. Endangered Kemp Ridley sea turtles also nest here and are closely protected.

3 Dude Ranches, Bandera

The area around Bandera hosts more than a dozen dude (or guest) ranches. Don't expect cattle drives; do expect daily horseback rides, hay wagons, swimming holes, rodeos and at least one chuckwagon breakfast or outdoor barbecue per stay.

4 Buffalo Bayou Park, Houston

This sinuous 160-acre park follows Buffalo Bayou west from downtown. Park highlights include the colony of 250,000 Mexican bats under the Waugh Dr Bridge and the lush walks of the Green Tree Nature Area.

5 The Alamo, San Antonio

Find out why the Alamo can rouse a Texan's sense of state pride like few other things. For many, it's not so much a tourist attraction as a pilgrimage. From the main chapel you can set off for a free history talk in the Cavalry Courtyard or browse the museum in the Long Barrack.

6 Hill Country vineyards

In spring the roadsides and fields of enchanting Hill Country are coloured with Indian paintbrushes, black-eyed susans and Texas bluebonnets, but all year you'll find a tranquil ranch, a pretty vineyard or a friendly dance hall round the next bend.

7 Clarksdale Blues

Clarksdale is the Delta's most useful base – it's within a couple of hours of all the blues sights, and big-name blues acts are regular weekend visitors. Head straight to Red's, Clarksdale's best juke joint and the place to see bluesmen do their thing.

8 Natchez Trace Parkway

This 444-mile trail follows a ridge line that was widely utilised by prehistoric animals as a grazing route; later, the area became a trading route used by Native American tribes. Today, it's a scenic drive that traverses a panoply of Southern landscapes: forests, wetlands, and gentle hill country.

9 Frenchmen St, New Orleans

Known as the 'locals' Bourbon St', Frenchmen is where New Orleanians listen to music. Bars and clubs are arrayed back to back for several city

Dude Ranches, Bandera: Ranches typically comprise a huge ranch house and stables set on hundreds of acres.

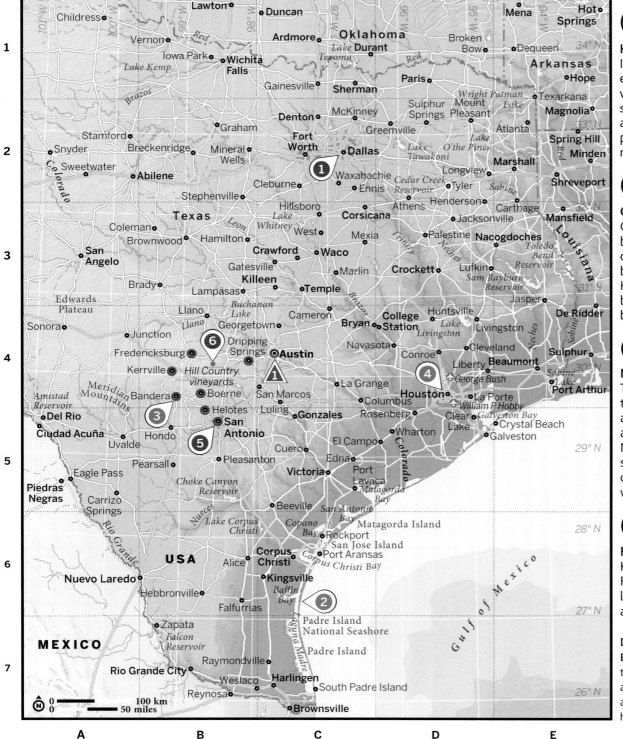

10-day itinerary
Austin, Hill Country and San Antonio

Start your trip with two days in **Austin**. Don't miss the Texas State History Museum or eating along quirky South Congress Ave. Next, head west to the countryside for one night in **Dripping Springs**, home of microbreweries and cool Hamilton Pool. Continue on to **Fredericksburg**; area activities include wine tasting or a musical pilgrimage to Luckenbach.

Skirt the Guadalupe River and lunch in **Kerrville** before overnighting in **Bandera** where a trail ride at a dude ranch and a drink at the 11th Street Cowboy Bar are must-dos. Go antique hunting in **Boerne** on your way to **San Antonio** to follow the Mission Trail and feast on Mexican food. Finally, catch a live local act at John T Floore's Country Store in **Helotes**.

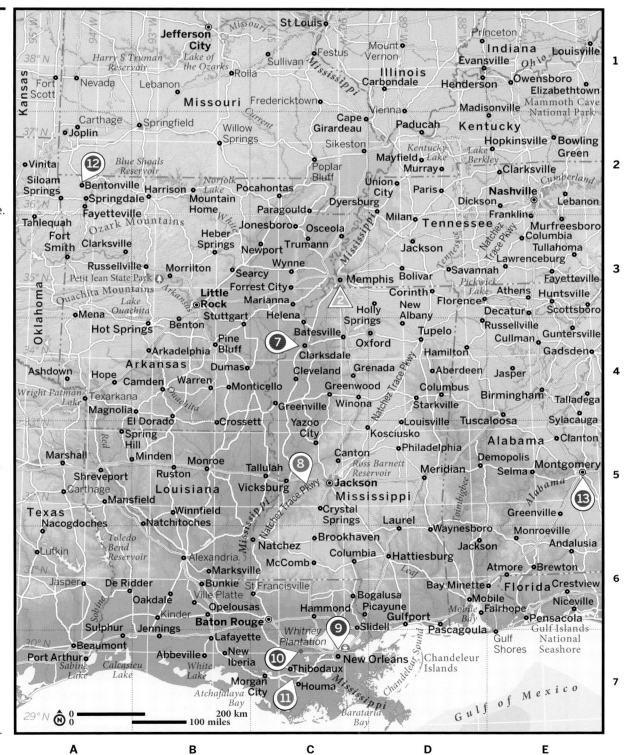

7-day itinerary
Southern Arts Tour

Start off in **Memphis**: enjoy some blues guitar on Beale Street, learn about Elvis' legacy at Graceland, and stuff yourself silly on dry-rubbed barbecue ribs. Head south to stately **Oxford**, one of Mississippi's most literary cities. Visit the University of Mississippi Museum, and take the half-mile trail through the woods to Rowan Oak, William Faulkner's

former home. Move on to **Jackson** to check out the funky arts scene in the Fondren District, the expansive Mississippi Museum of Art and the Eudora Welty House. Pay homage to the birthplace of American music in **Clarksdale**, the hub of Delta-blues country. Visit Muddy Waters' childhood cabin at the Delta Blues Museum and see a show at Red's. Then pass through

historic **Natchez**, the oldest post-European contact settlement on the Mississippi River, before crossing into Louisiana. Last stop is storied **New Orleans**, a city with an arts legacy nearly unrivalled in the US. Head to LaFitte's Blacksmith shop, one of Tennessee Williams' old haunts, before dancing the night away on Frenchmen St, one of the top music corridors in the city.

blocks in what may well be the best concentration of live-music venues in the country.

Whitney Plantation
The Whitney is the first plantation in the Louisiana to focus on slavery rather than the story of the 'big house'. Here the emphasis is given to the hundreds who died to keep the residents of the big house comfortable.

Louisiana Bayou
The best way to experience bayou culture is to take a swamp tour and afterwards tuck into a big plate of fresh-caught crawfish. Stop in Houma or drive to Thibodaux, where you can learn about Cajun culture in the wetlands region.

Crystal Bridges Museum of American Art
This enormous art museum, sprawling across a series of creek ponds fed by mountain streams, is an unexpected find – the curved pavilions that house the extensive collections are connected by magnificent glass-encased tunnels.

National Memorial for Peace and Justice, Montgomery
This powerful memorial pays tribute to the thousands of African-American victims of lynching. A sobering reminder of the country's history of racial inequality, it also includes information on the slave trade, civil rights era and modern police violence.

1 Grand Teton

The birthplace of American mountaineering, the chiselled and weathered Grand is among America's premier climbing destinations. A guided ascent is a two-day affair that starts with a steep 7-mile approach past wildflower and waterfalls. Rest up, because a 3am wake-up call heralds summit day, with views of the sprawling wilderness of three states.

2 Bechler Basin Waterfalls, Yellowstone National Park

Hidden in the southwest corner of Yellowstone, Bechler hides the park's most spectacular collection of waterfalls. Colonnade, Union, Dunanda and Cave Falls are the better-known but there are dozens of thundering falls, feathery cascades and hidden hot springs that entice hikers to brave the mosquitoes and boggy trails.

3 Old Faithful & Upper Geyser Basin, Yellowstone National Park

The world's most famous geyser erupts every 90 minutes or so, so you have plenty of time to view it from several angles – from the boardwalk, from the balcony of the Old Faithful Inn and from Observation Hill. The surrounding geyser basin offers dozens of other spouters; some that erupt just once a day, others that thrash continuously.

Upper Geyser Basin: This area contains the largest concentration of geysers in the world, including many of the world's largest.

4 Jackson Hole

Winter is the perfect time to combine a National Park visit with some serious mountain fun. The region's downhill action shines in Jackson Hole, Wyoming. Don't limit yourself to skiing though, there are backcountry yurts, and even heli-skiing options.

5 Lamar Valley, Yellowstone National Park

Known as the 'Serengeti of North America', the lush Lamar Valley is home to the densest collection of big animals in Yellowstone. A dozen lay-bys offer superb views over grazing bison and elk, but search the tree lines closely with binoculars and you might be lucky enough to see a grizzly on the prowl or a pack of wolves.

6 Sun Valley Resort

Occupying one of Idaho's more stunning natural locations, Sun Valley is a piece of ski history. It was the first purpose-built ski resort in the US and has been synonymous with skiing ever since, thanks to its luxury showcase lodge and the world's first chairlift.

7 Cheyenne Frontier Days

During the last full week in July, the world's largest outdoor rodeo and celebration of all things Wyoming features 10 days of roping, bucking, riding, singing and dancing between air shows, parades, melodramas, carnivals and chile cook-offs. There's also a lively Frontier Town and free 'slack' rodeos.

8 Rocky Mountain National Park

With elk grazing under granite walls, alpine meadows rife with wildflowers and a winding road inching over the Continental Divide, the natural splendour of Rocky Mountain National Park packs a punch. Trails cater to every ability, from epic outings up Longs Peak to family-friendly romps in the Bear Lake area. With a little effort, you can have the place all to yourself.

9 Mesa Verde National Park

You don't just walk into the past at Mesa Verde, the site of 600 ancient cliff dwellings. You scramble up 10ft ladders, scale a 60ft rock face, and crawl 12ft through a tunnel. It's one of the most exhilarating adventures in the Southwest.

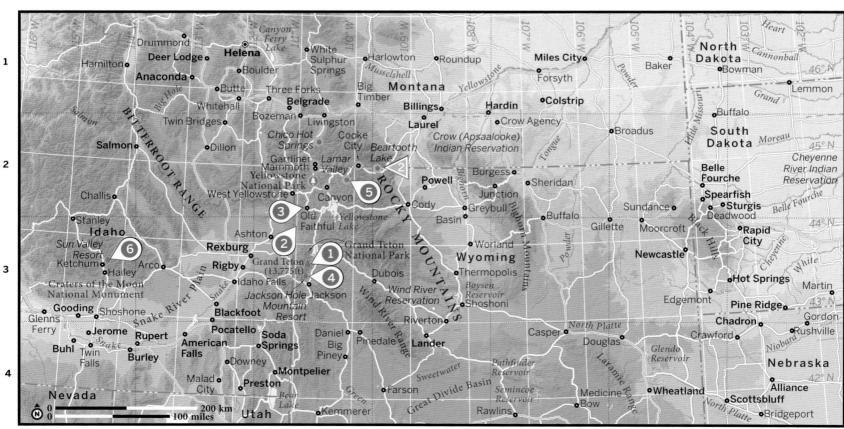

10-day itinerary
Southern Utah's Parklands

See the best of Utah's parks, with possible detours to the Grand Canyon and Monument Valley. Start in **Zion National Park**. See the highlights the first day and hike Angels Landing the next morning. Then spend an afternoon in East Zion. Travel north to say hello to hoodoos in **Bryce Canyon National Park** and Red Canyon. Begin your drive down scenic

Hwy 12, basing yourself in **Escalante** or **Boulder**, and squeeze through the slot canyons of **Grand Staircase-Escalante National Monument**. Head on down Hwy 12 to crack the geologists' code and go fruit-picking in the orchards of **Capitol Reef National Park**. Drive to **Moab** and spend three days in Arches, Canyonlands and on the nearby mountain-bike trails.

7-day itinerary
Yellowstone to Paradise

Drive the USA's most scenic 70 miles, the Beartooth Hwy, making a pitstop at **Beartooth Lake**. Overnight in **Cooke City**, then enter **Yellowstone National Park** for some early wildlife-watching in **Lamar Valley** and a hunt for petrified trees on the Fossil Forest Trail. Have lunch on the Yellowstone River Picnic Area hike and enjoy the views of the Narrows.

Head south to **Canyon** and take the South Rim Trail before overnighting in Canyon Village. The next morning try more wildlife-watching in Hayden Valley before hiking Elephant Back Mountain for great views of Yellowstone Lake. After a picnic on the sand bars around Gull Point, continue south to the hot springs of West Thumb Geyser Basin before heading

west across the Continental Divide. Spend a day visiting the geyser basins, before driving to **Mammoth**. Take a dusk hike to spot wildlife on the Beaver Ponds trail. Heading north, squeeze in a rafting trip or horseback ride from **Gardiner** before continuing north through Paradise Valley to relax with a hot soak at **Chico Hot Springs**.

Denver
Craft brewing has been elevated to a high art throughout Colorado. Each September Denver hosts the Great American Beer Festival, luring in 780-odd brewers and over 60,000 enthusiastic drinkers.

Arkansas River
Brace yourself for yet another icy splash swamping the raft as you plunge into a roaring set of big waves, or surrender to the power of the current as your shouting, thoroughly drenched crew

unintentionally spins backwards around a monster boulder. Adrenaline-charged fun guaranteed.

Vail
Vail resembles an elaborate amusement park for grown-ups, where every activity has been designed to send a tingle down your spine. As Colorado's best and most varied resort, Vail has 5000-plus acres of powdery back bowls, chutes and wickedly fun terrain. Whether it's your first time on a snowboard or you're flashing perfect telemark turns in the Outer Mongolia Bowl, this might very well be the ski trip of your dreams.

Fairyland Loop, Bryce Canyon National Park
Let your imagination work overtime on the aptly named Fairyland Loop, an all-day foray that gets up close and personal with wildly shaped hoodoos and millennial bristlecone pines.

Island in the Sky, Canyonlands National Park
This 6000ft-high flat-topped mesa drops precipitously on all sides, providing some of the longest, most enthralling vistas of the spectacular landscapes in southern Utah.

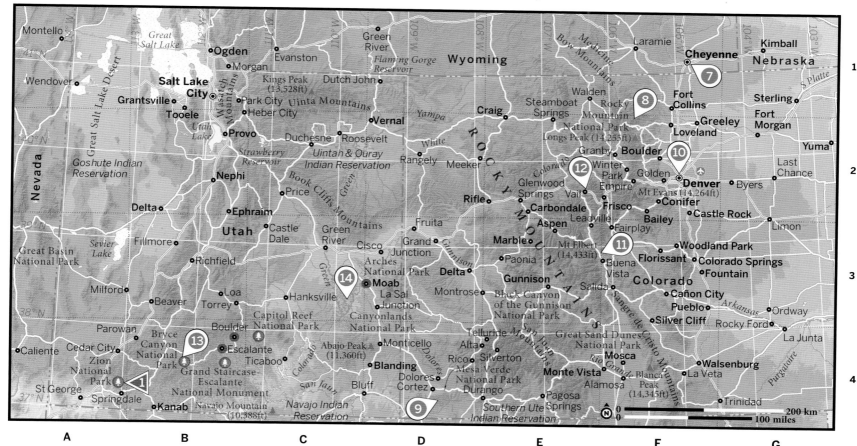

SIGHTS & ACTIVITIES

 SEE

DO

ITINERARY

▼ 1

▽ 2

Grand Canyon National Park

The scale of the Grand Canyon is what grabs you: it's a two-billion-year-old rip across the landscape that reveals the Earth's geological secrets. But it's Mother Nature's artistic touches – from sun-dappled ridges and striated cliffs to lush oasis and a ribbon-like river – that hold your attention.

Sedona

Many New Age types believe that Sedona's Red Rock Mountains are the centre of vortexes that radiate the earth's power. We like Airport Mesa, said to radiate electromagnetic energy; it's a great location for watching the spectacular red-rock sunset, too.

Flagstaff

Flagstaff is the perfect Southwest town. This outdoorsy mecca – there's hiking, biking, skiing and stargazing – has it all. Walk the vibrant downtown, loaded with ecofriendly restaurants, indie coffee shops, genial breweries and atmospheric hotels.

Heard Museum, Phoenix

Native American designs often have a ceremonial purpose or religious significance but the art that is crafted today puts a fresh spin on the ancient traditions. From Hopi *kachina* dolls and Navajo rugs to Zuni jewellery and the baskets of the White Mountain Apaches, art is a window into the heart of the native Southwest peoples.

Monument Valley Navajo Tribal Park

'May I walk in beauty' is the final line of a famous Navajo prayer. Beauty comes in many forms on the Navajo's vast reservation, but it makes its most famous appearance at Monument Valley, a majestic cluster of rugged buttes and stubborn spires.

Boothill Graveyard, Tombstone

'Murdered.' 'Shot.' 'Suicide.' 'Killed by Indians.' The epitaphs at Boothill Cemetery tell you everything you need to know about living – and dying – in Tombstone in the late 1800s. Some headstones are twistedly poetic: the oft-quoted epitaph for Lester Moore reads: 'Here lies Lester Moore, Four slugs from a .44, No Les, no More.'

White Sands National Monument

Undulating through the Tularosa Basin like something out of a dream, these ethereal dunes are a highlight of any trip to New Mexico, and a must on every landscape photographer's itinerary. Try to visit at sunrise or sunset, when the dazzlingly sea of sand is at its most magical.

Taos Pueblo

New Mexico's most extraordinary Native American site stands three miles northeast of Taos Plaza. An absolute must-see for anyone interested in Pueblo Indian life, history and culture, Taos Pueblo has been continuously inhabited for almost a thousand years, making it a strong contender to be the oldest community in the entire US.

Gila National Forest

For anyone in search of the isolated and undiscovered, the Gila ('hee-la') has it in spades. This rugged country is just right for black bears, mountain lions and the reintroduced Mexican gray wolves. Trickling creeks are home to four species of endangered fish, including the Gila trout. It was here that conservationist Aldo Leopold led a movement to establish the world's first designated wilderness area.

7-day itinerary
Native American Journey

In **Four Corners Monument** snap a picture with your hands and feet in four states. Head into New Mexico to see **Shiprock**, known to the Navajo as 'the rock with wings'. Overnight in Kokopelli's Cave, a B&B room 70ft underground. A rutted drive leads to the **Chaco Culture National Historical Park**. Marvel at the engineering and then camp out in the canyon. Pass through **Window Rock**, the capital of the Navajo Reservation. Then detour through the **Zuni Pueblo**. Next up? The **Canyon de Chelly National Monument**, an inhabited canyon with huts and sheep herds. Remember to breathe as you approach **Monument Valley Navajo Tribal Park**. Drive the 17-mile loop then camp overnight so you can gape at the sunrise.

7-day itinerary
Grand Tour

After ogling the art-deco style **Hoover Dam**, swoop into Arizona along Rte 66, which chases trains and roadside billboards as it unfurls between the historic towns of **Kingman** and **Williams**. Regroup in funky **Flagstaff** with caffeine and craft-beer fixes before venturing into **Grand Canyon National Park**, where a hike is a must-do. Swing through the red rocks of **Sedona** to chill a little while then head south for shabby-chic **Jerome**. Drive to **Phoenix** for a fix of shopping and museums then mellow out on 4th Ave, **Tucson**, study cacti at **Saguaro National Park** and fancy yourself a gunslinger in **Tombstone**. Next is New Mexico: sled down sand dunes and snap happy in **White Sands National Monument**, spend a day exploring caves at **Carlsbad Caverns National Park**, then head to **Roswell** to ponder its UFO mysteries. Hang out in **Santa Fe**, a foodie haven and art-fiend magnet. Atomic-age secrets are revealed at **Los Alamos** to the northwest. Finish up with the laid-back musings of hippies and ski bums just to the north in **Taos**.

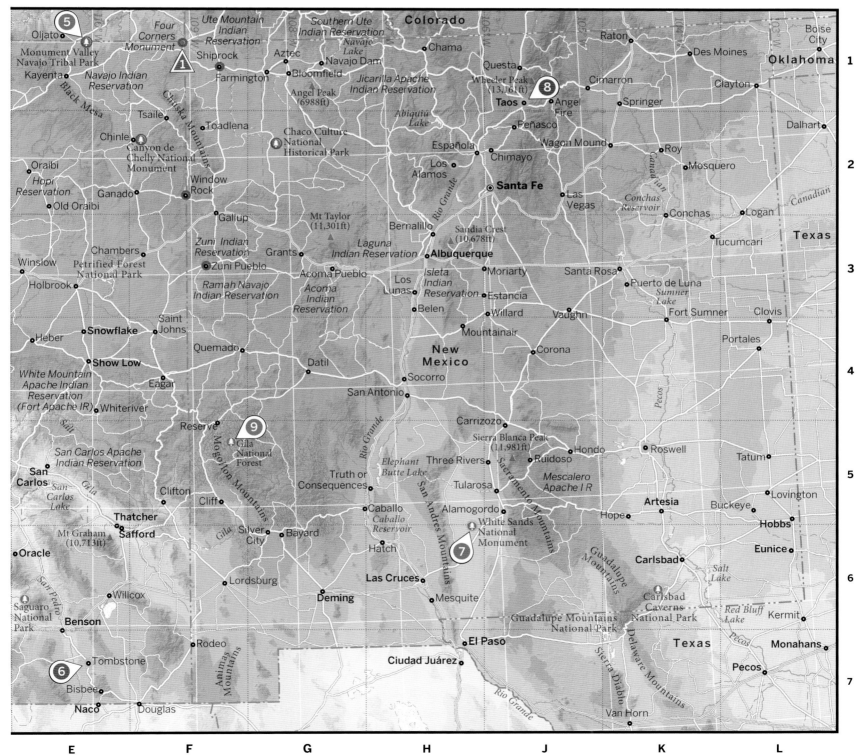

Las Vegas

Rolling into Vegas behind the wheel as a Sin City first-timer is a classic experience – arrive after dark and approach from the south for maximum 'wows' at the iconic Welcome to Fabulous Las Vegas sign, then cruise the 4.2-mile section of Las Vegas Blvd, known the world over as 'the Strip'.

Disneyland®, Anaheim

Where orange groves and walnut trees once grew in Anaheim, Walt Disney built his dream, a childlike universe of giant spinning teacups, selfie-snapping mice and glittery fireworks over a storybook castle. It's hard not to feel a pang for childhood.

Joshua Tree National Park

Joshua trees reach up towards heaven like a biblical prophet. You'll find no shortage in their namesake national park, where hiking trails lead you to even more natural wonders.

Palm Springs

Follow the lead of A-listers and hipsters: lounge by the pool at your mid-century-modern hotel, hit the galleries and vintage stores, then refresh with post-sunset cocktails. Too passive? Then break a sweat on hiking trails that wind through desert canyons and across Native American lands.

La Jolla

On what may be the most beautiful stretch of San Diego's coastline, you'll find nature-sculpted La Jolla Cove and, along the coast, the windswept Torrey Pines State Natural Reserve, where migratory whales swim.

Getty Center, Los Angeles

The Getty Center is a cultural citadel. Absorb that soul-lifting panorama, then explore the gardens, punctuated with flowers, sculptures and trickling water. The Richard Meier-designed museum showcases centuries of creativity, from medieval triptychs to starry Van Gogh skies.

Foxen Canyon Wine Trail

The Foxen Canyon Wine Trail is a must for oenophiles. Tread through fields of grapes, tipple Pinot Noir and graze on regional edibles. Start in Los Olivos' wine-tasting rooms and cafes, then follow country roads where big-name vineyards rub shoulders with risk-taking boutique winemakers.

Channel Islands National Park

The Channel Islands are SoCal's last outpost of civilisation. They support an abundance of marine life, from coral reefs to elephant seals. Get back to nature in Channel Islands National Park, a wildlife haven with fantastic sea kayaking and snorkelling, or go glam with a mod-con getaway to Med-style Catalina Island.

Death Valley National Park

The most surprising thing about Death Valley is how full of life it is. Spring wildflowers bloom across khaki hillsides and residents include coyotes and kit foxes. Hike up canyons hiding geological oddities, stand atop craters formed by prehistoric explosions or explore Wild West ghost towns.

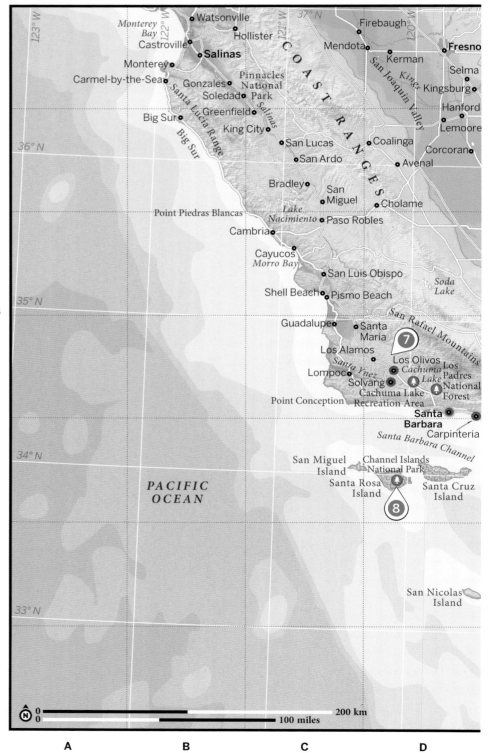

Balboa Park, San Diego

Balboa Park's 1200 acres are packed with dozens of museums, gardens and performance venues, including the San Diego Natural History Museum and the Japanese Friendship Garden.

4-day itinerary
Santa Barbara and Wine Country

A mild climate earns this stretch of SoCal coast the nickname of 'American Riviera'. Catch a ferry from **Ventura** to **Channel Islands National Park** and explore for a day. Back on land, oceanfront Ventura has a walkable downtown and mountainous **Ojai** is an inland Shangri-la. Head north and drop by **Carpinteria** for an afternoon on the beach. Indulge in **Santa Barbara**

for a few days before taking a scenic drive on San Marcos Pass Rd. Head past **Los Padres National Forest** and **Cachuma Lake Recreation Area** up to wine country. Drive west to Danish **Solvang**, with faux windmills and a historical mission, then north to the wine-tasting rooms of **Los Olivos** and the Foxen Canyon Wine Trail, which winds along rural roads past celebrated wineries.

10-day itinerary
Pacific Coast Hwy

Drop the convertible top, cue up 'California Girls' and step it for a road trip like no other. Before heading north from **San Diego** – the nation's eighth-largest and, acccording to its residents, finest city – soak up 360-degree views from **Point Loma**, buff surfers in **Mission Beach** and the underwater treasures of **La Jolla**. Head north

to Orange County and check out the secluded coves and craggy cliffs in **Laguna Beach**, the glitzy crowds in **Newport Beach** and the surf mecca that is **Huntington Beach**. Across the LA County line is **Long Beach**, home to a knockout aquarium and museum of Latin American art. Continue around **Palos Verdes Peninsula** before plunging into LA's

South Bay beach towns – boho-chic **Venice** and **Santa Monica** with its carnival pier and vibrant street life. Further north take in surreal ocean vistas en route to celebrity hideaway **Malibu**. Discreetly scan the surf for stars before winding up your trip in **Santa Barbara**, a seductive melange of red-tile roofs, lauded wineries and soul-lifting beaches.

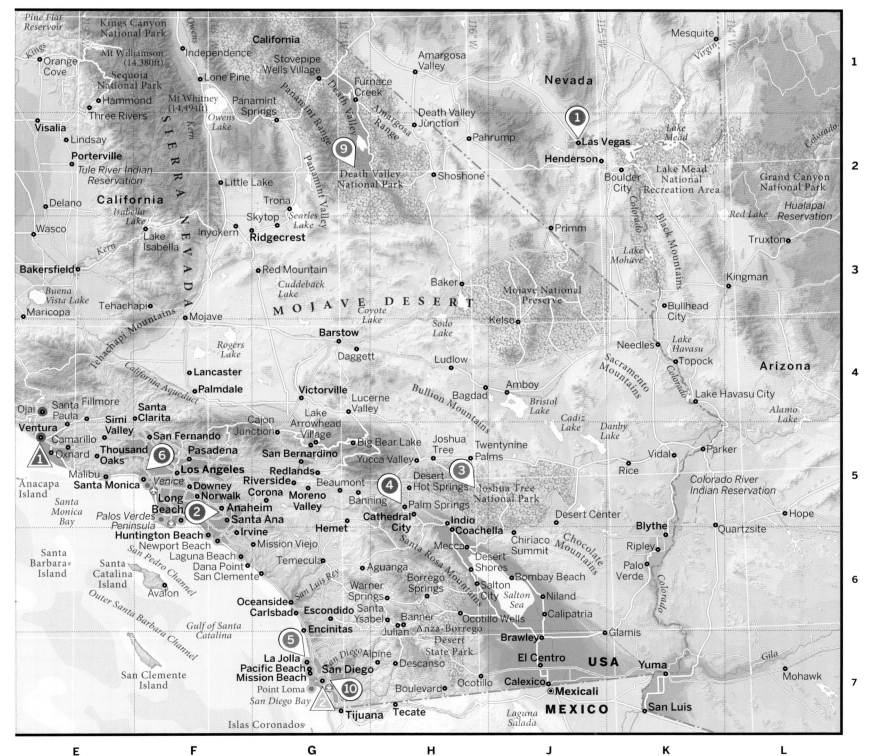

SIGHTS &
ACTIVITIES

SEE
DO

ITINERARY

1
2

Yosemite National
Park: Four million
annual visitors go
to Yosemite each
year to experience
its rivers, lakes,
forests and hulking
mountains.

Portland
Portland often tops lists of the USA's most bike-friendly cities, and it's true that the city is best seen by bicycle. With over a thousand miles of on-street bicycle routes checking out all the sights on two wheels is a breeze.

Willamette Valley
The mild climate and long summers in northern Willamette Valley foster the delicate Pinot Noir grape, as well as Pinot Gris, Chardonnay and Riesling. Check out the region's great wineries.

Crater Lake National Park
Oregon's only national park, Crater Lake is so blue that you'll catch your breath. And if you get to see it on a calm day, those deep waters reflect the surrounding cliffs like a mirror.

Rogue River
Famous for its turbulent grade-IV rapids, Rogue River departs civilisation at Grave Creek and winds for 40 wild miles through a remote canyon preserved within rugged Bureau of Land Management land and the Wild Rogue Wilderness. A typical rafting trip here takes three to four days, and hiring an outfitter is mandatory.

Redwood National & State Parks
Prepare to be impressed as some of the trees here have been standing since time immemorial, predating the Roman Empire by over 500 years. Pick up a map at the visitor centre and choose from a range of hikes.

Bend
Bend is where all lovers of the outdoors should live. Ski in the morning, paddle a kayak in the afternoon and play golf into the evening. Or try mountaineering, mountain biking, hiking, paddleboarding, rock climbing or fishing – all nearby and top drawer.

Calistoga
Calistoga is synonymous with mineral water bearing its name, bottled here since 1924, and its springs and geysers have earned it an appropriate nickname: 'Hot springs of the West'. The mud-bath emporiums in this folksy town use volcanic ash from nearby Mt St Helena.

Mt Heavenly, Lake Tahoe
The 'mother' of all Tahoe mountains boasts the most acreage, the longest run, great tree-skiing and the biggest vertical drop around. Follow the sun by skiing on the Nevada side in the morning, moving to the California side in the afternoon. Views of the lake and the high desert are heavenly indeed.

California Wine Country
The birthplace of modern-day Wine Country is famous for regal Cabernet Sauvignon, chateau-like wineries and fabulous food. The city of Napa anchors the valley while pretty towns include St Helena and Yountville.

Yosemite National Park
Eastern Yosemite Valley spreads out before you at the 7214ft Glacier Point. Half Dome looms at eye level and you can spot hikers on its summit. To the left lies the glacially carved Tenaya Canyon, and to the right are the white ribbons of Nevada and Vernal Falls. Hold on tight to the railing and peer 3200ft down at Half Dome Village.

Gold Country
Tens of thousands of immigrants arrived in the foothills of the Sierra Nevada range during California's gold rush. Wind past sleepy townships and abandoned mines on Hwy 49, also a gateway to swimming holes, white-water rafting and mountain biking runs.

Mendocino
Leading out to a gorgeous headland, Mendocino is the North Coast's salt-washed perfect village, with B&Bs surrounded by rose gardens, white-picket fences and water towers.

Lassen Volcanic National Park
This impressive park has steaming hydrothermal sulphur pools and cauldrons that can be seen from the boardwalk in Bumpass Hell. At 10,457ft, Lassen Peak is one of the world's largest plug-dome volcanoes. In total, the park has 150 miles of hiking trails, including a 17-mile section of the Pacific Crest Trail.

5-day itinerary
Sierra Nevada & Gold Country

Summer in the Sierra Nevada, brings wildflower meadows, alpine lakes and sun-catching peaks. Start in **Yosemite National Park**, where waterfalls and granite monoliths overhang a verdant valley. Soar over the Sierra Nevada's snowy rooftop on the high-elevation Tioga Rd. It's a quick trip to **Mammoth Lakes**, an all-seasons adventure base camp. Backtracking north, gaze out over **Mono Lake** and its bizarre tufa formations, then continue up Hwy 395. Sturdy vehicles can make a detour to **Bodie State Historic Park**, a gold-rush ghost town with 200 buildings frozen in time. Keep trucking north to the deep-blue jewel of **Lake Tahoe**, the USA's second-deepest lake.

5-day itinerary
Pacific Coast Road Trip

The stretch of Hwy 1 (and Hwy 101) between San Francisco and the Oregon border connects cute beach towns, rugged coastline and majestic redwood forests. Start in **San Francisco** where you'll need two days to do justice to the City by the Bay. Tap into Beat-poet culture in North Beach and wander through Golden Gate Park. Then hit the road north to stunning **Point Reyes National Seashore** and **Sonoma Coast State Beach** for picnicking, tide-pooling and whale watching before stopping for the night in **Mendocino**. Be sure to check out the town's galleries, boutiques and rocky headlands before journeying north. Cut inland to Hwy 101 at the Lost Coast, the North Coast's premier backpacking destination. Leave the main highway to follow the redwood-flanked **Avenue of the Giants** and keep going north. Detour for lunch in the Victorian village of **Ferndale**. Finally spend two days exploring **Redwood National & State Parks** and its mystic, awe-inspiring groves.

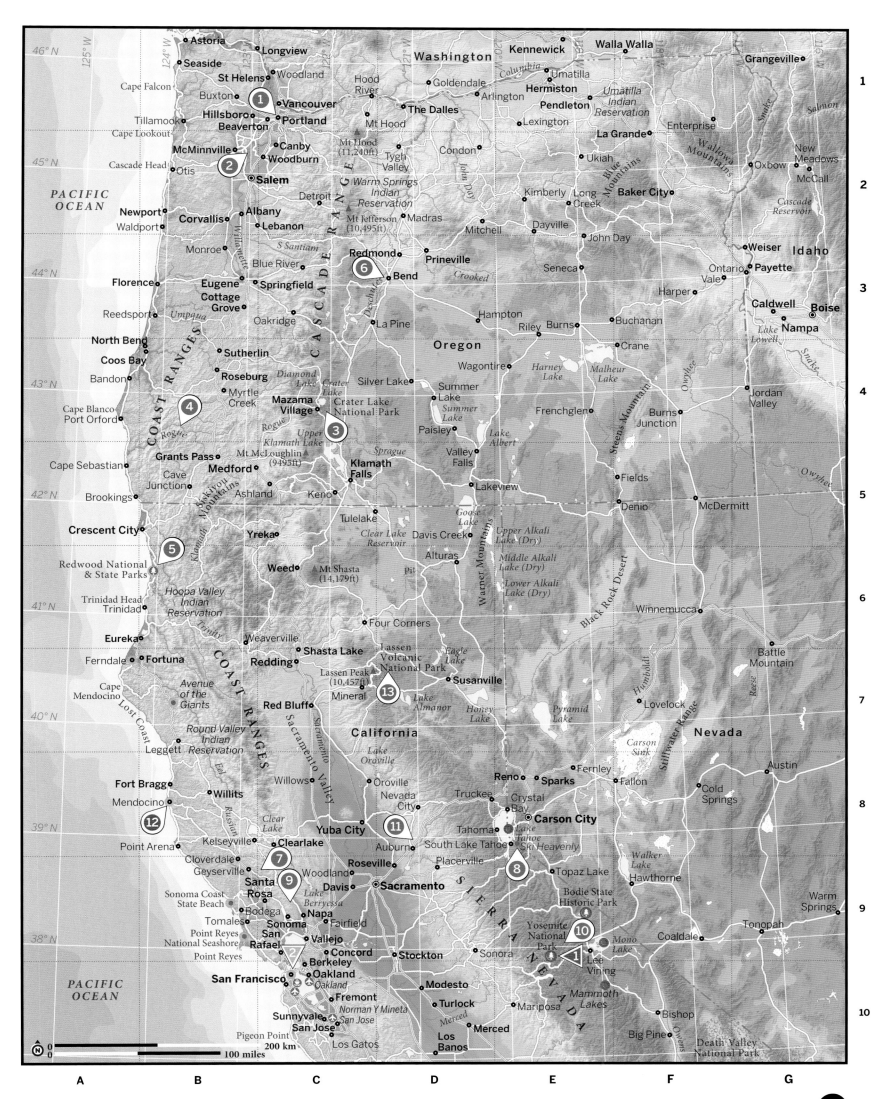

PACIFIC
OCEAN

46° N

125° W

124° W

Astoria
Longview
Seaside
St Helens   Woodland
Cape Falcon
Buxton
Vancouver
Hillsboro   Portland
Tillamook   Beaverton
Cape Lookout
McMinnville
Cascade Head   Otis
Salem
Canby
Woodburn

45° N

Washington
Kennewick   Walla Walla   Grangeville
Goldendale   Umatilla
Hood   Arlington   Hermiston
River   Pendleton   Umatilla
The Dalles   Lexington   Indian
Reservation
La Grande   Enterprise
New
Meadows
McCall
Mt Hood   Tygh
Condon   Wallowa
(11,240ft)   Valley   Mountains
Dayville   Baker City   Oxbow
Mitchell   Cascade
Reservoir
John Day   Weiser
Payette
Ukiah   Long
Kimberly   Creek   Ontario
Vale   Caldwell
Seneca   Boise
Harper   Idaho
Nampa

PACIFIC
OCEAN
Newport
Waldport
Corvallis
Albany
Lebanon
Monroe
Florence
Eugene
Cottage
Grove
Reedsport
Springfield
Oakridge
Detroit
Madras
Warm Springs
Indian
Reservation
Mt Jefferson
(10,495ft)
Redmond
Bend
Prineville
Crooked
Hampton
Lake
Lowell
Oregon

44° N

North Bend
Coos Bay
Bandon
Sutherlin
Roseburg
Myrtle
Creek
Diamond
Lake
Crater
Lake
Silver Lake
Summer
Lake
Wagontire
Riley   Burns
Buchanan
Crane
Jordan
Valley

43° N

Cape Blanco
Port Orford
Grants Pass
Cave
Junction
Medford
Mazama
Village
Crater Lake
National Park
Mt McLoughlin
(9495ft)
Upper
Klamath Lake
Sprague
Paisley
Lake
Albert
Frenchglen
Burns
Junction

42° N

Brookings
Ashland
Keno
Klamath
Falls
Valley
Falls
Lakeview
Fields
Owyhee

41° N

Crescent City
Redwood National
& State Parks
Yreka
Weed
Tulelake
Clear Lake
Reservoir
Davis Creek
Goose
Lake
Alturas
Upper Alkali
Lake (Dry)
Middle Alkali
Lake (Dry)
Lower Alkali
Lake (Dry)
Denio
McDermitt
Hoopa Valley
Indian
Reservation
Trinidad Head
Trinidad
Mt Shasta
(14,179ft)
Pit
Warner Mountains
Black Rock Desert
Winnemucca
Battle
Mountain

Eureka
Ferndale   Fortuna
Weaverville
Shasta Lake
Redding
Lassen
Volcanic
National Park
Lassen Peak
(10,457ft)
Mineral
Eagle
Lake
Susanville
Lake
Almanor
Honey
Lake
Pyramid
Lake
Lovelock
Humboldt
Reese

40° N

Cape
Mendocino
Avenue
of the
Giants
Red Bluff
California
Nevada

Leggett
Round Valley
Indian
Reservation
Willows
Lake
Oroville
Oroville
Nevada
City
Reno
Sparks
Fernley
Carson
Sink
Stillwater Range
Austin
Cold
Springs

Fort Bragg
Willits
Mendocino
Point Arena
Clear
Lake
Yuba City
Auburn
Truckee
Crystal
Bay
Carson City
Tahoma
Lake
Tahoe
South Lake Tahoe
Ski Heavenly
Placerville
Walker
Lake
Hawthorne
Warm
Springs

39° N

Cloverdale
Geyserville
Kelseyville
Clearlake
Santa
Rosa
Woodland
Roseville
Sacramento
Sonora
Topaz Lake
Bodie State
Historic Park
Yosemite
National
Park
Mono
Lake
Lee
Vining
Coaldale
Tonopah

38° N

Sonoma Coast
State Beach
Bodega
Tomales
Sonoma
Napa
Fairfield
Vallejo
Concord
Berkeley
Oakland
San
Rafael
Point Reyes
National Seashore
Point Reyes
San Francisco
Oakland
Fremont
Sunnyvale
San Jose
Pigeon Point
Davis
Lake
Berryessa
Stockton
Modesto
Turlock
Norman Y Mineta
San Jose
Los Gatos
Los
Banos
Merced
Merced
Mariposa
Mammoth
Lakes
Bishop
Big Pine
Owens
Death Valley
National Park

0   200 km
0   100 miles

1
2
3
4
5
6
7
8
9
10

A   B   C   D   E   F   G

331

SIGHTS & ACTIVITIES

 SEE

DO

ITINERARY

 1

2

1 Denali
What makes 20,310ft Denali one of the world's great scenic mountains is the sheer independent rise of its bulk. It begins at a base of just 2000ft, which means that on a clear day you will be transfixed by over 18,000ft of ascending rock, ice and snow. By contrast, Mt Everest rises 12,000ft from its base on the Tibetan Plateau.

2 Mendenhall Glacier
Mendenhall Glacier demands weak-kneed prose. Hike around this river of ice that flows from the mountains, stand in the mouth of an ice cave or watch the parade of icebergs that the glacier discharges into Mendenhall River. Come quick: scientists say most of it will be gone in 25 years.

3 Taku Glacier Lodge
The most popular tours in Juneau are flightseeing, glacier-viewing and salmon-bakes. A trip to this historic off-the-grid lodge combines all three. Wings Airways has a monopoly on access. Its trips include flying across a half-dozen glaciers to the lodge, where a meal of wild salmon awaits.

4 Katmai National Park & Preserve
Brown bears are abundant and well fed in Katmai National Park & Preserve where, thanks to the National Park Service, a well-protected ecosystem provides a supply of food. To see these brilliant beasts pluck spawning salmon out of Brooks Falls, hire a floatplane in July and head to Brooks Camp.

5 Anchorage
Who can go to bed when it's still light outside at 11pm? A bolt of energy surges through downtown Anchorage on any given weekend evening in the summer. Pushcart vendors hawk sausages on 4th Ave, frisbees glide through the air in Delaney Park and a line out the door at Chilkoot Charlie's waits for the house band to metaphorically blow the roof away.

7-day itinerary
Fairbanks to Seward by Train

Spend a day in **Fairbanks** exploring the museums and a night appreciating that the sun barely sets before hopping aboard the beautifully maintained Alaska Railroad to **Denali National Park**, where you can enjoy a good day's hiking on the Triple Lakes Trail. The next morning, take the extraordinary eight-hour ride to **Anchorage**. Along this stretch the tracks probe into asphalt-free wilderness, paralleling rivers instead of the highway, with the icy mass of Denali in view if you're lucky. In Anchorage enjoy the surprisingly sophisticated shopping and dining scene. Check out the world-class Anchorage Museum, or rev up for a salmon bake with a bike ride along the Coastal Trail. Then jump back on the train for another spectacular journey to **Seward**. Again, the train deviates from the road and takes you into the **Chugach Mountains**. Seward is the southern terminus of the railroad, ending in gorgeous **Resurrection Bay**.

6 Sealaska Heritage, Juneau
The essence of traditional culture lives on in Alaskan settlements. Most are a bush-plane flight away, but you can visit an urban cultural centre run by Alaska Natives. At the vanguard of an Alaska Native renaissance is Sealaska Heritage in Juneau.

7 Kenai Fjords National Park
Get an orca's-eye view of this marine ecosystem by kayaking through the waters of Kenai Fjords. As you paddle you might be treated to the thunder of calving glaciers, the honking and splashing of sea lions or the cacophony of a kittiwake rookery.

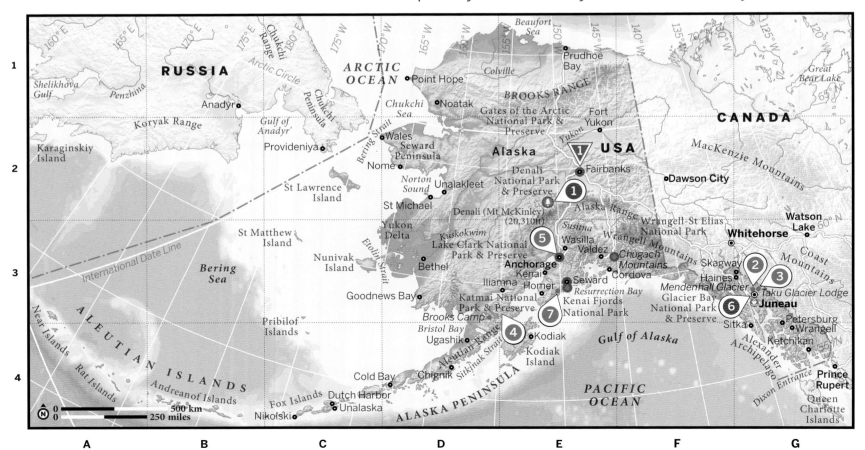

Pike Place Market, Seattle

A cavalcade of noise, smells, banter and urban theatre sprinkled around a waterside strip, Pike Place Market is Seattle in a bottle. In operation since 1907 and as soulful today as it was on day one, this experience highlights the city for what it really is: all-embracing, eclectic and proudly unique.

Mt Rainier

Majestic Mt Rainier is one of the country's most beguiling mountains. Part of a 368-sq-mile national park, the mountain's snow-capped summit and forested foothills boast numerous hiking trails, flower-carpeted meadows and a peak that presents a formidable challenge for climbers.

Lime Kiln Point State Park

Clinging to the rocky west coast of San Juan Island, this beautiful park overlooks the deep Haro Strait and is reputedly one of the best places in the world to view whales from the shoreline. Take a picnic and watch the killer whales feast on the salmon runs.

Walla Walla

Walla Walla has the ingredients to support a burgeoning wine culture: historic Main St, a handsome college,

10-day itinerary
Seattle and Washington

Start in **Seattle**, the largest city in the Pacific Northwest, to explore must-see attractions such as Pioneer Square, Pike Place Market, the Seattle Aquarium and the Space Needle, all under the lofty peak of majestic Mt Rainier. Hop a ferry to **Bainbridge Island**, then head north to **Port Townsend**. With its Victorian architecture and warm summer climate and a clutch of fine restaurants pairing wine and food. Due to its laid-back, small-town feel, excellent reds and plethora of unpretentious wineries, Walla Walla is the best place in the state to go wine touring. The blocks around Main St are crammed with tasting rooms.

location on the Strait of Juan de Fuca, this picturesque town is a magnet for artists and eclectic personalities. Work your way east along the Olympic Peninsula, perhaps stopping in **Port Angeles** for a day trip to Vancouver Island's capital, Victoria. **Olympic National Park** can't be missed. The coastal strip includes 57 miles of remote beaches; visit Rialto Beach for amazing views. Keep heading south to **Lake Quinault**, a gorgeous glacier-fed lake boasting a historic grand lodge. This is the place to go fishing, boating or swimming. Then drive to **Olympia**, Washington's lively capital that's a political, musical and outdoor powerhouse.

Hoh Rainforest

Meandering through the mist and getting up close and personal with a banana slug are highlights of the ecological wonderland that is the Hoh Rainforest. Tucked inside Olympic National Park, the Sitka spruce grow to giant size while mosses and ferns blanket every surface. If you only make one stop in the park, this should be it.

Glacier National Park

Few places on Earth are as pristine as Glacier, an ice-carved landscape of snowy peaks laced with waterfalls and turquoise lakes surrounded by dense forests. Bears still roam in abundance and smart park management has kept the place accessible but wild.

Trail of the Coeur d'Alenes

A 72-mile paved trail spanning the Idaho panhandle, from Plummer to Mullan, the scenic Trail of the Coeur d'Alenes skirts the shore of Lake Coeur d'Alene before connecting to the I-90 corridor through the mountains.

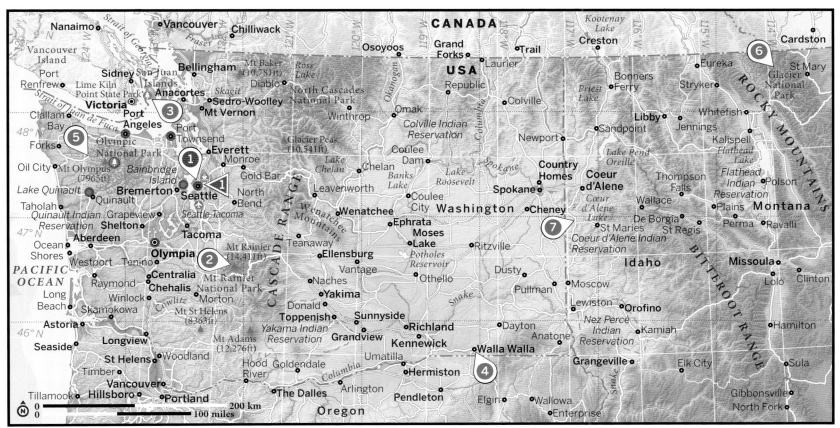

Hawai'i Volcanoes National Park
Set on the side of the world's most active volcano, this park reminds you that nature is alive and kicking. Hiking trails pass lava flows and tubes, steam vents and wild beaches, and plenty more geological marvels in between. Don't miss the overlook of the Halema'uma'u crater.

② Waikiki
By day, beach boys and girls surf legendary waves, and after sunset tiki torches light up the sand. Every night island musicians strum slack-key guitars and ukuleles as hula dancers sway to the rhythms.

③ Haleakalā National Park
Hike into Haleakalā's lunar landscape. The path continues through a tableau of stark lava, rainbow-coloured cinder cones and ever-changing clouds.

④ Pearl Harbor
For a reminder of why Hawaii remains strategically important to the US in the Pacific, tour O'ahu's USS *Arizona* Memorial, commemorating the 1941 attack on Pearl Harbor. Military history buffs can tour the Pacific Aviation Museum and stand on the decks of the 'Mighty Mo' battleship.

⑤ Mauna Kea
Up here, where night skies are clear, stars – even galaxies – sear the night white. Telescopes are set up for visitors to browse the sky's celestial glory. Get here by sunset for a heavenly double feature or show up during meteor showers for all-night star parties.

⑥ Waipi'o Valley
A stunning tropical valley. A mysterious green bowl full of ghosts and legends. A sacred site. Waipi'o's distillation of all these makes it irresistible. Trek down to the valley floor to stroll a black-sand beach and peer at distant waterfalls.

⑦ Na Pali Coast Wilderness State Park
Ke'e Beach is the entry point for the 11-mile Kalalau Trail along the Na Pali Coast. This famous trek will transport you to a place where verdant cliffs soar above a valley abundant with fruit trees, waterfalls and solace seekers.

⑧ Road to Hana
The Hana Hwy twists down into jungly valleys and along cliffs. Fifty-four one-lane bridges cross nearly as many waterfalls. Swim in a Zen-like pool, hike a ginger-scented trail and savour fresh guava.

⑨ Waimea Canyon
The 'Grand Canyon of the Pacific' stretches 10 miles long, one mile wide and more than 3600ft deep. Lookouts along a serpentine drive provide views of cliffs, buttes and gorges. Trails take hikers to the canyon floor.

⑩ Hanalei Bay
One of the USA's best beaches, this crescent bay delights lazy sunbathers and active beachgoers. Surfers charge massive (and some beginner) waves. Locals and visitors fire up barbecues and crack open cold brews at sunset.

⑪ O'ahu's North Shore
When giant rollers come crashing in, head to O'ahu's North Shore for a glimpse of Hawaii's surfing rock stars.

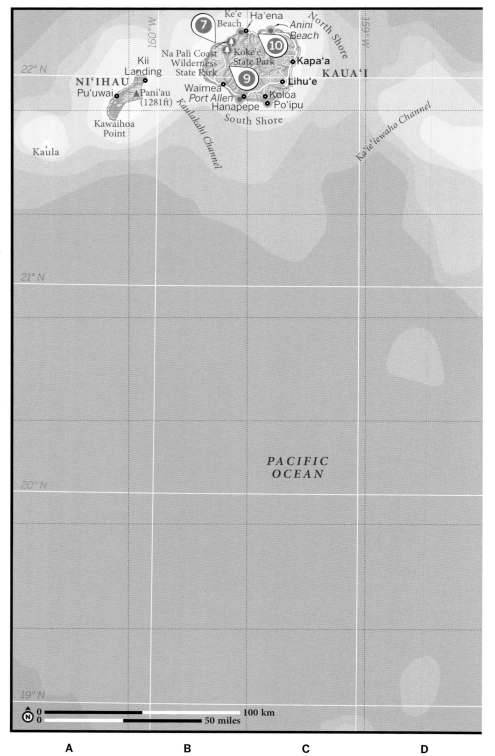

10-day itinerary
Lana'i and Moloka'i

Start in **Lana'i** and stay three nights at the Manele Bay resort. Laze on the sand before snorkeling at **Hulopo'e Beach**. To really get away from it all, take in the vistas on foot from the Munro Trail or rent a 4WD and head for the **Garden of the Gods**, **Shipwreck Beach** or down the dusty track to **Naha**. Devote the last part of your trip to Moloka'i. Bed

down at a beachfront B&B in small-town **Kaunakakai**. Explore East Moloka'i, checking out waterfalls and *heiau* (temple) ruins in **Halawa Valley**. Afterwards trek to the **Kalaupapa Peninsula** and munch macadamia nuts at Purdy's farm. Then head out to the remote beaches of the island's West End or penetrate the forests of the **Kamakou Preserve**.

10-day itinerary
O'ahu and Kaua'i

Start off in state capital, **Honolulu**, sleeping in style at the famous beach resort of Waikiki. Go bar- and gallery-hopping in Chinatown; visit the Bernice Pauahi Bishop Museum and 1882 'Iolani Palace; trace WWII history at Pearl Harbor's unique collection of war memorials and museums; hike up **Diamond Head** and tour Doris Duke's incomparable

Shangri La. Heading eastwards, snorkel at **Hanauma Bay** nature reserve – a perfect place for first-timers – and swim in **Waimanalo**, or surf and kayak at **Kailua**. Then wend your way along the Windward Coast, where you'll find a host of jungly hiking trails. For the next leg, hop on a plane to Kaua'i. Start in **Po'ipu**, enjoying a lazy day on the South Shore or head

over to **Port Allen** for a snorkelling trip. Then lace up your hiking boots for a day in **Koke'e State Park**. Back in Kaua'i's North Shore, swim or windsurf at **'Anini Beach**. Finally, kayak beside the sea cliffs at **Na Pali Coast Wilderness State Park** or backpack to **Ke'e Beach**. Either way, you'll agree that you've saved the best for last.

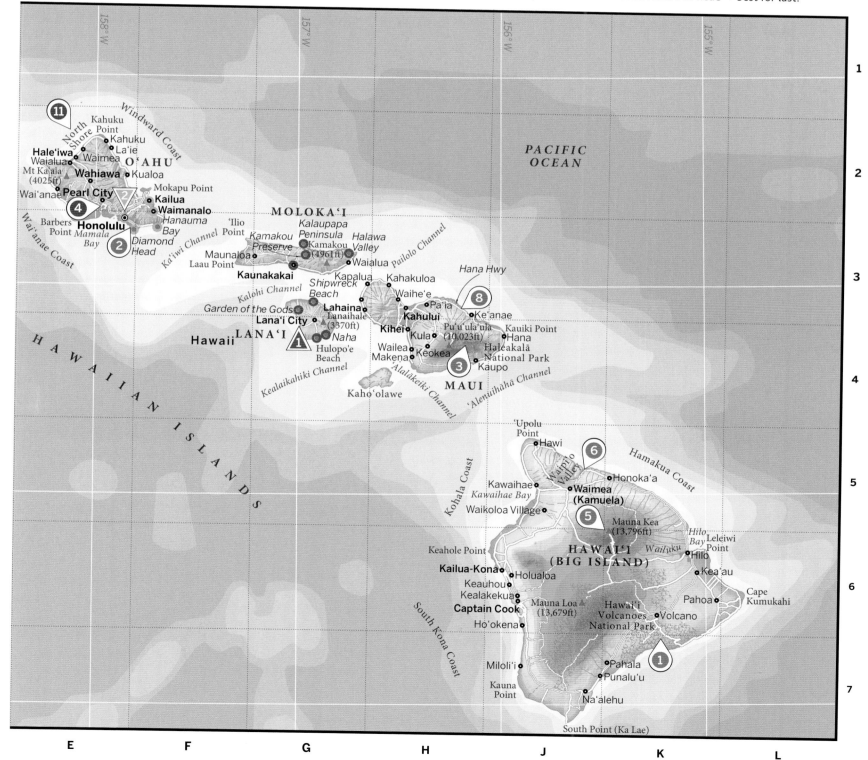

Mexico & Central America

With turquoise seas and ocean swells, lush forests, beaches, magnificent Maya ruins, towering volcanoes and flourishing farms and markets, Mexico and Central America are packed with opportunities to chill out – or thrill out. Equally rewarding are the interactions with its rich and dynamic mix of people and cultures. With more than 20 Maya languages spoken, Guatemala is the region's indigenous heartland. The Spanish left their mark throughout this land, with majestic colonial plazas, fervent beauty contests and silent hours of siesta. African culture permeates the Caribbean coast, from Congo rebel traditions to Garifuna drumbeats. It may be relatively small, but this region offers more than a lifetime's worth of explorations.

CLIMATE CHART

MEXICO CITY

RAINFALL
INCH/MM
—24/600
—16/400
—8/200
—0
D N O S A J J M A M F J

TEMP
°C/°F
40/104 —
30/86 —
20/68 —
10/50 —
0/32 —
J F M A M J J A S O N D

MANAGUA

RAINFALL
INCH/MM
—30/750
—24/600
—18/450
—12/300
—6/150
—0
D N O S A J J M A M F J

TEMP
°C/°F
40/104 —
30/86 —
20/68 —
10/50 —
0/32 —
-10/14 —
J F M A M J J A S O N D

WILDLIFE
You'll often be accompanied by a wild cast, whether birds, monkeys, whales or even swarms of butterflies. Hotspots include Península de Osa (Costa Rica), Refugio de Vida Silvestre La Flor (Nicaragua), Isla Bastimentos (Panama) or Reserva de la Biósfera Santuario Mariposa Monarca (Mexico).

RUINS
Enthralling ancient Maya ruins call for you to explore: Uxmal, and the pyramids at Calakmul and Chichén Itzá (Mexico); the lost temples of Tikal (Guatemala); the striking structures at Caracol (Belize); the jaguar carvings at Copán (Honduras); and the Tazumal site (El Salvador).

ADVENTURES
Dive the reef at Cabo Pulmo (Mexico); surf world-class waves at Santa Catalina (Panama); zip through the canopies at Parque Nacional Manuel Antonio (Costa Rica); descend into the sacred caves of Actun Tunichil Muknal (Belize); or mountain bike near Antigua (Guatemala).

BEACHES
With chilled-out Caribbean vibes on one side and monster Pacific swells on the other, Central America delivers the best of all worlds. Laze, gaze or blaze on Playa Norte (Mexico), Playa Grande (Costa Rica), Little Corn Island (Nicaragua), Playa El Tunco (El Salvador) or at Guna Yala (Panama).

Clockwise from top left: A squirrel monkey in Costa Rica's Corcovado National Park; Mundo Perdido temple and temple IV in Tikal National Park, Guatemala; a Costa Rican rufous-tailed hummingbird; fishing boats on Punta Allen beach, Mexico.

Transport hubs

With the region's largest airports and the world's most crossed border (that with the US), Mexico is the first port of call for most visitors. Flying in elsewhere is an option, though direct flights are rare unless departing from a handful of southern US cities. Arriving overland from South America isn't possible, but intrepid travellers can hop aboard small boats sailing from Cartagena to Panama. The Panama Canal facilitates cruises taking in both the Pacific and Caribbean coasts.

Mexico City
The sun in the Mexican solar system, this age-old capital is springing back to life with revamped public spaces, an exploding culinary scene and a flourishing cultural renaissance. Its airport is Latin America's largest, with incoming flights from around the globe.

Cancún
Cancún is a tale of two cities. There's a glitzy hotel zone with its famous white-sand beaches, party scene and sophisticated restaurants. Then there's the actual city itself, with taco joints and undeveloped beaches. The international airport is 8km south of downtown. Buses radiate across the country from a modern bus terminal.

Guadalajara
Guadalajara is as much a vanguard of the new Mexico as it is guardian of the old. Museums and theatres drive the cultural life forward and fusion chefs push culinary boundaries. Aeropuerto Internacional Miguel Hidalgo is 20km south of downtown. Its two bus stations link western, central and northern Mexico.

Belize City
The historical (if no longer the actual) capital of the nation, Belize City has two airports: Philip Goldson International Airport and the Municipal Airstrip.

San José
Chances are San José wasn't on your list when you started planning your trip, but the country's largest city and cultural capital has multidimensional appeal. International flights to Costa Rica arrive at Aeropuerto Internacional Juan Santamaría, 17km northwest of the city, in the town of Alajuela.

Guatemala City
Guatemala's capital city is home to the country's best museums and galleries. Aeropuerto La Aurora is the country's major international airport, and far-reaching buses link the rest of Guatemala and neighbouring countries.

Managua
Nicaragua's Managua is chaotic, poetic and mesmerising. Managua International Airport has connecting services to the southern USA and several Central American cities. The city has national bus and van terminals, plus some international bus lines.

Panama City
The most cosmopolitan capital in Central America, Panama City is both vibrant metropolis and gateway to tropical escapes. Most international flights arrive at Tocumen International Airport. Albrook Bus Terminal, near Albrook Airport, is a convenient and modern one-stop location for most buses leaving Panama City.

San Salvador
Surrounded by volcanoes, San Salvador is handsome indeed. Its Aeropuerto Internacional Comalpa is a major Latin American transport centre, and is also a gateway to the USA. It serves excellent networks of long-distance coaches and souped-up old American school buses.

San Pedro Sula
Honduras' business and industrial capital, it is served by the modern Aeropuerto Internacional Ramón Villeda Morales – domestic and international flights from cities in Central America and the USA land here. The Terminal Gran Central Metropolitana is a regional hub for buses.

Right: A typical Guatemalan 'chicken bus' (left), and (right) the Palacio de Bellas Artes in Mexico City.

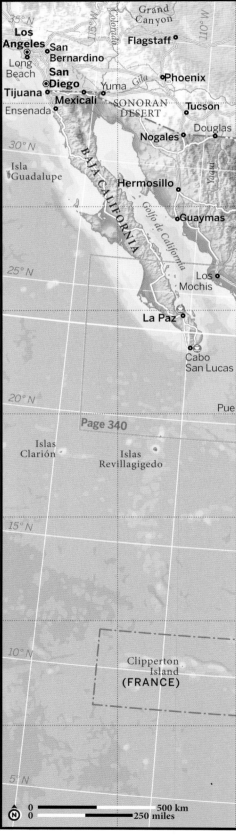

Page 340

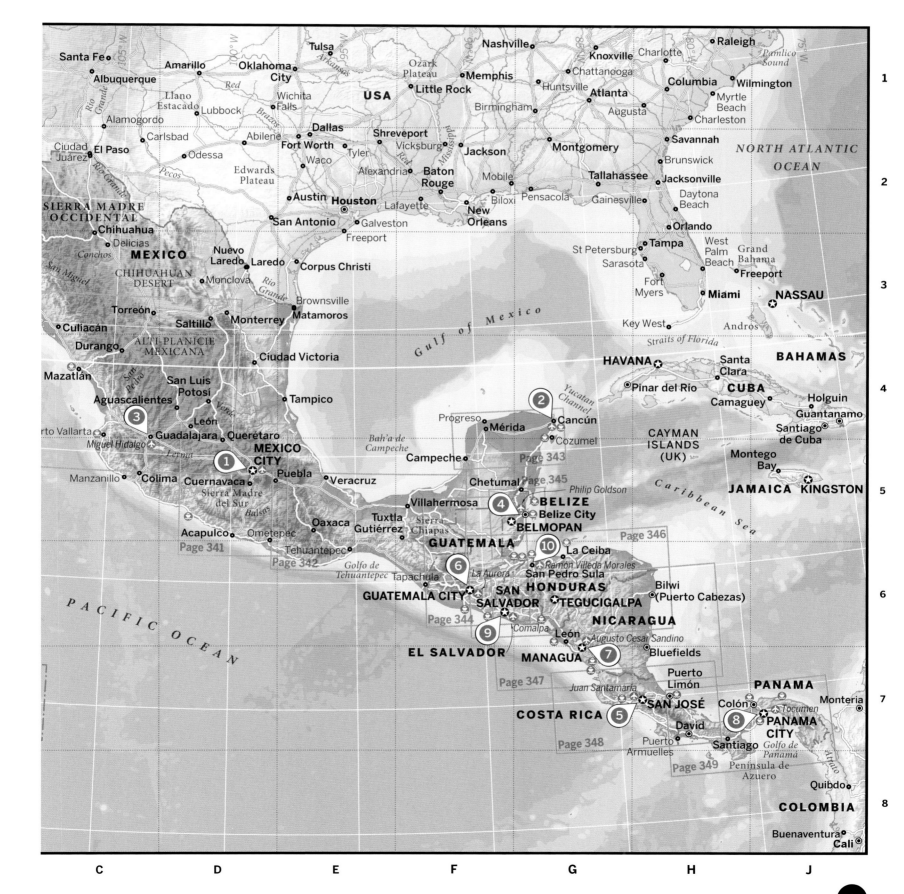

Santa Fe	Tulsa	Nashville	Knoxville	Charlotte	Raleigh	**1**
Albuquerque	Amarillo	Oklahoma City	Ozark Plateau	Memphis	Chattanooga	Columbia	Wilmington
	Llano Estacado	Wichita Falls	USA	Little Rock	Huntsville	Atlanta	Myrtle Beach
Alamogordo	Lubbock			Birmingham		Augusta	Charleston
Ciudad Juárez	El Paso	Carlsbad	Odessa	Dallas	Shreveport	Montgomery	Savannah

USA

SIERRA MADRE OCCIDENTAL

Chihuahua · Delicias

MEXICO

CHIHUAHUAN DESERT

Nuevo Laredo · Laredo · Corpus Christi

Torreón · Monclova · Rio Grande

Saltillo · Monterrey · Matamoros

Culiacán · Durango

ALTI PLANICIE MEXICANA

Mazatlán · Ciudad Victoria

Aguascalientes · San Luis Potosí · Tampico

③ León · Querétaro

Puerto Vallarta · Guadalajara

Miguel Hidalgo · ① **MEXICO CITY** · Puebla

Manzanillo · Colima · Cuernavaca · Veracruz

Acapulco · Ometepec · Oaxaca · Tuxtla Gutiérrez

Tehuantepec · Villahermosa · ④ **BELIZE**

Golfo de Tehuantepec · Tapachula · **GUATEMALA** · Belize City · **BELMOPAN**

⑥ · La Aurora · ⑩ La Ceiba

GUATEMALA CITY · San Pedro Sula · Ramón Villeda Morales

SAN SALVADOR · **HONDURAS** · Bilwi (Puerto Cabezas)

⑨ · **TEGUCIGALPA**

Comalpa · León · **NICARAGUA**

EL SALVADOR · Augusto Cesar Sandino · ⑦ Bluefields

MANAGUA

Puerto Limón · **PANAMA**

Juan Santamaría · Colón · Monteria

COSTA RICA · ⑤ **SAN JOSÉ** · Tocumen · ⑧ **PANAMA CITY**

David · Santiago · Golfo de Panamá

Puerto Armuelles · Peninsula de Azuero

COLOMBIA

Buenaventura · Cali

NORTH ATLANTIC OCEAN

Gulf of Mexico

Progreso · Mérida · Cancún · Cozumel

Campeche · Chetumal

HAVANA · Pinar del Río · Santa Clara · BAHAMAS · NASSAU · Andros

Straits of Florida · CUBA · Camaguey · Holguin · Guantanamo · Santiago de Cuba

CAYMAN ISLANDS (UK) · Montego Bay · JAMAICA · KINGSTON

Caribbean Sea

Philip Goldson

Key West · Miami · Freeport · Grand Bahama

West Palm Beach · Fort Myers · Daytona Beach · Orlando · Tampa · St Petersburg · Sarasota · Fort Myers

Tallahassee · Jacksonville · Gainesville · Pensacola · Biloxi · New Orleans

PACIFIC OCEAN

Page 341 · Page 342 · Page 343 · Page 344 · Page 345 · Page 346 · Page 347 · Page 348 · Page 349

| C | D | E | F | G | H | J |

SIGHTS & ACTIVITIES

 SEE

 DO

ITINERARY

 1

▽ 2

Espiritu Santo

A treasure of shallow azure inlets and sorbet-pink cliffs, Espiritu Santo is part of a Unesco-listed site compromising 244 Sea of Cortez islands and coastal areas. Kayak to spot sea turtles, dolphins and even whale sharks.

Puerto Vallarta's Old Town

Wander through the cobblestone streets savouring the tastes in small restaurants, markets and taco stands. With boutique shopping and traditional architecture, this Old Town slice of the city is like a little beach village amongst the grandeur of Puerto Vallarta.

Cabo San Lucas

Hop on a panga, kayak or SUP and head to El Arco, a jagged natural arch that partially fills with the tide. Paddle among pelicans and sea lions under the blue sky – it's magical.

4 Todos Santos

By far the prettiest town on the Baja, the boho-chic Todos Santos ('All Saints') is a quirky mix of locals, fishers, surfers and New Age spiritualists. Charming streets are lined with art galleries, romantic restaurants and cacti.

5 Plaza de los Mariachis, Guadalajara

This plaza in Guadalajara is the very birthplace of mariachi music. By day it's just a narrow walking street, flanked by charming old buildings. At night it gets lively, when patrons swill beer and listen to bands playing requests.

7-day itinerary
Southern Baja

Espiritu Santo: A paddleboarder in the shallows.

Start in quiet **San José del Cabo** with its colonial church, art galleries and clutch of restaurants. Go underwater for a closer glimpse of the reef at **Cabo Pulmo** – the only living reef in the Sea of Cortez, teeming with big-eyed jacks, whale sharks and more. Then try wild **Cabo San Lucas**: indulge in banana-boating and parasailing before hitting the bars, and take a boat to Land's

End to spy the stone arch. Next, stop at **Todos Santos**, a gorgeous town with galleries, sea turtle nesting grounds and historic buildings. Further north, enjoy the unspoiled charms of **La Paz**. Spend a day kayaking and snorkelling off the island of **Espiritu Santo** before detouring to **Puerto San Carlos** for a glimpse of leviathans during whale-watching season.

▽ 7-day itinerary
The Heartland

Get a feel for the country and its history at **Mexico City**'s famed Museo Nacional de Antropología – the Teotihuacán gallery is a primer on the America's first great state. Now make your way to the real ruins of **Teotihuacán**, about an hour northeast by bus or car. The pyramids of the sun and the moon are staggering in scale. Return to Mexico

City and head out northwest (by bus or car again) to the beautiful – if slightly unreal colonial town of **San Miguel de Allende**. Enjoy wandering the enchanting cobbled streets around the pink-hued Parroquia de San Miguel Arcángel. The town is also famed for its vibrant dining scene. Tear yourself away from the bars and restaurants

to continue to the former gold- and silver-mining city of **Guadalajara**. Its mineral wealth shows in the opulent colonial buildings, tree-filled plazas and handsome theatres. The entire city is on Unesco's World Heritage list. On the way back to Mexico City detour three hours' south for at least a day in elegant, centuries-old **Morelia**.

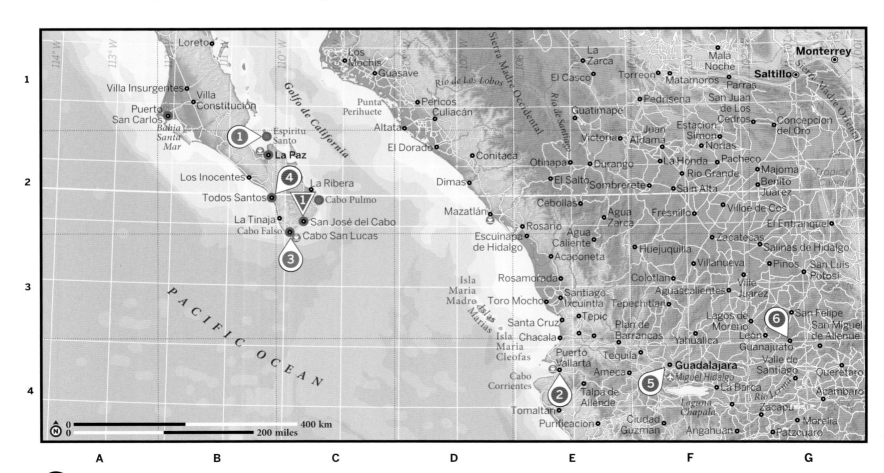

Festival Cervantino, Guanajuato

This is one of Latin America's foremost arts extravaganzas. Music, dance and theatre groups from around the globe perform (mostly non-Cervantes related) for two weeks in October.

Teotihuacán

Once among Meso-America's greatest cities, the immense Pirámide del Sol (Pyramid of the Sun) and Pirámide de la Luna (Pyramid of the Moon) dominate the remains of the ancient metropolis. Today it is a magnet for those seeking to soak up the mystical energies believed to converge here.

San Miguel de Allende

With its gorgeous colonial architecture, enchanting cobblestone streets and striking light, San Miguel de Allende has been popular with aesthetes and romantics for much of the past century. As such, it now has a cosmopolitan atmosphere seen in few other Mexican towns.

Playa Ventura

A long, pristine beach with soft white-and-gold sands, this seldom visited Mexican village leaves you no choice but to disconnect and surrender to its easy tempo and natural beauty.

Taxco

Surrounded by dramatic mountains and cliffs, Taxco's perfectly preserved colonial architecture and the twin belfries of its baroque masterpiece, Templo de Santa Prisca, make for one of the most beguiling views anywhere in the central highlands.

Zócalo, Mexico City

The veil of time is extremely thin in Mexico City's main square. Here you can witness the ceremonial centre of Aztec Tenochtitlán at Templo Mayor, the conquest of Cortés and the rise of Catholicism in the stunning cathedral and the modern flux of Mexican politics in the national buildings housing Diego Rivera's famous murals.

Puebla

Once a bastion of conservatism, Catholicism and tradition, Puebla has come out of its colonial-era shell. While the city retains a well-preserved centre – buildings adorned with painted Talavera tiles (for which Puebla is famous), a stunning cathedral and a wealth of beautiful churches – younger *poblanos* (people of Puebla) are embracing the city's increasingly thriving art and nightlife scenes.

Mineral del Chico

This charming old mining village, located near the 3000-hectare Parque Nacional El Chico, proffers wonderful views, fresh air and some great hiking among spectacular rock formations and beautiful waterfalls.

Teotihuacán:
Pyramids of the Sun and Moon on the Avenue of the Dead.

Troncones

With several world-class surf spots for experienced boarders, the one to chase is the left at Troncones Point. When it's small, the takeoff is right over the rocks (complete with sea urchins), but when it's big, it's beautiful and beefy and rolls halfway across the bay.

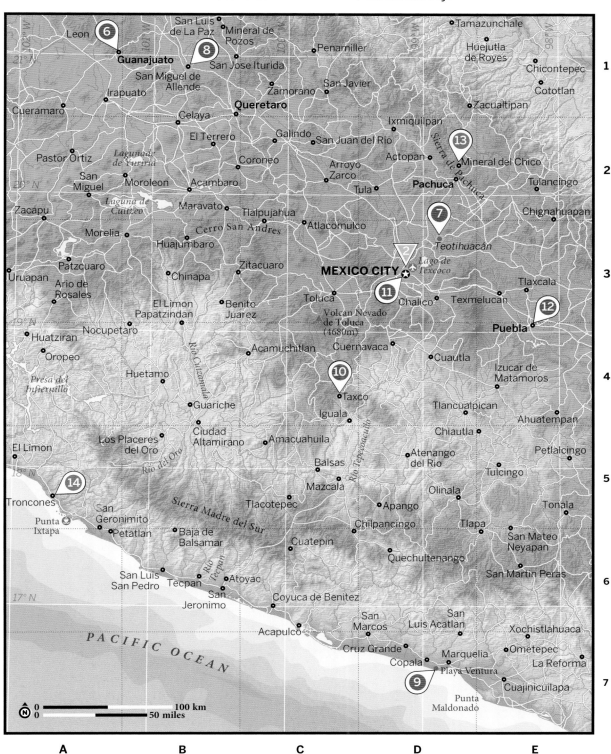

SIGHTS &
ACTIVITIES

 SEE

 DO

ITINERARY

 1

2

1 Playa Zicatela

Miles of golden sand and crashing waves are the attraction in Puerto Escondido, where surfboards are as ubiquitous as cell phones. The northern end is home to the Pipeline, arguably the best surfing in the country while the southern end has mellower surf and a vibe to go with it.

2 Pico de Orizaba

At a cloud-scraping and breathless 5611m, Pico de Orizaba is Mexico's tallest mountain. Rising high above the region, the snow-capped tip of this mighty volcano throws down a gauntlet to those who cannot resist the siren call of a peak not conquered. This is Mexico's ultimate trekking and climbing challenge (the ascent requires some technical skills) and the six-day, five-night summit treks start from the small village of Tlachichuca.

3 Playa Escobilla

This 15km-long beach is one of the world's major nesting grounds for the olive ridley turtle. Up to a million female olive ridleys a year arrive to lay their eggs, with numbers peaking at night for a period of about a week around the full moons from May to February – a spectacular phenomenon known as an *arribada* or *arribazón*.

Palenque: The Mayan ruin of El Palacio.

4 Pueblos Mancomunados

More than 100km of high-country trails run between eight remote villages protected under the umbrella of a unique ecotourism project. They offer great wilderness escapes and encounters with Zapotec village life.

5 Valles Centrales

A slightly rustic collection of towns and villages around Oaxaca City that tout some the state's biggest calling cards: ancient Meso-American ruins, indigenous crafts, industrious markets, riotous festivals and fields full of mezcal-producing agave plants.

6 Palenque

Ancient Palenque stands at the precise point where the first hills rise out of the Gulf coast plain, and the dense jungle covering these hills forms an evocative backdrop to some of Mexico's most exquisite Maya architecture.

7 Oaxaca City

Flowing through handsome yet tranquil streets, life pulsates in Oaxaca with an unadulterated regional flavour. See it in the colour palate of historic boutique hotels, a meet-the-producer artisan store or an intentionally grungy *mezcalería*. But the city also has a grittier edge that bubbles up in satirical street art, bohemian bars and been-around-forever street markets.

8 Parque Dos Ojos

The Maya considered cenotes sacred gateways to the underworld and once you visit one you'll better understand where they were coming from. Dos Ojos is one of the largest underwater cave systems in the world, with an extent of about 83km. Float past illuminated stalactites and stalagmites in an eerie wonderland.

9 Tulum

These dramatically situated ruins sit pretty atop a high cliff overlooking a spectacular white-sand beach. The tallest building in the complex is a watchtower named El Castillo. It is surrounded by elaborate temples, including one built shortly before the arrival of the Spanish. History lessons can be followed by swims in the Mexican Caribbean or a cenote.

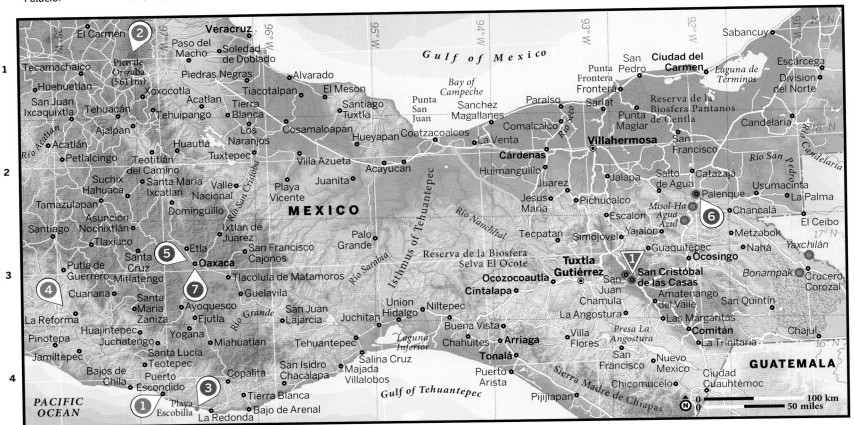

© Justin Foulkes / Lonely Planet

7-day itinerary
Tour Chiapas

In **San Cristóbal de las Casas**, marvel at the imposing 16th-century Templo de Santo Domingo, then stroll the crafts market to admire intricate textiles. Nearby **San Juan Chamula** is a village of fiercely independent Tzotzil people with unique religious practices. Make your way to **Palenque** where the mighty Maya temples are swept in morning jungle mist – it's also the perfect jumping-off point to explore the breathtaking **Agua Azul** and **Misol-Ha** waterfalls. Finally head to the wildly romantic ancient Maya cities of **Bonampak** and **Yaxchilán**. Bright tropical birds flit between crumbling monuments while monkeys hoot from the trees. At night the sky screams with stars and the air twinkles with fireflies.

10-day itinerary
Maya Country

The architectural and artistic achievements of the Maya are prominently displayed across the Yucatán peninsula. For background, visit the shiny Museo Maya de Cancún in the Zona Hotelera in **Cancún**. From there, head south to the cliff-top Mayan site of **Tulum** then hit the road for **Valladolid**, a former Maya ceremonial centre. Drop by **Cenote X'Kekén y Samulá** on your way and take a cool plunge. Next up is **Chichén Itzá**, one of the 'new seven wonders of the world'. Move on to **Oxkutzcab** and **Tekax**, which offer glimpses of traditional Maya life. While in Oxkutzcab, check out the **Grutas de Loltún**, the largest cave system on the peninsula. Then visit **Santa Elena** to explore the ruins of **Uxmal** and **Kabah** in the Puuc hills. Cross into Campeche and stop at **Hopelchén**, where you can witness the ancient art of herbal medicine. Campeche makes a good base for visiting **Edzná**'s five-storey temple. Finish your explorations in Chiapas with **Palenque**'s ruins and the contemporary Maya domain of **San Cristóbal de las Casas**.

Isla Holbox
Lying within Yum Balam reserve, this low-key island attracts more than 150 bird species, including roseate spoonbills, pelicans, herons and flamingos. In summer, whale sharks congregate nearby.

Chichén Itzá
The massive El Castillo pyramid, Chichén Itzá's iconic structure, will knock your socks off, especially at vernal and autumnal equinoxes, when morning and afternoon sunlight cast a shadow of a serpent on the staircase.

Mérida
Since the Spanish conquest, Mérida has been the cultural capital of the peninsula and it remains a rich and relaxed city to explore. Its colonial history has left a legacy of handsome, brightly painted buildings and grand plazas. Mérida is home to the Yucatán's best museums, including the Gran Museo del Mundo Maya, which is an accessible introduction to Mayan history. Food, art and music are prized here: the Parque Santa Lucía hosts Yucatecan serenades weekly. The town of Izamal, 70km east – also known as La Ciudad Amarilla (the Yellow City) – offers a similar colonial experience.

Campeche
Campeche is a colonial fairyland, its walled city centre a tight enclave of restored pastel buildings, narrow cobblestone streets, fortified ramparts and well-preserved mansions.

Uxmal
Easily ranking among the top Maya archaeological sites, Uxmal possesses some fascinating houses, temples and a pyramid in good condition and bearing a mass of ornamentation. Adding to its appeal is Uxmal's setting in the hilly Puuc region.

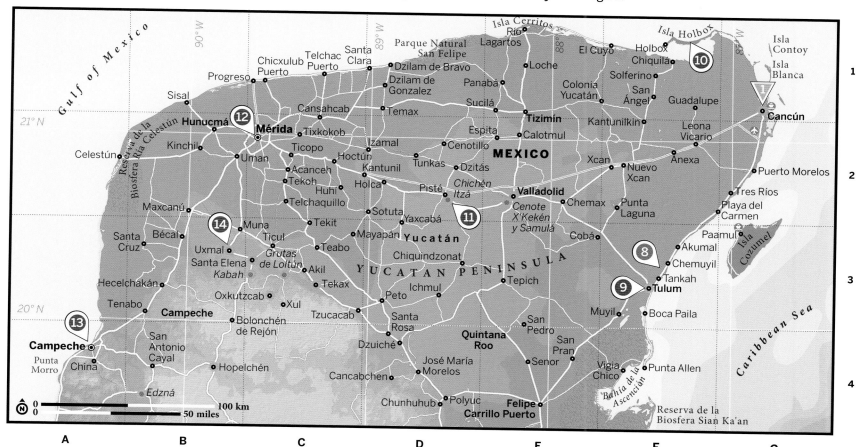

1 Antigua
A place of rare beauty, major historical significance and vibrant culture, Antigua is Guatemala's must-visit destination, and thanks to the dozens of Spanish-language schools that operate here, it's the perfect place to learn the lingo.

2 Reserva Natural Atitlán
A former coffee plantation being overtaken by natural vegetation, this reserve includes a butterfly enclosure and herb garden, an interpretive centre and an aviary. For more extreme thrills, there are various ziplines spanning canyons and forest.

3 Tikal
The restored temples standing in this corner of the jungle astonish for both their monumental size and architectural brilliance. Occupied for some 16 centuries, Tikal is an amazing testament to the cultural and artistic heights scaled by this civilisation.

4 El Mirador
Buried within the furthest reaches of the Petén jungle, this late-Preclassic metropolis contains the largest cluster of buildings of any single Maya site, among them the biggest pyramid ever built in the Maya world.

5 Chichicastenango
Chichicastenango can seem isolated from the rest of Guatemala, but the crowds of crafts vendors and visitors who flock to its markets lend it a much worldlier atmosphere. On Thursdays and Sundays villagers arrive at dawn and spread out their vegetables, textiles, pottery and other merchandise for sale.

6 Volcán Tajumulco
There are exciting volcano climbs to be done from Quetzaltenango. Tackle Volcán Tajumulco, which is a challenging trek to the highest point in Central America. Others include Volcán Santa María and the active Santiaguito, both of which can be done over long mornings.

7 Semuc Champey
Semuc Champey is famed for its great natural limestone bridge on top of which is a stepped series of pools with cool, flowing river water – perfect for a dip. The beauty of its setting and the turquoise perfection of the pools make it arguably the loveliest spot in Guatemala.

8 Caracol
Wander through what was once one of the most powerful cities in the entire Maya world. Caracol now lies enshrouded by jungle near the Guatemalan border. This is the largest Maya site in Belize – at its peak, the city's population approached 150,000.

9 Crooked Tree Wildlife Reserve
From December to May, migrating birds flock to the lagoons, rivers and swamps of this sanctuary managed by Belize Audubon Society. Boat-billed, chestnut-bellied and bare-throated tiger herons, Muscovy and black-bellied whistling ducks, ospreys, and all of Belize's five species of kingfisher are among the 276 species recorded here.

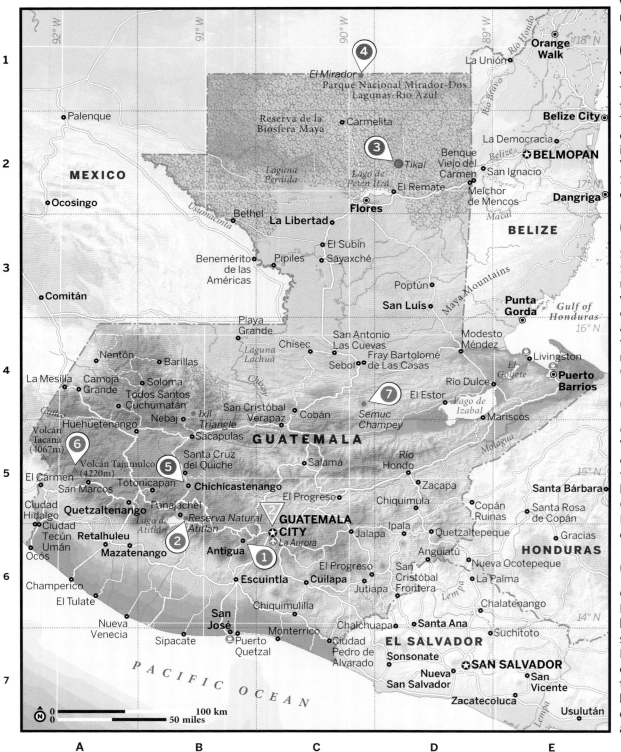

14-day itinerary
Surf and Turf in Belize

Antigua: Agua volcano behind Santa Catalina Arch.

Start your trip at San Pedro on **Ambergris Caye**. Snorkel or dive among coral gardens and observe the inhabitants of **Shark Ray Alley**. Use San Pedro as your launch pad for dives at **Blue Hole** and other atoll sites. After a week of sun and fun, make your way to dry land at **Belize City** and head out along the George Price Hwy. In Cayo, base yourself in **San Ignacio**. From here, you

can explore caves loaded with ancient remains, such as Actun Tunichil Muknal travel by canoe or inner-tube along jungle rivers; or dip beneath the waterfalls of the Mountain Pine Ridge. If you have the time, venture over the border into Guatemala, where you can visit the region's most significant Maya archaeological site at **Tikal**.

10-day itinerary
The Highlands of Guatemala

Guatemala's most spectacular scenery and strongest Maya traditions await. From **Guatemala City** head first to picturesque **Antigua**, enjoying the country's finest colonial architecture, the great restaurants and the language-student scene. From Antigua move on to **Panajachel** on volcano-ringed Lago de Atitlán. From the lake, hop a 'chicken bus' north

to **Chichicastenango** for its huge Thursday or Sunday market. From Chichicastenango follow the Interamericana Hwy to **Quetzaltenango**, Guatemala's second city with a host of intriguing villages, and natural wonders waiting within short bus rides away. From there, go further into the hills to **Todos Santos Cuchumatán**, a fascinating mountain

town with great walking possibilities. If you have extra time, push east to explore **Nebaj** and the **Ixil Triangle**, where you'll find stunning scenery and great hiking. A rough but passable road leads further eastward from here, providing a back-door route to Alta Verapaz, where you can check out **Cobán** or the turquoise pools of **Semuc Champey**.

Hol Chan Marine Reserve

Located at the southern end of Ambergris Caye, Hol Chan Marine Reserve is home to spectacular coral formations, sea-grass beds and mangroves all chock-full of diverse marine life. Hol Chan is Mayan for 'Little Channel', which refers to a natural break in the reef known as Hol Chan Cut.

Blue Hole

An incomparable natural wonder and a unique diving experience, this deep blue pupil with an aquamarine border has become a symbol of Belize. Almost 320m in diameter, this incredible void – lined with a dense forest of stalactites and stalagmites, and patrolled by reef sharks – plunges 125m straight down into the centre of Lighthouse Reef.

Xunantunich

Xunantunich is an accessible and impressive Maya site in Belize. Getting here is half the fun with a hand-cranked cable ferry taking you (and vehicles) across the Mopan River. Climb to the top of the 40m structure known as El Castillo to enjoy a fantastic view.

Nohoch Che'en Caves Branch Archaeological Reserve

This extensive network of limestone caves is popular for cave-tubing, kayaking and spelunking. The Caves Branch River flows through nine caves and side passages, one of which leads to the remarkable Crystal Cave.

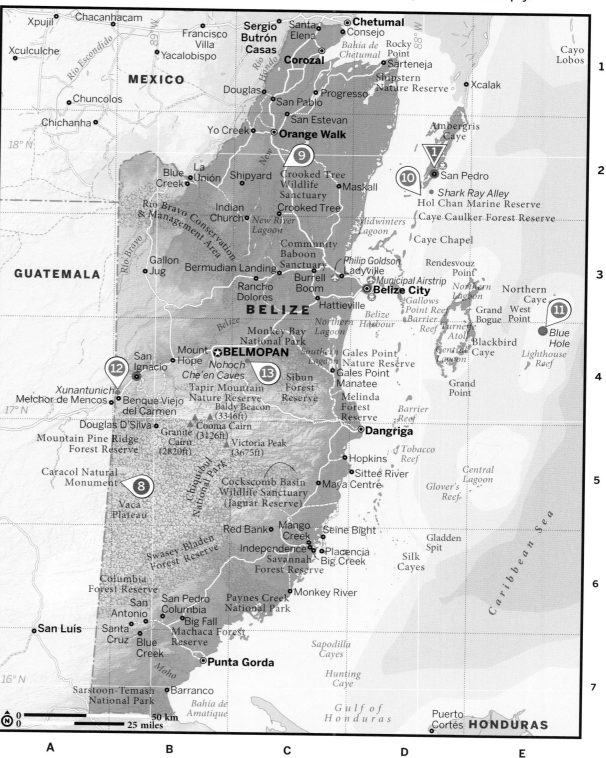

SIGHTS & ACTIVITIES

 SEE

DO

ITINERARY

1

2

Iglesia El Rosario, San Salvador

Designed by sculptor Ruben Martinez and completed in 1971, San Salvador's Iglesia El Rosario is radically beautiful. Arguably one of the finest churches in Central America, its concrete exterior conceals an arched roof and a rainbow of natural light rushing across the altar.

Playa El Tunco

Welcome to El Salvador's surfing paradise. El Tunco parties hard on weekends, but press on a few kilometres away from the city and you'll have the glistening ocean, awash with turtles, dolphins and leaping fish, all to yourself.

Suchitoto

Suchitoto is considered El Salvador's cultural capital and is home to a number of art shops and galleries. Visit Arte Añil, a cosy shop specialising in high-quality indigo-dyed pieces; visitors can also participate in dying workshops.

4

Utila

Utila is a charming island in El Salvador that has enjoyed a reputation for years as the place to learn to dive in Latin America. Explore life under the waves with Parrots Dive Center, which employs local instructors.

21-day itinerary
Crossing the Divide

Starting in **San Salvador**, first head south to the **Costa del Bálsamo**, sleeping at **Playa El Tunco**. Head north to **Ruta de las Flores** to sample coffee and culture in small artisanal towns. Sleep in **Juayúa**. Spend a day hiking nearby **Cerro Verde** or visit the Maya pyramids at **Tazumal**. Sleep in **San Salvador**, then explore the capital's galleries and museums. Next are the mountains and visits to **La Palma** and **Suchitoto**. From here take a bus to the Honduras border, before heading north to the stunning ruins of **Copán Ruinas**. Now make a short hop west to the atmospheric highland town of **Gracias** with its hot spring and Lencan villages. Then it's a long day on the road to the coastal city of **La Ceiba**. Set sail from here for either **Roatán** or **Utila** and indulge in some serious beach and reef time. Back on the mainland, raft down the exquisite **Río Cangrejal**, then it's south to the serene **Lago de Yojoa** for an artisan brew or two, hiking and boat trips. Finish off with a night in either tranquil **Comayagua** or **Tegucigalpa**.

El Boquerón

Hike up to El Boquerón (1893m), one of two peaks on Volcán San Salvador, for unbeatable views down over San Salvador. It also has a symetrically perfect 45m-high cone within its crater, which formed in 1917.

Parque Nacional La Tigra

This Honduran park is home to rugged forest, numerous rivers and waterfalls and a large population of mammals, including pumas, peccaries, agoutis and 350 species of birds. Hike here and it's impossible to miss the park's exuberant flora: lush trees, colourful mushrooms, and what seems like a million orchids.

Lago de Yojoa

Ringed by tropical forest, Lago de Yojoa in Honduras is exceptional. The lake's birdlife is world class, and you can hike to waterfalls, summit Montaña de Santa Bárbara, or kayak the calm waters. Be sure to grab a microbrew at D&D Brewery in Los Naranjos.

Copán Ruinas

One of the most important Maya civilisations lived, prospered, then mysteriously crumbled at this Honduran Unesco-listed site. The city dominated the region during the Classic period; you'll often be alone here, which makes it all the more haunting.

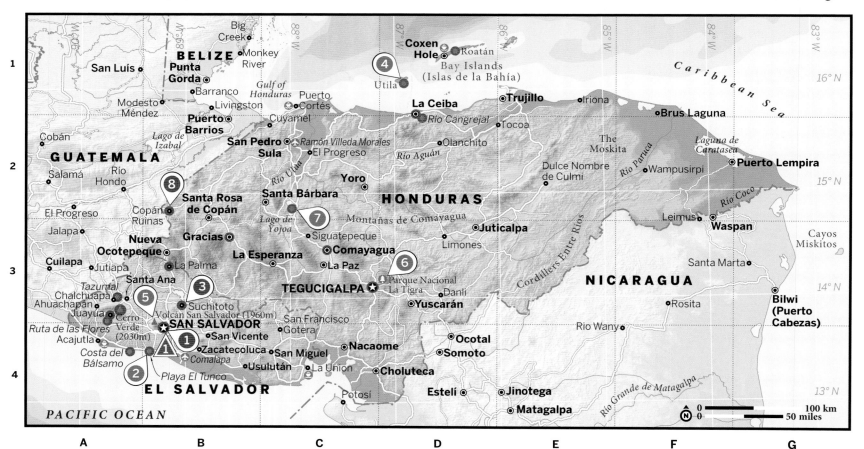

Parque Nacional Volcán Masaya

The craters that comprise this park are the most easily accessible active volcanoes in the country. You'll get a wonderful view of the surrounding countryside from Masaya's summit.

Granada

Granada is a town of palpable magnetism. At the heart of the city's charms are the picture-perfect cobbled streets, polychromatic colonial homes with splendid courtyards and churches. It is also a great base for day-trip adventures into the countryside.

Little Corn Island

A tiny, jungled, car-less jewel, this is a dreamy escape with imaginative bungalow properties encamped on otherwise virgin beaches. Try your hand at kitesurfing and soar over the turquoise waters.

Pearl Lagoon

At last, you've arrived in the real Caribbean – here are dirt roads and palm trees, reggae music, and a community that fishes the local waters for shrimp, fish and lobster. If your Caribbean dream is tinted turquoise, you can easily arrange a tour of the nearby Pearl Keys.

10-day itinerary
Cruise the Río San Juan

From **Managua** fly or bus it to **San Carlos**, where you can check out the Spanish fort and waterfront before taking the afternoon boat to enchanted **Islas Solentiname**. Spend a night on both Isla San Fernando and Isla Mancarrón, following jungle trails to petroglyphs and visiting local artisans. Next catch a riverboat down the Río San Juan to **Boca de Sábalos**. Visit the local chocolate factory or spot birds on the banks of the majestic river. After two nights in Sábalos, continue to **El Castillo**, where an imposing Spanish fort looms over the rapids. Spend two days here riding horses through the rolling hills and feasting on giant river shrimp. If you have a day to spare, detour north to **Refugio Bartola** biological station, with its swimming holes and hiking and kayaking routes. Then take a riverboat heading to **San Juan de Nicaragua**, where the Río San Juan meets the Caribbean Sea. Give yourself three days to explore the **Greytown** ruins and spot manatees in hidden lagoons. From San Juan de Nicaragua fly directly back to Managua.

Convento y Museo San Francisco, Granada

One of the oldest churches in Central America, the Convento y Museo San Francisco boasts a robin's egg-blue facade and houses a convent and one of the best museums in the region.

Museo Rubén Darío, León

Nicaragua's most famous poet, Rubén Dario, lived in this house for the first 14 years of his life. Of all the museums and monuments dedicated to the poet that are scattered across his doting homeland, this place seems like the one where you'd be most likely to run into his ghost.

Mercado de Artesanías de Masaya

Showcasing the highest-quality crafts in the country, this historic marketplace, a black-basalt Gothic structure with a Spanish-fortress motif, dates from 1888. It's one-stop shopping for Nicaraguan crafts of all kinds.

Isla de Ometepe

Ometepe never fails to impress. Its twin volcanic peaks rising up out of Lago de Nicaragua have captured the imagination of everyone from precolonial Aztecs to Mark Twain. And its clean waters, wide beaches, wildlife, archaeological sites and dramatic profile are equally enthralling.

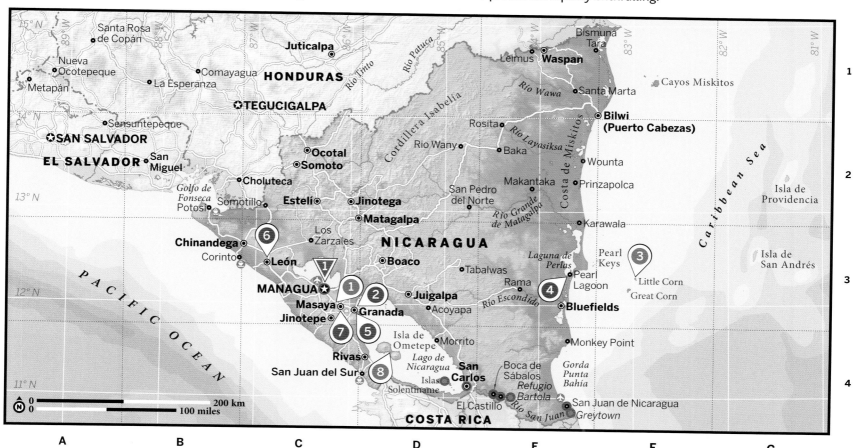

SIGHTS & ACTIVITIES

 SEE

DO

ITINERARY

 1

2

Reserva Santa Elena

Open since 1992, Santa Elena was one of the first community-managed conservation projects in the country. The exquisitely misty 310-hectare cloud forest has 12km of dewy trails. It's a more mellow respite to the famous Monteverde Cloud Forest nearby.

Punta Uva

Off a dirt road marked by Punta Uva Dive Center is an idyllic cove with a couple of locals renting out surfboards on the sand. The reef to the right of the cove is excellent for snorkelling and when the waves are up, this spot creates a forgiving, peeling right-hand wave.

③ Parque Nacional Manuel Antonio

The country's most popular national park is an absolute gem. Capuchin monkeys scurry across its beaches, brown pelicans dive-bomb its clear waters and sloths watch over its accessible trails.

④ Playa Hermosa

Regarded as one of the most consistent and powerful breaks in the whole country, Hermosa serves up serious surf. You need to know what you're doing in these parts – or sit back and watch the action.

7-day itinerary
Pacific Coast

Kick things off with **Parque Nacional Carara**, home to scarlet macaws. Then head south to **Quepos** and **Parque Nacional Manuel Antonio** which provides a refuge for rare animals, including the endangered squirrel monkey. Continue south, stopping to sample the roadside ceviche stands, and visit **Hacienda Barú National Wildlife Refuge** for some sloth spotting, or keep heading south to **Dominical** in search of waves. For deserted beach wandering, continue on to **Uvita**, where you can look for whales spouting offshore at Parque Nacional Marino Ballena. From Uvita, move further south to the far-flung **Península de Osa**, for journeys through the country's top national park for wildlife viewing and a bona fide jungle adventure. Emerge at the northern end in lush and remote **Bahía Drake**, where you'll swim in paradisaical coves among the dripping rainforest. Return to civilisation via ferry through Central America's longest stretch of mangroves to **Sierpe**, home to ancient stone spheres.

Hacienda Barú National Wildlife Refuge

With pristine beaches, mangrove estuaries, primary forests, tree plantations and pastures, this nature reserve is a key link in the Path of the Tapir biological corridor. Hike its well-kept trails and experience the rainforest canopy by tree climbing or ziplining.

San Isidro de Heredia

The divine Sibu Chocolate tour explains the culture and history surrounding Costa Rica's most decadent export. See cacao's story brought to life as you sample pre-Columbian-inspired hot chocolate and other treats.

Península de Osa

Osa Wild is the way to connect with Parque Nacional Corcovado and Osa. It's just what the area needed: a resource for travellers to connect with community-oriented initiatives that go to the heart of the real Osa through homestays, farm tours and sustainable cultural exchanges.

Parque Nacional Tortuguero

Canoeing the canals of this truly wild park is a boat-borne safari: thick jungle meets the water and you can get up close to shy caimans, river turtles, crowned night herons, monkeys and sloths.

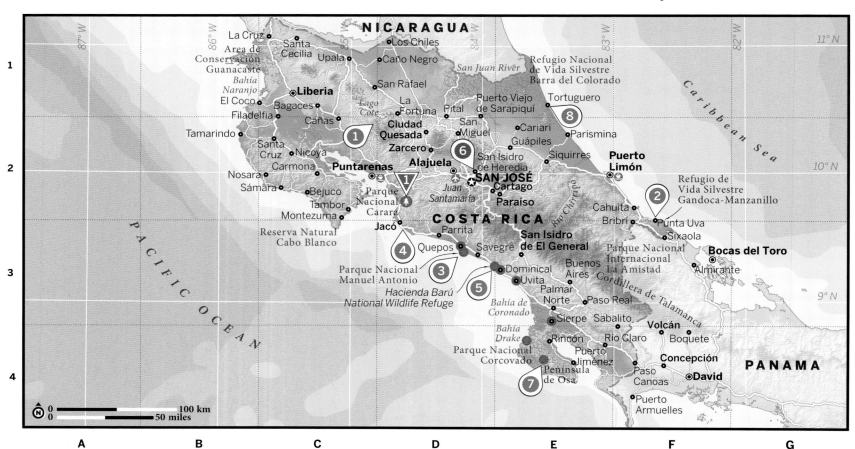

BioMuseo, Panama City
World-renowned architect Frank Gehry designed this landmark museum of crumpled multicolour forms as a visual feast that celebrates Panama's astonishing biodiversity. Gawk at its world-class exhibits and the botanical gardens.

Dario López Workshop, Parita
One of Panama's top artisans, Dario López has been making colourful masks for folkloric dancers since the 1960s. To visit his home workshop, look for the gas station near the Parita turnoff on Carretera Nacional.

Parque Nacional Marino Isla Bastimentos
Protecting 130 islands of the Bocas del Toro archipelago, including the coral-fringed Cayos Zapatillas and the wetlands in the centre of Isla Bastimentos, this marine park hosts mangroves, monkeys, sloths, and 28 species of amphibians and reptiles.

Panama City
Welcome to high-octane Latin America. Think ceviche, casinos, traffic and a stacked skyline. The beauty of Panama City lies in its underground rhythms, fiery sunsets and laid-back attitude.

14-day itinerary
Pacific Coast and Highlands

This route alternates between scenic beaches and highland cloud forests. Spend your first few days taking in **Panama City**, and then head west along the Interamericana to explore a string of Pacific beaches. Overnight at **Mamallena Ecolodge** in the sculpted foothills before heading to **El Valle**, a lush mountain retreat.

Return to the Interamericana, visiting Coclé province's roadside attractions, then detour for **Santa Fé**, a tiny highland town amid sparkling rivers and waterfalls. To surf, head to **Santa Catalina**. Another good reason to stop here is to connect to **Parque Nacional Coiba**, a pristine island in a vast marine park. Although there's minimal infrastructure, it's worth staying a few days. Head via David to **Boquete** in Chiriquí province, where you can hike and fill up on mountain-grown coffee. Retreat to a rainforest cabin before hiking the **Sendero Los Quetzales**, a trail through a cloud forest. To save time, fly back to Panama City from **David**.

Sendero Los Quetzales
One of Panama's most beautiful trails runs between Cerro Punta and Boquete, criss-crossing Río Caldera and offering travellers the chance to see remarkable orchids, tapirs and resplendent quetzals. The 8km route takes between four and six hours, and a guide is recommended.

Green Acres Chocolate Farm, Isla San Cristóbal
A tour at this chocolate farm will take you from cacao pod to candy bar. The grounds are teeming with flora and fauna including hundreds of orchid species and poison dart frogs

Miraflores Visitor Center
The best way to visit the Panama canal is to head to this modern visitors centre located just outside Panama City. It features a four-floor museum, viewing platforms and an excellent restaurant with panoramic views of canal transit.

Parque Nacional Coiba
Often compared to the Galápagos, this marine park is a veritable lost world of pristine ecosystems. You'll spy flocks of scarlet macaws, enormous schools of fish, migrating humpback whales with calves, and manta rays scuffing the ocean floor.

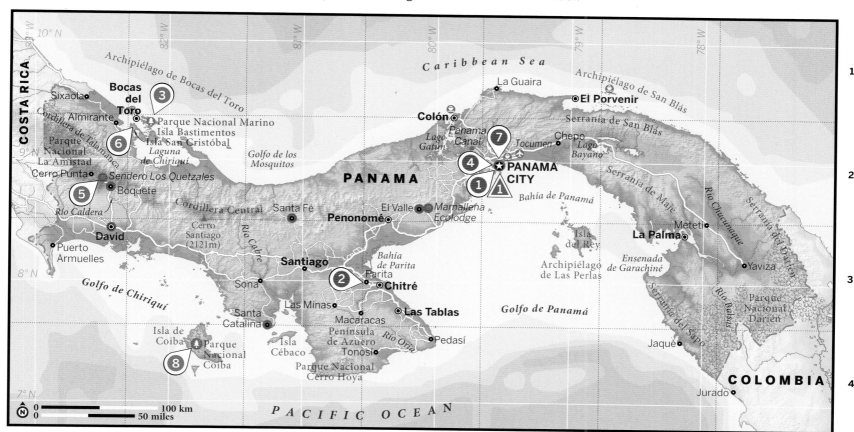

The Caribbean

From high mountain peaks to shimmering reefs, spicy salsa rhythms to deep rolling reggae, pirate hideouts to sugar-sand beaches, the Caribbean is dizzyingly diverse. The region is a joyous mosaic of islands beckoning paradise-hunters, an explosion of colour, fringed by beaches and soaked in rum. It's a lively and intoxicating profusion of people and places spread over 7000 islands (fewer than 10% are inhabited). But, for all they share, there's also much that makes them different. The region covers an impressive 2.75 million sq kilometres, and the people scattered across this archipelago speak a plethora of languages: English, Spanish, French, Dutch, Creole, Papamientu and many more.

CLIMATE CHART

HAVANA

RAINFALL
INCH/MM
—16/400
—12/300
—8/200
—4/100
—0
D N O S A J J M A M F J

TEMP
°C/°F
40/104—
30/86—
20/68—
10/50—
0/32—

KINGSTON

RAINFALL
INCH/MM
—20/500
—16/400
—12/300
—8/200
—4/100
—0
D N O S A J J M A M F J

TEMP
°C/°F
40/104—
30/86—
20/68—
10/50—
0/32—

BEACHES

Icons of the Caribbean, perfect stretches of powdery sand are found on almost every island. Enjoy St-Barthélemy's secluded Anse de Gouverneur, dig your toes into Grace Bay Beach in Turks & Caicos; sun yourself at Aruba's legendary Eagle Beach; or take in the turquoise water at Shoal Bay in Anguilla.

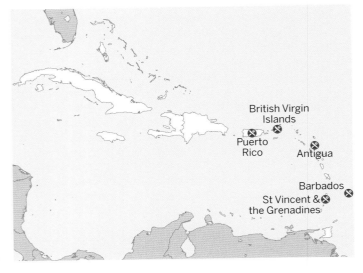

FOOD

Caribbean cuisine blends fruits, rice, seafood and spice. Sample pepperpot in Antigua, savory pumpkin soup in St Vincent and the Grenadines, *lechón asado* (spit-roasted pig) in Puerto Rico, Anegada lobster in the British Virgin Islands, and conkies in Barbados.

Clockwise from top left: Snorkelling in Grace Bay, Turks & Caicos; salsa singer in Cuba; Playa del Este near Havana, Cuba; Merengue dancers, Dominican Republic.

MUSIC

The Caribbean's beat is reason alone to make the trip. Head to Kingston, Jamaica for reggae and dancehall; hit Port of Spain, Trinidad for soca and steel-pan beats; rumba in the clubs of Havana, Cuba; merengue in Santo Domingo, Dominican Republic; and salsa in the streets of San Juan, Puerto Rico.

DIVING & SNORKELLING

The Caribbean is as enchanting underwater as it is above it. Explore the reef at the Bonaire National Marine Park; dive Grenada's shipwrecks; snorkel the shallows of the Exuma Cays in the Bahamas; deep-dive the pinnacles of Saba's marine park; and swim with the sea turtles at Curaçao's Playa Grandi.

Transport hubs

Most capital cities serve as transport hubs, though access varies. Many North American airlines fly direct to the more popular islands. UK airlines serve former British colonies like Barbados and Antigua; French airlines serve the French-speaking islands; and Dutch carriers fly to Aruba, Bonaire, Curaçao and Sint Maarten. There are no direct flights from Australia, New Zealand or Asia. Many cities here have ports for cruise ships, and inter-island ferries are widely available.

ELEVATION KEY

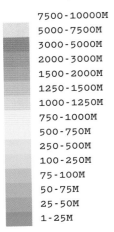

7500-10000M
5000-7500M
3000-5000M
2000-3000M
1500-2000M
1250-1500M
1000-1250M
750-1000M
500-750M
250-500M
100-250M
75-100M
50-75M
25-50M
1-25M

TRANSPORT

B3, B4, C1,
C2, C5, F7,
G4, H5, H7,
J6

B4, C1, C2,
C4, F4, F7,
G4, H5, H6,
H7, J6

 San Juan
San Juan is a mosaic of ever-evolving historic and modern neighborhoods. Luis Muñoz Marín International Airport is the city's main airport where almost all flights arrive or depart. San Juan is also the second-largest port for cruise ships in the western hemisphere (after Miami).

 Bridgetown
Wandering the sights and old colonial buildings of Bridgetown can easily occupy a day. Grantley Adams International Airport is the largest airport in the Eastern Caribbean and the major point of entry for the region. Cruise ships dock at Bridgetown.

 Nassau
Nassau is the vivacious alter ego to the relaxed character of most of the Bahamas. The majority of flights arrive in Nassau or Freeport where passengers will connect to another flight before continuing on to the Out Islands. Numerous cruise ships dock in Nassau and Grand Bahama.

 Havana
Havana's striking architecture and distinguished culture are what travel dreams are made of. Cuba's main airport, José Martí, is 25km southwest of the city. Some intra-country travel is done by air, but buses are more popular (and cheaper). The main bus company is Víazul.

 St George's
St George's is a fabulous place to explore on foot. Maurice Bishop International Airport has flights from North America, the UK, and regional Caribbean destinations. St George's is a port of call for many cruise ships.

 St John's
Antigua is the hub of regional airline LIAT, and VC Bird International Airport has frequent flights to St Kitts, Nevis, Sint Maarten, Dominica, Barbados and Puerto Rico. Antigua is also a major port of call for cruise ships. The cruise-ship pier in St John's Harbour is within walking distance of the town's premium sights.

 Willemstad
Willemstad feels like a Dutch city due to its waterways, street cafes and Unesco-protected architecture. Curaçao is part of southern Caribbean cruise-ship itineraries, and many ships call in Willemstad. Hato International Airport receives international flights from the Americas and Amsterdam.

 Santo Domingo
'La Capital' as it's typically called, is a collage of cultures and neighbourhoods. It's where the sounds of life – domino pieces slapped on tables, backfiring silencers and horns from chaotic traffic, merengue and bachata music blasting from corner stores – are most intense. It's home to two airports and the country's only international port.

 George Town
Supremely wealthy but surprisingly modest, the capital of the Cayman Islands is undoubtedly cosmopolitan. Tiny, tidy and pleasantly tropical, it is one of the world's busiest cruise ports.

 Kingston
Squeezed between the Blue Mountains and the world's seventh-largest natural harbour, Kingston both impresses you with its setting and overwhelms you with its noise and hustle. The airport is 27km southeast of town.

Above: A cruise ship departs Nassau, Bahamas (left); classic American cars in Havana, Cuba (right).

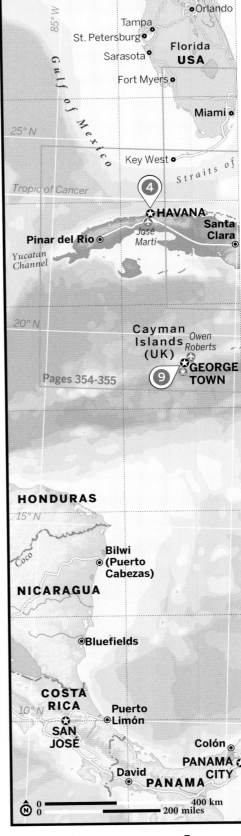

THE TRAVEL ATLAS

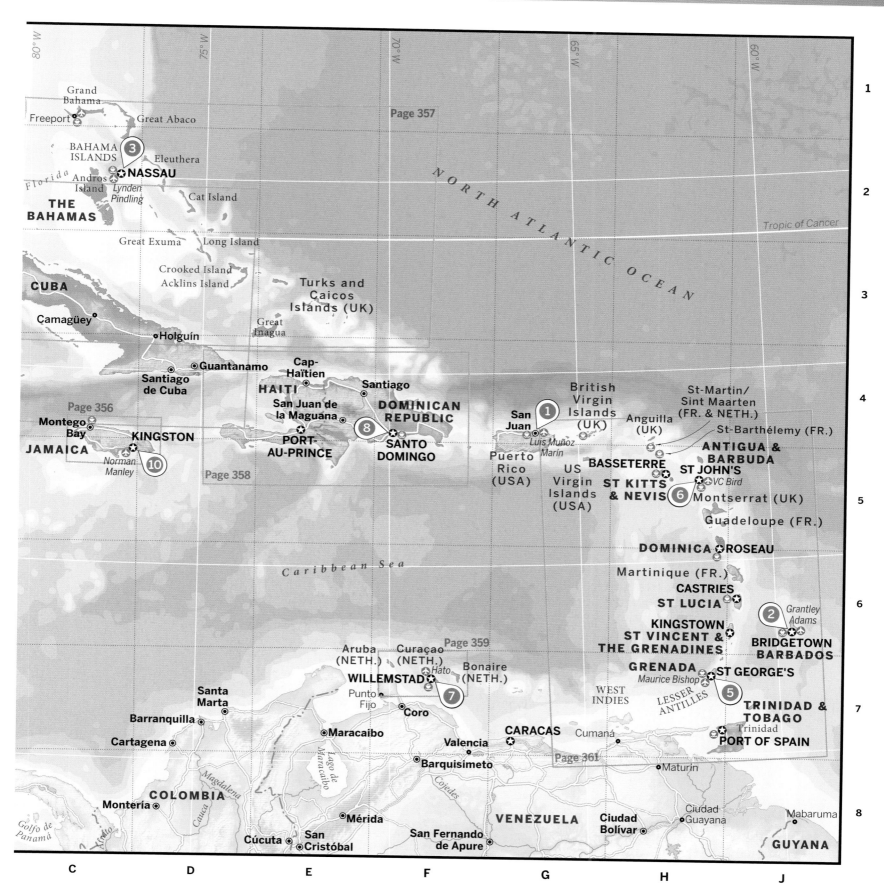

Ruth Peterkin / Shutterstock

Philip Lee Harvey / Lonely Planet

80° W

75° W

70° W

65° W

60° W

1

Page 357

Grand
Bahama

Freeport

Great Abaco

3

BAHAMA
ISLANDS

Eleuthera

NASSAU

Florida

Andros
Island

Lynden
Pindling

Cat Island

2

**THE
BAHAMAS**

Tropic of Cancer

Great Exuma

Long Island

Crooked Island

Acklins Island

CUBA

Camagüey

Holguín

Turks and
Caicos
Islands (UK)

3

Great
Inagua

N O R T H   A T L A N T I C   O C E A N

Santiago
de Cuba

Guantanamo

Cap-
Haïtien

Santiago

British
Virgin
Islands
(UK)

St-Martin/
Sint Maarten
(FR. & NETH.)

Page 356

HAITI

San Juan de
la Maguana

**DOMINICAN
REPUBLIC**

San
Juan

1

Anguilla
(UK)

St-Barthélemy (FR.)

4

Montego
Bay

KINGSTON

8

**SANTO
DOMINGO**

*Luis Muñoz
Marín*

BASSETERRE

**ANTIGUA &
BARBUDA**

ST JOHN'S

JAMAICA

Norman
Manley

10

**PORT-
AU-PRINCE**

Puerto
Rico
(USA)

US
Virgin
Islands
(USA)

**ST KITTS
& NEVIS**

VC Bird

Page 358

6

Montserrat (UK)

5

Guadeloupe (FR.)

Caribbean Sea

DOMINICA **ROSEAU**

Martinique (FR.)

CASTRIES

ST LUCIA

6

KINGSTOWN

*Grantley
Adams*

2

**ST VINCENT &
THE GRENADINES**

BRIDGETOWN

Page 359

Aruba
(NETH.)

Curaçao
(NETH.)

Bonaire
(NETH.)

BARBADOS

GRENADA

ST GEORGE'S

Santa
Marta

WILLEMSTAD

Hato

Maurice Bishop

WEST
INDIES

LESSER
ANTILLES

5

**TRINIDAD &
TOBAGO**

7

Punto
Fijo

Barranquilla

Coro

CARACAS

Cumaná

Trinidad

PORT OF SPAIN

Cartagena

Maracaibo

Valencia

Page 361

Maturín

Montería

*Lago de
Maracaibo*

Barquisimeto

COLOMBIA

Magdalena

Cauca

Mérida

VENEZUELA

Ciudad
Bolívar

Ciudad
Guayana

Mabaruma

8

*Golfo de
Panamá*

Cúcuta

San
Cristóbal

San Fernando
de Apure

Cojedes

GUYANA

C

D

E

F

G

H

J

THE TRAVEL ATLAS

SIGHTS & ACTIVITIES

 SEE

 DO

ITINERARY

 1

2

Habana Vieja, Havana

A detailed, meticulous, lovingly curated restoration process of Havana's Old Town has created one of the historical wonders of the Americas, a kind of Latin American 'Rome' where the past can be peeled off in layers. Walk its cobbled streets and evoke the ghosts of mega-rich sugar barons and sabre-rattling buccaneers.

Casa de Arte Jover, Camagüey

Home to two of Cuba's most creative and prodigious contemporary painters, Joel Jover and his wife Ileana Sánchez, this magnificent home in Plaza Agramonte functions as a gallery and piece of art in its own right.

Ciénaga de Zapata

The largest *ciénaga* (swamp) in the Caribbean, Ciénaga de Zapata is protected on multiple levels as the Gran Parque Natural Montemar, a Unesco Biosphere Reserve and a Ramsar Convention Site. Herein lies one of Cuba's most diverse ecosystems. Explore its steamy mix of wildlife-rich wetlands and briny salt flats.

Trinidad

Soporific Trinidad went to sleep in 1850 and never really woke up. This strange twist of fate is good news for modern travellers who can roam freely through the perfectly preserved mid-19th-century sugar town.

Comandancia de la Plata

Topping a crenellated mountain ridge amid thick cloud forest, this pioneering camp was established by Fidel Castro in 1958 after a year on the run in the Sierra Maestra. Well camouflaged and remote, the rebel HQ provides an evocative reminder of one of the most successful guerrilla campaigns in history. It remains much as it was left in the '50s.

El Yunque

Views from the summit (575m) of this moody, mysterious mountain are stupendous, as are the encounters with its birdlife and flora on the route up. Bank on seeing *tocororo* (Cuba's national bird), *zunzún* (the world's smallest bird), butterflies and *polymitas* (colourful endangered snails).

Parque Histórico Militar Morro-Cabaña

This unmissable military park, included in the Habana Vieja Unesco World Heritage site, is arguably the most formidable defensive complex in Spain's erstwhile colonial empire.

Playa las Tumbas

If they gave out awards for Cuban beaches, Las Tumbas might just win, edging out Playa Sirena on Cayo Largo del Sur (too busy) and Playa Pilar on Cayo Guillermo (recently blemished by an ugly hotel). It's certainly the nation's most isolated beach, 60km from the nearest population.

Valle de Viñales

With less traffic than 1940s Britain, Cuba is ideal for cycling and there's no better place to do it than the quintessentially rural Valle de Viñales. The valley offers all the ingredients of a tropical Tour de France, complete with spirit-lifting viewpoints at every turn.

Baracoa

Beguiling, outlandish and surreal, Baracoa's essence is addictive. On the wet and windy side of the Cuchillos del Toa mountains, Cuba's oldest and most isolated town exudes original atmosphere. Delve into its legends.

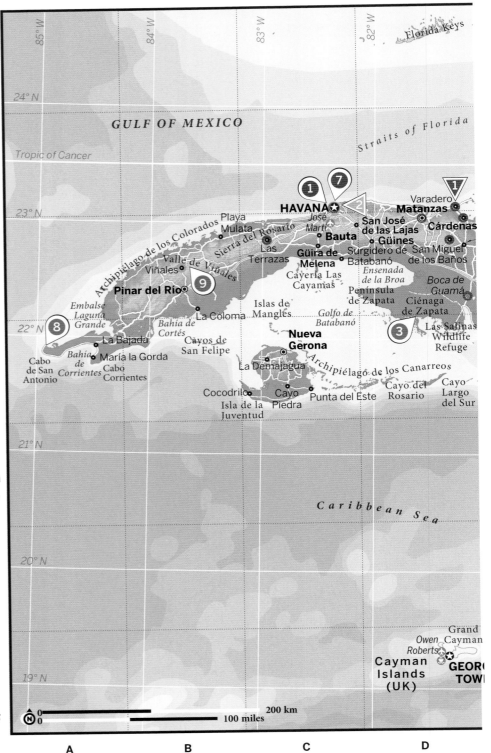

7-day itinerary
Escape from Varadero

Had your fill of **Varadero**? Bus west to **Matanzas** where Cuban reality will hit you like a slap to the face. Investigate the Museo Farmacéutico and peep inside the Teatro Sauto. Ride the Hershey train to **Havana** and watch as the lush fields of Mayabeque Province glide by. In the capital admire the copious sights of Habana Vieja. Next, head west to **Las Terrazas**, an eco-

resort. You can then bathe and birdwatch in the Baños del San Juan before turning east. Visit **Boca de Guamá** and procure a homestay in **Playa Girón**, where you can either dive or explore Ciénaga de Zapata. Further east lies the city of **Cienfuegos**, an elegant stopover for a sunset cruise on the bay. Lastly, see **San Miguel de los Baños** and **Cárdenas**' three superb museums.

14- to 18-day itinerary
Classic Cuba

Fall in love with classic Cuba in **Havana**, with its museums, forts and theatres. Travel west to the bucolic bliss of **Viñales** for a couple of days of hiking, caving and relaxing. Daily buses connect Viñales with French-flavoured **Cienfuegos**, an architectural monument to 19th-century neoclassicism. After a night of Gallic style and Cuban music, travel to colonial **Trinidad**. The *casas particulares*

(homestays) here resemble historical monuments, so stay three nights. On the second day choose between the beach (Playa Ancón) or the natural world (Topes de Collantes). **Santa Clara** is a rite of passage for Che Guevara pilgrims visiting his mausoleum but also a great place for luxurious private rooms and an upbeat nightlife. Further east, **Camagüey** invites further investigation

with its maze of Catholic churches and giant *tinajones* (clay pots). Laid-back **Bayamo** is where the revolution was ignited, and it has an equally sparky street festival every Saturday. Allow plenty of time for the cultural nexus of **Santiago de Cuba**. The Cuartel Moncada, Cementerio Santa Ifigenia and Morro Castle will fill a busy two days. Save the best till last with a stop at **Baracoa**.

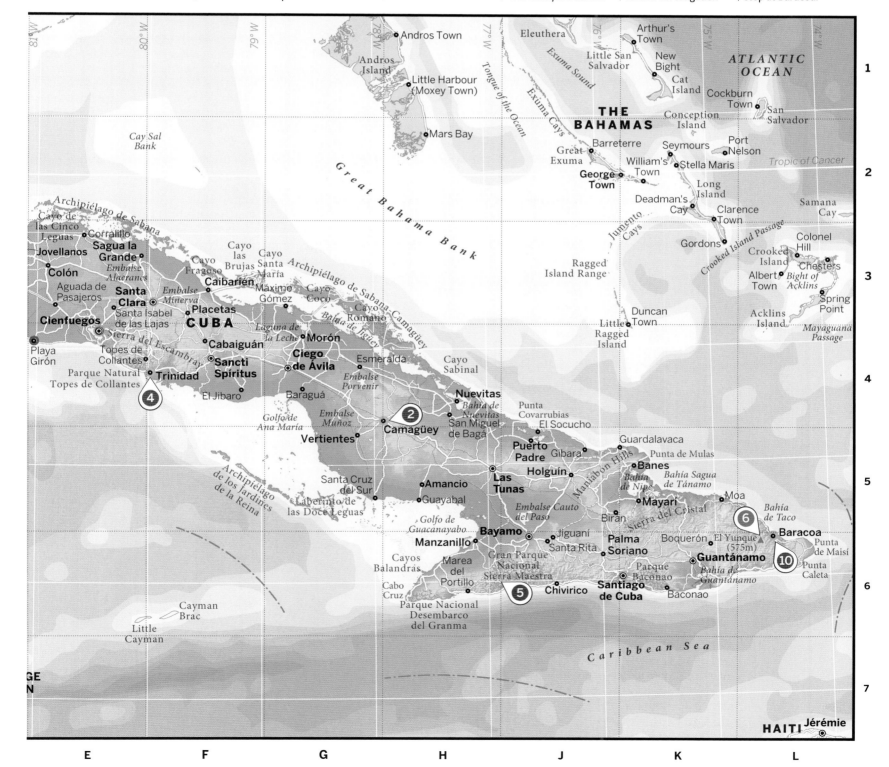

SIGHTS & ACTIVITIES

⦿ SEE

⦿ DO

ITINERARY

▽ 1

▽ 2

1 Blue Mountain Peak

Take a night hike to reach Jamaica's highest point by sunrise. As you climb, the vegetation becomes less and less tropical, until you're hiking amid giant ferns and stunted trees draped with lichen. In the predawn cold at the summit, wait in rapt silence as the first rays of the sun wash over the densely forested mountain peaks.

2 Irie Blue Hole

High on the White River, the heavenly Irie Blue Hole is an undisputed highlight of the north coast. You make your way up a series of magical falls and blue pools surrounded by forest, with ample opportunity to swim, dive and swing off ropes into the water.

3 Seven Mile Beach

Touted on tourism posters as 'seven miles of nothing but you and the sea', this is where sunbathers lie half submerged in the gentle surf while ganja smoke perfumes the breeze.

4 Jamnesia Surf Camp

Established by the indomitable Billy Wilmot, Jamaica's longest-running surf school offers lessons and board rental from its Bull Bay camp. There's a daily shuttle to the best surf.

▽ 10-day itinerary

Kingston, Blue Mountains and Portland

Touch down in **Kingston** for sightseeing, food and rip-roaring nightlife. Don't miss the art at National Gallery and Life Yard. Take in historic **Devon House**, enjoying Jamaica's best patties while there. After, head to the Bob Marley Museum. After hours indulge in some of the liveliest nightlife in the Caribbean at the Dub Club. For a captivating day trip, visit **Port Royal**, one-time haunt of pirates and privateers. Next, slip into the Blue Mountains. Enjoy breathtaking scenery and crisp mountain air from hiking trails in **Blue Mountains-John Crow National Park**. Then whizz down from the highlands on a bicycle tour or see how coffee rises from bean to brewery at a coffee plantation. Head on to Portland parish. Walk the atmospheric streets of **Port Antonio**, taking lodging in one of the many intimate spots to the east of town. You could go diving in the **Blue Lagoon** and stay at gorgeous Kanopi House, take a visit to **Boston Bay**, the home of jerk cooking, and stop in **Manchioneal**, a terrific base for visiting Reach Falls.

5 Boston Bay

Boston Bay is the supposed birthplace of jerk, the spice rub that is Jamaica's most famous contribution to the culinary arts. The turnoff to Boston Bay is lined with jerk stalls that produce smoked meats that redefine what heat and sweet can do as complementary gastronomic qualities.

6 Martha Brae River

Poled by a skilled guide, your bamboo raft will head through a green tunnel of jungle and vines. The river's upper reaches tumble at a good pace before slowing downriver, where you stop, swing and swim at 'Tarzan's Corner'.

7 Bob Marley Museum

Marley's creaky home is crammed with memorabilia, but the visitor is drawn to his untouched bedroom, adorned with objects of spiritual significance to the artist, the small kitchen where he cooked and the hammock in which he lay to seek inspiration from the distant mountains.

8 Reach Falls

On Jamaica's east coast, up in the hills and past stretches of jungle and beach that are completely off the radar of most tourists, a guide will help you find one of Jamaica's most beautiful waterfalls. A perfect place for a dip.

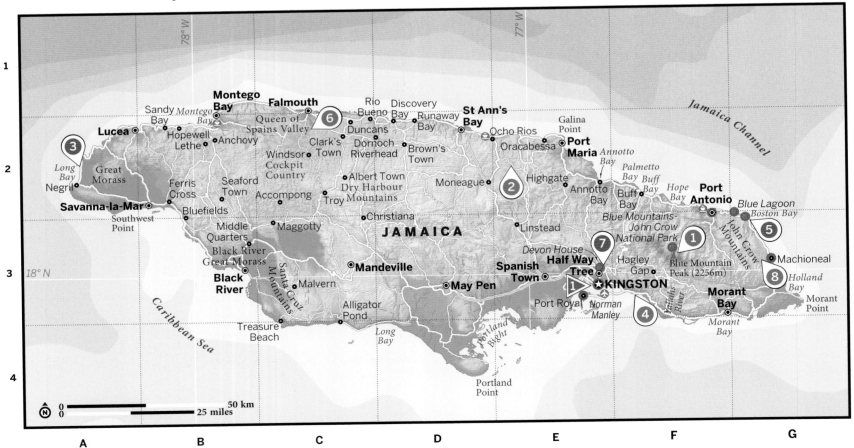

Garden of the Groves

This 5-hectare botanical garden in the Bahamas is a lush tropical refuge with a walking trail that meanders through tamarind groves and java plum trees, past cascading waterfalls, a lagoon and a tiny 19th-century hilltop chapel.

Blue Holes National Park

Blue Holes – deep vertical 'caves' formed by karst limestone subsidence that fill with rain and seawater – pit this Bahamian park's pine and coppice forest. Take your swimming gear if you fancy a plunge into Captain Bill's hole.

Exuma Cays Land & Sea Park

Founded as the world's first land-and-sea reserve in 1958, the Bahamas' stunning expanse of reef, cay and sea is world-famous among divers. All fishing and collecting is banned and the underwater adventure experience is accordingly out of this world.

Crossing Place Trail

Following the historic route connecting Middle Caicos with North Caicos, this coastal trail is a fantastic way to see beautiful Mudjin Harbour, the island's dramatic Atlantic coast and the resident birdlife. Join the trail at Conch Bar or Mudjin Harbor.

7-day itinerary
Turks & Caicos

Spend your first day in **Grace Bay** on Providenciales, lazing on the famous expanse of sand and checking out the bars and restaurants. Wake up early on day two for a stand-up paddleboard excursion to **'Iguana Island'** – Little Water Cay – then an afternoon learning to kiteboard on Long Bay Beach. Day three is deservedly more relaxed: take a tour to North Caicos to see the ruins of **Wade's Green Plantation** and to kayak through **East Bay Islands Reserve**. Next up are the historic islands of **Grand Turk** and **Salt Cay**. Fly to Grand Turk and spend a day on each (connections permitting) visiting the National Museum and Grand Turk's lighthouse, and the many relics of the days when salt and trade sustained these islands. The extensive reefs make for great diving, and you may be lucky enough to see humpback whales as they swim close to shore on their way south (this usually takes place around February and March).

Grace Bay Beach

Several miles long (the frequently boasted '12 miles' only applies if you measure the entire northern coast of Provo, which is, admittedly, one unbroken beach), this world-famous stretch of coast is powdered with white sand and is close enough to the reef wall to see the Atlantic breakers.

Cockburn Town

Brightly painted colonial buildings line the capital's roads and life goes on at a wonderfully slow pace miles away from the resorts of Providenciales. Wander past whitewashed stone walls and beneath traditional streetlamps.

Royal Naval Dockyard

When the British were no longer able to use ports in their former American colonies, they chose this site as their 'Gibraltar of the West'. In addition to the superb Bermuda Maritime Museum, Bermuda's largest fortifications comprise a Victorian victualling yard, barracks-turned-mall, restaurants, craft markets, and a comprehensive water-sports centre.

Jobson's Cove

This gorgeous pink-sand cove is framed by a perfect horseshoe of jagged cliffs. The swimming hole is one of Bermuda's loveliest.

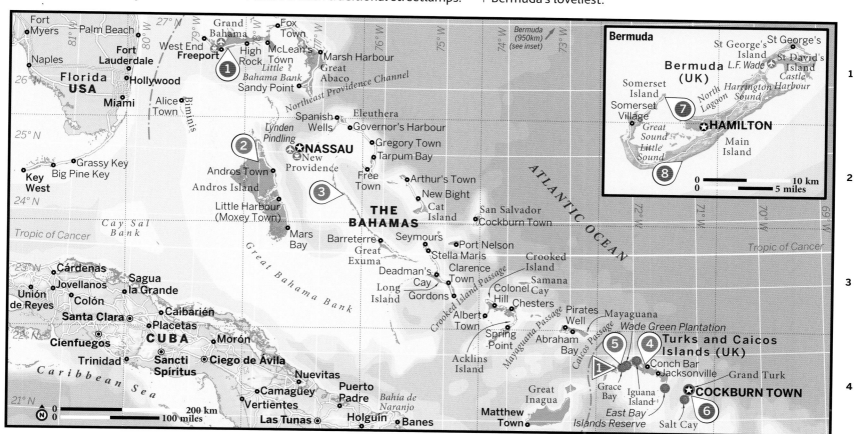

SIGHTS &
ACTIVITIES

◉ SEE

◉ DO

ITINERARY

▽ 1

▽ 2

Grand Rue Artists

A collective of Haitian sculptors and artists produces spectacular work in an unlikely setting, squeezed into the cinder-block houses on Grand Rue. In this Caribbean junkyard gone cyberpunk, the artists turn found objects into startling sculpture grounded in the preoccupations of daily Haitian life.

Bassin Bleu

Bassin Bleu is a series of three cobalt-blue pools (Bassin Clair, Bassin Bleu and Bassin Palmiste) linked by waterfalls that make up one of the prettiest swimming holes in Haiti. Bassin Clair is the most beautiful of the three, deep into the mountain at the bottom of the waterfall, sheltered and surrounded by smooth rocks draped with maidenhair and creeper ferns.

Citadelle Laferrière

Haitians call the Citadelle the eighth wonder of the world, and given this battleship-like fortress offers commanding views in every direction, you'll likely agree. Built to repel the French, it's a monument to the vision of Henri Christophe, who oversaw its construction. A visit here is an essential part of any trip to Haiti, and actually takes in two sites – the Unesco-listed fortress and the palace of Sans Souci.

14-day itinerary
Dominican Republic Circuit

This itinerary visits every major attraction in the DR, from the atmospheric capital and the adrenaline-packed central highlands to the country's best beaches. Start with two days exploring **Santo Domingo** and the Zona Colonial. On day three head to **Jarabacoa** – visit the waterfalls in the afternoon, with white-water rafting or canyoning the next day. Head north to **Cabarete** for world-class water sports and mountain biking, and spend several days diving and beach-bumming in nearby **Sosúa** and **Río San Juan**. Then bolt for whale-watching from **Península de Samaná** and take a boat trip to Parque Nacional Los Haitises to see mangroves and cave paintings. Spend two days hiking or boating to the beaches around dreamy **Las Galeras**. The southeast is perfect for some more relaxing beach time – go for either deserted **Playa Limón** or perennially popular Bávaro and Punta Cana. Then take the spectacular drive to **Barahona** to see the crocodiles in Lago Enriquillo.

Samaná

Seeing whales up close is hard to beat, and the Dominican Republic's Samaná is one of the world's top 10 whale-watching spots. Hit the water with Whale Samaná, the peninsula's most recommended whale-watching outfit.

Catedral Primada de América

The first stone of this cathedral in the Dominican Republic, the Western hemisphere's oldest standing, was set in 1514 by Diego Columbus. Numerous architects then worked on the church till 1540, which explains its Gothic vault, Romanesque arches and baroque ornamentation.

Bahía de Las Águilas

The Dominican Republic's Bahía de Las Águilas rewards visitors with a nearly deserted arc of shore between two prominent capes. The boat journey here from Playa Las Cuevas weaves in and out of rocky outcrops and past gorgeous cliffs.

Parque Nacional Los Haitises

This park contains coastal wetlands and lush hills jutting from the water. Los Haitises is home to more than 700 species of flora and 110 species of birds, making it one of the most biodiverse regions in the Caribbean.

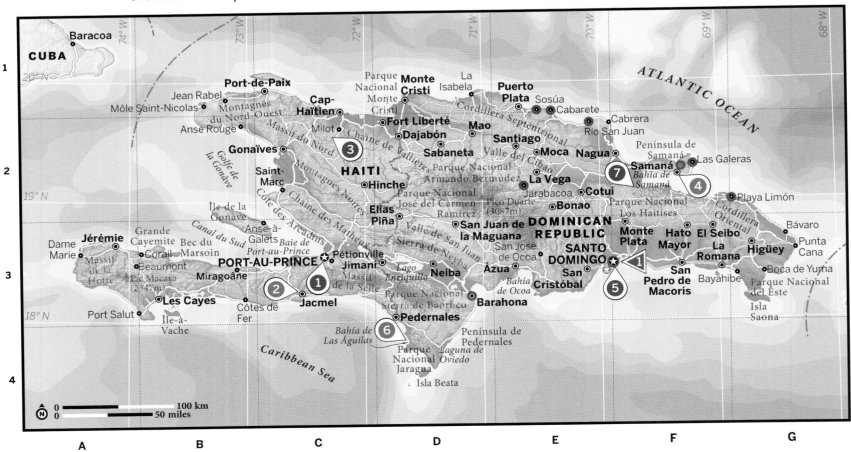

Eagle Beach

Fronting a stretch of the low-rise resorts just northwest of Oranjestad, Eagle Beach is a long stretch of white sand that regularly makes lists of the best in the world. There are shade trees in some areas and you can obtain every service you need here, from a lounger to a cold drink.

Arikok National Wildlife Park

Arid and rugged, this park is a vast, desolate stretch of desert wilderness covering much of the east coast. As you explore, you'll notice the peculiar flora, and keep your eyes peeled for wild donkeys and goats, electric-blue whiptail lizards, and a few dozen species of birds.

Lac Bay

The northern side of Bonaire's Lac Bay is sheltered by mangrove forests, where wetland birds breed and reef creatures mature, which explains why the mangrove is sometimes called a 'coral reef nursery'. It's a gem for paddlers and snorkellers, who can spot young fish, sea stars and sponges in the crystal clear waters. The Kaminda Lac – around the northern side of the bay – is a picturesque drive (and a popular cycling route) with views of dense mangroves and flocks of flamingos.

14-day itinerary
Aruba, Curaçao and Bonaire

The small size of all three islands means there'll be plenty of time for exploration and relaxation. Most places to stay, eat and play on Aruba are in the north, including relaxed **Eagle Beach**, Aruba's best. Amidst your beach time, take a day to explore **Arikok National Wildlife Park** and interesting **Oranjestad**. From Aruba, it's a quick hop over to **Curaçao**.

This is an island to take your time exploring. Stay in colonial **Willemstad**, then wander the coasts to the north, where national parks and a bevy of hidden beaches await. Count on three days at least to enjoy it all. Fly from Curaçao to Bonaire. One of the world's great diving locations, Bonaire's underwater splendour and 90 named dive sites

will keep you busy. Take a day to explore the starkly beautiful island: go flamingo-spotting; head to inviting **Rincon**, the island's second city (a village really); check out the horizon-spanning salt flats in the south where you can still see evidence of slavery and colonial traditions; and visit cute little **Kralendijk** to make the most of its good food and nightlife.

Bonaire National Marine Park

This park is the island's star attraction, and it attracts divers and snorkellers to explore miles of pristine coral reef. Between the two islands, there are about 90 named dive sites, many of which are accessible from shore.

Willemstad

Gazing across the bay at historic Willemstad's colourful townhouses, you might think that you're in a Dutch city, complete with waterways and street cafes. The architecture is rich, with stunning examples of 17th- and 18th-century fortifications and diverse building styles.

Christoffel National Park

This preserve has two driving routes and eight hiking trails that provide a variety of perspectives on the island's landscape, flora and fauna. It takes two to three hours to hike to the summit of Christoffel Mountain, Curaçao's highest point.

Playa Portomari

There's a lot to love about Playa Portomari, including the white coral sand and clear waters that shelter a unique double reef – excellent for snorkellers and divers alike. Onshore you'll find a dive shop, a restaurant, and three hiking trails.

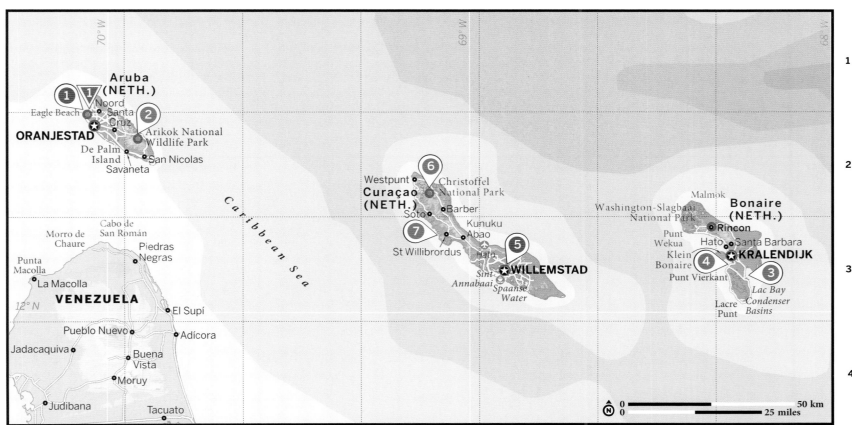

Nevis Heritage Trail
As you drive around the St Kitts & Nevis ring road, look for the blue road markers pointing out locations on the Nevis Heritage Trail, including churches, sugar estates, military installations and natural sites.

Nelson's Dockyard
Continuously in operation since 1745, this restored Georgian-era marina was made a Unesco World Heritage site in 2016. The Dockyard Museum relates tidbits about Antigua history, the dockyard and life at the forts.

Deshaies
This charming fishing village in Guadeloupe offers good eating and drinking options and a beach framed by green hills (but the best swimming beach is at nearby Grande Anse). Deshaies is popular with yachties.

Baie de Pompierre
Horseshoe-shaped Baie de Pompierre is perhaps Terre-de-Haut's loveliest: a reef-protected beach with golden sand. Tame goats mosey onto the beach and lie down next to sunbathers.

Grande Anse, Martinique
Crystalline Grande Anse des Salines in Martinique doesn't disappoint the bevy of swimmers who dabble in its depths or the sun worshippers who lie out on the ribbon of sand. There are food vans and snack shops along the beach, but otherwise it's wonderfully undeveloped, a slice of raw nature.

Sugar Beach: a view of Gros Piton from Sugar Beach, St Lucia.

Montserrat
In 1995, Montserrat's lower two thirds was devastated by eruptions of the Soufrière Hills Volcano. Two decades on this modern-day Pompeii is slowly recovering – learn more at the Montserrat Volcano Observatory.

Sugar Beach
The Pitons stand guard over Soufrière. Jutting from the sea, covered in vegetation, these rock towers are St Lucia's iconic landmarks. The island's famed Sugar Beach is situated between the two Pitons, ensuring phenomenal views from the sand and the water.

Mt Scenery
A dormant volcano that last erupted in 1640, Mt Scenery is the pinnacle of pyramid-shaped Saba. It's covered by cloud forest with 200-year-old trees smothered in orchids and bromeliads. A stairway climbs 1064 steps.

Tobago Cays
With five small islands ringed with coral reefs, Tobago Cays offer some of the Caribbean's best diving and snorkelling. The islands sit in a national park and are only accessible by boat on a day trip from one of the Grenadines.

Fort Duvernette
This eerie fort on St Vincent was built to defend Calliaqua and affords 360-degree views of the southern shoreline. At the top of a spiral staircase that has been carved into the rock, 200ft above sea level, you'll find cannons and a picnic area.

Barbados
Taste some of Barbados' best aged rum at the Mount Gay Visitors Center. Here you'll learn all about the rum-making process and get a chance to sample some of the island's favourites.

Underwater sculpture park
This underwater gallery, north of St George's in Molinière Bay, Grenada, is home to around 80 works, all encrusted with corals. The park is accessible to snorkellers and divers.

Carriacou
There are three islands in the nation of Grenada but you won't find cruise ships, big resorts or souvenir shops at Carriacou ('carry-a-cou'). This is Caribbean life the way it was 50 years ago: quiet, friendly and relaxed.

Carnival, Trinidad & Tobago
With roots in West Africa and Europe, Carnival is the ultimate indulgence before the sober disciplines of Lent – and everyone's welcome to participate in this big daddy of Caribbean festivals. Tens of thousands parade and dance in the streets with their mas bands, soca trucks with DJs, and steel bands.

7-day itinerary
Dominica to St Lucia

Begin in **Dominica**, one of the region's wildest and most natural islands. Delve into the rainforest at Morne Trois Pitons National Park, a Unesco World Heritage site – the walk to Middleham Falls is splendid. It's a quick hop to **Martinique**, where you should hit the beaches and restaurants of Les Anses d'Arlet,

followed by diving and a drink in the village of **Ste-Luce**. Next, take the scenic ferry to **St Lucia**, which emerges like a virescent monolith from the Caribbean as you home in. Stay in **Soufrière**, which has a dramatic position on a bay that's shadowed by the iconic peaks of the Pitons. You can hike these in the morning and dive in the afternoon.

7-day itinerary
St Vincent to Grenada

St Vincent is an island of boundless energy. Market days in **Kingstown** are joyfully chaotic as the streets teem with people. Explore some of the island's lush countryside and enjoy panoramic vistas on a hike to Dark View Falls. Catch a ferry to **Bequia**, the centre of beach fun and nightlife in the Grenadines and quite possibly the best all-

around little island in the Caribbean. Choose between fast and slow ferries and head down the Grenadines, stopping at one of the pretty islands of **Canouan**, **Mayreau** or **Union Island**. Take a day trip to snorkel amazing **Tobago Cays**. Catch a mail boat or hire a fishing boat and cross the aquatic border to **Carriacou**, the pint-sized sister

island to Grenada, which you will reach by ferry. Once there, immerse yourself in **St George's**, one of the Caribbean's most charming capital cities. Smell the local nutmeg in the air. With a flight from St Lucia to St Vincent, you could combine these two itineraries to make a real island-hopping adventure that explores the best of the Windward Isles.

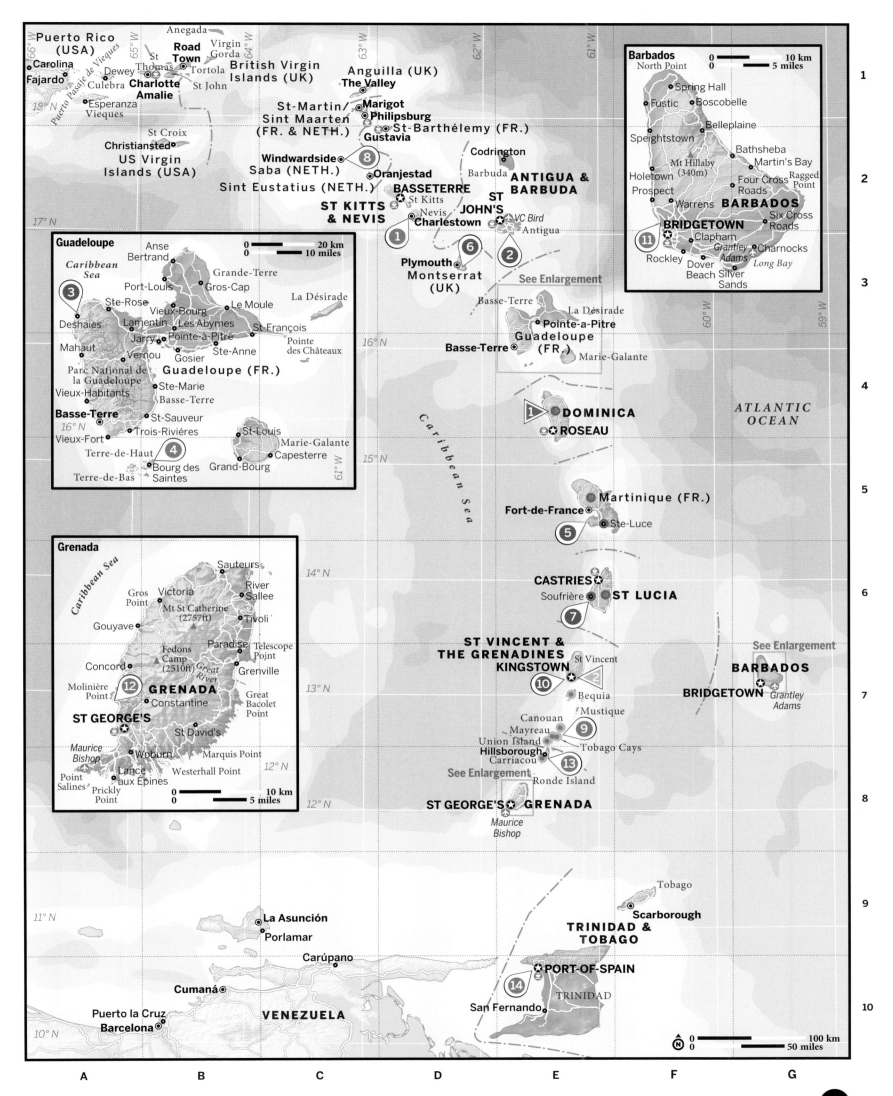

Puerto Rico
(USA)

Carolina

Fajardo

Dewey
Culebra
Esperanza
Vieques

Anegada

Road
Town

Virgin
Gorda

British Virgin
Islands (UK)

St
Thomas
Tortola

St John

Charlotte
Amalie

St Croix

Christiansted

US Virgin
Islands (USA)

Anguilla (UK)
The Valley

Marigot
St-Martin/
Sint Maarten
(FR. & NETH.)
Philipsburg
Gustavia
St-Barthélemy (FR.)

Windwardside **⑧**
Saba (NETH.)
Sint Eustatius (NETH.)
Oranjestad

Codrington

Barbuda

ANTIGUA &
BARBUDA

BASSETERRE
St Kitts

ST
JOHN'S

VC Bird

Nevis
Charlestown **①**
Antigua

Plymouth **⑥**
Montserrat
(UK)

②

See Enlargement

Basse-Terre
La Désirade
Pointe-à-Pitre
Guadeloupe
(FR.)
Basse-Terre
Marie-Galante

①
DOMINICA
✪ ROSEAU

ATLANTIC
OCEAN

Martinique (FR.)
Fort-de-France
Ste-Luce
⑤

CASTRIES
Soufrière **✪ ST LUCIA**
⑦

ST VINCENT &
THE GRENADINES
KINGSTOWN
⑩ St Vincent **②**
Bequia
Mustique
Canouan
Mayreau **⑨**
Union Island
Hillsborough **⑬**
Carriacou
Ronde Island

See Enlargement

ST GEORGE'S GRENADA
Maurice
Bishop

Tobago
Scarborough

TRINIDAD &
TOBAGO

PORT-OF-SPAIN
⑭
TRINIDAD
San Fernando

VENEZUELA

La Asunción
Porlamar

Carúpano

Cumaná

Puerto la Cruz
Barcelona

Guadeloupe

0 _____ 20 km
0 _____ 10 miles

Caribbean
Sea

Anse
Bertrand

Grande-Terre

③
Port-Louis
Gros-Cap

Ste-Rose
Le Moule

Deshaies
Vieux-Bourg
Lamentin Les Abymes
St-François

Jarry
Pointe-à-Pitre
La Désirade

Mahaut
Vernou
Gosier
Ste-Anne

Parc National de
la Guadeloupe
Guadeloupe (FR.)
Pointe
des Châteaux

Vieux-Habitants
Ste-Marie

Basse-Terre

Basse-Terre
St-Sauveur

Vieux-Fort
Trois-Riviéres
St-Louis

Terre-de-Haut
④
Marie-Galante
Capesterre

Terre-de-Bas
Bourg des
Saintes
Grand-Bourg

Grenada

Caribbean
Sea

Sauteurs

Gros
Point
Victoria
River
Sallee

Mt St Catherine
(2757ft)
Tivoli

Gouyave

Fedons
Camp
(2510ft)
Paradise
Telescope
Point

Concord
Grenville

Molinière
Point **⑫ GRENADA**
Great
Bacolet
Point

ST GEORGE'S
Constantine

St David's

Maurice
Bishop
Woburn
Marquis Point

Point
Salines
Lance
aux Épines
Westerhall Point

Prickly
Point

0 _____ 10 km
0 _____ 5 miles

Barbados

0 _____ 10 km
0 _____ 5 miles

North Point
Spring Hall
Fustic
Boscobelle

Belleplaine
Speightstown
Bathsheba
Mt Hillaby
(340m)
Martin's Bay
Holetown
Four Cross
Ragged
Prospect
Roads
Point
Warrens
BARBADOS

Six Cross
BRIDGETOWN
Roads
Clapham
Rockley
Grantley
Adams
Charnocks
Dover
Beach
Silver
Long Bay
Sands

See Enlargement

BARBADOS

BRIDGETOWN
Grantley
Adams

---

0 _____ 100 km
0 _____ 50 miles

1
2
3
4
5
6
7
8
9
10

A   B   C   D   E   F   G

Northern South America

Covered in mountains and vast swathes of jungle, fringed by exotic beaches and dotted with mesmerising relics of the ancient world, the northern half of South America is laden with a kaleidoscope of enticing (and unforgettable) sights, activities and adventures. And that is before you even bring its remarkable populace and rich cultures into the equation. Needless to say, the people you encounter, the meals you devour, the festivals you embrace and the roads you choose to take will all leave their mark on you. There is only one guarantee: you will be back.

CLIMATE CHART

BRASÍLIA

RAINFALL INCH/MM
—20/500
—16/400
—12/300
—8/200
—4/100
—0

J F M A M J J A S O N D

TEMP °C/°F
40/104
30/86
20/68
10/50
0/32

LIMA

RAINFALL INCH/MM
—12/300
—8/200
—4/100
—0

J F M A M J J A S O N D

TEMP °C/°F
40/104
30/86
20/68
10/50
0/32
-10/14

HISTORY AND CULTURE
With wilderness cloaking ancient sites such as Peru's Machu Picchu and Kuélap, and Colombia's Ciudad Perdida, history here is an adventure too. Learn of the region's colonial past at Barichara (Colombia), Cuenca (Ecuador), Potosí (Bolivia) and Trujillo (Peru), or make your own history at Rio's carnival.

TREKKING
There is no end to the trekking possibilities. In Peru, lace up your boots in Cañón del Colca, Cañón del Cotahuasi, the Cordillera Blanca or en route to Machu Picchu. Parque Nacional Natural El Cocuy (Colombia) and the Cordillera Real (Bolivia) are also prime trekking destinations.

BEACHES
Copacabana and Ipanema are rightly famous, but other sublime sands in Brazil lie at Ilha Grande and Alter do Chão. Colombia's Parque Nacional Natural Tayrona has magical beaches, while northeast Ecuador is a surfer's dream. On the Galápagos, sea iguanas can be spotted at Tortuga Bay.

JUNGLE AND WILDLIFE
The Amazon is a jungle wilderness carpeted and crawling with untold riches of biodiversity. Dive in at Coca in Ecuador or Manaus in Brazil, or explore the jungle's fringes in Parque Nacional Amboró in Bolivia. This region is also home to the Galápagos, famed for centuries for its truly unique wildlife.

Right: A spectacular view of Peru's 15th-century Incan city, Machu Picchu.

Transport hubs

Northern South America can be reached by air, land and sea. However, the vast majority of travellers fly into the region via the countless international flights serving São Paulo, Rio de Janeiro, Bogotá and Quito. There are many land crossings and buses linking the region to the continent's southern half, but the Darién Gap blocks any land access from Panama. The most popular route by sea is by private sailboat between Panama's San Blas Islands and Cartagena.

São Paulo
It is a monster. Enormous, intimidating and, at first glance at least, no great beauty. It's a difficult city for the traveller to master and one that may not seem worth the sweat. But it's the Brazilian hub for many international airlines, and thus it's the first stop for many visitors. Before buying a domestic ticket, check which of the city's airports the flight departs from, as GRU, the international airport, also serves many domestic flights.

Bogotá
This city is Colombia's beating heart, an engaging and vibrant capital cradled by chilly Andean peaks and steeped in sophisticated urban cool. Bogotá's shiny airport, Aeropuerto Internacional El Dorado, which handles nearly all domestic and international flights, is located 13km northwest of the city centre. The main bus terminal, La Terminal, about 5km west of centre, is one of South America's best.

Rio de Janeiro (see pp424-5 for city map)
Golden beaches and lush mountains, samba-fuelled nightlife and football matches: welcome to the Cidade Maravilhosa. Rio's Galeão international airport (Aeroporto Internacional Antônio Carlos Jobim) is 15km north of the city centre on Ilha do Governador. Buses leave from the sleek Rodoviária Novo Rio, 2km northwest of Centro.

Lima
After Cairo, this sprawling metropolis is the second-driest world capital, rising above a long coastline of crumbling cliffs. International flights arrive at Aeropuerto Internacional Jorge Chávez. There is no main bus terminal, instead several stations serve respective regional and international buses.

Quito
A capital city high in the Andes, Quito is dramatically situated, squeezed between mountain peaks whose greenery is concealed by the afternoon mist. Apartment buildings and concrete homes creep up their slopes, and busy commercial thoroughfares lined with shops and choked with traffic turn into peaceful neighbourhoods on Sundays. Aeropuerto Internacional Mariscal Sucre is 37km east of the city. There are two main bus terminals, both at least 30 minutes by taxi from the city centre.

Santa Cruz
Bolivia's largest city may surprise you with its small-town feeling, colonial buildings and a lightly buzzing, relaxed tropical atmosphere. Viru-Viru International Airport, 15km north of the centre, handles some domestic and international flights. The bimodal terminal, 1.5km east of the centre, is a combined long-distance bus and train station.

Cartagena
The undisputed queen of the Caribbean coast, Cartagena is a fairy-tale city of romance, legends and superbly preserved beauty lying within an impressive 13km of centuries-old colonial stone walls. Its Aeropuerto Internacional Rafael Núñez is connected to Panama, Miami, Fort Lauderdale and New York. Various boats arrive from Panama via the San Blas Archipelago and vice versa.

Georgetown
Georgetown's easy-to-navigate streets, dilapidated architecture and unkempt parks offer a laid-back feel amid real-life chaos. Several international flights arrive and depart from Cheddi Jagan International Airport, 41km south of Georgetown.

Right: A colourful bus in Cartagena, Colombia (left) and (right) Rio de Janeiro's Sugarloaf cable car.

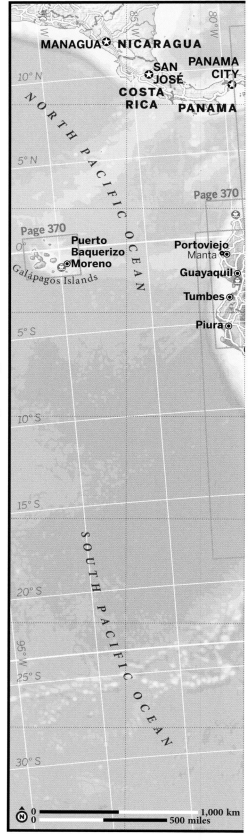

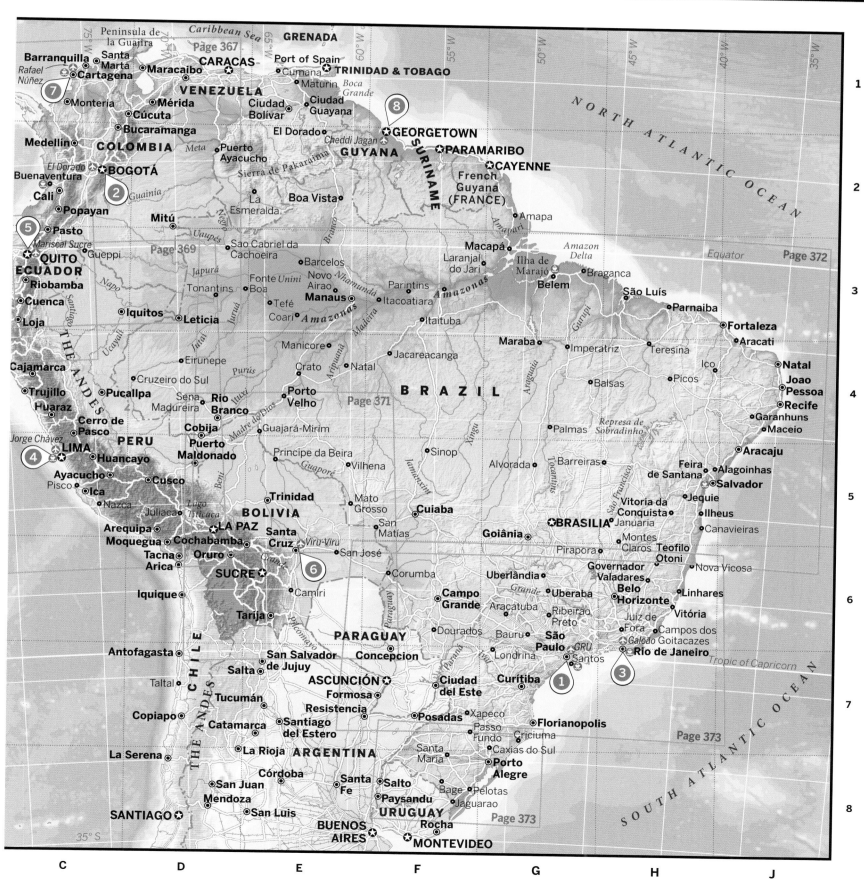

Peninsula de la Guajira

Caribbean Sea

GRENADA

Page 367

Barranquilla Santa Marta
Rafael Núñez
Cartagena ⑦
Monteria

CARACAS
Port of Spain
Cumana **TRINIDAD & TOBAGO**
Maturin Boca Grande

Mérida
Cúcuta
Bucaramanga

VENEZUELA
Ciudad Bolivar
Ciudad Guayana
⑧ ✪**GEORGETOWN**
Cheddi Jagan

Medellin
El Dorado
Buenaventura ✪**BOGOTÁ** ②
Cali
Popayan

COLOMBIA
Meta Puerto Ayacucho
El Dorado
Guainía
Mitú

GUYANA
Paramaribo
French Guyana (FRANCE)
✪**PARAMARIBO**
✪**CAYENNE**
Amapa

⑤ Pasto
Mariscal Sucre
✪**QUITO**
ECUADOR
Riobamba
Cuenca
Loja

Guppi
Page 369
Japurá
Napo
Sao Cabriel da Cachoeira
Barcelos
Novo Airao
Fonte Unini
Boa
Tonantins
Tefé
Coari

Macapá
Laranjal do Jari
Amazon Delta
Ilha de Marajó
Equator
Bragança
Page 372

Iquitos
Leticia
Tabatinga
Manaus
Itacoatiara
Parintins

Belem
São Luís
Parnaiba
Fortaleza
Aracati

Cajamarca
Cruzeiro do Sul
Eirunepe
Purús
Crato
Natal
Ico
Picos

Trujillo
Huaraz
Pucallpa
Sena Madureira
Rio Branco
Manicore
Jacareacanga

THE ANDES
Cerro de Pasco
Jorge Chávez
Lima ④
Huancayo
Ayacucho
Pisco Ica
Nazca
Juliaca

Cobija
Puerto Maldonado
Guajará-Mirim
Porto Velho
Page 371

B R A Z I L

Maraba
Imperatriz
Teresina
Balsas

Natal
Joao Pessoa
Recife
Garanhuns
Maceio

Aracaju
Alagoinhas
Feira de Santana Salvador
Jequie
Ilheus

Vitoria da Conquista
Januaria
Canavieiras

Cusco
Trinidad
Mato Grosso
San Matias
Cuiaba
Sinop
Alvorada
Barreiras
Palmas

BOLIVIA
✪**LA PAZ**
Santa Cruz
Viru-Viru
San José
⑥

Arequipa
Moquegua
Cochabamba
Tacna Oruro
Arica
✪**SUCRE**
Camiri

Goiânia
Pirapora
✪**BRASILIA**
Montes Claros
Teofilo Otoni
Nova Vicosa

Iquique
Tarija

Governador Valadares
Belo Horizonte
Linhares
Vitória

Antofagasta
San Salvador de Jujuy
Salta
Taltal

Uberlândia
Uberaba
Ribeirao Preto
Aracatuba
Bauru
São Paulo
Juiz de Fora
Campos dos Goitacazes
Galeão
Rio de Janeiro ③

Corumba
Campo Grande
Dourados
Londrina
GRU
Santos
① Curítiba
Tropic of Capricorn

PARAGUAY
Concepcion
✪**ASUNCIÓN**
Formosa
Resistencia
Posadas
Ciudad del Este

Copiapo
Tucumán
Catamarca
Santiago del Estero
Xapeco
Passo Fundo
Florianopolis
Criciuma

La Serena
La Rioja
ARGENTINA
Santa María
Caxias do Sul
Page 373

San Juan
Córdoba
Santa Fe
Salto
Paysandu
Bage Pelotas
Jaguarao
Porto Alegre

Mendoza
San Luis
SANTIAGO
BUENOS AIRES
URUGUAY
Rocha
Page 373
✪**MONTEVIDEO**

NORTH ATLANTIC OCEAN
SOUTH ATLANTIC OCEAN

1 2 3 4 5 6 7 8

C D E F G H J

SIGHTS & ACTIVITIES

 SEE

 DO

ITINERARY

1

2

1 Cartagena's Old Town

As visitors enter the walled old town of Cartagena, the hands of the clock on the Puerta del Reloj wind back 400 years in an instant. The pastel-toned balconies overflow with bougainvillea and the streets are abuzz with food stalls around magnificent Spanish-built churches, squares and historic mansions.

2 Ciudad Perdida

The thrilling multiday jungle walk to this ancient lost city is through some of the country's most majestic tropical scenery. Surging rivers pump faster than your pulse can keep pace as you ford them, waist deep, against the otherwise quiet beauty of the Sierra Nevada.

3 La Guajira Peninsula

Reaching this remote desert peninsula at South America's most northerly point can be fun (and arduous), but everyone who makes it here is blown away by the stunning simplicity of it all. Pink flamingos, mangrove swamps, sand-dune beaches and tiny Wayuu settlements dot the vast emptiness.

4 Caño Cristales

This series of remote rivers, waterfalls and streams within Parque Nacional Natural Sierra de La Macarena has been called everything from 'The River of Five Colours' to 'The Liquid Rainbow'. These names derive from a unique phenomenon that takes place for a couple of months between July and November when an eruption of aquatic life creates underwater blankets of bright red, yellow, green, black and blue.

Cartagena's Old Town: Flowers adorn the balconies of Cartagena's colonial houses.

5 Ensenada de Utría

Every year hundreds of humpback whales make an 8000km journey from the Antarctic to give birth and raise young in Colombia's Pacific waters. At Ensenada de Utría, they are known to come incredibly close to shore.

6 San Agustín

Scattered throughout rolling green hills, 500-plus ancient statues carved from volcanic rock are a magnificent window into pre-Columbian culture and one of the most important archaeological sights on the continent.

7 Parque Nacional Natural El Cocuy

This park is one of South America's most coveted trekking destinations, though strict environmental restrictions limit some access. The Sierra Nevada del Cocuy region is characterised by craggy peaks, and the *páramo* ecosystem of glacial valleys, mountain plains, high-altitude lakes and rare vegetation.

8 Cali

Cali didn't invent salsa, but this hardworking city has taken the genre to its heart and made it its own. Salsa is how *caleños* express themselves and there's nowhere better to learn.

9 Museo del Oro, Bogotá

There are few places in the world where you can get a sense of what finding a long-lost buried treasure might be like. This museum, one of South America's most astonishing, will floor you with a sensation of Indiana Jones proportions.

10 Barichara

With its rust-orange rooftops, symmetrically cobbled streets, whitewashed walls and pot-plant-adorned balconies contrasting with a backdrop of cinematic Andean green, Barichara is arguably Colombia's most picturesque colonial village.

11 Desierto de la Tatacoa

An otherworldly anomaly, this desert is a striking landscape of ochre and grey sands, sculpted cliffs and clumps of cactus. Surrounded by mountains, this is a silent, spiritual place with an ecosystem unlike any other in Colombia. It's also the best place in the country for stargazing, either with the naked eye or at the local observatory.

12 Zona Cafetera

Jump in a classic WWII 4WD and go on a caffeine-fuelled coffee-tasting adventure. Many of the best *fincas* (farms) are eager to show visitors what sets Colombian coffee apart and to share a little of their hardworking culture. Strap on a basket and head into the plantation to pick your own beans before returning to the traditional farmhouse to enjoy the end product, accompanied by the sounds of flowing rivers and birdsong.

14-day itinerary
Bogotá to Medellín

Take a day or two in **Bogotá**, admiring its colonial centre and the best of myriad museums, world-class food and nightlife. Next, visit the calming colonial villages of **Villa de Leyva** and **Barichara**, both miraculously preserved and picturesque. Take a day to walk the historic El Camino Real to **Guane**. Bus to **Santa**

Marta via **San Gil** to access **Parque Nacional Natural Tayrona** – linger on its otherworldly beaches for a few days. Continue southwest along the Caribbean coast to **Cartagena**. It's another long bus ride (or a quicker flight) to **Medellín**, where again you're faced with Colombia on overdrive: culture, cuisine and Pilsen, *paisa*-style.

14-day itinerary
Zona Cafetera

Start by spending a few days in the nature parks around **Manizales** – Los Yarumos, Recinto del Pensamiento and Reserva Ecológica Río Blanco, the latter a birdwatching favourite. Indulge in a coffee tour just outside town at Hacienda Venecia, which offers an excellent overview of all things coffee. Return to Manizales to organise a hiking

trip among snow-covered volcanic peaks in **Parque Nacional Natural Los Nevados**. Spend a night in the *páramo* (grasslands) beside the mystical **Laguna de Otún** before heading down the mountain to **Termales de Santa** Rosa to reinvigorate tired muscles. Suitably revitalised, pass through **Pereira** to spend four days in coffee-crazy

Salento, full of quaint charm and typical *bahareque* (adobe and reed) architecture. Take a classic jeep up to the impressive **Valle de Cocora,** one of Colombia's most beautiful half-day hikes. Finally, make the short trip to slow-paced **Filandia** and toast your tour from its *mirador*, which has some of the best views in coffee country.

© Jess Kraft / Shutterstock

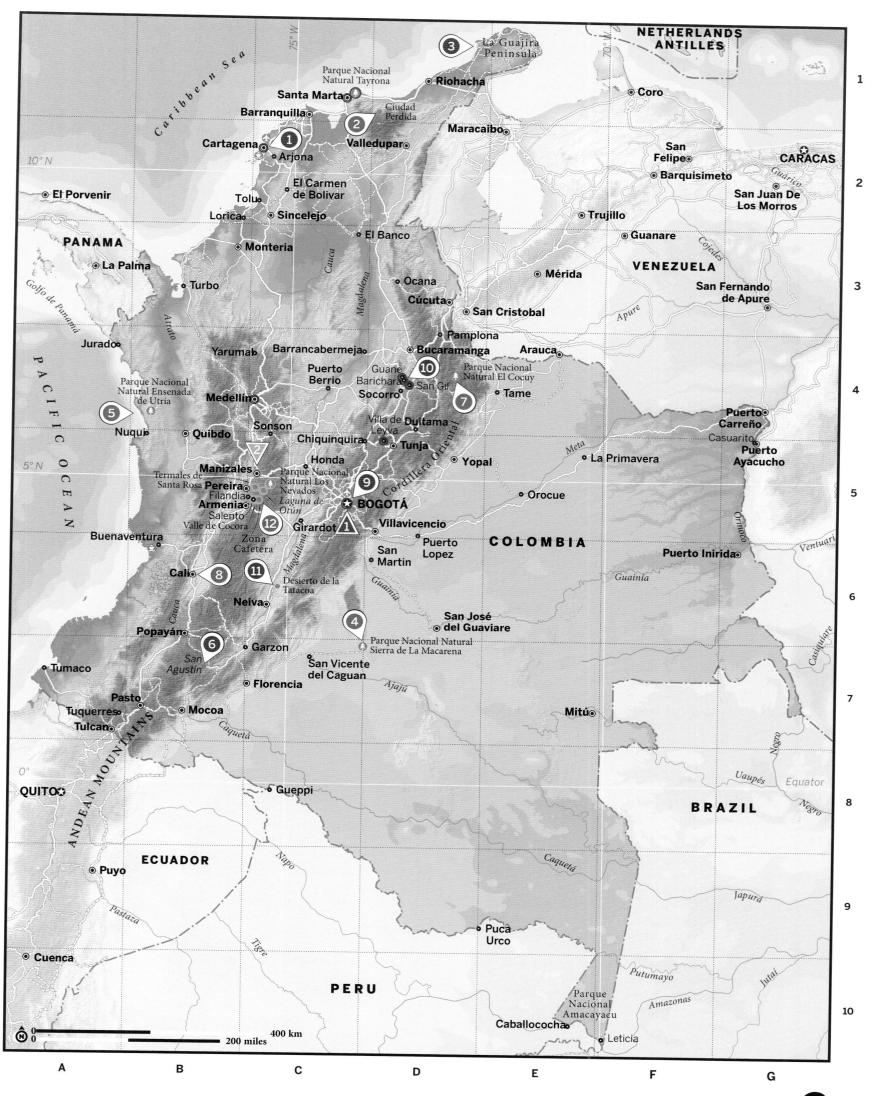

NETHERLANDS
ANTILLES

③ La Guajira
Peninsula

Caribbean Sea

Parque Nacional
Natural Tayrona

◉ Riohacha

Santa Marta ◉

Barranquilla ◉
Ciudad
Perdida

Cartagena ◉ ① ◎ Coro

◉ Arjona ② Valledupar

Maracaibo ◉

San
Felipe ◉ ☆ CARACAS

◉ El Porvenir ◉ Barquisimeto

San Juan De
Los Morros ◉

Tolu ◉
El Carmen
de Bolivar

PANAMA ◉ Trujillo

Lorica ◉ ◉ Sincelejo VENEZUELA

◉ Guanare

◉ Monteria ◉ El Banco ◉ Mérida
San Fernando
de Apure ◉

La Palma ◉ ◉ Ocana

◉ Turbo Cúcuta ◉ San Cristobal

Jurado ◉ ◉ Pamplona

Yarumal ◉ ◉ Barrancabermeja Bucaramanga ◉ ◉ Arauca

Guane ⑩
Barichara
◉ San Gil Parque Nacional
Natural El Cocuy

Parque Nacional
Natural Ensenada
de Utria

Puerto
Berrio Socorro ⑦ ◉ Tame

Puerto
Carreño ◉

Medellín ◉ Casuarito

⑤ Sonson Villa de
Leyva Duitama Puerto
Ayacucho ◉

Nuqui ◉ ◉ Quibdo Chiquinquira ◉ ◉ Tunja

◉ Honda ◉ Yopal

Termales de
Santa Rosa Manizales ② Parque Nacional
Natural Los
Nevados ⑨ ◉ La Primavera

Pereira ◉ ☆ BOGOTÁ

Filandia Laguna de
Otún ◉ Orocue

Armenia ◉ ⑫ Girardot ① Villavicencio ◉ COLOMBIA
Salento
Valle de Cocora

Buenaventura ◉ Zona
Cafetera San
Martin Puerto
Lopez Puerto Inirida ◉

Cali ◉ ⑧ ⑪ Desierto de la
Tatacoa

◉ Neiva

Popayán ◉ San José
del Guaviare ◉

⑥ ◉ Garzon

Tumaco ◉ San
Agustín San Vicente
del Caguan Mitú ◉

◉ Florencia

Pasto ◉
Tuquerres ◉ ◉ Mocoa

Tulcan ◉

ANDEAN MOUNTAINS

◉ Gueppi Equator BRAZIL

QUITO ◉

ECUADOR ◉ Puyo

◉ Cuenca
Puca
Urco ◉

PERU
Parque
Nacional
Amacayacu

Caballococha ◉ ◉ Leticia

N 0
0
400 km
200 miles

A B C D E F G

THE TRAVEL ATLAS

367

SIGHTS &
ACTIVITIES

◉ SEE
◉ DO

ITINERARY

▽ 1
▽ 2

1 Machu Picchu

A fantastic Inca citadel lost to the world until its rediscovery in the early 20th century, Machu Picchu stands as a ruin among ruins. With its emerald terraces, backed by steep peaks and Andean ridges that echo on the horizon, the sight simply surpasses all expectations. This marvel of engineering has withstood six centuries of earthquakes, foreign invasion and howling weather.

2 Floating reed islands, Lake Titicaca

First constructed centuries ago by the Uros people to escape more aggressive mainland ethnic groups, such as the Incas, these surreal floating islands are crafted entirely of tightly woven *totora* reeds. The reeds require near-constant renovation and are also used to build thatched homes, elegant boats and even archways and children's swing sets.

3 Arequipa

Crowned by dazzling baroque-*mestizo* architecture hewn out of the local *sillar* (white volcanic rock), Peru's second-largest metropolis is primarily a Spanish colonial city that hasn't strayed far from its original conception. It enjoys an ethereal natural setting, amid snoozing volcanoes and the high pampa.

4 Inca Trail

The continent's most famous pedestrian roadway, this trail snakes 43km, up stone steps and through thick cloud-forest mists. A true multiday pilgrimage, it ends at Intipunku – or Sun Gate – where you first glimpse the extravagant ruins at Machu Picchu.

Lake Titicaca: Tiny huts on a floating reed island, built by Peru's Uros people.

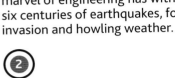

5 Sacred Valley

Ragtag Andean villages, crumbling Inca military outposts and agricultural terraces used since time immemorial are linked by the Río Urubamba as it curves and widens, coursing through this incredible valley.

6 Cordillera Blanca

These dramatic peaks stand sentinel over Huaraz and the surrounding region like an outrageously imposing granite Republican Guard. The range is the highest outside of the Himalaya, and 16 of its ostentatious summits breach 6000m. Glacial lakes, massive *Puya raimondii* plants and shards of sky-pointed rock all culminate in Parque Nacional Huascarán, where the Santa Cruz trek rewards the ambitious with a living museum of razor-sharp peaks.

7 Nazca Lines

Spread over 500-sq-km of arid, rock-strewn plain in the Pampa Colorada, the Nazca Lines are one of the world's great archaeological mysteries. Comprising more than 800 straight lines, 300 geometric figures and 70 animal and plant drawings, the lines are almost imperceptible on the ground. From above, they form a striking network of stylised figures and channels.

8 Kuélap

The extraordinary stone fortress at Kuélap is tucked away deep in cloud-forested territory at 3100m above the Río Urubamba near Chachapoyas. The remarkably preserved citadel is a testament to the enigmatic and strong-willed 'People of the Clouds'. Some 400 circular dwellings, some ornately adorned and surrounded by a towering rock wall, highlight this beautiful and mysterious stone beast in the clouds.

9 Trujillo

Rising from the sand-strewn desert like a kaleidoscopic mirage of colonial colour, old Trujillo boasts a dazzling display of preserved splendour. The city's historical centre is chock-full of elegant churches, mansions and otherwise unspoiled colonial constructions, which are steeped today in a modern motif that lends the city a lovely, liveable feel.

10 Cañón del Colca

Stretching 100km from end to end and plunging over 3400m at its deepest part, this canyon has been embellished with terraced agricultural fields, pastoral villages, Spanish colonial churches and ruins that date back to pre-Inca times. Hike it, bike it, raft it or zip-line it.

11 Lima

Lima is a city where life is often planned around the next meal. Dishes are a complex blend of Spanish, indigenous, African and Asian influences (both Chinese and Japanese).

▽

14- to 28-day itinerary
The Wild and Ancient North

From **Lima**, head to **Trujillo**, sampling the fiery coastal cuisine and exploring the ruins at **Chan Chan** and **Huacas del Sol y de la Luna**. Next is the scenic route to the lovely highland town of **Cajamarca** via the archaeological site of **Marcahuamachuco**. In the dry season, adventure on the slow, spectacular route to friendly **Celendín** and on

to **Leimebamba** to see the Marvelous Spatuletail Hummingbird. Continue on to **Chachapoyas** to see the fantastic fortress of **Kuélap**. From Chachapoyas, journey to **Tarapoto** to hike in lush forest to waterfalls. Next, fly to the jungle city of **Iquitos**, from where you can arrange boat trips that go deeper into the rainforest.

▽

14- to 28-day itinerary
Highlights of Peru

Leaving **Lima**, journey south to **Pisco** and **Paracas**, where you can boat to the wildlife-rich **Islas Ballestas**. Then it's on to **Ica**, Peru's wine and pisco capital, and the palm-fringed, dune-lined oasis of **Huacachina**, a place famous for sandboarding. Next is **Nazca** for a flight over the mysterious Nazca Lines. Turn inland for the 'White

City' of **Arequipa**, with its colonial architecture and stylish nightlife. Lace up your boots to trek the incredible **Cañón del Colca** or **Cañón del Cotahuasi** – perhaps the world's deepest – or climb **El Misti**, a postcard-perfect 5822m volcano. Continue upwards to **Puno**, Peru's port on Lake Titicaca, one of the world's highest navigable lakes.

From here you can boat to traditional islands and explore the strange *chullpas* (ancient funerary towers) at **Sillustani** and **Cutimbo**. Wind through the Andes to **Cuzco**, South America's oldest continuously inhabited city. Browse colourful markets and explore archaeological sites in the **Sacred Valley**, then make the trek to **Machu Picchu**.

© Philip Lee Harvey / Lonely Planet

0°

QUITO

Portoviejo

ECUADOR

Gueppi

COLOMBIA

Ambato

Nuevo
Rocafuerte

Río Putumayo

1

Riobamba

Río Napo

Puca
Urco

2

Cuenca

Río Pastaza

Río Tigre

Río Amazonas

Caballococha

Tumbes

Iquitos

Río Javari

Tabatinga

3

Máncora

La Tina

Río Marañón

Nauta

Talara

Sullana

5°S

Lagunas

Reserva Nacional
Pacaya-Samiria

Requena

Piura

San Ignacio

Huancabamba

Sechura

Olmos

Pedro Ruíz

Moyobamba

Yurimaguas

Chachapoyas

Kuélap

Tarapoto

Río Ucayali

4

BRAZIL

Chiclayo

⑧

Celendín

Leimebamba

Cajamarca

Juanjui

PERU

Pacasmayo

Puerto Chicama

⑨

Cajabamba

Marcahuamachuco

Contamana

Chan Chan

Otuzco

Trujillo

Huacas del Sol y de la Luna

Tayabamba

Tocache

Pucallpa

5

Alpamayo
(5947m)

Cordillera Blanca

Río Marañón

Río Huallaga

Chimbote

Huascarán
(6768m)

Casma

⑥

Huaraz

Huánuco

10°S

Huarmey

Puerto
Bermúdez

Río Juruá

Río Purús

Rio Branco

6

Yerupajá
(6634m)

Barranca

**Cerro de
Pasco**

Junín

La Merced

Río de las Piedras

Iñapari

Cobija

Huaura

Tarma

Satipo

Río Ucayali

Chancay

⑪

Jauja

Río Urubamba

Madre de Dios

Río de los Amigos

①

★ **LIMA**

Huancayo

Parque
Nacional
Manu

Boca
Manu

**Puerto
Maldonado**

Madre de Dios

7

②

Huancavelica

①

Quillabamba

Río Ucayali

Puerto
Heath

Ayacucho

Machu Picchu
Inca Trail

Aguas Calientes

Sacred Valley

⑤

Chincha Alta

CORDILLERA

④

Cuzco

Ausangate
(6384m)

Islas Ballestas

Paracas

Pisco

Abancay

8

Huacachina

Ica

DE

Sicuani

Nazca Lines

Nazca

Puquio

LOS

Ayaviri

⑦

Coracora

②

*Lake
Titicaca*

Cañón del
Cotahuasi

⑩

Cabanaconde

Juliaca

ANDES

BOLIVIA

Cañón
del Colca

Sillustani

Puno

Isla del Sol

9

Chala

Ampato
(6310m)

El Misti
(5822m)

Cutimbo

Copacabana

Arequipa

Desaguadero

Camaná

③

★ **LA PAZ**

Mollendo

Moquegua

Ilo

Charana

10

Tacna

N
0 ─── 400 km
0 ─── 200 miles

Arica

CHILE

A   B   C   D   E   F   G

SIGHTS &
ACTIVITIES

⊚ SEE
◉ DO

ITINERARY

▽ 1
▽ 2

① Galápagos Islands

This isolated group of volcanic islands and its fragile ecosystem has taken on almost mythological status as a showcase of biodiversity. And the creatures that call it home, many found nowhere else in the world, act as if humans are nothing more than slightly annoying paparazzi.

② Quilotoa Loop

Adventure begins at 3000m along this route, which runs through indigenous villages and painters' colonies to a deep-blue crater lake and into the heart of Ecuador's central highlands.

③ Parque Nacional Cotopaxi

The centrepiece of this park is the snow-capped and downright picture-perfect Volcán Cotopaxi (5897m). Around the volcano you'll find outstanding hiking opportunities and wildlife such as the Andean condor, white-tailed deer, little red brocket deer and wily *colpeo* (Andean fox).

④ Quito's Old Town

History lurks around every corner in vibrant Centro Histórico – it's packed with elaborate churches and old-time monasteries, people-packed plazas and looming bell towers.

⑤ Parque Nacional Yasuní

This vast tract of protected rainforest contains a simply dazzling biodiversity. Excitement-filled canoe trips through tiny overgrown creeks and hikes across the jungle floor with experienced guides reveal all manner of flowers, plants and creatures.

⑥ Cuenca

The fairy-tale colonial centre of Cuenca has been charming visitors since the 16th century. And while the cobblestone streets, polychrome building fronts and remarkably well-preserved cathedral will set your camera ablaze, it's the town's laid-back feel, friendly locals and bohemian spirit that will transfix you.

⑦ Northwest coast

Ecuador's northwest is packed with fishing villages, resort towns, surfer hangouts and pristine areas of golden sand. One of the best places for a sunny getaway is Canoa.

⑧ Papallacta

The beautifully maintained public baths just outside Papallacta offer one of Ecuador's best natural highs. At night, lie back and watch the stars fill the jet black sky.

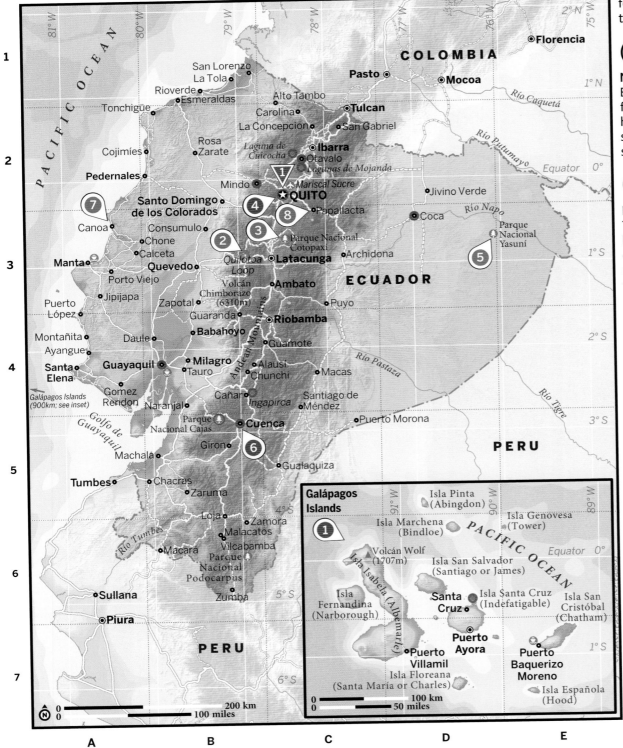

▽1 14-day itinerary
Best of Ecuador

Begin the trip in **Quito**. Spend two days soaking up the architectural gems of the Old Town, then go north to **Otavalo** for its famous market (best on Saturdays). Spend the night there and squeeze in a hike out to the stunning lakes **Laguna de Cuicocha** or **Lagunas de Mojanda**. On the fourth day, go west to the lush cloud forests of **Mindo**. Overnight in a riverside or mountaintop lodge, then return to Quito for a flight to **Cuenca**. Spend two days exploring and visiting **Parque Nacional Cajas**. If time allows, visit the Inca ruins of **Ingapirca** before continuing to **Guayaquil** for a flight to the **Galápagos Islands**. Spend four days there, wildlife watching and island hopping. For the final part of the adventure, fly back to Guayaquil and onward to **Coca** (via Quito), gateway to the Amazon. Spend three nights at a jungle lodge on the Lower Río Napo.

Salar de Uyuni

The vastness, austerity and crystalline perfection of the world's largest salt flat will inspire you. Explore its rock gardens, geyser fields and piping-hot springs on a chilly jeep tour, a defining experience of any Bolivian adventure.

Cordillera Real

Trek along ancient Incan paths that weave their way from the Andes into the Amazon Basin, through this remarkable skyward-bound wilderness. Along the way, dine with indigenous families, cool off beside cascading waterfalls and connect with Pachamama (Mother Earth).

Isla del Sol, Lake Titicaca

This island is considered to be the birthplace of Andean civilisation. Track down forgotten Inca roads to small archaeological sites, remote coves and intact indigenous communities. The lake itself has a magnetism, power and energy unique to this world.

Sucre

Proud, genteel and gleaming white in the Andean sun, Sucre is Bolivia's most beautiful city and the symbolic heart of the nation. It was here that independence was proclaimed.

Parque Nacional and Área de Uso Múltiple Amboró

One of Bolivia's most biodiverse and accessible protected areas, this explorer's haven is home to wonderful wildlife and breathtaking scenery. Here the lush, leafy Amazon kisses the thorny, dusty Chaco, and the sweaty lowlands greet the refreshing highlands.

La Paz markets

The whirling engine that feeds and fuels a nation, these markets are crazy, disjointed, colourful, mad, stinky and remarkable. Gaze at stalls packed with fruit, flowers, fish and even witchcraft.

Potosí

Said to be the highest city in the world, lofty Potosí once produced silver that funded the Spanish Empire for centuries. Imagine its wealthy past while observing the cracked brickwork of its ornate colonial-era buildings and the wonderfully preserved churches.

Tupiza

Cut from the pages of a Wild West novel, the polychromatic desert wonderlands and canyons around Tupiza are awesome places for heading off into the sunset (in a saddle, atop a mountain bike, on foot or in a 4WD).

14-day itinerary
Best of Bolivia

Start out with a day of acclimatisation in **La Paz**'s markets. History buffs can take a side trip to **Tiwanaku**. Next, head to **Lake Titicaca** to spend up to three days taking in the sites of Copacabana and Isla del Sol. From there, circle down the Altiplano (via La Paz) to the **Salar de Uyuni** for a bone-chatteringly cold three-day jeep tour. You can often extend your trip to take you to the former territory of Butch Cassidy in the town of **Tupiza**. Swing up to **Potosí**, a starkly beautiful Unesco World Heritage city, situated at 4070m, where you can visit the mint and mines. After a day or two, head to the white city of **Sucre** to hang out with students in grand plazas. Return to La Paz via **Cochabamba**, taking in the views along the way. On your last day in La Paz, consider a day of museum-hopping or take a mountain-bike ride down the World's Most Dangerous Road to **Coroico**.

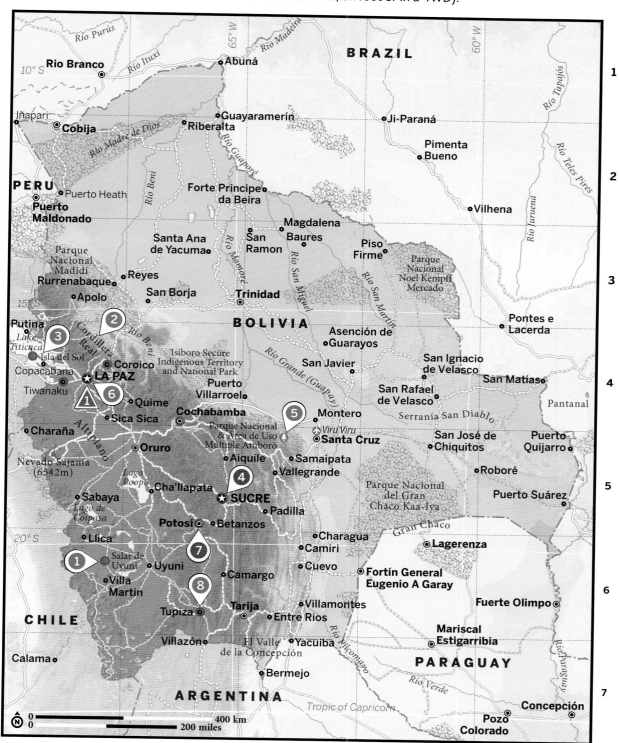

SIGHTS &
ACTIVITIES

 SEE

DO

ITINERARY

 1

2

14-day itinerary
Rio and the Southeast

Spend a few days discovering **Rio** before heading to **Paraty**. Next, stop in **Ubatuba** with its jungle-clad mountains and spectacular coastal scenery. Nearby **Ilhabela** is a car-free island of beaches, forests and waterfalls. Stop in **São Paulo** for high culture, then venture to exquisite **Tiradentes** and **Ouro Preto**. Afterwards, enjoy Mineira hospitality in **Belo Horizonte**. Before returning to Rio, visit the hiker's paradise of **Parque Nacional de Caparaó**, relish the beauty of **Parque Estadual da Pedra Azul** and embrace the dining and nightlife of **Búzios**.

21- to 28-day itinerary
Waterways of the Amazon

Begin in **Belém**, a culturally rich city at the river's mouth. From here, explore **Ilha de Marajó**, which has bird-filled forests, friendly locals and buffalo roaming the streets. Next dip south to **Palmas**, another ultra-planned city like Brasília, and jumping-off point for 4WD tours of rugged **Parque Estadual Jalapão**. Get a hammock and prepare yourself for a few hardy days of boat travel up the Amazon River. Stop in **Monte Alegre** to see ancient rock paintings. Upstream is **Santarém**, a pleasant city with many nearby attractions. Also reachable is the virgin rainforest of the **Floresta Nacional do Tapajós**, where you can lodge in simple *pousadas* and take rewarding hikes. Another stop worth making is at **Alter do Chão** for its picturesque lagoon with startling white-sand beaches. Continue to **Manaus**, Amazonia's largest city, to fly out. Or, with another week, continue west to **Reserva Baixo Rio Branco-Jauperi**, a rainforest reserve, before hitting **Tefé** and the nearby **Mamirauá Reserve**, home to dolphins, sloths, macaws, monkeys and more.

Amazon jungle
Needless to say, the best reason to visit the Amazon is to get out into the depths of the mighty jungle: to ply the winding waterways in a canoe, hike lush leafy trails, and scan the canopy for monkeys, sloths and other creatures. The world's biggest and best known rainforest has outdoor excursions of all sorts, and for all types of travellers: from easy nature hikes to scaling 50m trees, from luxury lodges to makeshift camps in the forest. Whatever your interest, experience, ability or budget, there's a jungle trip in the Amazon waiting to blow your mind.

Brasília
What the city of the future really needed to back up its claim to be the harbinger of Brazil's 'new dawn' was an architect capable of designing buildings that looked very much the part. In Oscar Niemeyer Brasilia found the right person for the job. The 'crown of thorns' Catedral Metropolitana is a religious masterwork and the interplanetary Teatro Nacional is truly out of this world. Brasília is a city overloaded with architectural gems designed by a genius who was inspired by the concept of creating a better future for his homeland.

Parque Nacional da Chapada Diamantina
A pristine outdoor wonderland of rushing waterfalls, crystal-blue pools, rugged hiking trails and natural waterslides, Chapada Diamantina is a deliciously unspoiled national park well off the beaten track.

Olinda
The colonial town of Olinda is full of creative types, and its twisting streets are brimming with galleries, artisans' workshops, museums, lovely churches and colourful old houses.

Iguazú Falls

The thunderous roar of 275 falls crashing across the Brazil and Argentina border floors even the most jaded traveller. Loud, angry, unstoppable and impossibly gorgeous, Iguaçu will leave you stunned and slack-jawed at the absolute power of Mother Nature.

Ilhabela

Rising steeply from the narrow strait that divides it from the continent, Ilhabela is home to volcanic peaks, beaches, tropical jungle and some 360 waterfalls. It shelters a remarkable profusion of flora and fauna, including toucans and capuchin monkeys. A haunt of pirates in the 16th and 17th centuries, its waters are scattered with shipwrecks, many of which make for excellent diving.

Ilha Grande

Spared from development due to its decades-long stint as an isolated prison and leper's colony, this remote island is now a true nature-lover's paradise – the jungle-clad slopes, aquamarine seas and dozens of beaches are some of Brazil's best preserved. Hike, snorkel or bask by a waterfall. With no motor vehicles to spoil the party, this is one clean, green island.

Iguazú Falls: The falls lie split between Brazil and Argentina in a national park, much of it teeming with flora and fauna.

Ouro Preto

With more ups and downs than a rollercoaster, Ouro Preto's historic streets veer precipitously between one baroque masterpiece and the next. View the sculpted gems of Aleijadinho, discover the 18th-century African tribal king turned folk hero Chico-Rei, and gaze upon opulent gilded churches.

Pantanal

Few places on earth can match the wildlife-watching experience provided by the Pantanal, a wondrously remote wetland. From cute capybaras and stately storks to the elusive jaguar, the animal life simply abounds.

Tiradentes

Wander the cobbled lanes of this incredibly preserved colonial town, moving past flower-draped walls and stunning colonial architecture. The many trails in the surrounding mountains are a hiker's delight.

Paraty

No place in Brazil offers such an enticing blend of colonial architecture and natural beauty as Paraty. Drop-dead gorgeous beaches and a stunning mountain backdrop jostle for attention with the multihued, cobblestoned charms of the 18th-century town centre. If you get bored with sunbathing and sightseeing, cool off with a caipirinha, go hurtling down a natural waterslide nearby, or whip up a gourmet Brazilian meal at the local cooking school.

São Paulo

Rivalling the frenetic pace of New York, the modernism of Tokyo and the prices of Moscow, but swamping all of them in options, São Paulo city is home to a pool of 20 million potential foodies, clubbers and cocktail connoisseurs and nearly 30,000 restaurants, bars and clubs to satiate them. It's a gluttonous avalanche of *bolinhos* (appetisers), booze and beats that outruns the sunrise on most nights.

Bonito

With a smorgasbord of aquatic adventures on offer in the jaw-dropping surroundings of the Serra da Bodoquena, Bonito offers you a wild wet-suited adventure like you've never experienced before. Try floating on the Rio da Prata or journeying to the centre of the earth at the Abismo de Añhumas.

Southern South America & Antarctica

From Andean peaks to Patagonian glaciers and the vast, empty Antarctica, this is a stage set for incredible adventures. Chile offers nature on a colossal scale, from the world's driest desert to vast glacial fields extending from the belly of South America to its foot. Argentina seduces with its streetside tango, *fútbol*, gaucho culture and the mighty Andes. Straddling both is Patagonia, a wild land that has seduced adventurers galore (plus Butch Cassidy and the Sundance Kid). Then there's Antarctica: the Great White Unknown, Earth's last wilderness and perhaps its greatest wonder.

LANDSCAPES
From Patagonia's pampas to the subtropical Argentine Chaco, from the summits of the Andes to the fjords and islands of Tierra del Fuego, few places are as geographically varied as this. Keep your camera ready – it's a paradise for landscape photographers.

NATIONAL PARKS
Watch waterfalls in Parque Nacional Iguazú, chart crashing glaciers in Parque Nacional Los Glaciares, hike through lunar landscapes in Parque Nacional Pali Aike or venture out to the island of Chiloé - the national parks of Argentina and Chile are stunning.

WILDLIFE
Nature-spotters are spoilt for choice. Glimpse right whales and orcas around the Península Valdés; see capybaras and caimans in the Parque Esteros del Iberá; watch Chilean flamingos around Lago Chungará; or travel into a truly wild world on the Antarctic Peninsula.

WINE
Together, Chile and Argentina make South America's finest wines. Follow the Ruta del Vino around Santa Cruz, taste your way around the Colchagua Valley, travel through Mendoza's endless vines or head for the little-known wineries of San Juan.

TREKKING
Mountains rumple the landscapes of Chile and Argentina, an irresistible magnet for hikers. El Chaltén, El Bolsón and Bariloche are Argentina's most popular areas; in Chile, you could trek through the Cerro Castillo, Parque Pumalín and Torres del Paine.

ICE
Ice is a constant feature this far south. Mighty ice sheets such as the Glacier Grey and Perito Moreno Glacier dazzle, but even they can't compare to the great expanses of Antarctica: the Ross Ice Shelf, the Polar Plateau and, of course, the storied South Pole itself.

Right: Teal waters and soaring peaks in Torres del Paine National Park.

Transport hubs

Chile and Argentina are well connected to the rest of the continent, as well as North America, Europe and Asia. The main hubs are the capitals, Santiago and Buenos Aires, but to reach more remote corners, such as Patagonia and Tierra del Fuego, requires more effort and expense. It's likely you'll pass through the small town of Punta Arenas if you're visiting Patagonia; it has become the region's travel nexus. Reaching Antarctica is another proposition altogether – pretty much the only option for non-explorers is to join an organised cruise from Ushuaia, or fly from Punta Arenas to King George Island, then join a ship there. It's worth the time and trouble: a voyage to Antarctica is one you'll remember as long as you live.

ELEVATION KEY

7500 - 10000M
5000 - 7500M
3000 - 5000M
2000 - 3000M
1500 - 2000M
1250 - 1500M
1000 - 1250M
750 - 1000M
500 - 750M
250 - 500M
100 - 250M
75 - 100M
50 - 75M
25 - 50M
1 - 25M

TRANSPORT

C2, C4, D2

C2, C3, C4,
D2, D4

Below: Dusk over the city of Valparaíso (left) and (right) a cruise ship in Antarctica.

Santiago

Chile has direct connections with North America, the UK, Europe, Israel, Australia and New Zealand. Long-distance flights to Chile arrive at Santiago, landing at Aeropuerto Internacional Arturo Merino Benítez. Chile's northern border touches Peru and Bolivia, while its vast eastern boundary hugs Argentina. Of the numerous border crossings, only a few are served by public transport.

Valparaíso

Frequent buses depart from the Terminal Rodoviario, about 20 blocks east of the town centre. Services to Santiago leave every 15 to 20 minutes. You can also reach Mendoza in Argentina by bus; some services continue to Buenos Aires.

Buenos Aires (see pp394-5 for city map)

Most international flights arrive at Buenos Aires' Aeropuerto Internacional Ministro Pistarini. There are numerous border crossings from neighbouring Bolivia, Brazil, Chile, Paraguay and Uruguay. Border formalities are generally straightforward as long as all your documents are in order. You can also travel between Uruguay and Buenos Aires by ferry or hydrofoil.

Mendoza

Mendoza has the only international airport in the central Andes, with regular flights to nearby Santiago in Chile. From Buenos Aires there are regular flights to Mendoza, San Juan, San Rafael and San Luis. There are two mountain passes between Argentina and Chile. Paso Internacional Los Libertadores is a major crossing a few hours from Mendoza, while El Paso de Agua Negra, in San Juan province, sees relatively few travellers.

Punta Arenas

Patagonia is synonymous with unmaintained *ripio* (gravel) roads, missing transport links and interminable bus rides, but flight options to Punta Arenas are expanding fast. Flying can be expensive, but it's an efficient way to see the area's highlights. Before skimping on your transport budget, bear in mind that Patagonia comprises a third of the world's eighth-largest country.

Ushuaia

The gateway to Antarctica, Ushuaia receives more than 90% of Antarctic-bound boats. Flights travel from Buenos Aires several times daily, sometimes stopping in El Calafate. A few private yachts charter trips around the Beagle Channel, to Cape Horn and Antarctica. For Puerto Williams (Chile), Ushuaia Boating goes daily in Zodiacs.

Antarctica

A journey to Antarctica is a once-in-a-lifetime adventure. The season runs from mid-October to mid-March, depending on ice conditions. Most visitors reach Antarctica via organised tours, generally on ships from Ushuaia, Argentina. All cruises and packages are also guided tours, with pre-determined itineraries. It is also possible to fly from Punta Arenas to Frei Station on King George Island, where you can transfer to a passenger ship to the South Shetlands and Antarctic Peninsula.

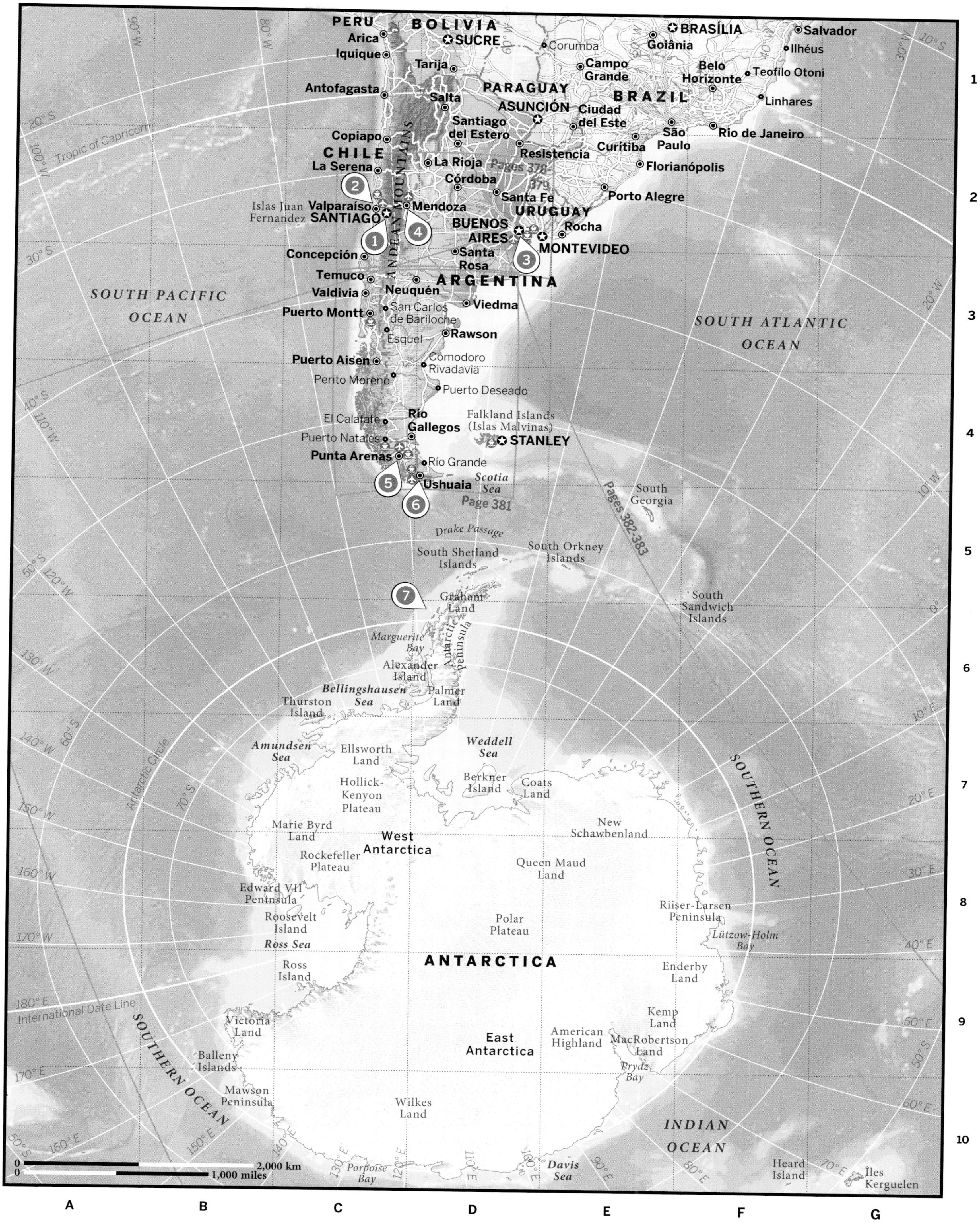
PERU
BOLIVIA
Arica
Iquique
SUCRE
Corumba
BRASÍLIA
Goiânia
Salvador
Ilhéus
Tarija
Campo Grande
Belo Horizonte
Teofilo Otoni
Antofagasta
PARAGUAY
Salta
BRAZIL
Linhares
ASUNCIÓN
Ciudad del Este
Santiago del Estero
São Paulo
Rio de Janeiro
Copiapo
Tropic of Capricorn
CHILE
Resistencia
Curítiba
La Rioja
La Serena
Florianópolis
Pages 378-379
Córdoba
ANDEAN MOUNTAINS
Santa Fe
Porto Alegre
Islas Juan Fernandez
Valparaíso
Mendoza
URUGUAY
SANTIAGO
BUENOS AIRES
Rocha
MONTEVIDEO
Concepción
Santa Rosa
Temuco
ARGENTINA
Neuquén
Valdivia
SOUTH PACIFIC OCEAN
San Carlos de Bariloche
Viedma
Puerto Montt
SOUTH ATLANTIC OCEAN
Esquel
Rawson
Puerto Aisen
Comodoro Rivadavia
Perito Moreno
Puerto Deseado
Río Gallegos
Falkland Islands (Islas Malvinas)
El Calafate
Puerto Natales
STANLEY
Punta Arenas
Río Grande
Ushuaia
Scotia Sea
Page 381
South Georgia
Pages 382-383
Drake Passage
South Shetland Islands
South Orkney Islands
Graham Land
South Sandwich Islands
Marguerite Bay
Antarctic Peninsula
Alexander Island
Bellingshausen Sea
Palmer Land
Thurston Island
Weddell Sea
Amundsen Sea
Ellsworth Land
Antarctic Circle
Hollick-Kenyon Plateau
Berkner Island
Coats Land
SOUTHERN OCEAN
Marie Byrd Land
New Schawbenland
West Antarctica
Rockefeller Plateau
Queen Maud Land
Edward VII Peninsula
Riiser-Larsen Peninsula
Roosevelt Island
Polar Plateau
Lützow-Holm Bay
Ross Sea
ANTARCTICA
Ross Island
Enderby Land
International Date Line
Kemp Land
Victoria Land
American Highland
MacRobertson Land
East Antarctica
Balleny Islands
Prydz Bay
SOUTHERN OCEAN
Mawson Peninsula
Wilkes Land
INDIAN OCEAN
Porpoise Bay
Davis Sea
Heard Island
Îles Kerguelen
0 2,000 km
0 1,000 miles
1 2 3 4 5 6 7 8 9 10
A B C D E F G

Mendoza

Thanks to a complex of river-fed aqueducts, land that was once desert now supports 70% of the country's wine production. Mendoza province is wine country, and many wineries near the capital offer tours and tasting. Malbec, of course, is the definitive Argentine wine.

Santiago

Surprising, cosmopolitan, energetic, sophisticated and worldly, Santiago is a city of syncopated cultural currents, madhouse parties, expansive museums and top-flight restaurants. Each neighbourhood has a unique flavour and tone.

Córdoba

With seven universities (and counting), Argentina's second city is one of the best places in the country for night owls, with many sidewalk bars, mega-discos and live-music venues. It's also the home of the *cuarteto* show – now popular all over the country, this music style was invented in Córdoba.

Parque Nacional Talampaya

The spectacular rock formations and canyons of this dusty desert national park are evidence of the erosive creativity of water. The sandstone cliffs are remarkable, as are the surrounding mountainscapes. A guided tour is included with the park's entrance fee.

Cerro Aconcagua

At 6960m, Aconcagua is the tallest peak in the western hemisphere and the 'roof of the Americas'. Italian-Swiss climber Matthias Zurbriggen made the first recorded ascent in 1897, but in 1985 the Club Andinista Mendoza discovered an Incan mummy at 5300m, proving it was used as an funerary site by ancient people.

Colchagua Valley

Protected by mountains on all sides, this sun-scorched parcel of vines and orchards produces Chile's best red wines. Today, the town of Santa Cruz serves as a central departure point for those heading to the countryside to visit eccentric vintners and experience the lyrical pull of wine country.

Valparaíso

Painters, philosophers and poets, including Pablo Neruda, have long been drawn to Chile's most unusual city. A maze of steep, sinuous streets, alleys and *escaleras* (stairways), this rough-and-ready port town has some of the best street art in Latin America.

Moai, Easter Island

The strikingly enigmatic *moai* (statues) oare the most pervasive image of Easter Island. Dotted all around the island, these massive carved figures stand on stone platforms, like colossal puppets on a supernatural stage.

Mar del Plata

'Mardel' is the classic Argentine beach destination. Once a glamorous seaside resort in the 1920s and 1930s, it has become a large and lively city, with stunning architecture, interesting museums and excellent seafood.

Elqui Valley

The heart of Chilean pisco production, the Elqui Valley is carpeted with a broad cover of striated green. Famous for its futuristic observatories, seekers of cosmic energies, UFO sightings and quaint villages, this is a truly enchanting – and enchanted – area.

SIGHTS & ACTIVITIES

⊚ SEE
⊚ DO

ITINERARY

▽ 1
▽ 2

7-day itinerary
Around Buenos Aires

After exploring **Buenos Aires**, head on to **Tigre**, with its hidden waterways and busy delta. Take a day trip to peaceful **San Antonio de Areco**, which has a history of gaucho culture, or tidy **La Plata**, with its huge cathedral. **Pinamar** and **Villa Gesell** make great summer escapes, as does **Mar del Plata**, the biggest Argentine beach destination of them

all. Or head inland to **Tandil**, a pretty town near scenic hills and a recreational reservoir. And then there's Uruguay, just a (relatively) short boat ride away. **Colonia del Sacramento** is truly charming; filled with cobbled streets and colonial buildings it makes a great day trip. Or stay overnight in **Montevideo**; like Buenos Aires' less frantic little sister.

14-day itinerary
Santiago & Wine Country

Start with a few nights in the happening Chilean capital, **Santiago**. Stroll around the historic centre, breaking for a lively seafood lunch in the clamouring Marcado Central. Sip sparkling wine at Boca Nariz or catch experimental dance at the Centro Gabriela Mistral. Venture to Santiago's outskirts to try its big-bodied local red wines; try commercial heavy

hitters Vina Concha y Toro and boutique winemakers Viña Aquitania. Next, head to **Valparaíso** to walk its steep hills and ride antique elevators, like Cerro Conceptión, the city's oldest. Wander the graffitied passageways, step into Neruda's La Sebastiana getaway and feast on freshly caught fish. Exhausted from the urban hiking? Unwind at

nearby Zapallar or Maitencillo for a quick beach getaway. Head south to Chile's best-known wine region, **Colchagua Valley**. Overnight in **Santa Cruz** with a morning visit to the Museo de Colchagua before a world-class prix-fixe lunch at Lapostolle. Finally, go surfing at relaxed party town **Pichilemu** or visit the lesser-known wineries of **Maule Valley**.

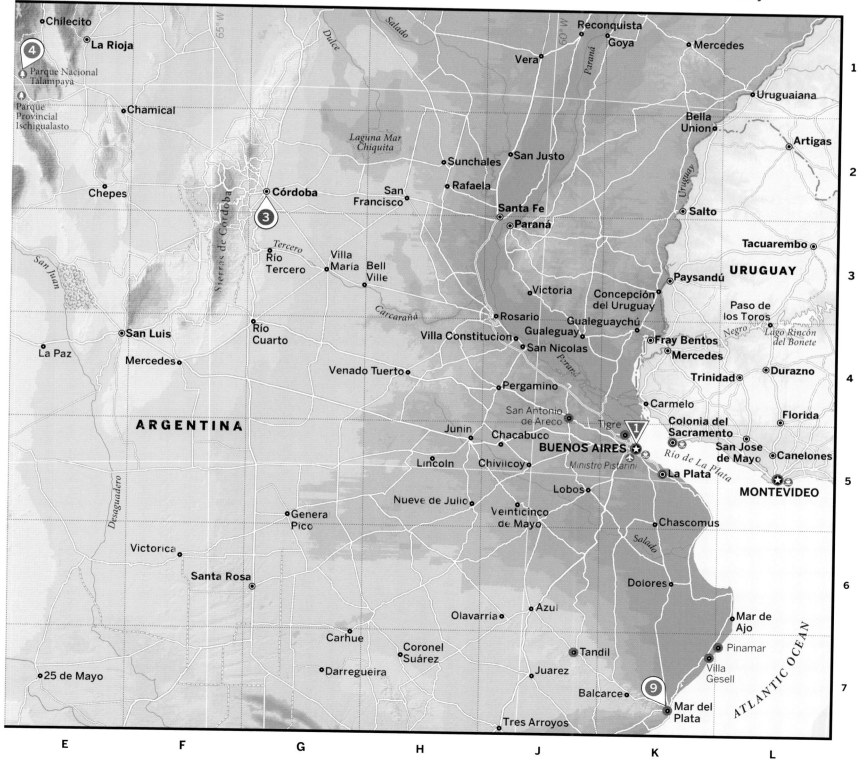

SIGHTS &
ACTIVITIES

● SEE
● DO

ITINERARY

▽ 1
▽ 2

① Parque Nacional Torres del Paine
Soaring 2000m above the Patagonian steppe, the granite pillars of Torres del Paine dominate the landscape of Patagonia's foremost national park, and inspire a mass pilgrimage of hikers from around the world. Part of Unesco's Biosphere Reserve system since 1978, the park is home to azure lakes, emerald forests, roaring rivers and the radiant Grey Glacier, as well as herds of guanaco, or wild llamas.

② Glaciar Perito Moreno
Among the Earth's most dynamic and accessible ice fields, Glaciar Perito Moreno is 30km long, 5km wide and 60m high, but what makes it exceptional in the world of ice is its constant advance – it creeps forward up to 2m per day, causing building-sized icebergs to calve from its face.

③ Parque Nacional Laguna San Rafael
Awesome and remote, this national park contains the 30,000-year-old San Valentín glacier in Chile's northern ice field, and 4058m Monte San Valentín, the southern Andes' highest peak. Most visitors use small boats or rafts to approach the glacier's 60m face.

④ Valle Chacabuco
This reformed *estancia* (grazing ranch) is home to flamingo, guanaco, huemul (endangered Andean deer), puma, viscacha and fox. Conservacion Patagonica began this initiative in 2004. Now dubbed as the Serengeti of the Southern Cone, the 690-sq-km park stretches from the Río Baker to the Argentine border.

El Chaltén: The village offers epic views of the jagged peaks of Mount Fitzroy and Cerro Torre.

⑤ Parque Nacional Pumalín
Verdant and pristine, this 2889-sq-km park encompasses vast extensions of temperate rainforest, clear rivers, seascapes and farmland. Created by American Doug Tompkins, it's one of the largest private parks in the world. After the 2008 eruption of Volcán Chaitén, the park closed for several years. It reopened in 2011, adding a spectacular trail to the new volcano.

⑥ El Chaltén
This village overlooks the northern sector of Parque Nacional Los Glaciares and its world-class trails. Founded in 1985, in a rush to beat Chile to the land claim, El Chaltén is still a frontier town; it is named for Cerro Fitz Roy's Tehuelche name, meaning 'peak of fire' or 'smoking mountain' – an apt description of the cloudy summit.

⑦ Reserva Nacional Jeinimeni
Turquoise lakes and the rusted hues of the steppe mark the rarely visited Reserva Nacional Jeinimeni, 52km southwest of Chile Chico. Its unusual wonders range from cave paintings to foxes and flamingos. In the transition zone to the Patagonian steppe, it covers 1610 sq km. Through-hikers can link to Valle Chacabuco via a three-day mountain traverse.

⑧ Carreterra Austral
The Carretera Austral runs 1240 mostly unpaved kilometres alongside ancient forests, glaciers, pioneer farmsteads, turquoise rivers and the crashing Pacific. Completed in 1996, it required an investment of US$300 million, took more than 20 years to build and cost 11 workers their lives.

⑨ Isla Magdalena
Thriving colonies of marching Magellanic penguins are the main attraction of a trip to the Monumento Natural Los Pingüinos on Isla Magdalena. The best way to see them is to join five-hour ferry tours departing from the mainland.

⑩ Caleta Tortel
Dedicated as a national monument, this fishing village cobbled around a steep escarpment is certainly unique. Seated between two ice fields at the mouth of Río Baker, it was first home to canoe-travelling Alacalufes (Qawashqar); colonists didn't arrive until 1955. Still isolated, locals live off tourism and cypress-wood extraction.

⑪ Parque Nacional Pali Aike
Rugged volcanic steppe pocked with craters, caves and twisted formations, Pali Aike means 'devil's country' in Tehuelche. This desolate landscape is a 50-sq-km park along the Argentine border. In the 1930s Junius Bird's excavations at 17m-deep Pali Aike Cave yielded the first artifacts associated with extinct New World fauna, such as the milodón and the native horse Onohippidium.

21-day itinerary
Classic Patagonia

Start in **Puerto Madryn** in springtime to see the wildlife at **Reserva Faunística Península Valdés**. Check out the world's largest dinosaur at the Museo Paleontológico Egidio Feruglio in **Trelew**, then fly south. Arrive in **Ushuaia** and hop on a boat to cruise around the **Beagle Channel** and hopefully see some penguins. Nearby **Parque Nacional Tierra del Fuego** offers hiking at the end of the world. Hop to **El Calafate** and lay your eyes on the **Glaciar Perito Moreno**. Outdoors-lovers can cross the border and trek in Chile's famous **Parque Nacional Torres del Paine**. Finish in **El Chaltén** for world-class hiking and camping.

28-day itinerary
Pioneer Patagonia

Leave **Puerto Montt** or **Puerto Varas** for the Cochamó or Río Puelo valleys, where you can hike or horseback ride, camp or stay at remote lodgings. From Puerto Montt, ferry to **Parque Nacional Pumalín** and explore ancient forests and climb to the steaming crater of **Volcán Chaitén**. Ramble the Carretera Austral to **Futaleufú**, for sweeping rural vistas and heart-pumping white water. Check out the hot springs near **Puyuhuapi** or camp under the hanging glacier at **Parque Nacional Queulat**. **Coyhaique** is the next hub. After making connections to **Chile Chico** on the enormous Lago General Carrera, hop the border to **Los Antiguos** and travel Argentina's Ruta 40 to **El Chaltén** for hiking around Cerro Fitz Roy. Take two days to visit **El Calafate** and glacier **Perito Moreno** in the **Parque Nacional Los Glaciares**. From El Calafate it's an easy connection to **Parque Nacional Torres del Paine** via **Puerto Natales**, where you can conclude with a hike along the 'W' route or the week-long circuit before heading home.

Lonquimay
Temuco
Zapala
Neuquén
General Roca
Río Colorado
Bahía Blanca
Tres Arroyos
Punta Alta
Necochea
Villarica
Choele Choel
Pedro Luro
Loncoche
Embalse Ezequiel Ramos Mexia
Villalonga
Valdivia
Los Lagos
General Conesa
Viedma
Río Bueno
Lago Ranco
Osorno
San Antonio Oeste
Puerto Varas
San Carlos de Bariloche
Ingeniero Jacobacci
Sierra Colorado
Ancud
Puerto Montt
El Bolsón
El Maiten
Parque Nacional Pumalin
Chico
Gastre
Telsen
Reserva Faunística Península Valdés
Puerto Madryn
Castro
Volcán Chaltén
Esquel
Trelew
Rawson
Quellon
Isla Grande de Chiloé
Futaleufú
Chubut

ANDEAN MOUNTAINS

ARGENTINA

La Junta
Parque Nacional Queulat
Alto Rio Sanguer
Puyuhuapi
Carreterra Austral
Chico
Puerto Aisen
Coyhaique
Paso Rio Mayo
Lago Musters
Lago Colhué Huapi
Comodoro Rivadavia
Monte San Valentin (4058m)
Reserva Nacional Jeinimeni
Chile Chico
Perito Moreno
San Valentin Glacier
Parque Nacional Laguna San Rafael
Valle Chacabuco
Los Antiguos
Deseado
Puerto Deseado
Caleta Tortel
Villa O'Higgins
Gobernador Gregores
Los Antiguos
Lago Cardiel
Puerto San Julián
El Chaltén
Chico
Parque Nacional Los Glaciares
Lago Viedma
Santa Cruz
Comondante Luis Piedrabuena
Glaciar Perito Moreno
El Calafate
Parque Nacional Torres del Paine
28 de Noviembre
Río Gallegos
Puerto Natales
Gallegos
Parque Nacional Pali Aike
Río Verde
Punta Arenas
Isla Magdalena
Río Grande
Ushuaia
Parque Nacional Tierra del Fuego
Puerto Williams
Beagle Channel

CHILE

SOUTH PACIFIC OCEAN

SOUTH ATLANTIC OCEAN

Fitz Roy Range

Isla Grande de Tierra del Fuego

FALKLAND ISLANDS (UK)
(ISLAS MALVINAS)
Fox Bay West
Stanley

75°W
70°W
65°W
60°W
40°S
45°S
50°S
55°S

0   400 km
0   200 miles
N

1
2
3
4
5
6
7
8
9
10

A   B   C   D   E   F   G

SIGHTS &
ACTIVITIES

◉ SEE
◉ DO

ITINERARY

▽ 1
▽ 2

1 Amundsen-Scott South Pole Station

First reached just over 100 years ago by explorer Roald Amundsen, the South Pole still embodies myth, hardship and glory. Today it is topped by a high-tech station surrounded by cutting-edge astrophysical observation equipment (including a neutrino detector array buried 1.9 km below the ice). A photo op with the globe-topped pole is a once-in-a-lifetime opportunity.

2 Shackleton's Hut

Shackleton erected this structure on his *Nimrod* expedition in February 1908. Fifteen men lived in the hut, which is much smaller than Scott's at Cape Evans. All of Shackleton's men left alive (unlike at Scott's hut), and apparently in a hurry: when members of the *Terra Nova* expedition visited in 1911, they found socks left hanging to dry and a meal still on the table.

3 Lemaire Channel

This sheer-sided channel – just 1600m wide – runs for 11km between the mountains of Booth Island and the nearby peninsula. So photogenic that it's been dubbed 'Kodak Gap', the passageway is only visible once you're nearly inside it. It was first navigated by the Belgian de Gerlache in 1898 and named after a Belgian explorer of the Congo. Basking Weddell seals, gentoo penguins and leopard seals are often seen here.

4 Deception Island

Easily recognised by its broken-ring shape, Deception Island's collapsed volcanic cone provides one of the safest natural harbours in the world, despite periodic eruptions. To reach this secret haven, however, vessels must navigate a tricky 230m-wide break in the volcano's walls, known since early-19th-century sealing days as Neptune's Bellows for the strong winds that blow through the strait.

5 Charlotte Bay & Cuverville Island

Cuverville Island is home to one of the largest gentoo rookeries on the Ice; several thousand pairs share their exquisite views with visitors. Nearby Charlotte Bay offers another spectacular photo opportunity, its inlet often studded with calved icebergs reflected on the smooth sea surface.

6 Paradise Harbor

The whalers who named this harbour were obviously quite taken with the stunning icebergs and reflections of the surrounding mountains. Gentoos and shags call the area home, with penguins nesting in the remains of Argentina's Brown Station.

7 McMurdo Station

Affectionately called Mac Town, Antarctica's largest base is operated by the US. Backed by the active volcano of Mt Erebus, the sprawling station is home to more than 1100 scientists and researchers during summer.

8 Antarctic Museum, Port Lockroy

Britain's Bransfield House was built at Port Lockroy during WWII. The museum's wooden skis, 1944 radio transmitter and wind-up HMV gramophone are evocative reminders of the explorers who lived for years at this wilderness outpost.

9 Ross Ice Shelf

This towering sheet of ice rising from the Ross Sea was the daunting barrier to many an Antarctic explorer. The floating ice shelf covers 520,000 sq km. Inland, where the glaciers meet it, the slab can be a kilometre thick.

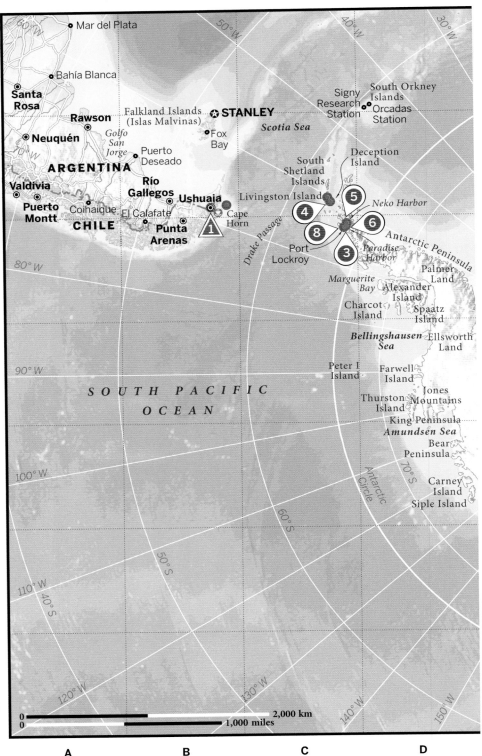

7- to 14-day itinerary
Antarctic Peninsula

The most popular trip to the Ice starts from **Ushuaia**, Argentina and crosses the Drake Passage. First landing is usually at one of the South Shetland Islands. Popular stops include **Deception Island**, an active volcano with a hidden 'amphitheatre', which is home to the largest chinstrap penguin rookery in the Peninsula region, and **Livingston Island**, with its penguins and wallowing elephant seals. Next, you'll steam down to the Peninsula. You could take a Zodiac cruise in aptly named **Paradise Harbor** or along the rumbling glaciers above **Neko Harbor**, and head to the museum at **Port Lockroy**. Homeward bound, keep an eye out for a glimpse of **Cape Horn** off the port side.

14- to 21-day itinerary
The Ross Sea

The Ross Sea was the explorers' gateway to the South Pole. Starting from an Australian or New Zealand port, cross the Southern Ocean, stopping at Macquarie Island, Campbell Island, or the Auckland Islands, all famous for their breeding seabirds and windswept aspects. After a cruise past the icebound coasts of the **Balleny Islands**, visit the enormous Adélie penguin rookery at **Cape Adare**. Turn to starboard and head south into the Ross Sea for a knockout view towards the floating, France-sized **Ross Ice Shelf**. You'll pass Cape Washington, with one of the largest emperor-penguin colonies in the world. Next, visit **Ross Island**, site of the Mt Erebus volcano. If you're fortunate – and pack ice permits – you'll be able to visit Scott's Discovery hut at **Hut Point**, Shackleton's Nimrod hut at **Cape Royds** and Scott's Terra Nova hut at **Cape Evans**. Most cruises also visit the sprawling US **McMurdo Station** and/or New Zealand's ecofriendly **Scott Base** for a look at Antarctic scientific research before returning north to warmer climes.

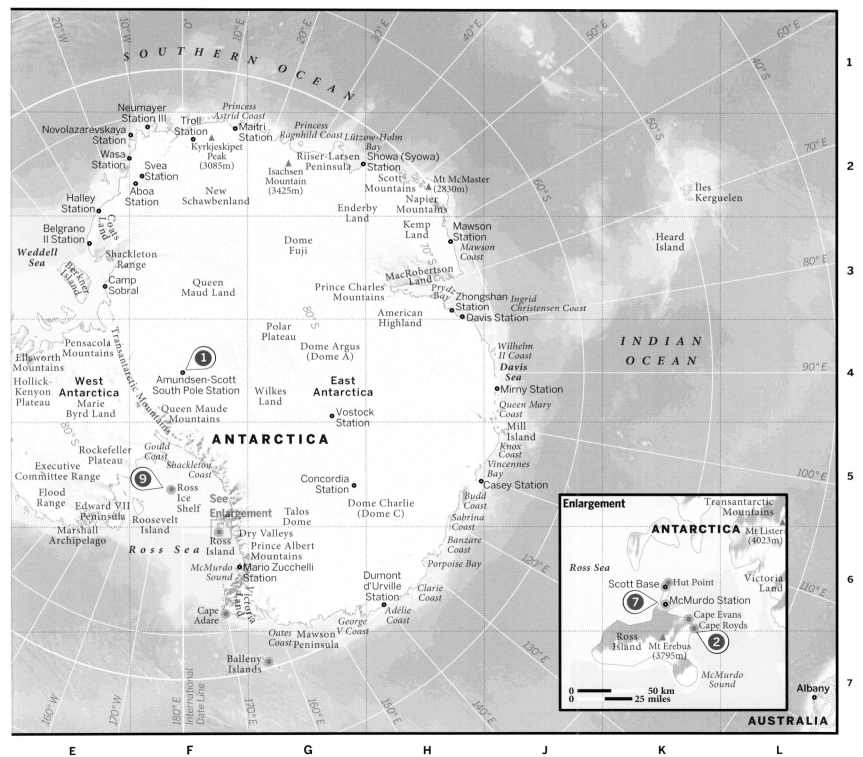

SIGHTS & ACTIVITIES

 SEE

 DO

ITINERARY

 1

 2

Rijksmuseum
Crowds huddle around Rembrandt's humongous *Night Watch* and Vermeer's *Kitchen Maid* in the Gallery of Honour, but that just means the the remaining 1.5km of rooms within the Netherlands' top treasure house are free for browsing savage-looking swords, crystal goblets and magic lanterns.

Van Gogh Museum
Housing the world's largest Vincent van Gogh collection, this museum is as much a tour through the driven painter's troubled mind as it is a tour through his body of work. Paintings by contemporaries Gauguin, Toulouse-Lautrec, Monet and Émile Bernard round out the retrospective.

Brown cafes
For a quintessential Amsterdam experience, pull up a stool in one of the famed *bruin cafés* (traditional Dutch pubs) such as In 't Aepjen. These cafes radiate a cosy vibe that prompts friends to linger and chat for hours over drinks – the same enchantment the cafes have cast for centuries.

Jordaan
The intimacy and *gezelligheid* (conviviality) of the old workers quarter is contagious, with modest old homes, offbeat galleries, tucked-away eateries, hidden courtyards, bustling markets and vintage shops peppering a grid of tiny lanes. This is the place for jovial bar singalongs and beery brown cafes.

Canal trips: A busy day on Oudezijds Voorburgwal, one of the city's oldest canals.

Vondelpark
Sublime for people-watching, this park is a sprawling urban oasis. Couples kiss on the grass, friends cradle beers at the outdoor cafes, while others trade songs on beat-up guitars. Street performers work the crowds, joggers and cyclists loop past, and kids romp in the playgrounds.

Albert Cuypmarkt
Amsterdam is market-mad and the Albert Cuypmarkt in De Pijp is king of the lot. Here stalls hawk rice cookers, spices and Dutch snacks, such as sweet *stroopwafels* (syrup-filled waffles).

Canal trips
Amsterdam has more canals than Venice and getting on the water is one of the best ways to feel the pulse of the city. Canal cruise operators depart from moorings at Centraal Station, Damrak, Rokin and opposite the Rijksmuseum.

Anne Frank Huis
Seeing Anne Frank's melancholy bedroom and her actual diary, preserved alone in its glass case, is a powerful experience. Step behind the bookcase that swings open to reveal the 'Secret Annexe' and go up the steep stairs into the living quarters.

Museum het Rembrandthuis
Housed in Rembrandt's former home, where the master painter spent his most successful years, painting big commissions such as *The Night Watch* and running the Netherlands' largest painting studio.

Oude Kerk
Dating back to around 1250, this Gothic-style church is Amsterdam's oldest building. Highlights include a stunning Müller organ, 15th-century choir stalls and the tombs of many famous Amsterdammers.

© Matt Munro / Lonely Planet

Day 1 itinerary
Begin with a tram to the Museum Quarter to ogle the masterpieces at the **Van Gogh Museum** and **Rijksmuseum** (make sure you've prebooked tickets). Modern-art buffs might want to swap the **Stedelijk Museum** for one of the others. They're all lined up in a walkable row. Then spend the afternoon in the **Medieval Centre**. Explore the secret courtyard and gardens at the **Begijnhof**. Walk up the street to the **Dam**, where the **Royal Palace**, **Nieuwe Kerk** and **Nationaal Monument** huddle and provide a dose of Dutch history. Bend over to sip your *jenever* (Dutch gin) like a local at **Wynand Fockink**. After dinner venture into the **Red Light District** before settling into a cosy brown cafe.

Days 2 and 3 itinerary
Start day two browsing the **Albert Cuypmarkt**, Amsterdam's largest street market. Then have brunch at **Bakers & Roasters** before crossing into the **Southern Canal Ring** to stroll along the grand **Golden Bend**. Visit **Museum Van Loon** for a peek into the opulent canal-house lifestyle, or get a dose of kitty quirk at the **Kattenkabinet**. Browse the **Bloemenmarkt** and behold the vast array of bulbs. When the sun sets, it's time to party at neon-lit square **Leidseplein**. On day three take a spin around beloved **Vondelpark** (all the better if you have a bicycle to zip by the ponds, gardens and sculptures). For lunch, head to the Western Canal Ring for timeless Dutch favourites at **Bistro Bij Ons**. Stay in the area to immerse yourself in the **Negen Straatjes**, a noughts-and-crosses board of speciality shops. The **Anne Frank Huis** is also in the neighbourhood, and it's a must. Spend your last evening in the **Jordaan**, the chummy district embodying the Amsterdam of yore. Hoist a glass on a canalside terrace at **'t Smalle** or join the houseboat party at **Café P 96**.

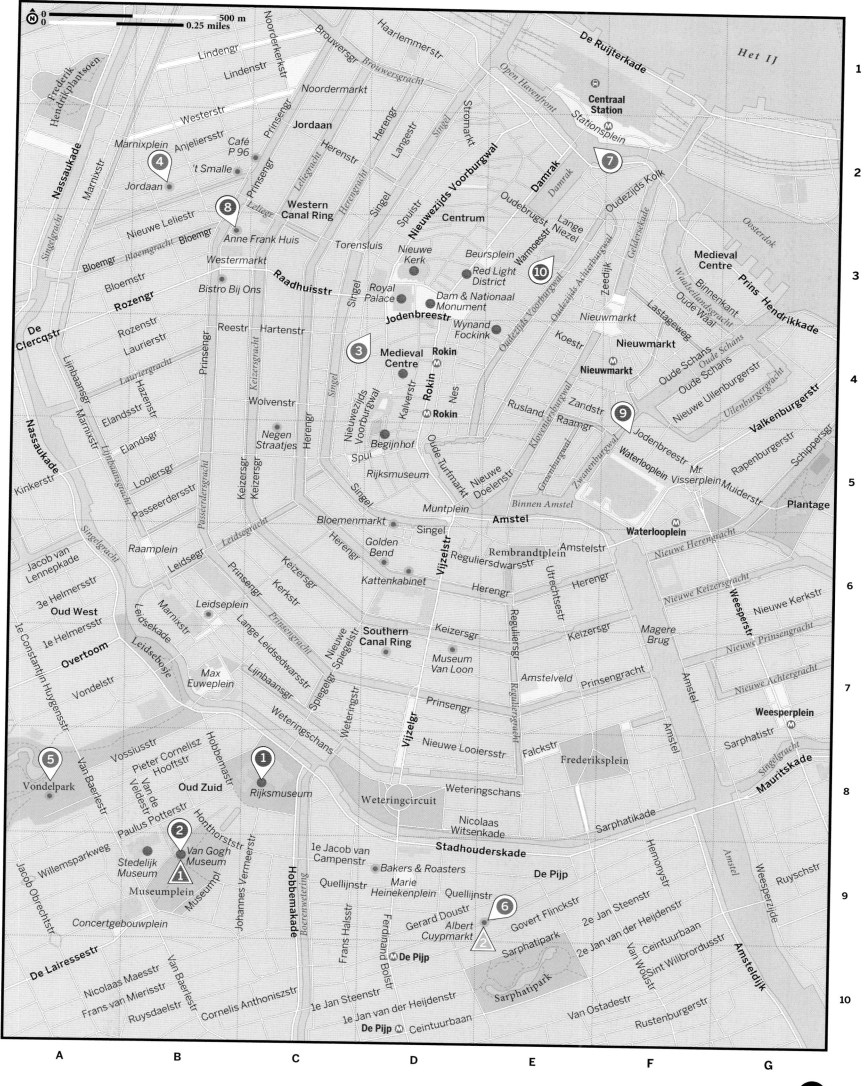

0 | **500 m**
0 | **0.25 miles**

Het IJ

De Ruijterkade

Open Havenfront

Centraal
Station

Stationsplein

Oosterdok

7

Noorderkerkst

Lindengr

Brouwersgr

Haarlemmerstr

Lindenstr

Westerstr

Noordermarkt

Brouwersgracht

Nieuwezijds Voorburgwal

Damrak

Oudezijds Kolk

Medieval
Centre

Prins Hendrikkade

Marnixplein

Anjeliersstr

Prinsengr

Jordaan

Herengr

Langestr

Stromarkt

Damrak

Gelderskade

Singel

4

Café
P 96

Herenstr

Herengracht

Centrum

Oudebrugst

Lange
Niezel

Zeedijk

Binnenkant

Walletjandgracht

Oude Waal

Jordaan

't Smalle

Prinsengr

Leliegracht

Singel

Spuistr

Oudezijds Voorburgwal

Warmoesstr

Lastageweg

Oude Schans

8

Nieuwe Leliestr

Leliegr

Western
Canal Ring

Beursplein

Oudezijds Achterburgwal

Nieuwmarkt

Oude Schans

Bloemgr

Anne Frank Huis

Torensluis

Nieuwe
Kerk

Red Light
District

10

Oudezijds Voorburgwal

Nieuwmarkt

Oude Schans

Bloemgracht

Bloemgr

Westermarkt

Royal
Palace

Dam & Nationaal
Monument

Nieuwe Uilenburgerstr

Bloemstr

Raadhuisstr

Singel

Jodenbreestr

Wynand
Fockink

Uilenburgergracht

Rozengr

Bistro Bij Ons

Klovenierswal

Nieuwmarkt

Valkenburgerstr

De
Clercqstr

Rozenstr

Reestr

Hartenstr

Medieval
Centre

Rokin

Koestr

9

Laurierstr

3

Rokin

Nes

Rusland

Zandstr

Jodenbreestr

Mr
Visserplein

Rapenburgerstr

Schippersgr

Hazenstr

Kalverstr

Raamgr

Waterlooplein

Muiderstr

Elandsstr

Wolvenstr

Nieuwezijds
Voorburgwal

Zwanenburgwal

Elandsgr

Negen
Straatjes

Herengr

Begijnhof

Oude Turfmarkt

Groenburgwal

Plantage

Looiersgr

Singel

Rijksmuseum

Nieuwe
Doelenstr

Binnen Amstel

Waterlooplein

Passeerdersstr

Keizersgr

Keizersgr

Spui

Muntplein

Amstel

Nieuwe Herengracht

Weesperstr

Nieuwe Kerkstr

Raamplein

Leidsegr

Bloemenmarkt

Singel

Rembrandtplein

Amstelstr

Jacob van
Lennepkade

Leidsegracht

Herengr

Golden
Bend

Vijzelstr

Reguliersdwarsstr

Utrechtsestr

Herengr

Nieuwe Keizersgracht

3e Helmersstr

Kerkstr

Kattenkabinet

Keizersgr

Keizersgr

Magere
Brug

Nieuwe Prinsengracht

1e Helmersstr

Marnixstr

Leidseplein

Prinsengr

Museum
Van Loon

Reguliersgr

Nieuwe Achtergracht

Oud West

Leidsekade

Lange Leidsedwarsstr

Southern
Canal Ring

Keizersgr

Prinsengracht

Weesperplein

Overtoom

Leidsebosje

Nieuwe
Spiegelstr

Reguliersgracht

Amstelveld

Amstel

Vondelstr

Max
Euweplein

Lijnbaansgr

Spiegelstr

Vijzelgr

Prinsengr

Sarphatistr

1e Constantijn Huygensstr

Weteringschans

Weteringstr

Nieuwe Looiersstr

Falckstr

Frederiksplein

Singelgracht

Mauritskade

5

Vossiusstr

Pieter Cornelisz
Hooftstr

Hobbemastr

1

Weteringschans

Vondelpark

Van Baerlestr

Van de
Veldestr

Oud Zuid

Rijksmuseum

Weteringcircuit

Nicolaas
Witsenkade

Stadhouderskade

Sarphatikade

Paulus Potterstr

2

Honthorststr

Van Gogh
Museum

1e Jacob van
Campenstr

Bakers & Roasters

De Pijp

Jacob Obrechtstr

Willemsparkweg

Stedelijk
Museum

1

Museumpl

Museumplein

Quellijnstr

Marie
Heinekenplein

Quellijnstr

Hemonystr

De Lairessestr

Johannes Vermeerstr

Gerard Doustr

Albert
Cuypmarkt

6

Govert Flinckstr

2e Jan Steenstr

Concertgebouwplein

Van Baerlestr

2

2e Jan van der Heijdenstr

Van Woustr

Sint Wilibrordusstr

Amsteldijk

Nicolaas Maesstr

Boerenwetering

Hobbemakade

Sarphatipark

Ceintuurbaan

Frans van Mierisstr

Ferdinand Bolstr

De Pijp

Sarphatipark

2e Jan van der Heijdenstr

Ruysdaelstr

Cornelis Anthoniszstr

Frans Halsstr

Quellijnstr

Van Ostadestr

Ruwschstr

Weesperzijde

De Pijp

Ceintuurbaan

1e Jan Steenstr

1e Jan van der Heijdenstr

Rustenburgerstr

① Open-air dining

Despite the modern conveniences of air-conditioning and contemporary cafes, some of the most memorable meals in the city (not coincidentally called the 'Big Mango') are had at the open-air markets and food stalls. In Bangkok locals snack throughout the day, packing away at least four meals before sunset. It would be rude not to join them. One of the top areas is Chinatown, which lures locals from across the city to eat at its many stalls.

② Jim Thompson's House

The late American entrepreneur used his traditional Thai-style home as a repository for age-old Thai traditions and artwork. He mysteriously disappeared in 1967 and today his home is a museum, one that every visitor secretly wishes to live in for a day or more. The garden is a miniature jungle of tropical plants and lotus ponds.

③ Banglamphu

Easily Bangkok's most charming neighbourhood, the city's former aristocratic enclave is now dominated by antique shophouses, backpackers seeking R&R on famous Th Khao San, bohemian artists and students, and vendor carts and classic restaurants.

④ Wat Phra Kaew

Architecturally fantastic, this temple complex is also the spiritual core of Thai Buddhism and the monarchy, symbolically united in what is the country's most holy image, the Emerald Buddha. Attached to the temple complex is the Grand Palace.

⑤ Wat Pho

Predating the city itself, Thailand's biggest temple is home to a 46m-long reclining Buddha figure. Symbolic of Buddha's death and passage into nirvana, the image is overlaid with gold leaf, making it truly larger than life.

⑥ Shopping

Bangkok's malls are just a warm-up for its markets, where footpaths are for additional retail space, not for pedestrians. In addition to Chatuchak Weekend Market – one of the world's largest markets – Bangkok is an established destination for bespoke tailoring. The strip of Th Sukhumvit between BTS stops at Nana and Asok in the neighbourhood of Thanon Sukhumvit is home to tonnes of tailors.

⑦ Mae Nam Chao Phraya

Mae Nam Chao Phraya (Chao Phraya River) is always teeming with activity: freighter boats trail behind tugs, river-crossing ferries skip across the wake, and children plunge into the muddy water. You can witness this from shore (ideally from Ko Ratanakosin or Thonburi), on a chartered long-tail boat or on a river taxi. As the blinding sun slips below the horizon, Bangkok suddenly looks serenely beautiful.

⑧ Chinatown

The neighbourhood's main artery, Th Yaowarat, is crowded with gold shops – sealed glass-front buildings that look more like Chinese altars than downtown jewellers. Likewise, the Buddha statue at Wat Traimit has more gold than you've likely ever seen in one place. And the pencil-thin lanes that branch off Talat Mai are decked with gold-leaf-coated goods. Throw in the blazing neon signs and smoky, open-air kitchens and you have an urban explorer's fantasy.

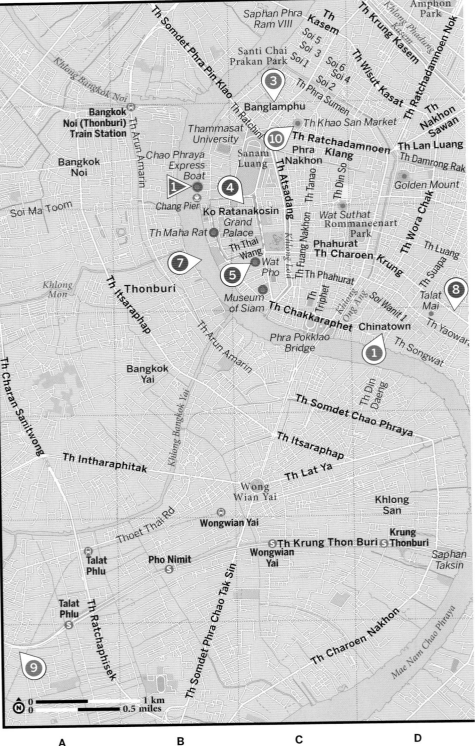

Day 1 itinerary

Get up early and take the **Chao Phraya Express Boat** north to Chang Pier to explore one of Ko Ratanakosin's museums, such as the **Museum of Siam**, as well as one of its must-see temples, like **Wat Pho**. After some street food for lunch on **Th Maha Rat**, freshen up with a spa treatment or Thai massage. Before dinner get a new perspective on Bangkok with a sunset rooftop cocktail at **Moon Bar**. Dine at **nahm**, which serves what is arguably the best Thai food in Bangkok, if not Thailand. If you've still got it in you, head over to **DJ Station**, **Telephone Pub** or any of the other bars and clubs in Bangkok's small but lively gay neighbourhood (Lower Silom).

Days 2 and 3 itinerary

Take the BTS (Skytrain) to **National Stadium** to start day two with a visit to **Jim Thompson's House**. Follow this by exploring the nearby canalside neighbourhood of **Baan Khrua** or by paying your respects at the **Erawan Shrine**. Next, walk through Bangkok's ultramodern commercial district, stopping off at its linked shopping centres, including **MBK Center**, **Siam Discovery**, **Siam Paragon** and **Siam Square**. Make time for a sweet snack or afternoon cuppa, or consider catching a Thai-boxing match at **Lumpinee Boxing Stadium**. Start day three by taking the **Chao Phraya Express Boat** to Chang Pier and set off on a long-tail boat tour of Thonburi's canals. Spend the afternoon shopping at the **Th Khao San Market** and visiting nearby sights, such as the **Golden Mount** and **Wat Suthat**. End the night with a Thai-themed cocktail at a cosy local, such as **WTF** or **Badmotel**, or a craft beer at **Hair of the Dog**. If it's still too early for you to turn in, pay a visit to a club such as **Glow** or **Beam**.

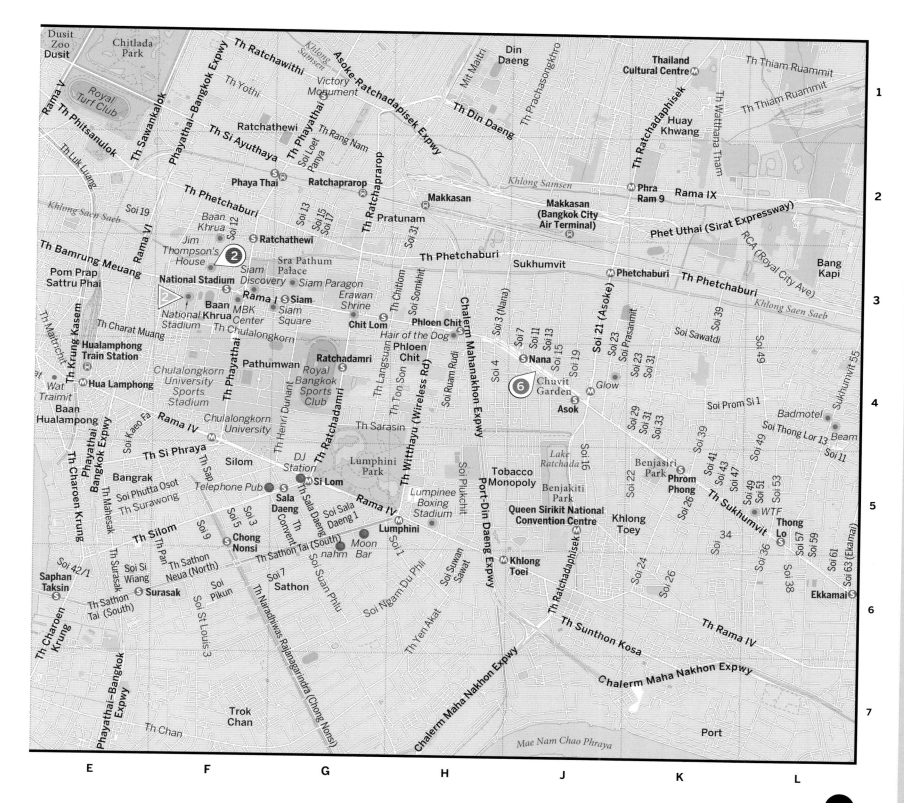

SIGHTS & ACTIVITIES

- SEE
- DO

ITINERARY

▽ 1

▽ 2

La Sagrada Família
This Modernista masterpiece remains a work in progress more than 90 years after the death of its creator, Antoni Gaudí. Fanciful and profound, inspired by nature and barely restrained by the Gothic style, Barcelona's quirky temple soars skyward with a playful majesty.

Modernista architecture
Weird and wonderful undulations of Antoni Gaudí's creations are echoed in countless Modernista flights of fancy across the city. You'll see shimmering mosaics, wild details and sculptural elements that reference nature, mythology and medieval days. One surely not to miss is Casa Batlló.

New Catalan cuisine
Barcelona's most celebrated chefs blend traditional Catalan recipes with new cooking techniques to create deliciously inventive masterpieces. The result is that Barcelona has become one of the world's great culinary destinations. La Ribera is a great place to start tasting – here you'll find these avant-garde chefs playing with fusion and technology cheek by jowl.

Museu Picasso
This museum – inside five contiguous medieval mansions – showcases perhaps the world's best collection of the master's early work. Picasso lived in Barcelona between the ages of 15 and 23, and elements of the city undoubtedly influenced his work. The courtyards, galleries and staircases are as delightful as the collection inside.

La Rambla: This broad pedestrian boulevard in Barcelona is flanked by plane trees.

Montjuïc
Head up this hill for fresh air and breathtaking views over the city, best enjoyed from the dizzy heights of a cable car. At any time of year it makes for a great day out, with endless parkland, themed gardens and museums to suit every taste.

Sant Antoni nightlife
Over the past few years the old Mercat Sant Antoni has truly bloomed. The opening of a few hip cafes sparked an influx of hipster pleasure-seekers and entrepreneurs, and this in turn has kick-started a slew of openings in the surrounding streets. There's now a lively strip of bars and restaurants.

Fundació Joan Miró
Joan Miró, the city's best-known 20th-century artistic progeny, bequeathed this art foundation to his hometown in 1971. Its light-filled buildings, designed by close friend Josep Lluís Sert are crammed with seminal works.

Mercat de la Boqueria
This temple of temptation is one of Europe's greatest permanent produce markets. Chefs stroll amid the endless bounty of glistening fruits and vegetables, gleaming fish counters, dangling rolls of smoked meats, pyramids of pungent cheeses and more.

La Rambla
This famous 1.2km-long pedestrian boulevard stretches towards the sea. It's pure sensory overload – with a parade of people amid open-air cafes, fragrant flower stands, a Miró mosaic and rather surreal human sculptures.

La Catedral
A masterpiece of Catalan Gothic architecture La Catedral is the main highlight of the Ciutat Vella (Old City). The facade dates from 1870 while the rest was built between 1298 and 1460. Wander wide-eyed through the shadow-filled interior, chapels, an eerie crypt and a garden-style cloister.

Day 1 itinerary

Spend the morning exploring the narrow medieval lanes of the **Barri Gòtic**. Have a peek inside **La Catedral** – not missing its geese-filled cloister – and stroll through the picturesque squares of **Plaça de Sant Josep Oriol** and **Plaça Reial**. Discover Barcelona's ancient roots in the fascinating **Museu d'Història de Barcelona**. Before lunch, have a wander down **La Rambla**. In the afternoon, head over to **La Ribera**, which is packed with architectural treasures. Visit the majestic **Basílica de Santa Maria del Mar** and the phenomenal **Museu Picasso**. Before having a customary late dinner, catch a show at the **Palau de la Música Catalana**, one of the city's great Modernista masterpieces.

Days 2 and 3 itinerary

Start day two with a visit to **La Sagrada Família** (it's worth paying a little extra for a guided tour, or audioguide). **Disfrutar**, which spreads a deliciously imaginative Catalan feast, is great for lunch. Next explore more of the great Modernista buildings by taking a turn down L'Eixample's **Passeig de Gràcia**. Have a look at the three most famous buildings that make up the **Manzana de la Discordia**. Then visit one of Gaudí's house museums on the street – either **Casa Batlló** or **La Pedrera** further up the avenue. In the evening check out the tapas bars in **El Born**. Start the third morning with a walk, jog or a bike ride along the waterfront. Post lunch, wander through Barceloneta, stopping for a glimpse inside the **Mercat de la Barceloneta** and for pastries at **Baluard**. Afterwards visit the **Museu d'Història de Catalunya**. The medieval streets of **El Call** make a magical setting for dinner. At night catch a live band in the Barri Gòtic – **Harlem Jazz Club** and **Jamboree** are good for jazz and world music. If you still have energy, check out a few bars off the beaten track, such as **L'Ascensor**.

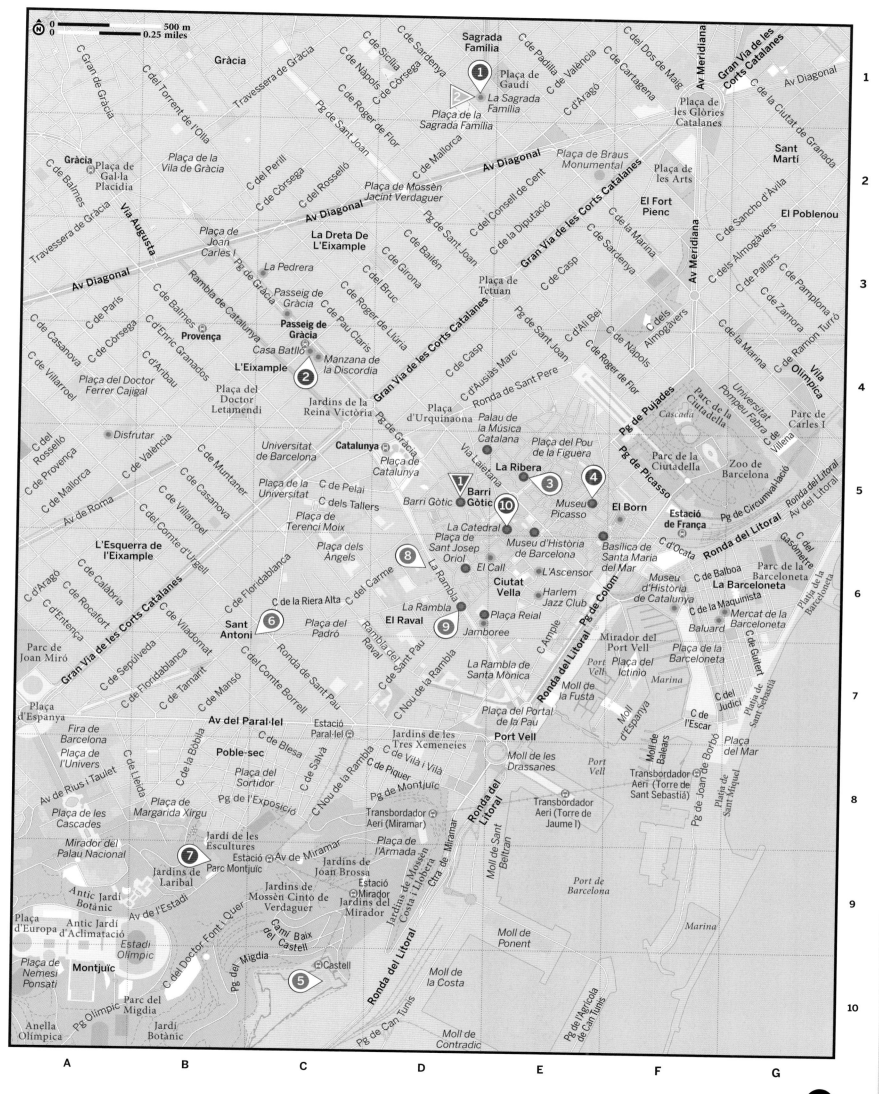

0
0
500 m
0.25 miles

1 Sagrada Família

C de Sicília
C de Sardenya
C del Dos de Maig
Av Meridiana
Gran Via de les Corts Catalanes

C de Padilla
C de València
C de Cartagena
Av Diagonal

1
Plaça de
Gaudí
C d'Aragó

2
La Sagrada
Família
Plaça de
les Glòries
Catalanes

Plaça de la
Sagrada Família

C de la Ciutat de Granada

Sant
Martí

Gràcia

C Gran de Gràcia
C del Torrent de l'Olla
Travessera de Gràcia

Plaça de la
Vila de Gràcia
C del Perill
C de Còrsega
C del Rosselló
C de Mallorca
Av Diagonal
Plaça de Braus
Monumental
Plaça de
les Arts

Gràcia
Plaça de
Gal·la
Placídia

C de Balmes

Via Augusta
Plaça de Mossèn
Jacint Verdaguer
Gran Via de les Corts Catalanes
El Fort
Pienc
C de Sancho d'Ávila
El Poblenou

Travessera de Gràcia
Av Diagonal
La Dreta De
L'Eixample
C de Bailén
C del Consell de Cent
C de la Diputació
C de la Marina
C de Casp
C de Sardenya
Av Meridiana
C dels Almogàvers
Vila
Olímpica

Plaça de
Joan
Carles I
La Pedrera
Rambla de Catalunya
Pg de Gràcia
C de Girona
C del Bruc
Plaça de
Tetuan
Pg de Sant Joan
C de Casp
C d'Ali Bei
C de Nàpols
C de la Marina
C de Ramon Turró
C de Zamora
C de Pamplona

Av Diagonal
C de París
C de Balmes
Passeig de
Gràcia
C de Roger de Llúria
C de Pau Claris
C dels
Almogàvers

C de Casanova
C d'Enric Granados
C d'Aribau
Provença
Passeig de
Gràcia
Casa Batlló
L'Eixample
2
Manzana de
la Discordia
C d'Ausiàs Marc
Ronda de Sant Pere
Pg de Sant Joan
Pg de Picasso

Plaça del Doctor
Ferrer Cajigal
Plaça del
Doctor
Letamendi
Jardins de la
Reina Victòria
Plaça
d'Urquinaona
Palau de
la Música
Catalana
Plaça del Pou
de la Figuera
Parc de la
Ciutadella
Cascada
Universitat
de Pompeu Fabra
Parc de
Carles I

C del
Rosselló
C de València
C de Provença
Disfrutar
Universitat
de Barcelona
Catalunya
Via Laietana
La Ribera
3
4
Museu
Picasso
Pg de Picasso
Parc de la
Ciutadella
Zoo de
Barcelona

C de Mallorca
C de Muntaner
C de Casanova
C de Villarroel
C del Comte d'Urgell
Plaça de
Catalunya
Plaça de la
Universitat
C de Pelai
C dels Tallers
1 Barri
Gòtic
10
Barri Gòtic
El Born
Estació
de França
Pg de Circumval·lació
Ronda del Litoral
Av del Litoral
Gasòmetre

Av de Roma
Plaça de
Terenci Moix
La Catedral
Plaça de
Sant Josep
Oriol
Museu d'Història
de Barcelona
Basílica de
Santa Maria
del Mar
C d'Ocata
Ronda del Litoral
Parc de la
Barceloneta

L'Esquerra de
l'Eixample
Plaça dels
Àngels
8
C del Carme
La Rambla
El Call
L'Ascensor
Museu
d'Història
de Catalunya
C de Balboa
La Barceloneta

C d'Aragó
C de Calàbria
C de Rocafort
C d'Entença
C de Floridablanca
C de la Riera Alta
Ciutat
Vella
La Rambla
Plaça Reial
Harlem
Jazz Club
C de la Maquinista
Baluard
Mercat de la
Barceloneta
Platja de la
Barceloneta

Gran Via de les Corts Catalanes
Sant
Antoni
6
Plaça del
Padró
Rambla del Raval
El Raval
La Rambla
9
Jamboree
Plaça del Portal
de la Pau
C Ample
Pg de Colom
Mirador del
Port Vell
Plaça de
la Barceloneta
C de Guiter
Platja de
Sant Sebastià

Parc de
Joan Miró
C de Sepúlveda
C de Floridablanca
C de Tamarit
C de Mansó
Ronda de Sant Pau
C Nou de la Rambla
La Rambla de
Santa Mònica
Ronda del Litoral
Plaça del
Ictinio
Marina
C de l'Escar
C del
Judici

Plaça
d'Espanya
Av del Paral·lel
Estació
Paral·lel
Jardins de les
Tres Xemeneies
Port Vell
Moll de les
Drassanes
Port
Vell
Transbordador
Aeri (Torre de
Sant Sebastià)
Plaça
del Mar

Fira de
Barcelona
Plaça de
l'Univers
C de la Bòbila
C de Blesa
C de Salva
Poble-sec
C de Vilà i Vilà
C de Piquer
Moll
d'Espanya
Moll de
Balears
Pg de Joan de Borbó
Platja de
Sant Miquel

Plaça de les
Cascades
Av de Rius i Taulet
C de Lleida
Plaça del
Sortidor
Pg de l'Exposició
C Nou de la Rambla
Pg de Montjuïc
Ronda del Litoral
Transbordador
Aeri (Torre de
Jaume I)
Port
Vell
Port de
Barcelona

Mirador del
Palau Nacional
Plaça de
Margarida Xirgu
Jardí de les
Escultures
7
Estació
Av de Miramar
Plaça de
l'Armada
Transbordador
Aeri (Miramar)
Moll de Sant Beltran
Moll de
Ponent

Jardins de
Laribal
Parc Montjuïc
Jardins de
Joan Brossa
Jardins de Mossèn
Costa i Llobera
Marina

Antic Jardí
Botànic
Av de l'Estadi
Estació
Mirador
Jardins de
Mossèn Cinto de
Verdaguer
Jardins del
Mirador

Plaça
d'Europa
Antic Jardí
d'Aclimatació
Estadi
Olímpic
Camí Baix
del Castell
Moll de
la Costa

Plaça de
Nemesi
Ponsati
Montjuïc
C del Doctor Font i Quer
Pg del Migdia
5 Castell
Ronda del Litoral
Ronda de Can Tunis

Anella
Olímpica
Pg Olímpic
Parc del
Migdia
Jardí
Botànic
Pg de Can Tunis
Moll de
Contradic
Pg de l'Agrícola
de Can Tunis

A   B   C   D   E   F   G

1   2   3   4   5   6   7   8   9   10

SIGHTS & ACTIVITIES

◉ SEE
◉ DO

ITINERARY

▽ 1
▽ 2

Forbidden City
The largest palace complex in the world, the Forbidden City encapsulates imperial Chinese grandeur, with imposing halls, splendid gates and age-old relics. No other place in Běijīng is invested with so much history, legend and intrigue.

Tiān'ānmén Square
The world's largest public square is a vast concrete desert at the heart of Běijīng. It's also a poignant epitaph to China's turbulent modern history. To stand in the middle, with kites flying high and the looming presence of the Forbidden City, is an experience unlike any other.

Běihǎi Park
Běihǎi Park is largely occupied by the North Sea (Běihǎi), a lake fringed by willows that freezes in winter and blooms with lotuses in summer. Old folk dance together outside temple halls and come twilight, young couples cuddle on benches. It's a restful place to stroll around, rent a rowing boat or watch calligraphers performing dìshū, inscribing characters on the ground with brushes and water.

Hútòng
The heart and soul of Běijīng are its hútòng: the alleyways that criss-cross the centre of the city. Still home for many locals, these intoxicating, unique lanes tie the capital to its historic past and a wander or cycle here offers the chance to experience street life in all its raucous glory.

Forbidden City: The Hall of Supreme Harmony is the largest structure in the Forbidden City.

Temple of Heaven Park
The ultimate expression of the eternal Chinese quest for order, Temple of Heaven Park is geometric perfection: a series of stunning shrines – including the iconic Hall of Prayer for Good Harvests – where the sons of heaven, China's emperors, came to pray for divine guidance.

National Museum of China
Běijīng's premier museum is housed in an immense 1950s Soviet-style building. You could spend a couple of hours in the Ancient China exhibition alone, with priceless artefacts, including ceramics, calligraphy, jade and bronze pieces.

Lama Temple
Central Běijīng's largest, most important and atmospheric Buddhist temple, this serene site used to be home to legions of monks from Mongolia and Tibet and was where the reincarnation of the Panchen Lama was determined.

Drum and Bell Towers
Standing watch over one of Běijīng's most charming corners, these two magnificent ancient towers were the city's timekeeper. Climb the Drum Tower to listen to a body-rumbling performance or ascend either for a perfect view of the surrounding hútòng.

Hòuhǎi Lakes
These three interconnected lakes are one of the city's great outdoor areas and a prime spot to join locals at play. In summer, flotillas of pedalos take to the water. During winter, the lakes transform to ice rinks. Then there's fishing, kayaking and swimming (for the brave).

Hóngqiáo Pearl Market
Hóngqiáo is home to more pearls than the South Sea. The range is huge (freshwater, seawater, white and black) and prices vary incredibly depending on quality. Vendors all speak some English.

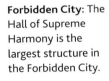

Day 1 itinerary

Head for **Temple of Heaven Park** at the crack of dawn, a time when it's filled with locals rather than tourists. Don't miss the park's crowning edifice, the magnificent **Hall of Prayer for Good Harvests** – Ming dynasty architectural perfection. After Peking duck for lunch, join the crowds of domestic tourists on their pilgrimage-like tour of China's most famous public space, **Tiān'ānmén Square**, before spending the afternoon exploring the immense palace grounds of the **Forbidden City**. It's a short walk to cute courtyard restaurant Little Yúnnán. Start your evening with cocktails in **Mao Mao Chong Bar**, north of **Little Yúnnán**, before catching some live music at **Yúgōng Yíshān** or **School Bar**.

Days 2 and 3 itinerary

Ease yourself into day two with a calming stroll around the incense-filled courtyards of the **Lama Temple** before visiting the equally peaceful and historic **Confucius Temple**. After coffee and lunch, wander through the hútòng to the magnificent **Drum Tower**. Catch one of the drumming performances here before hopping across the square to climb the equally majestic **Bell Tower**. Try lunch at the tranquil **Bǎihé Vegetarian Restaurant**, popular with the monks from the Lama Temple. In the late afternoon, locals congregate in the square for formation dancing and you're welcome to join in. Have a few drinks after dinner by the lakeside on the **Hòuhǎi Bar Strip**. Spend day three touring the lakes in the eastern part of the city. Take in **Běihǎi Park** first, perhaps spending an hour or more floating around its lake before striking out through the park's north gate to take in the sights and hútòng scattered around the **Hòuhǎi Lakes**. Once night falls, eat at one of the many restaurants close to the lakes and then join the crowds promenading around them, stopping in for a drink at the many bars lining the shores.

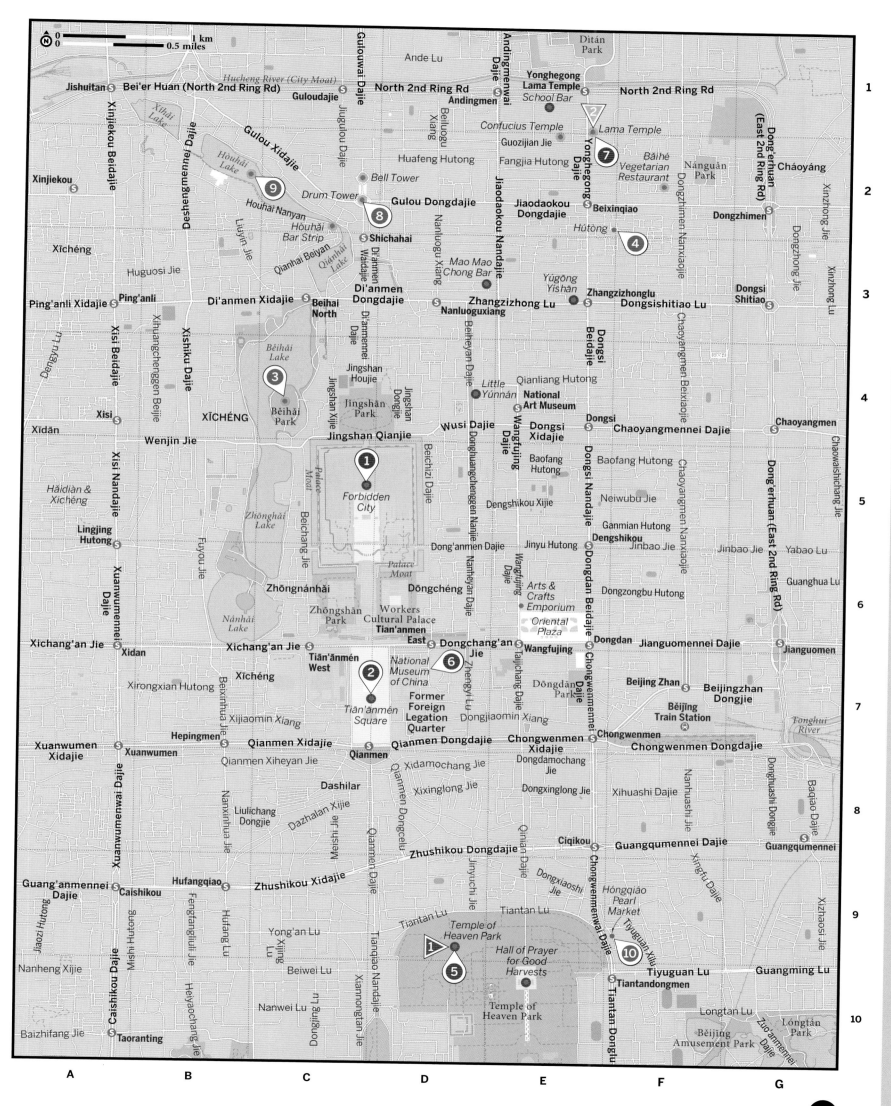

Map labels

1

0 — 1 km
0 — 0.5 miles

Ande Lu

Ditán Park

Hucheng River (City Moat)

Jishuitan · Bei'er Huan (North 2nd Ring Rd) · Guloudajie · North 2nd Ring Rd · Andingmen · North 2nd Ring Rd

Andingmenwai Dajie

Yonghegong Lama Temple

School Bar

2 Lama Temple

Xinjiekou Beidajie

Xihǎi Lake

Gulou Xidajie

Confucius Temple

Guozijian Jie

Fangjia Hutong

Bǎihé Vegetarian Restaurant

Nánguān Park

Dong'erhuan (East 2nd Ring Rd)

Cháoyáng

Xinzhong Jie

7 Yonghegong Dajie

Xinjiekou

Hòuhǎi Lake

9

Drum Tower **8**

Bell Tower

Gulou Dongdajie

Jiaodaokou Dongdajie

Beixinqiao

Dongzhimen

Houhai Nanyan

Hòuhǎi Bar Strip

Shichahai

Di'anmen Waidajie

Nanluogu Xiang

Hútòng **4**

Dongzhimen Nanxiaojie

Dongsi Shitiao

Xīchéng

Huguosi Jie

Qianhai Beiyan

Qiánhǎi Lake

Mao Mao Chong Bar

Yūgōng Yíshān

Dongzhong Lu

Ping'anli Xidajie · Ping'anli

Di'anmen Xidajie

Beihai North

Di'anmen Dongdajie

Zhangzizhong Lu

Zhangzizhonglu

Dongsishitiao Lu

Dongsi Shitiao

Dengqu Lu

Xihuangchenggen Beijie

Xishiku Dajie

XĪCHÉNG

Bĕihǎi Lake

3

Bĕihǎi Park

Jingshan Houjie

Jingshan Park

Jingshan Dongjie

Nanluoguxiang

Qianliang Hutong

Dongsi

National Art Museum

Dongsi Beidajie

Chaoyangmen Beixiaojie

Chaoyangmen

Xisi

Xisi Nandajie

Wenjin Jie

Jingshan Qianjie

Wusi Dajie

Dongsi Xidajie

Chaoyangmennei Dajie

Chaowaishichang Jie

Xīdān

Hǎidiàn & Xīchéng

Beichizi Dajie

Dong'anmennei Nanjie

Dongsi Nandajie

Baofang Hutong

Dengshikou Xijie

Neiwubu Jie

Ganmian Hutong

Lingjing Hutong

1 Forbidden City

Palace Moat

Zhōnghǎi Lake

Beichang Jie

Dengshikou

Jinbao Jie

Jinbao Jie

Yabao Lu

Dong'erhuan (East 2nd Ring Rd)

Fuyou Jie

Zhōngnánhǎi

Palace Moat

Dong'anmen Dajie

Nanheyan Dajie

Jinyu Hutong

Guanghua Lu

Zhōngshān Park

Workers Cultural Palace

Tian'anmen

Arts & Crafts Emporium

Dongzongbu Hutong

Nánhǎi Lake

Oriental Plaza

Dongdan Beidajie

Xichang'an Jie

Xidan

Xichang'an Jie

Tian'anmen East

Dongchang'an Jie **6**

Wangfujing

Dongdan

Jianguomennei Dajie

Jianguomen

Tiān'ānmén West

2

National Museum of China

Tiān'ānmén Square

Zhengyi Lu

Tajichang Dajie

Dōngdān Park

Chongwenmennei

Beijing Zhan

Beijing Train Station

Beijingzhan Dongjie

Xirongxian Hutong

XĪCHÉNG

Beixinhua Jie

Former Foreign Legation Quarter

Dongjiaomin Xiang

Tonghui River

Xuanwumen Xidajie

Xuanwumen

Xijiaomin Xiang

Hepingmen

Qianmen Xidajie

Qianmen Dongdajie

Chongwenmen Xidajie

Chongwenmen

Chongwenmen Dongdajie

Qianmen Xiheyan Jie

Qianmen

Dashilar

Xidamochang Jie

Dongdamochang Jie

Xihuashi Dajie

Nanhuashi Jie

Donghuashi Dongjie

Baqiao Dajie

Liulichang Dongjie

Dazhalan Xijie

Nanxinhua Jie

Xixinglong Jie

Dongxinglong Jie

Ciqikou

Guangqumennei Dajie

Guangqumennei

Zhushikou Dongdajie

Qinan Dajie

Chongwenmenwai Dajie

Xingfu Dajie

Xizhaosi Jie

Guang'anmennei Dajie

Caishikou

Hufangqiao

Zhushikou Xidajie

Qianmen Dongcelu

Hóngqiáo Pearl Market

Tiyuguan Xilu

Fengfangliuli Jie

Jinyuchi Jie

Dongxiaoshi Jie

10 Tiyuguan Lu

Guang'anmennei Dajie

Jiaozi Hutong

Mishi Hutong

Hufang Lu

Tiantan Lu

Tiantan Lu

Temple of Heaven Park

Hall of Prayer for Good Harvests

Tiyuguan Lu · Tiantandongmen

Guangming Lu

Nanheng Xijie

Yong'an Lu

Yong'an Lu Xijing Lu

1

5

Tiantan Dongli

Longtan Lu

Lóngtán Park

Caishikou Dajie

Nanheng Xijie

Beiwei Lu

Xiannongtan Jie

Temple of Heaven Park

Bĕijīng Amusement Park

Zuo'anmennei Dajie

Baizhifang Jie

Taoranting

Nanwei Lu

Heiyaochang Jie

Tiangiao Nandajie

1 · 2 · 3 · 4 · 5 · 6 · 7 · 8 · 9 · 10

A · B · C · D · E · F · G

SIGHTS & ACTIVITIES

 SEE

 DO

ITINERARY

 1

 2

1 Brandenburg Gate
Prussian kings, Napoleon and Hitler have marched through this neoclassical royal city gate that was once trapped east of the Berlin Wall. Since 1989 it has gone from a symbol of division and oppression to the symbol of unification.

2 Reichstag
Before its current iteration as the home of the German parliament and the focal point of the reunited country's government quarter, this historic landmark – now topped with a dazzling glass dome – has been set on fire, bombed, left to crumble, and even wrapped in fabric as part of an art installation.

3 Berlin Wall
Although little is left of the physical barrier that separated East from West between 1961 and 1989, its legacy lives on in the imagination, and in such places as Checkpoint Charlie, the Gedenkstätte Berliner Mauer and the East Side Gallery.

4 Nightlife
The techno temple Berghain (named after the neighbourhood it calls home) may be Berlin's most famous club, but nightlife booms everywhere: gothic raves to hip-hop hoedowns, craft-beer pubs to riverside bars, beer gardens to underground dives.

5 Museumsinsel
Berlin's 'Louvre on the Spree', this imposing ensemble of five treasure houses is the undisputed highlight of the city's museum landscape. Declared a Unesco World Heritage site, Museum Island represents 6000 years of art and cultural history.

6 Potsdamer Platz
No other area better reflects the 'New Berlin' than this quarter forged from the death strip that separated East and West Berlin. It's a postmodern take on the historic area that was once Berlin's equivalent of Times Square. A cluster of plazas, offices, museums, cinemas, theatres, hotels and flats, it shows off the talents of seminal architects of our times, including Helmut Jahn and Renzo Piano.

7 Holocaust Memorial
Listen to the sound of your footsteps and feel the presence of uncounted souls as you walk through the massive warped labyrinth that is Germany's central memorial to the Jewish victims of the Nazi-orchestrated genocide.

8 Counter-culture
Berlin has a uniquely unbridled climate of openness and tolerance that fosters experimentation, a DIY ethos and a thriving subculture. Hip and funky Kreuzberg, Friedrichshain and northern Neukölln are all trendsetting laboratories of diversity and creativity.

9 Schloss Charlottenburg
Berlin's largest and loveliest remaining royal palace, this late-baroque jewel was inspired by Versailles. It backs up against an idyllic park, complete with carp pond, rhododendron-lined paths, two smaller palaces and a mausoleum.

10 Kulturforum
West Berlin's answer to Museumsinsel, and a similarly enthralling cluster of cultural venues, Kulturforum hosts one of the city's most important art museums, the Gemäldegalerie. It wows fans with Old Masters from Rembrandt to Vermeer.

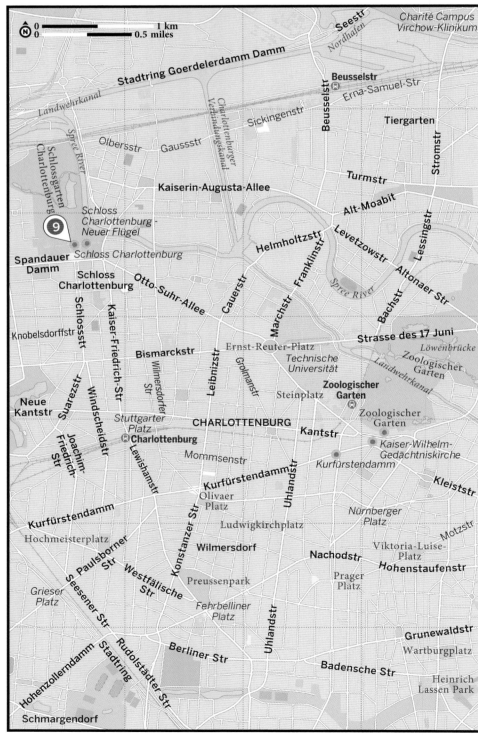

Day 1 itinerary

Having booked ahead, visit the **Reichstag** early, then snap a picture of the **Brandenburg Gate** before absorbing the **Holocaust Memorial**. It's a short walk to admire the contemporary architecture of **Potsdamer Platz**. View the **Berlin Wall** remnants, then head to **Checkpoint Charlie** to ponder the Cold War madness.

After lunch, soak up the glory of **Gendarmenmarkt**, drop by **Rausch Schokoladenhaus** for a chocolate treat and get a dose of retail therapy at the **Friedrichstadtpassagen**. Then follow **Unter den Linden** east to the **Museumsinsel** and marvel at the antiquities in the **Pergamonmuseum**. After dinner, stroll over to **Clärchens Ballhaus** for a dance.

Days 2 and 3 itinerary

Begin the second day by spending a couple of hours coming to grips with what life in Berlin was like when the Wall still stood by exploring the **Gedenkstätte Berliner Mauer**. Take a quick spin around **Mauerpark**, then poke around the boutiques on **Kastanienallee**. Start the afternoon at the stunning **Neues Museum**, then relax on a river cruise around Museumsinsel. After dinner, go bar-hopping around **Kottbusser Tor**. Day three starts at **Schloss Charlottenburg**, where the **Neuer Flügel** (New Wing) and the palace garden are essential stops. Take the bus to **Zoologischer Garten** and meditate upon the futility of war at the **Kaiser-Wilhelm-Gedächtniskirche**, then satisfy your shopping cravings along **Kurfürstendamm**. In the afternoon visit the amazing Daniel Libeskind–designed **Jüdisches Museum**, before heading down to the wide open fields of **Tempelhofer Feld** to see how an old airport can be recycled into a sustainable park and playground. Finish the day at the bars on **Weserstrasse** and its side streets.

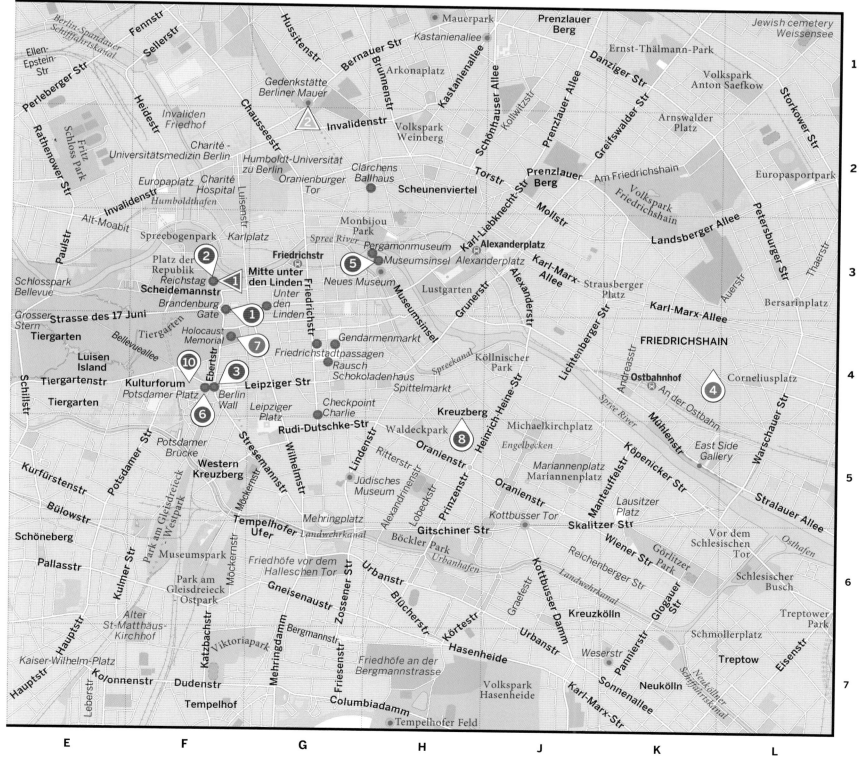

SIGHTS & ACTIVITIES

 SEE

 DO

ITINERARY

 1

 2

Cementerio de la Recoleta

Meander through the maze of narrow lanes lined with elaborate mausoleums in what must be the world's most ostentatious necropolis. Some of Argentina's most illustrious historical figures are buried in this 'city of the dead', including Eva Perón ('Evita').

Tango

Nothing captures the essence of Buenos Aires like the sensual and melancholy tango, and no visit to the city is complete without experiencing it in some form. Head to a *milonga* (dance event), held at dozens of venues, or take a class. La Catedral, south of Palermo, is the perfect place to take your first step.

Plaza de Mayo

Founded in 1580 and home to Casa Rosada presidential palace, this is the stage on which many of the dramatic events in Argentina's history were played out, from military bombings in 1955 and Evita's emotional speeches to massive union demonstrations (still going today).

Watching football

Fútbol inspires near-religious passion in *porteños*, clearing the streets and sending spectators into fits of ecstasy and anguish as they huddle around TV screens. Join them, or brave the explosive and boisterous crowds at La Bombonera Stadium to watch the Boca Juniors kick off. On match days the streets around La Bombonera are a sea of yellow and blue.

Cycling: Jacaranda trees in Buenos Aires bloom in vivid lilac come springtime.

Steak in Palermo Viejo

Believe the hype: Argentine beef is some of the best in the world. Eat, drink and be merry at a *parrilla* (steakhouse), where a leisurely meal begins with waiters pouring malbec and carving generous slabs of prime beef. The sub-neighbourhood of Palermo Viejo is home to dozens of restaurants.

San Telmo

This neighbourhood is a beguiling mix of faded grandeur and bohemian spirit. Wander along Defensa or Balcarce streets toward leafy Parque Lezama, taking in picturesque vistas of romantic facades and drooping balconies as you window-shop for antiques. Come on Sunday for the famous street fair.

Street art

Buenos Aires has become a canvas for talented street artists from all over the world, who come here to paint in collaboration with local graffiti superstars. Some of the best examples are found in leafy San Telmo.

Cycling

With an extensive network of cycle lanes and a free city bike programme, there is no better way to explore the city than on two wheels. A bike tour – especially around Palermo's green parks – is a relaxed way to get started. Here, miles of safe bike lanes exist.

Reserva Ecológica

In the shadow of Puerto Madero's shiny skyscrapers, an incredible nature reserve emerged from an area of abandoned, marshy wasteland. These days the remarkable park is home to hundreds of birds, colourful butterflies, turtles and iguanas. Take a walk along the paths that loop up past the coastline of the Río de la Plata and you'll soon feel far from the city amid refreshing river breezes, peace and a sense of space.

Day 1 itinerary

Start your BA experience with a stroll through San Telmo's cobbled streets while window-shopping. On Sunday, the famous **Feria de San Telmo** street market takes over the neighbourhood. Book a tour to the stunning **El Zanjón de Granados** for a peek into the city's origins. After lunch, explore the colourful corrugated houses along **El Caminito**. Art-lovers shouldn't miss **Fundación Proa**, a cutting-edge gallery, while football fans can head to **La Bombonera** and visit the **Museo de la Pasión Boquense**. If it's Wednesday, take a tango class in the evening then watch the dancing at **Maldita Milonga**. Or go drinking at a watering hole, such as the upscale cocktail bar **Doppelgänger**.

Days 2 and 3 itinerary

Spend your second morning walking or cycling the paths of Palermo's **Parque 3 de Febrero**. After lunch in a *parrilla*, visit **Museo de Arte Latinoamericano de Buenos Aires** (MALBA), a beautiful art museum. The **Museo Nacional de Arte Decorativo** is another must-see, as is **Museo Evita** for Eva Perón fans. Palermo is nightlife central, so begin with wine at **Pain et Vin** then head to **Uptown** for cocktails and dancing. On day three start from leafy **Plaza San Martín**, walking south on pedestrian **Florida** to experience the shopping and busking. Next, take in **Plaza de Mayo**, the heart of the city and surrounded by **Casa Rosada**, **Catedral Metropolitana** and **Cabildo**. After eating al fresco in **Puerto Madero**, check out the renovated old brick warehouses. The neighbourhood's pleasantly vehicle-free cobbled paths along the dykes are great for a stroll. Don't miss the eclectic **Colección de Arte Amalia Lacroze de Fortabat**. For a shot of nature, visit **Reserva Ecológica Costanera Sur**. Finish with an opera, ballet or classical-music show at **Teatro Colón**.

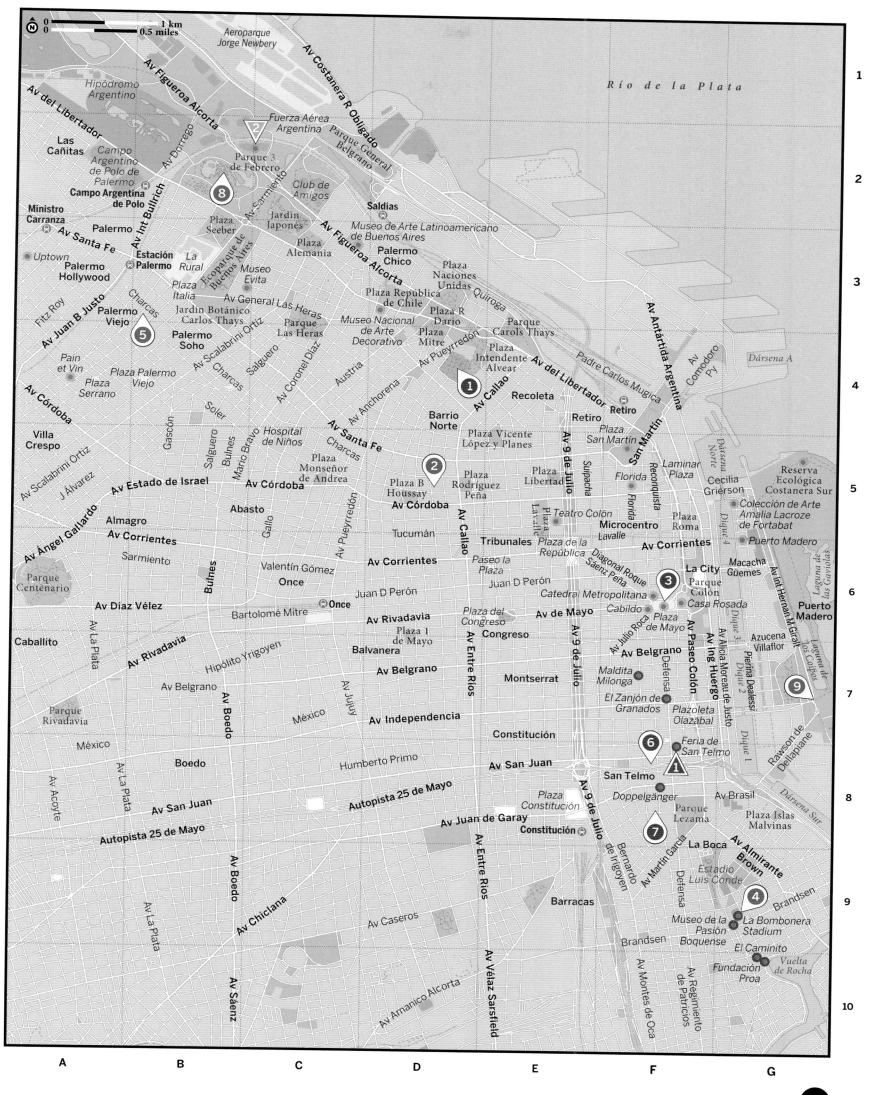

Río de la Plata

0   1 km
0   0.5 miles

Aeroparque
Jorge Newbery

Av Costanera R Obligado

Av Figueroa Alcorta

Hipódromo
Argentino

Av del Libertador

Las
Cañitas

Fuerza Aérea
Argentina

Parque General
Belgrano

Campo
Argentino
de Polo de
Palermo

Av Dorrego

Parque 3
de Febrero

Campo Argentina
de Polo

Ministro
Carranza

Palermo

Av Int Bullrich

Club de
Amigos

Saldías

Av Santa Fe

Uptown

Estación
Palermo

Plaza
Seeber

Jardín
Japonés

Av Sarmiento

Museo de Arte Latinoamericano
de Buenos Aires

Palermo
Hollywood

La
Rural

Ecoparque de
Buenos Aires

Plaza
Alemania

Av Figueroa Alcorta

Palermo
Chico

Plaza
Naciones
Unidas

Av Antártida Argentina

Fitz Roy

Plaza
Italia

Museo
Evita

Quiroga

Av Juan B Justo

Charcas

Palermo
Viejo

Jardín
Botánico
Carlos Thays

Plaza República
de Chile

Plaza R
Darío

Parque
Carols Thays

Av Comodoro Py

Dársena A

Paín
et Vin

Palermo
Soho

Parque
Las Heras

Museo Nacional
de Arte
Decorativo

Plaza
Mitre

Plaza
Intendente
Alvear

Padre Carlos Mugica

Av Córdoba

Plaza Palermo
Viejo

Av Scalabrini Ortiz

Charcas

Salguero

Austria

Av Anchorena

Av Puerrredón

Av Callao

Av del Libertador

Recoleta

Retiro

Plaza
San Martín

Retiro

Dársena
Norte

Reserva
Ecológica
Costanera Sur

Plaza
Serrano

Av Córdoba

Soler

Gascón

Av Coronel Díaz

Av Santa Fe

Barrio
Norte

Plaza Vicente
López y Planes

San Martín

Laminar
Plaza

Villa
Crespo

Av Scalabrini Ortiz

J Álvarez

Salguero

Bulnes

Mario Bravo

Hospital
de Niños

Charcas

Plaza
Monseñor
de Andrea

Plaza B
Houssay

Plaza
Rodríguez
Peña

Plaza
Libertad

Florida

Reconquista

Cecilia
Grierson

Colección de Arte
Amalia Lacroze
de Fortabat

Av Estado de Israel

Av Ángel Gallardo

Almagro

Abasto

Gallo

Av Córdoba

Tucumán

Av Callao

Teatro Colón

Microcentro

Florida

Plaza
Roma

Puerto Madero

Parque
Centenario

Av Corrientes

Sarmiento

Valentín Gómez

Once

Juan D Perón

Av Corrientes

Tribunales

Lavalle

Plaza
Lavalle

Av Corrientes

Macacha
Güemes

Av Díaz Vélez

Bulnes

Bartolomé Mitre

Once

Av Rivadavia

Paseo la
Plaza

Plaza de la
República

Juan D Perón

Diagonal Roque
Sáenz Peña

La City

Parque
Colón

Av Int Hernan M Giralt

Puerto
Madero

Caballito

Av La Plata

Av Rivadavia

Hipólito Yrigoyen

Plaza del
Congreso

Plaza 1
de Mayo

Av de Mayo

Catedral Metropolitana

Cabildo

Casa Rosada

Plaza
de Mayo

Azucena
Villaflor

Congreso

Balvanera

Av Belgrano

Av Entre Ríos

Av Belgrano

Montserrat

Av Julio Roca

Av Belgrano

Maldita
Milonga

Defensa

Av Paseo Colón

Av Ing Huergo

Pierina Dealessi

Parque
Rivadavia

Av Belgrano

Av Jujuy

México

Av Independencia

El Zanjón de
Granados

Plazoleta
Olazábal

México

Boedo

Av Boedo

Humberto Primo

Constitución

Feria de
San Telmo

Av San Juan

Av San Juan

Autopista 25 de Mayo

Plaza
Constitución

San Telmo

Doppelgänger

Av Brasil

Av Almirante Brown

Plaza Islas
Malvinas

Av Acoyte

Av La Plata

Av San Juan

Av Juan de Garay

Constitución

Av 9 de Julio

Parque
Lezama

Autopista 25 de Mayo

Av Boedo

México

Av Entre Ríos

La Boca

Estadio
Luis Conde

Defensa

Av Chiclana

Av Caseros

Barracas

Bernardo de Irigoyen

Av Martín García

Brandsen

Museo de la
Pasión
Boquense

La Bombonera
Stadium

Brandsen

Av La Plata

Av Sáenz

Av Amancio Alcorta

Av Vélaz Sarsfield

Av 9 de Julio

Av Montes de Oca

El Caminito

Fundación
Proa

Av Regimiento
de Patricios

Vuelta
de Rocha

Dársena Sur

Rawson de
Dellapiane

SIGHTS & ACTIVITIES

◉ SEE
◉ DO

ITINERARY

▽ 1
▽ 2

1 Table Mountain
Whether you ride the revolving cableway or put in the leg work and climb, reaching the summit of Table Mountain is a Capetonian rite of passage. Rewards are a panoramic view across the peninsula and a chance to experience some of the park's astonishing biodiversity.

2 Bo-Kaap
Painted in vivid colours straight out of a packet of liquorice allsorts, the jumble of crumbling and restored heritage houses and mosques along the cobblestoned streets of the Bo-Kaap are both visually captivating and a storybook of inner-city gentrification. The Bo-Kaap Museum provides an understanding of this former slave quarter. Try Cape Malay dishes at one of the area's several restaurants.

3 Cape of Good Hope
Make the spectacular journey out to this historic headland, and onward to Cape Point, the dramatic tip of the peninsula: rugged cliffs shoot down into the frothing waters of the Atlantic Ocean; giant waves crash over enormous boulders; and the Flying Dutchman Funicular runs up to the old lighthouse for fantastic views.

4 Kalk Bay
This delightful False Bay fishing village on the Cape Peninsula offers an abundance of antique, arts and craft shops and great cafes and restaurants, as well as a daily fish market at its harbour. Eat or drink at institutions such as the Brass Bell pub or Live Bait.

Robben Island: The island was used as a prison from the early days of the VOC (Dutch East India Company) until 1996.

5 Kirstenbosch National Botanical Garden
This historic garden is a spectacular showcase for the Cape Floral Kingdom, which was given Unesco World Heritage status for its incredible biodiversity. Take in the view from the treetop walkway known as the Boomslang.

6 Robben Island
This former prison and Unesco World Heritage site is a key location in South Africa's long walk to freedom. Many anti-apartheid heroes were incarcerated here, including Nelson Mandela for 18 years. The boat journey and the tour with former inmates provides a powerful insight into the country's history.

7 District Six Museum
More than 40 years on from when most of the homes in the inner-city suburb of District Six were demolished, and their multi-ethnic owners and tenants relocated to the blighted communities in the Cape Flats, the area remains largely barren. A visit to this illuminating museum provides an understanding of District Six's tragic history and the impact it has had on the lives of all of Capetonians. You can also arrange a walking tour of the area, led by a former resident.

8 V&A Waterfront
Big, busy and in a spectacular location, with Table Mountain as a backdrop, this waterfront offers a pirate's booty of opportunities: shopping in chic boutiques; cultural and educational experiences, including walking tours; the Two Oceans Aquarium, and the spectacular new Zeitz Museum of Contemporary African Art (MOCAA).

9 Kommetjie
A top surfing location on the Atlantic side of the Cape Peninsula, Kommetjie offers an assortment of reefs that hold a very big swell. Outer Kommetjie is a left point out from Slangkop Lighthouse, while Inner Kommetjie is a more protected, smaller left.

10 Constantia Wine Route
Spend a blissful afternoon exploring wineries. Target historic ones, such as Groot Constantia, which has a beautifully restored homestead and wine cellar, and Klein Constantia, producer of Napoleon's favourite tipple. The more contemporary Steenberg Farm has delicious wines and a wonderful bistro.

11 Guga S'Thebe Arts & Cultural Centre
Decorated with polychromatic ceramic murals, this is one of the most impressive buildings in the Cape townships – even more so now that it has a theatre, creatively constructed from recycled materials. Watch pottery being made, buy samples and enjoy performances by local groups.

Day 1 itinerary

Take the **Table Mountain Aerial Cableway**, its revolving car providing 360-degree views. From the upper cableway station it's about an hour's round-trip hike to the 1088m summit at **Maclear's Beacon**. Enjoy a postprandial stroll through the **Company's Garden**, pop into **St George's Cathedral** or the

Iziko Slave Lodge, then head uphill into the old Cape Malay quarter, the **Bo-Kaap**. Continue over into **De Waterkant** for more prettily restored cottages and the shops of the Cape Quarter mall. Catching the sunset with a cocktail in hand is a must – whether it be from along the **Sea Point Promenade** or the picturesque **Camps Bay Beach**.

Days 2 and 3 itinerary

Start day two at the 350-year-old **Castle of Good Hope**, then watch the noon key ceremony. Across the road is the handsome **Cape Town City Hall**, where Mandela made his famous speech after being released from prison. Next, take your time to absorb **District Six Museum** before checking out some contemporary art galleries and

the abundant street art around the **Woodstock Exchange**. Spend the rest of the afternoon at the **V&A Waterfront**, including the new **Zeitz MOCAA**, before boarding a sunset harbour cruise into Table Bay. On day three explore the beautiful **Kirstenbosch National Botanical Garden**, and wander around

lovely **Wynberg Village** and its old thatched-roof cottages. Following an afternoon on the **Constantia Wine Route**, head over Constantia Nek to enjoy the view of Hout Bay from the deck of the **Chapman's Peak Hotel** or beachside pub **Dunes**. If it's Friday night, the **Bay Harbour Market** will have live music and tasty eats.

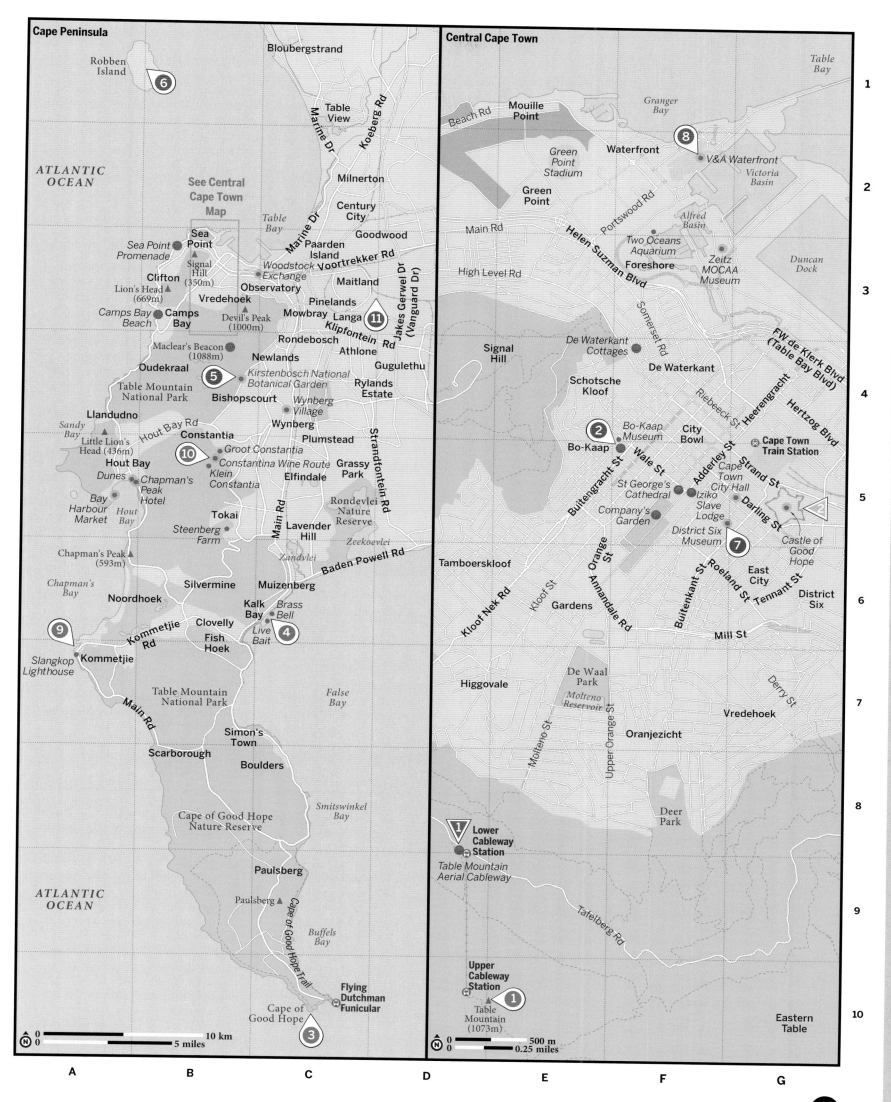

Cape Peninsula

Robben Island 6

Bloubergstrand

Table Bay

Table View

Marine Dr

Koeberg Rd

ATLANTIC OCEAN

See Central Cape Town Map

Milnerton

Century City

Goodwood

Table Bay

Sea Point Promenade

Sea Point

Signal Hill (350m)

Woodstock Exchange

Paarden Island

Voortrekker Rd

Clifton

Lion's Head (669m)

Vredehoek

Observatory

Maitland

Camps Bay Beach

Camps Bay

Devil's Peak (1000m)

Mowbray

Pinelands

Langa 11

Jakes Gerwel Dr (Vanguard Dr)

Maclear's Beacon (1088m)

Newlands

Rondebosch

Klipfontein Rd

Athlone

Gugulethu

Oudekraal

5

Kirstenbosch National Botanical Garden

Rylands Estate

Table Mountain National Park

Bishopscourt

Wynberg Village

Llandudno

Hout Bay Rd

Constantia

Wynberg

Plumstead

Sandy Bay

Little Lion's Head (436m)

10

Groot Constantia

Constantina Wine Route

Elfindale

Grassy Park

Hout Bay

Dunes

Klein Constantia

Strandfontein Rd

Chapman's Peak Hotel

Tokai

Lavender Hill

Rondevlei Nature Reserve

Bay Harbour Market

Hout Bay

Steenberg Farm

Zandvlei

Zeekoevlei

Chapman's Peak (593m)

Silvermine

Muizenberg

Baden Powell Rd

Chapman's Bay

Noordhoek

Kalk Bay

Brass Bell

9

Kommetjie Rd

Clovelly

Live Bait

4

Slangkop Lighthouse

Kommetjie

Fish Hoek

Table Mountain National Park

False Bay

Main Rd

Simon's Town

Scarborough

Boulders

ATLANTIC OCEAN

Cape of Good Hope Nature Reserve

Smitswinkel Bay

Paulsberg

Paulsberg

Buffels Bay

Cape of Good Hope Trail

Cape of Good Hope

Flying Dutchman Funicular

3

0   10 km
0   5 miles

Central Cape Town

Table Bay

Beach Rd

Mouille Point

Granger Bay

Waterfront

8

V&A Waterfront

Victoria Basin

Green Point Stadium

Green Point

Portswood Rd

Alfred Basin

Main Rd

Helen Suzman Blvd

Two Oceans Aquarium

Foreshore

Zeitz MOCAA Museum

Duncan Dock

High Level Rd

Sommerset Rd

FW de Klerk Blvd (Table Bay Blvd)

Signal Hill

De Waterkant Cottages

De Waterkant

Riebeeck St

Heerengracht

Hertzog Blvd

Schotsche Kloof

2

Bo-Kaap Museum

City Bowl

Cape Town Train Station

Bo-Kaap

Wale St

Adderley St

Strand St

Cape Town City Hall

Buitengracht St

St George's Cathedral

Iziko Slave Lodge

Darling St

2

Company's Garden

Orange St

District Six Museum

7

Castle of Good Hope

Tamboerskloof

Buitenkant St

Roeland St

East City

District Six

Kloof Nek Rd

Kloof St

Gardens

Annandale Rd

Mill St

Tennant St

Higgovale

De Waal Park

Derry St

Molteno St

Molteno Reservoir

Upper Orange St

Vredehoek

Oranjezicht

Deer Park

1

Lower Cableway Station

Table Mountain Aerial Cableway

Tafelberg Rd

Upper Cableway Station

1

Table Mountain (1073m)

Eastern Table

0   500 m
0   0.25 miles

A   B   C   D   E   F   G

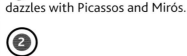

**SIGHTS &
ACTIVITIES**

◉ SEE
◉ DO

ITINERARY

▽ 1
▽ 2

① Art Institute of Chicago
The nation's second-largest art museum houses a treasure trove of global art. The collection of impressionist and post-impressionist paintings is second only to those in France, and the number of surrealist works is tremendous. Endless marble and glass corridors lead to Japanese prints, Grecian urns, suits of armour, Grant Wood's *American Gothic*, Edward Hopper's *Nighthawks* and one very big, dotted Seurat. The Modern Wing dazzles with Picassos and Mirós.

② Millennium Park
The playful heart of the city, this park shines with whimsical public art. Go head, walk under Anish Kapoor's *Cloud Gate* – aka 'the Bean' – and touch its silvery smoothness. Let the human gargoyles of Jaume Plensa's *Crown Fountain* gush water on you to cool down in summer. Unfurl a blanket by Frank Gehry's swooping silver band shell as the sun dips, wine corks pop and gorgeous music fills the twilight air. Or try to find the secret garden abloom with prairie flowers and a gurgling river.

③ Architecture cruises
There's no better way to feel Chicago's steely power than from low on the water looking up while cloud-poking towers glide by and iron bridges arch open to lead the way. The skyline takes on a surreal majesty when floating through its shadows on a river tour, and landmark after eye-popping landmark flashes by. Guides provide architecture lessons along the route, which enable visitors to tell the difference between beaux arts and International style by day's end.

Sky-high views:
The view south over Chicago and Lake Michigan from the 360 Chicago observation deck.

④ Wrigley Field
A tangible sense of history comes alive at this 100-plus-year-old baseball park, thanks to the hand-turned scoreboard, iconic neon entrance sign and time-honoured traditions that infuse games played here.

⑤ Sky-high views
For superlative seekers, Willis Tower is it: the city's tallest building (and one of the world's loftiest). After an ear-popping, 70-second elevator ride to the 103rd-floor Skydeck, stride into one of the glass-enclosed ledges that juts out in mid-air. Looking down is up to you.

⑥ Electric blues
In Chicago no genre is as iconic as the blues – the electric blues, to be exact. When Muddy Waters and friends plugged in their amps c 1950, guitar grooves reached new levels. The blues still fills clubs, especially Buddy Guy's.

⑦ Navy Pier
Stretching away from the skyline and a half-mile into the blue of Lake Michigan, this pier's charms unsurprisingly revolve around the cool breezes and sweet views, especially when riding its stomach-turning, 196ft Ferris wheel.

⑧ Public art downtown
Downtown is littered with extraordinary sculptures. The most heralded is Picasso's *Untitled*, which is set in Daley Plaza. Jean Dubuffet's abstract creation is officially titled *Monument with Standing Beast* but locals call it 'Snoopy in a Blender'. Marc Chagall's grand mosaic *Four Seasons* is more recognisable, depicting Chicago scenes.

⑨ Field Museum of Natural History
This massive museum houses some 30 million artefacts and includes beetles, mummies, gemstones and Bushman the stuffed ape – all tended by a slew of PhD-wielding scientists, as the Field remains an active research institution. The collection's rock star is Sue, the largest Tyrannosaurus Rex yet discovered. More incredible dinosaur exhibits are found in the Evolving Planet exhibit on the 2nd floor. The Hall of Gems and Inside Ancient Egypt exhibits are also worth exploring.

⑩ Museum of Science & Industry
This is the largest science museum in the Western Hemisphere. Highlights include a WWII German U-boat nestled in an underground display and the Science Storms exhibit with a mock tornado and tsunami. Other popular exhibits include the baby chick hatchery, the minuscule furnishings in Colleen Moore's fairy castle and the life-size shaft of a coal mine. The museum's main building served as the Palace of Fine Arts at the landmark 1893 World's Expo, which was set in the surrounding Jackson Park.

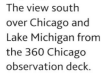

▽ Day 1 itinerary

Dive right in with the big stuff. Take a boat tour or walking tour with the **Chicago Architecture Foundation** and ogle some serious skyscrapers. Next, saunter over to **Millennium Park** for some fun in the sun. After lunch admire priceless painting after priceless painting in the **Art Institute of Chicago** before hitting the mighty

Willis Tower. Ride the elevator up 103 floors, then (if you're brave enough) step out onto the glass-floored ledge. If that didn't buckle your legs a little, a night eating, drinking and partying in the **West Loop** may do it. Find a patio, grab a drink and settle in. The **Haymarket Pub & Brewery** pours great beers and has the Drinking & Writing Theater inside.

▽ Days 2 and 3 itinerary

Start day two with a stroll on **Michigan Ave** before moseying over to **Navy Pier**. Wander the promenade, listen to some live music and then ride the Ferris wheel. Spend the afternoon at the Museum Campus taking in its many attractions: the **Field Museum**, with its dinosaurs and gemstones; the **Shedd Aquarium**, complete with

sharks; and the **Adler Planetarium**, where meteorites are on view. After dinner walk along **N Milwaukee Ave** and take your pick of booming bars, indie-rock clubs and hipster shops. On day three, dip your toes in Lake Michigan at **North Avenue Beach** before ambling northward through **Lincoln Park** – stop at its zoo and

then pop into its conservatory to smell exotic blooms. After lunch make your way north to **Wrigley Field** for a Cubs baseball game. Come evening, head into one of Andersonville's fine taverns, or see what's on at the **Neo-Futurists theatre**. Jazz hounds can venture into the highly acclaimed **Green Mill**, a timeless venue.

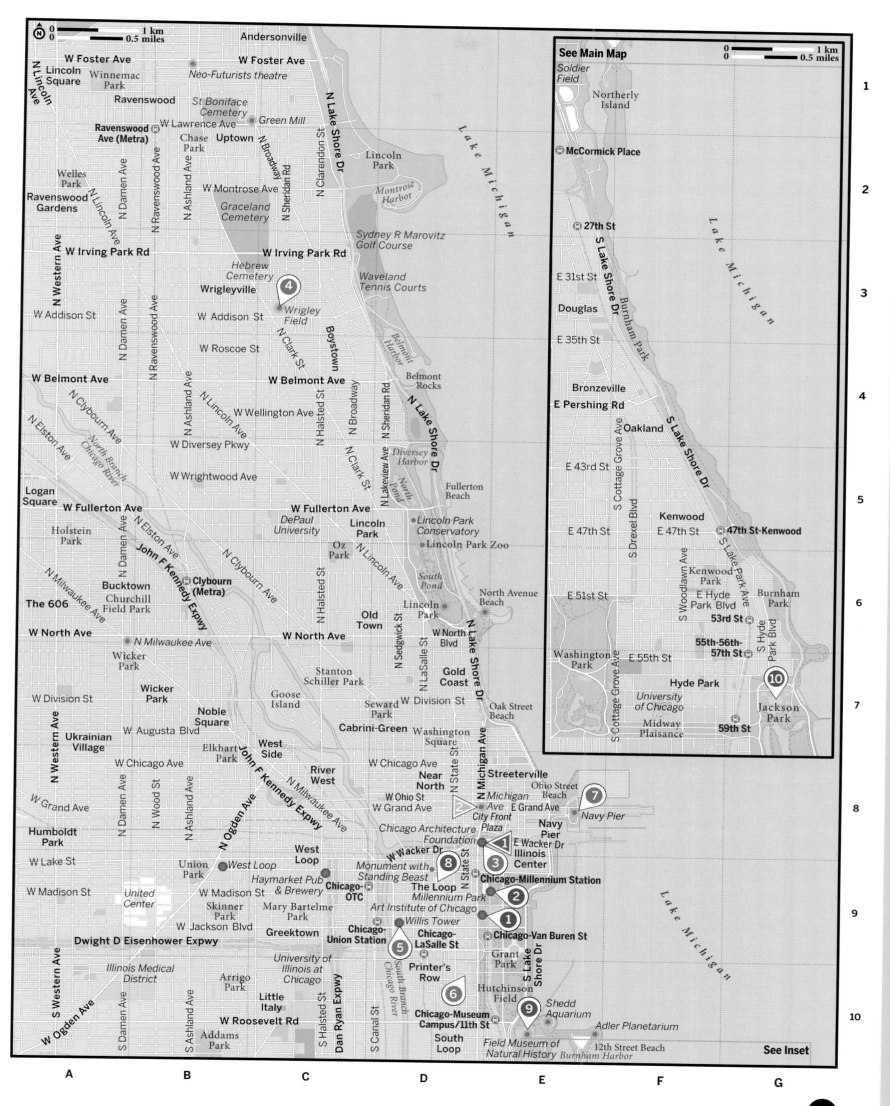

N
0 | 1 km
0 | 0.5 miles

Andersonville

W Foster Ave
N Lincoln Ave
Lincoln Square
Winnemac Park
W Foster Ave
Neo-Futurists theatre
Ravenswood
St Boniface Cemetery
Green Mill
Ravenswood Ave (Metra)
Chase Park
Uptown
W Lawrence Ave
Welles Park
N Damen Ave
N Ravenswood Ave
N Ashland Ave
N Broadway
N Sheridan Rd
N Clarendon St
N Lake Shore Dr
Lincoln Park

Ravenswood Gardens
N Lincoln Ave
W Montrose Ave
Graceland Cemetery
Montrose Harbor

N Western Ave
W Irving Park Rd
W Irving Park Rd
Sydney R Marovitz Golf Course

Hebrew Cemetery
Waveland Tennis Courts
Wrigleyville
4
W Addison St
W Addison St
Wrigley Field
N Clark St
Boystown

W Roscoe St

W Damen Ave
N Ravenswood Ave
W Belmont Ave
W Belmont Ave
N Halsted St
N Broadway
N Sheridan Rd
Belmont Harbor
Belmont Rocks

N Clybourn Ave
N Ashland Ave
N Lincoln Ave
W Wellington Ave
N Lake Shore Dr

N Elston Ave
W Diversey Pkwy
N Clark St
N Lakeview Ave

W Wrightwood Ave
Diversey Harbor

Logan Square
W Fullerton Ave
W Fullerton Ave
North Pond
Fullerton Beach

Holstein Park
N Elston Ave
N Damen Ave
N Clybourn Ave
DePaul University
Lincoln Park
N Lincoln Ave
Lincoln Park Conservatory
Lincoln Park

Bucktown
John F Kennedy Expwy
Clybourn (Metra)
Oz Park
Lincoln Park Zoo

The 606
N Milwaukee Ave
Churchill Field Park
N Halsted St
South Pond
North Avenue Beach

W North Ave
W North Ave
N Sedgwick St
N LaSalle St
Lincoln Park
W North Blvd
N Lake Shore Dr

Wicker Park
N Milwaukee Ave
Old Town
Oak Street Beach

Wicker Park
Stanton Schiller Park
Gold Coast

W Division St
Goose Island
Seward Park
W Division St

Ukrainian Village
Noble Square
Washington Square
Cabrini-Green

W Augusta Blvd
Elkhart Park
West Side
W Chicago Ave
W Chicago Ave
Near North
Streeterville
Ohio Street Beach

N Western Ave
N Damen Ave
N Wood St
N Ashland Ave
N Ogden Ave
N Milwaukee Ave
River West
W Ohio St
W Grand Ave
N State St
N Michigan Ave
N Michigan Ave
E Grand Ave
7
Navy Pier
Navy Pier

W Grand Ave
City Front Plaza
2
E Grand Ave

Humboldt Park
Chicago Architecture Foundation
1
E Wacker Dr
Illinois Center

W Wacker Dr
8
N State St
3

West Loop
Monument with Standing Beast
The Loop
Chicago-Millennium Station

Union Park
West Loop
Haymarket Pub & Brewery
Chicago-OTC
Millennium Park
2

W Lake St
W Madison St
W Madison St
Mary Bartelme Park
Art Institute of Chicago

United Center
Skinner Park
Willis Tower
1

Dwight D Eisenhower Expwy
Chicago-Union Station
Chicago-LaSalle St
Chicago-Van Buren St

S Western Ave
S Damen Ave
S Ashland Ave
S Halsted St
Dan Ryan Expwy
Greektown
5
Grant Park
S Lake Shore Dr

University of Illinois at Chicago
Printer's Row
Hutchinson Field

Illinois Medical District
Arrigo Park
South Branch Chicago River
6
Shedd Aquarium

Little Italy
S Canal St
Chicago-Museum Campus/11th St
9
Adler Planetarium

W Ogden Ave
W Roosevelt Rd
South Loop
Field Museum of Natural History
12th Street Beach
Burnham Harbor

Addams Park

See Main Map
0 | 1 km
0 | 0.5 miles

Soldier Field
Northerly Island
Lake Michigan

McCormick Place

27th St
Lake Michigan

E 31st St
S Lake Shore Dr
Burnham Park

Douglas
E 35th St

Bronzeville
E Pershing Rd
Oakland
S Lake Shore Dr

E 43rd St
S Cottage Grove Ave

Kenwood
E 47th St
S Drexel Blvd
E 47th St
47th St-Kenwood

E 51st St
S Woodlawn Ave
Kenwood Park
E Hyde Park Blvd
S Lake Shore Dr
Burnham Park

Washington Park
E 55th St
53rd St
55th-56th-57th St
S Hyde Park Blvd

Hyde Park
10

University of Chicago
Midway Plaisance
59th St
Jackson Park

S Cottage Grove Ave

Lake Michigan

See Inset

A　B　C　D　E　F　G

1　2　3　4　5　6　7　8　9　10

SIGHTS &
ACTIVITIES

 SEE
 DO

ITINERARY

 1
▽ 2

 Nationalmuseet
A visit to Denmark's veritable attic is a sprawling adventure that leads from prehistoric times to the enlightened nation we know today. Along the way at the country's biggest museum you'll stumble across ancient rune stones, bog bodies, Renaissance artworks, fashion and iconic modern design culture.

② **Designmuseum Danmark**
The 18th-century Frederiks Hospital is now the outstanding Denmark Design Museum. A must for fans of the applied arts and industrial design, its fairly extensive collection includes Danish textiles and fashion, as well as the iconic design pieces of modern innovators like Kaare Klint, Poul Henningsen and Arne Jacobsen.

③ **Torvehallerne KBH**
A feast for the eyes, nose and taste buds, the city's most celebrated market is a temple to all things seasonal, artisanal and scrumptious. Fill your bags with delish Danish delights and savour artful smørrebrød, sourdough pizza or a perfect espresso.

④ **Ny Carlsberg Glyptotek**
This museum is a love letter to the classical and the classics, from ancient Egyptian, Greek and Roman sculpture, to the thick, luscious brushstrokes of 19th-century European masters. Among the latter giants are Monet, Pissarro, Cézanne, Degas and Van Gogh. Its glorious, palm-graced winter garden is the perfect escape on a brooding, slate-grey Copenhagen day.

Tivoli Gardens: The twinkling pavilions and amusement rides of Tivoli are at their most romantic after dusk.

 Tivoli Gardens
Tivoli is an escapist fantasy of whimsical pavilions, romantic gardens and dreamy funfair rides. Squint a little and you could be by a Chinese lake, a Moorish palace, or in the mind of HG Wells.

⑥ **Rosenborg Slot**
Turreted, moated and the colour of gingerbread, this magnificent Dutch Renaissance palace is the stuff storybooks are made of. Step inside for three centuries of artworks, furnishings, crown jewels, curiosities and royal peepholes.

⑦ **Christiania**
A utopian commune founded by militant squatters in 1971, ramshackle Christiania remains one of Copenhagen's most distinctive corners. Part shambolic circus, part makeshift architectural expo, part urban oasis, this is the city's counterculture heart.

 Statens Museum for Kunst
Denmark's preeminent art museum spotlights six centuries of expression, reflection and provocation. It holds the world's finest collection of Danish 19th-century art and works by Matisse, Picasso, Per Kirkeby and Asger Jorn.

⑨ **Christiansborg Slot**
Burned down and rebuilt several times, the home of the national parliament, the Prime Minister's Office and the Supreme Court is an architectural phoenix. This palace's Royal Reception Rooms are a treat, as are the lavish interiors, royal oil paintings and tapestries.

⑩ **Christianshavn**
Copenhagen's dining scene leaves gourmands drooling. Christianshavn is the birthplace of Noma and the New Nordic cooking movement, a place where kitchens revel in all things innovative, daring and local.

 **Day 1 itinerary**

Pique your appetite at **Torvehallerne KBH** before indulging in a second breakfast. From here, it's an easy walk to **Kongens Have**, a former royal backyard turned city park. Snoop around the Hogwarts-worthy rooms of its 17th-century castle, **Rosenborg Slot**. After lunch continue east to salty **Nyhavn**, former haunt of Hans Christian Andersen. Capture the perfect snap of the colourful canal, then hop on a canal and harbour tour of the city. Alternatively, walk north along the harbourfront to royal pad **Amalienborg Slot**, the glorious church **Marmorkirken** and, further north, fortress **Kastellet**. Spend the evening swooning and screaming at **Tivoli Gardens**.

 Days 2 and 3 itinerary

Start day two by climbing **Rundetårn**, a 17th-century tower with views fit for its founder, Christian IV. The streets directly to the east are dotted with Nordic fashion boutiques and Scandi design stores. Alternatively, explore the historic Latin Quarter southwest of Rundetårn. Spend the afternoon at the **Nationalmuseet** or the nearby **Ny Carlsberg Glyptotek**. After dinner continue with wine, innovative cocktails or maybe a little late-night sax at **Jazzhus Montmartre**. Spend morning three exploring beautiful Christianshavn. If it's open, quickly pop into **Christians Kirke** to eye-up its theatre-like interior. Architectural curiosity also underscores **Vor Frelsers Kirke**, topped by a spiral wooden tower offering heavenly views. Both are within walking distance of **Christiania**. After lunch, cross **Knippelsbro** (Knippels Bridge) to reach **Christiansborg Slot**. For Danish sculpture and classical antiquities, drop into neighbouring **Thorvaldsens Museum**. After an industrious day of sightseeing, kick back with good grub and a fix of Copenhagen cool at **Kødbyen**, the still hip 'Meatpacking District'.

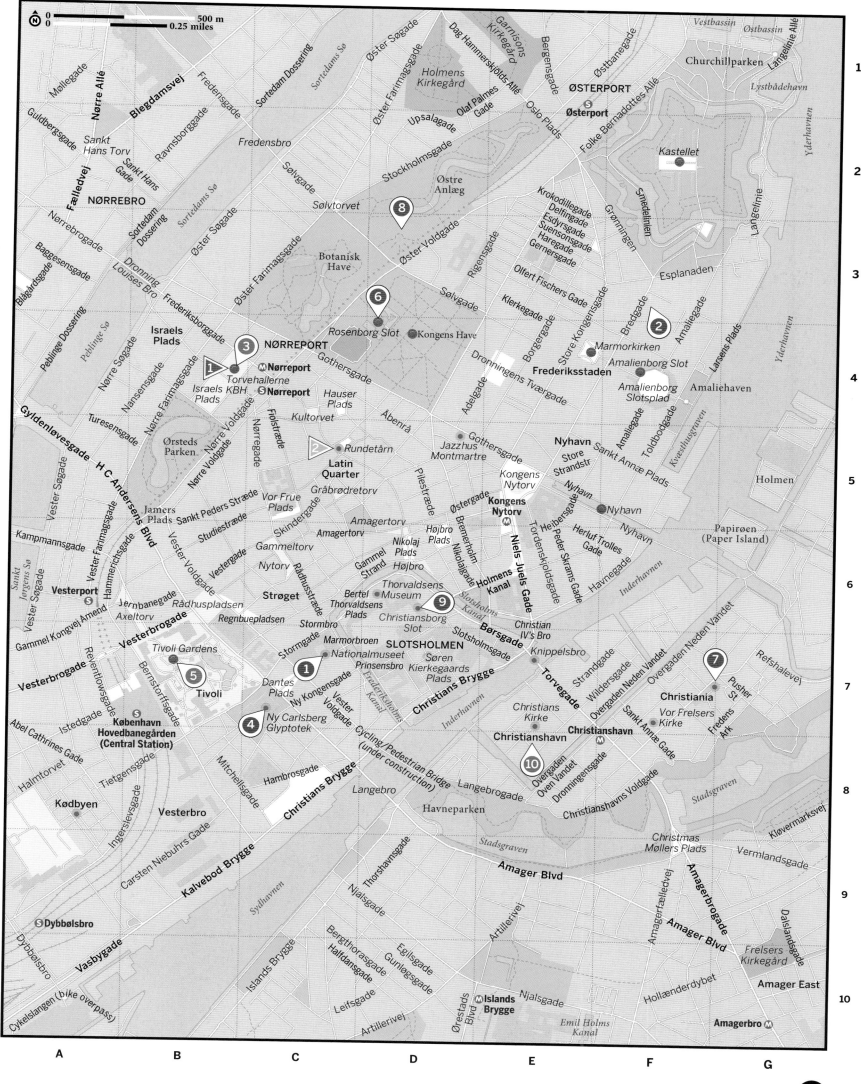

A   B   C   D   E   F   G

SIGHTS & ACTIVITIES

 SEE

DO

ITINERARY

1

2

Red Fort

Founded by Emperor Shah Jahan, this incredible fort with 18m-high walls took a decade to construct (1638–48). Decapitated bodies of prisoners were built into the foundations for luck, though this proved fruitless as the emperor was imprisoned by his disloyal son before he even managed to take up full residence here.

Humayun's Tomb

Thought to have been the inspiration for the Taj Mahal, this sublimely well-proportioned tomb seems to float above its symmetrical gardens. It marries Persian and Mughal elements, with restrained decoration enhancing the architecture.

Jama Masjid

A beautiful pocket of calm at the heart of Old Delhi's mayhem, India's largest mosque towers above the surrounding hubbub. It can hold a mind-blowing 25,000 people. This marble and red-sandstone 'Friday Mosque' was Shah Jahan's final architectural triumph, built between 1644 and 1658.

Qutb Minar Complex

Perhaps the capital's greatest ancient ruin, Delhi's first Islamic city is studded with tombs and monuments. The first group was erected by the sultans of Mehrauli, with subsequent rulers hiring the finest craftsmen and artisans to expand on the complex. The Qutb Festival of Indian classical music and dance takes place here every October/November.

Red Fort: A rickshaw rides past the walls of the Red Fort.

Gali Paratha Wali

This lane off Chandni Chowk has been dishing up delectable *parathas* (traditional flat bread) fresh off the *tawa* (hotplate) for generations, originally serving pilgrims at the time of the Mughals.

Hazrat Nizam-ud-din Dargah

Drink in the mystical atmosphere and hear *qawwali* (Islamic devotional singing) at this hallowed Sufi shrine. The *dargah* (shrine) is hidden away in a tangle of bazaars selling rose petals, *attars* (perfumes) and offerings.

Dawn cycle rides

Taking a rollicking, eye-opening bike ride through the city at dawn with DelhiByCycle. These cycle tours focus on specific neighbourhoods – Old Delhi, New Delhi, Nizamuddin, and the banks of the Yamuna – and start early to miss the worst of the traffic.

Mehrauli Archaeological Park

There are extraordinary riches scattered around Mehrauli, with more than 440 monuments – from the 10th century to the British era – dotting a forest and the village itself. Most impressive are the tombs of Balban and Quli Khan, his son.

Lodi Gardens

Roam around this tree-shaded garden that contains the 15th-century Bara Gumbad tomb and mosque, the strikingly different tombs of Mohammed Shah and Sikander Lodi, and the Athpula (eight-piered) bridge across the lake, which dates from Emperor Akbar's reign.

Shopping

Shahpur Jat urban village, just a 1km rickshaw ride northeast from Hauz Khas metro, is one of the best places in Delhi to buy independent designer threads. It's also home to bohemian restaurants such as artsy Bihari Potbelly and vegan organic Greenr.

Akshardham Temple

In the eastern suburbs, the Gujarati Hindu Swaminarayan Group's Akshardham Temple is breathtakingly lavish. Although built in 2005 the artisans used ancient techniques to carve the pale red sandstone into elaborate reliefs, including 20,000 deities, saints and mythical creatures.

Gurdwara Bangla Sahib

This huge, white-marble *gurdwara* (Sikh temple), topped by glinting golden onion domes, was constructed at the site where the eighth Sikh guru, Harkrishan Dev, stayed before his death in 1664. It's full of colour and life, yet tranquil, and live devotional songs waft over the compound. Despite his tender years, the six-year-old guru tended to victims of Delhi's cholera and smallpox epidemic, and waters here are said to have healing powers.

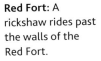

Days 1 and 2 itinerary

Spend your first day discovering Delhi's unexpectedly calm corners, such as lovely **Lodi Gardens**, the **National Museum**, **Gandhi Smriti** memorial and **Humayun's Tomb**. In the evening, have a cocktail at **1911** at the Imperial hotel, and dine out at **Khan Market** or on traditional North Indian dishes at **Pandara Market**. On day two, immerse yourself in **Old Delhi**. Take a ride with **DelhiByCycle**, or get to the **Red Fort** early to see it before the crowds, then plunge into the action-packed bazaars. Survey the mayhem from the minaret of **Jama Masjid**, then feast on sizzling kebabs at **Karim's** – it's been serving up Mughlai treats since 1913.

Days 3 and 4 itinerary

Follow the two-day itinerary, then start day three early to catch the ruins of the ancient Islamic city of **Qutb Minar** at dawn. Next, take a guided walk around **Mehrauli Archaeological Park**, including the Jamali Khamali mosque, attached to the tomb of the Sufi poet Jamali. Continue exploring, now in the ruins and boutiques of **Hauz Khas** and nearby **Shahpur Jat**. Listen to Sufi devotional songs at **Hazrat Nizam-ud-din Dargah** (if it's Thursday) or head to **Piano Man Jazz Club** in Safdarjung or the **Bandstand** for some live music. On day four, delve into the artistic splendours of embroidery, textiles and the Punjab cross-stitch at the laid-back **Crafts Museum**, then stop for quiet contemplation at Delhi's beautiful **Lotus Temple**, the **Bahai House of Worship**. Designed for tranquillity, it offers a rare moment of calm in the hectic city. Complete your stay with an meal at **Lakhori**, a restaurant in a restored *haveli* (mansion) that's especially atmospheric in the evening.

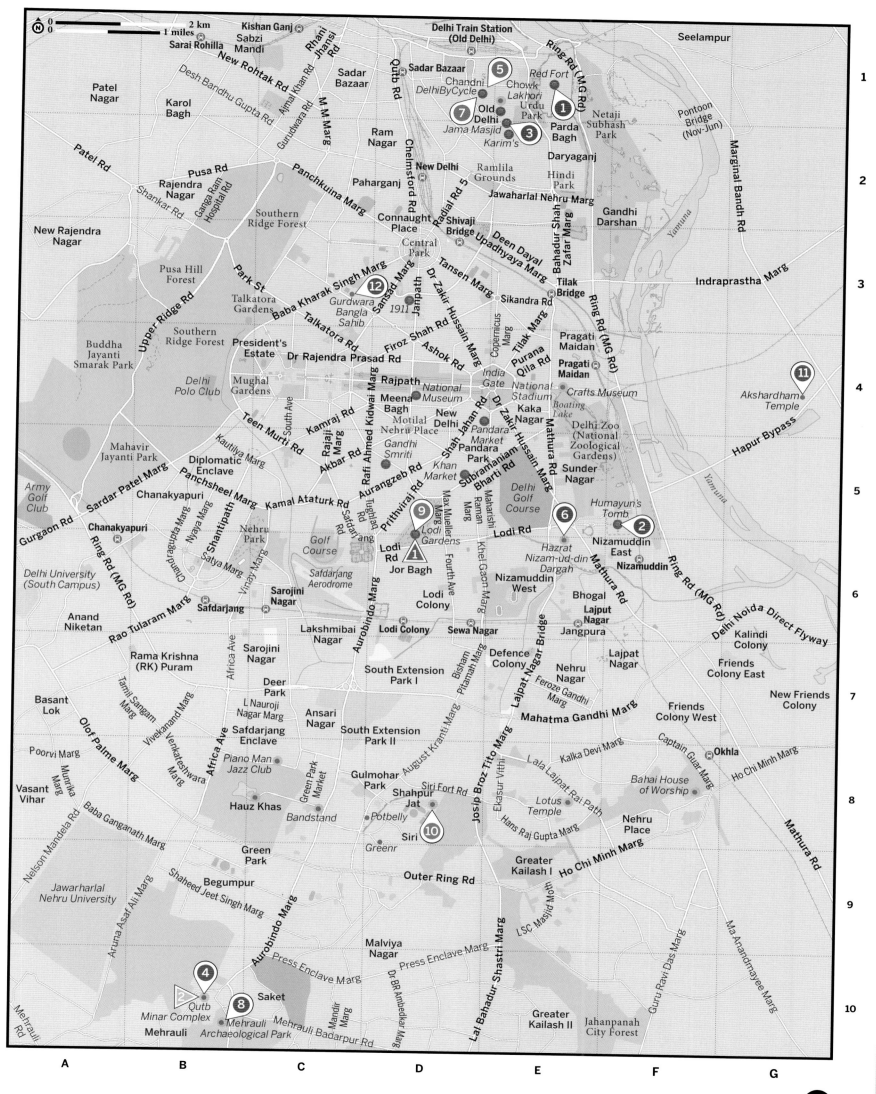

N
0   2 km
0   1 miles

SIGHTS & ACTIVITIES

 SEE

DO

ITINERARY

1

2

Trinity College
Since its foundation in 1592, Trinity College has become one of the world's most famous universities; it's the alma mater of Swift, Wilde and Beckett; it's where you'll find the most beautiful library in the whole country and the world's most famous illuminated Gospel, the *Book of Kells*. The college's 16 hectares are an oasis of aesthetic elegance, its cobbled quadrangles lined with handsome neoclassical buildings that lend an air of magisterial calm to the campus, evident as soon as you walk through Front Arch.

National Museum of Ireland
Since 1890, this museum has been the home of Ireland's key artefacts. It started with a fine collection of coins, medals and 'significant Irish antiquities', but it has since grown to house more than four million objects spread across three separate museum buildings.

Dublin City Gallery The Hugh Lane
Hanging on the walls of a magnificent Georgian pile is arguably the city's finest collection of modern and contemporary art, which runs the gamut from Impressionist masterpieces (Degas, Monet et al) to Irish artists. The gallery's extra-special treat is Dublin-born Francis Bacon's actual London studio, brought over piece by piece and painstakingly reassembled in all its glorious mess.

Kilmainham Gaol
Ireland's struggle for independence was a bloody and tempestuous journey, and this forbidding prison played a dark role in it for nearly 150 years. It's now a museum with an enthralling exhibit on the history of Irish nationalism.

Dining scene
Dublin's foodie scene is now one of the city's major highlights, with restaurants to suit every taste and budget. The most exciting ones are those defining Modern Irish cuisine, a fusion of basic ingredients and Irish recipes with culinary influences from around the globe. The area around Merrion Row is a culinary hotbed, for both casual and fine dining.

Guinness Storehouse
An old fermentation plant in the St James's Gate Brewery has been devoted to the history of Guinness, a beer as inextricably linked with Dublin as James Joyce. The top floor of seven houses the Gravity Bar, which has panoramic views.

St Stephen's Green
Dublin is blessed with green spaces, but none is so popular or so beloved as St Stephen's Green. When the sun burns through the cloud cover, join the students, lovers and workers who flock to its lush lawn.

National Gallery
An impressive collection of art history spread across six centuries and 54 separate galleries. The marquee names include Goya, Caravaggio and Van Gogh, but no less impressive are the paintings by luminaries such as Orpen, Reynolds and Van Dongen.

Chester Beatty Library
Alfred Chester Beatty was a mining magnate with exceptional taste, and the fruit of his aesthetic sensibility is gathered in this remarkable museum. Books, manuscripts and scrolls were his particular love, and it shows.

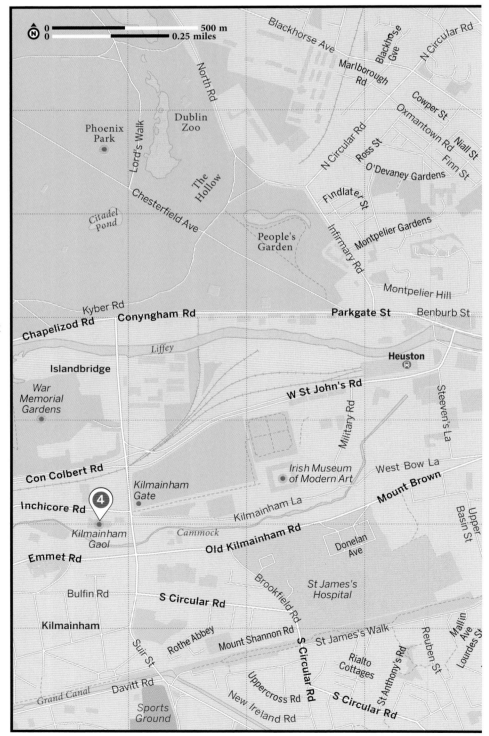

Day 1 itinerary

Start with an amble through the grounds of **Trinity College**, visiting the **Long Room** and the *Book of Kells* before ambling up Grafton St to **St Stephen's Green**. For more beautiful books and artefacts, drop into the **Chester Beatty Library**. On your way, you can do a spot of retailing in the boutiques west of Grafton St. In the afternoon pick your heavyweight institution, or visit all three: the **National Museum of Ireland – Archaeology**; the **National Gallery**; and the **Museum of Natural History**. **Temple Bar**, Dublin's one-time party zone, still likes to have a good time and it's definitely at its most animated in the evenings. Choose a traditional music session, some decent clubbing or a simple pint at any of the district's many pubs.

Days 2 and 3 itinerary

Begin day two with a little penance for your night at Temple Bar at either of Dublin's medieval cathedrals, **St Patrick's** or **Christ Church**, before hitting the **Guinness Storehouse**. In the afternoon go further west to Kilmainham, visiting the **Irish Museum of Modern Art** and then **Kilmainham Gaol**, the tour of which offers one of the most illuminating insights into Ireland's struggle for independence. If the weather is good, stroll in the **War Memorial Gardens**. After dinner take in a play at either the **Gate Theatre** or Ireland's national theatre, the **Abbey**. Day three starts with walking the length of O'Connell St – pause to inspect the bullet holes in the **General Post Office**. Explore the collection of the **Dublin City Gallery The Hugh Lane**, then stop at the **Old Jameson Distillery** to learn about (and taste) Irish whiskey. After sustenance, visit the **National Museum of Ireland – Decorative Arts & History**. Further west is Europe's largest city park, **Phoenix Park**. The biggest choice of nightlife in this area is in the streets around **Grafton St**. Or see what's on at the **Gaiety Theatre**.

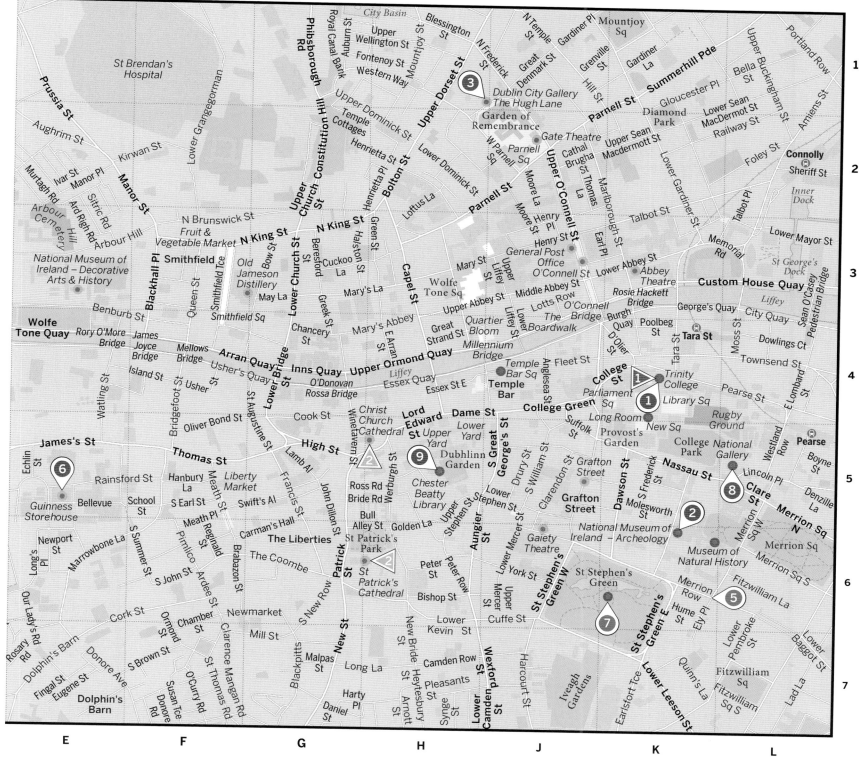

SIGHTS & ACTIVITIES

 SEE

 DO

ITINERARY

1

2

Edinburgh Castle

The brooding, black crags looming above the city gave birth to both Edinburgh and its stunning castle. The fortress has played a pivotal role in Scottish history, both as a royal residence – King Malcolm Canmore (r 1058–93) and Queen Margaret first made their home here in the 11th century – and as a military stronghold. The castle last saw military action in 1745; from then until the 1920s it served as the British army's main base in Scotland.

Royal Yacht Britannia

This yacht was the British royal family's floating holiday home during their travels from the time of her launch in 1953 until her decommissioning in 1997. The tour lifts the curtain on the everyday lives of the royals.

Arthur's Seat

A hike up this distinctive rocky peak (251m) – carved by ice sheets from the deeply eroded stump of a long-extinct volcano – offers wide-ranging views: west to the Forth Bridges, east to North Berwick Law and northwest to the Ochil Hills and the Highlands. From Holyrood, the hike takes 45 minutes.

Sandy Bell's

This unassuming pub is a stalwart of the traditional music scene (the founder's wife sang with the Corries). There's music almost every evening at 9pm, and from 3pm Saturday and Sunday, plus lots of impromptu sessions.

Arthur's Seat:
This craggy hill is a distinctive feature of Edinburgh's skyline.

Edinburgh Festival Fringe

When the first Edinburgh Festival was held in 1947, there were eight theatre companies who didn't make it on to the main programme. Undeterred, they held their own mini-festival and the Fringe was born. Today it's the biggest performing arts festival in the world, spread across more than 300 venues, nine of which are in Bristo Sq.

Real Mary King's Close

This subterranean labyrinth gives a fascinating insight into the everyday life of 17th-century Edinburgh. Before being opened to the public, the medieval alley was preserved for 250 years by the foundations of the 18th-century City Chambers.

Scottish Parliament Building

The Scottish parliament building, opened in 2004, was designed by Catalan architect Enric Miralles. The ground plan of the parliament complex is said to represent a 'flower of democracy rooted in Scottish soil'.

Surgeons' Hall Museums

Housed in a grand Ionic temple, these three fascinating museums were established as teaching collections. The History of Surgery Museum looks back to a time when barber-surgeons delved into bloodletting, amputations and other procedures.

National Museum of Scotland

Spread between two buildings, one modern, one Victorian – the golden stone and striking architecture of the former is one of the city's most distinctive landmarks. The collection traces the nation's history from its geological beginnings to the 1990s.

Royal Botanic Garden

The second-oldest institution of its kind in Britain, and one of world's most respected, features 28 landscaped hectares, splendid Victorian glasshouses, swaths of azalea and rhododendron and a rock garden. The cafe has a terrace with great views of Edinburgh Castle.

© Evan Hammonds / 500px

Day 1 itinerary

Spend at least the first two hours after it opens at **Edinburgh Castle**, then take a leisurely stroll down the **Royal Mile**, stopping off for a tour of **Real Mary King's Close**. At the bottom of the Mile, take a one-hour guided tour of the **Scottish Parliament Building**, before crossing the street to the **Palace of Holyroodhouse**. If the weather's fine, take an evening walk along **Radical Rd** at the foot of **Salisbury Crags**, or head up the stairs from nearby Calton Rd to the top of **Calton Hill**; both offer superb views. Dine at a restaurant with a vista such as **Tower**; or somewhere cosy, like Ondine. Post-dinner, scare yourself silly on a ghost tour of **Greyfriars Kirkyard**.

Days 2 and 3 itinerary

Start day two with a feast of culture at the **National Museum of Scotland**, followed by a short wander down the Mound – with great views across **Princes Street Gardens** and the New Town – to the iconic artworks of the **Scottish National Gallery**. Work off lunch by climbing the nearby **Scott Monument**, then catch a bus on Princes St to the **Royal Yacht Britannia**. Stay in Leith for a pint at **Teuchters Landing**, or head back to the city centre to sample some Edinburgh-brewed beer in the magnificent surroundings of the **Café Royal Circle Bar**. Begin day three with a visit to the **Scottish National Gallery of Modern Art**, then enjoy a surprisingly bucolic walk along the **Water of Leith Walkway** to **Stockbridge**. Spend an hour or so browsing the stalls at **Stockbridge Market** (Sundays only), then make the short journey to the **Royal Botanic Garden**. For the evening, see a show at the **Royal Lyceum** or the **Traverse**, or head for late-night Scottish folk music and dancing at **Ghillie Dhu**.

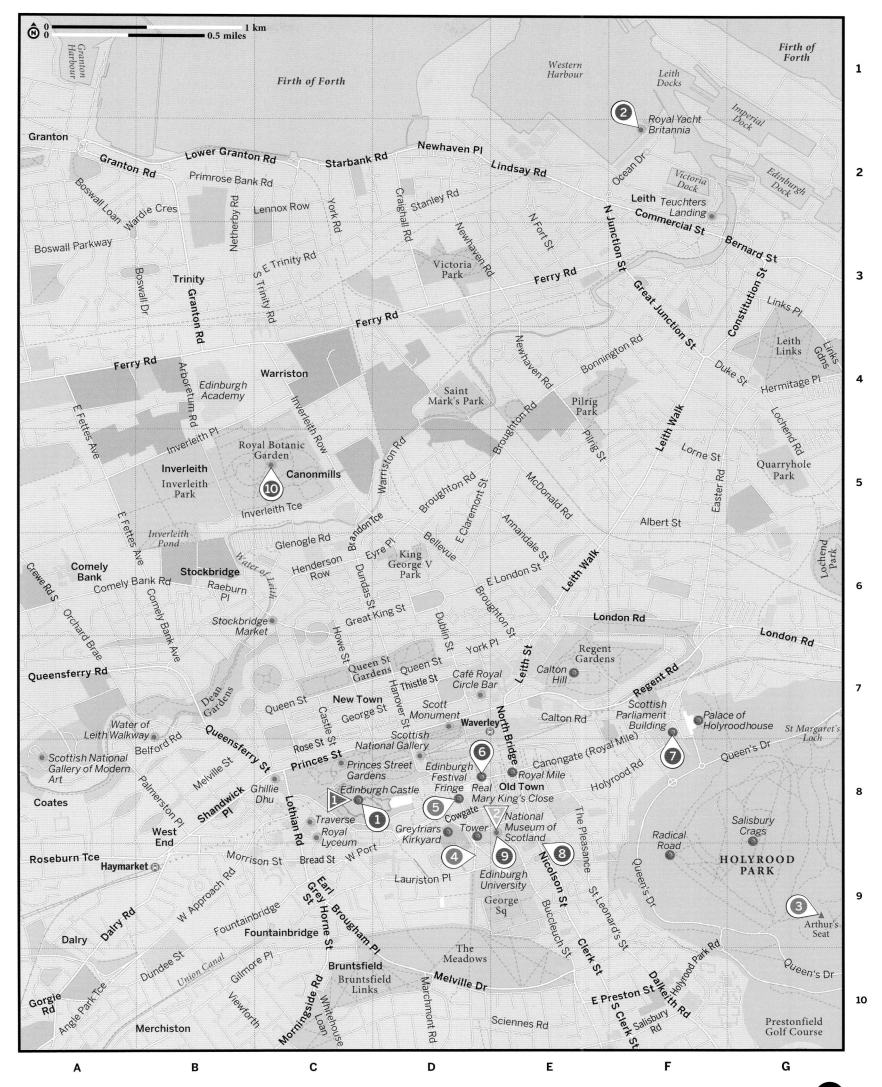

0 | 1 km
0 | 0.5 miles

Firth of Forth

Firth of Forth

Granton

Lower Granton Rd
Granton Rd
Starbank Rd
Newhaven Pl
Lindsay Rd

Western Harbour

Leith Docks

Imperial Dock

2 Royal Yacht Britannia

Ocean Dr

Victoria Dock

Edinburgh Dock

Primrose Bank Rd

Boswall Loan
Wardle Cres

Netherby Rd
Lennox Row

York Rd

Craighall Rd

Stanley Rd

N Fort St

Newhaven Rd

N Junction St

Leith Teuchters Landing
Commercial St

Bernard St

Boswall Parkway

S E Trinity Rd

Trinity

Boswall Dr
Granton Rd
S Trinity Rd

Ferry Rd

Victoria Park

Ferry Rd

Ferry Rd

Constitution St

Links Pl

Ferry Rd

Warriston

Edinburgh Academy

Arboretum Rd
E Fettes Ave
Inverleith Pl

Inverleith Row

Saint Mark's Park

Broughton Rd

Newhaven Rd

Bonnington Rd

Great Junction St

Duke St

Leith Links
Links Gdns

Hermitage Pl

Pilrig Park

Inverleith

Inverleith Park

Royal Botanic Garden

Canonmills

10

Inverleith Tce

Warriston Rd

Broughton Rd

Pilrig St

Leith Walk

Lorne St

Easter Rd

Quarryhole Park

Lochend Rd

Comely Bank

E Fettes Ave

Inverleith Pond

Glenogle Rd

Brandon Tce

Eyre Pl

Bellevue

King George V Park

E Claremont St

McDonald Rd

Albert St

Lochend Park

Crewe Rd S
Comely Bank Rd

Raeburn Pl

Henderson Row

Dundas St

E London St

Stockbridge

Water of Leith

Queensferry Rd

Orchard Brae

Comely Bank Ave

Stockbridge Market

Great King St

Howe St

Dublin St

Broughton St

E London St

London Rd

London Rd

Dean Gardens

Queen St Gardens

Queen St

York Pl

Leith St

Regent Gardens

Calton Hill

Regent Rd

Water of Leith Walkway

Belford Rd

Queensferry St

Queen St

George St

Thistle St

Hanover St

Scott Monument

Café Royal Circle Bar

Calton Rd

Scottish Parliament Building

7

Palace of Holyroodhouse

St Margaret's Loch

Scottish National Gallery of Modern Art

Melville St

Rose St

Castle St

Scottish National Gallery

Waverley

North Bridge

Canongate (Royal Mile)

Holyrood Rd

Queen's Dr

Coates

Shandwick Pl

Palmerston Pl

Princes St

Princes Street Gardens

6

Edinburgh Festival Fringe

Royal Mile

Old Town

Edinburgh Castle

1

Real Mary King's Close

Ghillie Dhu

1

Traverse Royal Lyceum

5

Cowgate

Greyfriars Kirkyard

Tower

2

National Museum of Scotland

The Pleasance

Radical Road

Salisbury Crags

HOLYROOD PARK

West End

Lothian Rd

Morrison St

Bread St

W Port

4

9

8

Nicolson St

Clerk St

Haymarket

Dalry Rd

W Approach Rd

Lauriston Pl

Edinburgh University

George Sq

Buccleuch St

St Leonard's St

Queen's Dr

3

Arthur's Seat

Roseburn Tce

Earl Grey St
Brougham Pl

Fountainbridge

Gorgie Rd

Angle Park Tce

Dundee St

Gilmore Pl

Morningside Rd
Whitehouse Loan

Bruntsfield

Bruntsfield Links

The Meadows

Melville Dr

Marchmont Rd

Dalkeith Rd

E Preston St
S Clerk St
Salisbury Rd

Holyrood Park Rd

Queen's Dr

Dalry

Merchiston

Union Canal

Viewforth

Sciennes Rd

Prestonfield Golf Course

SIGHTS & ACTIVITIES

 SEE

 DO

ITINERARY

 1

▽ 2

Star Ferry

A floating piece of Hong Kong heritage, this legendary ferry was founded in 1880 and plies the waters of Victoria Harbour in the service of commuters and visitors alike. With views of Hong Kong's iconic skyline, it must be one of the world's best-value cruises.

Victoria Peak

The highest point on Hong Kong Island and rising above its financial heart, Victoria Peak (552m) offers superlative views of the city and the mountainous countryside beyond, as well as some easy yet spectacular walks. Ride the hair-raising Peak Tram – Asia's first cable funicular, in operation since 1888 – to the cooler climes at the top.

Mong Kok markets

Mong Kok has an eclectic mix of speciality markets: the Ladies' Market, with everything from 'I Love HK' rugby shirts to granny swimwear; the flower market, with exotic seeds and fragrant florals; the goldfish market, alive with aquatic life; and vertical markets too – a buzzing computer mall, and a multistorey gadget-lovers' heaven.

Man Mo Temple

Permanently wreathed in sandalwood smoke, the famous temple is dedicated to Man (literature) and Mo (war) and the gods who govern them. Once a cultural and political focal point for the local Chinese, it now commands a wider following, including locals and tourists who come to perform age-old rites or have their fortunes told.

Victoria Peak: The Hong Kong cityscape views from this hill are superlative.

Wan Chai dining

If you were to hurl yourself, eyes closed, into a random neighbourhood and hope to emerge smacking your lips, you'd stand the best chance in Wan Chai. Regional Chinese cooking, European cuisines, Asian kitchens, East–West fusion, this is Hong Kong's food capital.

Temple Street Night Market

Beneath the glare of naked bulbs, hundreds of stalls sell a vast array of booty, from sex toys to Nepalese daggers. Browse for handy gadgets or quirky souvenirs, and test your bargaining skills. When hunger strikes, the many open-air stalls offer snacks and seafood feasts.

Hong Kong Museum of History

For an overview of the territory's archaeology, ethnography, and natural and local history, this museum is worth a visit, not just to learn more about the subject but to understand how Hong Kong presents its stories to the world.

Tsim Sha Tsui East Promenade

This promenade offers a famous view of Hong Kong – gleaming skyscrapers between emerald hills and a deep-blue harbour with criss-crossing boats. It's magical after sundown.

Hiking the Hong Kong Trail

Starting from Victoria Peak, this 50km route along the entire length of Hong Kong Island sweeps you into rolling hills, secluded woodland and lofty paths that afford sumptuous views of the rugged south and its wavy shore.

Shanghai Tang

This elegant four-level store is the place to go if you fancy a body-hugging *qípáo* (cheongsam) with a modern twist, a Chinese-style clutch or a lime-green mandarin jacket. Custom tailoring is available; it takes two weeks to a month and requires a fitting. Shanghai Tang also stocks cushions, picture frames, teapots, even mah-jong tile sets, designed in a modern chinoiserie style.

Day 1 itinerary

Catch the legendary **Peak Tram** up to **Victoria Peak** for stunning views of the city. Then descend and walk to **Sheung Wan**, checking out the shopping options along the way. Stop at **Man Mo Temple** for a taste of history and explore the burgeoning boho community on **Tai Ping Shan St**. After some dim sum for lunch, take the **Star Ferry** to Kowloon.

Enjoy the views along **Tsim Sha Tsui East Promenade** and savour your stroll to the **Museum of History** where you'll get some context on your day's impressions. For dinner, dunk and dip Hong Kong–style at hotpot heaven **Woo Cow**. Finish by hopping the tram to **Soho** for drinks, dancing and live music. **Club 71** is a favourite haunt of local artists.

Days 2 and 3 itinerary

Start day two by embracing (manufactured) nature at **Hong Kong Park** and checking out the **Museum of Teaware**, then head over to **Queen's Rd East** to explore the older part of Wan Chai. Take the tram to **Causeway Bay** for some shopping and lunch at **Fortune Kitchen**, serving delicious Cantonese home-cooking. In the afternoon visit the **Chungking Mansions** area, then head to Yau Ma Tei to see **Tin Hau Temple**, the **Jade Market** and traditional shops on **Shanghai St**. Dine at the **Temple Street Night Market**, then head out for a cocktail or two. Start your last day with a cruise on the lovely Aberdeen Harbour. Back in Kowloon make your way to **Mong Kok** to browse everthing from flowers to gadgets. If it's a clear night, hit the **Ritz Carlton** for early drinks and a view of the skyline at **Ozone**, one of Asia's highest bars. If it's cloudy, **Aqua** in Tsim Sha Tsui, is a fabulous alternative. After a few drinks, late-night dim sum at **One Dim Sum** may be music to your ears. Get in line and pick from the 45-item menu.

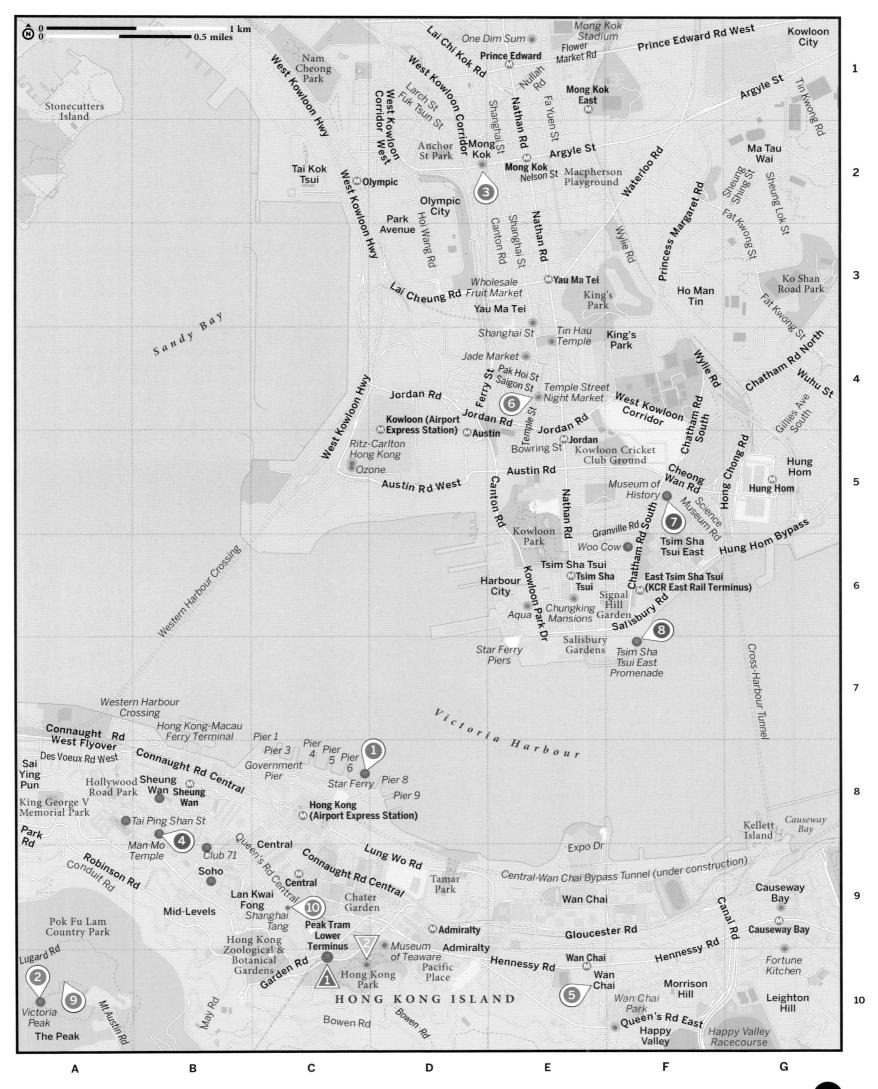

N
0 ——————— 1 km
0 ——————— 0.5 miles

Stonecutters
Island

Nam
Cheong
Park

Lai Chi Kok Rd

One Dim Sum

Mong Kok
Stadium

Flower
Market Rd

Prince Edward Rd West

Kowloon
City

West Kowloon Corridor

West Kowloon Corridor West

Larch St

Fuk Tsun St

Shanghai St

Nathan Rd

Fa Yuen St

Nullah Rd

Prince Edward

Mong Kok
East

Argyle St

Tin kwong Rd

Tai Kok
Tsui

Olympic

West Kowloon Hwy

Anchor
St Park

Mong Kok

Nelson St

Mong Kok

Argyle St

Macpherson
Playground

Waterloo Rd

Ma Tau
Wai

Sheung Shing St

Sheung Lok St

3

Olympic
City

Park
Avenue

Hoi Wang Rd

Canton Rd

Shanghai St

Nathan Rd

Wylie Rd

Princess Margaret Rd

Ho Man
Tin

Fat kwong St

Ko Shan
Road Park

Sandy Bay

Lai Cheung Rd

Wholesale
Fruit Market

Yau Ma Tei

King's
Park

Fat kwong St

Yau Ma Tei

Shanghai St

Tin Hau
Temple

King's
Park

Wylie Rd

Chatham Rd North

Wuhu St

Jade Market

Pak Hoi St
Saigon St

Temple Street
Night Market

West Kowloon
Corridor

Chatham Rd South

Gillies Ave South

Ferry St

Jordan Rd

Jordan Rd

6

Temple St

Jordan Rd

Hung
Hom

Kowloon (Airport
Express Station)

Austin

Bowring St

Jordan

Kowloon Cricket
Club Ground

Cheong Wan Rd

Hong Chong Rd

Hung Hom

Ritz-Carlton
Hong Kong

Ozone

Austin Rd West

Austin Rd

Canton Rd

Nathan Rd

Museum of
History

Science Museum Rd

7

Tsim Sha
Tsui East

Hung Hom Bypass

West Kowloon Hwy

Kowloon
Park

Granville Rd

Woo Cow

Chatham Rd South

Cross-Harbour Tunnel

Harbour
City

Kowloon Park Dr

Tsim Sha Tsui

Tsim Sha
Tsui

East Tsim Sha Tsui
(KCR East Rail Terminus)

Aqua

Chungking
Mansions

Signal
Hill
Garden

Salisbury Rd

8

Star Ferry
Piers

Salisbury
Gardens

Tsim Sha
Tsui East
Promenade

Victoria Harbour

Western Harbour Crossing

Western Harbour
Crossing

Hong Kong-Macau
Ferry Terminal

Pier 1

Pier 3

Pier 4
Pier 5
Pier 6

1

Star Ferry

Pier 8

Pier 9

Connaught Rd
West Flyover

Des Voeux Rd West

Connaught Rd Central

Government
Pier

Sai
Ying
Pun

Hollywood
Road Park

Sheung
Wan

Sheung
Wan

Hong Kong
(Airport Express Station)

Kellett
Island

Causeway
Bay

King George V
Memorial Park

Tai Ping Shan St

4

Central

Lung Wo Rd

Expo Dr

Central-Wan Chai Bypass Tunnel (under construction)

Park
Rd

Man Mo
Temple

Club 71

Queen's Rd Central

Connaught Rd Central

Tamar
Park

Causeway
Bay

Robinson Rd

Conduit Rd

Soho

Central

Wan Chai

Canal Rd

Causeway
Bay

Lan Kwai
Fong

Mid-Levels

Shanghai
Tang

Peak Tram
Lower
Terminus

10

Chater
Garden

Admiralty

Gloucester Rd

Hennessy Rd

Pok Fu Lam
Country Park

Hong Kong
Zoological &
Botanical
Gardens

Garden Rd

2

Museum
of Teaware

Admiralty

Wan Chai

Hennessy Rd

Wan Chai

Fortune
Kitchen

Lugard Rd

1

Hong Kong
Park

Pacific
Place

Morrison
Hill

Leighton
Hill

2

Victoria
Peak

The Peak

9

Mt Austin Rd

May Rd

Bowen Rd

Bowen Rd

HONG KONG ISLAND

5

Wan Chai
Park

Queen's Rd East

Happy
Valley

Happy Valley
Racecourse

1
2
3
4
5
6
7
8
9
10

A   B   C   D   E   F   G

SIGHTS &
ACTIVITIES

◉ SEE
◉ DO

ITINERARY

▽ 1
▽ 2

Aya Sofya

History resonates when you visit this majestic Byzantine basilica. Built by order of the Emperor Justinian in the 6th century, its soaring dome, huge nave and glittering gold mosaics contribute to its reputation as one of the world's most beautiful buildings.

Topkapı Palace

The secrets of the seraglio will be revealed during your visit to this opulent Ottoman palace complex. A series of mad, sad and downright bad sultans lived here with their concubines and courtiers between 1465 and 1830, and extravagant relics of their folly, intrigue, excess, patronage, diplomacy and war are everywhere you look.

Bosphorus ferry trip

A commuter ferry trip between Asia and Europe is a quintessential İstanbul experience, but a journey along the great strait from Eminönü towards the mouth of the Black Sea on a Bosphorus tourist ferry is even better. You'll view palaces, parks and ornate timber mansions on both continent's shores.

Blue Mosque: Visitors to the mosque must use the south door; only worshippers are admitted through the main entrance.

Grand Bazaar

This colourful and chaotic bazaar has been the heart of İstanbul's Old City for centuries. Starting as a small vaulted *bedesten* (covered market) in 1461, it grew to encompass the vast area seen today. Explore its labyrinthine lanes and hidden *hans* (caravanserais) for a shopping experience like no other.

Süleymaniye Mosque

Dominating the skyline, Süleyman the Magnificent's most notable architectural legacy certainly lives up to its patron's name. Built between 1550 and 1557, its extensive *külliye* (mosque complex) buildings illustrate aspects of daily Ottoman life and are still used by the local community. In the garden behind the mosque is a terrace offering lovely views of the Golden Horn and Bosphorus. The street underneath once housed the mosque complex's *arasta* (street of shops), which was built into the retaining wall of the terrace

Hamams

İstanbul's hamams offer a unique opportunity to simultaneously immerse yourself in Ottoman history and society, 16th-century architecture and soap suds. A treatment is a refreshing (and often invigorating) finale to any day. Kılıç Ali Paşa Hamamı in Beyoğlu is our top choice.

Beyoğlu

Breathtaking views of the Bosphorus and Old City from the rooftop terraces of a constellation of bars are just one of the enticements on offer in Beyoğlu.

Blue Mosque

The city's signature building was the grand project of Sultan Ahmet I. The mosque's 17th-century exterior features a cascade of domes and six tapering minarets. Inside, the huge space is encrusted with thousands of the blue İznik tiles that give Sultanahmet Camii its unofficial but commonly used name.

Basilica Cistern

This extraordinary Byzantine subterranean cistern features a wildly atmospheric forest of columns (336 to be exact), vaulted brick ceilings, mysterious carved Medusa-head capitals and ghostly patrols of carp.

Day 1 itinerary

Start with the showstoppers: **Aya Sofya**, the **Blue Mosque** and the **Basilica Cistern**. Next, wander through the **Hippodrome**, where ancient chariot races were held. Join local workers for lunch at one of the humble *lokantas* (eateries serving ready-made dishes), then walk down into the **Küçük Ayasofya** neighbourhood. Afterwards, source some souvenirs in the historic **Arasta Bazaar**. After dinner, claim a table at **Derviş Aile Çay Bahçesi** or **Cafe Meşale**, where you can enjoy tea, nargile (water pipe) and a whirling dervish performance. A treatment at one of the Old City's Ottoman-era hamams is a relaxing way to finish the day, particularly in winter.

Days 2 and 3 itinerary

Spend your second morning touring **Topkapı Palace**'s Harem, Treasury and pavilion-filled grounds. Investigate the excellent cheap eateries on Sirkeci's **Hocapaşa Sokak** for lunch, before exploring the streets, cafes and boutiques of **Galata, Tophane, Karaköy** and **Çukurcuma**. Head into **Beyoğlu**, the city's eating and drinking hotspot for a pre-dinner drink and a meal. Finish by hitting the bars and clubs in **Asmalımescit**, on İstiklal Caddesi or in **Cihangir**. Those who are still hungry should instead head to Karaköy for a late-night baklava fix at Karaköy Güllüoğlu. On day three explore the city's famous Bazaar District. After visiting the most magnificent of all Ottoman mosques, the **Süleymaniye**, make for the **Grand Bazaar** to pick up a few treasures for home. After lunch wind your way down the hill to the **Spice Bazaar**. While there, seek out the exquisite **Rüstem Paşa Mosque** – it's camouflaged in the midst of a busy produce market. After dinner in Beyoğlu, finish with an evening cruise on the **Bosphorus**.

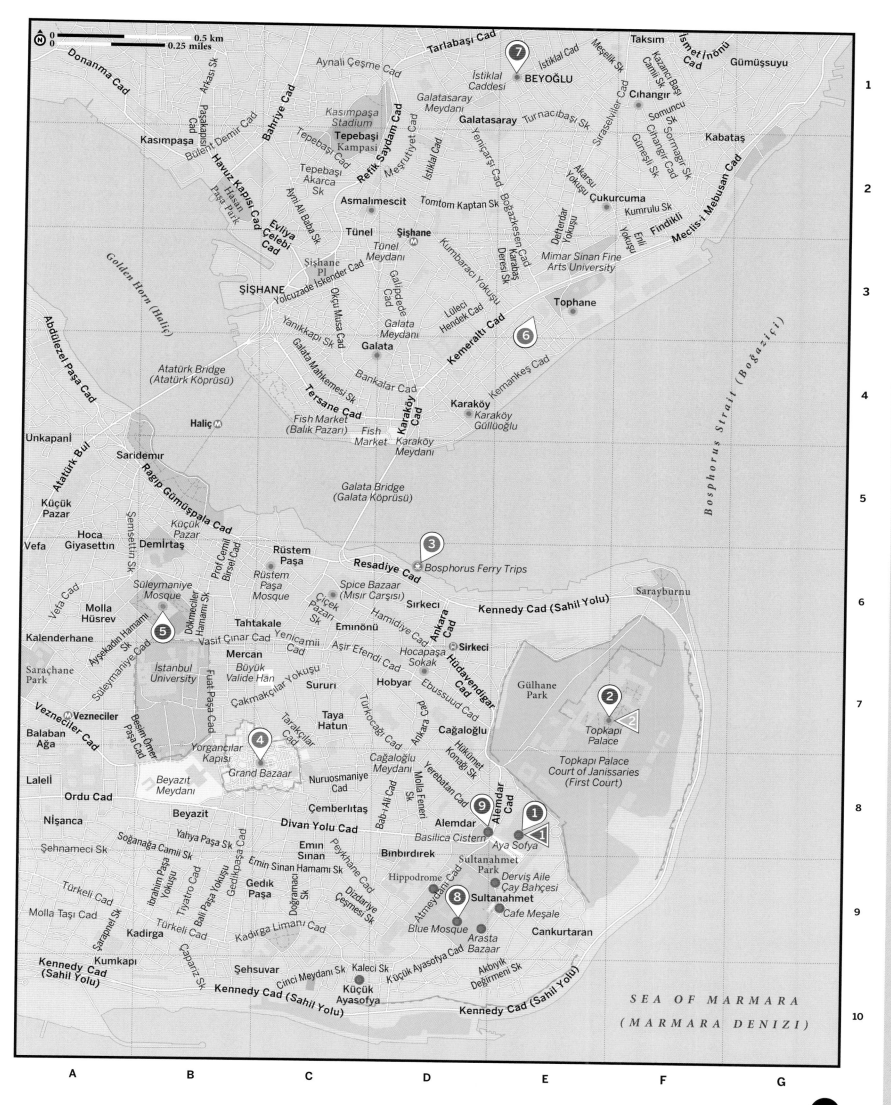

N
0
0
0.5 km
0.25 miles

Donanma Cad

Arkası Sk

Paşakapısı Cad

Bülent Demir Cad

Kasımpaşa

Havuz Kapısı Cad

Bahriye Cad

Tepebaşı Cad

Kasımpaşa Stadium

Tepebaşı Kampası

Tarlabaşı Cad

Aynalı Çeşme Cad

İstiklal Caddesi

BEYOĞLU

İstiklal Cad

Galatasaray Meydanı

Galatasaray

Turnacıbaşı Sk

Taksim

Meşelik Sk

İsmet İnönü Cad

Kazancı Başı

Camii Sk

Sıraselviler Cad

Somuncu Sk

Cihangir Cad Sk

Güneşli Sk

Cıhangır

Gümüşsuyu

Kabataş

Tepebaşı

Hasan Paşa Park

Tepebaşı Akarca Sk

Evliya Çelebi Cad

Havuz Kapısı Cad

Refik Saydam Cad

Meşrutiyet Cad

Asmalımescit

Aynı Ali Baba Sk

İstiklal Cad

Tomtom Kaptan Sk

Yeniçarşı Cad

Boğazkesen Cad

Karabaş Deresi Sk

Akarsu Yokuşu

Çukurcuma

Kumrulu Sk

Findikli

Defterdar Yokuşu

Emi Yokuşu

Meclis-i Mebusan Cad

Tünel

Şişhane

Tünel Meydanı

Şişhane Pl

Yolcuzade İskender Sk

Galipdede Cad

Okçu Musa Cad

Kumbaracı Yokuşu

Mimar Sinan Fine Arts University

SİSHANE

Yanıkkapı Sk

Galata Mahkemesi Sk

Galata Meydanı

Galata

Lüleci Hendek Cad

Kemeraltı Cad

Tophane

○3

Golden Horn (Haliç)

Abdülezel Paşa Cad

Paşa Cad

Atatürk Bridge (Atatürk Köprüsü)

Bankalar Cad

Tersane Cad

Karaköy Cad

Kemankeş Cad

Karaköy

Karaköy Güllüoğlu

○6

Bosphorus Strait (Boğaziçi)

Unkapanı

Haliç Ⓜ

Fish Market (Balık Pazarı)

Fish Market

Karaköy Meydanı

Sarıdemır

Atatürk Bul

Ragıp Gümüşpala Cad

Galata Bridge (Galata Köprüsü)

Küçük Pazar

Vefa

Hoca Giyasettın

Demırtaş

Şemsettin Sk

Küçük Pazar

Prof Cemil Birsel Cad

Rüstem Paşa

Reşadiye Cad

Bosphorus Ferry Trips

○3

Vefa Cad

Süleymaniye Mosque

Rüstem Paşa Mosque

Spice Bazaar (Mısır Çarşısı)

Çiçek Pazarı Sk

Sirkeci

Ankara Cad

Kennedy Cad (Sahil Yolu)

Sarayburnu

Molla Hüsrev

○5

Dökmeciler Hamamı Sk

Tahtakale

Vasıf Çınar Cad

Eminönü

Hamidiye Cad

Gülhane Park

Kalenderhane

Ayşekadın Hamamı Sk

İstanbul University

Mercan

Büyük Valide Han

Çakmakçılar Yokuşu

Yenicamii Cad

Hobyar

Aşır Efendi Cad

Hocapaşa Sokak

Sirkeci ○

Ebussuud Cad

Hüdavendigar Cad

○2

Topkapı Palace

△2

Saraçhane Park

Süleymaniye Cad

Fuat Paşa Cad

Sururı

Taya Hatun

Türkocağı Cad

Ankara Cad

Cağaloğlu

Hükümet Konağı Sk

Vezneciler

Vezneciler Cad

Besim Ömer Paşa Cad

Yorgancılar Kapısı

Tarakçılar Cad

○4

Grand Bazaar

Cağaloğlu Meydanı

Bab-ı Ali Cad

Yerebatan Cad

Molla Fenerı

Topkapı Palace Court of Janissaries (First Court)

Balaban Ağa

Lalelı

Ordu Cad

Beyazıt Meydanı

Beyazit

Nuruosmaniye Cad

Divan Yolu Cad

Çemberlıtaş

Bab-ı Ali Cad

Alemdar

○9

Basilica Cistern

○1

Aya Sofya

△1

Alemdar Cad

Nişanca

Soğanağa Camii Sk

Yahya Paşa Sk

Emin Sınan

Peykhane Cad

Emin Sinan Hamamı Sk

Binbirdirek

Sultanahmet Park

Derviş Aile Çay Bahçesi

Şehnameci Sk

İbrahim Paşa Yokuşu

Tiyatro Cad

Bali Paşa Yokuşu

Gedik Paşa

Doğramacı Sk

Dizdariye Çeşmesi Sk

Hippodrome

Atmeydanı Cad

○8

Sultanahmet

Cafe Meşale

Türkeli Cad

Molla Taşı Cad

Gedikpaşa Cad

Kadirga

Kadırga Limanı Cad

Blue Mosque

Arasta Bazaar

Küçük Ayasofya Cad

Cankurtaran

Kennedy Cad (Sahil Yolu)

Kumkapı

Şehsuvar

Çapariz Sk

Cinci Meydanı Sk

Kaleci Sk

Küçük Ayasofya

Akbıyık Değirmeni Sk

Kennedy Cad (Sahil Yolu)

SEA OF MARMARA
(MARMARA DENIZI)

A   B   C   D   E   F   G

1
2
3
4
5
6
7
8
9
10

SIGHTS &
ACTIVITIES

◉ SEE
◉ DO

ITINERARY

▽ 1
▽ 2

① Petronas Towers

It's impossible to resist the magnetic allure of the Petronas Towers: the 452m-high structure is beautiful to look at, as well as being the embodiment of Malaysia's transformation into a developed nation. Designed by architect César Pelli, this glistening, steel-wrapped structure is the focal point of the Kuala Lumpur City Centre (KLCC), a 40-hectare development that also includes an imaginatively designed tropical park, a fun aquarium, an excellent kids' museum and a world-class concert hall.

② Islamic Arts Museum

This museum – with its Iranian-tiled facade and beautifully decorated domes – is a stunning example of exquisite craftsmanship. Inside, the galleries are filled with natural light and a dazzling collection of works gathered from around the Islamic world. Don't miss the architecture gallery, with models of some of the major Islamic buildings.

③ Chinatown

Plumes of smoke curl upwards from smouldering coils of incense, flower garlands hang like pearls from the necks of Hindu statues; and the call to prayer punctuates the honk of traffic. The temples and mosques of the city's Hindus, Muslims and Chinese Buddhists are crammed shoulder to shoulder in this atmospheric neighbourhood along the Klang river – where KL was born. Don't miss eating at the daytime Madras Lane hawker stalls or savouring the bustle and fun of the night market along Jln Petaling.

④ Pavilion KL

Pavilion sets the gold standard in KL's shopping scene, with great local options including British India for fashion and the more affordable Padini Concept Store. For a quick trip to Japan, head to the 6th floor Tokyo Street stalls.

⑤ Tun Abdul Razak Heritage Park

This 173-hectare lush, landscaped park is also known, and more aptly described, by its colonial-era moniker: the Lake Gardens. This is KL's largest green space, and you can spend hours exploring the rolling terrain. Don't miss its sprawling Bird Park. It also hosts the National Planetarium, KL Butterfly Park and the striking National Monument.

⑥ Street food

Some of the best KL dining experiences will happen on the street. Delicious, freshly cooked meals served from mobile carts, stalls and humble shophouse *kopitiam* (coffee shops) are unforgettable for all the right reasons. Jalan Alor is the city's most famous eat street, with great food and atmosphere, but prices are higher than the more locally patronised hawker gourmet destinations such as Lucky Gardens, Glutton Street or the stalls scattered around Brickfields.

⑦ Merdeka Square

The huge open square where Malaysian independence was declared in 1957 is ringed by heritage buildings, such as the magnificent Sultan Abdul Samad Building, decorated with copper-clad domes and barley-sugar-twist columns, and St Mary's Anglican Cathedral, both designed by AC Norman. It also has an enormous flagpole and a fluttering Malaysian flag. In the British era, the square was used as a cricket pitch and called the Padang (field).

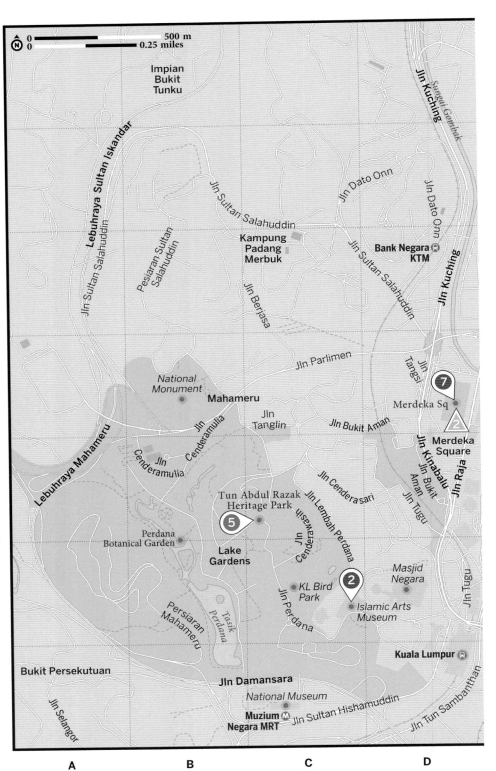

Day 1 itinerary

Head up the **Petronas Towers** before browsing the shops in **Suria KLCC** and seeing a free art exhibition at the excellent **Galeri Petronas**. For lunch join local office workers for a vegetarian meal at the **Dharma Realm Guan Yin Sagely Monastery Canteen**. Take a post-lunch stroll around KLCC Park, admiring the view of the towers, then take a look at contemporary Malaysian art at the **ILHAM**. Join the 3pm tour of the Malay-style wooden house **Rumah Penghulu Abu Seman** next to **Badan Warisan Malaysia** or learn about sea life at **Aquaria KLCC**. Find some street eat treats for dinner on **Jln Alor**. Finish your evening by heading to **Changkat Bukit Bintang** and **Jln Mesui** for the bars.

Days 2 and 3 itinerary

First off on day two is memorable **Merdeka Square**. Then cycle or taxi to **Tun Abdul Razak Heritage Park**. Start at the **National Monument**, then walk through the **Perdana Botanical Garden** to the **National Museum**. After some street food, enjoy the **KL Bird Park**. Save a couple of hours for the splendid **Islamic Arts Museum**, then admire the architecture of **Masjid Negara** and **KL Railway Station**. In the evening hit **Central Market** and Chinatown's **Petaling Street Market**. Start day three ambling past traditional wooden houses and flower gardens in the Malay area of **Kampung Baru**. After lunch, walk from **Masjid India** to **Bukit Nanas**, the oldest protected piece of jungle in Malaysia, and traverse the canopy walkway of **KL Forest Eco Park**. For another panoramic perspective, take the lift to the observation deck of **Menara KL**, a 421m telecommunications tower offering 360-degree views of the city and a sky-high revolving restaurant. At the tower's base are plenty of attractions, and a 150-year-old Jelutong tree.

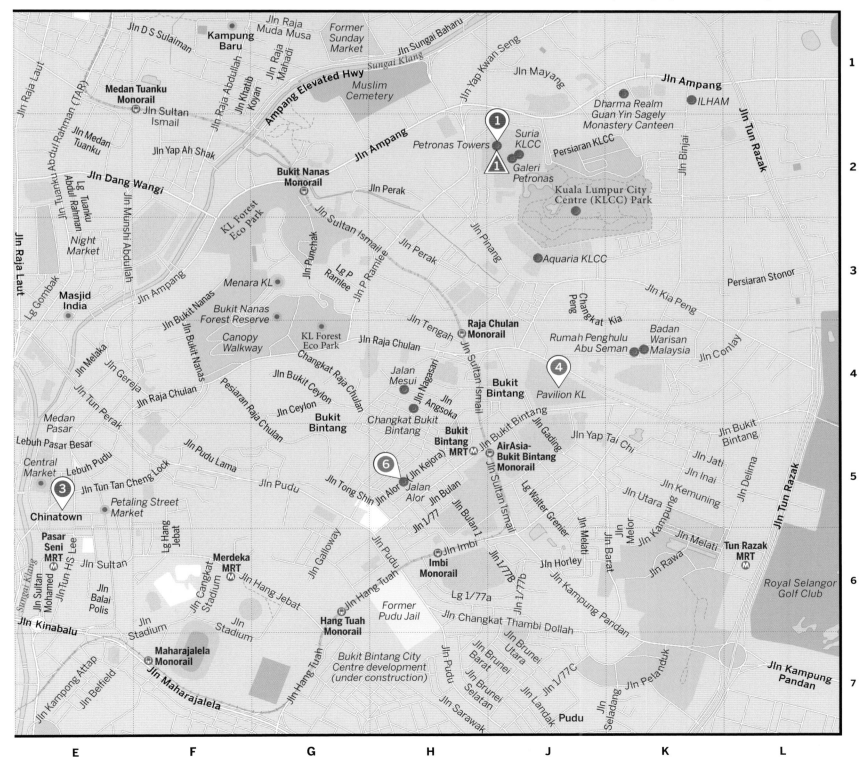

British Museum

You could spend a lifetime in this vast and hallowed collection of artefacts, art and age-old antiquity, and still make daily discoveries. Make sure you glimpse the Rosetta Stone, key to deciphering hieroglyphics, and the other-worldly mummies.

The South Bank

A must-visit area for art-lovers, theatre-goers and culture hounds, this riverside area pumps with energy. Besides the renowned Tate Modern, it proffers iconic views of the Thames and St Paul's Cathedral, great food markets, dollops of history and striking examples of modern architecture.

National Gallery

This superlative collection of art in the heart of London provides a roll call of some of the world's most outstanding artists: Leonardo da Vinci, Michelangelo, Turner, Monet, Renoir and Van Gogh – it's a bravura performance and one not to be missed.

Hyde Park & Kensington Gardens

London's urban parkland is virtually second to none and this duo provides everything you could want: a central London setting, a royal palace, extravagant Victoriana, boating opportunities, open-air concerts, art galleries, magnificent trees and the gleaming Albert Memorial.

Culinary London

The city has long been a shining light in culinary excellence, with a kaleidoscope of foreign cuisines unrivalled in Europe. However, don't miss the opportunity of trying traditional or Modern British cuisine, either in a good gastropub or one of the finer restaurants. East London's quickly evolving eating scene is worth an exploratory taste or two.

Tate Modern

The favourite museum of Londoners (and quite possibly the world), this contemporary art collection enjoys a triumphant position right on the River Thames. Housed in the former Bankside Power Station, Tate Modern is a vigorous statement of modernity, architectural renewal and accessibility.

Shakespeare's Globe

Few London experiences can beat a Bard's-eye view of the stage at the re-created Globe, a triumph of authenticity. Get a standing ticket to watch from the open-air yard in front of the stage for an unusual Elizabethan-style experience.

Victoria & Albert Museum

The world's leading collection of decorative arts has something for everyone, from Islamic textiles to antique Chinese ceramics, photography, fashion, works by Raphael and modern design classics from iMacs to Nike shoes.

Natural History Museum

With its thunderous, animatronic *Tyrannosaurus rex*, riveting displays about planet Earth, the outstanding Darwin Centre and architecture from a Gothic fairy tale, it is quite simply a work of great curatorial imagination.

Tower of London

This titanic fortress beside the Thames is steeped in history and legend. A former prison, armoury and royal residence, this castle now hosts the crown jewels, one of the world's largest diamonds and a dazzling array of armour and weaponry.

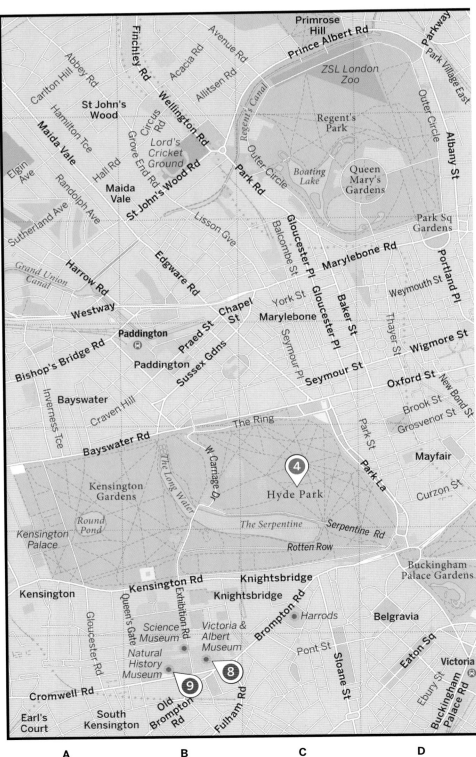

Day 1 itinerary

First stop, **Buckingham Palace** for the Changing of the Guard. Walk up the Mall to **Trafalgar Square** for its architectural grandeur and an exploration of the **National Gallery**. Now wander down **Whitehall** (and past **10 Downing Street**) for **Big Ben**, the **Houses of Parliament** and **Westminster Abbey**. Next circle the sky in the **London Eye**,

then stroll along the South Bank to **Tate Modern**. After touring some of its free displays, cross the elegant **Millennium Bridge** for a close up of **St Paul's Cathedral**. Make a return trip over the bridge for a performance at **Shakespeare's Globe** or join the post-work crowd in the pubs around **London Bridge** for real ales and historical surroundings.

Days 2 and 3 itinerary

Start day two within the ancient **Tower of London**. When you've seen it all, stroll across the iconic **Tower Bridge** before taking lunch. Next hop on a double-decker to the **British Museum** for a shot of world culture. If you fancy soaking up the atmosphere, an evening amble through **Chinatown** and **Soho** to **Leicester Sq** will do the trick. There

are literally dozens of pubs, bars and cocktail bars along the way from which to choose. The next morning hop on the tube to Knightsbridge. Keen shoppers will want to stroll down Old Brompton Rd and pop into **Harrods**, the famous department store. Culture vultures should save their energy for the nearby **Victoria & Albert Museum**,

the **Natural History Museum** or the **Science Museum**. If the pubs around Knightsbridge and South Kensington are too staid for you, hop over to **Shoreditch** where east London's multiculturalism has ensured that its food and drink scene stretches from some fantastic low-key options to gastropubs and more upmarket restaurants, too.

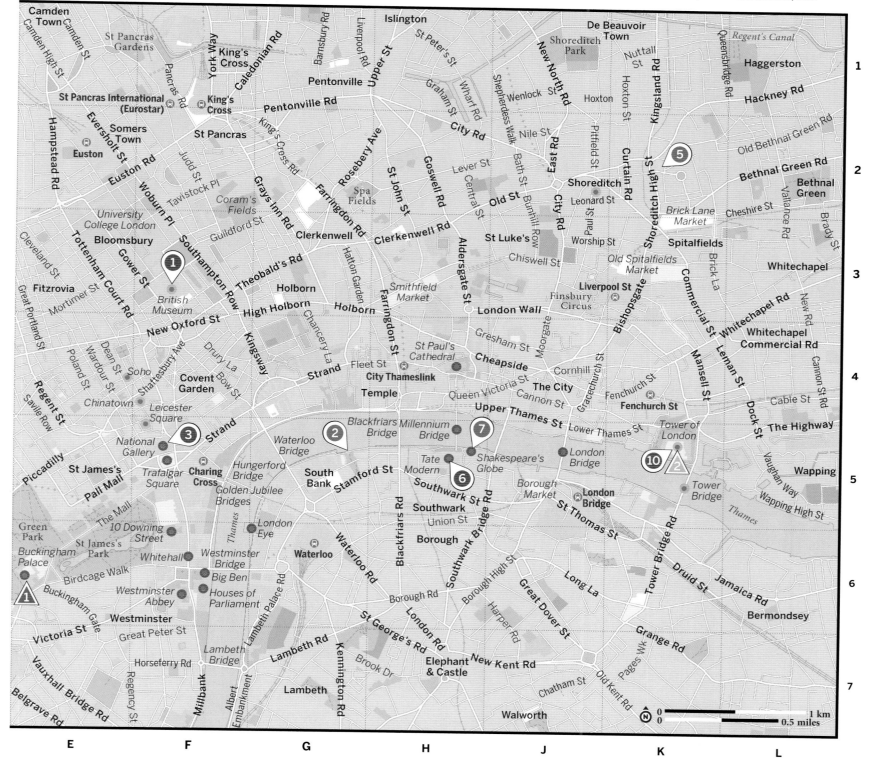

SIGHTS &
ACTIVITIES

◉ SEE
◉ DO

ITINERARY

▽ 1
▽ 2

Royal Botanic Gardens

Stretching for 38 glorious hectares on the south bank of the Yarra River, the Royal Botanic Gardens are one of the world's best examples of Victorian-era garden landscaping. Wander, sprawl on the extensive lawns for a picnic and then return to watch cinema or theatre under the stars.

City laneways and arcades

Nothing screams Melbourne quite as loudly as a graffiti-covered lane – preferably one hiding a cafe, basement bar or sought-after restaurant. The most famous (and most photographed) of them all is Hosier Lane.

National Gallery of Victoria International

Housed in a vast, brutally beautiful building, NGV International has an expansive collection that runs the gamut from the ancient to the bleeding edge. Key works include a Rembrandt self-portrait, Tiepolo's *The Banquet of Cleopatra*, Turner's otherworldly *Falls of Schaffhausen* and Picasso's *Weeping Woman*.

Melbourne Cricket Ground

The MCG is sacred ground to many Melburnians, carrying within its bulky frame the treasured hope of Grand Final glory for their beloved Aussie Rules footy team. If you can't make it to a cricket or footy match, entertaining guided tours are available. The excellent National Sports Museum also lies within.

St Kilda: Kite surfers on the beach at St Kilda.

Shrine of Remembrance

Taking the form of an ancient Greek temple, this secular shrine memorialises those who lost their lives during WWI. The views from the top of the monument are outstanding, and there's a museum beneath.

Melbourne Museum and Royal Exhibition Building

Victoria's cultural, social and natural history are given their due at this highly interesting museum, occupying a striking modern building at the heart of Carlton Gardens. The museum shares the gardens with the exquisite Royal Exhibition Building.

Culinary wizardry

Melbourne's exceptional dining scene, embraced by a discerning populace, has been shaped by immigrants from all over the world. Whether seeking memorable cheap eats or extraordinary fine fare, your palate will be rewarded. Head to Prahran Market to browse stalls of gourmet deli items.

Abbotsford Convent

No nuns remain at this 19th-century convent, but there are plenty of artsy types enjoying its lawns, galleries and cafes as well as its bakery and bar.

St Kilda

This seaside suburb has a roguish charm. A stroll along its pier offers wonderful panoramic views of Melbourne's skyline, and you might even catch a glimpse of one St Kilda's most charming denizens – penguins.

Coffee culture

Aussies and Kiwis lead the world in the dark arts of the espresso machine. Declaring it may risk an international incident, but Melbourne is the coffee capital of the world. Fitzroy is a prime hunting ground, along with nearby Collingwood and Abbotsford.

Day 1 itinerary

Start at **Federation Sq**, spending the morning exploring the **Ian Potter Centre: NGV Australia**, the **Australian Centre for the Moving Image** and the **Koorie Heritage Trust**. Then wander across Flinders St to **Hosier Lane** for Melbourne's most prominent street art. Dine at one of the great options along **Flinders Lane**. Jump on a tram heading north to **Carlton**. Have a good gawk at the **Royal Exhibition Building** before delving into the Melbourne Museum. Finish up with a stroll along **Lygon St** to soak up the old-school Melbourne Italian vibe and a memorable meal. If you're not finished yet, there are hip drinking options back around Flinders Lane.

Days 2 and 3 itinerary

Begin day two at **Queen Victoria Market**, then grab a takeaway flat white for a walk through **Flagstaff Gardens**. Head down William St to the grand Mint building and stop to explore the excellent **Hellenic Museum** within. Wander back up to Flagstaff station and take a train to Jolimont station. Pause for a deli lunch in **Richmond**. Next head to **Yarra Park** to the **Melbourne Cricket Ground**. Continue on to **Fitzroy Gardens** and seek out the **Conservatory**, **Cooks' Cottage**, **Fairies Tree** and miniature **Tudor Village**. Fitzroy has plenty of choice for dinner and drinks. Start day three with a walk around the **Royal Botanic Gardens** and a visit to the **Shrine of Remembrance**. Catch a tram to **South Yarra** and window-shop along **Chapel St** and **Commercial Rd** before calling into **Prahran Market**. Continue the shopping spree on **Greville St** and then continue up Chapel St to **Windsor**. Jump on a tram to spend the afternoon and evening in **St Kilda**, perhaps catching a concert at the **Palais Theatre**. If nightlife is calling, hit **Fitzroy St**.

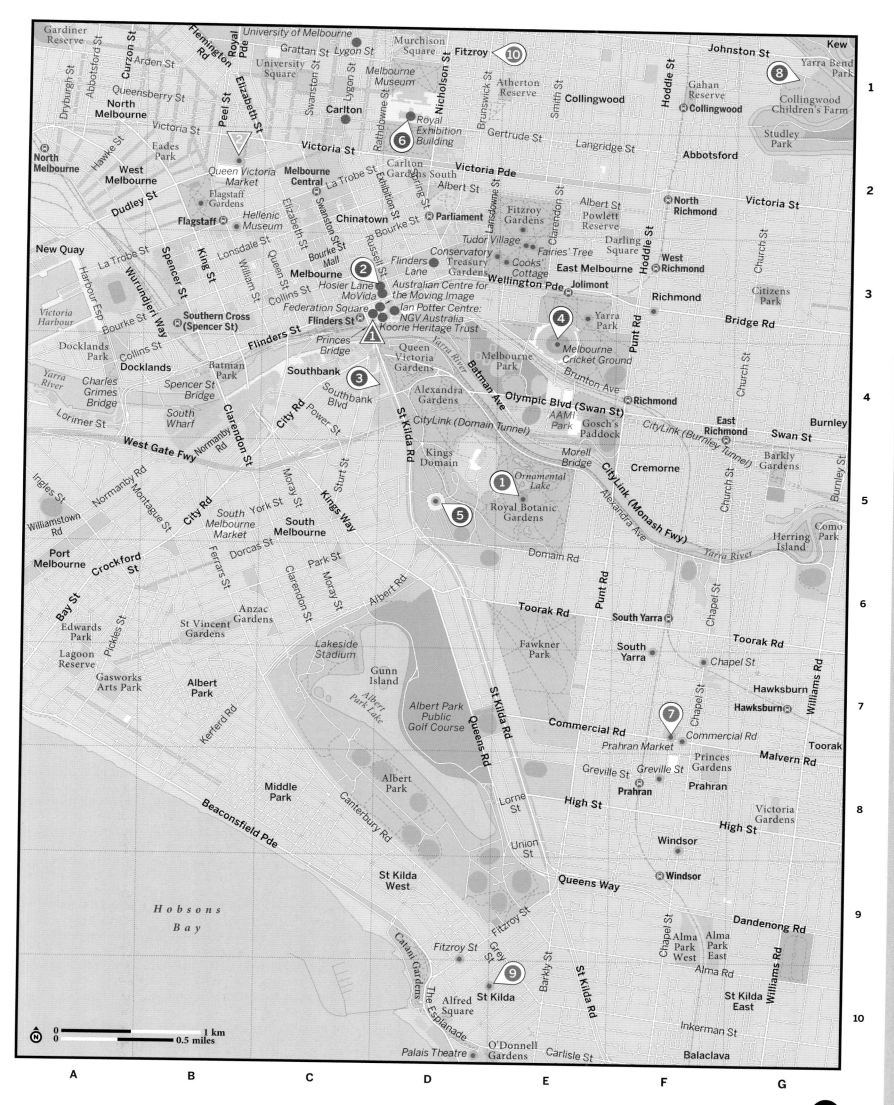

Gardiner
Reserve

Kew

University of Melbourne

Murchison
Square

Johnston St

Yarra Bend
Park

⑧

1

Dryburgh St
Abbotsford St
Curzon St
Arden St

Grattan St
Lygon St

Fitzroy ⑩

Studley
Park

Collingwood
Children's
Farm

Queensberry St

University
Square

Gahan
Reserve

**North
Melbourne**

Peel St
Elizabeth St
Flemington
Rd
Royal
Pde

Victoria St

Swanston St
Lygon St

Melbourne
Museum

Atherton
Reserve

Collingwood

Hoddle St

Abbotsford

Hawke St
Eades
Park
Victoria St

② ▽

Carlton

Rathdowne St
Nicholson St

Royal
Exhibition
Building

Brunswick St
Smith St

● **Collingwood**

**North
Melbourne**

**West
Melbourne**

Queen Victoria
Market

Victoria St

⑥

Gertrude St

Langridge St

2

Dudley St

Flagstaff
Gardens

Melbourne
Gardens

Carlton
Gardens
South

Victoria Pde

Albert St
Powlett
Reserve

**North
Richmond**

Victoria St

New Quay

Flagstaff ⓡ
Hellenic
Museum

Melbourne
Central

La Trobe St
Exhibition St

Albert St

Fitzroy
Gardens

Clarendon St

Darling
Square

**West
Richmond**

La Trobe St

Elizabeth St
Swanston St
Russell St
Bourke St

Chinatown

Lansdowne St

Tudor Village

Fairies' Tree

Hoddle St

Spencer St

Lonsdale St

Bourke St

ⓡ Parliament

Conservatory

Cooks'
Cottage

East Melbourne

3

King St
William St

Bourke St
Mall

Flinders
Lane

Treasury
Gardens

Wellington Pde

Jolimont

Richmond

Church St

Melbourne
②

Hosier Lane
MoVida

Australian Centre for
the Moving Image

Citizens
Park

Victoria
Harbour

ⓡ **Southern Cross
(Spencer St)**

Federation Square

Ian Potter Centre:
NGV Australia

Yarra Park

Punt Rd

Richmond

Bridge Rd

Flinders St ⓡ

Koorie Heritage Trust

① △

Flinders St

Princes
Bridge

Queen
Victoria
Gardens

Melbourne
Cricket Ground

④

Yarra Park

4

Docklands
Park

Collins St

Docklands

Batman
Park

Spencer St
Bridge

Southbank

Southbank
Blvd

Alexandra
Gardens

Olympic Blvd (Swan St)

Brunton Ave

ⓡ **Richmond**

East
Richmond

Burnley

Yarra
River

Charles
Grimes
Bridge

South
Wharf

③

City Rd
Power St
Sturt St

St Kilda Rd

CityLink (Domain Tunnel)

AAMI
Park

Gosch's
Paddock

CityLink (Burnley Tunnel)

Swan St

Church St
Barkly
Gardens

Lorimer St

West Gate Fwy

Normanby Rd
Clarendon St

Morell
Bridge

Cremorne

Burnley St

Ingles St

Normanby Rd
Montague St

Kings
Domain

Kings
Way

① ①

Ornamental
Lake

Alexandra Ave
CityLink (Monash Fwy)

Yarra River

Herring
Island

Como
Park

5

Williamstown
Rd

South
Melbourne
Market

York St
Moray St

**South
Melbourne**

⑤

**Royal Botanic
Gardens**

Port
Melbourne

Crockford
St

Dorcas St

Domain Rd

6

Bay St

Edwards
Park

Pickles St

St Vincent
Gardens

Anzac
Gardens

Albert Rd

Clarendon St
Moray St

Park St

Toorak Rd

Punt Rd

ⓡ **South Yarra**

Toorak Rd

Lagoon
Reserve

Gasworks
Arts Park

**Albert
Park**

Lakeside
Stadium

Gunn
Island

Fawkner
Park

**South
Yarra**

Chapel St

Hawksburn

Kerferd Rd

Albert
Park
Lake

Albert Park
Public
Golf Course

Queens Rd

⑦

Commercial Rd

Commercial Rd

Hawksburn ⓡ

Malvern Rd

Toorak

7

Canterbury Rd

Prahran Market

Chapel St

Princes
Gardens

Middle
Park

Albert
Park

St Kilda Rd

Lorne
St

Greville St

Greville St

Prahran

8

Beaconsfield Pde

Union
St

High St

ⓡ **Prahran**

High St

Victoria
Gardens

Windsor

**St Kilda
West**

Queens Way

ⓡ Windsor

Chapel St

Dandenong Rd

9

Fitzroy St
Grey St

Alma
Park
West

Alma
Park
East

*Hobsons
Bay*

Catani Gardens

Fitzroy St

⑨

Barkly St

St Kilda Rd

Alma Rd

St Kilda
East

Williams Rd

The Esplanade

St Kilda

Alfred
Square

Inkerman St

10

⬆
N

0 _____ 1 km
0 _____ 0.5 miles

Palais Theatre

O'Donnell
Gardens

Carlisle St

Balaclava

A   B   C   D   E   F   G

SIGHTS &
ACTIVITIES

◉ SEE
◉ DO

ITINERARY

▽ 1
▽ 2

Brooklyn Bridge:
This New York icon
links the island of
Manhattan with
Brooklyn.

Central Park
One of the world's most renowned
green spaces, comprises rolling
meadows, boulder-studded outcrops,
elm-lined walkways, manicured
European-style gardens, a lake and a
reservoir – not to mention an outdoor
theatre, a memorial to John Lennon,
an idyllic waterside eatery (the Loeb
Boathouse) and one very famous
statue of Alice in Wonderland. The big
challenge? Figuring out where to begin.

The High Line
A resounding triumph of urban
renewal, this park was once a dingy rail
line that anchored a rather unsavoury
district of slaughterhouses. Today,
it's an unfurled emerald necklace and
one of New York's best-loved green
spaces. Come to stroll, sit and picnic
30ft above the city – while enjoying
fabulous views of Manhattan's ever-
changing urban landscape.

Broadway & Times Square
Sizzling lights, electrifying energy:
Broadway is NYC's dream factory,
a place where romance, betrayal,
murder and triumph come with glittery
costumes and stirring scores. The
district's star is Times Square.

National September 11 Memorial
Rising from the ashes of Ground Zero,
this memorial is a beautiful, dignified
response to the city's darkest chapter.
Where the Twin Towers once soared,
two reflecting pools now weep like
dark, elegant waterfalls. Framing them
are the names of those who lost their
lives here.

One World Observatory
New York's tallest and most
anticipated skyscraper has arrived – a
soaring 104-storey landmark that
looms like a beacon above Lower
Manhattan. Take a high-speed ride in a
'sky pod' to the top for fabulous views.

New York City's food scene
The sheer variety of restaurants is
staggering. In a single neighbourhood
such as Queens you'll find vintage-
filled gastropubs, sushi counters, tapas
bars, French bistros, barbecue joints,
pizza parlours, vegan cafes, food trucks
and good old-fashioned delis.

Metropolitan Museum of Art
With more than two million objects in its
collections, the Met is dazzling. Its works
span the world, from the sculptures of
ancient Greece to the evocative carvings
of Papua New Guinea.

Brooklyn
If you want to see the real New
York, you need to head to Brooklyn.
This borough is home to some of
NYC's most interesting, historic and
culturally diverse neighborhoods, with
singularly fantastic dining, drinking,
shopping and entertainment options.

Statue of Liberty & Ellis Island
Since 1886 Lady Liberty has
welcomed millions of immigrants,
sailing into New York Harbor in the
hope of a better life. Contemplate
that while absorbing one of the Big
Apple's finest views from her crown.
Nearby Ellis Island has a moving
museum, which pays tribute to the
indelible courage of those arrivals.

Empire State Building
The striking art-deco skyscraper
may no longer be New York's tallest
building, but it remains one of its
most recognisable icons and still
provides one of the best views in town
– particularly around sunset when the
twinkling lights of the city switch on.

Brooklyn Bridge
This Gothic Revival masterpiece
has inspired poetry (Jack Kerouac's
'Brooklyn Bridge Blues'), music (Frank
Sinatra's 'Brooklyn Bridge') and plenty
of art (Walker Evans' photography). It's
also the most scenic way to pass from
Manhattan into Brooklyn. Run, walk
or cycle across at sunrise, when you'll
have it to yourself.

Museum of Modern Art
For art buffs, it's Valhalla. For the
uninitiated, it's a thrilling crash course
in all that is beautiful and addictive
about art. This superstar of the
modern-art scene scintillates with
heavyweights: Van Gogh, Matisse,
Picasso, Warhol, Lichtenstein, Rothko
and Pollock. Put simply, MoMA is
quite possibly the greatest hoarder of
modern masterpieces on earth.

**Day 1
itinerary**

Spend the morning
exploring **Central
Park**. Start at
Columbus Circle,
then take in the
zoo, the **Bethesda
Fountain**, the
Conservatory Water
and **Strawberry
Fields**. Then check
out the dinosaurs
at the **American
Museum of Natural
History** before
renting a rowboat at
the **Loeb Boathouse**.
After a picnic lunch,
uncover some of the

city's architectural
wonders: **Grand
Central Terminal**,
the **Chrysler
Building**, the **New
York Public Library**
and **Rockefeller
Center**. Round off
the afternoon with
a visit to the city's
museum darling:
MoMA. While away
the evening under
the starry lights of
Broadway, checking
out a show or just
soaking up **Times
Square**.

**Days 2 &3
itinerary**

Start day two at
the **Metropolitan
Museum of Art** by
wandering through
the Egyptian and
Roman collections,
then take in
European masters
before hitting the
roof for a view
over Central Park.
Afterwards, visit the
nearby **Neue Galerie**
for a feast of German
and Austrian art in a
1914 mansion. Come
afternoon, hit **SoHo**
for some shopping

and **Chinatown**
for some Buddhist
inspiration. In the
evening take in a
symphony, ballet
or opera at **Lincoln
Center**. Start your
last day by catching
the East River Ferry
over to **Dumbo**,
and admire the
magnificent view
of Manhattan from
the lush **Brooklyn
Bridge Park**.
Afterwards, stroll
through Dumbo's
cobblestone streets,

browsing bookshops,
boutiques and
cafes. On summer
Sundays be sure
to check out the
Brooklyn Flea inside
a giant archway
under Manhattan
Bridge. Next up,
take a meander
in **McCarren Park**
and, as night falls,
hit the bars of
Williamsburg. Start
with oysters and
cocktails and end at
a rooftop bar with
views over the city.

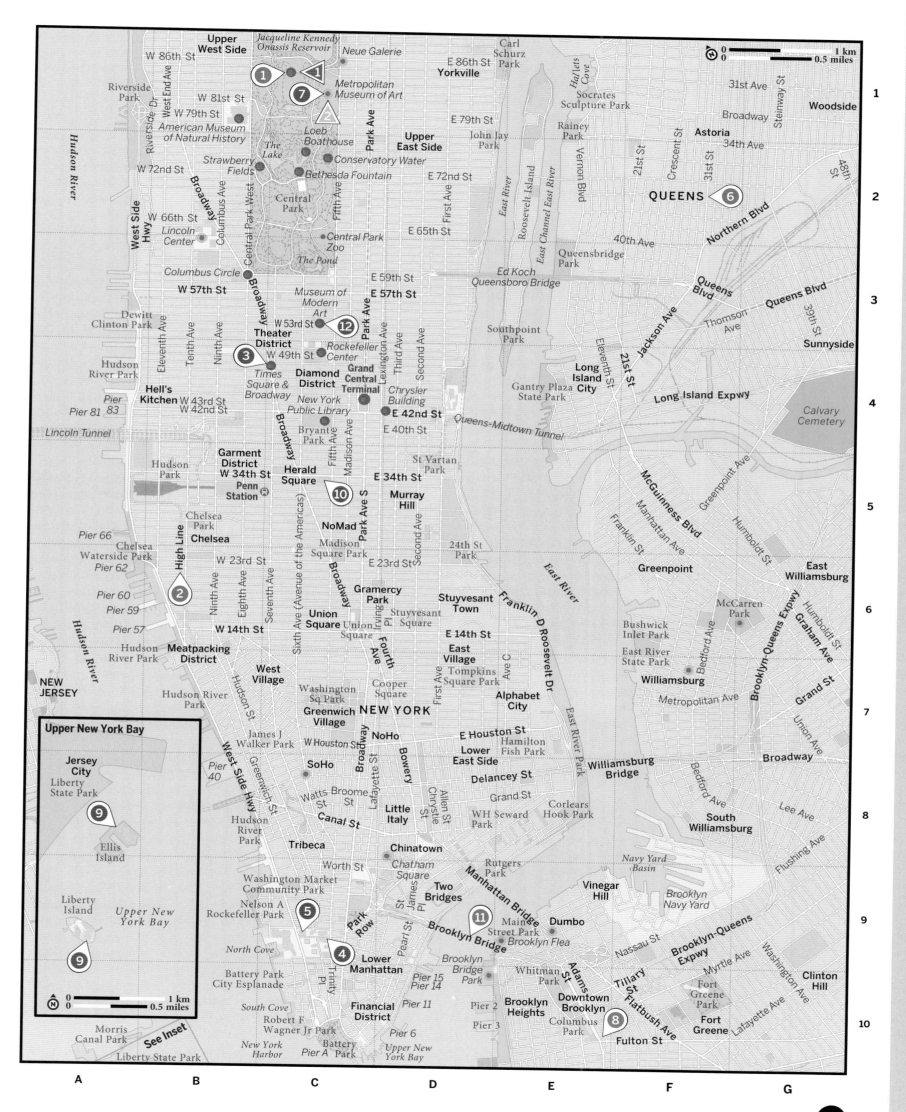

W 86th St

Upper
West Side

Riverside
Park

West End Ave

Jacqueline Kennedy
Onassis Reservoir

Neue Galerie

Carl
Schurz
Park

E 86th St

Yorkville

Halets Cove

Socrates
Sculpture Park

Rainey
Park

31st Ave

Broadway

Steinway St

34th Ave

Woodside

1

1

1

7

2

W 81st St

W 79th St

American Museum
of Natural History

Metropolitan
Museum of Art

Loeb
Boathouse

Park Ave

Upper
East Side

E 79th St

John Jay
Park

Astoria

21st St

Crescent St

31st St

48th St

The Lake

Strawberry
Fields

Conservatory Water

Bethesda Fountain

E 72nd Ave

Fifth Ave

First Ave

Vernon Blvd

Hudson River

Riverside Dr

W 72nd St

Central Park West

Columbus Ave

Broadway

Central
Park

Roosevelt Island

East River

East Channel East River

QUEENS

6

Northern Blvd

2

West Side Hwy

W 66th St

Lincoln
Center

Central Park
Zoo

E 65th St

40th Ave

Queensbridge
Park

Queens
Blvd

Queens Blvd

39th St

Dewitt
Clinton Park

Columbus Circle

W 57th St

Broadway

The Pond

Museum of
Modern
Art

E 59th St

E 57th St

Ed Koch
Queensboro Bridge

Southpoint
Park

Jackson Ave

Thomson
Ave

3

Sunnyside

3

12

W 53rd St

Theater
District

W 49th St

Rockefeller
Center

Lexington Ave

Third Ave

Second Ave

Long
Island
City

Gantry Plaza
State Park

Eleventh St

21st St

Long Island Expwy

Hudson
River Park

Eleventh Ave

Tenth Ave

Ninth Ave

Times
Square &
Broadway

Diamond
District

Grand
Central
Terminal

Chrysler
Building

Calvary
Cemetery

4

Pier
83

Pier 81

Hell's
Kitchen

W 43rd St

W 42nd St

New York
Public Library

E 42nd St

E 40th St

Queens-Midtown Tunnel

Lincoln Tunnel

Bryant
Park

Madison Ave

Fifth Ave

St Vartan
Park

Hudson
Park

Garment
District
W 34th St
Penn
Station

Broadway

Herald
Square

E 34th St

Murray
Hill

McGuinness Blvd

Greenpoint Ave

10

Chelsea
Park

NoMad

Madison
Square Park

24th St
Park

Manhattan Ave

Franklin St

Humboldt St

East
Williamsburg

5

Pier 66

High Line

Chelsea
Waterside Park
Pier 62

W 23rd St

E 23rd St

Second Ave

Greenpoint

McCarren
Park

Bedford Ave

Brooklyn-Queens Expwy

Humboldt St

Graham Ave

6

Pier 60

Pier 59

Pier 57

2

Ninth Ave

Eighth Ave

Seventh Ave

Sixth Ave (Avenue of the Americas)

Broadway

Union
Square

Gramercy
Park

Union
Square

Irving Pl

Stuyvesant
Square

Stuyvesant
Town

E 14th St

Franklin D Roosevelt Dr

East River

Bushwick
Inlet Park

East River
State Park

Williamsburg

Metropolitan Ave

Grand St

Union Ave

Broadway

7

Hudson River

NEW
JERSEY

Hudson River
Park

Meatpacking
District

West
Village

Washington
Sq Park

Cooper
Square

East
Village

Tompkins
Square Park

Alphabet
City

First Ave

Ave C

Williamsburg
Bridge

Bedford Ave

Lee Ave

Greenwich
Village

NEW YORK

NoHo

E Houston St

Hamilton
Fish Park

South
Williamsburg

8

See Inset

Upper New York Bay

Jersey
City

Liberty
State Park

9

Ellis
Island

James J
Walker Park

W Houston St

Pier
40

SoHo

Lower
East Side

Lafayette St

Bowery

Delancey St

Allen St

Chrystie St

Grand St

WH Seward
Park

Corlears
Hook Park

Navy Yard
Basin

Flushing Ave

West Side Hwy

Greenwich St

Watts St

Broome
St

Canal St

Little
Italy

Tribeca

Chinatown

Vinegar
Hill

Brooklyn
Navy Yard

Liberty
Island

Liberty Island

Upper New
York Bay

9

Worth St

Washington Market
Community Park

Nelson A
Rockefeller Park

North Cove

5

Chatham
Square

Rutgers
Park

Manhattan Bridge

Dumbo

Brooklyn
Flea

Brooklyn-Queens
Expwy

Nassau St

Washington Ave

Clinton
Hill

9

1 km
0.5 miles

4

Park Row

Two
Bridges

11

Maine
Street Park

Brooklyn Bridge

Brooklyn
Bridge
Park

Whitman
Park

Downtown
Brooklyn

Tillary
St

Fort
Greene
Park

Fort
Greene

Battery Park
City Esplanade

South Cove

Lower
Manhattan

Pearl St

James St

Trinity St

Pier 15
Pier 14

Pier 11

Brooklyn
Heights

Columbus
Park

Flatbush Ave

Adams St

Lafayette Ave

8

Myrtle Ave

Morris
Canal Park

See Inset

Financial
District

Pier 6

Pier 2

Pier 3

Brooklyn-Queens
Expwy

Fulton St

10

Liberty State Park

New York
Harbor

Pier A

Battery Park

Robert F
Wagner Jr Park

Upper New
York Bay

A   B   C   D   E   F   G

SIGHTS &
ACTIVITIES

◉ SEE
◉ DO

ITINERARY

▽ 1
▽ 2

Parisian dining

France pioneered the most influential style of cooking in the Western world and Paris is its showcase par excellence. In the area west of place de la République, you'll find young chefs heading up some of the most exciting dining venues in Paris today. Do as Parisians do: take your time and savour every moment.

Eiffel Tower

No one could imagine Paris without it. But Gustave Eiffel only constructed this graceful spire as a temporary exhibit for the 1889 Exposition Universelle. Luckily, its popularity (and radiotelegraphy antennas) assured its survival.

Arc de Triomphe

If anything rivals the Eiffel Tower as the symbol of Paris, it's this magnificent monument to Napoléon's 1805 victory at Austerlitz. The intricately sculpted triumphal arch stands sentinel in the centre of the Étoile (star) roundabout. Some of the best vistas in Paris radiate from the top.

Cathédrale Notre Dame de Paris

A vision of stained-glass rose windows, flying buttresses and frightening gargoyles, Paris' glorious Gothic wonder took nearly 200 years to build and is the city's geographic and spiritual heart. Climb its 400-odd spiralling steps for magical rooftop views.

Musée du Louvre

The *Mona Lisa* and the *Venus de Milo* are just two of the priceless treasures housed inside the fortress turned royal palace turned France's first national museum. Without the nine months needed to glance at everything, follow its thematic trails, from the 'Art of Eating' to 'Love in the Louvre'.

Jardin du Luxembourg

This inner-city oasis of formal terraces, chestnut groves and lush lawns offers a snapshot of Parisian life. Couples stroll. Children sail toy wooden boats around the pond. Old men play chess on weathered tables. Students pore over books. Office workers snatch some sun. And friends meet and make plans to meet again.

Musée Rodin

This is the most romantic of Paris' museums. Auguste Rodin's former workshop and showroom, the 1730-built, beautifully restored Hôtel Biron, is filled with his own sculptural masterpieces like *The Kiss*, as well as works by Monet, Van Gogh and Renoir.

Street markets

Cheeses, stacked baguettes, sun-ripened tomatoes, horse-meat sausages, quail eggs, chanterelle mushrooms and knobbly truffles: street markets, such as the wonderful Marché Bastille, are a feast for the senses.

The Seine

Paris' most beautiful 'boulevard' of all, the Seine, flows through the city's heart, flanked by Parisian-as-it-gets landmarks such as the Eiffel Tower, the Louvre and Notre Dame. A cruise or Batobus ferry is an idyllic way to acquaint yourself with the city.

Montmartre

Crowned by the Sacré-Cœur basilica, this is Paris' steepest *quartier* (quarter). To walk its slinking streets lined with crooked ivy-clad buildings is to embrace its fairy-tale charm. The lofty views over Paris are equally captivating.

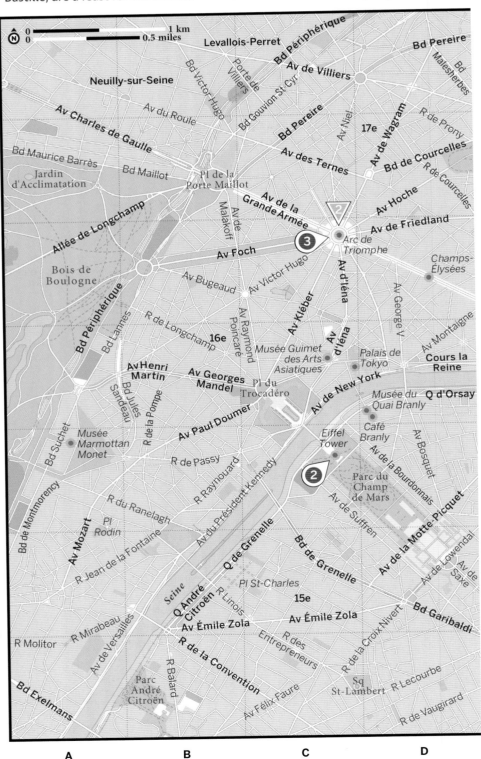

Day 1 itinerary

Start with a stroll through **Jardin des Tuileries**, stopping to view Monet's enormous *Water Lilies* at the **Musée de l'Orangerie**. Now, the **Louvre**! Dive in headfirst at IM Pei's glass pyramid. When lunch calls, nip out for French bistro fare before returning to the museum. Next up, browse **Jardin du Palais Royal** and the beautiful **Église St-Eustache**. Tap into the soul of the former Les Halles wholesale markets at backstreet legacies such as the former oyster market, **rue Montorgueil**. Linger for a drink on **rue Montmartre**, then head to the late-opening **Centre Pompidou** for its contemporary art and rooftop views. Afterwards grab a bite and hit the bars of **Le Marais**.

Days 2 and 3 itinerary

Day two starts with a climb up the **Arc de Triomphe** for a pinch-yourself Parisian panorama. Promenade down the **Champs-Élysées**, before touring Paris' opulent opera house, the **Palais Garnier**. Lunch at **Café Branly**, then check out **Musée du Quai Branly**, **Musée Marmottan-Monet**, **Palais de Tokyo** or **Musée Guimet**. Sunset is the best time to ascend the **Eiffel Tower**. Dine nearby then go for a drink at a historic Montparnasse brasserie like **Le Select**, or continue straight to the Seine to party at the hip bars on **quai d'Austerlitz**. Start day three at **Notre Dame**, then (for even more beautiful stained glass) step inside nearby **Sainte-Chapelle**. Now cross the Pont St-Louis to buy an ice cream at **Berthillon** before browsing the **Île St-Louis'** boutiques. Take lunch at the deliciously Parisian hang-out **Café Saint Régis**. Next, swoon over impressionist masterpieces in the magnificent **Musée d'Orsay** before lazing in the lovely **Jardin du Luxembourg**. Finish by spilling out into the **Latin Quarter** for its bars, cafes and pubs.

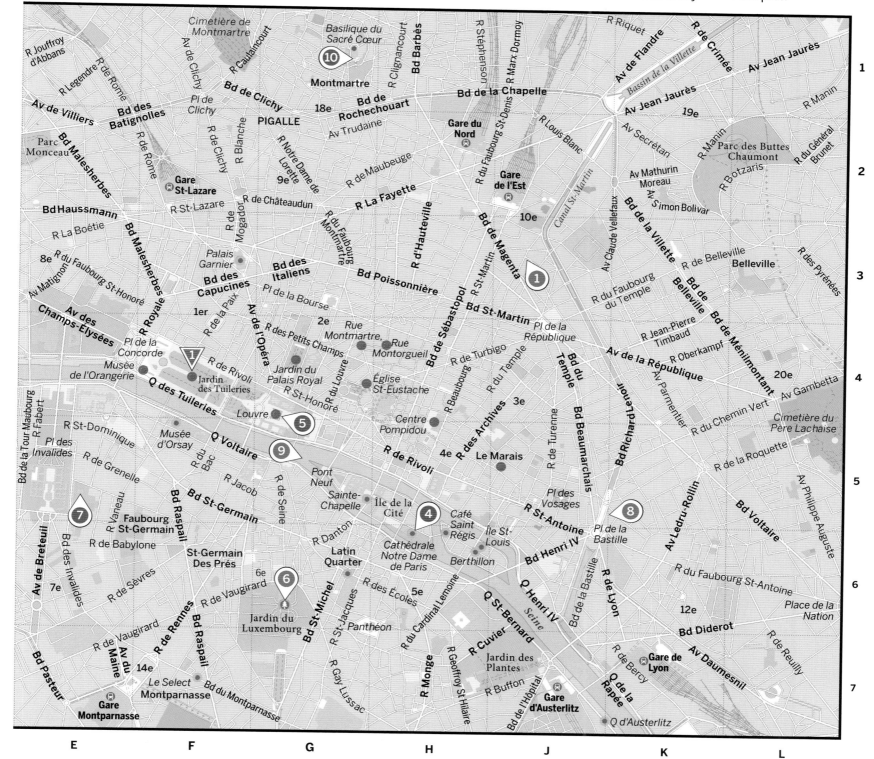

SIGHTS &
ACTIVITIES

 SEE

 DO

ITINERARY

▽ 1

▽ 2

Charles Bridge

Whether you visit alone in the early morning mist or shoulder your way through the afternoon crowds, crossing this fairy-tale bridge is the quintessential Prague experience. Built in 1357, its 16 elegant arches withstood wheeled traffic for 500-odd years – thanks, legend claims, to eggs mixed into the mortar – until it was made pedestrian-only after WWII. Its parade of baroque statues purvey mystery and magic to those who walk beneath.

Old Town Square

One of Europe's biggest and most beautiful urban spaces, Staroměstské náměstí has been Prague's principal public square since the 10th century. Famed for its intriguing Astronomical Clock, which 'performs' for 45 seconds on the hour.

St Vitus Cathedral

Occupying the site of a 10th-century Romanesque rotunda built by the Good King Wenceslas of Christmas carol fame, this cathedral was built over a time span of almost 600 years. It remains one of the most richly endowed cathedrals in central Europe, and it is pivotal to the nation's religious and cultural life. Admire the soaring spires and bell tower, then walk inside to gape at the gorgeous Gothic nave, stained glass and priceless treasures.

Prague Jewish Museum

Telling the poignant story of Prague's Jewish community, from the 16th-century creator of the Golem, Rabbi Loew, to the horrors of Nazi persecution, this museum encompasses ancient synagogues, a ceremonial hall and former mortuary, and the powerful and melancholic Old Jewish Cemetery.

Architecture

Malá Strana, Prague Castle and the city centre are a textbook display of 900 years of architectural evolution – Romanesque, Gothic, elegant Renaissance and dazzling baroque, plus 19th-century revivals of them all. And, incredibly, all unaltered by the modern world. And that's before you get started on the 20th century's sleek and sensual art nouveau, and Prague's uniquely Czech cubist and rondocubist buildings.

Veletržní Palác

This vast, ocean-liner-like building can lay claim to being one of Prague's best (and biggest) galleries, showing works by Van Gogh, Picasso, Klimt, Mucha and the impressionists, as well as masterpieces by Czech expressionist, cubist and surrealist artists.

Prague Castle

A thousand years of history is cradled within the walls of this hilltop castle, a complex of churches, towers, halls and palaces that is almost a village in its own right. This is the cultural and historical heart of the Czech Republic.

Wenceslas Square

Watched over by its equestrian statue of St Wenceslas, Prague's biggest square throbs with commerce. Wander past big-name chains rubbing shoulders with art-nouveau architecture, and follow mirrored art-deco arcades to stylish cafes and hidden gardens.

Žižkov pub crawl

The neighbourhood of Žižkov is famous for having more pubs per head of population than any other city district in Europe, and – depending on your tastes – offers the most authentic pub-crawling experience in Prague.

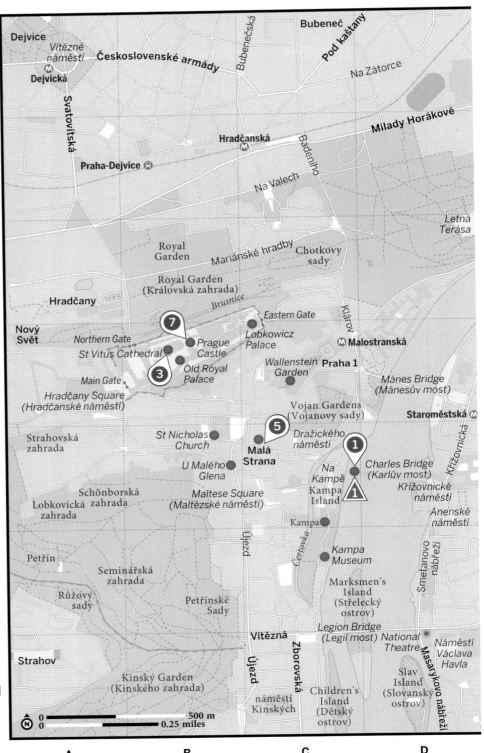

Day 1 itinerary

Rise before dawn to walk over **Charles Bridge** – you won't regret it. Next, wander the courtyards of **Prague Castle** before the main sights open, then tour **St Vitus Cathedral**, the **Old Royal Palace** and the **Lobkowicz Palace** (changing of the guard is at noon). After lunch with a view at Lobkowicz Palace Café, head to **Malá Strana** to admire the baroque beauty of **St Nicholas Church**. From here, visit the **Wallenstein Garden** for some peace and quiet, then follow the backstreets south to **Kampa**. Hang out in the park, or visit the **Kampa Museum**. As day fades, return to Charles Bridge. After dinner, head to Malá Strana, which is full of buzzy bars. Try **U Malého Glena**, a classic Prague bar and jazz club, with live music every night.

Days 2 and 3 itinerary

Start in the **Old Town Square**, watch the Astronomical Clock do its thing, then climb to the top of the **Old Town Hall Tower** for a great view of the square. Head to the **Municipal House** and have a coffee while you admire its art-nouveau decor. Dedicate the afternoon to visiting the half-dozen monuments that comprise the **Prague Jewish Museum**. In the evening, attend a concert in the Municipal House's **Smetana Hall** or the Klementinum's **Chapel of Mirrors**. Afterwards, explore the Old Town's cocktail joints. Day three starts by exploring the area around **Wenceslas Square**, especially **Lucerna Palace** and the **Franciscan Garden**. Then take in the **National Museum**, the **Prague City Museum** or the marvels of the **Mucha Museum**. In the afternoon, take a trip over the river to the **Veletržní Palác** where a fine collection of masterpieces of the 19th, 20th and 21st centuries are spread out over four floors. Walk back to the city centre . After dinner head to the New Town to catch a performance at the **National Theatre** or the **Prague State Opera**.

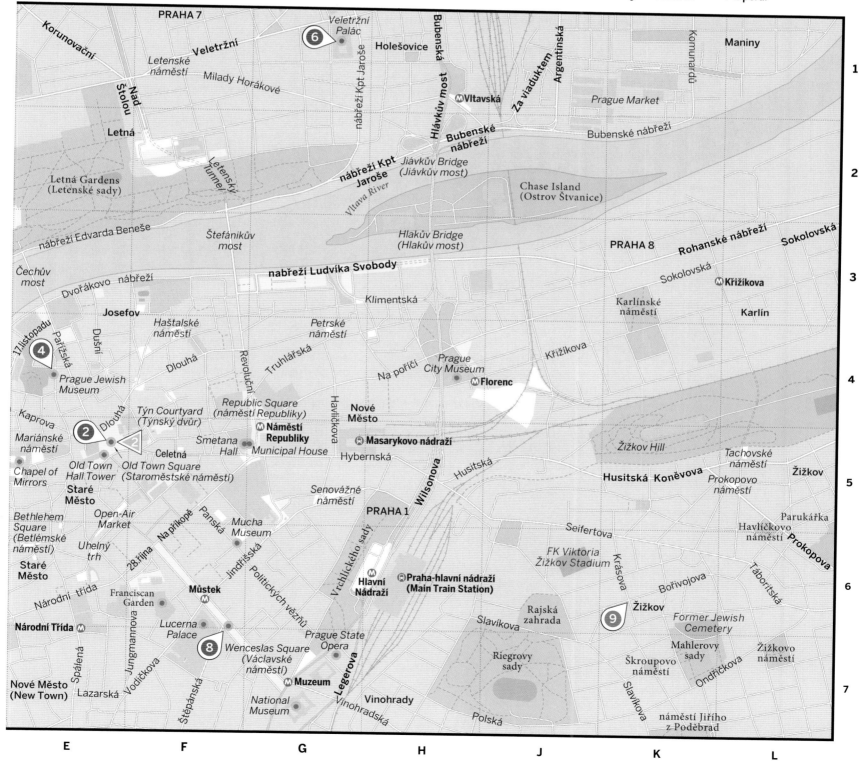

SIGHTS & ACTIVITIES

- ◉ SEE
- ◉ DO

ITINERARY

- ▽ 1
- ▽ 2

Ipanema Beach: This long stretch of sand teems with life, especially as the sun sets.

① Copacabana Beach

The Copacabana experience is about many things: rising early and going for a run along the sands; playing in the waves on a sun-drenched afternoon; or whiling away the evening over cocktails and appetisers at a beachfront kiosk. Regardless, you'll probably notice the incredibly seductive view: 4km of wide, curving sands framed by Rio's green peaks.

② Pão de Açúcar

At the top of Sugarloaf Mountain the city unfolds beneath you, with Corcovado mountain and Cristo Redentor off to the west, and Copacabana Beach to the south. You'll never look at Rio in the same way again. Come for sunset. Take the all-glass aerial trams, or rock climb your way to the summit.

③ Cristo Redentor

Standing atop Corcovado mountain (710m), Cristo Redentor gazes out over a mesmerising panorama of rainforest, beaches, islands, ocean, bay and verdant peaks. At night the brightly lit 38m-high open-armed statue is visible from nearly every part of the city.

④ Carnaval

Rio knows how to party. Whether you call it *joie de vivre*, *Lebensfreude* or lust for life, *cariocas* (residents of Rio) have it in spades. Carnaval is the most obvious manifestation of this celebratory spirit, with hundreds of street parties as well as costume balls and samba-fuelled parades attracting revellers from around the globe.

⑤ Escadaria Selarón

One of Rio's best loved attractions, the steps leading up from Rua Joaquim Silva became a work of art when Chilean-born artist Jorge Selarón decided to cover the steps with colourful mosaics.

⑥ Ipanema Beach

Eat, drink and people-watch at this enchanting beachfront. It attracts a wide mix of *cariocas* – surfers, volleyballers, bohemians, muscle boys – congregate at each section, or *posto*, including famous Posto 9 where Ipanema's young and beautiful frolic. Roaming vendors will come to you on the beach itself, and *barracas* (beach stalls) set you up with chairs, umbrellas and caipirinhas.

⑦ Maracanã Stadium

For a quasi-psychedelic experience, go to a *futebol* match at Maracanã, Brazil's temple to football (soccer). Matches here rate among the most exciting in the world, particularly during a championship game or when local rivals Flamengo, Vasco da Gama, Fluminense or Botafogo go head-to-head. Games take place year-round and generally happen on a Wednesday, Thursday, Saturday or Sunday.

⑧ Lagoa Rodrigo de Freitas

'Saltwater lagoon' may not be the first thing you think of when you hear the words 'Rio de Janeiro', but this picturesque body of water plays a key role in the city's psyche. By day *cariocas* cycle, jog and stroll the 7km path that loops around it. By nightfall a different crowd arrives to eat and drink in the open-air kiosks scattered along the shore. In December Lagoa is home to a massive floating Christmas tree – its glittering lights and nightly displays are pure magic for kids and adults alike.

⑨ Botafogo

The dining scene has exploded in this neighbourhood recently, with some of Rio's most creative restaurants opening up on its tree-lined back streets. A great street for browsing is Rua Nelson Mandela, which is lined with casual open-air eating and drinking spots.

⑩ Sunset drinks

One of the most magical settings for a sundowner is along the historic Travessa do Comércio. The sidewalk tables on this narrow, cobbled lane are packed on weekday nights, particularly as the weekend nears – Thursday is always a good bet.

⑪ Parque do Flamengo

The park spreads all the way from downtown Rio through Glória, Catete and Flamengo, and on around to Botafogo. The 1.2 sq km of land reclaimed from the sea stages every manner of *carioca* outdoor activity.

▽1 Day 1 itinerary

Spend the first day soaking up the rays on **Ipanema Beach**. Be sure to hydrate with *maté* (cold, sweetened tea) and *agua de côco* (coconut water), and sample a few beach snacks. Take a scenic stroll down to **Leblon**. In the afternoon, have a wander through the streets of **Ipanema**, doing some window-shopping on **Rua Garcia** d'Ávila, stopping for ice cream or coffee on the way.. After dinner catch a concert at **Vinícius Show Bar**, an intimate space for bossa nova and live jazz. Afterwards, head up the street to **Barzin**, a festive bar and live-music venue that always draws a crowd. End the night crawling the lounges, *botecos* (small open-air bars) and clubs of Leblon.

▽2 Days 2 and 3 itinerary

Take the cog train up Corcovado to marvel at the view beneath **Cristo Redentor**. Next, check out colourful folk art from Brazil and beyond at nearby **Museu Internacional de Arte Naïf do Brasil**. Lunch in **Santa Teresa**, Rio's most atmospheric neighbourhood, then go for a wander. Browse for handicrafts, admire scenic **Parque das Ruínas** and take in the eclectic art collection and lush gardens of **Museu Chácara do Céu**. Come evening hail a taxi downhill to **Lapa** for a late night of samba and caipirinhas. For the morning of day three, go for a hike along the forest-lined trails in **Parque Nacional da Tijuca**. In the afternoon, soak up the sun and surf on **Copacabana Beach** before strolling south to **Forte de Copacabana**. Here you'll find a small museum and several relaxing open-air cafes, each with memorable views. Enjoy a meal of tapas and sangria in buzzing **Baixo Copa** then drink up creative cocktails and vistas on the shore of **Lagoa Rodrigo de Freitas**.

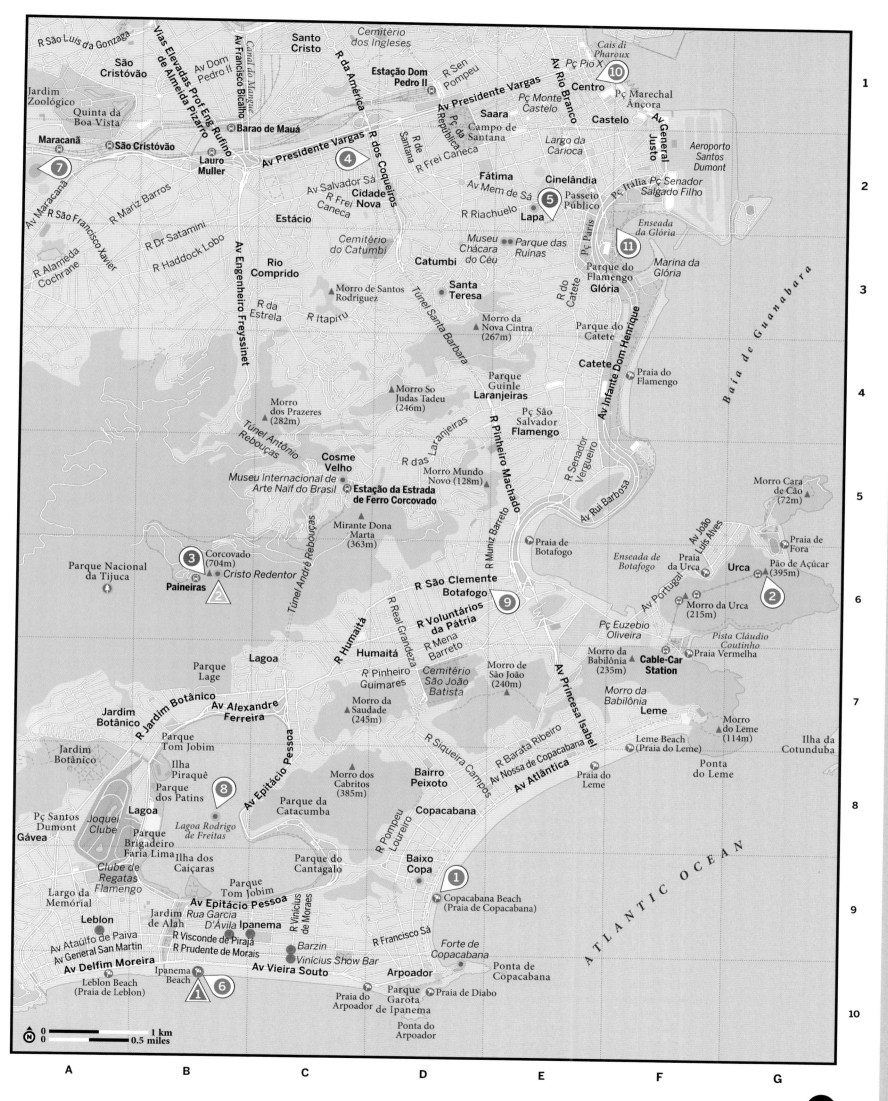

R São Luís da Gonzaga

São Cristóvão

Jardim
Zoológico

Quinta da
Boa Vista

Maracanã

São Cristóvão

R Mariz Barros

R São Francisco Xavier

R Alameda
Cochrane

Av Maracanã

Vias Elevadas Prof Eng Rufino
de Almeida Pizarro

Av Dom
Pedro II

Av Francisco Bicalho

Canal do Mangue

Barao de Mauá

Lauro
Muller

Santo
Cristo

R da América

Estação Dom
Pedro II

R Sen
Pompeu

Cemitério
dos Ingleses

Av Presidente Vargas

Av Presidente Vargas

R dos Coqueiros

Pç da
República

R de
Santana

R de
Santana

R Frei Caneca

Av Salvador Sá

R Frei
Caneca

Cidade
Nova

Estácio

Saara

Campo de
Santana

Fátima

Av Mem de Sá

Cais di
Pharoux

Pç Pio X

Av Rio Branco

Centro

Pç Monte
Castelo

Castelo

Pç Marechal
Âncora

Aeroporto
Santos
Dumont

Largo da
Carioca

Cinelândia

R Riachuelo

Lapa

Passeio
Público

Pç Pâris

Pç Itália Pç Senador
Salgado Filho

Av General
Justo

Enseada
da Glória

R Dr Satamini

R Haddock Lobo

Av Engenheiro Freyssinet

Rio
Comprido

R da
Estrela

R Itapiru

Cemitério
do Catumbi

Catumbi

Santa
Teresa

Morro de Santos
Rodriguez

Tünel Santa Barbara

Museu
Chácara
do Céu

Parque das
Ruínas

Glória

Parque do
Flamengo

R do Catete

Marina da
Glória

Parque do
Catete

Catete

Praia do
Flamengo

Baía de Guanabara

Túnel Antônio
Rebouças

Morro
dos Prazeres
(282m)

Morro So
Judas Tadeu
(246m)

Cosme
Velho

Museu Internacional de
Arte Naïf do Brasil

Estação da Estrada
de Ferro Corcovado

Morró Mundo
Novo (128m)

R das Laranjeiras

Parque
Guinle

Laranjeiras

Pç São
Salvador

Flamengo

R Pinheiro Machado

R Senador
Vergueiro

R Rui Barbosa

Av Infante Dom Henrique

Morro Cara
de Cão
(72m)

Parque Nacional
da Tijuca

Corcovado
(704m)

Cristo Redentor

Paineiras

Túnel André Rebouças

Mirante Dona
Marta
(363m)

R Muniz Barreto

R São Clemente

Botafogo

R Voluntários
da Pátria

Praia de
Botafogo

Enseada de
Botafogo

Av Rui Barbosa

Praia
da Urca

Av João
Luís Alves

Urca

Praia de
Fora

Pão de Açúcar
(395m)

Av Portugal

Morro da Urca
(215m)

R Humaitá

R Real Grandeza

Humaitá

R Mena
Barreto

Pç Euzebio
Oliveira

Praia Vermelha

Pista Cláudio
Coutinho

Parque
Lage

Lagoa

R Pinheiro
Guimares

Cemitério
São João
Batista

Morro de
São João
(240m)

Morro da
Babilônia
(235m)

Cable-Car
Station

Morro da
Babilônia

Jardim
Botânico

R Jardim Botânico

Av Alexandre
Ferreira

Morro da
Saudade
(245m)

R Siqueira Campos

Av Princesa Isabel

Leme

Morro
do Leme
(114m)

Ilha da
Cotunduba

Jardim
Botânico

Parque
Tom Jobim

Ilha
Piraquê

Parque
dos Patins

Av Epitácio Pessoa

Parque da
Catacumba

Morro dos
Cabritos
(385m)

Bairro
Peixoto

R Barata Ribeiro

Av Nossa de Copacabana

Av Atlântica

Praia do
Leme

Leme Beach
(Praia do Leme)

Ponta
do Leme

Pç Santos
Dumont

Joquei
Clube

Lagoa
Rodrigo
de Freitas

Lagoa

Parque
Brigadeiro
Faria Lima

Ilha dos
Caiçaras

Parque do
Cantagalo

Copacabana

Gávea

Parque
Tom Jobim

R Pompeu
Loureiro

Baixo
Copa

Clube de
Regatas
Flamengo

Largo da
Memórial

Leblon

Av Ataúlfo de Paiva

Av General San Martin

Av Delfim Moreira

Av Epitácio Pessoa

Jardim
de Alah

Rua Garcia
D'Ávila

Ipanema

R Visconde de Piraja

R Prudente de Morais

R Vinícius
de Moraes

Barzin

Vinícius Show Bar

Av Vieira Souto

R Francisco Sá

Forte de
Copacabana

Arpoador

Parque
Garota
de Ipanema

Praia de Diabo

Ponta de
Copacabana

Copacabana Beach
(Praia de Copacabana)

ATLANTIC OCEAN

Leblon Beach
(Praia de Leblon)

Ipanema
Beach

Praia do
Arpoador

Ponta do
Arpoador

0   1 km
0   0.5 miles

A   B   C   D   E   F   G

1
2
3
4
5
6
7
8
9
10

SIGHTS &
ACTIVITIES

 SEE
DO

ITINERARY

 1
2

Colosseum

No photograph can prepare you for the thrill of seeing Rome's great gladiatorial arena for the first time. More than any other monument, this 50,000-seat icon symbolises the power and drama of ancient Rome, and still today it's an electrifying sight.

Museo e Galleria Borghese

The greatest gallery you've never heard of, the Borghese houses some of Rome's most remarkable works of art, such as a series of sensational baroque sculptures by Gian Lorenzo Bernini, as well as a celebrated statue by Canova and paintings by the likes of Caravaggio, Raphael and Titian.

Pantheon

A 2000-year-old temple, now a church, the Pantheon is the best preserved of Rome's ancient monuments and one of the most influential buildings in the Western world. Pass through its vast bronze doors, gaze up at the largest unreinforced concrete dome ever built and marvel at the shafts of light streaming in through the central oculus.

Vatican Museums

Founded by Pope Julius II in the early 16th century, this is now one of the world's greatest art collections. Exhibitions stretch along some 7km of halls and corridors, ranging from Egyptian mummies and Etruscan bronzes to ancient busts, a suite of rooms frescoed by Raphael, and the Michelangelo-painted Sistine Chapel.

St Peter's Basilica

You don't have to be a believer to be bowled over by St Peter's Basilica, Rome's largest and most spectacular church. Everything about the place is astonishing, from the sweeping piazza that announces it, to the grandiose facade and opulent interior.

Trevi Fountain

A stop at Rome's most famous fountain is a rite of passage for visitors. The fountain, designed by Nicola Salvi in the 18th century, is a gloriously over-the-top rococo affair depicting wild horses, mythical figures and rock falls.

Capitoline Museums

Dating to 1471, the Capitoline Museums are the world's oldest public museums. Their collection of classical sculpture is one of Italy's finest, including crowd-pleasers such as the Lupa Capitolina (Capitoline Wolf).

Trastevere

One of the great joys of Rome is eating and drinking well, especially in summer when it's warm enough to dine al fresco and the city's animated streets are packed until the early hours. And nowhere is better than the picture-perfect neighbourhood of Trastevere.

Roman Forum

To walk through the tumbledown remnants of the Roman Forum – a grandiose district of temples, basilicas and vibrant public spaces – is to retrace the footsteps of the great figures of Roman history, people like Julius Caesar, Augustus and Pompey.

Piazza Navona

For sheer jaw-dropping beauty, no piazza beats Navona. In the heart of the city's historic centre, it's the picture of elegant baroque styling with its three ornamental fountains, domed church and handsome *palazzi* (mansions).

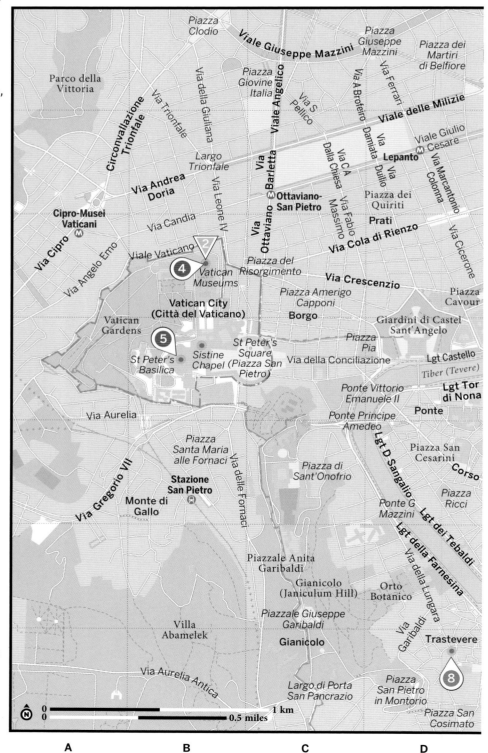

**Day 1
itinerary**

Start early at the **Colosseum**, Rome's huge gladiatorial arena, then head down to the **Palatino** to poke around crumbling ruins and admire sweeping views. Follow on to the **Roman Forum** for further pre-lunch explorations. In the afternoon climb up to Piazza del Campidoglio and the **Capitoline Museums**, where you'll find some sensational ancient sculpture on display. When you're done there, enjoy great views from the **Vittoriano** before pushing on to the *centro storico* (historic centre) to explore its labyrinthine medieval streets and headline sights such as the **Pantheon** and the stunning **Piazza Navona**. After dinner get a taste of *dolce vita* bar life near Piazza Navona.

**Days 2 and 3
itinerary**

On day two, hit the **Vatican Museums**. and the mind-blowing **Sistine Chapel**, then on to tour **St Peter's Basilica**. Climb its Michelangelo-designed dome for fantastic views over the entire city. After lunch jump on the metro to **Piazza di Spagna** and the **Spanish Steps**, before pushing on to the famous 18th-century **Trevi Fountain**. Next, head up the hill to catch the sunset on **Piazza del Quirinale** in front of the presidential palace, Palazzo del Quirinale. Spend the evening in the buzzing area around **Campo de' Fiori**. Day three starts with a trip to the **Museo e Galleria Borghese** for its outstanding statues and paintings. Afterwards, stroll through **Villa Borghese**, Rome's most celebrated park, down to **La Galleria Nazionale** for an injection of modern art. In the afternoon visit the **Basilica di Santa Maria del Popolo**, which is a magnificent repository of art. Next, browse the designer boutiques in the upscale streets off **Via del Corso**. Finish by dining and drinking in vivacious **Trastevere**.

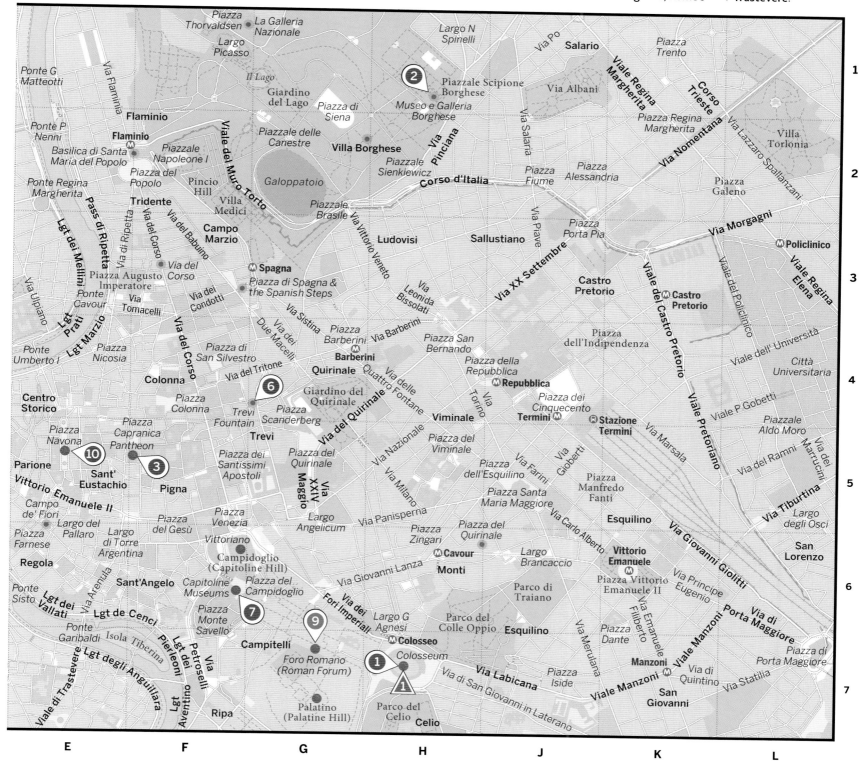

SIGHTS &
ACTIVITIES

◉ SEE
◎ DO

ITINERARY

▽ 1
▽ 2

Golden Gate Bridge

On sunny days, the world's most iconic suspension bridge transfixes crowds with its radiant glow. When afternoon fog rolls in, the bridge performs its disappearing act: now you see it, now you don't. For the closest view, hike or bike the 1.7-mile span along its sidewalks.

Alcatraz

From its 19th-century founding to detain Civil War deserters and Native American dissidents until its closure by Bobby Kennedy in 1963, the island of Alcatraz was America's most notorious jail. No prisoner is known to have escaped alive – but, once you enter D-Block solitary and hear carefree city life humming across the bay, the 1.25-mile swim through riptides seems worth a shot.

Ferry Building

Hedonism is alive and well at this transit hub turned gourmet emporium, where foodies happily miss their ferries over Sonoma oysters and bubbly, SF craft beer and Marin-raised beef burgers, or locally roasted coffee and freshly baked cupcakes. Star chefs are frequently spotted at the farmers market that wraps around the building all year.

Golden Gate Park

All that San Franciscans hold dear is here: free spirits, free music, redwoods, Frisbee, protests, fine art, bonsai and buffalo. The park is filled with flora from around the world and amazing sights, including the de Young Museum, California Academy of Sciences, San Francisco Botanical Garden, Japanese Tea Garden, Conservatory of Flowers and Stow Lake.

Barbary Coast nights

In the mid-19th century a bar crawl along North Beach's Barbary Coast saloons could end up with a patron involuntarily working on a vessel bound for Patagonia. These days visitors can relax – the hardest bit is just picking your poison: historically correct cocktails at Comstock Saloon, cult California wines at California Wine Merchant and/or enough microbrewed beer at Magnolia to keep you snoring to Patagonia and back.

Mission murals

The Mission district is an urban-art showstopper, featuring more than 400 murals. Balmy Alley has some of the oldest, while 24th St and the landmark San Francisco Women's Building are covered with glorious portrayals of community pride and political dissent.

Castro district

Somewhere over the rainbow crosswalk, you'll realise you've arrived in Castro. For more than 50 years this has been the most out and proud neighbourhood on earth. Learn more at America's first LGBT History Museum.

Cable cars

Carnival rides simply can't compare to the time-travelling thrills of cable cars, SF's vintage form of public transit. Slide into a stranger's lap, or follow locals' lead by gripping the leather hand straps, leaning back and riding the downhill plunges like a pro surfer.

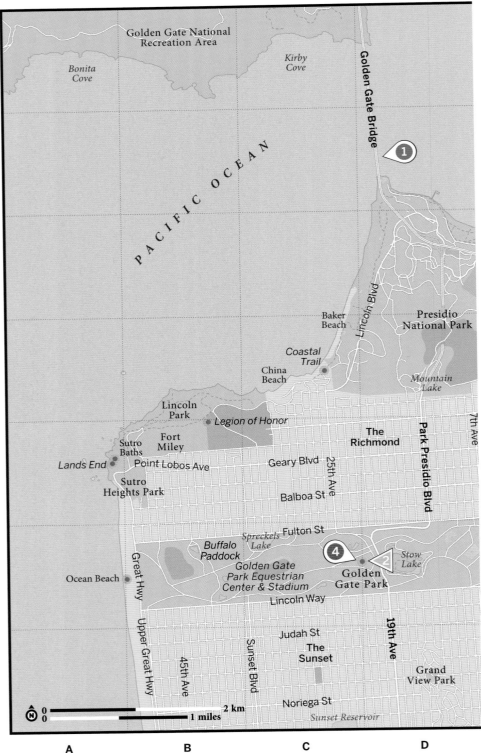

Coit Tower

The art-deco exclamation mark on San Francisco's skyline is Coit Tower. Its wraparound murals and panoramic viewing platform show San Francisco at its best: a city of broad perspectives, outlandish and inspiring.

Day 1 itinerary

Take the Powell-Mason cable car from Powell St to hop off at **Washington Square Park**, where parrots squawk encouragement for your hike up to **Coit Tower**. Next, take scenic **Filbert Street Steps** to the **Embarcadero** to wander across Fog Bridge and explore the freaky Tactile Dome at the **Exploratorium**. Try local oysters and Dungeness crab at the **Ferry Building**, then catch your ferry (complete with Golden Gate views) to **Alcatraz**. Return to ride the Powell-Mason cable car to **North Beach** for the free-speech landmark City Lights and to mingle with SF's freest spirits at the **Beat Museum**. Come evening, enjoy **Cobb's Comedy Club** or razor-sharp satire at **Beach Blanket Babylon**.

Days 2 and 3 itinerary

Start day two among many wonders of **Golden Gate Park**. Dining options line the Avenues here, from bargain hot spots to California-cuisine destinations. Then beachcomb **Ocean Beach** before following the **Coastal Trail** past **Sutro Baths** and **Land's End** for Golden Gate Bridge vistas and priceless paper artworks at the **Legion of Honor**. After a Pacific seafood feast, wade into rock music's past, present and future at the **Fillmore Auditorium**. Start day three by taking the California cable car to pagoda-topped **Grant Ave** for an eye-opening Red Blossom tea tasting and then a jaw-dropping history of Chinatown at the **Chinese Historical Society of America**. Wander temple-lined **Waverly Place** and notorious Ross before dining on dim sum. Take the Powell-Hyde cable car past zigzagging **Lombard Street** to the San Francisco **Maritime National Historical Park**, then watch sea lions cavort as the sun fades over **Pier 39**. After dinner browse **Hayes Valley** boutiques before a concert at the **SF Symphony**. Finish by toasting your good fortune in a high-rolling wine bar.

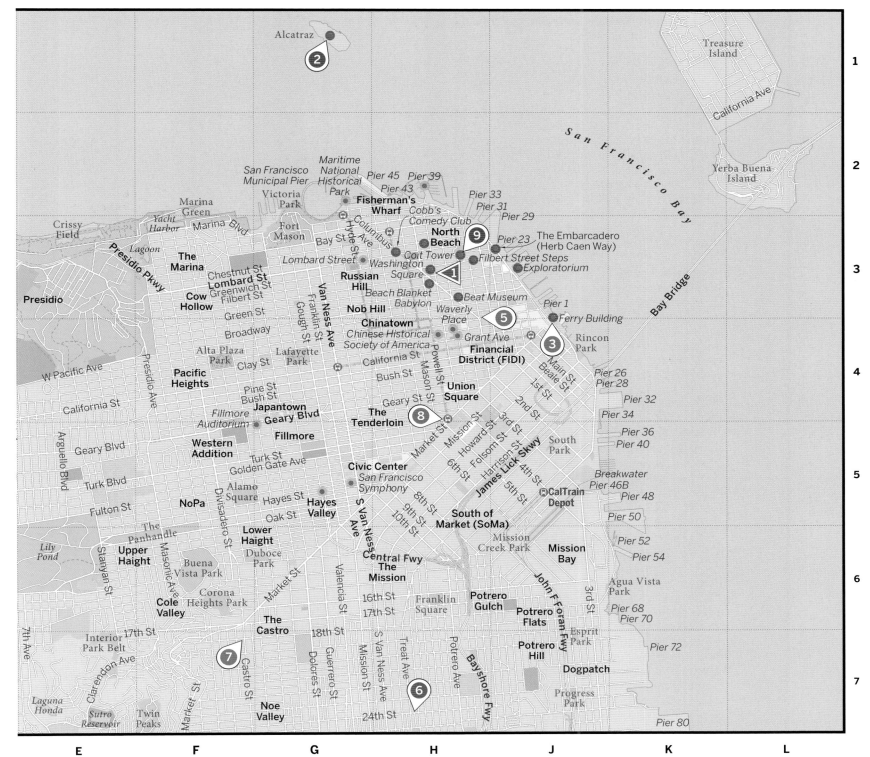

SIGHTS & ACTIVITIES

- ◉ SEE
- ◉ DO

ITINERARY

- ▽ 1
- ▽ 2

Cheong-gye-cheon

Long buried under a raised highway, this 'daylighted' stream has transformed Seoul's centre, creating a riverside park with walkways, footbridges, waterfalls and a variety of public artworks – it's a calm respite from the surrounding commercial hubbub.

Bukchon Hanok Village

In a city at the cutting edge of 21st-century technology and high-rise living, this neighbourhood stands as a testament to an age of craftsmanship when Seoulites lived in one-storey wooden *hanok*, complete with graceful tiled roofs and internal courtyard gardens.

Changdeokgung

The most beautiful and graceful of Seoul's five main palaces, the 'Palace of Illustrious Virtue' was built in the early 15th century and has been lived in by royal family members well into the 20th century. The most charming section is the Huwon, a 'secret garden' that is a royal horticultural idyll.

Gyeongbokgung

Like a phoenix, Seoul's premier palace has risen several times from the ashes of destruction. Watch the changing of the guard ceremonies, then indulge in the compound's museums, ornamental gardens and some of Seoul's grandest architectural sights.

Gwangjang Market

At night this market really comes into its own, when its alleys fill up with vendors selling all manner of street eats: golden fried *nokdu bindaetteok* (mung-bean pancake), *bibimbap* or *boribap* (mixed rice and barley topped with a selection of veggies), stewed pig trotters and snouts and more.

Namsan

Protected by parkland and crowned by the monumental N Seoul Tower, Namsan is the most central of the city's four guardian mountains. Join locals who actively patronise the park to keep fit and take in the cooler, sweeter air on hiking paths to the scenic summit.

Deoksugung

One of Seoul's five grand palaces built during the Joseon dynasty, Deoksugung is the only one you can visit in the evening and see the buildings illuminated. It first served as a palace in 1593 and is a mix of Korean and western neoclassical structures.

Lotus Lantern Festival

This spectacular festival celebrates Buddha's birthday each May. Temples are strung with rainbow-hued paper lanterns, and a dazzling night-time parade – involving thousands – snakes its way through the city.

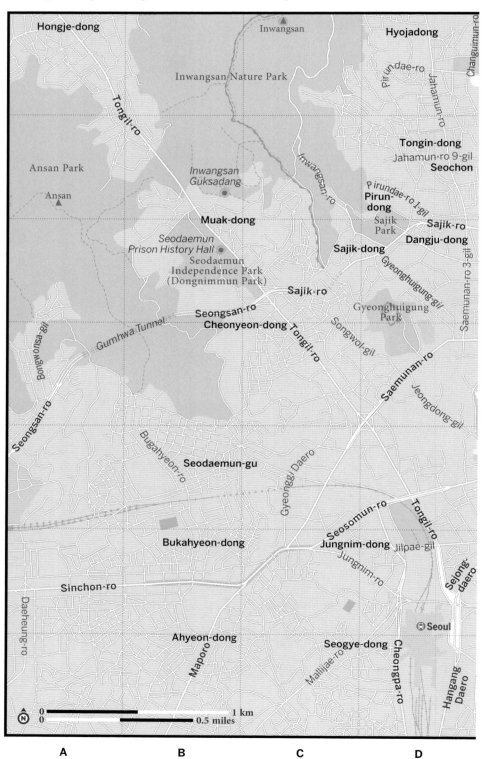

Dongdaemun

Historical and contemporary Seoul stand side by side in this eternally buzzing and sprawling market area. A facelift to Heunginjimun (aka Dongdaemun) has left the old east gate to the city looking grander than it has done in decades. Sections of the old city walls that the gate was once connected to have been uncovered and form part of the Dongdaemun History & Culture Park. Rising up behind this is the sleek, silvery form of the Zaha Hadid–designed Dongdaemun Design Plaza & Park, an architectural show stopper that could hardly be more 21st century in its conception.

Day 1 itinerary

Start your day at the palace of **Gyeongbokgung**, and be sure to observe the changing of the guard at the main gate (on the hour). Next, wander the winding streets of **Bukchon Hanok Village** and **Insa-dong**, pausing for refreshments at a teahouse. Join the afternoon tour of **Changdeokgung** before exploring the wooded grounds of the venerable shrine **Jongmyo**, housing the spirit tablets of the Joseon kings and queens. Korean street food at **Gwangjang Market** is perfect for dinner. Next take your seat at a fun nonverbal show such as **Jump**. Be dazzled by the bright lights and retail overload of **Myeong-dong** and neighbouring **Namdaemun Market**, where the stalls stay open all night.

Days 2 and 3 itinerary

On day two strike out on a circuit of **Namsan Park**. Hike, bus or cable car up to iconic **N Seoul Tower** and the Bongsudae and enjoy being at the geographical heart of Seoul. Grab some refreshments and then pick up the **City Wall trail** down to pretty Joongang Park. On the left is the **Ahn Jung-geun Memorial Hall**. Finish up by taking a look at the reconstruction of **Sungnyemun**. In the early afternoon head to **Deoksugung** for the changing of the guard (at 2pm and 3:30pm), an impressive ceremony involving 50 participants. Visit nearby **City Hall** and stick around for the evening free concerts (May to August only). Start day three by reflecting on the struggles and sacrifices of Koreans to overcome colonialism and create a modern country at **Seodaemun Prison History Hall**. Afterwards, hike up nearby **Inwangsan** for fabulous views, surreal rock formations and the other-worldly shamanistic rituals of **Inwangsan Guksadang**. In the evening head to **Dongdaemun**, where the night market will just be starting to crank up.

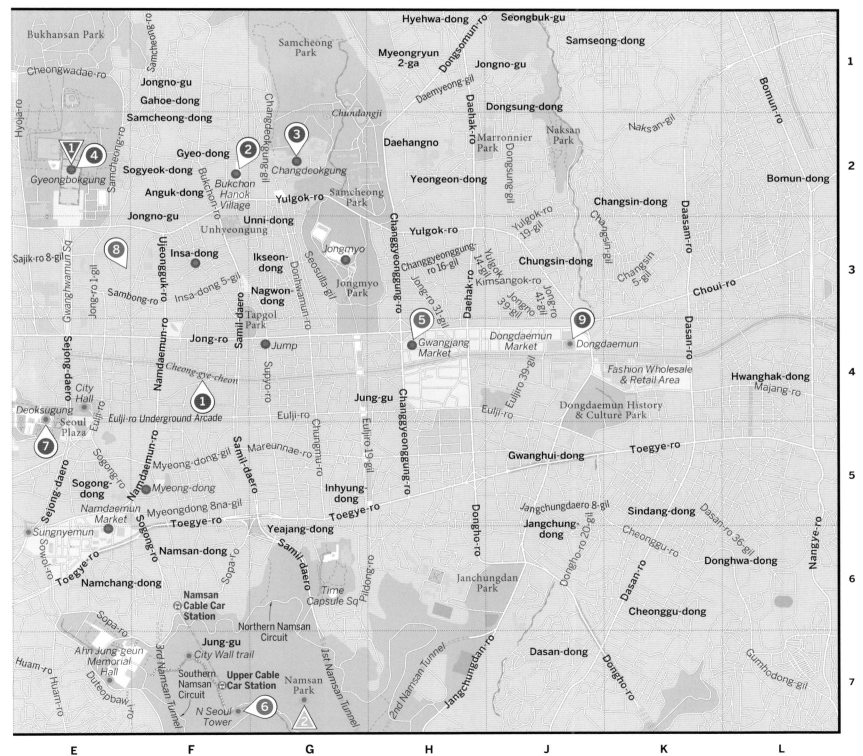

SIGHTS & ACTIVITIES

 SEE

DO

ITINERARY

 1

2

Asian Civilisations Museum
Travel back in time at this engrossing ode to Singapore's cross-cultural connections, developed through its position and history as a port city. You'll find the region's most comprehensive collection of pan-Asian treasures within its walls, and the recently recovered treasures from the Tang Shipwreck need to be seen to be believed, including a 1000-year-old bronze mirror.

Hawker food
Singapore's hawker food is the stuff of legend, with a dazzling array of cheap, lip-smacking dishes available – some stalls have even received Michelin stars. There's no better place to look than in Chinatown.

Gardens by the Bay
This 101-hectare, US$1 billion 'super park' is Singapore's hottest horticultural asset, a fantasy land of space-age bio-domes, high-tech Supertrees, whimsical sculptures and some 400,000 plants.

National Gallery Singapore
Connected by a striking aluminium and glass canopy, Singapore's historic City Hall and Old Supreme Court buildings form the city's breathtaking National Gallery. Its 8000-plus collection of world-class colonial and post-colonial Southeast Asian art fills two major gallery spaces. The museum's free one-hour tours covering the highlights of the galleries and the building architecture are recommended.

Gardens by the Bay: The OCBC Skyway connects two of the Supertrees and offers superb views of the gardens, city and South China Sea.

Marina Bay Sands
Love it or hate it, it's hard not to admire the sheer audacity of Singapore's S$5.7 billion Marina Bay Sands. Perched on the southern bank of Marina Bay, the sprawling hotel, casino, theatre, exhibition centre, mall and museum is the work of Israeli-born architect Moshe Safdie.

Singapore Botanic Gardens
This is a sprawling oasis laced with elegant lakes and themed gardens, and has no shortage of perfect spots for picnics and people-watching. Stroll through the orchid gardens, looking out for Vanda Miss Joaquim, Singapore's national flower, or cool down in a rare slice of ancient rainforest.

Orchard Road
Once lined with nutmeg and pepper plantations, this road is now the domain of Singapore's elite and those lured here by shopping centres, restaurants and nightspots. There are a few cultural sights that don't demand a credit card.

Chinatown Heritage Centre
The Chinatown Heritage Centre lifts the lid off Chinatown's chaotic, colourful and often scandalous past. Its endearing jumble of old photographs, personal anecdotes and recreated environments delivers an evocative stroll through the neighbourhood's highs and lows.

Little India
The most atmospheric of Singapore's historic quarters is as close as it gets to the city's old chaotic days. Experience it with the masses on the weekends when it gets packed to the gills with Indian workers craving a slice of home.

National Museum of Singapore
Imaginative and brilliantly designed, Singapore's National Museum is good enough to warrant two visits. The space ditches staid exhibits for lively multimedia galleries that bring Singapore's jam-packed biography to life. Afterwards, enjoy a wander around Fort Canning Park, where some of Singapore's historic events took place.

Day 1 itinerary

Start your Singapore fling with a local breakfast of *kaya* (coconut jam) toast, runny eggs and strong *kopi* (coffee) before taking a riverside stroll at the **Quays** for a jaw-dropping panorama of brazen skyscrapers and refined colonial buildings. Dive into the brilliant **Asian Civilisations Museum** or keep walking to the **National Museum of Singapore**, and the **Peranakan Museum**. After lunch take in the **Sri Mariamman Temple**, **Buddha Tooth Relic Temple** and **Thian Hock Keng Temple**. Before dinner head up **Pinnacle@Duxton** for a bird's-eye view of the city skyline and beyond. After an early dinner, catch a taxi to the Night Safari experience in northern Singapore.

Days 2 and 3 itinerary

Start day two in **Little India**, where weathered tailors stitch and sew by the side of the road, and the air is thick with cumin and Bollywood soundtracks. Absorb the essence of the **Sri Veeramakaliamman Temple** and learn about the area's fascinating backstory at the **Indian Heritage Centre**. Escape the afternoon heat in the air-conditioned comfort of **Orchard Rd**. Have dinner in **Gardens by the Bay**, then give yourself plenty of time to explore the incredible futuristic botanic gardens, including the Flower Dome and Cloud Forest conservatories. The gardens' Supertrees are especially spectacular. On day three move on to the pure, unadulterated fun of Singapore's pleasure island, **Sentosa**. Tackle rollercoaster rides at **Universal Studios**, or eye up creatures at the **SEA Aquarium**. Alternatively, ride artificial waves at **Wave House** or indoor skydive at **iFly**. End the day at the rooftop bar atop the **National Gallery Singapore**, where you can enjoy views of the Marina Bay Sands spectacular light-and-laser show.

© wsboon images / Getty Images

432

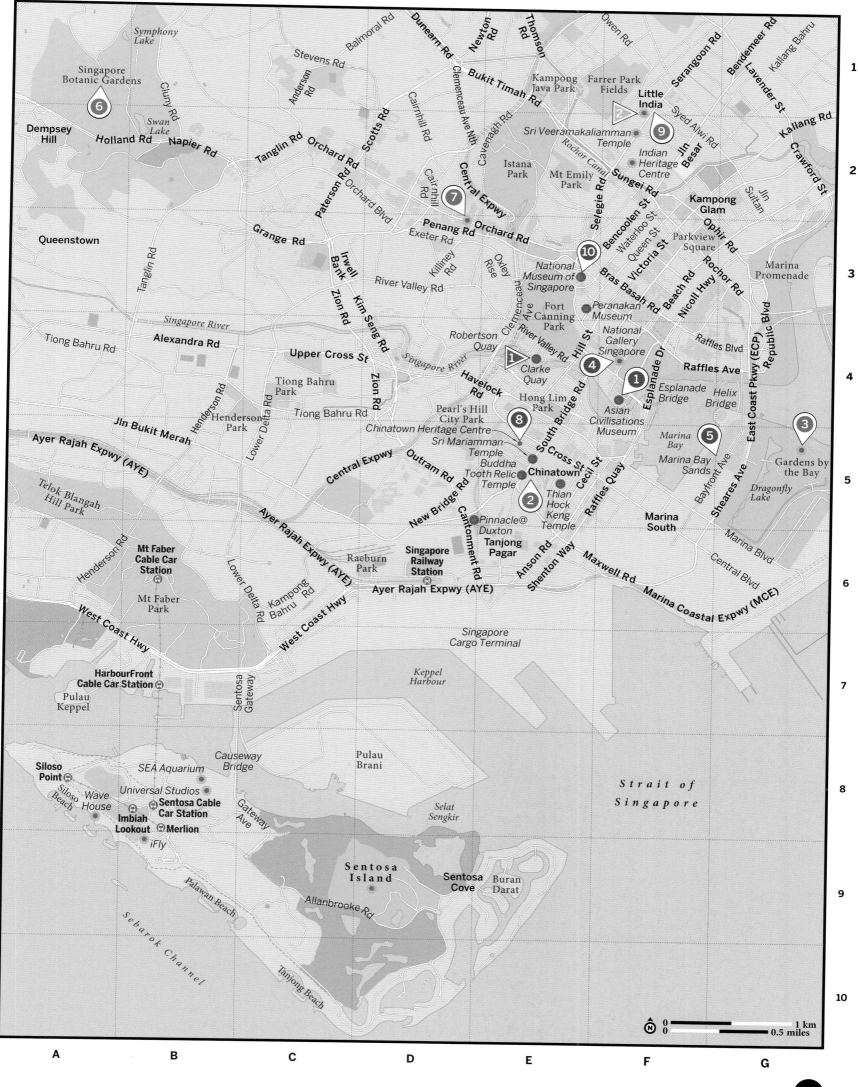

1

Symphony Lake

Singapore Botanic Gardens

6

Swan Lake

Dempsey Hill

Holland Rd   Napier Rd

Queenstown

Stevens Rd

Balmoral Rd

Anderson Rd

Cluny Rd

Scotts Rd

Cairnhill Rd

Tanglin Rd   Orchard Rd

Paterson Rd   Orchard Blvd

Cairnhill Rd

Grange Rd

Tanglin Rd

Irwell Bank

Kim Seng Rd

River Valley Rd

Killiney Rd

Zion Rd

Duneam Rd

Newton Rd

Clemenceau Ave Nth

Bukit Timah Rd

Cavenagh Rd

Central Expwy

Penang Rd

Exeter Rd

Oxley Rise

Clemenceau Ave

Thomson Rd

Owen Rd

Kampong Java Park

Istana Park

Mt Emily Park

7

Orchard Rd

Farrer Park Fields

2

Little India

Sri Veeramakaliamman Temple

9

Rochor Canal

Serangoon Rd

Syed Alwi Rd

Jln Besar

Indian Heritage Centre

Selegie Rd

Sungei Rd

Bencoolen St

Waterloo St

Queen St

Victoria St

Kampong Glam

Ophir Rd

Jln Sultan

Bendemeer Rd

Lavender St

Kallang Rd

Crawford St

Kallang Bahru

1

2

Marina Promenade

National Museum of Singapore

10

Bras Basah Rd

Beach Rd

Rochor Rd

Nicoll Hwy

Parkview Square

Marina Promenade

3

Tiong Bahru Rd

Alexandra Rd

Upper Cross St

Singapore River

Zion Rd

Fort Canning Park

Peranakan Museum

National Gallery Singapore

Hill St

Raffles Blvd

East Coast Pkwy (ECP)

Republic Blvd

4

Henderson Rd

Tiong Bahru Park

Tiong Bahru Rd

Henderson Park

Jln Bukit Merah

Ayer Rajah Expwy (AYE)

Lower Delta Rd

Central Expwy

Robertson Quay

Havelock Rd

Hong Lim Park

1

Clarke Quay

South Bridge Rd

4

Asian Civilisations Museum

1

Esplanade Dr

Esplanade Bridge

Helix Bridge

Raffles Ave

Marina Bay

3

Gardens by the Bay

5

Pearl's Hill City Park

Chinatown Heritage Centre

Sri Mariamman Temple

8

Buddha Tooth Relic Temple

Cross St

Chinatown

2

Thian Hock Keng Temple

Cecil St

Raffles Quay

Marina Bay Sands

5

Marina South

Bayfront Ave

Sheares Ave

Dragonfly Lake

Telok Blangah Hill Park

Henderson Rd

Mt Faber Cable Car Station

Mt Faber Park

West Coast Hwy

Lower Delta Rd

Kampong Bahru

Raeburn Park

New Bridge Rd

Outram Rd

Ayer Rajah Expwy (AYE)

Singapore Railway Station

Cantonment Rd

Pinnacle@Duxton

Tanjong Pagar

Anson Rd

Shenton Way

Maxwell Rd

Marina Coastal Expwy (MCE)

Marina Blvd

Central Blvd

6

West Coast Hwy

Sentosa Gateway

Singapore Cargo Terminal

Keppel Harbour

7

HarbourFront Cable Car Station

Pulau Keppel

Causeway Bridge

Pulau Brani

Strait of Singapore

8

Siloso Point

SEA Aquarium

Universal Studios

Siloso Beach

Wave House

Imbiah Lookout

Sentosa Cable Car Station

Merlion

iFly

Gateway Ave

Selat Sengkir

9

Sentosa Island

Allanbrooke Rd

Sentosa Cove

Buran Darat

Palawan Beach

Sebarok Channel

Tanjong Beach

10

N   0   1 km
     0   0.5 miles

A   B   C   D   E   F   G

SIGHTS & ACTIVITIES

◉ SEE
◉ DO

ITINERARY

▽ 1
▽ 2

Sydney Opera House: Beside Sydney's most recognisable icon is the popular open-air Opera Bar.

Sydney Opera House

Striking, unique, curvalicious – is there a sexier building on the planet? Seeing such a recognisable sight for the first time is always an odd experience. Depending on where you stand, the Opera House can seem smaller or bigger than you think it's going to be. It confounds expectations but is never disappointing.

Sydney Harbour National Park

Spread out around the harbour, this unusual national park offers a widely varied set of experiences, all with a blissful watery view. In this park, it's equally possible to separate yourself from civilisation or to be surrounded by traffic. It incorporates harbour islands, secluded beaches, ancient rock art, lighthouses, untouched headlands and, right in the middle of the city, a historic cottage. You can kayak into otherwise inaccessible coves, plan your own ferry-hike combinations or cycle along well-tended paths. Pack a picnic and disappear along the bushy trails.

③ Sydney Harbour Bridge

Like the Opera House, Sydney's second-most-loved construction inhabits the intersection of practicality and great beauty. The centrepiece of the city's biggest celebrations, the bridge is at its best on New Year's Eve when it erupts in pyrotechnics and the image is beamed into sitting rooms the world over. Its sheer size is impressive, and as you explore Sydney there's always some intriguing new view of it. And the views it provides are magnificent, whether you're walking over it or joining a BridgeClimb expedition up and over its central rainbow of steel.

Bondi Beach

Bondi offers fabulous opportunities for lazing on the sand, lingering in cafes, carving up surf, splashing in the shallows and swimming in sheltered pools. Every summer the world comes to Bondi and lets its hair down.

⑤ Royal Botanic Garden

Whether you're content to spread out a picnic on the lawn, stroll with glorious harbour perspectives or study the signs on the botanical specimens from around the globe, this superbly tranquil garden is an idyllic place.

⑥ Art Gallery of NSW

The Art Gallery of NSW's stately neoclassical building doesn't divulge the creative exuberance of the collection it contains. Step inside and a colourful portal opens into Sydney's history, Indigenous Australian heritage, the outback and distant lands.

⑦ The Rocks

Australia's convict history began here with a squalid canvas shanty town on a rocky shore. Its raucous reputation lives on in atmospheric lanes lined with historic buildings, more than a few of them still operating as pubs.

Aboriginal rock art

It inevitably comes as a surprise to stumble across an art form that's so ancient in such a modern city, yet Sydney is built on top of a giant gallery. Until recently not much attention was paid to such things and much was covered over or destroyed. But with dot paintings from distant deserts being celebrated, Sydneysiders have started to wake up to the treasure trove in their own backyard. Look for evidence of it on headlands around the harbour and on the coast between Bondi and Coogee.

⑨ Manly

With both a charming harbourside and a glorious ocean beach, Manly is Sydney's only ferry destination with surf. The journey here is fantastic, as are the activities: following the Manly Scenic Walkway, hiking the North Head section of Sydney Harbour National Park, kayaking at Store Beach and surfing from its namesake beach. There are also appealing bars and eateries and, as the gateway to the Northern Beaches, Manly makes a popular base for the board-riding brigade.

⑩ Sydney's food scene

Sydney's dining scene has never been more diverse, inventive and downright exciting. Sure, it can be pretentious, faddish and a little too obsessed with celebrity chefs, but it wouldn't be Sydney if it weren't. But it's assuredly not a case of style over substance – Sydney's quite capable of juggling both. Surry Hills is Sydney's foodie nirvana, though Newtown's King St and Enmore Rd are among the city's most diverse eat streets.

Day 1 itinerary

Why postpone joy? Start at **Circular Quay** and head directly to **Sydney Opera House**. Circle it, then follow the shoreline into the **Royal Botanic Garden**. Have a good gander and continue around **Mrs Macquaries Point** to **Woolloomooloo**. Grab a pie for lunch at **Harry's Cafe de Wheels**, a Sydney institution. Next, hit the **Art**

Gallery of NSW for outstanding Indigenous works and paintings by the likes of Picasso, then wander past **Parliament House**, **The Mint** and **Hyde Park Barracks**. Walk through **Hyde Park** and see the Anzac Memorial. After dinner, take in a play at **Belvoir St Theatre**, or stroll along **Crown St** to one of its many good pubs.

Days 2 and 3 itinerary

Grab your swimming gear and head to the beach. Catch the bus to **Bondi** and spend some time pottering about and soaking it all in. Now walk the clifftop path to **Tamarama** and **Bronte**. Have lunch at Bronte's excellent Three Blue Ducks, then continue on the coastal path south, pausing for a swim or snorkel at **Clovelly**. Finish with a drink on the

rooftop of **Coogee Pavilion** before boarding a bus back to **Bondi Junction**. Dine in **Chinatown** and stroll a few blocks north to check out some of the city's small bars. Start day three with a scenic ferry ride to **Watsons Bay**. Walk up to the **Gap** to watch the waves pounding against the cliffs, then take a dip at **Camp Cove**. The **South Head**

Heritage Trail offers sublime city views. After lunch head back to Circular Quay and spend the afternoon exploring **The Rocks** and its museums. Make this a glamorous night out by booking a show at **Sydney Opera House** or **Walsh Bay**, or head straight to **Opera Bar** to be mesmerised by the lights sparkling on the water.

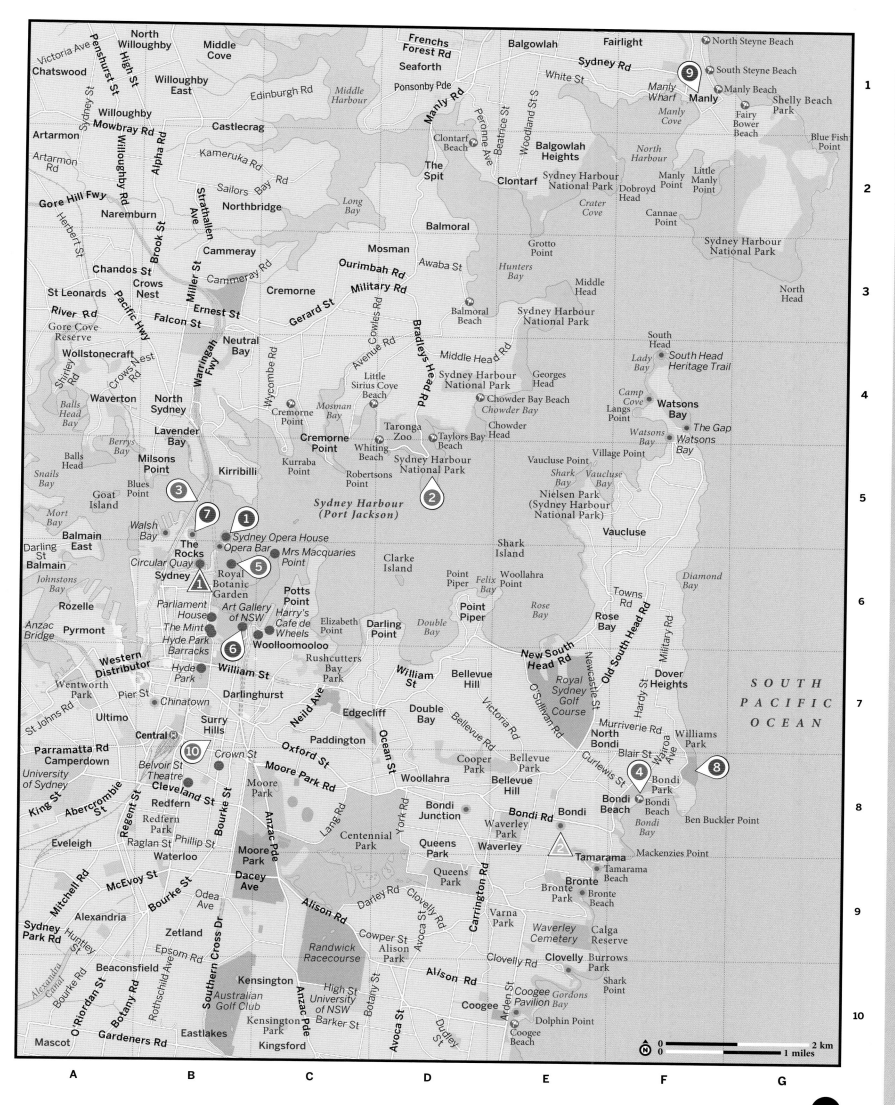

North Steyne Beach
South Steyne Beach
Manly Beach
Shelly Beach Park
North Willoughby
Victoria Ave
Penshurst St
High St
Sydney St
Middle Cove
Frenchs Forest Rd
Balgowlah
Fairlight
Sydney Rd
Chatswood
Willoughby East
Seaforth
White St
Woodland St
Manly Wharf
Manly
Manly Cove
Fairy Bower Beach
Artarmon
Mowbray Rd
Willoughby
Edinburgh Rd
Middle Harbour
Ponsonby Pde
Manly Rd
Perronne Ave
Beatrice St
Clontarf Beach
Balgowlah Heights
North Harbour
Manly Point
Little Manly Point
Blue Fish Point
Artarmon Rd
Castlecrag
The Spit
Clontarf
Sydney Harbour National Park
Dobroyd Head
Crater Cove
Gore Hill Fwy
Herbert St
Alpha Rd
Willoughby Rd
Kameruka Rd
Sailors Bay Rd
Cannae Point
Naremburn
Strathallen Ave
Northbridge
Balmoral
Mosman
Awaba St
Hunters Bay
Grotto Point
Sydney Harbour National Park
North Head
Cammeray
Ourimbah Rd
Middle Head
Chandos St
Brook St
Miller St
Cammeray Rd
Cremorne
Gerard St
Military Rd
St Leonards
Crows Nest
Ernest St
Falcon St
Bradleys Head Rd
Balmoral Beach
Sydney Harbour National Park
Georges Head
South Head
River Rd
Pacific Hwy
Middle Head Rd
Sydney Harbour National Park
Lady Bay
South Head Heritage Trail
Gore Cove Reserve
Neutral Bay
Avenue Rd
Chowder Bay Beach
Chowder Bay
Camp Cove
Wollstonecraft
Shirley Rd
Crows Nest Rd
Wycombe Rd
Little Sirius Cove Beach
Chowder Head
Langs Point
Watsons Bay
Waverton
Balls Head Bay
North Sydney
Mosman Bay
Cremorne Point
Taronga Zoo
Taylors Bay Beach
Watsons Bay
The Gap
Watsons Bay
Lavender Bay
Cremorne Point
Kurraba Point
Whiting Beach
Sydney Harbour National Park
Village Point
Vaucluse Point
Shark Bay
Balls Head
Berrys Bay
Milsons Point
Kirribilli
Robertsons Point
Nielsen Park (Sydney Harbour National Park)
Vaucluse Bay
Diamond Bay
Snails Bay
Mort Bay
Goat Island
Blues Point
③
⑦
①
Sydney Harbour (Port Jackson)
②
Shark Island
Vaucluse
Walsh Bay
Sydney Opera House
Opera Bar
Mrs Macquaries Point
Clarke Island
Woollahra Point
Balmain East
Darling St
The Rocks
Circular Quay
Sydney
⑤
Point Piper
Felix Bay
Diamond Bay
Balmain
Johnstons Bay
△1
Royal Botanic Garden
Potts Point
Point Piper
Double Bay
Rose Bay
Rozelle
Parliament House
Art Gallery of NSW
Harry's Cafe de Wheels
Elizabeth Point
Darling Point
Point Piper
Rose Bay
Towns Rd
Anzac Bridge
Pyrmont
The Mint
Hyde Park Barracks
⑥
Woolloomooloo
Rushcutters Bay Park
William St
Bellevue Hill
New South Head Rd
Rose Bay
Old South Head Rd
Military Rd
Dover Heights
Western Distributor
Hyde Park
William St
Darling St
Newcastle St
Wentworth Park
Pier St
Chinatown
Darlinghurst
Edgecliff
Double Bay
Bellevue Rd
Victoria Rd
O'Sullivan Rd
Royal Sydney Golf Course
Hardy St
Murriverie Rd
SOUTH PACIFIC OCEAN
St Johns Rd
Ultimo
Surry Hills
Paddington
Ocean St
Woollahra
Bellevue Hill
North Bondi
Curlewis St
Williams Park
⑧
Central
⑩
Crown St
Oxford St
Moore Park Rd
Cooper Park
Bellevue Hill
Blair St
④
Bondi Park
Parramatta Rd
Camperdown
Belvoir St Theatre
Moore Park
Moore Park
Woollahra
Bondi Junction
Bondi Rd
Bondi
Bondi Beach
Bondi Beach
Ben Buckler Point
University of Sydney
Cleveland St
Redfern
Redfern Park
Centennial Park
York St
Waverley Rd
Waverley
△2
Tamarama
Mackenzies Point
King St
Abercrombie St
Regent St
Bourke St
Phillip St
Lang Rd
Queens Park
Tamarama Beach
Eveleigh
Raglan St
Moore Park
Dacey Ave
Darley Rd
Clovelly Rd
Bronte Park
Bronte
Bronte Beach
Waterloo
Queens Park
Carrington Rd
Varna Park
Mitchell Rd
McEvoy St
Bourke St
Odea Ave
Alison Rd
Cowper St
Avoca St
Waverley Cemetery
Calga Reserve
Sydney Park Rd
Alexandria
Zetland
Epsom Rd
Randwick Racecourse
Alison Park
Alison Rd
Clovelly
Burrows Park
Shark Point
Beaconsfield
O'Riordan St
Botany Rd
Rothschild Ave
Southern Cross Dr
Anzac Pde
Kensington
Australian Golf Club
High St University of NSW
Barker St
Botany St
Clovelly Rd
Coogee
Coogee Pavilion
Gordons Bay
Mascot
Gardeners Rd
Eastlakes
Kensington Park
Kingsford
Avoca St
Dudley St
Coogee Beach
Dolphin Point

0 — 2 km
0 — 1 miles

A   B   C   D   E   F   G

1 2 3 4 5 6 7 8 9 10

SIGHTS &
ACTIVITIES

SEE

DO

ITINERARY

1

2

Shinjuku nightlife

Shinjuku is the biggest, brashest nightlife district in the land of the rising neon sun. There is truly something for everyone: the anachronistic shanty bars of Golden Gai; camp dance bars of Tokyo's gay quarter, Shinjuku-nichōme; risqué cabarets of Kabukichō; and then there are the sky-high lounges, all-night karaoke parlours and jazz dens.

Tokyo cityscape

Tokyo's cityscape takes on a surreal beauty when viewed from a few hundred metres in the air. By night it almost appears reversed, with the glittering stars below. Your best bet are the (free) observatories at the Tokyo Metropolitan Government Building.

Tsukiji Outer Market

Here, tightly packed rows of vendors hawk market and culinary-related goods, such as dried fish, seaweed, kitchen knives and crockery. It's also a fantastic place to eat, with great street food and countless seafood restaurants and cafes. The area is being redeveloped for the 2020 Olympics.

Meiji-jingū

Tokyo's largest and most famous Shintō shrine feels a world away from the city. It's reached via a long, rambling forest path marked by towering *torii* (gates). The grounds are vast, enveloping the classic wooden shrine buildings and a landscaped garden in a thick coat of green.

Roppongi Art Triangle

Roppongi was transformed into a polished gem by the opening of three high-profile museums: the Mori Art Museum, the Suntory Museum of Art and the National Art Center Tokyo. Within the triangle there are several smaller museums and galleries, too.

Akihabara pop culture

Venture into the belly of the pop culture beast that is Akihabara, the centre of Tokyo's *otaku* (geek) subculture. You don't have to obsess about manga or anime to enjoy this quirky neighbourhood. It's equal parts sensory overload, cultural mind-bender and just plain fun.

Kabukiza

The flamboyant facade of this venerable theatre makes a strong impression. It is a good indication of the extravagant dramatic flourishes that are integral to the traditional performing art of kabuki.

Sensō-ji

The spiritual home of Tokyo's ancestors, this Buddhist temple was founded over one thousand years before the city got its start. Today it retains an alluring, lively atmosphere redolent of Edo (old Tokyo) and the merchant quarters of yesteryear.

Sumo wrestling

From the ancient rituals to the thrill of the quick bouts, sumo is a fascinating spectacle. Tournaments take place in Tokyo three times a year; outside of tournament season you can catch a morning practice session at one of the stables where wrestlers live and train.

Shibuya Crossing

This is the Tokyo you've dreamed about and seen in movies: the frenetic pace, the mind-boggling crowds, the twinkling neon lights and the giant video screens beaming larger-than-life celebrities over the streets.

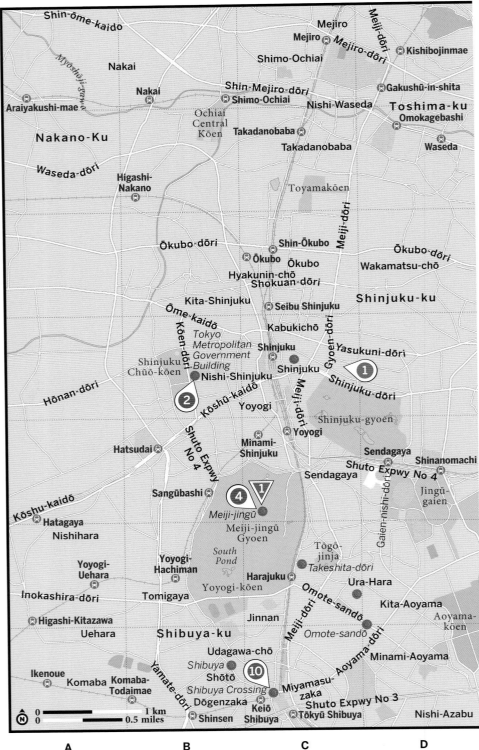

Day 1 itinerary

Start with a visit to **Meiji-jingū**, then walk down **Omote-sandō** to check out the jaw-dropping contemporary architecture along this stylish boulevard. Work (and shop) your way back through the side streets of **Ura-Hara**, and then up **Takeshita-dōri**, the famous teen fashion bazaar. Lunch on dumplings before heading down to **Shibuya** to continue your schooling in Tokyo pop culture. Don't miss Shibuya Center-gai, the main shopping drag, and the mural, *Myth of Tomorrow*, in the train station. Stick around until dusk to see **Shibuya Crossing** all lit up. After dinner take the train to **Shinjuku** for some full-on nightlife, then visit the **Tokyo Metropolitan Government Building** observatories.

Days 2 and 3 itinerary

Start with breakfast at **Tsukiji Outer Market**. From here it's an easy walk to the landscaped garden **Hama-rikyū Onshi-teien**. Continue to **Ginza**, home to boutiques and art galleries, before breaking for lunch. Walk as far as **Hibiya** to see the edge of the **Imperial Palace**, then hop on the subway to **Kabukiza**, Tokyo's premier kabuki theatre. After dining on ramen, finish the day by walking up Namiki-dōri and pretty, tree-lined Naka-dōri to **Marunouchi**. In nearby **Yūrakuchō**, stop for sake, beer and small plates of food under the train tracks. Spend morning three exploring the many attractions of Ueno-kōen: **Tokyo National Museum**, centuries-old temples and shrines, and the **Ueno Zoo**. Then stroll through the old-fashioned, open-air market, **Ameya-yokochō**, and the historical neighbourhood of **Yanaka**. In the afternoon, catch **Sensō-ji**, the shrine **Asakusa-jinja** and the maze of old-world alleys that surround these sights. Fill up on steaming *oden* at 100-year-old **Otafuku** for dinner, then enjoy **Asakusa's** fun, low-key nightlife.

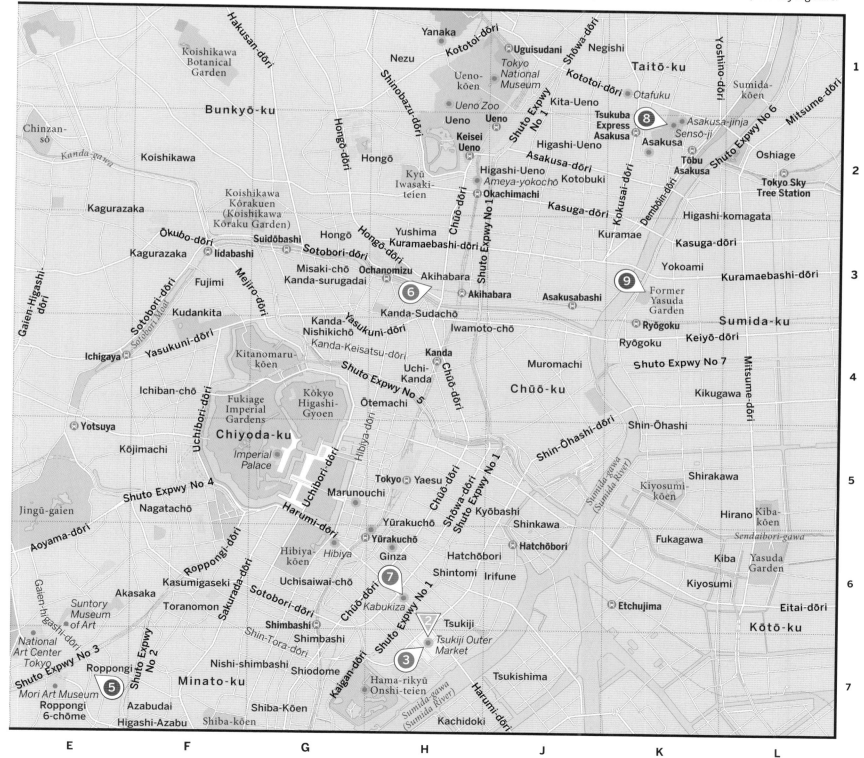

SIGHTS &
ACTIVITIES

◉ SEE
◉ DO

ITINERARY

▽ 1
▽ 2

① Royal Ontario Museum

The multidisciplinary ROM is Canada's biggest natural history museum and one of the largest museums in North America. You'll either love or loathe the synergy between the original heritage buildings at the main entrance on Bloor St and the 2007 addition of 'the Crystal', which appears to pierce the original structure and juts out into the street like a massive shard. Inside, the permanent collection features over 6 million specimens and artefacts, divided between two main galleries: Natural History and World Culture.

② CN Tower

Toronto's iconic CN Tower, once the world's highest freestanding structure, may be a communications hub, but that role takes a backseat to visitors riding glass elevators, peering from the SkyPod and now walking along its outer limits on the EdgeWalk. On a clear day, the views are astounding.

③ Toronto International Film Festival

Since its inception in 1976, TIFF has grown to be the crowning jewel of the Toronto festival scene and a key player in the world film circuit. Attracting over 400,000 eager cinephiles to the red-carpet celebrity frenzy of its 10-day run, the festival has become an important forum for showcasing (and watching) new films.

CN Tower:
Toronto's CN Tower is a marvel of 1970s engineering.

④ 401 Richmond

Inside an early-20th-century lithographer's warehouse, this 18,500-sq-m New York–style artist collective hums with the creative vibes of 130 diverse contemporary galleries showcasing works in almost any artistic medium you can think of. Grab a snack and a latte at the ground-floor cafe and enjoy it on the expansive roof garden: a little-known oasis in the summer.

⑤ Distillery District

Centered on the 1832 Gooderham and Worts distillery – once the British Empire's largest – this district is home to Victorian industrial warehouses that have been converted into soaring galleries, artists' studios, design boutiques, cafes and eateries. In summer, expect live jazz, activities, exhibitions and foodie events.

⑥ St Lawrence Market

Old York's sensational St Lawrence Market has been a neighbourhood meeting place for over two centuries. The restored, high-trussed South Market houses dozens of speciality food stalls: cheese vendors, fishmongers, butchers, bakers and pasta-makers.

⑦ Hockey games

Step inside the Air Canada Centre to witness the Toronto Maple Leafs play Canada's beloved game of hockey (the term 'ice hockey' is distinctly un-Canadian) in front of thousands as part of the National Hockey League.

⑧ Spadina Museum

This gracious home and its Victorian-Edwardian gardens were built in 1866 as a country estate for financier James Austin. Donated to the city in 1978, it became a museum in 1984 and was painstakingly transformed to evoke the heady age of the 1920s and '30s.

⑨ Elgin and Winter Garden Theatre

Tour this restored masterpiece, which is the world's last operating Edwardian double-decker theatre. The Winter Garden was built as the flagship for a vaudeville chain, while the downstairs Elgin was converted into a movie house in the 1920s.

▽ Day 1 itinerary

For the ultimate introduction to the city, take a rocket-ride up the **CN Tower** – as high as Torontonians can get without wings. Brave the EdgeWalk if you dare; on a clear day the views are outstanding. Lunch at **St Lawrence Market**, then head up to **Bloor-Yorkville** to window-shop. Once inspired, max out your style-to-value ratio in **Kensington Market** followed by an early dinner of dumplings in **Chinatown**. Come evening head over to **The Annex**, Toronto's largest downtown residential neighbourhood, which is favoured by students and academics. The number of pubs, organic grocery stores and spiritual venues should come as no surprise. Some of Toronto's most majestic architecture is here, too.

▽ Days 2 and 3 itinerary

Start early on day two and check out the amazing **Royal Ontario Museum**, or the **Art Gallery of Ontario**. Highlights of the permanent collection include Québecois religious statuary, First Nations and Inuit carvings and stunningly presented works by Canadian greats. Afterwards take a long lunch in **Baldwin Village**. then ride the ferry to the **Toronto Islands** and bike until the sun sets. Back on the mainland, relax with a pint in one of the breweries of the atmospheric **Distillery District** before catching a show or hitting the dancefloor in the **Entertainment District** or **Church-Wellesley Village**. Devote the whole of day three to exploring the boutiques, bars and eateries along **Queen West**, **Trinity-Bellwoods** and **West Queen West**. Once your retail cravings have been sated, catch the Toronto Blue Jays playing Major League Baseball at the **Rogers Centre** or, if hockey is more your style, the Maple Leafs playing at the **Air Canada Centre**, or both for half the price at **Wayne Gretzky's**, a pub once part-owned by Canada's favourite hockey legend.

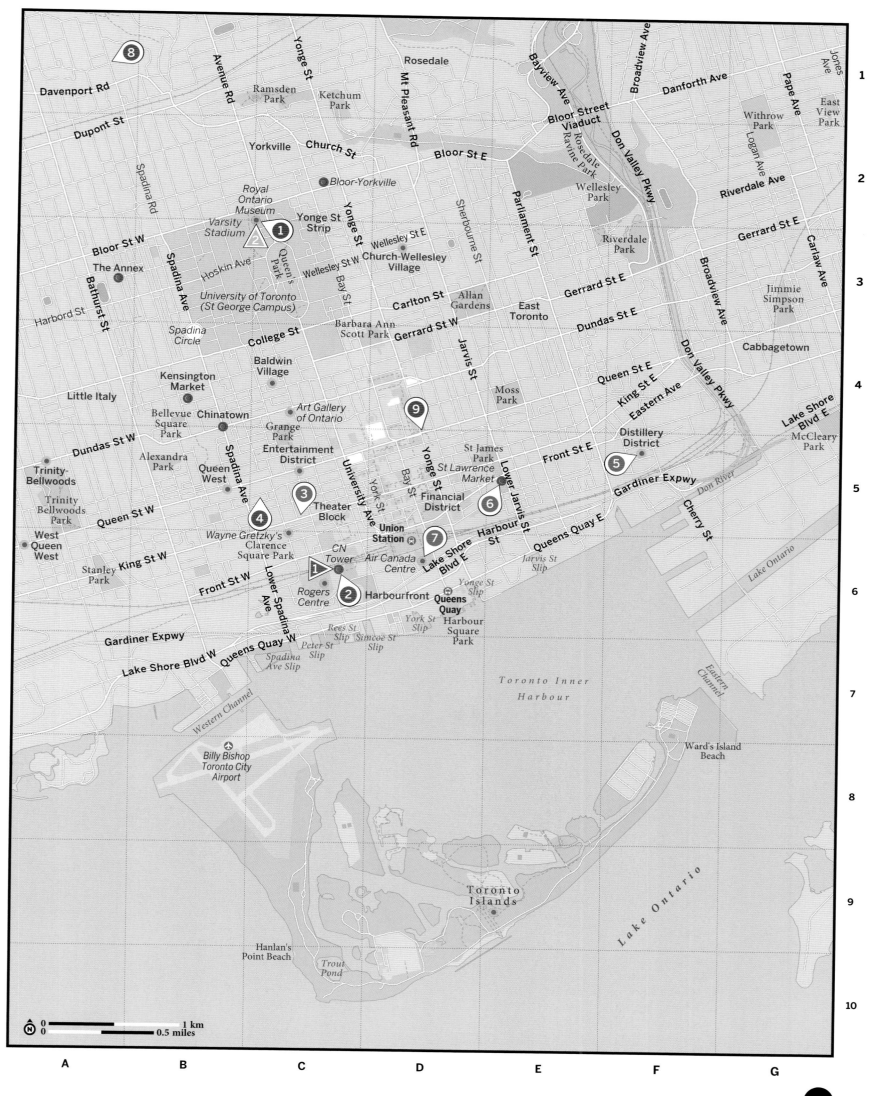

1 Rosedale

Davenport Rd

Dupont St

Yorkville

Ramsden Park

Ketchum Park

Mt Pleasant Rd

Bayview Ave

Broadview Ave

Danforth Ave

Pape Ave

Jones Ave

East View Park

Bloor Street Viaduct

Withrow Park

Logan Ave

Spadina Rd

Avenue Rd

Yonge St

Church St

Bloor St E

Rosedale Ravine Park

Don Valley Pkwy

Riverdale Ave

Bloor St W

Royal Ontario Museum

Bloor-Yorkville

Yonge St Strip

Wellesley Park

Gerrard St E

The Annex

Varsity Stadium

2 **1**

Hoskin Ave

Queen's Park

Yonge St

Wellesley St E

Sherbourne St

Parliament St

Wellesley Park

Riverdale Park

Carlaw Ave

Bathurst St

Spadina Ave

Wellesley St W

Bay St

Church-Wellesley Village

Riverdale Park

Jimmie Simpson Park

Harbord St

University of Toronto (St George Campus)

Carlton St

Allan Gardens

East Toronto

Gerrard St E

Spadina Circle

College St

Barbara Ann Scott Park

Gerrard St W

Dundas St E

Cabbagetown

Baldwin Village

Jarvis St

Moss Park

Queen St E

Broadview Ave

Kensington Market

Art Gallery of Ontario

9

King St E

Eastern Ave

Lake Shore Blvd E

Little Italy

Bellevue Square Park

Chinatown

Grange Park

St James Park

Front St E

Distillery District

McCleary Park

Alexandra Park

Entertainment District

St Lawrence Market

Gardiner Expwy

Trinity-Bellwoods

Dundas St W

Queen West

3

University Ave

Yonge St

6

5

Don River

Trinity Bellwoods Park

Spadina Ave

4

Theater Block

York St

Bay St

Financial District

Lower Jarvis St

Queens Quay E

Cherry St

Queen St W

Wayne Gretzky's

Clarence Square Park

Union Station

7

Harbour St

West Queen West

Stanley King St W

1

CN Tower

Air Canada Centre

Lake Shore Blvd E

Lake Ontario

Park

Front St W

2

Harbourfront

Queens Quay

Jarvis St Slip

Rogers Centre

Yonge St Slip

Gardiner Expwy

Lower Spadina Ave

Queens Quay W

Rees St Slip

Simcoe St Slip

York St Slip

Harbour Square Park

Eastern Channel

Lake Shore Blvd W

Peter St Slip

Spadina Ave Slip

Toronto Inner Harbour

Western Channel

Billy Bishop Toronto City Airport

Ward's Island Beach

Toronto Islands

Hanlan's Point Beach

Trout Pond

Lake Ontario

8

0   1 km
0   0.5 miles

A   B   C   D   E   F   G

1 2 3 4 5 6 7 8 9 10

THE TRAVEL ATLAS

THE TRAVEL ATLAS

THE TRAVEL ATLAS
THE ULTIMATE ATLAS FOR GLOBETROTTERS

Chapter editors/writers:
Oliver Berry (Spain & Portugal; Italy, Corsica & Malta; Central Europe; the Nordic Countries; Russia, Caucasus & Central Asia; the Middle East; Northeast Asia; Mainland Southeast Asia, Maritime Southeast Asia; Australia & New Zealand; Pacific Islands; Canada; Northern South America; Southern South America)
Joe Bindloss (Indian Subcontinent)
Bailey Freeman (USA, Mexico & Central America, the Caribbean)
Anne Mason (France)
Matt Phillips (Northern Africa, Southern Africa; Mexico & Central

America, the Caribbean, Cities)
Trisha Ping (USA)
Sarah Stocking (USA)
Brana Vladisavljevic (Southeastern Europe; Eastern Europe & the Baltics)

Cartography Project Lead & Design:
Wayne Murphy

Lead Cartographers:
Hunor Csutoros, Anthony Phelan

Cartographers:
Julie Dodkins, Michael Garrett, Mark Griffiths, Corey Hutchinson, Rachel Imeson, Valentina Kremenchutskaya, Alison Lyall, Julie Sheridan, Diana Von Holdt

Cartographic Support:
Piotr Czajkowski, Chris Lee Ack, Liam McGrellis

Map editors:
William Allen, Shona Gray, Kate Kiely, Jenna Myers, Rachel Rawling, Kathryn Rowan, Saralinda Turner, Amanda Williamson

1st Edition

Managing Director, Publishing
Piers Pickard

Associate Publisher & Commissioning Editor
Robin Barton

Editors
Dora Ball, Jessica Cole, Monica Woods

Indexers
Sandie Kestell, Monica Woods

Art Direction and Design
Daniel di Paolo

Print Production
Nigel Longuet, Jean-Pierre Masclef

Thanks
Laura Lindsay, Darren O'Connell, the Destination Editors

Published in 2018 by Lonely Planet Global Limited
ABN 36 005 607 983
www.lonelyplanet.com

Australia
The Malt Store, Level 3,
551 Swanston St,
Carlton, Victoria 3053
T: 03 8379 8000

Ireland
Digital Depot, Roe Lane, Digital Hub,
Dublin 8, D08 TCV4

USA
124 Linden St, Oakland, CA 94607
T: 510 250 6400

UK
240 Blackfriars Rd, London SE1 8NW
T: 020 3771 5100

Stay in touch
lonelyplanet.com/contact

ISBN 978 1 78701 6965
10 9 8 7 6 5 4 3 2 1

Text & maps © Lonely Planet Pty Ltd 2018 Photos © as indicated 2018
Printed in Singapore

Maps throughout this book were created using ArcGIS® software by Esri. Copyright © Esri. Mapping data made available by the U.S. Geological Survey and the Land Processes Distributed Active Archive Center (LP DAAC), located at USGS/EROS, Sioux Falls, SD.

Although the authors and Lonely Planet have taken all reasonable care in preparing this book, we make no warranty about the accuracy or completeness of its content and, to the maximum extent permitted, disclaim all liability arising from its use.

Paper in this book is certified against the Forest Stewardship Council™ standards. FSC™ promotes environmentally responsible, socially beneficial and economically viable management of the world's forests.

Cover images: © Lonely Planet